Praise for
Novel & Short Story Writer's Market

"This is the book every fiction writer needs. From its superior listings to its interviews with leading industry experts and bestselling authors, NSSWM should never be more than an arm's length away."
—Peter Blocksom, Editor, Fiction Writer

"Instead of buying half a dozen how-to-write and how-to-sell books, now writers can concentrate all their efforts through this one professional guide." **—Hutton Publications**

"This book is indispensible for budding authors who know what they want to say but can't get anyone to listen to them." **—The Advocate**

"An invaluable sourcebook for fiction writers—an education on the marketplace between hard covers." **—Janet Fitch, author of White Oleander**

"*Novel & Short Story Writer's Market* is an information-packed reference for fiction writers trying to find the right markets for their work—and increase their earnings." **—Writer's Write**

2000
NOVEL & SHORT STORY WRITER'S MARKET

2,000 PLACES TO SELL YOUR FICTION

EDITED BY
BARBARA KUROFF
ASSISTED BY
TRICIA WADDELL

WRITER'S DIGEST BOOKS
CINCINNATI, OHIO

If you are a publisher of fiction and would like to be considered for a listing in the next edition of *Novel & Short Story Writer's Market*, send a SASE (or SAE and IRC) with your request for a questionnaire to *Novel & Short Story Writer's Market*—QR, 1507 Dana Ave., Cincinnati OH 45207. Questionnaires received after July 15, 2000, will be held for the 2001 edition.

Managing Editor, Annuals Department: Cindy Laufenberg
Production Editor: Tricia Waddell

Writer's Digest Books website: www.writersdigest.com

International Standard Serial Number 0897-9812
International Standard Book Number 0-89879-934-1

Cover designed by Clare Finney
Cover illustration by Jeffrey Pelo

Attention Booksellers: This is an annual directory of F&W Publications. Return deadline for this edition is April 30, 2001.

contents at a glance

Contents

The Markets

Resources

From the Editor

On the threshold of the 21st Century, I am amazed at the balance that has surrounded us since the beginning of time. Days, years, seasons and millennia come and go with a precision no man-made technology could order. Perhaps it is a symptom of "millennium fever," but I noticed a surprising number of writers and editors interviewed for this edition of *Novel & Short Story Writer's Market* talk about or allude to the need for balance in their writing lives.

Writer Heidi Julavits (page 375) shares her experiences identifying the conditions that provide her with the balance she needs do her best writing: time of day, place, caffeine or no caffeine. Pinckney Benedict (page 35) alludes to the balance he has had to strike between writing fiction, where density of well-chosen details is valued, and writing screenplays, where the same details would be considered "mellifluous prose." Beginning on page 32, Russell Banks talks about the balance between time spent alone in a room writing and the time he spends on the road promoting his books and movies based on his books.

In this millennium edition of *Novel & Short Story Writer's Market*, we've worked hard to provide a balance of information for you, no matter what type of fiction you write, whether you are just beginning or already published. For beginning writers, Paul Raymond Martin offers Seven Secrets for New Writers (page 17). For those who are already published, Martin gives invaluable tips on Self-Promotion for Writers (page 99).

Part of the successful fiction writer's balance includes being savvy about the business aspects of writing. In our Getting Published section, we've included important articles on the Elements of the All-Important Query Letter (page 81) and Elements of a Successful Synopsis, both written by Blythe Camenson and Marshall J. Cook.

We include lots of inspiration and inside information for writers, too—in the articles, interviews and Insider Reports with editors and writers scattered throughout the book. Jonathan Galassi, editor-in-chief at Farrar, Straus & Giroux and editor of Tom Wolfe and Alice McDermott, talks about the important balance of a writer-editor relationship (page 20). Then, beginning on page 25, we balance Galassi's comments with the writer's viewpoint from Alice McDermott, author of *Charming Billy*, winner of the 1998 National Book Award. Among the Insider Reports, Janet Fitch had the good fortune of having to maintain balance as a person and a writer after Oprah Winfrey picked *White Oleander*, Fitch's first novel, as an Oprah Book Club™ selection and sent it skyrocketing in one day to the top of the bestseller lists.

There is much more in this 2000 edition of *Novel & Short Story Writer's Market*. That's why I suggest you take a minute right now to read through the Table of Contents and let it guide you to articles, interviews and markets that will help you achieve the balance necessary to be the best writer you can possibly be and find the right markets for your fiction in this, the first year of the 21st Century.

Barbara Kuroff

Editor
nsswm@fwpubs.com

The "Quick-Start" Guide to Publishing Your Fiction

To make the most of *Novel & Short Story Writer's Market* you need to know how to use it. And with more than 600 pages of fiction publishing markets and resources, a writer could easily get lost amidst the plethora of information. But, fear not. This "quick-start" guide will help you wind your way through the pages of *Novel & Short Story Writer's Market*, as well as the fiction publishing process, and emerge with your dream accomplished—to see your fiction in print.

1. Read, read, read.

Read numerous magazines, fiction collections and novels to determine if your fiction compares favorably with work currently being published. If your fiction is at least the same caliber as that you're reading, then move on to step two. If not, postpone submitting your work and spend your time polishing your fiction. Writing and reading the work of others are the best ways to improve craft.

For help with craft and critique of your work:

- You'll find articles on the craft and business aspects of writing fiction in the Craft & Technique section, beginning on page 6 and in the Getting Published section, beginning on page 81.
- If you're a genre writer, you will find information in For Mystery Writers, beginning on page 46, For Romance Writers, beginning on page 55 and For Science Fiction & Fantasy Writers, beginning on page 67.
- You'll find Conference & Workshop listings beginning on page 570.
- You'll find Organizations for fiction writers on page 608.

2. Analyze your fiction.

Determine the type of fiction you write to best target your submissions to markets most suitable to your work. Do you write literary, genre, mainstream or one of many other categories of fiction? There are magazines and presses seeking specialized work in each of these areas as well as numerous others.

For editors and publishers with specialized interests, see the Category Index beginning on page 632.

3. Learn about the market.

Read *Fiction Writer* and *Writer's Digest* magazines (both published by F&W Publications, Inc.), *Poet's & Writers* and *Byline*. Also read *Publishers Weekly*, the trade magazine of the publishing industry and *Independent Publisher* containing information about small- to medium-sized independent presses. And don't forget to utilize the Internet. There are a number of sites for writers, including www.fictionwritermag.com and www.writersdigest.com (see page 621 for Websites of Interest).

4. Find markets for your work.

There are a variety of ways to locate markets for fiction. The periodicals sections of bookstores and libraries are great places to discover new journals and magazines that might be open to your type of short stories. Read writing-related magazines and newsletters for information about new markets and publications seeking fiction submissions. Also, frequently browse bookstore shelves to see what novels and short story collections are being published and by whom. Check acknowledgment pages for names of editors and agents, too. Online journals often have links to the websites of other journals that may publish fiction. And last but certainly not least, read the listings found here in *Novel & Short Story Writer's Market*.

Also, don't forget to utilize the Category Indexes at the back of this book to help you target your fiction to the right market.

5. Send for guidelines.

In the listings in this book, we try to include as much submission information as we can glean from editors and publishers. Over the course of the year, however, editors' expectations and needs may change. Therefore, it is best to request submission guidelines by sending a self-addressed stamped envelope (SASE). You can also check the websites of magazines and presses which usually contain a page with guideline information.

6. Begin your publishing efforts with journals and contests open to beginners.

If this is your first attempt at publishing your work, your best bet is to begin with local publications or with publications that you know are open to beginning writers. Then, after you have built a publication history, you can try the more prestigious and nationally distributed magazines. For publications and contests most open to beginners, look for the ◻ symbol preceding listing titles. Also, look for the ◪ symbol that identifies markets open to exceptional work from beginners as well as work from experienced, previously published writers.

7. Submit your fiction in a professional manner.

Take the time to show editors that you care about your work and are serious about publishing. By following a publication's or book publisher's submission guidelines and practicing standard submission etiquette, you can better ensure your chances that an editor will want to take the time to read your work and consider it for publication. Remember, first impressions last, and a carelessly assembled submission packet can jeopardize your chances before your story or novel manuscript has had a chance to speak for itself.

For help with preparing submissions:
- Read The Business of Fiction Writing, beginning on page 104.
- Read Elements of the All-Important Query Letter, beginning on page 81, and Elements of a Successful Synopsis, beginning on page 91.

8. Keep track of your submissions.

Know when and where you have sent fiction and how long you need to wait before expecting a reply. If an editor does not respond by the time indicated in his market listing or guidelines, wait a few more weeks and then follow up with a letter (and SASE) asking when the editor anticipates making a decision. If you still do not receive a reply from the editor within a reasonable amount of time, send a letter withdrawing your work from consideration and move on to the next market on your list.

9. Learn from rejection.

Rejection is the hardest part of the publication process. Unfortunately, rejection happens to every writer and every writer needs to learn to deal with the negativity involved. On the other hand, rejection can be valuable when used as a teaching tool rather than a reason to doubt yourself and your work. If an editor offers suggestions with his or her rejection slip, take those comments into consideration. You don't have to automatically agree with an editor's opinion of your work. It may be that the editor has a different perspective on the piece than you do. Or, you may find that the editor's suggestions give you new insight into your work and help you improve your craft.

10. Don't give up.

The best advice for writers trying to get published is be persistent and to always believe in themselves and their work. By continually reading other writers' work, constantly working on the craft of fiction writing and relentlessly submitting your work, you will eventually find that magazine or book publisher that's the perfect match for your fiction. And, *Novel & Short Story Writer's Market* will be here to help you every step of the way.

GUIDE TO LISTING FEATURES

Below you will find an example of the market listings contained in *Novel & Short Story Writer's Market*. Also included are callouts identifying the various format features of the listings. (For an explanation of the symbols used, see the front and back covers of this book.)

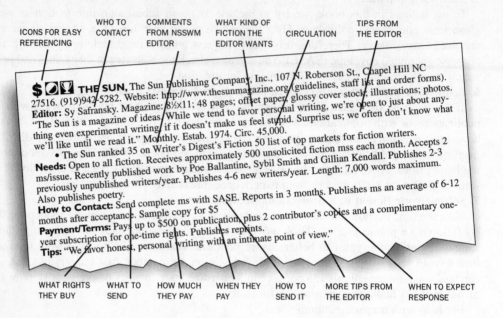

ICONS FOR EASY REFERENCING

WHO TO CONTACT

COMMENTS FROM NSSWM EDITOR

WHAT KIND OF FICTION THE EDITOR WANTS

CIRCULATION

TIPS FROM THE EDITOR

$ ⊘ ▢ ▨ THE SUN, The Sun Publishing Company, Inc., 107 N. Roberson St., Chapel Hill NC 27516. (919)942-5282. Website: http://www.thesunmagazine.org (guidelines, staff list and order forms). **Editor:** Sy Safransky. Magazine: 8½x11; 48 pages; offset paper; glossy cover stock; illustrations; photos. "The Sun is a magazine of ideas. While we tend to favor personal writing, we're open to just about anything even experimental writing if it doesn't make us feel stupid. Surprise us; we often don't know what we'll like until we read it." Monthly. Estab. 1974. Circ. 45,000.

• The Sun ranked 35 on Writer's Digest's Fiction 50 list of top markets for fiction writers.

Needs: Open to all fiction. Receives approximately 500 unsolicited fiction mss each month. Accepts 2 ms/issue. Recently published work by Poe Ballantine, Sybil Smith and Gillian Kendall. Publishes 2-3 previously unpublished writers/year. Publishes 4-6 new writers/year. Length: 7,000 words maximum. Also publishes poetry.

How to Contact: Send complete ms with SASE. Reports in 3 months. Publishes ms an average of 6-12 months after acceptance. Sample copy for $5

Payment/Terms: Pays up to $500 on publication, plus 2 contributor's copies and a complimentary one-year subscription for one-time rights. Publishes reprints.

Tips: "We favor honest, personal writing with an intimate point of view."

WHAT RIGHTS THEY BUY

WHAT TO SEND

HOW MUCH THEY PAY

WHEN THEY PAY

HOW TO SEND IT

MORE TIPS FROM THE EDITOR

WHEN TO EXPECT RESPONSE

Writing Fiction

Best Reads of the Century

BY JOANNE MILLER

More than 17 million books were published in the U.S. since 1900. Is it possible to label a few "the best"? *Novel & Short Story Writer's Market* looked at four groups who tried: The ten-member editorial board of Modern Library—Random House's literary reprint line—named their top 100, as did 217,520 respondents to a separate Modern Library website questionnaire. In another survey, readers of the trade publication *Library Journal* forwarded "hundreds of submissions, with entries from both individuals and groups of librarians . . . by e-mail and by post." The Modern Library and *Library Journal* groups concentrated on fiction; a five-member panel gathered by the theme-based quarterly, *Hungry Mind Review*, cited both fiction and nonfiction among their favorites.

According to Modern Library's managing director Ian Jackman, "Any group of ten people . . . will create an interesting list. But our editorial board, made up of literary superstars A. S. Byatt, Shelby Foote, Gore Vidal, and others has read a *lot* of books. . . ." Both the Modern Library board and respondents to the Internet survey were asked to choose books they considered "important works of literature and thought." However, the Internet survey result radically expanded Modern Library's definition of "important work."

Readers of *Library Journal* chose books they deemed "highly influential, either in the larger world or in their impact on the reader personally." Favorites included beloved childhood tales *Charlotte's Web* (E.B. White) and *The Hobbit* (J.R.R. Tolkien), as well as titles from contemporary authors such as Barbara Kingsolver (*The Bean Trees*), E.L. Doctorow (*Ragtime*) and Amy Tan (*The Joy Luck Club*). However, *Library Journal* readers and the two Modern Library groups all tended to favor male authors published prior to 1970.

The *Hungry Mind Review* panel, consisting of a multicultural group of Minnesotan writers, made the broadest choices. They cited classic titles as well as male and female contemporary authors from a variety of ethnic backgrounds. Editor Bart Schneider explains, "Our criteria were pretty loose; something like this is always arbitrary." Several short story collections (by John Cheever, Grace Paley, and others) and a smattering of nonfiction (essay collections by Joan Didion and Gore Vidal, and the recent *Slaves in the Family*, by Edward Ball) also made *Hungry Mind's* top 100. Unlike the other list makers, this panel didn't assign numbers to their picks; all were of equal value.

Using titles from all four lists, the following is a compendium of the century's best reads.

The top ten titles, in alphabetical order, were on all four lists:

Catch 22, Joseph Heller (1961)
The Catcher in the Rye, J.D. Salinger (1951)
The Grapes of Wrath, John Steinbeck (1939)
The Great Gatsby, F. Scott Fitzgerald (1925)
The Invisible Man, Ralph Ellison (1952)
Lolita, Vladimir Nabokov (1955)
On the Road, Jack Kerouac (1957)

JOANNE MILLER *is author of the* Pennsylvania Handbook *and the upcoming* Maryland-Delaware Handbook. *She's also working on a suspense/romance novel set in Victorian San Francisco.*

Slaughterhouse-Five, Kurt Vonnegut Jr. (1969)
The Sound and the Fury, William Faulkner (1929)
The Sun Also Rises, Ernest Hemingway (1926)

These titles were on three of four lists:

1984, George Orwell (1949)
As I Lay Dying, William Faulkner (1930)
Beloved, Toni Morrison (1987)
Brave New World, Aldous Huxley (1932)
The Call of the Wild, Jack London (1903)
A Clockwork Orange, Anthony Burgess (1962)
A Farewell to Arms, Ernest Hemingway (1929)
The Heart is a Lonely Hunter, Carson McCullers (1940)
Heart of Darkness, Joseph Conrad (1902)
I, Claudius, Robert Graves (1934)
Lord of the Flies, William Golding (1954)
The Moviegoer, Walker Percy (1961)
Native Son, Richard Wright (1940)
Of Human Bondage, W. Somerset Maugham (1915)
One Flew Over the Cuckoo's Nest, Ken Kesey (1962)
Portnoy's Complaint, Philip Roth (1969)
A Portrait of the Artist as a Young Man, James Joyce (1916)
The Sheltering Sky, Paul Bowles (1948)
Sophie's Choice, William Styron (1979)
To Kill a Mockingbird, Harper Lee (1960)
To the Lighthouse, Virginia Woolf (1927)
Tropic of Cancer, Henry Miller (1934)
Ulysses, James Joyce (1922)
USA, John Dos Passos (1919, 1936, 1938)
Winesburg, Ohio, Sherwood Anderson (1919)

These titles were on two of four lists:

The Age of Innocence, Edith Wharton (1920)
All the King's Men, Robert Penn Warren (1946)
An American Tragedy, Theodore Dreiser (1925)
Angle of Repose, Wallace Stegner (1971)
Animal Farm, George Orwell (1954)
Babbit, Sinclair Lewis (1922)
Brideshead Revisited, Evelyn Waugh (1945)
The Color Purple, Alice Walker (1982)
Day of the Locust, Nathanael West (1939)
Death Comes for the Archbishop, Willa Cather (1927)
Fahrenheit 451, Ray Bradbury (1952)
The Fountainhead, Ayn Rand (1943)
From Here to Eternity, James Jones (1951)
Go Tell It on the Mountain, James Baldwin (1953)
A Good Man is Hard to Find, Flannery O'Connor (1955)
The Good Soldier, Ford Maddox Ford (1927)
Gone with the Wind, Margaret Mitchell (1936)
The Handmaid's Tale, Margaret Atwood (1986)
Light in August, William Faulkner (1932)

Lord of the Rings, J.R.R. Tolkien (1956)
The Magus, John Fowles (1965)
The Naked and the Dead, Norman Mailer (1948)
A Passage to India, E.M. Forster (1924)
The Prime of Miss Jean Brodie, Muriel Spark (1962)
Rabbit Run, John Updike (1960)
Roots, Alex Haley (1976)
Sister Carrie, Theodore Dreiser (1900)
Stranger in a Strange Land, Robert A. Heinlein (1961)
Their Eyes Were Watching God, Zora Neale Hurston (1937)
Under the Volcano, Malcolm Lowry (1947)
The Wings of the Dove, Henry James (1902)
Women in Love, D.H. Lawrence (1920)

To see each list in its entirety, contact:

- Modern Library, www.randomhouse.com, (212)751-2600 (ask for a live person at Modern Library—messages may not get a reply).
- *Library Journal*, www.bookwire.com/ljdigital/, (212)463-6819.
- *Hungry Mind Review*, www.hungrymind.com, (651)699-2610.

Writers As Readers

BY ROBERT OLMSTEAD

Bear with me. Recently I had an encounter that has left me absolutely flummoxed. Well, not really. My friends will tell you that I am un-flummox-able. So too, I am unflappable and imperturbable, known by all as someone to call in an emergency and as one who is not immune to the lure of a challenge. I will concede to becoming apoplectic from time to time, and do wish God had blessed me with more patience, but nonetheless, allow me to proceed.

Robert Olmstead

Where I teach, a composition and rhetoric professor had the audacity to observe that the best way to become a writer is to write. He advises students that if they want to be writers, they should take composition and rhetoric courses instead of literature courses. Presumably, if one wants to become a writer, one should study writing as a discipline.

I know. It is hard to believe that advice could be so poor and right now you yourself are no doubt borderline flummoxed. But perhaps it is not so obvious. Perhaps you are not as thunderstruck as I was by that notion. Perhaps you too have been on the receiving end of similar advice and the individual advocating such had several initials after his name also, making him one of your more educated and intimidating observers on how best to become a writer.

I will tell you straight up, I do not know a single writer who did not learn to write by reading, who is not downright helpless when it comes to the seduction that is reading and, if you ask them, they will tell you so. I do not know a single writer who would rather be writing a book than reading a book. After all, reading was our first love and, no matter how old and rheumy we become, or how very much in love, we are forever still in love with our first.

Even as I sit here, there is to my left a stack of books whispering my name. They are calling to me, making outrageous promises and unseemly gestures and I cannot help but want to run away with all of them. I could list them for you, but right now I consider it to be a private matter between me and them.

So from this point forward, think of every book you read, for better or worse, to be a lesson in writing. This is to say that if you want to be a better writer, read better books and read them with intention.

BE A GOOD READER

But how do you do this? Consider for a moment that it could be your very talent as a reader that prevents you from learning about writing while you read. Good readers do not read every word. They are taught to read groups and sets of words. Good readers travel quickly because they want to find out what happens next and because they usually have two or three books

ROBERT OLMSTEAD *is the author of three novels—*America By Land *(Random House, 1993),* Soft Water *(Vintage, 1988), and* A Trail of Heart's Blood Wherever We Go *(Random House, 1990)—as well as a collection of short stories,* River Dogs, *and his memoir* Stay Here With Me *(Metropolitan Books, 1996). His work has appeared in* Fiction Writer, Granta, Cutbank, Black Warrior Review, Epoch, Ploughshares, Graywolf, Weber Studies *and* Sports Afield.

waiting to be held. Good readers do not just think about what is before them on the page. They understand what they are reading in the context of what they have already read while anticipating what they have yet to read. Good readers think while they read.

It could also be that those pesky emotions of yours prevent you from learning about writing while you read. The old love-hate thing. It is no easy task when you are laughing or weeping, terrified or enrapt to start parsing the prose. When the meaning of all that is or ever was is turned inside out and you are set to the task of questioning the worth of your own existence, when a writer causes you to do that, you are not apt to stop and say, 'Wait a minute buster, just how did you do that to me?'

It is not a wonder that we are terribly confused about the place of literature in our lives and that the relationship between reading and writing is somewhat opaque. Too much teaching is ignorant of the writer's experience when creating. Too much of writing study is focused on parts and forms. Name the plot. Name the theme. Name the protagonist. But books are not car engines. They do not have a necessarily common anatomy or psychology. They are art and no less confounding and challenging than any other art form. Moby Dick is no more a fish story than Picasso's "La Vie" is some blue people standing around.

READ THE WRITING

So here are some things to try, ways to hold your talented and emotional reader-self in check so you might observe what the writer is doing. Every novel and short story you read is a lesson in how to write. They are not only about their characters and events, they are also about writing. I suggest you do these things days after enjoying the book. God forbid you should deny yourself that pleasure. Also, a warning. With the best writing, it will be near impossible to do most of these activities with even the glimmer of conclusion. The best writers, as with the best magicians, leave no trace behind. One small note: What follows are not strategies and come with no suggestion whatsoever of guarantee. Think of these as habits or behaviors that are meant to run concurrently with your own reading and writing.

- Read aloud. This is how you first came to books, and the beginning of your learning to read and being read to was your favorite activity as a child. It is how you drifted off to sleep every afternoon and every night for many years, in the company of warmth and love and a book. So read aloud to hear the passages you admire. Learn to read them smoothly and as intended to be read. Do it until you have it right. There is no need to be dramatic. In fact, avoid such. Do this with your own work, again avoiding the histrionics so as not to bluff yourself into believing you have more than you really do. Read evenly so the words and their stitch might be apparent. Read so you can hear.

- Read randomly. Turn to any page and begin reading. Do this to step from the stream of events that are compelling you forward. In the best work you will not be as lost as you might think. You will soon begin to feel fully immersed in the prose and soon after the fullness of the story. How could this be? It's because good writing is always offering up a full experience. It withholds nothing.

- Look for elements and transitions. There will be dialogue, narrative, description, action, flashback, backstory and stuff like that. Clearly, there are times when words are used to do different things: words intended to be heard; words intended to make an image; words intended to be mulled over and understood. A writer must change words to go from one intention to another. Sometimes these transitions are easy to find, for instance going from narrative to dialogue, or back to narrative once the dialogue is concluded. Often they are difficult because a writer is doing so many things at once.

- Look for words. In an interview Don DeLillo talked about what Hemingway meant to him as a writer. DeLillo said that whatever you might think, Hemingway is about the conjunction *and*. Think about it.

- Change perspective. Do you know why art galleries have those signs about not touching paintings, objects, sculptures? Because people like me and you want to touch them, perhaps even have a need to touch them. My cousin is an artist. I like going to galleries with her because she likes to smell the paintings. She sees the brush work that I cannot and she tells me about it. She teaches me about painting by getting me close to it. Do the same. Parse a few sentences for how they are constructed.

- Go back. Say you find yourself in tears over something you have read. Or, you are laughing. Chances are the emotion you are experiencing did not begin and take effect all at once. It was given life and made to grow. Go back and find out where it started. Ask yourself, where did the writer begin this movement that has brought me to such a powerful feeling? Track the movement of that intention and see if you can identify how it grew to full effect.

- Copy passages in your own hand. If for no other reason, this is a good habit to have so you might always have a record of your reading and a collection of those sentences that, for one reason or another, are important to you. I know several writers who have notebooks dedicated to this practice and another writer who keeps an index card file of such quotes to use when teaching. It need not even be a passage. Let it be a list of vocabulary words, verbs or nouns.

- Look for firsts and lasts. Read the first sentence of each chapter or the first sentence of each story in a collection. Read the last sentence of each chapter or story. Read the first line of dialogue. Read the first sentence that begins the making of a character. Read the sentence before a line break and then the sentence that comes after it. Read these in isolation. Then read the sentences that follow or precede the sentence you have isolated.

- Scan and count. This can be useful. Simply thumb through the pages and see what they look like. Note the length of paragraphs and the ratio of dialogue to narrative. How many chapters are there and how many pages is each? Count the words on several random pages, multiply by the number of pages and see what the total word count is.

- Read widely. Read what you are not likely to read and don't be a wimp about it. A writer should read everything. Travel through time and place and genre and gender and culture. Read everything, including poetry and biography, science and natural history. Read the ancients and the brand-news. Read cookbooks and catalogues. Read them for how they are written and for the stories they tell and do not stop there. Visit an art gallery and look at work that has lasted for 500 years. This always helps me. Learn to love the symphony and go often. Attend the opera and the theater. These, too, I have found to be a great help. It takes a long time for writing to get better, but at least you can do better things while you are waiting around for it to not be so bad.

Sometimes I do get angry at such bad advice as implies the study of writing is enough and more important than reading. This is rather new thinking and as I talk to other writers at colleges and universities, it is seemingly pervasive and on the increase. But not to fret. What is of more concern is the bad idea that somehow writing is not an art form. I find this thinking either ignorant or arrogant, depending on the thinker. The ignorant know no better and the arrogant ought to. I think there is a simple explanation. Writing is the only art form that shares its medium with its audience, its critics and its teachers. We can all write a sentence, but few of us can draw. We respond to writing in words, but are not likely to respond to a film by making a film. Could it be that this familiarity makes for complacency? Could it be that we underestimate how near to impossible it is to write something worth reading? To say that one learns to write by writing would be the same as asking the student of music to stop listening to music, or the painter to refrain from visiting galleries. However radical an artist might seem, you can rest assured they know intimately the work of those who came before them.

I would conclude by returning to what I know best—my own experience. When I was growing up what spoke to me were books. They were a means of conveyance. They lifted and moved, made me think better than I could, made me think outside myself, made me smarter. My father was a reader and took me to the library. When I was old enough, I'd ride my bicycle there every Saturday. Getting my hands on books was an adventure. Peddling those seven miles became the way to everywhere for me. Sometimes I think being a writer is merely the finest excuse to be surrounded by books, for the objects they are, for the feel of them, for the way they make odd stacks and decorate a room and, of course, for all that they contain. They are all that is left of my boyhood: not trains, not mineral collections, not toy soldiers, not even baseball and glove. They are the clear path that leads me back into childhood where they pause for my remembering mind and then break me through and into the forever past and remember for me again all that I never knew.

The Ugly Duckling Grows Up: Short Stories Are Hot

BY JOANNE MILLER

In 1998, *New York Times* arts/cultural desk columnist Marty Arnold began his report by writing, "It's like trying to sell Joyce. Few things make publishers and agents scurry away faster than short stories. Well, maybe poetry does, since occasionally a short story becomes a movie." Carefully chewing and swallowing his own words, Arnold devoted the remainder of his column to a then-revolutionary act in book publishing: Viking Penguin's purchase—for a package including a $275,000 advance—of a collection of short stories. Not only that, Viking was forced to bid against eight other publishers at auction: a lot of hullabaloo for the ugly duckling of the publishing world. The focal point of this pricey bidding war was a series of stories by author Melissa Bank, a former advertising copywriter with only a few literary journal clips to her credit. Her short story collection *The Girls' Guide to Hunting and Fishing* was brought to the table by agent Molly Friedrich.

Joanne Miller

Photo by Bonnie Kamin

THE SURE THING

Short stories have a long tradition in the literary landscape, and American short stories are distinctive in their own right. Carson McCullers, Flannery O'Connor, F. Scott Fitzgerald, Eudora Welty, James Joyce and Ernest Hemingway all published short stories, although then a writer could make a decent living on short story sales, and there was a bit more prestige in publishing. That was also a time when the word "publishing" was usually followed by "house" rather than "industry," and literary merit, for the most part, took priority over profitability. During the last 10 to 15 years, publishers have favored collections by well-known authors such as Stephen King, Garrison Keillor and Louis L'Amour—names that could be relied upon to make house accountants rub their hands with glee. Bantam published the 21st collection of L'Amour's short stories in May, 1999, bringing the total number of that author's short story collections in print to 25 million. Though King and L'Amour were brought to the attention of the reading public by their novels, other bestselling short story authors such as John Cheever and Ray Bradbury have consistently worked in short format. Is it the author or story style that should receive credit for such popularity? Probably both.

A CHANGE IN FORM—LORRIE MOORE

In the late 1970s and early 1980s, a groundswell of interest in the short story form by writers such as Raymond Carver, Ann Beattie, Barry Hannah, Bobbie Ann Mason and Lorrie Moore led to publication in spite of the preponderance of novels. Each author reconstructed the American

---

JOANNE MILLER *is the author of the* Pennsylvania Handbook *and* Maryland-Delaware Handbook *for Moon Publications. She is currently working on a suspense novel set in Victorian San Francisco.*

short story in a unique way. Lorrie Moore was one of several authors who developed a following for her literary short stories. As a child, she says, "I was always writing a little bit, but not in a serious way. As for reading, it was typical little-girl stuff. I remember thinking there would be no reason to read a book if it wasn't a mystery."

In the mid-1970s, she attended St. Lawrence University, where she studied creative writing under fiction writer and critic Joe David Bellamy. "I loved it," she says. "I would stay up all night writing." Bellamy edited an anthology called *Superfiction*, and, Moore says, these "were the first short stories I remember reading that really startled me. There was a Gilbert Sorrentino story, 'The Moon in its Flight,' that I read about 15 times." In 1976, Moore won *Seventeen* magazine's story contest, ". . . but once I got out of college I thought, well, that was fun, but now I have to be real. I had no sense of how you went from being a student taking creative writing classes to being a real writer. It seemed impossible."

Moore took a 50-plus hours-a-week job as a paralegal in Manhattan, but found little satisfaction in it. She enrolled in Cornell's M.F.A. program, where she caught the attention of Allison Lurie, a novelist and academic whose encouragement convinced Moore she should write for a living. "I was in this situation where I could just get up and read and write all day. I couldn't believe it, it was such a gift."

At Cornell, Moore wrote a series of what she calls "mock-imperative narratives," counseling readers on "How to Be the Other Woman," "How to Talk to Your Mother" and simply, "How." Lurie recommended her to agent Melanie Jackson, who sent Moore's stories to Knopf editor Victoria Wilson. Knopf not only published the story collection as *Self-Help* in 1985, but also brought out her subsequent books: two novels (*Anagrams*, 1986, and *Who Will Run The Frog Hospital?*, 1994) and two other short story collections (*Like Life*, 1990, and the highly acclaimed *Birds of America*, 1998). "All but two or three of the stories in *Self-Help* were rejected by magazines. It was a fluke that I got the book published," says Moore. Her struggle for recognition seems a thing of the past; a decade after the publication of *Self-Help*, most of her stories from *Birds of America* were published in *The New Yorker* before being gathered into a collection. Her work has appeared in *The Best American Short Stories* and *Prize Stories: The O. Henry Awards*.

Moore is currently working on a novel, but writes short stories during the process. "Novels are like boarders . . . you can ignore them for a while and they'll still be there. But stories are like weekend guests who need a lot of attention or else will disappear. I've written what seems like whole books of stories while I was supposed to be working on a novel."

THE SHORT STORY AS NOVEL—MELISSA BANK

What makes Melissa Bank's short story collection worth more than a quarter of a million dollars? In discussing the book and its sale, Bank's agent Molly Friedrich says, "I don't really like short stories. I hate learning a world and being told that it's over in a very short period of time. Melissa is a friend and a former assistant of Aaron's (Aaron Priest, the founder of the eponymous literary agency). I know her very well. She left the office when she got a scholarship to Cornell for a two-year writing program. When she returned, she became an ad copywriter and sold stories to small literary journals. When she had a collection, she came to me." What was the appeal? "The stories were all connected, in that the main character appears in each one, at a different stage of life. In fact, one of the reviews (*Kirkus*) called it a novel, rather than a collection of stories." (See the Insider Report with Molly Friedrich, page 130).

Friedrich submitted the collection, *A Girls' Guide to Hunting and Fishing*, to a carefully chosen group of editors, and almost all of them wanted to buy it. She set up an auction, and the bidding bolted from $30,000 to $130,000 in one jump. Friedrich also had Bank meet the editors, so they would have direct access to her humor and personality. "Not something I would do with just anybody," she says. Viking agreed with Friedrich's assessment, citing the linked stories and central character as important factors; the book reads somewhat like a narrative, though each story stands on its own. Friedrich says, "In Melissa's book, the character is an adolescent in the first story, but her seasoned, ironic, intelligent voice—very likeable—carries through the whole book." It is, in fact, Bank's humor that wins over many readers, drawing parallels to an American-style *Bridget Jones's Diary*, by British author Helen Fielding. (See the Insider Report with author Melissa Bank, page 478).

ONE THING LEADS TO ANOTHER

Linking short stories is a venerable literary form. Marty Arnold noted in his column that Hemingway linked his Nick Adams stories, and author Alex Haley concentrated his early writing efforts on short stories and wrote *Roots* as a series of linked vignettes. Agents will frequently try to persuade their clients to link a group of their stories because they sell more easily. Few agents will touch a single short story since there's considerable foot- and phone-work involved, and little or no money on publication. Writers must sell their own single short stories, and the market continues to be limited to literary periodicals and a few high-end markets. Glossy publications like *The New Yorker*, *Harper's* and *The Atlantic Monthly* take pride in their literary short stories, and pay accordingly—but the competition is fierce. *The New Yorker* receives roughly 500 short stories over the transom in a single week. Bill Buford, literary editor of *The New Yorker*, buys 50 to 60 short stories a year.

EXCEPTION TO THE NEW RULE—NATHAN ENGLANDER

An exception to the linked-stories rule, Nathan Englander's recently published collection of short stories attracted big money and an equal amount of praise. In late 1998, Alfred A. Knopf paid a reported $350,000 for the collection and a novel not yet written, an astonishing sum for an unknown writer's first work. *For the Relief of Unbearable Urges* deciphers and shares the insular world of Jewish Orthodoxy—subject matter that might be construed as far too narrow for a national audience. Knopf is gambling on the universality of its stories, and on Englander's smooth style. Englander grew up in the United States as an Orthodox Jew, though he now lives a secular life in Jerusalem: "I write about a very specific world, but I don't think that should have anything to do with who reads the book." Though most of his stories revolve around Orthodox characters; the subtexts delve into the universal themes of love, frustration and fear.

Two of the stories in the collection appeared in the now-defunct literary magazine *Story*. *Story* editor Lois Rosenthal first met Englander two years ago at the Iowa Writers Workshop. She says, "I think his writing is risky and daring and has humor and is engaging and is political, all rolled into very readable stories." A story by Englander received the Pushcart Prize in 1998, awarded to work published by the best of the small presses.

Writing success didn't come easily to Englander. His Orthodox teachers emphasized Judaic studies, giving short shrift to secular topics. As a result, Englander reached college unable to punctuate a sentence properly; he dismissed the concept of personal creativity entirely. In 1989, he journeyed to Israel to spend a year studying, where he met secular Jews who expressed their spirituality through culture and music; the exposure changed his point of view, though it took several years for him to begin writing fulltime. "This was what I wanted to do. Yet even though it was a great discovery to realize it was an option to live life differently, the feeling of not living the life I was supposed to live as an Orthodox Jew was still prohibitive," he says. Once Englander made the commitment, Alfred A. Knopf handsomely recognized the merit of his work.

GETTING NOTICED

Publication of individual stories is still an excellent way to garner the attention of agents and editors. Englander was not alone in being "discovered" through the medium of one or two published short stories: Aimee Bender was an M.F.A. student at the University of California at Irvine when a book editor spotted one of her short stories in a local literary magazine and signed her. Doubleday published her collection, *The Girl in the Flammable Skirt*, in 1998. Like Bender and Englander, Stacey Richter had published in small literary journals, and her first collection sparked a bidding war among publishers—Scribner won the rights to *My Date with Satan*.

"A writer can make an impact with a collection," Scribner editor Nan Graham was quoted as saying in the Arnold article. "A lot of people write short stories before novels. We are investing in their future, but you have to love the present, and love the collection, which sometimes gets fabulous reviews." Marty Arnold says, "By investing in the future, Graham means the publisher wants the short story writer's novel next." He reports that the print runs for favored collections are generally between 6,000 and 10,000 copies, and the advances range from about $10,000 to $25,000 (which often is not covered by sales of the book). Says Graham, "Sometimes the short stories get great reviews and the writer goes into the novel with those reviews—it makes a hard sell easier."

SHORT-STORY SIGHTEDNESS

Though Molly Friedrich says, "Novels are still the form of choice for agents and editors," major publishing houses—Scribner's, Doubleday and Alfred A. Knopf—are bidding against each other for short story collections, linked and single. Writers fortunate enough to be the target of these auctions stand to make substantial sums, but the message is clear: collections may be an appetizing introduction for an author, but the novel that comes next is the real meat of the meal. But this shouldn't scare those whose talents lie in creating what author Isabel Allende (*The Stories of Eva Luna*) called "little jewels, perfect, complete in themselves." In Cornell's graduate writing program, Lorrie Moore's mentor would take her aside after her fellow students had dissected her innovative stories. "Allison [Lurie] said, 'Just don't pay attention to them.' So I didn't. And I realized that to be an artist you have to be stubborn in this kind of stupid way . . . you write from what's in your heart. You write from what's on your mind." Molly Friedrich agrees, "If you're good enough, you can break every rule."

A LIFE OF THEIR OWN

Individual stories can lead to a book contract, but are also recognized for their own merit. *Best American Short Stories* has been published since 1915, the oldest annual anthology in the country. Marketing sources for Houghton Mifflin say that since 1996, each edition has outsold the previous by a wide margin. Where do they find the stories they feature? Series editor Katrina Kenison reads more than 300 U.S. and Canadian literary magazines—roughly 3,000 stories a year—and submits the top 120 to a guest editor, who changes with each edition. From those stories, 20 are selected to be republished, and the remaining 100 are listed in the back of the book as 'notables.'

"It's a vocation," says Kenison, who has edited the anthology for ten years. "I love to read, and when I receive these beautifully produced literary magazines, I know that each one is the result of a vision and a labor of love." *Ploughshares*, *Granta*, *Iowa Review*, *Chicago Review*, *Bomb Magazine*, *Carolina Review*, *Boulevard*, *Agni* and the *Klackamas Review* are a few of the literary publications she peruses in her search. "I think it's encouraging to authors to know that their work may not end with a single publication in a small magazine."

In fact, it may go much further than that. Houghton Mifflin released *The Best American Short Stories of the Century* in early April, 1999. The initial print run of 100,000 copies was sold out before the end of the month. In that short period of time, the book reached number 18 on the *New York Times* bestseller list.

As author and teacher Allan Gurganus wrote in his introduction to *The Henfield Prize Stories*: "It must be remembered that the short story is, thanks to Poe, Hawthorne, and Irving, credited as a particularly American form." The great American short story is finally being celebrated for its beauty, power, and grace.

Seven Secrets for New Writers

BY PAUL RAYMOND MARTIN

Every writer craves the kiss of the Muse—that moment of glorious epiphany when a plot or character problem is resolved. Even more so, every writer craves the embrace of the Muse—that moment of glorious epiphany when a secret about writing is revealed. Ah, but the Muse reveals her secrets about writing only on one condition: that the secrets be shared.

Paul Raymond Martin

1. *You don't have to write the beginning of a story first.* In fact, stories are seldom written in the order in which they are read. Chris Adrian titled one of his stories with the phrase that inspired it: "Every night for a thousand years," the first six words of a caption for a medical illustration which intrigued him. The story was published in *The New Yorker*, but with an opening altogether different from the phrase used to trigger the writing process:

> He dreamed his brother's death at Fredericksburg. General Burnside appeared as an angel at the foot of his bed to announce the tragedy. "The Army regrets to inform you that your brother George Washington Whitman was shot in the head by a lewd fellow from Charleston."

So start with whatever you have: a character of circumstance, a moment of decision, a place of feeling, a snatch of dialogue. Write forward from that point. Later you can write the scenes that come earlier. The order in which the story should be presented to the reader will become clear as you continue writing. The important thing is to start.

2. *You don't have to know the whole story before you begin.* More often than not, it is in the act of writing that the story emerges. In an interview in *Southwest Review*, William Gass described the process this way: "When I'm writing fiction, it's very intuitive, so that what happens . . . or how it gets organized, is pretty much a process of discovery."

In ten years of writing fulltime, a story has come to me full-blown only once. I hopped off the lawn tractor, skedaddled to my computer and wrote the story from start to finish in one draft. "Killer Frog at the ATM" won first prize for short-short fiction in a contest sponsored by *Scavenger's Newsletter*.

So yes, a story can spring to mind as a whole piece, if only once in a great while. In the meantime, you and I must write without knowing exactly where we're going. As E.L. Doctorow put it, "Writing a novel is like driving at night. You can see ahead only as far as your headlights, but you can make the whole trip that way."

3. *You don't need to outline before you begin.* Please, please don't tell the nuns or Christian Brothers I told you so. Outlining makes it easier to try out new characters or plot twists, of

---

PAUL RAYMOND MARTIN *is the author of* The Writer's Little Instruction Book: 385 Secrets for Writing Well & Getting Published *(Writer's World Press 1998). Known as "a writer's writer," he has published dozens of articles on writing and more than 200 stories, poems and nonfiction pieces. Among the awards he has won for his writing, Martin most treasures the Froggy statuette he was awarded by* Scavenger's Newsletter *for his parody of a horror story, "Killer Frog at the ATM."*

course. And no doubt writing without an outline is not efficient. But don't let the lack of an outline keep you from writing. As Tony Hillerman said, "You don't have to be able to outline a plot if you have a reasonably long life expectancy."

Some writers begin with an outline. Some dive right in and write until the fever abates. Some writers carry stories around in their heads for weeks or months before putting a word on paper or screen. Whatever your approach, however, you *do* need to outline at some point, to check for completeness and consistency.

4. *You don't have to fill in all the details.* Reading is a creative process, too. Let me say that again. Reading is a creative process, too. The reader participates in creating the story. Your job is to include just enough detail to stimulate the reader's imagination.

Think of your story as a coloring book, with characters and scenes at first presented only as line drawings. As the story unfolds, the reader colors each character and scene based on his or her particular knowledge, experience and attitudes. In truth, every story you write will be created anew by each reader.

The details you provide will influence the reader's choice of crayons, of course, especially in genre fiction. Consider this passage from the opening paragraph of P.D. James' *Devices and Desires*:

> She saw with horror that the lights on their high poles shone down on a bleached and silent emptiness and, dashing to the corner, was in time to see the bus already half-way up the hill.

James doesn't mention the red tail lights of the departing bus, but did you color them in anyway? And in the evening's false light, what color did you paint the bus.

When we read, we hold a scene in abeyance, and the writer enables us to gradually color it in. When you write, offer your readers a coloring book and a few well-chosen crayons.

5. *You don't have to know a lot of fancy words or writing techniques.* Writing that calls attention to the writer is *not* good writing. Write simply. No need to sound "writerly." If the reader thinks, "I could have written that," you have written well.

Bobbie Ann Mason, author of *In Country*, says her style "imitates that country speech that I hear in my ear. It's plain speech, matter-of-fact, not romantic language." So next time you sit down with your tablet or keyboard, write as if you were writing a letter to an intelligent but uninformed friend. For therein lies your voice as a writer.

6. *You don't have to make it perfect on the first try.* You don't even have to make it *good* on the first try. Or the second try or the third. As Carole Maso, author of *The American Woman in the Chinese Hat*, puts it, "Books are human documents, which means they should have 'fingerprints' on them, evidence that a mess went into creating them."

Sometimes you have to write your way through the crummy stuff to get to the good stuff. Every writer has experienced this and you will, too. In truth, we all write poorly in order to learn to write well. Good writing always reads as if it were easy to create. For most writers, it takes several re-writes. I usually re-write a story at least half a dozen times, more often a dozen times, sometimes more.

7. *You don't have to live an exciting life or travel to exotic places to be a writer.* In a *Publishers Weekly* interview, Octavia Butler said, "I write about things that interest me, and I'm not the most unique person on earth. So I figure what will interest me will interest other people."

Right now, you are feeling some emotions as keenly as you will ever feel them in your life. Your emotions, your experiences, your understandings of other people and of the world are worth writing about. True, your writing may become more polished as you continue to write, but today's writing is not merely practice for the future. Today's writing is worthwhile in its own right. What you have to say is important and valid.

You must be able to work alone. You must read far and wide. You must believe in yourself and keep trying.

You can peek behind the refrigerator, search the attic, rattle through the junk drawer. You won't find time to write. You must *make* opportunities to write. As novelist J.A. Jance reminds us, "A writer is someone who has written today."

Bonus Secret: *Concentrate not on publishing, but on writing.* If your goal is to be published, you may be frustrated by circumstances you cannot control. If your goal is to write well, you can attain that goal no matter what the circumstances of the marketplace. Take joy in the accomplishment of writing well.

May you receive a kiss and a hug from the Muse—and pass it on.

Editor-in-Chief Jonathan Galassi on the Writer-Editor Relationship

BY ANNE BOWLING

When the pages of Alice McDermott's first novel landed on Jonathan Galassi's desk, he had no way of knowing that in picking up that author for Houghton Mifflin, he was picking up a future National Book Award winner. Nor would it have mattered to him, in all likelihood. In his 27 years in publishing—at Houghton Mifflin, Random House and now as editor-in-chief of Farrar, Straus & Giroux—Galassi has earned a reputation as an editor of refined instincts and discerning eye, to whom industry accolades and commercial success are not as important as publishing books of substance. In the case of McDermott's first submission to Galassi, which became *A Bigamist's Daughter*, Galassi says, "The voice there was very secure, and that was certainly clear in the pages . . . that's an editor's greatest gift, if he can find something that's truly new. That is very, very exciting."

Jonathan Galassi

Photo © Miriam Berkley

Not that the authors Galassi has edited have gone begging for attention, from readers or the publishing community. McDermott's *Charming Billy* won the National Book Award in 1998, narrowly passing Tom Wolfe's *A Man in Full*, also edited by Galassi. And the editor does not restrict his talents to fiction. The National Book Award nonfiction winner, Edward Ball's *Slaves in the Family*, was acquired by Galassi, who also counts Nobel prize winner Seamus Heaney and poet laureate Robert Pinsky among those he has edited. And there's the tale of Scott Turow. Like McDermott, Turow was picked up by Galassi as an untested author, and his bestselling first novel *Presumed Innocent* set sales records in publishing, launching a wave of renewed interest in the legal thriller genre.

"Jonathan bought my first novel on the strength of the first 100 pages," says McDermott (see the Alice McDermott interview on page 25). "And on that strength and a conversation we had about my plans for the rest of the novel, he took the risk. So a sense of trust has been there from the beginning. Jonathan has many wonderful qualities, but probably foremost is he trusts me to know what I'm doing. He does not impose himself or his will on my work, and I trust his opinion as an excellent reader. So when I'm ready to have a reader, I know he's a good person to go to."

Galassi is noted for his instincts and diplomacy as well as his restraint, evidenced in the told and retold story of Galassi's work with Tom Wolfe on *A Man in Full*. Wolfe had reached an impasse in the novel, and over lunch, Galassi suggested Wolfe set the book entirely in Atlanta. The suggestion required that Wolfe, eight years and nearly 1,000 pages into the book, eliminate New York as a setting and dump hundreds of pages of manuscript. Wolfe agreed. But despite Galassi's literary instincts and influence, he declines to be tagged as his generation's Maxwell Perkins, legendary editor of F. Scott Fitzgerald, Thomas Wolfe, Ernest Hemingway, Marjorie

---

ANNE BOWLING *is production editor for* Writer's Market, *contributing editor to* Fiction Writer *magazine, and a frequent contributor to* Writer's Digest Books. *She is also the author of the interview with National Book Award winner Alice McDermott in this edition of* Novel & Short Story Writer's Market.

K. Rowlings and other top writers of the 20th century. In an interview in *Harvard Magazine*, Galassi says: "The Maxwell Perkins myth . . . glorifies the editor, but the real creative figure in a book is the author. The better a book is, the less it needs an editor."

Galassi came to editing in 1973, as an editorial intern at Houghton Mifflin. The publishing industry moved more slowly then, he says, with greater interest in cultivating long-term writer-editor relationships. "There was a sense of loyalty to a house, working for a house for a long time, and building a list of authors," Galassi says. One of the first manuscripts he was given to read was Robert Stone's National Book Award-winning *Dog Soldiers*. Galassi moved to Random House in 1981, which he left for Farrar, Straus & Giroux in 1986, where, *Harvard Magazine* says, "He felt instantly, totally at home."

Galassi has created a second home for himself in poetry, as president of the Academy of American Poets and a published poet and translator. His most recent title, *Eugenio Montale, Collected Poems: 1920-1954* (FSG, 1998), was a 14-year-long labor of love. That 625-page volume of the works of the Italian modernist poet, which *The New Yorker* called "a model of its kind," was a finalist for a PEN/Faulkner Award for poetry translation. Preceding that title were two other volumes of Montale translations, and a volume of Galassi's own poetry, *Morning Run* (Paris Review Editions, 1988). "Poetry is something I know about," says Galassi in a *Chicago Tribune* interview. But will he ever tackle a novel? "I just don't know if I have the time to do a novel. And I don't know if I have the talent."

Here Galassi takes time out to share his views on strong writer-editor relationships, and how industry consolidation is bringing long-term changes to the business of publishing fiction.

Can you credit the current publishing climate with creating a renaissance in fiction writing, in that the much-publicized "death of the midlist author" has opened doors previously closed to new writers?

First of all, I don't think it's true that midlist is dead. You can't just publish bestsellers. You have to publish other books. You do still have to build authors, and even though people try to get around that system, I think that's how it really works. Midlist is still the meat and potatoes of publishing. People seem to think publishers don't want midlist books, but if you look across the board, that's what they are publishing by and large, because that's what they've got. That's what people write and that's what the market really bears.

Do you see more room now in publishing for experimentation with both the novel and short story forms?

I think there's more openness to experimentation across the board. I don't think you're going to see a lot of short stories on the bestseller list, but people are more willing to try unfamiliar things. I think there's more openness to foreign books, and more tolerance for experimentation. For instance, we published Michael Cunningham's *The Hours* late last year, which is quite an experimental book. It won the Pulitzer Prize, and we've now sold over 140,000 copies of that experimental novel, which people have responded to very, very strongly. So I think that the reading public for literary books is quite sophisticated. *The Hours* is not a book that has bestseller written all over it. But it's a very beautiful, original, substantial book that has garnered a huge amount of attention and sold very well.

You've been widely compared to legendary editor Maxwell Perkins for your similarities in style and close working relationships with high-profile authors. Yet you've been quoted as saying the Perkins myth "hangs like a cloud over editing" by elevating the status of the editor to that of the writer. Does that speak to your overall philosophy of the editor's role in the development of a writer?

In the case of Perkins, there were some writers, especially Thomas Wolfe, who needed a special kind of editing, which amounted to carving books out of manuscripts. This is very seldom what really goes on in editing, and I think it's true that a kind of mythology of the editor grew out of that relationship which is grandiose. I don't think most editors do anything like that, and most books don't call for that kind of thing.

I think a more realistic vision of what an editor does is that an editor is like a shrink—he or she listens to the book, listens to what the author is trying to do, and in the end gets the author to see what needs to happen. A really good shrink doesn't fix you, you fix yourself through the shrink, and I think that's what an editor should be doing.

You've edited Alice McDermott's novels from her first, *A Bigamist's Daughter*, through her most recent National Book Award winner *Charming Billy*. From an editor's perspective, what's it like to find a really promising manuscript from a previously unpublished author? And what does an editor look for?

There's something about the excitement of starting out together—starting out with an author on her first work—that is among the most exciting things an editor can do. I think what it takes, especially, is open-mindedness, an ability to hear something that hasn't been heard before, to spot something fresh.

With Alice McDermott, I had not a whole manuscript, but pages, which is not always how it happens. But the voice there was very secure, and fresh, and assured, and so we decided to publish the novel. Her voice was there, from the beginning. She's often quoted saying that a teacher once told her, 'I've got bad news for you—you're a writer.' And you could just tell. It was clear from the get-go that she had a voice, and that was certainly there in the pages—her sardonic humor, and crispness, and tone.

What is it about your relationship with authors such as McDermott, Scott Turow and Tom Wolfe that keeps them with you?

On my side, what keeps me with them is my admiration for their gifts, for their talent, their incredible devotion to what they're doing, and their seriousness about it. Writing is such a lonely, hard occupation. It's all about delayed gratification, and you have to have a special sense of mission. You have to have confidence in yourself. I think the greatest thing that writers have is the grit to keep writing. That's true of great writers, middling writers and not-so-great writers. For many writers it didn't just happen right away. They worked their way into their talent. In many cases, the difference between success and the lack of it is belief in yourself. I think that's true in life in general. If you can somehow convince yourself that you're going to be a writer, sometimes you can. Not always. But all these people who became great writers started out with one thing: desire. They also ended up having talent. You have to have both to make it. But the grit to keep writing is something I really respect greatly.

What does a writer need to be prepared to bring into a successful writer-editor relationship?

A writer should be prepared to be open-minded, to listen with as little prejudice as possible to what the editor has to say about the work, and be willing to consider the opinions of the editor. That doesn't mean you should blindly follow what the editor suggests, because editors are fallible people. But I think the best relationships between editor and author are where the editor feels free to be as honest as possible, and where the author then knows that he or she has the freedom to respond as openly as possible. In other words, when there is as little diffidence between them as possible.

I think the editor has to be prepared to bring the same things, to be open to what the author is really doing, to try to respond to that as fully as possible, and not try to twist the author's book to suit some idea that he or she has. They're both ideally working toward the same thing, which is getting this book in the best possible shape it can be for the public.

How has the spate of mergers, acquisitions and consolidations among publishing houses in the last five years affected the writer-editor relationship? Do you believe that has had a negative impact?

In a way, that would be like complaining about TV. We have to deal with reality. And I think what people really want to hear about is not what's wrong with the situation, but what to do about it. When I was trained at Houghton Mifflin in the '70s, an editor's career was somewhat less entrepreneurial than it is today. There's more a sense now of editors as quasi-independent operatives who are trying to strike gold fast, and I think there's more movement among authors and editors. The real stable element in an author's career is an agent rather than the publisher. I think that that's not the ideal situation.

Ideally, an author, agent and editor should settle down for a long winter's nap together. That's the ideal situation for building a career. Because the trouble with a fast shot is if it doesn't work, you've got a problem. You hear a lot about big deals for first novels, and the problem is, what if it doesn't work? Where is the author with the publisher the next time around? They lose the continuity, the history, the building. Let's face it, very few writers now can count on a career where that building happens. I think that's what's needed, but I think that's very hard to come by today.

At the Jerusalem International Book Fair last year, where you were a moderator, the keynote speaker addressed this question: How can young people who enter publishing with idealism be progressive forces in a world in which serving the marketplace has become the standard for a new 'excellence' in a world in which the owners mostly no longer care what is published? What's your take on that?

You have to start out with the right kind of philosophy in the publishing house. A publishing house is only as good as the fostering it does of the relationship with authors. So if a publisher doesn't care what's published, you're in trouble. But I don't think that's true, by and large. I think most major publishers are interested in quality, because quality is the only thing that sells in the long run.

But then, I do think that editors have to be good ambassadors for authors in the publishing house; they have to explain to the rest of the team why these books are important, why they are good. If they're good, they will sell. They may not sell a million, but good books have a market. It's part of their definition. So I think there's plenty of room for idealism in publishing today. There's also room for people to pursue their interests and their passions within the context of the marketplace, because in a shrinking market quality is more important than ever.

How do you view the long-term effects of mergers, acquisitions and restructurings on the publishing industry?

There has been more change in the time I've been in publishing than there was in the past 200 years in the way business is done, and the rate of change seems to be exponential. I think consolidation is something that causes a lot of concern, because if you're an agent and you're trying to place a book, the number of options you have is being limited by the consolidations. Even if you still have a lot of editors in different units of a big company, still the number of clear shots you have at different houses is smaller. Agents and authors are losing options, freedom, alternatives. The consolidation has gone very, very far.

Has it worked to homogenize the industry?

I would say that the companies that result from the homogenization tend to be more like one another than they would have been had they remained independent. I think that's undeniable. There's a theory in war that you end up becoming like your enemy so you can fight your enemy better, and I think some of that applies in this situation.

What are your predictions for changes in publishing in the early part of the 21st century?

I think change is the way we live today—we live in a technological society where change is a constant, so there definitely will be a huge amount of continued change in publishing in our lifetime. I think many of these changes are positive: books will be available in many different formats, they will be instantly available, there will be no out-of-print books. We're living in an information bath now—we drown in information—and books are part of that. And I think books will continue to have a very important role in our culture, because there is no substitute. Film and visual media cannot convey the complex information that books can. So we're not in danger of losing books.

The way books are sold, and the way they're published, that's bound to change. It's changing as we speak. Publishers will change, because they're really going to be brands for books more than anything else. That's already true today. If you go online, you can see how many people are self-publishing books, so the publishers are going to be the filters, the guardians of quality. But as far as what that all mean for writers—it's hard to know. I guess the real question is how is the world going to know about the individual writers—how are the writers going to stand out in this? That's what publishers are going to be there for, to discriminate.

Alice McDermott: Courting the "Difficult Muse" of Fiction

BY ANNE BOWLING

Alice McDermott

Photo © Jane E. Levine

In the nine months since Alice McDermott's Charming Billy *won the 1998 National Book Award, life has changed somewhat for the Maryland-based writer. "I've acquired a new job—I'm my own appointment secretary," McDermott says with her characteristic dry humor. Touring for the paperback edition of her book, and attending to a crowded schedule of speaking engagements, writers' conferences and lectures has prompted other changes, as well: "I've returned to my early days of being a fiction writer, writing late at night. I'm back to trying to eke out some time to write."*

McDermott's first shot at publication was a 100-page portion of the novel which would become A Bigamist's Daughter *(Random House). That submission ended up on the desk of editor Jonathan Galassi, then at Houghton Mifflin, who was impressed by the strength of her voice in the pages, which he called "secure, fresh and crisp." (See the interview with Jonathan Galassi, editor-in-chief of Farrar, Straus & Giroux, page 20). When Galassi moved to Random House after acquiring that book, McDermott followed him, beginning a relationship that would last through Galassi's next move to Farrar, Straus & Giroux and four novels. "I knew fairly early on to stay with a good thing, and so it just seemed right," McDermott says of that relationship.*

To readers looking forward to her fifth novel, McDermott offers nothing definitive. When her schedule permits, she is at work on two novels, "and I'm not sure which one I'm going to complete first," she says. "I'm still figuring out both of them, so there's nothing I can say reliably."

This interview, which first appeared in Fiction Writer *(April, 1999), was conducted a week after McDermott's* Charming Billy *won the National Book Award. Although her Bethesda home had been temporarily transformed into a media hub, she shared a morning talking with us about her development as a writer, and how her fiction succeeds.*

Had Alice McDermott had a say in the matter, she probably would not have become a fiction writer. The work is too hard, she says, and the rewards too few for writing to be anything other than a last resort among career options. So difficult does McDermott find the muse of fiction that she counsels her writing students at Johns Hopkins University: "If you can do anything else with your life and be content with it, you should do it."

"For those of us who are going to spend our lives in this way, it has to be the only thing you can do," says McDermott, a two-time Pulitzer Prize finalist and winner of the 1998 National Book Award. "I talked about going to law school, I tried working in publishing, I resisted and

---

ANNE BOWLING *is production editor for* Writer's Market, *contributing editor for* Fiction Writer *magazine, and a frequent contributor to* Writer's Digest Books. *She is also the author of the interview with Jonathan Galassi, editor-in-chief of Farrar, Straus & Giroux, in this edition of* Novel & Short Story Writer's Market.

resisted, but I knew that nothing was sufficiently satisfying except writing."

While the writing may be personally punishing, the labor doesn't show in prose critics have called "lyric" and "bewitching." Critical acclaim followed McDermott through publication of her first three novels: *A Bigamist's Daughter* (Random House, 1982), *That Night* (Farrar, Straus & Giroux, 1987) and *At Weddings and Wakes* (FSG, 1991). *That Night* was a finalist for both the Pulitzer Prize and the National Book Award, and the PEN/Faulkner and Los Angeles Times book awards as well. *At Weddings and Wakes*, which *The Wall Street Journal*'s Bruce Bawer called "exquisitely written, impeccably constructed," was also a Pulitzer finalist.

By the time her most recent novel, *Charming Billy* (FSG, 1998) was published, there were not enough superlatives to go around. That unassuming, 280-page novel slipped past Tom Wolfe's much-ballyhooed tome *A Man in Full* to scoop up the 1998 National Book Award, and perhaps no one was as surprised as McDermott. "I was joking with my editor that a second nomination wasn't the time to win," she says, "that you had to sort of accrue a few more nominations and suffer through it a few more times before you get to win."

Begun immediately after the title character's funeral, *Charming Billy* reaches backward to explore three generations of Irish Americans in Queens, from the Second World War to the present—the lives Billy Lynch and his legendary drinking had touched and transformed. "Billy had drunk himself to death," the narrator recalls. "He had at some point ripped apart, ploughed through, as alcoholics tend to do, the great, deep, tightly woven fabric of affection that was some part of the emotional life, the life of love, of everyone in the room."

Interested less in the actual events of Billy's life than in her character's perceptions of them, McDermott takes a circuitous route guided by memory to tell her story. The result is what Rand Richards Cooper in *Commonweal* called "incorrigibly digressive, brash with time, intricately layered and crammed full of life." McDermott's unchronological approach—employed in *At Weddings and Wakes* and *That Night*, as well—can be initially disorienting. Readers find themselves moving from room to room in her characters' memories, a little unsure of whom they're meeting and where they are in time, but as the layers accumulate the story becomes clear, and begins to deepen and resonate.

"McDermott keeps surprising you with a voice you haven't heard before, yet the reader experiences instant recognition," wrote Donn Fry in *The Seattle Times* of *That Night*. "As if it were a pearl seed, McDermott adds layer upon layer of memory, finally creating a jewel of shimmering luster."

Nice praise for a modest, self-deprecating woman from Long Island who was quoted two short novels ago as saying the hardest thing about writing was believing people would want to read her stories. Four novels into a promising career, have her doubts subsided?

"I don't think you ever overcome the doubts," McDermott says. "But I don't think you can be ambivalent about writing. It's a blessing and a curse. It's a blessing to know it, and a curse to live it, but you can't do anything else and feel right with yourself and the world."

When you first started serious fiction writing, which elements were effortless and which did you find took the most attention?

I don't think any of it ever felt effortless. I still don't. I think when I first began to write for someone to read, when I got to college and was writing something that I knew was going to have an audience, I was initially very startled to see that I had done something that elicited a reaction. Because it was all so hard for me. I think by that stage, part of the reason I did not think about writing as a career was because I thought it was supposed to come easily if it was going to be a career. And it never felt like it came easily to me. The act of writing did, I had no problems with sitting down with pen and paper, that was sort of the way I worked things out from an early age. But to write for an audience and to try to say something to that audience seemed to me to be tremendously difficult. That difficulty at first was an indication to me that this sure isn't something you can spend your life doing. It's just too hard.

I think a lot of readers and a lot of new writers have that feeling—you read something wonderful and you think "it's so easy to read, and it seems so perfect, that it must have just come out that way." Then I worked with Dr. Paul Briand who was a writing teacher at Oswego (campus of the State University of New York) in a one-on-one tutorial. He quite literally taught me how hard it is. I would bring in drafts of essays and stories I was writing, and he would go word by word, sentence by sentence, through everything I had written. He would ask "is that the best word, is that really what you wanted to say? Why did you say red instead of yellow? What does red mean? Shouldn't it be yellow? Why didn't you decide on yellow? Think about it every step of the way—does this sentence really follow that sentence, or does it only repeat it? Do you really need it? Does this paragraph seemed tied to the paragraph before it?" He taught me the nuts and bolts and the hard, hard work of slugging it out in prose. Once I accepted that, I could accept the idea that maybe I could have a career doing it.

How would you describe your evolution as a novelist from *A Bigamist's Daughter* to *Charming Billy*? Are you a different writer now?

Every novel is different, just like every short story is different. You're really a novice each time you begin, because it's a new story and you have to find a new way to tell it and it makes its own demands. And you hope you've never told it before. So I don't feel personally that I'm accumulating anything here. I'm really sort of stumbling from one novel to another and learning all over again with each novel.

When I started *A Bigamist's Daughter*, I had only written short stories. And I had the impression that writing short stories was exercise for writing a novel, that with each short story you learned a little bit more so that you were coming closer to being able to write a novel. I very quickly learned when I began trying to write a novel that short stories hadn't taught me anything because it's entirely different. Pacing is different, character development is different, structure is different, it's just a different thing, and you don't really gain any benefits from what you've learned in another form.

So I approached my first novel as "I'm going to learn how to write a novel, whether I publish it or not is another thing." And that was my main intention, simply to learn how to write a novel—how do you pace it, how do you structure it, and so on. And when it was finished and published, I thought the second one was going to be that much easier because hey, I learned how to write a novel. But I quickly learned that that was that novel and this is this one, and in a way you have to kind of let go of any hope of acquiring expertise. You acquire your expertise all over again with each new work.

On the other hand, with each novel I've had more life experience. I've gotten older, and the demands that I make of myself and my writing probably have increased with each novel, so maybe that's the thing that accumulates or changes. But as far as the craft goes, it's a new game every time, and you're just kidding yourself if you think it's otherwise.

While you were learning your craft, were there writers whose work inspired and influenced you?

I don't understand how anyone becomes a writer who isn't first an avid reader. You read and you see what writing does, and you want to try your hand at it. So writers got me into this in the first place. Novels got me into this. Everything you read and admire I think in some way influences you. But then there are writers who I recognized early on as craftspeople, and those are the writers I go back and look at again and again. I would say first among those is Vladimir Nabokov. I will go back just to admire the craft, and sometimes too, on dark days, to remember why you're doing this in the first place. Because I do think that's where it begins—that admiration for someone who writes well and whose work has touched you remains a driving force.

Many critics use the adjective 'prismatic' to describe the overall effect of your prose. Do you think they draw this description from the breadth of your sentence structure, or from your lack of chronology in plot?

I think the two are definitely related, sure. One of the things that interests me in fiction is to be able to see ordinary things, ordinary moments, in a variety of ways. Clearly that would give my writing the sense of being prismatic, to look at it again and again. I think one of the things that fiction writers can do for us is open our eyes, they can do the work that we don't always in the crux of life have time to do, and that is to look carefully, to really see. Fiction writers can help us see in ways we'd be crazy if we even tried to on our own.

There's a kind of meditation that goes on in the making of a worthy piece of fiction, and I think fiction writers hand us the fruits of that meditation—to look at the world we all see every day and we all encounter, but to see it in new ways, or to see it again, in a way that we've forgotten how to look at it. I think that's a great gift that fiction writers give us. And having been given that gift myself, obviously, it's something that I try to give to my readers as well. It's a new way to see, to open up life a little bit, and glimpse it in a different way. So I think the sense of a prism is really a way of seeing, and the language reflects that. And I do have a tendency—it's one I often have to struggle with—of trying to say everything at once, and simple sentences don't quite have it, so I tend to pile up the clauses.

You've said that you're interested in structure as a novelist, and that straight, realistic narrative leaves something out for you. "I like the puzzle of it," you've been quoted as saying. What does that mean about the actual process of constructing a novel for you? And what does the lack of chronology add to the final piece?

I love chronological narrative when I read it, I just find in composing my own work that it doesn't satisfy my need. I find it more challenging to play with time. But I think a lot of my work is about memory and storytelling, and it's much more about what characters have to say about what has happened to them and the people around them, rather than the things that have happened themselves. It seems to me that memory is seldom chronological, and even anecdote as we talk about ourselves is very seldom chronological. One event recalls another, and we look back through time at something and see it differently because of intervening events. So I think if I'm writing to give a sense of the importance and validity of not just what has happened to us but what we say about it and how we felt about it, then it seems to me chronology immediately goes out the window. When we tell our own stories we tell them in a variety of ways and very seldom go from A to B to C. So I think it reflects more thematic things I'm trying to do, but it also gives me kind of the puzzle of the structure. If I'm not telling a story Sunday, Monday, Tuesday, Wednesday, then how do I tell it? And how can it work? How can I make Sunday flow into Friday, and then back again into Tuesday, in a pleasing way? That's a challenge, but it's fun on another level. It's intriguing to me.

Then how do you end up, for example, starting with Billy's death and working backward in time? From a technical standpoint, do you start chronologically and then shuffle your events and characters like cards?

No. I couldn't do it that self-consciously. I suppose I kind of circle around a story for awhile, myself. With *Charming Billy* in particular, I knew that Billy alone was not the story. It was really the story of the people who surrounded him and made his life possible, so I wanted to hear from them first. Right away chronology goes out the window, because I don't want to hear about the first thing first. I want to hear about the people who know Billy's life in total and what they say about it. So having the characters around him begin speaking after he is gone freed them to say what they wanted to say about him. What I needed to hear about this character so I begin to understand him I had to get from the people around him. And the best way to do that, I knew, was to sit them down, pour drinks and make sure Billy wasn't in the room. Well if there were drinks around, Billy was going to be in the room, unless he was dead. So there you go.

How do your characters form for you?

It's different every time. With Billy, I was conscious of him as a stock character, and a character I had not dealt with in *At Weddings and Wakes*, despite all the stock characters that peopled that book, and he was appealing to me. I found him interesting and I couldn't let him pass. That hasn't happened that way with other books.

At Weddings and Wakes I approached more on a thematic level. I was interested in what goes on between and among generations in a given family, not so much in what gets passed on but what gets lost, what isn't conveyed from one generation to the next. And I just had to cast about for quite awhile to find a story and characters who could help to convey that. I really knew very little about the characters in *At Weddings and Wakes* when I began to write it. I didn't have a central character as I had with Billy. It was really a "create the world first and see who the characters are who live it in." So literally when in the first chapter I took the three children and their mother to their grandmother's apartment in Brooklyn, I didn't know who was going to answer the door until I wrote it. I found myself describing a woman opening the door, and as the children file past her she bends from the waist like a nun. It was really just a way to picture her, but as soon as I wrote that her whole character opened up for me. And I thought "oh, she did that like a nun because she was a nun, and she's not a nun anymore. I don't know why—I'll have to write some more and find out." So that was very much organic. It developed through the writing and I didn't bring a lot of ready-made decisions to the book. The writing helped me to discover them.

So this relates back to your earlier point that each novel is different. Each also comes from a different place—some are thematic approaches, others are character-driven.

Sure. And with *That Night*, it was voice. That's all. That's really all I had when I started that. I knew I wanted to write about someone looking back trying to define across time, a certain time and place. And that's all I had—I knew I had a voice. I had a first person narrator telling a story.

I read that your inspiration for the Brooklyn apartment setting in *At Weddings and Wakes* came from a poster for Maurice Sendak's *In the Night Kitchen* in your son's bedroom, and it strikes me that you're a very atmospheric writer. Yet while your settings are very evocative, they're equally light-handed. As a character from *Charming Billy* says, "enough is as good as a feast." Is there a technique behind that? Is that something you can teach a writer to do?

I see this with my own students. Often young writers don't recognize what they've already accomplished in their work. It's not excess, it's just that they tend in their enthusiasm and determination to say what they have to say to miss that they've already said it and keep going. So I don't know if it's so much a technique you can teach, but certainly it's something that young writers need to look at in their work—to see when they've succeeded, be able to recognize when they've succeeded. Maybe the lesson is "give your reader more credit. The reader has caught on by this sentence. We don't need the next two paragraphs. You've made your point and it's there and it's beautifully done. Don't dilute it with repetition." It's a very difficult thing to learn to do, to trust yourself and your reader, to trust the images. If they evoke something for you as you write them, then trust that they're going to evoke something for the reader as well.

Are there novels in your mind that haven't come to fruition? False starts you've abandoned or put away temporarily?

I have some things I've started and lost interest in or abandoned for whatever good reason. I think that's all a part of the process. Even if something doesn't pan out, if you've been working on something and it's not working or you lose interest in it or your energy flags or whatever, I feel you've gained something. I never feel a book I began and didn't pursue is in some way a failure. I think the more you write the more ideas you have for stories and novels. I'm not the kind of writer who can think up great story lines outside of writing. The writing itself generates stories for me, and that's all part of the process. The things that begin and don't continue continue in another form elsewhere. You still have discovered some things. You still have looked at some things in the careful way you have to look at them as a story is developing and you use it elsewhere, whether you're aware of it or not.

Most of us would like to believe you can do a lot of writing when you're not actually writing— you know, "I'm not writing but I'm thinking about writing"—as if that does anybody any good at all. And it doesn't. It's totally meaningless, and we just tell ourselves that to make ourselves feel a little less guilty for the time we spend away from our desks. But really the only thing that counts is when you start to put the words on the page, and then everything counts, whether it turns out to appear in print or not. When you're writing, I do believe everything ultimately counts, and all the stuff you do outside of writing doesn't.

Is there any advice you could share with fiction writers developing their craft?

One thing I think is really important, and that is reading and understanding at least on a very basic level what it is you're trying to do. If you read and recognize work that pleases you immensely, I don't think it's a bad idea to formulate some idea of what it is that pleases you, so you know what you're after. I think young writers are very hesitant to set goals for themselves, to come out and say "I want to do this, I want to leave behind a thing of beauty." You know, why are you doing this? What are you really after? I think it's not a bad idea to recognize that and to raise the stakes for yourself, and not just say "well, I'd like to see if I can write." I think the way to do that is to read and reread the fiction that moves you, and to understand what's happening there and to aspire to the same thing.

Russell Banks: Voice Arises From What's Heard

BY PAULA DEIMLING

. . . We all at times have buzzing in our heads a whole range of voices, some of them heard early on and retained, some of them taken from the ether, the broadcast ether. I mean it literally. I can hear John F. Kennedy's voice in a second. I can hear my father's voice; I can hear the voices of people I have met only once on the street. So I think the voices are buzzing around in an aural memory bank, and you can tap into them the way you can tap into forgotten visual memories. . . .

Russell Banks
The Paris Review
Summer 1998 Edition

Russell Banks

Photo by Arturo Patten

"We know voice when we hear it and see it, but it's elusive and difficult to define, or describe," says novelist Russell Banks, speaking to an attentive audience at a library in Cincinnati, Ohio. "Where does voice originate?"

He reads a passage from Eudora Welty's *One Writer's Beginnings*: "Ever since I was first read to, then started reading to myself, there has never been a line read that I didn't hear. As my eyes followed the sentence, a voice was saying it silently to me. It isn't my mother's voice, or the voice of any person I can identify, certainly not my own. It is human, but inward, and it is inwardly that I listen to it. It is to me the voice of the story or the poem itself."

"Reader. Voice," Banks says, his hands in the air about a foot apart, palms facing the audience of 200. "I hear my own words. I have always trusted this voice."

Banks' speaking voice is precise, passionate, caring. And yet the voice that draws people to his lectures, and book signings, is best heard in Banks' nine novels and four collections of short stories. "Voice in a work of fiction arises from what the author hears, not from what the author says. It's in the ears, not the mouth," he points out. "Until a writer can hear his or her characters and narrators speak—and even third-person objective narrators have speaking voices—the writer will remain voiceless, in the same way that a ventriloquist speaking through a dummy is voiceless. And the characters, too, will be voiceless, just as the dummy is."

THE ACT OF WRITING

Ninety-nine percent of a writer's time is spent alone in a room writing and listening, not lecturing or promoting books, Banks says. The occasional book tour reaffirms for him how "readers take stories into their lives in a personal intimate way," but he's not able to write when

---

PAULA DEIMLING *is a full-time writer, and former editor of* Writer's Market. *She is one of the authors of* The Writer's Essential Desk Reference *(Writer's Digest Books). Past interviews have included Jane Smiley, Isaac Asimov, Peter Davidson, Molly Peacock and William Zinnser.*

on the road promoting his books and, recently, the movies based on his books. There are just too many interruptions, he says.

Banks writes best in his studio, a remodeled sugar shack, a short walk downhill from his home in upstate New York's Adirondack Mountains. Mornings—four to five hours—are set aside for writing. Sometimes he writes longhand and then types the work into a computer; other times he writes at the computer. In ten years, he has produced four serious and ambitious novels, a feat that many writers would envy.

As a literary novelist, Banks never expected to earn a living or support a family from his writing. He never expected to become as commercially successful as he has, and for many years, balanced writing and teaching. In 1998, after 16 years, he was able to leave Princeton University's creative writing program to write full-time. The turning point in his career was *Continental Drift* (HarperCollins, 1985), a novel with dual points of view that confronts issues of immigration and affluence at a time when there was widespread anxiety about these issues. Banks was 45 then; his 6 published books hadn't sold more than 10,000 to 12,000 copies each in hardcover. "One of the things that mattered in gaining a wider audience was that it was set in a world that mattered to people," says Banks now, looking back. The hardcover print run of his most recent novel, *Cloudsplitter* (HarperCollins, 1998), was 100,000.

About seven years ago, Banks decided to write a historical novel. "Old Brown," or abolitionist John Brown, kept turning up in his reading. Coincidentally, Banks's writing studio is about 12 miles from where Brown lived, farmed and was buried. Brown's life raised questions for Banks, and as the years passed, these questions continued to pique his interest. Was John Brown a visionary or a fanatic? Where does an obsession with a cause become fanaticism?

Banks needed to decide whose point of view to use in the novel. With an omniscient point of view, the voice of history would have come from the present rather than the past, he says. "I'll do anything to avoid taking on that [omniscient] mantle." As fortune would have it, in Columbia University's Rare Book Room in seven dusty boxes, Banks found transcripts of interviews done for the book *John Brown: A Biography Fifty Years After*. These early-1900s documents included statements given by Brown's surviving children, and the details they provided. Pure narration. Banks says he heard a distinct mid-19th century middle-class voice and thus found his narrator, his voice and point of view for *Cloudsplitter*. "I would become Owen Brown's voice piece."

In order to capture the voice of Owen for his novel, Banks imagined himself as the transcriptionist listening to the long, extended letters that Brown's aged son, Owen, wrote for the transcriptionist. "I try to avoid feeling as if I'm speaking through the character," Banks says. "I want to be sure I'm listening to that character. That's the gateway for voice in fiction."

FINDING CHARACTERS, PROJECTS

Banks doesn't deliberately set out to look for subjects for a next book. "Sometimes the door opens because of a character that I've imagined or seen or taken off from; sometimes a newspaper clipping." He is now working on a contemporary novel set in West Africa. "I'm following my own curiosity and anxieties and concerns and obsessions, I suppose, without regard to however widely they may be shared. If it turns out they are widely shared, well and good, and if it turns out they're not, I can live with that. But I have to be faithful to myself and my own intuitions."

After completing *Cloudsplitter*, he took a year off "to let the well refill." It was the first time in his career he felt he needed a break. But during that time, he wrote essays, screenplays based on his novels *Continental Drift* and *Rule of the Bone*, and a libretto for an opera. Through these, he says, "You learn disciplines and forms of attention that you will apply to writing fiction in the future."

Banks's ambition as a novelist is to help readers see themselves, human beings and the world a little differently, and more clearly. That's the case when he's writing short stories, too. "My world is made a little larger by it, by having written it. I know that's what happens when, for instance, I read a Grace Paley story or a Raymond Carver story," Banks says. "And therefore it's what I want to happen when I write a Russell Banks story."

Over the years, he has written hundreds of short stories. In May 2000, HarperCollins will publish a volume of 24 stories from Banks' previous collections, and nine "new" previously uncollected stories. For each story that has been published in a magazine, "there must have been several that were not," he says. "Especially back when I was starting out, I often wrote a story, or started a story, just to see how it worked, or didn't work. One of the things you learn as you grow older is not how to be a better writer but how to recognize a dead end without having to go there first. Consequently, I don't abandon nearly as many stories now as I used to. I don't have to."

Aspects of the short story form that can stymie an aspiring writer's work are different for every writer, Banks has observed. And he says this with the wisdom of having taught not only at Princeton, but at Sarah Lawrence College, Columbia University and New York University. "Usually, though, one stumbles over, or overlooks, whichever aspect of the story most reflects one's anxious relation to the material at hand. Almost all problems in writing arise from the problems that exist in the writer's relation to the thing written about. Style is character, after all. And character arises from our relation to the larger world. We pick a piece of it to write about, and if our relation to that piece is troubled, it will show up in structure, syntax, tone, plot, whatever. You don't 'fix' a story by straightening out the structure, syntax, tone, etc.; you fix it by attending to your relation to the thing written about."

BANKS ON STRUCTURE

The ending of a novel is something that most novelists know when they begin the novel, says Banks. And it's important to get a first draft written before attempting to revise it in order to determine how certain parts will fit in. With a novel like *Cloudsplitter*—revolving around the 1859 raid on Harpers Ferry—the outcome of the incident was already known. How did that affect the writing of this novel?

"You know whether it's going to end in a fire or a wedding; what you don't know is the *meaning* of that event and you write the novel to try to understand what the meaning of that event—that wedding or that fire—really is," he says, citing E.M. Forster's *Aspects of the Novel*. This gives the reader two kinds of suspense: what's going to happen and the meaning of what's going to happen. "That second kind of suspense matters most to the serious writer and the serious reader. Serious literary fiction worries about the second kind of suspense—the meaning of the ending."

Structurally, the short story and novel forms each bear greatly different relations to time, Banks told *Paris Review* interviewer Robert Faggen. "The novel, I think, has a mimetic—or imitative—relation to time. The novel simulates the flow of time, so once you get very far into a novel, you forget where you began—just as you do in real time. Whereas with a short story the point is not to forget the beginning. The ending only makes sense if you can remember the beginning. I think the proper length for a short story is to go as far as you can without going so far that you have forgotten the beginning."

Banks thinks of fiction as "a controlled hallucination. That kind of hallucination is something I'm conscious of trying to induce." Examine your own reading process, he points out. You forget about the unbalanced checkbook and the hissing of the radiator. "Dialogue is an oral hallucination. Exposition and description create visual hallucinations."

How does Banks balance simplicity and complexity within a paragraph and a story? "I'm not sure I'm trying to do that, balance simplicity and complexity. It just comes out that way. I do know that I'm trying above all to be as clear and direct as possible at all times, and naturally, because of the complex nature of our experience, one's sentences will often be quite complex. But if at the same time one is trying to be clear and direct, even a complex, and very long, sentence will feel simple," he says. "Just as a very short sentence, if written by a person who is trying to be obscure and indirect, can seem very complex. Witness all the lesser members of the so-called minimalist school offiction in the late '80s."

Through the comments of readers—both at readings and through letters—Banks has come to know some work in a way he couldn't have imagined. Sometimes the reader and critic can know a writer's work better than an author can—the critic knows how the work applies to the whole of literature, the reader knows how the book or story applies to his or her own life. "Sarah Cole: A Type of Love Story" is one example. The story grew from Banks' casual observation of a homely woman approached in a bar by an attractive man—a reverse of the Frog Prince theme. *The Atlantic Monthly, Esquire* and *The New Yorker* had turned down the story; it was sitting, unpublished, in Banks' desk drawer when *The Missouri Review* asked Banks for a story. After *The Missouri Review* published "Sarah Cole," Banks began hearing from female readers touched by it. And since publication, the story has been taught in high school and college classes, and translated into 10 or 12 languages. Banks was surprised, and quite pleased. "I didn't know what the story was about, necessarily; I didn't know its depths," says Banks, who usually writes about—and is known for—male characters. The story eventually was included in the 1985 *The Best American Short Stories* and *The Pushcart Prize: Anthology,*1985, and won an O. Henry Award and a Best of the Stories of the 1980s Award.

BANKS'S JOURNEY AS A WRITER

Banks's early life—and journey as a writer—unfolded far from an Ivy League world. In high school, Banks wanted to be an artist/painter. He dropped out of Colgate University after the first nine weeks, then hitchhiked across the country. "I was living a kind of beatnik life," he admits— but by age 22 he was reading obsessively and had decided to write a novel.

A native New Englander, Banks was working as a plumber when he attended the Bread Loaf Writers' Conference, and eventually found his way to the University of North Carolina, where he earned a degree. (Banks's protagonist in a July 1999 story in *Esquire* is a construction "super." As with many of his characters, Banks has not forgotten his working-class roots.) Banks quotes author Toni Morrison's advice to her students: "The first job of a writer is to get a job," and he did so. Banks's apprenticeship as a writer extended into his early thirties. An apprenticeship, he acknowledges, needs three components: a mentor (his was Nelson Algren), a group of peers, and a means of income. As an aspiring writer, Banks was drawn to writers who had an articulated sense of structure and form, like Ernest Hemingway and James Joyce. As the years passed, Banks realized he had certain needs to meet in character and recognition of character, then the naturalist writers, like Theodore Dreiser and Sherwood Anderson, came to be of more importance. Later, the influence was on quality of voice. "You have to keep moving and shifting and changing. Otherwise you get stuck and are just repeating yourself so your influences have to change . . . You keep discovering new openings and ways to think about your work."

Some time ago, while visiting Paris, Banks had dinner with retired HarperCollins editor Ted Solotaroff. Solotaroff had just completed a memoir, and in conversation was looking back on his days as a book editor. Solotaroff told Banks: "If I had tried to write this memoir when I was a young man, I would have been a much better editor."

"Isn't that nice to know—and to hear?" Banks says, genuinely pleased as he looks back on that moment. "It's so damn hard to write a good book," Banks said, quoting Solotaroff. "As an editor, you forget that sometimes, how hard it is to write a good book."

At times in Banks's career, there have been editors who preferred that he write more in the vein of his previous book, but HarperCollins has continued to publish his books, and Banks has remained true to his own writerly intuition. "Your career is something you can have no control over; your work is the one thing only you do have control over," says Banks. Sometimes writers reverse these concepts, thinking they have no control over their work. "As an artist, you cannot give up control of your work to an industry. You lose all authority then." If that happens, your voice, and your characters' voices, won't be heard.

Pinckney Benedict: Transforming Fiction for Film

BY BRAD VICE

"Beware of the wise who are young and gifted," wrote novelist Russell Banks. "They quickly become irreplaceable." The particular wise man Banks had in mind when he penned this phrase was then 23-year-old West Virginian and recent Princeton graduate Pinckney Benedict. Benedict's first collection of short stories, *Town Smokes*, had just been published to rave reviews, and many like Banks thought of him as nothing less than a short fiction prodigy. Now, over 10 years later, Pinckney Benedict has proven Banks nothing less than a prophet.

Pinckney Benedict

By struggling to diversify his skills as a story writer, Benedict has managed to make a major contribution to almost every prose publishing niche worth inhabiting. To date Benedict has published another book of short stories called *The Wrecking Yard*, a novel, *Dogs of God*, and countless interviews, book reviews, and non-fiction articles in magazines like *Bomb* and *Esquire*. And with last summer's release of the new feature film *Four Days* starring Colm Meany (*Star Trek, The Commitments*) William Forsythe (*Raising Arizona, Once Upon A Time In America*) and Lolita Davidovich (*Blaze, Cobb*), Benedict has made a serious leap in proving himself an "irreplaceable" screenwriter as well. But although in the world of fiction writing he achieved early success, Benedict was quick to admit that it took much longer to find himself as a writer for the big screen.

"I was given my first job screenwriting by David Milch, the producer of *NYPD Blue*," Benedict says. "He had come to Iowa where I was getting my M.F.A. to recruit writers for a new TV series he was going to produce, a spin-off of *Hill Street Blues* called *Beverly Hills Buntz*. It starred Dennis Franz, probably the only TV show he's done that wasn't a big hit. Nothing I wrote ever made it to the screen. That's what a horrible screenwriter I was. Mainly, I wrote about pigs, since I was writing about pigs a lot in those days, and there was little room for pigs in the series."

It is this combination of Benedict's elemental good-old-boy wit, self-effacing charm, and ability to produce beautiful language that is responsible for the success of his stories, but it soon became clear to the author that writing too beautifully could be more a hindrance than a help to his screen career. "I soon found out that if I was writing about a man wearing a hat, it was useless to describe the 'lush green fedora'," he says. "This works in a book, because the book is a totally visual medium. In screenwriting, nobody cares about mellifluous prose. In fact, all that density of detail we learn to write as fiction writers to make our work believable—for people who read scripts it gets in the way. They are looking for clarity. They just want 'the man is wearing a hat.' "

BRAD VICE *is a graduate student at the University of Cincinnati. His articles have appeared in the* Guide to Literary Agents *(Writer's Digest Books). His fiction has appeared in* The Southern Review, Hayden's Ferry Review *and* New Stories from the South.

But, Benedict adds, writing for clarity is not enough. To be a polished screenwriter, one must understand that scriptwriting as a medium of communication is fundamentally different from novel writing. "When reading a book there is a kind of conversation going on between the author and the reader, a model of one-on-one communication. Writing a screenplay or a teleplay is more like a musical score. I am not the performer and I am not trying to communicate to the audience; rather I am communicating to an orchestra of other people who are responsible for the performance—the cast, the costume people, the director."

Having learned how to shift gears from fiction to film and back again, Benedict has recently taken a job that allows him to showcase both of his talents. As a new associate professor of creative writing at Hollins University in Roanoke, Virginia, a small liberal arts school only a few miles away from the author's hometown, Benedict teaches both workshops for fiction writing and screenwriting, as well as an occasional class on literature in film.

During this conversation, Benedict is gracious enough to share anecdotes about the development of his career, what it was like to adapt the script of *Four Days* from the book by Canadian novelist John Buell, and talk about his experiences as a teacher.

Tell me what happened to you after working for TV producer David Milch. How did your screenwriting career evolve?

I was contacted by WNPG, a West Virginia public TV affiliate that was known for an excellent series of documentaries on mountain people. They were doing another series of half-hour dramatic shows, adapting work from West Virginian writers. They wanted to know if they could turn one of my stories from *The Wrecking Yard*, "Leaving Arnette," into a show. My wife Laura is a writer too, and did most of the writing on the adaptation. The West Virginia theater department made up the cast. Of course, there wasn't any real money for production. But they were so good, it kind of looked like some money was involved. The NETA is a big awards ceremony for public TV, and later that year their episode of "Leaving Arnette" co-won an award.

What was it like seeing something you had written transformed onto the screen?

It was exciting and fun. It was also a little strange because at the time I had finished that story quite a few years ago. So it was a little odd to see work you've put behind you get a second life. We have it on tape, and every so often my little girl comes up to me and says, "Daddy can we watch 'Arnette' again?" I get a kick out of that.

Your first movie, *Four Days*, has been out in theaters for a few months. How did you get involved with that project? What was it like writing your first movie-length screenplay?

A creative team from Toronto known as Amerique Films, made up of two guys, Greg Dummett and Curtis Wehrfritz, had acquired the rights to *Four Days*. One of them had read my novel *Dogs of God*, and thought, 'Hey, this guy might be good for the script.' So they brought me to Toronto, and we spent sometime kicking around ideas for how the adaptation should go. At first the idea was to shoot a low-budget, 15-minute vignette and use that to try and raise money. I went home and wrote a 20-page script. By then, they had changed their minds about the vignette and decided to go ahead and try to raise money for the entire feature. They gave me feedback on my 20 pages, and then I went to work on the whole screenplay.

I gave them the full-length and they gave me more suggestions for revision. Then the distributor got hold of the script, and he gave me more suggestions. Before it was all over with I did six major revisions and any number of smaller ones. The first script was 157 pages long and the version they used for shooting was down to 87. So if I had it to do over again, I'd know how to be more compact.

Four Days is based on a novel by John Buell. How closely did you stick to the book?

The novel is very different from the screenplay; it was a very free adaptation. The book is narrated from the point of view of a very isolated and lonely 14-year-old boy who has an almost obsessive loyalty to his father. The dad, who is played by William Forsythe, is a petty criminal, and wants one big score to be able to free his son from this life of crime. Of course, the father is killed during the robbery and the kid winds up with all the money. The kid spends four days attempting to carry out the post-robbery plan, all the while being chased by his father's partner (Colm Meany). Partway through his journey the kid is picked up by Kristel Nick (Lolita Davidovich) and they begin a love affair. She is a good example of how the movie differs from the novel. In the book her character occupied only three pages. But I found her interesting, so she kind of expanded in my imagination. Really the book is only a launching pad. It's easy to make a bad film if you feel too much allegiance to the source. The book is very internal, and we can't film that.

Did the author have much input with the film?

I met the author, John Buell, and he was a very nice guy. He's a retired professor who has written several novels. Another one had been turned into a movie called _The Pyx_ back in the '70s. There had been several other attempts to turn _Four Days_ into a movie before, and he seemed pretty happy the project was finally getting off the ground. We wanted him to be happy. We didn't want him to feel betrayed, but I wanted a certain amount of freedom to depart from the book. So I didn't consult with him too much. The one extended meeting I had with him was very funny actually. I remember at one point he was describing all these misguided attempts other screenwriters had made adapting the book. He said to me, 'and there was this one guy who took this obscure character from the middle of the book and wanted to make her the love interest. Can you believe that? Ha ha.' I just stood there with my mouth hanging open. I didn't say a word.

But then again, if I have one bit of advice to give it's this: When you sign away your work into someone else's hands, don't gripe if they do something asinine to it. At all times be a professional.

You recently took a job as a professor of creative writing at Hollins University, which offers an M.A. in screenwriting. How is teaching screenwriting different from teaching a fiction workshop?

Not all that different. Most of it is getting the format down. So the first part of the class is more technically oriented. The students are better prepared because we live in a film culture; they know what good film looks like. That is not necessarily a virtue, but it's true. Most films have a basic three-act structure; we spend some time talking about that. There are several software programs you can buy that really help with format. I use Scriptware, but it is expensive. So it's good to shop around. Once we get through the mechanical stuff, they take to it like ducks to water. Students in the screenwriting classes are pretty serious, because they feel like, 'Hey, I could do this for a living.'

Other than that, I talk about what I like to call hand-built art. Whether we're talking about fiction or screenwriting or any other kind of writing, I encourage my students to ask themselves, 'Why am I the only person who can tell this story?' I'd much rather watch a Blaxploitation movie from the '70s, or even something truly horrific like _The Texas Chainsaw Massacre_, than most of the action pictures made today. I mean, Bruce Willis is never going to make an interesting mistake. In most low-budget movies, even if they are imperfect, you get the sense that not just anybody could have made this movie. That's why I love post-apocalyptic literature too. It always makes you think, 'How will we rebuild the world?' That's what writers should always be asking themselves.

What are you working on now?

I am working on an original screenplay, but I'd rather keep that under my hat since I am still in the middle of it. I am also working on another novel tentatively titled *Wild Bleeding Hearts*, as well as a screen adaptation of my last novel *Dogs of God*. It was optioned a few years ago by a London Production Company, but at the time I didn't know as much about writing for the screen. So, actually I am the second screenwriter to get a shot at it. Now I know what it's like to be John Buell—only I am both the desecrator and the desecrated.

I found *Dogs of God* to be a very interesting read because it seemed to be playing with ideas of genre, especially action-adventures. The book is kind of like three or four B-movies held together with some pretty polished prose. The mixture of low-brow subject matter with highbrow prose reminded me of Conrad's *Lord Jim*. In *Lord Jim*, Conrad plays on the 19th-century boy's sea-adventure genre. They made a movie of *Lord Jim* in the '60s, trying to capitalize on the success of "Lawrence of Arabia." Because the filmmakers could not capture the high/low irony, "Lord Jim" the movie was a rather dull boy's sea-adventure. Going into the screenwriting of *Dogs of God*, what is your strategy to prevent something like that from happening?

It's funny you should make a Conrad connection. I was reading *Heart of Darkness* all the way through the writing of *Dogs of God*. All I can say is that maybe *Dogs of God* was a little too clever for its own good. The filmmakers have been clear that the movie needs to be more straight. But it came as no surprise to me that the book did better in England than in America. And it was no surprise to me that a London company bought the rights, because English culture takes a more ironic view of everything.

On the other hand, Conrad is not my only model. Many of the writers I really love are genre writers like Philip K. Dick, H.P Lovecraft, and especially Stephen King because they all have the ability to write about actual things—objects, cars, houses, whatever, but then there is this inexplicable other world too that superimposes itself. I love that. As far as movie making goes, all I can say is that the most important thing is to surround yourself with people who have the same vision. If I write a script, I want to feel confident that the director and producer can translate what I have written to film. But really once the writing's done, it's out of the writer's hands. After that you're going on faith.

So do you see film influencing your fiction, or vice versa?

I was pretty set as a fiction writer by the time I started with film. For me there is a fairly natural confluence.

Teaching, film, fiction—how do you juggle it all?

I never take a vacation, unless I am dragged away from my word processor. I respond well to deadlines. As a writer, deadly pressure should come from some project at all times. I don't want to belong to any one thing for too long. I want to be creative outside the academy, but the academy allows me a certain freedom from the demands of my creative work. I need both. I often wonder what I would do if all my dreams came true and I made all the money I would ever need with my writing. To tell you the truth, I don't think I would change a thing.

First Bylines

BY PAMALA SHIELDS

At times, self-doubt and fear of failure can paralyze the budding writer. Am I good writer? Have I crafted an interesting story? Will my work get noticed by an editor? The process of writing and getting your work published can seem overwhelming, but it is not necessarily an unattainable achievement. There *is* light at the end of the tunnel.

The following four writers, of varying backgrounds, share their writing and publishing experiences, the bad along with the good. Each has a unique and admirable story to tell that will inspire you to forge ahead and never stop writing. They lend insight into what it took to get their first novels or stories published—belief in themselves as writers, perseverance and the ability to write a good story.

LAUREN BELFER
City of Light, *Dial Press*

Lauren Belfer says she can't remember a time when she did not want to be a writer. "When I was six years old, I was already scribbling away at fantasy stories." In high school she wrote poetry and received rejections from all the best magazines. But she says, "Rejection letters never deterred me. I just kept working." The first story she published was rejected 42 times before it was accepted by the *Michigan Quarterly Review*.

Photo © Marion Ettlinger

This persistent determination paid off with the publication of her much lauded first novel, *City of Light*. Dial Press was so enthusiastic they supported the book with a $200,000 marketing campaign that included extensive national print advertising and an author tour. The book was chosen as a main selection in the Book-of-the-Month Club, foreign rights were sold and Barnes and Noble selected it for its "Discover New Writers" program.

To complete the work, Belfer worked on a computer in the corner of her living room, rising at 5:45 a.m. every day, including Sundays and holidays. "I could work for at least an hour before my son woke up, while my mind was still clear and fresh," she says. "I believe I did my most creative work during these early morning hours, and often I would find myself typing scenes I hadn't planned or even thought about the night before. The notion of 'finding time' to write has never been an issue for me; writing is what I do, and I simply do it."

Before beginning *City of Light*, Belfer took a slight detour from writing but still kept close ties to the profession. She worked for more than a decade in television documentary film production. She says, "Working on television documentaries taught me how to structure a story." She gave up her career in the late 1980s to begin work on an M.F.A. degree at Columbia where she honed her craft. "At Columbia I learned about voice, point of view, dialogue." Her studies at Columbia entailed a good deal of autobiographical writing. But, she says, "When I finished my degree, I very much wanted to find a topic outside of my own life. Beginning writers are often

---

PAMALA SHIELDS *is the production editor for* Children's Writer's & Illustrator's Market *and* Photographer's Market.

told to 'write what you know,' but I believe you write what you know and what you want to discover."

Writers often write experientially or conceptually. But the idea for *City of Light* came to Belfer in a flash of inspiration. While visiting her parents in her hometown of Buffalo, New York, she wandered into a deserted exhibit at the historical museum. "What I saw was like a revelation to me. Buffalo, at the dawn of this century, had been a place of immense wealth, sophistication and technological innovation—truly the Silicon Valley of its day. I realized Buffalo, at the turn of the century, would make an extraordinary setting for a novel." Thus began six years of detailed research and writing. Belfer did not mind the historical research. Her father was a history teacher and love for history came naturally to her. "When I was young, facts and questions of history were the things that would always gain my father's attention." Not suprisingly, she went on to receive a B.A. in medieval studies and art history from Swarthmore College. Her investigation into the history of Buffalo led her to discover that many issues relevant today—environmentalism, equality for women and African-Americans—were significant at the turn of the century.

The novel went through five complete rewrites before publication. Belfer says, "I believe that often I only figure out what I'm trying to write through the process of writing. I might do 20 pages of a scene before finally figuring out how to present that scene and its characters." She worked alone because getting feedback from a writing group was not helpful. "Chapters in a novel are not the same as short stories and so the critiquing process of a group did not work for me. I found I had to fight out the difficult parts myself."

Belfer was reluctant to show her work-in-progress to anyone in publishing. "I was too afraid of rejection," she says. But her experience ultimately proved to be a positive one. When she had accomplished as much as she thought she could with the manuscript, she wrote a query letter to an agent who had called her ten years before. The agent had been interested in an essay Belfer had written for a magazine and suggested she stay in touch with her. The agent responded immediately to the query. After a few minor changes the book was sold within the week. Belfer says, "I realize I have been very lucky, indeed blessed, by my publishing experience. But it's important to remember that this luck was the result of years and years of hard work."

To promote *City of Light*, Belfer is making bookstore appearances. She says she loves the commitment, enthusiasm and personal involvement expressed by the people who attend her readings. She is also researching her next novel, "shaping it bit by bit," and creating a world she hopes to explore for the next few years.

AMANDA DAVIS
Circling the Drain, *Rob Weisbach Books (Morrow)*

Amanda Davis did not pursue writing in earnest until after graduating from Wesleyan University with a B.A. in theater. Living in New York at the time, she began to write stories and eventually summoned the courage to show them to a trusted friend who was encouraging. After enrolling in a workshop at The New School, she applied to M.F.A. programs. "By then, I had realized that even if being a writer seemed impossible, I wanted to try." She was admitted to the M.F.A. program at Brooklyn College but still lacked confidence in her writing ability. A turning point came when she applied to the Bread Loaf Writers' Conference, held in rural Vermont, and won a scholarship. "It was one of the best things I ever did," Davis says. Besides workshopping with good writers, and attending classes and publishing seminars, the Bread Loaf workshop experience also allowed one-on-one conferences with the teachers. Davis adds, "I studied with Gloria Naylor and she was incredibly encouraging."

Photo by Michael Darter

Naylor urged Davis to submit her work for publication. "I had not been very serious about the whole process and hadn't really known what I was doing." She learned a great deal about writing and submitting from the classes and seminars and from talking to published writers, like Naylor. She returned home, she says, "feeling like I had a whole new perspective on what I was doing and what I wanted to do. And I began to think of myself as a writer." Thus Davis enthusiastically suggests finding a mentor or joining a writers' group. "Finding people who do what you do and whose work and insight you respect can be extremely helpful."

And a bona fide writer Davis became. In 1997 she won first place in STORY's Short, Short Story contest and a 1998 Heekin Foundation Tara Fellowship for a short story. After earning an M.F.A. from Brooklyn College, she published, with the help of an agent, *Circling the Drain*, a collection of short stories that took over two years to write. *New York Magazine* said of the work, "Amanda Davis delivers the stuff of good short stories: passionate writing, empathetic characters, themes of alienation and loss, and beautiful language that keeps stinging long after you read it." To Davis, a good short story raises questions, unlike a novel that sets out to answer questions. She says, "I would point to Alice Munro's (my favorite short story writer) collection *Open Secrets* as an example. Her work often leads you to a place where you end up with more questions than answers, but it is really satisfying. Her stories are very, very tight, every element accounted for and relevant, no matter how subtle."

Interestingly, many of Davis's story ideas are literally stuff that dreams are made of. "I often write from dreams and for years I've kept a dream journal. I've gotten so good at waking to write things down that I sometimes find fragments in there I don't remember writing. The fragments are often good leaping-off places for stories." Davis tries to write first thing every morning, before she has a chance to face the world and all its distractions. She also admits she is "a wickedly talented" procrastinator. "Though my goal is to have just two hours of actual sit-down-face-the-beast writing time each day, it sometimes takes me ten hours to squeeze out those two hours." But she says she feels saner when she can write every day. Davis has held innumerable jobs that have been rich sources for her stories including producing commercials, writing press copy, reading fiction for *Esquire*, editing for *Brooklyn Review*, baby-sitting, dish-washing, computer consulting, bartending and waitressing. Davis recently took another interesting job in the pursuit of writing a good story. She toured the eastern part of the country with a small circus to research a novel she is currently working on.

Davis has not written much that has not seen major revisions. "Often," she says, "I'll put a story away and come back to it. I think time brings great clarity, or at least it allows you to be more ruthless in revising, because you're not quite as emotionally attached to what you've written."

When the writer has whipped a story into shape and is ready to submit, Davis advises her or him to become familiar with the kind of work particular publications publish. Read several issues. She says that when she worked in the fiction department at *Esquire*, they often got "interesting, well-written stories that were just incredibly wrong for our demographic and that's very frustrating if you're reading submissions." In the end the writer is the loser. Even if the work is good, it won't get accepted if it's not right for the publication.

After publication of *Circling the Drain*, Davis was dazed for a while. "To have worked for so long towards a goal and then suddenly achieve it was pretty overwhelming and it took a few months for me to feel normal again." Since then, she has attended numerous readings and book signings that are particularly thrilling to her. "It's a pretty amazing feeling to read from your own book in a bookstore. I'm still not used to that."

ROBERT DRAPER
Hadrian's Walls, *Knopf*

Fortunately for Robert Draper all he has ever wanted to do is write, since, he says, he is aptitudinally challenged—unable to comprehend the sciences and lacking in manual skills. "Since the second grade, I've known that I wanted to write for a living and my conviction has never wavered. I can't honestly say whether I have a pathological need to express myself, or to order the world on paper, or to obey some other rogue compulsion. But writing is all I have ever done, all I've ever wanted to do and all I know how to do." Early on, teachers singled him out and offered encouragement with his writing. His parents have always been supportive, with a special nod going to his mother. Likewise, a significant source of ambitious inspiration was provided by his grandfather, former Watergate special prosecutor, Leon Jaworski. From Jaworski, Draper learned "greatness was absolutely attainable, provided one worked slavishly and single-mindedly and was not deterred by long odds."

Draper freelanced for six years, then took a position as an investigative reporter and writer with *Texas Monthly* for seven years and is currently a staff writer for *GQ* Magazine. Draper believes it is a privilege, not a right, to write for a living. "The years of rejection winnow out the less committed." He advises, "When an opportunity arrives to advance yourself, do not disappoint, no excuses." In embracing a writing career for himself, he says, "I've managed to avoid honest work for most of my adult life."

As far as writing fiction goes, he experienced a dormant period of about five years. However, after spending a month at Bennington Writing Workshop a desire to put pen to paper was renewed. He relates that, "Such workshops provide the opportunity to immerse one's self in the writing life, to fall under the tutelage of experienced (though usually not commercially successful, which is itself instructive) writers and most importantly to encounter a host of like-minded souls."

Draper spends much of his time on the road for *GQ* or satisfying his "Italophilia in Venice or Rome." It was in Venice, Italy, while on a four-month unpaid leave from *Texas Monthly*, that he wrote his first published novel, *Hadrian's Walls*. The novel has debuted to positive reviews. *Publisher's Weekly* calls it, "an ambitious novel that explores the irony, pathos and contradictions inherent in our conceptions both of freedom versus captivity and of good versus evil," and *Booklist* says it is "a compelling novel." Completion of the book was dependent on extricating himself from the journalistic trade. He found combining journalism and writing fiction in the same time frame incompatible. "I knew for sure that I would have to go away to write the novel. The experience is psychically impossible. To create requires an uncluttered mind." He says he loves writing magazine stories and the opportunity to step into worlds he was "hitherto not privy is a deeply enriching experience." However, he says, "The opportunity to create a world and infuse it with depth, meaning and all-too-humanness is a pleasure for which there is no equivalent, nor any substitute." Draper thoroughly enjoyed the intensity of the novel writing experience. He wrote six days a week, five to ten hours a day, to complete the manuscript and usually began by rewriting what he had written the day before. The work flow varied from dozens of pages to sometimes only one. He says, "There was no way to govern the process, apart from committing myself to facing a blank page each morning."

Draper is a character-driven writer who wants to "clarify human truths that lurk obscured within us." He says it was most important to convey the concept of "finding and apprehending the spirit of the characters. I suppose at the root of my stories there is a character wrestling with some conflict that has preoccupied me at one time or another. Hadrian Coleman, the protagonist from my novel, is a man obsessed with his failings—something which I have fallen prey to at certain junctures of my life. I liked the idea of staging his struggles in a prison town that lies on the fault line of guilt and innocence."

Getting the novel published proved a positive experience for Draper this time around. Previously, he had written two novels his then-agent was unable or unwilling to sell. Draper subsequently acquired a new agent but worked on the novel for nine more months before sending it to him. Six days after his agent received the manuscript, there were four offers from major publishing houses. Draper liked what the editor at Knopf had to say about improvements to the manuscript and thus chose them to publish *Hadrian's Walls*. After two revisions, the final draft was submitted in August 1998 and the book was published in May 1999. He says quite sweepingly, "I was blessed with a good idea, with the proper circumstances in which the idea could come alive, with an enormously supportive agent and with the best editor with the best publishing house in America. I'd be a jackass to want more."

The biggest challenge Draper encountered after publication was to not take the reviews too seriously. "I can't control what people say or how others react. Accepting that reality and maintaining equanimity throughout the rollercoaster ride is what's critical." Fortunately, for him, the reviews have been notable.

Draper toured to promote *Hadrian's Walls* and enjoyed meeting strangers who had become fans of his writing. He is now working on a new novel about an underachieving attorney who gets caught up in an international swindle. Where *Hadrian's Walls* explored the themes of guilt and innocence, the new work will delve into the issues of identity and deception. His wish for the future is to "live out my days writing novels and magazine articles. I can't imagine a more gratifying existence for myself."

JOHN SON
"This Close," *Zoetrope*

Four years after he decided to start writing, John Son says he kept asking himself, "Now what do I do?" Then he picked up a book of poems (*Wild Iris*, by Louise Gluck) and experienced an epiphany. "Somehow that book showed me a glimpse of what writing was about." He relates that for a few years after, he churned out some mediocre poetry. But later, when he tried his hand at fiction, the world of writing opened up to him. He discovered "it was with fiction that I felt more comfortable. I felt like I was in the driver's seat."

The desire to write was not always a motivating factor for Son. Even though he was encouraged by a high school teacher to write, he did not take her, or writing, seriously at the time. While attending the University of Texas at Austin, he was unable to determine what he wanted to do with his life and unable to settle on a major. Finally, he decided to pursue a degree in English and thus began taking writing more seriously. After holding a variety of jobs, including flipping burgers, he secured a position as an assistant editor at Random House.

Now Son makes time for writing fiction, albeit, not as much as he would like. He writes after work and on weekends. However he did find time to write "This Close," a short story published by *Zoetrope* in July 1999. Son says his writing style is conceptual. "I place a character, or a group of characters, in an interesting situation and then see how they react." In this piece of short fiction, the protagonist must deal with the violent death of his beloved. He is "trying to come closer to what happened, trying to understand and/or accept what happened." Son tells the story in short titled episodes, moving from the past to the present with a revealing ending that touches the reader. According to Son, a story should "grab you, primarily through language and plot. Then it should come at you from the side—surprise you—again and again, until you come away from a story looking at the world differently."

Son tries to work on more than one project at a time. "When I work on one story for too long, I just end up getting sick of it. Periodically, I have to step away and let it stew somewhere in the back of my mind, then come back to it with a fresh perspective and renewed interest." Often, however, much of what he writes ends up being an exercise in what works and what does not. Still, he says, "The important thing is that I learn something from every single line I write."

According to Son, an author must write as much as possible to improve skills." When you have slaved away at something long enough and feel you might have a finished story on your hands, just submit to whomever you want and don't expect to hear back from them." Then just keep plugging away, keep writing and repeat the process. He relates that "it is an agonizing, demoralizing process and few people will envy you. But if you truly enjoy the act of writing, of creating a story, nothing can be more rewarding."

A writing group can also be a constructive tool. Son feels explaining or defending your work to others helps the writer focus. But having to explain or defend too much most likely reveals the writer is doing something wrong. In the end, though, "you realize that each person reads your story differently and that you can't please everyone's personal taste and ultimately you have to go with what feels right."

Son says he got lucky with "This Close." *Zoetrope* was the only market to which he submitted the story. Earlier he had hastily submitted a piece, he felt was not quite finished, in an effort to win a *Zoetrope* writing workshop scholarship. He did not win, but *Zoetrope* was impressed enough with his work that they asked him to send them something else. Of course living in New York and working for a publishing house affords him the advantage of knowing who the 'right' people are to read and appreciate his work. Even though he has the perspectives of those who publish and those who want to be published, he says, "It still makes me realize how slow a process writing, submitting and publishing can be." Submitting stories like, "This Close," does not require an agent, but Son advises, "If you're a novelist or have a collection of stories you want to get published, get an agent. The logic being that if you're good enough for an agent, then you might be good enough for a publisher."

Son has a story in submission and is working on several others. His goal is to publish a collection of his stories.

Genre Markets

The Mystery Market Today

BY BARBARA D'AMATO, President, Mystery Writers of America

At the opening of the new millennium, we are in the leading edge of the greatest revolution in the production and distribution of the written word since Gutenberg. For fiction readers there will be more types of material available than ever before. And for writers, there will be more outlets for work than we have ever dreamed of.

Photo by Jerry Bauer

Mystery short story sites are already open on the Internet. These will proliferate and differentiate, soon giving rise to sub-categories, such as hard-boiled, cozy, fantasy, historical mysteries, and so on. Where previously a publisher of a mystery magazine had to put large amounts of money into printing and paper, and then depend on distribution and point-of-sale visibility for survival, it will be possible for publishers simply to buy stories, post them, and let the world know the nature of their cyber-magazine. Readers will find it through key words.

Barbara D'Amato

The same will be true of mystery novels. Downloaded from certain suppliers, they may be read on e-books—book-sized cyber-readers that can be carried in a pocket.

This is not to say that paper or bookstores will vanish. Most readers enjoy browsing in bookstores and reading real books on real paper.

"Books on demand" printing machines produce books on-site from a disk, while you wait. Because of their small size, the disks can be stored almost anywhere. Distributors and neighborhood bookstores will be able to maintain a stock literally thousands of times more than they are now able to shelve. Because there will not be a need for publishers to maintain expensive physical stocks of books and pay for both storage and taxes on them, there will be no financial pressure for the backlist to go out of print and out of availability.

The new technology will benefit smaller bookstores because they will not need to stock multiple copies of individual books. They may shelve browsing copies of many, many titles and either sell the copy on hand and order another, or print one for the customer with on-demand printing. As readers, we will be able to buy long-unavailable mysteries from lesser-known writers, right in our neighborhood bookstores.

Paradoxically, the increased availability of old books will not, I believe, hurt the chances of new authors to be published. For new writers, the fact that they need not sell in hundreds of thousands is good news. At last writers who appeal to a limited audience, or new writers of untested appeal, will be publishable. At present, major publishers need to sell several thousand copies of a paperback per month in order for it to be economical to keep a title in print. No more. Soon, if a reader wants a historical mystery set in the West during the Civil War, for instance, or a techno-mystery involving cyber-crime set in the U.K., he can simply search and call up a list of titles. And as a writer, you can sell into your chosen mini-market.

This revolution is coming whether we like it or not. It's new and somewhat scary. However, for

BARBARA D'AMATO *is author of the Cat Marsala mystery series (Scribner) and the Suze Figuero Chicago cop series (Forge). She has won the Carl Sandberg Award for Literary Excellence and the Anthony and the Agatha awards. D'Amato is currently president of the Mystery Writers of America and past president of Sisters in Crime.*

a writer, there is no way a vastly increased number of fiction outlets—and a vastly increased search method for readers to find that writer—is going to be a bad thing in the long run.

To be sure, problems exist. Most importantly, how can we be certain the writer is paid, and how can we maintain gatekeeping functions? Payment is being solved to a certain extent already with encrypted access codes and other cyber-methods. Gatekeeping will be far more difficult. When anything can be cyber-published for very little money, including the collected stories of Mrs. Smith's eighth grade English class, how can a reader know what's good?

Existing publishing companies, will, of course, retain their selection, editing and validating functions. The new companies that spring up will develop reputations for certain types of fiction and a given quality of stories. There will be turmoil, but it will only increase the opportunities for new writers.

All this is coming at a time when the mystery field was already into a wonderful flowering. The period beginning in the early 1980s is being called the Second Golden Age of Mystery. The first Golden Age extended roughly from the mid 1920s to the mid 1950s, when the giants of mystery fiction—Agatha Christie, Dorothy L. Sayers, Dashiell Hammett, Ellery Queen, Raymond Chandler and others—were at their peak of production. It established the mystery novel as we now know it and developed a very high standard of writing and plotting, which laid the groundwork for the perennial sales of crime, mystery and suspense fiction.

But despite the high quality, the Golden Age was quite narrow. If you picked a mystery novel at random from a bookshelf in 1940, it was probably either a traditional puzzle novel with clues, most likely written by a woman living in the U.K., or a hard-boiled private eye story written by a man living in the U.S. If the book was set in the U.S., it probably took place in New York or Los Angeles. The ethnicity of the authors and detectives was most often white northern European. There were some exceptions, of course, but this was the general picture.

In the Golden Age we are experiencing today, mysteries are set from the Maine coast to the Pacific northwest, Canada to the Florida Keys, in large cities, small towns and wilderness areas. There is scarcely a city in the nation without one or more mystery series set there. The ethnicities of the authors and their detectives have broadened tremendously, with many African-American detectives, Native American detectives, Hispanic detectives and Asian detectives. There are now many gay and lesbian detectives. Women detectives today are varied and realistic, real people with real lives and professions, and the upsurge in their stories is sometimes credited with triggering the new Golden Age. There is also large and growing body of thoroughly researched historical detective novels set in the past in the U.S. and other countries.

Virtually every profession and hobby is represented: quilt makers, caterers, forensic pathologists, reporters, art appraisers, women cops, herbalists. Perhaps more surprisingly, there are many new hybrid fantasy mysteries and science fiction mysteries.

The result is this: Almost anything you as a writer have an interest in, anyone you are, anywhere you live, or any place and any time you would like to have lived is now fair game to write about. The richness in the field is extraordinary.

The corollary is this: The mystery least likely to appeal to readers is a generic, formulaic story. The mystery writer today needs to be fresh. Your best asset is your own voice and your own genuine interest in your material.

The new diversity in mysteries has produced a burgeoning market for crime and mystery novels. Short stories have many more outlets than 15 years ago. While most of the anthologies being published today are invitational, quite often the editors try to leave room for a couple of new voices. Several general magazines publish short mysteries. There are a number of mystery magazines, both old favorites, like *Ellery Queen* and *Alfred Hitchcock*, new magazines, and reborn old ones such as the *Strand*.

A tremendous expansion of the types of mysteries—plus a tremendous expansion of the potential market—means there has never been a better time to be a mystery writer. Or reader, of course, and we are all readers first, aren't we?

The Art, Craft and Selling of the Mystery Short Story

BY STUART M. KAMINSKY

Let's start with a few opening thoughts that may make the writing process easier for you to get into.

First, don't sit down to write art. If you write what you believe in, write it well and with knowledge of the field, others will decide whether you have written "art." If you start out trying to achieve a story that will live forever and win awards, you are probably doomed to fail. Besides, who wants to start writing with the raven of posterity looking down at them from the top of the computer or the window ledge?

Stuart M. Kaminsky

Photo by Vern Sawyer

Second, think of yourself as a storyteller who wants to hold the attention of an audience for only the duration of their reading experience with you. Write only what you yourself would want to read, not what you would be willing to read, but what you would really look forward to reading.

If you are not one of your own best fans, you're in trouble. When I write, I sometimes laugh out loud or frighten myself so badly that I have to stop, turn on more lights and be with people.

Third, write what you want to write. Don't try to outguess the market. Don't try to find a new gimmick, although if there is something unusual you are interested in or have discovered, your chances are certainly better than if you revisit old ground.

Fourth, do not begin writing short stories because you want to make money, be famous or win awards. Write because you can't help telling stories. There is certainly nothing wrong with wanting to be published. But any honorable market will do. It's quite an accomplishment to be published after being judged worthy by an editor or group of editors.

Eventually, if you are published enough and what you publish is good enough, you build up a resume that makes larger markets take an interest in your work.

Many people want to be writers for the wrong reasons. You can be taught the craft, and that is essential. You can learn and enjoy the literature, but it is difficult—some say impossible—to make you have the imagination necessary to be an author. Stories have teemed and tumbled in my mind, grown, changed, shifted and distracted me since I was about 14 years old, probably much younger. They still do. I have trouble holding them back. I want to get them out. I want to see them on paper (or the screen).

I want to share them with others. That is essential.

And remember this—in spite of what others may tell you, writing a short story is not more difficult than writing a novel. It does require a special precision and attention so that every word is precise, every phrase the perfect one. But don't let that intimidate you—just write the story. And you should have plenty of stories from which to choose.

STUART KAMINSKY, *past president of the Mystery Writers of America, won the Edgar Allan Poe Award for Best Novel for* A Cold Red Sunrise. *He has been nominated for five Edgar Awards. His stories have appeared in major anthologies of best short stories. He has published more than 40 books and over 50 short stories.*

I have more story ideas than I can ever use. If you don't have stories screaming to be written, forget about being a writer.

WRITING YOUR STORY: FROM IDEA TO "THE END"

Here are 18 practical suggestions to help you get your story written.

1. Keep a notebook, something small that will fit into a pocket or purse. When you get an idea, write it down. If you don't, you'll probably forget it. You can get ideas from listening to other people's conversations, newspapers, movies, television shows, books. A minor character in a film, for example, can get your imagination going. You may throw away most of those notes later, but write them now.

A situation may start your fantasy. You see a well-dressed, handsome woman in the mall. She is carrying a designer purse and a coarse brown bag that looks as if it had been pulled from the trash. What's in that bag? Why is she carrying it? I see things like this all the time. I make notes. I imagine.

2. Start the process with either a character or situation. You see a small Latino child wander into a store ahead of his mother who is talking to a friend. She doesn't notice the child. What happens in that store? What could happen? Who might be involved in what happens? Situations are constantly presenting themselves. Put them in your notebook. Dream about them. Create a character or discover one. You think your old high school algebra teacher might make a good central figure in your story? Fine. Let the teacher become whatever you want him or her to be. Let that character come to life, be real to you. When the imaginative process is working well, the characters you create will come to life and have a history you instantly know and can call upon. If they are roughly based on real people, they need not conform to who those people were or are. Let them come to new life in our imagination.

3. Keep your story idea simple. A novel or screenplay may have two or more story lines to follow. I suggest you concentrate on only one story line. Think in terms of a 25- or 30-page story (double spaced, 14-point type). Set that as your goal.

4. In a paragraph or two and only for yourself, outline what you are going to write, just a simple telling of the tale. Then spend time imagining your characters in that story.

5. Think of a first line or two. I spend a great deal of time thinking about that first line. It is my jumping off point, and my point of return. I don't try to think of deathless prose, just a first sentence or two that will grab or at least wink at the reader.

6. Let your imagination work as you write your story. Listen to your characters. Let them live and breathe. If they say something you didn't plan, let them speak. My bet is your unconscious mind will remember that two-paragraph outline you did and get you reasonably back to it or to an even better ending.

7. Writing the short story is a trip of imagination. Start. Put your characters into the situation and setting you have created and just listen to them. Describe what they are doing, and possibly what they are thinking. See yourself as a reporter of the tale you see unfolding in your imagination. Your characters should have their own phrasing, inflection and mannerisms. If your imagination is working, you don't have to be consciously aware of these things. You will just hear the characters and write what they say and how they say it. If your characters all sound and think like you, you are not letting them come to life. Also bear in mind if your characters are to come alive, they cannot be simply good or bad. Give every character, great or small, good or bad, his or her best shot. You are not recording the imagined tale.

8. As you write, don't worry about whether others will think your story is good or bad. In fact, don't worry about whether you think your story is good or bad. Let it happen. It's not magic, though it may feel like it when the process is going well. It's imagination.

9. Limit the number of characters in your short story. A small, clean, clear number, three to six, is easier for you to write and easier for your readers to absorb.

10. Limit your locations to no more than four or five. Again, keep it simple.

11. Know how much time your story will take and keep the time period short. My short stories usually cover less than a day. Most of my stories take place within a few hours.

12. Keep descriptions of your characters to a minimum. Do not open your story with the description of your main character. I know it has been done and done brilliantly by many writers. It is better to draw your reader into the story and then give a very brief description of your central character and each character as he or she appears. The more important the character, the more space you give him or her. Even the main character should get very little. Example: "The man who called himself Harry Ritsman was about 50, of average height, more stocky than muscular. His blonde hair was thinning. His smile was non-existent and his eyes were blue and cold and narrow. There was the look of a well-fed wary cat about him." Or, if he is a minor character, "Harry Ritsman was 50, of average height, a bit on the stocky side. His features were narrow like those of a wary cat." Or, a very minor character, "The woman was wealthy, wrinkled from too much sun and thin from too much desperate exercise."

13. Keep your paragraphs short. Shoot for a five- or six-line maximum.

14. Within four paragraphs have your reader asking the big question, the one that will keep him reading to get the answer. It can be simple and it should never be posed as a question. Some examples of 'big questions': "When she was 12, Sara saw something that made her decide never to speak again." What did Sara see? Another example: "When Sommes entered the dark building, he was sure that something, something large and without clear form undulated in the shadows by the stairs. And then he was just as sure that he was imagining things." What was it he saw?

15. Yes, the big question should keep the reader going, but even more important than the question are your characters. If you haven't created characters who are alive and interesting, no question is going to keep your reader going.

16. Your story should take you no more than four days for a first draft. I've known people who have agonized for months over a story. Don't do it. Get it written. Write whether you feel like it or not. Set a daily goal and meet it whether you feel like it or not. Don't wait or hope for inspiration. It may never come. Writing is fun and creative, but it is also work. Lawyers don't stay home because they are not inspired. They go to work. So do professional writers.

17. When your first draft is done, fix the clear problems such as characters who repeat themselves or contradictions of information. Make your story consistent. Oddly enough, life isn't consistent but our fiction better be. If it isn't, readers will reject it. Characters are expected to be consistent in fiction. People are often inconsistent in life.

Check your spelling, of course, and your grammar. Make small improvements, but set a time limit. For a 25-page story, you should take no more than four hours to make corrections. You probably don't need a second draft at this point.

18. If you haven't done so by this time, pick a title. I collect titles, make lists. Don't agonize over a title. Usually what you think of first works just fine. Here are some titles I've used for short stories or plan to use: Justice, Punishment, Hidden, Dead Cat On Gila Street, Joyce's Children, Blowout In Little Man Flats, What You Don't Know, Explosion In Lipman's Glass Factory, The Alien Who Hated Cats, Snow.

There is no consistency at all to those titles. The kind of story I wrote led me to a title. On occasion I'll even think of a title I like and launch into a story it suggests. Explosion In Lipman's Glass Factory is a good example.

Now you're ready to submit your story for publication. You can show it to friends, relatives, enemies, but I suggest you pay attention only to the errors they point out that you agree with. Pay little attention to their qualitative judgments. They are too close to you to give you any kind of criticism separate from whom they know you to be.

GETTING PUBLISHED

I've known two people who have actually started their own magazines or journals so they could get published. Nothing wrong with that if you can afford it.

If you can't start your own publication, you might want to take a course from a published short story writer near you. They may give you great advice or bad advice, but they may be able to make contacts for you or suggest markets for your work that you haven't considered. However, don't become an amateur fiction course enrollee. You should be writing, not taking courses. One decent short course is enough.

The same goes for books on writing. Find one good one by a successful professional writer, read it, and then read no more books on writing, not even mine.

If you are going to read, read short stories. Absorb them. Learn from them. Look for the questions raised by the writer. Examine the short strokes with which characters are created. Say the dialogue out loud. How much time is covered in the story? How many characters are there? How many locations are there? Read stories, not books about writing stories.

And then get a list of college and university periodicals, independent magazines and journals that publish fiction in the bigger paying market. Get on the Internet and search the lists, or have them before you in *Novel & Short Story Writers' Market*. Enter short story contests, also found on the Internet.

When you do submit, be sure to match your story to the interests of the publication. Read what they say about submissions. If possible, go to your local bookstore and take a look at some of the better known little magazines. If your story fits a specialized market, go for those markets first—horror, romance, mystery, science fiction, Western, whatever.

Many publications will say they don't want multiple submissions, meaning they don't want you to send your story to other publications till they make a decision. At the risk of offending some of those publications, I advise you to submit your story to as many as ten publications at a time. If you submit to only one publication and wait for an answer, it may take you years to make the rounds.

Keep your cover letter brief. Not more than one page, three short paragraphs. One short paragraph should tell who you are and what experience you've had as a writer or as anything else. You might want to include a sentence about your educational background. Another short paragraph should summarize your story. Don't hold back a strong ending because you want to surprise the editor. Tell them the story. Tell it in four or five sentences.

Indicate where you can be reached. End of letter.

Of course, you must include a stamped envelope with your return address on it.

Then you wait.

KEEP WRITING

Do not just write a story, send it out and sit back hoping for publication. While your story is out, write another one. Then write another. Keep writing. You should improve with each story. By the time you start getting your first one back, you may decide you have improved so much that you want to file that first story or two away for a later look or consignment to oblivion.

The market is not easy at any level. The chances of your getting published and then continuing to get published are very small, but someone has to make it. Have confidence in your work and stick it out. You have one life. If you are driven to write, write. Let others quit because the odds are slim.

Mystery Markets Appearing in This Book

Below is a list of mystery markets appearing in this edition of *Novel & Short Story Writer's Market*. To find page numbers of particular magazines or book publishing markets, go first to the General Index beginning on page 663 of this book. Then turn to the pages those listings appear on for complete information, including who to contact and how to submit your mystery short story or novel manuscript.

Magazines

SPSM&H
State of Being
Storyteller, The
Street Beat Quarterly
Tale Spinner, The
"Teak" Roundup
Thema
32 Pages
Threshold, The
Timber Creek Review
Tucumcari Literary Review
Urban Spaghetti
Vintage Northwest
VQ
Weber Studies
West Wind Review
Wicked Mystic
Wilmington Blues
Woman's World Magazine
Words of Wisdom
Writer's Head, The
Writes of Passage
Yellow Sticky Notes

Book Publishers

Alexander Books
Arcade Publishing
Avalon Books
Avon Books
Avon Books for Young Readers
Avon Twilight
Bancroft Press
Bantam Books
Beggar's Press
Berkley Publishing Group, The
British Book Company, Inc., The
Carroll & Graf Publishers, Inc.
Cartwheel Books
Centennial Publications
Chinook Press
Cumberland House Publishing
Dell Publishing Island
Doubleday Adult Trade
Dunne Books, Thomas
Fawcett
Forge Books
Foul Play Press

Gryphon Publications
Harcourt Inc.
Harlequin Enterprises, Ltd.
HarperCollins Publishers
HarperPaperbacks
Harris Literary Agency
Harvest House Publishers
Holt & Company, Henry
Houghton Mifflin Books for Children
Houghton Mifflin Company
Ivy League Press, Inc.
Kaeden Books
Kensington Publishing Corp.
Minotaur
Morrow and Company, Inc., William
Multnomah Publishers, Inc.
Mysterious Press, The
Palari Publishing
Peachtree Publishers, Ltd.
Philomel Books
Presidio Press
Press Gang Publishers
Pride and Imprints
Publishers Syndication, International
Putnam's Sons, G.P.
Rainbow Books, Inc.
Random House Books for Young Readers
Random House, Inc.
Random House, Inc. Juvenile Books
Rio Grande Press
St. Martin's Press
Scherf Books
Seniors Market, The
Soho Press
Stonewall Inn
Story Line Press
Tailored Tours Publications, Inc.
Toby Press Ltd., The
Tor Books
Tropical Press, Inc.
Turnstone Press
University of Nevada Press
Van Neste Books
Vista Publishing, Inc.
Walker and Company
Warner Books
Write Way Publishing

Resources for Mystery Writers

Below is a list of invaluable resources specifically for mystery writers. For more information on the magazines and organizations listed below, check the General Index and the Publications of Interest and Organizations sections of this book. To order any of the Writer's Digest Books titles or to get a consumer book catalog, call 1-800-289-0963. You may also order Writer's Digest Books selections through www.writersdigest.com, Amazon.com or www.barnesandnoble.com.

MAGAZINES:
- *The Armchair Detective*, P.O. Box 929, Bound Brook NJ 08805-0929
- *Fiction Writer*, 1507 Dana Ave., Cincinnati OH 45207
- *Mystery Readers Journal*, Mystery Readers International, P.O. Box 8116, Berkeley CA 94707
- *Writer's Digest*, 1507 Dana Ave., Cincinnati OH 45207

BOOKS:
Howdunit series (Writer's Digest Books):
- *Missing Persons: A Writer's Guide to Finding the Lost, the Abducted and the Escaped*
- *Murder One: A Writer's Guide to Homicide*
- *Armed and Dangerous: A Writer's Guide to Weapons*
- *Deadly Doses: A Writer's Guide to Poisons*
- *Cause of Death: A Writer's Guide to Death, Murder & Forensic Medicine*
- *Scene of the Crime: A Writer's Guide to Crime Scene Investigation*
- *Private Eyes: A Writer's Guide to Private Investigators*
- *Police Procedural: A Writer's Guide to the Police and How They Work*
- *Modus Operandi: A Writer's Guide to How Criminals Work*
- *Malicious Intent: A Writer's Guide to How Criminals Think*
- *Body Trauma: A Writer's Guide to Wounds and Injuries*
- *Amateur Detectives: A Writer's Guide to How Private Citizens Solve Criminal Cases*
- *Just the Facts, Ma'am: A Writer's Guide to Investigators and Investigation Techniques*
- *Rip-off: A Writer's Guide to Crimes of Deception*

Other Writer's Digest books for mystery writers:
- *How to Write Mysteries*
- *The Writer's Complete Crime Reference Book*
- *Writing the Modern Mystery*
- *Writing Mysteries: A Handbook by the Mystery Writers of America*
- *Writing the Private Eye Novel: A Handbook by the Private Eye Writers of America*
- *You Can Write a Mystery*

ORGANIZATIONS & ONLINE:
- The Mystery Writers' Forum: www.zott.com/mysforum/default.html (See complete listing in the Websites of Interest section of this book.)
- Mystery Writers of America, 17 E. 47th St., 6th Floor, New York NY 10017
- The Private Eye Writers of America, 407 W. Third St., Moorestown NJ 08057
- Sisters in Crime, P.O. Box 442124, Lawrence KS 66044-8933

The Romance Market Today

BY JO ANN FERGUSON, President, Romance Writers of America

Jo Ann Ferguson

Romance is hot!

You don't have to look any farther than your morning newspaper's entertainment section to see that. Hollywood and television are rediscovering what romance authors and readers have known for a long time—everyone loves a good love story.

Don't believe it? Look at the numbers gathered by Romance Writers of America (RWA) during a survey done in Spring 1999. More than 31 million women in America read romance fiction. Add to that the 3.5 million men who make up 9% of the romance readership, and you have a market that is hungry for books. Last year, 1,900 romance titles were released. Romance is the only genre (and that includes more than just fiction) where sales continue to rise slowly. All other genres are slipping each year. And the good news is publishers are buying from first-time authors.

Romance readers range from teenagers to senior citizens. Readers want an escape from their lives when they read romance. They are looking for a break, a chance to spend a few hours with a dynamic hero and an equally compelling heroine. These two characters are the very heart (pardon the pun) of a romance novel, because romances are character-driven stories. Readers read them for the characters and to experience how the hero and heroine overcome their problems, fall in love, and make a life commitment to one another. Romance heroes and heroines are most definitely not perfect people. They have weaknesses, but, by working together and daring to love, they can overcome those weaknesses and build a life together.

Our heroes are usually dashing, but they may be brooding or troubled or trying to atone for a past mistake. A hero may be a risk-taker with a powerful motorcycle or the nice guy next door who knows how to fix a dripping faucet. He may be a ruthless undercover agent or the knight in often-tarnished armor who has come to claim the heroine's castle and hand in marriage. But the hero must have a motivation for what he is doing, a motivation the reader can accept as the heroine does. Heroes are unquestioningly honorable. What is most important, however, is that the hero is a man the reader can fall in love with at the same time the heroine does.

Our heroines deal with the problems facing today's readers—whether the heroines are set in a contemporary or historical setting. Heroines can be single parents or responsible for an aging parent or trying to keep the family business (or castle) from falling apart. She does not need to be looking for love. In fact, a relationship with a man might be the last thing she thinks she has time for in her busy life. But that changes when the hero comes into her life, complicating it in

---

JO ANN FERGUSON *is the bestselling lead author of Regencies and historicals for Kensington; paranormals for ImaJinn (as J.A. Ferguson); and historicals for Berkley (as Joanna Hampton), Harper, New Concepts Publishing and Tudor. She also writes inspirational contemporaries for Mountain View Publishing (as Jo Ann Brown). Ferguson sold a historical suspense to M. Evans and contributed to an encyclopedia published by Garland on the English Regency period. The Counterfeit Count, May 1999 Zebra Regency, won the ARTemis Award for Regency from RWA. The editor of Now That You've Sold Your Book . . . What's Next?, Ferguson had 15 new titles released in 1999. She is the current national president of RWA.*

ways she could not have guessed. She must be as strong emotionally as the hero. Thank goodness weak heroines who wait for the hero to rescue them off the railroad tracks are long gone.

Once you have your characters, you need to decide what romance subgenre you want to put them in. If you don't know the subgenres of romance, look at your own stack of reading material and see which books you most enjoy reading.

Oh, by the way, if you don't read romance, put down this article and go to the bookstore and buy a bunch of titles that interest you before you try writing one yourself. Almost all successful romance authors are also romance readers. If you haven't read a romance in a while, you need to read lots of them now because they have evolved. There are certain parameters of the genre first-time writers are expected to meet, including a one man/one woman story (they may have had other lovers in the past, but, once they meet, they are not in a physical relationship with anyone else) and a happy-ever-after ending.

Most romances are either set in the ever-present today (contemporary) or between 1066 and 1899 (historical). There are some exceptions with time travel and other-worldly romances. The following are the subgenres that RWA uses to define different romances:

1. Traditional romance—short, contemporary romances usually without love scenes. (I use love scenes to mean when the hero and heroine make love.) Publishers include Harlequin and Silhouette.
2. Short contemporary romance—approximately 50,000-65,000 words. Some of these really sizzle. Publishers include Harlequin, Silhouette and Kensington.
3. Long contemporary romance—70,000-85,000 words. More secondary characters. Love scenes, but sensuality ranges from sensual to sizzle. Publishers include Harlequin, Silhouette and Kensington.
4. Contemporary single title—longer books that are not part of a publisher's line. May have multiple story lines and secondary characters. Publishers include Avon, Berkley, Kensington and Mira.
5. Romantic suspense—include shorter novels in Harlequin Intrigue line as well as single titles published by, for example, Avon, Kensington, Berkley, Bantam and Warner. These books have a suspense/mystery to be solved along with the hero and heroine falling in love. The balance between romance and suspense is different for each publisher.
6. Ethnic—primarily contemporary at this time, but some historicals are published. For African-American, BET Arabesque (editorial at Kensington) is the primary line. For Hispanic stories, Kensington has recently launched Encanto, published in both English and Spanish. Other publishers publish ethnic books as part of their regular list.
7. Historical—85,000-100,000 words. Set usually in England, Scotland, Wales or the United States, these books customarily take place during the years from 1066-1899. There are exceptions to those "rules," but a writer increases her chances of selling a first book by sticking to those parameters. Varying levels of sensuality. Publishers include Kensington, Avon, Berkley, Dell, Warner, Harlequin and Harper.
8. Regency—65,000-75,000 words. If you love Jane Austen, then Regencies may be the books for you. Set in the period of the English Regency (1811-1820), these are comedies of manners, usually without love scenes. Publishers include Kensington and Signet.
9. Paranormal—length varies. These are the books that don't fit elsewhere because they have elements that deal with time travel, witchcraft, science fiction, ghosts and other unearthly aspects. Publishers include ImaJinn, Dorchester/Leisure, Berkley/Jove and Warner.
10. Inspirational—length varies. Books with a religious element—usually Christian. They are both contemporary and historical. Publishers include Barbour, Waterbrook, Multnomah and Tyndale.
11. Young Adult—aimed at middle school readers. These usually are part of a packaged line. Very few stand alone titles published.

Some publishers will provide tip sheets (guidelines for writers on the lines they publish), if you send a SASE. Check listings in this guide for publishers who offer tip sheets.

I urge anyone who is serious about writing and selling romance novels to join RWA. Information on RWA can be found at www.rwanational.com or by e-mailing info@rwanational.com. The mailing address is: Romance Writers of America, 3707 FM 1960 West, Suite 555, Houston TX 77068. Phone: (281)440-6885. With chapters throughout North America and in Australia, RWA offers members the opportunity to network and learn. Each year, a national conference is held in July. In 2000, it will be held in Washington, DC. Contests are held for the best unpublished and best published works in each subgenre. A monthly journal, *Romance Writers' Report*, contains articles on writing, publishing and the writing life, as well as market updates.

So, after reading all this, you want to write romance? The best advice I can give after having sold over 40 titles is read and read and read in the subgenre you wish to write, then write the book you want to read with a heroine whom you admire and a hero you would love to fall in love with. Be funny, be serious, be yourself and let your unique voice shine through. That is the recipe for writing a book that will catch an editor's eye, and bring you an offer for publication.

An Award-Winning Romance Novelist Shares Surprising Secrets

BY MARY COX

Store clerks and car salesmen must be baffled by Alison Hart, a mysterious customer who browses their shops and showrooms. There's something about the deliberate way she slips into sandals and smart sedans that makes them snap to attention, poised for the sure sale. They watch as she makes her way through racks of designer suits, lingering over a luxurious fabric or examining the detail on a button or the cut of a lapel. They hover while she squeezes dozens of pretty bulbs at their perfume counters, eyes narrowing as she sniffs the air. When a final spritz brings a satisfied smile to Hart's face, it's no wonder clerks smell a sale. When car salesmen catch her adjusting the rear view mirror of a sports car, getting the feel of the wheel, they wink at each other confidently, preparing to close the deal. But, instead of whipping out a checkbook, Hart whips out a notebook and begins scribbling.

Alison Hart

This is no ordinary customer. Alison Hart is a bestselling novelist on a mission—she's busy falling in love with the characters in her next work of fiction.

"If I'm going to spend three months with these characters, I have to find out who they are, what makes them tick. I've found the best way to get to know them is to find out what clothes they might wear, what car they drive—what they stash in their glove compartments!" says Alison Hart, who as 'Jennifer Greene,' 'Jeanne Grant,' and 'Jessica Massey' has written more than 57 contemporary romance novels in the past 20 years. Hart's work has earned her a long list of awards, including three RITAs from the Romance Writers of America (RWA), a coveted spot in the RWA Hall of Fame and loyal readers around the world. Her work has been translated into 20 languages, including Portuguese and Japanese.

Reviewers and readers alike marvel at Hart's ability to create women of substance and three-dimensional, "to die for" leading men who possess brains and hearts along with their physical appeal. Her fellow writers wonder, "How does she do it?" What they don't know is that over the years Hart has developed a system for creating heroines women identify with and wonderful supportive men who set their pulses racing.

"It may not work for every writer, but I find picking out my characters' wardrobes, or imagining what cars they drive really helps me get a handle on their personalities," says Hart. "For example, I'm a blonde, but if I decide to make my heroine a redhead, I've got to put myself in her shoes. What colors dominate her closet? What shade of lipstick would she wear? What does she keep in her purse? How does she wear her hair?" Hart even searches through hair color packages on drugstore shelves to pinpoint the exact shade of vibrant auburn to match a character's feisty personality and green eyes.

Deciding her character would wear a short bob with spikey bangs instead of a soft shoulder-

---

MARY COX *is editor of* Artist's & Graphic Designer's Market, *and a frequent contributor to Writer's Digest Books.*

length style might lead Hart to picture her heroine wearing an up-to-the-minute short suit instead of a classic flowing skirt and cashmere sweater. Trying on shoes helps Hart "see" her redhead striding swiftly to her desk in snappy pumps, rather than gliding gracefully through the door in delicate t-straps. Each seemingly insignificant detail leads to another, becoming links in a chain of hundreds of traits that, put together, begin to define her character.

The same theory holds true for the men in Hart's fiction. If her "guy" is an architect with a quirky sense of humor, what kind of car would he drive? Would he enter the redhead's life wearing an Armani suit or a red-and-black flannel jacket? Is he addicted to soccer or *Star Trek*?

Once she's got a character's "look," Hart has some concrete information to build on. The details begin to contribute to making a whole picture. Emotional traits begin to emerge. That's when Hart concentrates on what her character might do for a living. She's got a few tricks up her sleeve for that, too.

The postal carrier who delivers to Hart's Michigan farm is undoubtedly just as perplexed as the clerks Hart encounters on her shopping sprees. Why would a seemingly quiet farm couple subscribe to *Fire Chief, Police Times* and *Nurse Week*? Trade magazines allow Hart to "eavesdrop" on her characters at work. Each profession has its own buzz words, says Hart. Characters sound more convincing if those words are used correctly, and sound natural in dialogue. How might interior designers or doctors sound when speaking to colleagues casually and comfortably in the argot of their professions? What do they talk about at the water cooler? What issues frustrate or fascinate them?

Hart suggests you try this trick, too. If your character is an architect, you should read *Architectural Digest*. If he's a fireman, subscribe to *Firefighter*. Before writing about a lawyer, read a few issues of *The Lawyers Weekly*. If your heroine enters her horse in competitions, *Dressage Today* will help you describe the trophies your character might proudly display on her mantelpiece. Hart swears by police procedural books for lending accuracy to dialogue when one of her heroines gets into a scrape, or falls madly in love with a cop. "The procedurals published by Writer's Digest Books are wonderful for bringing authentic details into your writing."

For detail in setting, Hart advises building several short business trips/vacations into your yearly schedule to help you set the scene for your novel. Stay in a town long enough to get the feel of the climate, the look of the sunsets and to get a handle on the architecture, the flowers and the foliage. (Be sure to keep all your receipts so you can deduct them later as business expenses, says Hart.)

Because smells trigger memories, Hart also makes it a point to bring home a fragrant souvenir—a scent that will remind her of her intended setting. A favorite trick is scooping a handful of earth or sand into a plastic bag. Or perhaps she'll bring back a cinnamon stick to remind her of a dessert she enjoyed in a certain town. Back home at the keyboard, one sniff transports her back to the setting and helps her write about it. Music and sound also help her hold onto the mood of a place. If a certain melody or rhythm—such as a country song or the sound of a Dixieland band or classical guitar—calls forth memories of her setting, she'll pop it into her CD player before she starts writing.

"I love choosing a theme when I start a novel," says Hart, almost apologizing for using that "old-fashioned high school English word." Her reasons are far from academic, insists Hart. It's all part of her plan to transport readers out of their daily lives and plunge them into a different world.

As a reader, Hart loves to come away from a novel having learned something new without even realizing it. Hart points out it is no coincidence that most bestsellers offer in-depth views of some fascinating environment or profession—such as the world of commerce, medicine, art or antiques, Hollywood, Chinatown—any subject will do, as long as it's one most readers know nothing about. So for each book, Hart researches several topics she can weave into her plots that resonate with the character's growth.

In *The Unwilling Bride*, Hart's heroine is a sculptor who carves cameos from jade and coral.

Hart researched cameos and precious stones for months so she could describe the jet, tortoise shell, amber, mother-of-pearl, jade and coral her character chisels to form each cameo. Hart researched the tools her character would use, and made a study of the colors and textures of each precious stone to determine which characteristics a sculptor would prize in the rarest and most perfect of all cameos.

Hart's descriptions of the flawless two-toned coral, in rich cherry-red colors the Italians call *rosso scuro* coupled with her explanation of how coral divers search for it in the deepest waters off the coast of Sardinia, makes for fascinating reading. But more than that, her descriptions dovetail beautifully with the lead character's obsessive search for the perfect stone for a special cameo she's carving to give her shy sister. The description of precious coral found only by "diving in deepest waters" resonates with the heroine's blossoming relationship with Stefan, an exuberant Russian who brings humor and spontaneity to her overly disciplined existence. He's someone willing to dive deep to find the treasure that lies beyond her cool exterior.

Although Hart is serious about plot and theme, she's quick to point out that "characters are the most important ingredient in romantic fiction. Your main character must go through a growth process." Hart's complicated heroines often struggle to overcome internal insecurities to find a new strength before the novel's end. It is the triumph of her women characters that keeps reader coming back for more.

Strong women in a romance novel? "Of course," says Hart. It rankles her when people stereotype the romance genre as "anti-feminist," she says, because the genre is very much pro-women. As one who deeply believes in the women's movement, Hart chose to work in the romance genre because she had a desire to help women: "I knew that by writing for this genre, I could reach more women readers than through any other type of writing."

In romance novels, Hart sees a great opportunity to show women how to be strong without preaching to them. While enjoying a warm romance, readers also find role models—strong women characters who stand up for themselves and who expect their men to be equal partners who respect them and are supportive of their dreams.

Within the context of a love story, Hart can expose women to a new kind of romance heroine—a strong woman who loves her career and leads a full life even before Mr. Right enters the picture. "In all my books, the heroine solves her own problems. A man doesn't come along on a white horse and instantly solve them for her." That Hart's characters happen to find a supportive soul mate along the way is the icing on the cake. "On the surface it may be a love story," says Hart, "but on a deeper level, it is the story of how one woman changes and grows and gains self-esteem through confronting a crisis or turning point in her life."

Hart doesn't flinch when writing about women's lives. Working within a genre other writers sometimes label as lightweight, she isn't afraid to tackle heavy-hitting issues such as date rape, alcoholism and impotence. "I think it is really important to bring these problems out in the open," says Hart.

"When my readers see how a strong woman deals with problems—how she acts in a relationship with an equal partner who respects her and is supportive of her dreams—I hope these concepts teach them to stand up for themselves. The story hopefully offers a model for discussing difficult or sensitive issues in their relationships."

But what about those who need a role model for being a romance writer? That's easy, Hart says. Before you start writing your first romance novel, "the very first thing you should do is to go to a secondhand book store, and fill a giant box full of paperbacks of all types of romances." Pick out historical and contemporary romances, and everything in between. There are so many genres-within-genres to choose from.

"To the outsider they all sound alike, but just as there are niches within the mystery genre—from the cozy on down—there are niches within the romance field." Some romances are light and humorous, others dark and heavy with lots of drama. Some are contemporary, others historical. As you read, you'll find some that appeal to you, others that don't.

After you zero in on the kind of romance you want to write, Hart advises you notice page length, number of chapters and other elements, such as the amount of dialogue used, which tend to stay fairly consistent within sub-genres. (Hart offers a favorite clue for writing good dialogue: "Say it out loud!")

Even though you are writing romances, Hart urges writers to continue reading outside the genre. A voracious reader who devours romances by Emilie Richards, Nora Roberts, Sandra Canfield and Jennifer Crusie, Hart also reads Pat Conroy, Susan Elizabeth Phillips and Michael Crichton, paying close attention to pacing and point of view. "I learned a lot about suspense from Michael Crichton—I believe even a romance should be a page-turner!"

The key is to "write what you love to write," says Hart, "while sticking to the few informal rules within your chosen genre. The 'rules' for each sub-genre are easy to pick up through reading them closely." (Remember that giant box?) Once you settle on a sub-genre, then research which publishers and editors are likely to want what you write.

To market your writing you have to be attuned to the differences in tone of romances published by various publishing houses. Not only should you be familiar with which houses publish *your* type of romance; you have to be familiar with each particular line within those publishing houses, and preferably become savvy enough to pinpoint which editors would be most receptive to your fiction. "I'm lucky in writing for Silhouette. Editors at Silhouette can buy for all lines, but that's not necessarily true of all publishers," says Hart.

This is where RWA, writers' groups and online newsgroups come in. In today's market, it is really necessary to join RWA, attend conferences and network with other writers, says Hart. In the years after she began writing, while her children were little, Hart didn't have that advantage. She wrote in isolation for years before selling her first manuscript. Today, she says, beginning writers can find out crucial information about marketing through the RWA.

"When I found RWA my whole world opened up," says Hart. "RWA conferences would be good for any writer—not just those in the romance genre. The panels are wonderful." There are publisher-specific sessions called "Spotlight on Bantam," "Spotlight on Warner" or "Spotlight on Harlequin," as well as other publishers, where panels of editors tell what they are buying. Sessions aren't limited to marketing, says Hart. RWA offers helpful sessions on polishing your craft and other topics, too. "I once attended a discussion by a panel of cops who answered questions about their work. I've also attended fascinating sessions on medieval food and weapons."

The mention of RWA brings up memories of Hart's first RITA award for contemporary fiction. At the RWA awards dinner, so sure she didn't have a chance at winning, Hart had kicked off her heels under the table. "I almost took to the stage in my stocking feet." When her name was called Hart grabbed hold of her editor's hand and scrambled to slip back into her shoes, whispering to her friend that she hadn't prepared a speech. Hart, the prolific writer, known for her characters' witty dialogue, was finally out of words. "Alison," her editor whispered as they walked up to the podium, "You'd better start thinking!" Ever true to her inventive nature, she did.

Ann Leslie: Bringing Passion to Romance Writing

BY HEIDI L. WINDMILLER

"Our authors must have a passion, a real excitement for the field of romance writing," says Silhouette associate editor Ann Leslie. "I know I am very excited about being an editor at Silhouette, and I wake up each morning and look forward to work. Likewise, I think writers must feel that writing romances is what they really want to do, and love what they are doing. That passion will translate to the editor."

Ann Leslie

Leslie first entered publishing as a reference book editor at Scribners. But her love of reading romance led her to a job at Silhouette. "I realized that (this kind of) fiction was what I really wanted to do, and it had always been my dream to nurture my own base of authors," she says. "I had always read women's fiction, and I wanted to edit and publish the type of fiction I was actually reading." Leslie's first position, as a freelance reader reviewing unsolicited manuscripts, led to a promotion to assistant editor and later to her current position of associate editor.

"In acquiring and editing romance books, I have about 28 authors I directly work with, and I am involved in all stages, from finding new talent to working with authors who are already with us," Leslie says. "It is really exciting to go from the point of discovering a special manuscript in a writing contest or helping an author find their next story to seeing it on the shelf."

Here she takes time out of her editing schedule to discuss what Silhouette editors look for in manuscripts, and how writers might break into the market.

Do you prefer to contract previously unpublished writers for more than one novel?

Generally, if it is an author who is previously unpublished, we would start with a one book contract. Unlike other houses, we often contract the author's next book before we have sales figures on the first titles in an attempt to build the author's presence in a line. Then authors work their way up. It all depends upon the author's track record and it is very specific to that author.

Do you usually solicit writers or do they contact you?

We do a little bit of both in the sense that we will go to conferences and take editor/author appointments. From the conference, I will be sent the manuscripts and I'll evaluate them and see if they work for us. Because we are so well known in the romance industry, we get letters every day pitching projects from unpublished authors and agents.

Do most of your writers have agents?

No, they don't. It depends on what the author feels her publishing needs are. Some feel very comfortable having an agent, others feel just as comfortable not having the agent. It's probably 50/50.

HEIDI L. WINDMILLER *is an editorial intern for Writer's Digest Books.*

Can you offer writers any tips for writing strong query letters?

Familiarity with our books is important because we publish category romance, and there are certain needs we're going to have that are very different from mainstream. Also, tell me about yourself as a writer: have you entered contests? How long you have been writing? Include anything that tells me you have a commitment to your writing career. Include a brief synopsis, hitting on the high points such as who the characters are and the emotional conflict.

What specifically are you looking for in a synopsis?

I am not averse to receiving a detailed synopsis. I want to see a sense of the story setup, who the characters are, the backstory, the story opening, key scenes and how they advance and develop the emotional conflict, and how the story resolves itself. I am not too concerned with length, but obviously a 40-page synopsis could be a bit off-putting.

What makes a manuscript stand out?

I think first and foremost it is the writer's voice that makes a manuscript stand out, and that is a hard element to describe. A writer can know all the elements in a story, but it is really her voice and the life she brings to these story elements that make a story special. Well-developed backstories for the protagonists also make a story special—then we know who the characters are and how they would respond in situations. Also, the writer needs to know our market and what our readers want, and integrate those needs into the context of the story.

Where do most manuscripts fall short of your expectations?

There are several areas. Pacing is one of them. The author needs to hook the reader immediately, come up with a captivating story, and then keep the pacing tight throughout her romance. We look for a strong emotional conflict—something that is going to sustain the length of the romance novel. Because everyone knows how these books end, the author has to set up obstacles and resolve them skillfully. I think the other thing is a lack of fantasy. There can be a real tendency to develop something dark, that makes you sit back and wonder, "Where is the fantasy?"

Do you think writers should stick to one category of romance, or should they try their skills in a variety of categories?

If I start working with a writer, I am trying to develop her in a line. And if she starts out writing romantic suspense, I really want to see her stay with romantic suspense so we can build reader recognition for her name. Whereas, if she starts writing for different lines there will be different readers for each line, so she is not going to get a chance to really develop her name.

What kinds of romance novels are you looking for now?

All the same classic themes such as boss/secretary, sheik books, marriage of convenience, stolen nights of passion, and pretend engagements. I am also looking for inspirational romances for the Steeple Hill Love Inspired line focusing on Christian characters facing challenges of life and love.

What is your advice to writers who want to get their work published by Silhouette?

Know the market. I can't stress enough the importance of reading our stories. I also think the writer must be persistent and dedicated and believe in the story she is writing. But there must also be a degree of realism when a story isn't working. When that happens, maybe it is time to put it aside and start on a new one.

Romance Markets Appearing in This Book

Below is a list of romance markets appearing in this edition of *Novel & Short Story Writer's Market*. To find page numbers of particular magazines or book publishing markets, go first to the General Index beginning on page 663 of this book. Then turn to the pages those listings appear on for complete information, including who to contact and how to submit your romance short story or novel manuscript.

Magazines

About Such Things
Advocate, PKA's Publication
Aguilar Expression, The
Amherst Review, The
Axe Factory Review
Bibliophilos
Blue Skunk Companion, The
Bridal Guides
Brilliant Corners
Brobdingnagian Times, The
Chat
Cochran's Corner
Cosmopolitan Magazine
CZ's Magazine
Dan River Anthology
Dialogue
Disenchanted
Downstate Story
Dream International/Quarterly
Drinkin' Buddy Magazine, The
Eternity Magazine
Eureka Literary Magazine
Evansville Review
Eyes
Fugue
Gathering of the Tribes, A
Gotta Write Network Litmag
Grit
Hayden's Ferry Review
Home Times
Jeopardy
Lamplight, The
Lynx Eye
Matriarch's Way: Journal of Female Supremacy
Medicinal Purposes
Merlyn's Pen
Musing Place, The
My Legacy
My Weekly
New England Writers' Network
New Writing
Nite-Writer's International Literary Arts Journal
Northwoods Journal
Ohio Teachers Write
Outer Darkness

Palo Alto Review
Penny-A-Liner
PeopleNet DisAbility DateNet Home Page
Poetry Forum Short Stories
Poskisnolt Press
Post, The
Potpourri
PSI
Reader's Break
Rejected Quarterly, The
Romantic Hearts
Rose & Thorn Literary E-Zine, The
Rosebud™
St. Anthony Messenger
San Diego Writers' Monthly
Shades Of December
Short Story Writers Showcase
Short Stuff Magazine for Grown-Ups
Skylark
Spoonfed
SPSM&H
State of Being
Storyteller, The
Tale Spinner, The
"Teak" Roundup
Threshold, The
Virginia Quarterly Review
VQ
West Wind Review
Woman's World Magazine
Writer's Head, The
Writes of Passage
Yellow Sticky Notes

Book Publishers

Avalon Books
Avon Books
Bantam Books
Beggar's Press
Berkley Publishing Group, The
British Book Company, Inc., The
Dan River Press
Dell Publishing Island
Doubleday Adult Trade
Dutton Plume
Edge Science Fiction and Fantasy Publishing

Fanfare
GoldenIsle Publishers Inc.
Harlequin Enterprises, Ltd.
Harlequin Mills & Boon Ltd.
HarperPaperbacks
Harvest House Publishers
Heartsong Presents
Kaeden Books
Kensington Publishing Corp.
Leisure Books
Lemeac Editeur Inc.
LionHearted Publishing, Inc.

Love Spell
Orpheus Romance
Red Sage Publishing, Inc.
St. Martin's Press
Scherf Books
Seniors Market, The
Silhouette Books
Steeple Hill
Thorndike Press
Vista Publishing, Inc.
Warner Books
Zebra Books

Resources for Romance Writers

Below is a list of invaluable resources specifically for romance writers. For more information on the magazines and organizations listed below, check the General Index and the Publications of Interest and Organizations sections of this book. To order any of the Writer's Digest Books titles or to get a consumer book catalog, call 1-800-289-0963. You may also order Writer's Digest Books selections through www.writersdigest.com, Amazon.com or www.barnesandnoble.com.

MAGAZINES:

- *Fiction Writer*, 1507 Dana Ave., Cincinnati OH 45207
- *Romance Writers Report*, Romance Writers of America, 3707 FM 1960 West, Suite 555, Houston TX 77014. (281)440-6885. Fax: (281)440-7510. E-mail: infobox@rwanational. com
- *Romantic Times Magazine*, 55 Bergen St., Brooklyn NY 11201. (718)237-1097. Website: www.romantictimes.com
- *Writer's Digest*, 1507 Dana Ave., Cincinnati OH 45207

BOOKS:

- *How To Write Romances (Revised and Updated)*, Writer's Digest Books
- *Keys to Success: A Professional Writer's Career Handbook*, Attention: Handbook, Romance Writers of America, 13700 Veterans Memorial, Suite 315, Houston TX 77014-1023. (281)440-6885, ext. 21. Fax: (281)440-7510. E-mail: infobox@rwanational.com
- *Romance Writer's Sourcebook: Where to Sell Your Manuscripts*, Writer's Digest Books
- *The Writer's Guide to Everyday Life in Regency and Victorian England*, Writer's Digest Books
- *Writing Romances: A Handbook by the Romance Writers of America*, Writer's Digest Books
- *You Can Write a Romance*, Writer's Digest Books

ORGANIZATIONS & ONLINE

- Romance Writers of America, Inc. (RWA), 3703 FM 1960 West, Suite 555, Houston TX 77068. (281)440-6885, ext. 21. Fax: (281)440-7510. E-mail: infobox@rwanational.com
- Romance Writers of America regional chapters. Contact National Office (address above) for information on the chapter nearest you.
- Romance Central website: romance-central.com. Offers workshops and forum where romance writers share ideas and exchange advice about romance writing. (See complete listing in the Websites of Interest section of this book.)

The Science Fiction & Fantasy Market Today

BY SHARON LEE, Executive Director, Science Fiction and Fantasy Writers of America

Sharon Lee

Trying to explain where science fiction and fantasy publishing is at any given moment is like doing an intricate, interconnected series of good-news/bad-news skits.

At first glance, the current trends in science fiction and fantasy publishing look discouraging, if not downright terrifying. Last year, the publishing industry trembled in the face of several corporate mergers. Bertelsmann AG, which already owned Bantam Doubleday Dell, purchased Random House, with its dozens of imprints, including Del Rey, Ballantine and Knopf. A dozen more imprints were consolidated under the Penguin Putnam umbrella. In other news, HarperCollins merged with William Morrow & Co. and Avon.

All of this would seem to argue for a decrease in actual books being bought and published, right?

Not necessarily.

After a couple of years in decline, the number of new SF/F books published in 1998 increased. Mass market paperbacks, once the field's bread and butter, saw a decrease in numbers, true enough—but the numbers for trade paperback and hardcover originals increased. Some genre experts see this trend away from mass market publication as a validation of the literature; a sign that speculative fiction is "growing up."

There's also good news for those who write short fiction: After three years in which the number of stories published in professional genre magazines fell, the numbers are rising. Even more encouraging for writers is the range of solid semi-pro zines that have grown up over the last couple years. Most magazines are eager to work with new writers.

In an effort to cut down on the amount of slush landing on editorial desks, some publishing houses have instituted an "agented manuscripts only" policy. At first glance, this policy seems to make the barrier to publishing for new, unagented writers insurmountable.

Look again.

Though some houses have stopped reading unagented material, Ace, Avon Eos, Baen, Bantam Spectra and Tor will look at the first three chapters and a synopsis of your novel. Roc, DAW and St. Martin's will read the whole manuscript. That's plenty to start with. And there's no law that says you can't be agent-shopping—an arduous process in itself—while your book is out for consideration.

SHARON LEE *has been publishing speculative fiction for 20 years. Her first professional sale was to* Amazing Stories, *in 1980. She is co-author, with Steve Miller, of the* Liaden Universe *books, first published by Del Rey in 1988 and 1989. Meisha Merlin Publishing has bought the rights to seven* Liaden *novels. Her most recent short fiction appears in* Catfantastic V *and in* Absolute Magnitude. *In August 1997, she was hired by the Science Fiction and Fantasy Writers of America, Inc. to be the organization's executive director and first full-time employee.*

A word here about the Good Old Days.

Some older writers tend to wax nostalgic about the past and will cheerfully tell new writers about the good ol' days and how "easy" it was to get published, way back in '93 or '90 or '88. On first hearing, these fond tales of yesterday seem reasonable, because, in fact, more paperback originals were published in 1988 than in 1998.

The truth is that it's never been "easy" to get published. Authors today are doing the same thing authors were doing five, eight, and ten years ago. They're writing the very best stories they can write, and sending them out, over and over, until they sell. This remains a constant, among all the changes that have swept through the field.

The biggest changes overtaking our field—and every other field within sight—are those wrought by electronic communication: e-zines, e-books, CD-ROMs, and who knows what else we'll have by next Wednesday. The electronic environment is changing so fast, no one's quite sure yet where or how the money will manifest. This has resulted in some rather odd contracts, as publishing houses try to maximize their investments.

As always, writers should read their contracts closely, and be clear about which rights are sold and which are retained. Particular attention needs to be paid to the reversion clause. Find out what happens when the book goes out of print. Find out what the publisher means when they say "out of print," since the reality of print-on-demand technology has thrown this seemingly straightforward phrase into a tailspin.

Some publishers are exploring the opportunity of e-zines and online publishing. Again, authors need to be certain of the rights they are selling. As a general rule of thumb, an author selling first electronic rights should negotiate a set time during which his story will be displayed, and possibly another length of time when the story is archived on the magazine's website, before rights revert.

As the electronic world and the Internet are expanding the opportunities for writers and publishers, they have also, unfortunately, given rise to a number of dangers. These dangers are not specific to SF/F writers, but to new or unexperienced writers.

Scam agents and bogus publishing houses have taken to the Internet like ducks to water. For God's sake, be careful.

The Association of Authors Representatives (AAR) has a list of questions for writers to ask agents, as well as a list of their members, posted on the web at: www.bookwire.com/AAR/homepage.html (For those who are not web-capable, write to AAR at 10 Astor Place, Third Floor, New York, NY 10003. Enclose a SASE).

In general, be wary of publishers who want you to provide a "stake" in publishing your book. The book *is* your stake. In the usual way of things, the publisher pays the author for the right to publish the author's book, not the other way around. If you do choose to self-publish your work, be very clear that this is your intent.

And, the last, the unchanging, warning: *Don't sign bad contracts*. It's hard, with that sale hanging in the balance, to take the time to cool-headedly read the contract and pay attention to what the publisher is buying. It *is* hard—but do it anyway. If the contract contains unacceptable clauses, try to negotiate them into more favorable form. If the unacceptable clauses are non-negotiable, take the time to seriously consider if you can live with those terms. If you can't, don't sign.

As difficult as it may be to believe in this age of mega-mergers, the publishing of speculative fiction started out as a small-time operation. The pulp magazines which printed SF/F stories enjoyed, let us say, a less-than-favorable position in the literary pecking order; novels serialized in the pulps were very rarely issued in book form (among those novels was Isaac Asimov's *Foundation* series). It thus fell to the enthusiasts of the genre to take publishing into their own hands. This they did with a will, and some of the houses they founded are still listed as viable markets in this guide.

Today, we find it hard to believe that there ever was a void—a time when stories of otherwhen and elsewhere were not easily obtainable. Today, the language and the images of speculative fiction have to a certain extent permeated our everyday lives. There's talk that SF/F is becoming "homogenized," "mundane." Some critics say that its work is done, its sun setting.

This is nonsense.

Speculative fiction is the genre that asks "What if?"

The answers to that question—the stories of the far future, the near future, and the magical never-was—have helped shape the present we stand in today. But the future is still before us. We have problems ahead that must be solved, joys to embrace and puzzles to unravel. We need stories that teach us how to solve problems creatively, to think outrageously; stories that illuminate the human condition in places strange and far from home—or on the next street over.

The work of our genre is just beginning.

Octavia Butler: Pushing the Boundaries of the Future

BY TRICIA WADDELL

Octavia Butler has always had a mind of her own when it comes to fiction. "It never occurred to me to ask, 'If no one else is doing it, do I dare to do it?' But I realize that a lot of people think if there's no model, then maybe there's some reason not to do something," she said in a 1988 interview in the anthology *Across the Wounded Galaxies*. Today, this award-winning author of 11 novels and a short story collection is still breaking the mold and challenging readers with provocative sociological and speculative fiction. Particularly known for her dystopian vision and unique explorations of race and gender issues, Butler's work is adored by fans, taught in college classrooms and critically debated in science fiction, African-American and feminist journals alike. *Ms. Magazine* called Butler's work "a literature of survival" and the *Village Voice* wrote, "Butler's

Octavia Butler

Photo by Miriam Berkley

books are exceptional . . . [She] is a realist, writing the most detailed social criticism and creating some of the most fascinating female characters in the genre."

The confidence and determination to follow her own mind has been the force behind Butler's 25-year publishing career and a crucial part of her makeup since she was a little girl. She started writing when she was 10 and began submitting stories for publication at the age of 13. Raised on dimestore science fiction paperbacks and comic books, Butler was influenced most by the classic SF writers she read growing up in Pasadena. Theodore Sturgeon, Harlan Ellison, John Brunner, Marion Zimmer Bradley, Eric Frank Russell, J.T. Macintosh and James Schmidt are just of few of the writers that shaped the imagination of the shy young author. But it was her training at the Writer's Guild of America West classes and the Clarion Science Fiction Writer's Workshop where she honed her craft. At Clarion, she was taught by Harlan Ellison who later became her mentor and life-long friend. And in 1970, after 10 years of persistence, Butler sold her first short story at the age of 23.

Butler published her first book, *Patternmaster* (Doubleday), in 1976. Originally based on an idea she had when she was 12, *Patternmaster* was the first in a five-volume series about an elite group of mentally linked telepaths. Her most popular novel, *Kindred* (Doubleday), about a contemporary black woman sent back in time to a slave plantation in the antebellum South, was published in 1979. Next Butler published her *Xenogenisis* trilogy (Warner Books) in the late 1980s, exploring the self-destructive human tendency toward hierarchical behavior. Her most recent novel series began with *Parable of the Sower* (Four Walls Eight Windows, 1993), named a *New York Times* Notable Book of the Year. In 1998 she published a sequel, *Parable of the Talents* (Seven Stories Press), named one of the best books of 1998 by *Publishers Weekly*. Butler's short story collection of previously published works, *Bloodchild and Other Stories* (Four Walls Eight Windows, 1995), includes her Hugo and Nebula Award-winning novella

TRICIA WADDELL *is production editor for* Novel & Short Story Writer's Market *and* Artist's & Graphic Designer's Market, *and a frequent contributor to Writer's Digest Books.*

"Bloodchild" and her short story, "Speech Sounds," which also won the Hugo Award. In 1995, Butler was awarded a $295,000 MacArthur Foundation fellowship "Genius Award" for her ongoing literary contribution in creating a body of work that constantly challenges our idea of the near and distant future.

Shunning marketing labels that confine her to being narrowly categorized as a science fiction writer, an African-American writer, or a feminist writer, Butler says "a good story is a good story, no matter what genre or non-genre it fits into." In a 1997 interview in *Poets & Writers Magazine* she explained, "I write about people who do extraordinary things. It just turned out that it was called science fiction." Butler, who refers to writing as her "positive obsession," takes a break from writing the next book in the *Parable* series to talk about her publishing career, changes in the science fiction genre and the craft of creating the literature of the future.

You sold your first three novels without an agent. How did you choose Doubleday as your first publisher?

I began with Doubleday in 1975, because it was big. It was willing to take a chance publishing new writers because it had a subscription arrangement with schools and libraries. All three books were almost completely written by the time Doubleday took my first book. I had been laid off and between looking for another job and writing as fast as I could I managed to get two and a half novels done in one year. It was the only time that ever happened.

I had been working on these novels in bits and pieces for many years. I got the idea for *Patternmaster* when I was 12 and the idea for *Mind of My Mind* when I was 15. I wrote a version of *Survivor* when I was 19. I wasn't just starting from scratch. I think most new writers begin with a trunk, either a physical trunk with their old novels in it or a mental trunk of ideas. This was my trunk.

Your novel *Kindred* is not science fiction, even though you are categorized as a science fiction writer. Did you have any trouble selling it to a publisher?

Kindred sold to Doubleday's general fiction department. I tried to sell it elsewhere because I was only offered an advance of $1,750 each for my first three books. I was just dying to get out. Meanwhile an agent from Writer's House wrote asking if I needed an agent. She wound up handling *Kindred*. She submitted it all over the place but couldn't sell it because people couldn't figure out where to place it. Publishers didn't know how to sell it. It's obviously not science fiction although people tend to assume it is because it involves time travel. It went through about 15 different publishers before my agent finally sold it back to Doubleday.

Your *Xenogenisis* trilogy was published by Warner. How was your experience working with another large publisher?

Warner paid me a decent advance, but I got very little advertising except as science fiction. I had been trying to convince people since *Kindred* that I had more than a science fiction audience. I had a new agent, Marrillee Heifitz, at Writer's House. She told me about a new small press called Four Walls Eight Windows. I did *Parable of the Sower* and *Bloodchild and Other Stories* with them. They were willing to market my work to whomever as opposed to just keeping me in science fiction. That was really important. Their books were reviewed by people who might not normally review science fiction. And they were willing to send me out on tour and no one had done that before. I reached a lot of audiences I wouldn't have otherwise if I had stayed with one of the strictly science fiction publishers. Then my editor left and I followed him to Seven Stories Press.

How do you create the titles for your books?

What I generally do, and this was back in typewriter days, I would roll in a piece of paper and just pop off a number of titles as fast as I could. If that didn't work I would pull out quotation books and dictionaries. I love specialized dictionaries, and own about a hundred of them. I just start going through them looking for something that grabs me. Sometimes just finding a title is real work. A title is a piece of advertising. It's also a piece of seduction. If you've got a dull title you may not have to worry if anybody likes your story because most of them won't even read it.

There have been many changes in the science fiction field since you first began publishing in the 1970s. How have those changes affected your career?

Many schools that never discussed science fiction now use my books in the classroom. *Kindred* is the one most often used, also *Dawn, Parable of the Sower* and *Wild Seed*. But it's still possible to get totally ignored because you write science fiction, especially with reviewers in newspapers and non-science fiction magazines. I don't mind a poor review if it's an honest review. What I mind is being ignored completely because they don't take science fiction seriously.

You have commented that you have three different audiences: a science fiction audience, a feminist audience and an African-American audience. These audiences also overlap. How do your different audiences affect you as a writer or inform your work?

I write from my own interests. Considering feminism, if you were reading science fiction back in the 50s and 60s, you got a lot of sexist stuff. Lots of cliché and prize women, women who weren't really there, literally and figuratively. One of the things I do is write myself in as female and black into the various universes I write about. When I did *Dawn* for instance, I was responding to some old clichés in science fiction. If you study history and anthropology, you realize no society could run without the women's contribution.

How has the writing process changed for you over the years?

My first book, *Patternmaster*, was something I had lived with for many years. The novels I'm writing now are novels I have to come up with. The backlog is gone. It takes a lot longer to get a novel out. I have to create the world and live in it a little bit before I can write about it.

What is your research process for providing historical, social and scientific credibility to your writing?

I try to show the situation and make it real without getting so technical as to bore somebody. One thing I tell new writers is don't gloss over things that would obviously be a problem. When I come up with a situation I need to feel it on my own body. Some people see things. I hear and feel them. I don't visualize well, but dialogue needs to feel right to me, needs to feel like something someone would actually say. Places and situations need to be believable. Plus, I'm not the kind of writer who does all the research and then sits down to write the book. The research and the writing of the book are happening at the same time. One is goosing the other. I get an idea from the research and it goes right into the novel. I'm working on the novel, I hit a question and go do more research.

You once said, "Every story I create, creates me. I write to create myself." How do you create yourself through your writing?

I write about characteristics I admire. I have to find a way to know my characters and like them. It helps if they have some aspect of themselves that I find admirable and perhaps missing or not that strong in me. For instance, when I wrote about Mary Larkin in *Mind of My Mind*, I didn't know how to write about that kind of person. She is not fearless, but she's the kind of person who takes action. My tendency is to go around the trouble. Her tendency is to confront it. I had to think about those people in my life who were likely to confront the trouble, and figure out what they would do and then cut that to fit Mary Larkin. By the time I was done with the novel, I was a bit more like Mary Larkin than I had been when I began it just because I had to learn how to build her.

What is your advice to new writers in regard to publishing?

Pay attention to the markets. What amazes me is there are still people who try to sell stories to magazines and other publications they've never bothered to read. Something I can't stress enough is people should spend a lot of time at their public library. The library is where I made use of writers' magazines early on because I couldn't afford to buy them. A big part of the problem is new writers haven't got a clue what's out there.

Jennifer Brehl: An Editor's Inside Scoop on Science Fiction

BY IAN BESSLER

"I am, first and foremost, an editor," says Jennifer Brehl, science fiction editor for Avon. "A true writer burns with the passion of writing; I don't have that passion. I *do*, however, have incredible passion for other people's work. All my energy and all my spare time go into other people's work. I dream about it. I wake up at night thinking, 'Aha, that's how so-and-so should work out that plot twist . . .' "

Brehl entered the editorial world immediately after graduating from William Smith College with a degree in English Literature. She took a job as an "in-house floater" with Doubleday, working in various editorial departments, book clubs, production and in the art department. She eventually settled into a position as an editorial secretary. "It was at that time that I had the good fortune to meet Isaac Asimov, who would become a major figure in my professional life. It was he who encouraged me as a young editor; I worked with him for the final eight years of his life."

Brehl came early to her love of science fiction. "I had always liked science fiction, and read it from childhood, just as I'd liked and read other types of literature. What engages me most about science fiction is its challenge to the reader to think 'outside the box,' to put aside preconceived notions about how things are, or how things can be, and really stretch one's imagination," says Brehl, who counts Asimov, Harlan Ellison, Ursula K. Le Guin, Connie Ellis and Ray Bradbury among her favorite authors. "And I like both the short story form and the novel equally, but for different reasons. A short story is more of a snapshot, whereas in a novel the author can really dig in, delve into his themes."

After six years with Doubleday, Brehl left publishing for a stint as a manager with a market research firm. She edged back into the publishing world by taking a job with Bantam Doubleday Dell Direct identifying and developing books for series release, which provided her with a satisfying mix of editing and marketing. However, she found she missed the routines of interacting with authors and the processes of guiding a book from inception to publication. Her return to editorial work was complete when, in November of 1995, Avon lured her away to work on its science fiction line, including the development of a new science fiction anthology for future release.

Despite her hectic daily schedule of meetings, manuscripts and discussions with authors, Brehl took some time to talk about the health of the science fiction genre, and advice for writers trying to break in.

While waiting for replies to queries and manuscripts, a lot of writers grow curious about what goes on in an editor's office. What should writers know about an average day at the office?

My day is pretty much filled up with various meetings—editorial, cover conference, publicity launch, paging and pricing, print order, marketing—you name it, it's got a meeting attached to

---

IAN BESSLER *is production editor for* Poet's Market *and* Guide to Literary Agents, *and a regular contributor to* Writer's Digest Books.

it! In between meetings, I attend to the various details of getting books done—going over copy-edited manuscripts, talking to authors, talking to sales reps, writing letters to key accounts about upcoming books, going over publicity releases, etc. A typical day is largely unscripted, so many things just pop up. An author might call with a crisis, or the art director may ask me to drop everything to comment on a cover concept—any number of things can and do happen with alarming regularity. If I don't have a business lunch with an agent or author, I tend to eat at my desk, during which time I go over sales reports, bestseller lists, read *Publishers Weekly*, *Locus*, the *New York Times Book Review* and publicity clippings.

I'm pretty exhausted by the time I leave in the evening, but I do the actual editorial work outside of the office, so I tend to read on the train ride home, then work for an hour or so at home each night. I also spend at least one full weekend day reading and editing manuscripts at home.

Submissions are logged in by my assistant. Either she or associate editor Diana Gill do the first read, unless something comes in from an author I know, or from an agent I know and trust, and who has called me about the particular project.

What is your view on the state of science fiction as a genre, especially how it has manifested itself in the manuscripts you've been reviewing for possible inclusion in the anthology?

I'm not sure if science fiction is particularly strong right now. It doesn't seem to me there's been any "oomph" lately. And I don't think that commercially it is doing terribly well, unless you count *Star Wars*, *Star Trek*, *X-Files*, etc. Senior vice-president/publisher Lou Aronica, Diana Gill and I are still working on putting together our as-yet-unnamed science fiction/fantasy anthology. We've bought a few stories—six thus far, I believe. We're very behind in our reading, as we've been inundated with submissions on top of our usual load. This is very frustrating to us, but we're getting to them one by one. To acquire a story for the anthology, each of us has to read it and like it. We are three very different people with distinct tastes, and so some lively discussion has been engendered! The quality of the submissions has been mixed. Not many seem to be "going out on a limb" thematically.

What sort of things cause you to accept or reject a manuscript? How often do problems with manuscript format result in a rejection?

As for acceptance versus rejection, good writing is numero uno in an acceptable manuscript. Clarity in voice, attention to detail and style, etc. I respond to strong characterization, and a story or a novel must, I think, challenge me in some way, whether it's the way I look at something or think about something. I like to *learn* from science fiction. As far as manuscript format for submissions, the basics really do apply: double space, check your spelling and punctuation, be clear and concise in your cover letter, etc.

Is it helpful for a writer to bring an agent on board when looking for a publisher?

Agents are extremely important in the acquisition of a manuscript. Agents know the editors, and can guide an author to the correct editor. As well, an agent can help you do a "pre-polish" to your submission material, to help it stand out from the rest. There are certain agents with whom I do a lot of business because I know they've taken the time to learn what appeals to me. They don't insist I look at something they know probably won't work for me. I think an author should get an agent as soon as possible. But—and this is important—having no agent is better than having a bad agent.

What sort of advice do you have for writers seeking to break into the science fiction field?

Make sure you have the passion and conviction to stay the course. It is not easy being a writer. Very few writers have writing as a full-time job. If possible, get an agent. Be patient. Believe in yourself.

Science Fiction & Fantasy Markets Appearing in This Book

Below is a list of science fiction and fantasy markets appearing in this edition of *Novel & Short Story Writer's Market*. To find page numbers of particular magazines or book publishing markets, go first to the General Index beginning on page 663 of this book. Then turn to the pages those listings appear on for complete information, including who to contact and how to submit your science fiction or fantasy short story or novel manuscript.

Magazines (Fantasy)

About Such Things
Adventures of Sword & Sorcery
Advocate, PKA's Publication
Allegheny Review
Altair
Amazing Stories
Amelia
Anotherealm
Anthology
Armchair Aesthete, The
Art Times
Art:Mag
Asimov's Science Fiction
Axe Factory Review
Barbaric Yawp
Blue Skunk Companion, The
Brutarian
Cafe Irreal, The
Capers Aweigh
Challenging Destiny
Chiricú
Climbing Art, The
Companion in Zeor, A
Compleat Nurse, The
Contact Advertising
CZ's Magazine
Dagger of the Mind
Dan River Anthology
Dargonzine
Dark Moon Rising
Deadly Nightshade
Dialogue
Disenchanted
Dream International/Quarterly
Dreams & Nightmares
Dreams & Visions
Drinkin' Buddy Magazine, The
Eternal Voice
Eternity Magazine
Eureka Literary Magazine
Evansville Review
Faultline
Fish Drum Magazine
Flying Island, The
Forbidden Donut

Fugue
Gotta Write Network Litmag
Grasslands Review
Green's Magazine
Happy
Hawaii Pacific Review
Hayden's Ferry Review
Heist Magazine
Implosion
Indigenous Fiction
Interbang
Interzone
Jackhammer E-Zine
Jupiter's Freedom
Lamp-Post, The
Leapings Literary Magazine
Lines in the Sand
Lite
Lost Worlds
Lynx Eye
MacGuffin, The
Magazine of Fantasy and Science Fiction
Matriarch's Way: Journal of Female Supremacy
Medicinal Purposes
Merlyn's Pen
Millennium Science Fiction & Fantasy
Minas Tirith Evening-Star
Mind in Motion
Mississippi Review
Mobius
Musing Place, The
My Legacy
Nassau Review
Nightly Gathering
Northwoods Journal
Oak, The
Of Unicorns and Space Stations
Office Number One
Ohio Teachers Write
On Spec
Once Upon a World
Orphic Chronicle, The
Outer Darkness
Pablo Lennis
Palo Alto Review
Parsec

Penny Dreadful
Penny-a-Liner
Pirate Writings
Play the Odds
Playboy Magazine
Poetry Forum Short Stories
Poet's Fantasy
Portland Review
Poskisnolt Press
Potpourri
Primavera
Prisoners of the Night
Queen's Quarterly
Rag Mag
Reader's Break
Rejected Quarterly, The
Rockford Review, The
Rose & Thorn Literary E-Zine, The
Samsara
San Diego Writers' Monthly
Seattle Review, The
Seductive Torture
Sepulchre
Shades of December
Short Story Writers Showcase
Skylark
Slate and Style
Songs of Innocence
Southern Humanities Review
Space and Time
SPSM&H
State of Being
Street Beat Quarterly
Tale Spinner, The
Talebones
Tampa Review
32 Pages
Threshold, The
Thresholds Quarterly
Twilight Showcase
Ulitarra
Urban Spaghetti
Urbanite, The
Vintage Northwest
VQ
Weber Studies
Weird Tales
West Wind Review
Wicked Mystic
Writer's Head, The
Writes of Passage
Xoddity
Yellow Silk
Yellow Sticky Notes

Magazines (Science Fiction)

About Such Things
Advocate, PKA's Publication
Allegheny Review
Altair
Amazing Stories
Amelia
Analog Science Fiction & Fact

Anotherealm
Anthology
Armchair Aesthete, The
Art Times
Artemis Magazine
Art:Mag
Asimov's Science Fiction
Axe Factory Review
Barbaric Yawp
Bear Essential Deluxe, The
BEEF
Black Petals
Blue Skunk Companion, The
Breakfast All Day
Brobdingnagian Times, The
Brownstone Review, The
Burning Sky
Cafe Irreal, The
Callaloo
Capers Aweigh
Challenging Destiny
Chat
Chiricú
Chrysalis Reader
Climbing Art, The
Cochran's Corner
Companion in Zeor, A
Compleat Nurse, The
Contraband
Cozy Detective, The
Dagger of the Mind
Dan River Anthology
Dark Matter
Dark Moon Rising
Deep Outside SFFH
Devil Blossoms
Dialogue
Disenchanted
Downstate Story
Dream International/Quarterly
Dreams & Nightmares
Dreams & Visions
Drinkin' Buddy Magazine, The
Eternal Voice
Eternity Magazine
Eureka Literary Magazine
Evansville Review
First Class
Fish Drum Magazine
Flying Island, The
Forbidden Donut
Fugue
Gathering of the Tribes, A
Georgetown Review
Gotta Write Network Litmag
Grasslands Review
Green's Magazine
Grit
Happy
Hawaii Pacific Review
Hayden's Ferry Review
Heist Magazine
Hurricane Alice
Iconoclast, The
Implosion

Interbang
Intertext
Interzone
Jackhammer E-Zine
Jeopardy
Jewish Vegetarian Newsletter
Jupiter's Freedom
Lamp-Post, The
Leapings Literary Magazine
Left Curve
Lines in the Sand
Lite
Lost Worlds
Lynx Eye
MacGuffin, The
Magazine of Fantasy and Science Fiction
Matriarch's Way: Journal of Female Supremacy
Medicinal Purposes
Mediphors
Merlyn's Pen
Mesechabe
Millennium Science Fiction & Fantasy
Mind in Motion
Mobius
Murderous Intent
Musing Place, The
My Legacy
Neverworlds
Nightly Gathering
Nimrod
Northwoods Journal
Of Unicorns and Space Stations
Ohio Teachers Write
On Spec
Once Upon a World
Orphic Chronicle, The
Outer Darkness
Pablo Lennis
Pacific Coast Journal
Palo Alto Review
Parsec
Penny-a-Liner
Pirate Writings
Play the Odds
Playboy Magazine
Poetry Forum Short Stories
Portland Review
Potpourri
Primavera
Prisoners of the Night
Queen's Quarterly
Reader's Break
RE:AL
Rejected Quarterly, The
Rockford Review, The
Rose & Thorn Literary E-Zine, The
Rosebud™
Samsara
San Diego Writers' Monthly
Seattle Review, The
Shades of December
Short Story Writers Showcase
Silver Web, The
Skylark
Space and Time

Spindrift
Spoonfed
SPSM&H
State of Being
Storyteller, The
Struggle
Tale Spinner, The
Talebones
Talus & Scree
Terra Incognita
Thema
32 Pages
Threshold, The
Thresholds Quarterly
Ulitarra
Urban Spaghetti
VQ
Weber Studies
West Wind Review
Wicked Mystic
Wilmington Blues
Writer's Head, The
Writes of Passage
Xenith
Xoddity
Yellow Silk
Yellow Sticky Notes

Book Publishers (Fantasy)

Ace Science Fiction
Artemis Creations Publishing
Avon Eos
Baen Books
Bantam Books
Berkley Publishing Group, The
Carroll & Graf Publishers, Inc.
Cartwheel Books
Chinook Press
Circlet Press
Dan River Press
Daw Books, Inc.
Del Rey Books
Dutton Plume
Edge Science Fiction and Fantasy Publishing
Geringer Books, Laura
HarperCollins Publishers
Hollow Earth Publishing
Houghton Mifflin Company
Kaeden Books
Our Child Press
Philomel Books
Pride and Imprints
Random House, Inc.
Random House, Inc. Juvenile Books
Red Dragon Press
Rio Grande Press
ROC
St. Martin's Press
Scherf Books
Spectra Books
Tor Books
TSR, Inc.
Ultramarine Publishing Co., Inc.

W.W. Publications
Warner Aspect
Warner Books
Write Way Publishing

Book Publishers (Science Fiction)

Ace Science Fiction
Alexander Books
Artemis Creations Publishing
Avon Books
Avon Eos
Baen Books
Bancroft Press
Bantam Books
Berkley Publishing Group, The
Black Heron Press
Brownout Laboratories
Carroll & Graf Publishers, Inc.
Cartwheel Books
Chinook Press
Circlet Press
Dan River Press
Daw Books, Inc.
Del Rey Books
Dutton Plume

Edge Science Fiction and Fantasy Publishing
Farthest Star
FC2
Feminist Press at the City University of New York, The
Gryphon Publications
HarperCollins Publishers
Harris Literary Agency
Kaeden Books
Morrow and Company, Inc., William
Pig Iron Press
Random House, Inc. Juvenile Books
Red Dragon Press
ROC
St. Martin's Press
Scherf Books
Smith, Publisher/Peregrine Smith, Gibbs
Spectra Books
Tor Books
TSR, Inc.
Ultramarine Publishing Co., Inc.
W.W. Publications
Warner Aspect
Warner Books
Wesleyan University Press
Write Way Publishing
Writers Direct

Resources for Science Fiction & Fantasy Writers

Below is a list of invaluable resources specifically for science fiction and fantasy writers. For more information on the magazines and organizations listed below, check the General Index and the Publications of Interest and Organizations sections of this book. To order any of the Writer's Digest Books titles or to get a consumer book catalog, call 1-800-289-0963. You may also order Writer's Digest Books selections through www.writersdigest.com, Amazon.com or www.barnesa ndnoble.com.

MAGAZINES:
- *Fiction Writer*, 1507 Dana Ave., Cincinnati OH 45207
- *Locus*, P.O. Box 13305, Oakland CA 94661
- *Science Fiction Chronicle*, P.O. Box 022730, Brooklyn NY 11202-0056. (718)643-9011. Fax: (718)522-3308. E-mail: sf_chronicle@compuserve.com
- *Writer's Digest*, 1507 Dana Ave., Cincinnati OH 45207

BOOKS:
Science Fiction Writing series (Writer's Digest Books)
- *Aliens and Alien Societies: A Writer's Guide to Creating Extraterrestrial Life-forms*
- *Space Travel: A Writer's Guide to the Science of Interplanetary and Interstellar Travel*
- *Time Travel: A Writer's Guide to the Real Science of Plausible Time Travel*
- *World-Building: A Writer's Guide to Constructing Star Systems and Life-supporting Planets*

Other Writer's Digest books for science fiction & fantasy writers:
- *The Craft of Writing Science Fiction That Sells*
- *How to Write Science Fiction and Fantasy*
- *How to Write Tales of Horror, Fantasy & Science Fiction*
- *Science Fiction and Fantasy Writer's Sourcebook, 2nd Edition*
- *The Writer's Complete Fantasy Reference*
- *The Writer's Guide to Creating a Science Fiction Universe*

ORGANIZATIONS & ONLINE:
- Science Fiction & Fantasy Writers of America, Inc., P.O. Box 171, Unity ME 04988-0171. E-mail: execdir@sfwa.org. Website: www.sfwa.org/
- Con-Tour: www.con-tour.com (See complete listing in the Websites of Interest section of this book.)
- Books and Writing Online: www.interzone.com/Books/books.html

Elements of the All-Important Query Letter

BY BLYTHE CAMENSON AND MARSHALL J. COOK

Many of the book publishers listed in this book ask that writers submit a query letter before submitting their manuscript. The function of the all-important query letter becomes that of selling your idea for a novel to an editor or agent who will then extend you permission to submit your manuscript for review.

In the following excerpt from their new book Your Novel Proposal *(Writer's Digest Books), Blythe Camenson and Marshall J. Cook take the angst and mystery out of writing query letters. Whether you're querying agents and editors for the first time, or hoping to get another chance to submit your manuscript, Camenson and Cook's step-by-step informed approach will help you write a query letter guaranteed to pique an agent or editor's interest in seeing your manuscript.*

THE ELEMENTS OF A QUERY LETTER

Although there are four main approaches you can take with formulating your query letter (and we will cover all of them), all query letters should contain the following elements:

the hook	your credits
the handle	what you're offering
a mini-synopsis	the closing
your credentials	

Let's look at each required element individually.

The hook

Ideally, every novel should have a hook: a special plot detail or unique approach, a twist that grabs the readers' attention and makes them want to read more. It can be something that will make them say "ooh" when they hear it. A hook is a concept, an intriguing idea that readers would find compelling.

And if your novel has that hook, it must be evident in your query letter. If you can't identify that hook, it probably means you didn't build it in when you sat down to write your novel. It could be time to go back to the "plotting board" to rectify matters.

In Blythe's query letter for her novel *Parker's Angel* she reveals the hook in the first line of paragraph three: "Unlucky in love, Parker Ann Bell wouldn't recognize an angel if she pulled

BLYTHE CAMENSON *is a full-time writer with 37 books and numerous articles to her credit. She is director of Fiction Writer's Connection, as well as an instructor for AOL's Online Campus, where she teaches courses on writing query letters and submissions.*
MARSHALL J. COOK, *also the author of* Freeing Your Creativity: A Writer's Guide *and* How to Write With the Skill of a Master and the Genius of a Child, *teaches writing, editing and creativity at the University of Wisconsin. He is a frequent speaker at conferences nationwide and has recently published his own novel,* The Year of the Buffalo.

one back to earth with her—which is exactly what happens." Ooh.

In that one line we know what to expect from the book: romance and angels. It's a matter of taste if the topic interests you or not, but making your hook clear will help the agent or editor know right away if it's something for them.

The handle

While the hook grabs the readers (i.e., agents or editors), the handle gives them something to hold onto. In other words, it's something they can use to determine if it's a book project they can sell.

To provide a handle you can identify your novel's theme—e.g., unrequited love, domestic violence, race relations—and also compare your book to something that's already out there. Agent Nancy Yost wants to learn from your query letter what kind of book it is and see a comparison of your book to similar titles. "The latter piece of information always helps because it tells me they know what's out there and they're current."

Agent Peter Rubie says, "Write what you want to write and how you want to write it. And then sit down at that point and decide 'How can I make what I have done commercial?' " When you've done that, you've provided a handle.

It could be in part identifying who your audience is. But this is another tricky part. Sometimes the audience is obvious. You don't have to go digging up statistics to tell romance editors that romance readers are female and between the ages of eighteen and ninety-eight. They already know all that. But, if you have written a book with a particular topic or theme that would be of interest to a particular segment of the population, then you should, indeed, mention it.

Anne Kinsman Fisher is the author of two novels: *The Legend of Tommy Morris* (Amber-Allen Publishing) and *The Masters of the Spirit* (HarperSanFrancisco, a division of HarperCollins). She hit the ground running, getting an acceptance within forty-eight hours of contacting an editor. There are two things to which she attributes her success: tailoring the topic for a specific editor and providing that editor with a handle to sell the book.

"It is possible to write your book specifically for an editor so you know that you've got precisely what they want," Fisher says. "An author friend was submitting a golf book and he got rejected by HarperSanFrancisco. The editor told him, 'Gosh, while I like your book, it's not the spiritual golf novel I've always been looking for.'

"I thought, 'Good golly. An editor who's looking for something!' I came up with an idea based on her words 'spiritual golf novel.' " And she sold it, too.

But Fisher didn't stop with just coming up with the right topic. She helped give the editor—and everyone on the editorial board—a handle, so they felt convinced the book would sell in the bookstores.

"I include a special section in my query/proposal on market research," Fisher says. "I tell my editor who will buy the book, specific numbers for the marketplace (e.g., for my book, women golfers are a growing audience). I include relevant articles about the popularity of my genre. I explain which other books are like mine and what they have sold. So, when my editor goes to her editorial meeting, she is prepared. Most writers worry only about getting an editor to like their work. They forget that the book actually needs to sell off the bookstore shelves."

Agent Evan Marshall says, "I really want to hear how the writer feels the book fits the market. I want to know that he has targeted his book for a certain audience, that he's done his homework. I realize that's largely my job, but I think all that has to start with the writer much more than it used to. If they are readers and are writing what they love to read, then chances are they know that the niche exists. Often the easiest way is to compare what they're doing with what's out there—a Mary Higgins Clark type women-in-jeopardy [novel], for example. Or they could just say they're writing a historical romance or a techno-thriller."

A mini-synopsis

In the synopsis part of your query you'll give an overview of your plot and introduce your main characters and their core conflict. Include a few plot high points, make the setting and time period clear and you're done.

Sound easy?

It isn't. Many successful authors will tell you that writing the novel was a lot easier than composing a query or a synopsis. In chapter six we cover synopsis writing in depth, and you'll get lots of helpful tips for making the synopsis section of your query letter effective.

In the meantime, just remember to not get too detailed—you can't put a complete blow by blow in two to four paragraphs. On the other hand, don't be so vague that the reader has no idea what you're hinting at.

Don't, for example, say, "Heroine X battles a multitude of problems before she solves the biggest one of all." This sentence includes what we call "empty phrases" and offers no information at all.

Do say, "Heroine X must cope with the abandonment by her husband, and a crooked judge hell-bent on revenge, before she can be reunited with the child he abducted." This version gives us a much better picture of what your book is about—and that's the sole purpose of the query letter's synopsis section.

Your credentials

The purpose of the credentials section of your query letter is to convey knowledge of your subject matter and to give a little information about yourself.

Give this aspect of your proposal some creative thought before you decide you don't have anything to say. No, by "creative" we're not suggesting you make things up. (Save that for the novel!) If you're a lawyer working on a legal thriller, tell them. Been coaching Little League for thirty years? Tell them that, too, but only if your novel concerns Little League.

Agents and editors want to know who you are and how you came to write this novel. Agent Julie Castiglia says, "It annoys me when people don't include any information about themselves—what was the motivation for the book? If they want to write a book about Russia, I want to know why. Why are they qualified? Why are they interested?"

When discussing who you are, it's important not to get carried away. "Do not include your life's story, unless it's pertinent to what you've written," editor Marjorie Braman says.

Credentials could also include membership in writers organizations, awards or contests won, attendance at writing seminars and workshops or completion of writing courses. But here's where you need to tread carefully. Some agents and editors don't put much stock in this sort of thing. Editor Michael Seidman says, "Telling me of the award you won from a contest is beside the point. I've judged too many of them to take them that seriously as validation. I don't think you should mention awards unless they are from professional peer organizations."

Omitting mention of your degree in creative writing might be the safest course, too. Some editors and agents will be gratified to hear it. Others will try not to hold it against you.

Under the credentials section of your query letter you can also mention any access to sources you have. Almost all fiction projects require some research. The plot may be pure fabrication, but details of setting, for example, had better be dead-on accurate. If your book is set in the Middle East and you lived there for several years, mention that. But if you have no experience in that part of the world, your book's setting will be a harder sell.

No matter what other credentials you have—and even if you can't think of a single relevant scrap of experience that might help you—your best credential, the only one you absolutely must have, is a good proposal sent to the right person. If you've got this one, you've got a chance. Don't let any supposed deficiency stop you.

Your credits

If you're a brand-new writer just starting out, you might not have any credits. That's OK. Just don't bring attention to it in a negative way. Don't apologize or even mention it—that's a surefire way of pointing out your amateur status. Michael Seidman says, "If you don't mention any fiction credits in your query letter, I'll assume it is a first novel; that has no bearing on when I read it or how carefully." The recipient of your query letter will infer that this is your first novel, and most agents and editors won't hold it against you.

Some put more stock in credits, and this could just mean that those aren't the right people for you to be querying. Agent Martha Millard says she prefers to look at potential clients who have a track record with published books to their credit, but any kind of credit—including publication of short stories or nonfiction in national magazines—is a step in the right direction. "Anyone who wants to interest an agent in reading her or his work should mention publishing credits right at the beginning of the query letter. There have certainly been times I have taken on writers with no publishing credits. In fact, I'm handling one right now. But if I spent all my time reading query letters and manuscripts from people who want to be published, believe me, I wouldn't have time to do anything else. When I turn down a query letter, it is because of the writer's credits and how he/she phrases the letter. If the letter isn't well written, it gives me a good idea that the book isn't going to be any good, either."

There are plenty of others, though, who are more than open to new writers and always looking for fresh talent. So don't worry if you lack a string of credits. Your writing will speak for itself.

And if you do have credits? Now is the time for a little horn tooting. Don't be shy, but don't be Barnum and Bailey, either. State your truth simply and directly.

Let's look at which credits to include and which might not be worth mentioning or might even go against you.

Of course, if you have any fiction credits, mention them: "My short stories have appeared in [names of the magazines]."

Blythe had one student, though, who had a slew of fiction credits, but was embarrassed to mention where they had appeared—in a series of erotica magazines. No reason not to mention those—look at Anne Rice and the work she has produced under a variety of pen names. But if, for whatever reason, you feel too shy, then just say, "My short stories have appeared in a variety of magazines," and don't mention their titles.

If you have any nonfiction publication credits, say so. "Any writing experience at all is of interest," says agent Jane Chelius.

If all the topics of your published work are irrelevant to your novel, just avoid going into too much detail. It's enough to say you're published. Period.

But if your current work of fiction is set during the Civil War, for example, and you have also published nonfiction pieces on the same topic, then definitely get specific about that.

There might be a few credits *not* worth mentioning—a letter to the editor of your local newspaper, an essay posted on an on-line message board, an article for your high school yearbook.

The point of listing credits is to show you have a track record, others have found your work acceptable, you are a professional and you have had experience working with editors.

What you're offering

Make sure you give the title of your book, its word count and the genre. To do that you'll need to know what category or kind of book you've written.

Basic categories of fiction include:

action/adventure	experimental
children's	fantasy
espionage	gay/lesbian/bisexual
erotic	historical

horror	science fiction
humor	suspense
inspirational/religious/spiritual	thriller (political/legal/medical)
military	western
mystery	women's
romance	young adult (YA)

Many of these categories also have subgenres. The broad category of romance, for instance, includes subgenres such as contemporary, sweet, historical and Regency. Within the thriller category you will find medical, political, techno- and legal thrillers. Mysteries cover a wide range, too—cozies, police procedurals and detective.

If you can't find yourself in any of these categories, you may have a mainstream or literary novel on your hands.

Defining *mainstream*, though, is no easy task. Agent Kathleen Anderson says mainstream novels are "books people like to read. However, *mainstream* can also refer to general women's fiction, for example. Mainstream women's fiction generally takes a contemporary subject and writes about domestic/romantic situations. But, in fact, mainstream is becoming an outdated concept. It really refers to a straightforward narrative with no poetic twists, and that is not finding a large audience these days."

Editor Elisa Wares says, "I dislike the word *mainstream* because you can't go into a bookstore and find a shelf for a noncategory book. So, I would say mainstream is a book that doesn't fit into a category. Unless it is a best-seller (Grisham or King), a writer should try to find a category that can be shelved. I decide what category goes on the spines of all my books. If I think it has a greater or 'breakout' audience than a specific genre would have, I will put *fiction* on the spine."

When looking at the difference between category romance and mainstream romance, agent Evan Marshall says, "Category romance deals with slighter issues, and most important, centers completely on the developing romance between the man and the woman. Mainstream romance has many other things going on in the story, other subplots and issues—and these issues are bigger, more momentous. It boils down to weightiness of story."

Literary fiction is identified by the style of writing—the deep tones and textures it contains—in addition to its subject matter.

If you don't know the genre or if you're just not sure, leave it out. It is not always necessary to state it, especially if there are too many crossovers. (Blythe, for example, considers her novel *Parker's Angel* to fall into the mainstream/romantic/suspense/comedy/women's fiction genre with a hint of New Age—but she wouldn't tell an agent or editor that.) In the handle section of your query letter, comparing your book to another author's can be sufficient to categorize it.

The closing

At the end of the query letter you offer to send more—the complete manuscript for a novel. Do not offer a choice. Do not offer to send sample chapters *or* the complete manuscript. Offer only the completed manuscript. (You shouldn't be querying if your manuscript isn't complete.) If they want to see more, they will tell you. They will also tell you what to send—sample chapters or the complete manuscript and a synopsis. You'll find information on how to prepare your proposal packet in part two of this book.

In closing your letter, less is more. Simply say, "May I send you the complete manuscript?" If you haven't made the title, genre and word count clear earlier, you can say instead, "May I send you my completed 100,000-word mainstream novel [title]?"

Titles, by the way, should be typed in italics (or underlined if you don't have an italic typeface) in your query letters. Don't use quotation marks or all caps.

There is no need to thank the editors and agents for their time and consideration or tell them you'll wait for their response or that you eagerly look forward to hearing from them. They know that, and such sentiments just take up room.

BUILDING KILLER QUERY LETTERS

Now it's time to sit down and actually compose one. For some this might seem like a daunting task; writing the novel was so much easier. But it doesn't have to be difficult. Look at it as a writing exercise. Compose your first draft, put it aside for awhile, then come back to it with fresh eyes. For your second read, replace your writer's cap with an editor's one and look for and correct any trouble spots.

ELEVEN QUERY LETTER TIPS

1. The style in your query should reflect the style of the project you are proposing.
2. Make sure you state your novel's word count. This is important information in deciding how to market your book—and if it can be marketed. Editor Michael Seidman points out that he absolutely needs to know word count. "At Walker & Company I'm stuck with very strict length guidelines—70,000 words—so it helps me to know what I'm dealing with. If the length is just slightly over or under, it's workable, but with something like a 97,000-word manuscript, I'd say no right from the git-go and not waste my time or yours."
3. Don't say you write like a particular best-selling writer. You should just say you write in the same genre as that author or in a style similar to hers. It's a fine distinction, but knowing the difference can prevent your annoying some editors and agents.
4. Avoid mentioning how many people have read and loved your book. The opinions of Aunt Mary and Uncle Fred won't help build your case. The agents and editors would prefer to decide for themselves.
5. Stay clear of self-glorifying adjectives (save those for the book reviewers). Don't give into the temptation of describing your work as dazzling, dramatic, exciting, fast-paced or anything else. Say, "My book is an account of . . .," not "My book is a fascinating account of. . . ."

    "I have a letter from someone that said something to the effect that 'I am the next major literary writer of my generation. You cannot afford to not read my book," agent Peter Rubie says. "I sent him a standard rejection slip, but my personal reaction was 'This is absurd.' If you're not published yet, you're not the best judge of your own material. I represent some very solid writers—they've won awards and have achieved a lot—but they don't come across like that, even though they're far closer to that level."
6. Avoid predicting your book's climb up the best-seller lists (no one can predict that). "It's a good idea not to mention in your letter that you think your novel is going to be Avon's next best-seller," editor Marjorie Braman says. "Publishers are never sure about that. I don't know how an author can be sure."

    The grander the brag and boast, the bigger the turnoff.
7. Propose only one project in a single query. You can mention that you have other books in the works (if you do), but don't go into too much detail on those in this particular query letter. Agents and editors want to know you're not a one-book wonder, but don't cloud the waters with too many projects in one query letter.

    If you are writing a series, say so, but your query should propose book one. Sending out a query for book two before book one has been accepted tells agents and editors that the first book didn't fly. "If you are submitting the third novel in a series to me, I'd like to know that there were two before it," notes agent Richard Henshaw. "I'd also like to know what your plans are down the road."

    In fact, this information may be the most important thing you can say. "I like to handle an author for their career, not by the book," Henshaw says. "If I liked the writing of this particular project but didn't find it commercial enough to take on, a good pitch on the next project might encourage me to ask for a look when it's ready."

8. Don't put yourself down in a query letter. Ever. Don't say it's your first book or you hope they'll like it. Of course, it is; of course, you do.

9. Don't tell the editor or agent his business. While you need to be market savvy and show you know the market for your book, there's a fine line to walk here. Michael Seidman says, "Nothing gets me angrier than seeing something like "Female PIs are selling big, so you'll love my book." Your impression of the market is based on what's there now, not on the sales we're seeing or the comments we get from wholesalers and jobbers." Just state what your book is about, what niche it falls into, but unless you have actual current sales statistics at hand, don't dig a hole for yourself.

10. Be nice. Don't discuss the advance you envision, the rights you are prepared to offer or any demands of any sort. Nothing will turn off an editor or agent faster than a show of arrogance. "You'd be amazed at how many query letters I receive that are out-and-out rude," agent Nancy Yost says.

11. Don't show your desperation. You've written ten previous novels, all unpublished. You have completely rewritten this one three times. You have polished it twenty. And if this one doesn't fly, your plan is to chuck writing forever and find the nearest bridge, nunnery or French Foreign Legion recruitment office. This is information that no agent or editor wants to know; it can only undermine your efforts.

Query Letter Checklist

Here's a checklist of items to watch for and fix.
- ☐ Weak lead sentence
- ☐ Wordiness
- ☐ Awkward phrasings
- ☐ Lack of clarity
- ☐ Illogical paragraph organization
- ☐ Repetitiveness
- ☐ Weak verbs
- ☐ Clichés
- ☐ Lack of rhythm
- ☐ Overusing adjectives and adverbs
- ☐ No transitions (or weak ones) between paragraphs
- ☐ Weak plotting (as related in the query)
- ☐ Incorrect punctuation, grammar and spelling

What follows are two drafts for a query letter written by a new author. The first draft is the original. With the above checklist in mind, read through it and see how many problem areas you can find. Then go on to the final, polished draft. Our comments point out what works and why we think so.

Although we get a sense that this query speaks for a compelling, literate book, we'd like to know more about what the protagonist's conflict is—what it is that will hook us and keep us reading.

We are more confused than intrigued, and we want to be intrigued. We want to say, "Ooh, this is a book to read." But right now, there's no grit to sink our teeth into. Why does Adam pass out—what is happening to him? If we knew that we'd probably want to read this book. We want an idea of what to expect. The writer is teasing too much.

In addition, the query is too long.

This query letter went through several more drafts before reaching this final version. In the final draft, our editorial comments point out what works and why.

FIRST DRAFT OF QUERY LETTER FOR *CHORDS OF FIRE*

February 17, 2000

Mr. John Smith
John Smith Literary Agency
1234 Main St., Suite 5
New York, NY 10001

Dear Mr. Smith,

Perhaps no other musical oeuvre has inspired as much passion worldwide, in aristocrats and commoners alike, as that of Beethoven. In my mainstream novel, *Chords of Fire*, Beethoven's music drives the protagonist as if it ❶ were a character itself.

Those who love this music often find in it an almost religious "meaning." ❷ Hearing Beethoven's Seventh Symphony at the age of sixteen gave Adam Faulke, an ordinary teenager and a lousy cellist, his first taste of religious majesty. This experience set him in motion and changed his life. ❸

At the opening of *Chords of Fire*, Adam, now an accomplished musician, is the principal cellist of the Philadelphia Orchestra. The book's first mystery ❹ begins to unfold at the orchestra's gala opening concert, when, to Adam's great dismay, he passes out while the orchestra is playing to an audience of three thousand people. Of all things, they are playing Beethoven's Seventh Symphony.

To his friends, he says, "It was the heat." But it wasn't the heat, any more than it was the position of the moon or what he had ❺ for dinner. It was the first in a series of unfathomable occurrences which plunge Adam into a growing confusion, one which ❻ threatens to derail his fledgling solo career and to sabotage his previously placid life. ❼

After the opening night debacle, Adam begins to have odd dreams, dreams ❽ in which he is playing a piece of unknown but intricate music on an old piano. From chapter sixteen, "The Ghost Music": "Before long the mad music dream came, with more delirious impact than ever before. My fingers bored into the piano, milking bewitchment from its innards. My hands ranged crazily over the keys, drawing ghostly wails and howls of protest. Not music, but a pact with God, or maybe the devil." ❾

continued on next page

1. Not clear what the *it* refers to. The way this is constructed, *it* refers to the protagonist.
2. Do not put *meaning* in quotes.
3. The opening line of the query leads us to think the novel is about Beethoven. Here we see it isn't. The writer needs to be clear right up front who this is about.
4. Although mainstream novels can have an element of mystery to them, this might make the reader think this is a mystery novel.
5. Should be "what he'd had."
6. Both "whichs" in sentence should be "that," not "which."
7. Repetitive. The point about the "first mystery" has already been made. We need more meat, fewer hints.
8. Second *dreams* is repetitive. In addition, *opening* has been used three times.
9. Not clear that writer is quoting her own work. Delete excerpt.

FIRST DRAFT OF QUERY LETTER FOR *CHORDS OF FIRE* (continued)

Chords of Fire, while not New Age fiction, shares with *The Celestine Prophecy* a quest for ageless spiritual "truths" which ⑩ transcend the banality of everyday life. ⑪

The protagonist's eventual realizations speak to a creeping ennui, one from which many people today are awakening with the question, "But isn't there something more?"

Chords of Fire is a story of urgency, friendship, and love. And ultimately, it is a story of discovery—of one's own purpose, of what it is to be an artist and of what it is to be human. By the story's end, Adam answers his burning questions, and the answers set him free.

May I send you the completed manuscript?

Sincerely,

Julie Goldman Connard

10. Which should be that.
11. More genre confusion: It isn't New Age, yet the writer compares it to a New Age novel. Previously she called it mainstream, then threw in mysteries. The best bet is to let the agent decide for himself.

FINAL DRAFT OF QUERY LETTER FOR *CHORDS OF FIRE*

February 17, 2000

Mr. John Smith
John Smith Literary Agency
1234 Main St., Suite 5
New York, NY 10001

Dear Mr. Smith:

In my mainstream novel, *Chords of Fire*, Beethoven's music drives the protagonist, cellist Adam Faulke, as if the music were a character itself. ❶

Those who love this music often find in it an almost religious meaning. Hearing Beethoven's Seventh Symphony at the age of sixteen gave Adam, an ordinary teenager and a lousy cellist, his first taste of religious majesty. This experience catalyzed his reach for musical excellence. ❷

At the beginning of *Chords of Fire*, Adam, now an accomplished performer, is the principal cellist of the Philadelphia Orchestra. The book's drama unfolds at the orchestra's gala opening concert, when, to Adam's great dismay, he passes out while the orchestra is playing to an audience of three thousand. Of all things, they are playing Beethoven's Seventh Symphony.

To his friends, he says, "It was the heat." But it wasn't the heat, any more than it was the position of the moon or what he'd had for dinner. It was the first in a series of occurrences that plunge Adam into a growing confusion, one that threatens to derail his fledgling solo career and to sabotage his previously placid life.

After the opening night debacle, Adam has an odd dream in which he is playing a piece of unknown but intricate music on an old piano. Adam's hands range madly over the instrument, "milking bewitchment from its innards." His fingers draw "ghostly wails and howls of protest."

He becomes obsessed with finding this music, which he begins to suspect is real. And find it he does—in Europe. These and other events lead Adam to conclude that he has lived before, in another time and place. But for Adam, acknowledging this thought is tantamount to admitting he's crazy. ❸

To resolve the confusion eroding his focus, his relationships and his love of making music, Adam must first confront those haunting traces from another life. By the story's end, Adam answers his questions about the past, and the answers set him free.

Chords of Fire shares with *The Celestine Prophecy* a quest for ageless spiritual truths that transcend the banality of everyday life. ❹

Adam's eventual realizations speak to a creeping ennui, one from which many people today are awakening with the question, "But isn't there something more?" Through music and the help of a woman, Adam learns that there is.

May I send you the completed manuscript?

Sincerely,

Julie Goldman Connard

1. This is a good, straightforward opening—much clearer than in the original draft.
2. Good characterization—"ordinary teenager and lousy cellist."
3. Now we are getting a better sense of what the mysteries are that were only hinted at in the first draft.
4. The writer provides the agent with a good handle here.

Elements of a Successful Synopsis

BY BLYTHE CAMENSON AND MARSHALL J. COOK

Many of the book publishers listed in this book ask for a synopsis to accompany sample chapters of a novel manuscript. The synopsis is a concise selling tool for your novel, a summary meant to make an agent or editor want to read your manuscript from beginning to end.

In the following excerpt from their new book Your Novel Proposal *(Writer's Digest books), Blythe Camenson and Marshall J. Cook guide you through the steps to writing a synopsis guaranteed to make an agent or editor want to read your novel manuscript.*

"The goal [of a synopsis] is not to explain the entire book," says novelist James Scott Bell (*The Darwin Conspiracy, Circumstantial Evidence*). "The goal is to get the editor, agent or reader hooked enough to read the sample chapters and to see the market potential."

You need to convey a clear idea of what your book is about, what characters we'll care about (including the ones we'll hate), what's at stake for the main character(s), and how the conflict comes out.

"Basically, we're reading for a sense of characters, conflict—internal and external—and some indication of the setting," says editor Karen Taylor Richman.

Understanding these key elements "can help potential authors write brief but effective synopses instead of dry summarizations of the plot," Bell says.

Your synopsis should usually include
- an opening hook
- quick sketches of the main characters
- plot high points
- the core conflict
- the conclusion

Let's look at each section.

The hook

James A. Ritchie (*The Last Free Range*) reminds us of just how important a good beginning is. "It's the first chapter that matters most," he says. "And perhaps the first page of the first chapter matters most of all. I have a hunch many editors stop reading if the first page or two doesn't hold their interest. So I work on this above all else. Get the opening sentence perfect, make it ask a question the editor/reader wants answered, and you're well on the way to selling a novel."

And as with the novel, so with the novel synopsis. You must start strong. Agents and editors

BLYTHE CAMENSON *is a full-time writer with 37 books and numerous articles to her credit. She is director of Fiction Writer's Connection, as well as an instructor for AOL's Online Campus, where she teaches courses on writing query letters and submissions.*

MARSHALL J. COOK, *also the author of* Freeing Your Creativity: A Writer's Guide *and* How to Write With the Skill of a Master and the Genius of a Child, *teaches writing, editing and creativity at the University of Wisconsin. He is a frequent speaker at conferences nationwide and has recently published his own novel,* The Year of the Buffalo.

want to be engaged when they're up late at night, plowing through submissions. If they don't like the opening, they won't get through the rest of it.

"Open with a hook, just as you would in a novel," says Marilyn Campbell (*Pretty Maids in a Row, See How They Run*). Your opening few sentences should pull the editor or agent into the synopsis just as your first scene must pull the reader into the novel.

The hook you create for your synopsis probably won't be the opening scene in your novel, but it has to be every bit as involving and engaging as that opening scene. You might use the same opening hook that you provided in your query letter.

Barbara Parker (*Suspicion of Guilt, Suspicion of Innocence, Criminal Justice*) gives her editor a double hook—"a super short spoonful you can gulp down in ten seconds" and then "an expanded version to nibble on."

Here's her "super short spoonful" for the novel *Blood Relations*, published by Dutton.

> The woman whom attorney Thomas Gage loved, then abandoned over twenty years ago, begs him to defend her daughter, a young fashion model charged with murdering the owner of a South Beach night club. Then another murder occurs, and Tom has to confront his past and the recent suicide of his only son to discover the truth.

We've got two murders, family conflict and back story all in two crisp sentences, fifty-seven words.

John Tigges (*The Curse, Evil Dreams*) doesn't waste any time getting to the action with his hook for the synopsis of *Monster*.

> Mal and Jonna Evans, in an effort to save their marriage, which has been jeopardized by Jonna's extramarital affair, go backpacking near Garibaldi Provincial Park, British Columbia. On their first night, while preparing their evening meal, a Sasquatch barges into their camp and grabs Jonna.

And we're off.

In the first two sentences, we've got exotic setting (Garibaldi Provincial Park, British Columbia), conflict (a marriage at risk), back story (Jonna's extramarital affair), and, oh yes, the monster.

Robert W. Walker (*Fatal Instinct, Razor's Edge*) uses this grabber for *Darkest Instinct*.

> FBI Medical Examiner Dr. Jessica Coran must stare into the oldest and darkest instinct known to mankind—murderous rage—to unmask a vicious, phantom killer who leaves his victims in the water, mangled and mutilated. The monster has turned loose his venom against young women in seaside towns and cities along Florida's coastal waters, turning dark the sun. A population is terrorized, unsure when or where the Night Crawler will strike next.

Character sketches

You need to provide a sense of your main characters' motivations, especially those that will bring the characters into conflict with one another. Most writers simply weave these motivations into the plot summary. Others provide separate thumbnail portraits of their characters.

"The characters' physical descriptions are not vital, but their motivations are," Marilyn Campbell says.

Here's how she describes her *Blood Relations* protagonist:

> Like many successful men who have hit forty-something, Thomas Gage found out how hollow his success really was. By the time Matthew died, Tom was already about to topple. Losing Matthew sent him in the wrong direction: toward disintegration. A second chance with Susan will help to turn him around. He betrayed her love for him when they were young. Now he has to make her believe it isn't too late.

Here's how Peggy Hoffmann describes the heroine for her novel *Wanted: Wife* (Harlequin Temptation):

Elise Sinclair is in love with love—perfect qualifications for a wedding consultant. From a crumbling Victorian townhouse in Chicago's Old Town, Elise runs her wedding consulting business, A Tasteful Affair. In addition to dealing with tasteless clients, Elise's happiness is hindered by a leaky roof, a temperamental heating system, inconsistent cash flow and two demanding and aloof Persian cats named Clorinda and Thisbe.

She is, Hoffmann tells us, a "hopeless romantic"—a characteristic Hoffmann will reveal in the novel through action and dialogue without ever labeling her.

Plot highlights

Once you've captured interest with an effective hook, you must sustain it with the body of your synopsis. Your hook has made a promise; now you must make good on that promise.

"Detail the beginning and ending scenes and one or two in the middle that give an indication of the kind of emotional intensity or type of action to be expected," Marilyn Campbell says. "Be clear about the type of action in your book. If your story contains explicitly graphic sex or violence, that should be obvious in the synopsis."

"I try to present each major scene in the book by following this form: incident, reaction, decision," Peggy Hoffmann says.

Ah, but which are the major scenes? Here are two guidelines to apply in auditioning a scene for possible inclusion in the synopsis:

1. Do I need this scene to make the primary plot hang together?
2. Do I need this scene for the ending to make sense?

Barbara Parker has a simple rule for picking out plot highlights: "I have gone back to my first rule of novel writing, which is 'How can we make the protagonist(s) suffer?' "

Your synopsis reveals how much and what kind of trouble your poor protagonist is going to encounter.

Core Conflict

If you don't have a conflict, you don't have a story to tell—or to sell. That's why you need to make sure your book's core conflict is clear in your synopsis.

Ideally, your hook will contain your conflict. In Barbara Parker's "super short spoonful," quoted above, we have protagonist Thomas Gage's double conflict made clear—while solving two murders, he must also confront a past love and the suicide of his only son. In the same way, the opening sentences of John Tigges's synopsis establish an emotional conflict (saving a troubled marriage) and a physical one (the sudden appearance of the monster Sasquatch).

If your conflict isn't implicit in your hook, spell it out. As with your pitch line, you should be able to state your core conflict in a single sentence.

For practice, take a few novels you've read recently and see if you can put the core conflict of each into a sentence.

If you're familiar with these classics of American literature, try the same exercise with each of them:

> *To Kill a Mockingbird*, by Harper Lee
> *The Old Man and the Sea*, by Ernest Hemingway
> *The Great Gatsby*, by F. Scott Fitzgerald
> *Invisible Man*, by Ralph Ellison
> *Gone With the Wind*, by Margaret Mitchell
> *One Flew Over the Cuckoo's Nest*, by Ken Kesey

Did you give them a try? The more you practice, the better you'll get. Here's how we would state the core conflicts for the classic tales.

To Kill a Mockingbird, by Harper Lee: Attorney Atticus Finch fights the bigotry of the small-town South to defend a Black man falsely accused of rape.

The Old Man and the Sea, by Ernest Hemingway: Aging fisherman Santiago battles to save his great catch from sharks.

The Great Gatsby, by F. Scott Fitzgerald: Millionaire Jay Gatsby remains hopelessly in love with his married ex-lover, Daisy Buchanan.

Invisible Man, by Ralph Ellison: Young Black man struggles to define himself in a racist society that insists he deny his authentic self.

Gone With the Wind, by Margaret Mitchell: Headstrong, spoiled Scarlett O'Hara loves her cousin Melanie's husband, Ashley Wilkes, and is in turn loved by the opportunistic and dashing Rhett Butler.

One Flew Over the Cuckoo's Nest, by Ken Kesey: Brash inmate Randall McMurphy fights the oppressive "Big Nurse" in a mental institution.

You'll have an easier time developing and defining your core conflict if you think in terms of one or more of these four traditional categories:

1. person vs. person
2. person vs. nature
3. person vs. society
4. person vs. self

Your core conflict may, of course, overlap categories and could even touch on all four. Here's an example:

Tortured by grief and loss (person vs. self) and fleeing a wrongful conviction for a crime he didn't commit (person vs. society), Dr. Richard Kimble struggles to survive (person vs. nature) while fleeing the relentless lawman who pursues him (person vs. person).

That, of course, states the core conflicts for *The Fugitive*.

If you can't come up with a core conflict to describe your novel, the problem may be with the book rather than the synopsis. Your book must have conflict. If you can't find it, you can't expect an agent or editor to find it, either.

The Conclusion

A synopsis is not a quiz or a puzzle. Don't close with a cliff-hanger.

Revealing the ending to your novel won't spoil the story for the editor or agent. It will show that you know how to successfully conclude your plot.

"Make sure every loose thread is tied up, and never leave an editor guessing about anything," Marilyn Campbell says.

"Don't try to be cute and leave us guessing what is going to happen in the story," says editor Karen Taylor Richman. "The whole purpose of this process is to determine if the story is anything that might work for us."

Literary agent Pesha Rubinstein stresses this point. "I cannot stand teasers saying, 'Well, you'll just have to read the manuscript to find out what the end is.' I need to know the whole story in order to see if it makes sense."

If your novel is one of a series, your ending can point to the sequel, as Robert W. Walker does in his outline for *Darkest Instinct*:

Santiva then tells her about another case he wants her to attend to, one that will take her to London, where a madman is killing people for their eyes. She'll be working alongside the man who helped them track Patric Allain.

HOW TO STRUCTURE YOUR SYNOPSIS

After having worked with editors at five different publishing houses in three different genres—contemporary, paranormal romance and contemporary category romance—Marilyn Campbell says she's learned that "there are no set guidelines for the perfect synopsis."

Develop a format that best lets you tell your story.

Most synopses, especially the shorter ones, weave character and conflict into a tight narrative. Each paragraph must flow naturally from the paragraph before it.

Some writers deal with the conflict in one paragraph, plot highlights in a second paragraph, a paragraph for each major character and then the resolution.

Peggy Hoffmann uses this basic outline for each synopsis.

First paragraph: hook, story setup

Second paragraph: heroine's story goal; motivation; physical description; internal and external conflicts; back story, as needed

Third paragraph: hero's story goal, motivation, physical description, internal and external conflicts, back story

Following paragraphs: story development and conclusion

Carla Anderson, who writes Silhouette romances as Jessica Barkley (*Into the Sunset, Montana Man*), devotes a tight paragraph each to:

the setting

the heroine

the hero

the beginning

the romance (internal conflicts)

the external conflict

the complication

the ending

Whatever format you use, if you've enclosed the first three chapters in your submission packet, don't begin your synopsis at chapter four. Let the agent or editor get an accurate sense of your story from the beginning.

FOUR WAYS TO AVOID "SYNOPSIS SPEAK"

Your synopsis is not the place for promotional-style book jacket copy, a medley of adjectives and adverbs, or every possible scene and background detail. But don't settle for a dry plot summary. If your synopsis is flat and stilted, the agent or editor will assume that your manuscript is, too.

Here are four ways to make the synopsis sing:

1. Select the right tense and person. No matter what choices you've made for the novel itself, write the synopsis in present tense and third person. ("Ahab harpoons the whale.") Third person works well for summary, and present tense creates immediacy and drama.

2. Use an appropriate writing style. Stick with the same writing style you use in your novel. Dark, brooding novel? You want a dark, brooding synopsis. A chatty, upbeat novel begets chatty, upbeat synopsis.

Dull, plodding novel? Rewrite the novel.

3. Write with nouns and verbs. Make strong action verbs and specific, concrete nouns carry the weight. Use adjectives and adverbs sparingly.

Remember, the synopsis is not a book review, and it's not a book jacket blurb. Eliminate opinion words and phrases ("in the next scintillating plot twist, which will have the reader on the edge of the chair . . ."). Just tell your story. Let the editor or agent judge it.

4. Use dialogue sparingly, if at all. Many successful synopses contain no dialogue. Include dialogue only if it's essential to reveal character or further the plot or create dramatic intensity.

HOW LONG IS LONG ENOUGH?

"The length of the synopsis depends on the complexity of the story's premise, background and motivations," says Harlequin Toronto editor Paula Eykelhof.

"As long as I know where the story is going—the beginning, the middle, the end—I'm not concerned with its length," says editor John Scognamiglio.

But editors and agents agree that shorter is generally better. They want to be able to see at a glance what your book is about.

"I recently heard a great description of a synopsis," says editor Michael Seidman. "Make it read as if you were explaining a movie to a ten-year-old. The more complex you make it, the more holes will open."

Agent Russell Galen looks for about 1,500 words. Karen Taylor Richman wants two to three pages, double-spaced. Editor Jennifer Brehl wants a synopsis of no more than "three pages for the entire book, beginning to end."

A one-page synopsis is often the best bet. It's a chance to show how tight your writing is; it won't put them to sleep; and the shorter the synopsis, the easier it is to refrain from making mistakes.

But a one-page synopsis just won't do the job in many contexts. Your agent or editor might prefer a longer, more detailed synopsis or even a full chapter outline. As in all things, follow our basic philosophy: Give them what they want—no more, no less.

BUILDING YOUR ONE-PAGE SYNOPSIS

In chapter three [of *Your Novel Proposal*] we revised a query letter to demonstrate how writers can shape and sharpen their work. Now we'll do the same with a synopsis by Kathleen Casey.

Synopsis Checklist

Here is a checklist of elements to look for in the following synopsis drafts and in your own.
- [ ] Strong lead sentence
- [ ] Logical paragraph organization
- [ ] Concise expression of ideas with no repetition
- [ ] Introduction of main characters—and their core conflicts
- [ ] Plot high points
- [ ] Narrative writing in the present tense
- [ ] Transitions between ideas
- [ ] Strong verbs
- [ ] Minimal use of adjectives and adverbs
- [ ] Correct punctuation, grammar and spelling
- [ ] The story's conclusion

Read through the original version of Casey's synopsis carefully, noting our suggestions to the author. Then, we'll reveal the final edited synopsis and why it works.

Here's our overall assessment: This is very good, very close. We've made a few suggestions about the wording and punctuation. We are concerned, though, that the author too often repeats that Colman leaves the heroine to go about his business. It might be a flaw in the plotting—that he is only available when the author needs him to be. The author must make the reason for his unavailability clearer and avoid the repetition.

The next page shows the final draft with our comments, including our thoughts as to why we feel it's a concise, powerful synopsis. Compare the two synopses.

You may disagree with some of our comments and suggestions. That's fine. The important point for you to take away from this exercise is the need to establish character and tone and capture plot—story plus conflict—in a few words.

Sanctuary From Wolves
Historical Novel
by Kathleen Casey

Brandwitha is a Frankish girl who longs for more than her inevitable fate: marriage into a family like hers, where violence and cruelty are commonplace, and the quest for power and wealth is paramount. Her life is a journey toward artistic fulfillment, but the ambition and betrayal of others made ❶ it a tortuous and dangerous path.

Two travelers happen upon the family villa outside of Paris in A.D. 596. Peter is a priest and teacher from Rome, who stays just long enough to teach Brandwitha to read. Colman is a youth from Ireland who soon travels on to his uncle's monastery, but not before winning her friendship. They both open her eyes to the existence of another world, one of kindness and books. Peter becomes like a father to her, and it hurts her deeply when he leaves for Britain to help found a church. Recognizing Brandwitha's intellect and promise, ❷ he makes her promise him that ❸ she will go into a nunnery.

When Brandwitha is almost a woman, the monk Wolfram teaches her the art of book illumination, but for a terrible price: She must become his concubine. The consequences of their bargain— pregnancy and miscarriage, resulting in sterility—almost destroy her and set into motion her desperate search for a way to both survive and create the art that has become an integral part of her.

This search takes her first to a nunnery in Soissons, where she is content to be a scribe, although she comes to realize she is not devout enough to be a nun. Even here she cannot escape the violent political machinations of the outside world, and she is wrongly accused of treason and cast out.

Alone and afraid in a church sanctuary, the only place she can go, Colman finds her. ❹ As he comes to her aid, their friendship is rekindled. He reluctantly leaves her to go on about his business, fooled into thinking that with his help she will now go to her mother's family in Burgundy. Instead, she makes a dangerous journey to Peter's monastery in England.

In the guise of a monk, she realizes her dream of making books, until her sex ❺ is discovered and she is forced to leave.

Once again Colman comes to her—in Dover, where Peter has found a place for her to stay. Colman is on his way home to Ireland to return to his life as a goldsmith, ❻ and has come to say good-bye.

Brandwitha, desperately unhappy where she is, asks him to help her once more and allow her to come with him. She is surprised when he agrees. ❼

In the strange, beautiful land of Leinster, Brandwitha tries to come to terms with her changed circumstances, as Colman tries to show her that there's more than one way to be an artist, and more than one kind of love. Before she can learn this, Brandwitha must make peace with her past—and with herself.

1. Should be *make* to maintain present tense.
2. Change the first *promise* to *potential* to avoid the repetition.
3. Delete unnecessary *that.*
4. *The introductory phrase seems to modify Colman here.*
5. *Gender* is more accurate.
6. No change in subject. No comma.
7. Why is she surprised? The author hasn't shown us earlier that she should be surprised. If it's important, this element should come up earlier in the synopsis. If it isn't, leave her surprise out.

Sanctuary From Wolves
Historical Novel
by Kathleen Casey

Brandwitha is a Frankish girl who longs for more than her inevitable fate: marriage into a family like hers, where violence and cruelty are commonplace, and the quest for power and wealth is paramount. Her life is a journey toward artistic fulfillment, but the ambition and betrayal of others make it a tortuous and dangerous path. ❶

Two travelers happen upon the family villa outside of Paris in A.D. 596. Peter is a priest and teacher from Rome, who stays just long enough to teach Brandwitha to read. Colman is a youth from Ireland who soon travels on to his uncle's monastery, but not before winning her friendship. They both open her eyes to the existence of another world, one of kindness and books. Peter becomes like a father to her, and it hurts her deeply when he leaves for Britain to help found a church. Recognizing Brandwitha's intellect and potential, he makes her promise him she will go into a nunnery. ❷

When Brandwitha is almost a woman, the monk Wolfram teaches her the art of book illumination, but for a terrible price: She must become his concubine. The consequences of their bargain—pregnancy and miscarriage, resulting in sterility—almost destroy her and set into motion her desperate search for a way to both survive and create the art that has become an integral part of her. ❸

This search takes her first to a nunnery in Soissons, where she is content to be a scribe, although she comes to realize she is not devout enough to be a nun. Even here she cannot escape the violent political machinations of the outside world, and she is wrongly accused of treason and cast out. ❹

Alone and afraid in a church sanctuary, the only place she can go, Brandwitha is surprised and ashamed to encounter Colman, on a fact-finding mission for his uncle. He is appalled to find her here among thieves and murderers. Colman comes to her aid, at first taking her on as simply a "holy duty." Soon it becomes more, their friendship rekindled as they fight Brandwitha's treacherous family together.

He leaves her to go on about his business, fooled into thinking that with his help she will now go to her mother's family in Burgundy. ❺

Instead, she makes a dangerous journey to Peter's monastery in England. In the guise of a monk, Brandwitha realizes her dream of making books, until her gender is discovered and she is forced to leave.

Peter finds a place for her in Dover, a house of holy women waiting for a nunnery to be built. She is desperately unhappy there but tells herself she cannot expect more. One night, to her shock, Colman comes to see her. He is on his way home to Ireland to return to his life as a goldsmith. He doesn't tell her that he sought Peter out first to learn of her fate: He left his uncle's monastery because of his strong feelings for her, which helped him reclaim his own identity as an artist. Brandwitha only knows that this opportunity is her last chance; although she feels she will be a burden to him again, as well as a stranger in exile, she asks him to allow her to come with him to Ireland.

In the strange, beautiful land of Leinster, as Brandwitha tries to come to terms with her changed circumstances, Colman tries to show her that there's more than one way to be an artist and more than one kind of love. Before she can learn this, Brandwitha must make peace with her past—and with herself. ❻

1. We start strong with the core conflict—Brandwitha seeks artistic fulfillment but will face betrayal and danger.
2. Good, clear focus. We learn about Peter and Colman only as they relate to the protagonist and the core conflict.
3. Shows a wealth of conflict and tension. Notice the economy with which Casey narrates all this disaster.
4. Conflict and tension keep increasing.
5. Now we understand why Colman leaves, opening Brandwitha's life to further conflict.
6. The author resolves the core conflict and reveals the novel's theme without beating us over the head with it. Story must come first; meaning or interpretation, second.

Self-Promotion for Writers

BY PAUL RAYMOND MARTIN

Congratulations! Your book is about to be published.

Now you have to sell the darn thing.

Whether you are working with a big house or a small publisher, you will be expected to promote your book. The good news? No one is better qualified than you to promote your book.

Of course, book promotion starts with the writing. A splashy campaign or author notoriety may create an initial buzz, but won't carry a book if it isn't well-written. As you write, it's okay to fantasize about book signings, author receptions and award presentations. It may help motivate you to keep writing! But if the thought of public appearances chills your soul, fear not. There are less public ways to promote your book as well. Choose activities that are a natural outgrowth of your personality, talents and interests. Not everything will work, of course, but some things will work beyond your expectations.

Paul Raymond Martin "selling the darn thing."

SELF-PROMOTION FOR THE BRAVE OF HEART

Open yourself to opportunities that have nothing to do with your book. I once spoke at a workshop for college registrars, not about writing, but about leaving regular employment to pursue a dream. At the book signing which followed I was mobbed, to my surprise and delight.

Here are some additional ways of thinking about self-promotion for the brave of heart. Remember, whatever you think is over the top in self-promotion—isn't.

- Arrange invitation-only book signings in the homes of friends and relatives.
- Enclose your book's praise sheet (endorsements) and order form with holiday greetings or family newsletters.
- Design a bookmark as a giveaway, or ask your publisher to design one featuring several books, including yours.
- Purchase your book at a discount from the publisher and resell it at presentations at

PAUL RAYMOND MARTIN *is the author of* The Writer's Little Instruction Book: 385 Secrets for Writing Well & Getting Published *(*Writer's World Press 1998*). Known as "a writer's writer," he has published dozens of articles on writing and more than 200 stories, poems and nonfiction pieces. Among the awards he has won for his writing, Martin most treasures the Froggy statuette he was awarded by* Scavenger's Newsletter *for his parody of a horror story, "Killer Frog at the ATM."*

libraries, service clubs, schools, trade association meetings, alumni gatherings, readers' groups, etc.
- Attend author fairs in your area, introduce yourself to the coordinator and ask to be invited to next year's fair.
- Parlay your expert status (You've been published!) into paid speaking assignments. Speaking fees often exceed royalties from book sales at such events.
- Solicit a commercial sponsor for a book tour.

SELF-PROMOTION FOR THE NOT SO BRAVE OF HEART

Many writers hate making personal appearances or putting themselves forward in social situations. Maybe that's one of the reasons you write. Okay, but you can still promote your book. Here are some suggestions.
- Provide your publisher with a mailing list of friends and relatives for mail-order solicitations.
- Provide your publisher with a list of contacts in the publishing industry who should receive review copies.
- Send announcements about your book to alumni associations, service clubs, trade unions or other organizations of which you are a member. Better yet, write a short feature for the organization's publication on some aspect of the book or the writing process.
- Publish short articles or stand-alone excerpts, with the book's title and publisher mentioned in the author tagline.
- Offer your book as a prize in a contest sponsored by a magazine, newsletter or website.
- Set up a website with excerpts, endorsements, reviews, author notes, ordering information and a link to your publisher's website.
- Invite friends and relatives to write reviews for bookstore websites such as Amazon. com.

SETTING UP BOOKSTORE SIGNINGS

The most frequent form of author self-promotion is the personal appearance. But a national book tour, arranged and paid for by a publisher, is about as rare as a polished first draft. More likely, the publisher will ask you to share travel costs or piggy-back signings onto your personal travel. Or the publisher may ask you to set up a series of signings within a day's drive of your home.

If you telephone the bookstore, ask for the person who handles signings, usually the manager or community relations coordinator (CRC). Introduce yourself, give the title of your book and the publisher's name. Offer to do a presentation or demonstration with Q&A and a signing. The more useful or intriguing the presentation, the better your draw. At my signings for *The Writer's Little Instruction Book*, the presentation which has drawn best is "How to Publish Something Every Ten Days."

If you've arranged signings at stores in the same chain in that area, say so. If you haven't been to the store, ask for directions and check the directions against a map. If you visit the store in person, show a copy of your book. Give the manager or CRC a flyer with endorsements and publishing information, and business cards for you and your publisher.

The manager or CRC will ask for the ISBN and check the store's computer to see if your book can be ordered. If your publisher is using a regional distributor, give the distributor's name and contact information.

Most signings are scheduled two or three months in advance. Telephone the bookstore at least a week in advance of your signing to confirm that they are expecting you and your books are in stock. Remember, you may be speaking with a clerk who has a line of people waiting at the cash register or a manager who has six things crashing in on her. You must remain patient, pleasant and professional with *all* your contacts in the bookstores. Still, you must make sure your books are in stock or on order. Be persistent but not pushy.

If you arrange a signing in a bookstore that publishes a newsletter, request a signing in the middle of the month. The calendar is usually not available until near the end of the previous month, so a signing early in the month might not get much advance notice. And by the end of the month, newsletter readers may have forgotten about your signing.

Before your signing, draft at least three sample inscriptions. An inscription is simply a personal message you write to accompany your autograph. I often use an excerpt from my book, such as, "No fair hiding stuff in the drawer," for writers who are uneasy about sending their work out to market. Or, "Don't deny the world your talent," for reluctant writers.

Check your materials against the list in the sidebar on page 103, sleep well, eat lightly, dress professionally and tear 'em up.

BUILDING AN AUDIENCE

In addition to offering presentations or demonstrations, you and your publisher can build an audience for your signings in several ways.

- Arrange local radio and television interviews on the day of the signing, especially in smaller markets. For example, my publisher arranged appearances on KAIT-TV in Jonesboro, Arkansas, for each of two signings at Hastings Books-Music-Video, and several customers mentioned the interviews at my signings.
- Loan the store one or two 8×10 counter signs with a photo of you and/or your book cover, with the caption, "Have you met our visiting author?"
- As you travel, mention your appearance at motels, restaurants and shops, particularly on the day of the signing. At a small-town restaurant in Arkansas, I introduced myself to a teacher leading a group of high school students on a field trip. After lunch, she brought the whole troop over to my signing at a nearby bookstore.
- Alert friends and relatives that you'll be signing at a bookstore in their area. Even if they already have copies of your book, invite them to stop by. Las Vegas casinos sometimes use "shills," house employees, to attract players to empty gaming tables. One or two friends examining your book and talking about it will help draw passers-by to your table.
- Wear a "Visiting Author" name tag as you walk through the mall and whenever you take a break.

Don't *expect* bookstores to promote your signings, but be prepared to offer suggestions. Depending on budget and the manager's enthusiasm, the bookstore may:

- Mail out postcards to your friends and relatives in the area, using address labels you provide.
- Publicize your signing in the store's newsletter or mailer.
- Display a poster on the day of your signing and perhaps for several days in advance. Mall bookstores also will sometimes display posters at mall entrances and at the food court. You or your publisher provide the poster, or the bookstore may print it using your photo and cover flat.
- Display a notice of your signing where your book is shelved.
- Provide information on your signing to local media, especially the events calendar for local newspapers. At the Davis-Kidd Bookstore in Memphis, a store employee announced my signing on his weekly radio spot.
- Include information about your signing in their regular advertising. Do *not* expect the store to place advertisements specifically to promote your signing.
- Insert "bag stuffers" with customer purchases for several days prior to your signing.
- Display your book at the cash register, help desk or "Staff Recommendations" shelf prior to your signing.
- Make in-store announcements during your signing.
- Mention your signing to customers at the cash register and help desk, particularly if your are not in a highly visible location.

AT THE SIGNING

As I approached a BookStar outlet in Nashville, housed in a vintage movie theater, I was delighted to see my signing announced on the marquee. My name in lights!

Your reception at a bookstore will vary from wine-and-cheese, balloons, fresh flowers, linen tablecloths and scented candles to, "What is your book again? Let me see if we have it in the back room."

When you arrive at the bookstore for your signing, introduce yourself to staff members but don't intrude upon their work. The manager or CRC may not be on duty the day of your signing. Don't expect someone to be there to hold your hand, unless you bring along your own personal hand-holder, which is not a bad idea.

Your host at the bookstore may present you with a gift in appreciation of your visit, perhaps a T-shirt, coffee mug, one-day discount or free beverages. Page One, an independent bookstore in Albuquerque, presented me with a distinctive pen with a southwest motif.

You may be asked to sign a guest book or pose for a photo (ask for a print!). The CRC at a Barnes & Noble outlet in Louisville invited me to sign a wall in the back office. Mary Gay Shipley, owner of That Bookstore in Blytheville, Arkansas, asked me to sign one of her folding wooden chairs. All the slats on the chair signed by John Grisham were already taken, but what great fun!

During your presentation, invite questions and welcome passers-by to join in. If your appearance is for a signing only, ask for a set-up near the main entrance, cash register or help desk. In mall stores, ask to be set up at the entrance so you can engage passers-by.

Sit, don't stand. Greet passers-by. "Hi, I'm signing my book today!" Invite passers-by to look at some specific feature of the book. Make eye contact. Ask questions of prospective buyers, related to your book. At signings for *The Writer's Little Instruction Book*, I ask, "Are you writing something now? Is there someone in your life who writes? What kind of writing?" If nothing else, you can ask, "What are you reading these days?"

Be prepared for light traffic. There is no way of predicting success, but weekends are better than weekdays. Make no assumptions about who will buy. Make yourself approachable to everyone.

On one occasion, a bookstore scheduled a tarot card reader at the same time as my book signing. I was stationed at the entrance and she was buried in the back of the store. All afternoon, she was packing them in while I struggled. So it goes sometimes.

Be prepared for a wide variety of responses to you and your book. Ignore the negative; it likely has nothing to do with you. Remain courteous. Thank those who look but don't buy. Some will return to buy, maybe just because you said, "Thanks for looking!"

Customers frequently ask, "Have you written anything else?" Or, "How much is your book?" Some will mistake you for a store employee and ask if you have a certain book. They also will ask, "Are these free?" and "Where are the restrooms?" One prospective customer looked over multiple copies of my book and asked, "Did you write all these?" Honest. But my favorite customer question at signings, asked more often than you would suppose, is "Did you write this book?"

Invite customers to sign your mailing list. If the customer buys the book as a gift, ask the customer to list the name and address of the person who will receive the book. Put a heading of PLEASE PRINT on the mailing list. Start it with a dummy entry, so your first customer does not appear to be the first.

Check the spelling of each customer's or gift recipient's name before inscribing the book. And check the customer's address on the mailing list for legibility before the customer leaves your table.

Develop a code for different categories of buyers and note this on your mailing list. To gauge my market for *The Writer's Little Instruction Book*, I classified each customer as teacher, writer, young writer, gift for writer or gift for young writer.

Before leaving, sign and attach "autographed-by-author" stickers on as many copies as the manager or CRC requests. Ask the manager or CRC if you may keep any posters announcing your signing; they make great gifts.

Take joy in the process—remind yourself that you are doing what you dreamed of doing as you wrote the book.

FOLLOW-UP TO SIGNINGS

Mail a handwritten thank-you note to your contact at the bookstore after each signing. Your publisher or editor may want to do so as well. If you can, re-visit the stores where you've offered signings, say hello to staff members, and check on the display of your book. If your book is displayed spine out, turn it face out.

You will have to give up something in order to make time to promote your book. What's usually given up is writing time. Be wary of giving up time with family and friends, or all your leisure time. Promotion is an insatiable beast. You will never be able to do all that is possible to promote your book. It is easy to get so caught up in promoting a book that you lose track of priorities. Set limits on the time you devote to promotion. Keep your balance.

And the best way to keep your sanity while trying to sell the darn thing is to write the next darn thing.

The More-Complete-Than-You-Need Checklist for Book Signings

☐ Name of bookstore, address, telephone number, map and directions, contact's name
☐ Binder with notes regarding arrangements with this store and notes from previous signings at this store
☐ Extra copies of your book(s)
☐ Notes and hand-outs for presentation
☐ Tablecloth and small boxes to place under the tablecloth, making platforms to display your book
☐ Pens and writing tablets
☐ Scratch pad for spelling customers' names before signing
☐ Bookstands, name plate, name tag, signage
☐ Poster with your photo and book cover and signs for cash register and/or help desk
☐ Watch, breath mints, hand lotion, tissues, seat cushion, camera and film, candy and candy dish
☐ Bookmarks or other give-aways
☐ Excerpts or samples of your work for giveaway
☐ Regional or local author stickers and autographed-by-author stickers
☐ Business cards for you and your publisher
☐ Order forms and praise sheet (endorsements) for your book, permission-to-quote form (for additional endorsements)
☐ Flyers or brochures for upcoming appearances at workshops or conferences
☐ Brochures or flyers for other books from your publisher

The Business of Fiction Writing

It's true there are no substitutes for talent and hard work. A writer's first concern must always be attention to craft. No matter how well presented, a poorly written story or novel has little chance of being published. On the other hand, a well-written piece may be equally hard to sell in today's competitive publishing market. Talent alone is just not enough.

To be successful, writers need to study the field and pay careful attention to finding the right market. While the hours spent perfecting your writing are usually hours spent alone, you're not alone when it comes to developing your marketing plan. *Novel & Short Story Writer's Market* provides you with detailed listings containing the essential information you'll need to locate and contact the markets most suitable for your work.

Once you've determined where to send your work, you must turn your attention to presentation. We can help here, too. We've included the basics of manuscript preparation, along with a compilation of information on submission procedures and approaching markets. In addition we provide information on setting up and giving readings. We also include tips on promoting your work. No matter where you're from or what level of experience you have, you'll find useful information here on everything from presentation to mailing to selling rights to promoting your work—the "business" of fiction.

APPROACHING MAGAZINE MARKETS

While it is essential for nonfiction markets, a query letter by itself is usually not needed by most magazine fiction editors. If you are approaching a magazine to find out if fiction is accepted, a query is fine, but editors looking for short fiction want to see *how* you write. A cover letter can be useful as a letter of introduction, but it must be accompanied by the actual piece. Include basic information in your cover letter—name, address, a brief list of previous publications—if you have any—and two or three sentences about the piece (why you are sending it to *this* magazine or how your experience influenced your story). Keep it to one page and remember to include a self-addressed, stamped envelope (SASE) for reply. See the Sample Short Story Cover Letter on page 106.

Agents: Agents are not usually needed for short fiction and most do not handle it unless they already have a working relationship with you. For novels, you may want to consider working with an agent, especially if marketing to publishers who do not look at unsolicited submissions. For more on approaching agents and listings of agents willing to work with beginning and established writers, see our Literary Agents section beginning on page 115. For information on over 500 agents, see *Guide to Literary Agents* (Writer's Digest Books).

APPROACHING BOOK PUBLISHERS

Some book publishers do ask for queries first, but most want a query plus sample chapters or an outline or, occasionally, the complete manuscript. Again, make your letter brief. Include the essentials about yourself—name, address, phone number and publishing experience. Include only the personal information related to your story. Show that you have researched the market with a few sentences about why you chose this publisher. See the Sample Book Query Cover Letter on page 107.

THE SAMPLE COVER LETTER

A successful cover letter is no more than one page (20 lb. bond paper), single spaced with a double space between paragraphs, proofread carefully, and neatly typed in a standard typeface (not script or italic). The writer's name, address and phone number appear at the top, and it is addressed, ideally, to a specific editor. (If the editor's name is unavailable, address to "Fiction Editor.")

The body of a successful cover letter contains the name and word count of the story, the reason you are submitting to this particular publication, a short overview of the story, and some brief biographical information, especially when relevant to your story. Mention that you have enclosed a self-addressed, stamped envelope or postcard for reply. Also let the editor know if you are sending a disposable manuscript that doesn't need to be returned. (More and more editors prefer disposable manuscripts that save them time and save you postage.) When sending a computer disk, identify the program you are using. Remember, however, that even editors who appreciate receiving your story on a disk usually also want a printed copy. Finally, don't forget to thank the editor for considering your story. See the sample cover letters on pages 106 and 107.

BOOK PROPOSALS

A book proposal is a package sent to a publisher that includes a cover letter and one or more of the following: sample chapters, outline, synopsis, author bio, publications list. When asked to send sample chapters, send up to three *consecutive* chapters. An **outline** covers the highlights of your book chapter by chapter. Be sure to include details on main characters, the plot and subplots. Outlines can run up to 30 pages, depending on the length of your novel. The object is to tell what happens in a concise, but clear, manner. A **synopsis** is a very brief description of what happens in the story. Keep it to two or three pages. The terms synopsis and outline are sometimes used interchangeably, so be sure to find out exactly what each publisher wants. For detailed information on writing a synopsis, see Elements of a Successful Synopsis, by Blythe Camenson and Marshall J. Cook, beginning on page 91.

MANUSCRIPT MECHANICS

A professionally presented manuscript will not guarantee publication. But a sloppy, hard-to-read manuscript will not be read—publishers simply do not have the time. Here's a list of suggested submission techniques for polished manuscript presentation:

- **Use white, 8½ × 11 bond paper,** preferably 16 or 20 lb. weight. The paper should be heavy enough so it will not show pages underneath it and strong enough to take handling by several people.
- **Type your manuscript** on a computer using a laser or ink jet printer, or on a typewriter using a new ribbon.
- **Proofread carefully.** An occasional white-out is okay, but don't send a marked-up manuscript with many typos. Keep a dictionary, thesaurus and stylebook handy and use the spellcheck function of your computer.
- **Always double space and leave a 1¼ inch margin** on all sides of the page.
- **For a short story manuscript,** your first page should include your name, address and phone number (single-spaced) in the upper left corner. In the upper right, indicate an approximate word count. Center the name of your story about one-third of the way down, skip two or three lines and center your byline (byline is optional). Skip three lines and begin your story. On subsequent pages, put last name and page number in the upper right hand corner.
- **For book manuscripts,** use a separate cover sheet. Put your name, address and phone number in the upper left corner and word count in the upper right. Some writers list their agent's name and address in the upper right (word count is then placed at the bottom of the page). Center your title and byline about halfway down the page. Start your first chapter on the next page. Center the chapter number and title (if there is one) one-third of the way down the page. Include

SAMPLE SHORT STORY COVER LETTER

Jennifer Williamson
8822 Rose Petal Ct.
Norwood OH 45212

January 15, 2000

Rebecca Rossdale
Young Woman Magazine
4234 Market St.
Chicago IL 60606

Dear Ms. Rossdale,

As a teacher and former assistant camp director I have witnessed many a summer romance between teens working at camp. One romance in particular touched me because the young people involved helped each other through a very difficult summer. It inspired me to write the enclosed 8,000-word short story, "Summer Love," a love story about two teens, both from troubled families, who find love and support while working at a camp in upstate New York.

I think the story will fit nicely into your Summer Reading issue. My publishing credits include stories in *Youth Today* and *Sparkle* magazines as well as publications for adults. I am also working on a historical romance.

I look forward to hearing from you.

Sincerely,

Jennifer Williamson
(513)555-5555

Encl.: Manuscript
        SASE

SAMPLE BOOK QUERY COVER LETTER

Bonnie Booth
1453 Nuance Blvd.
Norwood OH 45212

April 12, 2000

Ms. Thelma Collins
Bradford House Publishing
187 72nd St., Fifth Floor
New York NY 10101

Dear Ms. Collins:

I am a published mystery writer whose short stories have appeared in *Modern Mystery* and *Doyle's Mystery Magazine*. I am also a law student and professional hair designer and have brought these interests together in *Only Skin Deep*, my 60,000-word novel set in the glamorous world of beauty care, featuring hair designer to the stars and amateur detective Norma Haines.

In *Only Skin Deep*, Haines is helping to put together the state's largest hair design show when she gets a call from a friend at the local police station. The body of famed designer Lynette LaSalle has been found in an Indianapolis motel room. She's been strangled and her legendary blonde mane has been shaved off. Later, when the bodies of two other designers are discovered also with shaven heads, it's clear their shared occupation is more than a coincidence.

Your successful series by Ann Smythe and the bestseller *The Gas Pump Murders*, by Marc Crawford, point to the continued popularity of amateur detectives. *Only Skin Deep* would make a strong addition to your line.

I look forward to hearing from you.

Sincerely,

Bonnie Booth
(513)555-5555

Encl.: three sample chapters
synopsis
SASE

your last name and page number in the upper right of this page and each page to follow. Start each chapter with a new page.

• **Include a word count.** If you work on a computer, chances are your word processing program can give you a word count. If you are using a typewriter, there are a number of ways to count the number of words in your piece. One way is to count the words in five lines and divide that number by five to find an average. Then count the number of lines and multiply to find the total words. For long pieces, you may want to count the words in the first three pages, divide by three and multiply by the number of pages you have.

• **Always keep a copy.** Manuscripts do get lost. To avoid expensive mailing costs, send only what is required. If you are including artwork or photos, but you are not positive they will be used, send photocopies. Artwork is hard to replace.

• **Suggest art where applicable.** Most publishers do not expect you to provide artwork and some insist on selecting their own illustrators, but if you have suggestions, please let them know. Magazine publishers work in a very visual field and are usually open to ideas.

• **Enclose a self-addressed, stamped envelope (SASE)** if you want a reply or if you want your manuscript returned. For most letters, a business-size (#10) envelope will do. Avoid using any envelope too small for an 8½ × 11 sheet of paper. For manuscripts, be sure to include enough postage and an envelope large enough to contain it.

• **Consider sending a disposable manuscript** that saves editors time and saves you money. If you are requesting a sample copy of a magazine or a book publisher's catalog, send an envelope big enough to fit.

• **When sending electronic (disk or modem) submissions,** *contact the publisher first for specific information and follow the directions carefully.* Always include a printed copy with any disk submission. *Fax or e-mail your submissions only with prior approval of the publisher.*

• **Keep accurate records.** This can be done in a number of ways, but be sure to keep track of where your stories are and how long they have been "out." Write down submission dates. If you do not hear about your submission for a long time—about three weeks to one month longer than the reporting time stated in the listing—you may want to contact the publisher. When you do, you will need an accurate record for reference.

MAILING TIPS

When mailing short correspondence or short manuscripts:

• Fold manuscripts under five pages into thirds and send in a business-size (#10) envelope.

• Mail manuscripts five pages or more unfolded in a 9 × 12 or 10 × 13 envelope.

• Mark envelopes in all caps, FIRST CLASS MAIL or SPECIAL FOURTH CLASS MANU-SCRIPT RATE.

• For return envelope, fold it in half, address it to yourself and add a stamp or, if going to a foreign country, International Reply Coupons (available for $1.05 each at the main branch of your local post office).

• Don't send by certified mail. This is a sign of a paranoid amateur and publishers do not appreciate receiving unsolicited manuscripts this way.

When mailing book-length manuscripts:

FIRST CLASS MAIL over 11 ounces (@ 65 8½ × 11 20 lb.-weight pages) automatically becomes **PRIORITY MAIL.**

METERED MAIL may be dropped in any post office box, but meter strips on SASEs should not be dated.

The Postal Service provides, free of charge, tape, boxes and envelopes to hold up to two pounds for those using PRIORITY and EXPRESS MAIL.

Requirements for mailing FOURTH CLASS and PARCEL POST have not changed.

Current Mailing Costs for First Class Postage Versus Priority	
FIRST CLASS MAIL:	**PRIORITY MAIL:**
1 ounce = 33 cents	12 oz.-2 lbs. = $3.20
2 ounces = 55 cents	2 lbs.-3 lbs. = $4.30
each additional ounce	3 lbs.-4 lbs. = $5.40
up to 16 ounces = 22 cents	4 lbs.-5 lbs. = $6.50

Main branches of local banks will cash foreign checks, but keep in mind payment quoted in our listings by publishers in other countries is usually payment in their currency. Also note reporting time is longer in most overseas markets. To save time and money, you may want to include a return postcard (and IRC) with your submission and forgo asking for a manuscript to be returned. If you live in Canada, see Canadian Writers Take Note on page 626.

RIGHTS

Know what rights you are selling. The Copyright Law states that writers are selling one-time rights (in almost all cases) unless they and the publisher have agreed otherwise. A list of various rights follows. Be sure you know exactly what rights you are selling before you agree to the sale.

• **Copyright** is the legal right to exclusive publication, sale or distribution of a literary work. As the writer or creator of a written work, you need simply to include your name, date and the copyright symbol © on your piece in order to copyright it. Be aware, however, that most editors today consider placing the copyright symbol on your work the sign of an amateur and many are even offended by it.

To get specific answers to questions about copyright (but not legal advice), you can call the Copyright Public Information Office at (202)707-3000 weekdays between 8:30 a.m. and 5 p.m. EST. Publications listed in *Novel & Short Story Writer's Market* are copyrighted *unless* otherwise stated. In the case of magazines that are not copyrighted, be sure to keep a copy of your manuscript with your notice printed on it. For more information on copyrighting your work see *The Copyright Handbook: How to Protect and Use Written Works* by Stephen Fishman (Nolo Press, 1992).

Some people are under the mistaken impression that copyright is something they have to send away for, and that their writing is not properly protected until they have "received" their copyright from the government. The fact is, you don't have to register your work with the Copyright Office in order for your work to be copyrighted; any piece of writing is copyrighted the moment it is put to paper. Registration of your work does, however, offer some additional protection (specifically, the possibility of recovering punitive damages in an infringement suit) as well as legal proof of the date of copyright.

Registration is a matter of filling out an application form (for writers, that's generally Form TX) and sending the completed form, a nonreturnable copy of the work in question and a check for $30 to the Library of Congress, Copyright Office, Register of Copyrights, 101 Independence Ave. SE, Washington DC 20559-6000. If the thought of paying $30 each to register every piece you write does not appeal to you, you can cut costs by registering a group of your works with one form, under one title for one $30 fee.

Most magazines are registered with the Copyright Office as single collective entities themselves; that is, the individual works that make up the magazine are *not* copyrighted individually in the names of the authors. You'll need to register your article yourself if you wish to have the additional protection of copyright registration.

• **First Serial Rights**—This means the writer offers a newspaper or magazine the right to publish the article, story or poem for the first time in any periodical. All other rights to the material remain with the writer. The qualifier "North American" is often added to this phrase to specify a geographical limit to the license.

When material is excerpted from a book scheduled to be published and it appears in a magazine or newspaper prior to book publication, this is also called first serial rights.

• **One-time Rights**—A periodical that licenses one-time rights to a work (also known as simultaneous rights) buys the *nonexclusive* right to publish the work once. That is, there is nothing to stop the author from selling the work to other publications at the same time. Simultaneous sales would typically be to periodicals without overlapping audiences.

• **Second Serial (Reprint) Rights**—This gives a newspaper or magazine the opportunity to print an article, poem or story after it has already appeared in another newspaper or magazine. Second serial rights are nonexclusive—that is, they can be licensed to more than one market.

• **All Rights**—This is just what it sounds like. All Rights means a publisher may use the manuscript anywhere and in any form, including movie and book club sales, without further payment to the writer (although such a transfer, or *assignment*, of rights will terminate after 35 years). If you think you'll want to use the material later, you must avoid submitting to such markets or refuse payment and withdraw your material. Ask the editor whether he is willing to buy first rights instead of all rights before you agree to an assignment or sale. Some editors will reassign rights to a writer after a given period, such as one year. It's worth an inquiry in writing.

• **Subsidiary Rights**—These are the rights, other than book publication rights, that should be covered in a book contract. These may include various serial rights; movie, television, audiotape and other electronic rights; translation rights, etc. The book contract should specify who controls these rights (author or publisher) and what percentage of sales from the licensing of these sub rights goes to the author. For more information, see Selling Subsidiary Rights.

• **Dramatic, Television and Motion Picture Rights**—This means the writer is selling his material for use on the stage, in television or in the movies. Often a one-year option to buy such rights is offered (generally for 10% of the total price). The interested party then tries to sell the idea to other people—actors, directors, studios or television networks, etc. Some properties are optioned over and over again, but most fail to become dramatic productions. In such cases, the writer can sell his rights again and again—as long as there is interest in the material. Though dramatic, TV and motion picture rights are more important to the fiction writer than the nonfiction writer, producers today are increasingly interested in nonfiction material; many biographies, topical books and true stories are being dramatized.

• **Electronic Rights**—These rights cover usage in a broad range of electronic media, from online magazines and databases to CD-ROM magazine anthologies and interactive games. The editor should specify in writing if—and which—electronic rights are being requested. The presumption is that unspecified rights are kept by the writer.

Compensation for electronic rights is a major source of conflict between writers and publishers, as many book publishers seek control of them and many magazines routinely include electronic rights in the purchase of all rights, often with no additional payment. Alternative ways of handling this issue include an additional 15% added to the amount to purchase first rights to a royalty system based on the number of times an article is accessed from an electronic database.

PROMOTION TIPS

Everyone agrees writing is hard work whether you are published or not. Yet, once you arrive at the published side of the equation the work changes. Most published authors will tell you the work is still hard but it is different. Now, not only do you continue working on your next project, you must also concern yourself with getting your book into the hands of readers. It becomes time to switch hats from artist to salesperson.

While even bestselling authors whose publishers have committed big bucks to promotion are asked to help in promoting their books, new authors may have to take it upon themselves to plan and initiate some of their own promotion, sometimes dipping into their own pockets. While this does not mean that every author is expected to go on tour, sometimes at their own expense, it does mean authors should be prepared to offer suggestions for promoting their books. For lots of great information on promoting your book, see Self-Promotion for Writers, by Paul Raymond Martin, beginning on page 99.

Depending on the time, money and the personal preferences of the author and publisher, a promotional campaign could mean anything from mailing out press releases to setting up book signings to hitting the talk-show circuit. Most writers can contribute to their own promotion by

About Our Policies

We occasionally receive letters asking why a certain magazine, publisher or contest is not in the book. Sometimes when we contact a listing, the editor does not want to be listed because they: do not use very much fiction; are overwhelmed with submissions; are having financial difficulty or have been recently sold; use only solicited material; accept work from a select group of writers only; do not have the staff or time for the many unsolicited submissions a listing may bring.

Some of the listings do not appear because we have chosen not to list them. We investigate complaints of unprofessional conduct in editors' dealings with writers and misrepresentation of information provided to us by editors and publishers. If we find these reports to be true, after a thorough investigation, we will delete the listing from future editions. See Important Listing Information on page 114 for more about our listing policies.

If a listing appeared in our book last year but is no longer listed, we list it in the General Index, beginning on page 663, with a code explaining why it is not listed. The key to those codes is given in the introduction to the General Index. Sometimes the listing does not appear because the editor did not respond in time for our press deadline, or it may not appear for any of the reasons previously mentioned above.

There is no charge to the companies that list in this book. Listings appearing in Novel & Short Story Writer's Market are compiled from detailed questionnaires, phone interviews and information provided by editors, publishers and awards directors. The publishing industry is volatile and changes of address, editor, policies and needs happen frequently. To keep up with the changes between editions of the book, we suggest you check the monthly Markets columns in Writer's Digest and Fiction Writer magazines (both by Writer's Digest). Also check the market information on the Writer's Digest website at: www.writersdigest.com or Fiction Writer at www. fictionwritermag.com.

Club newsletters and small magazines devoted to helping writers also list market information. For those writers with access to online services, several offer writers' bulletin boards, message centers and chat lines with up-to-the-minute changes and happenings in the writing community. Some of these resources are listed in our Websites of Interest (page 621). Many magazine and book publishers offer updated information for writers on their websites. Check individual listings for those website addresses.

We rely on our readers, as well, for new markets and information about market conditions. Write us if you have any new information or if you have suggestions on how to improve our listings to better suit your writing needs.

providing contact names—reviewers, home-town newspapers, civic groups, organizations—that might have a special interest in the book or the writer.

Above all, when it comes to promotion, be creative. What is your book about? Try to capitalize on it. For example, if you've written a mystery whose protagonist is a wine connoisseur, you might give a reading at a local wine-tasting or try to set something up at one of the national wine events. For more suggestions on promoting your work see *The Writer's Guide to Promotion & Publicity*, by Elane Feldman (Writer's Digest Books).

The Markets

Important Listing Information

- Listings are not advertisements. Although the information here is as accurate as possible, the listings are not endorsed or guaranteed by the editor of *Novel & Short Story Writer's Market*.
- *Novel & Short Story Writer's Market* reserves the right to exclude any listing that does not meet its requirements.

Key to Symbols and Abbreviations

N New listing in all sections

�★ Canadian listing

🌐 International listing

A Agented material only

✔ Listing includes change in contact name, address or phone

▣ Online publication

Y Award-winning publication

$ Market pays money

Ø Accepts no submissions

◐ Actively seeking beginning writers

◑ Seeking new and established writers

◕ Prefers working with established writers, mostly referrals

◎ Only handles specific types of work

★ Market offers greater opportunities for unpublished writers

▢ Cable TV market (in Screenwriting section)

● Comment by editor of *Novel & Short Story Writer's Market*

ms—manuscript; **mss**-manuscripts

b&w—black and white

SASE—self-addressed, stamped envelope

SAE—self-addressed envelope

IRC—International Reply Coupon, for use on reply mail from other countries

(See Glossary for definitions of words and expressions used in writing and publishing.)

Complaint Procedure

If you feel you have not been treated fairly by a listing in *Novel & Short Story Writer's Market*, we advise you to take the following steps:

- First try to contact the listing. Sometimes one phone call or a letter can quickly clear up the matter.
- Document all your correspondence with the listing. When you write to us with a complaint, provide the details of your submission, the date of your first contact with the listing and the nature of your subsequent correspondence.
- We will enter your letter into our files and attempt to contact the listing.
- The number and severity of complaints will be considered in our decision whether or not to delete the listing from the next edition.

Literary Agents

Many publishers are willing to look at unsolicited submissions, but most feel having an agent is to the writer's best advantage. In this section we include 60 + agents who specialize in fiction, or publish a significant amount of fiction. These agents were also selected because of their openness to submissions from writers.

The commercial fiction field has become increasingly competitive. Many publishers have smaller staffs and less time. For that reason, more book publishers are relying on agents for new talent. Some publishers are even relying on agents as "first readers" who must wade through the deluge of submissions from writers to find the very best. For writers, a good agent can be a foot in the door—someone willing to do the necessary work to put your manuscript in the right editor's hands.

Agents' growing role not only includes discovering new writers who might otherwise get lost in the burgeoning slush piles of publishing houses. Along with smaller presses, agents are taking on midlist and otherwise "known," but not big-selling, authors who have been dropped by recent mergers of large publishing houses into even bigger publishing conglomerates.

It would seem today that finding a good agent is as hard as finding a good publisher. Many writers see agents as just one more roadblock to publication. Yet those writers who have agents say they are invaluable. Not only can a good agent help you make your work more marketable, an agent acts as your business manager and adviser, keeping your interests up front during and even after contract negotiations.

Still, finding an agent can be very difficult for a new writer. If you are already published in magazines, you have a better chance than someone with no publishing credits. (Many agents routinely read periodicals searching for new writers.) Although many agents do read queries and manuscripts from unpublished authors without introduction, referrals from their writer clients can be a big help. If you don't know any published authors with agents, you may want to attend a conference as a way of meeting agents. Some agents even set aside time at conferences to meet new writers.

All the agents listed here have said they are open to working with new, previously unpublished writers as well as published writers. Most do not charge a fee to cover the time and effort involved in reviewing a manuscript or a synopsis and chapters.

USING THE LISTINGS

It is especially important when contacting these busy agents that you read individual listings carefully before submitting anything. The first information after the company name includes the address and phone, fax and e-mail address (when available). **Member Agents** gives the names of individual agents working at that company (specific types of fiction an agent handles are indicated in parenthesis after that agent's name). The **Handles** section lists the types of fiction the agency works with. **Needs** includes any specific types of fiction the agency is currently looking for, as well as what they do not want to see. Reading the **Recent Sales** gives you the names of writers an agent is currently working with and, very importantly, publishers the agent has placed manuscripts with. **Writers' Conferences** identifies conferences an agent attends (and where you might possibly meet that agent). **Tips** presents advice directly from the agent to authors.

N ☩ ◪ ACACIA HOUSE PUBLISHING SERVICES LTD., 51 Acacia Rd., Toronto, Ontario M4S 2K6 Canada. Phone/fax: (416)484-8356. **Contact:** (Ms.) Frances Hanna. Estab. 1985. Represents 30 clients. **Works**

with a small number of new/unpublished authors. Specializes in contemporary fiction: literary or commercial (no horror, occult or science fiction); nonfiction. Currently handles: 30% nonfiction books; 70% novels.

● Ms. Hanna has been in the publishing business for 30 years, first in London (UK) as a fiction editor with Barrie & Jenkins and Pan Books, and as a senior editor with a packager of mainly illustrated books. She was condensed books editor for 6 years for *Reader's Digest* in Montreal, senior editor and foreign rights manager for (the then) Wm. Collins & Sons (now HarperCollins) in Toronto.

Represents: Nonfiction books, novels. **Considers these fiction areas:** action/adventure; detective/police/crime; literary; mainstream; mystery/suspense; thriller/espionage.

How to Contact: Query with outline. Prefers to be only reader. *No unsolicited mss.* Reports in 6 weeks on queries. Returns materials only with SASE.

Needs: Actively seeking "outstanding first novels with literary merit."

Recent Sales: Sold 20 titles in the last year and numerous international rights sales. Prefers not to share client or sales data.

Terms: Agent receives 15% commission on English language sales; 20% on dramatic sales; 25-30% on foreign language sales. Charges for photocopying.

Writers' Conferences: London International Book Fair (England); BEA (Chicago); Frankfurt Book Fair (Germany).

Tips: "I prefer that writers be previously published, with at least a few articles to their credit. Strongest consideration will be given to those with, say, three or more published books. However, I *would* take on an unpublished writer of outstanding talent."

🅽 🔘 ALIVE COMMUNICATIONS, INC., 1465 Kelly Johnson Blvd., Suite 320, Colorado Springs CO 80920. (719)260-7080. Fax: (719)260-8223. Website: www.alivecom.com. Estab. 1989. Member of AAR, CBA. Represents 100 clients. **5% of clients are new/unpublished writers.** Currently handles: 40% nonfiction books; 10% juvenile books; 4% short story collections; 40% novels; 1% syndicated material; 5% novellas.

Member Agent(s): Rick Christian (blockbusters, bestsellers); Greg Johnson (popular/commercial nonfiction and fiction); Kathy Yanni (literary nonfiction and fiction); Jerry "Chip" MacGregor (popular/commercial nonfiction and fiction, new authors with breakout potential).

Represents: Nonfiction books, juvenile books, novels, novellas, poetry, short story collections. **Considers these fiction areas:** action/adventure; contemporary issues; detective/police/crime; family saga; historical; humor/satire; juvenile; literary; mainstream; mystery/suspense; religious/inspirational; thriller/espionage; westerns/frontier; young adult.

How to Contact: Send outline and 3 sample chapters. Include bio/résumé, publishing history and SASE. Considers simultaneous submissions, "if clearly noted in cover letter." Reports in 2 weeks on queries; 1 month on mss. Returns materials only with SASE.

Needs Actively seeking inspirational/literary/mainstream fiction and work from authors with established track record and platforms. Does not want to receive poetry, young adult paperback, scripts, dark themes. Obtains new clients through recommendations from clients and publishers.

Recent Sales: Sold 300 titles in the last year. *Left Behind* series, by Tim LaHaye and Jerry B. Jenkins (Tyndale); *Jerusalem Vigil*, by Bodie and Brock Thoene (Viking).

Terms: Agent receives 15% commission on domestic sales; 15-30% on foreign sales. Offers written contract. 60 days written notice must be given to terminate contract.

Reading List: Reads literary, religious and mainstream journals to find new clients. "Our goal is always the same—to find writers whose use of language is riveting and powerful."

Tips: "Rewrite and polish until the words on the page shine. Provide us with as much personal and publishing history information as possible. Endorsements and great connections may help, provided you can write with power and passion. Alive Communications, Inc. has established itself as a premiere literary agency and speakers bureau. Based in Colorado Springs, we serve an elite group of authors and speakers, who are critically acclaimed and commercially successful in both Christian and general markets."

🅽 🔘 JAMES ALLEN, LITERARY AGENT, P.O. Box 278, Milford PA 18337-0278. **Contact:** James Allen. Estab. 1974. Signatory of WGA. Represents 40 clients. **10% of clients are new/previously unpublished writers.** "I handle all kinds of genre fiction (except westerns) and specialize in science fiction and fantasy." Currently handles: 2% nonfiction books; 8% juvenile books; 90% novels.

Represents: Nonfiction books, novels. **Considers these fiction areas:** action/adventure; detective/police/crime; family saga; fantasy; glitz; historical; horror; mainstream; mystery/suspense; romance (contemporary, historical); science fiction; young adult.

How to Contact: Query. Responds in 1 week on queries; 2 months on mss. "I prefer first contact to be a query letter with two- to three-page plot synopsis and SASE with a response time of one week. If my interest is piqued, I then ask for the first four chapters, response time within a month. If I'm impressed by the writing, I then ask for the balance of the manuscript, response time about two months."

Needs: Actively seeking "well-written work by people who at least have their foot in the door and are looking for someone to take them to the next (and subsequent) levels." Does not want to receive "petitions for representation from people who do not yet have even one booklength credit."

Recent Sales: Sold about 35 titles in the last year. *China Sea*, by David Poyer (St. Martin's Press), *Aranur's Tale*, by Tara K. Harper (Del Rey), *The Devil in Ol' Rosie*, by Louise Moeri (Atheneum/S&S). Other clients include Doug Allyn, Judi Lind, Robert Trout, Juanita Coulson and Jan Clark.

Terms: Agent receives 10% commission on domestic print sales; 20% on film sales; 20% on foreign sales. Offers written contract, binding for 3 years "automatically renewed. No reading fees or other up-front charges. I reserve the right to charge for extraordinary expenses (in practice, only the cost of book purchases when I need copies to market a title abroad). I do not bill the author but deduct the charges from incoming earnings."

Tips: *"First time at book length need NOT* apply—only taking on authors who have the foundations of their writing careers in place and can use help in building the rest. A cogent, to-the-point query letter is necessary, laying out the author's track record and giving a brief blurb for the book. The response to a mere 'I have written a novel, will you look at it?' is universally 'NO!' "

MARCIA AMSTERDAM AGENCY, 41 W. 82nd St., New York NY 10024-5613. (212)873-4945. **Contact:** Marcia Amsterdam. Estab. 1970. Signatory of WGA. Currently handles: 15% nonfiction books; 70% novels; 10% movie scripts; 5% TV scripts.

- Prior to opening her agency, Ms. Amsterdam was an editor.

Represents: Nonfiction, novels. **Considers these fiction areas:** action/adventure; detective; horror; humor; mainstream; mystery/suspense; romance (contemporary, historical); science fiction; thriller/espionage; westerns/frontier; young adult.

Also Handles: Feature film, TV MOW, sitcom. **Considers these script subject areas:** comedy, mainstream, mystery/suspense, romance (comedy, drama).

How to Contact: Send outline plus first 3 sample chapters and SASE. Reports in 1 month on queries.

Recent Sales: *Rosey In the Present Tense*, by Louise Hawes (Walker); *Flash Factor*, by William H. Lovejoy (Kensington). *TV scripts optioned/sold: Mad About You*, by Jenna Bruce (Columbia Tristar TV).

Terms: Agent receives 15% commission on domestic sales; 20% on foreign sales, 10% on scripts. Offers written contract, binding for 1 year, "renewable." Charges for extra office expenses, foreign postage, copying, legal fees (when agreed upon).

Tips: "We are always looking for interesting literary voices."

C G & W ASSOCIATES, 252 Stanford Ave. (or P.O. Box 7613), Menlo Park CA 94025-6328. (650)854-1020. Fax: (650)854-1020. E-mail: sallyconley@msn.com. **Contact:** Sally Conley. Estab. 1996. Represents 12 clients. **72% of clients are new/unpublished writers.** Specializes in literary and commercial mainstream fiction. Currently handles: 10% nonfiction books; 90% novels.

- Prior to opening her agency, Ms. Conley spent 20 years as co-owner of The Guild Bookstore (Menlo Park, CA) and was a Peace Corps volunteer for women in development from 1993-96.

Represents: Literary and commercial mainstream fiction. **Considers these fiction areas:** action/adventure; confessional; contemporary issues; detective/police/crime; ethnic; family saga; glitz; historical; literary; mainstream; mystery/suspense; regional; romance (contemporary, historical); thriller/espionage.

How to Contact: Query "with first 30 pages and SASE large enough to return pages." Accepts queries by fax. Considers simultaneous queries. Reports in 2 weeks on queries; 2-4 weeks on mss. Returns materials only with SASE.

Needs: Actively seeking "writers with a highly original voice."

Recent Sales: Prefers not to share information on specific sales. Clients include Karl Luntta.

Terms: Agent receives 15% commission on domestic sales; 20% on foreign sales. Offers written contract. 30 days written notice must be given to terminate contract.

MARIA CARVAINIS AGENCY, INC., 235 West End Ave., New York NY 10023. (212)580-1559. Fax: (212)877-3486. **Contact:** Maria Carvainis. Estab. 1977. Member of AAR, Authors Guild, ABA, MWA, RWA, signatory of WGA. Represents 35 clients. **10% of clients are new/previously unpublished writers.** Currently handles: 34% nonfiction books; 65% novels; 1% poetry books.

- Prior to opening her agency, Ms. Carvainis spent more than 10 years in the publishing industry as a senior editor with Macmillan Publishing, Basic Books, Avon Books, where she worked closely with Peter Mayer and Crown Publishers. Ms. Carvainis has served as a member of the AAR Board of Directors and AAR Treasurer, as well as serving as chair of the AAR Contracts Committee. She presently serves on the AAR Royalty Committee.

Represents: Nonfiction books, novels. **Considers these fiction areas:** fantasy; historical; literary; mainstream; mystery/suspense; romance; thriller; children's; young adult.

MARKET CONDITIONS are constantly changing! If you're still using this book and it is 2001 or later, buy the newest edition of *Novel & Short Story Writer's Market* at your favorite bookstore or order from Writer's Digest Books at (800)289-0963.

How to Contact: Query first with SASE. Reports within 3 weeks on queries; 3 months on solicited mss.
Needs: Does not want to receive science fiction. "60% of new clients derived from recommendations or conferences. 40% of new clients derived from letters of query."
Recent Sales: *The Alibi* and *Standoff*, by Sandra Brown (Warner Books); *Bearing Witness*, by Michael Kahn (TOR/Forge); *Dark of the Moon*, by P.J. Parrish (Kensington); *Heroin*, by Charlie Smith (W.W. Norton). Other clients include Mary Balogh, David Bottoms, Pam Conrad, Cindy Gerard, Sarah Zsidore, Samantha James, Jerome Loving, Kristine Rolofson, William Sessions and Jose Yglesias.
Terms: Agent receives 15% commission on domestic sales; 20% on foreign sales. Offers written contract, binding for 2 years "on a book-by-book basis." Charges for foreign postage and bulk copying.
Writers' Conferences: BEA; Frankfurt Book Fair.

N **◐** **HY COHEN LITERARY AGENCY LTD.**, P.O. Box 43770, Upper Montclair NJ 07043. (973)783-9494. Fax: (973)783-9867. E-mail: cogency@home.com. **Contact:** Hy Cohen. Estab. 1975. Represents 25 clients. **50% of clients are new/previously unpublished writers.** Currently handles: 20% nonfiction books; 5% juvenile books; 75% novels.
Represents: Nonfiction books, novels. **Considers all categories of fiction.**
How to Contact: Send 100 pages with SASE. Reports in about 2 weeks (on 100-page submission).
Needs: Obtains new clients through recommendations from others and unsolicited submissions.
Recent Sales: Prefers not to share information on specific sales.
Terms: Agent receives 10% commission.
Tips: "Send double-spaced, legible scripts and SASE. Good writing helps."

N **◒** **DON CONGDON ASSOCIATES INC.**, 156 Fifth Ave., Suite 625, New York NY 10010-7002. **Contact:** Don Congdon, Michael Congdon, Susan Ramer. Estab. 1983. Member of AAR, signatory of WGA. Represents approximately 100 clients. Currently handles: 50% fiction; 50% nonfiction books.
Represents: Nonfiction books, novels. **Considers all fiction areas, especially literary fiction.**
How to Contact: Query. Include SASE. "If interested, we ask for sample chapters and outline." Reports in 1 week on queries; 1 month on mss.
Needs: Obtains new clients through referrals from other authors.
Recent Sales: *The Return of Little Big Man*, by Thomas Berger (Little, Brown); *Pulse*, by Edna Buchanan (Avon Books).
Terms: Agent receives 10% commission on domestic sales. Charges for overnight mail, postage and photocopying.
Tips: "Writing a query letter with a self-addressed stamped envelope is a must."

N **◒** **CONNOR LITERARY AGENCY**, 2911 West 71st St., Richfield MN 55423. (612)866-1426. Fax: (612)869-4074. **Contact:** Marlene Connor Lynch. Estab. 1985. Represents 50 clients. **30% of clients are new/previously unpublished writers.** Specializes in popular fiction and nonfiction. Currently handles: 50% nonfiction books; 50% novels.
  • Prior to opening her agency, Ms. Connor served at the Literary Guild of America, Simon and Schuster and Random House.
Member Agents: Amy Jensen (children's books); Richard Zanders (assistant).
Represents: Nonfiction books, novels, children's books (especially with a minority slant). **Considers these fiction areas:** contemporary issues; detective/police/crime; ethnic; experimental; family saga; horror; literary; mystery/suspense; thriller/espionage.
How to Contact: Query with outline/proposal and SASE. Reports in 1 month on queries; 6 weeks on mss.
Needs: Obtains new clients through "queries, recommendations, conferences, grapevine, etc."
Recent Sales: *Essence: 25 Years of Celebrating the Black Woman* (Abrams); *The Marital Compatibility Test*, by Susan Adams (Carol Publishing Group); *We Are Overcome*, by Bonnie Allen (Crown).
Terms: Agent receives 15% commission on domestic sales; 25% on foreign sales. Offers a written contract, binding for 1 year.
Writers' Conferences: Howard University Publishing Institute; BEA; Detroit Writer's Conference; Mid-West Romance Writer's Conference.
Tips: "Seeking previously published writers with good sales records and new writers with real talent."

N **◒** **CRAWFORD LITERARY AGENCY**, 94 Evans Rd., Barnstead NH 03218. (603)269-5851. Fax: (603)269-2533. **Contact:** Susan Crawford. Estab. 1988. Represents 40 clients. **10% of clients are new/previously unpublished writers.** Specializes in celebrity and/or media-based books and authors. Currently handles: 50% nonfiction books; 50% novels.
Member Agents: Susan Crawford, Lorne Crawford (commercial fiction); Scott Neister (scientific/techno thrillers); Kristen Hales (parenting, psychology, New Age, self help).
Represents: Commercial fiction.
How to Contact: Query with SASE. No queries by fax. Considers simultaneous queries; no simultaneous ms submissions. Reports in 3 weeks on queries. Returns materials only with SASE.

Needs: Actively seeking action/adventure stories, medical thrillers, suspense thrillers, celebrity projects, self-help, inspirational, how-to and women's issues. Does not want to receive short stories or poetry. Obtains new clients through recommendations, conferences, and queries.

Recent Sales: *Housebroken*, by Richard Karn and George Mair (HarperCollins); *Psi/Net*, by Billy Dee Williams and Rob MacGregor (TOR/Forge). Other clients include Dr. Avner Hershlag, M.D., John Travolta, Richard Karn, Billy Dee Williams, Ruby Dee and Ossie Davis.

Terms: Agent receives 15% commission on domestic sales; 20% on foreign sales. Offers written contract, binding for 90 days. 100% of business is derived from commissions on sales.

Writers' Conferences: International Film & Writers Workshop (Rockport ME).

N **◙** **RICHARD CURTIS ASSOCIATES, INC.**, 171 E. 74th St., Suite 2, New York NY 10021. (212)772-7363. Fax: (212)772-7393. E-mail: ltucker@curtisagency.com. Website: www/curtisagency.com. **Contact:** Pam Valvera. Estab. 1969. Member of AAR, RWA, MWA, WWA, SFWA, signatory of WGA. Represents 100 clients. **5% of clients are new/previously unpublished writers.** Specializes in general and literary fiction and nonfiction, as well as genre fiction such as science fiction, women's romance, horror, fantasy, action-adventure. Currently handles: 50% nonfiction books; 50% novels.
  • Prior to opening his agency, Mr. Curtis was an agent with the Scott Meredith Literary Agency for 7 years and has authored over 50 published books.

Member Agents: Amy Victoria Meo, Laura Tucker, Richard Curtis.

Represents: Nonfiction books, scholarly books, novels. **Considers all fiction areas.**

How to Contact: No fax or e-mail queries. Conventional queries (outline and 3 sample chapters) must be accompanied by SASE. Reports in 1 month on queries; 1 month on mss.

Needs: Obtains new clients through recommendations from others, solicitations and conferences.

Recent Sales: Sold 100 titles in the last year. *Darwin's Radio*, by Greg Bear (Del Rey/Random House); *Expendable*, by James Gardner (Avon). Other clients include Dan Simmons, Jennifer Blake, Leonard Maltin, Earl Mindell and Barbara Parker.

Terms: Agent receives 15% commission on domestic sales; 20% on foreign sales. Offers written contract, binding on a "book by book basis." Charges for photocopying, express, fax, international postage, book orders.

Writers' Conferences: Romance Writers of America; Nebula Science Fiction Conference.

◙ **DARHANSOFF & VERRILL LITERARY AGENTS**, 179 Franklin St., 4th Floor, New York NY 10013. (212)334-5980. Fax: (212)334-5470. Estab. 1975. Member of AAR. Represents 100 clients. **10% of clients are new/previously unpublished writers.** Specializes in literary fiction. Currently handles: 25% nonfiction books; 60% novels; 15% short story collections.

Member Agents: Liz Darhansoff, Charles Verrill, Leigh Feldman.

Represents: Nonfiction books, novels, short story collections. **Considers literary and thriller fiction.**

How to Contact: Query letter only. Reports in 2 weeks on queries.

Needs: Obtains new clients through recommendations from others.

Recent Sales: *Cold Mountain*, by Charles Frazier (Atlantic Monthly Press); *At Home in Mitford*, by Jan Karon (Viking).

N **◙** **JOAN DAVES AGENCY**, 21 W. 26th St., New York NY 10010. (212)685-2663. Fax: (212)685-1781. **Contact:** Jennifer Lyons, director; Heather Currier, assistant. Estab. 1960. Member of AAR. Represents 100 clients. **10% of clients are new/previously unpublished writers.** Specializes in literary fiction and nonfiction, also commercial fiction.

Represents: Nonfiction books, novels. **Considers these fiction areas:** ethnic, family saga; gay; literary; mainstream.

How to Contact: Query. Considers simultaneous submissions. Reports in 3 weeks on queries; 6 weeks on mss. Returns materials only with SASE.

Needs: Obtains new clients through editors' and author clients' recommendations. "A few queries translate into representation."

Recent Sales: Sold 70 titles in the last year. *Strange Fire*, by Melvin Jules Bukiet (W.W. Norton); *JLVT! Growing Up Female with a Bad Reputation*, by Leora Tannenbaum; *Candor and Perversion*, by Roger Shattuck (W.W. Norton).

Terms: Agent receives 15% commission on domestic sales; 20% on foreign sales. Offers written contract, on a per book basis. Charges for office expenses. 100% of business is derived from commissions on sales.

Reading List: Reads *The Paris Review, Missouri Review*, and *Voice Literary Supplement* to find new clients.

N **◙** **◎** **DHS LITERARY, INC.**, 6060 N. Central Expwy., Suite 624, Dallas TX 75206-5209. (214)363-4422. Fax: (214)363-4423. **Contact:** David Hale Smith, president. Estab. 1994. Represents 40 clients. **50% of clients are new/previously unpublished writers.** Specializes in commercial fiction and nonfiction for adult trade market. Currently handles: 50% nonfiction books; 50% novels.
  • Prior to opening his agency, Mr. Smith was an editor at a newswire service.

Represents: Nonfiction books, novels. **Considers these fiction areas:** detective/police/crime; erotica; ethnic;

feminist; gay; historical; horror; literary; mainstream; mystery/suspense; sports; thriller/espionage; westerns/frontier.

How to Contact: Query. Considers simultaneous queries. Reports in 1 month on queries; 4 months on mss. Returns materials only with SASE, otherwise discards.

Needs: Actively seeking thrillers, mysteries, suspense, etc., and narrative nonfiction. Does not want to receive poetry, short fiction, children's books. Obtains new clients through referrals from other clients, editors and agents, presentations at writers conferences and via unsolicited submissions.

Recent Sales: Sold 29 titles in the last year. *Shooting At Midnight*, by Greg Rucka (Bantam); *Food & Mood*, by Elizabeth Somer (Holt).

Terms: Agent receives 15% commission on domestic sales; 25% on foreign sales. Offers written contract, with 10-day cancellation clause or upon mutual consent. Charges for client expenses, i.e., postage, photocopying. 100% of business is derived from commissions on sales.

Reading List: Reads *Outside Magazine*, STORY, *Texas Monthly, Kenyon Review, Missouri Review* and *Mississippi Mud* to find new clients. "I like to see good writing in many formats. So I'll often call a writer who has written a good short story, for example, to see if she has a novel."

Tips: "Remember to be courteous and professional, and to treat marketing your work and approaching an agent as you would any formal business matter. When in doubt, always query first—in writing—with SASE."

DONADIO AND OLSON, INC., (formerly Donadio and Ashworth), 121 W. 27th St., Suite 704, New York NY 10001. (212)691-8077. Fax: (212)633-2837. **Contact:** Neil Olson. Estab. 1970. Member of AAR. Represents approximately 100 clients. Specializes in literary fiction and nonfiction. Currently handles: 40% nonfiction; 50% novels; 10% short story collections.

Member Agents: Edward Hibbert (literary fiction); Neil Olson; Ira Silverberg; Peter Steinberg.

Represents: Nonfiction books, novels, short story collections.

How to Contact: Query with 50 pages and SASE. Considers simultaneous queries and submissions. Returns materials only with SASE.

Recent Sales: Sold over 15 titles in the last year. Prefers not to share information on specific sales.

Terms: Agent receives 15% commission on domestic sales; 20% on foreign sales.

ETHAN ELLENBERG LITERARY AGENCY, 548 Broadway, #5-E, New York NY 10012. (212)431-4554. Fax: (212)941-4652. E-mail: eellenberg@aol.com. **Contact:** Ethan Ellenberg. Estab. 1983. Represents 70 clients. **10% of clients are new/previously unpublished writers.** Specializes in commercial fiction, especially thrillers and romance/women's fiction. "We also do a lot of children's books." Currently handles: 25% nonfiction books; 75% novels.

● Prior to opening his agency, Mr. Ellenberg was contracts manager of Berkley/Jove and associate contracts manager for Bantam.

Represents: Nonfiction books, novels. **Considers these fiction areas:** detective/police/crime; family saga; fantasy; historical; humor; juvenile; literary; mainstream; mystery/suspense; picture book; romance; science fiction; thriller/espionage; young adult.

How to Contact: Send outline plus 3 sample chapters. Accepts queries by e-mail. No fax queries. Considers simultaneous queries and submissions. Reports in 10 days on queries; 1 month on mss. Returns materials only with SASE.

Needs: Commercial and literary fiction, children's books, break-through nonfiction. Does not want to receive poetry, westerns, autobiographies.

Recent Sales: Sold over 100 titles in the last year. 2 untitled historical romances, by Bertrice Small (Ballantine and Zebra); *The Prairie Train*, illustrated by Eric Rohmann (Crown); *The Hero of the Herd*, by John McCormack (Crown); *Consulting Demons*, by Louis Pinault (HarperCollins); *Puppy and Me* series, by Julia Noonan (Scholastic); *Threat From The Sea* series, by Mel Odom (Wizards of the Coast); *Soul Collector*, by Maureen Child (Hearst Entertainment/CBS).

Terms: Agent receives 15% on domestic sales; 10% on foreign sales. Offers written contract, "flexible." Charges for "direct expenses only: photocopying, postage."

Writers' Conferences: Attends RWA National and Novelists, Inc.

Tips: "We do consider new material from unsolicited authors. Write a good clear letter with a succinct description of your book. We prefer the first three chapters when we consider fiction. For all submissions you must include SASE for return or the material is discarded. It's always hard to break in, but talent will find a home. We continue to see natural storytellers and nonfiction writers with important books."

NICHOLAS ELLISON, INC., 55 Fifth Ave., 15th Floor, New York NY 10003. (212)206-6050. Fax: (212)463-8718. Affiliated with Sanford J. Greenburger Associates. **Contact:** Elizabeth Ziemska, Jane Mendle. Estab. 1983. Represents 70 clients. Currently handles: 25% nonfiction books; 75% novels.

● Prior to becoming an agent, Mr. Ellison was an editor at Minerva Editions, Harper & Row and editor-in-chief at Delacorte.

Member Agents: Alicka Pistek (foreign rights); Elizabeth Ziemska, Jane Mendle.

Represents: Nonfiction, novels. **Considers literary and mainstream fiction.**

How to Contact: Query with SASE. Reporting time varies on queries.

Needs: Does not want biography or self-help. Usually obtains new clients from word-of-mouth referrals.

Recent Sales: *Plum Island*, by Nelson DeMille (Warner); *The Mermaids Singing*; by Lisa Carey (Avon). Other clients include Olivia Goldsmith, P.T. Deutermann, James Webb.

Terms: Agent receives 15% commission on domestic sales; 20% commission on foreign sales.

[N] [●] MARY EVANS INC., 242 E. Fifth St., New York NY 10003. (212)979-0880. Fax: (212)979-5344. E-mail: merrylit@aol.com. **Contact:** Tanya McKinnon or Laura Albritton. Member of AAR. Represents 45 clients. Specializes in literary fiction and serious nonfiction. Currently handles: 45% nonfiction books; 5% story collections; 50% novels.

Member Agents: Tanya McKinnon, Mary Evans.

Represents: Nonfiction books, novels. **Considers these fiction areas:** contemporary issues; ethnic; gay; literary.

How to Contact: Query. Reports in 1 month on queries; 2 months on mss.

Needs: Actively seeking "professional well-researched nonfiction proposals; literary novels." No children's books. Obtains new clients through recommendations from others.

Recent Sales: *Whiteouts*, by Michael Blaire (Rob Weisbach Books); *Biorealism*, by Robert Frenay (Farrar, Straus & Giroux); *Venus Rituals*, by Vendela Vida (St. Martin's Press).

Terms: Agent receives 15% commission on domestic sales; 20% on foreign sales.

[N] [●] JUSTIN E. FERNANDEZ, AGENT/ATTORNEY, (formerly Justin E. Fernandez Attorney/Agent—Agency for the Digital & Literary Arts, Inc.), P.O. Box 20038, Cincinnati OH 45220. E-mail: lit4@aol.com. **Contact:** Justin E. Fernandez. Estab. 1996. Represents 10-15 clients. **50% of clients are new/previously unpublished writers.** Currently handles: 25% nonfiction; 65% fiction; 5% digital/multimedia, 5% other. "We are presently an affiliate agency of AEI, Inc. AEI has offices in Beverly Hills and New York. AEI's web address is www.aeionline.com."

• Prior to opening his agency, Mr. Fernandez, a 1992 graduate of the University of Cincinnati College of Law, served as a law clerk with the Ohio Court of Appeals, Second Appellate District (1992-94), and as a literary agent for Paraview, Inc., New York (1995-96).

Member Agents: Paul A. Franc (associate agent).

Represents: Nonfiction, fiction, screen/teleplays and digital art (virtual reality, music, software, multimedia/Internet-related products). **Considers most fiction genres.**

How to Contact: Query first with SASE (e-mail encouraged). Considers simultaneous queries and submissions. When hard copy is requested, be sure to include a container for the manuscript, with return address and sufficient postage affixed unless recycling is an option.

Needs: Mainstream fiction; pop culture; women's fiction; thrillers; histories; biographies; literary fiction and nonfiction; children's books; computer and Internet-related books; romance novels; African-American and Hispanic fiction; science fiction; gift and humor books; photography, art and design books; popular/mainstream science and philosophy, political science, Eastern religion, gay/lesbian fiction and nonfiction; and material for syndication (columns, cartoon strips, etc.). Usually obtains new clients through referrals or queries from listings.

Recent Sales: Sold 4 titles last year. *By Way of a Wager* and *Seeking Celeste*, by Hayley Ann Solomon (Kensington/Zebra).

Terms: Agent receives 10% commission on domestic sales; 15% on foreign sales; 25% with foreign co-agent. Offers written contract. No fees. Expenses deducted from monies received per contract terms.

Tips: "Proofread, proofread, proofread—50% of submissions have typos, usage errors, or clichés in the first several pages. Manuscripts should be double spaced, with 1-inch margins, 12 point font, and be accompanied by a return package, with sufficient postage attached (not loose) to the package. When sending e-mail follow-up messages, don't assume your name is enough information—identify the submission by title and date and method submitted."

[N] [●] GOODMAN-ANDREW-AGENCY, INC., 1275 N. Harper, #7, West Hollywood CA 90046. (323)656-3785. Fax: (323)656-3975. **Contact:** Sasha Goodman. Estab. 1992. Represents 25 clients. **50% of clients are new/previously unpublished writers.** Currently handles: 50% nonfiction books; 50% novels.

Represents: Nonfiction books, novels. **Considers these fiction areas:** contemporary issues; ethnic; gay; lesbian; literary; mainstream. "Not big on genre fiction."

How to Contact: Send outline and 2 sample chapters. Considers simultaneous queries and submissions. Reports in 3 weeks on queries; 3 months on mss. Returns materials only with SASE.

Recent Sales: Sold 10 titles in the last year. *Person or Persons Unknown*, by Bruce Alexander (Putnam).

Terms: Agent receives 15% commission. Offers written contract. Charges for postage.

Writers' Conferences: Pacific Northwest (Seattle, July).

Tips: "Query with 1-page letter, brief synopsis and 2 chapters. Patience, patience, patience. Always enclose return postage/SASE if you want your material returned. Otherwise, say you do not. Remember the agent is receiving dozens of submissions per week so try to understand this, and be patient and courteous."

[N] [●] RANDALL ELISHA GREENE, LITERARY AGENT, 620 S. Broadway, Suite 210, Lexington KY 40508-3150. (606)225-1388. **Contact:** Randall Elisha Greene. Estab. 1987. Represents 20 clients. **30% of clients**

are new/previously unpublished writers. Specializes in adult fiction and nonfiction only. No juvenile or children's books. Currently handles: 50% nonfiction books; 50% novels.

● Prior to opening his agency, Mr. Greene worked at Doubleday & Co. as an editor.

Represents: Nonfiction books, novels. **Considers these fiction areas:** contemporary issues; detective/police/crime; ethnic; family saga; humor/satire; literary; mainstream; mystery/suspense; regional; romance (contemporary); thriller/espionage.

How to Contact: Query with SASE only. Reports in 1 month on queries; 2 months on mss. *No unsolicited mss.*

Recent Sales: Prefers not to share information on specific sales.

Terms: Agent receives 15% commission on domestic sales; 20% on foreign sales and performance rights. Charges for extraordinary expenses such as photocopying and foreign postage.

 REECE HALSEY, 98 Main St., PMB 704, Tiburon CA 94920. (415)789-9191. Fax: (415)789-9177. E-mail: bookgirl@worldnet.att.net. **Contact:** Kimberley Cameron. Estab. 1957. Member of AAR, signatory of WGA. Represents 40 clients. **30% of clients are new/previously unpublished writers.** Specializes in mystery, literary and mainstream fiction, excellent writing. Currently handles: 30% nonfiction books; 70% fiction.

● The Reese Halsey Agency has an illustrious client list largely of established writers, including the estate of Aldous Huxley and has represented Upton Sinclair, William Faulkner and Henry Miller. Ms. Cameron has recently opened a Northern California office and all queries should be addressed to her at the Tiburon office.

Member Agents: Doris Halsey (by referral only, LA office); Kimberley Cameron (Reese Halsey North).

Represents: Fiction and nonfiction. **Considers these fiction areas:** action/adventure; contemporary issues; detective/police/crime; ethnic; family saga; historical; literary; mainstream; mystery/suspense; science fiction; thriller/espionage; women's fiction.

How to Contact: Query with SASE. Reports in 3 weeks on queries; 3 months on mss.

Recent Sales: Prefers not to share information on specific sales.

Terms: Agent receives 15% commission on domestic sales of books. Offers written contract, binding for 1 year. Requests 6 copies of ms if representing an author.

Writers' Conferences: BEA and various writer conferences, Maui Writers Conference.

Reading List: Reads *Glimmer Train*, *The Sun* and *The New Yorker* to find new clients. Looks for "writing that touches the heart."

Tips: Obtains new clients through recommendations from others and solicitation. "Please send a polite, well-written query and include a SASE with it!"

N ◎ **HARRIS LITERARY AGENCY**, P.O. Box 6023, San Diego CA 92166. (619)697-0600. Fax: (619)697-0610. E-mail: hlit@adnc.com. Website: www.HarrisLiterary.com. **Contact:** Barbara J. Harris. Estab. 1998. Represents 60 clients. **65% of clients are new/previously unpublished writers.** Specializes in mainstream fiction. Currently handles: 40% nonfiction books; 60% novels.

Member Agents: Barbara J. Harris (nonfiction); Norman J. Rudenberg (fiction).

Represents: Nonfiction books, novels. **Considers these fiction areas:** action/adventure; detective/police/crime; humor/satire; juvenile; mainstream; mystery/suspense; science fiction; thriller/espionage.

How to Contact: Query with SASE. "The initial query should contain a one- to two-page description plus the author's pertinent biography, neatly typed in 12 point font with accurate spelling and proper punctuation. Make sure it is clear and succinct. Tell what the work is about and do not add hype. Include the ending and tell us how many words and pages are in your work." Accepts queries by e-mail. "Do not query by sending long e-mail messages. Tell about your work in 200-300 words." Reports in 2 weeks on queries; 1 month on mss. Returns materials only with SASE.

Needs: Usually obtains new clients through directory, recommendations and internet listing.

Recent Sales: Sold 6 titles in the last year.

Terms: Agent receives 15% commission on domestic sales; 20% on foreign sales. Offers written contract. 30 days notice must be given to terminate contract. Charges for photocopying, postage.

Writers' Conferences: BEA (Chicago, June), BEA (Los Angeles, May).

Tips: "Professional guidance is imperative in bringing along new writers. In the highly competitive publishing arena, strict guidelines must be adhered to."

N ◎ **THE JOY HARRIS LITERARY AGENCY, INC.**, 156 Fifth Ave., Suite 617, New York NY 10010. (212)924-6269. Fax: (212)924-6609. E-mail: jhlitagent@aol.com. **Contact:** Joy Harris. Member of AAR. Represents 150 clients. Currently handles: 50% nonfiction books; 50% novels.

● **A BULLET INTRODUCES COMMENTS** by the editor of *Novel & Short Story Writer's Market* indicating special information about the listing.

Member Agents: Kassandra Duane, Leslie Daniels.

Represents: Considers all fiction areas except fantasy; juvenile; science fiction; westerns/frontier.

How to Contact: Query with outline/proposal and SASE. Reports in 2 months on queries. *No unsolicited mss*; queries only.

Needs: Obtains new clients through recommendations from clients and editors.

Recent Sales: Sold 10 titles in the last year. Prefers not to share information on specific sales.

Terms: Agent receives 15% commission on domestic sales; 20% on foreign sales. Charges for extra office expenses.

RICHARD HENSHAW GROUP, 132 W. 22nd St., 4th Floor, New York NY 10011. (212)414-1172. Fax: (212)721-4208. E-mail: rhgagents@aol.com. Website: www.rich.henshaw.com. **Contact:** Rich Henshaw. Estab. 1995. Member of AAR, SinC, MWA, HWA, SFWA. Represents 35 clients. **20% of clients are new/ previously unpublished writers.** Specializes in thrillers, mysteries, science fiction, fantasy and horror. Currently handles: 20% nonfiction books; 10% juvenile books; 70% novels.

• Prior to opening his agency, Mr. Henshaw served as an agent with Richard Curtis Associates, Inc.

Represents: Nonfiction books, juvenile books, novels. **Considers these fiction areas:** action/adventure; detective/police/crime; ethnic; family saga; fantasy; glitz; historical; horror; humor/satire; juvenile; literary; mainstream; psychic/supernatural; science fiction; sports; thriller/espionage; young adult.

How to Contact: Query with SASE. Reports in 3 weeks on queries; 6 weeks on mss.

Needs: Obtains new clients through recommendations from others, solicitation, at conferences and query letters.

Recent Sales: Sold 17 titles in the last year. *Out For Blood*, by Dana Stabenow (Dutton/Signet); *Deadstick*, by Megan Mallory Rust (Berkley); *And Then There Were None*, by Stephen Solomita (Bantam).

Terms: Agent receives 15% commission on domestic sales; 20% on foreign sales. No written contract. Charges for photocopying manuscripts and book orders. 100% of business is derived from commission on sales.

Tips: "Always include SASE with correct return postage."

HOPKINS LITERARY ASSOCIATES, PMB 327, 2117, Buffalo Rd., Rochester NY 14624-1507. (716)429-6559. E-mail: pamhopkins@aol.com. **Contact:** Pam Hopkins. Estab. 1996. Member of AAR, RWA. Represents 30 clients. **5% of clients are new/unpublished writers.** Specializes in women's fiction particularly historical, contemporary and category romance as well as mainstream work. Currently handles: 100% novels.

Represents: Novels. **Considers these fiction areas:** historical; mainstream; romance.

How to Contact: Send outline and 3 sample chapters. No queries by e-mail. Considers simultaneous queries and submissions. Reports in 2 weeks on queries; 1 month on mss. Returns material only with SASE.

Needs: Obtains new clients through recommendations from others, solicitations and conferences.

Recent Sales: Sold 50 titles in the last year. *Winds of Autumn*, by Merline Lovelace (MIRA); *Love in the Shadows*, by Madeline Archer (Bantam); *The Doctor's Wife*, by Cheryl St. John (Harlequin); *Great Caesar's Ghost*, by Cynthia Sterling (Berkley). Other clients include Maggie Price, Shari Anton, Lynda Cooper, Jodi O'Donnell, Victoria Malvey and Jillian Hart.

Terms: Agent receives 15% commission on domestic sales; 20% on foreign sales. No written contract. 30 day written notice must be given to terminate verbal contract.

Writer's Conferences: Romance Writers of America.

INTERNATIONAL CREATIVE MANAGEMENT, 40 W. 57th St., New York NY 10019. (212)556-5600. Fax: (212)556-5665. West Coast office: 8942 Wilshire Blvd., Beverly Hills CA 90211. (310)550-4000. Fax: (310)550-4100. **Contact:** Literary Department. Member of AAR, signatory of WGA.

Member Agents: Esther Newberg and Amanda Urban, department heads; Lisa Bankoff; Kristine Dahl; Mitch Douglas; Suzanne Gluck; Sloan Harris; Heather Schroder; Denise Shannon; Richard Abate.

Terms: Agent receives 10% commission on domestic sales; 15% on UK sales; 20% on translations.

J DE S ASSOCIATES INC., 9 Shagbark Rd., Wilson Point, South Norwalk CT 06854. (203)838-7571. **Contact:** Jacques de Spoelberch. Estab. 1975. Represents 50 clients. Currently handles: 50% nonfiction books; 50% novels.

• Prior to opening his agency, Mr. de Spoelberch was an editor at Houghton Mifflin.

Represents: Nonfiction books, novels. **Considers these fiction areas:** detective/police/crime; historical; juvenile; literary; mainstream; mystery/suspense; New Age; westerns/frontier; young adult.

How to Contact: Query with SASE. Reports in 2 months on queries.

Needs: Obtains new clients through recommendations from authors and other clients.

Recent Sales: Prefers not to share information on specific sales.

Terms: Agent receives 15% commission on domestic sales; 20% on foreign sales. Charges for foreign postage and photocopying.

JABBERWOCKY LITERARY AGENCY, P.O. Box 4558, Sunnyside NY 11104-0558. (718)392-5985. **Contact:** Joshua Bilmes. Estab. 1994. Member of SFWA. Represents 40 clients. **25% of clients are new/ previously unpublished writers.** "Agency represents quite a lot of genre fiction and is actively seeking to increase amount of nonfiction projects." Currently handles: 25% nonfiction books; 5% scholarly books; 65% novel; 5% other.

Represents: Nonfiction books, scholarly books, novels. **Considers these fiction areas:** action/adventure; cartoon/comic; contemporary issues; detective/police/crime; ethnic; family saga; fantasy; gay; glitz; historical; horror; humor/satire; lesbian; literary; mainstream; psychic/supernatural; regional; science fiction; sports; thriller/espionage.

How to Contact: Query with SASE. Considers simultaneous queries and submissions. Reports in 2 weeks on queries. Returns materials only with SASE.

Needs: Obtains new clients through recommendation by current clients, solicitation, "and through intriguing queries by new authors."

Recent Sales: Sold 20 titles in the last year. *Shakespeare's Christmas*, by Charlaine Harris (Dell); *Deathstalker Destiny*, by Simon Green (Roc); *Chance of Command*, by Elizabeth Moon. Other clients include Tanya Hutt, Kristine Smith, Edo van Belkom.

Terms: Agent receives 12.5% commission on domestic sales; 20% on foreign sales. Offers written contract, binding for 1 year. Charges for book purchases, photocopying, international book/ms mailing, international long distance.

Writers' Conferences: Malice Domestic (Washington DC, May); World SF Convention (Chicago, August); Icon (Stony Brook NY, April).

Reading list: Reads *New Republic*, *Analog* and various newspapers to find new clients.

Tips: "In approaching with a query, the most important things to me are your credits and your biographical background to the extent its relevant to your work. I (and most agents I believe) will ignore the adjectives you may choose to describe your own work. Please send query letter only with SASE; no manuscript material unless requested."

N **JCA LITERARY AGENCY**, 27 W. 20th St., Suite 1103, New York NY 10011. (212)807-0888. Fax: (212)807-0461. **Contact:** Jeff Gerecke, Tony Outhwaite. Estab. 1978. Member of AAR. Represents 100 clients. **20% of clients are new/unpublished writers.** Currently handles: 48% nonfiction books; 2% scholarly books; 50% novels.

Member Agents: Jeff Gerecke; Tony Outhwaite.

Represents: Nonfiction books, scholarly books, novels. **Considers these fiction areas:** action/adventure; confessional; contemporary issues; detective/police/crime; ethnic; experimental; family saga; feminist; gay/lesbian; glitz; historical; horror; humor/satire; literary; mainstream; mystery; sports; thriller/espionage; westerns/frontier.

How to Contact: Query with SASE. No queries by fax or e-mail. Considers simultaneous queries and submissions. "We occasionally may ask for an exclusive look." Reports in 2 weeks on queries; 6 weeks on mss. Returns materials only with SASE.

Needs: Does not want to receive screenplays, poetry, children's books, science fiction/fantasy, genre romance. Obtains new clients through recommendations, solicitations, conferences.

Recent Sales: *The Lost Glass Plates of Wilfred Eng*, by Thomas Orton (Counterpoint); *Sharp Shooter*, by David Healey (The Berkley Publishing Group/Jove); *A Healthy Place to Die*, by Peter King (St. Martin's Press). Other clients include Ernest J. Gaines, W.E.B. Griffin, Polly Whitney, David J. Garrow.

Terms: Agent receives 15% commission on domestic sales; 20% on foreign sales. No written contract. "We work with our clients on a handshake basis." Charges for postage on overseas submissions, photocopying, mss for submission, books purchased for subrights submission, and bank charges, where applicable. "We deduct the cost from payments received from publishers."

Tips: "We do not ourselves provide legal, accounting, or public relations services for our clients, although some of the advice we give falls somewhat into these realms. In cases where it seems necessary we will recommend obtaining outside advice or assistance in these areas from professionals who are not in any way connected to the agency."

N **VIRGINIA KIDD AGENCY, INC.**, 538 E. Harford St., P.O. Box 278, Milford PA 18337-0728. (717)296-6205. Fax: (717)296-7266. **Contact:** James Allen. Estab. 1965. Member of SFWA, SFRA, SFTA. Represents 80 clients. Specializes in "science fiction but we do not limit ourselves to it."

● Prior to opening her agency, Ms. Kidd was a ghost writer, pulp writer and poet.

Member Agents: Virginia Kidd; James Allen; Christine Cohen.

Represents: Fiction. **Considers these fiction areas:** speculative fiction, science fiction, fantasy (special interest in non-traditional fantasy), mystery, literary, mainstream, feminist, glitz, suspense, historical, young adult. **Specializes in science fiction.**

How to Contact: Query with SASE. Reports in 1 week on queries; 6 weeks on mss.

Needs: Occasionally obtains new clients through recommendations from others.

Recent Sales: Sold about 50 titles in the last year. *The Telling*, by Ursula K. Le Guin (Harcourt Brace); *The Tower and the Hive*, by Anne McCaffrey (Del Rey); *Midas*, by Wolfgang Jeschke (Tor-Forge); *Interlopers*, by Alan Dean Foster (Penguin Putnam); also film rights to the Company series by Kage Baker to Showtime. Other clients include Gene Wolfe, R.A. Lafferty, Joe L. Hensley, William Tenn, Al Coppel and Allan W. Eckert.

Terms: Agent receives 10% commission on domestic sales; 20% on foreign sales. Offers written contract,

binding until canceled by either party. 30 days notice must be given to terminate contract.
Tips: "If you have a novel of speculative fiction, romance, or mainstream that is *really extraordinary*, please query me, including a synopsis, a cv and a SASE."

N **KIDDE, HOYT & PICARD**, 335 E. 51st St., New York NY 10022. (212)755-9461. Fax: (212)223-2501. **Contact:** Katharine Kidde, Laura Langlie. Estab. 1980. Member of AAR. Represents 80 clients. Specializes in mainstream fiction and nonfiction. Currently handles: 15% nonfiction books; 5% juvenile books; 80% novels.
   • Prior to becoming agents, Ms. Kidde was an editor/senior editor at Harcourt Brace, New American Library and Putnam; Ms. Langlie worked in production and editorial at Kensington and Carroll & Graf.
Member Agents: Kay Kidde (mainstream fiction, general nonfiction, romances, literary fiction); Laura Langlie (romances, mysteries, literary fiction, general nonfiction).
Represents: Nonfiction books, novels. **Considers these fiction areas:** contemporary; detective/police/crime; feminist; gay; glitz; historical; humor; lesbian; literary; mainstream; mystery/suspense; romance (contemporary, historical, regency); thriller.
How to Contact: Query. Reports in a few weeks on queries; 1 month on mss. Returns materials only with SASE.
Needs: Actively seeking "strong mainstream fiction." Does not want to receive "male adventure, science fiction, juvenile, porn, plays or poetry." Obtains new clients through query letters, recommendations from others, "former authors from when I was an editor at NAL, Harcourt, etc.; listings in *LMP*, writers' guides."
Recent Sales: *Night Bus*, by Janice Law (Forge/TOR); *False Witness*, by Lelia Kelly (Kensington); *She Captains*, by Joan Druett (Simon & Schuster); *Tying Down the Wind*, by Eric Pinder (Tarcher/Putnam). Other clients include Michael Cadmum, Jim Oliver, Patricia Cabot, Bethany Campbell, Robin Hathaway, Mignon F. Ballard and Mark Miano.
Reading List: Reads literary journals and magazines, *Harper's*, STORY, *DoubleTake*, etc. to find new clients.
Terms: Agent receives 15% commission on domestic sales; 20% on foreign sales. Charges for photocopying.
Tips: "We look for beautiful stylistic writing, and that elusive treasure, a good book (mostly fiction). As former editors, we can help launch authors."

N **THE KNIGHT AGENCY**, P.O. Box 550648, Atlanta GA 30355. Or: 2407 Matthews St., Atlanta GA 30319. (404)816-9620. E-mail: deidremk@aol.com. Website: www.knightagency.net. **Contact:** Deidre Knight. Estab. 1996. Member of RWA, AAR, Author's Guild. Represents 30 clients. **40% of clients are new/previously unpublished writers.** Currently handles: 50% nonfiction books; 50% novels.
Represents: Nonfiction books, novels. **Considers these fiction areas:** ethnic; literary; mainstream; mystery/suspense; regional; religious/inspirational; romance (contemporary, historical, inspirational); women's fiction; commercial fiction.
How to Contact: Query with SASE. Considers simultaneous queries and submissions. Reports in 2 weeks on queries; 6 weeks on mss.
Recent Sales: Sold 20 titles in the last year.
Terms: Agent receives 15% commission on domestic sales; 25% on foreign sales. Offers written contract, binding for 1 year. 60 days notice must be given to terminate contract. "Charge clients for photocopying, postage, overnight courier expenses.
Tips: "We are looking for a wide variety of fiction and nonfiction. In fiction, we're always looking for romance, women's fiction, ethnic and commercial fiction."

ELAINE KOSTER LITERARY AGENCY, LLC, 55 Central Park West, Suite 6, New York NY 10023. (212)362-9488. Fax: (212)712-0164. **Contact:** Elaine Koster. Member of Women's Media Group and Publishers' Lunch Club. Represents 30 clients. **25% of clients are new/unpublished writers.** Specializes in quality fiction and nonfiction. Currently handles: 30% nonfiction books; 70% novels.
   • Prior to opening her agency, Ms. Koster was president and publisher of Dutton/NAL.
Represents: Nonfiction books, novels. **Considers these fiction areas:** action/adventure; confessional; contemporary issues; detective/police/crime; ethnic; family saga; feminist; gay/lesbian; glitz; historical; literary; mainstream; mystery (amateur sleuth, cozy, culinary, malice domestic); regional; suspense; thriller/espionage.
How to Contact: Query with outline, 3 sample chapters and SASE. No queries by e-mail or fax. Prefers to be only reader. Reports in 3 weeks on queries; 1 month on mss. Returns materials only with SASE.
Needs: No juvenile, screenplays. Obtains new clients through recommendations from others.
Recent Sales: *Brown-Eyed Girl*, by Virginia Swift (HarperCollins); *Colors of the Mountain*, by Da Chen (Random House); *The Beryllium Murder*, by Camille Minichino (Morrow).
Terms: Agent receives 15% commission on domestic sales; 20% on foreign sales. Offers written contract, 60 days notice must be given to terminate contract. Charges for photocopying, messengers, express mail, books and book galley, ordered from publisher to exploit other rights, overseas shipment of mss and books, overseas phone and fax charges.
Tips: Obtains new clients through recommendation from others.

N **IRENE KRAAS AGENCY**, 220 Copper Trail, Santa Fe NM 87505. (505)474-6212. Fax: (505)474-6216. Estab. 1990. Member of Authors Guild. Represents 30 clients. **75% of clients are new/unpublished**

writers. Specializes in fiction only, middle grade through adult. No romance, short stories, plays or poetry. Currently handles: 30% juvenile books; 70% novels.

Represents: Fiction—adult and juvenile (middle grade and up). **Considers these fiction areas:** action/adventure; detective/police/crime; ethnic; family saga; juvenile; literary; mainstream; mystery/suspense; science fiction; thriller/espionage; young adult.

How to Contact: Send cover letter and first 30 pages. Must include return postage and/or SASE. No e-mail queries. Considers simultaneous submissions. Returns materials only with SASE.

Needs: Actively seeking "books that are well written with commercial potential." Obtains new clients through recommendations from others, conferences.

Recent Sales: *Songs of Power*, by Hilari Bell (Hyperion); *The Astrologer* series, by Denise Vitola (Ace). Other clients include Brett Davis, Linda George, Christopher Farran, Terry England and Duncan Long.

Terms: Agent receives 15% commission on domestic sales; 20% on foreign sales. Offers written contract, binding for 1 year "but can be terminated at any time for any reason with written notice." Charges for photocopying and postage.

Writers' Conferences: Southwest Writers Conference (Albuquerque); Pacific Northwest Conference (Seattle); Vancouver Writers Conference (Vancouver BC).

[N] [◐] PETER LAMPACK AGENCY, INC., 551 Fifth Ave., Suite 1613, New York NY 10176-0187. (212)687-9106. Fax: (212)687-9109. E-mail: renbopla@aol.com. **Contact:** Loren G. Soeiro. Estab. 1977. Represents 50 clients. **10% of clients are new/previously unpublished writers.** Specializes in commercial fiction, male-oriented action/adventure, thrillers/suspense, contemporary relationships, distinguished literary fiction, nonfiction by a recognized expert in a given field. Currently handles: 20% nonfiction books; 80% novels.

Member Agents: Peter Lampack (psychological suspense, action/adventure, literary fiction, nonfiction, contemporary relationships); Sandra Blanton (foreign rights); Loren G. Soeiro (literary and commercial fiction, mystery, suspense, nonfiction, narrative nonfiction, high-concept thrillers).

Represents: Nonfiction books, novels. **Considers these fiction areas:** action/adventure; contemporary relationships; detective/police/crime; family saga; historical; literary; mainstream; mystery/suspense; thriller/espionage.

How to Contact: Query with SASE. *No unsolicited mss.* No queries by fax. Reports in 3 weeks on queries; 2 months on mss.

Needs: Actively seeking literary and commercial fiction, thrillers, mysteries, suspense, psychological thrillers, high-concept. Does not want to receive romance, science fiction, western, academic material. Obtains new clients from referrals made by clients.

Recent Sales: *Atlantis Found*, by Clive Cussler (Putnam); *The Lamorna Wink*, by Martha Grimes (Viking); *Give Me Liberty*, by Gerry Spence (St. Martin's); *After the Fall* by Judith Kelman.

Terms: Agent receives 15% commission on domestic sales; 20% on foreign sales.

Writers' Conferences: BEA (Chicago, June).

Tips: "Submit only your best work for consideration. Have a very specific agenda of goals you wish your prospective agent to accomplish for you. Provide the agent with a comprehensive statement of your credentials: educational and professional."

[N] [◐] RAY LINCOLN LITERARY AGENCY, Elkins Park House, Suite 107-B, 7900 Old York Rd., Elkins Park PA 19027. (215)635-0827. **Contact:** Mrs. Ray Lincoln. Estab. 1974. Represents 30 clients. **35% of clients are new/previously unpublished writers.** Specializes in biography, nature, the sciences, fiction in both adult and children's categories. Currently handles: 30% nonfiction books; 20% juvenile books; 50% novels.

Member Agents: Jerome A. Lincoln.

Represents: Nonfiction books, scholarly books, juvenile books, novels. **Considers these fiction areas:** action/adventure; contemporary issues; detective/police/crime; ethnic; family saga; fantasy; feminist; gay; historical; humor/satire; juvenile; lesbian; literary; mainstream; mystery/suspense; psychic/supernatural; regional; romance (contemporary, gothic, historical); sports; thriller/espionage; young adult.

How to Contact: Query first with SASE, then on request send outline, 2 sample chapters and SASE. "I send for balance of manuscript if it is a likely project." Reports in 2 weeks on queries; 1 month on mss.

Needs: Obtains new clients usually from recommendations.

Recent Sales: *Best Halloween Ever*, by Barbara Robinson (HarperCollins); *Daddy and Me*, by Jerry Spinelli (Knopf); *The Mummy's Smile*, by Susan Katz (Simon & Schuster).

Terms: Agent receives 15% commission on domestic sales; 20% on foreign sales. Offers written contract, binding "but with notice, may be cancelled." Charges only for overseas telephone calls. "I request authors to do manuscript photocopying themselves. Postage, or shipping charge, on manuscripts accepted for representation by agency."

Tips: "I always look for polished writing style, fresh points of view and professional attitudes."

[◐] LINDSTROM LITERARY GROUP, 871 N. Greenbrier St., Arlington VA 22205-1220. (703)522-4730. Fax: (703)527-7624. E-mail: lindlitgrp@aol.com. **Contact:** Kristin Lindstrom. Estab. 1994. Represents 13 clients. **30% of clients are new/previously unpublished writers.** Currently handles: 50% nonfiction books; 50% novels.

Represents: Nonfiction books; novels. **Considers these fiction areas:** action/adventure; contemporary issues; detective/police/crime; ethnic; historical; mainstream; thriller/espionage.
How to Contact: For fiction, send first 3 chapters and outline with SASE to cover return of ms if desired. Reports in 2 months on queries; 10 weeks on mss.
Needs: Obtains new clients through references, guide listing.
Recent Sales: *Lucky Man*, by Tony Dunbar (Dell Publishing); *Five Card Stud*, by Elizabeth Gunn (Walker & Co.).
Terms: Agent receives 15% commission on domestic sales; 20% on foreign sales; 20% on performance rights sales. Offers written contract. Charges for marketing and mailing expense, express mail, UPS, etc.
Tips: "Include biography of writer. Send enough material for an overall review of project scope."

STERLING LORD LITERISTIC, INC., 65 Bleecker St., New York NY 10012. (212)780-6050. Fax: (212)780-6095. **Contact:** Peter Matson. Estab. 1952. Signatory of WGA. Represents over 600 clients. Currently handles: 50% nonfiction books, 50% novels.
Member Agents: Peter Matson; Sterling Lord; Jody Hotchkiss (film scripts); Philippa Brophy; Chris Calhoun; Jennifer Hengen; Charlotte Sheedy; George Nicholson; Neeti Madan.
Represents: Nonfiction books, novels. "Literary value considered first."
How to Contact: Query. Reports in 1 month on mss.
Needs: Obtains new clients through recommendations from others.
Recent Sales: Prefers not to share information on specific sales.
Terms: Agent receives 15% commission on domestic sales; 20% on foreign sales. Offers written contract. Charges for photocopying.

DONALD MAASS LITERARY AGENCY, 157 W. 57th St., Suite 703, New York NY 10019. (212)757-7755. **Contact:** Donald Maass, Jennifer Jackson or Michelle Brummer. Estab. 1980. Member of AAR, SFWA, MWA, RWA. Represents over 100 clients. **5% of clients are new/previously unpublished writers.** Specializes in commercial fiction, especially science fiction, fantasy, mystery, romance, suspense. Currently handles: 100% novels.
  • Prior to opening his agency, Mr. Maass served as an editor at Dell Publishing (NY) and as a reader at Gollancz (London).
Member Agents: Donald Maass (mainstream, literary, mystery/suspense, science fiction); Jennifer Jackson (commercial fiction: especially romance, science fiction, fantasy, mystery/suspense); Michelle Brummer (fiction: literary, contemporary, feminist, science fiction, fantasy).
Represents: Novels. **Considers these fiction areas:** detective/police/crime; fantasy; historical; horror; literary; mainstream; mystery/suspense; psychic/supernatural; romance (historical, paranormal, time travel); science fiction; thriller/espionage.
How to Contact: Query with SASE. Considers simultaneous queries and submissions. Returns materials only with SASE. Reports in 2 weeks on queries, 3 months on mss (if requested following query).
Needs: Actively seeking "to expand the literary portion of our list and expand in romance and women's fiction." Does not want to receive nonfiction, children's or poetry.
Recent Sales: Sold over 100 titles in the last year. *The Twisted Root*, by Anne Perry (Fawcett Columbine); *A Clue for the Puzzle Lady*, by Parnell Hall (Bantam); *Midnight Robber*, by Nalo Hopkinson (Warner Aspect); *The Avalanche Soldier*, by Susan Matthews (Avon Eos); *Confluence II: Ancient of Days*, by Paul McAuley (Avon Eos).
Terms: Agent receives 15% commission on domestic sales; 20% on foreign sales. Charges for large photocopying orders and book samples, "after consultation with author."
Writers' Conferences: Donald Maass: World Science Fiction Convention, Frankfurt Book Fair, Pacific Northwest Writers Conference, Bouchercon, and others. Jennifer Jackson: World Science Fiction and Fantasy Convention, RWA National, and others. Michelle Brummer: ReaderCon, World Science Fiction Convention and Luna Con.
Tips: "We are fiction specialists, also noted for our innovative approach to career planning. Few new clients are accepted, but interested authors should query with SASE. Subagents in all principle foreign countries and Hollywood. No nonfiction or juvenile works considered."

ELAINE MARKSON LITERARY AGENCY, 44 Greenwich Ave., New York NY 10011. (212)243-8480. Fax: (212)691-9014. Estab. 1972. Member of AAR and WGA. Represents 200 clients. **10% of clients are new/unpublished writers.** Specializes in literary fiction, commercial fiction, trade nonfiction. Currently handles: 35% nonfiction books; 55% novels; 10% juvenile books.
Member Agents: Geri Thoma, Sally Wofford-Girand, Elizabeth Sheinkman, Elaine Markson.
Represents: Quality fiction and nonfiction.
How to Contact: Obtains new clients by recommendation only.
Recent Sales: *The First Horseman*, by John Case (Ballantine); *Life, the Movie*, by Neal Gabler (Knopf); *The Hidden Jesus*, by Donald Spoto (St. Martins).
Terms: Agent receives 15% commission on domestic sales; 20% on foreign sales. Charges for postage, photocopying, foreign mailing, faxing, and other special expenses.

THE EVAN MARSHALL AGENCY, 6 Tristam Place, Pine Brook NJ 07058-9445. (973)882-1122. Fax: (973)882-3099. E-mail: evanmarshall@thenovelist.com. Website: www.thenovelist.com. **Contact:** Evan Marshall. Estab. 1987. Currently handles: 50% nonfiction books; 50% novels.

● Prior to opening his agency, Mr. Marshall served as an editor with New American Library, Everest House, and Dodd, Mead & Co., and then worked as a literary agent at The Sterling Lord Agency.

Represents: Nonfiction books, novels. **Considers these fiction areas:** action/adventure; contemporary issues; detective/police/crime; erotica; ethnic; family saga; glitz; historical; horror; humor/satire; literary; mainstream; mystery/suspense; psychic/supernatural; religious/inspirational; romance (contemporary, gothic, historical, regency); science fiction; thriller/espionage; westerns/frontier.

How to Contact: Query with SASE. Reports in 1 week on queries; 2 months on mss.

Needs: Obtains many new clients through referrals from clients and editors.

Recent Sales: *All Fall Down*, by Erica Spindler (Mira); *The Brides of Durango: Elise*, by Bobbi Smith (Leisure); *The Resurrectionist*, by Mark Graham (Avon); *Hook*, by C.J. Songer (Scribner); *Mood to Murder*, by Joyce Christmas (Fawcett).

Terms: Agent receives 15% on domestic sales; 20% on foreign sales. Offers written contract.

DORIS S. MICHAELS LITERARY AGENCY, INC., 1841 Broadway, Suite #903, New York NY 10023. (212)265-9474. **Contact:** Doris S. Michaels. Estab. 1994. Member of WNBA, AAR. Represents 30 clients. **50% of clients are new/previously unpublished writers.** Currently handles: 40% nonfiction books; 60% novels.

● Prior to opening her agency, Ms. Michaels was an editor for Prentice-Hall, consultant for Prudential-Bache, and an international consultant for the Union Bank of Switzerland.

Member Agents: Faye Bender.

Represents: Nonfiction books, novels. **Considers these fiction areas:** action/adventure; contemporary issues; family saga; feminist; historical; literary; mainstream.

How to Contact: Query with SASE. Considers simultaneous queries. *No phone calls or unsolicited mss.* Reports ASAP on queries with SASE; no answer without SASE. Returns materials only with SASE.

Needs: Obtains new clients through recommendations from others, solicitation and at conferences.

Recent Sales: Clients include Maury Allen, Wendy Rue, Karin Abarbanel and Eva Shaw.

Terms: Agent receives 15% commission on domestic sales; 20% on foreign sales. Offers written contract, binding for 1 year, with 30-day cancellation clause. Charges for office expenses including deliveries, postage, photocopying and fax. 100% of business is derived from commissions on sales.

Writers' Conferences: BEA (Chicago, June); Frankfurt Book Fair (Germany, October); London Book Fair; Society of Southwestern Authors; San Diego State University Writers' Conference; Willamette Writers' Conference; International Women's Writing Guild; American Society of Journalists and Authors.

MARTHA MILLARD LITERARY AGENCY, 293 Greenwood Ave., Florham Park NJ 07932. (973)593-9233. Fax: (973)593-9235. E-mail: marmillink@aol.com. **Contact:** Martha Millard. Estab. 1980. Member of AAR, SFWA. Represents 50 clients. **2% of clients are new/unpublished writers.** Currently handles: 25% nonfiction books, 10% story collections, 65% novels.

● Prior to opening her agency, Ms. Millard worked in editorial departments of several publishers and was vice president at another agency for four and a half years.

Represents: Nonfiction books, novels. Considers fiction depending on writer's credits and skills.

How to Contact: Query with SASE. No queries by fax or e-mail. Reports in 2 weeks on queries; 1 month on mss. Returns materials only with SASE.

Needs: Obtains new clients through referrals from other clients or editors.

Recent Sales: Sold 45 titles in the last year. *The Old Bone Road*, by M. Swanwick (Avon); *3 Fishing Mysteries*, by V. Houston (Berkley Prime Crime); *Chainsaw*, by John Byrne (Harper Business); *Crisis of the Real*, by Andy Crundberg (Aperture). Other clients include Elizabeth Hand, Denise Lang, William Gibson, Dr. Marc Weissbluth, Julia Scully, Sean Stewart, Peter Heck, Shirley Rousseau-Murphy.

Terms: Agent receives 15% commission on domestic sales; 20% on foreign sales. Offers written contract, negotiated individually.

WILLIAM MORRIS AGENCY, INC., 1325 Ave. of the Americas, New York NY 10019. (212)586-5100. West Coast Office: 151 El Camino Dr., Beverly Hills CA 90212. **Contact:** Mel Berger, vice president. Member of AAR.

Member Agents: Owen Laster; Robert Gottlieb; Mel Berger; Matt Bialer; Claudia Cross; Joni Evans; Tracy Fisher; Marcy Posner; Dan Strone; Helen Breitwieser.
Represents: Nonfiction books, novels.
How to Contact: Query with SASE. Does not accept queries by fax or e-mail.
Recent Sales: Prefers not to share information on specific sales.
Terms: Agent receives 10% commission on domestic sales; 20% on foreign sales.

HENRY MORRISON, INC., 105 S. Bedford Rd., Suite 306A, Mt. Kisco NY 10549. (914)666-3500. Fax: (914)241-7846. **Contact:** Henry Morrison. Estab. 1965. Signatory of WGA. Represents 48 clients. **5% of clients are new/previously unpublished writers.** Currently handles: 5% nonfiction books; 5% juvenile books; 85% novels; 5% movie scripts.
Represents: Nonfiction books, novels. **Considers these fiction areas:** action/adventure; detective/police/crime; family saga.
How to Contact: Query. Reports in 2 weeks on queries; 3 months on mss.
Needs: Obtains new clients through recommendations from others.
Recent Sales: Sold 10 titles in the last year. *Untitled*, by Robert Ludlum (St. Martin's); *The Pearl*, by Eric Lustbader (TOR); *Burnt Sienna*, by David Morrell (Warner Books); *Rock & Scissors*, by Steve Samuel (Simon & Schuster). Other clients include Joe Gores, Samuel R. Delany, Beverly Byrnne, Patricia Keneally-Morrison and Molly Katz.
Terms: Agent receives 15% commission on domestic sales; 25% on foreign sales. Charges for ms copies, bound galleys and finished books for submission to publishers, movie producers, foreign publishers.

HAROLD OBER ASSOCIATES, 425 Madison Ave., New York NY 10017. (212)759-8600. Fax: (212)759-9428. Estab. 1929. Member of AAR. Represents 250 clients. **10% of clients are new/previously unpublished writers.** Currently handles: 35% nonfiction books; 15% juvenile books; 50% novels.
Member Agents: Phyllis Westberg, Wendy Schmalz, Emma Sweeney, Chris Byrne.
Represents: Nonfiction books, juvenile books, novels. **Considers all fiction areas.**
How to Contact: Query letter *only* with SASE. No queries by fax. Reports in 1 week on queries; 3 weeks on mss.
Needs: Obtains new clients through recommendations from others.
Recent Sales: Prefers not to share information on specific sales.
Terms: Agent receives 15% commission on domestic sales; 20% on foreign sales. Charges for photocopying and express mail or package services.

PINDER LANE & GARON-BROOKE ASSOCIATES, LTD., 159 W. 53rd St., Suite 14E, New York NY 10019-6005. (212)489-0880. **Contact:** Jean Free, vice president. Member of AAR, signatory of WGA. Represents 80 clients. **20% of clients are new/previously unpublished writers.** Specializes in mainstream fiction and nonfiction. Currently handles: 25% nonfiction books; 75% novels.
Member Agents: Nancy Coffey, Dick Duane, Robert Thixton, Jean Free.
Represents: Nonfiction books, novels. **Considers these fiction areas:** contemporary issues; detective/police/crime; family saga; fantasy; gay; literary; mainstream; mystery/suspense; romance; science fiction.
How to Contact: Query with SASE. Reports in 3 weeks on queries; 2 months on mss.
Needs: Does not want to receive screenplays, TV series teleplays or dramatic plays. Obtains new clients through referrals and from queries.
Recent Sales: Sold 15 titles in the last year. *Nobody's Safe*, by Richard Steinberg (Doubleday); *The Kill Box*, by Chris Stewart (M. Evans); *Return to Christmas*, by Chris Heimerdinger (Ballantine).
Terms: Agent receives 15% on domestic sales; 30% on foreign sales. Offers written contract, binding for 3-5 years.
Tips: "With our literary and media experience, our agency is uniquely positioned for the current and future direction publishing is taking. Send query letter first giving the essence of the manuscript and a personal or career bio with SASE."

AARON M. PRIEST LITERARY AGENCY, 708 Third Ave., 23rd Floor, New York NY 10017. (212)818-0344. Fax: (212)573-9417. **Contact:** Aaron Priest or Molly Friedrich. Estab. 1974. Member of AAR. Currently handles: 25% nonfiction books; 75% fiction.
Member Agents: Lisa Erbach Vance, Paul Cirone, Wendy Sherman.
Represents: Nonfiction books, fiction.
How to Contact: Query only (must be accompanied by SASE). Unsolicited mss will be returned unread.
Recent Sales: *Absolute Power*, by David Baldacci (Warner); *Three To Get Deadly*, by Janet Evanovich (Scribner); *How Stella Got Her Groove Back*, by Terry McMillan (Viking); *Day After Tomorrow*, by Allan Folsom (Little, Brown); *Angela's Ashes*, by Frank McCourt (Scribner); *M as in Malice*, by Sue Grafton (Henry Holt).
Terms: Agent receives 15% commission on domestic sales. Charges for photocopying, foreign postage expenses.

ANGELA RINALDI LITERARY AGENCY, P.O. Box 7877, Beverly Hills CA 90212-7877. (310)842-7665. Fax: (310)837-8143. E-mail: e2arinaldi@aol.com. **Contact:** Angela Rinaldi. Estab. 1994. Mem-

An interview with powerhouse agent Molly Friedrich

Molly Friedrich is one of a handful of literary agents in New York who has the power to propel her clients from the breadline to the bank line. Over the past 21 years, she's made dozens of megadollar deals and has become one of the most sought-after representatives in the literary world. Her client list is heavy with household names.

Friedrich's first job in the industry was as an intern with Doubleday; later, she worked in Anchor Press's publicity department. Agent Aaron Priest—making it very clear that he didn't intend to train another agent for his office—hired her as his assistant in January, 1978. Friedrich carried out a clandestine apprenticeship, observing her boss at work and acquainting herself with key players at each publishing house. A few months after Friedrich was hired, her boss drove cross-country with his family to explore a possible move to California. When he reached his destination, he called his assistant for an office update; what she told him changed her job description abruptly. In the time it took him to drive coast-to-coast, she had sold three books.

The contacts Friedrich made as an assistant became the foundation of her success as an agent. "This is a very social business," she says. "The absolute job of the agent is to know who's buying what and what's happening with them; if I didn't know that, I might as well not get up in the morning. You have to know who's on a honeymoon, who's just lost an auction and is flush with money to spend. All this is done over lunch."

Friedrich chooses her potential buyers very carefully, and the market varies with every book. After carefully assessing a book's potential, she selects a small group of editors who are appropriate for the manuscript. If several are interested, she'll set up an auction where each editor offers a confidential bid to Friedrich. "I'm working for the author, and the author has final say over which bid will be taken. Money isn't the only factor. Sometimes an author will meet with an editor and feel they don't have a mutual understanding of the material—then that publisher would be out of the running."

Friedrich receives about 200 queries a week, either an introductory-letter-plus-synopsis or a letter that combines the two. Of these, five percent will be good, and of those, four percent "are just not for me," says Friedrich. She will recommend other agents in this case, though she's cautious about making promises that are beyond her control. "When I read a manuscript, I know in the first five pages whether I'll take it on," she says. "When I read the single-spaced manuscript of Frank McCourt's *Angela's Ashes*, I set it down after a few pages and said, 'This is it, this is why I'm an agent.' It's that quick." If she feels a book shows great potential but needs more work, she'll send it to up to three editors and get their feedback for the author.

Meeting and representing great writers requires building a reputation over time, developing "different arteries. My writers come to me in complex and elaborate ways," says Friedrich. "The first short story collection I sold, by Maxine Claire, is an example. She did a reading of her work somewhere and a woman came up to her and said, 'Do you have more of those? If so, send them to Molly Friedrich. Tell her that Jackie sent you.' I read the stories—I really loved them—and I sent the manuscript out to four or five editors and got offers. To this day, I still don't know who Jackie is."

Author Frances Park sent queries on her tale of two Korean girls, *When My Sister Was Cleopatra Moon* to several agents, including Friedrich. "She knew her stuff," says Friedrich. "She knew who my clients were and what I had been doing. Some authors really do keep up with *Publishers Weekly*!" Two other agents wanted the book, but Park chose to wait for Friedrich to finish reading the manuscript. "You're my dream agent," Park wrote. Friedrich liked the "aggressively charming" story and placed the book within a few weeks.

Friedrich has worked with several first-time authors. New writers often come to her notice via query letters. "Not the ones with pale purple script or a photo of an author holding up her cat," says Friedrich. "People have sent macadamia nuts, artwork—any number of things to get us to look at their manuscripts. But it's the writing that counts. I look for queries that aren't generic; if it's personable and interesting, I'll read it. A good query should be like the letter you write to the sister you still get along with, telling her about the novel you've written and why it works for you. It shows your personality."

Friedrich believes a good author will not have to wait to be published posthumously. "Unfortunately, a lot of bad writing is published, and that confuses people; some authors see bad writing and wonder why their work isn't on the bookstands. Writers need to read the best examples of published work and strive for it. A great writer will be published, and a great book stays in your mind. I read *To Kill a Mockingbird* when I was very young, and I still remember it. But if you ask me to tell you the plot, I'd ramble on about a lawyer in the South, big case, etc. Why does an outstanding book stay in our memories? It's a combination of plot, characters, and an original voice." Friedrich further defines her three touchstones: "By plot, I mean a fresh cast on a plot—there are no new plots; characters that are fully realized; and, most important, an original voice. Read any passage from *Bonfire of the Vanities*, any passage—whether he's describing furniture or the weather—and you'll know within minutes that it's Tom Wolfe. That's an original voice."

Though Friedrich favors "long, flawed, ambitious novels," she's placed two short story collections. "They were so good, I had to represent them." (One of those short story collections was *The Girls' Guide to Hunting and Fishing*, for which author Melissa Bank received a $275,000 advance from Viking. See the interview with Bank on page 478 of this book.) At some point, Friedrich believes, a good author will reach critical mass, so anything he or she writes will sell, and people will ask each other if they've read the new "Lorrie Moore" rather than referring to the book by title. "That's the agent's dream," she says.

To what does Friedrich attribute her great success? "If you have good material even a bad agent can sell it. A good agent can do a little better, and a great agent can make a difference in a writer's life."

With all her success, Friedrich chivalrously rejects naming a favorite author or book she has represented. "How could I choose between Terry Macmillan's *Mama* or Jane Smiley's *A Thousand Acres*? I loved both those books. I only represent books I love. My client list is closed, but if I come upon something good enough, I'll represent it. A good agent has to be accessible."

When submitting work to an agent, Friedrich suggests, "Writers should think of quality first, rather than form. A great writer is destined to be published, and if you're good enough, you can break every rule."

— *Joanne Miller*

ber of AAR. Represents 40 clients. Currently handles: 50% nonfiction books; 50% novels.

● Prior to opening her agency, Ms. Rinaldi was an editor at New American Library, Pocket Books and Bantam, and the manager of book development of *The Los Angeles Times.*

Represents: Nonfiction books, novels, TV and motion picture rights. **Considers literary and commercial fiction.**

How to Contact: For fiction, send the first 100 pages and brief synopsis with SASE. Reports in 6 weeks. Accepts queries by e-mail. Considers simultaneous queries and submissions. "Please advise if this is a multiple submission to another agent." Returns materials only with SASE.

Needs: Actively seeking commercial and literary fiction. Does not want to receive scripts, category romances, children's books, westerns, science fiction/fantasy and cookbooks.

Recent Sales: *The Starlite Drive-In,* by Marjorie Reynolds (William Morrow & Co.); *Quiet Time,* by Stephanie Kane (Bantam).

Terms: Agent receives 15% commission on domestic sales; 20% on foreign sales. Offers written contract. Charges for photocopying ("if client doesn't supply copies for submissions"). 100% of business is derived from commissions on sales. Foreign, TV and motion picture rights for clients only.

N◑ JANE ROTROSEN AGENCY LLC, 318 E. 51st St., New York NY 10022. (212)593-4330. Fax: (212)935-6985. E-mail: jrotrosen@aol.com. **Contact:** Jane Rotrosen. Estab. 1974. Member of AAR and Authors Guild. Represents over 100 clients. Currently handles: 30% nonfiction books; 70% novels.

Member Agents: Andrea Cirillo; Ruth Kagle; Annelise Robey; Margaret Ruley; Stephanie Tade.

Represents: Nonfiction books, novels. **Considers these fiction areas:** action/adventure; detective/police/crime; family saga; historical; horror; mainstream; mystery; romance; thriller/espionage; women's fiction.

How to Contact: Query with SASE. No queries by fax or e-mail. Considers simultaneous queries and submissions. Reports in 2 weeks on queries; 7 weeks on mss. Returns materials only with SASE.

Recent Sales: Sold 120 titles in the last year. Prefers not to share information on specific sales.

Terms: Agent receives 15% commission on domestic sales; 20% on foreign sales. Offers written contract, binding for 3 years. 60-days notice must be given to terminate contract. Charges for photocopying, express mail, overseas postage and book purchases.

◑ THE DAMARIS ROWLAND AGENCY, 510 E. 23rd St., #8-G, New York NY 10010-5020. (212)475-8942. Fax: (212)358-9411. **Contact:** Damaris Rowland or Steve Axelrod. Estab. 1994. Member of AAR. Represents 50 clients. **10% of clients are new/previously unpublished writers.** Specializes in women's fiction. Currently handles: 75% novels, 25% nonfiction.

Represents: Nonfiction books, novels. **Considers these fiction areas:** detective/police/crime; historical; literary; mainstream; psychic/supernatural; romance (contemporary, gothic, historical, regency).

How to Contact: Send outline/proposal with SASE. Reports in 6 weeks.

Needs: Obtains new clients through recommendations from others, at conferences.

Recent Sales: *The Perfect Husband,* by Lisa Gardner (Bantam); *My Dearest Enemy,* by Connie Brockway (Dell).

Terms: Agent receives 15% commission on domestic sales; 20% on foreign sales. Offers written contract, with 30 day cancellation clause. Charges only if extraordinary expenses have been incurred, e.g., photocopying and mailing 15 ms to Europe for a foreign sale. 100% of business is derived from commissions on sales.

Writers' Conferences: Novelists Inc. (Denver, October); RWA National (Texas, July), Pacific Northwest Writers Conference.

N◑ PESHA RUBINSTEIN LITERARY AGENCY, INC., 1392 Rugby Rd., Teaneck NJ 07666-2839. (201)862-1174. Fax: (201)862-1180. E-mail: peshalit@aol.com. **Contact:** Pesha Rubinstein. Estab. 1990. Member of AAR, RWA, MWA, SCBWI. Represents 35 clients. **25% of clients are new/previously unpublished writers.** Specializes in commercial fiction and nonfiction and children's books. Currently handles: 30% juvenile books; 70% novels.

● Prior to opening her agency, Ms. Rubenstein served as an editor at Zebra and Leisure Books.

Represents: Commercial fiction, juvenile books, picture book illustration. **Considers these fiction areas:** detective/police/crime; ethnic; glitz; humor; juvenile; mainstream; mystery/suspense; picture book; psychic/supernatural; romance (contemporary, historical); spiritual adventures.

How to Contact: Send query, first 10 pages and SASE. Reports in 2 weeks on queries; 6 weeks on requested mss.

Needs: Does not want to receive poetry or westerns.

Recent Sales: *Freedom School,* by Amy Littlesugar (Philomel); *Excavation,* by James Rollins (Avon).

Terms: Agent receives 15% commission on domestic sales; 20% on foreign sales. Offers written contract. Charges for photocopying and overseas postage. No weekend or collect calls accepted.

Tips: "Keep the query letter and synopsis short. Please send first ten pages of manuscript rather than selected chapters from the manuscript. I am a stickler for correct grammar, spelling and punctuation. The work speaks for itself better than any description can. Never send originals. A phone call after one month is acceptable. Always include a SASE covering return of the entire package with the submission."

● VICTORIA SANDERS LITERARY AGENCY, 241 Avenue of the Americas, New York NY 10014-4822. (212)633-8811. Fax: (212)633-0525. **Contact:** Victoria Sanders and/or Diane Dickensheid. Estab. 1993. Member of AAR, signatory of WGA. Represents 75 clients. **25% of clients are new/previously unpublished writers.** Currently handles: 50% nonfiction books; 50% novels.
Represents: Nonfiction, novels. **Considers these fiction areas:** action/adventure; contemporary issues; ethnic; family saga; feminist; gay; lesbian; literary; thriller/espionage.
How to Contact: Query with SASE. Considers simultaneous queries. Reports in 1 week on queries; 1 month on mss. Returns materials only with SASE.
Needs: Obtains new clients through recommendations, "or I find them through my reading and pursue."
Recent Sales: Sold 15 titles in the last year. *Blindsighted*, by Karin Slaughter (Morrow); *Redemption Song*, by Dr. Bertice Berry (Doubleday).
Terms: Agent receives 15% commission on domestic sales; 20% on foreign sales. Offers written contract binding at will. Charges for photocopying, ms, messenger, express mail and extraordinary fees. If in excess of $100, client approval is required.
Tips: "Limit query to letter, no calls, and give it your best shot. A good query is going to get a good response."

🅽 ● ROSALIE SIEGEL, INTERNATIONAL LITERARY AGENCY, INC., 1 Abey Dr., Pennington NJ 08534. (609)737-1007. Fax: (609)737-3708. **Contact:** Rosalie Siegel. Estab. 1977. Member of AAR. Represents 35 clients. **10% of clients are new/previously unpublished writers.** Specializes in foreign authors, especially French, though diminishing. Currently handles: 45% nonfiction books; 45% novels; 10% young adult books and short story collections for current clients.
Needs: Obtains new clients through referrals from writers and friends.
Recent Sales: Prefers not to share information on specific sales.
Terms: Agent receives 15% commission on domestic sales; 20% on foreign sales. Offers written contract, with 60-day cancellation clause. Charges for photocopying. 100% of business is derived from commissions.
Tips: "I'm not looking for new authors in an active way."

🅽 ● SPECTRUM LITERARY AGENCY, (formerly Blassingame Spectrum Corp.), 111 Eighth Ave., Suite 1501, New York NY 10011. (212)691-7556. **Contact:** Eleanor Wood, president. Represents 75 clients. Currently handles: 90% fiction; 10% nonfiction books.
Member Agents: Lucienne Diver.
Represents: Considers these fiction areas: contemporary issues; fantasy; historical; romance; mainstream; mystery/suspense; science fiction.
How to Contact: Query with SASE. Reports in 2 months on queries.
Needs: Obtains new clients through recommendations from authors and others.
Recent Sales: Prefers not to share information on specific sales.
Terms: Agent receives 10% commission on domestic sales. Charges for photocopying and book orders.

🅽 ● PHILIP G. SPITZER LITERARY AGENCY, 50 Talmage Farm Lane, East Hampton NY 11937. (516)329-3650. Fax: (516)329-3651. E-mail: spitzer516@aol.com. **Contact:** Philip Spitzer. Estab. 1969. Member of AAR. Represents 60 clients. **10% of clients are new/previously unpublished writers.** Specializes in mystery/suspense, literary fiction, sports, general nonfiction (no how-to). Currently handles: 50% nonfiction books; 50% novels.
● Prior to opening his agency, Mr. Spitzer served at New York University Press, McGraw-Hill and the John Cushman Associates literary agency.
Represents: Nonfiction books, novels. **Considers these fiction areas:** contemporary issues; detective/police/crime; literary; mainstream; mystery/suspense; sports; thriller/espionage.
How to Contact: Send outline, 1 sample chapter and SASE. Reports in 1 week on queries; 6 weeks on mss.
Needs: Usually obtains new clients on referral.
Recent Sales: *Angels Flight*, by Michael Connelly (Little, Brown); *Heartwood*, by James Lee Burke (Hyperion); *Dancing After Hours*, by Andre Dubus (Knopf).
Terms: Agent receives 15% commission on domestic sales; 20% on foreign sales. Charges for photocopying.
Writers' Conferences: BEA (Chicago).

🅽 ● STERNIG & BYRNE LITERARY AGENCY, 3209 S. 55, Milwaukee WI 53219-4433. (414)328-8034. Fax: (414)328-8034. E-mail: jackbyrne@aol.com. **Contact:** Jack Byrne. Estab. 1950s. Member of SFWA and MWA. Represents 30 clients. **20% of clients are new/unpublished writers.** Sold 12 titles in the last year. "We have a small, friendly, personal, hands-on teamwork approach to marketing." Currently handles: 5% nonfiction books; 40% juvenile books; 50% novels; 5% short stories.
Member Agents: Jack Byrne.
Represents: Nonfiction books, juvenile books, novels. **Considers these fiction areas:** action/adventure; fantasy; glitz; horror; juvenile; mystery/suspense; psychic/supernatural; religious/inspirational; science fiction; thriller/espionage; young adult.
How to Contact: Query with SASE. Considers simultaneous queries; no simultaneous submissions. Reports

in 3 weeks on queries; 3 months on mss. Returns materials only with SASE. "No SASE equals no return."
Needs: Actively seeking science fiction/fantasy. Does not want to receive romance, poetry, textbooks, highly specialized nonfiction.
Recent Sales: Sold 12 titles in the last year. Prefers not to share information on specific sales. Clients include Betty Ren Wright, Lyn McComchie, Lenard Daniel Houarner, Andre Norton.
Terms: Agent receives 15% commission on domestic sales; 20% on foreign sales. Offers written contract, open/non binding. 60 days notice must be given to terminate contract.
Reading List: Reads *Publishers Weekly*, *Locus*, *Science Fiction Chronicles*, etc. to find new clients. Looks for "whatever catches my eye."
Tips: "Don't send first drafts; have a professional presentation . . . including cover letter; know your field (read what's been done . . . good and bad)."

N: ◘ **THE JOHN TALBOT AGENCY**, 540 W. Boston Post Rd., PMB 266, Mamaroneck NY 10543-3437. (914)381-9463. **Contact:** John Talbot. Estab. 1998. Member of the Authors Guild. Represents 40 clients. **15% of clients are new/unpublished writers.** Specializes in literary and commercial fiction, and general nonfiction. Currently handles: 35% nonfiction books; 65% novels.
• Prior to becoming an agent, Mr. Talbot was a book editor at Simon & Schuster and Putnam Berkley.
One of Mr. Talbot's clients recently had her novel selected for the Book of the Month Club.
Represents: Nonfiction books, novels. **Considers these fiction areas:** literary; suspense.
How to Contact: Query with SASE. No queries by fax or e-mail. Considers simultaneous queries. Reports in 1 month on queries; 2 months on mss.
Needs: Actively seeking suspense and literary fiction, "particularly by writers who are beginning to publish in magazines and literary journals." Does not want to receive children's books, science fiction, fantasy, westerns, poetry or screenplays. Obtains new clients through referrals, queries and conferences.
Recent Sales: Sold 25 titles in the last year. *Deep Sound Channel*, by Joe Buff (Bantam); *Lily of the Valley*, by Suzanne Strempek Sheen (Pocket Books); *The Fuck-Up*, by Arthur Nersesian (Pocket Books/MTV). Other clients include Robert Drake, Julio Esquivel, Charles Jaco, Clarence Major, Doris Meredith, Peter Telep, Barrett Tillman.
Terms: Agent receives 15% commission on domestic sales; 20% on foreign sales. Offers written contract. 2 weeks notice must be given to terminate contract. Charges for photocopying, overnight delivery, additional copies of books needed for use in sale of subsidiary rights, and fees incurred for submitting mss or books overseas.
Writer's Conferences: Florida Suncoast Writers Conference (St. Petersburg FL, February).
Tips: "I run an editorially-driven agency and bring the perspective of having been in the corporate book publishing industry for 14 years."

N: ◙ **PATRICIA TEAL LITERARY AGENCY**, 2036 Vista Del Rosa, Fullerton CA 92831-1336. (714)738-8333. **Contact:** Patricia Teal. Estab. 1978. Member of AAR, RWA, Authors Guild. Represents 60 clients. Specializes in women's fiction and commercial how-to and self-help nonfiction. Currently handles: 10% nonfiction books; 90% novels.
Represents: Nonfiction books, novels. **Considers these fiction areas:** glitz, mainstream, mystery/suspense, romance (contemporary, historical).
How to Contact: Published authors only. Query with SASE. Considers simultaneous queries. Reports in 10 days on queries; 6 weeks on requested mss. Returns materials only with SASE.
Needs: Does not want to receive poetry, short stories, articles, science fiction, fantasy, regency romance. Usually obtains new clients through recommendations from authors and editors or at conferences.
Recent Sales: Sold 35 titles in the last year. *The Orchid Hunter*, by Jill Marie Landis (Jove); *A Thanksgiving to Remember*, by Margaret Watson (Harlequin/Silhouette).
Terms: Agent receives 10-15% commission on domestic sales; 20% on foreign sales. Offers written contract, binding for 1 year. Charges $35 postage fee for first book, none thereafter.
Writers' Conferences: Romance Writers of America conferences; Asilomar (California Writers Club); Bouchercon; BEA (Chicago, June); California State University San Diego (January); Hawaii Writers Conference (Maui).
Reading List: Reads *Publishers Weekly*, *Romance Report* and *Romantic Times* to find new clients. "I read the reviews of books and excerpts from authors' books."
Tips: "Include SASE with all correspondence."

N: ◖ **THE VINES AGENCY, INC.**, 648 Broadway, Suite 901, New York NY 10012. (212)777-5522. Fax: (212)777-5978. E-mail: jvtva@mindspring.com. **Contact:** James C. Vines or Gary Neuwirth. Estab. 1995. Member of AAR, signatory of WGA. Represents 52 clients. **2% of clients are new/previously unpublished writers.** Specializes in mystery, suspense, science fiction, mainstream novels, screenplays, teleplays. Currently handles: 50% nonfiction books; 50% novels.
• Prior to opening his agency, Mr. Vines served as an agent with the Virginia Literary Agency.
Member Agents: James C. Vines; Gary Neuwirth; Ali Ryan (women's fiction and nonfiction, mainstream).
Represents: Nonfiction books, novels. **Considers these fiction areas:** action/adventure; contemporary issues; detective/police/crime; ethnic; feminist; horror; humor/satire; experimental; family saga; gay; lesbian; historical;

literary; mainstream; mystery/suspense; psychic/supernatural; regional; romance (contemporary, historical); science fiction; sports; thriller/espionage; westerns/frontier; women's fiction.
Also Handles: Feature film, TV scripts, stage plays. **Considers these script subject areas:** action/adventure; comedy; detective/police/crime; ethnic; experimental; feminist; gay; historical; horror; lesbian; mainstream; mystery/suspense; romance (comedy, drama); science fiction; teen; thriller; westerns/frontier.
How to Contact: Send outline and first 3 chapters with SASE. Accepts queries by fax and e-mail. "Maximum of one page by fax or e-mail." Considers simultaneous queries and submissions. Reports in 2 weeks on queries; 1 month on mss. Returns materials only with SASE.
Needs: Obtains new clients through query letters, recommendations from others, reading short stories in magazines and soliciting conferences.
Recent Sales: Sold 46 book titles and 5 script projects in the last year. *California Fire and Life*, by Don Winslow (Random House); *Sugar*, by Bernice McFadden (Doubleday). *Script(s) optioned/sold: Ninth Life*, by Jay Colvin (Miramax).
Terms: Agent receives 15% commission on domestic sales; 20% on foreign sales. Offers written contract, binding for 1 year, with 30-day cancellation clause. Charges for foreign postage, messenger services and photocopying. 100% of business is derived from commissions on sales.
Writers' Conferences: Maui Writer's Conference.
Tips: "Do not follow up on submissions with phone calls to the agency. The agency will read and respond by mail only. Do not pack your manuscript in plastic 'peanuts' that will make us have to vacuum the office after opening the package containing your manuscript. Always enclose return postage."

N ◐ **WATKINS LOOMIS AGENCY, INC.**, 133 E. 35th St., Suite 1, New York NY 10016. (212)532-0080. Fax: (212)889-0506. **Contact:** Katherine Fausset. Estab. 1908. Represents 150 clients. Specializes in literary fiction, London/UK translations, nonfiction.
Member Agents: Nicole Aragi (associate); Gloria Loomis (president); Katherine Fausset (assistant agent).
Represents: Nonfiction books, novels. **Considers these fiction areas:** contemporary issues; ethnic; gay; literary; mainstream; mystery/suspense.
How to Contact: Query with SASE. Reports within 1 month on queries.
Recent Sales: Prefers not to share information on specific sales. Clients include Walter Mosley, Edwidge Danticat, Katharine Weber and Junot Díaz.
Terms: Agent receives 15% commission on domestic sales; 20% on foreign sales.

N ◐ **SANDRA WATT & ASSOCIATES**, 1750 N. Sierra Bonita, Hollywood CA 90046-2423. (323)851-1021. Fax: (323)851-1046. E-mail: rondvart@aol.com. Estab. 1977. Signatory of WGA. Represents 55 clients. **15% of clients are new/previously unpublished writers.** Specializes in "books to film" and scripts: film noir; family; romantic comedies; books: women's fiction, young adult, mystery, commercial nonfiction. Currently handles: 40% nonfiction books; 60% novels.
 • Prior to opening her agency, Ms. Watt was vice president of an educational publishing company.
Member Agents: Sandra Watt (scripts, nonfiction, novels); Pricilla Palmer (adult, YA, children's).
Represents: Nonfiction books, novels. **Considers these fiction areas:** contemporary issues; detective/police/crime; family saga; mainstream; mystery/suspense; regional; religious/inspirational; thriller/espionage; women's mainstream novels.
How to Contact: Query with SASE. Accepts queries by fax and e-mail. Considers simultaneous queries and submissions. Reports in 2 weeks on queries; 2 months on mss. Returns materials only with SASE.
Needs: Does not want to receive "first 'ideas' for finished work." Obtains new clients through recommendations from others, referrals and "from wonderful query letters. Don't forget the SASE!"
Recent Sales: Sold 8 titles in the last year. *Risk Factor*, by Charles Atkins (St. Martin's Press); *Love is the Only Answer* (Putnam).
Terms: Agent receives 15% commission on domestic sales; 25% on foreign sales. Offers written contract, binding for 1 year. Charges one-time nonrefundable marketing fee of $100 *for unpublished authors.*

N ◐ **WIESER & WIESER, INC.**, 25 E. 21 St., 6th Floor, New York NY 10010. (212)260-0860. **Contact:** Olga Wieser. Estab. 1975. **30% of clients are new/previously unpublished writers.** Specializes in mainstream fiction and nonfiction. Currently handles: 50% nonfiction books; 50% novels.
Member Agents: Jake Elwell (history, military, mysteries, romance, sports, thrillers); Olga Wieser (psychology, fiction, pop medical, literary fiction).
Represents: Nonfiction books, novels. **Considers these fiction areas:** contemporary issues; detective/police/crime; historical; literary; mainstream; mystery/suspense; romance; thriller/espionage.

A BULLET INTRODUCES COMMENTS by the editor of *Novel & Short Story Writer's Market* indicating special information about the listing.

How to Contact: Query with outline/proposal and SASE. Reports in 2 weeks on queries.

Needs: Obtains new clients through queries, authors' recommendations and industry professionals.

Recent Sales: *Cutting*, by Steven Levenkron (Norton); *Hocus Corpus*, by James N. Tucker, M.D. (Dutton/Signet); *Grinning in Her Mashed Potatoes*, by Margaret Moseley (Berkley); *The Kamikazes*, by Edwin P. Hoyt (Burford Books); *Angels & Demons*, by Dan Brown (Pocket).

Terms: Agent receives 15% commission on domestic sales; 20% on foreign sales. Offers written contract. "No charge to our clients or potential clients." Charges for photocopying and overseas mailing.

Writers' Conferences: BEA; Frankfurt Book Fair.

N ○ WITHERSPOON & ASSOCIATES, INC., 157 W. 57th St., #700, New York NY 10019. (212)889-8626. Fax: (212)696-0650. **Contact:** Ross Kramer. Estab. 1990. Represents 150 clients. **20% of clients are new/previously unpublished writers.** Currently handles: 50% nonfiction books; 45% novels; 5% short story collections.

● Prior to becoming an agent Ms. Witherspoon was a writer and magazine consultant.

Member Agents: Maria Massie; Kimberly Witherspoon; David Forrer; Ross Kramer.

Represents: Nonfiction books, novels. **Considers these fiction areas:** contemporary issues; detective/police/crime; ethnic; family saga; feminist; gay; historical; lesbian; literary; mainstream; mystery/suspense; thriller/espionage.

How to Contact: Query with SASE. Reports in 3 weeks on queries; no unsolicited mss.

Needs: Obtains new clients through recommendations from others, solicitation and conferences.

Recent Sales: Prefers not to share information on specific sales.

Terms: Agent receives 15% commission on domestic sales; 20% on foreign sales. Offers written contract.

Writers' Conferences: BEA (Chicago, June); Frankfurt (Germany, October).

N ○ WRITERS HOUSE, 21 W. 26th St., New York NY 10010. (212)685-2400. Fax: (212)685-1781. Estab. 1974. Member of AAR. Represents 280 clients. **50% of clients were new/unpublished writers.** Specializes in all types of popular fiction and nonfiction. No scholarly, professional, poetry or screenplays. Currently handles: 25% nonfiction books; 35% juvenile books; 40% novels.

Member Agents: Albert Zuckerman (major novels, thrillers, women's fiction, important nonfiction); Amy Berkower (major juvenile authors, women's fiction, art and decorating, psychology); Merrilee Heifetz (quality children's fiction, science fiction and fantasy, popular culture, literary fiction); Susan Cohen (juvenile and young adult fiction and nonfiction, Judaism, women's issues); Susan Ginsburg (serious and popular fiction, true crime, narrative nonfiction, personality books, cookbooks); Fran Lebowitz (juvenile and young adult, popular culture); Michele Rubin (serious nonfiction); Karen Solem (contemporary and historical romance, women's fiction, narrative nonfiction, horse and animal books); Robin Rue (commercial fiction and nonfiction, YA fiction); Jennifer Lyons (literary, commercial fiction, international fiction, nonfiction and illustrated).

Represents: Nonfiction books, juvenile books, novels. **Considers any fiction area.** "Quality is everything."

How to Contact: Query. Reports in 1 month on queries.

Needs: Obtains new clients through recommendations from others.

Recent Sales: *The New New Thing*, by Michael Lewis (Norton); *The First Victim*, by Ridley Pearson (Hyperion); *Into the Garden*, by V.C. Andrews (Pocket); *Fearless*, by Francine Pascal (Pocket).

Terms: Agent receives 15% commission on domestic sales; 20% on foreign sales. Offers written contract, binding for 1 year.

Tips: "Do not send manuscripts. Write a compelling letter. If you do, we'll ask to see your work."

○ SUSAN ZECKENDORF ASSOC. INC., 171 W. 57th St., New York NY 10019. (212)245-2928. **Contact:** Susan Zeckendorf. Estab. 1979. Member of AAR. Represents 15 clients. **25% of clients are new/previously unpublished writers.** Currently handles: 50% nonfiction books; 50% fiction.

● Prior to opening her agency, Ms. Zeckendorf was a counseling psychologist.

Represents: Nonfiction books, novels. **Considers these fiction areas:** contemporary issues; detective/police/crime; ethnic; family saga; glitz; historical; literary; mainstream; mystery/suspense; thriller/espionage.

How to Contact: Query with SASE. Considers simultaneous queries and submissions. Reports in 10 days on queries; 3 weeks mss. Obtains new clients through recommendations, listings in writer's manuals. Returns materials only with SASE.

Needs: Actively seeking mysteries, literary fiction, mainstream fiction, thrillers, social history, parenting, classical music, biography. Does not want to receive science fiction, romance. "No children's books."

Recent Sales: Sold 6 titles in the last year. *The Four Hundred: New York in the Gilded Age*, by Jerry E. Patterson (Rizzoli); *The Power of Myth in Storytelling*, by James N. Frey (St. Martin's).

Terms: Agent receives 15% commission on domestic sales; 20% on foreign sales. Charges for photocopying, messenger services.

Writers' Conferences: Central Valley Writers Conference; the Tucson Publishers Association Conference; Writer's Connection; Frontiers in Writing Conference (Amarillo, TX); Golden Triangle Writers Conference (Beaumont TX); Oklahoma Festival of Books (Claremont OK); Mary Mount Writers Conference.

Tips: "We are a small agency giving lots of individual attention. We respond quickly to submissions."

Literary Agents Category Index

Agents listed in the preceeding section are indexed below according to the categories of fiction they represent. Use it to find agents who handle the specific kind of fiction you write. Then turn to those listings in the alphabetical Literary Agents section for complete contact and submission information.

Action/Adventure
Acacia House Publishing Services Ltd.
Allen, Literary Agent, James
Amsterdam Agency, Marcia
C G & W Associates
Crawford Literary Agency
Halsey, Reece
Harris Literary Agency
Harris Literary Agency, Inc., The Joy
Henshaw Group, Richard
Jabberwocky Literary Agency
JCA Literary Agency, Inc.
Koster Literary Agency, LLC, Elaine
Kraas Agency, Irene
Lampack Agency, Inc., Peter
Lincoln Literary Agency, Ray
Lindstrom Literary Group
Marshall Agency, The Evan
Michaels Literary Agency, Inc., Doris S.
Morrison, Inc., Henry
Rotrosen Agency LLC, Jane
Sanders Literary Agency, Victoria
Sternig & Byrne Literary Agency
Vines Agency, Inc., The
Zeckendorf Assoc. Inc., Susan

Cartoon/Comic
Harris Literary Agency, Inc., The Joy
Jabberwocky Literary Agency
Vines Agency, Inc., The

Confessional
C G & W Associates
Harris Literary Agency, Inc., The Joy
JCA Literary Agency, Inc.
Koster Literary Agency, LLC, Elaine

Contemporary Issues
Alive Communications, Inc.
C G & W Associates
Connor Literary Agency
Goodman-Andrew-Agency, Inc.
Greene, Literary Agent, Randall Elisha

Halsey, Reece
Harris Literary Agency, Inc., The Joy
Jabberwocky Literary Agency
JCA Literary Agency, Inc.
Kidde, Hoyt & Picard
Koster Literary Agency, LLC, Elaine
Lampack Agency, Inc., Peter
Lincoln Literary Agency, Ray
Lindstrom Literary Group
Marshall Agency, The Evan
Michaels Literary Agency, Inc., Doris S.
Pinder Lane & Garon-Brooke Associates, Ltd.
Sanders Literary Agency, Victoria
Spectrum Literary Agency
Spitzer Literary Agency, Philip G.
Vines Agency, Inc., The
Watkins Loomis Agency, Inc.
Watt & Associates, Sandra
Wieser & Wieser, Inc.
Witherspoon & Associates, Inc.
Zeckendorf Assoc. Inc., Susan

Detective/Police/Crime
Acacia House Publishing Services Ltd.
Alive Communications, Inc.
Allen, Literary Agent, James
Amsterdam Agency, Marcia
C G & W Associates
Connor Literary Agency
DHS Literary, Inc.
Ellenberg Literary Agency, Ethan
Greene, Literary Agent, Randall Elisha
Halsey, Reece
Harris Literary Agency
Harris Literary Agency, Inc., The Joy
Henshaw Group, Richard
J de S Associates Inc.
Jabberwocky Literary Agency
JCA Literary Agency, Inc.
Kidde, Hoyt & Picard
Koster Literary Agency, LLC, Elaine
Kraas Agency, Irene
Lampack Agency, Inc., Peter
Lincoln Literary Agency, Ray

Lindstrom Literary Group
Maass Literary Agency, Donald
Marshall Agency, The Evan
Morrison, Inc., Henry
Pinder Lane & Garon-Brooke Associates, Ltd.
Rotrosen Agency LLC, Jane
Rowland Agency, The Damaris
Rubenstein Literary Agency, Inc., Pesha
Spitzer Literary Agency, Philip G.
Vines Agency, Inc., The
Watt & Associates, Sandra
Wieser & Wieser, Inc.
Witherspoon & Associates, Inc.
Zeckendorf Assoc. Inc., Susan

Erotica
DHS Literary, Inc.
Harris Literary Agency, Inc., The Joy
Marshall Agency, The Evan

Ethnic
C G & W Associates
Connor Literary Agency
Daves Agency, Joan
DHS Literary, Inc.
Evans Inc., Mary
Goodman-Andrew-Agency, Inc.
Greene, Literary Agent, Randall Elisha
Halsey, Reece
Harris Literary Agency, Inc., The Joy
Henshaw Group, Richard
Jabberwocky Literary Agency
JCA Literary Agency, Inc.
Knight Agency, The
Koster Literary Agency, LLC, Elaine
Kraas Agency, Irene
Lincoln Literary Agency, Ray
Lindstrom Literary Group
Marshall Agency, The Evan
Rubenstein Literary Agency, Inc., Pesha
Sanders Literary Agency, Victoria
Vines Agency, Inc., The
Watkins Loomis Agency, Inc.
Witherspoon & Associates, Inc.
Zeckendorf Assoc. Inc., Susan

Experimental
Connor Literary Agency
Harris Literary Agency, Inc., The Joy
JCA Literary Agency, Inc.
Kidd Agency, Inc., Virginia
Vines Agency, Inc., The

Family Saga
Alive Communications, Inc.
Allen, Literary Agent, James
C G & W Associates
Connor Literary Agency
Daves Agency, Joan
Ellenberg Literary Agency, Ethan
Greene, Literary Agent, Randall Elisha
Halsey, Reece
Harris Literary Agency, Inc., The Joy
Henshaw Group, Richard
Jabberwocky Literary Agency
JCA Literary Agency, Inc.
Koster Literary Agency, LLC, Elaine
Kraas Agency, Irene
Lampack Agency, Inc., Peter
Lincoln Literary Agency, Ray
Marshall Agency, The Evan
Michaels Literary Agency, Inc., Doris S.
Morrison, Inc., Henry
Pinder Lane & Garon-Brooke Associates, Ltd.
Rotrosen Agency LLC, Jane
Sanders Literary Agency, Victoria
Vines Agency, Inc., The
Watt & Associates, Sandra
Witherspoon & Associates, Inc.
Zeckendorf Assoc. Inc., Susan

Fantasy
Allen, Literary Agent, James
Carvainis Agency, Inc., Maria
Ellenberg Literary Agency, Ethan
Henshaw Group, Richard
Jabberwocky Literary Agency
Kidd Agency, Inc., Virginia
Lincoln Literary Agency, Ray
Maass Literary Agency, Donald
Pinder Lane & Garon-Brooke Associates, Ltd.
Spectrum Literary Agency
Sternig & Byrne Literary Agency

Feminist
DHS Literary, Inc.
Harris Literary Agency, Inc., The Joy
JCA Literary Agency, Inc.
Kidd Agency, Inc., Virginia
Kidde, Hoyt & Picard
Koster Literary Agency, Elaine, LLC
Lincoln Literary Agency, Ray
Michaels Literary Agency, Inc., Doris S.
Sanders Literary Agency, Victoria
Vines Agency, Inc., The
Witherspoon & Associates, Inc.

Gay

Daves Agency, Joan
DHS Literary, Inc.
Evans Inc., Mary
Goodman-Andrew-Agency, Inc.
Harris Literary Agency, Inc., The Joy
Jabberwocky Literary Agency
JCA Literary Agency, Inc.
Kidde, Hoyt & Picard
Koster Literary Agency, LLC, Elaine
Lincoln Literary Agency, Ray
Pinder Lane & Garon-Brooke Associates, Ltd.
Sanders Literary Agency, Victoria
Vines Agency, Inc., The
Watkins Loomis Agency, Inc.
Witherspoon & Associates, Inc.

Glitz

Allen, Literary Agent, James
C G & W Associates
Harris Literary Agency, Inc., The Joy
Henshaw Group, Richard
Jabberwocky Literary Agency
JCA Literary Agency, Inc.
Kidd Agency, Inc., Virginia
Kidde, Hoyt & Picard
Koster Literary Agency, LLC, Elaine
Marshall Agency, The Evan
Rubenstein Literary Agency, Inc., Pesha
Sternig & Byrne Literary Agency
Teal Literary Agency, Patricia
Zeckendorf Assoc. Inc., Susan

Historical

Alive Communications, Inc.
Allen, Literary Agent, James
C G & W Associates
Carvainis Agency, Inc., Maria
DHS Literary, Inc.
Ellenberg Literary Agency, Ethan
Halsey, Reece
Harris Literary Agency, Inc., The Joy
Henshaw Group, Richard
Hopkins Literary Associates
J de S Associates Inc.
Jabberwocky Literary Agency
JCA Literary Agency, Inc.
Kidd Agency, Inc., Virginia
Kidde, Hoyt & Picard
Koster Literary Agency, LLC, Elaine
Lampack Agency, Inc., Peter
Lincoln Literary Agency, Ray
Lindstrom Literary Group
Maass Literary Agency, Donald

Marshall Agency, The Evan
Michaels Literary Agency, Inc., Doris S.
Rotrosen Agency LLC, Jane
Rowland Agency, The Damaris
Spectrum Literary Agency
Vines Agency, Inc., The
Wieser & Wieser, Inc.
Witherspoon & Associates, Inc.
Zeckendorf Assoc. Inc., Susan

Horror

Alive Communications, Inc.
Allen, Literary Agent, James
Amsterdam Agency, Marcia
Carvainis Agency, Inc., Maria
Connor Literary Agency
DHS Literary, Inc.
Ellenberg Literary Agency, Ethan
Harris Literary Agency, Inc., The Joy
Henshaw Group, Richard
J de S Associates Inc.
Jabberwocky Literary Agency
JCA Literary Agency, Inc.
Kidd Agency, Inc., Virginia
Kraas Agency, Irene
Lincoln Literary Agency, Ray
Maass Literary Agency, Donald
Marshall Agency, The Evan
Rotrosen Agency LLC, Jane
Sternig & Byrne Literary Agency
Vines Agency, Inc., The

Humor/Satire

Alive Communications, Inc.
Amsterdam Agency, Marcia
Greene, Literary Agent, Randall Elisha
Harris Literary Agency
Henshaw Group, Richard
Jabberwocky Literary Agency
JCA Literary Agency, Inc.
Kidde, Hoyt & Picard
Lincoln Literary Agency, Ray
Marshall Agency, The Evan
Rubenstein Literary Agency, Inc., Pesha
Vines Agency, Inc., The

Juvenile

Alive Communications, Inc.
Ellenberg Literary Agency, Ethan
Harris Literary Agency
Henshaw Group, Richard
J de S Associates Inc.
Kraas Agency, Irene

Lincoln Literary Agency, Ray
Rubenstein Literary Agency, Inc., Pesha
Sternig & Byrne Literary Agency
Vines Agency, Inc., The

Open to All Fiction Categories

Allen, Literary Agent, James
Amsterdam Agency, Marcia
C G & W Associates
Carvainis Agency, Inc., Maria
Cohen Literary Agency Ltd., Hy
Congdon Associates, Inc., Don
Curtis Associates, Inc., Richard
Ellenberg Literary Agency, Ethan
Fernandez Agent/Attorney, Justin E.
Greene, Literary Agent, Randall Elisha
Harris Literary Agency, Inc., The Joy
Hopkins Literary Associates
Kidde, Hoyt & Picard
Knight Agency, The
Lincoln Literary Agency, Ray
Maass Literary Agency, Donald
Marshall Agency, The Evan
Ober Associates, Harold
Pinder Lane & Garon-Brooke Associates, Ltd.
Rotrosen Agency LLC, Jane
Rowland Agency, The Damaris
Rubenstein Literary Agency, Inc., Pesha
Teal Literary Agency, Patricia
Vines Agency, Inc., The
Wieser & Wieser, Inc.
Writers House

Religious/Inspiration

Goodman-Andrew-Agency, Inc.
Harris Literary Agency, Inc., The Joy
Jabberwocky Literary Agency
Kidde, Hoyt & Picard
Koster Literary Agency, LLC, Elaine
Lincoln Literary Agency, Ray
Sanders Literary Agency, Victoria
Vines Agency, Inc., The
Witherspoon & Associates, Inc.

Romance

Acacia House Publishing Services Ltd.
Alive Communications, Inc.
C G & W Associates
Carvainis Agency, Inc., Maria
Congdon Associates, Inc., Don
Connor Literary Agency
Darhansoff & Verrill Literary Agents
Daves Agency, Joan

DHS Literary, Inc.
Ellenberg Literary Agency, Ethan
Ellison Inc., Nicholas
Evans Inc., Mary
Goodman-Andrew-Agency, Inc.
Greene, Literary Agent, Randall Elisha
Halsey, Reece
Harris Literary Agency, Inc., The Joy
Henshaw Group, Richard
J de S Associates Inc.
Jabberwocky Literary Agency
JCA Literary Agency, Inc.
Kidd Agency, Inc., Virginia
Kidde, Hoyt & Picard
Knight Agency, The
Koster Literary Agency, LLC, Elaine
Kraas Agency, Irene
Lampack Agency, Inc., Peter
Lincoln Literary Agency, Ray
Maass Literary Agency, Donald
Markson Literary Agency, Elaine
Marshall Agency, The Evan
Michaels Literary Agency, Inc., Doris S.
Pinder Lane & Garon-Brooke Associates, Ltd.
Rowland Agency, The Damaris
Sanders Literary Agency, Victoria
Spitzer Literary Agency, Philip G.
Talbot Agency, The John
Vines Agency, Inc., The
Watkins Loomis Agency, Inc.
Wieser & Wieser, Inc.
Witherspoon & Associates, Inc.
Zeckendorf Assoc. Inc., Susan

Science Fiction

Acacia House Publishing Services Ltd.
Alive Communications, Inc.
Allen, Literary Agent, James
Amsterdam Agency, Marcia
C G & W Associates
Carvainis Agency, Inc., Maria
Crawford Literary Agency
Daves Agency, Joan
DHS Literary, Inc.
Ellenberg Literary Agency, Ethan
Ellison Inc., Nicholas
Goodman-Andrew-Agency, Inc.
Greene, Literary Agent, Randall Elisha
Halsey, Reece
Harris Literary Agency
Harris Literary Agency, Inc., The Joy
Henshaw Group, Richard
Hopkins Literary Associates
J de S Associates Inc.
Jabberwocky Literary Agency

Sports

Thriller/Espionage

Westerns/Frontier

Young Adult

Literary Magazines

This section contains markets for your literary short fiction. Although definitions of what constitutes "literary" writing vary, editors of literary journals agree they want to publish the "best" fiction available today. Qualities they look for in stories include creativity, style, flawless mechanics, and careful attention to detail in content and manuscript preparation. Most of the authors writing such fiction are well-read and well-educated, and many are students and graduates of university creative writing programs.

STEPPING STONES TO RECOGNITION

Some well-established literary journals pay several hundred or even several thousand dollars for a short story. Most, though, can only pay with contributor's copies or a subscription to their publication. However, being published in literary journals offers the important benefits of experience, exposure and prestige. Agents and major book publishers regularly read literary magazines in search of new writers. Work from among these journals is also selected for inclusion in annual prize anthologies such as *The Best American Short Stories*, *Prize Stories: The O. Henry Awards*, *Pushcart Prize: Best of the Small Presses*, and *New Stories from the South: The Year's Best*.

You'll find most of the well-known prestigious literary journals listed here. Many, including *Carolina Quarterly* and *Ploughshares*, are associated with universities, while others such as *The Paris Review* are independently published.

You will also find electronic literary magazines, an increasingly common trend at a time when paper and publishing costs rise while funding to university presses continues to be cut back or eliminated altogether. These electronic outlets for literary fiction also benefit writers by eliminating copying and postage costs and providing the opportunity for much quicker responses to submissions. *Also notice that some magazines with websites give specific information about what they offer on their websites, including updated writers guidelines and sample fiction from their publications.*

SELECTING THE RIGHT LITERARY JOURNAL

Once you have browsed through this section and have a list of journals you might like to submit to, read those listings again, carefully. Remember that this is information editors present to help you in submitting work that fits their needs. The "Quick Start" Guide to Publishing Your Fiction, starting on page 2, will guide you through the process of finding markets for your fiction.

This is the only section in which you will find magazines that do not read submissions all year long. Whether limited reading periods are tied to a university schedule or meant to accommodate the capabilities of a very small staff, those periods are noted within listings. The staffs of university journals are usually made up of student editors and a managing editor who is also a faculty member. These staffs often change every year. Whenever possible, we indicate this in listings and give the name of the current editor and the length of that editor's term. Also be aware that the schedule of a university journal usually coincides with that university's academic year, meaning that the editors of most university publications are difficult or impossible to reach during the summer.

FURTHERING YOUR SEARCH

It cannot be stressed enough that reading the listings for literary journals is only the first part of developing your marketing plan. The second part, equally important, is to obtain fiction guidelines and read the actual magazine. Reading copies of a magazine helps you determine the fine points of the magazine's publishing style and philosophy. There is no substitute for this type of hands-on research.

Unlike commercial periodicals available at most newsstands and bookstores, it requires a little more effort to obtain some of the magazines listed here. The new super chain bookstores are doing a better job these days of stocking literaries and you can find some in independent and college bookstores, especially those published in your area. You may, however, need to send for a sample copy. We include sample copy prices in the listings whenever possible.

Another way to find out more about literary magazines is to check out the various prize anthologies and take note of journals whose fiction is being selected for publication there. Studying prize anthologies not only lets you know which magazines are publishing award-winning work, but it also provides a valuable overview of what is considered to be the best fiction published today. Those anthologies include:

- *Best American Short Stories*, published by Houghton Mifflin, 222 Berkeley St., Boston MA 02116.
- *New Stories from the South: The Year's Best*, published by Algonquin Books of Chapel Hill, P.O. Box 2225, Chapel Hill NC 27515.
- *Prize Stories: The O. Henry Awards*, published by Doubleday/Anchor, 1540 Broadway, New York NY 10036.
- *Pushcart Prize: Best of the Small Presses*, published by Pushcart Press, Box 380, Wainscott NY 11975.

At the beginnings of listings, we include symbols to help you in narrowing your search. Keys to those symbols can be found on the inside front and back covers of this book.

For More Information

If you're interested in learning more about literary and small magazines, you may want to look at *The International Directory of Little Magazines and Small Presses* (Dustbooks, Box 100, Paradise CA 95967); the *Directory of Literary Magazines*, published by the Council of Literary Magazines and Presses (3-C, 154 Christopher St., New York NY 10014-2839); or *The Association of American University Presses Directory* (584 Broadway, New York NY 10012).

The well-respected *Poet* magazine (published by Cooper House Publishing Inc., P.O. Box 54947, Oklahoma City OK 73154) annually honors the best literary magazines (those publishing both fiction and poetry). The program is titled The American Literary Magazine Awards and most recipients of editorial content awards have listings in this section. To find out more about the awards, see the *Poet*'s fall issue.

☑ ◌ ABOUT SUCH THINGS, Literary Magazine, 1701 Delancey St., Philadelphia PA 19103. (215)849-1583. E-mail: aboutsuch@juno.com. Website: world.std.com/~pduggan/ast/astroot.html (includes writer's guidelines, samples of writing and art, subscription information, contact information). Editor: Laurel Webster Garver. **Fiction Editor:** E. Louise Lindinger. Magazine: 8⅜ × 10¾; 28-32 pages; 24 lb. paper; 80 lb. cover stock; illustrations. "We seek to provide a forum for Christian authors to publish work. We receive editorial guidance from a Presbyterian church in Philadelphia. Our audience is primarily educated, professional, church-going intellectuals." Semiannually. Estab. 1996. Circ. 400.

Needs: Ethnic/multicultural, fantasy, historical, humor/satire (particularly with religious/inspirational elements), literary, regional, religious/inspirational, romance, science fiction (soft/sociological), allegory. No erotica, horror, occult, feminist, gay. Receives 15 unsolicited mss/month. Accepts 1-3 mss/issue; 2-6 mss/year. Does not read

February-April and August-October. Publishes ms 3 months after acceptance. Recently published work by Myrtle Archer, M. Jean Bowdy, Jeffrey Miller and Marleah D. Peabody. Length: 2,000 words average; 300 words minimum; 3,000 words maximum. Publishes short shorts. Also publishes cultural essays, book and film reviews and poetry. Always critiques or comments on rejected mss.

How to Contact: Send complete ms with a cover letter. Include estimated word count, SASE, address, phone number, e-mail and submission on diskette in ASCII text. Reports on mss in 12 months. Send SASE for return of ms. Simultaneous submissions and reprints OK. Sample copy for $3 and 9 × 12 SAE with 99¢ postage. Fiction guidelines for #10 SASE.

Payment/Terms: Pays 2 contributor's copies for one-time rights; additional copies for $3. Sends galleys to author. Not copyrighted.

Advice: "We look for high quality in content, clarity, tone and characterization; also for impact, snappy dialogue, many-faceted and growing characters. Let any moral or spiritual lesson be an outgrowth of a solid plot and real characters. Be willing to let the story have resonance and tension by not tying up every loose end too tightly. Avoid making 'good' characters stereotypically 'churchy.' "

[N] ★ ◯ ▣ THE ABSINTHE LITERARY REVIEW. E-mail: absinthe@execpc.com. Website: www.exe cpc.com/~absinthe. **Editor:** Charles Allen Wyman. Electronic literary magazine. "We publish short stories, novel excerpts, poems and occasionally essays. Our target audience is the literate individual who enjoys creative language use, character-driven fiction and the clashing of worlds-real and imagined, poetic and prosaic, archaic and modern."

Needs: "*ALR* has a special affection for the blending of archaic materials with modern subjects. Elements of myth, archetype and symobolism should figure heavily in most submissions. We favor the surrealist, the poet and the philosopher over the storyteller even in our fiction choices. More than anything else, we desire submissions from highly educated writers whose work is too dense, florid or learned for other markets. At the very least, your work should show an odd turn or a disaffected viewpoint. We abhor minimalist fiction simply because of its abundance in the present marketplace, be we can still appreciate a spare, well-done piece. Any genre work must substantially transcend traditional limitations of the form to be considered; and plot based fiction should be significantly odd." **Publishes 30-50 new writers/year.**

How to Contact: E-mail submissions only. See website for specific guidelines.

Payment/Terms: "We believe that writers should be paid for their work and will attempt to remit a small gratuity upon publication (usually in the $5-10 range) when funds are available. There is, however, no guarantee of payment. We are a nonprofit organization."

Advice: "Be erudite but daring in your writing. Draw from the past to drag meaning from the present. Kill cliché. Invest your work with layers of meaning that subtly reveal multiple realities. Do not submit pieces that are riddled with spelling errors and grammatical snafus."

[N] ◎ ▼ THE ACORN, a Journal of the Western Sierra, Hot Pepper Press, P.O. Box 1266, El Dorado CA 95623-1266. (530)621-1833. Fax: (530)621-3939. E-mail: theacorn@briefcase.com. **Editor:** Judy Graham and committee. Magazine: 8½ × 5½; 44 pages. *The Acorn* primarily publishes work about the "western slope of Sierra Nevada and rural lifestyle, but encourages the submission of any and all good writing." Quarterly. Estab. 1993. Circ. 200.

● A work from *The Acorn* received first place for Best Western Short Fiction from the Western Writers of America.

Needs: Adventure, historical, humor/satire, literary, mainstream/contemporary, regional, senior citizen/retire-ment. "No porn or erotica." "We usually try to choose subjects or topics that fit the season. Historical fiction is attractive to us, but we like to see all forms of fiction." Receives 5-10 unsolicited mss/month. Accepts 5-6 mss/issue; 24 mss/year. Publishes ms 1 month after acceptance. Recently published work by Allen Bristow, Wayne Myers, J.K. Colvin and Harlon Stafford. **Publishes 5 new writers/year.** Length: 4,000 words maximum. Publishes short shorts. Also publishes literary essays and poetry. Often critiques or comments on rejected mss. Sponsors contest; send SASE for information.

How to Contact: Send complete ms with a cover letter. Include 1-paragraph bio and list of publications. Accepts queries/mss by e-mail. Reports in 4 months on mss. Send SASE for reply, return of ms or send a disposable copy of ms. No simultaneous submissions; reprints OK. Electronic submissions encouraged. Sample copy for $4. Fiction guidelines for #10 SASE.

Payment/Terms: Pays 2 contributor's copy on publication; additional copies for $3.75. Acquires one-time rights.

Advice: Looks for "memorable work that captures the flavor of our region—its history, landforms and wildlife and rural lifestyle. Good writing helps too. If we remember a story the next day, if we find ourselves thinking about the story or a character while driving around in our car, you've struck a nerve and taken a huge first step. Proper formatting will at least get your story read—fancy fonts, italics and clip art are distracting and a short cut to rejection. We encourage electronic submissions of manuscripts. Since we use an editorial board approach and have 5-6 editors reviewing each submission, electronic submissions allow us to save time and money, as well as accelerating the review process."

ACORN WHISTLE, 907 Brewster Ave., Beloit WI 53511-5621. E-mail: burwellf@lib.beloit.edu. Website: www.acornwhistle.com (includes writer's guidelines, contact info, covers and table of contents of each issue, sample writing and information on our press). **Editor-in-Chief:** Fred Burwell. Magazine: 8½ × 11; 75-100 pages; uncoated paper; light card cover; illustrations; photos. "*Acorn Whistle* seeks accessible and personal writing, art and photography that appeals to readers on both emotional and intellectual levels. Our intended audience is the educated non-academic. Connecting writers with readers is our foremost goal. We also encourage a friendly working relationship between editors and writers. We seek accessible and humane literary fiction for an audience that reads for pleasure and edification." Semiannually. Estab. 1995. Circ. 500.

Needs: Ethnic/multicultural, feminist, historical (general), humor/satire, literary, mainstream/contemporary, regional. No erotica, experimental, fantasy, horror, religious or science fiction. Would like to see more "stories with vivid characterization, compassion for its characters, vivid sense of place. Writing with a commitment to readership." Accepts 5-7 mss/issue; 10-15 mss/year. Publishes ms within a year after acceptance. Recently published work by Mary Waters, Dan May, Elizabeth Gargano and James Hudson. **Publishes 2-6 new writers/ year.** Length: open. Publishes short shorts. Also publishes memoir and poetry. Often critiques or comments on rejected ms.

How to Contact: Send complete ms. Reports in 2 weeks on queries; 1-12 weeks on mss. Send SASE for reply, return of ms or send a disposable copy of ms. Simultaneous submissions OK. Sample copy for $7. Fiction guidelines for #10 SASE.

Payment/Terms: Pays 2 contributor's copies. Acquires first North American serial rights. Features expanded contributor's notes with personal comments from each author.

Advice: "We look for writing that is direct and human and makes the reader care—writing that communicates and illuminates the shared human experience, yet includes a variety of voices and backgrounds. Write what matters to you, rather than trying to impress an imaginary audience. Writing fueled by an author's passion *will* reach readers. Don't let rejections discourage you. And, if an editor says, "try again," try again . . . and again!"

$ ADVENTURES OF SWORD & SORCERY, Double Star Press, P.O. Box 807, Xenia OH 45385. E-mail: double_star@yahoo.com. **Editor:** Randy Dannenfelser. Magazine: 8½ × 11; 80 pages; slick cover stock; illustrations. "We publish sword and sorcery, heroic and high fantasy fiction." Quarterly. Estab. 1995. Circ. 7,000.

Needs: Sword and sorcery, heroic and high fantasy fiction. "We want fiction with an emphasis on action and adventure, but still cognizant of the struggles within as they play against the struggles without. Include sexual content only as required by the story, but not excessive/porn." Receives approximately 250 unsolicited mss/ month. Accepts 9 mss/issue; 36 mss/year. Publishes ms 1 year after acceptance. Agented fiction 5%. Recently published work by Mike Resnick, Stephen Baxter and Darrell Schweitzer. **Publishes 8 new writers/year.** Length: 5,000 words average; 1,000 words minimum; 20,000 words maximum. Also publishes literary criticism and book reviews (only solicited). Always critiques or comments on rejected mss.

How to Contact: Send complete ms with a cover letter. Include estimated word count, Social Security number, list of publications, phone number and e-mail address. Reports in 1 month on queries; 2 months on mss. Send SASE for reply, return of ms. No simultaneous submissions. Electronic submissions (e-mail, disk or modem) OK. Sample copy $6. Fiction guidelines for #10 SASE. Reviews novels and short story collections.

Payment/Terms: Pays 3-6¢/word on acceptance and 3 contributor's copies; additional copies 40% discount plus shipping. Acquires first North American serial rights. Sends galleys to author.

Advice: "Recently we are looking for more adventuresome work with settings other than generic medieval Europe. We look for real emotion in the prose. Think about the audience we are targeted at, and send us appropriate stories."

ADVOCATE, PKA'S PUBLICATION, PKA Publications, 301A Rolling Hills Park, Prattsville NY 12468. (518)299-3103. Tabloid: 9⅜ × 12¼; 32 pages; newsprint paper; line drawings; b&w photographs. "Eclectic for a general audience." Bimonthly. Estab. 1987. Publishes 12,000 copies.

● *PKA's Advocate* editors tend to like positive, upbeat, entertaining material.

Needs: Adventure, contemporary, ethnic, experimental, fantasy, feminist, historical, humor/satire, juvenile (5-9 years), literary, mainstream, mystery/suspense, prose poem, regional, romance, science fiction, senior citizen/ retirement, sports, western, young adult/teen (10-18 years). "Currently looking for equine (horses) stories, poetry, art, photos and cartoons. The *Gaited Horse Newsletter* is currently published within the pages of *PKA's Advocate.*" Nothing religious, pornographic, violent, erotic, pro-drug or anti-environment. Receives 60 unsolicited mss/ month. Accepts 6-8 mss/issue; 36-48 mss/year. Publishes ms 4 months to 1 year after acceptance. Length: 1,000 words preferred; 1,500 words maximum. Sometimes critiques rejected mss.

How to Contact: Send complete ms with cover letter. Reports in 2 weeks on queries; 2 months on mss. SASE. No simultaneous submissions. Sample copy for $4 (US currency for inside US; $5.25 US currency for Canada). Writers guidelines for SASE.

Payment/Terms: Pays contributor's copies. Acquires first rights.

Advice: "The highest criterion in selecting a work is its entertainment value. It must first be enjoyable reading. It must, of course, be original. To stand out, it must be thought provoking or strongly emotive, or very cleverly plotted. Will consider only previously unpublished works by writers who do not earn their living principally through writing."

AETHLON, East Tennessee State University, Box 70, 683, Johnson City TN 37614-0683. (423)439-5994. E-mail: morefiel@access.etsu.edu. **Fiction Editor:** John Morefield. Magazine: 6×9; 180-240 pages; illustrations and photographs. "Theme: Literary treatment of sport. We publish articles on that theme, critical studies of author's treatment of sport and original fiction and poetry with sport themes. Most of our readers are academics." Semiannually. Estab. 1983. Circ. 800.

Needs: Sport. No fantasy, science fiction or horror. "Stories must have a sport-related theme and subject; otherwise, we're wide open. No personal memoirs, mystery, sci-fi, horror, 'trick ending,' etc." Receives 15-20 fiction mss/month. Accepts 6-10 fiction mss/issue; 12-20 fiction mss/year. Publishes ms "about 1 year" after acceptance. Recently published work by Pat Reid, Adam Berlin, Enrico Raulli, Peter Martinez, Gary King, James G. Van Belle, Dinah Miller and Mary Waters. **Publishes 3-4 new writers/year.** Length: 2,500-5,000 words average; 500 words minimum; 7,500 words maximum. Also publishes literary essays, literary criticism, poetry. Sometimes critiques rejected mss.

How to Contact: Send complete ms and brief cover letter with 1-2 lines for a contributor's note. Reports in 4-6 months. SASE in size to fit ms. No simultaneous submissions. Electronic disk submissions OK. Final copy must be submitted on disk (WordPerfect). Sample copy for $12.50. Reviews novels and short story collections. Send books to Prof. Joe Dewey, Dept. of English, University of Pittsburgh-Johnstown, Johnstown PA 15601.

Payment/Terms: Pays 1 contributor's copy and 5 offprints.

Advice: "We are looking for well-written, insightful stories. The only criterion is literary excellence. A story should begin immediately to develop tension or conflict. It should have strong characters and a well-drawn setting. Don't be afraid to be experimental. Take more care with your manuscript. Please send a legible manuscript free of grammatical errors. Be willing to revise."

☑ $☑ AFRICAN AMERICAN REVIEW, Indiana State University, Department of English, Root Hall A220, Terre Haute IN 47809. (812)237-2968. Fax: (812)237-3156. E-mail: ascleco@amber.indstate.edu. **Editor:** Joe Weixlmann. Magazine: 7×10; 176 pages; 60#, acid-free paper; 100# skid stock cover; illustrations and photos. "*African American Review* publishes stories and poetry by African American writers, and essays about African American literature and culture." Quarterly. Estab. 1967. Circ. 4,200.

● *African American Review* is the official publication of the Division of Black American Literature and Culture of the Modern Language Association. The magazine received American Literary Magazine Awards in 1994 and 1995.

Needs: Ethnic/Multicultural: experimental, feminist, literary, mainstream/contemporary. "No children's/juvenile/young adult/teen." Receives 50 unsolicited mss/month. Accepts 40 mss/year. Publishes ms 1 year after acceptance. Agented fiction 10%. Published work by Clarence Major, Ann Allen Shockley, Ishmael Reed. Length: 3,000 words average. Also publishes literary essays, literary criticism, poetry. Sometimes critiques or comments on rejected mss.

How to Contact: Send complete ms with a cover letter. Reports in 2 weeks on queries; 3 months on mss. Send SASE for reply, return of ms or send a disposable copy of ms. Sample copy for $6. Fiction guidelines for #10 SASE. Reviews novels and short story collections. Send books to Keneth Kinnamon, Dept. of English, Univ. of Arkansas, Fayetteville, AR 72701.

Payment/Terms: Pays $25-100 and 10 contributor's copies on publication for first North American serial rights. Sends galleys to author.

☑ $☑ ☑ AGNI, Creative Writing Program, Boston University, 236 Bay State Rd., Boston MA 02215. (617)353-7135. Fax: (617)353-7136. E-mail: agni@bu.edu. Website: www.webdelsol.com/AGNI (includes names of editors, short fiction, poetry and interviews with authors). **Editor-in-Chief:** Askold Melnyczuk. Magazine: 5½×8½; 320 pages; 55 lb. booktext paper; recycled cover stock; occasional art portfolios. "Eclectic literary magazine publishing first-rate poems and stories." Biannually. Estab. 1972.

● Work from *Agni* has been selected regularly for inclusion in both *Pushcart Prize* and *Best American Short Stories* anthologies. "We tend to be backlogged with fiction. We will not be accepting unsolicited submissions until Fall 2000."

Needs: Stories, excerpted novels, prose poems and translations. No science fiction or romance. Receives more than 250 unsolicited fiction mss/month. Accepts 4-7 mss/issue, 8-12 mss/year. Reading period October 1 through April 30 only. No reading period 1999 to 2000. Recently published work by Adrienne Rich, Seamus Heaney,

READ THE BUSINESS OF FICTION WRITING section for information on manuscript preparation, mailing tips, rights and more.

Robert Pinsky, Frederick Basch and Thom Kennedy. **Publishes 3-4 new writers/year.** Never critiques rejected mss.

How to Contact: Send complete ms with SASE and cover letter listing previous publications. Simultaneous and electronic (disk) submissions OK. Reports in up to 5 months. Sample copy for $9.

Payment/Terms: Pays $10/page up to $150; 2 contributor's copies; one-year subscription. Pays on publication for first North American serial rights. Sends galleys to author. Copyright reverts to author upon publication.

Advice: "Read *Agni* carefully to understand the kinds of stories we publish. Read—everything, classics, literary journals, bestsellers. People need to read and subscribe to the magazines before sending their work. It's important for artists to support the arts."

$◻ THE AGUILAR EXPRESSION, 1329 Gilmore Ave., Donora PA 15033. (724)379-8019. **Editor:** Xavier F. Aguilar. Magazine: 8½×11; 10-16 pages; 20 lb. bond paper; illustrations. "We are open to all writers of a general theme—something that may appeal to everyone." Semiannually. Estab. 1989. Circ. 150.

• The editor is particularly interested in stories about the homeless in the U.S. but publishes fiction on other topics as well.

Needs: Adventure, ethnic/multicultural, experimental, horror, mainstream/contemporary, mystery/suspense (romantic suspense), romance (contemporary). No religious or first-person stories. Want more current social issues. Will publish annual special fiction issue or anthology in the future. Receives 10 unsolicited mss/month. Accepts 1-2 mss/issue; 2-4 mss/year. Publishes ms 1 month to 1 year after acceptance. Published work by Michael D. Cohen, R.G. Cantalupo and Kent Braithwaite. **Publishes 90% new writers.** Length: 1,000 words average; 750 words minimum; 1,500 words maximum. Also publishes poetry.

How to Contact: Send complete ms with cover letter. Reports on queries in 1 week; mss in 1 month. Send SASE for reply to a query or send a disposable copy of ms. No simultaneous submissions. Sample copy for $6. Fiction guidelines for #10 SASE.

Payment/Terms: Pays $10 and 1 contributor's copy for lead story; additional copies at a reduced rate of $3. Acquires one-time rights. Not copyrighted. Write to publication for details on contests, awards or grants.

Advice: "Clean, clear copy makes a manuscript stand out."

$◻ ▨ ALASKA QUARTERLY REVIEW, University of Alaska—Anchorage, 3211 Providence Dr., Anchorage AK 99508. (907)786-6916. E-mail: ayaqr@uaa.alaska.edu. Website: www.uaa.alaska.edu/aqr. **Fiction Editor:** Ronald Spatz. Magazine: 6×9; 260 pages; 60 lb. Glatfelter paper; 10 pt. C15 black ink varnish cover stock; photos on cover only. *AQR* "publishes fiction, poetry, literary nonfiction and short plays in traditional and experimental styles." Semiannually. Estab. 1982. Circ. 2,200.

• Work appearing in the *Alaska Quarterly Review* has been selected for the *Prize Stories: The O. Henry Awards*, *Best American Essays*, *Best American Poetry*, *Beacon Best* and *Pushcart Prize* anthologies. *The Washington Post* calls the *Alaska Quarterly Review*, "one of the nation's best literary magazines."

Needs: Contemporary, experimental, literary, prose poem, translations. Receives 200 unsolicited fiction mss/ month. Accepts 7-13 mss/issue, 15-24 mss/year. Does not read mss May 15 through August 15. Length: not exceeding 90 pages. Recently published work by Richard Ford, William H. Gass, Patricia Hampl, Stuart Dybek, Alan Lightman and Hayden Carruth. **Published 4 new writers within the last year.** Publishes short shorts.

How to Contact: Send complete mss with SASE. Accepts queries by e-mail. Simultaneous submissions "undesirable, but will accept if indicated." Reports in 2-3 months "but during peak periods a reply may take up to 6 months." Publishes ms 6 months to 1 year after acceptance. Sample copy for $5.

Payment/Terms: Pays 1 contributor's copy and a year's subscription. Pays $50-200 honorarium when grant funding permits. Acquires first rights.

Advice: "We have made a significant investment in fiction. The reason is quality; serious fiction *needs* a market. Try to have everything build to a singleness of effect."

◎ ALLEGHENY REVIEW, Box 32, Allegheny College, Meadville PA 16335. (814)332-6553. E-mail: review @alleg.edu. Website: www.alleg.edu/StudentLife/Organizations/AllegReview (includes writer's guidelines, ordering information, information about the editors and the prize winning poem and short story of the previous issue). Editors: Amy Augustyn, Jason Ramsey. Poetry Editor: Beth Hunter. Magazine: 8×5; 82 pages; white paper; illustrations and photos. "The *Allegheny Review* provides a national forum for undergraduate fiction writing. We accept all genres of fiction. Our intended audience is college students, professors and interested readers." Annually. Estab. 1983. Circ. 500.

Needs: Adventure, ethnic/multicultural, experimental, fantasy, feminist, gay, historical (general), horror, humor/ satire, lesbian, literary, mainstream/contemporary, mystery/suspense, psychic/supernatural/occult, regional, religious/inspirational, science fiction (soft/sociological), westerns. Receives 40 unsolicited mss/month. Buys 7 mss/ issue; 7 mss/year. Does not read mss May-August. Publishes ms 2 months after deadline. Published work by David Bernardy and Ander S. Monson. **Publishes 2-3 new writers/year.** Length: 2,000 words average; 3,000 words maximum. Publishes short shorts. Also publishes poetry.

How to Contact: *Open to work by undergraduate writers only.* Sometimes critiques or comments on rejected ms. Send complete ms with a cover letter. Should include 1 page bio. SASE for reply. Sample copy for $5.

Payment/Terms: Pays free subscription and 1 contributor's copy; additional copies for $4.

Advice: "The story told matters less than the telling. We have no preconceptions of what is publishable or not. Don't moralize. Tell your story and rely on the reader to interpret your work in their own way. The best writing has many interpretations."

★ ⬚ ◎ ⊻ **ALPHA BEAT PRESS**, 31 Waterloo St., New Hope PA 18938. (215)862-0299. **Editor:** Dave Christy. Magazine: 7½×9; 95-125 pages; illustrations. "Beat and modern literature—prose, reviews and poetry." Semiannually. Estab. 1987. Circ. 600.

• Work from *Alpha Beat Press* has appeared in *Pushcart Prize* anthologies. *Alpha Beat Press* also publishes poetry chapbooks and supplements. The magazine is known for writings associated with modern and beat culture. Also see listing for *Bouillabaisse* by same editor.

Needs: Erotica, experimental, literary and prose poem. No religious. Recently published work by Joseph Verrilli, John Gallo, t.k. splake and Laurence Lasky. **Publishes 25% new writers.** Length: 600 words minimum; 1,000 words maximum. Also publishes literary essays, literary criticism, poetry.

How to Contact: Query first. Reports on queries within 2 weeks. SASE. Simultaneous and reprint submissions OK. Sample copy for $10. Reviews novels and short story collections.

Payment/Terms: Pays in contributor's copies. Rights remain with author.

Advice: "*ABP* is the finest journal of its kind available today, having, with 20 issues, published the widest range of published and unpublished writers you'll find in the small press scene."

Ⓝ ♡ **THE ALSOP REVIEW**. E-mail: jwasserman@alsopreview.com. Website: www.alsopreview.com. **Managing Editor:** Jamie Wasserman. "*The Alsop Review* publishes only the best poetry and fiction. We are not a zine since we do not publish regular issues, rather we are a permanent showcase."

Needs: Literary, experimental. "No genre work or humor for its own sake. No pornography." Would like to see more "experimental and unconventional works. Surprise me." Recently published work by Kyle Jarrard, Dennis Must, Kristy Nielsen, Steve Watkins and Linda Sue Park. Length: no restriction.

How to Contact: Submit via e-mail only.

Payment/Terms: "None. We offer a permanent 'home' on the Web for writers and will pull and add material to their pages upon request. We accept previously published work."

Advice: "Read, read, read. Treat submissions to Web zines as carefully as you would to a print magazine. Research the market first. For every great Web zine, there are a hundred mediocre ones. Remember that once your work is on the Web, chances are it will be there for a very long time. Put your best stuff out there are take advantage of opportunities to re-publish work from print magazines."

🌐 ★ $ ◙ **AMBIT, Poetry/Art/Short Fiction**, 17 Priory Gardens, London, N6 5QY, United Kingdom. Phone: 0181 3403566. Website: www.AMBIT.CO.UK (includes writer's guidelines, names of editors, short fiction, subscription info). Editor: Martin Bax. **Fiction Editors:** Geoff Nicholson, J.G. Ballard. Magazine: 240cm×170cm; 100 pages; removable cover; illustrations and photos. Publishes "avant-garde material; short stories only, no novels." Quarterly. Estab. 1959. Circ. 3,000.

Needs: Erotica, ethnic/multicultural, experimental, contemporary, translations. No fantasy/horror/science fiction. No genre fiction. Receives 80 unsolicited mss/month. Accepts 5 mss/issue; 20 mss/year. Publishes ms up to 1 year after acceptance. Agented fiction under 1%. Recently published works by Scott Nicholson, E.A. Marckham and Heather Reyes. **Publishes 10 new fiction writers/year.** Length: 3,000 words average; 1,000 words minimum, 5,000 words maximum. Also publishes poetry.

How to Contact: Send 1-2 stories. Reports in 3 months. "No crits given." Send SASE with UK stamps or IRCs for reply, return of ms. Sample copy for $16. Fiction guidelines free.

Payment/Terms: Pays approx. £5/printed page and 2 contributor's copies on publication; additional copies $12. Acknowledgment if reprinted. Not copyrighted.

Advice: Chooses a ms for publication "if it involves you straight away—if it makes you ask questions of it and look for answers. Know how to edit your own work and remember your readers are not patient and do not know you."

★ $ ◙ ⊻ **AMELIA**, 329 E St., Bakersfield CA 93304. (805)323-4064. **Editor-in-Chief:** Frederick A. Raborg, Jr. Magazine: 5½×8½; 124-136 pages; perfect-bound; 60 lb. high-quality moistrite matte paper; kromekote cover; four-color covers; original illustrations; b&w photos. "A general review using fine fiction, poetry, criticism, belles lettres, one-act plays, fine pen-and-ink sketches and line drawings, sophisticated cartoons, book reviews and translations of both fiction and poetry for general readers with eclectic tastes for quality writing." Quarterly. Plans special fiction issue each July. Estab. 1984. Circ. 1,750.

• *Amelia* sponsors a long list of fiction awards. It ranked #18 on *Writer's Digest*'s Fiction 50 list of top markets for fiction writers.

Needs: Adventure, contemporary, erotica, ethnic, experimental, fantasy, feminist, gay, historical, humor/satire, lesbian, literary, mainstream, mystery/suspense, prose poem, regional, science fiction, senior citizen/retirement, sports, translations, western. Nothing "obviously pornographic or patently religious." Receives 160-180 unsolicited mss/month. Accepts up to 9 mss/issue; 25-36 mss/year. Published work by Michael Bugeja, Jack Curtis, Thomas F. Wilson, Maxine Kumin, Eugene Dubnov, Matt Mulhern and Merrill Joan Gerber. **Published new**

writers within the last year. Length: 3,000 words average; 1,000 words minimum; 5,000 words maximum. Usually critiques rejected mss.

How to Contact: Send complete ms with cover letter with previous credits if applicable to *Amelia* and perhaps a brief personal comment to show personality and experience. Reports in 1 week on queries; 2 weeks to 3 months on mss. SASE. Sample copy for $9.95. Fiction guidelines for #10 SASE. Sends galleys to author "when deadline permits."

Payment/Terms: Pays $35-50 on acceptance for first North American serial rights plus 2 contributor's copies; extras with 20% discount.

Advice: "Write carefully and well, but have a strong story to relate. I look for depth of plot and uniqueness, and strong characterization. Study manuscript mechanics and submission procedures. Neatness does count. There is a sameness—a cloning process—among most magazines today that tends to dull the senses. Magazines like *Amelia* will awaken those senses while offering stories and poems of lasting value."

AMERICAN LITERARY REVIEW, University of North Texas, P.O. Box 311307, Denton TX 76203-1307. (940)565-2755. Website: www.engl.unt.edu/alr/ (includes short fiction, essays, poetry, subscription information, writer's guidelines, contest details). **Editor:** Lee Martin. Magazine: 7×10; 128 pages; 70 lb. Mohawk paper; 67 lb. Wausau Vellum cover. "Publishes quality, contemporary poems and stories." Semiannually. Estab. 1990. Circ. 900.

Needs: Mainstream and literary only. No genre works. Receives 50-75 unsolicited fiction mss/month. Accepts 4-8 mss/issue; 8-16 mss/year. Reading period: September 1-May 1. Publishes ms within 2 years after acceptance. Published work by Jason Brown, Lex Williford, Lucy Ferriss and Mark Jacobs. Length: less than 7,500 words. Critiques or comments on rejected mss when possible. Also accepts poetry and essays.

How to Contact: Send complete ms with cover letter. Accepts queries/mss by fax. Reports in 2-3 months. SASE. Simultaneous submissions OK. Sample copy for $8. Fiction guidelines free.

Payment/Terms: Pays in contributor's copies. Acquires one-time rights.

Advice: "We like to see stories that illuminate the various layers of characters and their situations with great artistry. Give us distinctive character-driven stories that explore the complexities of human existance." Looks for "the small moments that contain more than at first appears possible, that surprise us with more truth than we thought we had a right to expect."

AMERICAN WRITING; A Magazine, Nierika Editions, 4343 Manayunk Ave., Philadelphia PA 19128. **Editor:** Alexandra Grilikhes. Magazine: $8\frac{1}{2} \times 5\frac{1}{2}$; 96 pages; matte paper and cover stock; photos. "We publish new writing that takes risks with form, point of view, language, ways of perceiving. We are interested in the voice of the loner, the artist as shaman, the powers of intuition, exceptional work of all kinds." Semiannually. Estab. 1990. Circ. 2,500.

Needs: Contemporary, excerpted novel, ethnic/multicultural, experimental, feminist, gay, lesbian, literary, translations. "We're looking for more literary, experimental, contemporary writing—writing that drives you to write it." No mainstream, romance. Receives 350 unsolicited mss/month. Accepts 4-5 mss/issue; 25 mss/year. Does not read mss June, December, January. Publishes ms 6-12 months after acceptance. Agented fiction less than 1%. Recently published work by Cris Mazza, Hugh Fox, Myla Goldberg, Peter Constantine, Emil Draitser and Jim Janko. **Publishes 4-6 new writers/year.** Length: 3,500 words average; 5,000 words maximum. Publishes short shorts. Also publishes literary essays, personal essays, literary criticism, poetry. Critiques or comments on rejected mss "when there is time."

How to Contact: Send complete ms with a brief cover letter. Include brief bio and list of publications if applicable. "No full-length books. Send one ms at a time." Reports in 4 months. Send SASE for reply, return of ms or send a disposable copy of ms. Simultaneous submissions OK. Sample copy for $6; fiction guidelines for #10 SASE.

Payment/Terms: Pays 2 contributor's copies; additional copies at half price. Acquires first rights or one-time rights.

Advice: "We look for intensity, vision, imaginative use of language, freshness, craft, sophistication; stories that delve. Read not just current stuff, but the old masters—Dostoyevsky, Chekhov and Hesse. Learn about subtlty and depth. Reading helps you to know who you are as a writer, writing makes you more that person, if you're lucky. Read one or two issues of the magazine *carefully.*"

THE AMERICAS REVIEW, A Review of Hispanic Literature and Art of the USA, University of Washington, Romance Languages, Box 354360, Seattle WA 98195-4360. (206)543-4343. Fax: (206)543-2020. E-mail: lflores@u.washington.edu. **Editors:** Lauro Flores and Evangelina Vigil-Pinon. Magazine: $5\frac{1}{2} \times 8\frac{1}{2}$; 128 pages; illustrations and photographs. "*The Americas Review* publishes contemporary fiction written by U.S. Hispanics—Mexican Americans, Puerto Ricans, Cuban Americans, etc." Triannually. Estab. 1972.

Needs: Contemporary, ethnic, literary, women's, hispanic literature. No novels. Receives 12-15 fiction mss/ month. Accepts 2-3 mss/issue; 8-12 mss/year. Publishes mss 6 months to 1 year after acceptance. Published work by Nash Candelaria, Roberto Fernández, Sheila Ortiz Taylor, Omar Castañeda, Kathleen Alcala and Daniel Orozco. Length: 3,000-4,500 average number of words; 1,500 words minimum; 6,000 words maximum (30 pages maximum, double-spaced). Publishes short shorts. Sometimes critiques rejected mss.

How to Contact: "*You must subscribe upon submitting materials.*" Send complete ms. Reports in 3-4 months. SASE. No simultaneous submissions. Accepts electronic submissions via IBM compatible disk. Sample copy for $5; $10 double issue.

Payment/Terms: Pays $50-200; 2 contributor's copies on acceptance for first rights, and rights to 40% of fees if story is reprinted. Sponsors award for fiction writers.

Advice: "There has been a noticeable increase in quality in U.S. Hispanic literature."

THE AMETHYST REVIEW, Marcasite Press, 23 Riverside Ave., Truro, Nova Scotia B2N 4G2 Canada. (902)895-1345. E-mail: amethyst@col.auracom.com. Website: www.col.auracom.com/~amethyst (includes writer's guidelines, names of editors, fiction excerpts, subscription info, contest guidelines, Editor's Picks and suggested reading). **Editors:** Penny Ferguson and Lenora Steele. Magazine: $8\frac{1}{4} \times 6\frac{3}{4}$; 84 pages; book weight paper; card stock cover; illustrations. "We publish quality contemporary fiction and poetry of interest to the literary reader." Semiannually. Estab. 1993. Circ. 150-200.

● *The Amethyst Review* has received grants from the Nova Scotia Department of Education and Culture.

Needs: Literary. Receives 25 unsolicited mss/month. Accepts 2-3 mss/issue; 4-6 mss/year. Publishes ms maximum 6 months after acceptance, "usually much sooner." Recently published work by Dana P. Tierney, Kath MacLean, Marilyn Grear Pilling, Eve Mills Nash, Joan Touenati, Laura Best, A.S. Penne and J.J. Steinfeld. **Publishes 50% new writers.** Length: 5,000 words maximum. Publishes short shorts. Also publishes poetry. Sponsors contest; send SASE for information.

How to Contact: Send complete ms with cover letter. Include estimated word count, a 50-word bio and list of publications. Reports in 2-28 weeks on mss. Send SASE or SAE and IRCs for reply, return of mss or send a disposable copy of ms. Sample copy for $6 (current) or $4 (back issues). Fiction guidelines for SASE or SAE and IRCs. "Please do not send American stamps! We are no longer replying to submissions without adequate return postage." Reviews novels and short story collections "only by people we have published."

Payment/Terms: Pays 1 contributor's copy; additional copies $6. Pays on publication. Acquires first North American serial rights.

Advice: "For us, a story must be memorable because it touches the reader's heart or imagination. Quality is our criterion. Try to delight us with originality and craft. Send for guidelines and sample. We don't look for a specific type of story. We publish the *best* of what we receive. We are seeking literary quality and accessibility. A story that stands out gives the reader a 'tingle' and stays in your mind for days to come. Pay attention to detail, don't be sloppy. Care about your subjects because if you don't neither will the reader. Dazzle us with quality instead of trying to shock us!"

THE AMHERST REVIEW, Box 2172, Amherst College, Amherst MA 01002. (413)542-2000. E-mail: review@amherst.edu. **Editor:** Steven Lee. Magazine: $7\frac{1}{2} \times 8\frac{1}{2}$; 60-70 pages; illustrations and photographs. "We are a college literary magazine publishing work by students, faculty and professionals. We seek submissions of poetry, fiction, and essay for the college community." Annually.

Needs: Adventure, confession, contemporary, ethnic, experimental, feminist, gay, historical (general), horror, humor/satire, lesbian, mainstream, prose poem, regional, romance, mystery/suspense, science fiction, translations, western. Wants more postmodernist, regional, historical and science. Receives 10-20 unsolicited mss/month. Does not read mss March-August. Recently published Deanne Bayer, Jene Beardsley, Diane Locke, Ze'ev Aviezer, Halcyon Marcuso and Kathleen Spivak. **Publishes 5 new writers/year.** Length: 4,500 words; 7,200 words maximum.

How to Contact: Send complete ms with cover letter and SASE. Reports in 4 months on mss. Sample copy for $6.

Payment/Terms: Pays 1 contributor's copy; $6 charge for extras. Acquires first rights.

Advice: We have "no set criteria. Writing with a quiet but firm voice behind it often stands out."

AMNESIA, P.O. Box 661441, Los Angeles CA 90066. **Editor:** Monica Rex. Magazine: 8×11; 50 pages; illustrations and photos. "*Amnesia* is an experimental arts magazine: literary, visual, performance, mail art. Intended audience: the adventurous. Amnesia is involved with a global network of artists and writers—we attempt to present the best and most adventurous of what we receive." Published "as possible." Estab. 1989. Circ. 500.

Needs: All themes/categories considered; short fiction. Legible mss in 8×11 format (for duplication in b&w or color); presented as received. Submissions cannot be returned. Length: 5,000 words maximum. Accepts 2 mss/year. **Publishes 5-10 new writers/year.** Recently published work by Robin Carr, Magdalena Rey, Astriana Zarot and D-APHID. Length: 5,000 words maximum. Publishes short shorts. Also publishes literary essays, literary criticism, poetry.

How to Contact: Send complete ms with a cover letter. Include bio (100 words maximum). Send disposable copy of ms. Simultaneous and reprint submissions OK. Sample copy for $5, 9×12 SASE. Reviews novels, short story collections and nonfiction books of interest to writers. Send books to editor.

Payment/Terms: Pays 2 contributor's copies. Acquires rights per issue and additional printing of same issue.

Advice: "*Amnesia* approaches each issue as a collage of the best available work and is unique each time it comes together. It is approached as an art object itself, for careful presentation of artists. Look for a unique artistic voice, good use of skills and legible presentation. Be yourself, drop conventions. The commercial fiction market has the ability to promote its artists, but it also homogenizes what is available to read. We provide a place for those that want to push the envelope creatively."

☑ $ ▨ ◎ ♟ **ANTIETAM REVIEW**, Washington County Arts Council, 41 S. Potomac St., Hagerstown MD 21740. Phone/fax: (301)791-3132. Editor: Ethan Fischer. **Fiction Editors:** Susanne Kass and Ann Knox. Magazine: 8½×11; 54-68 pages; glossy paper; light card cover; photos. A literary journal of short fiction, poetry and black-and-white photographs. "Our audience is primarily in the six state region. Urban, suburban and rural writers and readers, but copies are purchased nationwide, both by libraries as well as individuals. Sales and submissions increase yearly." Annually. Estab. 1982. Circ. 1,800.

> • *Antietam Review* has received several awards including First-runner Up (1993-94) for Editorial Content from the American Literary Magazine Awards. Work published in the magazine has been included in the *Pushcart Prize* anthology and *Best American Short Stories.* The magazine also received a grant from the Maryland State Arts Council and Washington County Arts Council.

Needs: Condensed/excerpted novel, contemporary, ethnic, experimental, feminist, literary and prose poem. Wants more contemporary, ethnic, experimental. "We read manuscripts from our region only—Delaware, Maryland, Pennsylvania, Virginia, West Virginia and Washington D.C. only. We read from September 1 through February 1." No horror, romance, inspirational, pornography. Receives about 100 unsolicited mss/month. Buys 8-10 stories/year. Publishes ms 2-3 months after acceptance. Recently published work by Marc Bookman, Tom Glenn, Richard Plan, Shirley G. Cochran, Judy Wilson and Jamie Holland. **Publishes 2-3 new writers/year.** Length: 3,000 words average. Also publishes poetry.

How to Contact: "Send ms and SASE with a cover letter. Let us know if you have published before and where." Accepts queries by e-mail. Include estimated word count, 1-paragraph bio and list of publications. Reports in 2-4 months. "If we hold a story, we let the writer know. Occasionally we critique returned ms or ask for rewrites." Sample copy for $5.25. Back issue $3.15. Guidelines for legal SAE.

Payment/Terms: "We believe it is a matter of dignity that writers and poets be paid. We have been able to give $50-100 a story and $25 a poem, but this depends on funding. Also 2 copies." Buys first North American serial rights. Sends galleys to author if requested.

Advice: "We seek high quality, well-crafted work with significant character development and shift. We seek no specific theme. We look for work that is interesting involves the reader, and teaches us a new way to view the world. A manuscript stands out because of its energy and flow. Most of our submissions reflect the times (i.e. the news, current events) more than industry trends. We also seek a compelling voice, originality, magic. We now require *accepted* stories to be put on disk by the author to cut down on printing costs. We are seeing an increase of first person narrative stories."

▨ $ ▨ **THE ANTIGONISH REVIEW**, St. Francis Xavier University, P.O. Box 5000, Antigonish, Nova Scotia B2G 2W5 Canada. (902)867-3962. Fax: (902)867-5563. E-mail: tar@stfx.ca. Website: www.antigonish. com/review/. **Editor:** George Sanderson. Literary magazine for educated and creative readers. Quarterly. Estab. 1970. Circ. 800.

Needs: Literary, contemporary, prose poem, translations. No erotic or political material. Accepts 6 mss/issue. Receives 50 unsolicited fiction mss each month. Published work by Arnold Bloch, Richard Butts and Helen Barolini. **Published new writers within the last year.** Length: 1,000-6,000 words. Sometimes comments briefly on rejected mss.

How to Contact: Send complete ms with cover letter. SASE ("U.S. postage not acceptable"). No simultaneous submissions. Electronic (disk compatible with WordPerfect/IBM and Windows or e-mail) submissions OK. Prefers hard copy with disk submission. Reports in 6 months. Publishes ms 3-8 months after acceptance. Sample copy $4. Guidelines free.

Payment/Terms: Pays $50 for stories. Authors retain copyright. Acquires first serial rights.

Advice: "Learn the fundamentals and do not deluge an editor."

$ ▨ **ANTIOCH REVIEW**, Box 148, Yellow Springs OH 45387-0148. (937)767-6389. Website: www.antioc h.edu/review (includes guidelines, awards, authors, titles and excerpts of current and upcoming issue, history of the Review, subscription info). **Editor:** Robert S. Fogarty. Associate Editor: Nolan Miller. Magazine: 6×9; 128 pages; 50 lb. book offset paper; coated cover stock; illustrations "seldom." "Literary and cultural review of contemporary issues in politics, American and international studies, and literature for general readership." Quarterly. Published special fiction issue last year; plans another. Estab. 1941. Circ. 5,100.

Needs: Literary, contemporary, experimental, translations. No children's, science fiction or popular market. Accepts 5-6 mss/issue, 20-24 mss/year. Receives approximately 275 unsolicited fiction mss each month. Approximately 1-2% of fiction agented. Recently published work by Gordon Lish, Jean Ross Justice, Peter LaSalle, Sylvia Foley, Josie Milliken, Teresa Svoboda, Joseph Caldwell, Richard Stern, Emily Cerf and Carolyn Osborn. **Published 1-2 new writers/year.** Length: generally under 8,000 words.

How to Contact: Send complete ms with SASE, preferably mailed flat. Reports in 2 months. Publishes ms 6-9 months after acceptance. Sample copy for $6. Guidelines for SASE.

Payment/Terms: Pays $10/page; 2 contributor's copies. $3.90 for extras. Pays on publication for first and one-time rights (rights returned to author on request).

Advice: "Our best advice, always, is to *read* the *Antioch Review* to see what type of material we publish. Quality fiction requires an engagement of the reader's intellectual interest supported by mature emotional relevance, written in a style that is rich and rewarding without being freaky. The great number of stories submitted to us indicates that fiction still has great appeal. We assume that if so many are writing fiction, many must be reading it."

N **⊙** **APOSTROPHE: University of South Carolina Beaufort Journal of the Arts**, 801 Carteret St., Beaufort SC 29902. (843)521-4158. Fax: (843)522-9733. E-mail: sjtombe@gwm.sc.edu. Editor: Sheila Tombe. **Fiction Editor:** Ellen Malphrus. Magazine: 8×5; 70 pages. Annually. Estab. 1996. Circ. 250-300.
Needs: Literary. Does not want anything "poorly written" or "in bad taste." Receives 3 unsolicited mss/month. Accepts 3-4 mss/issue; 3-4 mss/year. Does not read mss "during semester." Publishes ms 1-2 months after acceptance. **Publishes 2 new writers/year.** Publishes short shorts. Also publishes literary essays, literary criticism, poetry. Sometimes critiques or comments on rejected mss.
How to Contact: Send complete ms with a cover letter. Include short bio. Reports in 2 weeks on queries; 8-10 months on mss. Send SASE for reply, return of ms or send a disposable copy of ms. Simultaneous submissions and reprints OK. Sample copy for $3, 8×5 SAE and 2 first-class stamps. Fiction guidelines free for letter-size SASE.
Payment/Terms: Pays 2 contributor's copies; additional copies $5. Pays on publication. Acquires one-time rights. Not copyrighted.
Advice: Looks for "excellent prose style; nothing trite or clichéd; nothing 'crafted' à la college fiction writing course. Don't be afraid to ignore your writing instructors, when appropriate."

✓ **⊙** **APPALACHIAN HERITAGE**, Hutchins Library, Berea College, Berea KY 40404. (606)986-9341. Fax: (606)986-9494. E-mail: sidney-farr@berea.edu. **Editor:** James E. Gage. Magazine: 6×9; 80 pages; 60 lb. stock; 10 pt. Warrenflo cover; drawings and b&w photos. "*Appalachian Heritage* is a southern Appalachian literary magazine. We try to keep a balance of fiction, poetry, essays, scholarly works, etc., for a general audience and/or those interested in the Appalachian mountains." Quarterly. Estab. 1973. Circ. approximately 600.
Needs: Regional, literary, historical. "We do not want to see fiction that has no ties to Southern Appalachia." Receives 6-8 unsolicited mss/month. Accepts 2-3 mss/issue; 12-15 mss/year. Publishes ms 1-2 years after acceptance. Published work by Bettie Sellers, Robert Morgan, James Still and Wilma Dykeman. **Published new writers within the last year.** Length: 3,000 words maximum. Publishes short shorts. Length: 500 words. Occasionally critiques rejected mss.
How to Contact: Send complete ms with cover letter. Include estimated word count, 2-3-sentence bio and list of publications. Reports in 3-4 weeks on queries; 4-6 weeks on mss. Send SASE for reply, return of ms or send a disposable copy of ms. Simultaneous and electronic submissions OK. Sample copy for $6. Guidelines free.
Payment/Terms: Pays 3 contributor's copies; $6 charge for extras. Acquires first North American serial rights.
Advice: "Get acquainted with *Appalachian Heritage*, as you should with any publication before submitting your work."

N **🌐** **AQUARIUS**, Flat 4, Room-B, 116 Sutherland Ave., Maida-Vale, London W92QP England. Phone: 0171-289-4338. **Editor:** Eddie Linden. Semiannual. Estab. 1969. Circ. 3,000. Publishes 5 stories/issue. Interested in humor/satire, literary, prose poem and serialized/excerpted novels. "We publish prose and poetry and reviews." Receives 1,000 unsolicited mss/month. Length: 1,000 words minimum. Payment is by agreement. "We only suggest changes. Most stories are taken on merit." Price in UK £5 plus postage and packing; in US $18 plus $3 postage. "We like writers who buy the magazine to get an idea of what we publish."

N **⊙** **◎** **ARBA SICULA**, St John's University, Jamaica NY 11439. Editor: Gaetano Cipolla. Magazine: 5½×8½; 85 pages; top-grade paper; good quality cover stock; illustrations; photos. Bilingual ethnic literary review (Sicilian-English) dedicated to the dissemination of Sicilian culture. Published twice a year. Plans special fiction issue. Estab. 1979. Circ. 2,500.
Needs: Accepts ethnic literary material consisting of various forms of folklore, stories both contemporary and classical, regional, romance (contemporary, historical, young adult) and senior citizen. Material submitted must be in the Sicilian language, with English translation desirable or in English on Sicilian topics. **Published new writers within the last year.** Critiques rejected mss when there is time. Sometimes recommends other markets.
How to Contact: Send complete ms with SASE and bio. Reports in 2 months. Publishes ms 1-3 years after acceptance. Simultaneous submissions and reprints OK. Sample copy for $8 with 8½×11 SASE and 90¢ postage.
Payment/Terms: 5 free author's copies. $4 for extra copies. Acquires all rights.
Advice: "This review is a must for those who nurture a love of the Sicilian language."

◒ **▣** **ARCHIPELAGO, An International Journal On-Line of Literature, Art and Opinion**, Box 2485, Charlottesville VA 22902-2485. (804)979-5292. E-mail: editor@archipelago.org. Website: www.archipelago.org. **Editor:** Katherine McNamara. Electronic magazine: 50-60 pages in download (print) edition, available from website. "Literary (print-based, in spirit) work, meaning well-formed, fine writing, on diverse subjects and in various genres with an international tone. Readership is educated, well-read, international." Quarterly. Estab. 1997. Circ. 23 countries, 6,000 hits/month.

Needs: Literary. "No academic, self-involved, 'hip' fiction." Receives several unsolicited mss/month. Accepts 1 ms/issue. Does not read mss in the month before publication. Usually publishes ms in next issue after acceptance. Recently published work by Benjamin Cheever and Anna Maria Ortese. Publishes short shorts. Also publishes literary essays, literary criticism, poetry. Sometimes critiques or comments on rejected ms if requested.

How to Contact: Query first. Accepts queries by e-mail. Include brief bio. Reports in 1 month on queries; 2 months on mss. Send SASE for reply, return of ms. Simultaneous and reprint submissions OK. Reviews novels, short story collections and nonfiction books of interest to writers.

Payment/Terms: No payment. Acquires first rights and first electronic rights. Sends galleys to author. Copyright reverts to author on publication.

Advice: "We look for superb writing; engaged, adult imagination. As big publishing becomes more and more part of the entertainment industry, I look for writers deeply read, thoughtful, uncontaminated by pop culture and commercial plot-lines."

✅ 🅞 **ARKANSAS REVIEW, A Journal of Delta Studies**, Department of English and Philosophy, P.O. Box 1890, Arkansas State University, State University AR 72467-1890. (501)972-3043. Fax: (501)972-2795. E-mail: delta@toltec.astate.com. Website: www.clt.astate.edu/arkreview (includes guidelines, names of editors, ordering information, tables of contents). Editor: William C. Clements. **Fiction Editor:** Norman Stafford. Magazine: 8¼ × 11; 64-100 pages; coated, matte paper; matte, 4-color cover stock; illustrations and photos. Publishes articles, fiction, poetry, essays, interviews, reviews, visual art evocative of or responsive to the Mississippi River Delta. Triannually. Estab. 1996. Circ. 700.

Needs: Regional short stories, literary essays, literary criticism. "No genre fiction. Must have a Delta focus." Receives 30-50 unsolicited mss/month. Accepts 2-3 mss/issue; 5-7 mss/year. Publishes ms 6-12 months after acceptance. Agented fiction 1%. Recently published work by Chalana Oueles, Deborah Elliott Deutschmann, Mark Sindecuse and Craig Black. **Publishes 3-4 new writers/year.** Also publishes literary essays and poetry. Always critiques or comments on rejected mss.

How to Contact: Send complete ms with cover letter. Accepts queries/mss by e-mail and fax. Include bio. Reports in 1 week on queries; 4 months on mss. Send SASE for reply, return of ms or send a disposable copy of ms. Sample copy for $7.50. Fiction guidelines free for #10 SASE.

Payment/Terms: Pays 5 contributor's copies; additional copies for $5. Acquires first North American serial rights.

Advice: "We publish new writers in every issue. We look for distinguished, mature writing, surprises, a perfect ending and a story that means more than merely what went on in it. We don't like recognizable imitations of currently fashionable writers."

🅞 **THE ARMCHAIR AESTHETE**, Pickle Gas Press, 59 Vinal Ave., Rochester NY 14609. (716)342-6331. E-mail: bypaul@netacc.net. **Editor:** Paul Agosto. Magazine: 5½ × 8½; 40-65 pages; 20 lb. paper; 110 lb. card stock color cover. *The Armchair Aesthete* seeks quality writing that enlightens and entertains a thoughtful audience (ages 9-90) with a "good read." Quarterly. Estab. 1996. Circ. 100.

Needs: Adventure, fantasy (science fantasy, sword and sorcery), historical (general), horror, humor/satire, mainstream/contemporary, mystery/suspense (amateur sleuth, cozy, police procedural, private eye/hardboiled, romantic suspense), science fiction (soft/sociological), westerns (frontier, traditional). No racist, pornographic, advert gore or material intended for children. Plans to publish special fiction issue. Receives 50 unsolicited mss/month. Accepts 8-15 mss/issue; 32-60 mss/year. Publishes ms 3-9 months after acceptance. Agented fiction less than 5%. Recently published work by Don Stockard, Valerie W. Corderman, Joseph Segriff, C.B. Thatcher and Mikhammad Abdel-Ishara. **Publishes 4-6 new writers/year.** Length: 2,000 words average; 3,000 words maximum. Publishes short shorts. Also publishes poetry. Sometimes critiques or comments on rejected mss.

How to Contact: Send complete ms with a cover letter. Include estimated word count, 50-100 word bio and list of publications. Reports in 2-3 weeks on queries; 1-3 months on mss. Send SASE for reply, return of ms or send a disposable copy of ms. Simultaneous submissions, reprints and electronic submissions OK. Sample copy for $3 and 2 first-class stamps. Fiction guidelines free for #10 SASE. Reviews novels and short story collections.

Payment/Terms: Pays 1 contributor's copy on publication; additional copies for $3. Acquires one-time rights. Accepted works are automatically eligible for an annual contest.

Advice: "Clever, compelling storytelling has a good chance here. We look for a clever plot, thought-out characters, something that surprises or catches us off guard. Write on innovative subjects and situations. Submissions should be professionally presented and technically sound."

✅ $🅞 **ARTFUL DODGE**, Dept. of English, College of Wooster, Wooster OH 44691. (330)263-2577. Website: www.wooster.edu/artfuldodge (includes writer's guidelines, editor's bios, interviews with authors, subscription information, history of the magazine). **Editor-in-Chief:** Daniel Bourne. Magazine: 150-200 pages; illustrations; photos. "There is no theme in this magazine, except literary power. We also have an ongoing interest in translations from Eastern Europe and elsewhere." Annually. Estab. 1979. Circ. 1,000.

Needs: Experimental, literary, prose poem, translations. "We judge by literary quality, not by genre. We are especially interested in fine English translations of significant contemporary prose writers. Translations should be submitted with original texts." Receives 40 unsolicited fiction mss/month. Accepts 5 mss/year. Published fiction by Edward Kleinschmidt, Terese Svoboda, David Surface, Leslie Pietrzyk and Zbigniew Herbert; and interviews with Tim O'Brien, Lee Smith, Michael Dorris and Stuart Dybek. **Published 1 new writer within the last year.** Length: 10,000 words maximum; 2,500 words average. Also publishes literary essays, literary criticism, poetry. Occasionally critiques rejected mss.

How to Contact: Send complete ms with SASE. Do not send more than 30 pages at a time. Reports in 1 week to 8 months. No simultaneous or reprint submissions. Sample copies are $5 for older issues; $7 for current issues. Fiction guidelines for #10 SASE.

Payment/Terms: Pays 2 contributor's copies and honorarium of $5/page. Acquires first North American serial rights.

Advice: "If we take time to offer criticism, do not subsequently flood us with other stories no better than the first. If starting out, get as many *good* readers as possible. Above all, read contemporary fiction and the magazine you are trying to publish in."

✓ ◑ ◎ **ASIAN PACIFIC AMERICAN JOURNAL**, The Asian American Writers' Workshop, 37 St. Marks Place, New York NY 10003-7801. (212)228-6718. Fax: (212)228-7718. E-mail: aaww@panix.com. Website: www.aaww.org. **Editors:** Hanya Yaragihara and Jerome Chou. Magazine: 5½ × 8½; 200 pages; illustrations. "We are interested in publishing works by writers from all segments of the Asian Pacific American community. The journal appeals to all interested in Asian-American literature and culture." Semiannually. Estab. 1992. Circ. 1,500.

● *Asian Pacific American Journal* received a NEA grant in 1995.

Needs: Condensed/excerpted novel, erotica, ethnic/multicultural, experimental, feminist, gay, historical (general), humor/satire, lesbian, literary, mainstream/contemporary, regional, serialized novel, translations, Asian-American themes. "We are interested in anything related to the Asian American community." Receives 75 unsolicited mss/month. Accepts 15 mss/issue; 30 mss/year. Publishes ms 4-6 months after acceptance. Agented fiction 5%. Recently published work by David Henry Hwang, Chitra Banerjee Divakarvni, Kimiko Hahn and Bino A. Realuyo. Length: 3,000 words average. Also publishes short shorts. Also publishes literary essays, poetry.

How to Contact: Send SASE for guidelines. Should include estimated word count, 3-5 sentence bio, list of publications. Reports in 1 month on queries; 4 months on mss. SASE for reply or send a disposable copy of ms. Simultaneous, reprint, electronic (disk, Macintosh or IBM, preferably Microsoft Word 5 for Mac) submissions OK. Sample copy for $10. Fiction guidelines for SASE.

Payment/Terms: Pays 2 contributor's copies; additional copies at 40% discount. Acquires one-time rights. Sponsors contests, awards or grants for fiction writers. "Send query with SASE."

Ⓝ ◑ **ATOM MIND**, Mother Road Publications, P.O. Box 22068, Albuquerque NM 87154. Editor: Gregory Smith. Magazine: 8½ × 11; 128 pages; 60 lb. paper; 80 lb. cover; illustrations and photos. "*Atom Mind* reflects the spirit of the 1960s; it is dedicated to the memory of Steinbeck, Hemingway, Kerouac, Bukowski et al." Quarterly. Estab. 1992. Circ. 1,000.

Needs: Condensed/excerpted novel, erotica, ethnic/multicultural, experimental, humor/satire, literary, mainstream/contemporary, serialized novel, translations. No juvenile, romance, science fiction or young adult/teen. Receives 200-300 unsolicited mss/month. Accepts 5-6 mss/issue; 20 mss/year. Publishes ms 1-2 years after acceptance. Published work by Michael Phillips, Al Masarik, Rick Kempa and Jerry Kamstra. Length: 1,000 words minimum; 6,000 words maximum. Also publishes literary essays, literary criticism, poetry. Sometimes critiques or comments on rejected mss.

How to Contact: Send complete ms with a cover letter. Include estimated word count. Reports in 2 weeks on queries; 1-2 months on mss. Send SASE for reply, return of ms or send a disposable copy of ms. Reprint submissions OK. Sample copy $6. Fiction guidelines free.

Payment/Terms: Pays in contributor's copies. Cash awards to "best of issue," (to subscribers only) as determined by the results of a random readers' poll. Acquires first North American serial rights.

Advice: "*Atom Mind* is very much a one-man operation and therefore subject to the whims and personal biases of the editor. I would like to see more satirical short fiction. Read at least one issue of any magazine you intend to submit to. Writers can save an immense amount of time and money by sending their work ONLY to those journals for which it is suitable—study the markets!"

Ⓝ **AXE FACTORY REVIEW**, P.O. Box 4069, Philadelphia PA 19107. **Editor:** Joseph Farley. Magazine: 8½ × 11 folded; 40-70 pages; 20 lb. stock paper; 30-40 lb. cover; illustrations and photos. "We like eclectic fiction. Basically, read an issue or two first. Editor publishes what he likes. The view from the top is a little off-center." Published "at least twice a year, sometimes more." Estab. 1986. Circ. 100.

Needs: Adventure, children's/juvenile (adventure, fantasy, historical), comics/graphic novels, erotica, ethnic/multicultural (general, Asian), experimental, fantasy (space fantasy, sword and sorcery, crossover), feminist, gay, historical (general), horror (dark fantasy, futuristic, psychological, supernatural, crossover), humor satire, lesbian, literary, mainstream, military/war, mystery/suspense (amateur sleuth, private eye/hardboiled), New Age, psychic/supernatural/occult, regional (Asian/Asia related), religious (inspirational, religious fantasy, religious mystery/

suspense, religious thriller), romance, science fiction (hard science/technological, soft/sociological, mixed genre), translations, western (crossover genre), young adult/teen (adventure, fantasy/science fiction, historical, horror), mixed genre, the bizarre, the new, the non-dull. "No reruns, repeats, duller than dishwasher water TV makeovers." Receives 1 unsolicited ms/month. Accepts 0-2 mss/issue; 0-5 mss/year. Recently published work by Ron Androla, Joseph Farley and Arthur Winfield Knight. Length: 1,000 words average; 500 words minimum; 9,000 words maximum. Publishes short shorts "only if they work as prose poems." Also publishes literary essays, literary criticism, poetry. Often critiques or comments on rejected mss.

How to Contact: "Read an issue at a library or send for a copy, or chance a manuscript in the mail. Include a cover letter describing why you write. What motivates you? What school/philosophy do you adhere to (if any) with relation to your writing? How does this reflect on the story?" Reports in 1 month. SASE for reply. Simultaneous submissions and reprints OK. Sample copy for $5, 8½ × 11 SAE and 5 first-class stamps or 3 IRCs. Reviews novels, short story collections and nonfiction books of interest to writers. "Send to the editor. Books will not be returned unless SASE is enclosed with proper postage."

Payment/Terms: Pays 1-2 contributor's copies; additional copies $8. "Free subscriptions are sometimes given—if we really like the work." Pays on publication. Acquires one-time rights and reserve rights to reprint in best of anthology.

Advice: "A good story can work on a number of levels. A story can be a prose poem at heart that bases its success on language and imagery over plot. It can be a teaching tool that edifies the reader and editor. Or, it can be a damned good yarn. Despite this, I still prefer things that are off the wall. Read our publication before submitting."

THE AZOREAN EXPRESS, Seven Buffaloes Press, Box 249, Big Timber MT 59011. **Editor:** Art Cuelho. Magazine: 6¾ × 8¼; 32 pages; 60 lb. book paper; 3-6 illustrations/issue; photos rarely. "My overall theme is rural; I also focus on working people (the sweating professions); the American Indian and Hobo; the Dustbowl era; and I am also trying to expand with non-rural material. For rural and library and professor/student, blue collar workers, etc." Semiannually. Estab. 1985. Circ. 600.

Needs: Contemporary, ethnic, experimental, humor/satire, literary, regional, western, rural, working people. Receives 10-20 unsolicited mss/month. Accepts 2-3 mss/issue; 4-6 mss/year. Publishes ms 1-6 months after acceptance. Length: 1,000-3,000 words. Also publishes short shorts, 500-1,000 words. "I take what I like; length sometimes does not matter, even when longer than usual. I'm flexible."

How to Contact: "Send cover letter with ms; general information, but it can be personal, more in line with the submitted story. Not long rambling letters." Reports in 1-4 weeks. SASE. Sample copy for $7.75 postpaid. Fiction guidelines for SASE.

Payment/Terms: Pays in contributor's copies. "Depends on the amount of support author gives my press." Acquires first North American serial rights. "If I decide to use material in anthology form later, I have that right." Sends galleys to the author upon request.

Advice: "There would not be magazines like mine if I was not optimistic. But literary optimism is a two-way street. Without young fiction writers supporting fiction magazines the future is bleak because the commercial magazines allow only formula or name writers within their pages. My own publications receive no grants. Sole support is from writers, libraries and individuals."

THE BALTIMORE REVIEW, Baltimore Writers' Alliance, P.O. Box 410, Riderwood MD 21139. (410)377-5265. Fax: (410)377-4325. E-mail: hdiehl@bcpl.net. Website: members.aol.com/baltopen/index.htm (includes guidelines, info about Baltimore Writers' Alliance and Writer's Forum). **Editor:** Barbara Diehl. Magazine: 6 × 9; 136 pages; 60 lb. paper; 10 pt. CS1 gloss film cover. Showcase for the best short stories and poetry by writers in the Baltimore area and beyond. Semiannually. Estab. 1996.

Needs: Ethnic/multicultural, experimental, literary, mainstream/contemporary. "Would like to see more well-written literary and somewhat traditional stories." No science fiction, westerns, children's, romance, etc. Accepts 8-12 mss/issue; 16-24 mss/year. Publishes ms 1-9 months after acceptance. Recently published work by Curt Leviant, Gary Wilson and Tom Glenn. **Publishes "at least a few" new writers/year.** Length: 3,000 words average; short shorts to 6,000 words maximum. Also publishes poetry.

How to Contact: Send complete ms with a cover letter. Include estimated word count, brief bio and list of publications. Reports in 1-3 months. Send SASE for reply, return of ms or send a disposable copy of ms. Simultaneous submissions OK. Sample copy for $8. Fiction guidelines free for #10 SASE. No e-mail or fax submissions.

Payment/Terms: Pays 2 contributor's copies on publication. Acquires first North American serial rights.

Advice: "We look for compelling stories and a masterful use of the English language. We want to feel that we have never heard this story, or this voice, before. Read the kinds of publications you want your work to appear in. Make your reader believe, and care."

BARBARIC YAWP, Bone World Publishing, 3700 County Rt. 24, Russell NY 13684. (315)347-2609. Editor: John Berbrich. **Fiction Editor:** Nancy Berbrich. Magazine: digest-size; 60 pages; 24 lb. paper; matte cover stock. "We are not preachers of any particular poetic or literary school. We publish any type of quality material appropriate for our intelligent and wide-awake audience." Quarterly. Estab. 1997. Circ. 100.

Needs: Adventure, experimental, fantasy (science, sword and sorcery), historical, horror, humor/satire, literary, mainstream/contemporary, psychic/supernatural/occult, regional, religious/inspirational, science fiction (hard, soft/sociological). Wants more humor, satire and adventure. "We don't want any pornography, gratuitous violence or hining." Receives 30-40 unsolicited mss/month. Accepts 10-12 mss/issue; 40-48 mss/year. Publishes ms within 6 months after acceptance. **Publishes 6-10 new writers/year.** Recently published work by Mark Spitzer, Errol Miller and David Flynn. Length: 600 words average; 1,000 words maximum. Publishes short shorts. Also publishes literary essays, literary criticism, poetry. Often critiques or comments on rejected mss.
How to Contact: Send complete ms with a cover letter. Include estimated word count, brief bio and list of publications. Reports in 2 weeks on queries; 1-4 months on mss. Send SASE for reply, return of ms or send a disposable copy of ms. Simultaneous submissions and reprints OK. Sample copy for $3. Fiction guidelines for #10 SASE.
Payment and Terms: Pays 1 contributor's copy; additional copies $3. Acquires one-time rights.
Advice: "We are primarily concerned with work that means something to the author, but which is able to transcend the personal into the larger world. Send whatever is important to you. We will use Yin and Yang. Work must hold my interest and be well-crafted. Read, read, read; write, write, write—then send us your best. Don't get discouraged. Believe in yourself. Take risks. Do not fear rejection."

THE BARCELONA REVIEW, Correu Vell 12 - 2, 08002 Barcelona, Spain. Phone/fax: (00) 34 93 319 15 96. E-mail: bar_rev@retemail.es. Website: www.barcelonareview.com. **Editor:** Jill Adams. "The *BR* is an international review of contemporary, cutting-edge fiction published in English and Spanish with some Catalan. Our aim is to bring both new and established writers to the attention of a larger audience."
• *The Barcelona Review* ranked #49 on Writer's Digest's Fiction 50 list of top markets for fiction writers.
Needs: Short fiction and drama. Length: 4,000 words maximum. Also publishes articles and essays, book and film reviews and author interviews. "Most, but not all of our fiction lies somewhere out of the mainstream. Our bias is towards potent and powerful cutting-edge material; given that general criteria we are open to all styles and techniques and all genres. No slice-of-life stories, vignettes, raw autobiography posing as fiction." Published 8 new writers in first year; "we would like to quadruple that figure for 1999." Published work by Irvine Welsh, Alan Warner, A.M. Homes, Douglas Coupland and Poppy Z. Brite.
How to Contact: Send submissions by e-mail as an attached file. Hard copies accepted via mail but cannot be returned.
Payment/Terms: "In lieu of pay we offer a highly professional Spanish translation to English-language writers and vice versa to Spanish writers."
Advice: "We're after original, potent and powerful writing with a '90s feel that is literarily sound. We'd like to see more risks being taken, more writing with imaginative distinction."

BATHTUB GIN, Pathwise Press, P.O. Box 2392, Bloomington IN 47402. (812)323-2985. E-mail: charter@bluemarble.net. Website: www.bluemarble.net/~charter/btgin.htm (includes guidelines, news, links and catalogue). **Editors:** Chris Harter, Tom Maxedon. Magazine: 8½×5½; 48-52 pages; recycled 20-lb. paper; 60-lb. card cover; illustrations and photos. "*Bathtub Gin* is looking for work that has some kick to it. We are very eclectic and publish a wide range of styles. Audience is anyone interested in new writing and art that is not being presented in larger magazines." Semiannually. Estab. 1997. Circ. 150.
Needs: Condensed/excerpted novel, experimental, gay, humor/satire, lesbian, literary. "No horror, science fiction, historical unless they go beyond the usual formula." Want more experimental fiction. Receives 20 unsolicited mss/month. Accepts 2-3 mss/issue. Does not read mss September 15-December 1 and March 15-July 1; "we publish in mid-October and mid-April." Recently published work by B.Z. Niditch, Hugh Fox and Leslie Woolf Hedley. **Publishes 50% new writers.** Length: 10 double-spaced pages maximum. Publishes short shorts. Also publishes literary essays, literary criticism, poetry. Often critiques or comments on rejected ms.
How to Contact: Send complete ms with a cover letter. Include estimated word count, 3-5 line bio. Accepts queries by e-mail. Reports in 1-2 months. Send SASE for reply, return of ms or send a disposable copy of ms. Simultaneous, reprint and electronic submissions (modem) OK. Sample copy for $6 with 6×9 SAE and 4 first-class stamps. Fiction guidelines for #10 SASE. Reviews novels and short story collections.
Payment/Terms: Pays 1 contributor's copy; discount on additional copies. Rights revert to author upon publication.
Advice: "We are looking for writing that contains strong imagery, is complex, and is willing to take a chance with form and structure. Query first and obtain a sample of a magazine to see what it is looking for and if you really want to be published there."

BAYBURY REVIEW, 40 High St., Highwood IL 60040. (847)433-6259. E-mail: baybury@flash.net. Editor: Janet St. John. **Fiction Editor:** Pamela Sourelis. Magazine: 5½×8½; 80-120 pages; glossy card cover, perfect-bound; b&w line art. "*Baybury Review* publishes quality fiction, poetry and nonfiction by emerging and established writers." Annually. Estab. 1997. Circ. 400.
Needs: Literary fiction. No erotica, horror or children's fiction. Wants more short shorts and non-linear narratives. Receives 800 mss/year. Accepts 3-4 mss/year. Recently published work by Curtis Smith, Greg Melaik and

Michael Cook. **Publishes 2-6 new writers/year.** Length: 5,000 words maximum. Publishes short shorts. Also publishes prose poetry and book reviews.

How to Contact: Open to unsolicited mss from June 1 through December 1 only. Accepts queries by e-mail. Send complete ms with SASE and optional cover letter. Reports in 3 months. Simultaneous submissions OK (please notify of acceptance elsewhere). Publishes ms up to 1 year after acceptance. Sample copy for $7.25.

Payment/Terms: Pays 2 contributor's copies. Acquires first North American serial rights.

Advice: "We are particularly interested in writers who explore the boundaries of conventional form. Read and look through many different literary journals. Find the best 'home' for your work—where it seems to fit best. We are somewhat discouraged by the fact that many money-making, established and grant-supported literary journals keep repeat publishing well-known writers when they could be supporting more unrecognized and talented writers. We are dedicated to publishing these lesser known writers."

BBR MAGAZINE, P.O. Box 625, Sheffield, S1 3GY, United Kingdom. E-mail: magazine@bbr-online.com. Website: www.bbr-online.com/magazine (includes names of editors, writer's guidelines and more). **Editor:** Chris Reed. Annually. Circ. 3,000. Publishes 20,000-30,000 words/issue.

Needs: "*Back Brain Recluse*, the award-winning British fiction magazine, actively seeks new fiction that ignores genre pigeonholes. We tread the thin line between experimental speculative fiction and avant-garde literary fiction." No genre fiction, or science fiction, fantasy or horror.

How to Contact: Enclose a SASE for the return of your manuscript if it is not accepted. Accepts queries by e-mail. "We are unable to reply to writers who do not send return postage. We recommend two IRCs plus disposable ms for non-UK submissions. One US$ is an acceptable (and cheaper!) alternative to IRCs. Please send all submissions to Chris Reed, BBR, P.O. Box 625, Sheffield S1 3GY, UK. We aim to reply to all submissions within 2 months, but sometimes circumstances beyond our control may cause us to take longer. Please enclose SAE if enquiring about a manuscript's status. No responsibility can be accepted for loss or damage to unsolicited material, howsoever caused."

Payment/Terms: "We are currently reading for issue #24, for which we will pay £10 ($15) per 1,000 words on publication. Familiarity with the magazine is strongly advised." Sample copy available in US for $10 from BBR, % Anne Marsden, 31192 Paseo Amapola, San Juan Capistrano CA 92675-2227. (Checks payable to Anne Marsden).

Tips: "Guidelines are not there for the editor's amusement. If you're serious about being published, pay attention to what the guidelines say."

$ **THE BELLINGHAM REVIEW**, Western Washington University, MS9053, Bellingham WA 98225. Website: www.wwu.edu/~bhreview (includes guidelines, poetry, fiction, nonfiction). **Editor:** Robin Hemley. Magazine: 5½×8; 120 pages; 60 lb. white paper; varied cover stock. "A literary magazine featuring original short stories, novel excerpts, essays, short plays and poetry of palpable quality." Semiannually. Estab. 1977. Circ. 1,500.

• The editors would like to see more humor and literary fiction.

Needs: All genres/subjects considered. Accepts 1-2 mss/issue. Does not read between May 2 and September 30. Publishes short shorts. Published work by Sharon Solwitz, Michael Martone, Lee Upton and Bret Lott. **Publishes 8-10 new writers/year.** Length: 10,000 words or less. Also publishes poetry.

How to Contact: Send complete ms. Reports in 3-6 months. Publishes ms an average of 6 months after acceptance. Sample copy for $5. Reviews novels and short story collections.

Payment/Terms: Pays 1 contributor's copy plus 2-issue subscription and $250. Charges $2.50 for extra copy. Acquires first North American serial and one-time rights.

Advice: "We look for work that is ambitious, vital, and challenging both to the spirit and the intellect. We hope to publish important works from around the world, works by older, neglected writers, and works by unheralded but talented new writers."

BELLOWING ARK, A Literary Tabloid, P.O. Box 45637, Seattle WA 98145. (206)440-0791. **Editor:** R.R. Ward. Tabloid: 11½×17½; 28 pages; electro-brite paper and cover stock; illustrations; photos. "We publish material which we feel addresses the human situation in an affirmative way. We do not publish academic fiction." Bimonthly. Estab. 1984. Circ. 500.

• Work from *Bellowing Ark* has appeared in the *Pushcart Prize* anthology. The editor says he's using much more short fiction and prefers positive, life-affirming work. Remember, he likes a traditional, narrative approach and "abhors" minimalist and post-modern work.

Needs: Contemporary, literary, mainstream, serialized/excerpted novel. "Anything we publish will be true." No science fiction or fantasy. Receives 600-800 unsolicited fiction mss/year. Accepts 2-3 mss/issue; 12-18 mss/year. Time varies, but publishes ms not longer than 6 months after acceptance. Recently published work by Dave Ross, James Bernhard, Ann Applegarth and Susan Montag. **Publishes 10-50 new writers/year.** Length: 3,000-5,000 words average ("but no length restriction"). Publishes short shorts. Also publishes literary essays, literary criticism, poetry. Sometimes critiques rejected mss.

How to Contact: No queries. Send complete ms with cover letter and short bio. "Prefer cover letters that tell something about the writer. Listing credits doesn't help." No simultaneous submissions. Reports in 6 weeks on mss. SASE. Sample copy for $3, 9×12 SAE and $1.21 postage.

Payment/Terms: Pays in contributor's copies. Acquires all rights, reverts on request.

Advice: "*Bellowing Ark* began as (and remains) an alternative to the despair and negativity of the Workshop/ Academic literary scene; we believe that life has meaning and is worth living—the work we publish reflects that belief. Learn how to tell a story before submitting. Avoid 'trick' endings—they have all been done before and better. *Bellowing Ark* is interested in publishing writers who will develop with the magazine, as in an extended community. We find *good* writers and stick with them. This is why the magazine has grown from 12 to 28 pages."

BELOIT FICTION JOURNAL, Box 11, Beloit College WI 53511. (608)363-2577. E-mail: darlingr@ beloit.edu. **Editor:** Clint McCown. Magazine: 6×9; 150 pages; 60 lb. paper; 10 pt. C1S cover stock; illustrations and photos on cover. "We are interested in publishing the best contemporary fiction and are open to all themes except those involving pornographic, religiously dogmatic or politically propagandistic representations. Our magazine is for general readership, though most of our readers will probably have a specific interest in literary magazines." Semiannually. Estab. 1985.

● Work first appearing in *Beloit Fiction Journal* has been reprinted in award-winning collections, including the *Flannery O'Connor* and the *Milkweed Fiction Prize* collections.

Needs: Contemporary, literary, mainstream, prose poem, spiritual and sports. Wants more experimental and short shorts. No pornography, religious dogma, science fiction, horror, political propaganda. Receives 400 unsolicited fiction mss/month. Accepts 8-10 mss/issue; 16-20 mss/year. Replies take longer in summer. Publishes ms within 9 months after acceptance. Published work by Rita Ciresi, David Evanier and Marisa Silver. **Publishes 3 new writers/year.** Length: 5,000 words average; 250 words minimum; 10,000 words maximum. Sometimes critiques rejected mss and recommends other markets.

How to Contact: Send complete ms with cover letter. Reports in 1 week on queries; 2-8 weeks on mss. SASE for ms. Simultaneous submissions OK if identified as such. Sample copy for $6. Fiction guidelines for #10 SASE.

Advice: "We're looking for a whizz-bang opening paragraph, interesting narrative line, compelling voice and unusual subject matter. Many of our contributors are writers whose work we have previously rejected. Don't let one rejection slip turn you away from our—or any—magazine."

BERKELEY FICTION REVIEW, 201 Heller-ASUC Publications Library, University of California, Berkeley CA 94720. (510)642-2892. E-mail: naners@uclink4.berkeley.edu. Website: www.OCF.Berkeley.EDU/~bfr/ (includes guidelines, contest info and short fiction). **Editors:** Elaine Wong and Alex Wedemeyer. Magazine: 5½×8½; 180 pages; perfect-bound; glossy cover; some b&w art; photographs. "The mission of *Berkeley Fiction Review* is to provide a forum for new and emerging writers as well as writers already established. We publish a wide variety of contemporary short fiction for a literary audience." Biannually. Estab. 1981. Circ. 1,000.

Needs: Contemporary/mainstream, literary, experimental. "Quality, inventive short fiction. No poetry or formula fiction." Receives 60 unsolicited mss/month. Accepts 10-20 mss/issue. Recently published work by Dewitt Henry, Wayne Harrison and G. Davis Jandrey. **Publishes work by 5-10 new writers/year.** Also publishes short shorts. Occasionally comments on rejected mss.

How to Contact: Send complete ms to "Editor" with very brief cover letter and SASE. Accepts queries by e-mail. Simultaneous submission OK. Usually reports in 3-4 months, longer in summer. Sample copy for $9.50. Guidelines for SASE.

Payment/Terms: Pays 1 contributor's copy. Acquires first rights. Sponsors short story contest with $100 first prize. Entry fee: $6. Send SASE for guidelines.

Advice: "Our criteria is fiction that resonates. Voices that are strong and move a reader. Clear, powerful prose (either voice or rendering of subject) with a point. Unique ways of telling stories—these capture the editors. Work hard, don't give up. Don't let your friends or family critique your work. Get someone honest to point out your writing weaknesses, and then work on them. Don't submit thinly veiled autobiographical stories—it's been done before—and better. With the proliferation of computers, everyone thinks they're a writer. Not true, unfortunately. The plus side though is ease of transmission and layout and the diversity and range of new work."

BIBLIOPHILOS, A Journal for Literati, Savants, Bibliophiles, Amantes Artium, and Those Who Love Animals, 200 Security Building, Fairmont WV 26554-2834. (304)366-8107. Fax: (304)366-8461. **Editor:** Gerald J. Bobango, Ph.D. Literary magazine: 5½×8; 64-72 pages; white glossy paper; illustrations and photos. Magazine "for literate persons who are academically and scholastically oriented, focused on the liberal arts, ⅓ fiction. Nonfiction includes criticism, history, art, music, theology, philosophy, educational theory, economics." Estab. 1981. Circ. 200.

Needs: Adventure, ethnic/multicultural, family saga, historical (general, US, Eastern Europe), horror (psychological, supernatural), humor satire, literary, mainstream/contemporary, military/war, mystery/suspense (police procedural, private eye/hardboiled, courtroom, regional (New England, Middle Atlantic), romance (gothic, historical, regency period), short story collections, thriller/espionage, translations, western (frontier saga, traditional), Civil War, US ethnic history, immigration, 19th century politics. "No science fiction, high technology, Erma Bombeck material, or 'how I found Jesus and it changed my life.' " Receives 5-10 unsolicited mss/month. Accepts 1 ms/

issue; 4 mss/year. Publishes ms 1-2 months after acceptance. **Publishes 2-3 new writers/year.** Recently published work by Grace Gmeindl, George Stanton, Christy Vennam. Length: 1,500-3,500 words. Publishes short shorts. Length: 1,000 words. Also publishes literary essays, literary criticism and poetry. Often critiques or comments on rejected ms.

How to Contact: Query with clips of published work. Include bio, SASE and $5 for sample issue. Reports in 2 weeks on queries. Simultaneous and reprint submissions OK. Sample copy for $5. Guidelines for SASE. Reviews novels, short story collections and nonfiction books of interest to writers. Send books to editor.

Payment/Terms: Pays subscription to magazine and 4-5 contributor's copies; additional copies $5. Acquire first North American serial rights.

Advice: "Use correct English, correctly written and punctuated. No jargon, cant, or short-cut language. Type the manuscript on a typewriter, not on a word-processor or computer and you'll have an advantage over other contributors from the start. Scholarly magazines and journals are becoming a rarity. If you use 'feel' rather than 'think' as your verb of choice, better look elsewhere."

BLACK JACK, Seven Buffaloes Press, Box 249, Big Timber MT 59011. **Editor:** Art Cuelho. "Main theme: Rural. Publishes material on the American Indian, farm and ranch, American hobo, the common working man, folklore, the Southwest, Okies, Montana, humor, Central California, etc. for people who make their living off the land. The writers write about their roots, experiences and values they receive from the American soil." Annually. Estab. 1973. Circ. 750.

Needs: Literary, contemporary, western, adventure, humor, American Indian, American hobo, and parts of novels and long short stories. "Anything that strikes me as being amateurish, without depth, without craft, I refuse. Actually, I'm not opposed to any kind of writing if the author is genuine and has spent his lifetime dedicated to the written word." Receives approximately 10-15 unsolicited fiction mss/month. Accepts 5-10 mss/year. Length: 3,500-5,000 words (there can be exceptions).

How to Contact: Query for current theme with SASE. Reports in 1 month on queries and mss. Sample copy for $7.75 postpaid.

Payment/Terms: Pays 1-2 contributor's copies. Acquires first North American serial rights and reserves the right to reprint material in an anthology or future *Black Jack* publications. Rights revert to author after publication.

Advice: "Enthusiasm should be matched with skill as a craftsman. That's not saying that we don't continue to learn, but every writer must have enough command of the language to compete with other proven writers. Save postage by writing first to find out the editor's needs. A small press magazine always has specific needs at any given time. I sometimes accept material from writers that aren't that good at punctuation and grammar but make up for it with life's experience. This is not a highbrow publication; it belongs to the salt-of-the-earth people."

BLACK LACE, BLK Publishing Co., P.O. Box 83912, Los Angeles CA 90083-0912. (310)410-0808. Fax: (310)410-9250. E-mail: newsroom@blk.com. Website: www.blk.com. **Editor:** Alycee Lane. Magazine: 8⅛×10⅞; 48 pages; book stock; color glossy cover; illustrations and photographs. "*Black Lace* is a lifestyle magazine for African-American lesbians. Published quarterly, its content ranges from erotic imagery to political commentary." Estab. 1991.

• Member of COSMEP. The editor would like to see more full-length erotic fiction, politically-focused articles on lesbians and the African-American community as a whole, and nostalgia and humor pieces.

Needs: Ethnic/multicultural, lesbian. "Avoid interracial stories or idealized pornography." Accepts 4 mss/year. Published work by Nicole King, Wanda Thompson, Lynn K. Pannell, Sheree Ann Slaughter, Lyn Lifshin, JoJo and Drew Alise Timmens. Publishes short shorts. Also publishes literary essays, literary criticism, poetry.

How to Contact: Query first with clips of published work or send complete ms with a cover letter. Should include bio (3 sentences). Send a disposable copy of ms. No simultaneous submissions. Electronic submissions OK. Sample copy for $7. Fiction guidelines free.

Payment/Terms: Pays 2 contributor's copies. Acquires first North American serial rights and right to anthologize.

Advice: *Black Lace* seeks erotic material of the highest quality. The most important thing is that the work be erotic and that it feature black lesbians or themes. Study the magazine to see what we do and how we do it. Some fiction is very romantic, other is highly sexual. Most articles in *Black Lace* cater to black lesbians between these two extremes."

☑ $ ◖ ▼ BLACK WARRIOR REVIEW, Box 862936, Tuscaloosa AL 35486-0027. (205)348-4518. Website: www.sa.ua.edu/osm/bwr (includes writer's guidelines, names of editors, short fiction). **Editor-in-Chief:** Laura Didyk. **Fiction Editor:** Christopher Manlove. Magazine: 6×9; 200 pages; illustrations and photos. "We

---

MARKET CONDITIONS are constantly changing! If you're still using this book and it is 2001 or later, buy the newest edition of *Novel & Short Story Writer's Market* at your favorite bookstore or order from Writer's Digest Books at (800)289-0963.

publish contemporary fiction, poetry, reviews, essays, photography and interviews for a literary audience. We strive to publish the most compelling, best written work that we can find regardless of genre or type, for a literate audience." Semiannually. Estab. 1974. Circ. 2,000.

● Work that appeared in the *Black Warrior Review* has been included in the *Pushcart Prize* anthology, *The Year's Best Fantasy & Horror, Harper's Magazine, Best American Short Stories, Best American Poetry* and in *New Short Stories from the South.*

Needs: Contemporary, literary, short and short-short fiction. Want "work that is conscious of form, good experimental writing, short-short fiction, writing that is more than competent—that sings." No genre fiction please. Receives 200 unsolicited fiction mss/month. Accepts 5 mss/issue, 10 mss/year. Approximately 5% of fiction is agented. Recently published work by Barry Hannah, Noy Holland, Jane Buchbinder, Mark Wisniewski and Rob Trucks. **Publishes 5 new writers/year.** Length: 7,500 words maximum; 2,000-5,000 words average. Also publishes essays, poetry. Occasionally critiques rejected mss. Unsolicited novel excerpts are not considered unless the novel is already contracted for publication.

How to Contact: Send complete ms with SASE (1 story per submission). Simultaneous submissions OK. Reports in 1-4 months. Publishes ms 2-5 months after acceptance. Sample copy for $8. Fiction guidelines for SASE. Reviews novels and short story collections.

Payment/Terms: Pays up to $100 per story and 2 contributor's copies. Pays on publication.

Advice: "We look for attention to the language, freshness, honesty. Also, send us a clean, well-printed, typo-free manuscript. Become familiar with the magazine prior to submission. We're increasingly interested in considering good experimental writing and in reading short-short fiction. We read year round. We get a good number of stories, many of them competent but lacking a truly new vision or aesthetic. The stories we publish pay particular attention to language. They're fresh and honest. Read. Read. Read. Sometimes people forget the symbiotic relationship between reading good stories and writing good stories. Also, become familiar with the magazine prior to submission. The traditional 20-page short story is on the verge of becoming a dinosaur. Very short fiction (1-7 pages or so) and creative nonfiction seem to be asserting themselves as viable forms. We'd like to see more quality work in these new 'genres.' "

BLUE MESA REVIEW, University of New Mexico, Dept. of English, Humanities Bldg., Room 217, Albuquerque NM 87131. (505)277-6155. Fax: (505)277-5573. E-mail: bluemesa@unm.edu. Website: www.unm.edu/~english/mesa/ (includes writer's guidelines, names of editors, short fiction). **Editor:** James Colbert. Magazine: 6×9; 300 pages; 55 lb. paper; 10 pt CS1; photos. "*Blue Mesa Review* publishes the best/most current creative writing on the market." Annually. Estab. 1989. Circ. 1,200.

Needs: Adventure, ethnic/multicultural, experimental, feminist, gay, historical, humor/satire, lesbian, literary, mainstream/contemporary, regional, westerns. Contact for list of upcoming themes. Receives 300 unsolicited mss/year. Accepts 100 mss/year. Accepts mss July 1-October 1; all submissions must be postmarked by October 1; reads mss November-December; responds in January. Publishes ms 5-6 months after acceptance. Published work by Kathleen Spivack, Roberta Swann and Tony Mares. Publishes short shorts. Also publishes literary essays, poetry.

How to Contact: Send 2 copies of complete ms with a cover letter. Send SASE for reply. Sample copy for $12. Reviews novels, short story collections, poetry and nonfiction.

Payment/Terms: Pays 1 contributor copy for First North American serial rights.

Advice: "Contact us for complete guidelines. All submissions must follow our guidelines."

THE BLUE MOON REVIEW, P.O. Box 48, Ivy VA 22945-0045. E-mail: editor@thebluemoon.com; fiction@thebluemoon.com. Website: www.TheBlueMoon.com. **Editor:** Doug Lawson. Electronic magazine: Illustrations and photos. Quarterly. Estab. 1994. Circ. 16,000.

● *Blue Moon Review* ranked #39 on *Writer's Digest*'s Fiction 50 list of top markets for fiction writers.

Needs: Experimental, feminist, gay, lesbian, literary, mainstream/contemporary, regional, translations. No genre fiction or condensed novels. Receives 40-70 unsolicited mss/month. Accepts 7-10 mss/issue; 51-60 mss/year. Publishes ms up to 9 months after acceptance. Published work by Edward Falco, Deborah Eisenberg, Robert Sward and Eva Shaderowfsky. Length: 3,000 words maximum. Publishes short shorts. Also publishes literary essays, literary criticism, poetry. Sometimes critiques or comments on rejected mss.

How to Contact: Send complete ms with a cover letter. Include a brief bio, list of publications and e-mail address if available. Reports in 1-2 months on mss. Send SASE for reply, return of ms or send a disposable copy of ms. Simultaneous and electronic submissions OK. Sample copy and fiction guidelines available at above website. Reviews novels and short story collections.

Payment/Terms: Offers prizes for fiction and poetry. Acquires first North American serial rights. Rights revert to author upon request.

Advice: "We look for strong use of language or strong characterization. Manuscripts stand out by their ability to engage a reader on an intellectual or emotional level. Present characters with depth regardless of age and introduce intelligent concepts that have resonance and relevance. We recommend our writers be electronically connected to the Internet."

THE BLUE SKUNK COMPANION, The Blue Skunk Society Inc., P.O. Box 8400, MSU 59, Mankato MN 56002-8400. (507)625-7176. Editor: Scott Welvaert. **Fiction Editor:** Blake Hoena. Magazine: 8×11; 35-45 pages; illustrations and photographs. "We publish fiction, poetry, nonfiction and essays that are inspired by life, not by classic literature, periods or styles. We intend to reach readers that wish to be entertained and moved no matter their age, race or culture." Semiannually. Estab. 1997. Circ. 100-500.

Needs: Adventure, condensed/excerpted novel, ethnic/multicultural, experimental, fantasy (contemporary), historical (general), horror, humor/satire, literary, mainstream/contemporary, mystery/suspense (contemporary), psychic/supernatural/occult, regional, romance (contemporary), science fiction (contemporary), translations. "We do not want fiction/prose that falls into clichés." Receives 10-20 unsolicited mss/month. Accepts 5-7 mss/issue; 10-14 mss/year. Publishes ms 4-6 months after acceptance. Published work by Roger Sheffer, Brian Batt, Samuel Dollar and Kevin Langton. Length: 1,000-4,000 words average; 1,000 words minimum; 7,000 words maximum. Also publishes literary essays, literary criticism, poetry. Often critiques or comments on rejected mss.

How to Contact: Send complete ms with a cover letter. Include estimated word count, ½-1-page bio and list of publications. Reports in 1 month on queries; 2-3 months on mss. SASE. Simultaneous submissions OK. Sample copy for $5 and 9×12 SAE with 6 first-class stamps. Fiction guidelines for 4×12 SASE. Reviews novels and short story collections.

Payment/Terms: Pays free subscription to the magazine; additional copies for $5. Pays on publication. Acquires first rights. Not copyrighted.

Advice: "We look for a voice that sounds like a 'person' and not like a 'writer.' Good use of language as function, taste and art; not a boastful vocabulary. Try to avoid genre until you have a good grasp of mainstream and contemporary prose. Once that has been achieved, then your genre fiction will be much better. Always be fresh with ideas and themes. We feel that good fiction/prose can be found on the back shelves of bookstores and not on the bestsellers list."

BLUELINE, English Dept., SUNY, Potsdam NY 13676. (315)267-2043. E-mail: blueline@potsdam.edu. Website: www.potsdam.edu/engl/blueline.html. **Editor:** Rick Henry. Magazine: 6×9; 180 pages; 70 lb. white stock paper; 65 lb. smooth cover stock; illustrations; photos. "*Blueline* is interested in quality writing about the Adirondacks or other places similar in geography and spirit. We publish fiction, poetry, personal essays, book reviews and oral history for those interested in the Adirondacks, nature in general, and well-crafted writing." Annually. Estab. 1979. Circ. 400.

Needs: Adventure, contemporary, humor/satire, literary, prose poem, regional, reminiscences, oral history, nature/outdoors. Receives 8-10 unsolicited fiction mss/month. Accepts 6-8 mss/issue. Does not read January through August. Publishes ms 3-6 months after acceptance. Published fiction by Jeffrey Clapp. Published new writers within the last year. Length: 500 words minimum; 3,000 words maximum; 2,500 words average. Also publishes literary essays, poetry. Occasionally critiques rejected mss.

How to Contact: Send complete ms with SASE, word count and brief bio. Submit mss August through November 30. Reports in 2-10 weeks. Sample copy for $6. Fiction guidelines for 5×10 SASE.

Payment/Terms: Pays 1 contributor's copy for first rights. Charges $7 each for 3 or more extra copies.

Advice: "We look for concise, clear, concrete prose that tells a story and touches upon a universal theme or situation. We prefer realism to romanticism but will consider nostalgia if well done. Pay attention to grammar and syntax. Avoid murky language, sentimentality, cuteness or folksiness. We would like to see more good fiction related to the Adirondacks. If manuscript has potential, we work with author to improve and reconsider for publication. Our readers prefer fiction to poetry (in general) or reviews. Write from your own experience, be specific and factual (within the bounds of your story) and if you write about universal features such as love, death, change, etc., write about them in a fresh way. Triteness and mediocrity are the hallmarks of the majority of stories seen today."

BOGG, A Magazine of British & North American Writing, Bogg Publications, 422 N. Cleveland St., Arlington VA 22201. (703)243-6019. **U.S. Editor:** John Elsberg. Magazine: 6×9; 64-68 pages; 70 lb. white paper; 70 lb. cover stock; line illustrations. "American and British poetry, prose poems, experimental short 'fictions,' reviews, and essays on small press." Published "two or three times a year." Estab. 1968. Circ. 850.

● The editors at *Bogg* are most interested in short, wry or semi-surreal fiction.

Needs: Very short experimental fiction and prose poems. "We are always looking for work with British/Commonwealth themes and/or references." Receives 25 unsolicited fiction mss/month. Accepts 1-2 mss/issue; 3-6 mss/year. Publishes ms 3-18 months after acceptance. Published work by Nigel Hinshelwood. **Publishes 50% new writers/last year.** Length: 300 words maximum. Also publishes literary essays, literary criticism, poetry. Occasionally critiques rejected mss.

How to Contact: Query first or send ms (2-6 pieces) with SASE. Reports in 1 week on queries; 2 weeks on mss. Sample copy for $3.50 or $4.50 (current issue). Reviews novels and short story collections.

Payment/Terms: Pays 2 contributor's copies; reduced charge for extras. Acquires one-time rights.

Advice: "Read magazine first. We are most interested in prose work of experimental or wry nature to supplement poetry, and are always looking for innovative/imaginative uses of British themes and references."

☑ ◔ **BOTTOMFISH MAGAZINE**, De Anza College, 21250 Stevens Creek Blvd., Cupertino CA 95014. (408)864-8600. E-mail: splitter@cruzio.com. Website: www.deanza.fhda.edu/bottomfish/bottomfish.html (includes guidelines, names of editors, short fiction, authors, links). **Editor-in-Chief:** Randolph Splitter. Magazine: 6×9; 80-100 pages; White Bristol vellum cover; b&w high contrast illustrations and photos. "Contemporary poetry, fiction, creative nonfiction, b&w graphics, comics and photos." Annually. Estab. 1976. Circ. 500.

Needs: "Careful, thoughtful, personal writing. Diverse styles and voices." Receives 50-100 unsolicited fiction mss/month. Accepts 5-6 mss/issue. **Publishes 1-3 new writers/year.** Recently published work by Michelle Cacho-Negrete, Chitra Banerjee Divakaruni and Eleanor Swanson. Length: no minimum; 4,000 words maximum; 2,500 words average.

How to Contact: Reads mss September through February. Submission deadline: December 31; publication date: April. Accepts queries by e-mail (no mss). Submit 1 short story or up to 3 short shorts with cover letter, brief bio and SASE. "Sorry, we cannot return manuscripts." No reprints. Reports in 3-6 months. Publishes mss an average of 3 months after acceptance. Sample copy for $5.

Payment/Terms: Pays 2 contributor's copies. Acquires one-time rights.

Advice: "Write freely, rewrite carefully. Move beyond clichés and stereotypes."

★ ◐ ◎ ▼ **BOUILLABAISSE**, Alpha Beat Press, 31 Waterloo St., New Hope PA 18938. (215)862-0299. **Editor:** Dave Christy. Magazine: 11×17; 120 pages; bond paper; illustrations and photos. Publishes Beat Generation, post-Beat independent and other modern writings. Semiannually. Estab. 1986. Circ. 600.

● Work included in *Bouillabaisse* has been selected for inclusion in the *Pushcart Prize* anthology. Also see listing for *Alpha Beat Press* by same editor.

Needs: Beat generation and modern sub-cultures: adventure, condensed/excerpted novel, erotica, literary. No "suburbia" fiction. Wants more erotica. Receives 15 unsolicited mss/month. Accepts 2 mss/issue; 4 mss/year. Publishes ms 6 months after acceptance. Recently published work by Laurence Lasky, Raymond Mason, George Dowden and Daniel Crocker. **Publishes 25% new writers.** Length: no limit. Publishes short shorts. Also publishes literary essays, literary criticism, poetry. Sometimes critiques or comments on rejected mss.

How to Contact: Query first. Include bio with submission. Reports in 1 week. Send SASE for reply or return of ms. Simultaneous submissions OK. Sample copy for $10. Reviews novels and short story collections.

Payment/Terms: Pays 1 contributor's copy.

Advice: "Read a sample before submitting." Looks for "writing that is not forced with an interesting topic/story. Don't watch TV, concentrate on writing."

★ ☑ $ ◔ **BOULEVARD**, Opojaz Inc., PMB 332, 4579 Laclede Ave., St. Louis MO 63108-2103. (314)361-2986. **Editor:** Richard Burgin. Magazine: 5½×8½; 150-225 pages; excellent paper; high-quality cover stock; illustrations; photos. "*Boulevard* aspires to publish the best contemporary fiction, poetry and essays we can print. While we frequently publish writers with previous credits, we are very interested in publishing less experienced or unpublished writers with exceptional promise." Published 3 times/year. Estab. 1986. Circ. about 3,500.

Needs: Contemporary, experimental, literary. Does not want to see "anything whose first purpose is not literary." No genre fiction. Receives over 600 mss/month. Accepts about 10 mss/issue. Does not accept manuscripts between April 1 and October 1. Publishes ms less than 1 year after acceptance. Agented fiction ⅓-¼. Length: 5,000 words average; 8,000 words maximum. Publishes short shorts. Recently published work by Joyce Carol Oates, Billy Collins, Emily Fox Gordon, Yusef Komunyakaa and Charles Simic. **Publishes 10 new writers/year.** Also publishes literary essays, literary criticism, poetry. Sometimes critiques rejected mss and recommends other markets.

How to Contact: Send complete ms with cover letter. Reports in 2 weeks on queries; 3 months on mss. SASE for reply. Simultaneous submissions OK. Sample copy for $8 and SAE with 5 first-class stamps.

Payment/Terms: Pays $50-250; contributor's copies; charges for extras. Acquires first North American serial rights. Does not send galleys to author unless requested.

Advice: "Surprising, intelligent, eloquent work always makes an impression." We are open to different styles of imaginative and critical work and are mindful of Nabokov's dictum 'There is only one school, the school of talent.' Above all, when we consider the very diverse manuscripts submitted to us for publication, we value original sensibility, writing that causes the reader to experience a part of life in a new way. Originality, to us, has little to do with a writer intently trying to make each line or sentence odd, bizarre, or eccentric, merely for the sake of being 'different.' Rather, originality is the result of the character or vision of the writer; the writer's singular outlook and voice as it shines through in the totality of his or her work."

⊕ ◯ **BREAKFAST ALL DAY (aka BAD)**, 43 Kingsdown House, Amhurst Rd., London E8 2AS England. Phone: 0033 (0)2 35 40 33 26. **Editor:** Philip Boxall. Magazine: A4, 40 pages, 90 gsm bond paper; 100 gsm matt coated; illustrations and photos. *Breakfast All Day* publishes good quality writing in a wide range of subjects and styles and without regard to the previous publication credits of contributors. We draw contributions from Britain, mainland Europe and North America. The intended audience is intelligent, reflective and appreciative of dry humour." Quarterly. Estab. 1995. Circ. 300.

● Member National Small Press Centre.

Needs: Comics/graphic novels, ethnic/multicultural, gay, horror (psychological), humor/satire, literary, mainstream/contemporary, mystery/suspense, religious, science fiction (hard science), translations. No romantic fiction, sword and sorcery. Receives 10-15 unsolicited mss/month. Accepts 10 mss/issue; 40 mss/year. Publishes ms 3-6 months after acceptance. Published work by Gregory Arena, Linda Barnhart, William Borden, Kevin Decky, O'Neil De Noux, S.P. Elledge and Joel Ensana. Length: 2,500 words average; 500 words minimum; 4,000 words maximum. Also publishes literary essays, poetry. Sometimes critiques or comments on rejected ms.
How to Contact: Send complete ms with a cover letter. Include estimated word count, list of publications. Reports in 1 month on queries; 3 months on mss. SAE (or IRC). Send disposable copy of ms and copy on 3½″ disk (ASCII file). Simultaneous submissions OK. Sample copy for 6 IRCs. Fiction guidelines for 1 IRC. Send books to editor, 4 Rue Bonne Nouvelle, 76200 Dieppe, France.
Payment/Terms: Pays contributor's copies. Acquires first British serial rights.
Advice: "Aim for clear presentation and simplicity. Edit your work thoroughly to avoid redundancy."

N ★ ⊘ ▼ THE BRIAR CLIFF REVIEW, Briar Cliff College, 3303 Rebecca St., Sioux City IA 51104-0100. (712)279-1651 or 279-5321. Fax: (712) 279-5410. E-mail: currans@briar-cliff.edu. Website: www.briar-cliff.edu/bcreview (includes writer's guidelines, contest guidelines, previous contest winners and their winning poems/short stories and photos/art). Managing Editor: Tricia Currans-Sheehan. **Fiction Editor:** Phil Hey. Magazine: 8½×11; 80 pages; 70 lb. Finch Opaque cover stock; illustrations and photos. "*The Briar Cliff Review* is an eclectic literary and cultural magazine focusing on (but not limited to) Siouxland writers and subjects. We are happy to proclaim ourselves a regional publication. It doesn't diminish us; it enhances us." Annually. Estab. 1989. Circ. 500.
• *The Briar Cliff Review* has received The Gold Crown and Silver Crown awards from the Columbia Scholastic Press Association and the National Pacemaker Award from the Associated Collegiate Press.
Needs: Ethnic/multicultural, feminist, historical, humor/satire, literary, mainstream/contemporary, regional. No romance, mystery, horror or alien stories. Accepts 5 mss/year. Reads mss only between August 1 and November 1. Publishes ms 3-4 months after acceptance. Published work by Josip Novakovich, Diane Glancy, Diane Frank, Michael Carey, Sandra Adelmund and U Sam Oeur. **Publishes 10-14 new writers/year.** Length: 3,000 words average; 2,500 words minimum; 3,500 words maximum. Also publishes literary essays, literary criticism and poetry. Sometimes critiques or comments on rejected mss.
How to Contact: Send complete ms with a cover letter. Include estimated word count, bio and list of publications. Reports in 4-5 months on mss. Send a SASE for return of ms. Electronic submissions (disk) OK. Simultaneous submissions OK. Sample copy for $8 and 9×12 SAE. Fiction guidelines free for #10 SASE. Reviews novels and short story collections.
Payment/Terms: Pays 2 contributor's copies for first rights; additional copies available for $4.
Advice: "Send us your best. So many stories are just telling. I want some action. It has to move. We prefer stories in which there is no gimmick, no mechanical turn of events, no moral except the one I would draw privately."

⊘ THE BRIDGE, A Journal of Fiction & Poetry, 14050 Vernon St., Oak Park MI 48237. (248)547-6823. Editor: Jack Zucker. **Fiction Editor:** Helen Zucker. Magazine: 160 pages; matte cover. Semiannually. Estab. 1990.
• *The Bridge* has received grants from CLMP and Michigan Council of the Arts.
Needs: Serious, realistic. Publishes ms 12-18 months after acceptance. Recently published work by David Slavitt, Lynn Coffin and H.R. Francis. Length: 5,000-10,000 words average. Publishes short shorts. Also publishes literary essays, literary criticism, poetry.
How to Contact: Send complete ms with a cover letter. Reports in 4-8 months. SASE for reply, return of ms or send a disposable copy of ms. Simultaneous submissions OK. Sample copy for $7. Fiction guidelines for #10 SASE. Reviews novels and short story collections.
Payment/Terms: Pays 2 contributor's copies; additional copies for $7. Acquires first rights.

☑ ⊘ BRILLIANT CORNERS, A Journal of Jazz & Literature, Lycoming College, Williamsport PA 17701. (570)321-4279. Fax: (570)321-4090. E-mail: feinstei@lycoming.edu. Editor: Sascha Feinstein. Journal: 6×9; 100 pages; 70 lb. Cougar opaque, vellum, natural paper; photographs. "We publish jazz-related literature—fiction, poetry and nonfiction." Semiannually. Estab. 1996. Circ. 1,200.
Needs: Condensed/excerpted novel, ethnic/multicultural, experimental, literary, mainstream/contemporary, romance (contemporary). Receives 10-15 unsolicited mss/month. Accepts 1-2 mss/issue; 2-3 mss/year. Does not read mss May 15-September 1. Publishes ms 4-12 months after acceptance. Very little agented fiction. Publishes short shorts. Also publishes literary essays, literary criticism and poetry. Often critiques or comments on rejected mss.
How to Contact: Send complete ms with a cover letter. Include 1-paragraph bio and list of publications. Reports in 2 weeks on queries; 1-2 months on mss. SASE for return of ms or send a disposable copy of ms. Accepts unpublished work only. Sample copy for $7. Reviews novels and short story collections. Send books to editor.

insider report

The *Briar Cliff Review* provides a voice for Siouxland writers

After winning three Gold Crowns and two Silver Crowns from the Columbia Scholastic Press Association and one National Pacemaker award from the Associated Collegiate Press, *The Briar Cliff Review* began attracting attention.

But awards are not the goal of this small literary magazine located in Sioux City, Iowa, says Managing Editor Tricia Currans-Sheehan. Instead, the mission is to display the work of authors, artists and poets of the surrounding Siouxland, a term created by Frederick Manfred in his 1947 work *This is the Year* to describe the country. "Once more he was stirred by the strange troubled land," Manfred wrote. "It was hardly a wonder that the Indians had a wholesome respect for the rocks and rivers of Siouxland."

Tricia Currans-Sheehan

Siouxland includes the Big Sioux River basin in South Dakota, Minnesota, Iowa and Nebraska. It is this region that Currans-Sheehan promotes through the fiction, poetry, artwork, photographs and reviews in *The Briar Cliff Review*. "Eleven years ago we looked around the Siouxland area and saw there were very few places for writers to publish their works. That's when we, a few writers and poets on the Briar Cliff campus, decided to start a magazine," says Currans-Sheehan. "And when I started this thing I said it is not going to look cheap. People think, oh, Sioux City, Iowa, get out the copy machine and the stapler. It wasn't going to look like that."

After 11 years of publication and its myriad of awards, *The Briar Cliff Review* has indeed proved itself a professional magazine. Here Currans-Sheehan talks about her work as editor of this magazine that has not strayed from its original mission to cultivate and celebrate the work of regional artists.

How does being a regional publication affect the magazine?
That's always in our thoughts. We know our place and we want to make sure that's represented in the magazine. If I have to choose between two good stories, one from Davenport, Iowa, and the other from New Jersey, then I'll select the one from Iowa.

Are there any disadvantages of having a regional publication?
I know there is a sense in the literary world that regional is bad, and I disagree 100 percent. I think knowing our sense of place, knowing our focus, doesn't diminish us but enhances us. William Stafford wrote, "All events and experiences are local, somewhere." When talking about Greenwich Village, that is local, that is regional. So I think the name regional has been misused.

What is your process for reviewing submissions?

Most submissions come directly to me, the managing editor. I read everything. Then we meet as an editorial team five or six times each issue to review and select material.

What criteria are you looking for in a manuscript?

In fiction we are looking for a story that moves, that is a story. For us, something has to happen. Unfortunately, we see too many submissions where things don't happen.

Are there a lot of mistakes you see writers continuously making?

I don't like to see a writer show he is a beginning writer. You don't have to announce that you've never had anything published. Make sure everything is tight and include a cover letter. Just tell us what you are submitting and go from there. Also, in fiction submissions, we see a lot of problems with lack of development of plot and character.

Do you have any good tips for writing a cover letter?

I believe the simpler the better. I don't believe you have to give me a plot synopsis of what you are submitting. Just announce the story you are submitting, the title and number of words. In the cover letter tell me a little bit about your publishing background and that's it. Don't be cute. Sometimes writers are too cute. They're cracking jokes and making funny comments, and I am thinking it's false and flat. So just be simple. Be clear. Don't try to impress.

On your guidelines, there is list of awards that *Briar Cliff Review* has won. How important are these awards to you?

They are important because they affirm us. Being out here in Iowa we sometimes need that because we have a tendency to underestimate ourselves. We take the judges' comments seriously. If they recommend something we will look at it the next year and try to make changes. I think we have a stronger magazine because of it.

What do you see in the future of the literary magazine market?

I think literary markets right now are wonderful for beginning and advanced writers. More and more magazines are being launched, giving more writers a chance to be published. I see *Briar Cliff Review* playing a part in that. We have stronger writers in the magazine now and I think that is only going to increase. We get more and more submissions each year.

How does being a writer affect you as an editor?

It affects me all the time. Being a writer from the Midwest mailing my stuff out to the big magazines was one reason I started *Briar Cliff Review*. You realize you don't stand much of a chance as a beginning writer when the big markets—*Atlantic Monthly*, *The New Yorker* and *Harper's*, for instance—only take one story a month. Therein lies the importance of and need for small literary magazines. As a writer who is also an editor, I am always grateful for the manuscripts we receive and careful to show writers we are pleased they submitted to us. Since I am also sending out my own manuscripts every week, I am always concerned about the care we give to manuscripts we receive.

—*Heidi L. Windmiller*

Payment/Terms: Pays 2 contributor's copies. Acquires first North American serial rights. Sends galleys to author when possible.

Advice: "We look for clear, moving prose that demonstrates a love of both writing and jazz. We primarily publish established writers, but we read all submissions carefully and welcome work by outstanding young writers."

[N] [⊘] BROWNBAG PRESS, Hyacinth House Publications, P.O. Box 120, Fayetteville AR 72702-0120. **Editors:** Shannon Frach and Randal Seyler. Magazine: 30-55 pages; 20 lb. paper; cardstock cover; b&w illustrations. "*Brownbag Press* is a digest of poetry, fiction, and experimental writing that is seeking avant-garde, forceful, and often bizarre literature for a literate, adult audience that is bored to death with the standard offerings of modern mainstream fiction." Semiannually. Estab. 1989. Circ. 375.

● Hyacinth House Publications also publishes *Psychotrain* listed in this book. No need to send to both publications, says the editor, as submissions will be considered for both. Notice the editors have reduced the length to no more than 1,500 words. They are also currently overstocked with fiction. *No unsolicited mss!*

Needs: Condensed/excerpted novels, contemporary, erotica, ethnic, experimental, feminist, gay, humor/satire, lesbian, literary, prose poem, psychic/supernatural/occult, translations, "Punk, psychedelia, fringe culture, Dada, surrealism. A sense of dark humor is definitely a plus. No religious, romance, or criminally boring mainstream. No tedious formula fiction. No yuppie angst. Nothing saccharine." Accepts 4-6 ms/issue. Publishes ms 1 year after acceptance. Length: 100-1,500 words maximum. Publishes short shorts. Length: 100 words or longer. Sometimes critiques rejected mss and recommends other markets.

How to Contact: Send query letter. "*We are not accepting unsolicited manuscripts of any description. All unsolicited material will remain unread and unreturned.*" "Don't use a cover letter to brag about how great you are; if you're that good, I guarantee we'll have heard of you." Simultaneous and reprint submissions OK. Sample copy for $3 and 4 first-class stamps. Make checks out to "Hyacinth House Publications." Cash is also OK. Fiction guidelines for #10 SASE.

Payment/Terms: No payment. Acquires one-time rights.

Advice: "We're getting a lot of fiction that reads as if it were penned by the living dead. What we need, instead, is writing that is vigorous, unrepentant, and dynamically *alive*. We'd like to see *Brownbag* become more forceful and intense with every issue. Send us the strongest, most compelling material you've got. Keep the weak stuff at home. Short, tight stories always beat long, rambling ones. In fact, as we are nearly overstocked with longer fiction and are primarily interested in short shorts at present. International writers should try their best to obtain U.S. stamps for SASEs. Using IRCs will seriously delay response time. Also, we're receiving too many submissions with postage due. Despite the stacks of them we receive, we do not, under any circumstances, answer queries which arrive without SASE. A great deal of time and postage could be saved by writers if they would actually take the time to read market listings carefully. We receive material every day from people who claim to have seen our entries in this book, but who could not possibly have read them past the initial address."

[✓] [◁] THE BROWNSTONE REVIEW, 335 Court St., PMB 174, Brooklyn NY 11231. **Fiction Editor:** Aaron Scharf. Magazine: 5½ × 8½; 60 pages. "We publish any and all types of fiction, so long as the work is of highest quality. Our audience is primarily literary and expects a regular supply of excellent fiction." Semiannually. Estab. 1995. Circ. 250.

Needs: Literary, mainstream/contemporary. No romance, religious, children's stories or occult/gothic horror. Planning future special fiction issue or anthology. Receives 70 unsolicited mss/month. Accepts 3-6 mss/issue; 6-12 mss/year. Publishes ms 3-6 months after acceptance. Recently published work by William Keller, Jean Hey and Joe Evanisko. Length: 1,000-2,000 words average; 250 words minimum; 10,000 words maximum. Publishes short shorts. Also publishes poetry. Sometimes critiques or comments on rejected ms.

How to Contact: Send complete ms with a cover letter. Should include list of publications. Reports within 3 months. Send SASE for reply, return of ms or send a disposable copy of ms. Simultaneous submissions OK.

Payment/Terms: Pays 2 contributor's copies. Acquires first North American serial rights.

Advice: "Strong characters, natural (not expository) dialogue, a non-didactic tone, and a plot that reveals human nature in a way that doesn't clobber the reader over the head—these are qualities we look for in submissions. Avoid workshops and writing by committee. Read voraciously. Revise, revise, revise. We appreciate the drive towards multiple submissions, so long as writers are courteous about letting us know when a piece has been accepted elsewhere."

[N] [★] [▣] BURN. E-mail: clark@blindzero.com. Website: www.blindzero.com/burn/ (includes writer's guidelines). **Editor:** Clark Kline. "A literary e-zine with rotating themes." Quarterly.

Needs: Literary. "Unless we are having our Halloween themed issue, we shy away from supernatural and vampire/werewolf type stories." **Publishes 15 new writers/year.** Recently published work by Janet I. Buck, Joy Reid, Scott Holstad and Eve Rings.

How to Contact: Send queries/mss by e-mail. "Send in a .rtf or .doc file."

Advice: Looks for "fiction that rises above tradition. Tradition should be a part of the means, not the end. For instance, our last couple of issues had the theme of 'twisted nature' of man, however most submissions were about murder and/or sexual depravity while there are so many other ways to approach the theme. Stick to the theme which will be a little more strict in the coming issues. Otherwise, anything pretty much goes."

☑ ◯ **BUTTON, New England's Tiniest Magazine of Poetry, Fiction & Gracious Living**, 4222 Flora Place, St. Louis MO 63110. E-mail: buttonx26@aol.com. Editor: S. Cragin. **Fiction Editor:** W.M. Davies. Magazine: 4×5; 34 pages; bond paper; color cardstock cover; illustrations; photos. Semiannually. Estab. 1993. Circ. 1,500.

Needs: Literary. No genre fiction, science fiction, techno-thriller. Wants more of "anything Herman Melville, Henry James or Betty MacDonald would like to read." Receives 20-40 unsolicited mss/month. Accepts 1-2 mss/issue; 3-5 mss/year. Publishes ms 3-9 months after acceptance. Published work by Sven Birkerts, Stephen Mc-Cauley, Wayne Wilson, Romayne Dawney, Brendan Galvin, They Might Be Giants and Lawrence Millman. Length: 500-2,500 words. Also publishes literary essays, poetry. Sometimes critiques or comments on rejected mss "if it shows promise."

How to Contact: Request guidelines. Send ms with bio, list of publications and advise how you found magazine. Reports in 1 month on queries; 2-4 months on mss. SASE. Sample copy for $2. Fiction guidelines for SASE. Reviews novels and short story collections. Send book to editor. Sponsors poetry contest, for more info send SASE.

Payment/Terms: Pays honorarium and multiple free subscriptions to the magazine on publication. Acquires first North American serial rights. Sends galleys to author if there are editorial changes.

Advice: "What makes a manuscript stand out? Flannery O'Connor once said, 'Don't get subtle till the fourth page,' and I agree. We publish fiction in the 1,000-3,000 word category, and look for interesting, sympathetic, believable characters and careful setting. I'm really tired of stories that start strong and then devolve into dialogue uninterupted by further exposition. Also, no stories from a mad person's POV unless it's really tricky and skillful. Advice to prospective writers: continue to read at least ten times as much as you write. Read the best, and read intelligent criticism if you can find it. We welcome submissions, and are always glad to hear from people curious about *Button*. Please don't submit more than twice in a year—it's more important that you work on your craft rather than machine-gunning publications with samples, and don't submit more than 3 poems in a batch (this advice goes for other places, you'll find . . .)."

✪ $◯ **BYLINE**, Box 130596, Edmond OK 73013-0001. (405)348-5591. Website: www.bylinemag.com (includes writer's guidelines, names of editors, contest list and rules, ad rates and sample article from magazine). **Editor-in-Chief:** Marcia Preston. Monthly magazine "aimed at encouraging and motivating all writers toward success, with special information to help new writers. Articles center on how to write better, market smarter, sell your work." Estab. 1981.

• Byline ranked #25 on *Writer's Digest*'s Fiction 50 list of top markets for fiction writers.

Needs: Literary, genre, general fiction. Receives 100-200 unsolicited fiction mss/month. Does not want to see erotica or explicit graphic content. No science fiction or fantasy. Accepts 1 ms/issue; 11 mss/year. Recently published work by Lucrecia Guerrero, Linda Fitzgerald and Jeff Spelman. **Published many new writers within the last year.** Length: 4,000 words maximum; 2,000 words minimum. Also publishes poetry and articles.

How to Contact: Send complete ms with SASE. Simultaneous submissions OK, "if notified. For us, no cover letter is needed." Reports in 6-12 weeks. Publishes ms an average of 3 months after acceptance. Sample copy for $4. Guidelines for #10 SASE.

Payment/Terms: Pays $100 on acceptance and 3 contributor's copies for first North American rights.

Advice: "We look for good writing that draws the reader in; conflict and character movement by stories end. We're very open to new writers. Submit a well-written, professionally prepared ms with SASE. No erotica or senseless violence; otherwise, we'll consider most any theme. We also sponsor short story and poetry contests. Read what's being published. Find a good story, not just a narrative reflection. Keep submitting."

☑ $◯ ▨ ▣ **THE CAFE IRREAL, International Imagination**. E-mail: cafeirreal@iname.com. Website: home.sprynet.com/~awhit. **Editors:** Alice Whittenburg, G.S. Evans. E-zine; illustrations. "*The Cafe Irreal* is a webzine focusing on short stories and short shorts of an irreal nature." Semiannually.

• *The Cafe Irreal* has been named a "cool site" by the Open Directory Project (Netscape) and received the Karafiat Literature Outstanding E-Zine award.

Needs: Experimental, fantasy (literary), science fiction (literary), translations. "No horror or 'slice-of-life' stories; no genre or mainstream science fiction or fantasy." Accepts 10-15 mss/issue; 20-30 mss/year. Publishes mss 6 months after acceptance. Recently published translations of works by Faruk Ulay and Marion Palla. Length: no minimum; 2,000 words maximum (excerpts from longer works accepted). Publishes short shorts. Also publishes literary essays, literary criticism. Often critiques or comments on rejected ms.

How to Contact: "We only accept electronic submissions. E-mail us with complete manuscript as enclosed text, HTML or ASCII file." Include estimated word count. Reports in 2 months on mss. Reprint submissions OK. See website for sample copy and fiction guidelines.

Payment/Terms: Pays 1¢/word, $2 minimum on publication for first rights, one-time rights. Sends galleys (the html document via e-mail) to author.

Advice: "Forget formulas. Write about what you *don't* know, take me places I couldn't *possibly* go, don't try to make me care about the characters. Read short fiction by writers such as Kafka, Kobo Abe, Julio Cortazar, Leonard Carrington and Stanislaw Lem. Also read our website and guidelines.''

CALLALOO, A Journal of African-American and African Arts and Letters, Dept. of English, 322 Bryan Hall, University of Virginia, Charlottesville VA 22903. (804)924-6637. Fax: (804)924-6472. E-mail: callaloo@virginia.edu. Website: muse.jhu.edu/journals/callaloo (includes sample issues, copyright information, editorial information, submission guidelines). **Editor:** Charles H. Rowell. Magazine: 7×10; 250 pages. Scholarly magazine. Quarterly. "Devoted to publishing fiction, poetry, drama of the African diaspora, including North, Central and South America, the Caribbean, Europe and Africa. Visually beautiful and well-edited, the journal publishes 3-5 short stories in all forms and styles in each issue." Estab. 1976. Circ. 1,500.

• One of the leading voices in African-American literature, *Callaloo* has received NEA literature grants. Work published in *Callaloo* received a 1994 *Pushcart Prize* anthology nomination and inclusion in *Best American Short Stories*.

Needs: Contemporary, ethnic (black culture), feminist, historical, humor/satire, literary, prose poem, regional, science fiction, serialized/excerpted novel, translations. Also publishes poetry and drama. "Would like to see more well-crafted, literary fiction particularly dealing with the black middle class, immigrant communities and/or the black South." No romance, confessional. Themes for 1997-98: Dutch Antillean literature and emerging black male writers. Also a Sterling Brown special issue. Accepts 3-5 mss/issue; 10-20 mss/year. Length: 50 pages maximum. Published work by Chinua Achebe, Rita Dove, Reginald McKnight, Caryl Philips, Jewell Parker Rhodes and John Edgar Wideman. **Publishes 5-10 new writers/year.**

How to Contact: Submit complete ms in triplicate and cover letter with name, mailing address, e-mail address, if possible, and SASE. Accepts queries by e-mail and fax. Reports on queries in 2 weeks; 3-4 months on mss. Previously published work accepted "only as part of a special issue or if solicited." Sample copy for $10.

Payment/Terms: Pays in contributor's copies. Acquires all rights. Sends galleys to author.

Advice: "We strongly recommend looking at the journal before submitting."

CALYX, A Journal of Art & Literature by Women, Calyx, Inc., P.O. Box B, Corvallis OR 97339. (541)753-9384. Fax: (541)753-0515. E-mail: calyx@proaxis.com. Director: Margarita Donnelly. **Senior Editor:** Beverly McFarland. Magazine: 6×8; 128 pages per single issue; 60 lb. coated matte stock paper; 10 pt. chrome coat cover; original art. Publishes prose, poetry, art, essays, interviews and critical and review articles. "*Calyx* exists to publish women's literary and artistic work and is committed to publishing the work of all women, including women of color, older women, working class women, and other voices that need to be heard. We are committed to nurturing beginning writers." Biannually. Estab. 1976. Circ. 6,000.

• Work from *Calyx* was selected for the *Pushcart Prize* anthology in 1998.

Needs: Receives approximately 1,000 unsolicited prose and poetry mss when open. Accepts 4-8 prose mss/issue, 9-15 mss/year. Reads mss October 1-December 15; submit only during this period. Mss received when not reading will be returned. Published work by Margaret Willey, Chitrita Banerji, Torie Olsen, Catherine Brady, Deidre Duffy and Andrea Silva. **Publishes 10-20 new writers/year.** Length: 5,000 words maximum. Also publishes literary essays, literary criticism, poetry.

How to Contact: Send ms with SASE and bio. Accepts requests for guidelines by e-mail. Simultaneous submissions OK. Reports in up to 8 months on mss. Publishes ms an average of 8 months after acceptance. Sample copy for $9.50 plus $2 postage. Guidelines available for SASE. Reviews novels, short story collections, poetry and essays.

Payment/Terms: "Combination of payment, free issues and 1 volume subscription."

Advice: Most mss are rejected because "the writers are not familiar with *Calyx*—writers should read *Calyx* and be familiar with the publication."

CAMBRENSIS, 41 Heol Fach, Cornelly, Bridgend, Mid-Glamorgan, CF33 4LN Wales. **Editor:** Arthur Smith. Quarterly. Circ. 500.

Needs: "Devoted solely to the short story form, featuring short stories by writers born or resident in Wales or with some Welsh connection; receives grants from the Welsh Arts' Council and the Welsh Writers' Trust; uses artwork—cartoons, line-drawings, sketches etc." Length: 2,500 words maximum.

How to Contact: Writer has to have some connection with Wales. SAE and IRCs or similar should be enclosed with "Air mail" postage to avoid long delay.

Payment/Terms: Writers receive 3 copies of magazine. Send IRCs for a sample copy. Subscriptions via Blackwell's Periodicals, P.O. Box 40, Hythe Bridge Street, Oxford, OX1 2EU, UK or Swets & Zeitlinger B V, P.O. Box 800, 2160 S Z Lisse, Holland.

CAPERS AWEIGH, Cape Breton Poetry & Fiction, Capers Aweigh Press, 39 Water St., Glace Bay, Sydney, Nova Scotia B1A 1R6 Canada. (902)849-0822. E-mail: capersaweigh@hotmail.com. **Editor:** John MacNeil. Magazine: 5×8; 80 pages; bond paper; Cornwall-coated cover. "*Capers Aweigh* publishes poetry and fiction of, by and for Cape Bretoners." Publication frequency varies. Estab. 1992. Circ. 500.

Needs: Adventure, ethnic/multicultural, fantasy, feminist, historical, humor/satire, literary, mainstream, contemporary, mystery/suspense, psychic/supernatural/occult, regional, science fiction. List of upcoming themes available for SASE. Receives 2 unsolicited mss/month. Accepts 30 mss/issue. Publishes ms 9 months after acceptance. Published work by C. Fairn Kennedy and Shirley Kiju Kawi. Length: 2,500 words. Publishes short shorts. Also publishes literary criticism, poetry. Sponsors contests only to Cape Bretoners fiction writers.

How to Contact: Query first. Send SASE for reply or send a disposable copy of ms. Electronic submissions OK (IBM). Sample copy for $4.95 and 6×10 SAE.

Payment/Terms: Pays free subscription to the magazine and 1 contributor's copy; additional copies for $4.95. Acquires first North American serial rights. Sends galleys to author.

N ☯ $○ THE CAPILANO REVIEW, 2055 Purcell Way, North Vancouver, British Columbia V7J 3H5 Canada. (604)984-1712. Fax: (604)983-7520. E-mail: erains@capcollege.bc.ca. Website: www.capcollege.bc.ca/dept/TCR/tcr.html (includes guidelines, excerpts and complete bibliography of 25 years worth of contributors). **Editor:** Ryan Knighton. Magazine: 6×9; 90-120 pages; book paper; glossy cover; perfect-bound; illustrations and photos. Magazine of "fresh, innovative art and literature for literary/artistic audience." Triannually. Estab. 1972. Circ. 900.

Needs: Experimental, literary and drama. Receives 80 unsolicited mss/month. Accepts 3-4 mss/issue; 10 mss/year. Published work by Keith Harrison, Kim Echlin and Jack Hodgins. **Published new writers within the last year.** Length: 4,000 words average. Publishes short shorts. Also publishes literary essays, poetry. Occasionally recommends other markets.

How to Contact: Send complete ms with cover letter and SASE or IRC. Include 2- to 3-sentence bio and brief list of publications. Reports on mss in 2-4 months. Send SAE with IRCs for return of ms. Sample copy for $9 (Canadian).

Payment/Terms: Pays $50-200, 2 contributor's copies and one year subscription. Pays on publication. Acquires first North American serial rights.

Advice: "We are looking for exceptional, original style; strong thematic content; innovation and quality writing. Read several issues before submitting and make sure your work is technically perfect."

⊕ ✓ ◎ THE CARIBBEAN WRITER, The University of the Virgin Islands, RR 02, Box 10,000—Kingshill, St. Croix, Virgin Islands 00850. (340)692-4152. Fax: (340)692-4026. E-mail: qmars@uvi.edu. Website: www.uvi.edu/caribbeanWriter/ (includes excerpts). **Editor:** Erika J. Waters. Magazine: 6×9; 304 pages; 60 lb. paper; glossy cover stock; illustrations and photos. "*The Caribbean Writer* is an international magazine with a Caribbean focus. The Caribbean should be central to the work, or the work should reflect a Caribbean heritage, experience or perspective." Annually. Estab. 1987. Circ. 1,500.

Needs Contemporary, historical (general), humor/satire, literary, mainstream and prose poem. Receives 800 unsolicited mss/year. Accepts 60 mss/issue. Also accepts poetry, essays, translations, plays. Recently published work by E.A. Markham, Marvin E. Williams, Cynthia James, Lynn Halsey and Klaus de Albuquerque. **Publishes approximately 20% new writers.**

How to Contact: Send complete ms with cover letter. Accepts queries/mss by e-mail and fax. "Blind submissions only. Send name, address and title of manuscript on separate sheet. Title only on manuscript. Manuscripts will not be considered unless this procedure is followed." Reports "once a year." SASE (or IRC). Simultaneous submissions OK. Sample copy for $5 and $2 postage.

Payment/Terms: Pays 2 contributor's copies. Annual prizes for best story ($400); for best poem ($300); $100 for first publication.

Terms: Acquires one-time rights.

Advice: Looks for "fiction which reflects a Caribbean heritage, experience or perspective."

✓ ◐ ♈ CAROLINA QUARTERLY, Greenlaw Hall CB #3520, University of North Carolina, Chapel Hill NC 27599-3520. (919)962-0244. Fax: (919)962-3520. E-mail: cquarter@unc.edu. Website: www.unc.edu/student/orgs/cquarter (includes writer's guidelines, current contents, index to past contributors). **Editor-in-Chief:** Brian Carpenter. Literary journal: 70-90 pages; illustrations. Publishes fiction for a "general literary audience." Triannually. Estab. 1948. Circ. 1,400.

- Work published in *Carolina Quarterly* has been selected for inclusion in *Best American Short Stories*, in *New Stories from the South: The Year's Best*, and *Best of the South*. *Carolina Quarterly* received a North Carolina Arts Council grant for 1997-98 and a special mention in 1999 *Pushcart Prize* stories.

Needs: Literary. "We would like to see more short/micro-fiction and more stories by minority/ethnic writers." Receives 150-200 unsolicited fiction mss/month. Accepts 4-5 mss/issue; 14-16 mss/year. Publishes ms an average of 4 months after acceptance. Published work by Clyde Edgerton, Barry Hannah and Doris Betts. **Publishes 1-2 new writers/year.** Length: 7,000 words maximum; no minimum. Also publishes short shorts, literary essays, poetry. Occasionally critiques rejected mss.

How to Contact: Send complete ms with cover letter and SASE to fiction editor. Accepts queries by phone, fax and e-mail. No simultaneous submissions. Reports in 2-4 months. Sample copy for $5; writer's guidelines for SASE.

Payment/Terms: Pays in contributor's copies for first rights.

CAYO, A Chronicle of Life in the Keys, P.O. Box 4516, Key West FL 33041. (305)296-4286. **Editor:** Alyson Matley. Magazine: 8½×11; 40-48 pages; glossy paper; 70 lb. cover stock; illustrations and photos. Magazine on Keys-related topics or by Keys authors. Quarterly. Estab. 1993. Circ. 1,000.

Needs: Condensed/excerpted novel, experimental, literary, regional. Receives 4-5 unsolicited mss/month. Accepts 2-3 mss/issue; 8-12 mss/year. Published work by Alma Bond, Robin Shanley and Lawrence Ferlinghetti. Length: 3,000 words average; 800 words minimum; 3,000 words maximum. Publishes short shorts. Also publishes literary essays, poetry. Often critiques or comments on rejected mss.

How to Contact: Send complete ms with a cover letter. Include bio and list of publications with submission. Reports in 6 weeks on queries; 3 months on mss. Send SASE for reply, return of ms or send a disposable copy of ms. Simultaneous, reprint and electronic (ASCII text on disk) submissions OK. Sample copy for $4. Fiction guidelines for #10 SASE.

Payment/Terms: Pays in contributor's copies. Acquires one-time rights.

Advice: "The story has to stand on its own and move the reader."

CHANTEH, The Iranian Cross-Cultural Quarterly, P.O. Box 703, Falls Church VA 22046. (703)533-1727. Fax: (703)536-7853. **Editor:** Saïdeh Pakravan. Magazine: 8½×11; 80 pages; illustrations and photos. "A multicultural magazine for second-generation immigrants and exiles adapting to new environments." Quarterly. Estab. 1992. Circ. 1,200.

Needs: Ethnic/multicultural (general), historical (Middle East), humor/satire, literary, mainstream/contemporary. No romance, erotic, science fiction. Receives 100 unsolicited mss/month. Accepts 1-2 mss/issue; 10 mss/year. Publishes ms 3 months after acceptance. **Publishes 50% new writers.** Length: 3,000 words average; 2,000 words minimum; 7,500 words maximum. Publishes short shorts. Also publishes literary essays, literary criticism, poetry.

How to Contact: Send complete ms with a cover letter. Include 25-word bio. Reports in 6 weeks. Send disposable copy of ms. Simultaneous submissions OK. Reviews novels, short story collections and nonfiction books of interest to writers.

Payment/Terms: Pays 2 contributor's copies. Acquires first North American serial rights.

Advice: "The material should preferably, though not exclusively, relate to the cross-cultural experience. This is more a trend than a fast rule. An exceptional submission will always be considered on its own merit."

$ CHAPMAN, 4 Broughton Place, Edinburgh EH1 3RX Scotland. **Fiction Editor:** Joy Hendry. Phone: 0131 557 2207. Fax: 0131 556 9565. Website: www.compura/com.chapman (includes samples from current issues, guidelines, catalog). Quarterly. Circ. 2,000. Publishes 4-6 stories/issue. Estab. 1970.

Needs: "*Chapman*, Scotland's quality literary magazine, is a dynamic force in Scotland, publishing poetry, fiction, criticism, reviews; articles on theatre, politics, language and the arts." No horror, science fiction. Recently published work by Quim Monzo, Dilys Rose, Leslie Schenck. **Publishes up to 10 new writers/year.** Length: 1,000 words minimum; 6,000 words maximum.

How to Contact: Include SAE and return postage (or IRC) with submissions.

Payment/Terms: Pays £7/page. Sample copy available for £4 (includes postage).

$ THE CHARITON REVIEW, Truman State University, Kirksville MO 63552. (816)785-4499. Fax: (816)785-7486. **Editor:** Jim Barnes. Magazine: 6×9; approximately 100 pages; 60 lb. paper; 65 lb. cover stock; photographs on cover. "We demand only excellence in fiction and fiction translation for a general and college readership." Semiannually. Estab. 1975. Circ. 700.

Needs: Literary, contemporary, experimental, translations. Accepts 3-5 mss/issue; 6-10 mss/year. Published work by Ann Townsend, Glenn DelGrosso, Paul Ruffin and X.J. Kennedy. **Published new writers within the last year.** Length: 3,000-6,000 words. Also publishes literary essays, poetry. Critiques rejected mss when there is time.

How to Contact: Send complete ms with SASE. No book-length mss. No simultaneous submissions. Reports in less than 1 month on mss. Publishes ms an average of 6 months after acceptance. Sample copy for $5 with SASE. Reviews novels and short story collections.

Payment/Terms: Pays $5/page up to $50 maximum and contributor's copy on publication; additional copies for $5.50. Buys first North American serial rights; rights returned on request.

Advice: "Do not ask us for guidelines: the only guidelines are excellence in all matters. Write well and study the publication you are submitting to. We are interested only in the very best fiction and fiction translation. We are not interested in slick material. We do not read photocopies, dot-matrix, or carbon copies. Know the simple mechanics of submission—SASE, no paper clips, no odd-sized SASE, etc. Know the genre (short story, novella, etc.). Know the unwritten laws. There is too much manufactured fiction; assembly-lined, ego-centered personal essays offered as fiction."

CHASM, A Journal of the Macabre, P.O. Box 2549, Jamaica Plain MA 02130. Website: www.shore.net/~texas (includes writer's guidelines, names of editors, short fiction, interviews with authors, purchase information and stores where *Chasm* is available). **Editor:** Nat Panek. Magazine: 5×8½; 50-60 pages; 70 lb. vellum; illustrations and photos. "*Chasm* is a forum for high-quality, dark-themed fiction, poetry, literary journalism and artwork. Aimed at literate horror enthusiasts who want more from the genre than the mass media provide." Estab. 1995. Circ. 300.

Needs: Experimental, horror, psychic/supernatural/occult. Wants more "tight, well thought-out, surreal nature-of-reality stories." No "sword and sorcery fantasy." Receives 40 unsolicited mss/month. Accepts 5-6 mss/issue; 10-12 mss/year. Recently published work by K.S. Hardy, Ben Miller and William Sheldon. **Publishes 2-3 new writers/year.** Length: 5,000 words average; 100 words minimum; 6,000 words maximum. Publishes short shorts. Also publishes literary essays and poetry. Sometimes comments on or critiques rejected manuscripts.

How to Contact: Send complete manuscript with cover letter. Include 50-75 word bio and estimated word count. Reports in 2-4 weeks on queries; 2-3 months on manuscripts. Send SASE for reply, return of ms or send disposable copy of ms. Simultaneous and electronic (disk only) submissions OK. Sample copy for $5. Fiction guidelines for #10 SASE.

Payment/Terms: Pays 1 contributor's copy; additional copies $3. Sends galleys to author.

Advice: "Restrain your prose but not your imagination. Arresting language, imagery, characterization on the first page are key. Grabbing attention is the hard part—sustaining it only slightly less so. Mass market horror a la King, Barker, Koontz, etc. is a niche that is obviously full to overflowing, and needs no help from a small journal like *Chasm*. Writers who are further out on the fringes in terms of style and content—Harlan Ellison, Angela Carter, Lucius Shepard, Lisa Tuttle—are harder to find. That's where *Chasm* steps in."

$⊘☑ THE CHATTAHOOCHEE REVIEW, Georgia Perimeter College, 2101 Womack Rd., Dunwoody GA 30338. (770)551-3019. **Editor:** Lawrence Hetrick. Magazine: 6×9; 150 pages; 70 lb. paper; 80 lb. cover stock; illustrations; photographs. Quarterly. Estab. 1980. Circ. 1,250.

● Fiction from *The Chattahoochee Review* has been included in *Best New Stories of the South*.

Needs: Literary, mainstream. No juvenile, romance, science fiction. Receives 900 unsolicited mss/year. Accepts 5 mss/issue. Recently published work by Larry Brown, Terry Kay, Merrill Joan Gerber and Mary Ann Taylor-Hall. **Published new writers within the last year.** Length: 2,500 words average. Also publishes creative nonfiction, interviews with writers, poetry reviews, poetry. Sometimes critiques rejected mss.

How to Contact: Send complete ms with cover letter, which should include sufficient bio for notes on contributors' page. Reports in 2-4 months. SASE. May consider simultaneous submission "reluctantly." Sample copy for $5. Fiction and poetry guidelines available on request. Reviews novels and short story collections.

Payment/Terms: Pays $20/page fiction; $15/page nonfiction; $50/poem. Acquires first rights.

Advice: "Arrange to read magazine before you submit to it." Known for publishing Southern regional fiction.

$⊘☑ CHELSEA, Chelsea Associates, Inc., Box 773, Cooper Station, New York NY 10276-0773. E-mail: rafoerster@aol.com. **Editor:** Richard Foerster. Magazine: 6×9; 185-235 pages; 60 lb. white paper; glossy, full-color cover; artwork; occasional photos. "We have no consistent theme except for single special issues. Otherwise, we use general material of an eclectic nature: poetry, prose, artwork, etc., for a sophisticated, literate audience interested in avant-garde literature and current writing, both national and international." Annually. Estab. 1958. Circ. 1,800.

● *Chelsea* sponsors the Chelsea Awards. Entries to that contest will also be considered for the magazine, but writers may submit directly to the magazine as well. *Chelsea* was the recipient of a New York State Council for the Arts grant in 1998-1999. *Chelsea* has received the Beacon Best of 1999 for two authors and *Pushcart* nominations.

Needs: Literary, contemporary short fiction, poetry and translations. "No science fiction, romance, divorce, racist, sexist material or I-hate-my-mother stories. We look for serious, sophisticated literature from writers willing to take risks with language and narrative structure." Receives approximately 200 unsolicited fiction mss each month. Approximately 1% of fiction is agented. **Publishes 1-2 new writers/year.** Length: not over 25 printed pages. Publishes short shorts of 6 pages or less. Sponsors annual Chelsea Award, $1,000 (send SASE for guidelines).

How to Contact: Send complete ms with SASE and succinct cover letter with previous credits. No inquiries by e-mail. No simultaneous submissions. Reports in 5 months on mss. Publishes ms within a year after acceptance. Sample copy for $7.

Payment/Terms: Pays contributor's copies and $15 per printed page for first North American serial rights plus one-time non-exclusive reprint rights.

Advice: "Familiarize yourself with issues of the magazine for character of contributions. Manuscripts should be legible, clearly typed, with minimal number of typographical errors and cross-outs, sufficient return postage. Most manuscripts are rejected because they are conventional in theme and/or style, uninspired, contrived, etc. We see far too much of the amateurish love story or romance. We would like to see more fiction that is sophisticated, with attention paid to theme, setting, language as well as plot. Writers should say something that has never been said before or at least say something in a unique way. There is too much focus on instant fame and not enough attention to craft. Our audience is sophisticated, international, and expects freshness and originality."

☑ $⊘☑ CHICAGO REVIEW, 5801 S. Kenwood Ave., Chicago IL 60637. (773)702-0887. E-mail: chicago-review@uchicago.edu. Website: humanities.uchicago.edu (includes guidelines, editors' names, subscription information). **Fiction Editor:** William Martin. Magazine for a highly literate general audience: 6×9; 128

pages; offset white 60 lb. paper; illustrations; photos. Quarterly. Estab. 1946. Circ. 3,500.

- The *Chicago Review* has won two *Pushcart* prizes and an Illinois Arts Council Award.

Needs: Literary, contemporary and experimental. Accepts up to 5 mss/issue; 20 mss/year. Receives 80-100 unsolicited fiction mss each week. Recently published work by Hollis Seamon, Tom House, Rachel Klein and Doris Dörrie. **Publishes 2 new writers/year.** No preferred length, except will not accept book-length mss. Also publishes literary essays, literary criticism, poetry. Sometimes recommends other markets.

How to Contact: Send complete ms with cover letter. Accepts queries/mss by e-mail. SASE. No simultaneous submissions. Reports in 4-5 months on mss. Sample copy for $8. Guidelines with SASE. Reviews novels and short story collections. Send books to Book Review Editor.

Payment/Terms: Pays 3 contributor's copies and subscription.

Advice: "We look with interest at fiction that addresses subjects inventively, work that steers clear of clichéd treatments of themes. We're always eager to read writing that experiments with language, whether it be with characters' viewpoints, tone or style. We like a strong voice capable of rejecting gimmicks in favor of subtleties. We are most impressed by writers who have read both deeply and broadly, but display their own inventiveness. However, we have been receiving more submissions and are becoming more selective."

CHIRICÚ, Ballantine Hall 849, Indiana University, Bloomington IN 47405. (812)855-5257. **Managing Editor:** Barbara Santos. "We publish essays, translations, poetry, fiction, reviews, interviews and artwork (illustrations and photos) that are either by or about Latinos. We have no barriers on style, content or ideology, but would like to see well-written material. We accept manuscripts written in English, Spanish or Portuguese." Annually. Estab. 1976. Circ. 500.

Needs: Contemporary, ethnic, experimental, fantasy, feminist, humor/satire, literary, mainstream, prose poem, science fiction, serialized/excerpted novel, translations. **Published new writers within the last year.** Length: 7,000 words maximum; 3,000 words average. Occasionally critiques rejected mss.

How to Contact: Send complete ms with cover letter. "Include some personal information along with information about your story." SASE. No simultaneous submissions. Reports in 5 weeks. Publishes ms 6-12 months after acceptance. Sample copy for $5. Guidelines for #10 SASE.

Advice: "Realize that we are a Latino literary journal so, if you are not Latino, your work must reflect an interest in Latino issues or have a Latino focus." Mss rejected "because beginning writers force their language instead of writing from genuine sentiment, because of multiple grammatical errors."

CHIRON REVIEW, 702 N. Prairie, St. John KS 67576-1516. (316)549-6156. E-mail: chironreview@hotmail.com. Website: www.geocities.com/SoHo/Nook/1748 (includes writer's guidelines, names of editors, chat line, sample poems and contest info). **Editor:** Michael Hathaway. Tabloid: 10×13; minimum 24 pages; newsprint; illustrations; photos. Publishes "all types of material, no particular theme; traditional and off-beat, no taboos." Quarterly. Estab. 1982. Circ. 1,200.

- *Chiron Review* is known for publishing experimental and "sudden" fiction.

Needs: Contemporary, experimental, humor/satire, literary. No didactic, religious or overtly political writing. Receives 100 mss/month. Accepts 1-3 ms/issue; 4-12 mss/year. Publishes ms within 6-18 months of acceptance. Published work by Janice Eidus, David Newman, Craig Curtis, Jay Marvin and Ad Hudler. **Publishes 100 new writers and poets/year.** Length: 3,500 maximum. Publishes short shorts. Sometimes recommends other markets to writers of rejected mss.

How to Contact: Reports in 6-8 weeks. SASE. No simultaneous or reprint submissions. Deadlines: November 1 (Winter), February 1 (Spring), May 1 (Summer), August 1 (Autumn). Sample copy for $4 ($8 overseas). Fiction guidelines for #10 SASE.

Payment/Terms: Pays 1 contributor's copy; extra copies at 50% discount. Acquires first rights.

Advice: "Research markets thoroughly."

CHRISTIANITY AND THE ARTS, 1100 N. Lakeshore, #33-A, P.O. Box 118088, Chicago IL 60611. (312)642-8606. Fax: (312)266-7719. E-mail: chrnarts@aol.com. **Editor:** Marci Whitney-Schenck. Magazine: 8½×11; 52 pages; 60 lb. gloss paper; illustrations and photos. Publishes work on "Christian expression—visual arts, dance, music, literature, film. We reach Protestant, Catholic, and Orthodox readers throughout the United States and Canada. Our readers tend to be upscale and well-educated, with an interest in several disciplines, such as music and the visual arts." Quarterly. Estab. 1994. Circ. 4,000.

- *Christianity and the Arts* received an award from Associated Church Press in 1995 and 1996.

Needs: Mainstream/contemporary, religious/inspirational. No erotica. "We generally treat two themes in each issue." Receives 3-4 unsolicited mss/month. "We hope to publish one fiction manuscript per issue." Publishes ms 6 months after acceptance. Length: 3,000 words maximum. Publishes short shorts. Also publishes literary essays. Sometimes critiques or comments on rejected mss.

How to Contact: Send complete ms with a cover letter. Include bio, estimated word count and list of publications. SASE for reply. Simultaneous submissions OK. Sample copy for $6. Reviews novels and short story collections.

Payment/Terms: No payment. Sends galleys to author.

$ ▢ CHRYSALIS READER, Journal of the Swedenborg Foundation, The Swedenborg Foundation, P.O. Box 549, West Chester PA 19381-0549. (610)430-3222. Send mss to: Rt. 1, Box 184, Dillwyn VA 23936. (804)983-3021. **Editor:** Carol S. Lawson. Book series: 7½×10; 192 pages; archival paper; coated cover stock; illustrations; photos. "A literary magazine centered around one theme per issue. Publishes fiction, essays and poetry for intellectually curious readers interested in spiritual topics." Biannually. Estab. 1985. Circ. 3,000.
Needs: Fiction (leading to insight), contemporary, experimental, historical, literary, mainstream, mystery/suspense, science fiction, spiritual, sports. No religious, juvenile, preschool. Upcoming themes: "Serendipity" (September 2000). Receives 50 mss/month. Accepts 15-20 mss/issue; 20-40 mss/year. Publishes ms within 2 years of acceptance. Published work by Robert Bly, Larry Dossey, John Hitchcock, Barbara Marx Hubbard and Linda Pastan. Length: 2,000 words minimum; 3,500 words maximum. Also publishes literary essays, literary criticism, chapters of novels, poetry. Sometimes critiques rejected mss and recommends other markets.
How to Contact: Query first and send SASE for guidelines. Reports in 2 months. SASE. No simultaneous, reprinted or in-press material. Sample copy for $10. Fiction guidelines for #10 SASE.
Payment/Terms: Pays $75-250 and 5 contributor's copies on publication for one-time rights. Sends galleys to author.
Advice: Looking for "1. *Quality*; 2. appeal for our audience; 3. relevance to/illumination of an issue's theme."

$ ▢ ◎ CICADA, 329 "E" St., Bakersfield CA 93304. (805)323-4064. **Editor:** Frederick A. Raborg, Jr. Magazine: 5½×8¼; 24 pages; matte cover stock; illustrations and photos. "Oriental poetry and fiction related to the Orient for general readership and haiku enthusiasts." Quarterly. Estab. 1985. Circ. 700.
Needs: *All with Oriental slant*: Adventure, contemporary, erotica, ethnic, experimental, fantasy, feminist, historical (general), horror, humor/satire, lesbian, literary, mainstream, mystery/suspense, psychic/supernatural/occult, regional, contemporary romance, historical romance, young adult romance, science fiction, senior citizen/retirement and translations. "We look for strong fiction with Oriental (especially Japanese) content or flavor. Stories need not have 'happy' endings, and we are open to the experimental and/or avant-garde. Erotica is fine; pornography, no." Receives 30 unsolicited mss/month. Accepts 1 ms/issue; 4 mss/year. Publishes ms 6 months to 1 year after acceptance. Agented fiction 5%. Published work by Gilbert Garand, Frank Holland and Jim Mastro. Length: 2,000 words average; 500 words minimum; 3,000 words maximum. Critiques rejected ms when appropriate. Also publishes poetry.
How to Contact: Send complete ms with cover letter. Include Social Security number and appropriate information about the writer in relationship to the Orient. Reports in 2 weeks on queries; 3 months on mss (if seriously considered). SASE. Sample copy for $6. Fiction guidelines for #10 SASE.
Payment/Terms: Pays $10-25 and contributor's copies on publication for first North American serial rights; charges for additional copies. $5 kill fee.
Advice: Looks for "excellence and appropriate storyline. Strong characterization and knowledge of the Orient are musts. Neatness counts high on my list for first impressions. A writer should demonstrate a high degree of professionalism."

☑ $ ▢ CIMARRON REVIEW, Oklahoma State University, 205 Morrill, Stillwater OK 74074-0135. (405)744-9476. Website: cimarronreview.okstate.edu. **Associate Editors:** Todd Peterson and Jennifer Schell. Magazine: 6×9; 150 pages. "Poetry and fiction on contemporary themes; personal essay on contemporary issues that cope with life in the 20th century, for educated literary readers. We work hard to reflect quality. We are eager to receive manuscripts from both established and less experienced writers that intrigue us by their unusual perspective, language, imagery and character." Quarterly. Estab. 1967. Circ. 500.
Needs: Literary and contemporary. "Would like to see more work by Native American, African and Hispanic writers." No collegiate reminiscences, science fiction or juvenilia. Accepts 6-7 mss/issue, 24-28 mss/year. Published work by John Yau, Gordon Lish, Lee Martin and Jane Bradley. **Published "many" new writers within the last year.** Also publishes literary essays, literary criticism, poetry.
How to Contact: Send complete ms with SASE. "Short cover letters are appropriate but not essential, except for providing *CR* with the most recent mailing address available." No simultaneous submissions. Reports in 3 months on mss. Publishes ms within 1 year after acceptance. Sample copy with SASE and $5. Reviews novels, short story collections, and poetry collections.
Payment/Terms: Pays one-year subscription to author, plus $50 for each prose piece. Acquires all rights on publication. "Permission to reprint granted freely."
Advice: "Don't try to pass personal essays off as fiction. Short fiction is a genre uniquely suited to the modern world. *CR* seeks an individual, innovative style that focuses on contemporary themes."

[N] ○ CITY PRIMEVAL: Narratives of Urban Reality, P.O. Box 30064, Seattle WA 98103. (206)440-0791. **Editor:** David Ross. Magazine: 6×9; 72 pages; 60 lb. paper; card cover stock; illustrations; and photos. *City Primeval* "features work in the new genre: urban narrative (see guidelines)." Quarterly. Estab. 1995. Circ. 200.
Needs: Adventure, literary, military/war, mystery/suspense, thriller/espionage. Receives 30-50 unsolicited mss/ month. Accepts 6-10 mss/issue; 36-60 mss/year. Publishes ms 3-6 months after acceptance. **Publishes 6-10 new writers/year.** Recently published work by James Bernhard, Robert R. Ward, Lucas Doolin, Susan Montag and

Diane Trzcinski. Word length: 5,000 words average; 10,000 words maximum. Publishes short shorts. Also publishes literary essays and poetry. Sometimes comments on or critiques rejected ms.

How to Contact: Send complete ms with a cover letter. Include 6-12 line bio. Reports on mss in 6 weeks. Send SASE for return of ms. No simultaneous submissions. Sample copy for $5. Guidelines for SASE.

Payment/Terms: Pays 1 contributor's copy. Payment on publication. Acquires first North American serial rights.

Advice: "Must meet editorial requirements. Know the market."

THE CLAREMONT REVIEW, The Contemporary Magazine of Young Adult Writers, The Claremont Review Publishers, 4980 Wesley Rd., Victoria, British Columbia V8Y 1Y9 Canada. (604)658-5221. Fax: (604)658-5387. E-mail: aurora@home.com. **Editors:** Terence Young, Bill Stenson, Susan Stenson, Rob Filgate, Janice McCachen, Faro Sullivan and Susan Field. Magazine: 6×9; 110-120 pages; book paper; soft gloss cover; b&w illustrations. "We are dedicated to publishing emerging young writers aged 13-19 from anywhere in the English-speaking world, but primarily Canada and the U.S." Biannually. Estab. 1992. Circ. 700.

Needs: Young adult/teen ("their writing, not writing for them"). Plans special fiction issue or anthology. Receives 10-12 unsolicited mss/month. Accepts 10-12 mss/issue; 20-24 mss/year. Publishes ms 3 months after acceptance. Recently published work by Ami Drummand, Phoebe Wang, Courtney Myette and Nathan Hudon. Length: 1,500-3,000 words preferred; 5,000 words maximum. Publishes short shorts, prose and poetry. Always comments on rejected mss.

How to Contact: Send complete ms with cover letter. Include 2-line bio, list of publications and SASE. Reports in 6 weeks-3 months. Simultaneous and electronic (disk or modem) submissions OK. Sample copy for $6 with 6×9 SASE and $2 Canadian postage. Guidelines free with SASE.

Payment/Terms: Pays 1 contributor's copy on publication for first North American and one-time rights. Additional copies for $6.

Advice: Looking for "good concrete narratives with credible dialogue and solid use of original detail. It must be unique, honest and a glimpse of some truth. Send an error-free final draft with a short covering letter and bio; please, read us first to see what we publish."

THE CLIMBING ART, 6390 E. Floyd Dr., Denver CO 80222-7638. Phone/fax: (303)757-0541. E-mail: rmorrow@dnvr.uswest.net. **Editor:** Ron Morrow. Magazine: 5½×8½; 150 pages; illustrations and photos. "*The Climbing Art* publishes literature, poetry and art for and about the spirit of climbing." Semiannually. Estab. 1986. Circ. 1,200.

Needs: Adventure, condensed/excerpted novel, ethnic/multicultural, experimental, fantasy, historical, literary, mainstream/contemporary, mystery/suspense, regional, science fiction, sports, translations. "No religious, rhyming, or non-climbing related." Receives 50 unsolicited mss/month. Accepts 4-6 mss/issue; 10-15 mss/year. Publishes ms up to 1 year after acceptance. Agented fiction 10%. **Publishes 25-30 new writers/year.** Recently published work by Cameron Burns, Robert Walton and Gary Every. Length: 500 words minimum; 10,000 words maximum. Publishes short shorts. Also publishes literary essays, literary criticism, poetry. Sometimes critiques or comments on rejected mss. Sometimes sponsors contests.

How to Contact: Send complete ms with a cover letter. Include estimated word count, 1-paragraph bio and list of publications. Accepts queries/mss by fax or e-mail. Reports in 1 month on queries; 2-8 weeks on mss. SASE. Simultaneous and electronic submissions OK. Sample copy $7. Reviews novels and short story collections.

Payment/Terms: Pays free subscription and 2 contributor's copies; additional copies for $4. Acquires one-time rights.

Advice: Looks for knowledge of subject matter and love of the sport of climbing. "Read several issues first and make certain the material is related to climbing and the spirit of climbing. We have not seen enough literary excellence."

COLLAGES AND BRICOLAGES, The Journal of International Writing, P.O. Box 360, Shippenville PA 16254. E-mail: cb@penn.com. **Editor:** Marie-José Fortis. Magazine: 8½×11; 100-150 pages; illustrations. "The magazine includes essays, short stories, occasional interviews, short plays, poems that show innovative promise. It is often focus or issue oriented—themes can be either literary or socio-political." Annually. Estab. 1987.

Needs: Contemporary, ethnic, experimental, feminist, humor/satire, literary, philosophical works. "Also symbolist, surrealist b&w designs/illustrations are welcome." Receives about 60 unsolicited fiction mss/month. Publishes ms 6-9 months after acceptance. Recently published work by Rosette Lamont, Sharon Bourke, Daniella Gioseffi and John Fielding. **Published new writers within the last year.** Publishes short shorts. Also publishes literary essays, literary criticism, poetry. Critiques rejected ms "when great potential is manifest."

How to Contact: Send complete ms with cover letter that includes a short bio. Reports in 1-3 months. SASE. Sample copy for $10; older back issues $5. Reviews novels and short story collections. "How often and how many per issue depends on reviewers available. Only send material between August 15 and December 15."

Payment/Terms: Pays 2 contributor's copies. Acquires first rights. Rights revert to author after publication.

Advice: "Avoid following 'industry trends.' Do what you must do. Write what you must write. Write as if words were your bread, your water, a great vintage wine, salt, oxygen. Also, very few of us have a cornucopia budget, but it is a good idea to look at a publication before submitting."

$ ◨ COLORADO REVIEW, English Department, Colorado State University, Fort Collins CO 80523. (970)491-5449. E-mail: creview@vines.colostate.edu. **Editor:** David Milofsky. Literary journal: 200 pages; 70 lb. book weight paper. Triquarterly. Estab. as *Colorado State Review* 1966. Circ. 1,300.
● *Colorado Review*'s circulation has increased from 500 to 1,300.
Needs: Contemporary, ethnic, experimental, literary, mainstream, translations. No genre fiction. Receives 600 unsolicited fiction mss/month. Accepts 3-4 mss/issue. Recently published work by Robert Olen Butler, T. Alan Broughton, Elizabeth Gaffney, Ann Hood and Robert Boswell. **Published new writers within the last year.** Length: under 6,000 words. Does not read mss May through August. Also publishes literary essays, book reviews, poetry. Occasionally critiques rejected mss.
How to Contact: Send complete ms with SASE (or IRC) and brief bio with previous publications. Reports in 3 months. Publishes ms 6-12 months after acceptance. Sample copy for $10. Reviews novels or short story collections.
Payment/Terms: Pays $5/printed page for fiction; 2 contributor's copies; extras for $5. Pays on publication for first North American serial rights. "We assign copyright to author on request." Sends galleys to author.
Advice: "We are interested in manuscripts that show craft, imagination, and a convincing voice. If a story has reached a level of technical competence, we are receptive to the fiction working on its own terms. The oldest advice is still the best: persistence. Approach every aspect of the writing process with pride, conscientiousness—from word choice to manuscript appearance."

☑ ◨ COLUMBIA: A JOURNAL OF LITERATURE & ART, 415 Dodge Hall, Columbia University, New York NY 10027. (212)854-4216. E-mail: arts-litjournal@columbia.edu. Website: www.columbia.edu/cu/arts/writing/columbiajournal/index.html (includes writer's guidelines, themes, announcements, sample excerpts from past issues and annual contest). **Editors:** Max Fierst and Donald J. Modica. Prose Editor: Lillian Welch. Editors change each year. Magazine: 5¼ × 8¼; approximately 200 pages; coated cover stock; illustrations, photos. "We accept short stories, novel excerpts, translations, interviews, nonfiction, artwork and poetry." Biannually.
Needs: Literary and translations. "No genre unless it transcends the genre." Upcoming themes: "American History" (Summer 2000); "Millennium" (Winter 2000). Accepts 5-15 mss/issue. Receives approximately 125 unsolicited fiction mss each month. Does not read mss May 1 to August 31. Recently published work by Doris Dörrie, Ha Jin, Aimee Bender, Stephen Dixon and Jeanette Winterson. **Published 5-8 unpublished writers within the year.** Length: 25 pages maximum. Publishes short shorts.
How to Contact: Send complete ms with SASE. Accepts computer printout submissions. Reports in 2-3 months. Sample copy for $8.
Payment/Terms: Offers yearly contest with guest editors and cash awards. Offers one editor's award at $250/issue. Send SASE for guidelines.
Advice: "Because our staff changes each year, our specific tastes also change, so our best advice is to write what you want to write."

$ ◻ ◪ CONFRONTATION, English Dept., C.W. Post of Long Island University, Brookville NY 11548. (516)299-2391, (516)299-2720. Fax: (516)299-2735. Editor: Martin Tucker. **Associate Editor:** Jonna Semeiks. Magazine: 6 × 9; 190-250 pages; 70 lb. paper; 80 lb. cover; illustrations; photos. "We like to have a 'range' of subjects, form and style in each issue and are open to all forms. Quality is our major concern. Our audience is made up of literate, thinking people; formally or self-educated." Semiannually. Estab. 1968. Circ. 2,000.
● *Confrontation* has garnered a long list of awards and honors, including the Editor's Award for Distinguished Achievement from CCLM (now the Council of Literary Magazines and Presses) and NEA grants. Work from the magazine has appeared in numerous anthologies including the *Pushcart Prize, Best Short Stories* and *O. Henry Prize Stories*.
Needs: Literary, contemporary, prose poem, regional and translations. No "proseletyzing" literature. Accepts 30 mss/issue; 60 mss/year. Receives 400 unsolicited fiction mss each month. Does not read June through September. Approximately 10-15% of fiction is agented. Recently published work by Arthur Miller, Cynthia Ozick, Irving Fieldman, Nadine Gordimer and Stephen Dixon. **Publishes 20-25 new writers/year.** Length: 500-4,000 words. Publishes short shorts. Also publishes literary essays, poetry. Critiques rejected mss when there is time. Sometimes recommends other markets.
How to Contact: Send complete ms with SASE. "Cover letters acceptable, not necessary. We accept simultaneous submissions but do not prefer them." Accepts diskettes if accompanied by computer printout submissions. Reports in 6-8 weeks on mss. Publishes ms 6-12 months after acceptance. Sample copy for $3. Reviews novels, short story collections, poetry and literary criticism.
Payment/Terms: Pays $20-250 on publication for all rights "with transfer on request to author"; 1 contributor's copy; half price for extras.
Advice: "Keep trying."

N ☑ **COTTONWOOD**, Box J, 400 Kansas Union, University of Kansas, Lawrence KS 66045. (785)864-2528. E-mail: cottonwd@falcon.cc.ukans.edu. Editor: Tom Lorenz. **Fiction Editor:** Amy Stuber. Magazine: 6×9; 100 pages; illustrations and photos. "*Cottonwood* publishes high quality prose, poetry and artwork and is aimed at an audience that appreciates the same. We have a national scope and reputation while maintaining a strong regional flavor." Semiannually. Estab. 1965. Circ. 500.

• *Cottonwood* is a member of Council of Literary Magazines and Presses.

Needs: "We publish only literary prose and poetry." Receives 25-50 unsolicited mss/month. Accepts 5-6 mss/issue; 10-12 mss/year. Publishes ms 6-18 months after acceptance. Agented fiction 10%. **Publishes 1-3 new writers/year.** Recently published work by Connie May Fowler, Oakley Hall and Alan Brown. Length: 2,000-5,000 words average; 1,000 words minimum; 10,000 words maximum. Publishes short shorts. Length: 1,000 words. Rarely publishes literary essays; publishes literary criticism, poetry. Sometimes critiques or comments on rejected mss.

How to Contact: Send complete ms with a cover letter or submit through agent. Include 4-5 line bio and brief list of publications. Reports in 2-4 months. SASE for return of ms. Simultaneous submissions OK. Sample copy for $8.50, 9×12 SAE and $1.90. Reviews novels and short story collections. Send books to review editor at our Cottonwood address.

Payment/Terms: Pays 1 contributor's copy; additional copies $5. Pays on publication. Acquires one-time rights.

Advice: "We're looking for depth and/or originality of subject matter, engaging voice and style, emotional honesty, command of the material and the structure. *Cottonwood* publishes high quality literary fiction, but we are very open to the work of talented new writers. Write something honest and that you care about and write it as well as you can. Don't hesitate to keep trying us. We sometimes take a piece from a writer we've rejected a number of times. We generally don't like clever, gimmicky writing or writing overly concerned with style. The style should be engaging but not claim all the attention for itself."

☑ **COUNTRY FOLK**, HC77, Box 608, Pittsburg MO 65724. Phone/fax: (417)993-5944. **Editor:** Susan Salaki. Magazine: 8½×11; 40 pages; illustrations and photos. Bimonthly. Estab. 1988. Circ. 5,000.

Needs: "Folklore, humorous anecdotes, stories of hauntings from the past." Receives 20 unsolicited mss/month. Buys 1 ms/issue; 6 mss/year. Publishes ms-3 months after acceptance. Length: 750 words maximum. Also publishes local history and country humor.

How to Contact: Send complete ms. Include estimated word count and bio (100 words). Reports in 3 weeks. SASE for reply or send a disposable copy of ms. Sample copy for $4.

Payment/Terms: Pays contributor's copy on publication.

Advice: "Don't try to write. Just tell a story."

☑ **CRAB CREEK REVIEW**, 7265 S. 128th, Seattle WA 98178. (206)772-8489. Website: www.drizzle.com/~ccr. **Editors:** Kimberly Allison, Harris Levinson, Laura Sinai and Terri Stone. Magazine: 6×9 paperbound; 80-112 pgs., line drawings. "Magazine publishing poetry, short stories, and cover art for an audience interested in literary, visual and dramatic arts and in politics." Published twice yearly. Estab. 1983. Circ. 450.

Needs: Contemporary, humor/satire, literary and translations. No confession, erotica, horror, juvenile, preschool, religious/inspirational, romance or young adult. Receives 100 unsolicited mss/month. Recently published work by David Lee, Andrena Zawinski, Deborah Byrne and Judith Skillman. **Published new writers within the last year.** Length: 3,000 words average; 1,200 words minimum; 6,000 words maximum. Publishes short shorts.

How to Contact: Send complete ms with short list of credits. Reports in 2-4 months. SASE. No simultaneous submissions. Sample copy for $5. *Anniversary Anthology* $5.

Payment/Terms: Pays 2 contributor's copies; $4 charge for extras. Acquires first rights. Rarely buys reprints.

Advice: "We appreciate 'sudden fictions.' Type name and address on each piece. Enclose SASE. Send no more than one story in a packet (except for short shorts—no more than three, ten pages total). Know what you want to say and say it in an honest, clear, confident voice."

$ ☑ **⛫ CRAB ORCHARD REVIEW, A Journal of Creative Works**, Southern Illinois University at Carbondale, English Department, Faner Hall, Carbondale IL 62901. (618)453-6833. Fax: (618)453-3253. Website: www.siu.edu/~crborchd (includes contest information and guidelines). **Editor:** Richard Peterson. Prose Editor: Carolyn Alessio. Managing Editor: Jon Tribble. Magazine: 5½×8½; 250 pages; 55 lb. recycled paper, card cover; photo on cover. "This twice-yearly journal will feature the best in contemporary fiction, poetry, creative nonfiction, reviews and interviews. Estab. 1995. Circ. 800.

• Winner of a 1998 and a 1997 Illinois Arts Council Literary Award.

Needs: Condensed/excerpted novel, ethnic/multicultural, literary, translations. No science fiction, romance, west-

---

CHECK THE CATEGORY INDEXES, located at the back of the book, for publishers interested in specific fiction subjects.

ern, horror or children's. Wants more novel excerpts that also work as stand alone pieces. List of upcoming themes available on website. Receives 75 unsolicited mss/month. Accepts 5-10 mss/issue, 10-18 mss/year. Does not read during the summer. Publishes ms 9-12 months after acceptance. Agented fiction 5%. Recently published work by Susan Neville, Suzanne Kamata, Lee Martin, David Curry and Pete Fromm. **Publishes 2 new writers/ year.** Length: 2,500 words average; 1,000 word minimum; 6,500 words maximum. Also publishes literary essays and poetry. Rarely critiques or comments on rejected mss.

How to Contact: Send complete ms with a cover letter. Include brief bio and list of publications. Reports in 3 weeks on queries; 5-6 months on mss. Send SASE for reply, return of ms. Simultaneous submissions OK. Sample copy for $6. Fiction guidelines for #10 SASE. Reviews books, small press and university press novels and story collections only. Reviews done in house by staff. Send review copies to Managing Editor Jon Tribble.

Payment/Terms: Pays $100 minimum; $5/page maximum plus 2 contributor's copies for first North American serial rights, plus a year's subscription.

Advice: "We look for well-written, provocative, fully realized fiction that seeks to engage both the reader's senses and intellect. Don't sent too often to the same market, and don't send manuscripts that you haven't read over carefully. Writers can't rely on spell checkers to catch all errors. Always include a SASE. Read and support the journals you admire so they can continue to survive."

☑ ◎ **CRANIA, A Literary/Arts Magazine,** 1072 Palms Blvd., Venice CA 90291. E-mail: editor@crania.com. Website: www.crania.com. **Editor:** Dennis Hathaway. "To bring literary and visual works of art of the highest quality to an audience potentially much larger than the audience reached by print media."

Needs: Fiction, poetry, essays, reviews. No genre fiction. Recently published work by Alyson Hagy, Alvin Greenberg, Amy Gerstler and Alex Keegan.

How to Contact: Electronic submissions only. Send ms by e-mail.

Advice: "*Crania* welcomes submissions from new writers, but the magazine is not a bulletin board site where anyone can post their work. We urge potential contributors to read the magazine carefully, and to submit work that shows a facility with craft and a commitment to the idea of writing as an art."

$ ◎ ☒ **CRAZYHORSE,** Dept. of English, Univ. of Arkansas, Little Rock, AR 72204. (501)569-3161. Managing Editor: Zabelle Stodola. Fiction Editor: Judy Troy. Magazine: 6×9; 140 pages; cover illustration only. "Publishes original, quality literary fiction." Biannually. Estab. 1960. Circ. 1,000.

● Stories appearing in *Crazyhorse* regularly appear in the *Pushcart Prize* and *Best American Short Stories* anthologies.

Needs: Literary. No formula (science fiction, gothic, detective, etc.) fiction. Receives 100-150 unsolicited mss/ month. Buys 3-5 mss/issue; 8-10 mss/year. Does not read mss in summer. Published work by Lee K. Abbott, Frederick Busch, Andre Dubus, Pam Durban, H.E. Francis, James Hannah, Gordon Lish, Bobbie Ann Mason and Maura Stanton; published new writers within the last year. Length: Open. Publishes short shorts. Also publishes literary essays, literary criticism, poetry. "Rarely" critiques rejected mss.

How to Contact: Send complete ms with cover letter. Reports in 1-4 months. SASE. No simultaneous submissions. Sample copy for $5. Reviews novels and short story collections. Send books to fiction editor.

Payment/Terms: Pays $10/page and contributor's copies for first North American serial rights. *Crazyhorse* awards $500 to the author of the best work of fiction published in the magazine in a given year.

Advice: "Read a sample issue and submit work that you believe is as good as or better than the fiction we've published."

☑ ◎ **THE CREAM CITY REVIEW,** University of Wisconsin-Milwaukee, Box 413, Milwaukee WI 53201. (414)229-4708. E-mail: creamcity@csd.uwm.edu. Website: www.uwm.edu:80/Dept/English/CCR (includes writer's guidelines, names of editors, table of contents from past issues, cover art scanned and magazine's history). Editors-in-Chief: Kyoko Yoshida and Peter Whalen. **Fiction Editor:** Chris Fink. Editors rotate. Magazine: 5½×8½; 200-300 pages; 70 lb. offset/perfect-bound paper; 80 lb. cover stock; illustrations; photos. "General literary publication—an eclectic and electric selection of the best we receive." Semiannually. Estab. 1975. Circ. 2,000.

Needs: Ethnic, experimental, literary, prose poem, regional, translations. Does not want to see horror, formulaic, racist, sexist, pornographic, homophobic, science fiction, romance. Receives approximately 300 unsolicited fiction mss each month. Accepts 6-10 mss/issue. Does not read fiction or poetry May 1 through August 31. Recently published work by Gordon Lish, Ihab Hassan and William Stafford. **Publishes 6-7 new writers/year.** Length: 1,000-10,000 words. Publishes short shorts. Also publishes literary essays, literary criticism, poetry.

How to Contact: Send complete ms with SASE. Simultaneous submissions OK if notified. Reports in 6 months. Sample copy for $5 (back issue), $7 (current issue). Reviews novels and short story collections.

Payment/Terms: Pays 1 year subscription or in copies. Acquires first rights. Sends galleys to author. Rights revert to author after publication.

Advice: "Read as much as you write so that you can examine your own work in relation to where fiction has been and where fiction is going. We are looking for strong, consistent, fresh voices."

THE CRESCENT REVIEW, The Crescent Review, Inc., P.O. Box 15069, Chevy Chase MD 20825. (301)986-8788. Website: www.thecrescentreview.com (includes essays, interviews, guidelines, and more). **Editor:** J.T. Holland. Magazine: 6×9; 160 pages. Triannually. Estab. 1982.

● Work appearing in *The Crescent Review* has been included in *O. Henry Prize Stories, Best American Short Stories, Pushcart Prize* and *Black Southern Writers* anthologies and in the *New Stories from the South.*

Needs: "Well-crafted stories." Wants shorter-length pieces (though regularly publishes stories in the 6,000-9,000 word range). Wants stories where choice has consequences. Conducts two annual writers contests: The Renwick-Sumerwell Award (exclusively for new unpublished writers) and the Chekhov Award for Fine Storytelling. Does not read submissions May-June and November-December.

How to Contact: Reports in 1-4 months. SASE. Sample issue for $9.40.

Payment/Terms: Pays 2 contributor's copies; discount for contributors. Acquires first North American serial rights.

CRIMEWAVE, TTA Press, S. Martin's Lane, Witcham, Ely, Cambs CB6 2LB England. E-mail: ttapress@aol.com. **Fiction Editor:** Mat Coward. Magazine: 128 pages; lithographed, color paper; perfect bound. Magazine publishes "modern crime fiction from across the waterfront, from the misnamed cozy to the deceptively subtle hardboiled." Biannual.

Needs: Mystery (amateur sleuth, cozy, police procedural, private eye/hardboiled). Accepts 15 mss/issue.

How to Contact: Send complete ms with a cover letter. "Send one story at a time plus adequate return postage, or disposable ms plus 2 IRC's."

Payment/Terms: "Payment is modest, but increasing."

CRIPES!, 110 Bement Ave., Staten Island NY 10310. **Editors:** Jim Tolan and Aimee Record. Magazine: 5½×8½; 60 pages; card cover stock; illustrations; photos. "We look for poetry, prose, art, cartoons and many things in between—as long as it maintains a strong balance between passion (impulse) and craft. Estab. 1994. Circ. 300.

Needs: Condensed/excerpted novel, literary, mainstream/contemporary. Especially looking for short short fiction. No religious or westerns. Receives 20-30 unsolicited mss/month. Accepts 1-2 mss/issue; 4-6 mss/year. Publishes ms within 1 year after acceptance. Recently published work by Tom Whalen, Matthew Firth, Kendall Delacambre, John Fleming and Geezus Lee. Length: 1,500-2,000 words maximum. Publishes short shorts. Also publishes poetry. Often critiques or comments on rejected mss.

How to Contact: Send complete ms with a cover letter. Include a 1-paragraph bio and "tell us how you learned about us." Send SASE for reply or return of ms. Simultaneous submissions OK. Sample copy for $5.

Payment/Terms: Pays 1 contributor copy on publication. Acquires one-time rights.

Advice: Looks for "originality, unpredictability, fresh language, a carefully prepared manuscript, focus and playfullness. Look at *Cripes!* to see what we publish."

CROSSCONNECT, P.O. Box 2317, Philadelphia PA 19103. (215)898-5324. Fax: (215)898-9348. E-mail: xconnect@ccat.sas.upenn.edu. Website: ccat.sas.upenn.edu/xconnect. **Editor:** David Deifer. "*CrossConnect* publishes tri-annually on the World Wide Web and annually in print, with the best of our Web issues, plus nominated work from editors in the digital literary community. *xconnect: writers of the information age* is a nationally distributed, full color, journal sized book." 5½×8½; trade paper; 200 pages.

Needs: Literary and experimental fiction. "Our mission—like our name—is one of connection. *CrossConnect* seeks to promote and document the emergent creative artists as well as established artists who have made the transition to the new technologies of the Information Age." Recently published work by Bob Perelman, Paul Hoover and Yusef Komunyakaa. **Publishes 25 new writers/year.**

How to Contact: Electronic and traditional submissions accepted. "We prefer your submissions be cut and pasted into your mail readers and sent to us. No attached files unless requested." Send complete ms (up to three stories) with cover letter and short bio. Previously published and simultaneous submission OK. Rarely comments on rejections.

Payment/Terms: Pays 1 contributor's copy for use in print version. Author retains all rights. Regularly sends prepublication galleys.

Advice: "Persistence."

CRUCIBLE, English Dept., Barton College, College Station, Wilson NC 27893. (252)399-6456. Editor: Terrence L. Grimes. Magazine of fiction and poetry for a general, literary audience. Annually. Estab. 1964. Circ. 500.

Needs: Contemporary, ethnic, experimental, feminist, literary, regional. Receives 20 unsolicited mss/month. Accepts 5-6 mss/year. Publishes ms 4-5 months after acceptance. Does not normally read mss from April 30 to December 1. Published work by Mark Jacobs, William Hutchins and Guy Nancekeville. Length: 8,000 words maximum. Publishes short shorts.

How to Contact: Send 3 complete copies of ms unsigned with cover letter which should include a brief biography, "in case we publish." Reports in 6 weeks on queries; 3-4 months on mss (by June 15). SASE. Sample copy for $6. Fiction guidelines free.

Payment/Terms: Pays contributor's copies. Acquires first rights.

Advice: "Write about what you know. Experimentation is fine as long as the experiences portrayed come across as authentic, that is to say, plausible."

$\$$ ◻ **CURIO**, 81 Pondfield Rd., Suite 264, Bronxville NY 10708. (914)961-8649. Fax: (914)779-4033. Publisher: M. Teresa Lawrence. Editor and **Fiction Editor:** Mickey Z. Magazine: 8⅜ × 10½; 45 lb. glossy paper; 60 lb. cover; illustrations and photos. "Written for the young, fashionable and literate American trendsetters. Promotes new ideas, opinions, thoughts and interests through a variety of mixed media art and written words. Quarterly. Estab. 1996.

Needs: Ethnic/multicultural, experimental, gay, humor/satire, literary, psychic/supernatural/occult. List of upcoming themes available for SASE. Receives 300 unsolicited mss/month. Accepts 5-10 mss/issue; 20-40 mss/year. Does not read July 15 to August 31. Publishes ms 4 months after acceptance. Length: 100 words minimum; 3,000 words maximum. Publishes short shorts. Also publishes literary essays, literary criticism and poetry.

How to Contact: Send complete ms with a cover letter. Include estimated word count and Social Security number. Reports in 3 months. Send a disposable copy of ms. Simultaneous, reprint and electronic (disk) submissions OK. Reviews novels and short story collections. Send books to Mickey Z., P.O. Box 522, Bronxville NY 10708.

Payment/Terms: Pays $140/page on publication for first rights.

Advice: "It has to be something that I haven't read anywhere else and that moves me to laugh, cry or simply get outraged. I want people to think about social issues."

❖ ◑ **THE DALHOUSIE REVIEW**, Room 114, 1456 Henry St., Halifax, Nova Scotia B3H 3J5 Canada. Editor: Dr. Ronald Huebert. Magazine: 15cm × 23cm; approximately 140 pages; photographs sometimes. Publishes articles, book reviews, short stories and poetry. Published 3 times a year. Circ. 650.

Needs: Literary. Length: 5,000 words maximum. Also publishes essays on history, philosophy, etc., and poetry.

How to Contact: Send complete ms with cover letter. SASE (Canadian stamps). Sample copy for $10 (Canadian) including postage. Occasionally reviews novels and short story collections.

★ ☑ $\$$ ◻ **DAN RIVER ANTHOLOGY**, P.O. Box 298, S. Thomaston ME 04861. (207)354-0998. Fax: (207)354-8953. E-mail: cal@americanletters.org. Website: www.americanletters.org (includes writer's guidelines, catalogue). **Editor:** R. S. Danbury III. Book: 5½ × 8½; 180 pages; 60 lb. paper; gloss 65 lb. full-color cover; b&w illustrations. For general/adult audience. Annually. Estab. 1984. Circ. 800.

• The *Dan River Anthology* ranked #44 on *Writer's Digest's* Fiction 50 list of top markets for fiction.

Needs: Adventure, contemporary, ethnic, experimental, fantasy, historical, horror, humor/satire, literary, mainstream, prose poem, psychic/supernatural, regional, romance (contemporary and historical), science fiction, senior citizen/retirement, suspense/mystery and western. "Would like to see more first-person adventure." No "evangelical Christian, pornography or sentimentality." Receives 150 unsolicited fiction mss each submission period (January 1 through March 31). "We generally publish 12-15 pieces of fiction." Reads "mostly in April." Length: 2,000-2,400 words average; 800 words minimum; 2,500 words maximum. Also publishes poetry.

How to Contact: *Charges reading fee: $1 for poetry; $3 for prose* (cash only, no checks). Send complete ms with SASE. Reports by May 15 each year. No simultaneous submissions. Sample copy for $13.95 paperback, $42.20 cloth, plus $2.95 shipping. Fiction guidelines for #10 SASE or on website.

Payment/Terms: Pays $4/page, minimum *cash advance on acceptance* against royalties of 10% of all sales attributable to writer's influence: readings, mailings, autograph parties, etc., plus up to 50% discount on copies, plus other discounts to make total as high as 73%. Acquires first rights.

Advice: "Know your market. Don't submit without reading guidelines."

$\$$ ◑ ▼ **DENVER QUARTERLY**, University of Denver, Denver CO 80208. (303)871-2892. **Editor:** Bin Ramke. Magazine: 6 × 9; 144-160 pages; occasional illustrations. "We publish fiction, articles and poetry for a generally well-educated audience, primarily interested in literature and the literary experience. They read *DQ* to find something a little different from a strictly academic quarterly or a creative writing outlet." Quarterly. Estab. 1966. Circ. 2,000.

• *Denver Quarterly* received an Honorable Mention for Content from the American Literary Magazine Awards and selections have been anthologized in the *Pushcart Prize* anthologies.

Needs: "We are interested in experimental fiction (minimalism, magic realism, etc.) as well as in realistic fiction and in writing about fiction. No sentimental, science fiction, romance or spy thrillers. No stories longer than 15 pages!" Recently published work by Frederick Busch, Judith E. Johnson, Stephen Alter and Harriet Zinnes. **Published 5 new writers within the last year.** Also publishes poetry.

How to Contact: Send complete ms and brief cover letter with SASE. Does not read mss May-September 15. Do not query. Reports in 3 months on mss. Publishes ms within a year after acceptance. Electronic submissions (disk, Windows 7.0) OK. Simultaneous submissions OK. Sample copy $6.

Payment/Terms: Pays $5/page for fiction and poetry and 2 contributor's copies for first North American serial rights.

Advice: "We look for serious, realistic and experimental fiction; stories which appeal to intelligent, demanding readers who are not themselves fiction writers. Nothing so quickly disqualifies a manuscript as sloppy proofreading and mechanics. Read the magazine before submitting to it. We try to remain eclectic, but the odds for beginners are bound to be small considering the fact that we receive nearly 10,000 mss per year and publish only about ten short stories."

$ DESCANT, Descant Arts & Letters Foundation, P.O. Box 314, Station P, Toronto, Ontario M5S 2S8. (416)593-2557. **Editor:** Karen Mulhallen. Managing Editor: Michelle Maynes. Quarterly literary journal. Estab. 1970. Circ. 1,200.

Needs: Literary. Also publishes poetry and literary essays. Submit seasonal material 4 months in advance.

How to Contact: Send complete ms. Sample copy for $8. Writer's guidelines for SASE.

Payment/Terms: Pays $100 (Canadian). Pays on publication.

Advice: "Familiarize yourself with our magazine before submitting."

THE DICKINSON REVIEW, P.O. Box 1773, Carlisle PA 17013. (717)245-1847. Fax: (717)245-1942. E-mail: dsonrev@dickinson.edu. Editor: Jamie Bunce. **Fiction Editor:** Kristin Talka. Editors change each year. Magazine: 6×9; 80-120 pages; occasional photographs. *The Dickinson Review* "seeks engaging and well crafted fiction, with a strong, clear narrative voice." Annual. Estab. 1986. Circ. 300.

Needs: Literary. Receives 50 unsolicited mss/month. Accepts 6 mss/issue. Does not read mss March-August. Publishes ms 1-2 months after acceptance. "Small" percentage of agented fiction. **Publishes 25% new writers/ year.** Recently published work by Marvin Bell, Tess Gallagher, Chris Torockio and Stanley Lindberg. Word length: 2,000-4,000 words average; 6,000 words maximum. Publishes short shorts. Also publishes poetry. Sometimes comments on or critiques rejected ms.

How to Contact: Send complete ms with a cover letter. Inquiries by fax OK. Include brief bio and list of publications. Reports on mss within 4 months. Send SASE for reply, return of ms or send a disposable copy of ms. Simultaneous submissions OK. Sample copy and guidelines free.

Payment/Terms: Pays 2 contributor's copies; additional copies $5. Acquires first North American serial rights.

Advice: "It sounds obvious, but we're looking for well written stories. Solid prose makes it past the slush pile. Do not be experimental for the sake of being experimental."

DIRIGIBLE, Journal of Language Art, Dirigible Press, 101 Cottage St., New Haven CT 06511. (203)776-8446. E-mail: dirigibl@javanet.com. **Editors:** David Todd and Cynthia Conrad. Magazine: 4¼×7; 40-48 pages; 20 lb. white paper; card stock cover; illustrations. "We seek language-centered poetry, controlled experiments, fiction that is postmodern, paraliterary, nonlinear or subjective, and work that breaks with genre, convention, or form. Hybrid forms of writing and essays on aesthetics, poetics, reader experience and writing processes are also of interest to us." Quarterly. Estab. 1994. Circ. 500-800.

Needs: Experimental, literary, translations, avant garde. No realism or other mainstream genres. No "inspirational, moralizing or political work." Wants to see more "poetic prose, imaginative fiction that experiments with style, narrative technique, language." Accepts 2-3 mss/issue; 8-12 mss/year. Publishes ms 1-3 months after acceptance. Recently published work by Norman Lock, Mark E. Johnston, Peoria Melville, Matvei Yankelevich, Barbara Lefcowitz and John Lowther. **Publishes 4-6 new writers/year.** Length: 1,750 words average; 1 word minimum; 3,600 words maximum. Publishes short shorts. Also publishes literary essays, literary criticism, poetry.

How to Contact: Send complete ms with a cover letter. Reports in 1 month on queries; 2-4 months on mss. Send SASE for reply, return of ms or send a disposable copy of ms. No simultaneous submissions. Sample copy for $2 postage paid. Reviews novels and short story collections.

Payment/Terms: Pays 2 contributor's copies on publication; additional copies for $2 ppd. Acquires first rights.

Advice: "We are grinding an aesthetic ax and acceptance is dependent on our personal vision. Select markets that are looking for your type of writing. If in doubt, buy sample copies."

THE DISTILLERY: ARTISTIC SPIRITS OF THE SOUTH, Motlow St. Community College, P.O. Box 88100, Tullahoma TN 37388-8100. (931)393-1500. Fax: (931)393-1681. Website: mscc.cc.tn.us/www/ distillery (includes guidelines, contributor list and staff info). **Editor:** Niles Reddick. Magazine: 88 pages; color cover; color/b&w art and photographs. "The editors seek well-crafted, character-driven fiction. Several of us are writers, as well, so we want to see high-quality work that inspires us. In this postmodern-postmodern era, we think epiphanies are back in vogue." Semiannually. Estab. 1994. Circ. 500.

● Work from *The Distillery* has been anthologized in *Best New Stories of the South.*

Needs: Literary. Receives 50-60 unsolicited mss/month. Accepts 3-4 mss/issue; 6-8 mss/year. Does not read mss June 1-August 1. Publishes ms 6-12 months after acceptance. Recently published work by Janice Daugharty, Elaine Palencia and Virgil Suarez. **Publishes 50% new writers.** Length: 2,000-4,000 words average; 4,000 words maximum. Also publishes literary essays, literary criticism, poetry and book reviews.

How to Contact: Send complete ms with a cover letter. Include estimated word count, brief bio, list of publications. "No third-person bio, please." Reports 2 weeks on queries; 2-3 months on mss. SASE for reply.

Send a disposable copy of ms. Sample copy for $7.50. Fiction guidelines for SASE. Occasionally reviews novels, short story collections and poetry collections. Send books to editor.

Payment/Terms: Pays 2 contributor's copies on publication; additional copies for $7.50. Acquires first North American serial rights.

Advice: "We want fiction that inspires us, that moves us to laugh or weep. Even though we are jaded old teachers and editors, we still want to feel a chill run down our spines when we read a perfect description or evocative line of dialogue. Revise, revise, revise. Also, do not write for a 'market,' whatever that means. Find your voice. If that voice has something to say, others will find it too, eventually."

DODOBOBO, A Fiction Magazine of Washington D.C., Dodobobo Publications, P.O. Box 57214, Washington DC 20037. **Editor:** Brian Greene. Magazine: 5½ × 8½; 20-35 pages; illustrations and photos. "We're a literary fiction magazine which intends to give voice to writers the more well-known literary magazines would not be open to." Quarterly. Estab. 1994. Circ. 500.

Needs: Experimental and literary. Receives 20 unsolicited mss/month. Accepts 2-4 mss/issue; 8-16 mss/year. Publishes ms 1-12 months after acceptance. Length: 2,500 words maximum. Sometimes critiques or comments on rejected ms.

How to Contact: "Send complete ms, with or without cover letter." Reports in 2 months on mss. Send SASE for reply, return of ms or send a disposable copy of ms. Simultaneous and reprint submissions OK. Sample copy for $2 (including postage). Fiction guidelines for SASE.

Payment/Terms: Pays 2 contributor's copies. Acquires one-time rights. Sends galleys to author if requested.

Advice: "We like stories which illustrate the reality of the human experience—people's existential crises, their experiences with other people, with their own psyches. Get a copy or two of the magazine and read the stories we've printed."

$ **DOWNSTATE STORY,** 1825 Maple Ridge, Peoria IL 61614. (309)688-1409. E-mail: ehopkins@ prairienet.org. Website: www.wiu.bgu.edu/users/mfgeh/dss (includes guidelines, names of editors, short fiction and reviews). **Editor:** Elaine Hopkins. Magazine: illustrations. "Short fiction—some connection with Illinois or the Midwest." Annually. Estab. 1992. Circ. 500.

Needs: Adventure, ethnic/multicultural, experimental, historical, horror, humor/satire, literary, mainstream/contemporary, mystery/suspense, psychic/supernatural/occult, regional, romance, science fiction, westerns. No porn. Wants more political fiction. Accepts 10 mss/issue. Publishes ms up to 1 year after acceptance. Length: 300 words minimum; 2,000 words maximum. Publishes short shorts. Also publishes literary essays.

How to Contact: Send complete ms with a cover letter. Reports "ASAP." SASE for return of ms. Simultaneous submissions OK. Sample copy for $8. Fiction guidelines for SASE.

Payment/Terms: Pays $50 maximum on acceptance for first rights.

THE EDGE CITY REVIEW, Reston Review, Inc., 10912 Harpers Square Court, Reston VA 20191. Fax: (703)716-5752. E-mail: ponick@erols.com. **Editor:** T.L. Ponick. Magazine: 8½ × 11; 44-52 pages; 60 lb. paper; 65 lb. color cover. "We publish Formalist poetry, well-plotted artistic or literary fiction, literary essays and book reviews. Our editorial philosophy is right of center." Triannually. Estab. 1994. Circ. 500.

Needs: Humor/satire, literary, regional, serialized novel. "We see too much fiction that's riddled with four-letter words and needless vulgarity." Receives 10 unsolicited mss/month. Accepts 1-2 mss/issue; 3-6 mss/year. Publishes ms 4 months after acceptance. Length: 2,000 words average, 1,500 words minimum; 3,000 words maximum. Also publishes literary essays, literary criticism, poetry. Sometimes critiques or comments on rejected ms.

How to Contact: Send complete ms with a cover letter. Include estimated word count, 25-50 word bio, list of publications. Reports in 1 month on queries; 3-5 months on mss. Send SASE for reply, return of ms or send a disposable copy of ms. Electronic submissions (disk or modem) OK. Sample copy for $5. Reviews novels and short story collections. "No 'chapbooks' or self-published, please."

Payment/Terms: Pays 2 contributor's copies; additional copies $4. Acquires first North American serial rights. Sponsors contest; watch for announcements in major publications.

Advice: "We are looking for character-based fiction. Most fiction we receive does not grow out of its characters—but finely wrought characters, fully realized, are what we want to see."

1812, A Literary Arts Magazine, P.O. Box 1812, Amherst NY 14226-7812. E-mail: info@newwritin g.com. Website: www.newwriting.com. Fiction Editor: Richard Lynch. Magazine: Illustrations and photographs. "We want to publish work that has some *bang*." Annually. Estab. 1994.

● Work published in *1812* has been described as "experimental, surreal, bizarre."

Needs: Experimental, humor/satire, literary, mainstream/contemporary, translations. Does not want to see "stories about writers, stories about cancer, stories containing hospitals or stories that sound like they've been told before." Also publishes literary essays, literary criticism, poetry. Often critiques or comments on rejected mss.

How to Contact: Send complete ms with a cover letter. Include brief list of publications. Reports in 2 months. SASE for return of ms. Simultaneous, reprint and electronic submissions OK. Reviews novels and short story collections.

Payment/Terms: Payment is "arranged." Acquires one-time rights.

Advice: "Our philosophy can be summed up in the following quote from Beckett: 'I speak of an art turning from it in disgust, weary of its puny exploits, weary of pretending to be able, of being able, of doing a little better the same old thing, of going a little further along a dreary road.' Too many writers copy. We want to see writing by those who aren't on the 'dreary road.' "

N ★ ◐ ELYSIAN FIELDS QUARTERLY: The Baseball Review, 2034 Marshall Ave., St. Paul MN 55104-5744. (651)644-8558. Fax: (651)644-8086. E-mail: efq@citilink.com. Website: www.efqreview.com (includes ordering capabilities, back issues, affiliated products, sample stories, distribution information, e-mail addresses of staff and links). **Editor:** Stephen Lehman. Magazine: 6×9; 96 pages; 60 lb. paper; gloss/varnish cover; illustrations; and photos. *Elysian Fields Quarterly* is "unique because nobody covers baseball the way that we do, with such an offbeat, irreverent manner and yet with full appreciation for the game." Quarterly. Estab. 1992. Circ. 1,035.
Needs: "Any fiction piece about baseball will be considered. We do not want to see general fiction that tries to be a baseball story by making tangential connections to baseball, but in reality is not a fiction piece about baseball." Receives 3-5 unsolicited mss/month. Accepts 2-3 mss/issue; 10-15/year. Publishes ms 3-9 months after acceptance. **Publishes 10-12 new writers/year.** Recently published work by W.P. Kinsella, Donald Dewey, Rick Wilber, Lynn Rigney Schott, William McGill and George Bowering. Word length: 2,000-3,000 words average; 1,000 words minimum; 4,000 words maximum. Does not generally publish short shorts "but we don't rule out any good writing." Length: 750 words. Also publishes literary essays, literary criticism and poetry. Very rarely comments on or critiques rejected ms.
How to Contact: Send complete ms with a cover letter. Inquiries by e-mail OK. "E-mail submissions should be properly formatted or in readable attachments." Include 50 word bio. Reports in 2-3 months. Send SASE for reply, return of ms or send a disposable copy of ms. "Will occasionally consider" simultaneous and reprint submissions. Sample copy for $7.50. Guidelines free. "We review baseball books and novels of interest to our readership."
Payment/Terms: Pays 4 contributor's copies; additional copies $5.95. Acquires one-time rights and the right to reprint in any anthologies. Sponsors contest: Dave Moore Award for the "most important baseball book."
Advice: "Originality, creativity, believability—is it truly a baseball story? We do not pay attention to industry trends; we just try to publish good writing, not what is trendy."

◐ EMRYS JOURNAL, The Emrys Foundation, P.O. Box 8813, Greenville SC 29604. E-mail: jhn@ghs.org. **Editor:** Jeanine Halva-Neubauer. Catalog: 9×9¾; 120 pages; 80 lb. paper. "We publish short fiction, poetry, and essays. We are particularly interested in hearing from women and other minorities. We are mindful of the southeast but not limited to it." Annually. Estab. 1984. Circ. 400.
Needs: Contemporary, feminist, literary, mainstream and regional. Reading period: August 1-December 1, 2000. Accepts 18 mss/issue. Publishes mss in April. Length: 3,500 words average; 6,000 words maximum. Publishes short shorts. Recently published work by Colby Willis and Mary Sharratt.
How To Contact: Send complete ms with cover letter. Reports in 6 weeks. SASE. Sample copy for $15 and 7×10 SAE with 4 first-class stamps. Fiction guidelines for #10 SASE.
Payment/Terms: Pays in contributor's copies. Acquires first rights.
Advice: Looks for "fiction by women and minorities, especially but not exclusively southeastern."

$ ◐ ♥ EPOCH MAGAZINE, 251 Goldwin Smith Hall, Cornell University, Ithaca NY 14853. (607)255-3385. Fax: (607)255-6661. **Editor:** Michael Koch. Submissions should be sent to Michael Koch. Magazine: 6×9; 128 pages; good quality paper; good cover stock. "Top level fiction and poetry for people who are interested in good literature." Published 3 times a year. Estab. 1947. Circ. 1,000.
   ● *Epoch Magazine* won the premiere *O. Henry Magazine* Award for best magazine of 1997. Work originally appearing in this quality literary journal has appeared in numerous anthologies including *Best American Short Stories*, *Best American Poetry*, *Pushcart Prize*, *The O. Henry Prize Stories*, *Best of the West* and *New Stories from the South*.
Needs: Literary, contemporary and ethnic. Accepts 15-20 mss/issue. Receives 500 unsolicited fiction mss each month. Does not read in summer (April 15-September 15). Published work by Ron Hansen, Jessica Treat, Rick Bass, D.R. MacDonald and Victoria Radel. **Published new writers in the last year.** Length: no limit. Also publishes personal essays, poetry. Critiques rejected mss when there is time. Sometimes recommends other markets.
How to Contact: Send complete ms with SASE. No simultaneous submissions. Reports in 3-4 weeks on mss. Publishes ms an average of 6 months after acceptance. Sample copy for $5.
Payment/Terms: Pays $5-10/printed page and contributor copies on publication for first North American serial rights.
Advice: "Read the journals you're sending work to."

✓ ◐ EUREKA LITERARY MAGAZINE, 300 E. College Ave., Eureka College, Eureka IL 61530-1500. (309)467-6336. E-mail: llogsodon@eureka.edu. **Editor:** Loren Logsdon. **Fiction Editor:** Nancy Perkins. Magazine: 6×9; 100 pages; 70 lb. white offset paper; 80 lb. gloss cover; photographs (occasionally). "We seek to be open to the best stories that are submitted to us. We do not want to be narrow in a political sense of the word. Our audience is a combination of professors/writers and general readers." Semiannually. Estab. 1992. Circ. 500.

Needs: Adventure, ethnic/multicultural, experimental, fantasy (science), feminist, historical, humor/satire, literary, mainstream/contemporary, mystery/suspense (private eye/hardboiled, romantic), psychic/supernatural/occult, regional, romance (historical), science fiction (soft/sociological), translations. "We try to achieve a balance between the traditional and the experimental. We do favor the traditional, though. We look for the well-crafted story, but essentially any type of story that has depth and substance to it—any story that expands us as human beings and celebrates the mystery and miracle of the creation. Make sure you have a good beginning and ending, a strong voice, excellent use of language, good insight into the human condition, narrative skill, humor—if it is appropriate to the subject. No drug stories of any kind, stories with gratuitous violence or stories with heavy propaganda." Receives 30 unsolicited mss/month. Accepts 4 mss/issue; 8-9 mss/year. Does not read mss mainly in late summer (August). Recently published work by Gary Arpin, Marlene Dube, Andrew Cohen, Janis Bultman, Arliss Ryan, Carol Bergh Bennett, Steve Ousley, Suzanne De Cayette and Kathleen Zamloch. **Publishes 3-4 new writers/year.** Length: 4,500 words average; 7,000-8,000 words maximum. Publishes short shorts. Also publishes poetry.

How to Contact: Send complete ms with a cover letter. Should include estimated word count and bio (short paragraph). Reports in 1 week on queries; 4 months on mss. Send SASE for reply, return of ms or send a disposable copy of ms. Simultaneous submissions OK. Sample copy for $5.

Payment/Terms: Pays free subscription to the magazine and 2 contributor's copies. Acquires first rights or one-time rights.

Advice: "Does the writer tell a good story—one that would interest a general reader? Is the story provocative? Is its subject important? Does the story contain good insight into life or the human condition? We don't want anything so abstract that it seems unrelated to anything human. We appreciate humor and effective use of language, stories that have powerful, effective endings. Take pains with the beginning and ending of the story; both must work. Be sure the voice is genuine. Be sure the manuscript is free from serious surface errors and is easy to read. We would suggest that writers should avoid sending a manuscript that appears to have made the rounds. Always send an SASE. Send one story at a time unless the stories are very short."

EVANSVILLE REVIEW, University of Evansville, 1800 Lincoln Ave., Evansville IN 47722. (812)488-1114. Website: www.evansville.edu/~elrweb. **Editor:** Ingrid Jendrzejewski. Editors change every 1-2 years. Magazine: 6×9; 120-150 pages; 70 lb. white paper; heavy laminated 4-color cover. Annually. Estab. 1990. Circ. 2,500.

Needs: "We're open to all creativity. No discrimination. All fiction, screenplays, nonfiction, poetry, interviews, photo essays and anything in between." No children or young adult. List of upcoming themes available for SASE. Receives 300 unsolicited mss/year. Does not read mss February-August. Agented fiction 2%. Published work by John Updike, Lewis Turco, Felix Stefanile, Dana Gioia, Willis Barnstone, James Ragan, Rachel Hadas and Josephine Jacobsen. Also publishes literary essays, poetry.

How to Contact: Send complete ms with a cover letter, e-mail or fax. Include 150 word or less bio and list of publications. Reports in 2 weeks on queries; 3 months on mss. Send SASE for reply, return of ms or send a disposable copy of ms. Simultaneous and reprint submissions OK. Sample copy for $5. Fiction guidelines free; check website.

Payment/Terms: Pays 5 contributor's copies on publication. Acquires one-time rights. Sends galleys to author if requested. Not copyrighted.

Advice: "Because editorial staffs roll over every 1-2 years, the journal always has a new flavor."

EVENT, Douglas College, Box 2503, New Westminster, British Columbia V3L 5B2 Canada. Fax: (604)527-5095. **Editor:** Calvin Wharton. **Fiction Editor:** Christine Dewar. **Assistant Editor:** Bonnie Bauder. Magazine: 6×9; 144 pages; quality paper and cover stock. "Primarily a literary magazine, publishing poetry, fiction, reviews; for creative writers, artists, anyone interested in contemporary literature." Triannually. Estab. 1971. Circ. 1,000.

Needs: Literary, contemporary, feminist, humor, regional. "No technically poor or unoriginal pieces." Receives approximately 100 unsolicited fiction mss/month. Accepts 6-8 mss/issue. Recently published work by Julie Keith, Andrew Pyper and Kenneth Harvey. **Published new writers within the last year.** Length: 5,000 words maximum. Also publishes poetry.

How to Contact: Send complete ms, bio and SAE with Canadian postage or IRC. Reports in 1-4 months on mss. Publishes ms 6-12 months after acceptance. Sample copy for $5.

Payment/Terms: Pays $22/page and 2 contributor's copies on publication for first North American serial rights.

Advice: "A good narrative arc is hard to find."

THE EVERGREEN CHRONICLES, A Journal of Gay, Lesbian, Bisexual & Transgender Arts & Cultures, P.O. Box 8939, Minneapolis MN 55408-0939. (612)823-6638. E-mail: evergchron@aol.com. **Contact:** Managing Editor. Magazine: 7×8½; 90-100 pages; b&w line drawings and photos. "We look for work that addresses the complexities and diversities of gay, lesbian, bisexual and transgendered experiences." Triannually. Estab. 1985. Circ. 1,000.

● The magazine sponsors an annual novella contest; deadline September 30. Send SASE for guidelines.

Needs: Gay or lesbian: adventure, confession, contemporary, ethnic, experimental, feminist, humor/satire, literary, serialized/excerpted novel, suspense/mystery. "We are interested in works by artists in a wide variety of genres. The subject matter need not be specifically lesbian, gay, bisexual or transgender-themed, but we do look for a deep sensitivity to that experience. No sentimental, romantic stuff, fantasy or science fiction." Accepts 10-25 mss/issue; 30-52 mss/year. Publishes ms approximately 2 months after acceptance. Recently published work by Eileen Myles, Edward Cohen, Jane Eastwood, Eugene Kraft, Craig McWhorter and Mary Ann McFadden. **Publishes 10-15 new writers/year.** Length: 3,500-4,500 words average; no minimum; 5,200 words maximum. 25 pages double-spaced maximum on prose. Publishes short shorts. Sometimes comments on rejected mss.

How to Contact: Send 4 copies of complete ms with cover letter. Accepts queries by e-mail. "It helps to have some biographical information included." Submission deadlines: January 1 and July 1. Reports on queries in 3 weeks; on mss in 3-4 months. SASE. Electronic submissions (fax, e-mail) OK. Sample copy for $8 and $2 postage. Fiction guidelines for #10 SASE.

Payment/Terms: Pays $50 honorarium for one-time rights.

Advice: "We've seen a great increase in the number of unsolicited manuscripts sent to us for consideration. More and more competition in our specific genre of gay and lesbian writing. This means that the quality of the writing we publish is getting better—more readers and writers out there. We're looking for originality in perspective and/or language. Share your writing with others! Join writing groups."

N ★ ◑ ▣ EWGPRESENTS, 406 Shady Lane, Cayce SC 29033. (803)794-8869. E-mail: EWGBet@aol.com. Website: www.webpanache.com/EWGPresents/. **Fiction Editor:** donnag38@aol.com. Electronic zine. "A contemporary journal of literary quality by new and established writers. *EWGPresents* continues to provide an online forum for writers to present their works internationally, and to usher literature into the digital age."

Needs: Literary. "No pornography, or excessive violence and gore beyond the legitimate needs of a story. When in doubt, leave it out." **Publishes 50-60 new writers/year.** Recently published work by Tessa Nardi, L.C. Mohr, Mary Gordon, Jeffrey L. Jackson and Vasilis Afxentiou.

How to Contact: Send queries/mss by e-mail. No attachments. Submissions should be directed to specific departments with work on the body of the e-mail. Read and adhere to guidelines provided at the zine.

Advice: "We seek well-written, professionally executed fiction, with attention to basics—grammar, punctuation, usage. Be professional. Be creative. And above all, be yourself. A writer must speak with their own voice. Let us hear your voice. We have the means to reach a universal audience by the click of a mouse. Writers are gifted with a new medium of exposure and the future demands taking advantage of this format. Without a doubt, electronic publishing will be a major factor in gaining new audiences and recognition for today's writer."

★ ✓ ◑ EXPLORATIONS '99, UAS Explorations, University of Alaska Southeast, 11120 Glacier Highway, Juneau AK 99801. (907)465-6418. Fax: (907)465-6406. E-mail: jnamp@uas.alaska.edu. **Editor:** Art Petersen. Magazine: 5½×8¼; 60 pages; heavy cover stock; b&w illustrations and photographs. "Poetry, prose and art—we strive for artistic excellence." Annually. Estab. 1981. Circ. 750.

Needs: Experimental, humor/satire, traditional quality fiction, poetry, and art. Receives about 1,200 mss/year. Recently published work by Charles Bukowski, William Everson, David Ray, Ania Savage and Nicchia P. Leamer. **Publishes 75% new writers.**

How to Contact: *Reading/entry fee $6/story required.* Send name, address and short bio on *back* of first page of each submission. All submissions entered in contest. Submission postmark deadline is March 15. Reports in July. Mss cannot be returned. Simultaneous and reprint submissions OK. Sample copy for $5.

Payment/Terms: Pays 2 contributor's copies. Acquires one-time rights (rights remain with the author). Also awards 7 annual prizes of $1,000 for best story or poem, $500 for best story or poem in genre other than 1st Place, and more.

Advice: "It is best to send for full guidelines. Concerning poetry and prose, standard form as well as innovation are encouraged; appropriate and fresh *imagery* (allusions, metaphors, similes, symbols . . .) as well as standard or experimental form draw editorial attention. 'Language really spoken by men' and women and authentically rendered experience are encouraged. Unfortunately, requests for criticism usually cannot be met. The prizes for 1999 were awarded by the poet Richard Davenhauer."

N ★ ◑ ▣ THE FAIRFIELD REVIEW, (203)319-0039. Fax: (203)319-0049. E-mail: FairfieldReview@hpmd.com. Website: www.fairfieldreview.org. **Editors:** Edward and Janet Granger-Happ. Electronic magazine. "Our mission is to provide an outlet for poetry, short stories and essays, from both new and established writers and students, which are accessible to the general public."

Needs: Short stories, poetry, essays. Would like to see more stories "rich in lyrical imagery and those that are more humorous." **Publishes 50% new writers.** Recently published work by Joseph Conlin and Nathaniel Gillespie. Publishes over 20 new writers/year. "We encourage students and first-time writers to submit their work."

How to Contact: Electronic submissions preferred. Fax submissions accepted.

Advice: "In addition to the submission guidelines found in each issue on our website, we recommend reading the essay *Writing Qualities to Keep in Mind* from our Editors and Authors page at www.fairfieldreview.org/

fairfield/FairRevw.nsf/links/98General09.5?OpenDocument. Keep to small, directly experienced themes; write crisply using creative, poetic images; avoid the trite expression."

[N] ◧ ◎ FAN MAGAZINE, A Baseball Literary Magazine, 145 15th St. NE, #805, Atlanta GA 30361. (404)607-9489. Fax: (404)607-8639. Editor: Mike Schacht. Magazine: 5½×8½; 64 pages; 60 lb. paper; 65 lb. cover; illustrations and photos. "We believe everyone has a baseball story; we are out to capture the best in poetry, memoir and short fiction." Triannually. Estab. 1989. Circ. 400.

Needs: Historical, literary, sports, nostalgia, memoir. Receives 10 unsolicited mss/month. Accepts 3-5 mss/ issue, "depending on quality of submissions." Publishes ms 3 months to 1 year after acceptance. Recently published work by Gene Fehler and Paul Hemphill. Length: 1,500 words average. Publishes short shorts. Also publishes literary essays and poetry. Often critiques or comments on rejected mss.

How to Contact: Send complete ms with a cover letter. "A query for guidelines is appreciated." Include estimated word count and 1-2 paragraph bio. Reports in 2 weeks on queries; 2 months on mss. Send SASE for return of ms. Simultaneous submissions and reprints OK. Sample copy for $8. Fiction guidelines free.

Payment/Terms: Pays 2 contributor's copies.

Advice: "Please review sample copy and guidelines before submitting. Story must have baseball connection."

[N] ★ ◧ FAULTLINE, Journal of Art and Literature, P.O. Box 599-4960, Irvine CA 92716-4960. (949)824-1573. E-mail: caley@pacbell.net. Managing Editors: Caley O'Dwyer and Cullen Gerst. **Fiction Editor**: Cullen Gerst. Editors change in September each year. Literary magazine: 6×9; 105 pages; illustrations and photos. "We publish the very best of what we receive. Our interest is quality and literary merit." Annually. Estab. 1992. Circ. 375.

Needs: Erotica, ethnic/multicultural, experimental, fantasy, feminist, gay, humor satire, lesbian, literary, main-stream/contemporary. Receives 20-30 unsolicited mss/month. Accepts 6 mss/year. Does not read mss June-September. Publishes ms within 9 months after acceptance. Agented fiction 10-20%. **Publishes 30-40% new writers/year.** Recently published work by Phil Hay, Suzanne Lui, Julie Newman and Tom Fitts. Length: open. Publishes short shorts. Also publishes literary essays, poetry. Sometimes critiques or comments on rejected ms.

How to Contact: Send complete ms with a cover letter. Include estimated word count, 1-paragraph bio and list of publications. Reports in 2 weeks on queries; 2 weeks-4 months on mss. Send SASE for reply, return of ms or send a disposable copy of ms. Simultaneous and reprint submissions OK. Sample copy for $5. Fiction guidelines for business-size envelope.

Payment/Terms: Pays 2 contributor's copies on publication. Acquires one-time rights.

Advice: "Read a lot and practice, practice, practice."

◧ ◎ FEMINIST STUDIES, Department of Women's Studies, University of Maryland, College Park MD 20742. (301)405-7415. Fax: (301)314-9190. E-mail: femstud@umail.umd.edu. Website: www.inform.umd.edu/ femstud. Editor: Claire G. Moses. **Fiction Editor:** Shirley Lim. Magazine: journal-sized; about 200 pages; photographs. "Scholarly manuscripts, fiction, book review essays for professors, graduate/doctoral students; scholarly interdisciplinary feminist journal." Triannually. Estab. 1974. Circ. 7,500.

Needs: Contemporary, ethnic, feminist, gay, lesbian. Receives about 15 poetry and short story mss/month. Accepts 2-3 mss/issue. "We review fiction twice a year. Deadline dates are May 1 and December 1. Authors will receive notice of the board's decision by June 30 and January 30, respectively." Published work by Bell Chevigny, Betsy Gould Gibson and Joan Jacobson. Sometimes comments on rejected mss.

How to Contact: Send complete ms with cover letter. No simultaneous submissions. Sample copy for $15. Fiction guidelines free.

Payment/Terms: Pays 2 contributor's copies and 10 tearsheets. Sends galleys to authors.

✔ ◧ ⚑ FICTION, % Dept. of English, City College, 138th St. & Convent Ave., New York NY 10031. (212)650-6319/650-6317. **Editor:** Mark J. Mirsky. Managing Editor: Daniel W. Long. Magazine: 6×9; 150-250 pages; illustrations and occasionally photos. "As the name implies, we publish *only* fiction; we are looking for the best new writing available, leaning toward the unconventional. *Fiction* has traditionally attempted to make accessible the unaccessible, to bring the experimental to a broader audience." Biannually. Estab. 1972. Circ. 4,500.

● Stories first published in *Fiction* have been selected for inclusion in the *Pushcart Prize* and *Best of the Small Presses* anthologies.

Needs: Contemporary, experimental, humor/satire, literary and translations. No romance, science-fiction, etc. Receives 200 unsolicited mss/month. Accepts 12-20 mss/issue; 24-40 mss/year. Does not read mss May-October. Publishes ms 1-12 months after acceptance. Agented fiction 10-20%. Published work by Harold Brodkey, Joyce Carol Oates, Peter Handke, Max Frisch, Susan Minot and Adolfo Bioy-Casares. Length: 6,000 words maximum. Publishes short shorts. Sometimes critiques rejected mss and recommends other markets.

How to Contact: Send complete ms with cover letter. Reports in approximately 3 months on mss. SASE. Simultaneous submissions OK, but please advise. Sample copy for $5. Fiction guidelines for SASE.

Payment/Terms: Pays in contributor's copies. Acquires first rights.

Advice: "The guiding principle of *Fiction* has always been to go to terra incognita in the writing of the imagination and to ask that modern fiction set itself serious questions, if often in absurd and comic voices, interrogating the nature of the real and the fantastic. It represents no particular school of fiction, except the innovative. Its pages have often been a harbor for writers at odds with each other. As a result of its willingness to publish the difficult, experimental, unusual, while not excluding the well known, *Fiction* has a unique reputation in the U.S. and abroad as a journal of future directions."

THE FIDDLEHEAD, University of New Brunswick, Campus House, Box 4400, Fredericton, New Brunswick E3B 5A3 Canada. (506)453-3501. Editor: Ross Leckie. **Fiction Editor:** Norman Ravvin. Magazine: 6×9; 104-128 pages; ink illustrations; photos. "No criteria for publication except quality. For a general audience, including many poets and writers." Quarterly. Estab. 1945. Circ. 1,000.
Needs: Literary. No non-literary fiction. Receives 100-150 unsolicited mss/month. Buys 4-5 mss/issue; 20-40 mss/year. Publishes ms up to 1 year after acceptance. Small percent agented fiction. Recently published work by Eric Miller, Tony Steele and A.F. Moritz. **Publishes 30 new writers/year.** Length: 50-3,000 words average. Publishes short shorts. Occasionally critiques rejected mss.
How to Contact: Send complete ms with cover letter. Send SASE and *Canadian* stamps or IRCs for return of mss. Reprint submissions OK. No simultaneous submissions. Reports in 2-6 months. Sample copy for $7 (US). Reviews novels and short story collections—*Canadian only*.
Payment/Terms: Pays $10-12 (Canadian)/published page and 1 contributor's copy on publication for first or one-time rights.
Advice: "Less than 5% of the material received is published."

FIRST CLASS, Four-Sep Publications, P.O. Box 12434, Milwaukee WI 53212. E-mail: chriftor@ex ecpc.com. Website: www.execpc.com/~chriftor (includes all information regarding Four-Sep Publications). **Editor:** Christopher M. Magazine: 8½×11; 48-56 pages; 24 lb./60 lb. offset paper; craft cover; illustrations and photos. "*First Class* features short fiction and poetics from the cream of the small press and killer unknowns—mingling before your very hungry eyes. I publish plays, too." Triannually. Estab. 1995. Circ. 200-400.
Needs: Erotica, literary, mainstream, science fiction (soft/sociological), short story collections, post-modern. "No religious or traditional poetry." Receives 20-30 unsolicited mss/month. Accepts 3-4 mss/issue; 10-12 mss/year. Publishes ms 2-3 months after acceptance. **Publishes 5-6 new writers/year.** Recently published work by Gerald Locklin, John Bennett and B.Z. Niditch. Length: 2,000-3,000 words average; 5,000-8,000 words maximum. Publishes short shorts. Length: 500 words. Also publishes poetry. Sometimes critiques or comments on rejected mss.
How to Contact: Send complete ms with a cover letter. Accepts queries by e-mail. Include 1 page bio and SASE. Reports in 1 week on queries; 1-2 weeks on mss. Send SASE for reply, return of ms or send a disposable copy of ms. Simultaneous submissions and reprints OK. Sample copy for $5. Fiction guidelines free for #10 SASE. Reviews novels and short story collections. Send books to Christopher M.
Payment/Terms: Pays 1 contributor's copy; additional copies $4. Pays on publication. Acquires one-time rights.
Advice: "Don't bore me with puppy dogs and the morose/sappy feelings you have about death. Belt out a good, short, thought-provoking, graphic, uncommon piece."

FISH DRUM MAGAZINE, Murray Hill Station, P.O. Box 966, New York NY 10156. Fax: (212)947-2305. E-mail: fishdrum@earthlink.net. Website: www.fishdrum.com. **Editor:** Suzi Winson. Magazine: 6×9; 80-odd pages; glossy cover; illustrations and photographs. "Lively, emotional vernacular modern fiction, art and poetry." Annually. Estab. 1988 by Robert Winson (1959-1995). "*Fish Drum* includes lively, vernacular, prose and poetry that follows the working novel. Themes include Zen practice, the South West, et.al." Circ. 2,000.
Needs: Contemporary, erotica, ethnic, experimental, fantasy, literary, prose poem, regional, science fiction and Zen-oriented works. "Most of the fiction we've published is in the form of short, heightened prose-pieces." Recently published work by Tom Ireland, Herbert Genzmer, Judith Barry and Andrew Franck. Receives 6-10 unsolicited mss/month. Accepts 1-2 mss/issue. Also publishes literary essays, literary criticism, poetry.
How to Contact: No simultaneous submissions. Reports on mss in 2-3 months. SASE. Reviews novels and short story collections.
Payment/Terms: Pays in contributor's copies. Charges for extras. Acquires first North American serial rights. Sends galleys to author.

FIVE POINTS: A Journal of Literature and Art, Georgia State University, University Plaza, Atlanta GA 30303-3083. (404)651-0071. Fax: (404)651-3167. E-mail: msexton@gsu.edu. Website: www.g su.edu/fivepoints (includes excerpts from issue, guidelines, announcements and links). Editors: Pam Durban and David Bottoms. **Fiction Editor:** Pam Durban. Magazine: 6×9; 200 pages; cotton paper; glossy cover; and photos. *Five Points* is "committed to publishing work that compels the imagination through the use of fresh and convincing language." Triannually. Estab. 1996. Circ. 1,000.
• *Five Points* won the CELJ award for Best New Journal.
Needs: List of upcoming themes available for SASE. Receives more than 250 unsolicited mss/month. Accepts 4 mss/issue; 15-20 mss/year. Does not read mss May 31-September 1. Publishes ms up to 6 months after acceptance.

Recently published work by Charles Wright, Philip Levine, Jane Hirshfield, Frederick Busch, Ursula Hegi and Josie Raney. Word length: 7,500 words average. Publishes short shorts. Also publishes literary essays and poetry. Sometimes comments on or critiques rejected ms.

How to Contact: Send complete ms with a cover letter. Include 3-4 line bio and list of publications. Send SASE for reply to query. No simultaneous submissions. Sample copy $5. Guidelines free.

Payment/Terms: Pays $15/page minimum; $250 maximum, free subscription to magazine and 2 contributor's copies; additional copies $3. Acquires first North American serial rights. Sends galleys to author. Sponsors contest: Paul Bowles Prize, annual award for fiction published in *Five Points*.

Advice: "We place no limitations on style or content. Our only criterion is excellence. If your writing has an original voice, substance, and significance, send it to us. We will publish distinctive, intelligent writing that has something to say and says it in a way that captures and maintains our attention."

THE FLORIDA REVIEW, Dept. of English, University of Central Florida, Orlando FL 32816. (407)823-2038. Fax: (407)823-6582. Website: pegasus.cc.ucf.edu/~english/floridareview/home.htm (includes writer's guidelines, contest information and covers and table of contents of the six most recent issues. **Contact:** Russell Kesler. Magazine: 7 × 10; 120 pages; semigloss full-color cover; perfect-bound. "We publish fiction of high 'literary' quality—stories that delight, instruct and aren't afraid to take risks. Our audience consists of avid readers of contemporary fiction, poetry and personal essay." Semiannually. Estab. 1972. Circ. 1,000.

Needs: Contemporary, experimental and literary. "We welcome experimental fiction, so long as it doesn't make us feel lost or stupid. We aren't especially interested in genre fiction (science fiction, romance, adventure, etc.), though a good story can transcend any genre." Receives 200 mss/month. Accepts 4-6 mss/issue; 8-12 mss/year. Publishes ms within 3-6 months of acceptance. Recently published work by Richard Wirick, Daniel Ort and Debbie Lee Wesselmann. **Publishes 2-4 new writers/year.** Also publishes literary criticism, poetry and essays.

How to Contact: Send complete ms with cover letter. Reports in 2-4 months. SASE required. Simultaneous submissions OK. Sample copy for $6; fiction guidelines for SASE. Reviews novels and short story collections.

Payment/Terms: Pays in contributor's copies. Small honorarium occasionally available. "Copyright held by U.C.F.; reverts to author after publication. (In cases of reprints, we ask that a credit line indicate that the work first appeared in the *F.R.*)"

Tips: "We're looking for writers with a fresh voice, engaging situations and are not afraid to take risks. Read contemporary writers/literary magazines."

$FLYING HORSE, P.O. Box 445, Marblehead MA 01945. **Editor:** Dennis Must. Associate Editor: David Wagner. Magazine: 6 × 9; 100 pages; 50 lb. Finch Opaque paper; 70 lb. cover stock; illustrations; photographs. "*Flying Horse* is an alternative literary journal. Although we welcome contributions from all talented artists, we particularly hope to give voice to those often excluded from the dominant media. For example, we actively encourage submissions from inner city learning centers, community and public colleges, prisons, homeless shelters, social service agencies, unions, the military, hospitals, clinics or group homes, Indian reservations and minority studies programs." Semiannually. Estab. 1996. Circ. 1,000.

Needs: Condensed/excerpted novel, ethnic/multicultural, experimental, literary, mainstream/contemporary, translations. No science fiction or horror. Wants more literary fiction. Receives 75-100 unsolicited mss/month. Accepts 20 mss/issue; 40 mss/year. Publishes ms generally in the next issue. Recently published work by Joseph Hurka, Richard Schmitt, Elisa Biagini, Virgil Suarez and Irene Aubry Kellogg. **Publishes 20 new writers/year.** Length: 2,500-5,000 words average; 7,500 words maximum. Publishes short shorts. Also publishes literary essays, literary criticism and poetry. Occasionally critiques or comments on rejected ms.

How to Contact: Send complete ms with a cover letter. Include estimated word count and short bio with submission. Reports in 3 months on mss. Send SASE for reply, return of ms or send a disposable copy of ms. Simultaneous submissions OK. Sample copy for $4. Fiction guidelines for #10 SASE.

Payment/Terms: Pays $10-25 and 2 contributor's copies on publication for one-time rights. Sends galleys to author.

Advice: "*Flying Horse* seeks heterogeneity of voice. Circumstance, class and formal education are not weighed. Nor do we count writing credits. What moves us to say *yes* is the authority of a submitted work, its conviction and originality of expression. The reader will encounter authors from starkly diverse corners of our society in our journal. What unites us, our common fuel, is the *written word*, and our firmly held conviction in its powers of transformation. We are increasingly receiving more submissions from writers who have published at least one book, often more than one. I have to believe it is because of publishing trends; i.e., fewer outlets for short story collections."

THE FLYING ISLAND, Writers' Center of Indianapolis, P.O. Box 88386, Indianapolis IN 46208. (317)955-6336. E-mail: bgentry@uindy.edu. **Editor:** Bruce Gentry. Tabloid: 24 pages; illustrations and photos. "A magazine of fiction, essays, reviews and poetry by Indiana-connected writers, co-sponsored by the University of Indianapolis." Semiannually. Estab. 1979. Circ. 700.

Needs: Ethnic/multicultural, experimental, fantasy, feminist, gay, lesbian, literary, mainstream/contemporary, mystery/suspense, psychic/supernatural/occult, science fiction. Receives 1,000 unsolicited mss/year. Accepts 4-5 mss/issue; 8-10 mss/year. Does not read mss March-May and September-November. Publishes ms 2 months after acceptance. Length: 3,000 words average. Publishes short shorts. Also publishes literary essays, literary criticism and poetry.

How to Contact: Send two copies of complete ms with a cover letter. Should include short bio explaining Indiana connection. Write for guidelines. Reports in 3-5 months on mss. SASE for return of ms. Simultaneous submissions OK. Fiction guidelines for #10 SASE.

Payment/Terms: Pays 2 contributor's copies plus honorarium. Pays on publication.

Advice: "We have published work by high school and college students as well as work by 1994 Pulitzer Prize winner Yusef Komunyakaa and Edgar nominee Terence Faherty. Our readers enjoy a wide variety of settings and situations. We're looking for quality and we tend to overlook gimmicky and sentimental writing."

N ◙ **FOLIAGE, Short Story Quarterly**, Foliage Press, P.O. Box 687, Yarmouth ME 04096. E-mail: foliagemag@worldnet.att.net. Website: home.att.net/~foliagemag (includes writer's guidelines, name of editor, list of authors in most recent issue). **Editor:** Sarah Lepine. Magazine: 5½ × 8½; 52-60 pages; 24 lb. paper; heavy cover stock; some illustrations and photos. "*Foliage* publishes work by beginning and established writers. Theme and style are open, but we do prefer literary stories that explore the human condition—layers of character." Quarterly. Estab. 1999. Circ. 150.

Needs: Literary. Receives 100-200 unsolicited mss/month. Accepts 6 mss/issue; 24 mss/year. Also 2-4 poems/issue; 0-2 creative nonfiction. Publishes ms 1-6 months after acceptance. **Publishes 5-10 new writers/year.** Recently published work by Christopher Woods, David Michael Kaplan and Melanie Barton Zoltán. Length: 3,000 words average; 6,000 words maximum. Publishes short shorts. Also publishes literary essays and poetry. Sometimes critiques or comments on rejected mss.

How to Contact: Send complete ms with a cover letter. Include estimated word count, 50 word bio, list of publications and SASE. Reports in 1 month on queries/mss. SASE for reply, send a disposable copy of ms. Simultaneous submissions and reprints OK. Sample copy for $5. Fiction guidelines free for #10 SASE.

Payment/Terms: Pays 1 contributor's copy; additional copies $4 (20% discount). Pays on publication. Acquires one-time rights. Sends galleys to author "if edits are made."

Advice: "What stand out are good mechanics and structure, strong narrative and natural dialogue. A strong story is important, but themes and ideas are meaningful too. We want writing that touches us, haunts us after we have finished reading. Read good fiction. Write every day. And check your manuscript for grammar and punctuation errors; an editor does not want to stumble through the first page. Aside from that, know your story, its characters' needs. Apply to it a consistent style and tone, a powerful voice. Send us your best work—clear, honest writing that makes us feel."

N ◙ **FOLIO: A LITERARY JOURNAL**, Department of Literature, Washington DC 20016. (202)885-2990. Editor changes yearly. Send mss to attention: Editor. Magazine: 6 × 9; 64 pages. "Fiction is published if it is well written. We look for fresh language, engaging plot and character development." Semiannually. Estab. 1984.

Needs: Contemporary, literary, mainstream, prose poem, translations, essay, b&w art or photography. No pornography. Occasional theme-based issues. See guidelines for info. Receives 150 unsolicited mss/month. Accepts 3-5 mss/issue; 6-40 mss/year. Does not read mss during April-August. Published work by Henry Taylor, Kermit Moyer, Linda Pastan. **Publishes new writers.** Length: 2,500 words average; 4,500 words maximum. Publishes short shorts. Occasionally critiques rejected mss.

How to Contact: Send complete ms with cover letter. Include a brief bio. Reports in 1-2 months. SASE. Simultaneous and reprint submissions OK (if noted). Sample copy for $5. Guidelines for #10 SASE.

Payment/Terms: Pays in contributor's copies. Acquires first North American rights. "$100 award for best fiction, poetry and art. Query for guidelines."

☑ ◯ **FORBIDDEN DONUT**, 1538 Woodlawn Circle, Waconia MN 55387. (612)442-2964. E-mail: wwood @earthlink.net. Website: home.earthlink.net/~wwood. **Editors:** Brian Wood and Jon Cazares. Magazine: 8 × 10; 50 pages; illustrations and photos. "Our continuing mission is to seek out new writers and new artists, to explore strange new ideas and to boldly go where no editors have gone before." Quarterly. Estab. 1995. Circ. 500.

Needs: Adventure, experimental, fantasy (science fantasy, sword and sorcery), horror, humor/satire, literary, mainstream/contemporary, mystery/suspense (amateur sleuth, cozy, police procedural, private eye/hardboiled), psychic/supernatural/occult, science fiction (hard science/soft sociological). No romance or westerns. Receives 10-25 unsolicited mss/month. Accepts 5-10 mss/issue; 20-30 mss year. Publishes ms 1-3 months after acceptance. Length: 3,000 words average; 10,000 words maximum. Publishes short shorts. Also publishes literary essays and literary criticism. Critiques or comments on rejected mss at author's request.

How to Contact: Send complete ms with a cover letter. Include bio. Accepts queries by e-mail. Reports in 1-3 weeks on queries; 2-8 weeks on mss. Send a disposable copy of ms. Simultaneous, reprint and electronic submissions OK. Sample copy for $3. Fiction guidelines free. Reviews novel and short story collections. Send books "Attention: Z.H."

Payment/Terms: Pays $1 and 1 contributor's copy for one-time rights; additional copies $1.

Advice: "The best advice we can give as to what kind of story we might accept is conflict and dialogue. Conflict and dialogue tend to keep the story moving and keep the reader interested, while drawn-out descriptions of everything in sight cause the reader to bog down and become bored. Many great stories don't follow this rule, but those are much more difficult to write. We prefer not to get lengthy submissions through e-mail. Please send recommendations for illustrations or photography to accompany your stories."

FOURTEEN HILLS: The SFSU Review, Dept. of Creative Writing, San Francisco State University, 1600 Holloway Ave., San Francisco CA 94132. (415)338-3083. E-mail: hills@sfsu.edu. Website: mercury.sfsu. edu/~hills/14hills.html. Editors change each year. Magazine: 6×9; 160 pages; 60 lb. paper; 10 point C15 cover. *"Fourteen Hills publishes the highest quality innovative fiction and poetry for a literary audience."* Semiannually. Estab. 1994. Circ. 700.

• Two stories from *Fourteen Hills* were included in *Best American Gay Fiction 1997.*

Needs: Ethnic/multicultural, gay, humor/satire, lesbian, literary, mainstream/contemporary, translations. "No sexist or racist work, and no stories in which the plot has been chosen for its shock value. No genre fiction, please." Receives 100 unsolicited mss/month. Accepts 8-10 mss/issue; 16-20 mss/year. Does not usually read mss during the summer. Publishes ms 2-4 months after acceptance. Published work by Terese Svoboda, Peter Rock and Stephen Dixon. **Publishes 6 new writers/year.** Length: 7,000 words maximum. Publishes short shorts. Also publishes literary essays, poetry. Sometimes critiques or comments on rejected mss.

How to Contact: Send complete ms with a cover letter. Include brief bio and list of publications. Reports in 3-5 months on mss. SASE for return of ms. Simultaneous submissions OK. Sample copy for $5. Fiction guidelines for #10 SASE.

Payment/Terms: Pays 2 contributor's copies on publication. Acquires one-time rights. Sends galleys to author.

Advice: "Please read an issue of *Fourteen Hills* before submitting."

FRONTIERS: A Journal of Women Studies, Washington State University, Frontiers, Women's Studies, Box 644007, Pullman WA 99164-4007. (509)335-7268. Fax: (509)335-4377. E-mail: frontier@wsu.edu. **Contact:** Managing Editor. Magazine: 6×9; 200 pages; photos. "Women studies; academic articles in all disciplines; criticism; exceptional creative work (art, short fiction, photography, poetry)."

Needs: Feminist, lesbian. "We want to see fiction that deals with women's lives and experience from a feminist perspective." Receives 15 unsolicited mss/month. Accepts 7-12 mss/issue. Publishes ms 6-12 months after acceptance. Recently published work by Elizabeth Bell, Nadine Chapman, Tricia Currans-Sheehan and Alethea Eason. **Publishes 2 new writers/year.**

How to Contact: Send 3 copies of complete ms with cover letter. Queries by e-mail OK. Reports in 1 month on queries; 3-6 months on mss. SASE. Writer's guidelines for #10 SASE. Sample copy for $9.

Payment/Terms: Pays 2 contributor's copies. Acquires first North American serial rights.

Advice: "We are a *feminist* journal. *Frontiers* aims to make scholarship in women studies, and *exceptional* creative work, accessible to a cross-disciplinary audience inside and outside academia. Read short fiction in *Frontiers* before submitting."

$ **FUGUE, Literary Digest of the University of Idaho**, English Dept., Rm. 200, Brink Hall, University of Idaho, Moscow ID 83844-1102. (208)885-6156. Fax: (208)885-5944. E-mail: witt931@novell.uidaho.edu. Website: www.uidaho.edu/LS/Eng/Fugue (includes writer's guidelines, names of editors, short fiction). Managing Editor: Ryan Witt. Editors change frequently. **Contact:** Executive Editor. Magazine: 6×9; 60-100 pages; 20 lb. stock paper. "We are interested in all classifications of fiction—we are not interested in pretentious 'literary' stylizations. We expect stories to be written in a manner engaging for anyone, not just academics and literati. If we could put together an 'ideal' issue, we would probably have 6 or 7 pieces of fiction, each of which would run no more than 10 pages (printed—probably 15 or 16 manuscript pages), a modest essay, and maybe 10 or a dozen poems. The fiction would include a couple of solid 'mainstream/literary' stories, at least one 'regional/local' story (preferably by a writer from the inland Northwest), at least one story by an ethnic writer (Chicano, Native American, Asian-American, African-American), at least one story that had some sort of international or cosmopolitan angle (set, perhaps, in Hong Kong or Quito and written by someone who really knew what he or she was doing), and at least one story that would be 'experimental' (including postmodernism, fantasy, surrealism . . .). Wit and humor are always welcome." Semiannually. Estab. 1990. Circ. 300.

Needs: Adventure, ethnic/multicultural, experimental, fantasy, historical, humor/satire, literary, mainstream/contemporary, regional. "We're looking for good ethnic fiction by ethnic writers; work with a cosmopolitan/international flavor from writers who know what they're doing; and intelligent and sophisticated mainstream and postmodern work." Does not want to see Dungeons & Dragons, Sword & Sorcery, Harlequin, "Cowboy Adventure Stories," True Confessions, etc. No genre fiction. Receives 80 unsolicited mss/month. Accepts 4-8 mss/issue; 8-16 mss/year. Publishes ms 1 year after acceptance. Recently published work by Ed McClanahan, Sophia Dembling, Jacob M. Appel and Denise Haver. **Publishes 6-7 new writers/year.** Length: 3,000 words average; 50 words minimum; 6,000 words maximum. Publishes short shorts. Also publishes literary essays and poetry. Sometimes critiques or comments on rejected mss.

How to Contact: Send complete ms with cover letter. "Obtain guidelines first." Include estimated word count and list of publications. Report in 2 weeks on queries; 2-3 months on mss. SASE for a reply to a query or return of ms. No simultaneous submissions. Sample copy for $5. Fiction guidelines for #10 SASE.

Payment/Terms: Pays $10-20 on publication for first North American serial rights. All contributors receive a copy; extra copies available at a discount.

Advice: Looks for "competent writing, clarity and consideration for the reader; also stylistic flair/energy. Here are what we consider the characteristics of a 'good' story: distinct voice; the quality of strangeness; engaging, dynamic characters; engaging language, style, craftsmanship; emotional resonance ('snap'); and an un-put-down-ability. Be original and inventive. Take chances, but present your work as a professional. Proper manuscript format is essential."

N □ **GARGOYLE**, % Atticus Books, 2308 Mt. Vernon Ave., Alexandria VA 22301. (202)667-8148. Website: www.atticusbooks.com. **Editors:** Richard Peabody, Lucinda Ebersole, Maja Dravsnitz. Literary magazine: 6×9; 350 pages; illustrations and photos. "*Gargoyle* is a literary magazine for poets and writers who actually read and care about what their peers are writing. We're about ⅓ British these days and not stuck in a time warp." Annually. Estab. 1976. Circ. 3,000.

Needs: Erotica, ethnic/multicultural, experimental, gay, lesbian, literary, mainstream/contemporary, translations, "good short stories with sports and music backgrounds." No romance, horror, science fiction. Receives 50-100 unsolicited mss/month. Accepts 23 mss/issue. Does not read from Thanksgiving to March. Publishes ms 6-12 months after acceptance. Agented fiction 5%. **Publishes 5-6 new writers/year.** Recently published work by Kim Addonizio, Mary Caponegro, Billy Childish, Helen Schulman and Curtis White. Length: 5-10 pages average; 30 pages maximum. Publishes short shorts. Length: 2-3 pages. Also publishes literary essays, criticism and poetry. Sometimes critiques or comments on rejected ms.

How to Contact: Send complete ms with a cover letter. Reports in 1-2 weeks on queries; 2-3 months on mss. Send SASE for reply, return of ms or send a disposable copy of ms. No simultaneous submissions. Sample copy for $10.

Payment/Terms: Pays 1 contributor copy; additional copies for ½ price. Acquires first rights, first North American rights or first British rights. Sends prepublication galleys to author.

Advice: "Read a copy. Our favorite living writers are Paul Bowles and Jeanette Winterson. That should give you a clue. We are, as far as I can tell, one of the few magazines that likes both realism and experimental work. Both poles are welcome."

★ ✓ □ **A GATHERING OF THE TRIBES**, A Gathering of the Tribes, Inc., P.O. Box 20693, Tompkins Square Station, New York NY 10009. (212)674-3778. Fax: (212)388-9813. E-mail: info@tribes.org. Website: www.tribes.org (includes highlights from previous 7 issues, mission statement, events). **Editor:** Steve Cannon. Magazine: 8½×10; 130 pages; glossy paper and cover; illustrations and photos. A "multicultural and multigenerational publication featuring poetry, fiction, interviews, essays, visual art, musical scores. Audience is anyone interested in the arts from a diverse perspective." Estab. 1992. Circ. 2,000-3,000.

Needs: Erotica, ethnic/multicultural, experimental, fantasy (science), feminist, gay, historical, horror, humor/satire, lesbian, literary, mainstream/contemporary, romance (futuristic/time travel, gothic), science fiction (soft/sociological), senior citizen/retirement, translations. "Would like to see more satire/humor. We are open to all; just no poor writing/grammar/syntax." List of upcoming themes available for SASE. Receives 300 unsolicited mss/month. Publishes ms 3-6 months after acceptance. Published work of Carl Watson and Hanif Kureishi. **Publishes 60-70% new writers.** Length: 500 words average; 200 words minimum; 2,500 maximum. Publishes short shorts. Also publishes literary essays, literary criticism and poetry.

How to Contact: Send complete ms with a cover letter. Include estimated word count, half-page bio, list of publications, phone and fax numbers and address with submission. Send SASE for reply, return of ms or send a disposable copy of ms. Simultaneous and reprint submissions OK. Sample copy for $10. Reviews novels and short story collections.

Payment/Terms: Pays 1 contributor's copy; additional copies $12-50. Sponsors contests, awards or grants for fiction writers. "Watch for ads in *Poets & Writers* and *American Poetry Review*."

Advice: Looks for "unique tone and style, offbeat plots and characters, and ethnic and regional work. Type manuscript well: readable font (serif) and no typos. Make characters and their dialogue interesting. Experiment with style, and don't be conventional. Do not send dragged-out, self-indulgent philosophizing of life and the universe. Get specific. Make your characters soar!"

❀ ★ $□ ✿ **GEIST, The Canadian Magazine of Ideas and Culture**, The Geist Foundation, 103-1014 Homer St., Vancouver, British Columbia V6B 2W9 Canada. (604)681-9161. Fax: (604)669-8250. E-mail: geist@geist.com. Website: www.geist.com (includes guidelines, names of editors, short fiction, issue previews). **Editor:** Barbara Zatyko. Magazine: 8×10½; illustrations and photographs. "*Geist Magazine* is particularly interested in writing that blurs the boundary between fiction and nonfiction. Each issue and most of the writing in *Geist* explores the physical and mental landscape of Canada." Quarterly. Estab. 1990. Circ. 5,000.

● *Geist* was nominated for best regular column at the Western Magazine Awards.

Needs: Condensed/excerpted novel, literary. "Rarely publish works in passive voice." Upcoming themes: "Best of Geist" millenium project in 2000. Receives 25 unsolicited mss/month. Accepts 10 mss/issue; 40 mss/year. Publishes ms 2-12 weeks after acceptance. Recently published work by Myrna Kostash, Alberto Manguel and

Ann Diamond. **Publishes 20 new writers/year.** Length: 200 words minimum; 5,000 words maximum. Publishes short shorts.

How to Contact: Send complete ms with a cover letter. Accepts queries by e-mail. Prefer snail mail. Include estimated word count and 1-2 line bio. Reports in 1 week on queries; 1-2 months on mss. Send SASE for reply, return of ms or send a disposable copy of ms. Reprint submissions OK. Fiction guidelines for SASE. Reviews novels and short story collections. Send books to Shannon Emmerson.

Payment/Terms: Pays $50-250 on publication and 8 contributor's copies; additional copies for $2. Acquires first rights. Send a SASE requesting contest guidelines.

Advice: "Each issue of Geist is a meditation on the imaginary country that we inhabit. Often that imaginary country has something to do with some part of Canada. A sense of Canadian place is central to the work we publish. Recommended reading: George Orwell's essay "Politics and the English Language"; back issues of *Geist*; and *Granta*."

$ ⊠ **GEORGE & MERTIE'S PLACE: ROOMS WITH A VIEW**, Dick Diver Enterprises, P.O. Box 10335, Spokane WA 99209. (509)325-3738. **Editors:** George Thomas and Mertie Duncan. Magazine: 8½×11; 4-8 pages; heavy stock, colored paper; illustrations. "We want well-written fiction and poetry, political and philosophical debate, humor, satire and jeremiad. Our audience will be literate Americans who like to read and to think. They will enjoy the use of language." Monthly. Estab. 1995. Circ. 50.

Needs: Anything well written. Receives 20-30 unsolicited mss/month. Accepts 1-2 mss/issue; 10-15 mss/year. "We work 3 months ahead." Published work by John Taylor and Jeff Grimshaw. Length: 1,000 words average; 1 word minimum; 2,500 words maximum. Publishes short shorts. Also publishes essays, literary criticism, poetry. Comments on most rejected mss.

How to Contact: Send complete ms with a cover letter. Include word count and a very brief bio. Reports in 1-2 months. Send SASE for reply, return of ms or send a disposable copy of ms. No simultaneous submissions. Sample copy for $2 and SASE. Fiction guidelines for SASE.

Payment/Terms: Pays 1¢/word, at publication and 1 contributor's copy; additional copies for $1.50. Acquires first North American serial rights and republication in GMP anthology. Not copyrighted. Each issue has a $25 "best of issue" prize. Published work automatically entered.

Advice: "We look for style in the work and an interesting narrative persona. *GMP*'s leftist, existential editors enjoy Kerouac, Kafka, Carver, Austen, Yeats, Genet, Miller, Frost, Carlyle, Stafford, Nin, Steinbeck, Fellini, Chaucer, Mishima, Hanshan, Kubric, Lapham, all those Russians, and many more (even Pope and Swift)! Old dogs with new tricks, our goal is to create a short, scruffy, entertaining, sometimes querulous monthly bark with a bite that does tricks but won't roll over."

◐ GEORGETOWN REVIEW, P.O. Box 6309, Southern Station, Hattiesburg MS 39406-6309. Phone/fax: (601)582-8677. E-mail: gr@georgetownreview.com. Website: www.georgetownreview.com (includes masthead, short fiction, poetry, guidelines). Editor: Steve Conti. **Fiction Editor:** Victoria Lancelotta. Magazine: 5½×8½; 150-200 pages; smooth offset paper; 10 pt. CS1 cover. "We want to publish quality fiction and poetry." Published twice a year. Estab. 1993. Circ. 1,000.

Needs: Condensed/excerpted novel, ethnic/multicultural, experimental, feminist, gay, humor/satire, lesbian, literary, science fiction. Wants to see more character-driven fiction. No romance, juvenile, fantasy or genre. Receives 150 mss/month. Does not read mss May through August. Agented fiction 10%. Published work by Claudia Mon Pere McIsaac, Caroline Langston and John Wallace. Length: 3,000 words average; 300 words minimum; 6,500 words maximum. Publishes short shorts. Length: 300 words. Also publishes poetry.

How to Contact: Send complete ms with a cover letter. Reports in 2-4 months on mss. SASE. Simultaneous and electronic submissions OK. Sample copy for $8. Guidelines free for SAE and 1 first-class stamp.

Payment/Terms: Pays 2 contributor's copies. Acquires first rights. Sends galleys to author.

Advice: "We simply look for quality work, no matter what the subject or style. Don't follow trends. Write with honesty and heart."

$ ◐ ▼ **THE GEORGIA REVIEW**, The University of Georgia, Athens GA 30602-9009. (706)542-3481. Website: www.uga.edu/~garev. **Editor-in-Chief:** Stanley W. Lindberg. Associate Editor: Stephen Corey. Assistant Editor: Janet Wondra. Journal: 7×10; 208 pages (average); 50 lb. woven old-style paper; 80 lb. cover stock; illustrations; photos. "*The Georgia Review* is a journal of arts and letters, featuring a blend of the best in contemporary thought and literature—essays, fiction, poetry, visual art and book reviews for the intelligent nonspecialist as well as the specialist reader. We seek material that appeals across disciplinary lines by drawing from a wide range of interests." Quarterly. Estab. 1947. Circ. 6,000.

● This magazine has an excellent reputation for publishing and has repeatedly been a finalist for the National Magazine Award in Fiction. *The Georgia Review* won that award in 1986.

Needs: Experimental and literary. "We're looking for the highest quality fiction—work that is capable of sustaining subsequent readings, not throw-away pulp magazine entertainment. Nothing that fits too easily into a 'category.'" Receives about 400 unsolicited fiction mss/month. Accepts 3-4 mss/issue; 12-15 mss/year. Does not read unsolicited mss in June, July or August. Would prefer *not* to see novel excerpts. Published work by Louise Erdrich, Eudora Welthy, Tim Gautreaux, Marjorie Sandor and Gary Gildner. **Published new writers**

within the last year. Length: Open. Also publishes literary essays, literary criticism, poetry. Occasionally critiques rejected mss.

How to Contact: Send complete ms (one story) with SASE. No multiple submissions. Usually reports in 2-3 months. Sample copy for $6; guidelines for #10 SASE. Reviews short story collections.

Payment/Terms: Pays minimum $35/printed page on publication for first North American serial rights, 1 year complimentary subscription and 1 contributor's copy; reduced charge for additional copies. Sends galleys to author.

GERTRUDE: A Journal of Voice & Vision, P.O. Box 270814, Ft. Collins CO 80527-0814. **Editor:** Eric Delehoy. Magazine: 5×8½, 36-48 pages; 60 lb. paper; glossy card cover; illustrations; and photos. *Gertrude* is a "biannual publication featuring the voices and visions of the gay, lesbian, bisexual, transgender and supportive community." Estab. 1999. Circ. 350.

Needs: Ethnic/multicultural, feminist, gay, humor satire, lesbian, literary, mainstream. No erotica, pornography or science fiction. Receives 3-5 unsolicited mss/month. Accepts 2-3 mss/issue; 4-6 mss/year. Publishes ms 1-2 months after acceptance. **Publishes 5-7 new writers/year.** Recently published work by Jennifer Dick, Joe Plambeck, Craig Dietz, Vittoria Repetto, Susan Lovejoy and Elisabeth Tyler James. Word length: 2,000 words average; 200 words minimum; 3,000 words maximum. Publishes short shorts. Length: 250 words. Also publishes poetry. Often comments on or critiques rejected ms.

How to Contact: Send complete ms with a cover letter. Include estimated word count, 1 paragraph bio and list of publications. Reports on mss in 2-4 months. Send SASE for reply to query and a disposable copy of ms. No simultaneous submissions. Reprint submissions OK. Sample copy for $4.95, 6×9 SAE and 3 first class stamps. Guidelines for #10 SASE.

Payment/Terms: Pays 1-2 contributor's copies; additional copies $3.95. Payment on publication. Author retains rights upon publication. Not copyrighted. Sponsors contest: "The Gerty," editors choice award. All accepted work is automatically considered.

Advice: "We look for strong characters, vivid detail and believable dialogue. Show us through words—don't tell us. We look for work that conveys the strength of the human spirit whether seriously or comically. Spell check and have someone else read your work. Just because we might not accept your work doesn't mean it is poorly written. Much has to do with editorial tastes. We tend to be eclectic. We are concerned with the quality of work and what it has to say to our readers."

THE GETTYSBURG REVIEW, Gettysburg College, Gettysburg PA 17325. (717)337-6770. Fax: (717)337-6775. E-mail: mdrew@gettysburg.edu. Editor: Peter Stitt. **Assistant Editor:** Mark Drew. Magazine: 6¾×10; 170 pages; acid free paper; full color illustrations. "Quality of writing is our only criterion; we publish fiction, poetry, and essays." Quarterly. Estab. 1988. Circ. 4,500.

● Work appearing in *The Gettysburg Review* has also been included in *Prize Stories: The O. Henry Awards*, the *Pushcart Prize* anthology, *Best American Poetry*, *New Stories from the South*, *Harper's*, and elsewhere. It is also the recipient of a Lila Wallace-Reader's Digest grant and NEA grants.

Needs: Contemporary, experimental, historical, humor/satire, literary, mainstream, regional and serialized novel. "We require that fiction be intelligent, and aesthetically written. Want more funny, hip, post-modern fiction." Receives 500 mss/month. Accepts 4-6 mss/issue; 16-24 mss/year. Publishes ms within 1 year of acceptance. Published work by Robert Olen Butler, Joyce Carol Oates, Naeem Murr, Tom Perrotta, Jacoba Hood and Tom House. **Publishes 2-10 new writers/year.** Length: 3,000 words average; 1,000 words minimum; 20,000 words maximum. Occasionally publishes short shorts. Also publishes literary essays, some literary criticism, poetry. Sometimes critiques rejected mss.

How to Contact: Send complete ms with cover letter September through May. Reports in 3-6 months. SASE. No simultaneous submissions. Sample copy for $7 (postage paid). Does not review books per se. "We do essay-reviews, treating several books around a central theme." Send review copies to editor.

Payment/Terms: Pays $25/printed page, subscription to magazine and contributor's copy on publication for first North American serial rights. Charge for extra copies.

Advice: "Reporting time can take more than three months. It is helpful to look at a sample copy of *The Gettysburg Review* to see what kinds of fiction we publish before submitting."

GINOSKO, P.O. Box 246, Fairfax CA 94978. (415)460-8436. **Editor:** Robert Cesaretti. Magazine: 4×6; 50-60 pages; standard paper; card cover; illustrations and photographs. Published "when material permits."

Needs: Experimental, literary, existential. Does not want conventional work. Wants more work like Kate Braverman. Receives 20 unsolicited mss/month. Length: 30,000 words maximum. Publishes short shorts. Also publishes literary essays, poetry.

How to Contact: Send complete ms with a cover letter. Reports in 3 months on mss. SASE for return of ms. Simultaneous and reprint submissions OK.

Payment/Terms: Pays 1 contributor's copy. Acquires one-time rights.

Advice: "I am looking for a style that conveys spiritual hunger and depth yet avoids religiosity and convention—between literary vision and spiritual realities."

★ ☑ $◯ ▨ **GLIMMER TRAIN STORIES**, Glimmer Train Press, 710 SW Madison St., Suite 504, Portland OR 97205. (503)221-0836. E-mail: linda@glimmertrain.com. Website: www.glimmertrain.com (includes writer's guidelines, story excerpts and a Q&A section for writers). **Editors:** Susan Burmeister-Brown and Linda Burmeister Davies. Magazine: 6¾×9¼; 160 pages; recycled, acid-free paper; 20 illustrations; 12 photographs. Quarterly. Estab. 1991. Circ. 21,000.

● *Glimmer Train* was ranked #14 on *Writer's Digest's* Fiction 50 list of top markets for fiction writers. The magazine also sponsors an annual short story contest for new writers and a very short fiction contest.

Needs: Literary. Receives 3,000 unsolicited mss/month. Accepts 10 mss/issue; 40 mss/year. Reads in January, April, July, October. Publishes ms 6-12 months after acceptance. Agented fiction 20%. Recently published work by Judy Budnitz, Brian Champeau, Ellen Cooney, Andre Dubus III, Thomas Kennedy, Chris Offutt, Alberto Rios and Monica Wood. **Publishes 8 new writers/year.** Length: 1,200 words minimum; 8,000 words maximum.

How to Contact: Send complete ms with a cover letter. Include estimated word count. Reports in 3 months. Send SASE for return or send a disposable copy of ms (with stamped postcard or envelope for notification). Simultaneous submissions OK. Sample copy for $10. Fiction guidelines for #10 SASE.

Payment/Terms: Pays $500 and 10 contributor's copies on acceptance for first rights.

Advice: "If you're excited about a story you've written, send it to us! If you're not very excited about it, wait and send one that you are excited about. It's usually a good idea to do a lot of reading. This will often improve the quality of your own writing. When a story stays with us after the first reading, it gets another reading. Those stories that simply don't let us set them aside, get published. Read good fiction. It will often improve the quality of your own writing."

★ ★ ☑ $◯ ▨ **GRAIN**, Saskatchewan Writers' Guild, Box 1154, Regina, Saskatchewan S4P 3B4 Canada. (306)244-2828. Fax: (306)244-0255. E-mail: grain.mag@sk.sympatico.ca. Website: www.skwriter.com (includes history, news, subscription and contest information). Editor: Elizabeth Philips. **Fiction Editor:** Dianne Warren. Literary magazine: 6×9; 128 pages; Chinook offset printing; chrome-coated stock; illustrations; some photos. "Fiction and poetry for people who enjoy high quality writing." Quarterly. Estab. 1973. Circ. 1,300.

● *Grain* won magazine of the year-Saskatchewan at the Western Magazine awards and was ranked #48 on *Writer's Digest's* Fiction 50 list of top markets for fiction writers.

Needs: Contemporary, experimental, literary, mainstream and prose poem. Want to see more magic realism. "No propaganda—only artistic/literary writing." No genre fiction. No mss "that stay *within* the limits of conventions such as women's magazine type stories, science fiction; none that push a message." Receives 80 unsolicited fiction mss/month. Accepts 8-12 mss/issue; 32-48 mss/year. Recently published work by Douglas Glover, Cyril Dabydeen, Lewis Horne and Anita Shir-Jacob. Length: "No more than 30 pages." Also publishes poetry and creative nonfiction. Occasionally critiques rejected mss.

How to Contact: Send complete ms with SASE (or IRC) and brief letter. Queries by e-mail or fax OK. No simultaneous submissions. Reports within 4 months on mss. Publishes ms an average of 4 months after acceptance. Sample copy for $7.95 plus postage.

Payment/Terms: Pays $30-100 and 2 contributor's copies on publication for first Canadian serial rights. "We expect acknowledgment if the piece is republished elsewhere."

Advice: "Submit a story to us that will deepen the imaginative experience of our readers. *Grain* has established itself as a first-class magazine of serious fiction. We receive submissions from around the world. If Canada is a foreign country to you, we ask that you *do not* use U.S. postage stamps on your return envelope. If you live outside Canada and neglect the International Reply Coupons, we *will not* read or reply to your submission. We look for attention to detail, credibility, lucid use of language and metaphor and a confident, convincing voice. Sweat the small stuff. Make sure you have researched your piece, that the literal and metaphorical support one another."

🌐 ◯ **GRANTA, The Magazine of New Writing**, 2-3 Hanover Yard, Noel Rd., London N1 8BE England. Phone: 0171 704 9776. Fax: 0171 704 0474. E-mail: editorial@grantamag.co.uk. **Editor:** Ian Jack. Magazine: paperback, 270 pages approx.; photos. "*Granta* magazine publishes fiction, reportage, biography and autobiography, history, travel and documentary photography. It rarely publishes 'writing about writing.' The realistic narrative—the story—is its primary form." Quarterly. Estab. 1979. Circ. 90,000.

Needs: Literary. "No fantasy, science fiction, romance, historical, occult or other 'genre' fiction." Themes decided as deadline approaches. Receives 100 unsolicited mss/month. Accepts 0-1 ms/issue; 1-2 mss/year. Percentage of agented fiction varies. **Publishes 1-2 new writers/year.** Length: open. Rarely critiques or comments on rejected ms.

How to Contact: Query first. Reports in 1 month on queries; 3 months on mss. Send SAE and IRCs for reply, return of ms or send a disposable copy of ms. Simultaneous submissions OK. Sample copy £7.99.

Payment/Terms: Pays £75-5,000 and 3 contributor's copies. Acquires variable rights. Sends galleys to author.

Advice: "We are looking for the best in realistic stories; originality of voice; without jargon, connivance or self-conscious 'performance'—writing that endures."

★ ☑ ◯ **GRASSLANDS REVIEW**, P.O. Box 626, Berea OH 44017. E-mail: glreview@aol.com. Website: www.hometown.aol.com/glreview/prof/index.htm (includes guidelines, contest information, sample text, table of contents for latest issue). **Editor:** Laura B. Kennelly. Magazine: 6×9; 80 pages. *Grasslands Review* prints creative writing of all types; poetry, fiction, essays for a general audience. "Designed as a place for new writers to publish." Semiannually. Estab. 1989. Circ. 300.

Needs: Contemporary, ethnic, experimental, fantasy, horror, humor/satire, literary, mystery/suspense, prose poem, regional, science fiction and western. Nothing pornographic or overtly political or religious. Accepts 1-3 mss/issue. Reads only in October and March. Publishes ms 6 months after acceptance. Recently published work by Carole Chips Carlson and Yvonne Jackson. **Publishes 15 new writers/year.** Length: 100-3,500 words; 1,500 words average. Publishes short shorts (100-150 words). Also publishes poetry. Sometimes critiques rejected mss and recommends other markets.

How to Contact: Send complete ms in October or March *only* with cover letter. No simultaneous submissions. Reports on mss in 3 months. SASE. Sample copy for $4.

Payment/Terms: Pays in contributor's copies. Acquires one-time rights. Publication not copyrighted.

Advice: "A fresh approach, imagined by a reader for other readers, pleases our audience. We are looking for fiction which leaves a strong feeling or impression—or a new perspective on life. The *Review* began as an in-class exercise to allow experienced creative writing students to learn how a little magazine is produced. It now serves as an independent publication, attracting authors from as far away as the Ivory Coast, but its primary mission is to give unknown writers a start."

THE GREEN HILLS LITERARY LANTERN, Published by North Central Missouri College and co-published by The North Central Missouri Writer's Guild, P.O. Box 375, Trenton MO 64683. (660)359-3948, ext. 324. Fax: (660)359-3202. E-mail: jsmith@mail.ncmc.cc.mo.us. Editors: Jack Smith and Ken Reger. **Fiction Editor:** Sara King. Magazine: 6×9; 200 pages; good quality paper with glossy 4-color cover. "The mission of *GHLL* is to provide a literary market for quality fiction writers, both established and beginners, and to provide quality literature for readers from diverse backgrounds. We also see ourselves as a cultural resource for North Central Missouri. Our publication works to publish the highest quality fiction—dense, layered, subtle, and, at the same time, fiction which grabs the ordinary reader. We tend to publish traditional short stories, but we are open to experimental forms." Annually. Estab. 1990. Circ. 500.

● *The Green Hills Literary Lantern* received a Missouri Arts Council grant in 1999.

Needs: Ethnic/multicultural, experimental, feminist, humor/satire, literary, mainstream/contemporary and regional. "Fairly traditional short stories but we are open to experimental. Our main requirement is literary merit. Wants more quality fiction about rural culture." No adventure, crime, erotica, horror, inspirational, mystery/suspense, romance. Receives 30 unsolicited mss/month. Accepts 4-5 mss/issue. Publishes ms 6-12 months after acceptance. Recently published work by Walter Cummins, Karl Harshbarger, Joan Connor and Robert Garner McBrearty. **Publishes 0-1 new writer/year.** Length: 3,000 words average; 5,000 words maximum. Publishes short shorts. Also publishes poetry. Sometimes critiques or comments on rejected mss.

How to Contact: Send complete ms with a cover letter. Include bio (50-100 words) with list of publications. Accepts queries (only) by e-mail. Reports in 3-4 months on mss. SASE for return of ms. Simultaneous submissions OK. Sample copy for $7 (includes envelope and postage).

Payment/Terms: Pays two contributor's copies. Acquires one-time rights. Sends galleys to author.

Advice: "We look for strong character development, substantive plot and theme, visual and forceful language within a multilayered story. Make sure your work has the flavor of life—a sense of reality. A good story, well-crafted, will eventually get published. Find the right market for it, and above all, don't give up. The cost of funding a literary magazine prevents us from publishing longer pieces (over 5,000 words), and it also means we have to reject some publishable fiction due to space limitation."

$ GREEN MOUNTAINS REVIEW, Johnson State College, Box A-58, Johnson VT 05656. (802)635-1350. Editor-in-Chief: Neil Shepard. **Fiction Editor:** Tony Whedon. Magazine: digest-sized; 160-200 pages. Semiannually. Estab. 1975 (new series, 1987). Circ. 1,700.

● *Green Mountain Review* has received a Pushcart Prize and Editors Choice Award.

Needs: Adventure, contemporary, experimental, humor/satire, literary, mainstream, serialized/excerpted novel, translations. Receives 80 unsolicited mss/month. Accepts 6 mss/issue; 12 mss/year. Publishes ms 6-12 months after acceptance. Reads mss September 1 through May 1. Recently published work by Peter LaSalle and Norberto Luis Romero. **Publishes 0-4 new writers/year.** Length: 25 pages maximum. Publishes short shorts. Also publishes literary criticism, poetry. Sometimes critiques rejected mss.

How to Contact: Send complete ms with cover letter. "Manuscripts will not be read and will be returned between March 1 and September 1." Reports in 1 month on queries; 3-6 months on mss. SASE. Simultaneous submissions OK (if advised). Sample copy for $5.

Payment/Terms: Pays contributor's copies, 1-year subscription and small honorarium, depending on grants. Acquires first North American serial rights. Rights revert to author upon request. Sends galleys to author upon request.

Advice: "We're looking for more rich, textured, original fiction with cross-cultural themes. The editors are open to a wide spectrum of styles and subject matter as is apparent from a look at the list of fiction writers who have published in its pages. One issue was devoted to Vermont fiction, and another issue filled with new writing from the People's Republic of China. The Fall/Winter 1999 issue will be devoted to literary ethnography."

N ★ ⌀ ◎ ▣ THE GREEN TRICYCLE: "The fun-to-read lit mag!", Cayuse Press, P.O. Box 66003, Burien WA 98166-0003. E-mail: green_tricycle@cayuse-press.zzn.com. Website: www.cayuse-press.com ("The Cayuse Press website offers everything a writers needs for publication in the *Green Tricycle* or any of our other publications. You'll find guidelines, deadlines, current and archived issues, tools and tips for writers, freebies, and a lively poetry forum, open to all writers.") **Editor:** B. Benepe. Electronic magazine. "*The Green Tricycle* is an online thematic literary journal, with three themes per issue. Each piece is limited to 200 words. We accept poetry, micro-fiction, mini-essays, letters, and drama, as long as it addresses the theme in an original manner." Quarterly. Estab. 1999.

Needs: Literary. "No erotica, horror, or occult—too much of that is on the Internet already." List of upcoming themes available on website. Receives 40-100 unsolicited mss/month. Accepts 2-5 mss/issue; 8-10 mss/year. Publishes ms 1-3 months after acceptance. Agented fiction 10%. **Publishes 15 new writers/year.** Recently published work by Otis Luce, Jay Smith, Margret Watland and Cris Bisch. Word length: 175 words average; 100 words minimum; 200 words maximum. Also publishes literary essays and poetry. Sometimes comments on or critiques rejected ms.

How to Contact: Send complete ms with a cover letter. "Online submissions only. No attachments." Include estimated word count, 25-30 word bio and list of publications. Reports within 2 months. Simultaneous submissions and reprints OK. Sample copy and guidelines free. Reviews novels, short story collections and nonfiction books of interest to writers. Contact the publisher.

Payment/Terms: Acquires one-time rights. Sponsors contest: information on website.

Advice: "I look for originality. A creative approach to the theme catches my attention. Be original. Read the magazine. Sloppy mechanics are sickening. Write the best you can without using four-letter words."

❦ ★ ⌀ GREEN'S MAGAZINE, Fiction for the Family, Green's Educational Publications, Box 3236, Regina, Saskatchewan S4P 3H1 Canada. **Editor:** David Green. Magazine: 5¼ × 8½; 96 pages; 20 lb. bond paper; matte cover stock; line illustrations. Publishes "solid short fiction suitable for family reading." Quarterly. Estab. 1972.

Needs: Adventure, fantasy, humor/satire, literary, mainstream, mystery/suspense and science fiction. No erotic or sexually explicit fiction. Receives 20-30 mss/month. Accepts 10-12 mss/issue; 40-50 mss/year. Publishes ms within 3-6 months of acceptance. Agented fiction 2%. Recently published work by Robert Redding, Edward Wahl and Mary Wallace. **Publishes 10 new writers/year.** Length: 2,500 words preferred; 1,500 words minimum; 4,000 words maximum. Also publishes poetry. Sometimes critiques rejected mss.

How to Contact: Send complete ms. "Cover letters welcome but not necessary." Reports in 2 months. SASE (or IRC). No simultaneous submissions. Sample copy for $5. Fiction guidelines for #10 SASE (IRC). Reviews novels and short story collections.

Payment/Terms: Pays in contributor's copies. Acquires first North American serial rights.

Advice: "No topic is taboo, but we avoid sexuality for its own sake, and dislike material that is needlessly explicit or obscene. We look for strongly written stories that explore their characters through a subtle blending of conflicts. Plots should be appropriate, rather than overly ingenious or reliant on some *deus ex machina*. It must be a compression of experience or thoughts, in a form that is both challenging and rewarding to the reader. We have no form rejection slip. If we cannot use a submission, we try to offer constructive criticism in our personal reply. Often, such effort is rewarded with reports from our writers that following our suggestions has led to placement of the story or poem elsewhere."

☑ ⌀ ♥ THE GREENSBORO REVIEW, English Dept., 134 McIver Bldg., UNC Greensboro, P.O. Box 26170, Greensboro NC 27402-6170. (336)334-5459. E-mail: jlclark@uncg.edu. Website: www.uncg.edu/eng/mfa (includes writer's guidelines, literary awards guidelines, address, deadlines, subscription information). Editor: Jim Clark. **Fiction Editor:** Cassandra Gainer. Fiction editor changes each year. Send mss to the editor. Magazine: 6 × 9; approximately 128 pages; 60 lb. paper; 65 lb. cover. Literary magazine featuring fiction and poetry for readers interested in contemporary literature. Semiannually. Circ. 800.

● *The Greensboro Review* won Pushcart Prizes in 1997, 1998 and 1999. *New Stories from the South* selected a story for 1999.

Needs: Contemporary and experimental. Accepts 6-8 mss/issue, 12-16 mss/year. Recently published work by Robert Morgan, George Singleton, Robert Olmstead, Jean Ross Justice, Dale Ray Phillips and Kelly Cherry. Length: 7,500 words maximum.

How to Contact: Send complete ms with SASE. No simultaneous submissions or previously published works. Unsolicited manuscripts must arrive by September 15 to be considered for the spring issue and by February 15 to be considered for the fall issue. Manuscripts arriving after those dates may be held for the next consideration. Reports in 2-4 months. Sample copy for $5.

Payment/Terms: Pays in contributor's copies. Acquires first North American serial rights.

Advice: "We want to see the best being written regardless of theme, subject or style. Recent stories from *The Greensboro Review* have been included in *The Best American Short Stories*, *Prize Stories: The O. Henry Awards*, *New Stories from the South*, and *Pushcart Prize* anthologies recognizing the finest short stories being published."

$ ⊘ ⛉ GULF COAST, A Journal of Literature & Fine Arts, Dept. of English, University of Houston, Houston TX 77204-3012. (713)743-3223. Fax: (713)743-3215. **Fiction Editor:** Chris Haven. Editors change each year. Magazine: 6×9; 144 pages; stock paper; gloss cover; illustrations and photographs. "Innovative fiction for the literary-minded." Estab. 1984. Circ. 1,500.
  • Work published in *Gulf Coast* has been selected for inclusion in the *Pushcart Prize* anthology and *Best American Short Stories*.
Needs: Contemporary, ethnic, experimental, literary, regional, translations. Wants more "cutting-edge, experimental" fiction. No children's, genre, religious/inspirational. Receives 150 unsolicited mss/month. Accepts 8-10 mss/issue; 16-20 mss/year. Publishes ms 6 months-1 year after acceptance. Agented fiction 5%. Published work by Diana Joseph, Karen Mary Penn, J. David Stevens, Darren Defrain, Brian Leung and Karla Kuban. Length: no limit. Publishes short shorts. Sometimes critiques rejected mss.
How to Contact: Send complete ms with brief cover letter. "List previous publications; please notify us if the submission is being considered elsewhere." Reports in 3-6 months. Simultaneous submissions OK. Back issue for $6, 7×10 SAE and 4 first-class stamps. Fiction guidelines for #10 SASE.
Payment/Terms: Pays contributor's copies and *small* honorariam for one-time rights.
Advice: "Rotating editorship, so please be patient with replies. As always, please send one story at a time."

✓ ⊘ ⛉ GULF STREAM MAGAZINE, Florida International University, English Dept., North Miami Campus, N. Miami FL 33181. (305)919-5599. **Editor:** Lynne Barrett. Editors change every 1-2 years. Magazine: 5½×8½; 96 pages; recycled paper; 80 lb. glossy cover; cover illustrations. "We publish *good quality*—fiction, nonfiction and poetry for a predominately literary market." Semiannually. Estab. 1989. Circ. 500.
  • Awarded "Best Literary Journal" by *New Times*, Best of Miami issue, 1999.
Needs: Contemporary, literary, mainstream. Plans special issues. Receives 100 unsolicited mss/month. Accepts 5 mss/issue; 10 mss/year. Does not read mss during the summer. Publishes ms 3-6 months after acceptance. Published work by Christine Liotta, Jane McCafferty, Steven Almond and Charles Radke. **Publishes 2-5 new writers/year.** Length: 5,000 words average; 7,500 words maximum. "Usually longer stories do not get accepted. There are exceptions, however." Publishes short shorts. Also publishes poetry. Sometimes critiques rejected mss.
How to Contact: Send complete manuscript with cover letter including list of previous publications and a short bio. Reports in 3 months. SASE. Simultaneous submissions OK "if noted." Sample copy for $4. Free fiction guidelines.
Payment/Terms: Pays in gift subscriptions and contributor's copies. Acquires first North American serial rights.
Advice: "Looks for good concise writing—well plotted with interesting characters."

⊘ HABERSHAM REVIEW, Piedmont College, P.O. Box 10, Demorest GA 30535. (706)778-3000. E-mail: fgannon@piedmont.edu. **Editor:** Frank Gannon. Magazine. "General literary magazine with a regional (Southeastern U.S.) focus for a literate audience." Semiannually. Estab. 1991.
Needs: Contemporary, experimental, literary, mainstream, regional. Wants more fiction with a Southern focus. Receives 100 unsolicited mss/month. Acquires 6-10 mss/issue. Recently published work by Bettie Sellers, Barbara Brown Taylor and Phyllis Sanchez Gussler. **Publishes 6 new writers/year.** Publishes short shorts. Sometimes critiques rejected mss.
How to Contact: Send complete ms with cover letter. Accepts queries/mss by e-mail. Reports in 6 months on mss. SASE. No simultaneous submissions. Sample copy for $6.
Payment/Terms: Pays in contributor's copies. Acquires first rights.
Tips: "We look for fresh writing and technical skill. Keep working until you find your voice."

✓ ⊘ HALF TONES TO JUBILEE, English Dept., Pensacola Junior College, 1000 College Blvd., Pensacola FL 32504-8910. (850)484-1450. **Editor:** Walter Spara. Magazine: 6×9; approx. 100 pages. "No theme, all types published." Annually. Estab. 1985. Circ. 500.
Needs: Open. Accepts approx. 6 mss/issue. "We publish in September." Published work by Mark Spencer, Brenda Cook and Wanda Wood. Length: 1,500 words average. Publishes short shorts. Also publishes poetry.
How to Contact: Send complete ms with cover letter. SASE. Sample copy for $4. Free fiction guidelines.
Payment/Terms: Pays 1 contributor's copy. Acquires one-time rights.
Advice: "We are moving away from linear development; we are noted for innovation in style."

✪ $ ⊘ HAPPY, The Happy Organization, 240 E. 35th St., 11A, New York NY 10016. (212)689-3142. Fax: (212)683-1169. E-mail: bayardx@aol.com. **Editor:** Bayard. Magazine: 5½×8; 100 pages; 60 lb. text paper; 150 lb. cover; perfect-bound; illustrations and photos. Quarterly. Estab. 1995. Circ. 500.
  • *Happy* was ranked #3 in *Writer's Digest*'s Fiction 50 list of top markets for fiction writers.
Needs: Erotica, ethnic/multicultural, experimental, fantasy, feminist, gay, horror, humor/satire, lesbian, literary, psychic/supernatural/occult, science fiction. No "television rehash or religious nonsense." Want more work that is "strong, angry, empowering." Receives 300-500 unsolicited mss/month. Accepts 30-40 mss/issue; 100-150 mss/year. **Publishes 30-50% new writers.** Publishes ms 6-12 months after acceptance. Length: 1,000-3,500

words average; 6,000 words maximum. Publishes short shorts. Often critiques or comments on rejected mss.

How to Contact: Send complete ms with a cover letter. Include estimated word count. Accepts queries by e-mail. Reports in 1 week on mss. Send SASE for reply, return of ms or send a disposable copy of ms. Simultaneous submissions OK. Sample copy for $12.

Payment/Terms: Pays 1¢/word, minimum $5 on publication and 1 contributor's copy for one-time rights.

Advice: "No more grumbling about what you should be—become what you intended!"

HAWAII REVIEW, University of Hawaii English Dept., 1733 Donaghho Rd., Honolulu HI 96822. (808)956-3030. Fax: (808)956-9962. **Editor:** Kyle Koza. Magazine: 6½×9½; 150-250 pages; illustrations; photos. "We publish short stories as well as poetry and reviews by new and experienced writers. As an international literary journal, we hope to reflect the idea that cultural diversity is of universal interest." For residents of Hawaii and non-residents from the continental US and abroad. Twice per year. Estab. 1972. Circ. 1,000.

Needs: Contemporary, ethnic, humor/satire, literary, prose poem, regional and translations. No genre fiction. Receives 50-75 mss/month. No more than 40 mss/issue; 130 mss/year. Published work by Mathew Cashion, Lee A. Tonouchi, Ron Carlson and Andrea Cornachio. **Publishes 4 new writers/year.** Length: 4,000 words average; no minimum; 8,000 words maximum. Occasionally critiques mss. Also publishes poetry.

How to Contact: Send complete ms with SASE. Reports in 3-4 months on mss. Sample copy for $10. Fiction guidelines for SASE.

Payment/Terms: Pays 4 contributor's copies.

Advice: "We select fiction based on excellent story, good sentence level writing, attention to detail, no overused story lines, no self-conscious narratives. We like story character development—characters the reader feels for—and a strong voice. Also well-crafted language that propels the eye forward."

$ HAYDEN'S FERRY REVIEW, NSSWM Box 871502, Arizona State University, Tempe AZ 85287-1502. (480)965-1243. Fax: (480)965-6704. E-mail: hfr@asu.edu. Website: www.statepress.com/hfr. Editors change every 1-2 years. Magazine: 6×9; 128 pages; fine paper; illustrations and photographs. "Contemporary material by new and established writers for a varied audience." Semiannually. Estab. 1986. Circ. 1,300.

● Work from *Hayden's Ferry Review* has been selected for inclusion in *Pushcart Prize* anthologies.

Needs: Contemporary, experimental, literary, prose poem, regional. Possible special fiction issue. Receives 250 unsolicited mss/month. Accepts 5 mss/issue; 10 mss/year. Publishes mss 3-4 months after acceptance. Published work by T.C. Boyle, Raymond Carver, Ken Kesey, Rita Dove, Chuck Rosenthal and Rick Bass. Length: No preference. Publishes short shorts. Also publishes literary essays.

How to Contact: Send complete ms with cover letter. Reports in 3-5 months from deadline on mss. SASE. Sample copy for $6. Fiction guidelines for SAE.

Payment/Terms: Pays 2 contributor's copies; prose $25; poetry $15. Acquires first North American serial rights. Sends page proofs to author.

$ HIGH PLAINS LITERARY REVIEW, 180 Adams St., Suite 250, Denver CO 80206. (303)320-6828. Fax: (303)320-6828. **Editor-in-Chief:** Robert O. Greer, Jr. Magazine: 6×9; 135 pages; 70 lb. paper; heavy cover stock. "The *High Plains Literary Review* publishes poetry, fiction, essays, book reviews and interviews. The publication is designed to bridge the gap between high-caliber academic quarterlies and successful commercial reviews." Triannually. Estab. 1986. Circ. 1,100.

Needs: Most pressing need: outstanding essays, serious fiction, contemporary, humor/satire, literary, mainstream, regional. No true confessions, romance, pornographic, excessive violence. Receives approximately 400 unsolicited mss/month. Accepts 4-6 mss/issue; 12-18 mss/year. Publishes ms usually 6 months after acceptance. Recently published work by Michael Martone, Naton Leslie, Tony Ardizzone and Paula L. Woods. **Published new writers within the last year.** Length: 4,200 words average; 1,500 words minimum; 8,000 words maximum; prefers 3,000-6,000 words. Also publishes literary essays, literary criticism, poetry. Occasionally critiques rejected mss.

How to Contact: Send complete ms with cover letter. Include brief publishing history. Reports in 4 months. Send SASE for reply or return of ms. Simultaneous submissions OK. Sample copy for $4.

Payment/Terms: Pays $5/page for prose and 2 contributor's copies on publication for first North American serial rights. "Copyright reverts to author upon publication." Sends copy-edited proofs to the author.

Advice: "HPLR publishes *quality* writing. Send us your very best material. We will read it carefully and either accept it promptly, recommend changes or return it promptly. Do not start submitting your work until you learn the basic tenets of the game including some general knowledge about how to develop characters and plot and how to submit a manuscript. I think the most important thing for any new writer interested in the short story

● **A BULLET INTRODUCES COMMENTS** by the editor of *Novel & Short Story Writer's Market* indicating special information about the listing.

form is to have a voracious appetite for short fiction, to see who and what is being published, and to develop a personal style."

HILL AND HOLLER: Southern Appalachian Mountains, Seven Buffaloes Press, P.O. Box 249, Big Timber MT 59011. **Editor:** Art Cuelho. Magazine: 5½×8½; 80 pages; 70 lb. offset paper; 80 lb. cover stock; illustrations; photos rarely. "I use mostly rural Appalachian material: poems and stories, and some folklore and humor. I am interested in heritage, especially in connection with the farm." Annually. Published special fiction issue. Estab. 1983. Circ. 750.

Needs: Contemporary, ethnic, humor/satire, literary, regional, rural America farm. "I don't have any prejudices in style, but I don't like sentimental slant. Deep feelings in literature are fine, but they should be portrayed with tact and skill." Receives 10 unsolicited mss/month. Accepts 4-6 mss/issue. Publishes ms 6 months-1 year after acceptance. Length: 2,000-3,000 words average. Also publishes short shorts of 500-1,000 words.

How to Contact: Query first. Reports in 1 month on queries. SASE. Sample copy for $7.75 postpaid.

Payment/Terms: Pays in contributor's copies. Acquires first North American serial rights "and permission to reprint if my press publishes a special anthology." Sometimes sends galleys to author.

Advice: "In this Southern Appalachian rural series I can be optimistic about fiction. Appalachians are very responsive to their region's literature. I have taken work by beginners that had not been previously published. Be sure to send a double-spaced clean manuscript and SASE. I have the only rural press in North America; maybe even in the world. So perhaps we have a bond in common if your roots are rural."

HORIZON, Stationsstraat 232A, 1770 Liedekerke Belgium. **Fiction Editor:** Johnny Haelterman. Annually. Circ. 720. Publishes several stories/issue.

● The last issue of *Horizon* will be published in December 2000.

Needs: "*Horizon* is a cultural magazine for a general public, therefore fiction should be suitable for a general public." Published work by Louis Friedman, Marco Knauff, Geoff Jackson and Jim Miller. Length: 300 words minimum; 7,500 words maximum. "A realistic treatment is preferred but a touch of fantasy is sometimes acceptable. No extreme violence or sex."

How to Contact: Enclose money or IRCs if you want your work back. "Submitting outside your country is mainly the same as in your own country, except that the postage costs are higher."

Payment/Terms: Payment in Belgian funds for original fiction in Dutch only. No payment for fiction in other languages but the writers receive two copies in that case. English fiction can be translated into Dutch without payment (two copies). Sample copy available for $10 (US).

Advice: "Puns are usually not translatable, so avoid writing stories with an essential part based on puns if you want your work to be translated."

THE HORSETHIEF'S JOURNAL, Celebrating the Literature of the New West, Cayuse Press, P.O. Box 66003, Burien WA 98166-0003. E-mail: horsethief@cayuse-press.zzn.com. Website: www.cayuse-press.com (includes submission guidelines, deadlines, current and archived issues, tools and tips for writers and a poetry forum). **Editor-in-Chief**: Barbara Benepe. Electronic literary journal. "*The Horsethief's Journal* is a triannual online literary journal showcasing the best in contemporary poetry, short fiction and memoir for the general reader." Estab. 1998.

Needs: Adventure, ethnic/multicultural (general), historical, literary, mainstream, mystery/suspense, regional (western US), thriller/espionage, translations, cross-genre fiction. No erotica, horror, occult, children's, young adult. Receives 30 unsolicited mss/month. Accepts 2-5 mss/issue; 6-15/year. Publishes ms 1-3 months after acceptance. **Publishes 25 new writers/year.** Recently published work by Alan Kaufman, Jo Nelson, Robert James Berry, Grecia Luke, Cris Bisch, Sharon Carter, John Bush and more. Length: 1,500 words average; 200 words minimum; 3,000 words maximum. Publishes short shorts. Length: 300 words. Also publishes literary essays and poetry. Sometimes critiques or comments on rejected ms.

How to Contact: Send complete ms with a cover letter by e-mail only; no attachments. Include estimated word count, 100-200 word bio and list of publications. Reports in 1-2 months on mss. Simultaneous and reprint submissions OK. Guidelines available on website. Reviews novels, short story collections and nonfiction books of interest to writers. Send books to editor.

Payment/Terms: Acquires one-time rights.

Advice: "We're looking for stories with an original slant. No cliched plots, characters or themes. Polish. Polish. Polish. Poor diction, grammar errors—bad mechanics in general—will get you a rejection. Read the magazine. Be original."

THE HUDSON REVIEW, 684 Park Ave., New York NY 10021. (212)650-0020. Fax: (212)774-1911. **Editor:** Paula Deitz. Magazine: 4½×7½; 176 pages; 50 Basis Miami book vellum paper; 65 Basis Torchglow cover. "*The Hudson Review* is a sourcebook of American culture that explores the current trends in literature and the arts. Each issue features poetry and fiction, essays on literary and cultural topics, book reviews, reports from abroad, and chronicles covering recent developments in film, theater, dance, music and art. We encourage and publish new writing in order to bring the creative imagination of today to a varied, responsive audience."

Quarterly. Estab. 1948. Circ. 4,500. "Writers who wish to send unsolicited mss outside the normal reading period (June 1 to November 30) must have a subscription."

Needs: Literary. Receives 375 unsolicited mss/month. Accepts 1-2 mss/issue; 4-8 mss/year. Does not read from December 1 through May 31 (except for subscribers). Recently published work by Gary Krist, Barbara Haas and Joseph Epstein. Length: 8,000 words average; 10,000 words maximum. Also publishes literary essays, literary criticism and poetry.

How to Contact: Send complete ms with a cover letter. Include estimated word count. Reports in 6 weeks on queries; 12 weeks on mss. Send SASE for reply, return of ms or send disposable copy of ms. No simultaneous submissions. Sample copy for $8. Fiction guidelines free. Reviews novels and short story collections. Send book to editor.

Payment/Terms: Pays 2 contributor's copies; additional copies $4. Sends galleys to author.

Advice: "We do not specialize in publishing any particular 'type' of writing; our sole criterion for accepting unsolicited work is literary quality. The best way for you to get an idea of the range of work we publish is to read a current issue."

THE HUNTED NEWS, The Subourban Press, P.O. Box 9101, Warwick RI 02889. (401)826-7307. **Editor:** Mike Wood. Magazine: 8½×11; 30-35 pages; photocopied paper. "I am looking for good writers in the hope that I can help their voices be heard. Like most in the small press scene, I just wanted to create another option for writers who otherwise might not be heard." Annually. Estab. 1991. Circ. 200.

Needs: Experimental, historical, horror, literary, mainstream/contemporary, regional, religious/inspirational, translations. "No self-impressed work, shock or experimentation for its own sake." Would like to see more religious/spiritual fiction. Receives 50-60 unsolicited mss/month. Acquires 3 mss/issue. Publishes ms within 3-4 months after acceptance. Published work by Alfred Schwaid, Steve Richmond, Darryl Smyers and Charles Bukowski. **Publishes 10 new writers/year.** Length: 700 words maximum. Publishes short shorts. Also publishes literary essays, literary criticism and poetry. Often critiques or comments on rejected mss.

How to Contact: Send complete ms with cover letter. Reports in 1 month. Send SASE for return of ms. Simultaneous and reprint submissions OK. Sample copy for 8½×11 SAE and 3 first-class stamps. Fiction guidelines free. Reviews novels or short story collections.

Payment/Terms: Pays 3-5 contributor's copies. Acquires one-time rights.

Advice: "I look for an obvious love of language and a sense that there is something at stake in the story, a story that somehow needs to be told. Write what you need to write, say what you think you need to say, no matter the subject, and take a chance and send it to me. A writer will always find an audience if the work is true."

$ THE ICONOCLAST, 1675 Amazon Rd., Mohegan Lake NY 10547-1804. **Editor:** Phil Wagner. Journal. 8½×5½; 32-40 pages; 20 lb. white paper; 50 lb. cover stock; illustrations. "*The Iconoclast* is a self-supporting, independent, unaffiliated general interest magazine with an appreciation of the profound, absurd and joyful in life. Material is limited only by *its* quality and *our* space. We want readers and writers who are open-minded, unafraid to think, and actively engaged with the world." Published 8 times/year. Estab. 1992. Circ. 700-3,000 (special issues).

• *The Iconoclast* has grown from a 16-page newsletter to a 32-40-page journal and is buying more fiction.

Needs: Adventure, ethnic/multicultural, humor/satire, literary, mainstream/contemporary, science fiction. Wants to see more "literary fiction with plots." "Nothing militant, solipsistic, or silly." Receives 100 unsolicited mss/month. Accepts 3-6 mss/issue; 25-30 mss/year. Publishes ms 6-9 months after acceptance. Recently published work by W.P. Kinsella, Lilia Levin and E.G. Silverman. **Publishes 8-10 new writers/year.** Length: 2,000-2,500 words preferred; 100 words minimum; occasionally longer. Publishes short shorts. Also publishes essays, poetry. Sometimes critiques or comments on rejected mss.

How to Contact: Send complete ms. Reports in 1 month. Send SASE for reply, return of ms or send a disposable copy of the ms labeled as such. Sample copy for $2. Reviews novels and short story collections.

Payment/Terms: Pays 1¢/word on acceptance for subscribers and 2-5 contributor's copies; additional copies $1.20 (40% discount). Acquires one-time rights.

Advice: "We like fiction that has something to say (and not about its author). We hope for work that is observant, intense and multi-leveled. Follow Pound's advice—'make it new.' Write what you want in whatever style you want without being gross, sensational, or needlessly explicit—then pray there's someone who can appreciate your sensibility. Read good fiction. It's as fundamental as learning how to hit, throw and catch is to baseball. With the increasing American disinclination towards literature, stories must insist on being heard. Read what is being published—then write something better—and different. Do all rewrites before sending a story out. Few editors have time to work with writers on promising stories; only polished."

THE IDIOT, Anarchaos Press, 1706 S. Bedford St., Los Angeles CA 90035. E-mail: purple-hayes@juno.com. **Editor:** Sam Hayes. Magazine: 5½×8½; 48 pages; 20 lb. white paper; cardboard cover; illustrations. "For people who enjoy TV shows such as 'The Simpsons' and 'Dennis Miller Live' as well as those who like Woody Allen and S.J. Perelman. We're looking for black comedy to make our audience (mostly bitter misanthropes) laugh. I've had letters from engineers to teenagers saying they loved it, so you have to be both funny and weird and sophisticated all at once." Annually. Estab. 1993. Circ. 250-300.

Needs: Humor/satire. Wants more short, dark humor. Publishes ms 6-12 months after acceptance. Recently published work by Joe Deasy, Mark Lafferty, Brian Campbell and Margaret Magee. **Publishes 1-3 new writers/ year.** Length: 750 words average; 2,500 words maximum. Publishes short shorts. Also publishes poetry. Sometimes critiques or comments on rejected mss.

How to Contact: Send complete ms with a cover letter. Include estimated word count and bio (30-50 words). Accepts queries/mss by e-mail. Reports in 1 month on queries; 3 months on mss. Send SASE for reply, return of ms or send a disposable copy of ms. Simultaneous, reprint and electronic submissions OK. Sample copy for $5.

Payment/Terms: Pays 1 contributor copy. Acquires one-time rights. Sends galleys to author if time permits.

Advice: "Do not send anything if it isn't hilarious. If I don't laugh out loud by the second page I stop reading. It must be consistently funny—most submissions are merely 'cute.' Also, read the magazine to see what we're doing."

N **ILLUMINATIONS: An International Magazine of Contemporary Writing**, c/o Dept. of English, College of Charleston, 66 George St., Charleston SC 29424-0001. (843)953-1993. Fax: (843)953-3180. E-mail: lewiss@cofc.edu. Website: www.cofc.edu/~lewis/illums.html (includes writer's guidelines and information on back issues). **Editor:** Simon Lewis. Magazine: 5×8; 80 pages; illustrations. "*Illuminations* is one of the most challengingly eclectic little literary magazines around, having featured writers from the United States, Britain and Romania as well as Southern Africa." Annual. Estab. 1982. Circ. 400.

Needs: Literary. No "poor writing!" Receives 2 unsolicited mss/month. Accepts 2 mss/year. **Publishes 1 new writer/year.** Recently published work by Marlene van Nienerk, Ivan Vladislavic and Taban lo Liyong. Word length: 400 minimum; 1,500 maximum. Also publishes poetry. Sometimes comments on or critiques rejected ms.

How to Contact: Send complete ms with a cover letter. Inquiries by e-mail and fax OK. Include estimated word count and 50-word bio. Reports on queries in 2 weeks; 2 months on mss. Send SASE for reply, return of ms or send a disposable copy of ms. No simultaneous submissions. Sample copy for $10 and a 6×9 envelope. Guidelines free.

Payment/Terms: Pays 2 contributor's copies of current issue; 1 of subsequent issue. Acquires one-time rights.

✓ **$** **IMAGE, A Journal of the Arts & Religion**, The Center for Religious Humanism, 323 S. Broad St., P.O. Box 674, Kennett Square PA 19348. (302)652-8279. E-mail: gwolfe@imagejournal.org. Website: www.imagejournal.org. **Editor:** Greg Wolfe. Magazine: 7×10; 136 pages; glossy cover stock; illustrations and photos. "*Image* is a showcase for the encounter between religious faith and world-class contemporary art. Each issue features fiction, poetry, essays, memoirs, an in-depth interview and articles about visual artists, film, music, etc. and glossy 4-color plates of contemporary visual art." Quarterly. Estab. 1989. Circ. 6,000. Member CLMP.

Needs: Literary, humor/satire, regional, religious, translations. Receives 60 unsolicited mss/month. Accepts 2 mss/issue; 8 mss/year. Publishes ms within 1 year after acceptance. Agented fiction 5%. Recently published work by Romulus Linney, Tim Gautreaux, Clyde Edgerton, Tim Winton, Wally Lamb, Jon Hassler, Ron Hansen, Denise Giardina and Doris Betts. Length: 5,000 words average; 2,000 words minimum; 8,000 words maximum. Also publishes literary essays and poetry.

How to Contact: Send complete ms with a cover letter. Include bio. Reports in 1 month on queries; 3 months on mss. Send SASE for reply, return of ms or send a disposable copy of ms. No electronic submissions. Sample copy for $10. Reviews novels and short story collections.

Payment/Terms: Pays $10/page ($100 minimum) and 4 contributor's copies on publication; additional copies for $5. Sends galleys to author.

Advice: "Fiction must grapple with religious faith, though the settings and subjects need not be overtly religious."

$ **IMAGO**, School of Media & Journalism, QUT, GPO Box 2434, Brisbane 4001 Australia. Phone: (07)3289 1008. Fax: (07)3864 1810. E-mail: h.horton@qut.edu.au. Website: www.maj.arts.qut.edu.au/creative/home/htm. **Contact:** Dr. Philip Neilsen or Helen Horton. Published 3 times/year. Circ. 750. 30-50% fiction. *Imago* is a literary magazine publishing short stories, poetry, articles, interviews and book reviews.

Needs: "While content of articles and interviews should have some relevance either to Queensland or to writing, stories and poems may be on any subject. The main requirement is good writing." Length: 1,000 words minimum; 3,000 words maximum; 2,000 words preferred.

How to Contact: "Contributions should be typed double-spaced on one side of the paper, each page bearing the title, page number and author's name. Name and address of the writer should appear on a cover page of longer mss, or on the back, or bottom, of single page submissions. A SAE and IRCs with sufficient postage to cover the contents should be sent for the return of ms or for notification of acceptance or rejection. No responsibility is assumed for the loss of or damage to unsolicited manuscripts." Accepts queries/mss by e-mail. Sample copy available for $A9. Guidelines, as above, available on request.

Payment/Terms: Pays on publication: short stories, $A80 minimum; articles, $A80 minimum; poems $A30; reviews, $A50. Also provides contributor's copy.

✪ ✔ ◐ **IMPRINT: a Literary Journal**, (formerly *Huckleberry Press*), Imprint Publishers, 4053 Harlan St., Loft 314, Emeryville CA 94608. E-mail: imprint_editor@hotmail.com. **Editor:** Melanie Booth. Magazine: 5½×8½; 90 pages; 40 lb. bond paper; card stock cover; illustrations and photographs. "*Imprint* strives to promote creative individual talents that have not yet been discovered, silenced, or commercialized who speak with a distinctly literate and contemporary voice." Semiannually. Estab. 1999. Circ. 500.

Needs: Humor/satire, literary, mainstream/contemporary, regional. Wants to see more experimental narrative, travelogue and personal essay. No science fiction, horror, erotica, juvenile. Receives over 200 unsolicited mss/month. Accepts 4-6 mss/issue; 8-12 mss/year. Publishes ms 2-8 months after acceptance. Agented fiction 5%. **Publishes 10 new writers/year.** Length: 3,500 words average; 1,000 words minimum; 6,000 words maximum. Also publishes literary essays. Sometimes critiques or comments on rejected mss.

How to Contact: Send complete ms with a cover letter. Include estimated word count and 50-word bio. Reports 2 weeks on queries; 3 months on mss. SASE. Simultaneous submissions OK. Sample copy for $5 and 9×6 SASE with 5 first-class stamps. Fiction guidelines for #10 SASE or e-mail for guidelines. No e-mail submissions.

Payment/Terms: Pays 2 contributor's copies on publication; additional copies for $4. Acquires first North American serial rights.

Advice: "Don't try to distract the reader with concerts and techniques. Write with purpose. We want direct and uncompromising, literate writing."

✪ ✔ $ ◐ ✿ **INDIANA REVIEW**, 465 Ballantine, Bloomington IN 47405. (812)855-3439. **Fiction Editor:** Brian Leung. Editors change every 2 years. Magazine: 6×9; 160 pages; 50 lb. paper; Glatfelter cover stock. *Indiana Review* looks for stories which integrate theme, language, character and form. We like mature, sophisticated fiction which has consequence beyond the world of its narrator. Semiannually. Estab. 1976. Circ. 2,000.

• *Indiana Review* won the 1996 American Literary Magazine Award. Work published in *Indiana Review* was selected for inclusion in the *O. Henry Prize Stories* anthology. This publication ranked #30 on *Writer's Digest*'s Fiction 50 list of top markets for fiction writers.

Needs: Ethnic, literary, regional, translations. Also considers novel excerpts. No genre fiction. Receives 200 unsolicited mss each month. Accepts 7-9 prose mss/issue. Published work by Jason Brown, Dan Chaon, Stuart Dubek, Kathy Acker and Antonya Nebon. Length: 1-35 magazine pages. Also publishes literary essays, poetry and reviews.

How to Contact: Send complete ms with cover letter. Cover letters should be *brief* and demonstrate specific familiarity with the content of a recent issue of *Indiana Review*. SASE. Simultaneous submissions OK (if notified *immediately* of other publication). Reports in 3 months. Publishes ms an average of 3-6 months after acceptance. Does not read mid-December through mid-January. Sample copy for $8.

Payment/Terms: Pays $5/page and 2 contributor's copies for first North American serial rights.

Advice: "Because our editors change each year, so do our literary preferences. It's important that potential contributors are familiar with the most recent issue of *Indiana Review* via library, sample copy or subscription. Beyond that, we look for prose that is well crafted and socially relevant. Dig deep. Don't accept you first choice descriptions when you are revising. Cliché and easy images sink 90% of the stories we reject. Understand the magazines you send to—investigate! As people write more and more short-shorts, the beauty of longer pieces becomes even more apparent and attractive to us."

$ ◐ **INDIGENOUS FICTION**, I.F. Publishing, P.O. Box 2078, Redmond WA 98073-2078. E-mail: deckr@earthlink.net. **Publisher/Managing Editor:** Sherry Decker. Associate Editors: Evelyn Gratrix and Becky Warden. Magazine: 5½×8½; 60-70 pages; 20 lb. white paper; 4-color glossy cover; illustrations. "*I.F.* wants literary stories from all areas: fantasy, dark fantasy, science fiction, horror, mystery and mainstream." Triannual. Estab. 1998. Circ. 250 estimated.

Needs: Adventure, ethnic/multicultural, experimental, fantasy (science fantasy, sword and sorcery, contemporary), feminist, horror, humor/satire, literary, mainstream/contemporary, suspense, psychic/supernatural/occult, science fiction (soft/sociological, cross-genre). "No porn; children-physical/sexual abuse; hard-tech science fiction; gore; vignettes; it-was-all-a-dream; evil cats; unicorns; sweet nostalgia." Receives 100 unsolicited mss/month. Accepts 6-8 mss/issue; 16-24 mss/year. Publishes ms 1 year maximum after acceptance preferred. Recently published work by Stepan Chapman, Kathryn Kulpa, Jeff Vander Meer, Jeffrey Thomas and Mark McLaughlin. **Publishes 1-2 new writers/year.** Length: 4,500 words average; 500 words minimum; 8,000 words maximum. Also publishes poetry. Sometimes critiques or comments on rejected ms.

How to Contact: Send complete ms with a cover letter. Include estimated word count, brief bio and list of publications. Reports in 1 week on queries; 2 weeks on mss. Send SASE for reply, return of ms or send a disposable copy of ms. Accepts only queries by e-mail. Simultaneous submissions OK. Fiction guidelines for #10 SASE. Sample copy $6, $7 Canada, $8 overseas.

Payment/Terms: Pays $5-20 for work between 500-8,000 words. Accepted works of at least 1,500 words also receives contributor's copy. Additional copies $4.75. Sends galleys to authors.

Advice: "We want wonderful writing—unusual stories of the supernatural or the unexplained, dark moody stories, bizarre, odd occurrences mixed with stark reality." Looks for "distinctive writing, lack of adverbs, a sense of wonder and professional manuscript. There is not such thing as a 'born writer.' Take classes. Keep taking classes."

N ★ ⊘ INTERBANG: Dedicated to perfection in the art of writing, P.O. Box 1574, Venice CA 90294. (310)450-6372. Website: www.interbang.net (includes back issues and writer's guide). **Editor:** Heather Hoffman. Magazine: 8½×7; 30 pages; 60 lb. paper; card cover stock; illustrations; and photos. "We publish well-crafted writing on a variety of topics." Quarterly. Estab. 1995. Circ. 2,000.

Needs: Adventure, ethnic/multicultural, experimental, family saga, fantasy (space fantasy, sword and sorcery), feminist, gay, glitz, historical (general), horror (dark fantasy, futuristic, psychological, supernatural), humor satire, lesbian, literary, mainstream, military/war, mystery/suspense (amateur sleuth, cozy, police procedural, private eye/hardboiled), New Age, psychic/supernatural/occult, regional, science fiction (hard science/technological, soft/sociological), short story collections, thriller/espionage, translations. No children's. Receives 10 unsolicited mss/month. Accepts 5 mss/issue; 25 mss/year. Publishes ms 1 month after acceptance. Agented fiction 5%. **Publishes 20 new writers/year.** Recently published work by L. Fitzgerald Sjoberg and Nick Bischoff. Word length: 2,500 word average. Publishes short shorts. Also publishes literary essays. Sometimes comments on or critiques rejected ms.

How to Contact: Send complete ms with a cover letter. Inquiries by e-mail OK. Include estimated word count and bio. Reports on queries in 2 weeks; 3 months on mss. Send SASE for reply, return of ms or send a disposable copy of ms. Simultaneous submissions OK. Sample copy free. Reviews novels, short story collections and nonfiction books. Send books to editor.

Payment/Terms: Pays free subscription to the magazine, an *Interbang* T-shirt and 5 contributor's copies. Payment on publication. Acquires one-times rights.

Advice: "We're looking for well-written stories with strong, vivid descriptions, well-developed characters and complex themes. Focus on a consistent narrative style. We do not publish stories that read like a TV show. We want stories with style and depth."

✓ ⊘ INTERIM, Dept. of English, University of Nevada, Las Vegas NV 89154. (702)895-3458. **Editor:** Claudia Keelan. Magazine: 6×9; 100 pages; heavy paper; semigloss cover with illustration. Publishes "poetry and short fiction for a serious, educated audience." However, they focus more on poetry than fiction. Annually. Estab. 1944; revived 1986. Circ. 600-800.

Needs: Contemporary, experimental, literary. No science fiction, outdoor adventure. Accepts 1-2 mss/issue. Publishes ms 6 months to 1 year of acceptance. Recently published work by G.K. Wuori and Mark Wisniewski. Length: 7,500 words maximum.

How to Contact: Send 1 complete ms with cover letter. Reports on mss in 4-6 weeks. SASE. Sample copy for $8.

Payment/Terms: Pays in contributor's copies and two-year subscription to magazine.

Advice: "Don't send excerpts from novels or longer works. We like completed stories, written as such, with the ordinary virtues of the form: strong, interesting characters, movement, resolution, economy, intensity, or wholeness, harmony, radiance. *No simultaneous submissions in either poetry or fiction.* These are unfair to our volunteer, unpaid staff. We cannot study and debate your work only to find at the end that it's been accepted for publication somewhere else. We try to keep our end of the bargain by holding submissions no longer than 60 days."

N ⊘ INTERNATIONAL QUARTERLY, Essays, Fiction, Drama, Poetry, Art, Reviews, P.O. Box 10521, Tallahassee FL 32302-0521. (850)224-5078. Fax: (850)224-5127. Website: english.FSU/IQ. **Editor:** Van K. Brock. Magazine: 7½×10; 176 pages; 50 lb. text paper; 60 lb. gloss cover; fine art illustrations. "*International Quarterly* seeks to bridge boundaries between national, ethnic and cultural identities, and among creative disciplines, by providing a venue for dialogue between exceptional writers and artists and discriminating readers. We look for work that reveals character and place from within." Quarterly. Estab. 1993.

Needs: Ethnic/multicultural, experimental, humor/satire, literary, mainstream/contemporary, regional, translations. "We would consider work in any of the genres that transcends the genre through quality of language, characterization and development. Our sympathies are strongly feminist. Many of the genre categories imply simplistic and limited literary purposes. Any genre can transcend its limits. No issue is limited to work on its regional or thematic focus." Accepts 5 mss/issue; 20 mss/year. "We read all year, but fewer readers are active in July and August." Publishes ms 3-9 months after acceptance. Recently published work by Mark Apelman and Alyson Shaw. Publishes short shorts. Also publishes literary essays, literary criticism (for general readers), poetry. Sometimes critiques or comments on rejected mss.

How to Contact: Query first or send complete ms with a cover letter. Include estimated word count, bio, list of publications. Include rights available. "We prefer first rights for all original English texts." Reports in 1-2 weeks on queries; 2-4 months on mss. Send SASE for reply, return of ms or send a disposable copy of ms. Simultaneous, reprint (please specify) and electronic submissions OK. Sample copy for $6 (a reduced rate) and 4 first-class stamps. Fiction guidelines for #10 SASE. Reviews novels and short story collections. Send books to Book Review Editor.

Payment/Terms: Pays free subscription to magazine and 2 contributor's copies. Acquires first North American serial rights. Sends galleys to author.

Advice: "We would like to see more fiction break out of conventional thinking and set fictional modes without straining or trying to shock and fiction that presents the world of its characters from inside the skin of the culture, rather than those outside of the culture, tourists or short-termers, as it were, commenting on the world of a story's subjects from outside, lamenting that it has fallen into our consumerist ways, etc., lamentable as that may be. Works we publish do not have to be foreign, they may arise out of a profound understanding of any culture or locale, as long as they provide the reader with an authentic experience of that locale, whatever the origin of the author. We have no taboos, but we want writing that understands and creates understanding, writers who want to go beyond cultural givens."

$ ◯ **THE IOWA REVIEW,** University of Iowa, 308 EPB, Iowa City IA 52242. (319)335-0462. E-mail: iowa-review@uiowa.edu. Website: www.uiowa.edu/~iareview. **Editor:** David Hamilton. Magazine: 6×9; 200 pages; first-grade offset paper; Carolina CS1 10-pt. cover stock. "Stories, essays, poems for a general readership interested in contemporary literature." Triannually. Estab. 1970. Circ. 2,000.
● Work published in *Iowa Review* regularly has been selected for inclusion in the *Pushcart Prize* and *Best American Short Stories* anthologies.
Needs: "We always hope to be surprised by work we then think we need. We feel we are open to a range of styles and voices. We prefer either really good, mature, well developed stories with character, humanity, depth, insight and all that distinguished literature would be, or really surprising off-the-wall stuff that does not seem sophomoric." Receives 300-400 unsolicited fiction mss/month. Agented fiction less than 2%. Accepts 4-6 mss/issue, 12-18 mss/year. Does not read mss April-August. Recently published work by Cornelia Nixon, Bruce Holbert, Michael Joyce, Jorge Accame, Doran Larson, Sharon Wahl and Tamara Grogan. Published new writers within the last year. Also publishes literary essays, literary criticism, poetry.
How to Contact: Send complete ms with cover letter. "Don't bother with queries." SASE for return of ms. Simultaneous submissions OK. Reports in 2-4 months on mss. Publishes ms an average of 6-12 months after acceptance. Sample copy for $6. Fiction guidelines for SASE. Reviews novels and short story collections (3-6 books/year).
Payment/Terms: Pays $10/page ($25 minimum) on publication and 2 contributor's copies; additional copies 30% off cover price. Acquires first North American serial rights.
Advice: "Don't try to read my mind—show me yours. We have no set guidelines as to content or length; we look for what we consider to be the best writing available to us. In fact, we especially encourage new writers and are pleased when writers we believe we have discovered, from their unsolicited manuscripts, catch on with a wider range of readers. It is never a bad idea either to look through an issue or two of the magazine prior to a submission."

N ✪ ◯ ◎ **ipsissima verba, the very words,** Haypenny Press, 32 Forest St., New Britain CT 06052. (860)832-9550. Fax: (860)832-9566. E-mail: ipsiverba@aol.com. **Editor:** P.D. Jordan. Literary magazine: 8½×11; 65 pages; paper varies; illustrations and photos. "We are a quarterly journal of first person fiction and poetry. All submission must be written in first person singular." Estab. 1991.
Needs: "All categories of fiction except porn or children's as long as it's written in first person singular." Receives more than 100 unsolicited mss/month. Accepts 10 mss/issue; 40-50 mss/year. Publishes ms within 3 months of acceptance. **Publishes 40-50 new writers/year.** "We really encourage new writers." Recently published work by Thomas F. Wilson, Ron Watson, Jim Adams and Dennis Orlinski. Length: open. Publishes short shorts. Also publishes poetry. Sometimes critiques or comments on rejected ms.
How to Contact: Send complete ms with a cover letter. Include 1-paragraph bio. Reports in 1 month on mss. Send SASE for reply, return of ms or send disposable copy of ms. No simultaneous submissions. Reprint submissions OK. Sample copy for $5.
Payment/Terms: Pays in contributor's copies. Acquires one-time rights.
Advice: "Remember the first-person rule. The single factor most considered is the ease with which the writer 'speaks.' The more natural the voice, the more likely it will be published."

N ◯ ◎ **IRIS: A Journal About Women,** Box 323 HSC, University of Virginia, Charlottesville VA 22908. (804)924-4500. E-mail: iris@virginia.edu. Website: www.minerva.acc.virginia.edu/-womenctr/pubs/iris/irishome.html (includes last issue cover and table of contents). **Coordinating Editor:** Eileen Boris. Magazine: 8½×11; 80 pages; glossy paper; heavy cover; illustrations, artwork and photographs. "Material of particular interest to women. For a feminist audience, college educated and above." Semiannually. Estab. 1980. Circ. 3,500.
Needs: Experimental, feminist, lesbian, literary, mainstream. "I don't think what we're looking for particularly falls into the 'mainstream' category—we're just looking for well-written stories of interest to women (particularly feminist women)." Receives 300 unsolicited mss/year. Accepts 5 mss/year. Publishes ms within 1 year after acceptance. Recently published work by Sibyl Johston and Barbara Drake. **Publishes 1-2 new writers/year.** Length: 2,500-4,000 words average. Sometimes critiques rejected mss.
How to Contact: Send complete ms with cover letter. Include "previous publications, vocation, other points that pertain. Make it brief!" Accepts queries by e-mail. Reports in 3 months on mss. SASE. Simultaneous submissions OK. Accepts electronic submissions via disk or modem. Sample copy for $5. Fiction guidelines with SASE. Label: Fiction Editor.

Payment/Terms: Pays in contributor's copies and 1 year subscription. Acquires one-time rights.

Advice: "I select mss which are lively imagistically as well as in the here-and-now; I select for writing which challenges the reader. My major complaint is with stories that don't elevate the language above the bland sameness we hear on the television and everyday. Read the work of the outstanding women writers, such as Alice Munroe and Louise Erdrich."

N ⊕ ISLAND, P.O. Box 210, Sandy Bay 7005 Australia. 03 6226 2325. Fax: 03 6226 2765. E-mail: island@e nglish.utas.edu.au. Website: www.tased.edu.au/tasonline/island/island.html. Contact: Editor. Quarterly. Circ. 1,000. Publishes 6 stories/issue.

Needs: "*Island* is a quarterly of ideas, criticism, fiction and poetry." Length: 4,000 words maximum.

How to Contact: Send double-spaced laser print copy where possible. Include a brief cover letter and SASE. Inquiries by fax and e-mail OK.

Payment/Terms: Pays $100 (Australian) minimum. Sample copy available for $8.95 (Australian), back issues $5 plus postage.

Payment/Terms: Pays 2 contributor's copies; additional copies free. Acquires one-time rights.

Advice: "We are looking for quality work that may be of special interest to people of African descent."

★ ✓ $ ◐ ◎ JAPANOPHILE, Box 7977, Ann Arbor MI 48107. (734)930-1553. Fax: (734)930-9968. E-mail: jpnhand@japanophile.com. Website: www.japanophile.com (includes writer's guidelines, sample fiction). **Editors:** Susan Lapp and Ashby Kinch. Magazine: 5¼×8½; 58 pages; illustrations; photos. Magazine of "articles, photos, poetry, humor, short stories about Japanese culture, not necessarily set in Japan, for an adult audience, most with a college background and who like to travel." Quarterly. Estab. 1974. Circ. 800.

● Most of the work included in *Japanophile* is set in recent times, but the magazine will accept material set back as far as pre-WWII.

Needs: Adventure, historical, humor/satire, literary, mainstream, and mystery/suspense. No erotica, science fiction or horror. Published special fiction issue last year; plans another. Receives 40-100 unsolicited fiction mss/month. Accepts 12 ms/issue, 20-30 mss/year. Recently published work by Suzanne Kamata, Amy Chavez and Matt Malcomson. **Publishes 12 new writers/year.** Length: 3,200 words average; 2,000 words minimum; 6,000 words maximum. Also publishes essays, book reviews, literary criticism and poetry.

How to Contact: Send complete ms with SASE, cover letter, bio and information about story. Accepts queries/mss by e-mail and fax. Simultaneous and reprint submissions OK. Reports in 2 months on mss. Sample copy for $4; guidelines for #10 SASE.

Payment/Terms: Pays $20 on publication for all rights, first North American serial rights or one-time rights (depends on situation). Stories submitted to the magazine may be entered in the annual contest. *A $5 entry fee must accompany each submission* to enter contest. Prizes include $100 plus publication for the best short story. Deadline: December 31.

Advice: "We look for originality and sensitivity to cultural detail. Clarity and directness of expression make manuscripts stand out. Short stories usually involve Japanese and 'foreign' (non-Japanese) characters in a way that contributes to understanding of Japanese culture and the Japanese people. However, a *good* story dealing with Japan or Japanese cultural aspects anywhere in the world will be considered, even if it does not involve this encounter or meeting of Japanese and foreign characters. Some stories may also be published in an anthology with approval of the author and additional payment."

★ ✓ ◐ JEOPARDY, Literary Arts Magazine, CH 132, Western Washington University, Bellingham WA 98225. (360)650-3118. E-mail: jeopardy@cc.wwu.edu. Website: www.wwu.edu/~jeopardy (includes writer's guidelines, names of editors, short fiction, artwork, poetry, links to other online mags). **Editor:** Sarah McCarry. Editors change every year. Magazine: 6×9; 192 pages; 70 lb. paper; glossy cover stock; illustrations and photographs. "*Jeopardy Magazine*'s intended audience is an intelligent readership which enjoys risks, surprises and subtlety. Our philosophy is that reputation is nothing and words/images are everything." Annually. Estab. 1965. Circ. 1,000.

Needs: Adventure, contemporary, erotica, ethnic, experimental, feminist, gay, historical, humor/satire, lesbian, literary. No long stories. "We are not interested in conventional narratives, plot-driven fiction or formulaic genre fiction." Want more feminist, experimental, queer and multicultural. Receives 50-100 unsolicited mss/month. Accepts 4-8 mss/year. Reading period: September 15-April 15. Publishes ms 3 months after acceptance. Recently published work by James Bertolino, Omar Castañeda and Robin Hemley. **Publishes 15-20 new writers/year.** Length: 1,500 words average; 250 words minimum; 5,000 words maximum. Also publishes literary essays, poetry.

How to Contact: Send complete ms with cover letter and 50-word bio. SASE and disposable copy of the ms. Does not return mss. Simultaneous submissions OK. Reports in 1-6 months. Sample copy for $5. Fiction guidelines for #10 SASE.

Payment/Terms: Pays 2 contributor's copies. Acquires one-time rights.

Advice: "A clear, insightful voice and style are major considerations. Things that will get your manuscript recycled: tired representations of sex and/or death and/or angst. We like writers who take risks! Know your characters thoroughly—know why someone else would want to read about what they think or do. Then, submit your work and don't give up at initial failures. Don't send us stories about being a writer/artist and/or a college student/professor. We would like to see more fiction pieces which involve unique or unexpected situations and characters. We look for a strong voice, a willingness to take risks, and writers who are willing to push the boundaries of what's been done. Have something to say and say it well. Proofreading helps.''

THE JOURNAL, Dept of English, Ohio State University, 164 W. 17th St., Columbus OH 43210. (614)292-4076. Website: www.cohums.ohio-state.edu/english/journals/the-journal. **Editors:** Michelle Herman (fiction); Kathy Fagan (poetry). Magazine: 6×9; 150 pages. "We are open to all forms of quality fiction." For an educated, general adult audience. Semiannually. Estab. 1973. Circ. 1,500.
- One of the stories from *The Journal* was anthologized in the *Pushcart Prize*.
Needs: No romance, science fiction or religious/devotional. Accepts 2 mss/issue. Receives approximately 100 unsolicited fiction mss/month. "Usually" publishes ms within 1 year of acceptance. Agented fiction 10%. Recently published work by Stephen Dixon, Norma Rosen, Mark Jacobs and Liza Wieland. **Published new writers within the last year.** Length: Open. Also accepts poetry. Critiques rejected mss when there is time.
How to Contact: Send complete ms with cover letter. Reports "as soon as possible," usually 3 months. SASE. Sample copy for $7; fiction guidelines for SASE.
Payment/Terms: Pays $25 stipend when funds are available; contributor's copies; $7 charge for extras.
Terms: Acquires First North American serial rights. Sends galleys to author.
Advice: Mss are rejected because of "lack of understanding of the short story form, shallow plots, undeveloped characters. Cure: read as much well-written fiction as possible. Our readers prefer 'psychological' fiction rather than stories with intricate plots. Take care to present a clean, well-typed submission."

THE JOURNAL, Poetry Forum, 5713 Larchmont Dr., Erie PA 16509. Phone/fax: (814)866-2543. (Faxing hours: 8-10 a.m. and 5-8 p.m.) E-mail: 75562.670@compuserve.com. **Editor:** Gunvor Skogsholm. Journal: 5½×8½; 18-20 pages; light card cover. Looks for "good writing—for late teens to full adulthood." Quarterly. Estab. 1989. Circ. 200.
- *The Journal* is edited by Gunvor Skogsholm, the editor of *Poetry Forum Short Stories* and *Short Stories Bimonthly*. This magazine is not strictly a pay-for-publication, "subscribers come first.'
Needs: Mainstream. Plans annual special fiction issue. Want more "work born from the human condition rather than from so called trends." No extreme horror. Receives 25-30 unsolicited mss/month. Accepts 1 ms/issue; 7-10 mss/year. Publishes mss 2 weeks to 7 months after acceptance. Agented fiction 1%. **Publishes 60% new writers.** Length: 500 words preferred; 300 words average; 150 words minimum. Publishes short shorts. Length: 400 words. Sponsors contest. Send SASE for details.
How to Contact: Send complete ms. Accepts queries/mss by e-mail. Reports in 2 weeks to 7 months on mss. SASE. Simultaneous submissions OK. Accepts electronic disk submissions. Sample copy for $3. Fiction guidelines for SASE.
Payment/Terms: No payment. Acquires one-time rights. Not copyrighted.
Advice: "Subscribers come first!" Looks for "a good lead stating a theme, support of the theme throughout and an ending that rounds out the story or article. Make it believable, please don't preach, avoid propaganda, and don't say, 'This is a story about a retarded person'; instead, prove it by your writing. Show, don't tell. Avoid using 'slang expressions' and 'street' language (except for in a dialogue). Correct English is a must."

THE JOURNAL OF AFRICAN TRAVEL-WRITING, P.O. Box 346, Chapel Hill NC 27514-0346. (919)929-0419. E-mail: ottotwo@email.unc.edu. Website: www.unc.edu/~ottotwo/ (includes guidelines, selected texts, table of contents). **Editor:** Amber Vogel. Magazine: 7×10; 96 pages; 50 lb. paper; illustrations. *"The Journal of African Travel-Writing* presents materials in a variety of genres that explore Africa as a site of narrative." Semiannually. Estab. 1996. Circ. 600.
- Sponsors annual award for best piece published in the journal.
Needs: Adventure, condensed/excerpted novel, ethnic/multicultural, historical, literary, translations. Accepts 1-4 mss/issue. Publishes ms 4-6 months after acceptance. Recently published work by Eileen Drew, Lisa Fugard and Sandra Jackson-Opoku. Also publishes literary essays, literary criticism and poetry. Sometimes critiques or comments on rejected mss.
How to Contact: Send complete ms with a cover letter. Sample copy for $6. Reviews novels and short story collections. Send books to editor.
Payment/Terms: Pays 5 contributor's copies for first rights. Sends galleys to author.

$ KALEIDOSCOPE: International Magazine of Literature, Fine Arts, and Disability, 701 S. Main St., Akron OH 44311-1019. (330)762-9755. Fax: (330)762-0912. **Editor-in-Chief:** Darshan Perusek, Ph.D. Senior Editor: Gail Willmott. Magazine: 8½×11; 56-64 pages; non-coated paper; coated cover stock; illustrations (all media); photos. *"Kaleidoscope* Magazine has a creative focus that examines the experiences of disability through literature and the fine arts. Unique to the field of disability studies, this award-winning publication is not an advocacy or rehabilitation journal. *Kaleidoscope* expresses the experiences of disability from the perspective of individuals, families, healthcare professionals, and society as a whole. Each issue explores a specific theme which deals with disability. Readers include people with and without disabilities." Semiannually. Estab. 1979. Circ. 1,000.

- *Kaleidoscope* has received awards from the American Heart Association, the Great Lakes Awards Competition and Ohio Public Images. The editors are looking for more fiction .

Needs: Personal experience, drama, fiction, essay, artwork. "Would like to see more fiction with emphasis on character study instead of action." Upcoming theme: "Disability and Memoir/Biography" (deadline March 2000). No fiction that is sentimental, erotic, romantic or maudlin. Receives 20-25 unsolicited fiction mss/month. Accepts 10 mss/year. Approximately 1% of fiction is agented. Recently published work by Andre Dubus and Margaret Robison. **Published new writers within the last year.** Length: 5,000 words maximum. Also publishes poetry.

How to Contact: Query first or send complete ms and cover letter. Queries by fax are OK. Include author's educational and writing background and if author has a disability, how it has influenced the writing. Simultaneous submissions OK. Reports in 1 month on queries; 6 months on mss. Sample copy for $4. Guidelines for #10 SASE.

Payment/Terms: Pays $10-125 and 2 contributor's copies on publication; additional copies $5. Acquires first rights. Reprints permitted with credit given to original publication.

Advice: "Read the magazine and get submission guidelines. We prefer that writers with a disability offer original perspectives about their experiences; writers without disabilities should limit themselves to our focus in order to solidify a connection to our magazine's purpose. Do not use stereotypical, patronizing and sentimental attitudes about disability."

KALLIOPE, A Journal of Women's Art, Florida Community College at Jacksonville, 3939 Roosevelt Blvd., Jacksonville FL 32205. (904)381-3511. Website: www.fccj.org/Kalliope/Kalliope.htm. **Editor:** Mary Sue Koeppel. Magazine: 7¼×8¼; 76-88 pages; 70 lb. coated matte paper; Bristol cover; 16-18 halftones per issue. "A literary and visual arts journal for women, *Kalliope* celebrates women in the arts by publishing their work and by providing a forum for their ideas and opinions." Short stories, poems, plays, essays, reviews and visual art. Triannually. Estab. 1978. Circ. 1,550.

- *Kalliope* ranked #46 on *Writer's Digest's* Fiction 50 of top markets for fiction writers. *Kalliope* has received the Frances Buck Sherman Award from the local branch of the National League of Pen Women. The magazine has also received awards and grants for its poetry, grants from the Florida Department of Cultural Affairs and the Jacksonville Club Gallery of Superb Printing Award.

Needs: "Quality short fiction by women writers." Accepts 2-4 mss/issue. Receives approximately 100 unsolicited fiction mss each month. Recently published work by Glynis Kinnan, Rolaine Hoch Stein, Kathleen Spivack and Connie Mary Fowler. **Publishes 3 new writers/year.** Published new writers within the last year. Preferred length: 750-2,000 words, but occasionally publishes longer (and shorter) pieces. Also publishes poetry. Critiques rejected mss "when there is time and if requested."

How to Contact: Send complete ms with SASE and short contributor's note. No simultaneous submissions. Reports in 2-3 months on ms. Publishes an average of 1-3 months after acceptance. Sample copy: $7 for current issue; $4 for issues from '78-'88. Reviews short story collections.

Payment/Terms: Pays 2 contributor's copies or 1-years subscription for first rights. Discount for extras. "We accept only unpublished work. Copyright returned to author upon request."

Advice: "Read our magazine. The work we consider for publication will be well written and the characters and dialogue will be convincing. We like a fresh approach and are interested in new or unusual forms. Make us believe your characters; give readers an insight which they might not have had if they had not read you. We would like to publish more work by minority writers." Manuscripts are rejected because "1) nothing *happens*!, 2) it is thinly disguised autobiography (richly disguised autobiography is OK), 3) ending is either too pat or else just trails off, 4) characterization is not developed, and 5) point of view falters."

KARAMU, English Department, Eastern Illinois University, 600 Lincoln Ave., Charleston IL 61920. (217)581-6297. **Editors:** Olga Abella and Lauren Smith. Literary magazine: 5×8; 132-136 pages; illustrations and photos. "*Karamu* is a literary magazine of ideas and artistic expression independently produced by the faculty members and associates of Eastern Illinois University. Contributions of essays, fiction, poetry and artwork of interest to a broadly educated audience are welcome." Annually. Estab. 1969. Circ. 400.

Needs: Adventure, ethnic/multicultural, experimental, feminist, gay, historical, humor satire, lesbian, literary, mainstream/contemporary, regional. List of upcoming editorial themes available for SASE. Receives 20-25 unsolicited mss/month. Accepts 7-10 mss/issue. Does not read mss May 1-September 1. Publishes ms 1 year after acceptance. **Publishes 2-5 new writers/year.** Recently published work by Lorraine Bodger, B.A. Andrews, Fred Martich and Marilyn Zuckerman. Length: 3,500 words maximum. Publishes short shorts. Also publishes literary criticism and poetry. Sometimes critiques or comments on rejected ms.

How to Contact: Query first. Includes estimated word count, 1-paragraph bio and list of publications. Reports in 1 week on queries. Send SASE for reply. Simultaneous submissions OK. Sample copy for $7.50 or $6 for back issues. Guidelines for SASE.

Payment/Terms: Pays 1 contributor's copy; additional copies for $3.75. Acquires one-time rights.

Advice: Looks for "development of characters, strong voice and original story line."

[N] ★ ◯ KARAWANE, Or, the Temporary Death of the Bruitist, 402 S. Cedar Lake Rd., Minneapolis MN 55405. (612)381-1229. **Editor:** Laura Winton. Magazine: 8×10; 7-20 pages; newsprint paper and cover; illustrations. "All contributors must read/perform their work in public. But work must also hold up in print. We like modern/post-modern, surrealist, experimental work a lot." Semiannually. Estab. 1997. Press run 1,000.
Needs: Ethnic/multicultural, experimental, literary. "No genre: mystery, sci-fi, romance, horror." Accepts 0-1 mss/issue; 1-2 mss/year. Publishes ms 1-8 months after acceptance. **Publishes more than 20 new writers/year.** Recently published work by Ed McGarrity, Karyn Milos and Neil Levy. Length: 2,500 words maximum. Publishes short shorts. Also publishes literary essays, literary criticism, poetry. Sometimes critiques or comments on rejected mss.
How to Contact: Send complete ms with a cover letter. Include estimated word count; 1 paragraph bio and list of publications. Reports in 1-6 month on mss. "Queries take longer than manuscripts." Send SASE for reply, return of ms or send a disposable copy of ms. Simultaneous submissions and reprints OK. "We encourage both!" Sample copy for $1, 9×12 SAE with 2 first-class stamps.
Payment/Terms: Pays 3-5 contributor's copies; additional copies $1. Pays on publication. Acquires one-time rights.
Advice: "Simply, readability (do I make it to the end?), interesting writing style/form. Work that breaks genres interests me more and more. If your writing makes me jealous, you're in! Don't wait around for your big break. Network, perform, publish yourself and your cronies. If you can't support small presses with cash, get out there and help your favorite small presses and lit mags with your time and energy. Look at the Beats, Dadas, etc. A strong community that gets literature out there succeeds!"

◯ ◎ KELSEY REVIEW, Mercer County College, P.O. Box B, Trenton NJ 08690. (609)586-4800. E-mail: kelsey.review@mccc.edu. Website: www.mccc.edu (includes deadlines and writer's guidelines). **Editor-in-Chief:** Robin Schore. Magazine: 7×14; 80 pages; glossy paper; soft cover. "Must live or work in Mercer County, NJ." Annually. Estab. 1988. Circ. 1,750.
Needs: Open. Regional (Mercer County only). Receives 120 unsolicited mss/year. Accepts 24 mss/issue. Reads mss only in May. Publishes ms 1-2 months after acceptance. Recently published work by Brandi Scollins, Beatrice Cohen and Robert Baum. **Publishes 5-6 new writers/year.** Length: 2,000 words maximum. Publishes short shorts. Also publishes literary essays, literary criticism and poetry. Always critiques or comments on rejected mss.
How to Contact: Send complete ms with cover letter. SASE for return of ms. Accepts queries/mss by e-mail. No simultaneous submissions. Reports in 1-2 months. Sample copy free.
Payment/Terms: Pays 5 contributor's copies. Rights revert to author on publication.
Advice: Looks for "quality, intellect, grace and guts. Avoid sentimentality, overwriting and self-indulgence. Work on clarity, depth and originality."

$ ◯ ⛏ THE KENYON REVIEW, Kenyon College, Gambier OH 43022. (740)427-5208. Fax: (740)427-5417. E-mail: kenyonreview@kenyon.edu. Website: www.kenyonreview.com (includes excerpts, advertising information, issue highlights, writer's guidelines, summer programs and author bios and photos). **Editor:** David H. Lynn. "Fiction, poetry, essays, book reviews." Triannually. Estab. 1939. Circ. 5,000.
• *Kenyon Review currently has a backlog of accepted manuscripts. Not reading unsolicited material until September 2000. Work published in the Kenyon Review has been selected for inclusion in Pushcart Prize anthologies.*
Needs: Condensed/excerpted novel, contemporary, ethnic, experimental, feminist, gay, historical, humor/satire, lesbian, literary, mainstream, translations. Receives 400 unsolicited mss/month. Unsolicited mss typically read only from September 1 through March 31. Publishes ms 12-18 months after acceptance. Recently published work by Philip Levine, W.S. Merwin, Zbigniew Herbert and Nancy Zafris. Length: 3-15 typeset pages preferred.
How to Contact: Send complete ms with cover letter. Reports on mss in 3-4 months. SASE. No simultaneous submissions. Sample copy for $9.
Payment/Terms: Pays $10-15/page on publication for first-time rights. Sends copyedited version to author for approval.
Advice: "Read several issues of our publication. We remain invested in encouraging/reading/publishing work by writers of color, writers expanding the boundaries of their genre, and writers with unpredictable voices and points of view."

◎ KEREM, Creative Explorations in Judaism, Jewish Study Center Press, Inc., 3035 Porter St. NW, Washington DC 20008. (202)364-3006. Fax: (202)364-3806. Website: www.kerem.com. **Editors:** Sara R. Horowitz and Gilah Langner. Magazine: 6×9; 128 pages; 60 lb. offset paper; glossy cover; illustrations and photos. "*Kerem* publishes Jewish religious, creative, literary material—short stories, poetry, personal reflections, text study, prayers, rituals, etc." Annually. Estab. 1992. Circ. 2,000
Needs: Jewish: feminist, humor/satire, literary, religious/inspirational. Receives 10-12 unsolicited mss/month. Accepts 1-2 mss/issue. Publishes ms 2-10 months after acceptance. Recently published work by Marge Piercy, William Novak and Anita Diamant. Length: 6,000 words maximum. Also publishes literary essays, poetry.
How to Contact: Send complete ms with a cover letter. Should include 1-2 line bio. Reports in 2 months on

queries; 4-5 months on mss. Send SASE for reply, return of ms or send a disposable copy of ms. Simultaneous submissions OK. Sample copy for $8.50.

Payment/Terms: Pays free subscription and 2-10 contributor's copies. Acquires one-time rights.

Advice: "Should have a strong Jewish content. We want to be moved by reading the manuscript!"

N ⃝ KIDS' HIGHWAY, Oo! What a Ride!, P.O. Box 6275, Bryan TX 77805-6275. (409)778-7372. Fax: (409)778-0284. E-mail: kidshighway@att.net. Website: home.att.net~KidsHighway (includes mission statement, updated table of contents, contest information, writer's guidelines, short fiction, e-mail address and subscription information). Editor: Miranda Garza. **Fiction Editor:** Hector Cole Garza. Magazine: 8½ × 11; 22 pages; illustrations. "*Kids' Highway* is a literary magazine that has something for everyone. It has fiction for kids and a tear-out section for adults. We do publish nonfiction if it is timely." Published 5 times/year. Estab. 1999.

Needs: Adventure, children's/juvenile (adventure, animal, fantasy, mystery, series), mystery/suspense (amateur sleuth, cozy), young adult/teen (adventure, fantasy/science fiction, mystery/suspense, series, western). "We are looking for young writers as well as new ones. No ghosts, magic, occult, horror, problem novels, gay or lesbian." Accepts 5-6 mss/issue; 25-30 mss/year. Publishes ms up to 6 months after acceptance. Length: childrens stories, 1,200 words maximum; adult stories, 900-2,200 words. Publishes short shorts. Length: 50-400 words. Also publishes poetry. Often critiques or comments on rejected mss.

How to Contact: Send complete ms with a cover letter. "Send SASE for reply. Send disposable copy of manuscript or send adequate postage for return of manuscript." Accepts queries/mss by e-mail. Include estimated word count, 100 word maximum bio. "If student, include age in cover letter or on manuscript." Reports in 2 months. Send SASE for reply, return of ms or send a disposable copy of ms. Simultaneous submissions and reprints OK. Sample copy for $2.50, 9 × 12 SAE and 2 first-class stamps. Fiction guidelines free for #10 SASE. Reviews novels and short story collections. Send books to Miranda Garza (children's novels and juvenile fiction).

Payment/Terms: Pays 2 contributor's copies; additional copies $2. Pays on publication. Acquires one-time and reprint rights. Sends galleys to author "upon request and with SASE."

Advice: "We look for stories that are unique and entertaining. It has to be original and fun with a surprising and/or satisfying ending. Neatness counts as well as good grammar. Be different but not gross. Have fun with your story. Think 'entertaining' when writing it."

N ★ ⃝ ▣ KIMERA: A JOURNAL OF FINE WRITING, N. 1316 Hollis, Spokane WA 99201. E-mail: kimera@onramp.ior.com. Website: www.ior.com/kimera/. **Editor:** Jan Strever. Electronic magazine. "Kimera attempts to meet John Locke's challenge: Where is the head with no chimeras? We seek fiction that pushes the edge in terms of language use and craft."

Needs: Eclectic, energetic fiction. "Nothing badly conceived without attention to the muscularity of language." Published work by J. Bowers, L. Lynch and G. Thomas. **Publishes 25% new writers.**

How to Contact: Electronic submissions only.

Advice: "Pay attention to how sound echoes the senses in writing."

N ⃝ KIOSK, English Department, S.U.N.Y. at Buffalo, 306 Clemens Hall, Buffalo NY 14260. (716)645-2575. E-mail: ed-kiosk@acsu.buffalo.edu. Website: wings.buffalo.edu/kiosk (includes writer's guidelines, names of editors, representative fiction and poetry from issues). **Editor-in-Chief:** Kevin Grauke. Magazine: 5½ × 8½; 150 pages; 80 lb. cover; illustrations. "We seek innovative, non-formula fiction and poetry." Annually. Estab. 1986. Circ. 500.

Needs: Literary. "While we subscribe to no particular orthodoxy, we are most hospitable to stories with a strong sense of voice, narrative direction and craftsmanship." No genre fiction. Wants more experimental fiction. Receives 50 mss/month. Accepts 10-20 mss/issue. Publishes ms within 6 months of acceptance. Recently published work by Mark Jacobs, Jay Atkinson and Richard Russo. Published new writers within the last year. Length: 3,000 words preferred; 7,500 words maximum. Publishes short shorts, "the shorter the better." Also publishes poetry. Sometimes critiques rejected mss.

How to Contact: Send complete mss with cover letter. Accepts queries/mss by e-mail. Does not read from June through August. Reports in 3-4 months on mss. SASE. Simultaneous and reprint submissions OK. Sample copy for $5. Guidelines for SASE.

Payment/Terms: Pays in contributor's copies. Acquires one-time rights.

Advice: "First and foremost, *Kiosk* is interested in sharp writing. Make it new, but also make it worth the reader's effort. Demand our attention with the first paragraph and maintain it to the end. Read as many different journals as possible. See what people are writing and publishing."

N ★ ⃝ KOJA, 7314 21 Avenue #6E, Brooklyn NY 11204-5906. Website: www.monkeyfish.com/koja (includes sample writing from the premier issue). **Editor:** Mike Magazinnik. Magazine: 8½ × 11; 64 pages; color cover; illustrations. "The magazine is dedicated to experimental prose/poetry from American authors and Russian authors living in the US and writing in English. We publish only experimental works." Biennial. Estab. 1996. Circ. 300. "Authors need to buy a sample issue before submitting their works."

Needs: "We do not publish anything except for experimental literary fiction." Receives 20-30 unsolicited mss/ month. Accepts 5-10 mss/issue. Publishes ms up to 2 years after acceptance. **Publishes 10-15 new writers/year.**

Recently published work by Raymond Federman, Richard Vostelanetz, Doug Rice and Lance Olsen. Word length: no minimum; 3,000 words maximum. Publishes short shorts: "any length." Also publishes poetry. Sometimes comments on or critiques rejected ms.

How to Contact: Send complete ms with a cover letter. Include 1-2 paragraph bio. Reports on queries in 1 week; 3-4 months on mss. Send SASE for reply, return of ms or send a disposable copy of ms. No simultaneous submissions. Sample copy for $7. Reviews novels, short story collections and poetry of interest to writers. Send book to editor.

Payment/Terms: Pays 1 contributor's copy; additional copies $7. Acquires first North American serial rights.

Advice: "We look for a fresh approach to writing prose; challenging the boundaries of prose, as well as narrative structure. Please send only experimental work, and only after having seen a sample copy. We receive a lot of works unrelated to the mission of the magazine."

N ⊕ ◎ LA KANCERKLINIKO, 162 rue Paradis, 13006 Marseille France. Phone: 2-48-61-81-98. E-mail: a.lazarus-1.septier@wanadoo.fr. **Fiction Editor:** Laurent Septier. Circ. 300. Quarterly. Publishes 40 pages of fiction annually. "An esperanto magazine which appears 4 times annually. Each issue contains 32 pages. *La Kancerkliniko* is a political and cultural magazine."

Needs: General fiction. Short stories or very short novels. "The short story (or the very short novel) must be written only in esperanto, either original or translation from any other language." Wants more science fiction. Length: 15,000 words maximum.

How to Contact: Accepts queries/mss by e-mail and fax.

Payment/Terms: Pays in contributor's copies. Sample copy on request with 3 IRCs from Universal Postal Union.

◐ THE LAMPLIGHT, Beggar's Press, 8110 N. 38 St., Omaha NE 68112. (402)455-2615. Editor: Richard R. Carey. **Fiction Editor:** Sandy Johnsen. Magazine: 8½×11; 60 pages; 20 lb. bond paper; 65 lb. stock cover; some illustrations; a few photographs. "Our purpose is to establish a new literature drawn from the past. We relish foreign settings in the 19th century when human passions transcended computers and fax machines. We are literary but appeal to the common intellect and the mass soul of humanity." Semiannually.

Needs: Historical (general), humor/satire, literary, mystery/suspense (literary), romance (gothic, historical). "Settings in the past. Psychological stories." Plans special fiction issue or anthology in the future. Receives 120-140 unsolicited mss/month. Accepts 2 mss/issue; 4 mss/year. Publishes ms 4-12 months after acceptance. Published work by James Scoffield and Philip Sparacino. Length: 2,000 words preferred; 500 words minimum; 3,500 words maximum. Publishes short shorts. Length: 300 words. Also publishes literary criticism and poetry. Critiques or comments on rejected mss.

How to Contact: Send complete ms with cover letter. Include estimated word count, bio (a paragraph or two) and list of publications. Reports in 1 month on queries; 2½ months on mss. SASE. Simultaneous and reprint submission OK. Sample copy for $10.95, 9×12 SAE. Fiction guidelines for #10 SASE. Reviews novels and short story collections.

Payment/Terms: Pays 1 contributor's copy. Acquires first North American serial rights.

Advice: "We deal in classical masterpieces. Every piece must be timeless. It must live for five centuries or more. We judge on this basis. These are not easy to come by. But we want to stretch authors to their fullest capacity. They will have to dig deeper for us, and develop a style that is different from what is commonly read in today's market."

◑ ◎ THE LAMP-POST, of the Southern California C.S. Lewis Society, 29562 Westmont Ct., San Juan Capistrano CA 92675. (949)347-1255. E-mail: lamppost@ix.netcom.com. **Senior Editor:** James Prothero. Magazine: 5½×8½; 34 pages; 7 lb. paper; 8 lb. cover; illustrations. "We are a literary review focused on C.S. Lewis and like writers." Quarterly. Estab. 1977. Circ. 200.

• C.S. Lewis was an English novelist and essayist known for his science fiction and fantasy featuring Christian themes. He is especially well-known for his children's fantasy, *The Chronicles of Narnia*. So far, the magazine has found little fiction suitable to its focus, although they remain open.

Needs: "Literary fantasy and science fiction for children to adults." Publishes ms 9 months after acceptance. Recently published work by Rita Quinton and DJ Kolacki. **Publishes 3-5 new writers/year.** Length: 2,500 words average; 1,000 words minimum; 5,000 words maximum. Also publishes literary essays, literary criticism and poetry. Sometimes critiques or comments on rejected mss.

How to Contact: Query first or send complete ms with a cover letter. Accepts queries/mss by e-mail. Include 50-word bio. Reports in 6-8 weeks. Send SASE for reply, return of ms or send a disposable copy of ms. No simultaneous submissions. Reprints and electronic (disk) submissions OK. Sample copy for $3. Fiction guidelines for #10 SASE. Reviews fiction or criticism having to do with Lewis or in his vein. Send books to: Dr. David W. Landrum, book review editor, Cornerstone College, 1001 E. Beltline, NE, Grand Rapids MI 49525.

Payment/Terms: Pays 3 contributor's copies; additional copies $3. Acquires first North American serial rights or one-time rights.

Advice: "We look for fiction with the supernatural, mythic feel of the fiction of C.S. Lewis and Charles Williams. Our slant is Christian but we want work of literary quality. No inspirational. Is it the sort of thing Lewis, Tolkien and Williams would like—subtle, crafted fiction? If so, send it. Don't be too obvious or facile. Our readers aren't stupid.''

THE LAUREL REVIEW, Northwest Missouri State University, Dept. of English, Maryville MO 64468. (660)562-1265. **Co-editors:** William Trowbridge, David Slater and Beth Richards. Associate Editors: Nancy Vieira Couto, Randall R. Freisinger, Steve Heller. Reviewer: Peter Makuck. Magazine: 6×9; 124-128 pages; good quality paper. "We publish poetry and fiction of high quality, from the traditional to the avant-garde. We are eclectic, open and flexible. Good writing is all we seek." Biannually. Estab. 1960. Circ. 900.

• A story published in *The Laurel Review* in 1996 was selected for inclusion in the annual *Pushcart Prize* anthology. Two others received special mention.

Needs: Literary and contemporary. No genre or politically polemical fiction. Accepts 3-5 mss/issue, 6-10 mss/year. Receives approximately 120 unsolicited fiction mss each month. Approximately 1% of fiction is agented. Published work by Karla J. Kuban, Ian MacMillan, Richard Duggin and Becky Bradway. Length: 2,000-10,000 words. Sometimes publishes literary essays; also publishes poetry. Reads September to May.

How to Contact: Send complete ms with SASE. No simultaneous submissions. Reports in 1-4 months on mss. Publishes ms an average of 1-12 months after acceptance. Sample copy for $3.50.

Payment/Terms: Pays 2 contributor's copies and 1 year subscription. Acquires first rights. Copyright reverts to author upon request.

Advice: Send $3.50 for a back copy of the magazine.

LE FORUM, Supplement Littéraire, Franco-American Research Opportunity Group, University of Maine, Franco American Center, 164 College Ave., Orono ME 04473-1578. (207)581-3764. Fax: (207)581-1455. E-mail: lisa_michaud@umit.maine.edu. **Managing Editor:** Lisa Michaud. Tabloid size, magazine format: 36 pages; illustrations and photos. Publication was founded to stimulate and recognize creative expression among Franco-Americans, all types of readers, including literary and working class. This publication is used in classrooms. Circulated internationally. Quarterly. Estab. 1986. Circ. 5,000.

Needs: "We will consider any type of short fiction, poetry and critical essays having to do with Franco-American experience. They must be of good quality in French or English. We are also looking for Canadian writers with French-North American experiences." Receives about 10 unsolicited mss/month. Accepts 2-4 mss/issue. **Published new writers within the last year.** Length: 1,000 words average; 750 words minimum; 2,500 words maximum. Occasionally critiques rejected mss.

How to Contact: Send complete ms with cover letter. Include a short bio and list of previous publications. Reports in 3 weeks on queries; 1 month on mss. SASE. Simultaneous, reprint and electronic submissions (e-mail, fax) OK.

Payment/Terms: Pays $10 and 3 copies for one-time rights.

Advice: "Write honestly. Start with a strongly felt personal Franco-American experience. If you make us feel what you have felt, we will publish it. We stress that this publication deals specifically with the Franco-American experience."

LEAPINGS LITERARY MAGAZINE, 2455 Pinercrest Dr., Santa Rosa CA 95403. (707)544-4861. E-mail: 72144.3133@compuserve.com. Website: home.inreach.com/editserv/leapings.html (includes writer's guidelines). **Editor:** S.A. Warner. Magazine: 5×8; 40 pages; 20 lb. paper; glossy cover; illustrations and photos. "Eclectic magazine emphasizing diversity." Semiannually. Estab. 1998. Circ. 200.

Needs: Adventure, ethnic/multicultural, experimental, fantasy, feminist, humor satire, literary, mainstream, mystery/suspense, science fiction. Receives 20 unsolicited mss/month. Accepts 2 mss/issue; 4 mss/year. Publishes ms 6 months after acceptance. Less than 10% of fiction accepted is agented. **Publishes 5 new writers/year.** Publishes short shorts. Also publishes literary essays, literary criticism, poetry. Sometimes critiques or comments on rejected mss.

How to Contact: Send complete ms with a cover letter. Include estimated word count. Reports in 6 weeks. Send SASE for reply, return of ms or send a disposable copy of ms. No simultaneous submissions. Sample copy for $5. Fiction guidelines free for #10 SASE. Reviews novels and short story collections. Send books to S.A. Warner.

Payment/Terms: Pays 2 contributor's copies; additional copies $5. Pays on publication. Acquires first rights.

Advice: Looks for "good presentation and sound writing showing the writer has worked at his/her craft. Write and rewrite and only submit it when you've made the work as crisp and clear as possible."

LIBIDO, The Journal of Sex and Sensibility, Libido, Inc., P.O. Box 146721, Chicago IL 60614. (800)495-1988. Fax: (773)275-0752. E-mail: rune@mcs.com. **Submissions Editor:** J L Beck. Magazine:

SENDING TO A COUNTRY other than your own? Be sure to send International Reply Coupons instead of stamps for replies or return of your manuscript.

6½ × 9¼; 72-88 pages; 70 lb. coated; b&w illustrations and photographs. "*Libido*, to paraphrase Oscar Wilde, is the literary answer to a horizontal urge. Libido is about sex and sensibility—eroticism with reflection. Our audience is educated and liberated." Quarterly. Estab. 1988. Circ. 10,000.

- Specializing in "literary" erotica, this journal has attracted a number of top-name writers and was given a Venus Award from Good Vibrations, San Francisco and named Publication of the Year at the 6th annual erotic Oscars.

Needs: Condensed/excerpted novel, confession, erotica, gay, lesbian. "We'd like more well-written eroticism—orientation doesn't matter; writing quality does." No "dirty words for their own sake, violence or sexual exploitation." Receives 25-50 unsolicited mss/month. Accepts about 5 mss/issue; about 20 mss/year. Publishes ms up to 1 year after acceptance. Recently published work by Carol Queen and William Levy. **Publishes 5-10 new writers/ year.** Length: 1,000-3,000 words; 300 words minimum; 5,000 words maximum. Also publishes literary essays, literary criticism. Sometimes critiques rejected mss and recommends other markets.

How to Contact: Send complete ms with cover letter including Social Security number and brief bio for contributor's page. Reports in 6 months on mss. SASE. No simultaneous submissions. Reprint submissions OK. Sample copy for $8. Fiction guidelines for SASE. Reviews novels and short story collections.

Payment/Terms: Pays $25-100 and 1 contributor's copy on publication for one-time or anthology rights.

Advice: "Humor is a strong plus. There must be a strong erotic element, and it should celebrate the joy of sex. Also, stories should be well written, insightful and arousing. Bonus points given for accuracy of characterization and style."

✓ 🅞 **THE LICKING RIVER REVIEW**, University Center, Northern Kentucky University, Highland Heights KY 41076. (606)572-5416. E-mail: lrr@nku.edu. **Faculty Advisor:** Andrew Miller. Magazine: 7 × 11; 104 pages; photos. Annually. Estab. 1991. Circ. 1,500.

Needs: Experimental, literary, mainstream/contemporary. No erotica. Wants more experimental. Receives 40 unsolicited mss/month. Accepts 7-9 mss/year. Does not read mss January through July. Publishes ms 6 months after acceptance. Recently published work by Dallas Wiebe, George Malko, Laurie Jones Neighbor, Brett Weaver, Pax Riddle and dayna marie. Length: 5,000 words maximum. Publishes short shorts. Also publishes poetry.

How to Contact: Send complete ms with a cover letter. Accepts queries by e-mail. Include list of publications. Reports in 6 months on mss. SASE for return of manuscript or send disposable copy of ms. No simultaneous submissions. Sample copy for $5.

Payment/Terms: Pays 2 contributor's copies on publication.

Advice: Looks for "good writing and an interesting and well-told story. Read a sample copy first. Don't do what everybody else is doing. Be fresh, original. Write what you like—it will show."

🅞 **LIGHT MAGAZINE**, P.O. Box 7500, Chicago IL 60680. **Editor:** John Mella. Magazine: 6 × 9; 64 pages; Finch opaque (60 lb.) paper; 65 lb. color cover; illustrations. "Light and satiric verse and prose, witty but not sentimental. Audience: intelligent, educated, usually 'professional.' " Quarterly. Estab. 1992. Circ. 1,000.

Needs: Humor/satire, literary. Upcoming theme: Ogden Nash parody issue. Receives 10-40 unsolicited fiction mss/month. Accepts 2-4 mss/issue. Publishes ms 6-24 months after acceptance. Published work by X.J. Kennedy, J.F. Nims and John Updike. Length: 1,200 words preferred; 600 words minimum; 2,000 words maximum. Publishes short shorts. Also publishes literary essays, literary criticism and poetry. Sometimes critiques or comments on rejected mss.

How to Contact: Query first. Include estimated word count and list of publications. Reports in 1 month on queries; 2-4 months on mss. Send SASE for reply, return of ms or send a disposable copy of ms. No simultaneous submissions. Electronic submissions (disk only) OK. Sample copy for $6 (plus $2 for 1st class). Fiction guidelines for #10 SASE. Reviews novels and short story collections. Send review copies to review editor.

Payment/Terms: Pays contributor's copies (2 for domestic; 1 for foreign). Acquires first North American serial rights. Sends galleys to author.

Advice: Looks for "high literary quality; wit, allusiveness, a distinct (and distinctive) style. Read guidelines or issue first."

⊠ 🅞 **LINES IN THE SAND**, LeSand Publications, 890 Southgate Ave., Daly City CA 94015. (650)992-4770. E-mail: nsand415@aol.com. Website: members.aol.com/nsand415/index.html (includes writer's guidelines). Editor: Nina Z. Sanders. **Fiction Editors:** Nina Z. Sanders and Barbara J. Less. Magazine: 5½ × 8½; 32 pages; 20 lb. bond; King James cost-coated cover. "Stories should be well-written, entertaining and suitable for all ages. Our readers range in age from 7 to 90. No particular slant or philosophy." Bimonthly. Estab. 1992. Circ. 100.

- *Lines In The Sand* is known for quirky fiction with surprise endings. Humorous and slice-of-life fiction has a good chance here.

Needs: Adventure, experimental, fantasy, humor/satire, literary, mainstream/contemporary, mystery/suspense (private eye/hard-boiled, amateur sleuth, cozy, romantic), science fiction (soft/sociological), senior citizen/retirement, westerns (traditional, frontier, young adult), young adult/teen (10-18 years). "Would like to see more humorous, surprise endings. No erotica, horror or pornography." Receives 70-80 unsolicited mss/month. Accepts 8-10 mss/issue; 50-60 mss/year. Publishes ms 2-4 months after acceptance. Recently published work by

Jeff Webb, Laura Hosmer and Paul Perry. **Publishes 10 new writers/year.** Length: 1,200 words preferred; 250 words minimum; 2,000 words maximum. Publishes short shorts. Length: 250 words. Also publishes poetry. Often critiques or comments on rejected mss. Sponsors contests. To enter contest submit 2 copies of story, 2,000 words maximum, double-spaced, typed and $5 reading fee for each story submitted.

How to Contact: Send complete ms with cover letter containing estimated word count and bio (3-4 sentences). Reports in 2-6 months on mss. Send SASE for reply, return of ms or send disposable copy of themes. Simultaneous submissions OK. Sample copy for $3.50. Fiction guidelines for #10 SASE.

Payment/Terms: Pays one contributor's copy. Acquires first North American serial rights.

Advice: "Use fresh, original approach; 'show, don't tell'; use dialogue to move story along; and be grammatically correct. Stories should have some type of conflict. Read a sample copy (or two). Follow guidelines carefully. Use plain language; avoid flowery, 'big' words unless appropriate in dialogue. Make sure story has a beginning, a middle and an end. If it's a 'true' story, write it as though it were fiction. No essays, please!"

⊠ ◨ **LITE, Baltimore's Literary Newspaper**, P.O. Box 26162, Baltimore MD 21210. (410)719-7792. E-mail: pkinlock@bcpl.net. Website: LiteCircle.dragonfire.net (includes guidelines, current and back issues, literary news, staff contact information). **Editor:** David W. Kriebel. Tabloid: 11 × 14; 12 pages; 30 lb. newsprint paper; 2-4 illustrations; some photographs. "Poetry, short fiction, occasional nonfiction pieces, satire. Our audience is intelligent, literate, and imaginative. They have the ability to step back and look at the world from a different perspective." Bimonthly. Estab. 1989. Circ. 10,000.

Needs: Experimental, fantasy, historical (general), horror, humor/satire, literary, mystery/suspense (private eye), psychic/supernatural/occult, science fiction (hard science, soft/sociological). "No erotica, gay, lesbian. Nothing demeaning to any ethnic or religious group. No stories with an obvious or trite 'message.' No violence for its own sake." Receives 20-30 unsolicited mss/month. Accepts 1-2 mss/issue; 12-18 mss/year. Publishes mss 1-3 months after acceptance. Published work by Vonnie Crist, Barry Patrick Fitzsimmons and Elizabeth Ames. **Publishes more than 30 new writers/year.** Length: 1,500 words preferred; 3,000 words maximum (however, will consider serializing longer pieces). Publishes short shorts. Also publishes poetry. Comments on or critiques rejected mss if requested with SASE.

How to Contact: Request guidelines, then send ms and cover letter. Encourages electronic submissions. Include "information on the writer, focusing on what led him to write or create visual art. We want to know the person, both for our contributors guide 'Names in Lite' and to help build a network of creative people." Reports in 6-12 months. SASE. Simultaneous submissions OK, but prefer them not be sent to other Baltimore publications. Sample copy for 9 × 12 SAE and 3 first-class stamps. Fiction guidelines for #10 SASE.

Payment/Terms: Pays 5 contributor's copies; 5 extras for 9 × 12 SASE with 4 first-class stamps. Acquires one-time rights.

Advice: "We first look for quality writing, then we look at content and theme. It's not hard to tell a dedicated writer from someone who only works for money or recognition. Fiction that resonates in the heart makes us take notice. It's a joy to read such a story." Known for "offbeat, creative, but not overtly sexual or violent. We like characterization and the play of ideas. We don't like contrived plots or political propaganda masquerading as literature."

◨ ⚑ **THE LITERARY REVIEW, An International Journal of Contemporary Writing**, Fairleigh Dickinson University, 285 Madison Ave., Madison NJ 07940. Phone/fax: (973)443-8564. E-mail: tlr@fdu.edu. Website: www.webdelsol.com/tlr/ (includes subscription information, writer's guidelines, names of editors, chapbooks and selections from printed issues). **Editor-in-Chief:** Walter Cummins. Magazine: 6 × 9; 140 pages; professionally printed on textpaper; semigloss card cover; perfect-bound. "Literary magazine specializing in fiction, poetry, and essays with an international focus." Quarterly. Estab. 1957. Circ. 2,500.

● This magazine has received grants from a wide variety of international sources including the Spanish Consulate General in New York, the Program for Cultural Cooperation between Spain's Ministry of Culture and U.S. Universities, Pro Helvetia, the Swiss Center Foundation, The Luso-American Foundation, Japan-U.S. Friendship Commission. Work published in *The Literary Review* has been included in *Editor's Choice*, *Best American Short Stories* and *Pushcart Prize* anthologies. The editor would like to see more fiction with an international theme.

Needs: Works of high literary quality only. Receives 50-60 unsolicited fiction mss/month. Approximately 1-2% of fiction is agented. Recently published work by David Lida, Gladys Swan and Michael Zadoorian. **Published 3-4 new writers/year.** Length: 5,000 words maximum. Acquires 10-12 mss/year. Does not read submissions during June, July and August. Also publishes literary essays, literary criticism, poetry. Occasionally critiques rejected mss.

How to Contact: Send 1 complete ms with SASE. "Cover letter should include publication credits." Reports in 3 months on mss. Publishes ms an average of 1½-2 years after acceptance. Sample copy for $5; guidelines for SASE. Reviews novels and short story collections.

Payment/Terms: Pays 2 contributor's copies; 25% discount for extras. Acquires first rights.

Advice: "We want original dramatic situations with complex moral and intellectual resonance and vivid prose. We don't want versions of familiar plots and relationships. Too much of what we are seeing today is openly derivative in subject, plot and prose style. We pride ourselves on spotting new writers with fresh insight and approach."

⬛ 🔲 ⬛ **THE LITTLE MAGAZINE**, State University of New York at Albany, English Department, Albany NY 12222. E-mail: litmag@csc.albany.edu. Website: www.albany.edu/~litmag. **Editors:** Dimitri Anastasopoulos, Christina Milletti, Manny Savopoulos. "Web-based journal; publishes CD-ROM issue every 2 years. Includes fiction and poetry for a literary audience; also illustrations, photography, artwork. Fiction and poetry for a literary audience." Annually. Estab. 1965.

• *The Little Magazine* has published entirely on the Web since 1995.

Needs: Literary, multi-media, hypertext, experimental, feminist, humor/satire. No genre fiction or long pieces not suitable for web publication. Receives "roughly" 600 mss/issue over a 3-month reading period. Accepts 20 mss/issue. Does not read June through August. Submissions accepted on a rolling basis September through May. Publishes ms 6 months after acceptance. Recently published work by Stuart Moulthrop and Mark Amerika. **Publishes 10 new writers/year.** Length: no limit. Publishes short shorts.

How to Contact: Send complete ms with SASE (or IRC) *on disk* (IBM or Mac) or by e-mail. Hard copy submissions also accepted. Reports in 2 months on queries; in 4 months on mss. Simultaneous and reprint submissions OK. Sample copy for $15.

Payment/Terms: Pays 2 contributor's copies (when published on CD-ROM).

Terms: Acquires first North American serial rights.

Advice: "We're looking for high-quality fiction and poetry that has been conceived as, or lends itself to, multi-media or hypertext production."

⬛ ✅ ◐ **THE LONG STORY**, 18 Eaton St., Lawrence MA 01843. (978)686-7638. E-mail: rpbtls@aol.c om. Website: www.litline.org/html/thelongstory.html (includes writer's guidelines, cumulative index, editorials and a description of the magazine). **Editor:** R.P. Burnham. Magazine: 5½ × 8½; 150-200 pages; 60 lb. paper; 65 lb. cover stock; illustrations (b&w graphics). For serious, educated, literary people. No science fiction, adventure, romance, etc. "We publish high literary quality of any kind, but especially look for stories that have difficulty getting published elsewhere—committed fiction, working class settings, left-wing themes, etc." Annually. Estab. 1983. Circ. 1,200.

Needs: Contemporary, ethnic, feminist and literary. Receives 30-40 unsolicited mss/month. Accepts 6-7 mss/issue. **Publishes 50% new writers.** Length: 8,000 words minimum; 20,000 words maximum. Best length: 8,000-12,000 words.

How to Contact: Send complete ms with a brief cover letter. Reports in 2 months. Publishes ms an average of 3 months to 1 year after acceptance. SASE. May accept simultaneous submissions ("but not wild about it"). Sample copy for $6.

Payment/Terms: Pays 2 contributor's copies; $5 charge for extras. Acquires first rights.

Advice: "Read us first and make sure submitted material is the kind we're interested in. Send clear, legible manuscripts. We're not interested in commercial success; rather we want to provide a place for long stories, the most difficult literary form to publish in our country."

◐ **LOONFEATHER**, P.O. Box 1212, Bemidji MN 56619. (218)751-4869. **Editor:** Betty Rossi. Magazine: 5½ × 8½; 48 pages; 60 lb. Hammermill Cream woven paper; 65 lb. vellum cover stock; illustrations; occasional photos. A literary journal of short prose, poetry and graphics. Mostly a market for Northern Minnesota, Minnesota and Midwest writers. Semiannually. Estab. 1979. Circ. 250.

Needs: Well crafted short prose and poetry. Accepts 2-3 mss/issue, 4-6 mss/year. Reads mss from September 1 through May 31. **Published new writers within the last year.** Length: 600-1,500 words (prefers 1,500).

How to Contact: Send complete query, and short autobiographical sketch with SASE. Reports within 4 months. Sample copy for $4 back issue; $6 current issue.

Payment/Terms: 2 free author's copies. Acquires one-time rights.

Advice: "Send carefully crafted and literary fiction. The writer should familiarize himself/herself with the type of fiction published in literary magazines as opposed to family magazines, religious magazines, etc."

◐ ◎ **LOST AND FOUND TIMES**, Luna Bisonte Prods, 137 Leland Ave., Columbus OH 43214. (614)846-4126. **Editor:** John M. Bennett. Magazine: 5½ × 8½; 56 pages; good quality paper; good cover stock; illustrations; photos. Theme: experimental, avant-garde and folk literature, art. Published irregularly (twice yearly). Estab. 1975. Circ. 375.

Needs: Contemporary, experimental, literary, prose poem. Prefers short pieces. The editor would like to see more short, extremely experimental pieces. "No 'creative writing' workshop stories." Also publishes poetry. Accepts approximately 2 mss/issue. Published work by Spryszak, Steve McComas, Willie Smith, Rupert Wondolowski, Al Ackerman. **Published new writers within the last year.**

How to Contact: Query with clips of published work. SASE. No simultaneous submissions. Reports in 1 week on queries, 2 weeks on mss. Sample copy for $6.

Payment/Terms: Pays 1 contributor's copy. Rights revert to authors.

◑ ◎ **LOUISIANA LITERATURE, A Review of Literature and Humanities**, Southeastern Louisiana University, SLU 792, Hammond LA 70402. (504)549-5022. E-mail: jbedell@selu.edu. **Editor:** Jack Bedell. Magazine: 6¾×9¾; 150 pages; 70 lb. paper; card cover; illustrations. "Essays should be about Louisiana material; preference is given to fiction and poetry with Louisiana and Southern themes, but creative work can be set anywhere." Semiannually. Estab. 1984. Circ. 400 paid; 500-700 printed.

• The editor would like to see more stories with firm closure.

Needs: Literary, mainstream, regional. "No sloppy, ungrammatical manuscripts." Upcoming themes: Louisiana detective fiction, Tennessee Williams, music (jazz, Cajun, blues, etc.), and dog stories (planned for Fall 1997 through Spring 1999). Receives 100 unsolicited fiction mss/month. Accepts mss related to special topics issues. May not read mss June through July. Publishes ms 6-12 months maximum after acceptance. Recently published work by Robert Olen Butler, Patty Friedmann, Albert Davis and Robin Beeman. **Published new writers within the last year.** Length: 3,500 words preferred; 1,000 words minimum; 6,000 words maximum. Also publishes literary essays (Louisiana themes), literary criticism, poetry. Sometimes comments on rejected mss.

How to Contact: Send complete ms. Reports in 1-3 months on mss. SASE. Sample copy for $6. Reviews novels and short story collections (mainly those by Louisiana authors).

Payment/Terms: Pays usually in contributor's copies. Acquires one-time rights.

Advice: "Cut out everything that is not a functioning part of the story. Make sure your manuscript is professionally presented. Use relevant specific detail in every scene."

⭐ ✅ ◑ **LULLWATER REVIEW**, Emory University, P.O. Box 22036, Atlanta GA 30322. E-mail: lwolfso @emory.edu. Editor-in-Chief: Leah Wolfson. Associate Editor: Alicia Galindo. **Fiction Editor:** Robyn Turner. Magazine: 6×9; 100 pages; 60 lb. paper; photos. "We look for fiction that reflects the issues and lifestyles of today, in whatever form it might arrive, whether as a story, short story or a novel excerpt. We hope to reach the average person, someone who might not ordinarily read a publication like ours, but might be attracted by our philosophy." Semiannually. Circ. 2,000. Member of the Council of Literary Magazines and Presses.

Needs: Condensed/excerpted novel, ethnic/multicultural, experimental, feminist, gay, humor/satire, lesbian, literary, mainstream/contemporary, regional. "No romance or science fiction, please." Receives 75-115 unsolicited mss/month. Accepts 3-7 mss/issue; 6-14 mss/year. "Response time is slower in the summer, but we are always reading." Publishes ms within 2 months after acceptance. Recently published work by Greg Jenkins, Thomas Juvik, Jimmy Gleacher, Carla Vissers and Judith Sudnolt. **Publishes 25% new writers.** Length: 10 pages average; 30 pages maximum. Publishes short shorts. Length: 300-500 words. Also publishes poetry. Rarely critiques or comments on rejected mss. Sponsors contest; send SASE for information in early Fall.

How to Contact: Send complete ms with cover letter. Include bio and list of publications. Reports in 1-2 weeks on queries; 3-4 months on mss. Send SASE for reply, return of ms or send a disposable copy of ms. Simultaneous submissions OK. Sample copy for $5. Back copy $4. Fiction guidelines for SASE.

Payment/Terms: Pays 3 contributor's copies; additional copies for $5. Acquires first North American serial rights.

Advice: "We at the *Lullwater Review* look for clear cogent writing, strong character development and an engaging approach to the story in our fiction submissions. Stories with particularly strong voices and well-developed central themes are especially encouraged. Be sure that your manuscript is ready before mailing it off to us. Revise, revise, revise!"

◑ **LUMMOX JOURNAL**, Lummox Press, P.O. Box 5301, San Pedro CA 90733-5301. (562)439-9858. E-mail: lumoxraindog@earthlink.net. **Editor:** Raindog. Magazine: digest size; 20 pages; photocopy paper; illustrations and photos. "*The Lummox Journal* focuses on the process of creativity using interviews, reviews, articles and essays as exploratory tools. Lummox Press also publishes a series of poetry books entitled The Little Red Books. Audience: the curious literary bohemian." Estab. 1996. Circ. 200.

Needs: Experimental, historical, literary, regional, serialized novel. "Would like to see more 'micro' fiction that focuses on creativity." Publishes special fiction and poetry anthology. Receives 1-2 unsolicited mss/month. Accepts 2-3 mss/year. Recently published work by Jay Alamares and Scott Wannberg. Length: 750 words average; 900 words maximum. Publishes short shorts. Also publishes literary essays, literary criticism and poetry.

How to Contact: Query first. Accepts queries/mss by e-mail. Include brief bio and estimated word count. Reports in 1-2 months on queries. Send SASE for reply, return of ms or send disposable copy of ms. Simultaneous and electronic (disk only) submissions OK. Sample copy for $2 and a 6×9 SAE with 2 first-class stamps. Fiction guidelines for #10 SASE. Reviews poetry and short story collections. Send books to editor.

Payment/Terms: Pays 1 contributor's copy for one-time rights; additional copies $1. Not copyrighted.

Advice: Looks for "well-written, reality based emotion (not buzzword rants), strength and genuine believability. Make sure it's something you want to see in print."

⭐ ✅ $ ◑ ▼ **LYNX EYE**, ScribbleFest Literary Group, 1880 Hill Dr., Los Angeles CA 90041-1244. (323)550-8522. **Editors:** Pam McCully and Kathryn Morrison. Magazine: 5½×8½; 120 pages; 60 lb. book paper; varied cover stock. "*Lynx Eye* is dedicated to showcasing visionary writers and artists, particularly new voices." Quarterly. Estab. 1994. Circ. 500.

• A story from *Lynx Eye* has been chosen for reprint in the *Best Mystery Stories* anthology.

Needs: Adventure, condensed/excerpted novel, erotica, ethnic/multicultural, experimental, fantasy (science), feminist, gay, historical, horror, humor/satire, lesbian, literary, mainstream/contemporary, mystery/suspense, romance, science fiction, serialized novel, translations, westerns. No horror with gratuitous violence or YA stories. Receives 500 unsolicited mss/month. Accepts 30 mss/issue; 120 mss/year. Publishes ms approximately 3 months after acceptance (contract guarantees publication within 12 months or rights revert and payment is kept by author). Recently published work by Anjali Banerjee, Jean Ryan, Karen Wendy Gilbert, Jack Random and Robert R. Gass. **Publishes 30 new writers/year.** Length: 2,500 words average; 500 words minimum; 5,000 words maximum. Also publishes artwork, literary essays, poetry. Often critiques or comments on rejected mss.
How to Contact: Send complete ms with a cover letter. Include name and address on page one; name on *all* other pages. Reports in 2-3 months. Send SASE for reply, return of ms or send a disposable copy of ms. Simultaneous submissions OK. Sample copy for $7.95. Fiction guidelines for #10 SASE.
Payment/Terms: Pays $10 on acceptance and 3 contributor's copies for first North American serial rights; additional copies $3.95.
Advice: "We consider any well-written manuscript. Characters who speak naturally and who act or are acted upon are greatly appreciated. Your high school English teacher was correct. Basics matter. Imaginative, interesting ideas are sabotaged by lack of good grammar, spelling and punctuation skills. Most submissions are contemporary/mainstream. We could use some variety. Please do not confuse confessional autobiographies with fiction."

★ ✓ ◎ **THE MACGUFFIN**, Schoolcraft College, Department of English, 18600 Haggerty Rd., Livonia MI 48152. (734)462-4400, ext. 5292 or 5327. Fax: (734)462-4558. E-mail: alindenb@schoolcraft.cc.mi.us. Website: www.schoolcraft.cc.mi.us (includes samples, guidelines, editorial contacts and subscription information). Editor: Arthur J. Lindenberg. **Fiction Editor:** Wendy Shirilla. Magazine: 6×9; 160 pages; 60 lb. paper; 110 lb. cover; b&w illustrations and photos. "*The MacGuffin* is a literary magazine which publishes a range of material including poetry, nonfiction and fiction. Material ranges from traditional to experimental. We hope our periodical attracts a variety of people with many different interests." Triannual. Quality fiction a special need. Estab. 1984. Circ. 600.
Needs: Adventure, contemporary, ethnic, experimental, fantasy, historical (general), humor/satire, literary, mainstream, prose poem, psychic/supernatural/occult, science fiction, translations. No religious, inspirational, confession, romance, horror, pornography. Receives 25-40 unsolicited mss/month. Accepts 5-10 mss/issue; 10-30 mss/year. Does not read mss between July 1 and August 15. Publishes ms 6 months to 2 years after acceptance. Agented fiction: 10-15%. Recently published work by Jeda Bennet, Peter Love and Randall Garrison. **Published 30 new writers within the last year.** Length: 2,000-2,500 words average; 100 words minimum; 5,000 words maximum. Publishes short shorts. Also publishes literary essays. Occasionally critiques rejected mss and recommends other markets.
How to Contact: Send complete ms with cover letter, which should include: "1. *brief* biographical information; 2. note that this *is not* a simultaneous submission." Reports in 2-3 months. SASE. Reprint and electronic (disk) submissions OK. Sample copy for $5; current issue for $6. Fiction guidelines free.
Payment/Terms: Pays 2 contributor's copies. Acquires one-time rights.
Advice: "We want to give promising new fiction writers the opportunity to publish alongside recognized writers. Be persistent. If a story is rejected, try to send it somewhere else. When we reject a story, we may accept the next one you send us. When we make suggestions for a rewrite, we may accept the revision. There seems to be a great number of good authors of fiction, but there are far too few places for publication. However, I think this is changing. Make your characters come to life. Even the most ordinary people become fascinating if they live for your readers."

◎ **THE MADISON REVIEW**, Department of English, Helen C. White Hall, 600 N. Park St., University of Wisconsin, Madison WI 53706. (608)263-0566. **Managing Editors:** Dan Fitzsimons and Emily Benz. Poetry Editors: Erin Hanusa and Trevor Schaid. Magazine: 6×9; 180 pages. "Magazine of fiction and poetry with special emphasis on literary stories and some emphasis on Midwestern writers." Semiannually. Estab. 1978. Circ. 1,000.
Needs: Experimental and literary stories, prose poems, novel excerpts and stories in translation. No historical fiction. Receives 10-50 unsolicited fiction mss/month. Acquires approximately 6 mss/issue. Does not read mss May through September. Published work by Leslie Pietrzyk, Stephen Shugart and Ira Gold. Published new writers within the last year. Length: 4,000 words average. Also publishes poetry.
How to Contact: Send complete ms with cover letter and SASE. Include estimated word count, 1-page bio and list of publications. "The letters should give one or two sentences of relevant information about the writer— just enough to provide a context for the work." Reports in 6 months on mss. Publishes ms an average of 4 months after acceptance. Sample copy for $2.50.
Payment/Terms: Pays 3 contributor's copies; $2.50 charge for extras.
Terms: Acquires first North American serial rights.

✄ $ ☒ **MALAHAT REVIEW**, University of Victoria, P.O. Box 1700, STN CSC, Victoria, British Columbia V8W 2Y2 Canada. (250)721-8524. Website: web.uvic.ca/malahat (includes guidelines, contest info, names of editors and recent contributors). **Acting Editor:** Marlene Cookshaw. Quarterly. Circ. 1,800.

• *The Malahat Review* has received the National Magazine Award for poetry.

Needs: "General fiction and poetry." Reports in 3 months. Publishes 3-4 stories/issue. Recently published work by Robert Sherrin, Natasha Waxman, Leon Rooke and Russell Smith. Publishes 4-5 new writers/year. Length: 10,000 words maximum.

How to Contact: "Enclose proper postage on the SASE." Sample copy: $8 available through the mail; guidelines available upon request. No simultaneous submissions.

Payment/Terms: Pays $30/printed page and contributor's copies.

Advice: "We do encourage new writers to submit. Read the magazines you want to be published in, ask for their guidelines and follow them. Write for information on *Malahat*'s novella competitions."

N ⬛ **MANGROVE, Fiction, Interviews and Poetry from Around the World**, University of Miami, English Dept., Box 248145, Miami FL 33124-4632. (305)284-2182. **Contact:** Fiction Editor. Editors change each year. Magazine: 120 pages. *Mangrove* is "a literary magazine publishing short fiction, poetry, memoirs and interviews." Annually. Estab. 1994. Circ. 500.

Needs: Literary, ethnic/multicultural, mainstream/contemporary, regional, translations. Receives 60-100 unsolicited mss/month. Accepts 6 mss/year. Publishes in May. Notifies writers of acceptance in May. Reads ms August-December. Recently published work by Jamaica Kincaid, Tim O'Brien, Dale Peck and Donald Justice. Length: 5,000 words maximum. Publishes short shorts. Also publishes poetry. Sometimes critiques or comments on rejected ms.

How to Contact: Send complete ms. Include estimated word count, one-paragraph bio and list of publications with submission. SASE for reply. Simultaneous submissions OK. Sample copy for $6, SAE. Fiction guidelines for SASE.

Payment/Terms: Pays 2 contributor's copies. Acquires one-time rights.

Advice: "We look for stories with a distinct voice that make us look at the world in a different way. Send only one story at a time and send us your best."

$ ⬛ **Y** **MANOA, A Pacific Journal of International Writing**, English Dept., University of Hawaii, Honolulu HI 96822. (808)956-3070. Fax: (808)956-7808. E-mail: mjournal-1@hawaii.edu. Website: www.hawaii. edu/mjournal (includes writer's guidelines, names of editors, short fiction and poetry). Editor: Frank Stewart. **Fiction Editor:** Ian MacMillan. Magazine: 7×10; 240 pages. "An American literary magazine, emphasis on top US fiction and poetry, but each issue has a major guest-edited translated feature of recent writings from an Asian/Pacific country." Semiannually. Estab. 1989.

• *Manoa* has received numerous awards, and work published in the magazine has been selected for prize anthologies.

Needs: Contemporary, excerpted novel, literary, mainstream and translation (from US and nations in or bordering on the Pacific). "Part of our purpose is to present top U.S. fiction from throughout the U.S., not only to U.S. readers, but to readers in Asian and Pacific countries. Thus we are not limited to stories related to or set in the Pacific—in fact, we do not want exotic or adventure stories set in the Pacific, but good US literary fiction of any locale." Accepts 8-10 mss/issue; 16-20/year. Publishes ms 6 months-2 years after acceptance. Agented fiction 10%. Recently published work by Robert Olen Butler, Monica Wood and Barry Lopez. **Publishes 1-2 new writers/year.** Publishes short fiction. Also publishes essays, book reviews, poetry.

How to Contact: Send complete ms with cover letter or through agent. Reports in 4-6 months. SASE. Simultaneous submissions OK; query before sending e-mail. Sample copy for $10. Reviews novels and short story collections. Send books or reviews to Reviews Editor.

Payment/Terms: Pays "highly competitive rates so far," plus contributor's copies for first North American serial rights and one-time reprint rights. Sends galleys to author.

Advice: "*Manoa*'s readership is (and is intended to be) mostly national, not local. It also wants to represent top US writing to a new international market, in Asia and the Pacific. Altogether we hope our view is a fresh one; that is, not facing east toward Europe but west toward 'the other half of the world.' "

N 🌐 **MANUSHI, A Journal About Women and Society**, C/174 Lajpat Nagar 1, New Delhi 110024 India. E-mail: manushi@ndu.vsnl.in. **Editor:** Madhu Kishwar. Bimonthly. Circ. up to 8,000. Publishes one fiction story/issue. "*Manushi* is a magazine devoted to human rights and women's rights issues with a focus on the Indian subcontinent and the situation of Indian communities settled overseas. It includes poetry, fiction, historical and sociological studies, analysis of contemporary politics, review of mass media and literature, biographies, profiles and histories of various movements for social change." Length: 12,000 words maximum. Accepts queries/mss by e-mail. Duplicate mss preferred.

☑ ⬛ **MANY MOUNTAINS MOVING, a literary journal of diverse contemporary voices**, 420 22nd St., Boulder CO 80302-7909. (303)545-9942. Fax: (303)444-6510. E-mail: mmm@mmminc.org. Editor: Naomi Horii. **Fiction Editor:** Beth Nugent. Magazine: 6×8¾; 200 pages; recycled paper; color/heavy cover; illustrations and photos. "We publish fiction, poetry, general-interest essays and art. We try to seek contributors from all cultures." Triannually. Estab. 1994. Circ. 2,000.

• The editor would like to see more experimental, avant garde fiction.

Needs: Ethnic/multicultural, experimental, feminist, gay, historical, humor/satire, lesbian, literary, mainstream/contemporary, translations. No genre fiction. Plans special fiction issue or anthology. Receives 300 unsolicited mss/month. Accepts 4-6 mss/issue; 12-18 mss/year. Publishes ms 2-8 months after acceptance. Agented fiction 5%. Recently published work by Michael Dorsey, Daniela Kuper, Julie Shigekuni and Michael Ramos. "We try to **publish at least one new writer per issue**; more when possible." Length: 3,000-10,000 words average. Publishes short shorts. Also publishes literary essays, poetry. Sometimes critiques or comments on rejected mss. **How to Contact:** Send complete ms with a cover letter. Include estimated word count, list of publications. Reports in 2 weeks on queries; 1-3 months on mss. Send SASE for reply, return of ms or send a disposable copy of ms. Simultaneous submissions OK. Sample copy for $6.50 and enough IRCs for 1 pound of airmail/printed matter. Fiction guidelines for #10 SASE.
Payment/Terms: Pays 3 contributor's copies; additional copies for $3. Acquires first North American serial rights. Sends galleys to author "if requested." Sponsors a contest, $200 prize. Send SASE for guidelines. Deadline: December 31.
Advice: "We look for top-quality fiction with fresh voices and verve. Read at least one issue of our journal to get a feel for what kind of fiction we generally publish."

★ $ ◑ ▼ THE MASSACHUSETTS REVIEW, South College, University of Massachusetts, Amherst MA 01003. (413)545-2689. Fax: (413)577-0740. E-mail: massrev@external.umass.edu. Website: www.litline. org/html/massreview.html (includes general overview, information on editors, excerpts, guidelines). **Editors:** Mary Heath, Jules Chametzky, Paul Jenkins. Magazine: 6×9; 172 pages; 52 lb. paper; 65 lb. vellum cover; illustrations and photos. Quarterly. Estab. 1959. Circ. 1,200.
● Stories from the *Massachusetts Review* have been anthologized in the *100 Best American Short Stories of the Century* and the *Pushcart Prize* anthology. This magazine ranked #26 on *Writer's Digest's* Fiction 50 list of top markets for fiction writers.
Needs: Short stories. Wants more prose less than 30 pages. No mystery or science fiction. Does not read fiction mss June 1-October 1. Recently published work by Vern Rutsala, Peter Love and Neal Durando. **Publishes 3-5 new writers/year.** Approximately 5% of fiction is agented. Also accepts poetry. Critiques rejected mss when time permits.
How to Contact: Send complete ms. No ms returned without SASE. Simultaneous submissions OK, if noted. Reports in 2 months. Publishes ms an average of 9-12 months after acceptance. Sample copy for $8. Guidelines available for SASE.
Payment/Terms: Pays $50 maximum on publication for first North American serial rights.
Advice: "Shorter rather than longer stories preferred (up to 28-30 pages)." Looks for works that "stop us in our tracks." Manuscripts that stand out use "unexpected language, idiosyncrasy of outlook and are the opposite or ordinary."

★ ◑ MATRIARCH'S WAY: JOURNAL OF FEMALE SUPREMACY, Artemis Creations, 3395 Nostrand Ave., 2J, Brooklyn NY 11229-4053. Phone/fax: (718)648-8215. E-mail: mwjournal@aol.com. Website: members.aol.com/mwjournal (includes contest news, subscription info, purpose). **Editor:** Shirley Oliveira. Magazine: 5½×8½; illustrations and photos. *Matriarch's Way* is a "matriarchal feminist" publication. Quarterly. Estab. 1996.
Needs: Condensed/excerpted novel, erotica (quality), ethnic/multicultural, experimental, fantasy (science, sword and sorcery), feminist (radical), horror, humor/satire, literary, psychic/supernatural/occult, religious/inspirational, romance (futuristic/time travel, gothic, historical), science fiction (soft/sociological), serialized novel. "No Christian anything." Want more "femme dominant erotica and sci-fi." Upcoming themes: "Science of Matriarchy" and "What it Means to be a Female 'Other.'" Receives 10 unsolicited mss/week. Often critiques or comments on rejected mss. **Publishes 90% new writers.**
How to Contact: Query first, query with clips of published work or query with synopsis plus 1-3 chapters of novel. Accepts queries/mss by fax. Include estimated word count, bio and list of publications with submission. Reports in 1 week on queries; 6 weeks on mss. SASE for reply or send a disposable copy of ms. Sample copy for $8.50. Reviews novels and short story collections and excerpts "We need book reviewers desperately, original or reprints. We supply books."
Payment/Terms: Pays 1 copy of published issue. Acquires one-time rights.
Advice: Looks for "a knowledge of subject, originality and good writing style. If you can best Camille Paglia, you're on your way!" Looks for "professional writing—equates with our purpose/vision—brave and outspoken."

Ⓝ ⊕ MATTOID, School for Literary and Communication Studies, Deakin University, Geelong, Victoria 3217 Australia. E-mail: bje@deakin.edu.au. **Fiction Editor:** Prof. Brian Edwards. Published 3 times/year. Circ. 650. Publishes 5-7 stories/issue. "*Mattoid* publishes short fiction, poetry, essays, interviews, reviews and graphics. At present we are running a series of special issues ('Revisions in Romanticism,' 'Masculinities') but we are interested in innovative fiction." Upcoming themes: "The City" (mid 2000). Length: 300 words minimum; 3,000 words maximum. Pays in copies. "Our main criterion is interest value, though we are pleased to see innovative/experimental writing that is well-crafted. Take some care with the choice of destination. Research the writing.

Include a brief biographical statement." Single copies available for $18 overseas. Annual subscription (3 issues) $40.

⭐ $▢ ◉ ✇ MERLYN'S PEN: Fiction, Essays and Poem's by America's Teens, Grades 6-12, Box 1058, East Greenwich RI 02818. (401)885-5175. Fax: (401)885-5222. E-mail: merlynspen@aol.com. Website: www.merlynspen.com (includes writer's guidelines, the first page of most stories that appear in our anthology collection: *The American Teen Writer Series*). **Editor:** R. Jim Stahl. Magazine: 8⅜ × 10⅞; 100 pages; 70 lb. paper; 12 pt. gloss cover; illustrations; photos. Student writing only (grades 6 through 12) for libraries, homes and English classrooms. Annual (each November). Estab. 1985. Circ. 6,000.

• Winner of the Paul A. Witty Short Story Award and Selection on the New York Public Library's Book List of Recommended Reading.

Needs: Adventure, fantasy, historical, horror, humor/satire, literary, mainstream, mystery/suspense, romance, science fiction, western, young adult/teen. "Would like to see more humor." Also publishes editorial reviews, poetry. Must be written by students in grades 6-12. Receives 1,200 unsolicited fiction mss/month. Accepts 50 mss/issue; 50 mss/year. Publishes ms 3 months to 1 year after acceptance. **Publishes 50 new writers/year.** Length: 1,500 words average; 25 words minimum; no maximum. Publishes short shorts. Responds to rejected mss.

How to Contact: Send for cover-sheet template. Accepts queries/mss by fax. *Charges submission fee: $1/title. For an additional $4, authors receive an extended editorial critique (100 or more words) of their submission in addition to the standard yes/no response.* Reports in 10 weeks.

Payment/Terms: Three copies of *Merlyn's Pen* plus $10 (up to 1,000 words); $75 (over 1,000 words); $175 (over 3,000 words); $200 (over 5,000 words). Published works become the property of Merlyn's Pen, Inc.

Advice: "Write what you *know*; write where you are. We look for the authentic voice and experience of young adults."

▥ ◐ MESECHABE, The Journal of Surre(gion)alism, 1539 Crete St., New Orleans LA 70119-3006. (504)944-4823. E-mail: daf09@gnofn.org. **Editor:** Dennis Formento. Literary magazine: 8½ × 11; 32 pages; bond paper; card cover; illustrations and photos. *Mesechabe* is a "confluence of bioregionalism, surreal, beat and black mountain streams—underground rivers sprouting from the Mississippi (Mesechabe in the Choctaw tongue)—poetry, fiction, art, music." Semiannually. Estab. 1988. Circ. 1,000.

Needs: Erotica (ecorotica), ethnic/multicultural (Afro-Creole, African American, Native American), experimental (unconventional, counter culture), regional (bioregional and Mississippi Delta), science fiction (ecoscience fiction), translations, earth, air, fire, water. No "waiting room romance and 'ladies fiction.' " Publishes ms 2-6 months after acceptance. **Publishes 2-5 new writers/year.** Length: 2,000 words average; 500 words minimum; 6,000 words maximum. Publishes short shorts. Length: 500 words. Also publishes literary essays and poetry. Sometimes critiques or comments on rejected ms.

How to Contact: "Query with clips of published work or send complete ms with a cover letter. Include estimated word count. Reports in 6 weeks on queries and mss. Send SASE for reply, return of ms or send a disposable copy of ms. Sample copy for $5. Guidelines for SASE. Reviews novel, short story collections and nonfiction books of interest to writers. Send books to editor.

Payment/Terms: "Pays 2-5 contributor's copies; additional copies $2. Acquires one-time rights. Send prepublication galleys to author when possible.

Advice: Looks for "the unexpected. Don't cling to the bummer."

⭐ ◐ MESSAGES FROM THE HEART, P.O. Box 64840, Tucson AZ 85728. (520)577-0588. Fax: (520)529-9657. E-mail: lbsmith@theriver.com. Website: www.heartmessages.com. **Editor:** Lauren B. Smith. Magazine: 4¼ × 10½; 20 pages; text weight, various papers; illustrations and photos. "A publication of writings, specifically letters, which nurture understanding between people. Intended audience: mainstream public interested in letter writing." Quarterly. Estab. 1993. Circ. 500.

Needs: Short stories about or containing letters. "We welcome submissions from children and have a student page." No erotica, science fiction, psychic. Receives 150-250 mss/month. Accepts 100 mss/year. Publishes ms 9-12 months after acceptance. **Publishes 80 new writers/year.** Length: 800 words maximum. Publishes letters and short shorts. Also publishes literary essays, literary criticism, poetry.

How to Contact: Send complete ms with a cover letter. Accepts mss by e-mail. Reports in 3 weeks. Send SASE for return of ms and response. Simultaneous submissions OK. Sample copy $5. Fiction guidelines free with SASE. Reviews novels, short story collections and nonfiction books about letter writing.

Payment/Terms: Pays 3 contributor's copies; additional copies $2.75. Acquires one-time rights.

Advice: "Speak from the heart, honestly, no gimmicks."

$✇ MICHIGAN QUARTERLY REVIEW, University of Michigan, 3032 Rackham, Ann Arbor MI 48109-1070. (734)764-9265. E-mail: mqr@umich.edu. Website: www.umich.edu/~mqr (includes history and description of magazine; of current and forthcoming issues, subscription information). **Editor:** Laurence Goldstein. "An interdisciplinary journal which publishes mainly essays and reviews, with some high-quality fiction and poetry, for an intellectual, widely read audience." Quarterly. Estab. 1962. Circ. 1,800.

• Stories from *Michigan Quarterly Review* have been selected for inclusion in *The Best American Short Stories*.

Needs: Literary. No "genre" fiction written for a "market." "Would like to see more fiction about social, political, cultural matters, not just centered on a love relationship or dysfunctional family." Receives 200 unsolicited fiction mss/month. Accepts 2 mss/issue; 8 mss/year. Published work by Jonis Agee, Reginald Gibbons, George V. Higgins and Jennifer Moses. Length: 1,500 words minimum; 7,000 words maximum; 5,000 words average. Also publishes poetry, literary essays.

How to Contact: Send complete ms with cover letter. "I like to know if a writer is at the beginning, or further along, in his or her career. Don't offer plot summaries of the story, though a background comment is welcome." Reports in 6-8 weeks. SASE. No simultaneous submissions. Sample copy for $2.50 and 2 first-class stamps.

Payment/Terms: Pays $8-10/printed page on publication for first rights. Awards the Lawrence Foundation Prize of $1,000 for best story in *MQR* previous year.

Advice: "There's no beating a good plot and interesting characters, and a fresh use of the English language. (Most stories fail because they're written in such a bland manner, or in TV-speak.) Be ambitious, try to involve the social world in the personal one, be aware of what the best writing of today is doing, don't be satisfied with a small slice of life narrative but think how to go beyond the ordinary."

$🖉🅥 MID-AMERICAN REVIEW, Department of English, Bowling Green State University, Bowling Green OH 43403. (419)372-2725. Website: www.bgsu.edu/midamericanreview (includes submission guidelines, sample work and contest info). **Fiction Editor:** Michael Czyzniejewski. Magazine: 5½ × 8½; 100-150 pages; 60 lb. bond paper; coated cover stock. "We publish serious fiction and poetry, as well as critical studies in contemporary literature, translations and book reviews." Biannually. Estab. 1981.

• A story published in the magazine was reprinted in *Best American Short Stories of 1996* and *New Stories From the South* 1997.

Needs: Experimental, literary, memoir, prose poem, traditional and translations. Receives about 150 unsolicited fiction mss/month. Accepts 6-8 mss/issue. Approximately 5% of fiction is agented. Recently published work by Brian Evenson, Gary Lutz, David Foster Wallace, Michael Knight and Bonnie Jo Campbell. **Published 5-10 new writers within the last year.** Length: 25 pages maximum. Also publishes literary essays and poetry. Occasionally critiques rejected mss. Sponsors the Sherwood Anderson Short Fiction Award.

How to Contact: Send complete ms with SASE. No simultaneous submissions. Reports in about 2-6 months. Publishes ms an average of 6 months after acceptance. Sample copy for $5. Reviews novels and short story collections. Send books to editor-in-chief.

Payment/Terms: Payment offered pending funding; usually pays $10-50 on publication and 2 contributor's copies for one-time rights; charges for additional copies.

Advice: "We look for well-written stories that make the reader want to read on past the first line and page. Clichéd themes and sloppy writing turn us off immediately. Read literary journals to see what's being published in today's market. We tend to publish work that is more non-traditional in style and form, but are open to all literary non-genre submissions."

✓ ◎ MINAS TIRITH EVENING-STAR, W.W. Publications, Box 7871, Flint MI 48507. **Editor:** Philip Helms. Magazine: 8½ × 11; 16 pages; typewriter paper; black ink illustrations; photos. Magazine of J.R.R. Tolkien and fantasy—fiction, poetry, reviews, etc. for general audience. Quarterly. Published special fiction issue; plans another. Estab. 1967. Circ. 500.

Needs: "Fantasy and Tolkien." Receives 5 unsolicited mss/month. Accepts 1 ms/issue; 5 mss/year. Published new writers within the last year. Length: 1,000-1,200 words preferred; 5,000 words maximum. Publishes short shorts. Also publishes literary essays, literary criticism, poetry. Occasionally critiques rejected mss.

How to Contact: Send complete ms and bio. Reports in 1-2 months. SASE. No simultaneous submissions. Reprint submissions OK. Sample copy for $2. Reviews novels and short story collections.

Terms: Acquires first rights.

Advice: Goal is "to expand knowledge and enjoyment of J.R.R. Tolkien's and his son Christopher Tolkien's works and their worlds."

✓ 🖉 MIND IN MOTION, A Magazine of Poetry and Short Prose, P.O. Box 1701, Bishop CA 93515. **Editor:** Céleste Goyer. Magazine: 5½ × 8½; 64 pages; 20 lb. paper; 50 lb. cover. "We prefer to publish works of substantial brilliance that engage and encourage the reader's mind." Quarterly. Estab. 1985. Circ. 350.

• This magazine is known for surrealism and poetic language.

Needs: Experimental, fantasy, humor/satire, literary, prose poem, science fiction. No "mainstream, romance, nostalgia, un-poetic prose; anything with a slow pace or that won't stand up to re-reading." Receives 50 unsolicited mss/month. Accepts 10 mss/issue; 40 mss/year. Reads mss October through July. Publishes ms 2-12 weeks after acceptance. Published work by Elizabeth Howkins, Coral Hull, Bent Lorentzen and Mike Standish. Length: 2,000 words preferred; 250 words minimum; 3,500 words maximum. Also publishes poetry. Sometimes critiques rejected mss.

How to Contact: Send complete ms. "Cover letter or bio not necessary." SASE. Simultaneous (if notified) submissions OK. Sample copy for $3.50. Fiction guidelines for #10 SASE.

Mid-American Review: creating a home for experimental fiction

"The definition of 'literary fiction' I've heard from literature professors and other people pretty consistently is in literature there is a point to reading the story beyond finding out what happens next," explains Michael Czyzniejewski, fiction editor of the *Mid-American Review*. And the fiction published in *MAR*, the literary magazine of Bowling Green State University, is often as experimental in form and language as it is in plot.

Michael Czyzniejewski

"Probably every story we take, I read the first paragraph and I know there's a good chance we're going to take that story," Czyzniejewski says. While he has no strict definition of "quality fiction," Czyzniejewski is confident he can identify the best writing from the pile of submissions in his inbox. "You can tell fairly quickly if a story is good by how crisp the writing is, the sentence structure and distribution of length, the originality in what's happening and the word choice. Plot has a lot to do with it, though. If you've got a tired old plot and tired old characters that I've seen a thousand times, you're not going to do yourself any good. But if you have a thousand flying rhinoceroses, well OK, you have my attention now. You just have to carry it out for the next how many thousand words."

But Czyzniejewski is quick to explain that it's still possible to write a good story with a traditional theme. "I think you can write any story well, no matter what it is. You can write love stories. That's the oldest story there is, I guess. I think it all depends upon the handling of the writing." The handling of the writing is also what distinguishes the literary fiction *MAR* considers from genre fiction, which they don't publish. But the line between the two is sometimes thin. "I think if somebody sent in a magical realism detective story, I would consider it a literary detective story and we'd look at that," Czyzniejewski explains. He admits he is a big fan of magical realism.

He's also a big fan of writing that is sometimes difficult to categorize as fiction. "I guess it's up to the author," Czyzniejewski says. "If they send it to me, the fiction editor, then it's fiction." If the writing is sent to the poetry editor, it's considered prose poetry. "By no means do we take only nontraditional work," Czyzniejewski explains. "We just want the best work. But I think it's much easier to catch an editor's eye with nontraditional work because it sticks out. If I've learned anything from being an editor, I've learned that." Czyzniejewski says he's altered his own writing style towards the nontraditional since he's been at *MAR*.

The magazine, which was first published in 1980, is approaching its twentieth anniversary and the editors are planning a double issue. "I've read our first issue that came out in 1980," Czyzniejewski says. "It's just so different. It's so strange. I'm not saying the stories weren't good. It was just such a different aesthetic than we have now. If the first editors looked at the fiction we put in this last issue back then, I don't want to say it would blow their minds, but . . ." Czyzniejewski doubts they would even recognize some of the pieces as fiction.

He is excited by all the changes in short stories over the past 20 years. "I think playing with form is what makes today's fiction different from that written in 1980. Then, I think people were trying to write the blankest Raymond Carver story in the world. Now, instead of trying to copy somebody, people are trying to do something no one's done before. They're not afraid to say, 'well, why not. I'm going to write this story even though it seems totally absurd.' "

And *MAR* is not afraid to take a chance on new writers, who are just as likely to find their work published beside someone like David Foster Wallace as they are to be near another writer who's being published for the first time. "We've had issues where five out of the six stories are first publications," Czyzniejewski says. But he specifically solicits "name" authors to submit work as well. Despite *MAR*'s three-copy "payment," writers including Stuart Dybeck, Peter Ho Davies, Michael Knight and Michael Martone have sent in work.

"I think literary magazines are like the independent films of publications," Czyzniejewski explains. "I'm not saying that David Foster Wallace needs *Mid-American Review* in any way to legitimize his career, but I think it's interesting because a lot of people start with literary magazines. I think what he sent us, and what other writers send us, are things that big magazines aren't going to take yet. Like in independent films, we can do things that somebody who's looking out for corporate concerns won't let you do."

Czyzniejewski also hopes that writers send their work to *MAR* because there are more good stories out there than there are big magazines that will take them. "I think we have a reputation. We've been in all the major award publications like *Best American Short Stories*. So I think people read our magazine. Publishers read our magazine and we get agents calling us for writers' addresses."

While finding an agent because you were published in a small magazine is great, Czyzniejewski admits he would like to be able to pay his contributors. "We used to pay but our funding got cut," he explains. To remedy this, the magazine restructured its contest to generate revenue to pay writers. "This is the first year we've actually done a revenue contest," Czyzniejewski says. "Before, we'd just take the stories that were published that year and give a prize that wasn't really a prize." Now, the winner of the Sherwood Anderson Short Fiction Award will receive $300 and publication in the magazine. If there is enough money left over, *MAR* will start paying its contributors again.

On the verge of his magazine's anniversary and the turn of the millennium, Czyzniejewski is optimistic about the future of fiction. "It's why people watch soap operas, because their lives just aren't that interesting. Even people who have interesting lives want different interesting lives," he says. Literary magazines also provide an escape from loud media like TV and the Internet. "I think books are attractive. I think they're very personal. I think people want time by themselves," he says. And he's no longer afraid that paper books will be replaced by handheld computers and micro disks. "I just don't think so," he says. "Like I don't think we're going to eat food in capsules and just add water. I think people like to eat and I think people like to read from a book. Plus I think staring at a computer screen, whatever type, makes you go blind after a while."

—*Megan Lane*

Payment/Terms: Pays 1 contributor's copy; charge for additional copies. Acquires first North American serial rights.
Advice: "We're now taking more stories per issue, and they may be a bit longer, due to a format modification. *Mind in Motion* is noted for introspective, philosophical fiction with a great deal of energy and originality."

◖ THE MINNESOTA REVIEW, A Journal of Committed Writing, Dept. of English, University of Missouri, Columbia MO 65211. (919)328-6388. Fax: (919)328-4889. **Editor:** Jeffrey Williams. Magazine: 5¼×7½; approximately 200 pages; some illustrations; occasional photos. "We emphasize socially and politically engaged work." Semiannually. Estab. 1960. Circ. 1,500.
Needs: Experimental, feminist, gay, historical, lesbian, literary. Receives 50-75 mss/month. Accepts 3-4 mss/issue; 6-8 mss/year. Publishes ms within 6 months-1 year after acceptance. Published work by Laura Nixon Dawson, Jameson Currier, Jiqi Kajane and Stephen Guiterrez. Length: 1,500-6,000 words preferred. Publishes short shorts. Also publishes literary essays, literary criticism, poetry. Occasionally critiques rejected mss and recommends other markets.
How to Contact: Send complete ms with optional cover letter. Reports in 2-3 weeks on queries; 2-3 months on mss. SASE. Simultaneous submissions OK. Reviews novels and short story collections. Send books to book review editor.
Payment/Terms: Pays in contributor's copies. Charge for additional copies. Acquires first rights.
Advice: "We look for socially and politically engaged work, particularly short, striking work that stretches boundaries."

$◖ MISSISSIPPI MUD, 7119 Santa Fe Ave., Dallas TX 75223. Phone/fax: (214)321-8955. E-mail: chjw@swbell.net. **Editor:** Joel Weinstein. Magazine: 7¾×10; 96 pages; coated and uncoated paper; coated cover; illustrations; photographs. "*Mississippi Mud* publishes fiction, poetry and artworks reflecting life in America at the end of the 20th century. Good writing is its focus." Published irregularly. Estab. 1973. Circ. 1,600.
  • Editor would like to see more non-didactic political fiction.
Needs: Excerpted novel, ethnic/multicultural, experimental, literary, mainstream/contemporary, translations. "No religious or romance." Receives 40-50 unsolicited mss/month. Accepts 8-10 mss/year. Publishes ms 8-18 months after acceptance. Recently published work by Robert Gregory, Wendy Dutton, Willie Smith, Ursula K. Leguin, Matt Sharpe and Toni Graham. Length: 5,000 words average; 100 words minimum; 25,000 words maximum. Publishes short shorts. Also publishes poetry. Sometimes critiques or comments on rejected mss.
How to Contact: Send complete ms with a cover letter. Include list of publications. Reports in 6-8 weeks on queries; 4-6 months on mss. Send SASE for reply, return of ms or send a disposable copy of ms. Simultaneous and electronic (disk) submissions OK. Sample copy for $6.
Payment/Terms: $50-100 and 2 contributor's copies on publication for first North American serial rights.
Advice: "We want good writing, a good story, originality. Look for the right markets: magazines where your writing fits."

◖ MISSISSIPPI REVIEW, University of Southern Mississippi, Box 5144, Hattiesburg MS 39406-5144. (601)266-4321. E-mail: fb@netdoor.com. Website: www.sushi.st.usm.edu/mrw/. **Managing Editor:** Rie Fortenberry. "Literary publication for those interested in contemporary literature—writers, editors who read to be in touch with current modes." Semiannually. Estab. 1972. Circ. 1,500.
Needs: Literary, contemporary, fantasy, humor, translations, experimental, avant-garde and "art" fiction. Quality writing. No juvenile or genre fiction. Buys varied amount of mss/issue. Does not read mss in summer. Published work by Jason Brown, Terese Svoboda and Barry Hannah. Length: 30 pages maximum.
How to Contact: Not currently reading unsolicited work. Sample copy for $8.
Payment/Terms: Pays in contributor's copies. Acquires first North American serial rights.
Advice: "May I suggest that you enter our annual *Mississippi Review* Prize competition (see Contests section in this book) or submit the work via e-mail to our World Wide Web publication, which is a monthly (except August) and publishes more new work than we are able to in the print version. Send submissions to fb@netdoor.com as ASCII files in the text of your e-mail message, or as Microsoft Word of WordPerfect attachments to your message."

★ ✔ $◖ ▼ THE MISSOURI REVIEW, 1507 Hillcrest Hall, University of Missouri—Columbia, Columbia MO 65211. (573)882-4474. Fax: (573)884-4671. Website: www.missourireview.org (includes guidelines, contest information, staff photos, editorial column, short fiction, poetry, essays, interviews, features and book reviews). **Editor:** Speer Morgan. Magazine: 6×9; 212 pages. Theme: fiction, poetry, essays, reviews, interviews, cartoons, "all with a distinctly contemporary orientation. For writers, and the general reader with broad literary interests. We present nonestablished as well as established writers of excellence. The *Review* frequently runs feature sections or special issues dedicated to particular topics frequently related to fiction." Published 3 times/academic year. Estab. 1977. Circ. 6,800.
  • *The Missouri Review* ranked #28 on *Writer's Digest*'s Fiction 50 list of top markets for fiction writers. This magazine had stories anthologized in the *Pushcart Prize Anthology*, *Best American Short Stories*, *Best American Erotica* and *New Stories From the South*.

Needs: Condensed/excerpted novel, ethnic/multicultural, humor/satire, literary, contemporary. "No genre or flash fictions; no children's." Receives approximately 400 unsolicited fiction mss each month. Accepts 5-6 mss/issue; 15-20 mss/year. Recently published work by William Gay, Frederick Busch and Nicola Mason. Publishes 6-10 new writers/year. No preferred length. Also publishes personal essays, poetry. Often critiques rejected mss.

How to Contact: Send complete ms with SASE. Include brief bio and list of publications. Reports in 10 weeks. Send SASE for reply, return of ms or send disposable copy of ms. Sample copy for $7.

Payment/Terms: Pays $20/page minimum on signed contract for all rights.

Advice: Awards William Peden Prize in fiction; $1,000 to best story published in *Missouri Review* in a given year. Also sponsors Editors' Prize Contest with a prize of $1,500 for fiction, $1,000 for essays and the Larry Levis Editors' Prize for poetry, with a prize of $1,500; and the Tom McAfee Discovery Prize in poetry for poets who have not yet published a book.

N **MM REVIEW,** Finishing Line Press, P.O. Box 1016, Cincinnati OH 45201-1016. E-mail: finishingl@aol.com. Website: members.aol.com/finishingl (includes writer's guidelines, contests and books sales information). Editor: C.J. Morrison. **Fiction editor:** Elle Larkin. Magazine: 6×9; 35 pages; cotton paper; linen or cotton cover. "We are a literary magazine interested in publishing serious verse and excellent fiction, drama and essays." Semiannually. Estab. 1998. Circ. 500.

Needs: Literary. "No children's/juvenile or young adult/teen. No erotica." Receives 50 unsolicited mss/month. Accepts 1-4 mss/issue; 2-8 mss/year. Publishes ms 6 months after acceptance. **Publishes 20% new writers/year.** Recently published work by Alexandra Grilikhes, Rane Arroyo, Lean Maines, Tanya Preminger and Irene Sedeora. Word length: 500-700 words average. Publishes short shorts. Length: 500 words. Also publishes literary essays, poetry and drama. Often comments on or critiques rejected ms.

How to Contact: Send complete ms with a cover letter. "We want a cover letter and bio listing past publication credits, if any. Please no long bios, 50-75 words." Reports on queries in 1 month; mss in 6 months. Reviews novels, short story collections and nonfiction of interest to writers. Send books to Kevin Walzer, P.O. Box 1204, Cincinnati OH 45254-1204.

Payment/Terms: Pays 1 contributor's copy; additional copies $4. Payment on publication. Acquires one-time rights. "Rights revert back to authors after publication." Sends galleys to the author.

Advice: "Excellence is our only criteria. We enjoy 'pushing the envelope' and are interested in experimental and cutting edge writing. We do not want 'grandma stories.' Send a clean manuscript free of typos, spelling/grammar errors and/or coffee stains! Please do not send long bios listing every place you have been published since high school plus your cat's name! No 'cute' cover letters. Writing is a business."

MOBIUS, The Journal of Social Change, 1250 E. Dayton #3, Madison WI 53703. (608)255-4224. E-mail: smfred@aol.com. **Editor:** Fred Schepartz. Magazine: 8½×11; 32-64 pages; 60 lb. paper; 60 lb. cover. "Looking for fiction which uses social change as either a primary or secondary theme. This is broader than most people think. Need social relevance in one way or another. For an artistically and politically aware and curious audience." Quarterly. Estab. 1989. Circ. 1,500.

Needs: Contemporary, ethnic, experimental, fantasy, feminist, gay, historical, horror, humor/satire, lesbian, literary, mainstream, prose poem, science fiction. "No porn, no racist, sexist or any other kind of ist. No Christian or spiritually proselytizing fiction." Receives 15 unsolicited mss/month. Accepts 3-5 mss/issue. Publishes ms 3-9 months after acceptance. Published work by JoAnn Yolanda Hernández, Patricia Stevens and Rochelle Schwab. Length: 3,500 words preferred; 500 words minimum; 5,000 words maximum. Publishes short shorts. Length: 500 words. Always critiques rejected mss.

How to Contact: Send complete ms with cover letter. Reports in 2-4 months. SASE. Simultaneous and reprint submissions OK. Sample copy for $2, 9×12 SAE and 3 first-class stamps. Fiction guidelines for 9×12 SAE and 4-5 first-class stamps. "Please include return postage, not IRCs, in overseas submissions."

Payment/Terms: Pays contributor's copies. Acquires one-time rights and electronic rights for www version.

Advice: "We like high impact, we like plot and character-driven stories that function like theater of the mind." Looks for "first and foremost, good writing. Prose must be crisp and polished; the story must pique my interest and make me care due to a certain intellectual, emotional aspect. Second, *Mobius* is about social change. We want stories that make some statement about the society we live in, either on a macro or micro level. Not that your story needs to preach from a soapbox (actually, we prefer that it doesn't), but your story needs to have *something* to say."

$ **MUSHROOM DREAMS,** 14537 Longworth Ave., Norwalk CA 90650-4724. **Editor:** Jim Reagan. Magazine: 8½×5½; 32 pages; 20 lb. paper; heavy cover stock; illustrations. "Eclectic content with emphasis on literary quality." Semiannually. Estab. 1997. Circ. 100.

Needs: Literary. No gay, lesbian. Receives 10-15 unsolicited mss/month. Accepts 3 mss/issue; 6 mss/year. Publishes ms 6-12 months after acceptance. Recently published work by John M. Daniel, John Taylor and Jo-Ann Godfrey. Length: 1,500 words average; 250 words minimum; 1,800 words maximum. Publishes short shorts. Length: 250 words. Also publishes poetry. Often critiques or comments on rejected ms.

How to Contact: Send complete ms with a cover letter. Include estimated word count, short paragraph bio.

Reports in 1 week on queries; 6 weeks on mss. Send SASE for reply or return of ms. Simultaneous and reprint submissions OK. Sample copy $1. Fiction guidelines free.

Payment/Terms: Pays $2-20 and 2 contributor's copies on publication for first rights; additional copies $1.

THE MUSING PLACE, The Literary & Arts Magazine of Chicago's Mental Health Community, The Thresholds, 2700 N. Lakeview, Chicago IL 60614. (773)281-3800, ext. 2465. Fax: (773)281-8790. E-mail: lkrinsky@thn.thresholds.org. **Editor:** Linda Krinsky. Magazine: 8½×11; 36 pages; 60 lb. paper; glossy cover; illustrations. "We are mostly a poetry magazine by and for mental health consumers. We want to give a voice to those who are often not heard. All material is composed by mental health consumers. The only requirement for consideration of publication is having a history of mental illness." Semiannually. Estab. 1986. Circ. 1,000.

Needs: Adventure, condensed/excerpted novel, ethnic/multicultural, experimental, fantasy (science fantasy, sword and sorcery), feminist, gay, historical (general), horror, humor/satire, lesbian, literary, mainstream/contemporary, mystery/suspense, regional, romance, science fiction and serialized novel. Publishes ms up to 6 months after acceptance. Published work by Allen McNair, Donna Willey and Mark Gonciarz. Length: 500 words average; 700 words maximum. Length: 500 words. Also publishes poetry.

How to Contact: Send complete ms with a cover letter. Include bio (paragraph) and statement of having a history of mental illness. Reports in 6 months. Send a disposable copy of ms. Simultaneous and reprint submissions OK. Sample copy free.

Payment/Terms: Pays contributor's copies. Acquires one-time rights.

NASSAU REVIEW, Nassau Community College, State University of New York, Stewart Ave., Garden City NY 11530-6793. (516)572-7792. Editor: Paul A. Doyle. Magazine: 5½×8½; 80-120 pages; heavy stock paper; b&w illustrations and photographs. For "college teachers, libraries, educated college-level readers." Annually. Estab. 1964.

Needs: Contemporary, fantasy, historical (general), literary, mainstream, serialized novel. Receives 600-800 unsolicited mss/year. Accepts 15 mss/issue. Does not read mss August through November. Publishes ms 6 months after acceptance. Published work by Dick Wimmer, Louis Phillips and Norbert Petsch. Length: 800-1,500 words preferred; 1,000 words minimum; 1,500 words maximum. Publishes short shorts "occasionally."

How to Contact: Send complete ms with cover letter. Include basic publication data. Reports in 1 month on queries; 8 months on mss. SASE. No simultaneous submissions. Sample copy for 9×12 SAE.

Payment/Terms: No payment. Acquires first rights or one-time rights.

Advice: Looks for "imaginative, concrete writing on interesting characters and scenes. Avoid the bizarre."

NEBO, A Literary Journal, Arkansas Tech University, Dept. of English, Russellville AR 72801. (501)968-0256. Editors change each year. **Contact** Editor or Advisor: Dr. Michael Karl Ritchie. Literary, fiction and poetry magazine: 5×8; 50-60 pages. For a general, academic audience. Annually. Estab. 1983. Circ. 500.

Needs: Literary, mainstream, reviews. Upcoming theme: pop icon fiction and poetry (fiction and poetry that plays with the roles of pop icons). Receives 20-30 unsolicited fiction mss/month. Accepts 2 mss/issue; 6-10 mss/ year. Does not read mss May 1-September 1. Published work by Steven Sherrill, J.B. Bernstein, Jameson Currier, Tricia Lande and Joseph Nicholson. **Published new writers within the last year.** Length: 3,000 words maximum. Also publishes literary essays, literary criticism, poetry. Occasionally critiques rejected mss.

How to Contact: Send complete ms with SASE and cover letter with bio. No simultaneous submissions. Reports in 3 months on mss. Publishes ms an average of 6 months after acceptance. Sample copy for $6. "Submission deadlines for all work are November 15 and January 15 of each year." Reviews novels and short story collections.

Payment/Terms: Pays 1 contributor's copy. Acquires one-time rights.

Advice: "A writer should carefully edit his short story before submitting it. Write from the heart and put everything on the line. Don't write from a phony or fake perspective. Frankly, many of the manuscripts we receive should be publishable with a little polishing. Manuscripts should *never* be submitted with misspelled words or on 'onion skin' or colored paper."

THE NEBRASKA REVIEW, University of Nebraska at Omaha, Omaha NE 68182-0324. (402)554-3159. E-mail: jreed@fa-cpacs.unomaha.edu. **Fiction Editor:** James Reed. Magazine: 5½×8½; 104 pages; 60 lb. text paper; chrome coat cover stock. "*TNR* attempts to publish the finest available contemporary fiction and poetry for college and literary audiences." Publishes 2 issues/year. Estab. 1973. Circ. 1,000.

Needs: Contemporary, humor/satire, literary and mainstream. No genre fiction. Receives 40 unsolicited fiction mss/month. Accepts 4-5 mss/issue, 8-10 mss/year. Reads for the *Nebraska Review* Awards in Fiction and Poetry September 1 through November 30. Open to submissions January 1-April 30; does not read May 1-August 31. Published work by Cris Mazza, Mark Wisniewski, Stewart O'Nan, Gerda Saunders and Tom Franklin. **Published new writers within the last year.** Length: 5,000-6,000 words average. Also publishes poetry.

How to Contact: Send complete ms with SASE. Reports in 3-6 months. Publishes ms an average of 6-12 months after acceptance. Sample copy for $3.

Payment/Terms: Pays 2 contributor's copies plus 1 year subscription; $3 charge for extras. Acquires first North American serial rights.

Advice: "Write stories in which the lives of your characters are the primary reason for writing and techniques of craft serve to illuminate, not overshadow, the textures of those lives. Sponsors a $500 award/year—write for rules."

☑ ▣ ◎ **NEOTROPE**, Broken Boulder Press, P.O. Box 172, Lawrence KS 66044. E-mail: apowell10@hot mail.com. Website: www.brokenboulder.com (includes submission guidelines, ordering information and addresses, samples of published work, and general information about our press). **Editors:** Adam Powell and Paul Silvia. Magazine: 5½×8½; 90 pages; perfect-bound; illustrations and photos. "We view *Neotrope* as a deprogramming tool for refugees from MPW programs and fiction workshops. We are seeking highly original and aggressively experimental fiction. We publish new and progressive forms of fiction writing, stories that are experimental in structure, style, subject matter and execution. We don't target any specific groups, but trust our audience to define itself." Published annually in August. Estab. 1998. Circ. 1,000.

Needs: Experimental fiction and drama. "No genre fiction, nothing traditional." Receives 30-50 unsolicited mss/month. Accepts 12-16 mss/issue. Publishes ms up to 1 year after acceptance. Recently published works by Scott MacLeod, Charles White, Kenward Elmslie, Michael Lenhart and Bayard. **Publishes 1-16 new writers/ year.** Length: open. Publishes short shorts. Always critiques or comments on rejected ms.

How to Contact: Send complete ms with a cover letter and SASE. Reports in 2 weeks. Simultaneous submissions OK, "but if we accept it we will use it, regardless of any other magazine's decision." Sample copy for $5 postpaid. Fiction guidelines free.

Payment/Terms: Pays 2 contributor's copies; additional copies $5. Acquires one-time rights. Sometimes sends galleys to author.

Advice: "If it reminds me of something I've seen before, it's not ready for *Neotrope*. You can never take too much time to develop your art. I despise this unwritten code of honor among editors which prohibits all but the most general and impersonal replies with returned manuscripts. Most editors don't even bother to sign their names to a xeroxed rejection slip. Those people who are confident enough to set themselves up as the caretakers of contemporary literature have an obligation to prove their worth by helping other writers along."

◖ **NERVE COWBOY**, Liquid Paper Press, P.O. Box 4973, Austin TX 78765. **Editors:** Joseph Shields and Jerry Hagins. Magazine: 7×8½; 60-64 pages; 20 lb. paper; card stock cover; illustrations. "*Nerve Cowboy* publishes adventurous, comical, disturbing, thought-provoking, accessible poetry and fiction. We like to see work sensitive enough to make the hardest hard-ass cry, funny enough to make the most hopeless brooder laugh and disturbing enough to make us all glad we're not the author of the piece." Semiannually. Estab. 1996. Circ. 250.

● Sponsors an annual chapbook contest for fiction or poetry. Deadline January 31. Send SASE for details.

Needs: Literary. No "racist, sexist or overly offensive" work. Wants more "unusual stories with rich description and enough twists and turns that leaves the reader thinking." Receives 25 unsolicited mss/month. Accepts 2-3 mss/issue; 4-6 mss/year. Publishes ms 6-12 months after acceptance. Published work by Albert Huffstickler, Mark Smith, Catfish McDaris, Laurel Speer, Brian Prioleau, Marcy Shapiro, Susanne R. Bowers and Adam Gurvitch. **Publishes 5-10 new writers/year.** Length: 750-1,000 words average; 1,500 words maximum. Publishes short shorts. Also publishes poetry.

How to Contact: Send complete ms with a cover letter. Include bio and list of publications. Reports in 2 weeks on queries; 6-8 weeks on mss. Send SASE for reply, return of ms or send disposable copy of ms. No simultaneous submissions. Reprints OK. Sample copy for $4. Fiction guidelines for #10 SASE.

Payment/Terms: Pays 1 contributor's copy for one-time rights.

Advice: "We look for writing which is very direct and elicits a visceral reaction in the reader. Read magazines you submit to in order to get a feel for what the editors are looking for. Write simply and from the gut."

☑ ▣ ♔ **NEW DELTA REVIEW**, 15 Allen Hall, English Dept./Louisiana State University, Baton Rouge LA 70803-5001. (225)388-4079. E-mail: wwwndr@unix1.snce.lsu.edu. **Editors:** Andrew Spear and Ray Thibodeaux. **Fiction Editor:** Sean Cavanaugh. Editors change every year. Magazine: 6×9; 75-125 pages; high quality paper; glossy card cover; b&w illustrations and artwork. "No theme or style biases. Poetry, fiction primarily; also literary interviews and reviews." Semi-annual. Estab. 1984. Circ. 500.

● The magazine recently won a *Pushcart* Prize. *New Delta Review* also sponsors the Eyster Prizes for fiction and poetry. See the listing in the Contest and Awards Section of this book. Work from the magazine has been included in the *Pushcart Prize* anthology.

Needs: Contemporary, humor/satire, literary, mainstream, prose poem, translations. No novel excerpts, adventure, sci-fi, juvenile. Receives 200 unsolicited mss/ month. Accepts 3-4 mss/issue, 6-8 mss/year. Recently published work by George Berridge, Jr., Ted Graf, Hayley R. Mitchell and Rebecah Edwards. Published new writers within the last year. Length: 20 ms pages average; 250 words minimum. Publishes short shorts. Also publishes poetry. Rarely critiques rejected mss.

How to Contact: Send complete ms with cover letter. Cover letter should include estimated word count, bio, Social Security number and "credits, if any; no synopses, please." Accepts queries/mss by fax. No simultaneous submissions. Reports on queries in 3 weeks; 3 months on mss. SASE (or IRC). Mss deadlines September 1 for fall; February 15 for spring. Sample copy for $6. Reviews novels and short story collections.

Payment/Terms: Pays in contributor's copies. Charge for extras.

Terms: Acquires first North American serial rights. Sponsors award for fiction writers in each issue. Eyster Prize-$50 plus notice in magazine. Mss selected for publication are automatically considered.

Advice: "We want fiction that compels the reader to continue reading until the end. Keep reading what is being published in the small journals and 'Best of' anthologies, and write, and then rewrite."

$ ⊘ NEW ENGLAND REVIEW, Middlebury College, Middlebury VT 05753. (802)443-5075. E-mail: nereview@mail.middlebury.edu. Website: www.middlebury.edu/~nereview (includes guidelines, staff, ordering information, sample works from current and back issues). **Editor:** Stephen Donadio. Magazine: 7×10; 180 pages; 50 lb paper; coated cover stock. A literary quarterly publishing fiction, poetry and essays with special emphasis on contemporary cultural issues, both in the US and abroad. For general readers and professional writers. Quarterly. Estab. 1977. Circ. 2,000.

Needs: Literary. Receives 250 unsolicited fiction mss/month. Accepts 5 mss/issue; 20 mss/year. Does not read ms June-August. Recently published work by Tom Paine, George Singleton, Lucia Perillo, Cornelia Nixon and Steve Stern. **Publishes 1-2 new writers/year.** Publishes ms 3-9 months after acceptance. Agented fiction: less than 5%. Prose length: 10,000 words maximum, double spaced. Novellas: 30,000 words maximum. Publishes short shorts occasionally. Sometimes critiques rejected mss.

How to Contact: Send complete ms with cover letter. "Cover letters that demonstrate that the writer knows the magazine are the ones we want to read. We don't want hype, or hard-sell, or summaries of the author's intentions. Will consider simultaneous submissions, but must be stated as such." Reports in 12-15 weeks on mss. SASE.

Payment/Terms: Pays $10/page, $20 minimum and 2 contributor's copies on publication; charge for extras. Acquires first rights and reprint rights. Sends galleys to author.

Advice: "It's best to send one story at a time, and wait until you hear back from us to try again."

⊘ NEW LAUREL REVIEW, New Orleans Poetry Forum/New Laurel Review, P.O. Box 770257, New Orleans LA 70112. Phone/fax: (504)947-6001. **Editor:** Lee Meitzen Grue. Poetry Editor: Lenny Emmanuel. Magazine: 6½×8; 125 pages; 60 lb. white paper; illustrations and photos. Journal of poetry, fiction, critical articles and reviews. "We have published such internationally known writers as James Nolan, Tomris Uyar and Yevgeny Yevtushenko." Readership: "Literate, adult audiences as well as anyone interested in writing with significance, human interest, vitality, subtlety, etc." Published irregularly. Estab. 1970. Circ. 500. Member of Council of Editors of Learned Journals.

Needs: Literary, ethnic/multicultural, excerpted novel, translations, "cutting edge." No "dogmatic, excessively inspirational or political" material. No science fiction. Want more classic short story and experimental short story. Acquires 1-2 fiction mss/issue. Receives approximately 25 unsolicited fiction mss each month. Does not read mss during summer months and December. Agented fiction 10%. **Publishes 5 new writers/year.** Length: about 10 printed pages. Publishes short shorts. Also publishes literary essays and poetry. Critiques rejected mss when there is time.

How to Contact: Send complete ms with a cover letter. Include bio and list of publications. Reports in 3 months. Send SASE for reply or return of ms. No simultaneous submissions. Sample copy for $10. "Authors need to look at sample copy before submitting."

Payment/Terms: Pays 1 contributor's copy; additional copies $10, discounted. Acquires first rights.

Advice: "We are interested in fresh, original work that keeps a reader reading. Send a finished manuscript: clean."

$ ⊘ NEW LETTERS MAGAZINE, University of Missouri-Kansas City, University House, 5101 Rockhill Rd., Kansas City MO 64110. (816)235-1168. Fax: (816)235-2611. Website: www.umkc.edu/newletters. **Editor:** James McKinley. Magazine: 14 lb. cream paper; illustrations. Quarterly. Estab. 1971 (continuation of *University Review*, founded 1935). Circ. 2,500.

Needs: Contemporary, ethnic, experimental, humor/satire, literary, mainstream, translations. No "bad fiction in any genre." Published work by Tess Gallagher, Jimmy Carter and Amiri Baraka; **published work by new writers within the last year.** Agented fiction: 10%. Also publishes short shorts. Rarely critiques rejected mss.

How to Contact: Send complete ms with cover letter. Does not read mss May 15-October 15. Reports in 3 weeks on queries; 2-3 months on mss. SASE for ms. No simultaneous or multiple submissions. Sample copy $5.50 or on website.

Payment/Terms: Pays honorarium—depends on grant/award money; 2 contributor's copies. Sends galleys to author.

Advice: "Seek publication of representative chapters in high-quality magazines as a way to the book contract. Try literary magazines first."

✓ ⊘ ⚑ NEW ORLEANS REVIEW, Box 195, Loyola University, New Orleans LA 70118. (504)865-2295. Fax: (504)865-2294. E-mail: noreview@loyno.edu. **Editor:** Sophia Stone. Magazine: 8½×11; 160 pages; 60 lb. Scott offset paper; 12+ King James C1S cover stock; photos. "Publishes poetry, fiction, translations, photographs, nonfiction on literature and film. Readership: those interested in current culture, literature." Quarterly. Estab. 1968. Circ. 1,300.

● Work from the *New Orleans Review* has been anthologized in *Best American Short Stories*.

Needs: "Storytelling between traditional and experimental." No romance. Want more experimental fiction. Recently published work by Laurie Blauner, Valerie Martin, John Keegan, Sheila Mulligan Webb, R.M. Berry, Moira Crone and Charlotte Forbes. **Publishes 6-8 new writers/year.**

How to Contact: Send complete ms with SASE. Accepts queries/mss by fax. Does not accept simultaneous submissions. Accepts disk submissions; inquire about system compatibility. Prefers hard copy with disk submission. Reports in 2-12 weeks. Sample copy for $9.

Payment/Terms: "Inquire." Most payment in copies. Pays on publication for first North American serial rights.

N NEW VIRGINIA REVIEW, 2A, 1306 E. Cary St., Richmond VA 23219. (804)782-1043. Editor: Mary Flinn. Magazine: 6½×10; 180 pages; high quality paper; coated, color cover stock. "Authors are serious writers of contemporary fiction." Published January, May and October. Estab. 1978. Circ. 2,000.

Needs: Contemporary, experimental, literary, mainstream, serialized/excerpted novel. No blue, science fiction, romance, children's. Receives 50-100 unsolicited fiction mss/month. Accepts an average of 15 mss/issue. Does not read from April 1 to September 1. Publishes ms an average of 6-9 months after acceptance. Length: 5,000-6,500 words average; no minimum; 8,000 words maximum. Also publishes poetry. Sometimes critiques rejected mss.

How to Contact: Send complete ms with cover letter, name, address, telephone number, brief biographical comment. Reports in 6 weeks on queries; up to 6 months on mss. "Will answer questions on status of ms." SASE (or IRC). Sample copy for $7 and 9×12 SAE with 5 first-class stamps.

Payment/Terms: Pays $10/printed page; contributor's copies; charge for extras, ½ cover price.

Terms: Pays on publication for first North American serial rights. Sponsors contests and awards for Virginia writers only.

Advice: "Try to write good strong fiction, stick to it, and try again with another editor."

🌐 $ NEW WELSH REVIEW, Chapter Arts Centre, Market Rd., Cardiff Wales CF5 1QE United Kingdom. Phone: 01222 665529. Fax: 01222 665529. E-mail: robin@nwrc.demon.co.uk. **Editor:** Robin Reeves. "*NWR*, a literary quarterly ranked in the top five of British Literary magazines, publishes stories, poems and critical essays. The best of Welsh writing in English, past and present, is celebrated, discussed and debated. We seek poems, short stories, reviews, special features/articles and commentary." Accepts 16-20 mss/year.

Needs: Short fiction. "No extremes, such as extreme thriller, erotica etc. where emphasis is placed on sensationalizing." Length: 2,000-3,000 words. Recently published work by Sian James, Ron Berry, Alun Richard, Lloyd Rees, Roger Granelli and Herbert Williams. **Publishes 20% new writers.**

How to Contact: Accepts queries by e-mail. Do not send mss by e-mail.

Terms: Pays "cheque on publication and one free copy."

⭐ ✓ ○ ▣ NEW WRITING, A Literary Magazine for New Writers, P.O. Box 1812, Amherst NY 14226-7812. (716)834-1067. E-mail: 1812@newwriting.com. Website: www.newwriting.com. **Editor:** Sam Meade. Electronic magazine; illustrations and photographs. "We publish work that is deserving." Annually. Estab. 1994.

Needs: Work by new writers: action, experimental, horror, humor/satire, literary, mainstream/contemporary, romance, translations, westerns. Recently published work by Rob Roberge and Dom Leone. **Publishes 20 new writers/year.** Length: open. Publishes short shorts. Often critiques or comments on rejected mss. Sponsors an annual award.

How to Contact: Send complete ms with a cover letter. "When sending e-mail do not send attached files." Include *brief* list of publications and *short* cover letter. Reports in 1-2 months. Send SASE for return of ms. Simultaneous submissions OK. Reviews novels and short story collections.

Payment/Terms: Acquires one-time rights.

Advice: "Don't send first copies of *any* story. Always read over, and rewrite!" Avoid "stories with characters who are writers, stories that start with the character waking, and death and dying stories—we get too many of them."

🍁 ⭐ ✓ $○ ◎ NeWEST REVIEW, Box 394, R.P.O. University, Saskatoon, Saskatchewan S7N 4J8 Canada. (306)934-1444. Fax: (306)664-4515. E-mail: allison.muri@home.com. **Contact:** Allison Muri. Magazine: 40 pages; book stock; illustrations; photos. Magazine devoted to western Canada cultural and regional issues; "fiction, reviews, poetry for middle- to high-brow audience." Quarterly. Estab. 1975. Circ. 1,000.

Needs: "We want fiction of high literary quality, whatever its form and content. But we do have a heavy regional emphasis." No adventure or animal stories. Receives 15-20 unsolicited mss/month. Accepts 1 ms/issue; 10 mss/year. Recently published work by Jill Robinson, Richard Hetherton, Thomas Trofimuk and Don Gayton. **Publishes 12 new writers/year.** Length: 2,500 words average; 1,500 words minimum; 5,000 words maximum. Sometimes recommends other markets.

How to Contact: "We like *brief* cover letters." Accepts queries/mss by e-mail. Reports very promptly in a short letter. SAE, IRCs or Canadian postage. No multiple submissions. Electronic submissions (disk or e-mail) OK. Sample copy for $5.

Payment/Terms: Pays $100 maximum on publication for one-time rights.

Advice: "We don't want unpolished, careless submissions. We do want to be intrigued, entertained and stimulated. Polish your writing. Develop your story line. Give your characters presence. If we, the readers, are to care about the people you create, you too must take them seriously. Be bold and venturesome."

NEXUS, Wright State University, W016a Student Union, Dayton OH 45435. (937)775-5533. Editor: Larry Sawyer. Magazine: 7×10; 90-140 pages; good coated paper; heavy perfect-bound cover; b&w illustrations and photography. "International arts and literature for those interested." 3 times per year. Circ. 2,000.

Needs: Contemporary, experimental, literary, regional, translations. No sci-fi, western, romance. Receives 25-30 unsolicited mss/month. Accepts 2-3 mss/issue; 6-10 mss/year. Does not read mss June-Sept. Publishes ms 2-6 months after acceptance. Length: 4,000 words average; 500 words minimum; 7,500 words maximum. Publishes short shorts of any length. Also publishes literary essays, literary criticism and poetry. Sometimes critiques rejected mss and recommends other markets.

How to Contact: Send complete manuscript with cover letter including "any previous publishers of your work. *Do not* explain anything about the story." Reports in 2-4 weeks on queries; 1-2 months on mss. SASE. Simultaneous, photocopied and reprint submissions OK. Sample copy for $5. Fiction guidelines for #10 SASE.

Payment/Terms: Pays contributor's copies. Acquires first North American serial rights.

Advice: "Simplicity and a perfection of style (description, simile, dialogue) always make a lasting impression. Good, careful translations receive favored readings."

$ NIMROD, International Journal of Prose and Poetry, University of Tulsa, 600 S. College Ave., Tulsa OK 74104. (918)631-3080. E-mail: ringoldfl@centum.utulsa.edu. Website: www.utulsa.edu/nimrod/nimrod .html (includes writer's guidelines, excerpts from published work, contest rules). **Fiction Editor:** Gerry McLoud. Magazine: 6×9; 160 pages; 60 lb. white paper; illustrations; photos. "We publish one thematic issue and one awards issue each year. A recent theme was "The City," a compilation of poetry and prose from all over the world. We seek vigorous, imaginative, quality writing. Our mission is to discover new writers and publish experimental writers who have not yet found a 'home' for their work." Semiannually. Estab. 1956. Circ. 3,000.

Needs: "We accept contemporary poetry and/or prose. May submit adventure, ethnic, experimental, prose poem, science fiction or translations." Receives 120 unsolicited fiction mss/month. Published work by Linda Watanabe McFerris, Rea Nolan Martin, Lisa Harris, Rochelle Distelheim and Sheila Thorne. **Published 5-10 new writers within the last year.** Length: 7,500 words maximum. Also publishes poetry.

How to Contact: SASE for return of ms. Accepts queries by e-mail. Reports in 3-5 months. Sample copy: "to see what *Nimrod* is all about, send $10 for a back issue. To receive a recent awards issue, send $10 (includes postage).

Payment/Terms: Pays 2 contributor's copies, plus $5/page up to $25 total per author per issue for one-time rights, budget permitting.

Advice: "We have not changed our fiction needs: quality, vigor, distinctive voice. We have, however, increased the number of stories we print. See current issues. We look for fiction that is fresh, vigorous, distinctive, serious and humorous, seriously-humorous, unflinchingly serious, ironic—whatever. Just so it is quality. Strongly encourage writers to send #10 SASE for brochure for annual literary contest with prizes of $1,000 and $2,000."

96 Inc., P.O. Box 15559, Boston MA 02215-0011. (617)267-0543. Fax: (617)262-3568. **Fiction Editors:** Julie Anderson and Vera Gold. Magazine: 8½×11; 50 pages; 20 lb. paper; matte cover; illustrations and photos. "*96 Inc.* promotes the process; integrates beginning/young with established writers; reaches out to audiences of all ages and backgrounds." Annual. Estab. 1992. Circ. 3,000.

Needs: All types, styles and subjects. Receives 200 unsolicited mss/month. Accepts 12-15 mss/issue; 30 mss/year. Agented fiction 10%. Recently published work by Judith Stitzel, Aaron Alexander, Susan Green and Linda Goldberg. **Publishes 4-5 new writers/year.** Length: 1,000 words minimum; 7,000 words maximum. Publishes short shorts. Also publishes literary essays, literary criticism and poetry. Sometimes critiques or comments on rejected mss.

How to Contact: Query first. Include estimated word count, bio (100 words) and list of publications. Reports in 3 weeks on queries; 6-12 months on mss. Send SASE for reply, return of ms or send a disposable copy of ms. Simultaneous and electronic submissions OK. Sample copy for $7.50. Fiction guidelines for #10 SASE. Reviews novels and short story collections on occasion.

Payment/Terms: Pays modest sum if funds are available, not depending on length or merit, free subscription and 4 contributor's copies on publication for one-time rights.

Advice: Looks for "good writing in any style. Pays attention to the process. Read at least one issue. Be patient—it takes a very long time for readers to go through the thousands of manuscripts."

N NITE-WRITER'S INTERNATIONAL LITERARY ARTS JOURNAL, Nite Owl Press, 137 Pointview Rd., Suite 300, Pittsburgh PA 15227. (412)885-3798. E-mail: nitewrite2@aol.com. **Editor:** John A. Thompson, Sr. Assistant Editor: Bree A. Orner. Magazine: 8½×11; 30-50 pages; bond paper; illustrations. "*Nite-*

Writer's International Literary Arts Journal is dedicated to the emotional intellectual with a creative perception of life." Quarterly. Estab. 1993. Circ. 250.

Needs: Adventure, erotica, historical, humor/satire, literary, mainstream/contemporary, religious/inspirational, romance, senior citizen/retirement, sports, young adult/teen (adventure). Plans special fiction issue or anthology. Receives 3-5 unsolicited mss/month. Accepts 1-2 mss/issue; 5-8 mss/year. Publishes ms within 1 year after acceptance. Published work by Julia Klatt Singer, Jean Oscarson Schoell, Lawrence Keough and S. Anthony Smith. Length: 150 words average; 150 words minimum; 250 words maximum. Publishes short shorts. Also publishes literary essays, literary criticism, poetry. Often critiques or comments on rejected mss.

How to Contact: Send complete ms with a cover letter. Include estimated word count, 1-page bio, list of publications. Reports in 4-6 weeks. SASE for return of ms. Simultaneous submissions OK. Sample copy for $6, 9×13 SAE and 6 first-class stamps. Fiction guidelines for legal size SASE.

Payment/Terms: Does not pay. Acquires first North American serial rights. Sponsors contests.

Advice: "Read a lot of what you write, study the market; don't fear rejection, but use it as a learning tool to strengthen your work before resubmitting. Express what the heart feels."

★ ✔ ◑ **NO EXPERIENCE REQUIRED**, D J Creations, P.O. Box 7573, The Woodlands TX 77387-7573. (281)367-3603. Fax: (281)367-7292. E-mail: nerzine@excite.com Website: www.members.tripod.com/~JCP12/index.html (includes guidelines). **Contact:** Editor. Editor changes each issue. Magazine: 5½×8½; 40-48 pages; marble text 24 lb. paper; 80 lb. cover stock; illustrations and photos. "We have no specific theme. Our philosophy is simple: we want to help new writers break into publication." Triannually. Estab. 1997. Circ. 350.

Needs: "We will consider most categories. No pornographic, erotica, racial/religious denegration." Wants more humor. Receives 20 mss/month. Accepts 12-15 mss/issue; 35-50 mss/year. Published work by Michael McFarland, Doré Hevenor, Martha James, Joseph Burns and Helen Ciancimino. **Publishes 30 new writers/year.** Length: 1,200 words maximum. Publishes short shorts. Also publishes poetry. Provides short critiques or comments on rejected ms.

How to Contact: Send complete ms with cover letter. Include estimated word count, phone, net/e-mail address if applicable. Reports in 3-4 weeks on queries; 3-4 months on mss. Send SASE for reply, return of ms or send a disposable copy of ms. Simultaneous, reprint and electronic (disk or modem) submissions OK. Sample copy $3 and $1 postage. Fiction guidelines for #10 SASE.

Payment/Terms: Pays 2 contributor's copies; additional copies $3. Acquires one-time rights; rights revert to author.

Advice: "We want interesting, compelling stories with proper use of grammar and clear, concise writing. We just want to encourage writers, who may have become discouraged by rejections elsewhere."

Ⓝ **THE NORTH AMERICAN REVIEW**, University of Northern Iowa, Cedar Falls IA 50614. (319)273-6455. E-mail: nar@uni.edu. Website: www.webdelsol.com/NorthAmRev/NAR. Editor: Robley Wilson. "The NAR is the oldest literary magazine in America and one of the most respected; though we have no prejudices about the subject matter of material sent to us, our first concern is quality." Bimonthly. Estab. 1815. Circ. 4,000.

Needs: Open (literary). Reads mss from January 1 to April 1 only.

How to Contact: Send complete ms with SASE. No simultaneous submissions. Sample copy for $5.

Payment/Terms: Pays approximately $12/printed page; 2 contributor's copies on publication for first North American serial rights. $4.50 charge for extras.

Advice: "We stress literary excellence and read 3,000 manuscripts a year to find an average of 35 stories that we publish. Please *read* the magazine first. Please don't mail your work to us in a Tyvek envelope; it defies letter-openers. Otherwise, our mechanical requirements are the usual ones. Material sent to us must be accompanied by a stamped, self-addressed envelope; the envelope should be large enough to accommodate the manuscript, and the postage should be sufficient to cover the cost of its return to you. If you don't supply postage, or if the envelope isn't large enough to contain the manuscript, we assume that you don't want your work sent back."

◑ ♈ **NORTH DAKOTA QUARTERLY**, University of North Dakota, Box 7209, University Station, Grand Forks ND 58202. (701)777-3322. Fax: (701)777-3650. E-mail: ndq@sage.und.nodak.edu. Website: www.192.41.6.160/ndq (includes editors, samples of published work and covers). Editor: Robert W. Lewis. **Fiction Editor:** William Borden. Poetry Editor: Jay Meek. Magazine: 6×9; 200 pages; bond paper; illustrations; photos. Magazine publishing "essays in humanities; some short stories; some poetry." University audience. Quarterly. Estab. 1911. Circ. 700.

• Work published in *North Dakota Quarterly* was selected for inclusion in *The O. Henry Awards* anthology. The editors are especially interested in work by Native American writers.

Needs: Contemporary, ethnic, experimental, feminist, historical, humor/satire, literary. Receives 100-120 unsolicited mss/month. Accepts 4 mss/issue; 16 mss/year. Recently published work by Debra Marquort, Andrew Dillon, Richard Broderick, Robert Wrigley, Phillip Dacey, Adrian C. Louis and Nancy L. Walker. **Publishes 4-5 new writers/year.** Length: 3,000-4,000 words average. Also publishes literary essays, literary criticism, poetry. Sometimes comments on or critiques rejected ms.

How to Contact: Send complete ms with cover letter. Include one-paragraph bio. "But it need not be much more than hello; please read this story; I've published (if so, best examples) . . ." SASE. Reports in 3 months.

Publishes ms an average of 1 year after acceptance. Sample copy for $8. Reviews novels and short story collections.

Payment/Terms: Pays 2-4 contributor's copies; 30% discount for extras. Acquires one-time rights. Sends galleys to author.

★ ◨ NORTHEAST ARTS MAGAZINE, P.O. Box 94, Kittery ME 03904. **Editor:** Mr. Leigh Donaldson.
Magazine: 6½×9½; 32-40 pages; matte finish paper; card stock cover; illustrations and photographs. Bimonthly. Estab. 1990. Circ. 750.

Needs: Ethnic, gay, historical, literary, mystery/suspense (private eye), prose poem (under 2,000 words). No obscenity, racism, sexism, etc. Receives 50 unsolicited mss/month. Accepts 1-2 mss/issue; 5-7 mss/year. Publishes ms 2-4 months after acceptance. Agented fiction 20%. Length: 750 words preferred. Publishes short shorts. Sometimes critiques rejected mss.

How to Contact: Send complete ms with cover letter. Include short bio. Reports in 1 month on queries; 2-4 months on mss. SASE. Simultaneous submissions OK. Sample copy for $4.50, SAE and 75¢ postage. Fiction guidelines free.

Payment/Terms: Pays 2 contributor's copies. Acquires first North American serial rights. Sometimes sends galleys to author.

Advice: Looks for "creative/innovative use of language and style. Unusual themes and topics."

★ $ ◨ ▼ NORTHEAST CORRIDOR, Beaver College, 450 S. Easton Rd., Glenside PA 19038.
(215)572-2870. E-mail: balee@beaver.edu. Editor: Susan Balée. **Fiction Editor:** Deborah Goldschmidt. Magazine: 6¾×10; 120-220 pages; 60 lb. white paper; glossy, perfect-bound cover; illustrations and photos. "Interested in writers and themes treating the Northeast Corridor region of America. Literary fiction, poetry, drama, essays, interviews with writers." Annually. Estab. 1993. Circ. 1,000.

• *Northeast Corridor* has received grants from the Daphne Foundation, the Ruth and Robert Satter Foundation, the Cottonwood Foundation and the Nicholas Roerich Museum. An essay it published was listed in *Best American Essays.*

Needs: Literary: excerpted novel, ethnic/multicultural, feminist, humor/satire, literary, regional, translations. No religious, western, young adult, science fiction, juvenile, horror. "Needs literary stories with humor." List of upcoming themes available for SASE. Planning future special memoir issue or anthology. Receives 100 unsolicited mss/month. Accepts 2-6 mss/issue; 4-12 mss/year. Reads mss infrequently during June, July and August. Publishes ms 6 months after acceptance. Recently published work by Joe Evanisko, Mark Winegardner and Jim Quinn and Lisa Borders. **Publishes 12 new writers/year.** Length: 2,500 words average; 1,000 words minimum; 4,500 words maximum. Publishes literary essays, interviews and poetry. Often critiques or comments on rejected mss.

How to Contact: Send complete ms with a cover letter. Include word count, 1-2 line bio and publications list. Reports in 2-4 months on mss. SASE for reply, return of ms or send a disposable copy of ms. Simultaneous submissions OK if indicated. Sample copy for $7, 9×12 SAE and $1.21 postage. Fiction guidelines for #10 SASE.

Payment/Terms: Payment in contributor's copies on publication for first North American serial rights until additional grant money received; additional copies for $7/copy.

Advice: "In selecting fiction we look for love of language, developed characters, believable conflict, metaphorical prose, satisfying resolution. Read everything from Chekov to Alice Munro and write at least 10-20 stories before you start trying to send them out. We would like to see more humor. Writers should avoid sending work that is 'therapy' rather than 'art.' The best fiction is still to be found in small journals. The small tale well told appears here where it can be appreciated if not remunerated."

Ⓝ ◎ ▣ THE NORTHERN MICHIGAN JOURNAL. (231)256-2829. E-mail: nmj@leelanau.com. Website: www.leelanau.com/nmj. **Editor:** Andrew L. McFarlane. Electronic magazine. Publishes "new work from writers that deals (primarily) with what it is to live, visit or love the Northern Michigan area."

Needs: Historical, regional. Wants more historical fiction. No pornographic or erotic. **Publishes 7-10 new writers/year.** Recently published work by Jim Rink, Dan Foley, David Sutherland and Mark Smith. Also publishes poetry.

How to Contact: Send queries/mss by e-mail (straight text format preferred or MS Word).

Advice: "Read *NMJ*, then submit something you think I'll like."

◨ ▼ NORTHWEST REVIEW, 369 PLC, University of Oregon, Eugene OR 97403. (503)346-3957. Website: darkwing.uoregon.edu/~engl/deptinfo/NWR.html. **Editor:** John Witte. **Fiction Editor:** Janice MacCrae.
Magazine: 6×9; 140-160 pages; high quality cover stock; illustrations; photos. "A general literary review featuring poems, stories, essays and reviews, circulated nationally and internationally. For a literate audience in avant-garde as well as traditional literary forms; interested in the important writers who have not yet achieved their readership." Triannually. Estab. 1957. Circ. 1,200.

• *Northwest Review* has received the Oregon Governor's Award for the Arts. The work included in *Northwest Review* tends to be literary, heavy on character and theme.

Needs: Contemporary, experimental, feminist, literary and translations. Accepts 4-5 mss/issue, 12-15 mss/year. Receives approximately 100 unsolicited fiction mss each month. Published work by Diana Abu-Jaber, Madison Smartt Bell, Maria Flook and Charles Marvin. Published new writers within the last year. Length: "Mss longer than 40 pages are at a disadvantage." Also publishes literary essays, literary criticism, poetry. Critiques rejected mss when there is time. Sometimes recommends other markets.

How to Contact: Send complete ms with SASE. "No simultaneous submissions are considered." Reports in 3-4 months. Sample copy for $4. Reviews novels and short story collections. Send books to John Witte.

Payment/Terms: Pays 3 contributor's copies and one-year subscription; 40% discount on extras. Acquires first rights.

★ ✓ $ ◐ NORTHWOODS JOURNAL, A Magazine for Writers, Conservatory of American Letters, P.O. Box 298, Thomaston ME 04861. (207)354-0998. Fax: (207)354-8953. E-mail: cal@americanletters.org. Website: www.americanletters.org (includes guidelines and catalogue). Editor: R.W. Olmsted. **Fiction Editor:** Ken Sieben (submit fiction to Ken Sieben, 253 Ocean Ave., Sea Bright NJ 07760). Magazine: 5½×8½; 32-64 pages; white paper; 70 lb. text cover; offset printing; some illustrations and photographs. "No theme, no philosophy—for people who read for entertainment." Quarterly. Estab. 1993. Circ. 500.

Needs: Adventure, experimental, fantasy (science fantasy, sword and sorcery), literary, mainstream/contemporary, mystery/suspense (amateur sleuth, police procedural, private eye/hard-boiled, romantic suspense), psychic/supernatural/occult, regional, romance (gothic, historical), science fiction (hard science, soft/sociological), sports, westerns (frontier, traditional). Publishes special fiction issue or anthology. "Would like to see more first-person adventure." No porn or evangelical. Receives 40 unsolicited mss/month. Accepts 12-15 mss/year. Recently published work by Paul A. Jurvie, Richard Vaughn, Bryn C. Gray and Sandra Thompson. **Publishes 15 new writers/years.** Length: 2,500 words maximum. Also publishes literary essays, literary criticism and poetry.

How to Contact: *Charges $3 reading fee per 2,500 words.* Read guidelines *before* submitting. Send complete ms with a cover letter. Include word count and list of publications. There is a $3 fee per story (make checks payable to Ken Sieben. The magazine gets none of the reading fee). Reports in 1-2 days on queries; by next deadline plus 5 days on mss. Send SASE for reply, return of ms or send a disposable copy of ms. No simultaneous submissions. No electronic submissions. Sample copies: $5.50 next issue, $8.45 current issue, $12.50 back issue (if available), all postage paid. Fiction guidelines for #10 SASE. Reviews novels, short story collections and poetry.

Payment/Terms: Varies, "minimum $4/published page on acceptance for first North American serial rights."

Advice: "Read guidelines, read the things we've published. Know your market."

$ ◐ NOTRE DAME REVIEW, University of Notre Dame, English Department, Creative Writing, Notre Dame IN 46556. (219)631-6952. Fax: (219)631-4268. E-mail: english.ndreview.1@nd.edu. Website: www.nd. edu/~ndr/review.htm (includes guidelines, editors, additional poetry, fiction, book reviews, art, audio clips of authors and photos). **Editors:** William O'Rourke and John Matthias. Literary magazine: 6×9; 115 pages; 50 lb. smooth paper; illustrations and photographs. "The *Notre Dame Review* is an independent, non-commercial magazine of contemporary American and international fiction, poetry, criticism and art. We are especially interested in work that takes on big issues by making the invisible seen, that gives voice to the voiceless. In addition to showcasing celebrated authors like Seamus Heaney and Czelaw Milosz, the *Notre Dame Review* introduces readers to authors they may have never encountered before, but who are doing innovative and important work. In conjunction with the *Notre Dame Review*, the on-line companion to the printed magazine, the *Notre Dame Re-view* engages readers as a community centered in literary rather than commercial concerns, a community we reach out to through critique and commentary as well as aesthetic experience." Semiannually. Estab. 1995. Circ. 2,000.

Needs: "We're eclectic." No genre fiction. Upcoming theme issues planned. List of upcoming themes or editorial calendar available for SASE. Receives 75 unsolicited fiction mss/month. Accepts 4-5 mss/issue; 10 mss/year. Does not read mss May through August. Publishes ms 6 months after acceptance. Recently published work by Seamus Heaney, Denise Levertov and Czeslaw Milosz. **Publishes 2 new writers/year.** Length: 3,000 words maximum. Publishes short shorts. Also publishes literary criticism and poetry. Sometimes comments on rejected ms.

How to Contact: Send complete ms with cover letter. Include 4-sentence bio. Reports in 3-4 months. Send SASE for response, return of ms, or send a disposable copy of ms. Simultaneous submissions OK. Sample copy for $6.

Payment/Terms: Pays $5-25 and contributor's copies. Pays on publication. Acquires first North American serial rights.

Advice: "We're looking for high quality work that takes on big issues in a literary way. Please read our back issues before submitting."

$ ◉ NOW & THEN, Center for Appalachian Studies and Services, East Tennessee State University, Box 70556, Johnson City TN 37614-0556. Phone/fax: (423)439-5348. Website: www.cass.etsu.edu/n&t/guidelin.htm. **Contact:** Editor. Magazine: 8½×11; 36-52 pages; coated paper and cover stock; illustrations; photographs. Publication focuses on Appalachian culture, present and past. Readers are mostly people in the region involved with Appalachian issues, literature, education." Triannually. Estab. 1984. Circ. 1,250.

Needs: Ethnic, literary, regional, serialized/excerpted novel, prose poem. "Absolutely has to relate to Appalachian theme. Can be about adjustment to new environment, themes of leaving and returning, for instance. Nothing unrelated to region." Upcoming themes: "Appalachian Accents" (about language in Appalachia, Summer 2000, deadline March 1, 2000); "Appalachian Museums and Archives" (Winter 2000, deadline July 1, 2000). Buys 2-3 mss/issue. Publishes ms 3-4 months after acceptance. Published work by Lee Smith, Pinckney Benedict, Gurney Norman, George Ella Lyon; **published new writers within the last year.** Length: 3,000 words maximum. Publishes short shorts. Also publishes literary essays, poetry.

How to Contact: Send complete ms with cover letter. Reports in 3 months. Include "information we can use for contributor's note." SASE (or IRC). Simultaneous submissions OK, "but let us know when it has been accepted elsewhere right away." Sample copy for $5. Reviews novels and short story collections.

Payment/Terms: Pays up to $75 per story, contributor's copies.

Terms: Holds copyright.

Advice: "Keep in mind that *Now & Then* only publishes fiction related to the Appalachian region (all of West Virginia and parts of 12 other states from southern New York to northern Mississippi, Alabama and Georgia). Plus we only publish fiction that has some plausible connection to a specific issue's themes. Get the guidelines. We like to offer first-time publication to promising writers."

☑ $☑ OASIS, A Literary Magazine, P.O. Box 626, Largo FL 33779-0626. (727)449-2186. E-mail: oasislit@aol.com. Website: members.aol.com/wordthis/schvn.htm or www.litline.org/oasis/oasis.html (includes writer's guidelines, names of editors, short fiction). **Editor:** Neal Storrs. Magazine: 70 pages. "Literary magazine first, last and always—looking for styles that delight and amaze, that are polished and poised. Next to that, content considerations relatively unimportant—open to all." Quarterly. Estab. 1992. Circ. 500.

Needs: High-quality writing. Also publishes translations. Receives 150 unsolicited mss/month. Accepts 6 mss/issue; 24 mss/year. Publishes ms 4-6 months after acceptance. Recently published work by Wendell Mayo, Al Masarik and Mark Wisniewski. Publishes 2 new writers/year. Length: no minimum or maximum. Also publishes literary essays and poetry. Occasionally critiques or comments on rejected mss.

How to Contact: Send complete ms with or without a cover letter. Accepts queries/mss by e-mail. Usually reports same day. Send SASE for reply, return of ms or send a disposable copy of ms. Simultaneous, reprint and electronic (e-mail) submissions OK. Sample copy for $7.50. Fiction guidelines for #10 SASE.

Payment/Terms: Pays $15-30 and 1 contributor's copy on publication for first rights.

Advice: "If you want to write good stories, read good stories. Cultivate the critical ability to recognize what makes a story original and true to itself."

🌐 OASIS, Oasis Books, 12 Stevenage Rd., London SW6 6ES United Kingdom. **Editor:** Ian Robinson. Published 6 times/year. Circ. 400. Publishes usually 1 story/issue.

Needs: "Innovative, experimental fiction. No science fiction, fantasy, surreal. Wants non-standard, 'experimental' short stories." Recently published work by Eugenio de Andrade (Portugal), Sheila E. Murphy (USA), Henrikas Radauskas (Lithuania), D.F. Lewis (UK), Jay Woodman (S. Africa) and Neil Leadbeater (Scotland). Length: 1,800 words maximum.

Payment/Terms: Pays in copies. Sample copy available for $3.50 check (made payable to Robert Vas Dias) and 4 IRCs.

Advice: "Have a look at a copy of the magazine before submitting. We look for originality of thought and expression, and a willingness to take risks."

Ⓝ ✪ ◯ ◼ OF AGES PAST: The Online Magazine for Historical Fiction. E-mail: ofagespast@hotmail.com. Website: www.angelfire.com/il/ofagespast (includes writer's guidelines). **Editor:** Trace Edward Zaber. E-zine. "Magazine dedicated to the sorely-overlooked genre of historical fiction and promoting the hardworking authors of the genre." Monthly.

Needs: Historical, novel excerpts. "We require historical and historical only. The work can also include mystery, romance, suspense, etc., yet must include some historical content. Strictly contemporary pieces and poetry will not be considered." **Publishes 90-95% new writers.** Recently published work by Kinley MacGregor, Charlotte Boyett-Compo, Denise Dietz Wiley and Sherry-Anne Jacobs.

How to Contact: Send queries/mss by e-mail. "All submissions must be formatted according to the guidelines specified at the website." Reviews novels and short story collections.

Advice: "Follow the submission guidelines to the letter. Do not send any work that does not pertain to historical fiction. Also note that all work will be judged and edited according to our policies before it goes online. If major changes are needed, they will not be done without express written consent of the author. Minor changes will be applied according to editorial standards. The author, however, is allowed a 'preview' and approval of the work before it officially goes online. Unfortunately, due to the 'old corporate mentality' the print-publishing industry has grown stagnant. No one is willing to try anything new. The Internet, however, is the only place to play, to give authors the opportunity to gain publishing credits and hone their skills. Of Ages Past is only 6 months old, and already has been the winner of nearly 100 awards for design excellence, but more importantly for its uniqueness."

☑ $ ◎ **THE OHIO REVIEW**, 344 Scott Quad, Ohio University, Athens OH 45701-2979. (740)593-1900. Fax: (740)597-2967. **Editor:** Wayne Dodd. Magazine: 6×9; 200 pages; illustrations on cover. "We attempt to publish the best poetry and fiction written today. For a mainly literary audience." Semiannually. Estab. 1971. Circ. 3,000.
Needs: Contemporary, experimental, literary. "We lean toward contemporary on all subjects." Receives 150-200 unsolicited fiction mss/month. Accepts 5 mss/issue. Does not read mss June 1-September 15. Publishes ms 6 months after acceptance. Also publishes poetry. Sometimes critiques rejected mss and/or recommends other markets.
How to Contact: Query first or send complete ms with cover letter. Reports in 6 weeks. SASE. Sample copy for $6. Fiction guidelines for #10 SASE.
Payment/Terms: Pays $5/page, free subscription to magazine and 2 contributor's copies on publication for first North American serial rights. Sends galleys to author.
Advice: "We feel the short story is an important part of the contemporary writing field and value it highly. Read a copy of our publication to see if your fiction is of the same quality. So often people send us work that simply doesn't fit our needs."

☑ ◎ ◎ **OHIO TEACHERS WRITE**, Ohio Council of Teachers of English Language Arts, 1069 Edgewood Dr., Chillicothe OH 45601. (740)775-7494. Fax: (740)634-2890. E-mail: rmcclain@bright.net. **Editor:** Tom McCracken. Editors change every 2 years. Magazine: 8½×11; 50 pages; 60 lb. white offset paper; 65 lb. blue cover stock; illustrations and photos. "The purpose of the magazine is threefold: (1) to provide a collection of fine literature for the reading pleasure of teachers and other adult readers; (2) to encourage teachers to compose literary works along with their students; (3) to provide the literate citizens of Ohio a window into the world of educators not often seen by those outside the teaching profession." Annually. Estab. 1995. Circ. 1,000.
● Submissions are limited to Ohio educators.
Needs: Adventure, ethnic/multicultural, experimental, fantasy (science fantasy), feminist, gay, historical, humor/satire, lesbian, literary, mainstream/contemporary, regional, religious/inspirational, romance (contemporary), science fiction (hard science, soft/sociological), senior citizen/retirement, sports, westerns (frontier, traditional), teaching. Receives 2 unsolicited mss/month. Accepts 7 mss/issue. "We read only in May when editorial board meets." Publishes ms 3-4 months after acceptance. Published work by Lois Spencer, Harry R. Noden, Linda J. Rice and June Langford Berkley. Length: 2,000 words maximum. Publishes short shorts. Also publishes poetry. Often critiques or comments on rejected ms.
How to Contact: Send 6 copies of complete ms with a cover letter. Include 30-word bio. Reports by July 30th. Send SASE with postage clipped for return of ms or send a disposable copy of ms. Sample copy $6.
Payment/Terms: Pays 2 contributor's copies; additional copies $6. Acquires first rights.

Ⓝ ◎ 🌂 **OLD CROW REVIEW**, FKB Press, P.O.Box 403, Easthampton MA 01027-0403. **Editor:** John Gibney. Magazine: 5½×8½; 100 pages; 20 lb. paper; 90 lb. cover stock; illustrations and photos. Semiannually. Estab. 1991. Circ. 500.
● William Monahan's "Experiments in Vacuo" received a *Pushcart* Prize.
Needs: Erotica, experimental, literary, mainstream/contemporary, psychic/supernatural/occult, regional, translations. Receives 400-500 unsolicited mss/month. Accepts 3-5 mss/issue; 6-10 mss/year. Publishes ms 1-3 months after acceptance. Agented fiction 25%. Recently published work by Robert L. Mayne, Stephen Jones and Katherine Toy Miller. Length: 3,000 words average; 6,000 words maximum. Publishes short shorts. Also publishes literary essays, literary criticism and poetry.
How to Contact: Send complete ms with a cover letter. Should include estimated word count, bio (2-5 sentences) and list of publications. Reports in 1 month on queries; 2 months on mss. Send SASE for reply, return of ms or send a disposable copy of ms. Simultaneous and reprint submissions OK. Sample copy for $5; make check payable to Tawnya Kelley Tiskus. Fiction guidelines for #10 SASE.
Payment/Terms: Pays 1 contributor's copy; additional copies for $5.
Advice: "A piece must seem true to us. If it strikes us as a truth we never even suspected, we build an issue around it. Visions, or fragments of visions, of a new myth emerging at the millennial end are welcome. We haven't seen enough writers taking risks with their stories. Avoid sending pieces which sound just like somebody else's. Take the time to make a story tight and complete."

Ⓝ ◎ **OPEN SPACES QUARTERLY**, PMB 134, 6327 C SW Capitol Hwy., Portland OR 97201-1937. (503)227-5764. Fax: (503)227-3401. E-mail: info@open-spaces.com. Website: www.open-spaces.com (includes overview, contents of current and back issues, sample articles and creative writing, submission guidelines, contact information). Editor: Penny Harrison. **Fiction Editor:** A. Bradley. Magazine: 64 pages; illustrations and photos. "We are a high-quality, general-interest publication with an intelligent, well-educated readership appreciative of well-written, insightful work." Quarterly. Estab. 1997.
Needs: "Excellence is the issue—not subject matter." Accepts 2 mss/issue; 8 mss/year. Recently published work by William Kittredge, Terence O'Donnell, Pattiann Rogers and David James Duncan. Publishes short shorts. Also publishes literary essays and poetry. Sometimes critiques or comments on rejected mss.
How to Contact: Send complete ms with a cover letter. Accepts queries/mss by fax. Include short bio, social

security number and list of publications. SASE for return of ms or send a disposable copy of ms. Sample copy for $10. Fiction guidelines free for SASE.

Payment/Terms: Pays on publication.

Advice: "The surest way for a writer to determine whether his or her material is right for us is to read the magazine."

ORACLE STORY, Rising Star Publishers, 2105 Amherst Rd., Hyattsville MD 20783-2105. (301)422-2665. Fax: (301)422-2720. E-mail: ekwonna@aol.com. Editorial Director: Obi H. Ekwonna. **Senior Editor:** Sam Okere. Magazine: 5½×8½; 38 pages; white bond paper; 60 lb. Ibs cover. "Didactic well-made stories; basically adults and general public (mass market)." Quarterly. Estab. 1993. Circ. 500.

● *Oracle Story* is a member of the Association of African Writers. The editors are interested in all genres of fiction but with an African-cultural slant.

Needs: Condensed/excerpted novel, ethnic/multicultural, folklore (African), historical, horror, humor/satire, literary, mainstream/contemporary, mystery/suspense (romantic suspense), serialized novel, young adult/teen (horror and mystery). "No erotic, gay or lesbian writings." List of upcoming themes available for SASE. Publishes annual special fiction issue or anthology. Receives 60 unsolicited mss/month. Accepts 8 mss/issue; 26 mss/year. Publishes ms 6-12 months after acceptance. Recently published work by Joseph Manco. **Publishes 50 new writers/year.** Length: "not more than 20 typewritten pages." Publishes short shorts. Also publishes literary essays, literary criticism and poetry. Sometimes critiques or comments on rejected mss.

How to Contact: Send complete ms with a cover letter. Accepts queries/mss by fax. Include bio with SASE. Reports in 4-6 weeks. SASE for reply or return of ms. No simultaneous submissions. Electronic submissions OK (disks in WordPerfect 5.1, IBM readable format). Sample copy for $5 plus $1.50 postage. Fiction guidelines for SASE. Reviews novels and short story collections.

Payment/Terms: Pays contributor's copy. Acquires first North American seial rights.

Advice: Looks for work that is "well made, well written, and has good language. Take grammar classes." Especially interested in African folklore. "Manuscripts that come along with diskettes in WordPerfect are more likely to be given first priority."

OUTERBRIDGE, English 2S-218, The College of Staten Island (CUNY), 2800 Victory Blvd., Staten Island NY 10314. (718)982-3651. **Editor:** Charlotte Alexander. Magazine: 5½×8½; approximately 110 pages; 60 lb. white offset paper; 65 lb. cover stock. "We are a national literary magazine publishing mostly fiction and poetry. To date, we have had several special focus issues (the 'urban' and the 'rural' experience, 'Southern,' 'childhood,' 'nature and the environment,' 'animals,' 'love and friendship'). For anyone with enough interest in literature to look for writing of quality and writers on the contemporary scene who deserve attention. There probably is a growing circuit of writers, some academics, reading us by recommendations." Annually. Estab. 1975. Circ. 500-700.

Needs: Literary. "No *Reader's Digest* style; that is, very popularly oriented. We like to do interdisciplinary features, e.g., literature and music, literature and science and literature and the natural world." Accepts 8-10 mss/year. Does not read in July or August. Recently published work by Henry Alley, Gary Fricke, Max Ludwigton, Kyoko Yoshida and Cara Chamberlein. **Published new writers within the last year.** Length: 10-25 pages. Also publishes poetry. Sometimes recommends other markets.

How to Contact: Query. Send complete ms with cover letter. "Don't talk too much, 'explain' the work, or act apologetic or arrogant. If published, tell where, with a brief bio." SASE (or IRC). Reports in 8-10 weeks on queries and mss. No multiple submissions. Sample copy for $6 for annual issue.

Payment/Terms: Pays 2 contributor's copies. Charges ½ price of current issue for extras to its authors. Acquires one-time rights. Requests credits for further publication of material used by *OB*.

Advice: "Read our publication first. Don't send out blindly; get some idea of what the magazine might want. A *short* personal note with biography is appreciated. Competition is keen. Read an eclectic mix of classic and contemporary literature. Beware of untransformed autobiography, but *everything* in one's experience contributes."

THE OXFORD AMERICAN, The Southern Magazine of Good Writing, P.O. Box 1156, Oxford MS 38655. (601)236-1836. **Editor:** Marc Smirnoff. Magazine: 8½×11; 100 pages; glossy paper; glossy cover; illustrations and photos. Bimonthly. Estab. 1992. Circ. 25,000.

Needs: Regional (Southern); stories set in the South. Published work by Lewis Nordan, Julia Reed, Florence King and Tony Earley. Also publishes literary essays. Sometimes critiques or comments on rejected mss.

How to Contact: Send complete ms. Send SASE for reply, return of ms or send a disposable copy of ms. No simultaneous submissions. Sample copy for $4.50. "We review Southern novels or short story collections only."

Payment/Terms: Pays $100 minimum on publication for first rights; prices vary.

Advice: "I know you've heard it before—but we appreciate those writers who try to get into the spirit of the magazine which they can best accomplish by being familiar with it."

OXFORD MAGAZINE, Bachelor Hall, Miami University, Oxford OH 45056. (513)529-1954 or 529-5221. Editor: David Mitchell Goldberg. Editors change every year. **Send submissions to:** "Fiction Editor." Magazine: 6×9; 120 pages; illustrations. Annually. Estab. 1985. Circ. 1,000.

● *Oxford* has been awarded two Pushcart Prizes.

Needs: Literary, ethnic, experimental, humor/satire, feminist, gay/lesbian, translations. Receives 150 unsolicited mss/month. Reads mss September through January. Published work by Stephen Dixon, Andre Dubus and Stuart Dybek. **Published new writers within the last year.** Length: 2,000-4,000 words average. "We will accept long fiction (over 6,000 words) only in cases of exceptional quality." Publishes short shorts. Also publishes poetry.

How to Contact: Send complete ms with cover letter, which should include a short bio or interesting information. Simultaneous submissions OK, if notified. Reports in 1-2 months, depending upon time of submissions; mss received after January 31 will be returned. SASE. Sample copy for $5.

Payment/Terms: Pays in contributor's copies. Acquires one-time rights.

Advice: "*Oxford Magazine* is looking for humbly vivid fiction; that is to say, fiction that illuminates, which creates and inhabits an honest, carefully rendered reality populated by believable, three-dimensional characters. We want more stories—from undiscovered writers—that melt hair and offer the heat of a character at an emotional crossroads. Send us stories that are unique; we want fiction no one else but you could possibly have written."

★ ✓ ◐ ☿ ▣ **OYSTER BOY REVIEW OF FICTION AND POETRY**, P.O. Box 77842, San Francisco CA 94107-0842. E-mail: obr@levee67.com. Website: www.levee67.com (includes full contents of all issues; also related links). **Editor:** Damon Sauve. Electronic and print magazine. "An independent literary magazine of poetry and fiction published in North Carolina in print and electronic form. We're interested in the under-rated, the ignored, the misunderstood, and the varietal. We'll make some mistakes. The editors tend to select experimental and traditional narrative fiction. Our audience tends to be young, unpublished writers or writers of considerable talent who have published in the bigger little magazines but like the harder literary edge *Oyster Boy* promotes. We publish kick-ass, teeth-cracking stories."

● Work from *Oyster Boy* was selected for the *Pushcart Prize 1999* anthology.

Needs: "Fiction that revolves around characters in conflict with themselves or each other; a plot that has a beginning, a middle, and an end; a narrative with a strong moral center (not necessarily 'moralistic'); a story with a satisfying resolution to the conflict; and an ethereal something that contributes to the mystery of a question, but does not necessarily seek or contrive to answer it." No genre fiction. Recently published work by Michael Rumaker, Charlotte Morgan, Paul Dilsaver. **Publishes 20 new writers/year.**

How to Contact: Electronic and traditional submissions accepted. "E-mail submissions should be sent as the body-text of the e-mail message, or as an attached ASCII-text file.

Advice: "Keep writing, keep submitting, keep revising."

✓ ◐ **PACIFIC COAST JOURNAL**, French Bread Publications, P.O. Box 23868, San Jose CA 95153-3868. Website: www.bjt.net/~stgraham/pcj (includes guidelines, contest information, past published work). **Editor:** Stillson Graham. Fiction Editor: Stephanie Kylkis. Magazine: 5½×8½; 40 pages; 20 lb. paper; 67 lb. cover; illustrations; b&w photos. "Slight focus toward Western North America/Pacific Rim." Quarterly (or "whenever we have enough money"). Estab. 1992. Circ. 200.

Needs: Ethnic/multicultural, experimental, feminist, historical, humor/satire, literary, science fiction (soft/sociological, magical realism). Receives 30-40 unsolicited mss/month. Accepts 3-4 mss/issue; 10-12 mss/year. Publishes ms 6-18 months after acceptance. Recently published work by A.D. Winans, Joan Payne Kincaid and Errol Miller. **Publishes 3-5 new writers/year.** Length: 2,500 words preferred; 4,000 words maximum. Publishes short shorts. Also publishes literary essays and poetry. Sometimes critiques or comments on rejected mss. Sponsors contest. Send SASE for details.

How to Contact: Send complete ms with a cover letter. Include 3 other publication titles that are recommended as good for writers. Reports in 2-4 months. Send SASE for reply, return of ms or send a disposable copy of ms. Simultaneous, reprint and electronic submissions OK (Mac or IBM disks). Sample copy for $2.50, 6×9 SASE. Reviews novels and short story collections.

Payment/Terms: Pays 1 contributor's copy. Acquires one-time rights.

Advice: "We tend to comment more on a story not accepted for publication when an e-mail address is provided as the SASE. There are very few quality literary magazines that are not backed by big institutions. We don't have those kinds of resources so publishing anything is a struggle. We have to make each issue count."

◨ ◐ **PACIFIC ENTERPRISE, A Magazine for Enterprising Filipinos and Friends**, P.O. Box 1907, Fond du Lac WI 54936-1907. (920)922-9218. E-mail: rudyled@vbe.com. **Editor:** Rudy Ledesma. Magazine: 8½×11; 36-44 pages; 35 lb. stock newsprint paper; coated enamel cover; illustrations and photos. "*Pacific Enterprise* welcomes submissions of unpublished works from emerging and established writers. Although our primary audience is Filipino Americans, we welcome submissions from everyone. Our aim is to publish the best work we can find regardless of the author's country of origin." Triannually. Estab. 1998. Circ. 3,000-5,000.

Needs: Literary. "No fantasy, juvenile, western, romance, horror, science fiction." Receives about 10 unsolicited mss/month. Accepts 0-3 mss/issue; 6-9 mss/year. Publishes ms 6-12 months after acceptance. Recently published work by Val Vallejo and Holly Lalena Day. Length: 700 words minimum; 5,000 words maximum. Publishes short shorts. Length: 500 words. Also publishes literary essays, literary criticism, poetry. Sometimes critiques or comments on rejected mss.

How to Contact: Send complete ms with short bio. Accepts queries/mss by e-mail. Include estimated word count, 4-5 sentence bio and list of publications. Reports in 6 months "or longer." Send a disposable copy of ms. Simultaneous submissions OK. Sample copy for $4, 9×12 SAE and 3 first-class stamps. Fiction guidelines free. Reviews novels and short story collections. Send books to the editor at above address.

Payment/Terms: Pays 2 contributor's copies; additional copies $2.95 plus postage. Pays on publication. Acquires first North American serial rights. Sends galleys to author.

Advice: "We're looking for a strong command of language; something happening in the story; a story that surprises us. Request a sample copy and send in your work."

PACIFIC REVIEW, Dept. of English and Comparative Lit., San Diego State University, San Diego CA 92182-0295. **Editor-in-Chief:** Michael J. Grattan. Magazine: 6×9; 75-100 pages; book stock paper; paper back, extra heavy cover stock; b&w illustrations, b&w photos. "There is no designated theme. We publish high-quality fiction, poetry, and occasionally critical essays. The number of quality submissions determines the length of the issue. Generally, no more than three stories are published in each issue. Fiction is not used as filler." Annual. Estab. 1973. Circ. 1,000.

Needs: "We do not restrict or limit our fiction or poetry in any way other than quality. We are interested in all fiction, from the very traditional to the highly experimental. Acceptance is determined by the quality of submissions." Preference is given to experimental fiction. Published work by Derrick Pell and Gerald Butler. **Publishes 5-10 new writers/year.** Length: 4,000 words max. Publishes short shorts.

How to Contact: Send original ms with SASE or (preferably) ms with contact info on disc—MS Word format. Reports in 6 months on mss. Sample copy for $6.

Payment/Terms: 1 contributor's copy. "First serial rights are *Pacific Review*'s. All other rights revert to author."

Advice: "The current editor prefers experimental fiction that employs language in fresh, unique ways. Submissions that interrogate the issues of our age in light of technological advancement, mass media and the Internet in a thoughtful manner will gain special attention. We are looking for fiction that goes beyond the 'conventional' by examining the roles of men and women under the influence of twenty-first century hyper-media awareness and the displacement of morality."

PAINTED BRIDE QUARTERLY, Painted Bride Art Center, 230 Vine St., Philadelphia PA 19106. (215)925-9914. Website: www.libertynet.org/pbq~/. Fiction Editor: Kathy Volk-Miller. Literary magazine: 6×9; 96-100 pages; illustrations; photos. Quarterly. Estab. 1973. Circ. 1,000.

Needs: Contemporary, ethnic, experimental, feminist, gay, lesbian, literary, prose poem and translations. Published work by Lisa Borders, Jeannie Tietja, Kevin Miller, Mark LaMonda and Jennifer Moses. **Published new writers within the last year.** Length: 3,000 words average; 5,000 words maximum. Publishes short shorts. Also publishes literary essays, literary criticism, poetry. Occasionally critiques rejected mss.

How to Contact: Send complete ms. Reports in 6 months. SASE. Sample copy for $6. Reviews novels and short story collections. Send books to editor.

Payment/Terms: Pays $5/accepted piece and 1 contributor's copy, 1 year free subscription, 50% off additional copies. Acquires first North American serial rights.

Advice: Looks for "freshness of idea incorporated with high-quality writing. We receive an awful lot of nicely written work with worn-out plots. We want quality in whatever—we hold experimental work to as strict standards as anything else. Many of our readers write fiction; most of them enjoy a good reading. We hope to be an outlet for quality. A good story gives, first, enjoyment to the reader. We've seen a good many of them lately, and we've published the best of them."

PALO ALTO REVIEW, A Journal of Ideas, Palo Alto College, 1400 W. Villaret, San Antonio TX 78224. (210)921-5021. Fax: (210)921-5008. E-mail: eshull@accd.edu. **Editors:** Bob Richmond and Ellen Shull. Magazine: 8½×11; 60 pages; 60 lb. natural white paper (50% recycled); illustrations and photographs. "Not too experimental nor excessively avant-garde, just good stories (for fiction). Ideas are what we are after. We are interested in connecting the college and the community. We would hope that those who attempt these connections will choose startling topics and interesting angles with which to investigate the length and breadth of the teaching/learning spectrum, life itself." Semiannually (spring and fall). Estab. 1992. Circ. 500-600.

Needs: Adventure, ethnic/multicultural, experimental, fantasy, feminist, historical, humor/satire, literary, mainstream/contemporary, mystery/suspense, regional, romance, science fiction, translations, westerns. Upcoming themes: "Beginnings" (spring 2001). Upcoming themes available for SASE. Receives 100-150 unsolicited mss/month. Accepts 2-4 mss/issue; 4-8 mss/year. Does not read mss March-April and October-November when putting out each issue. Publishes ms 2-15 months after acceptance. Published work by Layle Silbert, Naomi Chase, Kenneth Emberly, C.J. Hannah, Tom Juvik, Kassie Fleisher and Paul Perry. **Publishes 30 new writers/year.** Length: 5,000 words maximum. Publishes short shorts. Also publishes articles, interviews, literary essays, literary criticism, poetry. Always critiques or comments on rejected mss.

How to Contact: Send complete ms with a cover letter. "Request sample copy and guidelines." Accepts queries by e-mail. Include brief bio and brief list of publications. Reports in 3-4 months. Send SASE for reply, return of ms or send a disposable copy of ms. Simultaneous and electronic (Macintosh disk) submissions OK. Sample copy for $5. Fiction guidelines for #10 SASE.

Payment/Terms: Pays 2 contributor's copies; additional copies for $5. Acquires first North American serial rights.

Advice: "Good short stories have interesting characters confronted by a dilemma working toward a solution. So often what we get is 'a moment in time,' not a story. Generally, characters are interesting because readers can identify with them. Edit judiciously. Cut out extraneous verbiage. Set up a choice that has to be made. Then create tension—who wants what and why they can't have it."

PANGOLIN PAPERS, Turtle Press, P.O. Box 241, Nordland WA 98358. (360)385-3626. **Editor:** Pat Britt. Magazine: 5½ × 8½; 120 pages; 24 lb. paper; 80 lb. cover. "Best quality literary fiction for an informed audience." Triannually. Estab. 1994. Circ. 500.

Needs: Condensed/excerpted novel, experimental, humor/satire, literary, translations. No "genre such as romance or science fiction." Plans to publish special fiction issues or anthologies in the future. Receives 20 unsolicited mss/month. Accepts 7-10 mss/issue; 20-30 mss/year. Publishes ms 4-12 months after acceptance. Agented fiction 10%. Published work by Jack Nisbet and Barry Gifford. **Publishes 3-4 new writers/year.** Length: 3,500 words average; 100 words minimum; 7,000 words maximum. Publishes short shorts. Length: 400 words. Also publishes literary essays. Sometimes critiques or comments on rejected mss.

How to Contact: Send complete ms with a cover letter. Include estimated word count and short bio. Reports in 2 weeks on queries; 2 months on mss. Send SASE for reply, return of ms or send a disposable copy of ms. No simultaneous submissions. Sample copy for $5 and $1.50 postage. Fiction guidelines for #10 SAE.

Payment/Terms: Pays 2 contributor's copies. Offers annual $200 prize for best story. Acquires first North American serial rights. Sometimes sends galleys to author.

Advice: "We are looking for original voices. Follow the rules and be honest in your work."

PAPERPLATES, a magazine for fifty readers,", Perkolator Kommunikation, 19 Kenwood Ave., Toronto, Ontario M6C 2R8 Canada. (416)651-2551. Fax: (416)651-2910. E-mail: paper@perkolator.com. Website: www.perkolater.com. **Editor:** Bernard Kelly. Electronic magazine. Published 2-3 times/year. Estab. 1990.

• *Paperplates* is now published entirely online.

Needs: Condensed/excerpted novel, ethnic/multicultural, feminist, gay, lesbian, literary, mainstream/contemporary, translations. "No science fiction, fantasy or horror." Receives 2-3 unsolicited mss/week. Accepts 2-3 mss/issue; 6-9 mss/year. Publishes ms 6-8 months after acceptance. Published work by Celia Lottridge, C.J. Lockett, Deirdre Kessler and Marvyne Jenoff. Length: 5,000 words average; 1,500 words minimum; 7,500 words maximum. Publishes short shorts. Also publishes literary essays, literary criticism and poetry.

How to Contact: Send complete ms with a cover letter. Reports in 6 weeks on queries; 3 months on mss. Send SASE for reply, return of ms or send a disposable copy of ms. Simultaneous submissions and electronic submissions OK. Fiction guidelines for #10 SASE.

Payment/Terms: Pays 2 contributor's copies on publication; additional copies for $5. Acquires first North American serial rights.

THE PARIS REVIEW, 45-39 171 Place, Flushing NY 11358 (*business office only, send mss to address below*). (212)861-0016. Fax: (212)861-4504. **Editor:** George A. Plimpton. Magazine: 5¼ × 8½; about 260 pages; illustrations and photographs (unsolicited artwork not accepted). "Fiction and poetry of superlative quality, whatever the genre, style or mode. Our contributors include prominent, as well as less well-known and previously unpublished writers. *The Art of Fiction, Art of Poetry, Art of Criticism* and *Art of Theater* interview series include important contemporary writers discussing their own work and the craft of writing." Quarterly.

Needs: Literary. Receives about 1,000 unsolicited fiction mss each month. Published work by Raymond Carver, Elizabeth Tallent, Rick Bass, John Koethe, Sharon Olds, Derek Walcott, Carolyn Kizer, Tess Gallagher, Peter Handke, Denis Johnson, Bobbie Ann Mason, Harold Brodkey, Joseph Brodsky, John Updike, Andre Dubus, Galway Kinnell, E.L. Doctorow and Philip Levine. **Published new writers within the last year.** No preferred length. Also publishes literary essays, poetry.

How to Contact: *Send complete ms with SASE to Fiction Editor, 541 E. 72nd St., New York NY 10021.* Reports in 6-8 months. Simultaneous submissions OK. Sample copy for $12. Writer's guidelines for #10 SASE (from Flushing office). Sponsors annual Aga Khan Fiction Contest award of $1,000.

Payment/Terms: Pays up to $1,000. Pays on publication for all rights. Sends galleys to author.

PARTING GIFTS, 3413 Wilshire, Greensboro NC 27408. E-mail: rbixby@aol.com. Website: users.aol.com/marchst (includes guidelines, samples, catalog, news, some artwork and a few java applets just for fun). **Editor:** Robert Bixby. Magazine: 5 × 7; 60 pages. "High-quality insightful fiction, very brief and on any theme." Semiannually. Estab. 1988.

Needs: "Brevity is the second most important criterion behind literary quality." Publishes ms within one year of acceptance. Published work by David Chorlton, Ben Miller, Deborah Bayer, Tessa Dratt, Mary Rohrer-Dann, Peter Markus and Ray Miller. Length: 250 words minimum; 1,000 words maximum. Also publishes poetry. Sometimes critiques rejected mss.

How to Contact: Send complete ms with cover letter. Simultaneous submissions OK. Reports in 1 day on queries; 1-7 days on mss. SASE.

Payment/Terms: Pays in contributor's copies. Acquires one-time rights.

Advice: "Read the works of Amy Hempel, Jim Harrison, Kelly Cherry, C.K. Williams and Janet Kauffman, all excellent writers who epitomize the writing *Parting Gifts* strives to promote. I need more than ever for my authors to be better read. I sense that many unaccepted writers have not put in the hours reading."

☒ ◯ PARTISAN REVIEW, 236 Bay State Rd., Boston MA 02215. (617)353-4260. E-mail: partisan@bu.e du. Website: www.webdelsol.com/Partisan_Review. Editor-in-Chief: William Phillips. **Editor:** Edith Kurzweil. Magazine: 6×9; 160 pages; 40 lb. paper; 60 lb. cover stock. "Theme is of world literature and contemporary culture: fiction, essays and poetry with emphasis on the arts and political and social commentary, for the general intellectual public and scholars." Quarterly. Estab. 1934. Circ. 8,000.

Needs: Contemporary, experimental, literary, prose poem, regional and translations. Receives 100 unsolicited fiction mss/month. Buys 1-2 mss/issue; 4-8 mss/year. Recently published work by Leonard Michaels, Janko Polic Kamov and Doris Lessing. **Published new writers within the last year.** Length: open.

How to Contact: Send complete ms with SASE and cover letter listing past credits. No simultaneous submissions. Reports in 4 months on mss. Sample copy for $6 and $1.50 postage.

Payment/Terms: Pays $25-200 and 1 contributor's copy. Pays on publication for first rights.

Advice: "Please, research the type of fiction we publish. Often we receive manuscripts which are entirely inappropriate for our journal. Sample copies are available for sale and this is a good way to determine audience."

◐ ◎ PASSAGER, A Journal of Remembrance and Discovery, University of Baltimore, 1420 N. Charles St., Baltimore MD 21201-5779. **Editors:** Kendra Kopelke and Mary Azrael. Magazine: 8¼ square; 32 pages; 70 lb. paper; 80 lb. cover; photographs. "We publish stories, poems, interviews with featured authors. One of our missions is to provide exposure for new older writers." Quarterly. Estab. 1990. Circ. 750.

Needs: "Special interest in discovering new older writers, but publishes all ages." Receives 200 unsolicited mss/month. Accepts 2-3 prose mss/issue; 8-12/year. "Publishes contest issues and theme issues." Does not read mss June through August. Publishes ms up to 18 months after acceptance. Length: 250 words minimum; 4,000 words maximum. Publishes short shorts. Also publishes poetry.

How to Contact: Sample copy for $4. "Send for fiction guidelines before submitting work with #10 SASE."

Payment/Terms: Pays subscription to magazine and 2 contributor's copies. Acquires first North American serial rights. Sometimes sends galleys to author.

Advice: "*Get a copy* so you can see the quality of the work we use. We seek powerful images of remembrance and discovery from writers of all ages. No stereotyped images of older people—we are interested in promoting complex images of aging that reveal the imagination and character of this stage of life."

✓ ◯ ♈ THE PATERSON LITERARY REVIEW, Passaic County Community College, One College Blvd., Paterson NJ 07505. (973)684-6555. Fax: (973)684-5843. E-mail: mgillan@pccc.cc.nj.us. **Editor:** Maria Mazziotti Gillan. Magazine: 6×9; 336 pages; 60 lb. paper; 70 lb. cover; illustrations; photos. Annually.

● Work from *PLR* has been anthologized in the *Pushcart Prize* anthology.

Needs: Contemporary, ethnic, literary. "We are interested in quality short stories, with no taboos on subject matter." Receives about 60 unsolicited mss/month. Publishes ms about 6 months to 1 year after acceptance. **Publishes 5% new writers.** Recently published work by Robert Mooney. Length: 1,500 maximum. Also publishes literary essays, literary criticism, poetry.

How to Contact: Submit no more than 1 story at a time. Submission deadline: March 1. Send SASE for reply or return of ms. "Indicate whether you want story returned." Simultaneous submissions OK. Sample copy for $12. Reviews novels and short story collections.

Payment/Terms: Pays in contributor's copies. Acquires first North American rights.

Advice: Looks for "clear, moving and specific work."

◯ ◎ PEARL, A Literary Magazine, Pearl, 3030 E. Second St., Long Beach CA 90803-5163. (562)434-4523. E-mail: mjohn5150@aol.com. **Editors:** Joan Jobe Smith, Marilyn Johnson and Barbara Hauk. Magazine: 5½×8½; 96 pages; 60 lb. recycled, acid-free paper; perfect-bound; coated cover; b&w drawings and graphics. "We are primarily a poetry magazine, but we do publish some *very short* fiction and nonfiction. We are interested in lively, readable prose that speaks to *real* people in direct, living language; for a general literary audience." Biannually. Estab. 1974. Circ. 600.

Needs: Contemporary, humor/satire, literary, mainstream, prose poem. "We will only consider short-short stories up to 1,200 words. Longer stories (up to 4,000 words) may only be submitted to our short story contest. All contest entries are considered for publication. Although we have no taboos stylistically or subject-wise, obscure, predictable, sentimental, or cliché-ridden stories are a turn-off." Publishes an all fiction issue each year. Receives 10-20 unsolicited mss/month. Accepts 1-10 mss/issue; 12-15 mss/year. Submissions accepted September-May *only*. Publishes ms 6 months to 1 year after acceptance. Recently published work by Gina Ochsner, Helena Maria Viramontes, Stephanie Dickinson, Lisa Glatt, Gerald Locklin and Dave Newman. **Publishes 1-5 new writers/**

year. Length: 1,000 words average; 500 words minimum; 1,200 words maximum. Also publishes poetry. Sponsors an annual short story contest. Send SASE for complete guidelines.

How to Contact: Send ms with cover letter including publishing credits and brief bio. Simultaneous submissions OK. Reports in 6-8 weeks on mss. SASE. Sample copy for $7 (postpaid). Fiction guidelines for #10 SASE.

Payment/Terms: Pays 2 contributor's copies. Acquires first North American serial rights. Sends galleys to author.

Advice: "We look for vivid, *dramatized* situations and characters, stories written in an original 'voice,' that make sense and follow a clear narrative line. What makes a manuscript stand out is more elusive, though—more to do with feeling and imagination than anything else . . ."

THE PEGASUS REVIEW, P.O. Box 88, Henderson MD 21640-0088. (410)482-6736. **Editor:** Art Bounds. Magazine: 5½ × 8½; 6-8 pages; illustrations. "*The Pegasus Review* is a bimonthly, done in a calligraphic format and occasionally illustrated. Each issue is based on a specific theme." Estab. 1980. Circ. 120.

• Because *The Pegasus Review* is done in calligraphy, fiction submissions must be very short. Two pages, says the editor, are the ideal length.

Needs: Humor/satire, literary, prose poem and religious/inspirational. Wants more short-shorts and theme-related fiction. Upcoming themes: "Music" (March/April); "Books & Reading" (May/June); "Theater" (July/August); "Memories" (September/October); "Faith" (November/December). Receives 35 unsolicited mss/month. Accepts "about" 50 mss/year. "Try to approach themes in various ways, rather than the traditional manner. Themes may be approached by means of poetry, short short fiction or essays . . . even an appropriate cartoon." Recently published work by Frederick Foote, Mildred Kadison, Judi Rypma and Patrick Flavin. **Publishes 10 new writers/ year.** Publishes short shorts of 2-3 pages; 500 words. Themes are subject to change, so query if in doubt. "Occasional critiques."

How to Contact: Send complete ms. SASE "a must." Brief cover letter with author's background, name and prior credits, if any. Simultaneous submissions acceptable, if so advised. Reports in 1-2 months. Sample copy for $2.50. Fiction guidelines for SAE. Subscription: $12/year.

Payment/Terms: Pays 2 contributor's copies. Occasional book awards. Acquires one-time rights.

Advice: "Study various writing publications. Pay strict attention to indicated guidelines. They serve a definite purpose. Join a local writers' group, especially one that does critiquing. Above all, don't be afraid of rewriting: it comes with the craft. Circulate your work and keep it circulating. Our publication is open to novice and professional writers alike."

PEMBROKE MAGAZINE, Box 1510, University of North Carolina at Pembroke, Pembroke NC 28372. (910)521-6358. Editor: Shelby Stephenson. **Managing Editor:** Fran Oxendine. Magazine: 6 × 9; approximately 200 pages; illustrations; photos. Magazine of poems and stories plus literary essays. Annually. Estab. 1969. Circ. 500.

Needs: Open. Receives 120 unsolicited mss/month. Publishes short shorts. Published work by Fred Chappell, Robert Morgan. **Published new writers within the last year.** Length: open. Occasionally critiques rejected mss and recommends other markets.

How to Contact: Send complete ms. No simultaneous submissions. Reports in up to 3 months. SASE. Sample copy for $8 and 9 × 10 SAE.

Payment/Terms: Pays 1 contributor's copy.

Advice: "Write with an end for *writing*, not publication."

PENNSYLVANIA ENGLISH, Penn State DuBois, College Place, DuBois PA 15801. (814)375-4814. Fax: (814)375-4784. E-mail: ajv2@psu.edu. **Editor:** Antonio Vallone. Magazine: 5½ × 8½; up to 180 pages; perfect bound; full color cover featuring the artwork of a Pennsylvania artist. "Our philosophy is quality. We publish literary fiction (and poetry and nonfiction). Our intended audience is literate, college-educated people." Annually. Estab. 1985. Circ. 300.

Needs: Literary, contemporary mainstream. No genre fiction or romance. Publishes ms within 12 months after acceptance. Recently published work by Dave Kress, Dan Leone and Paul West. **Publishes 1-2 new writers/ year.** Length: "no maximum or minimum." Publishes short shorts. Also publishes literary essays, literary criticism, poetry. Sometimes critiques rejected mss.

How to Contact: Send complete ms with cover letter. Reports in 2 months. SASE. Simultaneous submissions OK.

Payment/Terms: Pays in 3 contributor's copies. Acquires first North American serial rights.

Advice: "Quality of the writing is our only measure. We're not impressed by long-winded cover letters or résumés detailing awards and publications we've never heard of. Beginners and professionals have the same chance with us. We receive stacks of competently written but boring fiction. For a story to rise out of the rejection pile, it takes more than basic competence."

PEREGRINE, The Journal of Amherst Writers & Artists Press, AWA Press, P.O. Box 1076, Amherst MA 01004-1076. (413)253-7764. Fax: (413)253-7764. Website: www.javanet.com/~awapress. **Managing Edi-**

tor: Nancy Rose. Magazine: 6×9; 120 pages; 60 lb. white offset paper; glossy cover. "*Peregrine* has provided a forum for national and international writers for 18 years, and is committed to finding excellent work by new writers as well as established authors. We publish what we love, knowing that all editorial decisions are subjective, and that all work has a home somewhere." Annually.

Needs: Poetry and prose—short stories, short short stories, personal essays. No previously published work. No children's stories. Publishes 2 pages in each issue of work in translation. "We welcome work reflecting diversity of voice." Accepts 6-12 fiction mss/issue. Publishes ms an average of 4 months after acceptance. Recently published work by Roderick Townley, Catherine Strisik, George Kalamaras, Lisa Williams Kline and Bill Brown. **Published new writers within the last year.** "We like to be surprised. We look for writing that is honest, unpretentious, and memorable." Length: 3,000 words maximum. Short pieces have a better chance of publication. *Peregrine* sponsors an annual contest (The *Peregrine* Prize) and awards $500 each for fiction and poetry, and $100 "Best of the Nest" awarded to a local author.

How to Contact: Send #10 SASE to "Peregrine Guidelines" or visit website for writer's guidelines. Send ms with cover letter; include 40-word biographical note, prior publications and word count. Simultaneous submissions OK. Enclose sufficiently stamped SASE for return of ms; if disposable copy, enclose #10 SASE for response. Deadline for submission: April 1, 2000. Read October-April. Sample copy $8.

Payment/Terms: Pays contributor's copies. All rights return to writer upon publication.

Advice: "We look for heart and soul as well as technical expertise. Trust your own voice. Familiarize yourself with *Peregrine*." Every ms is read by three or more readers.

☑ **PHOEBE, An Interdisciplinary Journal of Feminist Scholarship**, Theory and Aesthetics, Women's Studies Department, State University of New York, College at Oneonta, Oneonta NY 13820-4015. (607)436-2014. Fax: (607)436-2656. E-mail: omarakk@oneonta.edu. **Editor:** Kathleen O'Mara. Journal: 7×9; 140 pages; 80 lb. paper; illustrations and photos. "Feminist material for feminist scholars and readers." Semiannually. Estab. 1989. Circ. 400.

● Editor would like to see more experimental fiction.

Needs: Feminist: ethnic, experimental, gay, humor/satire, lesbian, literary, translations. Receives 25 unsolicited mss/month. "One-third to one-half of each issue is short fiction and poetry." Does not read mss in summer. Publishes ms 3-4 months after acceptance. Published work by Elaine Hatfield, Betty A. Wilder, Jenny Potts, Kristan Ruona and Sylvia Van Nooten. **Publishes 4-6 new writers/year.** Length: 1,500-2,500 words preferred. Publishes short shorts. Sometimes critiques rejected mss and recommends other markets.

How to Contact: Send complete ms with cover letter. Reports in 1 month on queries; 15 weeks on mss. Electronic (WordPerfect/Microsoft Word disk, e-mail) submissions OK. Sample copy for $7.50. Fiction guidelines free.

Payment/Terms: Pays in contributor's copies. Acquires one-time rights.

Advice: "We look for writing with a feminist perspective. *Phoebe* was founded to provide a forum for cross-cultural feminist analysis, debate and exchange. The editors are committed to providing space for all disciplines and new areas of research, criticism and theory in feminist scholarship and aesthetics. *Phoebe* is not committed to any one conception of feminism. All work that is not sexist, racist, homophobic, or otherwise discriminatory, will be welcome. *Phoebe* is particularly committed to publishing work informed by a theoretical perspective which will enrich critical thinking."

N ◑ **PIEDMONT LITERARY REVIEW**, 25 W. Dale Dr., Lynchburg VA 24501. (804)385-8775. **Fiction Editor:** Olga Kronmeyer. Poetry Editor: Vito Victor. Magazine: 5½×8; 42 pages; 20 lb. bond paper; 65 lb. card stock cover. "Primarily a poetry journal, we include in each issue a prose/fiction piece." Quarterly. Estab. 1976. Circ. 240.

Needs: Humor/satire, literary, mainstream/contemporary. No erotica, experimental, juvenile, sci-fi. Receives 10-15 unsolicited mss/month. Accepts 1 ms/issue; 4 mss/year. Publishes ms 3 months after acceptance. Recently published work by Mary Chandler, Walter R. Smith and Paul F. Wolf. Length: 2,200 words average; 1,000 words minimum; 2,500 words maximum. Also publishes essays, articles, literary criticism, poetry. Sometimes critiques or comments on rejected mss.

How to Contact: Send complete ms with a short cover letter. Include estimated word count. Reports in 1 month on queries; 3 months on mss. SASE for reply, return of ms or send a disposable copy of ms. Simultaneous submissions OK if prompt notice is given of acceptance elsewhere. Sample copy for $4 domestic and Canada. Fiction guidelines free for #10 SASE.

Payment/Terms: Pays 1 contributor's copy on publication; additional copies for $3 pre-publication or $4 post-publication. Acquires first North American serial rights. Rights revert to author at publication.

Advice: "Stay within our 2,500 word limit, work on consistent character development and plot, come to satisfactory natural end."

$ ◑ **PIG IRON PRESS**, Box 237, Youngstown OH 44501. (330)747-6932. Fax: (330)747-0599. **Editor:** Jim Villani. Annual series: 8½×11; 144 pages; 60 lb. offset paper; 85 pt. coated cover stock; b&w illustrations; b&w 120 line photographs. "Contemporary literature by new and experimental writers." Annually. Estab. 1975. Circ. 1,000.

Needs: Literary and thematic. No mainstream. Accepts 60-70 mss/issue. Receives approximately 75-100 unsolicited mss/month. Published work by Judith Hemschemeyer, Andrena Zawinski, Gary Fincke and Rebecca Orr. Length: 8,000 words maximum. Also publishes literary nonfiction, poetry. Sponsors contest. Send SASE for details.

How to Contact: Send complete ms with SASE. No simultaneous submissions. Reports in 4 months. Sample copy for $5.

Payment/Terms: Pays $5/printed page and 2 contributor's copies on publication for first North American serial rights; $5 charge for extras.

Advice: "Looking for work that is polished, compelling and magical."

$ PLANET-THE WELSH INTERNATIONALIST, P.O. Box 44, Aberystwyth, Ceredigion, SY23 3ZZ Cymru/ Wales UK. Phone: 01970-611255. Fax: 01970-611197. **Fiction Editor:** John Barnie. Bimonthly. Circ. 1,400. Publishes 1-2 stories/issue.

Needs: "A literary/cultural/political journal centered on Welsh affairs but with a strong interest in minority cultures in Europe and elsewhere." Recently published work by Arthur Winfield Knight, Roger Granelli, Sian James, Jan Morris and Guy Vanderhaeghe. Length: 1,500-4,000 words maximum.

How to Contact: No submissions returned unless accompanied by an SAE. Writers submitting from abroad should send at least 3 IRCs for return of typescript; 1 IRC for reply only.

Payment/Terms: Writers receive 1 contributor's copy. Payment is at the rate of £40 per 1,000 words for prose; a minimum of £25 per poem (in the currency of the relevant country if the author lives outside the UK). Sample copy: cost (to USA & Canada) £2.87. Writers' guidelines for SAE.

Advice: "We do not look for fiction which necessarily has a 'Welsh' connection, which some writers assume from our title. We try to publish a broad range of fiction and our main criterion is quality. Try to read copies of any magazine you submit to. Don't write out of the blue to a magazine which might be completely inappropriate to your work. Recognize that you are likely to have a high rejection rate, as magazines tend to favor writers from their own countries."

THE PLAZA, A Space for Global Human Relations, U-Kan Inc., Yoyogi 2-32-1, Shibuya-ku, Tokyo 151-0053, Japan. Tel: +81-(3)-3379-3881. Fax: +81-(3)-3379-3882. E-mail: plaza@u-kan.co.jp. Website: u-kan.co.jp (includes contribution guide, contents of the current and back issues, representative works by *The Plaza* writers). Editor: Leo Shunji Nishida. **Fiction Editor:** Roger Lakhani. "*The Plaza* is an intercultural and bilingual magazine (English and Japanese). Our focus is the 'essence of being human.' All works are published in both Japanese and English (translations by our staff if necessary). The most important criteria is artistic level. We look for works that reflect simply 'being human.' Stories on intercultural (not international) relations are desired. *The Plaza* is devoted to offering a spiritual *Plaza* where people around the world can share their creative work. We introduce contemporary writers and artists as our generation's contribution to the continuing human heritage." Quarterly. Circ. 3,000.

Needs: Length: Less than 1,000 words, minimalist short stories are welcomed. Wants to see more fiction "of not human beings, but being human. Of not international, but intercultural. Of not social, but human relationships." No political themes: religious evangelism; social commentary. Publishes about 2 stories/issue. Recently published work by Michael Hoffman, Bun'ichirou Chino and Isabel Wendell. **Publishes 3 new writers/year.**

How to Contact: Send complete ms with cover letter. Sample copy and guidelines free. Accepts queries/mss by e-mail and fax. "The most important consideration is that which makes the writer motivated to write. If it is not moral but human, or if it is neither a wide knowledge nor a large computer-like memory, but rather a deep thinking like the quietness in the forest, it is acceptable. While the traditional culture of reading of some thousands of years may be destined to be extinct under the marvellous progress of civilization, *The Plaza* intends to present contemporary works as our global human heritage to readers of forthcoming generations."

$ PLEIADES, Department of English & Philosophy, Central Missouri State University, Martin 336, Warrensburg MO 64093. (660)543-4425. Fax: (660)543-8544. E-mail: rmk8708@cmsu2.cmsu.edu. Website: www.cmsu.edu/academics/arts&sciences/Engl/Phil/Pleiades (includes guidelines, editors, sample poetry or prose). **Executive & Fiction Editor:** R.M. Kinder. Poetry: Kevin Prufer. Magazine: 5½×8½; 120 pages; 60 lb. paper; perfect-bound; 8 pt. color cover. Sponsored in part by Missouri Arts Council. "*Pleiades* emphasizes cultural diversity, publishes poetry, fiction, essays, occasional drama, interviews and reviews for a general educated audience." Semiannually. Estab. 1939. Circ. 2,000.

● A work appearing in *Pleiades* won the Stanley Hawks Memorial Prize, sponsored by the St. Louis Poetry Center.

Needs: Ethnic/multicultural, experimental, especially cross-genre, feminist, gay, humor/satire, literary, mainstream/contemporary, regional, translations. "No westerns, romance, mystery, etc. Nothing pretentious, didactic or overly sentimental." Receives 100 unsolicited mss/month. Accepts 8 mss/issue; 16 mss/year. "We're slower at reading manuscripts in the summer." Publishes ms 6-12 months after acceptance. Recently published work by Jim Sanderson, Kay Sloan and Sandra Spatt Olsen. Length: 3,000-6,000 words average; 800 words minimum; 8,000 words maximum. Also publishes literary essays, literary criticism and poetry. Sometimes critiques or comments on rejected mss.

How to Contact: Send complete ms with a cover letter. Accepts queries by e-mail. Include 75-100 bio, Social Security number and list of publications. Reports in 3 weeks on queries; 4 months on mss. Send SASE for reply, return of ms or send a disposable copy of ms. Simultaneous submissions OK. Sample copy (including guidelines) for $6.

Payment/Terms: Pays $10 or subscription and 1 contributor's copy on publication. Acquires first North American serial rights.

Advice: Looks for "a blend of language and subject matter that entices from beginning to end. Send us your best work. Don't send us formula stories. While we appreciate and publish well-crafted traditional pieces, we constantly seek the story that risks, that breaks form and expectations and wins us over anyhow."

$ **PLOUGHSHARES**, Emerson College, 100 Beacon St., Boston MA 02116. (617)824-8753. Website: www.emerson.edu/ploughshares. **Editor:** Don Lee. "Our mission is to present dynamic, contrasting views on what is valid and important in contemporary literature, and to discover and advance significant literary talent. Each issue is guest-edited by a different writer. We no longer structure issues around preconceived themes." Triquarterly. Estab. 1971. Circ. 6,000.

● Work published in *Ploughshares* has been selected continuously for inclusion in the *Best American Short Stories* and *O. Henry Prize* anthologies. In fact the magazine has the honor of having the most stories selected from a single issue (three) to be included in *B.A.S.S.* Guest editors have included Richard Ford, Tim O'Brien and Ann Beattie. *Ploughshares* ranked #22 on *Writer's Digest*'s Fiction 50 list of top markets for fiction writers.

Needs: Literary. "No genre (science fiction, detective, gothic, adventure, etc.), popular formula or commercial fiction whose purpose is to entertain rather than to illuminate." Buys 30 mss/year. Receives 1,000 unsolicited fiction mss each month. Published work by Rick Bass, Joy Williams and Andre Dubus. **Published new writers within the last year.** Length: 300-6,000 words.

How to Contact: Reading period: postmarked August 1 to March 31. Cover letter should include "previous pubs." SASE. Reports in 3-5 months on mss. Sample copy for $8. (Please specify fiction issue sample.) Current issue for $9.95. Fiction guidelines for #10 SASE.

Payment/Terms: Pays $25/page, $50 minimum per title; $250 maximum, plus copies and a subscription on publication for first North American serial rights. Offers 50% kill fee for assigned ms not published.

Advice: "Be familiar with our fiction issues, fiction by our writers and by our various editors (e.g., Sue Miller, Tobias Wolff, Rosellen Brown, Richard Ford, Jayne Anne Phillips, James Alan McPherson) and more generally acquaint yourself with the best short fiction currently appearing in the literary quarterlies, and the annual prize anthologies (*Pushcart Prize, O. Henry Awards, Best American Short Stories*). Also realistically consider whether the work you are submitting is as good as or better than—in your own opinion—the work appearing in the magazine you're sending to. What is the level of competition? And what is its volume? Never send 'blindly' to a magazine, or without carefully weighing your prospect there against those elsewhere. Always keep a log and a copy of the work you submit."

THE PLOWMAN, Box 414, Whitby, Ontario L1N 5S4 Canada. **Editor:** Tony Scavetta. Tabloid: 20 pages; illustrations and photos. "An international journal publishing all holocaust, religion, didactic, ethnic, eclectic, love and other stories." Quarterly. Estab. 1988. Circ. 10,000.

Needs: No science fiction. Published work by B. Fleming, P. Larty, B. Lilley, B. McCann Jr., Y. Nair and D. Garza. **Publishes 50 new writers/year.** Length: 7,000 words maximum.

How to Contact: Send complete ms with cover letter. Reports in 1 week. Simultaneous and reprint submissions OK. Sample copy and fiction guidelines for SAE.

Payment/Terms: Pays in contributor's copies; charges for extras. Acquires one-time rights. Sends galleys to author.

Advice: "No satanic or rude language." Looks for "detail, excellent English and language as well as quality. Be patient and submit to different publishers."

POETIC SPACE, A Magazine of Poetry & Fiction, Poetic Space Press, P.O. Box 11157, Eugene OR 97440. E-mail: poeticspac@aol.com. Editor: Don Hildenbrand. **Fiction Editor:** Thomas Strand. Magazine: 8½×11; 32 pages; bond paper; heavy cover; b&w art. "Social, political, avant-garde, erotic, environmental material for a literary audience." Biannually (summer and winter). Estab. 1983. Circ. 600.

Needs: Erotica, ethnic, experimental, feminist, gay, lesbian, literary. Wants more contemporary, realistic and fantastic fiction. No sentimental, romance, mainstream. Receives about 20 unsolicited mss/month. Accepts 3-4 mss/issue; 8-10 mss/year. Publishes ms 6 months after acceptance. Recently published work by A.W. DeAnnuntis, Mitch Grabois and Seamus O'Bannion. **Publishes 25% of new writers.** Length: 10 double-spaced pages. Publishes short shorts. Also publishes literary essays, literary criticism, poetry. Often critiques rejected mss and recommends other markets.

How to Contact: Send complete ms with cover letter that includes estimated word count, short bio and list of publications. Queries/mss by e-mail OK. Reports in 1 week on queries; 2 months on mss. SASE. Simultaneous, reprint and electronic submissions OK. Sample copy for $3, 4×9 SAE and 45¢ postage. Fiction guidelines for

#10 SAE and 1 first-class stamp (or IRC). Reviews novels and short story collections. Send books to Don Hildenbrand.

Payment/Terms: Pays 1 contributor's copy. Acquires one-time rights or "reserves anthology rights."

Advice: Looks for "originality, risk taking and quality writing. Work hard every day, read contemporary fiction and experience life!"

POETRY FORUM SHORT STORIES, Poetry Forum, 5713 Larchmont Dr., Erie PA 16509. Phone/fax: (814)866-2543 (fax hours 8-10 a.m., 5-8 p.m.). E-mail: 75562.670@compuserve.com. **Editor:** Gunvor Skogsholm. Newspaper: 7×8½; 34 pages; card cover; illustrations. "Human interest themes (no sexually explicit or racially biased or blasphemous material) for the general public—from the grassroot to the intellectual." Quarterly. Estab. 1989. Circ. 400.

Needs: Confession, contemporary, ethnic, experimental, fantasy, feminist, historical, literary, mainstream, mystery/suspense, prose poem, religious/inspirational, romance, science fiction, senior citizen/retirement, young adult/teen. "No blasphemous, sexually explicit material." Publishes annual special fiction issue. Receives 50 unsolicited mss/month. Accepts 12 mss/issue; 40 mss/year. Publishes ms 6 months after acceptance. Agented fiction less than 1%. **Publishes 80% new writers.** Recently published work by Scott Fields and Frank Bland. Length: 2,000 words average; 500 words minimum; 5,000 words maximum. Also publishes literary essays, literary criticism, poetry.

How to Contact: *This magazine charges a "professional members" fee of $36 and prefers to work with subscribers.* The fee entitles you to publication of a maximum of 3,000 words. Send complete ms with cover letter. Accepts queries/mss by e-mail and fax. Reports in 3 weeks to 2 months on mss. SASE. Simultaneous and reprint submissions OK. "Accepts electronic submissions via disk gladly." Sample copy for $3. Fiction guidelines for SASE. Reviews novels and short story collections.

Payment/Terms: Preference given to submissions by subscribers. Acquires one-time rights.

Advice: "Tell your story with no padding as if telling it to a person standing with one hand on the door ready to run out to a meeting. Have a good lead. This is the 'alpha & omega' of all good story writing. Don't start with 'This is a story about a boy and a girl.' Avoid writing how life 'ought to be,' rather write how life is."

POET'S FANTASY, 227 Hatten Ave., Rice Lake WI 54868-2030. (715)236-3066. E-mail: stardome@chiba rdun.net. **Editor:** Gloria Stoeckel. Magazine: 8½×11; 44 pages; 20 lb. paper; colored stock cover; illustrations. *Poet's Fantasy* is a magazine of "fantasy, but not conclusive." Bimonthly. Estab. 1992. Circ. about 400.

Needs: Fantasy (science), literary. No stories about sex, love. "Wants to see more fantasy and science fiction." Receives 20-30 unsolicited mss/month. Accepts 60 mss/year. Recently published work by Michael C. Powell and Diana K. Rubin. Publishes "several hundred" new writers/year. Length: 1,000 words average; 500 words minimum; 1,500 words maximum. Publishes short shorts. Also publishes literary essays and poetry.

How to Contact: Send complete ms with a cover letter. Include estimated word count and list of publications. Accepts queries/mss by e-mail. Reports in 3 weeks. Send SASE for reply or return of ms. No simultaneous submissions. Sample copy for $5. Fiction guidelines free.

Payment/Terms: Pays $5 coupon on publication toward purchase of subscription for first North American serial rights. Subscribers are given preference.

Advice: "Fiction must include fantasy and have a surprise twist at the end." Wants fiction with "tight writing, action and ending twist. Edit and re-edit before sending."

THE POINTED CIRCLE, Portland Community College-Cascade, 705 N. Killingsworth St., Portland OR 97217. **Editors:** student editorial staff. Magazine: 80 pages; b&w illustrations and photographs. "Anything of interest to educationally/culturally mixed audience." Annually. Estab. 1980.

Needs: Contemporary, ethnic, literary, prose poem, regional. "We will read whatever is sent, but encourage writers to remember we are a quality literary/arts magazine intended to promote the arts in the community." Acquires 3-7 mss/year. Accepts submissions only December 1-February 15, for July 1 issue. Published work by Steve Slavin, Ernie Cooper and DC Palter. **Publishes several new writers/year.** Length: 3,000 words maximum.

How to Contact: Send complete ms with cover letter and brief bio, #10 SASE. "The editors consider all submissions without knowing the identities of the contributors, so please do not put your name on the works themselves." Sample copy for $4.50. Entry guidelines, send #10 SASE. Submitted materials will not be returned unless writer requests and provides SASE with adequate postage.

FOR EXPLANATIONS OF THESE SYMBOLS,
SEE THE INSIDE FRONT AND BACK COVERS OF THIS BOOK.

Payment/Terms: Pays 1 copy. Acquires one-time rights.

Advice: "Looks for quality—topicality—nothing trite. The author cares about language and acts responsibly toward the reader, honors the reader's investment of time and piques the reader's interest."

PORCUPINE LITERARY ARTS MAGAZINE, P.O. Box 259, Cedarburg WI 53012-0259. (414)375-3128. E-mail: ppine259@aol.com. Website: members.aol.com/ppine259 (includes writer's guidelines, cover art, subscription information, table of contents). Editor: W.A. Reed. **Fiction Editor:** Chris Skoczynski. Magazine: 5×8½; 100 pages; glossy color cover stock; illustrations and photos. Publishes "primarily poetry and short fiction. Novel excerpts are acceptable if self-contained. No restrictions as to theme or style." Semiannually. Estab. 1996. Circ. 1,500.

• *Porcupine Literary Arts Magazine* was named Best Literary/Arts Magazine by *Milwaukee Magazine* (1997).

Needs: Condensed/excerpted novel, ethnic/multicultural, literary, mainstream/contemporary. No pornographic or religious. Receives 10 unsolicited mss/month. Accepts 3 mss/issue; 6 mss/year. Publishes ms within 6 months of acceptance. Published work by Karen Sharp and Martha Highers. **Publishes 4-6 new writers/year.** Length: 3,500 words average; 2,000 words minimum; 7,500 words maximum. Publishes literary essays and poetry. Sometimes critiques or comments on rejected mss.

How to Contact: Send complete ms with a cover letter. Accepts queries/mss by e-mail. Include estimated word count, 5-line bio and list of publications. Reports in 2 weeks on queries; 2 months on mss. Send SASE for reply, return of ms or send a disposable copy of ms. No simultaneous submissions. Sample copy for $5. Fiction guidelines for #10 SASE.

Payment/Terms: Pays 1 contributor's copy on publication; additional copies for $8.95. Acquires one-time rights.

Advice: Looks for "believable dialogue and a narrator I can see and hear and smell. Form or join a writers' group. Read aloud. Rewrite extensively."

PORTLAND REVIEW, Portland State University, Box 347, Portland OR 97207-0347. (503)725-4533. Fax: (503)725-5860. E-mail: review@vanguard.vg.pdx.edu. Website: www.angelfire.com/in/portlandreview.com (includes writer's guidelines, e-mail and links to other journals). **Editor:** Barbara Mann. Magazine: 9×6; 200 pages; b&w drawings and photos. "We seek to publish fiction in which content takes precedence over style." Quarterly. Estab. 1955. Circ. 1,500.

• The editors say they are looking for experimental work "dealing with the human condition."

Needs: Adventure, ethnic/multicultural, experimental, fantasy (science), feminist, gay, historical, humor/satire, lesbian, literary, mainstream/contemporary, mystery/suspense, regional, science fiction. Wants more humor. Receives about 100 mss each month. Accepts 4-6 mss/issue; 25-30 mss/year. Also publishes critical essays, poetry, drama, interviews and reviews.

How to Contact: Submit complete ms with short bio. Accepts queries/mss by e-mail and fax. Manuscripts returned only if SASE is supplied. Simultaneous and electronic submissions OK (if noted). Reports in "several" months. Sample copy for $6 plus $1 postage.

Payment/Terms: Pays contributor's copies. Acquires one-time rights.

Advice: "Our editors, and thus our tastes/biases change annually, so keep trying us."

POSTCARD, P.O. Box 444, Tivoli NY 12583. (914)757-5484. **Editor:** Jenny Fowler. Magazine: 3×5; 10-20 pages; illustrations and photos. Published "whenever we can." Estab. 1995. Circ. 200.

Needs: "No long pieces." Length: 150 words average; 500 words maximum. Publishes short shorts. Also publishes poetry. Often critiques or comments on rejected mss.

How to Contact: Send complete ms with a cover letter. SASE for reply and return of ms. Simultaneous submissions and reprints OK. Sample copy for $1.50.

Payment/Terms: Pays 5 contributor's copies; additional copies $1. Acquires one-time rights.

POTOMAC REVIEW, The Quarterly with a Conscience—and a Lurking Sense of Humor, Potomac Review, Inc., P.O. Box 354, Port Tobacco MD 20677. (301)934-1412. E-mail: elilu@juno.com. Website: www.meral.com/potomac (includes editor's note, contents page, contact information, some sampling of stories, poems). **Editor:** Eli Flam. Magazine: 5½×8½; 128 pages; 50 lb. paper; 65 lb. cover; illustrations. *Potomac Review* "explores the topography and inner terrain of the Mid-Atlantic and beyond via a challenging diversity of prose, poetry and b&w artwork." Estab. 1994. Circ. 2,000.

Needs: Excerpted novel—"stories with a vivid, individual quality that get at 'the concealed side' of life. Regionally rooted, with a cross-cutting theme each issue (e.g., 'Twining Trails,' summer 1999); we also keep an eye on the wider world." No "overly experimental" fiction. Wants more "fiction that gets inside its characters." Upcoming themes (subject to change): "Up From the Underground Railroad" and "It's About Time." Receives 100 unsolicited mss/month, assigns some nonfiction pieces. Accepts 20-30 mss/issue of all sorts; 80-120 mss/year. Publishes ms within a year after acceptance as a rule. Agented fiction 5%. Recently published work by David B. Prather, Andrena Zawinski, Aleksandër Dardeli, Alvin Rosenbaum, Lee Smith and Ellen Dudley. **Publishes up to 24 new writers/year.** Length: 2,000 words average; 100 words minimum; 3,000 words maximum. Publishes short shorts. Length: 250 words. Also publishes poetry, essays and cogent, issue-oriented nonfiction. Humor is welcome.

How to Contact: Send complete ms with a cover letter. Include estimated word count, 2-3 sentence bio, list of publications and SASE. Reports in 2 weeks on queries; 2-3 months on mss. Send SASE for reply, return of ms or send a disposable copy of ms. Simultaneous and reprint submissions OK. Sample copy for $5. Submission guidelines for #10 SASE. Reviews novels, short story collections, other books.

Payment/Terms: Pays 1 or more contributor's copy; $75 for assigned nonfiction; additional copies for $3.

Advice: "Some kind of vision should be inherent in your writing, something to say *inter alia* about life in these or other times. Read all possible magazines that might take your work; work at your last, first and last, like an old-fashioned shoemaker, daily and with dedication. Learn, above all, to rewrite; and when to stop." Fiction selected must "educate, challenge and divert in fresh ways; have something to say, in an original voice; and convey ethical depth, and a corresponding vision."

POTPOURRI, P.O. Box 8278, Prairie Village KS 66208. (913)642-1503. Fax: (913)642-3128. E-mail: editor@potpourri.org. Website: Website: www.potpourri.com (includes guidelines, contents, reprints of fiction, author profiles). **Senior Editor:** Polly W. Swafford. Magazine: 8×11; 76 pages; glossy cover. "Literary magazine: short stories, verse, essays, travel, prose poetry for a general adult audience." Quarterly. Estab. 1989. Circ. 4,500.

Needs: Adventure, contemporary, ethnic, experimental, fantasy, historical (general), humor/satire, literary, mainstream, suspense, prose poem, romance (contemporary, historical, romantic suspense), science fiction (soft/sociological), western (frontier stories). "*Potpourri* accepts a broad genre; hence its name. Guidelines specify no religious, confessional, racial, political, erotic, abusive or sexual preference materials unless fictional and necessary to plot." Receives 75 unsolicited fiction mss/month. Accepts 10-12 fiction mss/issue; 60-80 prose mss/year. Publishes ms 10-12 months after acceptance. Agented fiction 1%. Recently published work by Walter Cummins, Deborah Shouse, Conger Beasley, Phil Choi and Judy Ray. **Publishes 2-3 new writers/year.** Length: 3,500 words maximum. Also publishes poetry and literary essays. Sometimes critiques rejected mss. *Potpourri* offers annual awards (of $100 each) for best of volume in fiction and poetry, more depending on grants received, and sponsors the Annual Council on National Literatures Award of $100 each for poetry and fiction on alternating years. "Manuscripts must celebrate our multicultural and/or historic background." Next fiction entry deadline: August 31, 2000. Reading fee: $5 per story. Send SASE for guidelines.

How to Contact: Send complete ms with cover letter. Accepts queries by e-mail and fax. Include "complete name, address, phone number, brief summary statement about submission, short author bio." Reports in 2-4 months. SASE. Simultaneous submissions OK when advised at time of submission. Sample copy for $4.95 with 9×12 envelope. Fiction guidelines for #10 SASE.

Payment/Terms: Pays contributor's copies. Acquires first rights.

Advice: "We look for well-crafted stories of literary value and stories with reader appeal. First, does the manuscript spark immediate interest and the introduction create the effect that will dominate? Second, does the action in dialogue or narration tell the story? Third, does the conclusion leave something with the reader to be long remembered? We look for the story with an original idea and an unusual twist. We are weary of excessive violence and depressing themes in fiction and are looking for originality in plots and some humorous pieces."

POTTERSFIELD PORTFOLIO, P.O. Box 40, Station A, Sydney, Nova Scotia B1P 6G9 Canada. Website: www.chebucto.ns.ca/culture/WFNS/Pottersfield/potters.html. **Editor:** Douglas Arthur Brown. Magazine: 8×11; 60 pages; illustrations. "Literary magazine interested in well-written fiction and poetry. No specific thematic interests or biases." Triannually. Estab. 1979. Circ. 1,000.

Needs: Receives 40-50 fiction mss/month. Buys 4-5 fiction mss/issue. Recently published work by David Adams Richards, Vivette Kady and M.J. Hull. Length: 4,000 words maximum. Sometimes comments on rejected mss.

How to Contact: Send complete ms with SASE and cover letter. Include estimated word count and 50-word bio. No simultaneous submissions. No fax or e-mail submissions. Reports in 3 months. SASE. Sample copy for $7 (US).

Payment/Terms: Pays contributor's copy plus $5 Canadian per printed page to a maximum of $25 on publication for first Canadian serial rights.

Advice: "Provide us with a clean, proofread copy of your story. Include a brief cover letter with biographical note, but don't try to sell the story to us. *Always* include a SASE with sufficient *Canadian* postage, or IRCs, for return of the manuscript or a reply from the editors."

THE PRAGUE REVUE, Bohemia's Journal of International Literature, Prague Publishers Group, V jámě 7, 110 00 Prague 1, Czech Republic. (00420)(2)24222383. Fax: (00420)(2)4221783. E-mail: revue@terminal.cz. Website: www.praguepivo.com (includes writer's guidelines and names of editors). Editor: Jason Penazzi-Russell. **Fiction Editors:** Max Munson and David Leslie Conhaim. Magazine: 130 pages; 80 weight paper; 180 weight cover stock with dust jacket; illustrations and photos. "Brings together both contemporary and lost classics into a single international volume." Biannually. Estab. 1995. Circ. 1,500.

● Recipient of a grant from the Czech Ministry of Culture. Member of the Prague Publishers Group.

Needs: "*The Prague Revue* is Bohemia's English language, international biannual of contemporary fiction, poetry, performance text and nonfiction. We will publish any genre. Editorial decisions are based solely on the quality of submissions. Our biannual English language issue brings Central European writers together with international writers for world exposure. We also publish non-English anthologies to bring the works to greater audiences." Recently published work by Janice Galloway, John Kinsella, Richard Zenith, Hanna Krall and Louis Armand. **Publishes 15 new writers/year.** Length: 6,000 words average.

How to Contact: Submit complete ms with a cover letter. Include estimated word count, 1-paragraph bio, Social Security number and list of publications. SASE for reply or send a disposable copy of the ms. Queries by e-mail OK. Reports in 3 weeks on queries; 4 months on mss. Simultaneous submissions, reprints and electronic submissions OK.

Payment/Terms: Pays $5-150 on acceptance "for those pieces which are also selected for our foreign language issues" and 2 contributor's copies; additional copies for $4. Sample copy available for $7. Fiction guidelines for SAE and IRCs.

Advice: "We keep an eye out for pieces which would contribute also to our foreign language anthologies—particularly our Czech language annual. Prague themes do not contribute to the piece's chances for publication."

PRAIRIE FIRE, Prairie Fire Press Inc., 100 Arthur St., Room 423, Winnipeg, Manitoba R3B 1H3 Canada. (204)943-9066. Fax: (204)942-1555. Managing Editor: Andris Taskans. Magazine: 6×9; 200 pages; offset bond paper; sturdy cover stock; illustrations; photos. "Essays, critical reviews, short fiction and poetry. For writers and readers interested in Canadian literature." Published 4 times/year. Estab. 1978. Circ. 1,500.

  • *Prairie Fire* recently received two Silver National Magazine Awards for poetry and personal journalism and was nominated for six Western Magazine Awards (Canada).

Needs: Literary, contemporary, experimental, prose poem, reviews. "We will consider work on any topic of artistic merit, including short chapters from novels-in-progress. We wish to avoid gothic, confession, religious, romance and pornography." Buys 3-6 mss/issue, 12-24 mss/year. Does not read mss in summer. Recently published work by Carol Shields, Robert Kroetsch, Greg Hollingshead and Lorna Crozier. Published new writers within the last year. Receives 100-120 unsolicited fiction mss each month. Publishes short shorts. Length: 5,000 words maximum; 2,500 words average. Also publishes literary essays, literary criticism, poetry. Critiques rejected mss "if requested and when there is time."

How to Contact: Send complete ms with IRC w/envelope and short bio. No simultaneous submissions. Reports in 6 months. Sample copy for $10 (Canadian). Reviews novels and short story collections. Send books to Andris Taskans.

Payment/Terms: Pays $40 for the first page, $35 for each additional page; 1 contributor copy; 60% of cover price for extras. Pays on publication for first North American serial rights. Rights revert to author on publication.

Advice: "We are publishing more fiction, and we are commissioning illustrations. Read our publication before submitting. We prefer Canadian material. Most mss are not ready for publication. Be neat, double space, and put your name and address on everything! Be the best writer you can be."

THE PRAIRIE JOURNAL OF CANADIAN LITERATURE, Prairie Journal Press, Box 61203, Brentwood Postal Services, Calgary, Alberta T2L 2K6 Canada. Website: www.geocities.com/athens/ithaca/4436. **Editor:** A.E. Burke. Journal: 7×8½; 50-60 pages; white bond paper; Cadillac cover stock; cover illustrations. Journal of creative writing and scholarly essays, reviews for literary audience. Semiannually. Published special fiction issue last year. Estab. 1983.

Needs: Contemporary, literary, prose poem, regional, excerpted novel, novella, double-spaced. Canadian authors given preference. Publishes "a variety of types of fiction—fantasy, psychological, character-driven, feminist, etc. We publish authors at all stages of their careers from well-known to first publication." No romance, erotica, pulp, westerns. Publishes anthology series open to submissions: *Prairie Journal Poetry II* and *Prairie Journal Fiction III*. Receives 50 unsolicited mss each month. Accepts 10-15 mss/issue; 20-30 mss/year. Suggests sample issue before submitting ms. Published work by Magie Dominic, Allison Kydd, Nancy Ellen Russell, Carla Mobley, Patrick Quinn. **Publishes 20 new writers/year.** Length: 2,500 words average; 100 words minimum; 3,000 words maximum. Suggested deadlines: April 1 for spring/summer issue; October 1 for fall/winter. Also publishes literary essays, literary criticism, poetry. Sometimes critiques rejected mss and recommends other markets.

How to Contact: Send complete ms. Reports in 1 month. SASE. Sample copy for $8 (Canadian) and SAE with $1.10 for postage or IRC. Include cover letter of past credits, if any. Reply to queries for SAE with 55¢ for postage or IRC. No American stamps. Reviews novels and short story collections.

Payment/Terms: Pays contributor's copies and modest honoraria. Acquires first North American serial rights. In Canada author retains copyright.

Advice: "We like character-driven rather than plot-centered fiction." Interested in "innovational work of quality. Beginning writers welcome. There is no point in simply republishing known authors or conventional, predictable plots. Of the genres we receive fiction is most often of the highest calibre. It is a very competitive field. Be proud of what you send. You're worth it."

PRAIRIE SCHOONER, University of Nebraska, English Department, 201 Andrews Hall, Lincoln NE 68588-0334. (402)472-0911. E-mail: lrandolp@unlinfo.unl.edu. Website: www.unl.edu/schooner/psmain.htm

(includes guidelines, editors, table of contents and excerpts of current issue). **Editor:** Hilda Raz. Magazine: 6×9; 200 pages; good stock paper; heavy cover stock. "A fine literary quarterly of stories, poems, essays and reviews for a general audience that reads for pleasure." Quarterly. Estab. 1926. Circ. 3,200.

● *Prairie Schooner*, one of the oldest publications in this book, has garnered several awards and honors over the years. Work appearing in the magazine has been selected for anthologies including *Pushcart Prize* and *Best American Short Stories*. *Prairie Schooner* ranked #34 on *Writer's Digest* Fiction 50 list of top markets for fiction writers.

Needs: Good fiction (literary). Accepts 4-5 mss/issue. Receives approximately 500 unsolicited fiction mss each month. Mss are read September through May only. Recently published work by Ursula Hegi, Josip Novakovitch, Rebecca Goldstein, Robin Hemley and Susan Fromberg Schaeffer. **Published new writers within the last year.** Length: varies. Also publishes poetry. Offers annual prize of $1,000 for best fiction, $500 for best new writer (poetry or fiction), two $500 awards for best poetry (for work published in the magazine in the previous year).

How to Contact: Send complete mss with SASE and cover letter listing previous publications—where, when. Accepts queries/mss by e-mail or fax. Reports in 3-4 months. Sample copy for $5. Reviews novels, poetry and short story collections.

Payment/Terms: Pays in contributor's copies and prize money awarded. Acquires all rights. Will reassign rights upon request after publication.

Advice: "*Prairie Schooner* is eager to see fiction from beginning and established writers. Be tenacious. Accept rejection as a temporary setback and send out rejected stories to other magazines. *Prairie Schooner* is not a magazine with a program. We look for good fiction in traditional narrative modes as well as experimental, meta-fiction or any other form or fashion a writer might try. Create striking detail, well-developed characters, fresh dialogue; let the images and the situations evoke the stories themes. Too much explication kills a lot of otherwise good stories. Be persistent. Keep writing and sending out new work. Be familiar with the tastes of the magazines where you're sending. We are receiving record numbers of submissions. Prospective contributors must sometimes wait longer to receive our reply."

$◙ PRESS, Daniel Roberts Inc., 2124 Broadway, Suite 323, New York NY 10023. (212)579-0873. Fax: (212)579-0776. E-mail: pressltd@aol.com. **Editor:** Daniel Roberts. Magazine: 6¾×10; 160 pages; cougap-opaque paper; loe cream cover. Features fiction, poetry and "articles about writing and writers; features that humanize literature, celebrate talent and beauty, and expose fraudulence and pomposity. *Press* will stand not only as the most absolute record of contemporary, American, literary talent, but as a means by which the public can commune with literature." Quarterly. Estab. 1996. Circ. 15,000.

Needs: Receives 800 unsolicited mss/month. Accepts 10 mss/issue; 40 mss/year. Publishes ms 6-10 weeks after acceptance. Agented fiction 10%. Published work by Joyce Carol Oates, Anthony Hecht, Philip Levine, William J. Cobb, James Gallant, Gordon Lish and Harry Mathews. Also publishes poetry. Sometimes comments on or critiques rejected mss.

How to Contact: Send complete ms with a cover letter. Include a short bio and list of publications. Reports in 2 months on queries; 4 months on mss. Send SASE for reply, return of ms or send a disposable copy of ms. Sample copy for $8. Fiction guidelines free.

Payment/Terms: Pays $100 minimum and 1 contributor's copy; additional copies for $6. Pays on acceptance for first rights, first North American serial rights or one-time rights. Sends galleys to the author.

Advice: "While almost all forms are acceptable, prose poems and more experimental writing (stories that don't actually tell a story) are discouraged. We are looking for a strong and specific plot (where 'something' actually happens); one that makes a reader want to turn the page. We want stories where the author's style does not interfere with the plot, but strengthens the expression of that plot."

◪ ◎ PRIMAVERA, Box 37-7547, Chicago IL 60637. (312)324-5920. Editorial Board. Magazine: 5½×8½; 128 pages; 60 lb. paper; glossy cover; illustrations; photos. Literature and graphics reflecting the experiences of women: poetry, short stories, photos, drawings. Readership: "an audience interested in women's ideas and experiences." Annually. Estab. 1975. Circ. 1,000.

● *Primavera* has won grants from the Illinois Arts Council, the Puffin Foundation and from Chicago Women in Publishing.

Needs: Literary, contemporary, fantasy, feminist, gay/lesbian, humor and science fiction. "We dislike slick stories packaged for more traditional women's magazines. We publish only work reflecting the experiences of women, but also publish manuscripts by men." Accepts 6-10 mss/issue. Receives approximately 40 unsolicited fiction mss each month. Published work by Amy Stuber, Carol Kopec, L. Hluchan Sintetos and Sucha Cardoza. **Published new writers within the last year.** Length: 25 pages maximum. Also publishes poetry. Critiques rejected mss when there is time. Often gives suggestions for revisions and invites re-submission of revised ms. Occasionally recommends other markets.

How to Contact: Send complete ms with SASE. No post cards. Cover letter not necessary. No simultaneous submissions. Reports in 1-6 months on mss. Publishes ms up to 1 year after acceptance. Sample copy for $5; $10 for recent issues. Guidelines for SASE.

Payment/Terms: Pays 2 contributor's copies. Acquires first rights.

Advice: "We're looking for artistry and deftness of untrendy, unhackneyed themes; an original slant on a well-known theme, an original use of language, and the highest literary quality we can find."

■ ★ ✓ $ ∅ ⛉ **PRISM INTERNATIONAL**, E462-1866 Main Mall, University of British Columbia, Vancouver, British Columbia V6T 1Z1 Canada. (604)822-2514. E-mail: prism@unixg.ubc.ca. Website: www.arts. ubc.ca/prism/ (includes entire year of issues, writer's guidelines, contest information, PRISM news and e-mail address). Executive Editor: Laisha Rosnad. **Editors:** Kiera Miller and Jennica Harper. Magazine: 6×9; 72-80 pages; Zephyr book paper; Cornwall, coated one side cover; photos on cover. "An international journal of contemporary writing—fiction, poetry, drama, creative nonfiction and translation." Readership: "public and university libraries, individual subscriptions, bookstores—a world-wide audience concerned with the contemporary in literature." Quarterly. Estab. 1959. Circ. 1,200.

● *PRISM international* has won numerous magazine awards and stories first published in *PRISM* have been included in the *Journey Prize Anthology* every year since 1991. *PRISM* ranked #45 in *Writer's Digest's* Fiction 50 list of top markets for fiction writers.

Needs: New writing that is contemporary and literary. Short stories and self-contained novel excerpts. Works of translation are eagerly sought and should be accompanied by a copy of the original. No gothic, confession, religious, romance, pornography, or sci-fi. Also looking for creative nonfiction that is literary, not journalistic, in scope and tone. Buys approximately 70 mss/year. Receives over 100 fiction unsolicted mss each month. "*PRISM* publishes both new and established writers; our contributors have included Franz Kafka, Gabriel Garcia Marquez, Michael Ondaatje, Margaret Laurence, Mark Anthony Jarman, Gail Anderson-Dargatz and Eden Robinson." Recently published works by Jane Eaton Hamilton, Anne Fleming, David Prall, Janice Levy and Vivette J. Kady. **Publishes 10% new writers.** Submissions should not exceed 5,000 words "though flexible for outstanding work" (only one long story per submission, please). Publishes short shorts. Also publishes poetry and drama. Sponsors annual short fiction contest with $2,000 (Canadian) grand prize: send SASE for details.

How to Contact: Send complete ms with SASE or SAE, IRC and cover letter with bio, information and publications list. Accepts mss by e-mail. "Keep it simple. U.S. contributors take note: Do note send U.S. stamps, they are not valid in Canada. Send International Reply Coupons instead." Reports in 2-6 months. Electronic submissions OK (e-mail, web). Sample copy for $5 (U.S./Canadian).

Payment/Terms: Pays $20 (Canadian)/printed page, 1 year's subscription on publication for first North American serial rights. Selected authors are paid an additional $10/page for digital rights.

Advice: "Read several issues of our magazine before submitting. We are committed to publishing outstanding literary work in all genres. We look for strong, believeable characters; real voices; attention to language; interesting ideas and plots. Send us fresh, innovative work which also shows a mastery of the basics of good prose writing. Poorly constructed or sloppy pieces will not receive serious consideration. We welcome e-mail submissions and are proud to be one of few print literary journals who offer additional payment to select writers for digital publication. Too many e-mail submissions, however, come to us unpolished and unprepared to be published. Writers should craft their work for e-mail submission as carefully as they would for submissions through traditional methods. They should send one piece at a time and wait for our reply before they send another."

○ **PROCREATION: A JOURNAL OF TRUTHTELLING IN POETRY & PROSE**, Silent Planet Publishing, Ltd., 6300-138 Creedmoor Rd., Raleigh NC 27612. (919)510-9010. Fax: (919)510-0210. E-mail: editor@ procreation.org. Website: www.procreation.org (includes writer's guidelines, full issue, editorials, subscription information and links). **Editor:** Stephen A. West. Journal: digest-sized; 48 pages; high-quality paper; matte card cover; photographs. "We are a literary journal dedicated to the pursuit and expression of artfully encapsulated truth. We believe that in creating we echo the Creator's own imaginative and creative activity and, so, become more fully human. We are interested in all kinds of truth, including spiritual truth, but we do not accept propaganda (however truthful), or religious or abstract prose not rooted in real-life experience." Biannually. Estab. 1997. Circ. 500.

Needs: Condensed/excerpted novel, experimental, humor/satire, literary, mainstream/contemporary, religious/ inspirational. No erotica, horror, political fiction, graphic violence or "preachy or sentimental fiction." Receives 100 unsolicited mss/month. Accepts 4 mss/issue; 12 mss/year. Publishes ms 6 months after acceptance. Recently published work by Gayle Chaney and John McFarland. Length: 1,500 words average; 250 words minimum; 3,000 words maximum. Publishes short shorts. Length: 250 words. Also publishes poetry. Often critiques or comments on rejected mss.

How to Contact: Send complete ms with a cover letter. Accepts queries/mss by fax. Include estimated word count, 1 page bio, list of publications "whether, if published, they desire to have contact information listed along with their byline. We seek interaction with the readership, if writers consent, so as to facilitate dialogue and community." Reports in 2 months. SASE for reply, return of ms or send a disposable copy of ms. Sample copy for $5 (US), $8 (foreign) and 5 first-class stamps or 2 IRCs. Fiction guidelines for #10 SASE or SAE and 1 IRC or by e-mail. Reviews novels and short story collections.

Payment/Terms: Pays 1 contributor's copy on publication; additional copies for $4.50. Acquires first North American serial rights.

Advice: "We look for strong imagery and well-written prose which reveals truth rather than simply states it in a didactic fashion. We are especially interested in fiction that strongly connects to human experience, whether tragic, comic or beautiful, yet which points to a larger truth outside itself, something transcendent. Look for the extraordinary in the ordinary. Write out of experience, with strong attention to the particulars of time, place, and character but at the same time capturing some universal, some shared truth, to which readers can relate."

N ★ □ THE PROSE MENAGERIE. E-mail: caras@reporters.net. Website: www.geocities.com/Sotto/Studios/5116/index.html. **Editor:** Cara Swann. E-zine. "*The Prose Menagerie* is a mixture of interesting prose, essays, articles as well as fiction (short stories/novellas/poetry)."

Needs: Literary. No erotica. Wants more "meaningful themes." **Publishes 1-2 new writers/weekly.** Recently published work by Allen Woodman, John K. Trammell and Zalman Velvel.

How to Contact: Send queries/mss by e-mail. Send in body of e-mail and/or attached as plain ASCII text file only. No MS Word files accepted.

Payment/Terms: "Since *The Prose Menagerie* is only available online, the writer maintains copyright; and while there is no payment, there is wide exposure for new and unknown writers, eagerly promoted along with those who do have name recognition."

Advice: "Submit a piece of writing that has meaning, whether it is poetry, fiction or articles. Also open to those who wish to present ideas for regular columns and book reviews."

$ ⬚ ⬚ PROVINCETOWN ARTS, Provincetown Arts, Inc., 650 Commercial St., P.O. Box 35, Provincetown MA 02657. (508)487-3167. Fax: (508)487-8634. **Editor:** Christopher Busa. Magazine: 9×12; 184 pages; 60 lb. coated paper; 12 pcs. cover; illustrations and photographs. "*PA* focuses broadly on the artists, writers and theater of America's oldest continuous art colony." Annually. Estab. 1985. Circ. 8,000.

 • *Provincetown Arts* is a recipient of a CLMP seed grant. Provincetown Arts Press has an award-winning poetry series.

Needs: Plans special fiction issue. Receives 300 unsolicited mss/year. Buys 5 mss/issue. Publishes ms 3 months after acceptance. Published work by Carole Maso and Hilary Masters. Length: 3,000 words average; 1,500 words minimum; 8,000 words maximum. Publishes short shorts. Also publishes literary essays, literary criticism, poetry. Sometimes critiques rejected mss and recommends other markets.

How to Contact: Send complete ms with cover letter including previous publications. No simultaneous submissions. Reports in 2 weeks on queries; 3 months on mss. SASE. Sample copy for $7.50. Reviews novels and short story collections.

Payment/Terms: Pays $75-300 on publication for first rights. Sends galleys to author.

★ ⬚ PUCKERBRUSH REVIEW, Puckerbrush Press, 76 Main St., Orono ME 04473. (207)866-4868/581-3832. **Editor:** Constance Hunting. Magazine: 9×12; 80-100 pages; illustrations. "We publish mostly new Maine writers; interviews, fiction, reviews, poetry for a literary audience." Semiannually. Estab. 1979. Circ. approx. 500.

Needs: Belles-lettres, experimental, gay (occasionally), literary. "Wants to see more original, quirky and well-written fiction." No genre fiction. "Nothing cliché." Receives 30 unsolicited mss/month. Accepts 6 mss/issue; 12 mss/year. Publishes ms 1 year after acceptance. Recently published work by Beth Lurie, Beth Round, Miriam Colwell, Christopher Fahy and Farnham Blair. **Publishes 10 new writers/year.** Sometimes publishes short shorts. Also publishes literary essays, literary criticism, poetry. Sometimes critiques rejected mss.

How to Contact: Send complete ms with cover letter. "No disks please!" Reports in 2 months. SASE. Simultaneous submissions OK. Sample copy for $2. Fiction guidelines for SASE. Sometimes reviews novels and short story collections.

Payment/Terms: Pays in contributor's copies.

Advice: "I don't want to see tired plots or treatments. I want to see respect for language—the right words. Be true to yourself, don't follow fashion."

⬚ PUERTO DEL SOL, New Mexico State University, Box 3E, Las Cruces NM 88003-0001. (505)646-3931. Fax: (505)646-7725. E-mail: kwest@nmsu.edu. **Editors:** Kay West, Antonya Nelson and Kevin McIlvoy. Magazine: 6×9; 200 pages; 60 lb. paper; 70 lb. cover stock; photos sometimes. "We publish quality material from anyone. Poetry, fiction, art, photos, interviews, reviews, parts-of-novels, long poems." Semiannually. Estab. 1961. Circ. 1,500.

Needs: Contemporary, ethnic, experimental, literary, mainstream, prose poem, excerpted novel and translations. Receives varied number of unsolicited fiction mss/month. Acquires 8-10 mss/issue; 12-15 mss/year. Does not read mss March through August. Published work by Dagobeuto Gilb, Wendell Mayo and William H. Cobb. **Publishes 8-10 new writers/year.** Also publishes poetry. Occasionally critiques rejected mss.

How to Contact: Send complete ms with SASE. Simultaneous submissions OK. Reports in 3 months. Sample copy for $7.

Payment/Terms: Pays 2 contributor's copies. Acquires one-time rights (rights revert to author).

Advice: "We are open to all forms of fiction, from the conventional to the wildly experimental, as long as they have integrity and are well written. Too often we receive very impressively 'polished' mss that will dazzle readers with their sheen but offer no character/reader experience of lasting value."

N Ø ▣ PULSE, Heartsounds Press, 17100 Bear Valley Rd. PMB 308, Victorville CA 92392. (760)243-8043. E-mail: lpinto3402@aol.com or mim47@aol.com. Website: www.heartsoundspress.com. **Fiction Editor:** Liz Pinto. Nonfiction Editor: Linda Peters. Poetry Editor: Carol Bockofner. E-zine specializing in literary short stories, essays and poetry. Quarterly. Estab. 1999.

Needs: Literary, mainstream. No "porn, romance, horror." Receives 25-30 unsolicited mss/month. Publishes ms 6 weeks after acceptance. **Publishes 5 new writers/year.** Recently published work by Frank Criscenti, Geraldine Tyler, Karen Wallace, Marcy Sheiner, David Steinberg and Lyn Lifshin. Word length: 3,000 words average; 5,000 words maximum. Also publishes literary essays, literary criticism and poetry. Sometimes comments on or critiques rejected ms.

How to Contact: Send complete ms with a cover letter. Inquiries by e-mail OK. Include estimated word count, 50-100 word bio and list of publications. Reports on ms in 6 weeks. Send SASE for reply, return on ms or send a disposable copy of ms. Simultaneous submissions OK. Fiction guidelines free for #10 SAE.

Payment/Terms: Pays "a pen with *Pulse* logo." Payment on publication. Rights revert to writer.

Advice: " 'Does it work?' is the only criteria I use. Ask yourself: 'Is this story the best it can be?' The print market continues to narrow. We work to give more writers a forum for their work."

N ⊕ QUADRANT, P.O. Box 1495, Collingwood, Victoria 3066 Australia. Fiction Editor: Mr. Les Murray. Ten issues/year. Circ. 6,000.

Needs: "Magazine of current affairs, culture, politics, economics, the arts, literature, ideas; stories: general and varied." Publishes 1-2 stories/issue. Length: 800 words minimum; 5,000 words maximum.

Payment/Terms: Pays contributor's copies and a minimum of $100 (Australian). For sample copy "write to us, enclosing cheque for $6 U.S. or equivalent."

✓ Ø ◎ QUARTER AFTER EIGHT, A Journal of Prose and Commentary, QAE, Ellis Hall, Ohio University, Athens OH 45701. (740)594-6085. Editors: Matthew Cooperman, Thom Conroy, Bonnie Proudfoot, Kristy Veladota. **Fiction Editor:** Tom Noyes. Magazine: 6×9; 310 pages; 20 lb. glossy cover stock; photos. "We look to publish work which somehow addresses, in its form and/or content, the boundaries between poetry and prose." Annually.

Needs: Condensed/excerpted novel, erotica, ethnic/multicultural, experimental, gay, humor/satire, lesbian, literary, mainstream/contemporary, translations. Send SASE for list of upcoming themes. Receives 50 unsolicited mss/month. Accepts 10 mss/issue. Does not read mss mid-March to mid-September. Publishes ms 6-9 months after acceptance. Agented fiction 15%. Recently published work by Colette Inez, Ray Gonzalez, Barbara Lefcowitz, Alexandr Kushner and Vivian Shipley. Length: 3,000 words average; 10,000 words maximum. Publishes short shorts. Also publishes literary essays, literary criticism, prose poetry. Also sponsors an annual prose contest: $500 award. Sometimes critiques or comments on rejected ms.

How to Contact: Send complete ms with a cover letter. Include short bio and list of publications. Reports in 6-8 weeks. Send SASE for return of ms or send a disposable copy of ms. Simultaneous submissions OK. Sample copy for $10, 8×11 SAE and $1.50 postage. Fiction guidelines for #10 SASE. Reviews novels and short story collections. Send books to fiction editor.

Payment/Terms: Pays 2 contributor's copies; additional copies $10. Acquires first North American serial rights. Sponsors contest. Send SASE for guidelines.

Advice: "We're interested in seeing more stories that push language and the traditional form to their limits."

★ $ Ø ♥ QUARTERLY WEST, University of Utah, 200 S. Central Campus Dr., Room 317, Salt Lake City UT 84112-9109. (801)581-3938. Website: chronicle.utah.edu/QW/QW.html (includes novella guidelines, submission guidelines, recent issues with samples of contributors' work). Editor: Margot Schilpp. **Fiction Editors:** Gerry Hart and Becky Lindberg. Editors change every 2 years. Magazine: 6×9; 200 pages; 60 lb. paper; 5-color cover stock; illustrations and photographs rarely. "We try to publish a variety of fiction and poetry from all over the country based not so much on the submitting author's reputation but on the merit of each piece. Our publication is aimed primarily at an educated audience interested in contemporary literature and criticism." Semiannually. "We sponsor a biennial novella competition." (Next competition held in 2000). Estab. 1976. Circ. 1,800.

• *Quarterly West* is a past recipient of grants from the NEA and was awarded First Place for Editorial Content from the American Literary Magazine Awards. Work published in the magazine has been selected for inclusion in the *Pushcart Prize* anthology and *The Best American Short Stories* anthology. *Quarterly West* ranked #29 on *Writer's Digest*'s Fiction 50 list of top markets for fiction writers.

Needs: Literary, contemporary, experimental, translations. Accepts 6-10 mss/issue, 12-20 mss/year. Receives 300 unsolicited fiction mss each month. Published work by H.E. Francis, Alan Cheuse, Ron Carlson, Cynthia Baughman, William T. Vollmann, David Kranes and Antonya Nelson. **Publishes 3-5 new writers/year.** No preferred length; interested in longer, "fuller" short stories, as well as short shorts. Critiques rejected mss when there is time.

How to Contact: Send complete ms. Brief cover letters welcome. Send SASE for reply or return of ms. Simultaneous submissions OK with notification. Reports in 2-3 months; "sooner, if possible." Sample copy for $7.50.

Payment/Terms: Pays $15-500 and 2 contributor's copies on publication for all rights (negotiable).
Advice: "We publish a special section of short shorts every issue, and we also sponsor a biennial novella contest. We are open to experimental work—potential contributors should read the magazine! We solicit occasionally, but tend more toward the surprises—unsolicited. Don't send more than one story per submission, but submit as often as you like."

☑ ⦿ **RAG MAG,** Box 12, Goodhue MN 55027-0012. (651)923-4590. **Publisher/Editor:** Beverly Voldseth. Magazine: 6×9; 60-112 pages; varied paper quality; illustrations; photos. "We are eager to print poetry, prose and art work. We are open to all styles." Semiannually. Estab. 1982. Circ. 300.
Needs: Adventure, comics, contemporary, erotica, ethnic, experimental, fantasy, feminist, literary, mainstream, prose poem, regional. "Anything well written is a possibility. It has to be a good adult story, tight, with plot and zip. I also like strange but well done. No extremely violent or pornographic writing." Receives 100 unsolicited mss/month. Accepts 4 mss/issue. Recently published work by Susan Thurston Hamerski, Sigi Leonhard, Paul Jensi and Steve Lange. **Published new writers within the last year.** Length: 1,000 words average; 2,200 words maximum. Novel chapters or excerpts 25 pages maximum (excerpts must stand alone).
How to Contact: Send short story or excerpt of novel, brief bio and brief cover letter. SASE. Reports in 3-4 weeks. Simultaneous and previously published submissions OK. Single copy for $6.
Payment/Terms: Pays 1 contributor's copy; $4 plus $2.50 s&h for up to 5 copies. Acquires one-time rights.
Advice: "Submit clean copy on regular typing paper (no tissue-thin stuff). We want fresh images, sparse language, words that will lift us out of our chairs. I like the short story form. I think it's powerful and has a definite place in the literary magazine."

⦿ **RAMBUNCTIOUS REVIEW,** Rambunctious Press, Inc., 1221 W. Pratt Blvd., Chicago IL 60626. (773)338-2439. **Editors:** Nancy Lennon, Richard Lennon and Elizabeth Hawsler. Magazine: 10×7; 48 pages; illustrations and photos. Annually. Estab. 1983. Circ. 300.
Needs: Experimental, feminist, humor/satire, literary, mainstream/contemporary. List of upcoming themes available for SASE. Receives 30 unsolicited mss/month. Accepts 4-5 mss/issue. Does not read mss May through August. Publishes ms 5-6 months after acceptance. Published work by Hugh Fox, Lyn Lifshin and Stephen Schroeder. **Publishes 6 new writers/year.** Length: 12 double-spaced pages. Publishes short shorts. Also publishes poetry. Sometimes critiques or comments on rejected mss. Sponsors contest. Send SASE for details.
How to Contact: Send complete ms with a cover letter. Include estimated word count. Reports in 9 months. Send SASE for reply, return of ms or send a disposable copy of ms. Simultaneous submissions OK. Sample copy for $4.
Payment/Terms: Pays 2 contributor's copies. Acquires one-time rights.

⦿ **RASKOLNIKOV'S CELLAR and THE LAMPLIGHT,** The Beggars's Press, 8110 N. 38th St., Omaha NE 68112-2018. (402)455-2615. Editor: Richard Carey. **Fiction Editor:** Danielle Staton. Magazine: 8½×12; 60-150 pages; 20 lb. bond paper; 12pt soft cover. "Our purpose is to encourage writing in the style of the past masters and to hold back illiteracy in our generation." Semiannually. Estab. 1952. Circ. 1,200.
● Member of the International Association of Independent Publishers and the Federation of Literary Publishers.
Needs: Historical, horror, humor/satire, literary, serialized novels, translations. No "religious, sentimental, folksy, science fiction or ultra modern." Publishes special fiction issue or anthologies. Receives 135 unsolicited mss/month. Accepts 15 mss/issue; 30-45 mss/year. Publishes ms 2-6 months after acceptance. Agented fiction 5%. Published work by James Scoffield, Richard Davignon and Philip Sparacino. Length: 1,500-2,000 words average; 50 words minimum; 3,000 words maximum. Publishes short shorts. Also publishes literary essays, literary criticism and poetry.
How to Contact: Send complete ms with a cover letter. Include estimated word count and 1 page bio. Reports in 2 months on queries; 4 months on mss. Simultaneous submissions OK. Sample copy for $10 plus 9×12 SAE with 2 first-class stamps. Fiction guidelines for #10 SAE with 2 first-class stamps. Reviews novels or short story collections. Send books to Danielle Staton.
Payment/Terms: Pays 1 contributor's copy for first North American serial rights.
Advice: "We judge on writing style as well as content. If your style of writing and your word usage do not attract us at once, there is faint hope of the content and the plot saving the story. Read and learn from the great writers of the past. Set your stories in the un-computer age, so your characters have time to think, to feel, to react. Use your glorious language to the fullest. Our subscribers can read quite well. The strongest way to say anything is to never quite say it."

[N] ✦ ⦿ ☑ **THE RAVEN CHRONICLES, A Magazine of Transcultural Art, Literature and the Spoken Word,** The Raven Chronicles, 1634 11th Ave., Seattle WA 98122. (206)323-4316. E-mail: ravenchron @speakeasy.org. Website: www.speakeasy.org/ravenchronicles (includes guidelines, editors, short fiction, prose, poetry, separate monthly topics for online publication). Managing Editor: Phoebe Bosché. **Fiction Editor:** Kathleen Alcala. Poetry Editors: Tiffany Midge and Jody Aliesan. Webmaster: Scott Martin. Magazine: 8½×11; 48-64 pages; 50 lb. book paper; glossy cover; b&w illustrations; photos. "*The Raven Chronicles* is designed to

promote transcultural art, literature and the spoken word." Triannually. Estab. 1991. Circ. 2,500-5,000.
- This magazine is a frequent winner of Bumbershoot Bookfair awards. The magazine also received grants from the Washington State Arts Commission, the Seattle Arts Commission, the King County Arts Commission and ATR, a foundation for social justice projects.

Needs: Ethnic/multicultural, literary, regional. No romance, fantasy, mystery or detective. Receives 300-400 mss/month. Buys 20-40 mss/issue; 60-120 mss/year. Publishes 3-6 months after acceptance. **Publishes 40% new writers.** Published work by David Romtvedt, Sherman Alexie, D.L. Birchfield, Nancy Redwine, Diane Glancy, Greg Hischak and Sharon Hashimoto. Length: 2,000 words average; 2,500 words maximum. Publishes short shorts. Length: 300-500 words. Also publishes literary essays, reviews, literary criticism, poetry. Sometimes critiques rejected mss.

How to Contact: Send complete ms with a cover letter. Include estimated word count. Accepts queries/mss by e-mail. Reports in 4-8 months on manuscripts. Send SASE for return of ms. Simultaneous submissions OK. Sample copy for $3. Fiction guidelines for #10 SASE.

Payment/Terms: Pays $10-40 plus 2 contributor's copies; additional copies at half cover cost. Pays on publication for first North American serial rights. Sends galleys to author.

Advice: Looks for "clean, direct language, written from the heart. Read sample copy, or look at *Before Columbus* anthologies and *Greywolf Annual* anthologies."

THE RAW SEED REVIEW, 780 Merion Greene, Charlottesville VA 22901. **Editor:** Sam Taylor. Magazine; digest-sized; 80 pages; quality paper; 4-color cover; illustrations and photos. "*The Raw Seed Review* aims to be a mecca of vision, exploration and urgency. We publish poetry, art, fiction and essays that in some way produce a closer encounter with the essence or origin of things—the 'raw seed,' the unknown." Semiannually. Estab. 1999. Circ. 500.

Needs: Condensed/excerpted novel, experimental, literary. "No genre fiction or anything unoriginal, uninspired or unedited." Receives 20 unsolicited mss/month. Accepts 2 mss/issue; 4 mss/year. Publishes ms 1-8 months after acceptance. Length: open, "but shorter pieces stand a better chance." Recently published work by Tom Whalen and Christopher Woods. Publishes short shorts. Also publishes literary essays, literary criticism, poetry. Sometimes critiques or comments on rejected ms.

How to Contact: Send complete ms with a cover letter. Include estimated word count, bio and list of publications. Reports in 1-12 weeks. SASE for return of ms. Simultaneous submissions OK. Sample copy $6.50.

Payment/Terms: Pays 1-3 contributor's copies. Acquires first rights. Sometimes sends galleys to author.

Advice: "We look for work that explores and creates the world, expands the mythological matrix of language and evokes the mystery. Write what is necessary—what surprises, distills, enlivens, transcends, mesmerizes. Work should resonate with imaginative clarity, though this does not necessarily mean it should be discursively understandable."

READER'S BREAK, Pine Grove Press, P.O. Box 85, Jamesville NY 13078. (315)423-9268. **Editor:** Gertrude S. Eiler. Annual anthology with an "emphasis on short stories written with style and ability. Our aim has always been to publish work of quality by authors with talent, whether previously published or not."

Needs: "We welcome stories about relationships, tales of action, adventure, science fiction and fantasy, romance, suspense and mystery. Themes and plots may be historical, contemporary or futuristic. No "pornography, sexual perversion, incest or stories for children." Recently published work by Bayard, Anjila Batia, Mike Lipstock, Don Stockland, Clara Stites and Glenn Coates. **Publishes 10-15 new writers/year.** Length: 3,500 words maximum. Also publishes "poems to 75 lines in any style or form and on any subject with the above exceptions."

How to Contact: Accepts unsolicited mss. Include SASE. Reports in 3-5 months "since the stories are considered by a number of editorial readers." Reviews novels. SASE for details.

Terms: Pays 1 contributor's copy for one-time rights; additional copies at 20% discount.

Advice: "We prefer fiction with a well-constructed plot and well-defined characters of any age or socio-economic group. Upbeat endings are not required. Please check the sequence of events, their cause-and-effect relationship, the motivation of your characters, and the resolution of plot. Keep writing and develop a thick skin to criticism."

REAL POETIK: A Little Magazine of the Internet, 840 W. Nickerson St. #11, Seattle WA 98119. (206)282-3776. E-mail: salasin@wln.com. Website: www.scn.org/arts/realpoetik. "This is an archive/ website for the mailing list/e-mail aspect of *Real Poetik*." **Editor:** Sal Salasin. E-zine. "We publish the new, lively, exciting and unexpected in vernacular English. Any vernacular will do." Weekly. Estab. 1993.

Needs: "We do not want to see anything that fits neatly into categories. We subvert categories." Publishes ms 2-4 months after acceptance. **Publishes 20-30 new writers/year.** Word length: 250-500 average. Publishes short shorts. Also publishes literary essays, literary criticism and poetry. Sometimes comments on or critiques rejected ms.

How to Contact: "E-mail to salsanis@scn.org." Reports on queries in 2-4 weeks. Send SASE for reply, return of ms or send a disposable copy of ms. No simultaneous submissions. Reviews novels, short story collections and poetry.

Payment/Terms: Acquires one-time rights. Sponsors contest.

Advice: "Be different, but interesting. Humor and consciousness are always helpful. Write short. We're a postmodern e-zine."

RE:AL, The Journal of Liberal Arts, Stephen F. Austin State University, P.O. Box 13007, Nacogdoches TX 75962-3007. (409)468-2059. Fax: (409)468-2614. E-mail: f_real@sfasu.edu. Website: www.libarts.sfasu.edu/REAL/index.html (includes writer's guidelines). **Editor:** W. Dale Hearell. Academic journal: 6×10; perfect-bound; 175-225 pages; "top" stock. Editorial content: 30% fiction, 30% poetry, 30% scholarly essays and criticism; an occasional play, book reviews (assigned after query) and interviews. "Work is reviewed based on the intrinsic merit of the scholarship and creative work and its appeal to a sophisticated international readership (U.S., Canada, Great Britain, Ireland, Brazil, Puerto Rico, Italy)." Semiannually. Estab. 1968. Circ. 400.

Needs: Adventure, contemporary, genre, feminist, science fiction, historical, experimental, regional. No pornographic material, romance or juvenile fiction. Want more speculative, experimental, feminist and contemporary. Receives 1,400-1,600 unsolicited mss/2 issues. Accepts 2-5 fiction mss/issue. Publishes 1-12 months after acceptance. Recently published work by Holly Kulak, Cyd Adams, John Dublin and Errol Miller. **Publishes 25 new writers/year.** Length: 1,000-5,000 words. Occasionally critiques rejected mss and conditionally accepts on basis of critiques and changes.

How to Contact: Send complete ms with cover letter. No simultaneous submissions. Reports in 2 weeks on queries; 3-4 weeks on mss. SASE. Sample copy and writer's guidelines for $12.50. Guidelines for SASE.

Payment/Terms: Pays 2 contributor's copies; charges for extras. Rights revert to author.

Advice: "Please study an issue. *RE:AL* seeks finely crafted stories that include individualistic ideas and approaches, allowing and encouraging deeper repeated readings. Have your work checked by a well-published writer—who is not a good friend. Also proofread for grammatical and typographical errors. A manuscript must show that the writer is conscious of what he or she is attempting to accomplish in plot, character and theme. A short story isn't written but constructed; the ability to manipulate certain aspects of a story is the sign of a conscious storyteller."

RECURSIVE ANGEL. (914)765-1156. Fax: (914)765-1157. E-mail: recangel@calldei.com. Website: www.recursiveangel.com. **Fiction Editor:** Paul Kloppenborg. E-zine. "*Recursive Angel* looks for and pays a fee for high quality, cutting edge fiction, poetry and art. We prefer the serious writer with a preference to the philosophical/experimental in works accepted."

Needs: Literary. "Wants experimental, no standard storyline or topic. Would like to see more of those stories that take risks with ones imagination as well as reach for broader world views." **Publishes 50-60 new writers/year.** Recently published work by Beth Spencer, Mark Budman and Coral Hull.

How to Contact: Send queries/mss by e-mail. "Our guidelines with the appropriate editorial contacts are listed on our web pages."

Payment/Terms: Pays $15/short story; $10/poem.

Advice: "Take a chance with your writing, push the envelope. Electronic publishing is alive and healthy! We see thousands of readers per month and have received positive write-ups/reviews from the *New York Times Online*, *Poets & Writers* and *The Boston Review*."

RED CEDAR REVIEW, Dept. of English, 17C Morrill Hall, Michigan State University, East Lansing MI 48824. (517)655-6307. E-mail: rcreview@msu.edu. Website: www.msu.edu/~rcreview (includes writer's guidelines, editors' names, subscription information). Editors change. **Fiction Editor:** David Sheridan. Magazine: 5½×8½; 100 pages. Theme: "literary—poetry and short fiction." Biannual. Estab. 1963. Circ. 400.

Needs: Literary. "Good stories with character, plot and style, any genre, but with a real tilt toward literary fiction." Accepts 3-4 mss/issue, 6-10 mss/year. Recently published work by Marc Bookman and Catherine Ryan Hyde. **Publishes 4 new writers/year.** Length: 5,000 words maximum.

How to Contact: Query with unpublished ms with SASE. No simultaneous submissions. Reports in 2-3 months on mss. Publishes ms up to 4 months after acceptance. Sample copy for $5.

Payment/Terms: Pays 2 contributor's copies. $5 charge for extras. Acquires first rights.

Advice: "It would be nice to see more stories that self-confidently further our literary tradition in some way, stories that 'marry artistic vision with moral insight.' What does your story discover about the human condition? What have you done with words and sentences that's new? Hundreds of journals get hundreds of manuscripts in the mail each month. Why does yours need to get printed? I don't want to learn yet again that innocent people suffer, that life is hollow, that the universe is meaningless. Nor do I want to be told that a warm kitten can save one from the abyss. I want an honest, well crafted exploration of where and what we are. Something after which I can no longer see the world in the same way."

REED MAGAZINE, % English Dept., San Jose State University, 1 Washington Square, San Jose CA 95192-0009. (408)924-4493. Website: www.SJSU.edu. Editors change each year. Magazine: 6×9; 140 pages; matte paper; textured cover; illustrations; photos. "We publish the highest quality material we can find." Annually. Estab. 1946. Circ. 700.

Needs: Experimental, humor/satire, literary, regional. "All quality work is considered." No genre romance or science fiction. Receives 150-200 unsolicited mss/month. Accepts 30-40 mss/issues. Does not read mss May through August. Publishes ms each May. Recently published work by Robert Phillips, P.J. Rondinore, R.T. Smith, Richard Burgin and Richard Kostelanetz. Length: 4,000 words average. Publishes short shorts. Also publishes literary essays and poetry.

How to Contact: Send complete ms with a cover letter. Include list of publications. Reports in 6 weeks on queries; 3 months on mss. Send SASE for reply, return of ms or send a disposable copy of ms. Sample copy for $4.95 and 6×9 SASE with 3 first-class stamps. Fiction guidelines given in the magazine.

Payment/Terms: Pays 2 contributor's copies. Author retains all rights.

Advice: Looks for "quality and originality. Most of all, we're looking for a distinctive voice. Read the best magazines and make yourself an expert in what makes a story work. We'd like to see more lovingly obsessive attention to detail. We don't want to see generic and undetailed five-page stories."

REFLECT, 1317-D Eagles Trace Path, Chesapeake VA 23320. (757)547-4464. Editor: W.S. Kennedy. Magazine: 5½×8½; 48 pages; pen & ink illustrations. "Spiral Mode fiction and poetry for writers and poets—professional and amateur." Quarterly. Estab. 1979.

Needs: Spiral fiction. "The four rules to the Spiral Mode fiction form are: (1) The story a situation or condition. (2) The outlining of the situation in the opening paragraphs. The story being told at once, the author is not overly-involved with dialogue and plot development, may concentrate on *sound*, *style*, *color*—the superior elements in art. (3) The use of a concise style with euphonic wording. Good poets may have the advantage here. (4) The involvement of Spiral Fiction themes—as opposed to Spiral Poetry themes—with love, and presented with the mystical overtones of the Mode." No "smut, bad taste, socialist." Accepts 2-6 mss/issue; 8-24 mss/year. Publishes ms 3 months after acceptance. Recently published work by Dr. Elaine Hatfield, Ruth Schuler, Joan P. Kincaid and Susan Tanaka. **Publishes 6 new writers/year.** Length: 1,500 words average; 2,500 words maximum. Publishes short shorts. Sometimes critiques rejected mss.

How to Contact: Send complete ms with cover letter. Reports in 2 months on mss. SASE. No simultaneous submissions. Sample copy for $2. (Make checks payable to W.S. Kennedy.) Fiction guidelines in each issue of *Reflect*.

Payment/Terms: Pays contributor's copies. Acquires one-time rights. Publication not copyrighted.

Advice: "Subject matter usually is not relevant to the successful writing of Spiral Fiction, as long as there is some element or type of *love* in the story, and provided that there are mystical references. (Though a dream-like style may qualify as 'mystical.')"

$ THE REJECTED QUARTERLY, A Journal of Quality Literature Rejected at Least Five Times, Black Plankton Press, P.O. Box 1351, Cobb CA 95426. E-mail: bplankton@juno.com. Editor: Daniel Weiss. **Fiction Editors:** Daniel Weiss, Jeff Ludecke. Magazine: 8½×11; 40 pages; 60 lb. paper; 8 pt. coated cover stock; illustrations. "We want the best literature possible, regardless of genre. We do, however, have a bias toward the unusual and toward speculative fiction. We aim for a literate, educated audience. *The Rejected Quarterly* believes in publishing the highest quality rejected fiction and other writing that doesn't fit anywhere else. We strive to be different, but will go for quality every time, whether conventional or not." Quarterly. Estab. 1998.

Needs: Experimental, fantasy, historical, humor/satire, literary, mainstream/contemporary, mystery/suspense, romance (futuristic/time travel only), science fiction (soft/sociological), sports. "No vampire fiction." Receives 30 unsolicited mss/month. Accepts 4-6 mss/issue; 16-24 mss/year. Publishes ms 1-12 months after acceptance. Recently published work by Vera Searles, Lance Carrey, Arthur Winefeld Knight, Kay Haugaard, Jessiyka Anya Blau and Thomas E. Kennedy. **Publishes 1-2 new writers/year.** Length: 5,000 words average; no mimimum; 8,000 words maximum. Publishes short shorts. Also publishes literary essays, literary criticism, poetry. Often critiques or comments on rejected ms.

How to Contact: Send complete ms with a cover letter and 5 rejection slips. Include estimated word count, 1-paragraph bio and list of publications. Accepts queries by e-mail. Reports in 1-2 weeks on queries; 1-3 months on mss. Send SASE for reply, return of ms or send a disposable copy of ms. Reprint submissions OK. Sample copy $6 (IRCs for foreign requests). Reviews novels, short story collections and nonfiction.

Payment/Terms: Pays $5 on acceptance and 1 contributor's copy for first rights; additional copies, one at cost, others $5. Sends galleys to author if possible.

Advice: "We are looking for high-quality writing that tells a story or expresses a coherent idea. We want unique stories, original viewpoints and unusual slants. We are getting far too many inappropriate submissions. Please be familiar with the magazine. Be sure to include your rejection slips! Send out quality rather than quantity. Work on one piece until it is as close to a masterpiece in your own eyes as you can get it. Find the right place for it. Be selective in ordering samples, but do be familiar with where you're sending your work."

$ REVIEW: LATIN AMERICAN LITERATURE AND ARTS, 680 Park Ave., New York NY 10021. (212)249-8950, ext. 366. **Editor:** Alfred MacAdam. Managing Editor: Daniel Shapiro. "Magazine of Latin American fiction, poetry and essays in translation for academic, corporate and general audience." Biannual.

Needs: Literary. No political or sociological mss. Receives 5 unsolicited mss/month. Length: 1,500-2,000 words average. Occasionally critiques rejected mss.

How to Contact: "Please submit query before sending any manuscripts. We will request manuscripts if interested." Reports in 3 months. "Submissions must be previously unpublished in English." Simultaneous submissions OK, if notified of acceptance elsewhere. Sample copy free. Reviews novels and short story collections. Send books to Daniel Shapiro, Managing Editor.

Payment/Terms: Pays $50-200 and 2-3 contributor's copies on publication.

Advice: "We are always looking for good translators."

RHINO, The Poetry Forum, P.O. Box 554, Winnetka IL 60093. Website: www.artic.edu/~ageorge/RHINO. **Editors:** Alice George, Deborah Nadler Rosen. Magazine: 5½×7½; 90-120 pages; glossy cover stock; illustrations and photos. "An eclectic magazine looking for strong voices and risk-taking." Annually. Estab. 1976.

Needs: Erotica, ethnic/multicultural, experimental, feminist, humor/satire, literary, mainstream/contemporary, regional. "No long stories—we only print short-shorts/flash fiction." Receives 20-30 unsolicited mss/month. Accepts 1-2 mss/issue. Publishes ms up to 9 months after acceptance. Published work by Anne Calcagno and David Starkey. Length: flash fiction/short shorts (under 500 words) only. Also publishes literary essays. Sometimes critiques or comments on rejected ms.

How to Contact: Send complete ms with a cover letter. Include bio. Reports in 1 month on queries; 3 months on mss. Send SASE for reply, return of ms or send a disposable copy of ms. Simultaneous submissions OK. Sample copy $5. Fiction guidelines free.

Payment/Terms: Pays 2 contributor's copies; additional copies $3.50. Acquires one-time rights. Sends galleys to author.

RIO GRANDE REVIEW, UT El Paso's literary magazine, Student publications, 105 E. Union, University of Texas at El Paso, El Paso TX 79968-0062. (915)747-5161. Fax: (915)747-8031. E-mail: rgr@mail.utep.edu. Website: www.utep.edu/proscmine/rgr/. **Editors:** Skipper Warson and Magdoline Asfahan. Editors change each year. Magazine: 6×9; approximately 200 pages; 70 lb. paper; 85 lb. cover stock; illustrations and photographs. "We publish any work that challenges writing and reading audiences alike. The intended audience isn't any one sect in particular; rather, the work forcing readers to think as opposed to couch reading is encouraged." Semiannually. Estab. 1984. Circ. 1,000.

Needs: Experimental, feminist, gay, humor/satire, lesbian, mainstream/contemporary, flash fiction, short drama, short fiction. No regional, "anything exclusionarily academic." Receives 40-45 unsolicited mss/month. Accepts 3-4 mss/issue; 6-8 mss/year. Publishes ms approximately 2 months after acceptance. Published work by Lawrence Dunning, James J. O'Keeffe and Carole Bubash. Length: 1,750 words average; 1,100 words minimum; 2,000 words maximum. Publishes short shorts. Also publishes poetry. Sometimes critiques or comments on rejected mss.

How to Contact: Send complete ms with a cover letter. Include estimated word count, 40-word bio and list of publications. Reports in 3 months on queries; 4 months on mss. Send SASE for reply and disposable copy of ms. Electronic submissions OK. Sample copy for $5.

Payment/Terms: Pays 2 contributor's copies on publication; additional copies for $5. Acquires "one-time rights that revert back to the author but the *Rio Grande Review* must be mentioned."

Advice: "Be patient. If the beginning fiction writer doesn't make it into the edition the first time, re-submit. Be persistent. One huge category that the *RGR* is branching into is flash fiction. Because the attention span of the nation is dwindling, thereby turning to such no-brain activities as television and movies, literature must change to accommodate as well."

N RIVER CITY, Dept. of English, The University of Memphis, Memphis TN 38152. (901)678-4509. **Editor:** Thomas Russell. Magazine: 7×10; 150 pages. Semiannually. Estab. 1980. Circ. 1,200.

Needs: Short stories. Recently published work by John Updike and Susan Minot; **published new writers within the last year.**

How to Contact: Send complete ms with SASE. Reports in 2 months on ms. Sample copy for $7.

Payment/Terms: Pays 2 contributor's copies. Acquires first North American serial rights.

Advice: "We're soliciting work from writers with a national reputation. I would prefer no cover letter. *River City* Writing Awards in Fiction: $2,000 1st prize, $500 2nd prize, $300 3rd prize. See magazine for details. Send SASE for upcoming topics and contest guidelines."

✓ $ RIVER STYX, Big River Association, 634 N. Grand Blvd., 12th Floor, St. Louis MO 63103-1218. **Editor:** Richard Newman. Magazine: 6×9; 100 pages; color card cover; perfect-bound; b&w visual art. "No theme restrictions; only high quality, intelligent work." Triannual. Estab. 1975.

Needs: Excerpted novel chapter, contemporary, ethnic, experimental, feminist, gay, satire, lesbian, literary, mainstream, prose poem, translations. No genre fiction, "less thinly veiled autobiography." Receives 150-200 unsolicited mss/month. Accepts 1-3 mss/issue; 3-8 mss/year. Reads only May through November. Published work by Richard Burgin, Lucia Perillo, Leslie Pietrzyk and Peggy Shinner. Length: no more than 20-30 manuscript pages. Publishes short shorts. Also publishes poetry. Sometimes critiques rejected mss and recommends other markets.

How to Contact: Send complete ms with name and address on every page. SASE required. Reports in 3-5 months on mss. Simultaneous submissions OK, "if a note is enclosed with your work and if we are notified immediately upon acceptance elsewhere." Sample copy for $7.

Payment/Terms: Pays 2 contributor's copies, 1-year subscription and $8/page "if funds available." Acquires first North American serial rights.

Advice: "We want high-powered stories with well-developed characters. We like strong plots, usually with at least three memorable scenes, and a subplot often helps. No thin, flimsy fiction with merely serviceable language. Short stories shouldn't be any different than poetry–every single word should count. One could argue every word counts more since we're being asked to read 10 to 30 pages."

N: ⬤ RIVERWIND, General Studies/Hocking College, 3301 Hocking Pkwy., Nelsonville OH 45764. (614)753-3591 (ext. 2375). Editors: Deni Naffziger and Jane Ann Devol-Fuller. **Fiction Editors:** Kris Williams and Jeff Hanson. Magazine: 7×7; 60 lb. paper; cover illustrations; "College press, small literary magazine." Annually. Estab. 1975.

    ● In addition to receiving funding from the Ohio Arts Council from 1985 to 1992, *Riverwind* has won the Septa Award and a Sepan Award.

Needs: Contemporary, ethnic, feminist, historical, humor/satire, literary, mainstream, prose poem, spiritual, sports, regional, translations. No juvenile/teen fiction. Receives 30 mss/month. Does not read during the summer. Published work by Greg Anderson and James Riley; **published new writers within the last year.** Sometimes critiques rejected mss.

How to Contact: Send complete ms with a cover letter. No simultaneous submissions. Reports on mss in 1-4 months. SASE. Sample back issue: $1.

Payment/Terms: Pays in contributor's copies.

Advice: "Your work must be strong, entertaining. It helps if you are an Ohio/West Virginia writer. We hope to print more fiction. We now publish mainly regional writers (Ohio, West Virginia, Kentucky)."

⬤ ROANOKE REVIEW, English Department, Roanoke College, Salem VA 24153. (703)375-2500. **Editor:** Robert R. Walter. Magazine: 6×9; 40-60 pages. Semiannually. Estab. 1967. Circ. 300.

Needs: Receives 50-60 unsolicited mss/month. Accepts 2-3 mss/issue; 4-6 mss/year. Publishes ms 6 months after acceptance. Length: 2,500 words minimum; 7,500 words maximum. Publishes short shorts. Occasionally critiques rejected mss.

How to Contact: Send complete ms with a cover letter. Reports in 1-2 weeks on queries; 10-12 weeks on mss. SASE for query. Sample copy for $3.

Payment/Terms: Pays in contributor's copies.

$⬤ ROCKET PRESS, P.O. Box 730, Greenport NY 11944-0730. E-mail: rocketusa@delphi.com. Website: www.people.delphi.com/rocketusa. **Editor:** Darren Johnson. 16-page newspaper. "A Rocket is a transcendental, celestial traveler—innovative and intelligent fiction and poetry aimed at opening minds—even into the next century." Biannually. Estab. 1993. Circ. 500-2,000.

Needs: Erotica, experimental, humor/satire, literary, special interests (prose poetry). "No historical, romance, academic." Publishes annual special fiction issue or anthology. Receives 20 unsolicited mss/month. Accepts 2-4 mss/issue; 8-16 mss/year. Published work by Chris Woods, Roger Lee Kenvin and Ben Ohmart. **Publishes 1 new writer/year.** Length: 1,000 words average; 500 words minimum; 2,000 words maximum. Publishes short shorts. Length: 400 words. Also publishes poetry. Sometimes critiques or comments on rejected mss.

How to Contact: Reports in 3 months on mss. Send SASE for reply, return of ms or send a disposable copy of ms. Simultaneous submissions OK. Current issue $2, past issue $1.

Payment/Terms: Pays 1¢/word. Acquires one-time rights.

Advice: "We've changed our dateline to 2050 A.D. and publish straight, newspaper-style stories that fit that time frame. Send anything that could also be publishable fifty years from now. Zany is okay. Also, too many writers come off as self-important. When writing a cover letter really try to talk to the editor—don't just rattle off a list of publications you've been in."

⬤ THE ROCKFORD REVIEW, The Rockford Writers Guild, Box 858, Rockford IL 61105. **Editor-in-Chief:** David Ross. Magazine: 5⅜×8½; 50 pages; b&w illustrations; b&w photos. "We look for prose and poetry with a fresh approach to old themes or new insights into the human condition." Triquarterly. Estab. 1971. Circ. 750.

Needs: Ethnic, experimental, fantasy, humor/satire, literary, regional, science fiction (hard science, soft/sociological). Published work by Kevin Mims, Bill Embly, William Gorman and Melanie Coronetz. Length: Up to 1,300 words. Also publishes one-acts and essays.

How to Contact: Send complete ms. "Include a short biographical note—no more than four sentences." Simultaneous submissions OK. Reports in 6-8 weeks on mss. SASE. Sample copy for $5. Fiction guidelines for SASE.

Payment/Terms: Pays contributor's copies. "Two $25 editor's choice cash prizes per issue." Acquires first North American serial rights.

Advice: "Any subject or theme goes as long as it enhances our understanding of our humanity." Wants more "satire and humor, good dialogue."

N ★ ◑ ☟ ▣ THE ROSE & THORN LITERARY E-ZINE, Showcasing Emerging and Established Writers and A Writer's Resource. E-mail: raven763@aol.com or amaznbella@aol.com. Website: members.aol/Raven763/index.html (includes writer's resources, current issue, submissions guidelines and staff information). Editor: Jasmin Randick. **Fiction Editor:** Barbara Quinn. E-zine specializing in literary works of fiction, poetry and essays: 35-40 pages; illustrations and photos. "We created *The Rose & Thorn Literary E-zine* for readers and writers alike. We offer inspiration from eclectic works of distinction and provide a forum for emerging and established voices. We blend contemporary writing with traditional prose and poetry in an effort to promote the literary arts and expand the venue of standard publishing." Quarterly. Estab. 1998. Circ. 12,000.

- The Rose & Thorn Literary E-zine has received the Page One Award For Literary Contribution (1998), Scars Publications Editor's Choice Award (1998), The Original Cool Site of the Day Award (1998) and the Home and Hearth Award of Excellence (1998).

Needs: Adventure, ethnic/multicultural (general), experimental, fantasy (space fantasy, sword and sorcery), historical, horror (dark fantasy, futuristic, psychological, supernatural), humor satire, literary, mainstream, mystery/suspense, New Age, regional, religious (inspirational, religious fantasy, religious mystery/suspense, religious thriller, religious romance), romance (contemporary, futuristic/time travel, gothic, historical, regency period, romantic suspense), science fiction (hard science/technological, soft/sociological), thriller/espionage, western. Receives "several hundred" unsolicited mss/month. Accepts 8-10 mss/issue; 40-50 mss/year. "We are very open to unpublished writers and encourage submissions by both emerging and established writers. **Publishes 50% new writers.**" Recently published work by Ibarionex R. Perello and Anjana Basu. Length: 250-750 words minimum; 2,000 words maximum. Publishes short shorts. Length: 250-750 words. Also publishes literary essays and poetry. Sometimes critiques or comments on rejected mss.

How to Contact: Send queries/mss by e-mail to Jasmin Randick, managing editor at raven763@aol.com or Barbara Quinn, co-managing editor at amaznbella@aol.com. Include estimated word count, 150 word bio, list of publications and authors byline. Reports in 1 week on queries; 1-4 weeks on mss. Simultaneous submissions and reprints OK. Sample copy and fiction guidelines free. Reviews novels and short story collections. Send books to Jasmin Randick, managing editor at raven763@aol.com.

Payment/Terms: "No payment except feedback from visitors and subscribers to the site. Writer retains all rights—our goal is to showcase exceptional writers." Sends galleys to author.

Advice: "Clarity, control of the language, evocative stories that tug at the heart and make their mark on the reader long after it's been read. We look for uniqueness in voice, style and characterization. New twists on old themes are always welcome. Use all aspects of good writing in your stories, including dynamic characters, strong, narrative voice and a riveting and original plot. We have eclectic tastes so go ahead and give us a shot. Read the publication and other quality, literary journals to see if your work would fit with our style. Always check your spelling and grammar before submitting. Reread your submission with a critical eye and ask yourself, does it evoke an emotional response? Have I completely captured my reader? Check your submission for 'it' and 'was' and see if you can come up with a better way to express yourself. Be unique."

N ★ ◯ THE ROUGHNECK REVIEW, P.O. Box 759, Duluth GA 30096. (770)381-6292. E-mail: savannahbooks@mindspring.com. Website: www.savannahbooks.com (includes writer's guidelines). Editor: Brian P. McQuilkin. **Fiction Editor:** Jamie Underwood. Magazine: 8½ × 11; 72 pages; uncoated index stock paper. "*The Roughneck Review* is dedicated to the work of new American authors and poets who might otherwise remain unpublished due to atypical writing styles or unpopular subject matter. We look for writers who not only choose the road less traveled, but dive into the woods and beat their own path. By bringing these writers and their work to the public, we hope to broaden the expectations of our readers in an ever narrowing and corporate market." Bimonthly. Estab. 1999.

Needs: Experimental, literary, mainstream. Receives 30 unsolicited mss/month. Accepts 12 mss/issue. Publishes ms 2-4 months after acceptance. **"Almost all" previously unpublished writers.** Word length: 2,500 words average; 250 words minimum; 7,500 words maximum. Publishes short shorts. Length: 250 words. Also publishes poetry. Often comments on or critiques rejected ms.

How to Contact: Send complete ms with a cover letter. Inquiries by fax and e-mail OK. Include estimated word count. Reports in 2 weeks on queries; 1 month on mss. Send SASE for reply, return of mss or send a disposable copy of ms. Simultaneous submissions OK. Guidelines free.

Payment/Terms: Pays subscription to the magazine and 5 contributor's copies; additional copies $2.50. Payment on publication. Acquires one-time rights.

Advice: "Our only criteria is that a submission be well-written, unique and fresh. Don't write something that you think a publisher would want you to write. Write what you like to write, not the same tripe that everyone else is writing. Many (but not all) publishers of short fiction appear to print only that which is commercially viable and trendy at the moment. *The Roughneck Review* looks for fiction and poetry that differs from the commonly published work which litters most reviews and magazines."

N 🖉 **THE ROUND TABLE, A Journal of Poetry and Fiction**, P.O. Box 18673, Rochester NY 14618. Editors: Alan and Barbara Lupack. Magazine: 6×9; 64 pages. "We publish serious poetry and fiction based on or alluding to the Arthurian legends." Annually. Estab. 1984. Circ. 150.
Needs: "Any approach with a link to Arthurian legends. The quality of the fiction is the most important criterion." Published new writers within the last year. Publishes ms about 9 months after acceptance. Publishes short shorts. Publishes chapbooks.
How to Contact: Send complete ms with cover letter. Reports usually in 3-4 months, but stories under consideration may be held longer. SASE for ms. Simultaneous submissions OK—if notified immediately upon acceptance elsewhere. Sample copy for $4 (specify fiction issue). Fiction guidelines for SASE.
Payment/Terms: Contributor's copy, reduced charge for extras.

N **SALMAGUNDI**, Skidmore College, Saratoga Springs NY 12866. (518)584-5000. **Editor**: Robert Boyers. Literary magazine: 5½×8½; 200 pages; photos. Quarterly. Estab. 1965. Circ. 5,000-8,000. Member of CLMP, PEN.
Needs: Literary. Also publishes literary criticism and poetry
How to Contact: Reports in 6 months on mss. Sample copy for $4.

☑ 🖉 **SALT HILL**, Salt Hill, English Dept., Syracuse University, Syracuse NY 13244-1170. (315)425-9371. Fax: (315)443-3660. E-mail: cbkoplik@syr.edu. Website: www.hypertext.com/sh (includes writer's guidelines, short fiction, links, audio). **Editor**: Caryn Koplik. Magazine: 5½×8½; 120 pages. 4-color cover; illustrations and photos. Publishes fiction with "fresh imagery, original language and tonal and structural experimentation." Semiannually. Estab. 1994. Circ. 1,000.
● Member of CLMP. Sponsors short short fiction contest. Deadline September 15. Send SASE for details.
Needs: Erotica, ethnic/multicultural, experimental, gay, humor/satire, lesbian, literary, translations. No genre fiction. Receives 40-50 unsolicited mss/month. Accepts 3-5 mss/issue; 6-10 mss/year. Publishes ms 2-8 months after acceptance. Recently published work by Christine Schutt, Edra Ziesk and Mark Kipniss. **Publishes 2 new writers/year.** Length: 4,500 words maximum. Publishes short shorts. Also publishes literary essays, literary criticism and poetry.
How to Contact: Send complete ms with a cover letter. Include 3-5 sentence bio and estimated word count. Accepts fiction queries/mss by e-mail. Reports in 2-6 months on mss. Send SASE for reply, return of ms or send disposable copy of ms. Simultaneous submissions OK. Sample copy for $8. Fiction guidelines for #10 SASE. Reviews novels or short story collections. Send books to "Book Review Editor."
Payment/Terms: Pays 1 contributor's copy for first North American serial rights and web rights; additional copies $7.
Tips: "Read everything you can, think about what you read, understand the structures, characters, etc.—then write, and write, and write again."

◎ **SAMSARA, The Magazine of Suffering**, P.O. Box 367, College Park MD 20741-0367. Website: members .aol.com/rdfgoalie/ (includes writer's guidelines and tips for writers). **Editor:** R. David Fulcher. Magazine: 8½×11; 50-80 pages; Xerox paper; poster stock cover; illustrations. "*Samsara* publishes only stories or poems relating to suffering." Semiannually. Estab. 1994. Circ. 250.
Needs: Condensed/excerpted novel, erotica, experimental, fantasy (science fantasy, sword and sorcery), horror, literary, mainstream/contemporary, science fiction (hard science, soft/sociological). Receives 80 unsolicited mss/month. Accepts 17-20 mss/issue; 40 mss/year. "*Samsara* closes to submission after the publication of each issue. However, this schedule is not fixed." Publishes ms 4 months after acceptance. Recently published work by D.F. Lewis, D. Ceder and Christopher Hivner. Length: 2,000 words average; no minimum or maximum. Publishes short shorts. Also publishes poetry. Sometimes critiques or comments on rejected ms.
How to Contact: Send complete ms with a cover letter. Include estimated word count, 1-page bio and list of publications. Reports in 6 months on queries. Send SASE for reply, return of ms or send a disposable copy of ms. Simultaneous and reprint submissions OK. Sample copy for $5.50. Fiction guidelines for #10 SASE.
Payment/Terms: Pays 1 contributor's copy. Acquires first North American serial rights and reprint rights.
Advice: "We seek out writers who make use of imagery and avoid over-writing. Symbolism and myth really make a manuscript stand out. Read a sample copy. Too many writers send work which does not pertain to the guidelines. Writers should avoid sending us splatter-punk or gore stories."

N **$** ◻ **SAN DIEGO WRITERS' MONTHLY**, 3910 Chapman St., San Diego CA 92101. (619)266-0986. E-mail: mcarthy@sandiego-online.com. Website: www.sandiego-online.com/entertainment/sdwm. Editor: Michael T. MacCarthy. **Fiction Editor**: Mark A. Clements. Literary magazine: 8×10; 32 pages; 60 lb. paper; illustrations and photos. "A publication dedicated to the San Diego writing community, San Diego Writers' Monthly will cross all genres and include columns, interviews, essays, feature, reviews, fiction and poetry written by San Diego County residents." Monthly. Estab. 1991. Circ. 500.
Needs: Adventure, ethnic/multicultural (general), family saga, fantasy (space fantasy), historical (general), horror (psychological), humor satire, literary, mainstream/contemporary, mystery/suspense (police procedural, private eye/hardboiled), New Age/mystic/spiritual, regional (south west US), religious (inspirational), romance (contem-

porary, futuristic/time travel, gothic, historical, romantic suspense), science fiction (soft/sociological), thriller/espionage, western (traditional), young adult/teen (adventure, fantasy/science fiction, historical, horror, mystery/suspense, western). No children's/juvenile, erotica, occult, translations. Receives 25-100 unsolicited mss/month. Accepts 2 mss/issue; 24 mss/year. **Publishes 50-80% new writers.** Length: 2,500 words minimum; 4,000 words maximum. Also publishes literary essays, criticism and poetry. Sometimes critiques or comments on rejected ms.
How to Contact: Send complete ms with a cover letter. Include estimated word count, 25-50 word bio, list of publications. Send SASE for reply and a disposable copy of ms. No simultaneous submissions. Reprint submissions OK. Sample copy for $4. Guidelines for SASE. Reviews novels, short story collections or nonfiction books of interest to writers. Send books to editor.
Payment/Terms: Pays $15-25 and 1 contributor's copy on publication for one-time rights.
Advice: Looks for "good, tight, entertaining writing. Follow the guidelines."

N ⬤ SANTA BARBARA REVIEW, Literary Arts Journal, P.O. Box 808, Summerland CA 93067-0808. (805)969-0861. Editor: Patricia Stockton Leddy. Magazine: 6×9; 240 pages, 60 lb. opaque paper; 10 pt. CS1; illustrations and photos. "The goal of *The Santa Barbara Review* is to find stories that entertain, surprise, and shed light on the vast human condition." Annual. Estab. 1993.
Needs: Literary. "No children's fiction. We try to avoid topics for their news value or political correctness." Receives 50-100 unsolicited fiction mss/month. Accepts 6-8 mss/issue; 24 mss/year. Publishes ms 1 year after acceptance. Length: 3,500-4,000 words average. Occasionally publishes short shorts. Length: 500 words. Also publishes literary essays and poetry. Often critiques or comments on rejected mss.
How to Contact: Send complete ms with a cover letter. Include 2-3 line bio and list of publications. "Always send a disk upon acceptance, Macintosh or IBM." Reports in 6 weeks on queries; 6 months on mss. Send SASE for reply, return of ms or send a disposable copy of ms. Electronic (disk) submissions OK. Sample copy for $7. Reviews novels and short story collections.
Payment/Terms: Pays 2 contributor's copies. Acquires one-time rights.
Advice: "First thing we look for is voice. Make every word count. We want to see immediate involvement, convincing dialogue, memorable characters. Show us connection between things we had previously thought disparate. The self-indulgent, feel sorry for yourself polemic we really don't like. We are very fond of humor that is not mean spirited and wish to see more."

N ⬤ SANTA MONICA REVIEW, Santa Monica College, 1900 Pico Blvd., Santa Monica CA 90405. (310)434-4242. **Editor:** Andrew Tonkovich. Magazine: 250 pages. "The editors are committed to fostering new talent as well as presenting new work by established writers. There is also a special emphasis on presenting and promoting writers who make their home in Southern California." Estab. 1989. Circ. 1,500.
Needs: Literary, experimental. No "genre writing, no TV, no clichés, no gimmicks." Want more "self conscious, smart, political, humorous, digressive, meta-fiction." Publishes special fiction issues or anthologies. Receives 250 unsolicited mss/month. Accepts 10 mss/issue; 20 mss/year. Agented fiction 10%. **Publishes 3-4 new writers/year.** Recently published work by Jim Krusoe, Aimee Bender, Gregg Bills, Judith Grossman and Amy Gerstler. Also publishes literary essays, memoirs and novel chapters.
How to Contact: Send complete ms with a cover letter. Reports in 3 months. Send a disposable copy of ms. Simultaneous submissions OK. Sample copy for $7.
Payment/Terms: Pays 2 contributor's copies for first North American serial rights. Sends galleys to author.

⬤ SATIRE, C&K Publications, P.O. Box 340, Hancock MD 21750-0340. (301)678-6999. E-mail: satire@intrepid.net. Website: www.intrepid.net/satire (includes guidelines, preview of issues, links for satire, ordering information). **Editor:** Larry Logan. Magazine: 8½×11; 60-70 pages; bond paper; illustrations. "We hope that our quarterly provides a home for contemporary literary satire that might make you laugh . . . make you squirm . . . and make you think." Quarterly. Estab. 1994. Circ. 500.
Needs: Humor/satire, literary. "We will consider all categories as long as a satiric treatment is incorporated. Would like more political satire." Receives 150 unsolicited mss/month. Accepts 20 mss/issue; 80 mss/year. Publishes ms within 6 months after acceptance. Published work by Frederick J. McGavran, Mark Gifford, Gene-Michael Higney, Terry Stawar, Barbara Lefcowitz, Dick Lancaster and Leslie Woolf Hedley. Length: 6,000 words maximum. Publishes short shorts. Also publishes literary essays, condensed/excerpted novel, poetry and 3-6 cartoons/issue. Sometimes critiques or comments on rejected mss.
How to Contact: Send complete ms with cover letter. Include estimated word count, a short bio and list of publications. Accepts queries by e-mail. Reports in 3 months on mss. Send SASE for reply, return of ms or send a disposable copy of ms. Simultaneous, reprint and electronic submissions OK. Sample copy for $5 and #10 SASE. Fiction guidelines free.
Payment/Terms: Pays 2 contributor's copies for works over 1 page; additional 5 copies at cost to authors. Acquires one-time rights. Sends galleys to author.
Advice: "When considering fiction, we ask does it make us laugh? Does it make us think? Does it make us say Wow! I never looked at it that way before! Clever humor and wit is prized within a well-developed story/essay/etc."

SCRIVENER CREATIVE REVIEW, 853 Sherbrooke St. W., Montreal, Quebec H3A 2T6 Canada. (514)398-6588. Fax: (514)398-8146. E-mail: bqgc@musicb.mcgillica. Coordinating Editors: Konstantine Stavrakos and Michelle Syba. **Fiction Editors:** Michael Bezuhly and Sarah Mynowski. Magazine: 8×9; 100 pages; matte paper; illustrations; b&w photos. "*Scrivener* is a creative journal publishing fiction, poetry, graphics, photography, reviews, interviews and scholarly articles. We publish the best of new and established writers. We examine how current trends in North American writing are rooted in a pervasive creative dynamic; our audience is mostly scholarly and in the writing field." Annually. Estab. 1980. Circ. 500.

Needs: Open, "good writing." Receives 10 unsolicited mss/month. Accepts 20 mss/year. Does not read mss May 1-Sept 1. Publishes ms 2 months after acceptance. Published work by Gail Scott, Heather Hermant and Leanne Fitzgerald. **Publishes 6 new writers/year.** Length: 25 pages maximum. Occasionally publishes short shorts. Also publishes literary essays, literary criticism, poetry. Often critiques rejected mss. Rarely recommends other markets.

How to Contact: Send complete ms with a cover letter and SASE. Include 50-100 word bio and list of publications. Accepts queries/mss by fax. "If piece is in simultaneous circulation, include the titles of the other journals/magazines." Order sample copy ($5); send complete ms with cover letter with "critical statements; where we can reach you; biographical data; education; previous publications." Reports in 4 months on queries and mss. SASE/IRC preferred but not required. Simultaneous and photocopied submissions OK. Accepts computer printouts. Sample copy for $5 (US in USA; Canadian in Canada). Fiction guidelines for SAE/IRC. Reviews novels and short story collections. Send books to Nonfiction Editor.

Payment/Terms: Pays contributor's copies; charges for extras. Rights retained by the author.

Advice: "Send us your best stuff. Don't be deterred by rejections. Sometimes a magazine just isn't looking for your *kind* of writing. Don't neglect the neatness of your presentation."

$ THE SEATTLE REVIEW, Padelford Hall Box 354330, University of Washington, Seattle WA 98195. (206)543-9865. E-mail: seaview@english.washington.edu. Website: www.weber.u.washington.edu/~engl/seavie w1.html (includes short fiction, guidelines, list of back issues, mission statement and visuals of covers). **Editor:** Colleen J. McElroy. Magazine: 6×9. "Includes general fiction, poetry, craft essays on writing, and one interview per issue with a Northwest writer." Semiannual. Published special fiction issue. Estab. 1978. Circ. 1,000.

Needs: Contemporary, ethnic, experimental, fantasy, feminist, gay, historical, horror, humor/satire, lesbian, literary, mainstream, prose poem, psychic/supernatural/occult, regional, science fiction, excerpted novel, mystery/suspense, translations, western. Wants more creative nonfiction. "We also publish a series called Writers and their Craft, which deals with aspects of writing fiction (also poetry)—point of view, characterization, etc., rather than literary criticism, each issue." Does not want to see "anything in bad taste (porn, racist, etc.)." Receives about 100 unsolicited mss/month. Buys about 3-6 mss/issue; about 4-10 mss/year. Does not read mss June through September. Agented fiction 25%. Recently published work by Daniel Orozco, Frederick Busch, Peter Bacho, Jewell Parker Rhodes and David Guterson; **published new writers within the last year.** Length: 3,500 words average; 500 words minimum; 10,000 words maximum. Publishes short shorts. Sometimes critiques rejected mss. Occasionally recommends other markets.

How to Contact: Send complete ms. Reports in 6-8 months. SASE. Sample copy "half-price if older than one year." Current issue for $6; some special issues $8.

Payment/Terms: Pays 0-$100, 2 contributor's copies; charge for extras. Pays on publication for first North American serial rights. Copyright reverts to writer on publication; "please request release of rights and cite *SR* in reprint publications." Sends galleys to author.

Advice: "Beginners do well in our magazine if they send clean, well-written manuscripts. We've published a lot of 'first stories' from all over the country and take pleasure in discovery."

SEED CAKE, 16966 129th Ave. SE, Renton WA 98058. E-mail: lvpurdy@earthlink.net. Website: home.earthlink.net/~lvpurdy/seedcake (includes digital chapbooks published through the website, writer's guidelines, etc.). **Editor:** Lisa Purdy. Literary e-zine. "Each issue is a self-contained file and includes a cover with the contents arranged as an A and B side like old 78 or 45 records." Estab. 1997. Circ. 5,000.

Needs: Comics/graphic novels, experimental, feminist, gay, humor satire, literary, short story collections. "We do not want to see genre fiction or fiction that can be easily classified. Receives 20 unsolicited mss/month. Accepts 2 mss/issue, 10 mss/year. Published ms 1 month after acceptance. **Publishes 1 new writer/year.** Length: 6,000 words average. No minimums or maximums. Also publishes literary essays. Often critiques or comments on rejected ms.

How to Contact: "We accept only e-mail submissions." Include bio. Reports in 1 week on queries, 1 month on mss. Simultaneous and reprint submissions OK. Sample copy and guidelines available free on website. Reviews novels, short story collections or nonfiction books of interest to writers. Send books to Matt Briggs at the above address.

Payment/Terms: Pays free subscription to the magazine. Acquires one-time rights and the right to reprint story "if we ever do an anthology." Send prepublication galleys to author.

Advice: "We look for writing with a distinctive voice or subject matter that can be arranged into a pair of short stories."

SEEMS, Lakeland College, Box 359, Sheboygan WI 53082-0359. (920)565-1276. Fax: (920)565-1206. E-mail: kelder@excel.net. **Editor:** Karl Elder. Magazine: 7×8½; 40 pages. "We publish fiction and poetry for an audience which tends to be highly literate. People read the publication, I suspect, for the sake of reading it." Published irregularly. Estab. 1971. Circ. 300.

Needs: Literary. Accepts 4 mss/issue. Receives 12 unsolicited fiction mss each month. Published work by Sapphire and other emerging writers. **Publishes 1-2 new writers/year.** Length: 5,000 words maximum. Publishes short shorts. Also publishes poetry. Critiques rejected mss when there is time.

How to Contact: Send complete ms with SASE. Reports in 2 months on mss. Publishes ms an average of 1-2 years after acceptance. Sample copy for $4.

Payment/Terms: Pays 1 contributor's copy; $4 charge for extras. Rights revert to author.

Advice: "Send clear, clean copies. Read the magazine in order to help determine the taste of the editor." Mss are rejected because of "lack of economical expression, or saying with many words what could be said in only a few. Good fiction contains all of the essential elements of poetry; study poetry and apply those elements to fiction. Our interest is shifting to story poems, the grey area between genres."

SENSATIONS MAGAZINE, 2 Radio Ave., A5, Secaucus NJ 07094-3843. E-mail: messineo@concentric.net. **Founder:** David Messineo. Magazine: 8½×11; 200 pages; 20 lb. paper; full color cover; color photography. "We publish short stories and poetry, no specific theme." Magazine also includes the Rediscovering America in Poetry research series. Semiannually. Estab. 1987.

● *Sensations Magazine* is one of the few markets accepting longer work. They would like to see more mysteries, well-researched historical fiction.

Needs: "We're interested in almost any theme/genre." Wants to see more "well-written mysteries, with great attention to period detail/research, science fiction and historical fiction." No sexually graphic work. "We're not into gratuitous profanity, pornography, or violence. Sometimes these are needed to properly tell the tale. We'll read anything unusual, providing it is submitted in accordance with our submission policies. No abstract works only the writer can understand." Theme for March 2000 issue: "Scenic New Jersey." Accepts 2-4 mss/issue. Publishes ms 2 months after acceptance. Recently published work by Don Lehmann, Vicki Moss, Bradd Saunders and Michael Pallotta. Length: 20 pages maximum.

How to Contact: Send SASE for guidelines. Simultaneous submissions OK. Accepts e-mail queries. *"Do not submit material before reading submission guidelines."*

Payment/Terms: Pays 1 copy on acceptance for one-time rights.

Advice: "Each story must have a strong beginning that grabs the reader's attention in the first two sentences. Characters have to be realistic and well-described. Readers must like, hate, or have some emotional response to your characters. Setting, plot, construction, attention to detail—all are important. We work with writers to help them improve in these areas, but the better the stories are written before they come to us, the greater the chance for publication. Purchase sample copy first and read the stories. Develop long-term relationships with five magazines whose editorial opinions you respect. Naturally, we'd like to be one of the five."

SEPIA, Poetry & Prose Magazine, Kawabata Press, Knill Cross House, Knill Cross, Millbrook, Nr Torpoint, Cornwall England. **Editor-in-Chief:** Colin David Webb. Published 3 times/year.

Needs: "Magazine for those interested in modern un-clichéd work." No science fiction, detective "or any typical genre." Contains 32 pages/issue. **Publishes 5-6 new writers/year.** Length: 200-4,000 words (for short stories).

How to Contact: Always include SAE with IRCs. Send $1 for sample copy and guidelines. Subscription $5; "no cheques!"

Payment/Terms: Pays 1 contributor's copy.

$ THE SEWANEE REVIEW, University of the South, 735 University Ave., Sewanee TN 37383-1000. (931)598-1246. E-mail: rjones@sewanee.edu. Website: www.sewanee.edu/sreview/home.html (includes extracts from recent and back issues, magazine's history, writers' guidelines, links to other literary sites). **Editor:** George Core. Magazine: 6×9; 192 pages. "A literary quarterly, publishing original fiction, poetry, essays on literary and related subjects, book reviews and book notices for well-educated readers who appreciate good American and English literature." Quarterly. Estab. 1892. Circ. 3,500.

Needs: Literary, contemporary. No erotica or excessively violent or profane material. Buys 10-15 mss/year. Receives 100 unsolicited fiction mss each month. Does not read mss June 1-August 31. **Publishes 2-3 new writers/year.** Recently published work by Ann Chidister, George V. Higgins, William Hoffman, Kent Nelson, Gladys Swan and William Trevor. Length: 6,000-7,500 words. Critiques rejected mss "when there is time." Sometimes recommends other markets.

How to Contact: Send complete ms with SASE and cover letter stating previous publications, if any. Reports in 6 weeks on mss. Sample copy for $6.25.

Payment/Terms: Pays $10-12/printed page; 2 contributor's copies; $4 charge for extras. Pays on publication for first North American serial rights and second serial rights by agreement. Writer's guidelines for SASE.

Advice: "Send only one story at a time, with a serious and sensible cover letter. We think fiction is of greater general interest than any other literary mode."

SHADES OF DECEMBER, Box 244, Selden NY 11784. E-mail: eilonwy@innocent.com. Website: www2. crosswinds.net/new-york/~shadesof12. **Editor:** Alexander Danner. Magazine: 8½ × 5½; 60 pages. "Good writing comes in all forms and should not be limited to overly specific or standard genres. Our intended audience is one that is varied in taste and open to the unorthodox." Quarterly. Estab. 1998. Circ. 200-300. Reading fee of $1 for non-electronic submissions.
Needs: Experimental, fantasy, humor/satire, literary, mainstream/contemporary, psychic/supernatural/occult, romance, science fiction. "We are not limited in the categories of writing that we will consider for publication." Accepts 1-3 mss/issue; 6-18 mss/year. Publishes ms 1-4 months after acceptance. Recently published work by Joe Lucia and Judy Thompson. Length: 2,500 words maximum. Publishes short shorts. Also publishes literary essays, poetry. Sometimes critiques or comments on rejected ms.
How to Contact: Send complete ms with a cover letter. Include bio (50 words or less) and list of publications. Reports in 6-8 weeks. Send SASE for reply, return of ms or send a disposable copy of ms. Simultaneous and reprint submissions OK. Electronic submissions preferred; $1 reading fee for nonelectronic submissions. Sample copy $3. Fiction guidelines for #10 SASE.
Payment/Terms: Pays 2 contributor's copies. Acquires one-time rights.
Advice: "We like to see work that strays from the conventional. While we print good writing in any form, we prefer to see work that takes risks."

THE SHALLOWEND EZINE, % Susan Matteson, 740 E. Mingus #2002, Cottonwood AZ 86326. (520)639-0933. E-mail: submissions@shallowend.org. Website: www.shallowend.org. **Editor:** Susan Matteson. E-zine. "Our goal is to publish literature on its own so that literature can be accessible to everyone and mean something different to each reader. Fiction, poetry and art should be an unintimidating part of our daily lives."
Needs: Literary. No "erotica, horror, or works with excessive profanity." **Publishes 40-60 new writers/year.** Recently published works by Michael Maiello, Scott Speck, Lisa Klassen and Joshua Matteson.
How to Contact: Prefers queries/mss by e-mail. Also accepts mss by snail mail. "Send writing submissions via e-mail in .txt, .doc or .html. Keep in mind line breaks or paragraph breaks may be changed when e-mailed, so put in [BR] or some equivolent notation. Please include a short tag line about author to be included in the credits (. . . and we mean about you—not what you've published). Also, please include any acompanying graphics preferences. Your e-mail address will be included in the credits unless you request it not to."
Advice: "We like very original, slightly offbeat work. We like to be entertained. We like to feel that we know something about you when we're done. We publish works in a very wide range of styles, genres and subject matters. Our best advice is to be yourself, through philosophy or character. Write in such a way that we know more about you when we are done reading your work. The world has such a variety of different and interesting voices that it is tiresome to read new writers who are trying to sound like other writers. Let your own original style and voice come through in the words."

SHATTERED WIG REVIEW, Shattered Wig Productions, 425 E. 31st, Baltimore MD 21218. (410)243-6888. **Editor:** Collective. Attn: Sonny Bodkin. Magazine: 8½ × 8½; 70 pages; "average" paper; cardstock cover; illustrations and photos. "Open forum for the discussion of the absurdo-miserablist aspects of everyday life. Fiction, poetry, graphics, essays, photos." Semiannually. Estab. 1988. Circ. 500.
Needs: Confession, contemporary, erotica, ethnic, experimental, feminist, gay, humor/satire, lesbian, literary, prose poem, psychic/supernatural/occult, regional. Does not want "anything by Ann Beattie or John Irving." Receives 15-20 unsolicited mss/month. Publishes ms 2-4 months after acceptance. Published work by Al Ackerman, Kim Harrison and Mok Hossfeld. **Published new writers within the last year.** Publishes short shorts. Also publishes literary criticism, poetry. Sometimes critiques rejected mss and recommends other markets.
How to Contact: Send complete ms with cover letter. Reports in 2 months. Send SASE for return of ms. Simultaneous and reprint submissions OK. Sample copy for $4.
Payment/Terms: Pays in contributor's copies. Acquires one-time rights.
Advice: "The arts have been reduced to imploding pus with the only material rewards reserved for vapid stylists and collegiate pod suckers. The only writing that counts has no barriers between imagination and reality, thought and action. Send us at least three pieces so we have a choice."

$ SHENANDOAH, The Washington and Lee Review, 2nd Floor, Troubadour Theater, Lexington VA 24450-0303. (540)463-8765. Fax: (540)463-8461. Website: www.wlu.edu/~shenando (includes samples, guidelines and contents). **Editor:** R.T. Smith. Magazine: 6 × 9; 124 pages. "We are a literary journal devoted to excellence." Quarterly. Estab. 1950. Circ. 2,000.
Needs: Literary. Receives 400-500 unsolicited fiction mss/month. Accepts 4 mss/issue; 16 mss/year. Does not read mss during summer. Publishes ms 6 months to 1 year after acceptance. Published work by Kent Nelson, Barry Gifford, Nicholas Delbanco and Reynolds Price. **Publishes 1 new writer/year.** Publishes short shorts. Also publishes literary essays, literary criticism and poetry.
How to Contact: Send complete ms with cover letter. Include a 3-sentence bio and list of publications ("just the highlights"). Reports in 10 weeks on mss. Send a disposable copy of ms. Sample copy for $5. Fiction guidelines for #10 SASE. Reviews novels and short story collections.

Payment/Terms: Pays $25/page, $2.50/line and free subscription to the magazine on publication. Acquires first North American serial rights. Sends galleys to author. Sponsors contest.
Advice: Looks for "thrift, precision, originality. As Frank O'Connor said, 'Get black on white.' "

◐ **SHORT STORIES BIMONTHLY**, Poetry Forum, 5713 Larchmont Dr., Erie PA 16509. Phone/fax: (814)866-2543. E-mail: 75562.670@compuserve.com. **Editor:** Gunvor Skogsholm. Newsletter: 11×17; 14 pages; 20 lb. paper; illustrations. Magazine "provides an outlet for the beginner writer, as well as the advanced to express their ideas to a greater audience." Estab. 1992. Circ. 400.
Needs: Literary, mainstream. No extreme horror. Wants more "deeply felt works, dealing with some aspect of the human condition." Receives 30 unsolicited mss/month. Accepts 8-10 mss/issue; 48-60 mss/year. Publishes ms 1-9 months after acceptance. Published work by Richard French, Tod Goldberg, David Ross and L.B. Sinnat. **Publishes 70% new writers.** Length: 1,800 words average; 600 words minimum; 4,000 words maximum. Publishes short shorts. Length: 600 words. Also publishes literary essays and literary criticism.
How to Contact: Send complete ms with a cover letter. Accepts queries/mss by e-mail and fax. Include estimated word count. Reports in 3 weeks to 6 months on mss. Send SASE for reply, return of ms or send a disposable copy of ms. Simultaneous and electronic submissions OK. Sample copy for $3. Fiction guidelines free. Favors submissions from subscribers. "We exist by subscriptions and advertising." Reviews novels and short story collections.
Payment/Terms: Acquires one-time rights. Sponsors contests, awards or grants for fiction writers. Send SASE.
Advice: "Be original, be honest. Write from your deepest sincerity—don't play games with the readers. Meaning: we don't want the last paragraph to tell us we have been fooled."

$ ◐ **SHORT STUFF MAGAZINE FOR GROWN-UPS**, Bowman Publications, P.O. Box 7057, Loveland CO 80537. (970)669-9139. **Editor:** Donna Bowman. Magazine: 8½×11; 40 pages; bond paper; enamel cover; b&w illustrations and photographs. "Nonfiction is regional—Colorado and adjacent states. Fiction and humor must be tasteful, but can be any subject. We are designed to be a 'Reader's Digest' of fiction. We are found in professional waiting rooms, etc." Publishes 6 issues/year.
Needs: Adventure, contemporary, historical, humor/satire, mainstream, mystery/suspense (amateur sleuth, English cozy, police procedural, private eye, romantic suspense), regional, romance (contemporary, gothic, historical), western (frontier). No erotica. Wants to see more humor or cozy mystery. "We use holiday themes. Need 3 month lead time. Issues are Valentine (February/March); Easter and St. Patrick's Day (April/May); Mom's and Dad's (June/July); Americana (August/September); Halloween (October/November); and Holiday (December/January). Receives 500 unsolicited mss/month. Accepts 9-12 mss/issue; 76 mss/year. Publishes accepted work immediately. Recently published work by Bill Hallstead, Eleanor Sherman, Guy Belleranti, Judith Grams, Gloria Amoury, Charles Langley, Erika Leck, Diane Sawyer and Jacque Hall. **Publishes 90% new writers.** Length: 1,000 words average; 1,600 words maximum.
How to Contact: Send complete ms with cover letter. SASE. Reports in 3-6 months. Sample copies for $1.50 and 9×12 SAE with $1.50 postage. Fiction guidelines for SASE.
Payment/Terms: Pays $10-50 "at our discretion" and subscription to magazine on publication for first North American serial rights. $1-5 for fillers (less than 500 words). "We do not pay for single jokes or poetry, but do give free subscription if published."
Advice: "We seek a potpourri of subjects each issue. A new slant, a different approach, fresh viewpoints—all of these excite us. We don't like gore, salacious humor or perverted tales. Prefer third person, past tense. Be sure it is a story with a beginning, middle and end. It must have dialogue. Many beginners do not know an essay from a short story. Essays frequently used if *humorous*. We'd like to see more young (25 and over) humor; 'clean' humor is hard to come by. Length is a big factor. Writers who can tell a good story in a thousand words are true artists and their work is highly prized by our readers. Stick to the guidelines. We get manuscripts of up to 10,000 words because the story is 'unique and deserving.' We don't even read these."

◐ ⊠ **SIDE SHOW, Short Story Anthology**, Somersault Press, P.O. Box 1428, El Cerrito CA 94530-1428. (510)215-2207. E-mail: jisom@crl.com. **Editors:** Shelley Anderson and Marjorie K. Jacobs. Book (paperback): 5½×8½; 300 pages; 50 lb. paper; semigloss card cover with color illustration; perfect-bound. "Quality short stories for a general, literary audience." Estab. 1991. Circ. 3,000.
● Previously published as an annual anthology, from now on *Side Show* will publish a book once they have the requisite number of publishable stories (approximately 20-25). There is no longer a yearly deadline. Stories are accepted year round. Work published in *Side Show* has been selected for inclusion in the *Pushcart Prize* anthology.
Needs: Contemporary, ethnic, feminist, gay, humor/satire, literary, mainstream. Nothing genre, religious, pornographic. Receives 50-60 unsolicited mss/month. Accepts 25-30 mss/issue. Publishes ms up to 9 months after acceptance. Recently published work by George Harrar, Elisa Jenkins and Miguel Rios. 25% of fiction by previously unpublished writers. **Publishes 5-10 new writers/per book.** Length: Open. Critiques rejected mss, if requested.
How to Contact: Accepts queries by e-mail. All submissions entered in contest. *$10 entry fee* (includes subscription to next *Side Show*). No guidelines. Send complete ms with cover letter and entry fee. Reports in 1

month on mss. SASE. Simultaneous submissions OK. Multiple submissions encouraged (entry fee covers all submissions mailed in same envelope). Sample copy for $10 and $2 postage and handling ($.83 sales tax CA residents).

Payment/Terms: Pays $5/printed page on publication for first North American serial rights. Sends galleys to author. All submissions entered in our contest for cash prizes of $200 (1st), $100 (2nd) and $75 (3rd).

Advice: Looks for "readability, vividness of characterization, coherence, inspiration, interesting subject matter, imagination, point of view, originality, plausibility. If your fiction isn't inspired, you probably won't be published by us (i.e., style and craft alone won't do it)."

SIDEWALKS, P.O. Box 321, Champlin MN 55316. (612)571-1390. **Editor:** Tom Heie. Magazine: 5½×8½; 60-75 pages; 60 lb. paper; textured recycled cover. "*Sidewalks* . . . place of discovery, of myth, power, incantation . . . places we continue to meet people, preoccupied, on our way somewhere . . . tense, dark, empty places . . . place we meet friends and strangers, neighborhood sidewalks, place full of memory, paths that bring us home." Semiannually. Estab. 1991. Circ. 500.

Needs: Experimental, humor/satire, literary, mainstream/contemporary, regional. No violent, pornographic kinky material. Accepts 6-8 mss/issue; 12-16 mss/year. Work is accepted for 2 annual deadlines: May 31 and December 31. Publishes ms 10 weeks after deadline. Published work by Sydney Harth, Ben Miller, Robert Haight and W.P. Strange. Length: 2,500 words preferred; 3,000 words maximum. Publishes short shorts. Also publishes poetry.

How to Contact: Send complete ms with cover letter. Include estimated word count, very brief bio, list of publications. Reports in 1 week on queries; 1 month after deadline on mss. Send SASE for reply, return of ms or send a disposable copy of ms. No simultaneous submissions. Accepts electronic submissions. Sample copy for $6.

Payment/Terms: Pays 1 contributor's copy. Acquires one-time rights.

Advice: "We look for a story with broad appeal, one that is well-crafted and has strong narrative voice, a story that leaves the reader thinking after the reading is over."

SIERRA NEVADA COLLEGE REVIEW, Sierra Nevada College, P.O. Box 4269, Incline Village NV 89450. (702)831-1314. **Editor:** June Sylvester. Magazine: 5½×8½; 50-100 pages; coated paper; card cover; saddle-stitched. "We are open to many kinds of work but avoid what we consider trite, sentimental, contrived. . . ." Annually. Estab. 1990. Circ. 200-250 (mostly college libraries).

● The majority of work published in this review is poetry.

Needs: Experimental, literary, mainstream/contemporary, regional. Receives about 50 unsolicited mss/month. Accepts 2-3 mss/year. Does not read mss April 1 through September 1. Work is published by next issue (published in May, annually). Published work by Jamie Andree and James Braziel. Length: 500 words average; 1,000 words maximum. Publishes short shorts. Also publishes literary essays, literary criticism and poetry. Sometimes critiques or comments on rejected mss.

How to Contact: Send complete ms with a cover letter. Include estimated word count and bio. Send SASE for reply, return of ms or send a disposable copy of ms. Simultaneous submissions OK. Sample copy for $2.50.

Payment/Terms: Pays 2 contributor's copies. Acquires one-time rights.

Advice: Looks for "memorable characters, close attention to detail which makes the story vivid. We are interested in flash fiction. Also regional work that catches the flavor of place and time—like strong characters. No moralizing, inspirational work. No science fiction. No children's stories. Tired of trite love stories—cynicism bores us."

THE SILVER WEB, A Magazine of the Surreal, Buzzcity Press, Box 38190, Tallahassee FL 32315. (850)385-8948. Fax: (850)385-4063. E-mail: annkl9@mail.idt.net. **Editor:** Ann Kennedy. Magazine: 8½×11; 80 pages; 20 lb. paper; full color; perfect bound; glossy cover; b&w illustrations and photographs. "Looking for unique character-based stories that are off-beat, off-center and strange, but not inaccessible." Semiannually. Estab. 1989. Circ. 2,000.

● Work published in *The Silver Web* has appeared in *The Year's Best Fantasy and Horror* (DAW Books) and *The Year's Best Fantastic Fiction*.

Needs: Experimental, horror, science fiction (soft/sociological). No "traditional storylines, monsters, vampires, werewolves, etc." *The Silver Web* publishes surrealistic fiction and poetry. Work too bizarre for mainstream, but perhaps too literary for genre. This is not a straight horror/sci-fi magazine. No typical storylines." Receives 500 unsolicited mss/month. Accepts 8-10 mss/issue; 16-20 mss/year. Does not read mss October through December. Publishes ms 6-12 months after acceptance. Recently published work by Brian Evenson, Jack Ketchum and Joel Lane. Length: 6,000 words average; 100 words minimum; 8,000 words maximum. Publishes short shorts. Also publishes poetry. Sometimes critiques rejected ms.

How to Contact: Send complete ms with a cover letter. Include estimated word count. Reports in 1 week on queries; 6-8 weeks on mss. Send SASE for reply, return of ms or send a disposable copy of ms plus SASE for reply. Simultaneous and reprint submissions OK. Sample copy for $7.20. Fiction guidelines for #10 SASE. Reviews novels and short story collections.

Payment/Terms: Pays 2-3¢/word and 2 contributor's copies; additional copies for $4. Acquires first North American serial rights, reprint rights or one-time rights.

Advice: "I have a reputation for publishing excellent fiction from newcomers next to talented, established writers, and for publishing cross-genre fiction. No traditional, standard storylines. I'm looking for beautiful writing with plots that are character-based. Tell a good story; tell it with beautiful words. I see too many writers writing for the marketplace and this fiction just doesn't ring true. I'd rather read fiction that comes straight from the heart of the writer." Read a copy of the magazine, at least get the writer's guidelines.

SILVERFISH REVIEW, Box 3541, Eugene OR 97403. (503)344-5060. E-mail: sfrpress@aol.com. Website: qhome.com/silverfish. Editor: Rodger Moody. High quality literary material for a general audience. Published in June and December. Estab. 1979. Circ. 1,000.
Needs: Literary. Accepts 1-2 mss/issue. Published work by Sherrie Flick, Lidia Yuknavitch and Dennis Duhamel. Also publishes literary essays, poetry, interviews, translations and reviews.
How to Contact: Send complete ms with SASE. No simultaneous submissions. Reports in 2-3 months on mss. Sample copy for $4 and $1.50 postage.
Payment/Terms: Pays 2 contributor's copies and one year subscription; $5/page when funding permits. Rights revert to author.
Advice: "We publish primarily poetry. We will, however, publish good quality fiction. *SR* is mainly interested in the short short story (one-minute and three-minute)."

SINISTER WISDOM, Box 3252, Berkeley CA 94703. **Editor:** Margo Mercedes Rivera-Weiss. Magazine: 5½×8½; 128-144 pages; 55 lb. stock; 10 pt C1S cover; illustrations; photos. Lesbian-feminist journal, providing fiction, poetry, drama, essays, journals and artwork. Triannually. Past issues included "Lesbians of Color," "Old Lesbians/Dykes" and "Lesbians and Religion." Estab. 1976. Circ. 2,000.
Needs: Lesbian: erotica, ethnic, experimental. No heterosexual or male-oriented fiction; no 70s amazon adventures; nothing that stereotypes or degrades women. List of upcoming themes available for SASE and on website. Receives 30 unsolicited mss/month. Accepts 6 mss/issue; 24 mss/year. Publishes ms 3 months to 1 year after acceptance. Published work by Jacqueline Miranda, Amanda Esteva and Sharon Bridgeforth; **published new writers within the last year.** Length: 2,000 words average; 500 words minimum; 4,000 words maximum. Publishes short shorts. Also publishes literary essays, literary criticism, poetry. Sometimes critiques rejected mss.
How to Contact: Send 1 copy of complete ms with cover letter, which should include a brief author's bio to be published when the work is published. Simultaneous submissions OK, if noted. Reports in 3-6 months. SASE. Sample copy for $7.50. Fiction guidelines for #10 SASE. Reviews novels and short story collections. Send books to "Attn: Book Review."
Payment/Terms: Pays 2 contributor's copies. Acquires one-time rights.
Advice: *Sinister Wisdom* is "a multicultural lesbian journal reflecting the art, writing and politics of our communities."

SKYLARK, Purdue University Calumet, 2200 169th St., Hammond IN 46323. (219)989-2273. Fax: (219)989-2165. E-mail: skylark@nwi.calumet.purdue.edu. **Editor-in-Chief:** Pamela Hunter. Magazine: 8½×11; 100 pages; illustrations; photos. "*Skylark* presents short stories, essays and poetry which capture a positive outlook on life through vivid imagery, well-developed characterization and unstylized plots. We publish adults, both beginners and professionals, and young authors side be side to complement the points of view of writers of all ages." Annually. Estab. 1971. Circ. 1,000.
Needs: Contemporary, ethnic, experimental, feminist, humor/satire, literary, mainstream, prose poem, spiritual and sports. Wants to see more experimental and avant garde fiction. No erotica, science fiction, overly-religious stories. Upcoming theme: "The American Worker" (submit by April 2000). Receives 20 mss/month. Accepts 8 mss/issue. Recently published work by Kevin Harris, Frank Scozzari and Vincent Ortega. **Publishes 5 new writers/year.** Length: 4,000 words maximum. Also publishes essays and poetry.
How to Contact: Send complete ms. Send SASE for return of ms. Accepts queries/mss by fax. Reports in 4 months. No simultaneous submissions. Sample copy for $8; back issue for $6.
Payment/Terms: Pays 3 contributor's copies. Acquires first rights. Copyright reverts to author.
Advice: "We seek fiction that presents effective imagery, strong plot, and well-developed characterization. Graphic passages concerning sex or violence are unacceptable. We're looking for dramatic, closely-edited short stories. Manuscript must require little editing both for content and syntax. Author must be sincere in the treatment of plot, characters and tone. Please state in your cover letter that the story is not being considered elsewhere. We live in one of the most industrialized sections of the country. We are looking for stories set in steel mills and refractories, etc. We especially need stories set in these areas but we rarely find such stories."

☑ ◖ ◎ **SLIPSTREAM**, Box 2071, New Market Station, Niagara Falls NY 14301. (716)282-2616. Website: www.slipstreampress.org (includes guidelines, editors, current needs, info on current and past releases, sample poems, contest info.). Editor: Dan Sicoli. **Fiction Editors:** R. Borgatti, D. Sicoli and Livio Farallo. Magazine: 7×8½; 80-100 pages; high quality paper; card cover; illustrations; photos. "We use poetry and short fiction with a contemporary urban feel." Estab. 1981. Circ. 500.

Needs: Contemporary, erotica, ethnic, experimental, humor/satire, literary, mainstream and prose poem. No religious, juvenile, young adult or romance. Occasionally publishes theme issues; query for information. Receives over 25 unsolicited mss/month. Accepts 2-4 mss/issue; 6 mss/year. Published work by Al Masarik, John Richards, Alan Catlin, Richard Kostelanetz and B.D. Love. Length: under 15 pages. Publishes short shorts. Rarely critiques rejected mss. Sometimes recommends other markets.

How to Contact: "Query before submitting." Reports within 2 months. Send SASE for reply or return of ms. Sample copy for $6. Fiction guidelines for #10 SASE.

Payment/Terms: Pays 2 contributor's copies. Acquires one-time rights.

Advice: "Writing should be honest, fresh; develop your own style. Check out a sample issue first. Don't write for the sake of writing, write from the gut as if it were a biological need. Write from experience and mean what you say, but say it in the fewest number of words."

◖ **THE SMALL POND MAGAZINE**, Box 664, Stratford CT 06615. (203)378-4066. **Editor:** Napoleon St. Cyr. Magazine: 5½×8½; 42 pages; 60 lb. offset paper; 65 lb. cover stock; illustrations (art). "Features contemporary poetry, the salt of the earth, peppered with short prose pieces of various kinds. The college educated and erudite read it for good poetry, prose and pleasure." Triannually. Estab. 1964. Circ. 300.

Needs: "Rarely use science fiction or the formula stories you'd find in *Cosmo*, *Redbook*, *Ladies Home Journal*, etc. Philosophy: Highest criteria, originality, even a bit quirky is OK. Don't mind O Henry endings but better be exceptional. Readership: College grads, and college staff, ⅓ of subscribers are college and university libraries." No science fiction, children's. Accepts 10-12 mss/year. Longer response time in July and August. Receives approximately 40 unsolicited fiction mss each month. Recently published work by Peter Baida, Stephen V. Smith, Stuart Mitchner, Margaret Haller and James Bellarosa. **Publishes 1-2 new writers/year.** Length: 200-2,500 words. Critiques rejected mss when there is time. Sometimes recommends other markets.

How to Contact: Send complete ms with SASE and short vita. Reports in 2 weeks to 3 months. Publishes ms an average of 2-18 months after acceptance. Sample copy for $4; $3 for back issues.

Payment/Terms: Pays 2 contributor's copies for all rights; $3/copy charge for extras, postage paid.

Advice: "Send for a sample copy first. All mss must be typed. Name and address and story title on front page, name of story on succeeding pages and paginated. I look for polished, smooth progression—no clumsy paragraphs or structures where you know the author didn't edit closely. Also, no poor grammar. Beginning and even established poets read and learn from reading lots of other's verse. Not a bad idea for fiction writers, in their genre, short or long fiction."

★ ☑ $ ◖ **SNOWY EGRET**, P.O. Box 9, Bowling Green IN 47833. E-mail: pcrepp@bsu.edu. Publisher: Karl Barnebey. **Editor:** Philip Repp. Magazine: 8½×11; 50 pages; text paper; heavier cover; illustrations. "Literary exploration of the abundance and beauty of nature and the ways human beings interact with it." Semiannually. Estab. 1922. Circ. 500.

● *Snowy Egret* ranked #40 on *Writer's Digest* Fiction 50 list of top markets for fiction writers.

Needs: Nature writing, including 'true' stories, eye-witness accounts, descriptive sketches and traditional fiction. "We are particularly interested in fiction that celebrates abundance and beauty of nature, encourages a love and respect for the natural world, and affirms the human connection to the environment. No works written for popular genres: horror, science fiction, romance, detective, western, etc." Receives 25 unsolicited mss/month. Accepts up to 6 mss/issue; up to 12 mss/year. Publishes ms 6 months to 1 year after acceptance. Published works by Jane Candia Coleman, Tama Janowitz, David Abrams and Suzanne Kamata. Length: 1,000-3,000 words preferred; 500 words minimum; 10,000 words maximum. Publishes short shorts. Length: 400-500 words. Sometimes critiques rejected mss.

How to Contact: Send complete ms with cover letter. "Cover letter optional: do not query." Reports in 2 months. SASE. Simultaneous (if noted) and electronic (Mac, ASCII) submissions OK. Sample back issues for $8 and 9×12 SAE. Send #10 SASE for writer's guidelines.

Payment/Terms: Pays $2/page and 2 contributor's copies on publication; charge for extras. Acquires first North American serial rights and reprint rights. Sends galleys to author.

Advice: Looks for "honest, freshly detailed pieces with plenty of description and/or dialogue which will allow the reader to identify with the characters and step into the setting. Characters who relate strongly to nature, either positively or negatively, and who, during the course of the story, grow in their understanding of themselves and the world around them."

Ⓝ ◯ ◼ **SNREVIEW: Starry Night Review—A Literary E-Zine**, 197 Fairchild Ave, Fairfield CT 06432-4856. E-mail: moxie0708@aol.com. Website: members.aol.com/jconlin1221/snreview.htm. **Editor:** Joseph Conlin. E-zine specializing in literary short stories, essays and poetry. "The *SNReview* searches for material that not only has strong characters and plot but also a devotion to imagery." Quarterly. Estab. 1999.

Needs: "We only want literary and mainstream." Receives 10 mss/month. Accepts 5 mss/issue; 20 mss/year. Publishes ms 6 months after acceptance. **Publishes 80% new writers/year.** Word length: 4,000 words average; 1,500 words minimum; 7,000 words maximum. Also publishes literary essays, literary criticism and poetry.

How to Contact: Send complete ms with a cover letter via e-mail only. Include 100 word bio and a list of publications. Reports in 1 month. Simultaneous and reprint submissions OK. Sample copy and guidelines free on website.

Payment/Terms: Acquires first rights. Sends prepublication webpages to the author.

SO TO SPEAK, A Feminist Journal of Language and Art, George Mason University, Sub1, Room 254A, 4400 University Dr., Fairfax VA 22030-4444. (703)993-3625. E-mail: sts@gmu.edu. **Fiction Editor:** Nolde Alexius. Editors change every 2 years. Magazine: 7×10; approximately 70 pages. "We are a feminist journal of high-quality material geared toward an academic/cultured audience." Semiannually. Estab. 1988. Circ. 1,300.

Needs: Ethnic/multicultural, experimental, feminist, lesbian, literary, mainstream/contemporary, regional, translations. "No science fiction, mystery, genre romance, porn (lesbian or straight)." Receives 100 unsolicited mss/month. Accepts 2-3 mss/issue; 6 mss/year. Publishes ms 6 months after acceptance. Published work by Deborah J.M. Owen and Sally Chandler. **Publishes 2 new writers/year.** Length: 4,000 words average; 6,000 words maximum. Publishes short shorts. Also publishes literary essays, literary criticism, book reviews and poetry. Sometimes critiques or comments on rejected mss.

How to Contact: Send complete ms with a cover letter. Include bio (50 words maximum) and SASE. Reports in 6 months on mss. SASE for return of ms or send a disposable copy of ms. Simultaneous submissions OK. Sample copy for $5. Fiction guidelines for #10 SASE.

Payment/Terms: Pays contributor's copies for first North American serial rights.

Advice: "Every writer has something they do exceptionally well; do that and it will shine through in the work. We look for quality prose with a definite appeal to a feminist audience. We are trying to move away from strict genre lines."

THE SOFT DOOR, 1800 U.S. Rt. 6 East, Bradner OH 43406. E-mail: terria@bgnet.bgsu.edu. **Editor:** T. Williams. Magazine: 8½×11; 100 pages; bond paper; heavy cover; illustrations and photos. "We publish works that explore human relationships and our relationship to the world." Irregularly.

Needs: Literary, mainstream/contemporary. No science fiction or romance. Receives 25 mss/month. Accepts 5 mss/year. Does not read mss November through December. Publishes ms up to 2 years after acceptance. Published work by Mark Sa Franko, Simon Peter Buehrer, E.S. Griggs, Jennifer Casteen and Jim Feltz. **Publishes 3 new writers/year.** Length: 5,000 words average; 10,000 words maximum. Publishes short shorts. Also publishes poetry. Sometimes critiques or comments on rejected mss.

How to Contact: Send complete ms with a cover letter. Include "short statement about who you are and why you write, along with any successes you have had. Please write to me like I am a human being." Send SASE for reply, return of ms or send a disposable copy of ms. "Please include SASE with all correspondence. Do not send postcards." Simultaneous submissions OK. Sample copy for $12. Make checks payable to T. Williams.

Payment/Terms: Pays 1 contributor's copy. Acquires one-time rights.

Advice: "Read as much contemporary fiction and poetry as you can get your hands on. Write about your deepest concerns. What you write can, and does, change lives. Always interested in works by Native American writers. I also don't get enough work by and about women. Be patient with the small presses. We work under terrific pressure. It's not about money; it's about the literature, caring about ideas that matter."

SONGS OF INNOCENCE, Pengradonian Publications, P.O. Box 719, New York NY 10101-0719. **Editor:** Michael Pendragon. Literary magazine/journal: 8½×5½; 52 pages; 60 lb. cover; illustrations. "A literary publication which celebrates the nobler aspects of humankind and the human experience. Along with sister-publication, *Penny Dreadful*, *Songs* seeks to provide a forum for poetry and fiction in the 19th century/Romantic/Victorian tradition." Triannually. Circ. estimated 350.

Needs: Fantasy, historical (19th century or earlier), literary, New Age, psychic/supernatural/occult. No "children's/young adult; tales mentioning 20th century persons, events, fads, etc; Christian (or anything dogmatic)." Receives 20 unsolicited mss/month. Accepts 5 mss/issue; 15 mss/year. Publishes ms up to 1 year after acceptance. Length: 500 words minimum; 2,500 words maximum. Publishes short shorts. Also publishes literary essays, literary criticism, poetry. Often critiques or comments on rejected mss.

How to Contact: Send complete ms with a cover letter. Include estimated word count, 1 page or less bio and list of publications. Reports in 3 weeks on queries; up to 3 months on mss. SASE for reply and send a disposable copy of ms. Simultaneous submissions and reprints OK. Sample copy for $5 and 9×6 SAE. Guidelines for SASE.

Payment/Terms: Pays 1 contributor's copy; additional copies $5 each. Pays on publication. Acquires one-time rights. Sends galleys to author. Sponsors contst: Awards certificate only. Writers appearing in a specific issue vote on their favorite tale and poem.

Advice: "We prefer tales set in 1910 or earlier (preferably earlier). We prefer prose in the 19th century/Victorian style. We do not like the terse, modern, post-Hemingway "see Dick run" style. Tales should transcend genres and include a spiritual supernatural element (without becoming fantasy). Avoid strong language, sex, etc. Include name and address on the title page. Include word count on title page. Double space, 12-pt. Times/Courier font, etc. (usual professional format). We select stories/poems that appeal to us and do not base selection on whether one has been published elsewhere.''

SOUTH CAROLINA REVIEW, Strode Tower, Clemson University, Clemson SC 29634-1503. (864)656-5399. Fax: (864)656-1345. E-mail: cwayne@clemson.edu. **Editor:** Wayne Chapman. Magazine: 6×9; 200 pages; 60 lb. cream white vellum paper; 65 lb. cream white vellum cover stock. Semiannually. Estab. 1967. Circ. 700. **Needs:** Literary and contemporary fiction, poetry, essays, reviews. Receives 50-60 unsolicited fiction mss each month. Does not read mss June through August or December. Published work by Joyce Carol Oates, Rosanne Coggeshall and Stephen Dixon. **Published new writers within the last year.** Rarely critiques rejected mss. **How to Contact:** Send complete ms with SASE. Requires text on disk upon acceptance in WordPerfect or Microsoft Word format. Reports in 3-4 months on mss. "No unsolicited reviews." Sample copy for $5. **Payment/Terms:** Pays in contributor's copies.

SOUTH DAKOTA REVIEW, University of South Dakota, Box 111, University Exchange, Vermillion SD 57069. (605)677-5966. Fax: (605)677-5298. E-mail: bbedard@sunbird.usd.edu. Website: www.usd.edu/englisdr/index.html (includes masthead page with editors' names and submission/subscription guidelines, sample covers, sample story and essay excerpts and poems). **Editor:** Brian Bedard. Editorial Assistant: Geraldine Sanford. Magazine: 6×9; 160-180 pages; book paper; glossy cover stock; illustrations sometimes; photos on cover. "Literary magazine for university and college audiences and their equivalent. Emphasis is often on the American West and its writers, but will accept mss from anywhere. Issues are generally essay, fiction, and poetry with some literary essays." Quarterly. Estab. 1963. Circ. 500. **Needs:** Literary, contemporary, ethnic, excerpted novel, regional. "We like very well-written, thematically ambitious, character-centered short fiction. Contemporary western American setting appeals, but not necessary. No formula stories, horror, or adolescent 'I' narrator." Receives 40 unsolicited fiction mss/month. Accepts about 40 mss/year. Assistant editor accepts mss in June through July, sometimes August. Agented fiction 5%. Publishes short shorts of 5 pages double-spaced typescript. Published work by Steve Heller, H.E. Francis, James Sallis, Ronna Wineberg, Lewis Horne and Rita Welty Bourke. **Publishes 3-5 new writers/year.** Length: 1,000-1,300 words minimum; 6,000 words maximum. (Has made exceptions, up to novella length.) Sometimes recommends other markets. **How to Contact:** Send complete ms with SASE. Accepts queries/mss by fax. "We like cover letters that are not boastful and do not attempt to sell the stories but rather provide some personal information about the writer." Reports in 6-10 weeks. Publishes ms an average of 1-6 months after acceptance. Sample copy for $5. **Payment/Terms:** Pays 1-year subscription, plus 2-4 contributor's copies, depending on length of ms; cover price charge for extras while issue is current, $3 when issue becomes a back issue.. Acquires first and reprint rights. **Advice:** Rejects mss because of "careless writing; often careless typing; stories too personal ('I' confessional), aimlessness, unclear or unresolved conflicts; subject matter that editor finds clichéd, sensationalized, pretentious or trivial. We are trying to use more fiction and more variety."

SOUTHERN CALIFORNIA ANTHOLOGY, University of Southern California, Waite Phillips Hall, Room 404, Los Angeles CA 90089-4034. (213)740-3252. Fax: (213)740-5775. **Contact:** Editor. Magazine: 5½×8½; 142 pages; semigloss cover stock. "The *Southern California Anthology* is a literary review that contains an eclectic collection of previously unpublished quality contemporary fiction, poetry and interviews with established literary people, published for adults of all professions; of particular interest to those interested in serious contemporary literature." Annually. Estab. 1983. Circ. 1,500. **Needs:** Contemporary, ethnic, experimental, feminist, historical, humor/satire, literary, mainstream, regional, serialized/excerpted novel. No juvenile, religious, confession, romance, science fiction or pornography. Receives 40 unsolicited fiction mss each month. Accepts 1-2 mss/issue. Does not read February through September. Publishes ms 4 months after acceptance. Recently published work by John Updike, Hubert Selby, Jr., Marge Piercy, Joyce Carol Oates and Gay Talese. Length: 10-15 pages average; 2 pages minimum; 25 pages maximum. Publishes short shorts. **How to Contact:** Send complete ms with cover letter or submit through agent. Cover letter should include list of previous publications. Reports on queries in 1 month; on mss in 4 months. Send SASE for reply or return of ms. Sample copy for $4. Fiction guidelines for #10 SASE. **Payment/Terms:** Pays in contributor's copies. Acquires first rights. **Advice:** "The *Anthology* pays particular attention to craft and style in its selection of narrative writing."

SOUTHERN HUMANITIES REVIEW, Auburn University, 9088 Haley Center, Auburn University AL 36849. **Co-editors:** Dan R. Latimer and Virginia M. Kouidis. Magazine: 6×9; 100 pages; 60 lb. neutral pH, natural paper; 65 lb. neutral pH med. coated cover stock; occasional illustrations and photos. "We publish essays, poetry, fiction and reviews. Our fiction has ranged from very traditional in form and content to very experimental.

Literate, college-educated audience. We hope they read our journal for both enlightenment and pleasure." Quarterly. Estab. 1967. Circ. 800.

Needs: Serious fiction, fantasy, feminist, humor and regional. Receives approximately 25 unsolicited fiction mss each month. Accepts 1-2 mss/issue, 4-6 mss/year. Slower reading time in summer. Published work by Anne Brashler, Heimito von Doderer and Ivo Andric; **published new writers within the last year.** Length: 3,500-15,000 words. Also publishes literary essays, literary criticism, poetry. Critiques rejected mss when there is time. Sometimes recommends other markets.

How to Contact: Send complete ms (one at a time) with SASE and cover letter with an explanation of topic chosen—"special, certain book, etc., a little about author if he/she has never submitted." Reports in 3 months. Sample copy for $5. Reviews novel and short story collections.

Payment/Terms: Pays 2 contributor's copies; $5 charge for extras. Rights revert to author upon publication. Sends galleys to author.

Advice: "Send us the ms with SASE. If we like it, we'll take it or we'll recommend changes. If we don't like it, we'll send it back as promptly as possible. Read the journal. Send typewritten, clean copy carefully proofread. We also award annually the Hoepfner Prize of $100 for the best published essay or short story of the year. Let someone whose opinion you respect read your story and give you an honest appraisal. Rewrite, if necessary, to get the most from your story."

THE SOUTHERN REVIEW, Louisiana State University, 43 Allen Hall, Baton Rouge LA 70803. (225)388-5108. Fax: (225)388-5098. E-mail: bmacon@lsu.edu. Website: www.lsu.edu/guests/wwwtsm (includes subscription information, staff, guidelines, current issue, table of contents). **Editors:** James Olney and Dave Smith. Magazine: 6¾×10; 240 pages; 50 lb. Glatfelter paper; 65 lb. #1 grade cover stock. "A literary quarterly publishing critical essays, poetry and fiction for a highly intellectual audience." Quarterly. Estab. 1935. Circ. 3,100.

Needs: Literary. "We emphasize style and substantial content. No mystery, fantasy or religious mss." Accepts 4-5 mss/issue. Receives approximately 300 unsolicited fiction mss each month. Does not read mss June through August. Publishes ms 6-9 months after acceptance. Agented fiction 1%. Published work by Rick Bass, Robert Olen Butler, Ellen Douglas, Pam Durban, Ehud Havazelet, Joyce Carol Oates, Richard Rubin, Gerald Shapiro, June Spence and Scott Ely. **Publishes 4-6 new writers/year.** Length: 2,000-10,000 words. Also publishes literary essays, literary criticism, poetry. Sponsors annual contest for best first collection of short stories published during the calendar year.

How to Contact: Send complete ms with cover letter and SASE. "Prefer brief letters giving information on author concerning where he/she has been published before, biographical info and what he/she is doing now." Reports in 2 months on mss. Sample copy for $8. Fiction guidelines free for SAE. Reviews novels and short story collections.

Payment/Terms: Pays $12/printed page; 2 contributor's copies on publication for first North American serial rights. Sends galleys to author.

Advice: "Develop a careful, clear style. Although willing to publish experimental writing that appears to have a valid artistic purpose, *The Southern Review* avoids extremism and sensationalism."

SOUTHWEST REVIEW, P.O. Box 750374, 307 Fondren Library West, Southern Methodist University, Dallas TX 75275-0374. (214)768-1037. **Editor:** Willard Spiegelman. Magazine: 6×9; 144 pages. "The majority of our readers are college-educated adults who wish to stay abreast of the latest and best in contemporary fiction, poetry, literary criticism and books in all but the most specialized disciplines." Quarterly. Estab. 1915. Circ. 1,600.

Needs: "High literary quality; no specific requirements as to subject matter, but cannot use sentimental, religious, western, poor science fiction, pornographic, true confession, mystery, juvenile or serialized or condensed novels." Receives approximately 200 unsolicited fiction mss each month. Published work by Bruce Berger, Thomas Larsen, Alice Hoffman, Matthew Sharpe, Floyd Skloot, Daniel Harris and Daniel Stern. Length: prefers 3,000-5,000 words. Also publishes literary essays and poetry. Occasionally critiques rejected mss.

How to Contact: Send complete ms with SASE. Reports in 6 months on mss. Publishes ms 6-12 months after acceptance. Sample copy for $6. Guidelines for SASE.

Payment/Terms: Payment varies; writers receive 3 contributor's copies. Pays on publication for first North American serial rights. Sends galleys to author.

Advice: "We have become less regional. A lot of time would be saved for us and for the writer if he or she looked at a copy of the *Southwest Review* before submitting. We like to receive a cover letter because it is some reassurance that the author has taken the time to check a current directory for the editor's name. When there isn't a cover letter, we wonder whether the same story is on 20 other desks around the country."

SOUTHWESTERN AMERICAN LITERATURE, Center for the Study of the Southwest, Southwest Texas State University, San Marcos TX 78666. (512)245-2232. Fax: (512)245-7462. E-mail: mb13@swt.edu. Editors: Mark Busby, D.M. Heaberlin. **Fiction Editor:** Mark Busby. Magazine: 6×9; 125 pages; 80 lb. cover stock. "We publish fiction, nonfiction, poetry, literary criticism and book reviews. Generally speaking, we want material concerning the Greater Southwest, or material written by southwestern writers." Semiannually. Estab. 1971. Circ. 300.

• A poem published in *Southwestern American Literature* was selected for the anthology, *Best Texas Writing 2.*

Needs: Ethnic/multicultural, literary, mainstream/contemporary, regional. No science fiction or romance. Receives 10-15 unsolicited mss/month. Accepts 1-2 mss/issue; 4-5 mss/year. Publishes ms up to 6 months after acceptance. Published work by Jerry Craven, Paul Ruffin, Robert Flynn and Philip Heldrich. **Publishes 1-2 new writers/year.** Length: 6,000 words average; 6,250 words maximum. Publishes short shorts. Also publishes literary essays, literary criticism, poetry. Sometimes critiques or comments on rejected ms.

How to Contact: Send complete ms with a cover letter. Include estimated word count, 200-word bio and list of publications. Accepts queries by e-mail. Reports in 1-2 months. SASE for return of ms. Simultaneous submissions OK. Sample copy $7. Fiction guidelines free. Reviews novels and short story collections. Send books to Mark Busby.

Payment/Terms: Pays 2 contributor's copies; additional copies $7. Acquires first rights.

Advice: "We look for crisp language, interesting approach to material; regional emphasis is desired but not required. Read widely, write often, revise carefully. We are looking for stories that probe the relationship between the tradition of Southwestern American literature and the writer's own imagination in creative ways. We seek stories that move beyond stereotype and approach the larger defining elements of regional literature with three qualities: originality, supple language, and humanity. We want stories with regional elements and also ones that, as William Faulkner noted in his Nobel Prize acceptance speech, treat subjects central to good literature—the old verities of the human heart such as honor and courage and pity and suffering, fear and humor, love and sorrow."

SOU'WESTER, Box 1438, Southern Illinois University—Edwardsville, Edwardsville IL 62026-1438. (618)692-3190. Managing Editor: Fred W. Robbins. Magazine: 6×9; 120 pages; Warren's Olde Style paper; 60 lb. cover. General magazine of poetry and fiction. Biannually. Estab. 1960. Circ. 300.

• The *Sou'wester* is known for publishing traditional, well-developed and carefully crafted short stories. Work published here has received an Illinois Arts Council Literary Award for "Best Illinois Fiction" and the Daniel Curley Award.

Needs: "The best work we can find, no matter who the author is." No science fiction or fantasy. Receives 50-100 unsolicited fiction mss/month. Accepts 6 mss/issue; 12 mss/year. Published work by Robert Wexelblatt, Julie Simon, John Pesta, Ellen Slezak and David Starkey. **Publishes 3-4 new writers/year.** Length: 10,000 words maximum. Also publishes poetry. Occasionally critiques rejected mss.

How to Contact: Send complete ms with SASE. Simultaneous submissions OK. Reports in 6-8 months. Publishes ms an average of 6 months after acceptance. Sample copy for $5.

Payment/Terms: Pays 2 contributor's copies; $5 charge for extras. Acquires first serial rights.

Advice: "Work on polishing your sentences."

SPARKS, E-mail: sparks@las.alfred.edu. Website: las.alfred.edu/~sparks. **Editor:** Jim Esch. Electronic magazine. "*Sparks* is aimed at creative, critically-aware people who thirst for quality and perspective."

Needs: Experimental, literary. "Literature of the imagination. Art is key. Beauty as cause and effect." No genre, fan or cliché fiction. Would like to see more experimental, character-rich realism and satire. Recently published work by Sherri Jilek, Alan Kaufman, Paul Ford, Michael Salinger and Tom Harmon. **Publishes 10-20 new writers/year.**

How to Contact: Electronic submissions only.

Advice: "Read back issues. Build your fiction around interesting, intriguing characters. Don't be afraid of imagery and imaginative exploration. A story has to spark the imagination or sizzle with linguistic zest. We like good honest old fashioned realism as much as we like wacked out experimentation. Intriguing, rich characters are always important, a distinctive narrative voice is a plus too."

$ SPELUNKER FLOPHOUSE, P.O. Box 617742, Chicago IL 60661. E-mail: spelunkerf@aol.com. Website: members.aol.com/spelunkerf/ (includes guidelines, excerpts, magazine history, how to subscribe, etc.). **Editors:** Chris Kubica and Wendy Morgan. Magazine: 8½×7; 96 pages; offset print; perfect-bound; 4-color glossy card cover. "We offer the best poetry, fiction and artwork we can in an inventive, original format. We cooperate regularly with other literary magazines." Quarterly. Estab. 1996. Press run: 1,500.

Needs: Ethnic/multicultural, experimental, feminist, humor/satire, literary, translations. "We are especially interested in fiction and poetry exploring small details of everyday life." No genre fiction. Receives 100 unsolicited mss/month. Accepts 3-6 mss/issue; 12-24 mss/year. Publishes ms 4 months after acceptance. Agented fiction: 5%. Published work by Edward Falco, Stephen Dixon, Julie Checkoway, Chris Mazza, W.P. Kinsella, Denise Duhamel and Carolyn Alessio. **Publishes 5-20 new writers/year.** Length: 100 words minimum; 10,000 words maximum. Publishes short shorts. Also publishes poetry. Often critiques or comments on rejected mss. Sponsors contest. Look for guidelines in the magazine.

How to Contact: Send complete ms with a cover letter. Include bio, list of publications if available and any brief interesting information about yourself. Reports in 4-10 weeks on mss. Send SASE for return of the ms or send a disposable copy of the ms. Simultaneous submissions OK, if noted. Sample copy for $6.95 postpaid. Fiction guidelines free with #10 SASE. Occasionally reviews fiction or poetry in book form.

Payment/Terms: Pays "depending on current cash flow" and 2 contributor's copies. Pays on publication. Acquires first North American serial rights. Sends galleys to author.

Advice: "We are interested in stories that have a strong sense of character, technique, language, realistic dialogue, unique style/voice, and (if possible) a plot. No restrictions on length or subject matter except no genre work or 'statements.' Nothing patently cute. Support this necessary forum for the arts by purchasing copies of literary magazines, reading them, and increasing local awareness of magazines/forums such as ours whenever possible. Study the market; then submit. And keep in touch. We love to hear from members/supporters of the literary community."

✔ ⊘ **SPINDRIFT**, Shoreline Community College, 16101 Greenwood Ave. North, Seattle WA 98133. (206)546-5864. **Editor:** Carol Orlock, adviser. Magazine: 140 pages; quality paper; photographs; b&w artwork. "We look for fresh, original work that is not forced or 'straining' to be literary." Annually. Estab. around 1967. Circ. 500.

   • *Spindrift* has received awards for "Best Literary Magazine" from the Community College Humanities Association both locally and nationally and awards from the Pacific Printing Industries.

Needs: Contemporary, ethnic, experimental, historical (general), prose poem, regional, science fiction, serialized/excerpted novel, translations. No romance, religious/inspirational. Receives up to 150 mss/year. Accepts up to 20 mss/issue. Does not read during spring/summer. Publishes ms 3-4 months after acceptance. Published work by David Halpern and Jana Harris; **published new writers within the last year.** Length: 250 words minimum; 3,500-4,500 words maximum. Publishes short shorts.

How to Contact: Send complete ms, and "bio, name, address, phone and list of titles submitted." Reports in 2 weeks on queries; juries after February 1 and responds by March 15 with SASE. Sample copy for $6.50, 8 × 10 SAE and $1 postage.

Payment/Terms: Pays in contributor's copies; charge for extras. Acquires first rights. Publication not copyrighted.

Advice: "The tighter the story the better. The more lyric values in the narrative the better. Read the magazine, keep working on craft. Submit by February 1."

⊘ **SPITBALL**, 5560 Fox Rd., Cincinnati OH 45239. (513)385-2268. **Editor:** Mike Shannon. Magazine: 5½ × 8½; 96 pages; 55 lb. Glatfelter Natural, neutral pH paper; 10 pt. CS1 cover stock; illustrations; photos. Magazine publishing "fiction and poetry about *baseball* exclusively for an educated, literary segment of the baseball fan population." Biannually. Estab. 1981. Circ. 1,000.

Needs: Confession, contemporary, experimental, historical, literary, mainstream and suspense. "Our only requirement concerning the type of fiction written is that the story be *primarily* about baseball." Receives 100 unsolicited fiction mss/year. Accepts 16-20 mss/year. Published work by Dallas Wiebe, Michael Gilmartin and W.P. Kinsella; **published new writers within the last year.** Length: 20 typed double-spaced pages. "The longer it is, the better it has to be."

How to Contact: Send complete ms with cover letter and SASE. Include brief bio about author. Reporting time varies. Publishes ms an average of 3 months after acceptance. *First-time submitters are required to purchase a sample copy for $6.*

Payment/Terms: "No monetary payment at present. We may offer nominal payment in the near future." 2 free contributor's copies per issue in which work appears. Acquires first North American serial rights.

Advice: "Our audience is mostly college educated and knowledgeable about baseball. The stories we have published so far have been very well written and displayed a firm grasp of the baseball world and its people. In short, audience response has been great because the stories are simply good as stories. Thus, mere use of baseball as subject is no guarantee of acceptance. We are always seeking submissions. Unlike many literary magazines, we have no backlog of accepted material. Fiction is a natural genre for our exclusive subject, baseball. There are great opportunities for writing in certain areas of fiction, baseball being one of them. Baseball has become the 'in' spectator sport among intellectuals, the general media and the 'yuppie' crowd. Consequently, as subject matter for adult fiction it has gained a much wider acceptance than it once enjoyed."

Ⓝ ⊘ ⊚ **SPOONFED**, P.O. Box 21036, Washington DC 20009-1036. (202)667-5248. E-mail: spoonfed99 @aol.com. Website: members.aol.com/spoonfed99/spoonfed1.html (includes contact information, mission statement, guidelines, themes, previous issues). Literary magazine: 7 × 7; 16-24 pages; white offset; illustrations and photos. "*Spoonfed* is a publication for queer writers and artists whose work is often considered out of the mainstream. Issues of critical examination include family, religion, politics, sex, identity and orientation, race, class, culture." Quarterly. Estab. 1995. Circ. 2,500.

Nees: Comics/graphic novels, erotica, experimental, feminist, gay, horror, humor satire, lesbian, New Age/mystic/spiritual, psychic/supernatural/occult, regional, romance (futuristic/time travel, gothic), science fiction (soft/sociological). Upcoming themes for 2000: "Fuck the Right/The Right to Fuck" (deadline Jan. 15); "For Queer Girls & Boys Who Have Considered Suicide When the Rainbow Flag Is Not Enough" (deadline April 15); "Dysfunction Junction: Childhood Issue(s)" (deadline Oct. 15); "Dildo-a Go-Go: The Auto Eroticism Issue" (deadline July 15). Receives 6 unsolicited mss/month. Accepts 3-4 mss/issue; approx. 12 mss/year. Publishes ms 3-6 months after acceptance. **Publishes 50% new writers.** Half the writers published each year are new. Recently published work by Jeff Bagato, Gigi Ross-Fowler, Stefen Styrsky, Michael Fantus, Mary Conley and Bert Menninga. Length: 1,000 words average; 250 words minimum; 1,500 words maximum. Publishes short shorts. Also publishes literary essays, criticism and poetry. Sometimes critiques or comments on rejected ms.

How to Contact: Send complete ms with a cover letter. Reports in 2-4 weeks. Send SASE for reply, return of ms or send a disposable copy of ms. Simultaneous and reprint submissions OK. Sample copy for $2 and a 9×12 envelope with 4 first-class stamps. Guidelines free.

Payment/Terms: Pays 3-5 contributor's copies; additional copies $2.

Advice: "Ask yourself is this work critical of the current political/societal/organizational systems? Does it meet the theme of the issue? Is it unusual or non-mainstream? Is the writing provocative/emotive? Is it good? Workshop your submission prior to sending it out. If you are willing to discuss editorial changes, indicate that to us."

SPOUT, Spout Press, 28 W. Robie St., St. Paul MN 55107. (612)379-7737. E-mail: colb0018@gold.tc.umn. edu. Editors: John Colburn and Michelle Filkins. **Fiction Editor:** Chris Watercott. Magazine: 8½×11; 40 pages; 70 lb. flat white paper; colored cover; illustrations. "We like the surprising, the surreal and the experimental. Our readers are well-read, often writers." Triannually. Estab. 1989. Circ. 300-500.

● *Spout* editors submit work to the *Pushcart* anthology. They would like to see more sudden fiction.

Needs: Condensed/excerpted novel, ethnic/multicultural, experimental, feminist, gay, humor/satire, lesbian, literary, regional, translations. No horror. Publishes special fiction issues or anthologies. Receives 25-30 unsolicited mss/month. Accepts 4-5 mss/issue; 15 mss/year. Publishes ms 1-3 months after acceptance. Agented fiction 5%. Published work by Mario Benedetti, Layle Silbert, Stephen Gutierrez and Michael Little. Publishes 5 new writers/year. Length: open. Publishes short shorts and "sudden" fiction. Also publishes poetry. Seldom comments on rejected mss.

How to Contact: Send complete ms with a cover letter. Include short bio and list of publications with submission. Reports in 1 month on queries; 2-3 months on mss. Send SASE for reply, return of ms or send a disposable copy of ms. Simultaneous submissions OK. Sample copy for $4, 8½×11 SAE and 5 first-class stamps. Fiction guidelines for SASE.

Payment/Terms: Pays 1 contributor's copy; additional copies for $3 plus postage. Acquires one-time rights.

Advice: Looks for "imagination, surprise and attention to language. We often publish writers on their third or fourth submission, so don't get discouraged. We need more weird, surreal fiction that lets the reader make his/her own meaning. Don't send moralistic, formulaic work."

$ **SPSM&H,** *Amelia* Magazine, 329 "E" St., Bakersfield CA 93304. (805)323-4064. **Editor:** Frederick A. Raborg, Jr. Magazine: 5½×8¼; 24 pages; matte cover stock; illustrations and photos. "*SPSM&H* publishes sonnets, sonnet sequences and fiction, articles and reviews related to the form (fiction may be romantic or Gothic) for a general readership and sonnet enthusiasts." Quarterly. Estab. 1985. Circ. 600.

● This magazine is edited by Frederick A. Raborg, Jr., who is also editor of *Amelia* and *Cicada*.

Needs: Adventure, confession, contemporary, erotica, ethnic, experimental, fantasy, feminist, gay, historical, horror, humor/satire, lesbian, literary, mainstream, mystery/suspense, regional, romance (contemporary, historical), science fiction, senior citizen/retirement, translations and western. All should have romantic element. "We look for strong fiction with romantic or Gothic content, or both. Stories need not have 'happy' endings, and we are open to the experimental and/or avant-garde. Erotica is fine; pornography, no." Receives 30 unsolicited mss/month. Accepts 1 ms/issue; 4 mss/year. Publishes ms 6 months to 1 year after acceptance. Agented fiction 5%. Published work by Brad Hooper, Mary Louise R. O'Hara and Clara Castelar Bjorlie. Length: 2,000 words average; 500 words minimum; 3,000 words maximum. Critiques rejected ms when appropriate; recommends other markets.

How to Contact: Send complete ms with cover letter. Include Social Security number. Reports in 2 weeks. SASE. Sample copy for $6. Fiction guidelines for #10 SASE.

Payment/Terms: Pays $10-25 and contributor's copies on publication for first North American serial rights; charge for extra copies.

Advice: "A good story line (plot) and strong characterization are vital. I want to know the writer has done his homework and is striving to become professional."

STAND MAGAZINE, School of English, University of Leeds, Leeds LS2 9JT England. Phone: (44)113 223 4794. Fax: (44)113 233 4791. E-mail: stand@english.novell.leeds.ac.uk. **Editors:** Michael Hulse and John Kinsella. "*Stand* is an international quarterly publishing poetry, short stories, reviews, criticism and translations." Circ. 4,500. Quarterly.

Needs: Literary. Recently published work by Michael Mott, Christopher Hope and Penelope. **Publishes 10 new writers/year.** Length: 5,000 words maximum.

How to Contact: "Read copies of the magazine before submitting. Enclose sufficient IRCs for return of mss/reply. No more than 6 poems or 2 short stories at any one time. Should not be under consideration elsewhere."

Payment/Terms: £75 per 1,000 words of prose on publication (or in US dollars); contributor's copies. Sponsors biennial short competition: First prize, £1,500. Send 2 IRCs for information. Sample copy: £11.

🌐 **STAPLE**, Tor Cottage 81, Cavendish Rd., Matlock DE4 3HD United Kingdom. **Fiction Editor:** Don Measham. Published 3 times/year. Circ. up to 600. Publishes up to 50% fiction. *Staple* is "about 90 pages, perfect-bound; beautifully designed and produced."

Needs: "Stories used by *Staple* have ranged from social realism (through autobiography, parody, prequel, parable) to visions and hallucinations. We don't use unmodified genre fiction, i.e., adventure, crime or westerns. We are interested in extracts from larger works—provided author does the extraction." Length: 200 words minimum; 5,000 words maximum.

How to Contact: Adequate IRCs and large envelope for return, if return is required. Otherwise IRC for decision only. Please note that *Staple* requires stories to be previously unpublished worldwide.

Payment/Terms: Pays complimentary copy plus subscription for US contributors. Get a specimen copy of one of the issues with strong prose representation. Send $10 for airmail dispatch, $5 for surface mail. "We require first use, world-wide."

✓ $⬚ ◎ 🏆 **STONE SOUP, The Magazine By Young Writers and Artists**, Children's Art Foundation, Box 83, Santa Cruz CA 95063. (831)426-5557. E-mail: gmandel@stonesoup.com. Website: www.stonesoup.com (includes writer's guidelines, sample copy, links, projects, international children's art). **Editor:** Ms. Gerry Mandel. Magazine: 7×10; 48 pages; high quality paper; photos. Stories, poems, book reviews and art by children through age 13. Readership: children, librarians, educators. Published 6 times/year. Estab. 1973. Circ. 20,000.

* This is known as "the literary journal for children." *Stone Soup* has previously won the Ed Press Golden Lamp Honor Award and the Parent's Choice Award.

Needs: Fiction by children on themes based on their own experiences, observations or special interests. Also, some fantasy, mystery, adventure. No clichés, no formulas, no writing exercises; original work only. Receives approximately 1,000 unsolicited fiction mss each month. Accepts approximately 15 mss/issue. **Published new writers within the last year.** Length: 150-2,500 words. Also publishes literary essays and poetry. Critiques rejected mss upon request.

How to Contact: Send complete ms with cover letter. "We like to learn a little about our young writers, why they like to write, and how they came to write the story they are submitting." SASE. No simultaneous submissions. Reports in 1 month on mss. Does not respond to mss that are not accompanied by an SASE. Publishes ms an average of 3-6 months after acceptance. Sample copy for $4. Guidelines for SASE. Reviews children's books.

Payment/Terms: Pays $25 plus 2 contributor's copies; $2.50 charge for extras. Buys all rights.

Advice: Mss are rejected because they are "derivatives of movies, TV, comic books; or classroom assignments or other formulas."

✓ ⊘ $ **STONEFLOWER LITERARY JOURNAL**, Stoneflower Press, Box 90507, San Antonio TX 78209. E-mail: stonflower@aol.com. Editor: Brenda Davidson-Shaddox. **Fiction Coordinator:** Coley Scott. Journal: 5½×4; 125 pages; 50 lb. white offset paper; 8 pt. carolina C1S cover stock; illustrations (ink drawings only) and photographs (b&w only). Annually. Estab. 1996.

* *Stoneflower Literary Journal* is not currently reading unsolicited manuscripts.

Needs: Recently published work by Carlos Brown, Jane Butkin Roth and Adina Sara. Publishes short shorts, poetry. "We also publish one interview or profile each issue. Subject should be writer, editor, agent, artist, publisher, photographer or other professional whose primary career is creative." Sometimes (but rarely) critiques or comments on rejected mss.

Payment/Terms: "Short story writers receive $10/story; interview $10/work; poetry $5/poem." Pays on publication. Acquires one-time rights. Sponsors contest; "send SASE (9″ envelope with one first-class stamp for guidelines. First place fiction winner $75; 2nd place $25. First place poetry $50; 2nd place $10. All honorable mentions receive free copy of journal. Winners names announced in the journal."

Advice: "Technically correct writing combined with colorful, exciting use of the language helps. A story must draw us in quickly. If we lose interest by the end of the first page, we quit reading. In addition to good writing, clean, professionally prepared manuscripts are a must. Will not read handwritten manuscripts. Don't use clichés. Watch spelling. Stay away from passive verbs. Don't choose an exotic topic; write about what people care about. Above all, study creative writing—either on your own or in classes—and read, read, read. Nothing improves one's writing more than exposure to other good writers."

🌐 ⬚ ◎ **STORYBOARD, A Journal of Pacific Imagery**, Division of English, University of Guam, Mangilao, Guam 96921. Phone: (671)735-2749. Fax: (671)734-0010. E-mail: jtalley@uoga.uog.edu. Website: www.uog2.uog.edu/strybrd/STORYBOARD. **Editor:** Jeannine E. Talley. Editors change each year. Magazine: 100 pages; illustrations and photographs. "A multilingual journal with a focus on Pacific writing and writers. We publish short fiction, creative nonfiction and poetry." Annually. Estab. 1991. Circ. 300. Member of Council of Literary Magazines and Presses.

* Material sent to *Storyboard* must relate to the Pacific region or be written by an indigenous Pacific writer.

Needs: Ethnic/multicultural (Pacific region), experimental, family saga, regional (Pacific region). Receives 10-15 unsolicited mss/month. Accepts 30-40 mss/issue. Publishes ms 6-12 months after acceptance. Agented fiction 50-75%. Length: 1,000 words average. Publishes short shorts. Also publishes poetry.

How to Contact: Send complete ms with a cover letter. Accepts queries/mss by e-mail. Include bio. Reports in 1-4 weeks on queries; 4-6 months on mss. Send SASE for reply, return of ms or send a disposable copy of ms. Sample copy $6 and 7×10 SAE. Fiction guidelines free.

Payment/Terms: Pays 2 contributor's copies; additional copies $7.50.

[N] STORYQUARTERLY, Box 1416, Northbrook IL 60065. (847)564-8891. E-mail: theloon@ameritech. net. **Co-editors:** Anne Brashler and Marie Hayes. Magazine: approximately 6×9; 300 pages; good quality paper; illustrations; photos. A magazine devoted to the short story and committed to a full range of styles and forms. Annually. Estab. 1975. Circ. 3,500.

• *StoryQuarterly* received honorable mention in *Best Essays* 1997.

Needs: "Great humor, serious and well-written stories about life." No sci-fi, horror, animal-oriented or sex-driven stories. Receives 300 unsolicited fiction mss/month. Accepts 20-35 mss/issue. Recently published work by Stephen Dixon, Pamela Painter, Melissa Pritchard, Alice Hoffman, Lois Hauselman, Oliver Broudy, Mark Halliday and S.L. Wisenberg. **Published new writers within the last year.**

How to Contact: Send complete ms with SASE. Simultaneous submissions OK. Reports in 3 months on mss. Sample copy for $5.

Payment/Terms: Pays 3 contributor's copies for one-time rights. Copyright reverts to author after publication.

Advice: "Send one manuscript at a time, subscribe to the magazine, send SASE." Fiction selected based on "the voice, the story and the author's control. Read. Read. Read. Don't be self-obsessed. Enjoy and be proud of being a writer. A sense of humor helps. Literary magazines (university affiliated and/or independent) deal with reality in ways the industry trends do not. We do not deal in fairy tale endings."

[●] STOVEPIPE, A Journal of Little Literary Value, P.O. Box 1076, Georgetown KY 40324. E-mail: troyteegarden@worldradio.org. Website: www.worldradio.org/soup.html. **Editor:** Troy Teegarden. Magazine: 8½×5½; 30-60 pages; 70 lb. paper; card stock cover; illustrations. "We like to have a good time with what we read. We publish fiction, nonfiction, poetry and black and white art." Quarterly. Estab. 1995. Circ. 250.

Needs: Comics/graphic novels, experimental, humor/satire, literary, short story collections. No religious, fantasy. Want more experimental, humor and fringe. Receives 50 unsolicited mss/month. Accepts 1-2 mss/issue; 4-8 mss/ year. Publishes ms 1-3 months after acceptance. **Publishes 4-8 new writers/year.** Recently published work by Mike Francis and Steven Carter. Length: 3,500 words maximum. Publishes short shorts. "We really dig short short stories." Also publishes poetry. Often critiques or comments on rejected ms.

How to Contact: Send complete ms with a cover letter. Accepts queries by e-mail. Include estimated word count, short but informative bio and list of publications. Reports in 1-2 weeks on queries; 1 month on mss. Send SASE for reply, return of ms. Sample copy $2 or send 5½×8½ SAE with 78¢ postage. Fiction guidelines for #10 SASE.

Payment/Terms: Pays 1-3 contributor's copies; additional copies $2. Acquires one-time rights.

Advice: "Stories must be interesting and new and they must offer something original to the reader. We don't see much fiction but would like to publish more. We look for originality, creativity, strong characters and unique perspectives. Write for yourself. Just because we don't publish it doesn't mean it's not good. We are very particular."

[✓] $ [●] STREET BEAT QUARTERLY, Wood Street Commons, 301 Third Ave., Pittsburgh PA 15222. (412)765-3302. Fax: (412)765-2187. **Editor:** Sharon Thorp. Magazine: 8½×11; 32 pages; newsprint paper; newsprint cover; illustrations and photos. "*Street Beat Quarterly* publishes (primarily) literary works by those who have experienced homelessness or poverty. We reach those interested in literary magazines and others interested in homelessness issues." Quarterly. Estab. 1990. Circ. 2,000-3,000.

Needs: Adventure, ethnic/multicultural, experimental, fantasy, feminist, historical, humor/satire, literary, mainstream/contemporary, mystery/suspense, stories by children. "No religious." Receives 2 unsolicited mss/month. Accepts 2-5 mss/issue. Publishes ms 1-3 months after acceptance. Published work by Freddy Posco, James Burroughs and Mel Spivak. Length: 750 words average; 100 words minimum; 10,000 words maximum. Publishes short shorts. Also publishes literary essays and poetry. Sometimes critiques or comments on rejected mss.

How to Contact: Send complete ms with a cover letter including bio. Reports in 1 month on mss. Send a disposable copy of ms. Simultaneous, reprint and electronic submissions OK. Sample copy for 3 first-class stamps.

Payment/Terms: Pays $3 plus 1 contributor's copy on publication for one-time rights.

Advice: "We are pretty flexible. Our mission is to publish work by those who have experienced homelessness and poverty; we will consider a limited amount of works by others if it is on the topic (homelessness/poverty). Don't be afraid of us! We are very much a grass-roots publication. Be patient with us; as we sometimes take a short while to respond. We publish some very polished work; we also publish some very 'rough' yet energetic work. We are looking for stories that truly capture the experience of homelessness and poverty on a personal level."

[●] STRUGGLE, A Magazine of Proletarian Revolutionary Literature, Box 13261, Detroit MI 48213-0261. (213)273-9039. E-mail: timhall@megsinet.net. **Editor:** Tim Hall. Magazine: 5½×8½; 36-72 pages; 20

lb. white bond paper; colored cover; illustrations; occasional photographs. Publishes material related to "the struggle of the working class and all progressive people against the rule of the rich—including their war policies, racism, exploitation of the workers, oppression of women, etc." Quarterly. Estab. 1985. Subscription: $10/year in US, $12 to libraries, $15 foreign.

Needs: Contemporary, ethnic, experimental, feminist, historical (general), humor/satire, literary, prose poem, regional, science fiction, senior citizen/retirement, translations, young adult/teen (10-18). "The theme can be approached in many ways, including plenty of categories not listed here. Would like to see more fiction that depicts the life, work and struggle of the working class of every background; also the struggles of the 1930s and 60s illustrated and brought to life." No romance, psychic, mystery, western, erotica, religious. Receives 10-12 unsolicited fiction mss/month. Publishes ms 6 months or less after acceptance. Recently published work by Greg Norton, David Poyner, Billie Louise Jones and Dennis Hammond. **Published new writers within the last year.** Length: 1,000-3,000 words average; 4,000 words maximum. Publishes short shorts. Normally critiques rejected mss.

How to Contact: Send complete ms; cover letter optional. "Tries to" report in 3-4 months. SASE. Simultaneous and reprint submissions OK. Sample copy for $2.50. Make checks payable to Tim Hall-Special Account.

Payment/Terms: Pays 2 contributor's copies. No rights acquired. Publication not copyrighted.

Advice: "Write about the oppression of the working people, the poor, the minorities, women, and if possible, their rebellion against it—we are not interested in anything which accepts the status quo. We are not too worried about plot and advanced technique (fine if we get them!)—we would probably accept things others would call sketches, provided they have life and struggle. For new writers: just describe for us a situation in which some real people confront some problem of oppression, however seemingly minor. Observe and put down the real facts. Experienced writers: try your 'committed'/experimental fiction on us. We get poetry all the time. We have increased our fiction portion of our content in the last few years. The quality of fiction that we have published has continued to improve. If your work raises an interesting issue of literature and politics, it may get discussed in letters and in my editorial. I suggest ordering a sample."

N ⚑ ◑ SUB-TERRAIN, P.O. Box 1575, Bentall Centre, Vancouver BC V6C 2P7 Canada. (604)876-8710. Fax: (604)879-2667. E-mail: subter@pinc.com. Fiction Editors: D.E. Bolen and Brian Kaufman. Magazine: 8½×11; 40 pages; offset printed paper; illustrations; photos. "*Sub-Terrain* provides a forum for work that pushes the boundaries in form or content." Estab. 1988.

Needs: "Primarily a literary magazine; also interested in erotica, experimental, humor/satire." Receives 100 unsolicited mss/month. Accepts 15-20 mss/issue. Publishes ms 1-4 months after acceptance. Publishes 6-10 new writers/year. Recently published work by Steven Heighton, Clark Timmins, J. Jill Robinson, Derek McCormack, Billie Livingston and Mark Jarman. Length: 200-3,000 words. Publishes short shorts. Length: 200 words. Also publishes literary essays, literary criticism, poetry. Sometimes critiques rejected mss and "at times" recommends other markets.

How to Contact: Send complete ms with cover letter. Simultaneous submissions OK, if notified when ms is accepted elsewhere. Reports in 3-4 weeks on queries; 2-3 months on mss. SASE. Sample copy for $5. Also features book review section. Send books marked "Review Copy, Managing Editor."

Payment/Terms: Pays (for solicited work) $25/page; $20/poem. Acquires one-time rights.

Advice: "We look for contemporary, modern fiction with something special in the voice or style, not simply something that is a well-written story—a new twist, a unique sense or vision of the world, the stuff that every mag is hoping to find. Read a sample copy before submitting."

◑ SULPHUR RIVER LITERARY REVIEW, P.O. Box 19228, Austin TX 78760-9228. (512)292-9456. **Editor:** James Michael Robbins. Magazine: 5½×8½; 145 pages; illustrations and photos. "*SRLR* publishes literature of quality—poetry and short fiction with appeal that transcends time. Audience includes a broad spectrum of readers, mostly educated, many of whom are writers, artists and educators." Semiannually. Estab. 1978. Circ. 400.

Needs: Ethnic/multicultural, experimental, feminist, humor/satire, literary, mainstream/contemporary and translations. No "religious, juvenile, teen, sports, romance or mystery." Receives 10-12 unsolicited mss/month. Accepts 2-3 mss/issue; 4-6 mss/year. Publishes ms 1-2 years after acceptance. Recently published work by Hugh Fox, Angela Hall, Rafael Courtoisie, Warren Carrier and Emilia Pardo Bazáu. **Publishes few new writers/year.** Publishes short shorts. Also publishes literary essays, literary criticism and poetry. Often critiques or comments on rejected mss.

How to Contact: Send complete ms with a cover letter. Include short bio and list of publications. Reports in 1 week on queries; 1 month on mss. Send SASE for reply, return of ms or send a disposable copy of ms. No simultaneous submissions. Sample copy for $7.

Payment/Terms: Pays 2 contributor's copies; additional copies for $7. Acquires first North American serial rights.

Advice: Looks for "originality, mastery of the language, imagination. Revise, revise, revise."

N ◑ A SUMMER'S READING, A Journal of Fiction, Nonfiction, Poetry & Art, 409 Lakeview Dr., Sherman IL 62864-9432. (217)496-3012. **Editor:** Ted Morrissey. Magazine: 5½×8½; 75 pages; 20 lb. paper;

card cover stock; b&w illustrations. "There is so much excellent writing being produced and, by comparison, so few opportunities to publish—we want to provide one more well-edited, attractive outlet." Annually. Estab. 1997. Circ. 150.

Needs: Excerpted novel, literary, translations (provide copy of original). "We have absolutely no taboos in subject matter or imagery. No genre." Prefers to read April to September. "One of our reasons for emerging in the summer is to provide a place for writers to send material when the majority of journals are not accepting submissions. We select, edit, produce and distribute during the 'academic' year." Receives 60-100 unsolicited mss/month. Publishes ms 1 year after acceptance. Recently published work by G.W. Clift, Kathryn Ma and Rebecca Phillips. Length: 3,500 words average; 100 words minimum; 8,000 words maximum. Publishes short shorts. Also publishes poetry and narrative nonfiction (e.g., autobiography, biography). Would like to see more translations. Sometimes critiques or comments on rejected mss.

How to Contact: Send complete ms with a concise cover letter. Include estimated word count, brief bio (25-50 words) and list of publications. "Do not explain the piece or what inspired it; allow it to speak for itself." Reports in 3-12 months on mss. Send SASE for return of ms or send a disposable copy of the ms. "No reply without SASE." Simultaneous submissions OK, "but please inform us." Sample copy for $5. Fiction guidelines for #10 SASE.

Payment/Terms: Pays 2 contributor's copies. Acquires one-time rights. Sends galleys to the author.

Advice: "We look for a combination of engaging plot and/or characters with a practical writing style."

☑ ◎ ▽ SYCAMORE REVIEW, Department of English, Purdue University, West Lafayette IN 47907. (765)494-3783. Fax: (765)494-3780. E-mail: sycamore@expert.cc.purdue.edu. Website: www.sla.purdue.edu/academic/engl/sycamore (includes back and current issues, index, submission guidelines, subscription information, journal library). **Editor-in-Chief:** Numsiric Kunakemakorn. Editors change every two years. Send fiction to Fiction Editor, poetry to Poetry Editor, all other correspondence to Editor-in-Chief. Magazine: 5½×8½; 150-200 pages; heavy, textured, uncoated paper; heavy laminated cover. "Journal devoted to contemporary literature. We publish both traditional and experimental fiction, personal essay, poetry, interviews, drama and graphic art. Novel excerpts welcome if they stand alone as a story." Semiannually. Estab. 1989. Circ. 1,000.

● Work published in *Sycamore Review* has been selected for inclusion in the *Pushcart Prize* anthology. The magazine was also named "The Best Magazine from Indiana" by the *Clockwatch Review*.

Needs: Contemporary, experimental, humor/satire, literary, mainstream, regional, translations. "We generally avoid genre literature, but maintain no formal restrictions on style or subject matter. No science fiction, romance, children's." Publishes ms 3 months to 1 year after acceptance. Recently published work by Susan Neville, Tibor Fischer, Richard Wagner and Carolyn Johnson Lewis. 10% of material published is by new writers. Length: 3,750 words preferred; 250 words minimum. Also publishes poetry, "this most recently included Billy Collins, Thomas Lux, Kathleen Peirce and Vandana Khanna." Sometimes critiques rejected mss and recommends other markets.

How to Contact: Send complete ms with cover letter. Cover letter should include previous publications and address changes. Does not read mss September through March 31. Reports in 4 months. SASE. Simultaneous submissions OK. Sample copy for $7. Fiction guidelines for #10 SASE.

Payment/Terms: Pays in contributor's copies; charge for extras. Acquires one-time rights.

Advice: "We publish both new and experienced authors but we're always looking for stories with strong emotional appeal, vivid characterization and a distinctive narrative voice; fiction that breaks new ground while still telling an interesting and significant story. Avoid gimmicks and trite, predictable outcomes. Write stories that have a ring of truth, the impact of felt emotion. Don't be afraid to submit, send your best."

🌐 ✕ $ TAKAHE, P.O. Box 13-335, Christchurch, New Zealand. **Fiction Editor:** Bernadette Hall. "A literary magazine which appears three or four times a year, and publishes short stories and poetry by both established and emerging writers. The publisher is the Takahe Collective Trust, a charitable trust formed by established writers to help new writers and get them into print."

Needs: Recently published work by Sarah Quigley, Michael Harlow, Kapka Kassabora, Fiona Farrell, David Hill and Mark Pirie. **Publishes 25 new writers/year.**

How to Contact: Send complete ms with bio. SASE with IRCs for overseas submissions.

Payment/Terms: "There is a small payment for work published."

Advice: "While insisting on correct British spelling (or recognised spellings in foreign languages), smart quotes, and at least internally-consistent punctuation, we, nonetheless, try to allow some latitude in presentation. Any use of foreign languages must be accompanied by an English translation."

◎ TALKING RIVER REVIEW, Lewis-Clark State College, Division of Literature and Languages, 500 8th Ave., Lewiston ID 83501. (208)799-2307. Fax: (208)799-2324. E-mail: triver@lcsc.edu. Editor: Dennis Held. **Fiction Editor:** Claire Davis. Magazine: 6×9; 150 pages; 60 lb. paper; coated, color cover; illustrations and photos. "We publish the best work by well-known and unknown authors; our audience is literary but unpretentious." Semiannually. Estab. 1994. Circ. 750.

Needs: Condensed/excerpted novel, ethnic/multicultural, feminist, historical, humor/satire, literary, mainstream/contemporary, regional. "Wants more well-written, character-driven stories that surprise and delight the reader with fresh, arresting yet unself-conscious language, imagery, metaphor, revelation." No surprise endings; plot-driven stories; or stories that are sexist, racist, homophobic, erotic for shock value, romance. Receives 200 unsolicited mss/month. Accepts 5-8 mss/issue; 10-15 mss/year. Does not read March to September. Publishes ms up to 1 year after acceptance. Agented fiction 10%. Recently published work by Gary Gildner, William Kittredge, David Long and Mary Clearman Blew. **Publishes 10 new writers/year.** Length: 3,000 words average; 7,500 words maximum. Rarely publishes short shorts. Also publishes literary essays and poetry. Sometimes critiques or comments on rejected mss.

How to Contact: Send complete manuscript with a cover letter. Include estimated word count, 2-sentence bio, Social Security number and list of publications. Reports in 3 months on mss. Send SASE for reply, return of ms or send disposable copy of ms. Simultaneous submissions OK if indicated. Sample copy for $5. Fiction guidelines for #10 SASE. Subscription: $14/year.

Payment/Terms: Pays 2 contributor's copies and a year's subscription for one-time rights; additional copies $4.

Advice: "Revise, revise, revise. Read more widely, including poetry."

N ⬛ **TALUS & SCREE**, International Literary Journal, P.O. Box 832, Newport OR 97365-0062. (541)574-7708. E-mail: ocrisc@pioneer.net. Website: www.teleport.com/~cbs/talus (includes excerpts from magazine, guidelines, contest information, contact names). **Fiction Editor**: Carla Perry. Literary magazine: 8½×11; 164 pages, 70 lb. paper; illustrations and photos. "We publish work that has fallen through the cracks—work too controversial, risky—humor, satire and erotica." Annual. Estab. 1996. Circ. 1,000.

Needs: Adventure, erotica, ethnic/multicultural, experimental, family saga, feminist, gay, humor satire, lesbian, literary, mainstream, New Age, psychic/supernatural/occult, science fiction (soft/sociological), short story collections, translations. "No religious dogma or pure academia." Receives 20-50 unsolicited mss/months. Accepts 5-20 mss/issue. Publishes ms after August 15 deadline each year. **Publishes 10 new writers/year.** Length: up to 3,000 words. Publishes short shorts. Also publishes literary essays and poetry. Always critiques or comments on rejected ms.

How to Contact: Send complete ms with a cover letter. Prefers submissions by e-mail. Include estimated word count and 50-word bio. Reports in 2 months on mss. Send SASE for reply, return of ms or send disposable copy of ms. Simultaneous and reprint submissions OK. Sample copy for $11. Fiction guidelines for SASE.

Payment/Terms: Pays 2 contributor's copies; additional copies for $10. Acquires one-time rights. Sponsors contest "follow guidelines for contest which are available on website or on request by e-mail or snail mail."

Advice: Looks for a "memorable, unique approach, humor, risks to author, stretches, well-written craft of words, odd slant. Read our guidelines-they are specific. Our focus is narrow."

✅ **$**⬜ **TAMEME, New writing from North America/Nueva literatura de Norteamérica**, Tameme, Inc., 199 First St., Suite 335, Los Altos CA 94022. (650)941-2037. Fax: (650)941-5338. E-mail: editor@tameme.org. Website: www.tameme.org (includes editor, contributors, writer's guidelines, staff, index of magazine). **Editor:** C.M. Mayo. Magazine: 6×9; 220 pages; good quality paper; heavy cover stock; illustrations; photos. "*Tameme* is an annual fully bilingual magazine dedicated to publishing new writing from North America in side-by-side English-Spanish format. *Tameme*'s goals are to play an instrumental role in introducing important new writing from Canada and the United States to Mexico, and vice versa, and to provide a forum for the art of literary translation." Estab. 1996. Circ. 1,500. Member Council of Literary Magazines and Presses (CLMP).

Needs: Ethnic/multicultural, literary, translations. No genre fiction. Plans special fiction issue or anthology. Receives 10-15 unsolicited mss/month. No romance, mystery or western. Accepts 3-4 mss/issue; 6-8 mss/year, "but we are a new magazine so these numbers may not be indicative of a year from now." Publishes ms 1 year after acceptance. Agented fiction 5%. Published work by Fabio Morábito, Margaret Atwood, Juan Villoro, Jaime Sabines, Edwidge Danticat, A. Manette Ansay, Douglas Glover and Marianne Toussaint. **Publishes 1-3 new writers/year.** Publishes short shorts. Also publishes literary essays and poetry. Sometimes critiques or comments on mss.

How to Contact: Send complete ms with a cover letter. Translators query or submit mss with cover letter, curriculum vita and samples of previous work. Include 1-paragraph bio and list of publications. Reports in 6 weeks on queries; 3 months on mss. Send SASE for reply, return of ms or send a disposable copy of ms. Simultaneous submissions OK, "if we are advised when the manuscript is submitted." Sample copy for $14.95. Fiction guidelines for SASE.

Payment/Terms: Pays 3 contributor's copies to writers; $20 per double-spaced WordPerfect page to translators. Pays on publication. Acquires one-time rights. Sends galleys to author.

Advice: "We're looking for whatever makes us want to stand up and shout YES! Read the magazine, send for guidelines (with SASE), then send only your best, with SASE."

$⬜ **TAMPA REVIEW**, 401 W. Kennedy Blvd., Box 19F, University of Tampa, Tampa FL 33606-1490. (813)253-6266. Fax: (813)258-7593. E-mail: utpress@alpha.utampa.edu. Editor: Richard Mathews. **Fiction Editors:** Lisa Birnbaum, Kathleen Ochshorn. Magazine: 7½×10½; hardback; approximately 70 pages; acid-free paper; visual art; photos. "Interested in fiction of distinctive literary quality." Semiannually. Estab. 1988.

Needs: Contemporary, ethnic, experimental, fantasy, historical, humor/satire, literary, mainstream, prose poem, translations. "We are far more interested in quality than in genre. Nothing sentimental as opposed to genuinely moving, nor self-conscious style at the expense of human truth." Buys 4-5 mss/issue. Publishes ms within 7 months-1 year of acceptance. Agented fiction 60%. Published work by Elizabeth Spencer, Lee K. Abbott, Lorrie Moore, Tim O'Connor and Kit Reed. Length: 250 words minimum; 10,000 words maximum. Publishes short shorts "if the story is good enough." Also publishes literary essays (must be labeled nonfiction), poetry.

How to Contact: Send complete ms with cover letter. Include brief bio. No simultaneous submissions. SASE. Reads September through December; reports January through March. Sample copy for $5 (includes postage) and 9×12 SAE. Fiction guidelines for #10 SASE.

Payment/Terms: Pays $10/printed page on publication for first North American serial rights. Sends galleys to author upon request.

Advice: "There are more good writers publishing in magazines today than there have been in many decades. Unfortunately, there are even more bad ones. In T. Gertler's *Elbowing the Seducer*, an editor advises a young writer that he wants to hear her voice completely, to tell (he means 'show') him in a story the truest thing she knows. We concur. Rather than a trendy workshop story or a minimalism that actually stems from not having much to say, we would like to see stories that make us believe they mattered to the writer and, more importantly, will matter to a reader. Trim until only the essential is left, and don't give up belief in yourself. And it might help to attend a good writers' conference, e.g. Wesleyan or Bennington."

TAPROOT LITERARY REVIEW, Taproot Writer's Workshop, Inc., Box 204, Ambridge PA 15003. (724)266-8476. E-mail: taproot10@aol.com. **Editor:** Tikvah Feinstein. Magazine: 5½×8½; 93 pages; #20 paper; hard cover; attractively printed; saddle-stitched. "We select on quality, not topic. Variety and quality are our appealing features." Annually. Estab. 1987. Circ. 500.

Needs: Literary. No pornography, religious fiction. "Want more multicultural-displaced people living among others in new places." The majority of mss published are received through their annual contest. Receives 20 unsolicited mss/month. Accepts 6 fiction mss/issue. Recently published work by Allan Izen, Henryk Skwanczynski, Sally Levin, Elise Ehrhard and Erlina Kravetz. **Publishes 20 new writers/year.** Publishes 20 new writers/year. Length: 2,000 words preferred; 250 words minimum; 3,000 words maximum (no longer than 10 pages, double-spaced maximum). Publishes short shorts. Length: 300 words preferred. Sometimes critiques or comments on rejected mss. Also publishes poetry. Sponsors annual contest. Entry fee: $10/story. Deadline: December 31. Send SASE for details.

How to Contact: Send for guidelines first. Send complete ms with a cover letter. Include estimated word count and bio. Accepts queries/mss by e-mail. Reports in 6 months. Send SASE for return of ms or send a disposable copy of ms. No simultaneous submissions. Sample copy for $5, 6×12 SAE and 5 first-class stamps. Fiction guidelines for #10 SASE.

Payment/Terms: Awards $25 in prize money for first place fiction and poetry winners each issue; certificate for 2nd and 3rd place; 1 contributor's copy. Acquires first rights.

Advice: "*Taproot* is getting more fiction submissions and everyone is read entirely. This takes time, so response can be delayed at busy times of year. Our contest is a good way to start publishing. Send for a sample copy and read it through. Ask for a critique and follow suggestions. Don't be offended by any suggestions—just take them or leave them and keep writing. Looks for a story that speaks in its unique voice, told in a well-crafted and complete, memorable style, a style of signature to the author. Follow writer's guidelines. Research markets. Send cover letter. Don't give up."

"TEAK" ROUNDUP, The International Quarterly, West Coast Paradise Publishing, #5-9060 Tronson Rd., Vernon, British Columbia V1H 1E7 Canada. (250)545-4186. Fax: (250)545-4194. E-mail: wcpp@junction.net. **Editors:** Yvonne and Robert Anstey. Magazine: 5½×8½; 60 pages; 20 lb. copy paper; card stock cover; illustrations and photos. " *'Teak' Roundup* is a general interest showcase for prose and poetry. No uncouth material." Quarterly. Estab. 1994. Circ. 200.

Needs: Adventure, children's/juvenile, condensed/excerpted novel, ethnic/multicultural, historical, humor/satire, literary, mainstream/contemporary, mystery/suspense (police procedural), regional, religious/inspirational, romance (contemporary, historical), sports, westerns, young adult/teen (adventure). "No uncouth or porn. No war or violence." List of upcoming themes available for SASE. Receives 25 unsolicited mss/month. Accepts 20 mss/issue. Publishes ms 3-6 weeks after acceptance. Recently published work by Ann Carson, Philip Fletcher and Rita Campbell. **Publishes 20 new writers/year.** Length: 1,000 words maximum. Also publishes literary essays, literary criticism and poetry. Often critiques or comments on rejected ms.

How to Contact: *Accepts work from subscribers only.* Subscription for $17 (Canadian); $13 (US). Query first or send complete ms with a cover letter. Include estimated word count and brief bio. Reports in 1 week. Send SASE for reply, return of ms or send a disposable copy of ms. Simultaneous, reprint and electronic submissions OK. Sample copy for $5 (Canadian); $3 (US). Fiction guidelines for #10 SASE. Reviews novels and short story collections.

Payment/Terms: Acquires one-time rights (unreserved reprint if "Best of" edition done later.)

Advice: "Subscribe and see popular work which is enjoyed by our growing audience. Many good writers favor us with participation in subscribers-only showcase for prose and poetry. No criticism of generous contributors."

$⊘ TEARS IN THE FENCE, 38 Hod View, Stourpaine, Nr. Blandford Forum, Dorset DT11 8TN England. Phone: 01258-456803. E-mail: poets@in2it.co.uk. **Editor:** David Caddy. Biannual. The editor looks for "the unusual, perceptive and risk-taking as well as the imaginistic and visionary."

• *Tears in the Fence* has expanded to 112 pages and is accepting more prose and prose poems.

Needs: A magazine of poetry, fiction, criticism and reviews, open to a variety of contemporary voices from around the world. Upcoming themes: "Identity" (June 2000). Recently published work by Virginia Charles, Kim Taplin, Nigel Barrett, Karen Rosenberg, Nigel Jarrett, Brian George and Sarah Connor. **Publishes 1-2 new writers/year.** Publishes short and long fiction. Publishes 4-5 stories/issue.

Payment/Terms: Pays £7.50 per story plus complimentary copy of the magazine. Sample copy for $5 (US).

Advice: "Look for firm narrative control with an economical style that takes the reader far beyond the obvious and inconsequential. Explore the market by buying sample copies."

⊘ THE TEXAS REVIEW, Texas Review Press at Sam Houston University, Huntsville TX 77341-2146. (409)294-1992. **Editor:** Paul Ruffin. Magazine: 6×9; 148-190 pages; best quality paper; 70 lb. cover stock; illustrations; photos. "We publish top quality poetry, fiction, articles, interviews and reviews for a general audience." Semiannually. Estab. 1976. Circ. 1,200.

Needs: Literary and contemporary fiction. "We are eager enough to consider fiction of quality, no matter what its theme or subject matter. No juvenile fiction." Accepts 4 mss/issue. Receives approximately 40-60 unsolicited fiction mss each month. Does not read June-August. Published work by George Garrett, Ellen Gilchrist and Fred Chappell; published new writers within the last year. Length: 500-10,000 words. Critiques rejected mss "when there is time." Recommends other markets.

How to Contact: Send complete ms, cover letter optional. SASE. Reports in 3 months on mss. Sample copy for $5.

Payment/Terms: Pays contributor's copies plus one year subscription. Acquires first North American serial rights. Sends galleys to author.

✪ ✓ ⊘ TEXTSHOP, A Collaborative Journal of Writing, Dept. of English, University of Regina, Regina, Sasketchewan S4S 0A2 Canada. (306)585-4827. **Editors:** Andrew Stubbs, Judy Chapman and Richelle Leonard. Magazine: 8½×11; 50 pages; illustrations. *Textshop* is "eclectic in form and open to fiction, poetry and mixed genres, including creative nonfiction." Annually. Estab. 1993.

Needs: Ethnic/multicultural, experimental, literary. Plans special fiction issues or anthologies. Receives 20-25 unsolicited mss/month. Accepts 15-20 mss/issue. Publishes ms in next issue after acceptance. **Publishes 15 new writers/year.** Length: 500 words minimum; 1,000 words maximum. Also publishes literary essays, literary criticism and poetry. Sometimes critiques or comments on rejected ms.

How to Contact: Send complete ms with a cover letter. Include estimated word count and 25-word bio with submission. Accepts queries/mss by e-mail. Reports in 1 month on queries; 3 months on mss. SASE. Sample copy for $10. Reviews material published in each issue.

Payment/Terms: Pays 1 contributor's copy; additional copies for $10. Rights remain with the writer.

Advice: Looks for "risk-taking, mixed genre, experimental fiction. Trust your own voice and idiom. Blur the distinction between life and writing."

✪ THALIA: Studies in Literary Humor, Thalia: Association for the Study of Literary Humor, English Dept., University of Ottawa, Ottawa, Ontario K1N 6N5 Canada. (613)230-9505. Fax: (613)565-5786. **Editor:** J. Tavernier-Courbin. Magazine: illustrations and photos. Semiannually. Estab. 1978. Circ. 500.

Needs: Humor/satire. Publishes short shorts. Also publishes literary essays, literary criticism and poetry. Often critiques or comments on rejected ms.

How to Contact: Send complete ms with a cover letter. Include list of publications. Reports in 4 months on mss. Send SASE for reply. Reviews novels and short story collections.

Payment/Terms: Acquires first rights.

✪ ✓ $⊘ ☲ THEMA, Box 8747, Metairie LA 70011-8747. (504)887-1263. E-mail: bothomos@juno.com. Website: www.litline.com (includes guidelines, list of upcoming themes and back issues). **Editor:** Virginia Howard. Magazine: 5½×8½; 200 pages; Grandee Strathmore cover stock; b&w illustrations. "Different specified theme for each issue—short stories, poems, b&w artwork must relate to that theme." Triannually. Estab. 1988.

• Ranked #8 on *Writer's Digest*'s Fiction 50 list of top markets for fiction writers. *Thema* received a Certificate for Excellence in the Arts from the Arts Council of New Orleans.

Needs: Adventure, contemporary, experimental, humor/satire, literary, mainstream, mystery/suspense, prose poem, psychic/supernatural/occult, regional, science fiction, sports, western. "Each issue is based on a specified premise—a different unique theme for each issue. Many types of fiction acceptable, but must fit the premise. No pornographic, scatologic, erotic fiction." Upcoming themes (deadlines for submission in 2000): "Addie hasn't been the same. . . ." (March 1); "Scraps" (July 1); and "Safety in Numbers" (November 1). Publishes ms within 6 months of acceptance. Recently published work by Suzanne Sutton, J.F. Peirce and Barbara Anton. **Publishes 10-15 new writers/year.** Length: fewer than 6,000 words preferred. Also publishes poetry. Sometimes critiques rejected mss and recommends other markets.

How to Contact: Send complete ms with cover letter, include "name and address, brief introduction, specifying the intended target issue for the mss." Accepts queries by e-mail. Simultaneous submissions OK. Reports on queries in 1 week; on mss in 5 months after deadline for specified issue. SASE. Sample copy for $8. Free fiction guidelines.

Payment/Terms: Pays $25; $10 for short shorts on acceptance for one-time rights.

Advice: "Do not submit a manuscript unless you have written it for a specified premise. If you don't know the upcoming themes, send for guidelines first, before sending a story. We need more stories told in the Mark Twain/O. Henry tradition in magazine fiction."

THIN AIR, Graduate Creative Writing Association of Northern Arizona University, P.O. Box 23549, Flagstaff AZ 86002. Website: www.nau.edu/~english/thinair. Contact: Fiction Editor. Editors change each year. Magazine: 8½×11; 50-60 pages; illustrations; photos. Publishes "contemporary voices for a literary-minded audience." Semiannually. Estab. 1995. Circ. 500.

Needs: Condensed/excerpted novel, ethnic/multicultural, experimental, literary, mainstream/contemporary. "No children's/juvenile." Editorial calendar available for SASE. Receives 75 unsolicited mss/month. Accepts 5-8 mss/issue; 10-15 mss/year. Does not read mss May-September. Publishes ms 6-9 months after acceptance. Solicited fiction 35%. Recently published work by Stephen Dixon, Henry H. Roth, Brian Evenson, Charles Bowden, Sean Caughlin, Patricia Lawrence and Craig Rullman. **Publishes 3-8 new writers/year.** Length: 6,000 words maximum. Publishes short shorts. Also publishes literary essays, literary criticism, creative nonfiction, poetry and interviews. Recent interviews include Thom Jones, Alan Lightman and Rick Bass

How to Contact: Send complete ms with a cover letter. Include estimated word count and list of publications. Reports in 1 month on queries; 3-5 months on mss. Send SASE for reply, return of ms or send a disposable copy of ms. Simultaneous submissions OK. Sample copy for $5. Fiction guidelines free. Reviews novels and short story collections.

Payment/Terms: Pays 2 contributor's copies; additional copies for $4. Pays on publication. Acquires first North American serial rights. Sponsors contest; send SASE for guidelines.

Advice: Looks for "writers who know how to create tension and successfully resolve it."

THE THIRD ALTERNATIVE, 5 Martins Lane, Witcham, Ely, Cambs CB6 2LB England. E-mail: ttapress@aol.com. **Fiction Editor:** Andy Cox. Quarterly. Publishes 8 stories/issue. A4, 68 pages, lithographed, color glossy.

Needs: "Modern fiction: no mainstream or genre clichés. Innovative, quality science fiction/fantasy/horror and slipstream material (cross-genre)." Length: No minimum; no maximum (no serials).

How to Contact: Only send one story at a time, mailed flat or folded no more than once. USA stamps are not acceptable as return postage (UK stamps, 2 IRCs or an e-mail address—but no submissions via e-mail). "A covering letter is appreciated." Standard ms format and SAE (overseas: disposable ms and 2 IRCs). No simultaneous submissions. Reprints only in exceptional circumstances.

Payment/Terms: Payment is £20 per 1,000 words. $6 sample copy, $22 four-issue subscription. US checks acceptable, payable to TTA Press.

THIRD COAST, Dept. of English, Western Michigan University, Kalamazoo MI 49008-5092. (616)387-2675. Fax: (616)387-2562. Website: www.umich.edu/thirdcoast (includes guidelines, editors names and samples of past fiction we have published are all available on the website). Managing Editor: Kathleen McGookey. **Fiction Editors:** Pedro Ponce and Chris Torockio. Magazine: 6×9; 150 pages. "We will consider many different types of fiction and favor that exhibiting a freshness of vision and approach." Semiannually. Estab. 1995. Circ. 600.

● *Third Coast* has received *Pushcart Prize* nominations. The editors of this publication change with the university year.

Needs: Literary. "While we don't want to see formulaic genre fiction, we will consider material that plays with or challenges generic forms." Receives approximately 100 unsolicited mss/month. Accepts 6-8 mss/issue; 15 mss/year. Publishes ms 3-6 months after acceptance. Recently published work by Peter Ho Davies, Sarah J. Smith, Wang Ping and Sara McAulay. Length: no preference. Publishes short shorts. Also publishes literary essays, poetry and interviews. Sometimes critiques or comments on rejected mss.

How to Contact: Send complete ms with a cover letter. Include list of publications. Reports in 2 months on queries; 5 months on mss. Send SASE for reply or return of ms. No simultaneous submissions. Sample copy for $6. Fiction guidelines for #10 SASE.

Payment/Terms: Pays 2 contributor's copies as well as 1 year subscription to the publication; additional copies for $4. Acquires first North American serial rights.

Advice: "Of course, the writing itself must be of the highest quality. We love to see work that explores non-western contexts, as well as fiction from all walks of American (and other) experience."

THE THIRD HALF MAGAZINE, "Amikeco," 16, Fane Close, Stamford, Lincolnshire PE9 1HG England. **Fiction Editor:** Kevin Troop. Published irregularly (when possible).

Needs: "*The Third Half* literary magazine publishes mostly poetry, but editorial policy is to publish as much *short* short story writing as possible in each issue." Recently published work by Steve Sneyd and Michael Newman. Length: 2,000 words maximum.

Payment/Terms: Pays in contributor's copies. Sample copy £4.95; £5.50 by post in England; £7 overseas.

✔ ◨ ◎ **13TH MOON, A Feminist Magazine**, Dept. of English, University at Albany, Albany NY 12222. (518)442-4181. Editor: Judith Johnson. **Fiction Editors:** Judith Fetterly and Hollis Seamon. Magazine: 6×9; 300 pages; 50 lb. paper; heavy cover stock; illustrations; photographs. "Feminist literary magazine for feminist women and men." Annually. Estab. 1972. Circ. 2,000.

Needs: Ethnic/multicultural, experimental, feminist, lesbian, literary, romance, science fiction, translations. No fiction by men. List of upcoming themes available for SASE. Receives 10 unsolicited mss/month. Accepts 30 mss/year. Does not read mss June-August. Time varies between acceptance and publication. Published work by F.R. Lewis, Jan Ramjerdi and Wilma Kahn. Length: Open. Publishes short shorts. Also publishes poetry. Sometimes critiques rejected mss.

How to Contact: Query first; send complete ms with cover letter and SASE (or IRC). Include bio and list of publications. Reports in 1 month of queries; 1 year on mss. SASE. Sample copy for $10. Guidelines for SASE.

Payment/Terms: Pays 2 contributor's copies.

Terms: Acquires first North American serial rights.

Advice: Looks for *"unusual* fiction with feminist appeal."

$◨ **32 PAGES**, Rain Crow Publishing, 2127 W. Pierce Ave. Apt. 2B, Chicago IL 60622-1824. (773)276-9005. E-mail: 32pp@rain-crow-publishing.com. Website: rain-crow-publishing.com/32pp/ (includes writer's guidelines, sample issue, back issue sales, advertising rates). **Editor:** Michael S. Manley. Magazine: 8½×11; 32 pages; 40 lb. white paper; illustrations. *"32 Pages* publishes new and experienced writers in many styles and genres. I look for eclectic, well-crafted, entertaining fiction aimed at those who enjoy literature for its pleasures." 4 to 6 issues per year. Estab. 1997. Circ. 1,000.

Needs: Adventure, erotica, ethnic/multicultural, experimental, fantasy, feminist, gay, historical (general), horror, humor/satire, lesbian, literary, mainstream/contemporary, mystery/suspense, regional, science fiction, translations. "No dogmatically religious, politically propagandistic or formulaic fiction. Not too interested in porn or juvenile, either." Receives 25-50 unsolicited mss/month. Accepts 3-4 mss/issue; 18-24 mss/year. Publishes ms within 6 months after acceptance. Published work by Susan Neville, Stanley Jenkins, William Stuckey, Peter Johnson, Murray Shugars, John McDermott, Carolyn Alessio, Christine Butterworth, Rob Davidson and Maija Kroeger. **Publishes several new writers/year.** Length: 4,000 words average; 250 words minimum; 8,000 words maximum. Publishes short shorts. Also publishes personal essays, poetry. Sometimes critiques or comments on rejected mss.

How to Contact: Send complete ms with a cover letter. May also e-mail submissions. Include estimated word count and brief bio. Reports in 3 months. Send SASE for reply, return of ms or send a disposable copy of ms. Simultaneous submissions, reprints and electronic submissions OK. Sample copy for $2.50. Fiction guidelines for #10 SASE (1 IRC).

Payment/Terms: Pays $5 per page on publication, free subscription to magazine and 2 contributor's copies; additional copies for $2. Acquires one-time rights and one-time electronic rights. Sends galleys to author. Sponsors "fiction chapbook contest annually. Watch for announcements in writer's publications and on our website."

Advice: "Is it a story I want to read again? Did it keep me locked into its fictional dream? A good manuscript makes me forget I'm reading a manuscript. I look for attention to craft: voice, language, character and plot working together to maximum effect. Unique yet credible settings and situations that entertain will get the most attention. Write to the best of your abilities and submit your best work. Present yourself and your work professionally. Get used to rejections. Literary magazines must change if they are to survive in today's market. Contemporary fiction must do the same."

🍁 ✔ $◨ ♈ **THIS MAGAZINE**, Red Maple Foundation, 401 Richmond St. W., Suite 396, Toronto, Ontario M5V 3A8 Canada. (416)979-8400. E-mail: thismag@web.net. Website: www.thismag.org (includes writer's guidelines). **Literary Editor:** Chris Chambers. Magazine: 8½×11; 48 pages; bond paper; non-coated cover; illustrations and photographs. "Alternative general interest magazine." Bimonthly. Estab. 1966. Circ. 7,000.

 • *This Magazine* has won national Canadian Magazine awards, and *Utne Reader's* alternative press awards for cultural coverage. *This Magazine* is not currently accepting unsolicited manuscripts.

Needs: Ethnic, contemporary, experimental, feminist, gay, lesbian, literary, regional. No "commercial/pulp fiction." Published work by Elise Levine, Stuart Ross, Lynn Coady, Allan Barr and Tony Burgess. Length: 2,000 words average; 3,000 words maximum.

How to Contact: "We no longer accept unsolicited poetry or fiction." Accepts queries by e-mail. Sample copy for $4.50 (plus GST). Fiction guidelines for #9 SASE with Canadian stamps or IRC.

Payment/Terms: Pays $150 minimum (Canadian) fiction; $50 minimum/poem published for one-time rights.

Advice: "It's best if you're familiar with the magazine when submitting work; a large number of mss that come into the office are inappropriate. Style guides are available. Manuscripts and queries that are clean and personalized really make a difference. Let your work speak for itself—don't try to convince us."

⭐ 💲 🗹 🗹 **THE THREEPENNY REVIEW**, P.O. Box 9131, Berkeley CA 94709. (510)849-4545. **Editor:** Wendy Lesser. Tabloid: 10×17; 40 pages; Electrobrite paper; white book cover; illustrations. "Serious fiction." Quarterly. Estab. 1980. Circ. 9,000.

• *The Threepenny Review* ranked #11 on *Writer's Digest*'s Fiction 50 list of top markets for fiction writers, and has received GE Writers Awards, CLMP Editor's Awards, NEA grants, Lila Wallace grants and inclusion of work in the *Pushcart Prize Anthology.*

Needs: Literary. "Nothing 'experimental' (ungrammatical)." Receives 300-400 mss/month. Accepts 3 mss/issue; 12 mss/year. Does *not* read mss June through August. Publishes 6-12 months after acceptance. Agented fiction 5%. Published Sigrid Nunez, Dagoberto Gilb, Gina Berriault and Leonard Michaels. Length: 5,000 words maximum. Publishes short shorts. Also publishes literary essays, literary criticism, poetry.

How to Contact: Send complete ms with a cover letter. Reports in 2-4 weeks on queries;1-2 months on mss. Send SASE for reply, return of ms or send a disposable copy of the ms. No simultaneous submissions. Sample copy for $7. Fiction guidelines for #10 SASE. Reviews novels and short story collections.

Payment/Terms: Pays $200 on acceptance plus free subscription to the magazine; additional copies at half price. Acquires first North American serial rights. Sends galleys to author.

🗹 💲 🗹 **TIMBER CREEK REVIEW**, 3283 UNCG Station, Greensboro NC 27413. (336)334-6970. E-mail: timber_creek_Review@hoopsmail.com. **Editor:** J.M. Freiermuth. Associate Editor: Celestine Woo. Newsletter: 5½×8½; 76-84 pages; copy paper; some illustrations and photographs. Quarterly. Circ. 150.

Needs: Adventure, contemporary, ethnic, feminist, historical, humor/satire, literary, mainstream, mystery/suspense (cozy, private eye), regional, western (adult, frontier, traditional). No religion, children's, gay, romance. Plans seventh "All Woman Author" issue (October 2000). Receives 40-60 unsolicited mss/month. Accepts 15-20 mss/issue; 70-75 mss/year. Publishes ms 3-12 months after acceptance. Recently published work by J. Michael Blue, Delray Dvoracek, Tod Golberg, Karl Nilsson, Catherine Uroff and Roslyn Willett. **Publishes 0-3 new writers/year.** Length: 3,500 words average; 1,500 words minimum; 10,000 words maximum. Sometimes critiques rejected mss. "If you don't like to hear the slightest bad news, mention that in your cover letter and I won't bother."

How to Contact: Send complete ms and/or DOS disk (uses MS Word). Cover letter required. "There are no automatons here, so don't treat us like machines. We recognize the names of a couple hundred writers on sight, but if you are not a dead white guy, we may not recognize your name at the top of the manuscript. A few lines about you break the ice. The names of three or four magazines that have published you in the last year would show your reality. A bio blurb of 37 +/- words including the names of two or three of the magazines you send the occasional subscription check (where you aspire to be?) could help. If you are not sending a check to some little magazine that is supported by subscriptions and the blood sweat and tears of the editors, why would you send your work to any of them and expect to receive a warm welcome? No requirement to subscribe or buy a sample, but they are available at $4.25 and encouraged. There are no phony contests and never a reading fee. Read all year long, but may take one to six months to respond." Simultaneous submissions OK but no reprints.

Payment/Terms: Pays $10-35. Pays subscription to magazine for first publication and contributor's copies for subsequent publications. Acquires one-time rights. Publication not copyrighted.

Advice: "Stop watching TV and read that book of stories your last manuscript appeared in. If you are not reading other people's stories, they are probably not reading yours either. If no one reads this stuff, was it worth wasting the tree? If your story has a spark of life or a degree of humor that brings a smile to my face, you may have a chance here. Most stories lack these ingredients. Write new stories. If you have 20 stories circulating, you have a better chance of having one published."

🅽 💲 🗹 **TIN HOUSE**, McCormack Communications, Box 10500, Portland OR 97296-0550. (503)274-4393. Fax: (503)222-1154. E-mail: tinhouse@europa.com. Editor: Win McCormack. **Fiction Editors**: Rob Spillman and Elissa Schappell. Literary magazine: 5¾×8¼; 200 pages, 50 lb. paper; glossy cover stock; illustrations and photos. Quarterly.

Needs: Experimental, literary. Accepts 3-4 mss/issue. Publishes ms up to one year after acceptance. Length: 3,500 words average; 2,000 words minimum; 5,000 words maximum. Publishes short shorts. Also publishes literary essays, literary criticism and poetry.

How to Contact: Send complete ms with a cover letter or submit through an agent. Include estimated word count. Reports in 6 weeks on mss. Send SASE for return of ms. Simultaneous submissions OK. Sample copy for $9.95. Guidelines for $2.

Payment/Terms: Pays $100-1,000 plus 2 contributor's copies for first North American serial and Anthology rights; additional copies for $9.95.

Advice: "Our criteria are boldness of concept, intense level of emotion and energy, precision of observation, deployment of imagination, grace of style. Any sentence read at random is impeccable and as good as any other in the work. Do not send anything that does not make you feel like laughing or crying, or both, when you read it yourself."

🗹 **TOUCHSTONE LITERARY JOURNAL**, P.O. Box 8308, Spring TX 77387-8308. E-mail: guidmj@flex. net. Editor/Publisher: William Laufer. Managing Editor: Guida Jackson. **Fiction Editor:** Julia Gomez-Rigas.

Magazine: 5½×8½; 56 pages; linen paper; kramkote cover; perfect bound; b&w illustrations; occasional photographs. "Literary and mainstream fiction, but enjoy experimental work and multicultural. Audience middle-class, heavily academic. We are eclectic and given to whims—i.e., two years ago we devoted a 104-page issue to West African women writers." Annually (with occasional special supplements). Estab. 1976. Circ. 1,000.

• Touchstone Press also publishes a chapbook series. Send a SASE for guidelines.

Needs: Humor/satire, literary, translations. No erotica, religious, juvenile, "stories written in creative writing programs that all sound alike." List of upcoming themes available for SASE. Publishes special fiction issue or anthology. Receives 20-30 mss/month. Accepts 3-4 mss/issue. Does not read mss in December. Publishes ms within the year after acceptance. Published work by Ann Alejandro, Lynn Bradley, Roy Fish and Julia Mercedes Castilla. Length: 2,500 words preferred; 250 words minimum; 5,000 words maximum. Publishes short shorts. Length: 300 words. Also publishes literary essays, literary criticism and poetry. Sometimes critiques or comments on rejected mss.

How to Contact: Send complete ms with a cover letter. Include estimated word count and 3-sentence bio. Reports in 6 weeks. Send SASE for return of ms. Simultaneous and electronic submissions OK. Sample copy for $3 or 10 first-class stamps. Fiction guidelines for #10 SASE.

Payment/Terms: Pays 2 contributor's copies; additional copies $5. Acquires one-time rights. Sends galleys to author (unless submitted on disk).

Advice: "We like to see fiction that doesn't read as if it had been composed in a creative writing class. If you can entertain, edify, or touch the reader, polish your story and send it in. Don't worry if it doesn't read like our other fiction."

TRIQUARTERLY, Northwestern University, 2020 Ridge Ave., Evanston IL 60208-4302. (847)491-7614. **Editor:** Susan Hahn. Magazine: 6×9¼; 240-272 pages; 60 lb. paper; heavy cover stock; illustration; photos. "A general literary quarterly especially devoted to fiction. We publish short stories, novellas or excerpts from novels, by American and foreign writers. Genre or style is not a primary consideration. We aim for the general but serious and sophisticated reader. Many of our readers are also writers." Triannual. Estab. 1964. Circ. 5,000.

• Stories from *Triquarterly* have been reprinted in *The Best American Short Stories*, *Pushcart Prizes* and *O'Henry Prize* Anthologies.

Needs: Literary, contemporary and translations. "No prejudices or preconceptions against anything *except* genre fiction (romance, science fiction, etc.)." Accepts 10 mss/issue, 30 mss/year. Receives approximately 500 unsolicited fiction mss each month. Does not read April 1 through September 30. Agented fiction 10%. Recently published work by John Barth, Chaim Potok, Joyce Carol Oates, Hélène Cixous, Charles Baxter, Margot Livesey and Robert Girardi. **Publishes 1-5 new writers/year.** Length: no requirement. Publishes short shorts.

How to Contact: Send complete ms with SASE. No simultaneous submissions. Reports in 4 months on mss. Publishes ms an average of 6-12 months after acceptance. Sample copy for $5.

Payment/Terms: Pays 2 contributor's copies on publication for first North American serial rights. Cover price less 40% discount for extras. Sends galleys to author. Honoraria vary, depending on grant support.

TUCUMCARI LITERARY REVIEW, 3108 W. Bellevue Ave., Los Angeles CA 90026. **Editor:** Troxey Kemper. Magazine: 5½×8½; about 40 pages; 20 lb. bond paper; 67 lb. cover stock; few illustrations; photocopied photographs. "Old-fashioned fiction that can be read and reread for pleasure; no weird, strange pipe dreams and no it-was-all-a-dream endings." Bimonthly. Estab. 1988. Circ. small.

Needs: Adventure, contemporary, ethnic, historical, humor/satire, literary, mainstream, mystery/suspense, regional (southwest USA), senior citizen/retirement, western (frontier stories). No "sci-fi, occult, violence, sex sex sex, dirty language for no reason or romance. Would like to see more Western, mystery and O. Henry endings." No drugs/acid rock, occult, pornography, horror, martial arts or children's stories. Accepts 6 or 8 mss/issue; 35-40 mss/year. Publishes ms 2-6 months after acceptance. Published work by Wilma Elizabeth McDaniel, Ruth Daniels, Andy Peterson, Jim Boone and Bobby Rivera. **Publishes 12 new writers/year.** Length: 400-1,200 words preferred. Also publishes rhyming poetry.

How to Contact: Send complete ms with or without cover letter. Reports in 2 weeks. SASE. Simultaneous and reprint submissions OK. Sample copy for $2. Fiction guidelines for #10 SASE.

Payment/Terms: Pays in contributor's copies. Acquires one-time rights. Publication not copyrighted.

Advice: "Computers/printers are 'nice' but sometimes handwritten work on 3-hole lined notebook paper is interesting, too. Think of some stories you read in English class when you were in grade school/high school. Try something, *but not the same story*, along those lines."

ULITARRA, Ulitarra Literary Association Inc. P.O. Box 195, Armidale, New South Wales 2350 Australia. (02)67729135. Editors: Michael Sharkey (coordinating editor), Stephen Harris and Winifred Belmont. "We also have a panel which referees academic submissions." Magazine: 210mm×150mm; 140 pages; 80 GSM paper; 240 GSM cover stock; illustrations and photos. "*Ulitarra* seeks original writing, predominantly by Australian writers (in Australia and abroad), but also publishes works by other writers. We particularly encourage Aboriginal writers and translations by Australian writers of works in other languages." Semiannually. Estab 1992, Circ. 600.

Needs: Adventure, erotica, ethnic/multicultural, excerpted novel, experimental, fantasy (science fantasy), feminist, gay, historical, humor/satire, lesbian, literary, mainstream/contemporary, science fiction (hard science), translations. Publishes special fiction issues or anthologies. Receives 30 unsolicited mss/month. Accepts 4-5 mss/issue; 8-10 mss/year. Publishes ms within 6 months after acceptance. Publishes 5-15 new writers/year. Recently published work by Morris Lurie, Ahmed Shamloo, Antonia Baldo, Ben Wilensky, Barney Roberts and Anita Heiss. Length: 3,500 words average; 1,200 words minimum; 5,000 words maximum. Publishes short shorts. Length: 3,500 words. Also publishes literary essays, literary criticism, poetry. Always critiques or comments on rejected mss.
How to Contact: Send compete ms with a cover letter and SASE (or IRCs). Include estimated word count and 3-line bio. Reports in 1 week on queries; 3 weeks on mss. Send SASE (or IRCs) for reply, return of ms or send a disposable copy of ms. Electronic submissions (disk or modem) OK. Sample copy for $15. Fiction guidelines free. Reviews novels and short story collections.
Payment/Terms: Pays $90 and 1 contributor's copy; additional copies $10 for overseas contributors. Pays on publication. Acquires first rights. Sends galleys to author. Sponsors contests. Writers can participate by buying a copy of January issue (for poetry prize) or July issue (for short story prize). Details and entry forms are in issue.
Advice: "We publish what *we* like; talent is what we're after. We don't follow fashion: we set it."

[N] [M] UNMUZZLED OX, Unmuzzled Ox Foundation Ltd., 105 Hudson St., New York NY 10013. (212)226-7170. E-mail: mandreox@aol.com. Editor: Michael Andre. Magazine: 5½×8½. "Magazine about life for an intelligent audience." Published irregularly. Estab. 1971. Circ. 7,000.
● Recent issues of this magazine have included poetry, essays and art only. You may want to check before sending submissions or expect a long response time.
Needs: Contemporary, literary, prose poem and translations. No commercial material. Receives 20-25 unsolicited mss/month. Also publishes poetry. Occasionally critiques rejected mss.
How to Contact: Not reading unsolicited mss until April 1998. "Please no phone calls. Correspondence by mail *only*. Cover letter is significant." Reports in 1 month. SASE. Sample copy for $10.
Payment/Terms: Contributor's copies.

[N] [O] URBAN SPAGHETTI, Literary Arts Journal, P.O. Box 5186, Mansfield OH 44901-5186. E-mail: editor@urban-spaghetti.com. Website: www.urban-spaghetti.com. Editor: Cheryl Dodds. **Fiction Editor**: Philip Richardson. Literary magazine: 8½×7; 50-90 pages; 60-80 lb. bond paper; illustrations and photos. "Our focus extends a hand to new writers and poets who share a sense of social responsibility in their writing and offer a fresh presentation and language which challenges us." Semiannually. Estab. 1998.
Needs: Adventure, ethnic/multicultural, experimental, fantasy, feminist, historical, horror, humor satire, literary, mainstream/contemporary, military/war, mystery/suspense, science fiction, western. Receives 20 unsolicited mss/month. Accepts 2-5 mss/issue; 4-10 mss/year. Does not read December-June. Publishes ms 2-5 months after acceptance. Length: 3,500 words maximum. Publishes short shorts. Also publishes literary essays, criticism and poetry. Often critiques or comments on rejected ms.
How to Contact: Send complete ms with a cover letter. Include estimated word count and 1-paragraph bio. Reports in 1 week on queries; 2 months on mss. Send SASE for reply or return of ms. Simultaneous and reprint submissions OK with notification. Sample copy for 9×12 SAE with 4 first-class stamps. Reviews short story collections and nonfiction books of interest to writers. Send books to editor.
Payment/Terms: Pays 2 contributor's copies; additional copies $5. Acquires first rights. Sends prepublication galleys to author. Not copyrighted. Sponsors contest: see website for details.
Advice: Looks for "excellent writing, strong voice, good characterization and craft. Proof read, use fresh language, do not use 'shock factor' without well-crafted purpose, make us believe. *Urban Spaghetti* wants to promote new writers. We want to be a resource for innovative new voices."

[★] [✓] [$] [◐] [◎] THE URBANITE, Surreal & Lively & Bizarre, Urban Legend Press, P.O. Box 4737, Davenport IA 52808. Website: members.tripod.com/theurbanite/ (includes information on current and upcoming issues and also features a fiction showcase). **Editor:** Mark McLaughlin. Magazine: 8½×11; 52-80 pages; bond paper; coated cover; saddle-stitched; illustrations. "We look for quality fiction with a surrealistic tone. We publish character-oriented, sophisticated fiction that expands the boundaries of the speculative genres. Our readers appreciate the best in imaginative fiction." Each issue includes a featured writer, a featured poet and a featured artist. Published three times a year. Estab. 1991. Circ. 500-1,000.
● *The Urbanite* ranked #10 on the *Writer's Digest* Fiction 50 list of top markets for fiction writers.
Needs: Experimental, fantasy (dark fantasy), horror, humor/satire, literary, psychic/supernatural/occult, science fiction (soft/sociological). "We love horror, but please, no tired, gore-ridden horror plots. Horror submissions must be subtle and sly. Want more unusual, stylish stories with a sense of 'voice.' Also, more bizarre humor." Upcoming themes: "The Zodiac" and "All Horror" issue. List of upcoming themes available for SASE. Receives over 800 unsolicited mss/month. Accepts 15 mss/issue; 45 mss/year. Publishes ms 6 months after acceptance. Published work by Basil Copper, Wilum Pugmire, Hertzan Chimera, Marni Scofidio Griffin, Alexa de Monterice and Thomas Ligotti. **Publishes at least 2-3 new writers/year.** Length: 2,000 words preferred; 500 words mini-

mum; 3,000 words maximum. Publishes short shorts. Length: 350 words preferred. Also publishes poetry. Sometimes critiques or comments on rejected mss.

How to Contact: Include estimated word count, 4- to 5-sentence bio, Social Security number and list of publications. Reports in 1 month on queries; 3-4 months on mss. Send large SASE for reply and return of ms, or send a stamped, self-addressed business-size envelope and a disposable copy of ms. Sample copy for $5. Fiction guidelines for #10 SASE.

Payment/Terms: Pays 2-3¢/word and 2 contributor's copies for first North American serial rights and nonexclusive rights for public readings. Featured authors receive 3¢/word, 6 contributor's copies and a lifetime subscription to the magazine. Authors of stories in our website's fiction showcase receive $25.

Advice: "The tone of our magazine is unique, and we strongly encourage writers to read an issue to ascertain the sort of material we accept. The number one reason we reject many stories is because they are inappropriate for our publication: in these cases, it is obvious that the writer is not familiar with *The Urbanite*. We are known for publishing quality horror—work from *The Urbanite* has been reprinted in *Year's Best Fantasy & Horror, The Year's Best Fantastic Fiction*, England's *Best New Horror*, volumes 7 and 8, and on the *Masters of Terror Website*. We want to see more bizarre (yet urbane and thought-provoking) humor. Excellence is priority number one. We simply want stories that are well-written, compelling and unique. Find your own 'voice.' Put your own style and personality into your work!"

WASAFIRI, Dept. of English, Queen Mary & Westfield College, University of London, Mile End Road, London EI4NS UK. Editor: Ms. Susheila Nasta. Bi-annual. Circ. 1,000. Publishes 2-3 short stories/issue. "Publishes critical articles, interviews, fiction and poetry by and about African, Asian, Caribbean, Pacific and Black British writers." Length: 500 words miminum; 2,000 words maximum. Pays contributor's copies. "We welcome any writing for consideration which falls into our areas of interest. Work from writers outside Britain is a major part of our interest. Articles should be double-spaced and follow MLA guidelines."

WASCANA REVIEW OF CONTEMPORARY POETRY AND SHORT FICTION, University of Regina, Regina, Saskatchewan S4S 0A2 Canada. (306)585-4299. E-mail: kathleen.wall@uregina.ca. Editor: Dr. Kathleen Wall. **Fiction Editor:** Dr. Jeanne Shaimi. "Literary criticism, fiction and poetry for readers of serious fiction." Semiannually. Estab. 1966. Circ. 500.

Needs: Literary and humor. Upcoming themes: "Landscape & Literature" and "Life Writing." Buys 8-10 mss/year. Receives approximately 20 unsolicited fiction mss/month. Agented fiction 5%. **Publishes 1-2 new writers/year.** Length: 2,000-6,000 words. Occasionally recommends other markets.

How to Contact: Accepts queries by e-mail. Send complete ms with SASE. Reports in 2 months on mss. Publishes ms an average of 6 months after acceptance. Sample copy for $5. Guidelines with SASE.

Payment/Terms: Pays $3/page for prose; $10/page for poetry; 2 contributor's copies on publication for first North American rights. Pays on publication.

Advice: "Stories are often technically incompetent or deal with trite subjects. Usually stories are longer than necessary by about one-third. Be more ruthless in cutting back on unnecessary verbiage. All approaches to fiction are welcomed by the *Review* editors—but we continue to seek the best in terms of style and technical expertise. As our calls for submission state, the *Wascana Review* continues to seek . . . short fiction that combines craft with risk, pressure with grace."

WASHINGTON SQUARE, Literary Review of New York University's Creative Writing Program, (formerly Ark/Angel Review), NYU Creative Writing Program, 19 University Place, 3rd Floor, Room 310, New York NY 10003-4556. (212)998-8816. Fax: (212)995-4017. Editor: Jennifer Keller. **Fiction Editor:** David Pucell. Editors change each year. Magazine: 5½×8½; 144 pages; photographs. "*Washington Square* is the literary review produced by New York University's Graduate Creative Writing Program. We publish outstanding works of fiction and poetry by the students and faculty of NYU as well as the work of writers across the country." Semiannually. Estab. 1996 (we were previously called Ark/Angel Review, estab. 1987). Circ. 1,000.

Needs: Condensed/excerpted novel, ethnic/multicultural, experimental, literary, mainstream/contemporary. No adventure, children's, erotica. Receives 75 unsolicited mss/month. Accepts 5 mss/issue; 10 mss/year. Publishes ms 3-5 months after acceptance. Agented fiction 20%. Published work by Dika Lam, Sarah Inman, Jessica Anya Blau, Irene Korenfeld. Length: 5,000 words average; 7,000 words maximum. Publishes short shorts. Also publishes poetry. Sometimes critiques or comments on rejected mss.

How to Contact: Send complete ms with a cover letter. Include estimated word count (only put name on first page). Reports in 2 weeks on queries; 6 weeks on mss. Send SASE for reply, return of ms or send a disposable copy of ms. Simultaneous submissions OK. Sample copy for $6.

Payment/Terms: Pays 3 contributor's copies; additional copies for $6. Acquires first North American serial rights. "Each fall we sponsor a short story contest. Send SASE for more info."

Advice: "We look for compelling, original, outstanding fiction. Please send polished, proofread manuscripts only."

WEB DEL SOL, E-mail: editor@webdelsol.com. Website: webdelsol.com. **Editor:** Michael Neff. Electronic magazine. "The goal of *Web Del Sol* is to use the medium of the Internet to bring the finest in contemporary literary arts to a larger audience. To that end, *WDS* not only webpublishes collections of work by accomplished writers and poets, but hosts other literary arts publications on the WWW such as *Ploughshares*, *AGNI, North American Review, Zyzzyva, Flashpoint, 5-Trope, Global City Review, The Literary Review* and *The Prose Poem*.

● *Web Del Sol* ranked #21 on *Writer's Digest*'s Fiction 50 list of top markets for fiction writers.

Needs: "*WDS* publishes work considered to be literary in nature, i.e., non-genre fiction. *WDS* also publishes poetry, prose poetry, essays and experimental types of writing." Publishes short shorts. Recently published work by Robert Olen Butler, Forrest Gander, Xue Di, Michael Buceja, Martine Billen and Roldey Wilson. **Publishes 30-40 new writers/year.** "Currently, *WDS* published Featured Writer/Poet websites, approximately 15 per year at this time; but hopes to increase that number substantially in the coming year. *WDS* also occasionally publishes individual works and plans to do more of these also."

How to Contact: "Submissions by e-mail from September through November and from January through March only. Submissions must contain some brief bio, list of prior publications (if any), and a short work or prortion of that work, neither to exceed 1,000 words. Editors will contact if the balance of work is required."

Advice: "*WDS* wants fiction that is absolutely cutting edge, unique and/or at a minimum, accomplished with a crisp style and concerning subjects not usually considered the objects of literary scrutiny. Read works in such publications as *Conjunctions* (www.conjunctions.com) and *North American Review* (webdelsol.com/NorthAmRe view/NAR) to get an idea what we are looking for."

WEST BRANCH, Bucknell Hall, Bucknell University, Lewisburg PA 17837. **Editors:** Karl Patten and Robert Love Taylor. Magazine: 5½ × 8½; 96-120 pages; quality paper; coated card cover; perfect-bound; illustrations; photos. Fiction and poetry for readers of contemporary literature. Biannually. Estab. 1977. Circ. 500.

● The next two issues of the magazine, #45 and #46 (fall 1999 and spring 2000), will be combined into a double issue celebrating *West Branch*'s 22 years of publication. The contents of this issue will be poems and stories reprinted from past issues of the magazine. Because *West Branch* #47, the next issue containing all new work, will not be published until the autumn of 2000, the editors will not be reading mss that are received between March 1, 1999 and May 1, 2000.

Needs: Literary, contemporary, prose poems and translations. No science fiction. Accepts 3-6 mss/issue. Recently published work by Daniel J. Bingley, Cynthia Elliott, Deborah Hodge, Leslie Pietrzyk, Darby Sanders, Steve Moncada Street, Kathleen Wakefield and Jo-Anne A. Watts. **Published new writers within the last year.** No preferred length. However, "the fiction we publish usually runs between 12-25 double-spaced pages."

How to Contact: Send complete ms with cover letter, "with information about writer's background, previous publications, etc." SASE. No simultaneous submissions. Reports in 6-8 weeks on mss. Sample copy for $3.

Payment/Terms: Pays 2 contributor's copies and one-year subscription; cover price less 25% discount charge for extras. Acquires first rights.

Advice: "Narrative art fulfills a basic human need—our dreams attest to this—and storytelling is therefore a high calling in any age. Find your own voice and vision. Make a story that speaks to your own mysteries. Cultivate simplicity in form, complexity in theme. Look and listen through your characters."

WEST COAST LINE, A Journal of Contemporary Writing & Criticism, 2027 E. Academic Annex, Simon Fraser University, Burnaby, British Columbia V5A 1S6 Canada. (604)291-4287. Fax: (604)291-4622. E-mail: wcl@sfu.ca. Website: www.sfu.ca/west-coast-line. **Managing Editor:** Jennifer Conroy. Magazine: 6 × 9; 128-144 pages. "Poetry, fiction, criticism—modern and contemporary, North American, cross-cultural. Readers include academics, writers, students." Triannual. Estab. 1990. Circ. 600.

Needs: Experimental, ethnic/multicultural, feminist, gay, literary. "We do not publish journalistic writing or strictly representational narrative." Receives 30-40 unsolicited mss/month. Accepts 2-3 mss/issue; 3-6 mss/year. Publishes ms 2-10 months after acceptance. Recently published work by Claire Harris, Ashok Mathur, Erin Mouré and Marwan Hassan. **Publishes 3 new writers/year.** Length: 3,000-4,000 words. Publishes short shorts. Length: 250-400 words. Also publishes literary essays and literary criticism.

How to Contact: Send complete ms with a cover letter. "We supply an information form for contributors." Reports in 3 months. Send SAE with IRCs, not US postage, for return of ms. No simultaneous submissions. Sample copy for $10. Fiction guidelines free.

Payment/Terms: Pays $3-8/page (Canadian); subscription; 2 contributor copies; additional copies for $6-8/copy, depending on quantity ordered. Pays on publication for one-time rights.

Advice: "Special concern for contemporary writers who are experimenting with, or expanding the boundaries of conventional forms of poetry, fiction and criticism; also interested in criticism and scholarship on Canadian and American modernist writers who are important sources for current writing. We recommend that potential

---

MARKET CONDITIONS are constantly changing! If you're still using this book and it is 2001 or later, buy the newest edition of *Novel & Short Story Writer's Market* at your favorite bookstore or order from Writer's Digest Books at (800)289-0963.

contributors send a letter of enquiry or read back issues before submitting a manuscript."

✓ ◯ WEST WIND REVIEW, 1250 Siskiyou Blvd., Ashland OR 97520. (503)552-6518. E-mail: westwind @tao.sou.edu. Website: www.sou/stu_affa/westwind.htm (includes guidelines, editors and short fiction). **Editor:** Dan Buck (1999-2000 school year). Editors change each year. Magazine: 5¾ × 8½; 150-250 pages; illustrations and photos. "Literary journal publishing prose/poetry/art. Encourages new writers, accepts established writers as well, with an audience of people who like to read challenging fiction." Annually. Estab. 1980. Circ. 500.
Needs: Adventure, erotica, ethnic/multicultural, experimental, fantasy, feminist, gay, historical (general), horror, humor/satire, lesbian, literary, mainstream/contemporary, mystery/suspense, psychic/supernatural/occult, regional, religious/inspirational, romance, science fiction, senior citizen/retirement, sports, translations—"just about anything." No pornography. "Would like to see more firction that flows from character rather than plot. Would like to see more fiction that takes stylistic risks." Receives 6-60 unsolicited mss/month. Accepts 15-20 mss/issue. Publishes ms almost immediately after acceptance. Recently published work by Carol Davitt, Jessica Barksdale and Rubba Nadda. **Publishes 5-10 new writers/year.** Length: 3,000 words maximum. Publishes short shorts. Also publishes literary essays and poetry. Sometimes critiques or comments on rejected ms.
How to Contact: Send complete ms with a cover letter. Include estimated word count and short bio. Reports in 2 weeks on queries; by March 1 on mss. Send SASE for reply, return of ms or send a disposable copy of ms. No simultaneous submissions. For fiction guidelines, visit our website or send SASE.
Payment/Terms: To enter prize contest include $1 with entry. First place winner in fiction wins $50. Accepted authors receive 1 free copy. Authors retain all rights.
Advice: "Good writing stands out. Content is important but style is essential. Clearly finished pieces with subtle action, reaction and transformation are what we like."

⊕ $ WESTERLY, English Dept., University of Western Australia, Nedlands, 6907 Australia. 08 9380 2101. Fax: 08 9380 1030. E-mail: westerly@uniwa.uwa.edu.au. Website: www.arts.uwa.edu.au/westerly (includes details of current issue, past issues, forthcoming issues and information about subscribing and contributing). Caroline Horobin, Administrator. Quarterly. Circ. 1,000.
Neds: "A quarterly of poetry, prose, reviews and articles of a literary and cultural kind, giving special attention to Australia and Southeast Asia." No romance, children's science fiction.
How to Contact: Queries by e-mail OK.
Payment/Terms: Pays $50 (AUS) minimum and 1 contributor's copy. Sample copy for $8 (AUS) plus postage.

N ◉ WESTERN HUMANITIES REVIEW, % University of Utah English Dept., 255 S. Central Campus Dr., Room 3500, Salt Lake City UT 84112-0494. (801)581-6070. Fax: (801)581-3392. Editor: Barry Weller. Fiction Editor: Karen Brennan. Magazine: 95-120 pages. Quarterly. Estab. 1947. Circ. 1,200.
Needs: Experimental, literary. Receives 75 unsolicited mss/month. Accepts 3-5 mss/issue; 15-20 mss/year. Does not read mss July-September. Publishes ms within 1-4 issues after acceptance. Recently published work by Stephen Dixon, Benjamin Wessman, Jeanne Schinto and Wendy Rawlings. Length: open. Publishes short shorts. Also publishes literary essays, literary criticism and poetry. Sometimes critiques or comments on rejected mss.
How to Contact: Send complete ms with a cover letter. Include list of publications. Reports in 3 weeks on queries; 1-6 months on mss. Send SASE for reply, return of ms or send a disposable copy of ms. Simultaneous submissions OK. Sample copy for $6.
Payment/Terms: Pays 2 contributor's copies; additional copies for $3.50. Acquires first North American serial rights. Sends galleys to author.

✓ ◉ WESTVIEW, A Journal of Western Oklahoma, Southwestern Oklahoma State University, 100 Campus Dr., Weatherford OK 73096-3098. (580)774-3168. **Editor:** Fred Alsberg. Magazine: 8½ × 11; 44 pages; 24 lb. paper; slick color cover; illustrations and photographs. Biannual. Estab. 1981. Circ. 400.
Needs: Contemporary, ethnic (especially Native American), humor, literary, prose poem. No pornography, violence, or gore. No overly sentimental. "We are particularly interested in writers of the Southwest; however, we accept work of quality from elsewhere." Receives 20 unsolicited mss/month. Accepts 5 mss/issue; 10 mss/year. Publishes ms 3-12 months after acceptance. Published work by Diane Glancy, Wendell Mayo, Jack Matthews, Mark Spencer and Pamela Rodgers. Length: 2,000 words average. Also publishes literary essays, literary criticism, poetry. Occasionally critiques rejected mss.
How to Contact: Simultaneous submissions OK. Send complete ms with SASE. Reports in 1-2 months. "We welcome submissions on a 3.5 disk formatted for WordPerfect 5.0, IBM or Macintosh. Please include a hard copy printout of your submission."
Payment/Terms: Pays contributor's copy for first rights.

N ◉ WHETSTONE, Barrington Area Arts Council, P.O. Box 1266, Barrington IL 60011. (847)382-5626. Co-Editors: Sandra Berris, Marsha Portnoy and Jean Tolle. Magazine: 9 × 6; 130 pages; heavy cover stock. "We try to publish the best quality nonfiction, fiction and poetry for the educated reader." Annually. Estab. 1984. Circ. 700. Member CLMP.
• *Whetstone* has received numerous Illinois Arts Council Awards.

Needs: Humor/satire, literary, mainstream/contemporary. "No genre, formula or plot driven fiction." Receives 100 unsolicited mss/month. Accepts 8-10 mss/year. Publishes ms by December 1 of year accepted. Recently published work by Barbara Croft, Ann Joslin Will, James Reed, Leslie Pietzyk and Scott Blackwood. **Publishes 1-2 new writers/year.** Length: 3,000 words average; 6,000 words maximum. Also publishes poetry. Sometimes comments on rejected mss "depending on the work. We often write out the readers' responses if they are helpful. A work gets a minimum of two readers and up to four or five."

How to Contact Send complete ms with a cover letter. Include a 50-word bio. Reports in 3-6 months on mss "or sooner depending on the time of the year." Send SASE for return of ms or reply only. Simultaneous submissions OK. Sample copy (including guidelines) for $5.

Payment/Terms: Pays a variable amount and 2 contributor's copies on publication. Acquires first North American serial rights. Sends galleys to author. "We frequently work with writers on their pieces. All works selected for publication are considered for the $500 Whetstone Prize and the $250 McGrath Award."

Advice: "We like strong characterization and a vivid use of language and, of course, a coherent plot. We like texture and a story which resonates. Read the journal and other small literary journals. Study good writing wherever you find it. Learn from editorial comments. Read. Read. Read, but do it as a writer reads. We're seeing too many childhood trauma stories. There are only so many of these we can accept."

◑ WHISKEY ISLAND MAGAZINE, Dept. of English, Cleveland State University, Cleveland OH 44115. (216)687-2056. Fax: (216)687-6943. E-mail: whiskeyisland@popmail.csuohio.edu. Website: www.csuohio.edu/whiskey_island (includes writer's guidelines, contest guidelines, staff information, history, short fiction, poetry, subscription information). Editors change each year. Magazine of fiction and poetry, including experimental works, with no specific theme. "We provide a forum for new writers and new work, for themes and points of view that are both meaningful and experimental, accessible and extreme." Biannually. Estab. 1978. Circ. 2,500.

Needs: "Would like to see more short shorts, flash fiction." Receives 100 unsolicited fiction mss/month. Accepts 4-6 mss/issue. Reads submissions September through April only. Published work by Vickie A. Carr and John Fulmer. **Publishes 5-10 new writers/year.** Length: 5,000 words maximum. Also publishes poetry (poetry submissions should contain no more than 10 pages).

How to Contact: Send complete ms with SASE. Accepts queries/mss by fax. No simultaneous or previously published submissions. Reports in 2-4 months on mss. Sample copy for $5.

Payment/Terms: Pays 2 contributor's copies. Acquires one-time rights.

Advice: "We seek a different voice, controlled language and strong opening. Also, learn to live with rejection. Even good work is turned away."

◪ WHITE WALL REVIEW, 63 Gould St., Toronto, Ontario M5B 1E9 Canada. (416)977-9924. E-mail: whitewal@acs.ryerson.ca. Editors change annually. Send mss to "Editors." Magazine: 5¾×8¾; 144-160 pages; professionally printed with glossy card cover; b&w photos and illustrations. "An annual using interesting, preferably spare art. No style is unacceptable." Annually. Estab. 1976. Circ. 500.

Needs: Nothing "boring, self-satisfied, gratuitously sexual, violent or indulgent." Accepts 10 mss/book. Accepts mss from September to 1st week in December of a given year. Published work by Terry Watada, Brendan Landers and Ruth Olsen Latta. Length: 3,000 words maximum.

How to Contact: Send complete ms with cover letter, SASE and *$5 non-refundable reading fee.* Include a short bio. Reports on mss "as soon as we can (usually in April or May)." Always comments on ms. No simultaneous submissions. Sample copy for $8.

Payment/Terms: Pays 1 contributor's copy. Acquires first or one-time rights.

Advice: "Keep it *short.* We look for creativity, but not to the point of obscurity."

Ⓝ ◪ ◎ WICKED MYSTIC, 532 La Guardia Place, #371, New York NY 10012. (718)638-1533. E-mail: wicksomyst@aol.com. Editor: Andre Scheluchin. Magazine: Full-sized; 80 pages; 20 lb. paper; 60 lb. 4-color cover. "Horror, gothic, gore, sex, violence, blood, death." Published 3 times/year. Estab. 1990. Circ. 10,000.

Needs: Explicit, gut-wrenching, brutally twisted, warped, sadistic, deathly, provocative, nasty horror. "No vampires." Receives 120 unsolicited mss/month. Acquires 10-15 mss/issue; 30-45 mss/year. Time between acceptance of the ms and publication varies. Recently published work by James Dorr, Tony Plank, Charlee Jacob and Donald Burleson. Length: 3,000 words preferred; 1,000 words minimum; 5,000 words maximum. Also publishes literary essays, literary criticism, art and poetry.

How to Contact: Send complete ms with cover letter. Include estimated word count, short and basic bio, list of publications. Reports in 2-12 weeks. Send SASE for reply, return of ms or send a disposable copy of the ms. No simultaneous submissions. Electronic submissions OK. Sample copy for $5.95. Free fiction guidelines.

Payment/Terms: Pays $1.25/word, 3 copies of the issue and a FREE ¼ page ad (a $50 value) for a product or service you are promoting. Acquires First North American serial rights..

Advice: "Your story must have a bizarre twist to it and involve both sex and death. No predictability and no slow-moving pieces."

$◪ THE WILLIAM AND MARY REVIEW, P.O. Box 8795, Campus Center, The College of William and Mary, Williamsburg VA 23187-8795. (757)221-3290. E-mail: bbhatl@mail.wm.edu. **Fiction Co-Editors:**

Dave Gunton and Amanda Petrusich. Magazine: 110 pages; graphics; photography. "We publish high quality fiction, poetry, interviews with writers, and art. Our audience is primarily academic." Annually. Estab. 1962. Circ. 3,500.

• This magazine has received numerous honors from the Columbia Scholastic Press Association's Golden Circle Awards.

Needs: Literary, contemporary. No horror, hardcore porn, romance. Receives approximately 90 unsolicited fiction mss/month. Accepts 9 mss/issue. Published work by Toni de Bonneval, Philip Cioffari and Martha Howard. **Publishes 2-3 new writers/year.** Length: 7,000 words maximum; no minimum. Also publishes poetry. Usually critiques rejected mss.

How to Contact: Send complete ms with SASE and cover letter with name, address and phone number. "Cover letter should be as brief as possible." Accepts queries by e-mail. Simultaneous submissions OK. Queries by e-mail OK; no mss. Reports in 2-4 months. All departments closed in June, July and August. Sample copy for $5.50. May review novels, poetry and short story collections.

Payment/Terms: Pays 5 contributor's copies; discounts thereafter. Acquires first rights.

Advice: "We look for powerful, tight writing that creates energy. We believe that, first and foremost, a work of fiction must be an entertaining and compelling story. Page allotment to fiction will rise in relation to the quality of fiction received."

☑ $ ◑ ☒ WILLOW SPRINGS, Eastern Washington University, 526 Fifth St., MS-1, Cheney WA 99201. (509)458-6429. **Editor:** David Lombardi. Magazine: 9×6; 128 pages; 80 lb. glossy cover. "*Willow Springs* publishes literary poetry and fiction of high quality, a mix of new and established writers." Semiannually. Estab. 1977. Circ. 1,200.

• *Willow Springs* is a member of the Council of Literary Magazines and Presses and AWP. The magazine has received grants from the NEA and a CLMP excellence award.

Needs: Parts of novels, short stories, literary, prose poems, poems and translations. "No genre fiction please." Receives 150 unsolicited mss/month. Accepts 2-4 mss/issue; 4-8 mss/year. Does not read mss May 15-September 15. Publishes ms 6 months to one year after acceptance. Recently published work by Alberto Rios, Madeline DeFrees and Robin Hemley; **published new writers within the last year.** Length: 5,000 words minimum; 11,000 words maximum. Also publishes literary essays, literary criticism and poetry. Rarely critiques rejected mss.

How to Contact: Send complete ms with cover letter. Include short bio. No simultaneous submissions. Reports in 2 weeks on queries. Sample copy for $5.50.

Payment/Terms: Pays $20-50 and 2 contributor's copies for first North American rights.

Advice: "We hope to attract good fiction writers to our magazine, and we've made a commitment to publish three-four stories per issue. We like fiction that exhibits a fresh approach to language. Our most recent issues, we feel, indicate the quality and level of our commitment."

ℕ ◑ WIND MAGAZINE, P.O. Box 24548, Lexington KY 40524. (606)885-5342. E-mail: wind@wind.org. **Editors:** Charlie Hughes and Leatha Kendrick. Magazine: 5½×8½; 100 pages. "Eclectic literary journal with stories, poems, book reviews from small presses, essays. Readership is students, professors, housewives, literary folk, adults." Semiannually. Estab. 1971. Circ. 450.

Needs: Literary, mainstream/contemporary, translations. Accepts 6 fiction mss/issue; 12 mss/year. Publishes ms less than 1 year after acceptance. Published work by Carolyn Osborn, Jane Stuart, David Shields, Lester Goldberg and Elisabeth Stevens. Length: 5,000 words maximum. Publishes short shorts, length: 300-400 words. Also publishes literary essays, literary criticism and poetry. Sometimes critiques or comments on rejected mss.

How to Contact: Send complete ms with a cover letter. Include estimated word count and 50-word bio. No e-mail submissions accepted. Reports in 2 weeks on queries; 2 months on mss. Send SASE for reply, return of ms or send a disposable copy of ms. No simultaneous submissions. Sample copy for $4.50. Reviews novels and short story collections from small presses.

Payment/Terms: Pays 1 contributor's copy; additional copies for $3.50. Acquires first North American serial rights and anthology reprint rights.

Advice: "The writing must have an impact on the reader; the reader must come away changed, perhaps haunted, or maybe smiling. There is nothing I like better than to be able to say 'I wish I had written that.' "

ℕ 🏵 ◑ WINDSOR REVIEW, A Journal of the Arts, Dept. of English, University of Windsor, Windsor, Ontario N9B 3P4 Canada. (519)253-3000, ext. 2332. Fax: (519)973-7050. E-mail: uwrevu@uwindsor.ca. **Editor:** Katherine Quinsey. **Fiction Editor:** Alistair MacLeod. Magazine/perfect bound book: 6×9; 110 pages; illustrations and photos. "We try to offer a balance of fiction and poetry distinguished by excellence." Semiannually. Estab. 1965. Circ. 250.

Needs: Literary. Publishes ms 6-9 months after acceptance. Accepts 1-4 unsolicited mss/issue. Publishes ms 6 months after acceptance. Recently published work by John B. Lee and Nadine McInnis. Length: 1,000 word minimum; 5,000 words maximum. Also publishes poetry. Sometimes critiques or comments on rejected mss.

How to Contact: Send complete ms with a cover letter. Accepts queries/mss by e-mail. Include estimated word count, bio, Social Security number and list of publications. Reports in 1 month on queries; 6 weeks on mss. Send

SASE for reply, return of ms or send a disposable copy of ms. No simultaneous submissions. Sample copy for $7 (US). Free fiction guidelines.

Payment/Terms: Pays $50 and 1 contributor's copy on publication for one-time rights; additional copies available for $10.

✓ ◯ **WISCONSIN REVIEW**, University of Wisconsin, Box 158, Radford Hall, Oshkosh WI 54901. (920)424-2267. **Editor:** Debbie Martin. Editors change every year. Send submissions to "Fiction Editor." Magazine: 6×9; 60-100 pages; illustrations. Literary prose and poetry. Triannual. Estab. 1966. Circ. 2,000.
Needs: Literary and experimental. Receives 30 unsolicited fiction mss each month. Publishes 3 new writers/year. Length: up to 5,000 words. Publishes short shorts.
How to Contact: Send complete ms with SASE and cover letter with bio notes. Simultaneous submissions OK. Reports in 2-6 months. Publishes ms an average of 1-3 months after acceptance. Sample copy for $4.
Payment/Terms: Pays 2 contributor's copies. Acquires first rights.
Advice: "We look for well-crafted work with carefully developed characters, plots and meaningful situations. The editors prefer work of original and fresh thought when considering a piece of experimental fiction."

N: ◯ **WITNESS**, OCC, 27055 Orchard Lake Rd., Farmington Hills MI 48334. (734)996-5732. **Editor:** Peter Stine. Magazine: 6×9; 192 pages; photos. "*Witness* highlights role of modern writer as witness to his/her times." Semiannually. Estab. 1987. Circ. 3,000.
Needs: Ethnic/multicultural, experimental, literary. Upcoming themes: "Crime In America" (deadline July 15, 2000). List of upcoming themes available for SASE. Receives 150 unsolicited mss/month. Accepts 12 mss/issue; 24 mss/year. Publishes ms 1-2 years after acceptance. Agented fiction 10%. Publishes 4 new writers/year. Recently published works by Richard Burgin, Therese Svoboda and Walt McDonald. Length: 4,000 words average; 1,000 words minimum; 7,000 words maximum. Publishes short shorts. Also publishes literary essays, poetry. Sometimes critiques or comments on rejected mss.
How to Contact: Send complete ms with a cover letter. Include estimated word count, list of publications. Reports in 1 month on queries; 3 month on mss. SASE for reply or send disposable copy of ms. Simultaneous submissions OK. Sample copy for $9. Fiction guidelines free.
Payment/Terms: Pays $6/page for prose; $10/page for poetry and 2 contributor's copies; additional copies $7. Payment on publication. Acquires one-time rights. Sponsors contest: send SASE for information.

✓ ◯ **THE WORCESTER REVIEW**, Worcester Country Poetry Association, Inc., 6 Chatham St., Worcester MA 01609. (508)797-4770. Website: www.geocities.com/paris/leftbank/6433. **Editor:** Rodger Martin. Magazine: 6×9; 100 pages; 60 lb. white offset paper; 10 pt. CS1 cover stock; illustrations and photos. "We like high quality, creative poetry, artwork and fiction. Critical articles should be connected to New England." Annually. Estab. 1972. Circ. 1,000.
Needs: Literary, prose poem. "We encourage New England writers in the hopes we will publish at least 30% New England but want the other 70% to show the best of writing from across the US." Receives 20-30 unsolicited fiction mss/month. Accepts 2-4 mss/issue. Publishes ms an average of 6 months to 1 year after acceptance. Agented fiction less than 10%. Published work by Toni Graham and Carol Glickfeld. Length: 2,000 words average; 1,000 words minimum; 4,000 words maximum. Publishes short shorts. Also publishes literary essays, literary criticism, poetry. Sometimes critiques rejected mss and recommends other markets.
How to Contact: Send complete ms with cover letter. Reports in 6-9 months on mss. SASE. Simultaneous submissions OK if other markets are clearly identified. Sample copy for $5; fiction guidelines free.
Payment/Terms: Pays 2 contributor's copies and honorarium if possible for one-time rights.
Advice: "Send only one short story—reading editors do not like to read two by the same author at the same time. We will use only one. We generally look for creative work with a blend of craftsmanship, insight and empathy. This does not exclude humor. We won't print work that is shoddy in any of these areas."

✓ ◯ **WORDS OF WISDOM**, 3283 UNCG Station, Greensboro NC 27413-1031. (336)334-6970. E-mail: wowmail@hoopsmail.com. **Editor:** Mikhammad Abdel-Ishara. Associate Editor: Celestine Woo. Newsletter: 5½×8½; 72-88 pages; computer generated on copy paper; saddle-stapled with 40 lb. colored paper cover; some illustrations. "Fiction, satire/humor, poetry and travel for a general audience." Estab. 1981. Circ. 150-160.
Needs: Adventure, contemporary, ethnic, feminist, historical, humor/satire, literary, mainstream, mystery/suspense (cozy, private eye), regional, western. No religion, children's, gay or romance. Fall 2000 issue to feature travel stories in foreign lands. Receives 500-600 unsolicited mss/year. Accepts 67-75 mss/year. Publishes ms 2-6 months after acceptance. Recently published work by Paul Agosto, Joyce S. Zaritsky, Toby Tucker Hecht, D.L. Nelson, Geoff Uark, Patricia Prime and Joseph S. Salemi. **Publishes 0-5 new writers/year.** Length: 3,000 words average; 1,200 words minimum; 6,000 words maximum. Publishes short shorts.
How to Contact: Cover letter required. "There are no automatons here, so don't treat us like machines. We may not recognize your name at the top of the manuscript. A few lines about yourself breaks the ice, the names of three or four magazines that have published you in the last year would show your reality, and a bio blurb of 37 +/- words including the names of two or three of the magazines you send the occasional subscription check (where you aspire to be?) could help. If you are not sending a check to some little magazine that is supported

by subscriptions and the blood, sweat and tears of the editors, why would you send your manuscript to any of them and expect to receive a warm welcome? No requirement to subscribe or buy a sample, but they are available at $4 and encouraged. There are no phony contests and never a reading fee. Read all year long, but may take one to six months to respond." Seldom comments on rejections. Simultaneous submissions OK but no reprints. Reviews short story collections.

Payment/Terms: Pays subscription to magazine for first story published. Acquires one-time rights. Publication not copyrighted.

Advice: "Stop watching TV and read that book of stories where your last manuscript appeared."

$☑ works & conversations, P.O. Box 5008, Berkeley CA 94705. (510)653-1146. E-mail: rwhit@jps.net. Website: www.conversations.org (includes magazine excerpts). Editor: Richard Whittaker. **Fiction Editor:** Wm. Dudley. Magazine: 8½ × 11; 64 pages; color cover, 60 lb. coated paper. "We publish art portfolios and interviews, primarily. But we also publish essays, articles, photographs, graphics, a little fiction and poetry, and anything else that strikes our fancy. We're interested in the interior aspects of art and artmaking from a broad perspective. Triquarterly. Evolved from earlier publication, *The Secret Alameda*." Estab. 1998.

Needs: Work that reflects upon issues of meaning in light of contemporary conditions. "We like work that feels grounded, in the writer's real experiences." Upcoming themes: "The desert" and "Outsider Art." Length: 100-2,000 words. Will consider longer works in special cases. Circ. 1,500-2,000.

How to Contact: Send complete ms with cover letter. Accepts queries by e-mail. Reports in 4-6 weeks. Simultaneous and reprint submissions OK. Sample copy for $5.

Payment/Terms: Pays a small honorarium plus contributor's copies. Acquires one-time rights.

Advice: "Really advise you to get a sample copy to understand our editorial interests."

☑ WRITERS' FORUM, University of Colorado at Colorado Springs, Colorado Springs CO 80933-7150. Fax: (719)262-4557. E-mail: kpellow@brain.uccs.edu. **Editor:** C. Kenneth Pellow. "Ten to fifteen short stories or self-contained novel excerpts published once a year along with 25-35 poems. Highest literary quality only: mainstream, avant-garde, with preference to western themes. For small press enthusiasts, teachers and students of creative writing, commercial agents/publishers, university libraries and departments interested in contemporary American literature." Estab. 1974.

Needs: Contemporary, ethnic (Chicano, Native American, not excluding others), literary and regional (West). Want more fiction "with pressing, relevant social/domestic issues and those with fully realized characters." Receives approximately 50 unsolicited fiction mss each month and will publish new as well as experienced authors. Recently published work by Toni Graham, Mark Lewandowski, Ben Brooks and Mary Clyde. **Publishes 1-3 new writers/year.** Length: 1,500-8,500 words. Also publishes literary essays, literary criticism, poetry. Critiques rejected mss "when there is time and perceived merit."

How to Contact: Send complete ms and letter with relevant career information with SASE. Accepts queries by e-mail. Submissions read year-round. Simultaneous submissions OK. Reports in 5-8 weeks on mss. Publishes ms an average of 6 months after acceptance. Sample back copy $8 to *NSSWM* readers. Current copy $10. Make checks payable to "Writers' Forum."

Payment/Terms: Pays 2 contributor's copies. Cover price less 50% discount for extras. Acquires one-time rights.

Advice: "Read our publication. Be prepared for constructive criticism. We especially seek submissions with a strong voice that show immersion in place (trans-Mississippi West) and development of credible characters. Probably the TV-influenced fiction with trivial dialogue and set-up plot is the most quickly rejected. Our format—a 5½ × 8½ professionally edited and printed paperback book—lends credibility to authors published in our imprint. Never consider a piece 'finished'; keep it in revision; keep it in circulation. Do not get discouraged!"

☑ ☑ ◎ WRITES OF PASSAGE, The Literary Journal for Teenagers, Writes of Passage USA, Inc., P.O. Box 1935, Livingston NJ 07039. (212)473-7564. E-mail: wopassage@aol.com. Website: www.writes.org. Editor: Laura Hoffman. Fiction Editor: Wendy Mass. Magazine: 5½ × 8½; 100 pages; 60 lb. offset paper; 10 pt. cover; illustrations/photos only on cover; no artwork within magazine. "*Writes of Passage* is designed to publish the creative writing (poems and short stories) of teenagers across the country. We review work from Senior high school and Junior high school students across the country on all topics." Now *Writes of Passage* also publishes submissions on "the largest teen website on the Internet." Semiannually. Estab. 1994. Circ. 2,000.

Needs: "We accept short stories on all topics written by preteens and teens." Adventure, children's/juvenile (10-12 years), ethnic/multicultural, experimental, fantasy, feminist, gay, historical, horror, humor/satire, lesbian, literary, mainstream/contemporary, mystery/suspense, psychic/supernatural/occult, regional, religious/inspirational, romance, science fiction, sports, westerns, young adult/teen. Receives 50 unsolicited mss/month. Accepts 50 mss/issue; 100 mss/year. "Issues are published in the fall and spring so publication of mss depend on when they are received." Length: 2,000 words average; 5,000 words maximum. Publishes short shorts. Also publishes poetry.

How to Contact: Send complete ms with a cover letter. Teachers may submit the work of their students as a group. Include bio with SASE and contact information. Send SASE for reply or send disposable copy of the ms. Simultaneous and electronic submissions OK. Sample copy for $6.

Payment/Terms: Pays 2 contributor's copies; additional copies $6 for each copy up to 10; 10 or more copies are $5 each. Rights revert back to the author.

Advice: "Write from your heart. We are looking for original work, clearly written, poignant subject matter for teen readers. We are interested in more short stories, particularly about teens."

WRITING FOR OUR LIVES, Running Deer Press, 647 N. Santa Cruz Ave., Annex, Los Gatos CA 95030-4350. (408)354-8604. **Editor:** Janet M. McEwan. Magazine: 5¼×8¼; 80 pages; 70 lb. recycled white paper; 80 lb. recycled cover. "*Writing For Our Lives* is a periodical which serves as a vessel for poems, short fiction, stories, letters, autobiographies, and journal excerpts from the life stories, experiences and spiritual journeys of women. Audience is women and friends of women." Annually. Estab. 1992. Circ. 600.

Needs: Ethnic/multicultural, experimental, feminist, humor/satire, lesbian, literary, translations, "autobiographical, breaking personal or historical silence on any concerns of women's lives. *Women writers only, please.* We have no preannounced themes." Receives 15-20 unsolicited mss/month. Accepts 10 mss/issue; 20 mss/year. Publishes ms 2-24 months after acceptance. Recently published work by Sabah Akbur, Anjali Banerjee, Debra Kay Viest, Eison M. Ortiz and Luci Yamamoto. **Publishes 3-5 new writers/year.** Length: 2,100 words maximum. Publishes short shorts. Also publishes poetry. Rarely critiques or comments on rejected mss.

How to Contact: Send complete ms and bio with a cover letter. "Publication date is October. Closing dates for mss are 2/15 and 8/15. Initial report immediate; next report, if any, in 1-18 months." Send 2 SASE's for reply, and one of them must be sufficient for return of ms if desired. Simultaneous and reprint submissions OK. Sample copy for $6-8 (in California add 8.25% sales tax), $9-11 overseas. Fiction guidelines for #10 SASE.

Payment/Terms: Pays 2 contributor's copies; additional copies for 50% discount and 1 year subscription at 50% discount. Acquires one-time rights in case of reprints and first worldwide English language serial rights.

Advice: "It is in our own personal stories that the real herstory of our time is told. This periodical is a place for exploring the boundaries of our empowerment to break long historical and personal silences. While honoring the writing which still needs to be held close to our hearts, we can begin to send some of our heartfelt words out into a wider circle."

XAVIER REVIEW, Xavier University, 7325 Palmetto St., Box 110C, New Orleans LA 70125-1098. (504)483-7303. Fax: (504)485-7197. E-mail: rskinner@mail.xula.edu (correspondence only—no mss). **Editor:** Thomas Bonner, Jr. Managing Editor: Robert E. Skinner. Assistant Editor: Patrice Melnick. Production Consultant: Mark Whitaker. Magazine: 6×9; 75 pages; 50 lb. paper; 12 pt. CS1 cover; photographs. Magazine of "poetry/fiction/nonfiction/reviews (contemporary literature) for professional writers/libraries/colleges/universities." Semiannually. Estab. 1980. Circ. 500.

Needs: Contemporary, ethnic, experimental, historical (general), literary, Latin American, prose poem, Southern, religious, serialized/excerpted novel, translations. Receives 100 unsolicited fiction mss/month. Accepts 2 mss/issue; 4 mss/year. Does not read mss during the summer months. Published work by Randall Ivey, Rita Porteau, John Goldfine and Christine Wiltz. Length: 10-15 pages. Publishes literary criticism, literary essays, books of creative writing and poetry. Occasionally critiques rejected mss.

How to Contact: Send complete ms. Include 2-3 sentence bio. SASE. Reports in 8-10 weeks. Sample copy for $5.

Payment/Terms: Pays 2 contributor's copies.

THE YALE REVIEW, Yale University/Blackwell Publishers Inc., P.O. Box 208243, New Haven CT 06520-8243. (203)432-0499. Fax: (203)432-0510. Editor: J.D. McClatchy. **Fiction Editor:** Susan Bianconi. Magazine: 9¼×6; 180-190 pages; book stock paper; glossy cover; illustrations and photographs. "*The Yale Review* is meant for the well-read general reader interested in a variety of topics in the arts and letters, in history, and in current affairs." Quarterly. Estab. 1911. Circ. 7,000.

Needs: Mainstream/contemporary. Receives 50-80 unsolicited mss/month. Accepts 1-3 mss/issue; 7-12 mss/year. Publishes ms 3 months after acceptance. Agented fiction 25%. Published work by Steven Millhauser, Deborah Eisenberg, Jeffrey Eugenides, Sheila Kohler, Joe Ashby Porter, Julie Orringer, John Barth and James McCourt. Publishes short shorts (but not frequently). Also publishes literary essays, poetry.

How to Contact: Send complete ms with a cover letter. Include estimated word count and list of publications. Reports in 1 month on queries; 2 months on mss. Send SASE for reply, return of ms or send a disposable copy of ms. Always include SASE. No simultaneous submissions. Reviews novels and short story collections. Send books to the editors.

Payment/Terms: Pays $300-400 on publication and 2 contributor's copies; additional copies for $7. Sends galleys to author. "Awards by the editors; cannot be applied for."

Advice: "We find that the most accomplished young writers seem to be people who keep their ears open to other voices; who read widely."

THE YALOBUSHA REVIEW, The Literary Journal of the University of Mississippi, University of Mississippi, P.O. Box 186, University MS 38677-0186. (601)232-7439. E-mail: yalobush@olemiss.edu. Editors change each year. Magazine: 5½×8½; 130 pages; 60 lb. off-white; card cover stock. "We look for high-quality fiction, poetry, and creative essays; and we seek a balance of regional and national writers." Annually. Estab. 1995. Circ. 500.

Needs: Literary. "No genre or formula fiction." List of upcoming themes available for SASE. Receives 30 unsolicited mss/month. Accepts 3-6 mss/issue. Does not read mss April through August. Published work by Larry Brown, Cynthia Shearer and Eric Miles Williamson. Length: 15 pages average; 35 pages maximum. Publishes short shorts. Also publishes literary essays and poetry. Sometimes critiques or comments on rejected mss.

How to Contact: Send complete ms with a cover letter. Reports in 1 month on queries; reporting time on mss varies. Send SASE for reply, return of ms or send a disposable copy of ms. Electronic submissions OK.

Payment/Terms: Pays 2 contributor's copies. Pays on publication. Acquires first North American serial rights.

Advice: "We look for writers with a strong, distinct voice and good stories to tell."

N ⚑ $ ◐ YELLOW SILK: Journal of Erotic Arts, Verygraphics, Box 6374, Albany CA 94706. (510)644-4188. Editor/Publisher: Lily Pond. "We are interested in nonpornographic erotic literature: joyous, mad, musical, elegant, passionate. 'All persuasions; no brutality' is our editorial policy. Literary excellence is a priority; innovative forms are welcomed, as well as traditional ones." Quarterly. Estab. 1981.

Needs: Erotica, ethnic, experimental, fantasy, feminist/lesbian, gay, humor/satire, literary, prose poem, science fiction and translations. No "blow-by-blow" descriptions; no hackneyed writing except when used for satirical purposes. Nothing containing brutality. Accepts 16-20 mss/year. Recently published work by Tobias Wolff, Richard Zimler and Jane Smiley. **Publishes 20 new writers/year.** Length: no preference. Occasionally critiques rejected ms.

How to Contact: Send complete ms with SASE and include short, *personal* bio notes. No queries. No pre-published material. No simultaneous submissions. Name, address and phone number on each page. Submissions on disk OK *with* hard copy only. Reports in 3 months on mss. Publishes ms up to 3 years after acceptance..

Payment/Terms: Competitive payment on publication for all periodical and anthology rights for one year following publication, at which time rights revert back to author; and nonexclusive reprint, electronic and anthology rights for the duration of the copyright.

Advice: "Read, read, read! Including our magazine—plus Nabokov, Ntozaké Shangé, Rimbaud, Virginia Woolf, William Kotzwinkle, James Joyce. Then send in your story! Trust that the magazine/editor will not rip you off—they don't. As they say, 'find your own voice,' then trust it. Most manuscripts I reject appear to be written by people without great amounts of writing experience. It takes years (frequently) to develop your work to publishable quality; it can take many rewrites on each individual piece. I also see many approaches to sexuality (for my magazine) that are trite and not fresh. The use of language is not original, and the people do not seem real. However, the gems come too, and what a wonderful moment that is. Please don't send me anything with blue eye shadow."

✓ ◐ YEMASSEE, The literary journal of the University of South Carolina, Department of English, University of South Carolina, Columbia SC 29208. (803)777-2085. Fax: (803)777-9064. Website: www.cla.sc. edu/ENGL/yemassee/index.htm (includes cover of latest issue, origin of name and subscription info). **Editor:** Lisa Kerr. Magazine: 5½×8½; 60-80 pages; 60 lb. natural paper; 65 lb. cover; cover illustration. "We are open to a variety of subjects and writing styles. *Yemassee* publishes primarily fiction and poetry, but we are also interested in one-act plays, brief excerpts of novels, essays, reviews and interviews with literary figures. Our essential consideration for acceptance is the quality of the work." Semiannually. Estab. 1993. Circ. 375.

Needs: Condensed/excerpted novel, ethnic/multicultural, experimental, feminist, gay, historical, humor/satire, lesbian, literary, regional. No romance, religious/inspirational, young adult/teen, children's/juvenile, erotica. Wants more experimental. Receives 10 unsolicited mss/month. Accepts 1-3 mss/issue; 2-6 mss/year. "We hold manuscripts until our reading periods—October 1 to November 15 and March 15 to April 30." Publishes ms 2-4 months after acceptance. Published work by Gene Able, Robert Coover, Chris Railey, Robert B. Kennedy, Nichole Potts and Michael Cody. **Publishes 6 new writers/year.** Length: 4,000 words or less. Publishes short shorts. Also publishes literary essays and poetry.

How to Contact: Send complete ms with a cover letter. Include estimated word count, brief bio, Social Security number and list of publications. Reports in 2 weeks on queries, 2-4 months after deadlines on mss. Send SASE for reply, return of ms or send disposable copy of ms. No simultaneous submissions. Sample copy for $5. Fiction guidelines for #10 SASE.

Payment/Terms: Pays 2 contributor's copies for first rights; additional copies $2.75. All submissions are considered for the *Yemassee* awards—$200 each for the best poetry and fiction in each issue when funding permits.

Advice: "Our criteria are based on what we perceive as quality. Generally that is work that is literary. We are interested in subtlety and originality, interesting or beautiful language; craft and precision. Read more, write more and revise more. Read our journal and any other journal before you submit to see if your work seems appropriate. Send for guidelines and make sure you follow them. Don't suck up in the cover letter. Be honest."

🌐 ◎ YORKSHIRE JOURNAL, Smith Settle Ltd., Ilkley Road, Otley, W. Yorkshire LS21 3JP England. 01943-467958. Fax: 01943-850057. Editor: Mark Whitley. Magazine: 245mm×175mm; 120 pages; matt art paper; art board cover stock; illustrations and photos. "We publish historical/factual articles, poetry and short stories by and about the county of Yorkshire in England." Quarterly. Estab. 1993. Circ. 3,000.

Needs: Regional, "anything about Yorkshire." Receives 2-4 unsolicited mss/month. Accepts 2-3 mss/year. Published work by Denis Yeadon, Neville Slack, Mary Walsh and Alex Marwood. Length: 1,500 words average. Often critiques or comments on rejected mss.

How to Contact: Query first. Include estimated word count and 50-word bio with submission. Reports in 6 weeks on queries; 10 weeks on mss. Send SASE (or IRCs) for reply, return of ms or send a disposable copy of ms. Reprints and electronic submissions (disk or modem) OK. Sample copy for $10. Fiction guidelines for SASE (or IRC).

Payment/Terms: Pay varies; includes 1 contributor's copy; additional copies $10. Pays on publication. Acquires first rights.

Advice: "Fiction must be about Yorkshire in some way. Send in an outline first, not the completed manuscript."

★ $✐ ▼ ZOETROPE: All-Story, AZX Publications, 1350 Avenue of the Americas, 24th Floor, New York NY 10019. (212)696-5720. Fax: (212)696-5845. Website: www.zoetrope-stories.com (includes online writer's workshop, monthly magazine that publishes the top two submissions each month and chats with writers, editors, etc.) **Editor:** Adrienne Brodeur. Magazine: 10½×14; 60 pages; illustrations and photos. Quarterly. "*Zoetrope: All-Story* bridges the worlds of fiction and film by publishing stories that have been or may be adapted for film." Estab. 1997. Circ. 40,000.

● Library Journal named *Zoetrope: All-Story* one of the ten best new magazines. Stories from *Zoetrope* have received the O. Henry Prize (plus six honorable mentions), the Pushcart Prize (plus six honorable mentions) and have been reprinted in *New Stories from the South* and received honorable mentions in *Best American Short Stories*. *Zoetrope: All-Story* was ranked #23 on the *Writer's Digest*'s Fiction 50 list of top markets for fiction writers.

Needs: Literary, mainstream/contemporary, one act plays. No excerpts from larger works. Receives 500 unsolicited mss/month. Accepts 7-8 mss/issue; 28-32 mss/year. Publishes ms 2-6 months after acceptance. Agented fiction 15%. Recently published work by Melissa Bank, Tim Gatreaux, David Mamet and T.C. Boyle. **Publishes 4-6 new writers/year.** Length: 7,000 words maximum.

How to Contact: Send complete manuscript (no more than 2) with a cover letter. Include estimated word count and list of publications. Simultaneous submissions OK. Sample copy for $5.95 and 9×12 SAE and $1.70 postage. Fiction guidelines for #10 SASE. *No unsolicited submissions from June 1-August 31.*

Payment/Terms: Pays $1,200 for first serial rights and 2 year option on movie rights for unsolicited submissions; $5,000 for commissioned works.

★ ✓ ✐ ZUZU'S PETALS QUARTERLY, P.O. Box 4853, Ithica NY 14852. (607)844-9009. E-mail: info@zuzu.com. Website: www.zuzu.com. Editor: T. Dunn. Internet magazine. "Arouse the senses; stimulate the mind." Estab. 1992.

● *Zuzu's Petals Quarterly* ranked #50 on *Writer's Digest*'s Fiction 50 list of top markets for fiction writers.

Needs: Ethnic/multicultural, feminist, gay, humor/satire, lesbian, literary, regional. No "romance, sci-fi, the banal, TV style plotting." Receives 110 unsolicited mss/month. Accepts 1-3 mss/issue; 4-12 mss/year. Publishes ms 4-6 months after acceptance. Agented fiction 10%. Published work by Norah Labiner, Jean Erhardt and LuAnn Jacobs. Length: 1,000 words minimum; 6,000 words maximum. Publishes short shorts. Length: 350 words. Also publishes literary essays, literary criticism and poetry. Sometimes critiques or comments on rejected mss.

How to Contact: Send complete ms with a cover letter. Include estimated word count and list of publications. Reports in 2 weeks on queries; 2 weeks to 2 months on mss. Send SASE (or IRC) for reply, return of ms or send a disposable copy of ms. Simultaneous and electronic submissions OK. Back issue for $5. Fiction guidelines free. Reviews novels and short story collections. Send to Doug DuCap, Reviewer.

Advice: Looks for "strong plotting and a sense of vision. Original situations and true to life reactions."

★ ✓ $✐ ◎ ZYZZYVA, the last word: west coast writers & artists, 41 Sutter St., PMB 1400, San Francisco CA 94104. (415)752-4393. Fax: (415)752-4391. E-mail: editor@zyzzyva.org. Website: www.zyzzyva.org (includes guidelines, names of editors, selections from current issues, editor's note). **Editor:** Howard Junker. Magazine: 6×9; 208 pages; graphics; photos. "Literate" magazine featuring West Coast writers and artists. Triquarterly. Estab. 1985. Circ. 4,000.

● *Zyzzyva* ranked #20 on *Writer's Digest*'s Fiction 50 list of top markets for fiction writers, and was recently profiled in *Poet's & Writer's* magazine.

Needs: Contemporary, experimental, literary, prose poem. West Coast US writers only. Receives 400 unsolicited mss/month. Accepts 5 fiction mss/issue; 20 mss/year. Agented fiction: 10%. Recently published work by Kathryn Chetkovich, Toni Miresovich and Ellen Slezak. **Publishes 20 new writers/year.** Length: varies. Also publishes literary essays.

How to Contact: Send complete ms. "Cover letters are of minimal importance." Reports in 2 weeks on mss. SASE. No simultaneous or reprint submissions. Sample copy for $5. Fiction guidelines on masthead page.

Payment/Terms: Pays $50 on acceptance for first North American serial rights.

Advice: "Keep the faith."

Small Circulation Magazines

This section of *Novel & Short Story Writer's Market* contains general interest, special interest, regional and genre magazines with circulations of under 10,000. Although these magazines vary greatly in size, theme, format and management, the editors are all looking for short stories for their respective publications. Their specific fiction needs present writers of all degrees of expertise and interests with an abundance of publishing opportunities.

Although not as high-paying as the large-circulation consumer magazines, many of the publications listed here do pay writers 1-5¢/word or more. Also unlike the big consumer magazines, these markets are very open to new writers and relatively easy to break into. Their only criteria is that your story be well written, well presented, and suitable for their particular readership.

DIVERSITY IN OPPORTUNITY

Among the diverse publications in this section are magazines devoted to almost every topic, every level of writing and every type of writer. Some of the markets listed here publish fiction about a particular geographic area or by authors who live in that locale. Even more specialized editorial needs than genre and regional fiction include *The Pipe Smoker's Ephemeris* and *Rosebud, For People Who Enjoy Writing*.

SELECTING THE RIGHT MARKET

Your chance for publication begins as you zero in on those markets most likely to be interested in your work. If you write genre fiction, check out specific sections for lists of magazines publishing in that genre (mystery, page 52; romance, page 64; science fiction and fantasy, page 76). For other types of fiction, begin by looking at the Category Index starting on page 632. If your work is more general, or, in fact, very specialized, you may wish to browse through the listings, perhaps looking up those magazines published in your state or region. Also check the Zine section for other specialized and genre publications.

In addition to browsing through the listings and using the Category Index, check the ranking codes at the beginning of listings to find those most likely to be receptive to your work. This is especially true for beginning writers, who should look for magazines that say they are especially open to new writers (□) and for those giving equal weight to both new and established writers (◩). The ◪ symbol indicates markets that offer writers greater opportunities by buying a large amount of freelance/unagented manuscripts, or by otherwise being very open to new writers. For more explanation about these codes, see the inside front and back covers of this book.

Once you have a list of magazines you might like to try, read their listings carefully. Much of the material within each listing carries clues that tell you more about the magazine. The "Quick Start" Guide to Publishing Your Fiction starting on page 2 describes in detail the listing information common to all the markets in our book.

The physical description appearing near the beginning of the listings can give you clues about the size and financial commitment to the publication. This is not always an indication of quality, but chances are a publication with expensive paper and four-color artwork on the cover has more prestige than a photocopied publication featuring a clip art self-cover. For more information on some of the paper, binding and printing terms used in these descriptions, see Printing and Production Terms Defined on page 627.

FURTHERING YOUR SEARCH

It cannot be stressed enough that reading the listing is only the first part of developing your marketing plan. The second part, equally important, is to obtain fiction guidelines and read the actual magazine. Reading copies of a magazine helps you determine the fine points of the magazine's publishing style and philosophy. There is no substitute for this type of hands-on research.

Unlike commercial magazines available at most newsstands and bookstores, it requires a little more effort to obtain some of the magazines listed here. You may need to send for a sample copy. We include sample copy prices in the listings whenever possible. See The Business of Fiction Writing for the specific mechanics of manuscript submission. Above all, editors appreciate a professional presentation. Include a brief cover letter and send a self-addressed envelope for a reply or a self-addressed envelope in a size large enough to accommodate your manuscript, if you would like it returned. Be sure to include enough stamps or International Reply Coupons (for replies from countries other than your own) to cover your manuscript's return. Many publishers today appreciate receiving a disposable manuscript, eliminating the cost to writers of return postage and saving editors the effort of repackaging manuscripts for return.

Most of the magazines listed here are published in the US. You will also find some English-speaking markets from around the world. These foreign publications are denoted with a 🌐 symbol at the beginning of listings. To make it easier to find Canadian markets, we include a 🍁 symbol at the start of those listings.

🌐 ⬤ **ALTAIR, Alternative Airings in Speculative Fiction**, Altair Publishing, P.O. Box 475, Blackwood, South Australia 5051. +61 (8)8278 8995. Fax: +61 (8)8278 5585. E-mail: altair@senet.com.au. Website: www.ozemail.com.ow/robsteph/fstguide.htm. **Editor:** Robert N. Stephenson. Magazine: A5; 152 pages; 80ssm bond paper; 250ssm glossy cover stock; illustrations. "We publish speculative fiction with a focus on science fiction and fantasy; a good mix of the two encouraged. We like character-driven stories."
Needs: Fantasy (science fantasy), mystery/suspense, science fiction (hard science, soft/sociological, some cyberpunk). Accepts 6-10 mss/issue; 12-70/year. Length: 5,000 words average; 2,000 words minimum; 6,500 words maximum. Publishes short shorts (length: 1,500 words). Sometimes critiques or comments on rejected mss.
How to Contact: Send complete ms with a cover letter. Include estimated word count and 5-line bio. "Return postage is essential or e-mail address; not read otherwise." Reports in 2 months on mss. SASE (or IRCs) for reply or return of ms. Sample copy for $10 (US) (includes international postage: air) and A5 SAE with 2 IRCs. As all copies are limited editions the price is projected by age." Fiction guidelines for SASE (or 1 IRC).
Payment/Terms: Pays 3 cents/word and 1 contributor's copy; additional copies $10. Acquires first world serial rights. Issue #1 is a large international competition open to all writers. Information available from website.
Advice: "We want strong characters, good, clear ideas and a believable plot. We are not interested in single-faceted work; localized slang is not good for an international audience. We are looking for cultural influences and this will show through the writer's talent."

✅ ⬤ **ANTHOLOGY**, Inkwell Press, P.O. Box 4411, Mesa AZ 85211-4411. (602)461-8200. E-mail: guidelines@inkwellpress.com. Website: www.inkwellpress.com. **Editor:** Sharon Skinner. Magazine: 8½×11; 20-28 pages; 20 lb. paper; 60-100 lb. cover stock; illustrations and photos. "Our intended audience is anyone who likes to read." Bimonthly. Estab. 1994. Circ. 500-1,000.
Needs: Adventure, children's/juvenile (5-9 and 10-12 years); fantasy (science fantasy, sword and sorcery), humor/satire, literary, mystery/suspense (amateur sleuth, police procedural, private eye/hardboiled), science fiction (hard science, soft/sociological). *Anthology* maintains an ongoing series of short stories based in the Mythical City of Haven. Information in guidelines. Receives 10-20 unsolicited mss/month. Accepts 2 mss/issue; 12 mss/year. Publishes ms 6-12 months after acceptance. Length: 3,000-6,000 words average; Haven stories 3,000-5,000 words. Publishes short shorts. Also publishes poetry.
How to Contact: Send complete ms with a cover letter. Include estimated word count. Reports in 4 weeks on queries; 2 months on mss. Send SASE for reply, return of ms or send disposable copy of ms. Simultaneous, reprint and electronic (disk or modem) submissions OK. Sample copy for $3.95. Fiction guidelines for 4½×9½ SASE. Reviews chapbooks and audio books.
Payment/Terms: Pays 1 contributor's copy; additional copies $2. Haven stories pay $5. Acquires one-time rights. *Anthology* retains rights to reprint any Haven story, however, author may submit the story elsewhere for simultaneous publication.
Advice: "Is there passion in the writing? Is there forethought? Will the story make an emotional connection to the reader? Send for guidelines and a sample issue. If you see that your work would not only fit into, but add something to *Anthology*, then send it."

N $ 🖉 ARCHAEOLOGY, P.O. Box 1264, Huntington WV 25714. Magazine: 8½×11; 24 pages; illustrations and photos. Authors are "archaeology writers who have a message for children and young adults." Quarterly. Estab. 1993. Circ. 9,000.

Needs: Children's/juvenile (adventure, historical, mystery, preschool, series), historical, mystery/suspense (procedural), young adult/teen (adventure, historical, mystery/suspense, series, western), archaeology. Receives 25 unsolicited mss/month. Accepts 1-2 mss/issue; 12-16 mss/year. Publishes ms 1-3 months after acceptance. Recently published work by Linda Lyons and Rocky Nivison. Length: 500 words minimum. Also publishes literary essays, criticism and poetry. Always critiques or comments on rejected ms.

How to Contact: Send complete ms with a cover letter. Include estimated word count, bio and list of publications. Replies in 1 month on queries; 2 months on mss. Send SASE for reply, return of ms or send disposable copy of ms. Simultaneous and reprint submissions OK. Sample copy for $3.50. Guidelines free.

Payment/Terms: Pays 1¢/word maximum plus 2 contributor's copies on acceptance for first rights. Sends prepublication galleys to author.

Advice: "Guidelines are the best reference to knowing if a manuscript or filler is acceptable for a magazine. Writers' time and resources can be saved by submitting their work to publications that need their style of writing. Guidelines for *Archaeology* are sent for a SASE."

N $ 🖉 ARTEMIS MAGAZINE, Science and Fiction for a Space-Faring Age, 1380 East 17th St., Suite 201, Brooklyn NY 11230-6011. E-mail: magazine@lrcpubs.com. Website: www.lrcpublications.com (includes writer's guidelines, names of editors, reviews, author information, letters, news, etc.). **Editor**: Ian Randal Strock. Magazine: 8½×11; 64 pages; glossy cover; illustrations. "The magazine is an even mix of science and fiction. We are a proud sponsor of the Artemis Project, which is constructing a commercial, manned moon base." Quarterly. Estab. 1999.

Needs: Adventure, science fiction, thriller/espionage. Receives 200 unsolicited mss/month. Accepts 4-7 mss/issue. Publishes ms 3-12 months after acceptance. Recently published work by Joseph J. Lazzaro, Fred Lerner, Ron Collins, Linda Dunn, Stanley Schmidt and Jack Williamson. Length: 2,000-8,000 words average; 1 word minimum; 15,000 words maximum. Publishes short shorts. Also publishes poetry. Often critiques or comments on rejected ms.

How to Contact: Send complete ms with a cover letter. Include estimated word count, 1-3-paragraph bio, Social Security number, list of publications. Reports in 1 month on mss. Send SASE for reply, return of ms or send a disposable copy of ms. Sample copy for $5 and a 9×12 SAE with 4 first-class stamps. Guidelines for SASE. Reviews novels, short story collections and nonfiction books of interest to writers. Send books to editor.

Payment/Terms: Pays 3-5¢/word and 3 contributor's copies on acceptance for first rights. Sends prepublication galleys to author.

Advice: "*Artemis Magazine* publishes the best science and science fiction based, in some way, on lunar development. The more closely related to the Project the better, but do not sacrifice a good story or informative article simply to get in a reference to the Project. Present lunar development in a positive, entertaining manner. The moon is an attractive goal, to which people want to go. Please remember that we are part of the Artemis Project, so stories about colonists bashing the company that got them there probably won't make the cut."

N $ ☐ ◎ THE BANNER, 2850 Kalamazoo SE, Grand Rapids MI 49560. (616)241-1691. Fax: (616)224-0834. E-mail: thebanner@crcna.org. Website: www.thebanner.org (includes sample articles and information about the publication). **Editor:** John Suk. Magazine: 8½×11; 40 pages; glossy paper; illustrations and photos. "*The Banner* is the official magazine of the Christian Reformed Church in North America and an organ for news, features, fiction and poetry that inform and uplift our members." Biweekly. Estab. 1866. Circ. 29,500.

Needs: Ethnic/multicultural ("religious and reformed fiction/poetry representing diverse voices is very welcome"), religious (children's religious, inspirational). Does not want to see "anything incompatible with Christian Reformed Church notions of morality." Accepts 2-3 mss/year. Publishes ms 3-4 months after acceptance. Length: 1,700 words average; 1,800 words maximum. Publishes short shorts. Also publishes poetry. Often critiques or comments on rejected ms.

How to Contact: Send complete ms with a cover letter. Include estimated word count, 100-word bio, social security number, picture. Reports in 2 weeks on queries; 1 months on mss. Send SASE for reply, return of ms or send disposable copy of ms. Sample copy for $2.25 and an 8½×11 envelope with 2 first-class stamps. Guidelines for SASE.

Payment/Terms: Pays $50-200 and 1 contributor's copy on acceptance for all rights; additional copies $2.25.

Advice: Looks for "relevance to our church audience, clarity, cohesion, simplicity. We're a bit more open to fiction than we used to be. Church audiences are coming to look for stories as well as information."

READ THE BUSINESS OF FICTION WRITING section for information on manuscript preparation, mailing tips, rights and more.

N $⊘ BASEBALL, P.O. Box 1264, Huntington WV 25714. Magazine: 8½×11; illustrations and photos. Quarterly. Estab. 1998. Circ. 9,000.

Needs: Children's/juvenile (sports), young adult/teen (sports), baseball. Length: 500 words minimum. Also publishes literary essays, criticism and poetry. Often critiques or comments on rejected ms.

How to Contact: Send complete ms with a cover letter. Include estimated word count, bio and list of publications. Replies in 1 month on queries; 2 months on mss. Send SASE for reply, return of ms or send disposable copy of ms. Simultaneous and reprint submissions OK. Sample copy for $3.50. Guidelines free.

Payment/Terms: Pays 1¢/word maximum plus contributor's copies on acceptance for first rights. Send prepublication galleys to author.

◎ BLACK BOOKS BULLETIN: WORDSWORK, Third World Press, P.O. Box 19730, Chicago IL 60619-0730. (773)651-0700. Fax: (773)651-7286. **Editor:** Haki R. Madhubuti. Magazine: 80 pages. *"Black Books Bulletin: WordsWork* publishes progressive material related to an enlightened African-American audience." Annually.

• In addition to publishing fiction, *Black Books Bulletin: WordsWork* is primarily a review publication covering nonfiction, fiction and poetry books by African-American authors.

Needs: Condensed/excerpted novel, ethnic/multicultural, feminist, historical (general). Receives 40 unsolicited mss/month. Accepts 2 mss/issue. Does not read mss January through June. Publishes ms 1 year after acceptance. Agented fiction 20%. Published work by Amiri Baraka, Keorapetse Kgositsile. Also publishes literary essays, literary criticism, poetry. Sometimes critiques or comments on rejected mss.

How to Contact: Query first. Include estimated word count and bio. Reports in 3 weeks on queries; 3 months on mss. Simultaneous and reprint submissions OK. Reviews novels and short story collections. Send books to Assistant Editor Melissa Moore.

Payment/Terms: Pays on publication. Acquires all rights.

▢ ◎ BLACKFIRE, BLK Publishing Co., P.O. Box 83912, Los Angeles CA 90083-0912. (310)410-0808. Fax: (310)410-9250. E-mail: newsroom@blk.com. Website: www.blk.com. **Editor:** Alan Bell. Magazine: 8⅛×10⅞; 68 pages; color glossy throughout; illustrations and photographs. Bimonthly magazine featuring the erotic images, experiences and fantasies of black gay and bisexual men. Estab. 1992.

• BLK is a member of COSMEP.

Needs: Ethnic/multicultural, gay. No interracial stories or idealized pornography. Accepts 4 mss/issue. Published work by Terrance 'Kenji' Evans, Geoff Adams, Shawn Hinds, Stefan Collins and Robert Wesley. Publishes short shorts. Also publishes poetry.

How to Contact: Query first, query with clips of published work or send complete ms with a cover letter. Should include bio (3 sentences). Send a disposable copy of ms. Simultaneous and electronic submissions OK. Sample copy for $7. Fiction guidelines free.

Payment/Terms: Pays $50-100, 5 contributor's copies. Acquires first North American serial rights and right to anthologize.

Advice: *"Blackfire* seeks erotic material of the highest quality. The most important thing is that the work be erotic and that it features black gay men or themes. Study the magazine to see what we do and how we do it. Some fiction is very romantic, other is highly sexual. Most articles in *Blackfire* cater to black gay/bisexual men between these two extremes."

$ ▢ ▼ BOY'S QUEST, The Bluffton News Publishing & Printing Co., P.O. Box 227, Bluffton OH 45817. (419)358-4610. Fax: (419)358-5027. **Editor:** Marilyn Edwards. Magazine: 7×9; 50 pages; enamel paper; illustrations and photos. Bimonthly. Estab. 1994.

• *Boy's Quest* received an EDPRESS Distinguished Achievement Award for Excellence in Educational Journalism, and a Silver Award-Gallery of Superb Printing.

Needs: Adventure, children's/juvenile (5-9 years, 10-12 years), ethnic/multicultural, historical, sports. Upcoming themes: astronomy, pets, unique and unusual, digging up the past, flying, boats, forest animals, and frogs, turtles and snakes. List of upcoming themes available for SASE. Receives 300-400 unsolicited mss/month. Accepts 20-40 mss/year. Agented fiction 2%. Published work by Jean Patrick, Eve Marar and Linda Herman. Length: 300-500 words average; 500 words maximum. Publishes short shorts. Length: 250-400 words. Also publishes poetry. Always critiques or comments on rejected mss.

How to Contact: Send complete ms with a cover letter. Include estimated word count, 1 page bio, Social Security number, list of publications. Reports in 2-4 weeks on queries; 6-10 weeks on mss. Simultaneous and reprint submissions OK. Sample copy for $3. Fiction guidelines for #10 SASE. Reviews novels and short story collections.

Payment/Terms: Pays 5¢/word and 1 contributor's copy on publication for first North American serial rights; additional copies $4, $2.50 for 10 or more.

N $⊘ BREAD FOR GOD'S CHILDREN, P.O. BOX 1017, Arcadia FL 34265-1017. (941)494-6214. Fax: (941)993-0154. E-mail: bread@desoto.net. **Editor:** Judith M. Gibbs. Magazine: 8×10½; 32 pages; 40 lb stock. *"Bread* is a teaching tool for Christian families. It is best used by the family together, but there are sections for children, youth and parents to use on their own." Bimonthly. Estab. 1972. Circ. 9,000.

Needs: Adventure, children's/juvenile (adventure, historical, sports), religious (children's religious, general religious, inspirational), young adult/teen (adventure, historical, sports). No "fantasy, science fiction or any other work not in line with Christian principles." Receives more than 50 unsolicited mss/month. Accepts 2 mss/issue; 12 mss/year. **Publishes 4-5 new writers/year.** Length: 500-1,700 words average; 500-900 words (children's stories); 900-1,700 words (teen stories). Also publishes poetry. Sometimes critiques or comments on rejected mss.

How to Contact: Send complete ms with a cover letter. Reports in 3 weeks on queries; 2 months on mss. SASE for reply or return of ms. Simultaneous submissions and reprints OK. Sample copies (2-3) for 9 × 12 SAE and 5 first-class stamps. Fiction guidelines for #10 SAE and 1 first-class stamp.

Payment/Terms: Pays $40-50 and 3 contributor's copies. Pays on publication. Not copyrighted.

Advice: "Primary criteria is the message of Christian principles underlying the theme or plot. Good writing and believable, well developed characters are essential. Know our publication—get and study sample copies. Know Jesus so the gospel message is presented clearly."

N $ **BRIDAL GUIDES**, P.O. Box 1264, Huntington WV 25714. Magazine: 8½ × 11; illustrations and photos. Quarterly. Estab. 1993. Circ. 9,000.

Needs: Children's/juvenile, romance, young adult/teen (romance), weddings. Receives 25 unsolicited mss/month. Accepts 1-4 mss/issue; 24-30 mss/year. Publishes ms 1-3 months after acceptance. Length: 500 words minimum. Also publishes literary essays, criticism and poetry. Always critiques or comments on rejected ms.

How to Contact: Send complete ms with a cover letter. Include estimated word count, bio and list of publications. Replies in 1 month on queries; 2 months on mss. Send SASE for reply, return of ms or send disposable copy of ms. Simultaneous and reprint submissions OK. Sample copy for $3.50. Guidelines free.

Payment/Terms: Pays 1¢/word plus 2 contributor's copies on acceptance for first rights. Send prepublication galleys to author.

N **BRUTARIAN**, P.O. Box 25222, Arlington VA 22202-9222. (703)360-2514. **Editor:** D.J. Salemi. Magazine: 8½ × 11; 84 pages; illustrations and photos. "Our theme is whatever doesn't fit we're interested in." Quarterly. Estab. 1991. Circ. 3,000.

Needs: Erotica, experimental, fantasy, feminist, gay, horror, humor/satire, lesbian, literary, mainstream/contemporary, mystery/suspense (police procedural, private eye/hardboiled), psychic/supernatural/occult. Receives 150 unsolicited mss/month. Accepts 2 mss/issue; 8 mss/year. Publishes ms 3 months after acceptance. Agented fiction 10%. Recently published work by Dennis Etchison and Jack Ketchum. Length: 2,000-3,000 words average; 500 words minimum; 5,000 words maximum. Publishes short shorts.

How to Contact: Send complete ms with a cover letter. Include estimated word count and list of publications. Reports in 2 weeks on queries, 2 months on mss. Send SASE for reply, return of ms or send a disposable copy of ms. No simultaneous and reprint submissions. Sample copy for $6. Reviews novels and short story collections.

Payment/Terms: Pays 10¢/word for well established writers and 3 contributor's copies; additional copies for $6.

Terms: Pays on publication for first rights. Sends galleys to author.

Advice: "The beauty of the language, the depth of ideas make a manuscript stand out. Rewrite it several times."

$ **CHALLENGING DESTINY, New Fantasy & Science Fiction**, Crystalline Sphere Publishing, R.R. #6, St. Marys Ontario N4X 1C8 Canada. (519)884-7557. E-mail: csp@golden.net. Website: home.golden.net/~csp/ (includes previews of published and upcoming magazines, writer's guidelines, interviews with authors, reviews of books, movies, soundtracks and games, links to other websites). **Editors:** David M. Switzer and Robert P. Switzer. Magazine: 8 × 5¼; 120 pages; Kallima 10 pt cover; illustrations. "We publish all kinds of science fiction and fantasy short stories." Quarterly. Estab. 1997. Circ. 300.

Needs: Fantasy, science fiction. No horror, short short stories. Receives 40 unsolicited mss/month. Accepts 6 mss/issue, 24 mss/year. Publishes ms 1-3 months after acceptance. Recently published work by Michael Mirolla, Stefano Donati, D. Sandy Nielsen, Hugh Cook, Leah Silverman and James A. Hartley. **Publishes 12 new writers/year.** Length: 6,000 words average; 2,000 words minimum; 10,000 words maximum. Often critiques or comments on rejected mss.

How to Contact: Send complete ms with a cover letter. Include estimated word count. Reports in 1 month on queries, 2 months on mss. Send SAE and IRC for reply, return of ms or send disposable copy of ms. Simultaneous submissions OK. Sample copy for $6.50. Guidelines for 1 IRC. Reviews novels and short story collections. Send books to James Schellenberg, R.R. #1, 4421 Spring Creek Rd., Vineland Ontario L0R 2C0 Canada.

Payment/Terms: Pays 1¢/word plus 2 contributor's copies for first North American serial rights. Sends galleys to author.

Advice: "Manuscripts with a good story and interesting characters stand out. We look for fiction that entertains and makes you think. If you're going to write short fiction, you need to read lots of it. Don't reinvent the wheel. Use your own voice."

THE CHINOOK QUARTERLY, Chinook Press, 1432 Yellowstone Ave., Billings MT 59102. (406)245-7704. **Editor:** Mary Ellen Westwood. Magazine: 7×8½; 60-80 pages; acid-free paper; card cover stock; illustrations; photos. *"The Chinook Quarterly* will be a catalyst for human change and understanding. We want forward-looking and challenging submissions that will be of use to readers in the West." Quarterly. Estab. 1996.
Needs: Adventure, children's/juvenile (10-12 years), condensed/excerpted novel, ethnic/multicultural, experimental, fantasy (science fantasy), feminist, historical, humor/satire, literary, mainstream/contemporary, mystery/suspense (all kinds), regional, romance (contemporary), futuristic/time travel), science fiction (hard science, soft/sociological), sports, translations, westerns, young adult/teen (all kinds). Especially interested in stories about the contemporary West. "No fiction that degrades or discounts human beings." Accepts 4-6 mss/issue; 16-24 mss/year. Publishes ms 1-12 months after acceptance. Length: 1,600 words average; 300 words minimum; 2,000 words maximum. Publishes short shorts. Also publishes literary essays, literary criticism and poetry. Often critiques or comments on rejected mss.
How to Contact: Send complete ms with a cover letter. Include estimated word count, 250-word bio, Social Security number, list of publications and explanation of the piece submitted (why did you write it?)." Send SASE for return of ms. Reprints OK. Sample copy for $7. Fiction guidelines for #10 SASE. Reviews novels and short story collections.
Payment/Terms: Pays $2/printed page and 4 contributor's copies on publication. Acquires one-time rights. Sends galleys to the author.
Advice: "I am looking for a fresh and daring approach and a thinking view of the world. I admire risk takers. I want writing about real people, not just academic musings. I want the true like experiences of humans, not some shallow misinterpretations. Edit, edit, edit . . . after you rewrite, of course."

CHRISTIAN COURIER, Reformed Faith Witness, Unit 4, 261 Martindale Rd., St. Catharines, Ontario L2W 1A1 Canada. (905)682-8311. Fax: (905)682-8313. E-mail: cceditor@aol.com. **Managing Editor:** Marian Van Til. Tabloid: 11½×14; 20 pages; newsprint; illustrations and photos. Bi-weekly. Estab. 1945. Circ. 4,000.
Needs: Adventure, children's/juvenile (10-12 years), historical, religious/inspirational, senior citizen/retirement, sports and translations. No "sentimental 'religious' stuff; superficial moralizing." Receives 5-10 unsolicited mss/month. Accepts 12 mss/year. Does not read mss from the end of July through early August. Publishes ms within a month after acceptance. Length: 1,200 words average; no minimum; 1,400 words maximum. Publishes short shorts. Length 500 words. Also publishes literary essays (if not too technical), literary criticism and poetry. Always critiques or comments on rejected mss.
How to Contact: Send complete ms with a cover letter. Include word count and bio (100 words maximum). Reports in 3 weeks on queries; 4-6 weeks on mss. Send a disposable copy of ms. Simultaneous, reprint and electronic submissions OK. Sample copy free. Fiction guidelines for SASE. Reviews novels and short story collections.
Payment/Terms: Pays $25-60 on publication and 1 contributor's copy (on request). Acquires one-time rights.
Advice: Looks for work "geared to a Christian audience but reflecting the real world, real dilemmas, without pat resolutions—written in an engaging, clear manner."

CLUBHOUSE MAGAZINE, Focus on the Family, 8605 Explorer Dr., Colorado Springs CO 80920. (719)531-3400, ext. 1860. Fax: (719)531-3499. **Editor:** Jesse Florea. Associate Editor: Annette Brashler Bourland. Magazine: 24 pages; illustrations and photos. Christian children's magazine. Monthly. Estab. 1987. Circ. 109,000.
● *Clubhouse Magazine* has received Evangelical Press Association awards for fiction and art.
Needs: Adventure, children's/juvenile (8-12 years), religious/inspirational, sports. No animal fiction or where the main character is not between the ages of 8-12 and dealing with issues appropriate to the age level. Would like to see more historical fiction with Bible-believing/Christian protagonist. Receives 100 unsolicited mss/month. Accepts 1 ms/issue; 12 mss/year. Recently published work by Nancy N. Rue, Sigmund Brouwer and Katherine Bond. **Publishes 8 new writers/year.** Length: 500-1,200 words average. Publishes short shorts.
How to Contact: Send complete ms with a cover letter. Include estimated word count, Social Security number and list of publications. Reports in 4-6 weeks on queries and mss. Send SASE for reply, return of ms or send disposable copy of ms. Simultaneous submissions OK. Sample copy for $1.50. Writer's guidelines free.
Payment/Terms: Pays $25 minimum; $250 maximum on acceptance and 5 contributor's copies for first rights.
Advice: *"Clubhouse* readers are 8- to 12-year-old boys and girls who desire to know more about God and the Bible. Their parents (who typically pay for the membership) want wholesome, educational material with scriptural or moral insight. The kids want excitement, adventure, action, humor or mystery. Your job as a writer is to please both the parent and child with each article."

COCHRAN'S CORNER, 1003 Tyler Court, Waldorf MD 20602-2964. Phone/fax: (301)870-1664. President: Ada Cochran. **Editor:** Jeanie Saunders. Magazine: 5½×8; 52 pages. "We publish fiction, nonfiction and poetry. Our only requirement is no strong language." For a "family" audience. Quarterly magazine. Estab. 1986. Circ. 500.
Needs: Adventure, children's/juvenile, historical, horror, humor/satire, mystery/suspense, religious/inspira-

tional, romance, science fiction, young adult/teen (10-18 years). Would like to see more mystery and romance fiction. "Mss must be free from language you wouldn't want your/our children to read." Plans a special fiction issue. Receives 50 mss/month. Accepts 4 mss/issue; 8 mss/year. Publishes ms by the next issue after acceptance. Published work by James Hughes, Ellen Sandry, James Bennet, Susan Lee and Judy Demers. **Publishes approximately 30 new writers/year.** Length: 500 words preferred; 300 words minimum; 1,000 words maximum. Also publishes literary essays, literary criticism, poetry.

How to Contact: "Right now we are forced to limit acceptance to *subscribers only*." Send complete ms with cover letter. Reports in 3 weeks on queries; 6-8 weeks on mss. SASE for manuscript. Simultaneous and reprint submissions OK. Sample copy for $5, 9×12 SAE and 90¢ postage. Fiction guidelines for #10 SASE.

Payment/Terms: Pays in contributor's copies. Acquires one-time rights.

Advice: "I feel the quality of fiction is getting better. The public is demanding a good read, instead of having sex or violence carry the story. I predict that fiction has a good future. We like to print the story as the writer submits it if possible. This way writers can compare their work with their peers and take the necessary steps to improve and go on to sell to bigger magazines. Stories from the heart desire a place to be published. We try to fill that need. Be willing to edit yourself. Polish your manuscript before submitting to editors."

COLD-DRILL MAGAZINE, English Dept., Boise State University, 1910 University Dr., Boise ID 83725. (208)426-3862. **Editor:** Tamara Shores. Faculty Advisor: Dr. Mitchell Wieland. Magazine: box format; various perfect and non-perfect bound inserts; illustrations and photos. For adult audiences. Annually. Estab. 1970. Circ. 500.

Needs: "The 2000 issue will not have a theme; it will be open to all forms of writing and artwork." Length: determined by submissions.

How to Contact: Query first. SASE.

Payment/Terms: Pays in contributor's copies. Acquires first rights.

THE COMPLEAT NURSE, A Voice of Independent Nursing, Dry Bones Press, P.O. Box 640345, San Francisco CA 94164-0345. Phone/fax: (415)292-7371. E-mail: jrankin@drybones.com. Website: www.drybones.com (includes current listings, guest book, online order placement, delays in publication schedule). **Editor/Publisher:** Jim Rankin. Newsletter: 8½×11; 4-6 pages; 60 lb. paper; illustrations and photographs. "We publish themes, ideas, and subjects of interest to nurses and their patients—a definition we view very broadly. Nurses seen as cultural individuals, who practice as well in a profession." Monthly. Estab. 1990.

● Member of PMA, SPAN.

Needs: Adventure, children's/juvenile, erotica, ethnic/multicultural, fantasy (sexuality and sexual issues), feminist, gay, historical, humor/satire, lesbian, mainstream/contemporary, mystery/suspense, regional, religious/inspirational (historical), science fiction, senior citizen/retirement, translations, young adult/teen, nurse or patient issues. Impact of health care infrastructure changes. Publishes special fiction issues or anthologies. Receives 2-3 unsolicited mss/month. Fiction mss accepted varies; 3-5 mss/year. Publishes ms almost immediately to 1 year after acceptance. Length: 1,500 words average; 3,000 words maximum. Publishes short shorts. Also publishes literary essays, literary criticism, poetry. Always critiques or comments on rejected mss.

How to Contact: Query first with clips of published work. Include estimated word count, bio, Social Security number and list of publications. Reports in 1 month on queries; 1-2 months on mss. Send SASE for reply, return of ms or send a disposable copy of ms. Simultaneous submissions, reprints and electronic submissions OK. Reviews novels and short story collections. Send books to editor.

Payment/Terms: Pays in contributor's copies on publication. Rights acquired negotiable. Sends galleys to author.

Advice: "Please consider basic human issues including humor and personal experience and write about those things. We are a shoestring small press—and authors need to work with us to build markets. But we can consider good things others pass up, or unique things."

CONTRABAND, P.O. Box 8565, Atlanta GA 31106. (404)572-9141. E-mail: louve@mindspring.com. **Editors:** Bill Campbell and Angela Wiens. Magazine: 8½×11; 64 pages; illustrations and photographs. "Genres are not important to us nor name and reputation. What we are looking for is thought-provoking material that says something about the world in which we live. We abhor yuppie angst, precocious children, and how tough it is to be a writer. Say something important and say it well." Quarterly. Estab. 1996. Circ. 600.

Needs: Condensed/excerpted novel, ethnic/multicultural, experimental, feminist, gay, historical (general), horror, humor/satire, lesbian, literary, magic realism, mainstream, psychic/supernatural/occult, science fiction (soft/sociological), serialized novel, translations. No romance, adventure. Receives 20 unsolicited mss/month. Accepts 3-5 mss/issue; 18-30 mss/year. Publishes ms 6-12 months after acceptance. Recently published work by Farnoosh Moshiri, Manning Marable, Yehezkel Lein and Kendra Fanconi.. Publishes short shorts. Also publishes literary essays, literary criticism, poetry. Often critiques or comments on rejected mss.

How to Contact: Send complete ms with a cover letter. Include estimated word count. Reports in 2-3 weeks on queries; 2 months on mss. Send SASE for reply, return of ms or send a disposable copy of ms. Simultaneous submissions, reprints and electronic submissions OK. Sample copy for $4. Fiction guidelines free. Reviews novels and short story collections.

Payment/Terms: Pays 2 contributor's copies on publication; additional copies for $4. Acquires rights to publish in our magazine and on website.

Advice: "We look for a vitality and intensity in any submission. It must say something important to our readers and say it in a unique way. It must intrigue and provoke and stay away from the cliché. I didn't believe this as a beginning writer, but, as an editor, I think it's extremely important to know the market in which one plans to submit. Many editors have unique tastes and are overworked. Purchasing a sample copy first often saves time, postage and fragile egos."

✓ ◯ THE COZY DETECTIVE, Mystery Magazine, Meager Ink Publishing, 686 Jakes Ct., McMinnville OR 97128. Phone/fax: (503)472-4896. E-mail: papercapers@yahoo.com. Editor: David Workman. **Fiction Editor:** Charlie Bradley. Magazine: 8½ × 5½; 80 pages; illustrations and photos. Publishes mystery/suspense fiction and true crime stories for mystery buffs. Quarterly. Estab. 1994. Circ. 2,000.

Needs: Condensed/excerpted novel, mystery/suspense (amateur sleuth, cozy, police procedural, private eye/hardboiled), science fiction (mystery), serialized novel, young adult (mystery). No "sex, violence or vulgarity." Publishes special fiction issues or anthologies. Receives 15-25 unsolicited mss/issue; 20 mss/year. Does not read mss June-August. Recently published work by Kris Neri, Wendy Dager, Ruth Latta, James Geisert, C. Lester Bradley and Robert W. Kreps. Length: 6,000 words maximum; will consider longer stories for two-part series. Publishes short shorts. Also publishes poetry. Sometimes critiques or comments on rejected ms.

How to Contact: Send complete ms with a cover letter. Include 1-paragraph bio and estimated word count. Reports in 2 months on queries; 1-6 months on mss. Send SASE for reply, return of ms or send disposable copy of ms. Simultaneous, reprint and electronic submissions OK. Sample copy for $2.95. Fiction guidelines for #10 SASE. Reviews novels and short story collections. Send books to "Review Editor."

Payment/Terms: Pays 2 contributor's copies for first North American serial rights; additional copies $1.50.

Advice: "Do your best work—don't rush. Try to make your plot secondary to characters in the story. We look for action, crisp dialogue and original use of old ideas. We love a good mystery."

✓ ◯ ▣ CZ'S MAGAZINE, CZA, 3300 St. Joachim, St. Ann MO 63074. (314)890-2060. E-mail: cz@cza.c om. Website: www.cza.com/ (includes guidelines, reader participation in giving comments on stories and poems). **Editor:** Loretta Nichols. Electronic magazine. "This publication is produced for writers who want to be published in a general subject magazine. We publish general topics and wholesome plots. Family reading. Inspirational type stories and poems." Triquarterly. Estab. 1997. Circ. 200.

Needs: Adventure, children's/juvenile (10-12 years), experimental, fantasy (science fantasy, sword and sorcery), feminist, humor/satire, literary, mainstream/contemporary, mystery/suspense (amateur sleuth, police procedural, romantic suspense), psychic/supernatural/occult, religious/inspirational, romance (contemporary, futuristic/time travel, gothic), young adult/teen (adventure, mystery, romance, science fiction), interviews. Would like to see more inspirational and romance fiction. "No porn." Receives 20 unsolicited mss/month. Accepts 3 mss/issue; 12 mss/year. Recently published work by Kenneth Goldman and Jack Fisher. **Publishes 10 new writers/year.** Length: 1,500 words average; 500 words minimum; 3,000 words maximum. Publishes short shorts. Also publishes literary essays, literary criticism and poetry. Sometimes critiques or comments on rejected mss.

How to Contact: Send complete ms with a cover letter. Accepts queries/mss by e-mail. Include estimated word count, bio and list of publications. Reports in 6 months. Send SASE for reply, return of ms or send a disposable copy of ms. Simultaneous submissions and reprints OK. Sample copy for $2. Fiction guidelines free. Reviews novels and short story collections. Send books to editor.

Payment/Terms: Varies.

Advice: "Send your work with SASE. I always publish unpublished authors first (unless their work is not fitting)."

$ ◹ DAGGER OF THE MIND, Beyond The Realms Of Imagination, K'yi-Lih Productions (a division of Breach Enterprises), 1317 Hookridge Dr., El Paso TX 79925-7808. (915)591-0541. **Executive Editor:** Arthur William Lloyd Breach. Magazine. 8½ × 11; 62-86 pages; hibright paper; high glossy cover; from 5-12 illustrations. "Our aim is to provide the reading, educated public with thought-provoking, intelligent fiction without graphic sex, violence and gore. We publish science fiction, fantasy, horror, mystery and parapsychological/fortean nonfiction material." Quarterly. Estab. 1990. Circ. 5,000.

● Do not send this publication "slasher" horror. The editor's preferences lean toward *Twilight Zone* and similar material. He says he added mystery to his needs but has received very little quality material in this genre.

Needs: Lovecraftian, *Twilight Zone* fiction. Intelligent, well-crafted and thought provoking exactly like the television series. Adventure, experimental, fantasy, horror, mystery/suspense (private eye, police procedural), science fiction (hard science, soft/sociological). Nothing sick and blasphemous, vulgar, obscene, racist, sexist, profane, humorous, weak, exploited women stories and those with idiotic puns. No westerns or slasher. Plans special paperback anthologies. Receives 500 unsolicited mss/month. Accepts 8-15 mss/issue; 90-100 mss/year depending upon length. Publishes ms 2 years after acceptance. Agented fiction 30%. Published work by Sidney Williams, Jessica Amanda Salmonson and Donald R. Burleson. **Publishes 1-2 new writers/year.** All lengths are acceptable; from short shorts to novelette lengths. Also publishes literary essays, literary criticism, poetry. Sometimes comments on rejected mss.

How to Contact: All mail should be addressed to Arthur Breach. Send complete manuscript with cover letter. "Include a bio and list of previously published credits with tearsheets. I also expect a brief synopsis of the story." Reports in 6 months on mss. SASE. Simultaneous submissions OK "as long as I am informed that they are such." Accepts electronic submissions. Sample copy for $3.50, 9×12 SAE and 5 first-class stamps. Fiction guidelines for #10 SASE.

Payment/Terms: Pays ½-1¢/word plus 1 contributor's copy on publication for first rights (possibly anthology rights as well).

Advice: "Do not send *revised* stories unless requested. I'm a big fan of the late H.P. Lovecraft. I love reading through Dunsanian and Cthulhu Mythos tales. I'm constantly on the lookout for this special brand of fiction. If you want to grab my attention immediately, write on the outside of the envelope 'Lovecraftian submission enclosed.' There are a number of things which make submissions stand out for me. Is there any sensitivity to the tale? I like sensitive material, so long as it doesn't become mushy. Another thing that grabs my attention are characters which leap out of the pages at you. Move me, bring a tear to my eye; make me stop and think about the world and people around me. Frighten me with little spoken of truths about the human condition. In short, show me that you can move me in such a way as I have never been moved before."

N $ ⃝ **DANCE**, P.O. Box 1264, Huntington WV 25714. Magazine: 8½×11; illustrations and photos. Quarterly. Estab. 1993. Circ. 9,000.

Needs: Children's/juvenile, young adult/teen, dance. Receives 25 unsolicited mss/month. Accepts 1-2 mss/issue; 12-16 mss/year. Publishes ms 1-3 months after acceptance. Length: 500 words minimum. Also publishes literary essays, criticism and poetry. Always critiques or comments on rejected ms.

How to Contact: Send complete ms with a cover letter. Include estimated word count, bio and list of publications. Replies in 1 month on queries; 2 months on mss. Send SASE for reply, return of ms or send disposable copy of ms. Simultaneous and reprint submissions OK. Sample copy for $3.50. Guidelines free.

Payment/Terms: Pays 1¢/word plus contributor's copies on acceptance for first rights. Send prepublication galleys to author.

N ⊕ **DARK HORIZONS**, 46 Oxford Rd., Acocks Green, Birmingham B27 6DT England. **Editors:** Peter Coleborn and Mike Chinn. Published 1-2 times/year. Circ. 500-700. Publishes 5-8 stories (and articles)/issue. "We are a small press fantasy magazine. Our definition of fantasy knows no bounds, covering science, heroic, dark and light fantasy and horror fiction. We also use occasional poetry." Length: 8,000-10,000 words maximum. Pays contributor's copies. Send ms with brief cover letter and IRCs for return of ms or acknowledgement. Sample copy, "if stock remains," for large SAE and five IRCs.

✓ ⃝ **DARK MATTER, A Chronicle of the Speculative Mind,** Sign of the Celtic Cross Press, 2222 Foothill Blvd., PMB E-216, La Canada CA 91011-1456. **Editor:** Cristopher Hennessey-DeRose. Magazine: full-sized; 30-40 pages; 24 lb. paper; gloss cover stock; illustrations. "*TwilightZone*-esque stories/art for a mature (not xxx-rated) audience." Published annually. Estab. 1998. Circ. 100.

Needs: Horror, humor/satire, psychic/supernatural/occult, science fiction (hard science, soft/sociological). "No fantasy, splatterpunk." Receives 50 unsolicited mss/month. Accepts 8-10 mss/year. Publishes ms 1 year after acceptance. Recently published work by D.F. Lewis, Charlee Jacob, D. Sandy Nielsen and John B. Rosenman. Length: 2,000 words average; 250 words minimum; 3,000 words maximum. Publishes short shorts. Also publishes literary essays. Sometimes critiques or comments on rejected ms.

How to Contact: Send complete ms with a cover letter. Include estimated word count, 50-word bio, social security number and list of publications. Reports in 3 months. Send SASE for return of ms or send a disposable copy of ms. Simultaneous submissions OK. Sample copy for $5.95. Fiction guidelines free.

Payment/Terms: Pays $5 on acceptance and 1 contributor's copy; additional copies $3.95. Acquires first North American serial rights and non-exclusive anthology reprint rights.

Advice: "Use proper manuscript format."

★ ⃝ ◎ **DREAM INTERNATIONAL/QUARTERLY,** U.S. Address: Charles I. Jones, #H-1, 411 14th St., Ramona CA 92065-2769. **Editor-in-Chief:** Charles I. Jones. Magazine: 8½×11; 140-165 pages; Xerox paper; parchment cover stock; some illustrations and photos. "Publishes fiction and nonfiction that is dream-related or clearly inspired by a dream. Also dream-related fantasy and poetry." Quarterly. Estab. 1981. Circ. 80-100.

Needs: Adventure, confession, contemporary, erotica, ethnic, experimental, fantasy, historical, horror, humor/

● **A BULLET INTRODUCES COMMENTS** by the editor of *Novel & Short Story Writer's Market* indicating special information about the listing.

satire, literary, mainstream, mystery/suspense, prose poem, psychic/supernatural/occult, romance, science fiction, translations, young adult/teen (10-18). "We would like to see submissions that deal with dreams that have an influence on the person's daily waking life. Suggestions for making dreams beneficial to the dreamer in his/her waking life. We would also like to see more submissions dealing with lucid dreaming." Receives 20-30 unsolicited mss/month. Publishes ms 8 months to 3 years after acceptance. **Publishes 40-50 new writers/year.** Length: 1,000 words minimum; 2,000 words maximum. Publishes short shorts. Recently published work by Tim Scott, Carmen M. Pursifull and Allen Underwood. Also publishes literary essays, poetry (poetry submissions to Carmen M. Pursifull, 809 W. Maple St., Champaign IL 61820-2810. Hard copy only for poetry. No electronic submissions please! Send SASE for poetry guidelines).

How to Contact: Submit ms. Reports in 6 weeks on queries; 3 months on mss. SASE. Simultaneous and reprint submissions OK. No electronic submissions. Sample copy for $13. Guidelines $2 with SAE and 2 first-class stamps. Subscription: $50 (1-year); $100 (2-year). "Accepted mss will not be returned unless requested at time of submission."

Payment/Terms: Pays in contributor's copies (contributors must pay $3 for postage and handling). Offers magazine subscription. Acquires one-time rights.

Advice: "Write about what you know. Make the reader 'stand up and take notice.' Avoid rambling and stay away from chichés in your writing unless, of course, it is of a humorous nature and is purposefully done to make a point."

$ DREAMS & VISIONS, New Frontiers in Christian Fiction, Skysong Press, 35 Peter St. S., Orillia, Ontario L3V 5AB Canada. Website: www.bconnex.net/~skysong. **Editor:** Steve Stanton. Magazine: 5½×8½; 56 pages; 20 lb. bond paper; glossy cover. "Contemporary Christian fiction in a variety of styles for adult Christians." Triannually. Estab. 1989. Circ. 200.

Needs: Contemporary, experimental, fantasy, humor/satire, literary, religious/inspirational, science fiction (soft/sociological). "All stories should portray a Christian world view or expand upon Biblical themes or ethics in an entertaining or enlightening manner." Receives 20 unsolicited mss/month. Accepts 7 mss/issue; 21 mss/year. Publishes ms 2-6 months after acceptance. Length: 2,500 words; 2,000 words minimum; 6,000 words maximum.

How to Contact: Send complete ms with cover letter. "Bio is optional: degrees held and in what specialties, publishing credits, service in the church, etc." Reports in 1 month on queries; 2-4 months on mss. SASE. Simultaneous submissions OK. Sample copy for $4.95. Fiction guidelines for SASE or on website.

Payment/Terms: Pays ½¢/word and contributor's copy. Acquires first North American serial rights and one-time, non-exclusive reprint rights.

Advice: "In general we look for work that has some literary value, that is in some way unique and relevant to Christian readers today. Our first priority is technical adequacy, though we will occasionally work with a beginning writer to polish a manuscript. Ultimately, we look for stories that glorify the Lord Jesus Christ, stories that build up rather than tear down, that exalt the sanctity of life, the holiness of God, and the value of the family."

THE ELOQUENT UMBRELLA, Linn-Benton Community College, 6500 SW Pacific Blvd., Albany OR 97321-3779. (541)753-3335. **Contact:** Linda Smith. Magazine: illustrations and photos. "*The Eloquent Umbrella*'s purpose is to showcase art, photography, poetry and prose of Linn and Benton Counties in Oregon." Annually. Estab. 1990. Circ. 500.

Needs: Regional. "No slander, pornography or other material unsuitable for community reading." Accepts 50-100 mss/issue. Deadline January 15 each year. Reads mss during winter term only; publishes in spring. Length: 2,000 words maximum. Publishes short shorts. Also publishes literary essays, literary criticism and poetry.

How to Contact: Send complete ms with cover letter. Include 1- to 5-line bio. Reports in 6 weeks on mss. SASE for return of ms or send a disposable copy of ms. Simultaneous submissions OK. Sample copy for $2 and 8½×11 SAE.

Payment/Terms: Rights remain with author.

Advice: "The magazine is created by a collective editorial board and production team in a literary publication class."

EYES, 3610 North Doncaster Ct., Apt. X7, Saginaw MI 48603-1862. (517)498-4112. E-mail: fjm3eyes@aol.com. Website: members.aol.com/fjm3eyes/index.html (includes guidelines). **Editor:** Frank J. Mueller, III. Magazine: 8½×11; 40 pages; 20 lb. paper; Antiqua parchment, blue 65 lb. cover. "No specific theme. Speculative fiction and surrealism most welcome. For a general, educated, not necessarily literary audience." Estab. 1991.

Needs: Contemporary, horror (psychological), mainstream, ghost story. "Especially looking for speculative fiction and surrealism. Would like to see more ghost stories, student writing. Dark fantasy OK, but not preferred." No sword/sorcery, no overt science fiction. Nothing pornographic; no preachiness; children's fiction discouraged. Accepts 5-9 mss/issue. Publishes ms up to 1 year or longer after acceptance. **Publishes 15-20 writers/year.** Length: up to 6,000 words. Sometimes critiques rejected mss.

How to Contact: Query first or send complete ms. A short bio is optional. Reports in 1 month (or less) on queries; 3 months or longer on mss. SASE. No simultaneous submissions. Sample copy for $4; extras $4. Subscriptions $14. (Checks to Frank J. Mueller III.) Fiction guidelines for #10 SASE.

Payment/Terms: Pays one contributor's copy. Acquires one-time rights.

Advice: "Pay attention to character. A strong plot alone, while important, may not be enough to get you in *Eyes*. Atmosphere and mood are also important. Please proofread. If you have a manuscript you like enough to see it in *Eyes*, send it to me. Above all, don't let rejections discourage you. I would encourage the purchase of a sample to get an idea of what I'm looking for. Read stories by authors such as Algernon Blackwood, Nathaniel Hawthorne, Shirley Jackson and Poe. Also, please write for information concerning chapbooks."

THE FIRST WORD BULLETIN, Domingo Fernandez 5, Box 500, 28036 Madrid, Spain. United States address: c/o Mary Swain, 2046 Lothbury Dr., Fayetteville NC 28304-5666. (910)426-0134. Fax: (910)426-5240. Magazine: 15 cm×21cm; 64 pages; slick paper; 160 grams, slick cover; illustrations. "We want to make the public acutely aware of problems concerning pollution of air, earth and water. Also man's inhumanity to man and animal." Publishes material on environment, ecology, nature, alternative medicine; young adult, retirement articles. Quarterly. Estab. 1995. Circ. 5,000.

Needs: Adventure, historical, humor/satire, literary, mainstream/contemporary, senior citizen/retirement, young adult/teen (adventure, western). No pornography, smut, dirty language; no mystery, science fiction (unless related to the world environment), detective stories or romance. Would like to see more "down-to-earth grass-roots stories; more alternatives to helping the poor." Receives 15-20 unsolicited mss/month. Accepts 6-8 mss/issue; 24-32 mss/year. Publishes ms 1-2 months after acceptance. Agented fiction 10%. Recently published work by Evelyn Horan (Israel-American), Richard Reeve (UK), May Lenzer (USA), Dorothy Eker (Canada) and Joyce Vath (Mexico). **Publishes 8 new writers/year.** Length: 800 words minimum; 4,000 words maximum. Publishes short shorts. Also publishes literary essays, literary criticism and poetry. Often critiques or comments on rejected mss.

How to Contact: Query. Include estimated word count, short bio, Social Security number, list of publications. Reports in 6 weeks on queries.

Payment/Terms: Pays 25¢/word minimum, $50 maximum plus 1 contributor's copy (writer pay postage, 4 IRCs) for one-time world rights.

Advice: "In fiction I like to see the two dogs and a bone theory, well crafted with attention to clarity and precision of language, that is a seamless read. We want to give exposure to emerging writers. First, write from the heart and then revise and revise until it is acceptable. You don't always have to write what you know about but if different pay close attention to detail from research. Study the market you are writing for. Most manuscripts that land on an editor's desk are not suitable because of not being familiar with the magazine or the editor's needs. Some are too long or of the wrong genre. Buy a copy and know the magazine."

FORESIGHT, 44 Brockhurst Rd., Hodge Hill, Birmingham B36 8JB England. 0121.783.0587. Editor: John Barklam. **Fiction Editor:** Judy Barklam. Quarterly.

Needs: Magazine including "new age material, world peace, psychic phenomena, research, occultism, spiritualism, mysticism, UFOs, philosophy, etc. Shorter articles required on a specific theme related to the subject matter of *Foresight* magazine." Length: 300-1,000 words.

How to Contact: Send SAE with IRC for return of ms.

Payment/Terms: Pays in contributor's copies. Sample copy for 75p and 50p postage.

FREE FOCUS/OSTENTATIOUS MIND, Wagner Press, Bowbridge Press, P.O. Box 7415, JAF Station, New York NY 10116-7415. **Editor:** Patricia Denise Coscia. Editors change each year. Magazine: 8×14; 10 pages; recycled paper; illustrations and photos. "*Free Focus* is a small-press magazine which focuses on the educated women of today, and *Ostentatious Mind* is designed to encourage the intense writer, the cutting reality." Bimonthly. Estab. 1985 and 1987. Circ. 100 each.

Needs: Experimental, feminist, humor/satire, literary, mainstream/contemporary, mystery/suspense (romantic), psychic/supernatural/occult, westerns (traditional), young adult/teen (adventure). "X-rated fiction is not accepted." List of upcoming themes available for SASE. Plans future special fiction issue or anthology. Receives 1,000 unsolicited mss/month. Does not read mss February to August. Publishes ms 3-6 months after acceptance. Published work by Edward Janz. **Publishes 200 new writers/year.** Length: 500 words average; 1,000 words maximum. Publishes short shorts. Also publishes literary essays, literary criticism and poetry. Always critiques or comments on rejected mss. Sponsors contest for work submitted to *Free Focus.*

How to Contact: Query with clips of published work or send complete ms with a cover letter. Should include 100-word bio and list of publications. Reports in 3 months. Send SASE for reply. Simultaneous submissions OK. Sample copy for $3, #10 SAE and $1 postage. Fiction guidelines for #10 SAE and $1 postage. Reviews novels and short story collections.

Payment/Terms: Pays $2.50-5 and 2 contributor's copies on publication for all rights; additional copies for $2. Sends galleys to author.

Advice: "This publication is for beginning writers. Do not get discouraged; submit your writing. We look for imagination and creativity; no x-rated writing."

GHOST TOWN, P.O. Box 1264, Huntington WV 25714. Magazine: 8½×11; illustrations and photos. Quarterly. Estab. 1999.

Needs: Children's/juvenile (historical), historical (ghost towns), western, young adult/teen (historical). Receives 25 unsolicited mss/month. Accepts 1-2 mss/issue; 12-16 mss/year. Publishes ms 1-3 months after acceptance. Length: 500 words minimum. Also publishes literary essays, criticism and poetry. Always critiques or comments on rejected ms.

How to Contact: Send complete ms with a cover letter. Include estimated word count, bio and list of publications. Replies in 1 month on queries; 2 months on mss. Send SASE for reply, return of ms or send disposable copy of ms. Simultaneous and reprint submissions OK. Sample copy for $3.50. Guidelines free.

Payment/Terms: Pays 1¢/word plus contributor's copies on acceptance for first rights. Send prepublication galleys to author.

GLOBAL TAPESTRY JOURNAL, BB Books, 1 Spring Bank, Longsight Rd., Copster Green, Blackburn, Lancashire BB1 9EU England. **Editor:** Dave Cunliffe. Magazine. Limited press run: 1,000-1,500/issue.

Needs: "Post-underground with avant-garde, experimental, alternative, counterculture, psychedelic, mystical, anarchist etc. fiction for a bohemian and counterculture audience." Published fiction by Andy Darlington, Sir Darren Subarton and A.D. Winans. **Published work by new writers within the last year.**

How to Contact: Accepts unsolicited mss. SAE, IRCs. Reports in 2-6 weeks.

Payment/Terms: Pays contributor's copy. Sample copy for $4 (Sterling Cheque, British Money Order or dollar currency).

GRUE MAGAZINE, Hell's Kitchen Productions, P.O. Box 370, New York NY 10108-0370. Phone/fax: (212)245-2329. E-mail: nadramia@panix.com. **Editor:** Peggy Nadramia. Magazine: 5½ × 8½; 96 pages; 60 lb. paper; 10 pt. C1S film laminate cover; illustrations; photos. "We look for quality short fiction centered on horror and dark fantasy—new traditions in the realms of the gothic and the macabre for horror fans well read in the genre, looking for something new and different, as well as horror novices looking for a good scare." Triannually. Estab. 1985.

Needs: Horror, psychic/supernatural/occult. No fantasy or science fiction. Receives 250 unsolicited fiction mss/month. Accepts 10 mss/issue; 25-30 mss/year. Publishes ms 1-2 years after acceptance. Recently published work by Wayne Allen Sallee, Kevin Filan, A.R. Morlan and Denise Dumars. **Publishes 10-15 new writers/year.** Length: 4,000 words average; 6,500 words maximum. Sometimes critiques rejected ms.

How to Contact: Send complete ms with cover letter. "I like to hear where the writer heard about *Grue*, his most recent or prestigious sales, and maybe a word or two about himself." Reports in 3 weeks on queries; 6 months on mss. Send SASE for return of ms. Sample copy for $5. Fiction guidelines for #10 SASE.

Payment/Terms: Pays ½¢/word on publication and 2 contributor's copies for first North American serial rights.

Advice: "Remember that readers of *Grue* are mainly seasoned horror fans, and *not* interested or excited by a straight vampire, werewolf or ghost story—they'll see all the signs, and guess where you're going long before you get there. Throw a new angle on what you're doing; put it in a new light. How? Well, what scares *you*? What's *your* personal phobia or anxiety? When the writer is genuinely, emotionally involved with his subject matter, and is totally honest with himself and his reader, then we can't help being involved, too, and that's where good writing begins and ends."

HARD ROW TO HOE DIVISION, Misty Hill Press, P.O. Box 541-I, Healdsburg CA 95448. (707)433-9786. **Editor:** Joe Armstrong. Newsletter: 8½ × 11; 12 pages; 60 lb. white paper; illustrations and photos. "Book reviews, short story and poetry of rural USA including environmental and nature subjects." Triannually. Estab. 1982. Circ. 150.

● *Hard Row to Hoe* was called "one of ten best literary newsletters in the U.S." by *Small Press* magazine.

Needs: Rural America. Receives 8-10 unsolicited mss/month. Acquires 1 ms/issue; 3-4 mss/year. Publishes ms 6-9 months after acceptance. Length: 1,500 words average; 2,000-2,200 words maximum. Publishes short shorts. Sometimes critiques rejected mss.

How to Contact: Send complete ms with cover letter. Reports in 3-4 weeks on mss. SASE. No simultaneous submissions. Sample copy for $2. Fiction guidelines for legal-size SASE.

Payment/Terms: Pays 2 contributor's copies. Acquires one-time rights.

Advice: "Be certain the subject fits the special need."

$ HARDBOILED, Gryphon Publications, P.O. Box 209, Brooklyn NY 11228-0209. **Editor:** Gary Lovisi. Magazine: Digest-sized; 100 pages; offset paper; color cover; illustrations. Publishes "cutting edge, hard, noir fiction with impact! Query on nonfiction and reviews." Quarterly. Estab. 1988.

● By "hardboiled" the editor does not mean rehashing of pulp detective fiction from the 1940s and 1950s but, rather, realistic, gritty material. Lovisi could be called a pulp fiction "afficionado," however. He also publishes *Paperback Parade* and holds an annual vintage paperback fiction convention each year.

Needs: Mystery/suspense (private eye, police procedural, noir). Receives 40-60 mss/month. Accepts 10-20 mss/year. Publishes ms within 6 months-2 years of acceptance. Published work by Andrew Vachss, Joe Lansdale, Bill Nolan, Richard Lupoff, Bill Pronzini and Eugene Izzi. **Published many new writers within the last year.** Length: 2,000 words minimum; 3,000 words maximum. Sometimes critiques rejected mss and recommends other markets.

How to Contact: Query first or send complete ms with cover letter. Query with SASE only on anything over 3,000 words. No full-length novels. Reports in 1 month on queries; 1-2 months on mss. SASE. Simultaneous submissions OK, but query first. Sample copy for $8. Subscriptions are 5 issues $35.

Payment/Terms: Pays $5-50 on publication and 2 contributor's copies for first North American serial rights. Copyright reverts to author.

N **HAWAII PACIFIC REVIEW** Hawaii Pacific University, 1060 Bishop St., Honolulu HI 96813. (808)544-1107. **Fiction Editor:** Catherine Sustana. Magazine: 6×9; 100-150 pages; quality paper; glossy cover; illustrations and original artwork. "The *Review* seeks to reflect the cultural diversity that is the hallmark of Hawaii Pacific University. Consequently, we welcome material on a wide variety of themes and we encourage experimental styles and narrative techniques. Categories: fiction, poetry, personal essays." Annually. Estab. "nationwide in 1988."

Needs: Adventure, contemporary, ethnic, experimental, fantasy, humor/satire, literary, mainstream, regional, science fiction, translations. No romance, confessions, religious or juvenile. Receives approx. 50 unsolicited fiction mss/month. Accepts 4-8 mss/issue. Reading period is September 1 through December 31. Publishes ms 3-12 months after acceptance. **Published new writers within the last year.** Length: 5,000 words maximum. Publishes short shorts. Also publishes literary essays, poetry. Sometimes critiques rejected mss or recommends other markets.

How to Contact: Send complete manuscript with cover letter, which should include a brief bio. Reports in 4 months. SASE. Simultaneous submissions OK. Fiction guidelines for #10 SASE.

Payment/Terms: Pays in contributor's copies. Acquires first North American serial rights. Rights revert to author upon publication.

N **HEIST MAGAZINE,** P.O. Box 2, Newcastle University Union, Callaghan NSW 2308 Australia. 0419-316-625. E-mail: matthew@mockfrog.com. Website: www.mockfrog.com/heist (includes writer's guidelines). **Editor:** Matthew Ward. Magazine : 32 pages; bond 80 gsm paper; 150 gsm gloss cover; illustrations and photographs. "*Heist Magazine* aims to capture the essense of male-dom through writing and art." Quarterly. Estab. 1998. Circ. 1,000.

• *Heist* has received the Mannering Prize for Fiction.

Needs: Adventure, erotica, experimental, family saga, fantasy (space fantasy, sword and sorcery), historical (general), horror (dark fantasy, futuristic, psychological, supernatural), humor satire, literary, mainstream, military/war, mystery/suspense (amateur sleuth, police procedural, private eye/hardboiled, Bindaburra), science fiction (hard science/technological, soft/sociological), short story collections, thriller/espionage, western (frontier saga, traditional), men. "We do not want chapters from unpublished novels. We want short stories in their entirety." Receives 50 unsolicited mss/month. Accepts 15 mss/issue; 60 mss/year. Publishes ms 3 months after acceptance. **Publishes 50% new writers.** Recently published work by Mark Crowley, Jeff Lancaster, Rob Riel and William A. Tyler. Length: 2,500 words average; 3,000 words maximum. Also publishes poetry. Sometimes critiques or comments on rejected mss.

How to Contact: Send complete ms with a cover letter. Accepts queries/mss by e-mail. Include estimated word count, 50 word bio, list of publications, SASE. Reports in 2 weeks on queries; 2 months on mss. Send SASE for reply, return of ms or send a disposable copy of ms. No simultaneous submissions. Sample copy for $5, A4 envelope and IRCs. Fiction guidelines available on website.

Payment/Terms: Pays 1 contributor's copy. Additional copies $5 each. Pays on publication. Acquires first rights. Sometimes sends galleys to author.

Advice: Looks for work "accessible to most readers, not too obscure. Enjoyable. *Heist* is a fiction mag. We usually get too much poetry, so send fiction. Don't send a chapter from that (as yet) unpublished novel. Try to send a slice of life! Read as many of other people's short stories as you can (try Chandler, Carver, Barthelm, Goldsworthy et. al.)."

$ **HOPSCOTCH: THE MAGAZINE FOR GIRLS,** The Bluffton News Publishing & Printing Co., P.O. Box 164, Bluffton OH 45817. (419)358-4610. Fax: (419)358-5027. **Editor:** Marilyn Edwards. Magazine: 7×9; 50 pages; enamel paper; pen & ink illustrations; photographs. Publishes stories for and about girls ages 5-12. Bimonthly. Estab. 1989. Circ. 9,000.

• *Hopscotch* is indexed in the *Children's Magazine Guide* and *Ed Press* and has received a Parents' Choice Gold Medal Award and Ed Press Awards.

Needs: Children's/juvenile (5-9, 10-12 years): adventure, ethnic/multicultural, fantasy, historical (general), sports. Upcoming themes: "Friendship;" "Penpals;" "Sisters;" "Pets;" "Poetry;" "Different Schools;" "Dolls;" "Hamsters;" "Names;" "The Circus;" "Horses;" and "Zoo Animals." "All writers should consult the theme list before sending in articles." Current theme list available for SASE. Receives 300-400 unsolicited mss/month. Accepts 20-40 mss/year. Agented fiction 2%. Published work by Lois Grambling, Betty Killion, Jean Patrick and VaDonna Jean Leaf. Length: 500-750 words preferred; 300 words minimum; 750 words maximum. Publishes short shorts. Length: 250-400 words. Also publishes poetry, puzzles, hidden pictures and crafts. Always comments on rejected mss.

How to Contact: Send complete ms with cover letter. Include estimated word count, 1-page bio, Social Security number and list of publications. Reports in 2-4 weeks on queries; 6-10 weeks on mss. Send SASE for reply, return of ms or send disposable copy of the ms. Simultaneous and reprint submissions OK. Sample copy for $3. Fiction guidelines for #10 SASE. Reviews novels and short story collections.

Payment/Terms: Pays 5¢/word (extra for usable photos or illustrations) before publication and 1 contributor's copy for first North American serial rights; additional copies $4; $2.50 for 10 or more.

Advice: "Make sure you have studied copies of our magazine to see what we like. Follow our theme list. We are looking for wholesome stories. This is what our publication is all about."

HURRICANE ALICE, A Feminist Quarterly, Hurricane Alice Fn., Inc., Dept. of English, Rhode Island College, Providence RI 02908. (401)456-8377. E-mail: mreddy@grog.ric.edu. **Executive Editor:** Maureen Reddy. Fiction is collectively edited. Tabloid: 11×17; 12-16 pages; newsprint stock; illustrations and photos. "We look for feminist fictions with a certain analytic snap, for serious readers, seriously interested in emerging forms of feminist art/artists." Quarterly. Estab. 1983. Circ. 600-700.

Needs: Experimental, feminist, gay, humor/satire, lesbian, science fiction, translations, work by young women. "No coming-out stories, defloration stories, abortion stories, dreary realism. Would like to see more speculative and experimental fiction." Receives 30 unsolicited mss/month. Publishes 8-10 stories annually. Publishes mss up to 1 year after acceptance. Published work by Vickie Nelson, Mary Sharratt and Kathryn Duhamel. **Publishes 4-5 new writers/year.** Length: up to 3,500 words maximum. Publishes short shorts. Occasionally critiques rejected mss.

How to Contact: Send complete ms with cover letter. "A brief biographical statement is never amiss. Writers should be sure to tell us if a piece was commissioned by one of the editors." Reports in 6-9 months. SASE for response. Simultaneous submissions OK, but must be identified as such. Sample copy for $2.50, 11×14 SAE and 2 first-class stamps.

Payment/Terms: Pays 6 contributor's copies. Acquires one-time rights.

Advice: "Fiction is a craft. Just because something happened, it isn't a story; it becomes a story when you transform it through your art, your craft."

$ IN THE FAMILY, The Magazine for Lesbians, Gays, Bisexuals and their Relations P.O. Box 5387, Takoma Park MD 20913. (301)270-4771. Fax: (301)270-4660. E-mail: helenalips@aol.com. Website: www.inthefamily.com (includes writer's guidelines, bulletin board, back issues and current issue descriptions). Editor: Laura Markowitz. **Fiction Editor:** Helena Lipstadt. Magazine: 8½×11, 32 pages; coated paper; coated cover; illustrations and photos. "We use a therapy lens to explore the diverse relationships and families of lesbians, gays, bisexuals and their straight relations." Quarterly. Estab. 1995. Circ. 2,000.

● Received 1997 Excellence in Media Award from the American Association for Marriage and Family Therapy. Member of IPA.

Needs: Ethnic/multicultural, feminist, gay, humor/satire, lesbian. No erotica. Would like to see more short stories. List of upcoming themes available for SASE. Receives 25 unsolicited mss/month. Accepts 1 ms/issue; 4 mss/ year. Publishes ms 3-6 months after acceptance. Published work by Ellen Hawley, Daniel Cox, Shoshana Daniel and Martha Davis. **Publishes 2 new writers/year.** Length: 2,000 words average; 2,500 words maximum. Publishes short shorts. Also publishes literary essays and poetry. Sometimes critiques or comments on rejected mss.

How to Contact: Send complete ms with a cover letter. Include estimated word count and 40-word bio. Reports in 6 weeks on queries and mss. Send SASE for reply, return of ms or send disposable copy of ms. Sample copy for $5.50. Fiction guidelines free. Reviews novels and short story collections. Send books to Book Review Editor.

Payment/Terms: Pays $25 minimum; $50 maximum plus free subscription to magazine and 5 contributor's copies for first rights.

Advice: "Story must relate to our theme of gay/lesbian/bi relationships and family in some way. Read a few issues and get a sense for what we publish. Shorter is better. Go deep, write from the gut, but not just your pain; also your joy and insight."

ITALIAN AMERICANA, URI/CCE 80 Washington St., Providence RI 02903-1803. (401)277-5306. Fax: (401)277-5100. Website: www.uri.edu/prov/italian/italian.html (includes writer's guidelines, names of editors). **Editors:** Carol Bonomo Albright and John Paul Russo. Poetry Editor: Dana Gioia. Magazine: 6×9; 200 pages; varnished cover; perfect-bound; photographs. "*Italian Americana* contains historical articles, fiction, poetry and memoirs, all concerning the Italian experience in the Americas." Semiannually. Estab. 1974. Circ. 1,200.

Needs: Italian American: literary. No nostalgia. Receives 10 mss/month. Accepts 3 mss/issue; 6-7 mss/year. Publishes up to 1 year after acceptance. Agented fiction 5%. Recently published work by Mary Caponegro and Tony Ardizzone. **Publishes 1-2 new writers/year.** Length: 20 double-spaced pages. Publishes short stories. Also publishes literary essays, literary criticism, poetry. Sometimes critiques rejected mss. Sponsors $500-1,000 literature prize annually.

How to Contact: Send complete ms (in triplicate) with a cover letter. Accepts queries/mss by fax. Include 3-5 line bio, list of publications. Reports in 1 month on queries; 2 months on mss. Send SASE for reply, return of ms or send a disposable copy of ms. No simultaneous submissions. Sample copy for $6. Fiction guidelines for

SASE. Reviews novels and short story collections. Send books to Professor John Paul Russo, English Dept., Univ. of Miami, Coral Gables, FL 33124.

Payment/Terms: Awards $250 to best fiction of year and 1 contributor's copy; additional copies $7. Acquires first North American serial rights.

Advice: "Please individualize characters, instead of presenting types (i.e., lovable uncle, etc.). No nostalgia."

JEWISH CURRENTS MAGAZINE, 22 E. 17th St., New York NY 10003-1919. Phone/fax: (212)924-5740. **Editor-in-Chief:** Morris U. Schappes. Magazine: 5½×8½; 48 pages. "We are a secular, progressive, independent Jewish monthly, pro-Israel though not Zionist, printing fiction, poetry articles and reviews on Jewish politics and history, Holocaust/Resistance; mideast peace process, Black-Jewish relations, labor struggles, women's issues. Audience left/progressive, Jewish." Monthly. Estab. 1946. Circ. 2,000.

● This magazine may be slow to respond. They continue to be backlogged.

Needs: Contemporary, ethnic, feminist, historical, humor/satire, literary, senior citizen/retirement, translations. "We are interested in *authentic* experience and readable prose; humanistic orientation. Must have Jewish theme. Could use more humor; short, smart, emotional and intellectual impact. No religious, sectarian; no porn or hard sex, no escapist stuff. Go easy on experimentation, but we're interested." Upcoming themes (submit at least 3 months in advance): "Black-Jewish Relations" (February); "Holocaust/Resistance" (April); "Israel" (May); "Jews in the USSR & Ex-USSR" (July-August). Receives 6-10 unsolicited fiction mss/month. Accepts 0-1 ms/issue; 8-10 mss/year. Published work by Grace Paley, Paul Robeson, Jr., Robert Meeropol and Andrew Furman. **Publishes 9-12 new writers/year.** Length: 1,000 words minimum; 3,000 words maximum; 1,800 words average. Also publishes literary essays, literary criticism, poetry.

How to Contact: Send complete ms with cover letter. "Writers should include brief biographical information, especially their publishing histories." SASE. No simultaneous submissions. Reports in 2 months on mss. Publishes ms 2-24 months after acceptance. Sample copy for $3 with SAE and 3 first-class stamps. Reviews novels and short story collections.

Payment/Terms: Pays complimentary one-year subscription and 6 contributor's copies. "We readily give reprint permission at no charge." Sends galleys to author.

Advice: Noted for "stories with Jewish content and personal Jewish experience—e.g., immigrant or Holocaust memories, assimilation dilemmas, dealing with Jewish conflicts OK. Space is increasingly a problem. Be intelligent, imaginative, intuitive and absolutely honest. Have a musical ear, and an ear for people: how they sound when they talk, and also hear what they don't say."

$JEWISH QUARTERLY, P.O. Box 2078, London W1A1JR England. E-mail: jewish.quarterly@ort.org. Website: www.ortnet.org/communit/jq/start.htm (includes magazine info, covers, excerpts from articles). **Editor:** Matthew Reisz. Quarterly. Publishes 1-3 contribution of fiction/issue.

Needs: "It deals in the broadest sense with all issues of Jewish interest." Length: 1,500 words minimum; 7,000 words maximum.

Payment/Terms: Payment for accepted items £50.

Advice: "Work should have either a Jewish theme in the widest interpretation of that phrase or a theme which would interest our readership. The question which contributors should ask is 'Why should it appear in the *Jewish Quarterly* and not in another periodical?'"

JEWISH VEGETARIAN NEWSLETTER, 6938 Reliance Road, Federalsburg MD 21632-2722. (410)754-5550. E-mail: imossman@skipjack.bluecrab.org. Website: www.orbyss.com (includes sample newsletter). Editor: Evan Mossman. **Fiction Editor:** Israel Mossman. Magazine: 8½×11; 16 pages; 50 lb. paper; 50 lb. cover; illustrations and photos. "Quarterly newsletter on Jewish vegetarianism in the U.S. Publishes short stories on animal rights and the environment." Estab. 1983. Circ. 800.

Needs: Ethnic/multicultural (Jewish), science fiction (environmental), young adult/teen, animal rights, environment, vegetarianism. Receives several unsolicited mss/month. Accepts 1 ms/issue, 4 mss/year. Publishes ms 3 month to 1 year after acceptance. **Publishes several new writers/year.** Length: 1 page, single spaced. Also publishes poetry.

How to Contact: Send complete ms with a cover letter. Include 3 sentence bio. Reports in 1 month on mss. Send SASE for reply, return of ms or send disposable copy of ms. Simultaneous and reprint submissions OK. Sample copy for #10 SAE with 2 first-class stamps.

Payment/Terms: Pays free subscription to magazine and 4 contributor's copies. Acquires first rights. Not copyrighted.

Advice: "Stories must not be graphic or bitter."

INTERESTED IN A PARTICULAR GENRE? Check our sections for: **Mystery/ Suspense**, page 46; **Romance**, page 55; **Science Fiction & Fantasy**, page 67.

JOURNAL OF POLYMORPHOUS PERVERSITY Wry-Bred Press, Inc., 10 Waterside Plaza, Suite 20-B, New York NY 10010. (212)689-5473. E-mail: info@psychhumor.com. Website: www.psychhumor.com. **Editor:** Glenn Ellenbogen. Magazine: 6¾×10; 24 pages; 60 lb. paper; antique india cover stock; illustrations with some articles. "*JPP* is a humorous and satirical journal of psychology, psychiatry, and the closely allied mental health disciplines." For "psychologists, psychiatrists, social workers, psychiatric nurses, *and* the psychologically sophisticated layman." Semiannally. Estab. 1984.

Needs: Humor/satire. "We only consider materials that are funny or that relate to psychology *or* behavior." Receives 50 unsolicited mss/month. Accepts 8 mss/issue; 16 mss/year. **"Most writers published last year were previously unpublished writers."** Length: 1,500 words average; 4,000 words maximum. Comments on rejected mss.

How to Contact: Send complete ms *in triplicate.* Include cover letter and SASE. Reports in 1-3 months on mss. SASE. Sample copy for $7. Fiction guidelines for #10 SASE.

Payment/Terms: Pays 2 contributor's copies; additional copies $7.

Advice: "We will *not* look at poetry. We only want to see intelligent spoofs of scholarly psychology and psychiatry articles written in scholarly scientific language. Take a look at *real* journals of psychology and try to lampoon their *style* as much as their content. There are few places to showcase satire of the social sciences, thus we provide one vehicle for injecting a dose of humor into this often too serious area. Occasionally, we will accept a piece of creative writing written in the first person, e.g. 'A Subjective Assessment of the Oral Doctoral Defense Process: I Don't Want to Talk About It, If You Want to Know the Truth' (the latter being a piece in which Holden Caulfield shares his experiences relating to obtaining his Ph.D. in Psychology). Other creative pieces have involved a psychodiagnostic evaluation of The Little Prince (as a psychiatric patient) and God being refused tenure (after having created the world) because of insufficient publications and teaching experience."

KRAX MAGAZINE, 63 Dixon Lane, Leeds LS12 4RR, Yorkshire, Britain, U.K. **Fiction Editor:** Andy Robson. Appears 1-2 times/year.

Needs: "We publish mostly poetry of a lighthearted nature but use comic or spoof fiction, witty and humorous essays." Publishes 1 story/issue. Length: 2,000 words maximum.

How to Contact: No specific guidelines.

Payment/Terms: Pays contributor's copies. Sample copy for $1 direct to editor.

Advice: "Don't spend too long on scene-setting or character construction as this inevitably produces an anticlimax in a short piece. Send IRCs or currency notes for return postal costs."

LEFT CURVE, P.O. Box 472, Oakland CA 94604. (510)763-7193. E-mail: leftcurv@wco.com. Website: www.ncal.verio.com/~leftcurv. **Editor:** Csaba Polony. Magazine: 8½×11; 130 pages; 60 lb. paper; 100 pt. C1S Durosheen cover; illustrations; photos. "*Left Curve* is an artist-produced journal addressing the problem(s) of cultural forms emerging from the crises of modernity that strive to be independent from the control of dominant institutions, based on the recognition of the destructiveness of commodity (capitalist) systems to all life." Published irregularly. Estab. 1974. Circ. 2,000.

Needs: Contemporary, ethnic, experimental, historical, literary, prose poem, regional, science fiction, translations, political. "We publish critical, open, social/political-conscious writing." Upcoming theme: "Cyber-space and Nature." Receives approximately 12 unsolicited fiction mss/month. Accepts approximately 1 ms/issue. Publishes ms a maximum of 12 months after acceptance. Published work by Pēter Lengyel and Michael Filas. Length: 1,200 words average; 500 words minimum; 2,500 words maximum. Publishes short shorts. Sometimes comments on rejected mss.

How to Contact: Send complete ms with cover letter. Include "statement of writer's intent, brief bio and reason for submitting to *Left Curve*." Electronic submissions OK; "prefer 3½ disk and hard copy, though we do accept e-mail submissions." Reports in 3-6 months. SASE. Sample copy for $10, 9×12 SAE and $1.24 postage. Fiction guidelines for 1 first-class stamp.

Payment/Terms: Pays in contributor's copies. Rights revert to author.

Advice: "Dig deep; no superficial personalisms, no corny satire. Be honest, realistic and gorge out the truth you wish to say. Understand yourself and the world. Have writing be a means to achieve or realize what is real."

LOST WORLDS, The Science Fiction and Fantasy Forum, HBD Publishing, P.O. Box 605, Concord NC 28026-0605. Phone/fax: (704)933-7998. **Editor:** Holley B. Drye. Newsletter: 8½×11; 48 pages; 24 lb. bond paper; full-color cover; b&w illustrations. "General interest science fiction and fantasy, as well as some specialized genre writing. For broad-spectrum age groups, anyone interested in newcomers." Monthly. Estab. 1988. Circ. 150.

Needs: Experimental, fantasy, horror, psychic/supernatural/occult, science fiction (hard science, soft/sociological), serialized novel. Publishes annual special fiction issue. Receives 35-45 unsolicited mss/month. Accepts 10-14 mss/issue; 100 and up mss/year. Publishes ms 1 year after acceptance (unless otherwise notified). Length: 3,000 words preferred; 2,000 words minimum; 5,500 words maximum. Publishes short shorts. Sometimes critiques rejected mss and recommends other markets. "Although we do not publish every type of genre fiction, I will, if asked, critique anyone who wishes to send me their work. There is no fee for reading or critiquing stories."

How to Contact: Query first. "Cover letters should include where and when to contact the author, a pen name, if one is preferred, as well as their real name, and whether or not they wish their real names to be kept confidential. Due to overwhelming response, we are currently unable to predict response time to mss or queries. Phone calls are welcome to check on manuscripts." SASE for return of ms. Simultaneous and reprint submissions OK. Accepts electronic submissions via disk or modem. Sample copy for $5. Fiction guidelines free.

Payment/Terms: Pays contributor's copies. Acquires one-time rights.

Advice: "I look for originality of story, good characterization and dialogue, well-written descriptive passages, and over-all story quality. The presentation of the work also makes a big impression, whether it be good or bad. Neat, typed manuscripts will always have a better chance than hand-written or badly typed ones. All manuscripts are read by either three or four different people, with an eye towards development of plot and comparison to other material within the writer's field of experience. Plagiarism is not tolerated, and we do look for it while reading a manuscript under consideration. If you have any questions, feel free to call—we honestly don't mind. Never be afraid to send us anything, we really are kind people."

MAIL CALL JOURNAL, Keeping the Spirit of the Civil War Soldier Alive!, Distant Frontier Press, P.O. Box 5031, Dept. N, South Hackensack NJ 07606. (201)296-0419. E-mail: mcj@historyonline.net. Website: www.historyonline.net. **Managing Editor:** Anna Pansini. Newsletter: 8½×11; 8 pages; 20 lb. paper; illustrations. *Mail Call Journal* focuses on the soldiers' lives during the Civil War and publishes Civil War soldiers' letters, diaries, memoirs and stories of the individual soldiers as well as poems. Bimonthly. Estab. 1990. Circ. 500.

Needs: Historical (American Civil War). Receives 20 unsolicited mss/month. Accepts 2 mss/issue; 10 mss/year. Publishes ms up to 2 years after acceptance. **Publishes 10 new writers/year.** Length: 500 words minimum; 1,500 words maximum. Also publishes literary essays, literary criticism and poetry. Sometimes critiques or comments on rejected ms.

How to Contact: Send complete ms with a cover letter mentioning "any relations from the Civil War period for reference only, not a determining factor." Accepts queries/mss by e-mail. Reports in 1 year. SASE for return of ms. Simultaneous, reprint and electronic (disk) submissions OK. Sample copy and fiction guidelines are included in a writer's packet for $5.

Payment/Terms: Pays in contributor's copies. Acquires one-time rights for print and Internet publication.

Advice: Wants more "personal accounts" and no "overused themes. Write from your heart but use your head. Our readers are knowledgeable about the basics of the Civil War, so go beyond that."

★ ○ ◎ **MAJESTIC BOOKS** P.O. Box 19097A, Johnston RI 02919-0097. **Fiction Editor:** Cindy MacDonald. Bound softcover short story anthologies; 5½×8½; 192 pages; 60 lb. paper; C1S cover stock. "Majestic Books is a small press which was formed to give children an outlet for their work. We publish softcover bound anthologies of fictional stories by children, for children and adults who enjoy the work of children." Triannually. Estab. 1993. Circ. 250.

Needs: Stories written on any subject by children (under 18) only. Children's/juvenile (10-12 years), young adult (13-18 years). Receives 50 unsolicited mss/month. Accepts 100 mss/year. Publishes ms 1 year maximum after acceptance. Published work by Jennie Alpert, Gregory Miller and Brian Freeman. **Publishes 100 new writers/year.** Length: 2,000 words maximum. Publishes short shorts. Also publishes literary essays.

How to Contact: Send complete ms with a cover letter. Include estimated word count and author's age. Reports in 3 weeks. Send SASE for reply. Simultaneous submissions OK. Sample copy for $5. Fiction guidelines for #10 SASE.

Payment/Terms: Pays 10% royalty for all books sold due to the author's inclusion.

Advice: "We love stories that will keep a reader thinking long after they have read the last word. Be original. We have received some manuscripts of shows we have seen on television or books we have read. Write from inside you and you'll be surprised at how much better your writing will be. Use *your* imagination."

Ⓝ ★ $ ○ **MAYHEM, The Magazine of Thriller & Suspense**, P.O. Box 827, Clifton Park NY 12065-0801. (518)664-3478. E-mail: mayhem@mediasi.com. Website: www.mediasi.com/chantingmonks (includes guidelines, highlights, features, story portions). **Editor:** Pamela Hazelton. Magazine: 6½×10¼; 48 pages; newsprint; glossy cover; illustrations and photos. "We feature only thriller, suspense and true crime. No anticipated endings." Quarterly. Estab. 1999. Circ. 2,000-3,000.

Needs: Mystery/suspense (amateur sleuth, police procedural, private eye/hardboiled). "No romance mysteries." Receives 70 unsolicited mss/month. Accepts 6-10 mss/issue; 35-40 mss/year. Publishes ms 3-9 months after acceptance. **Publishes 9-12 new writers/year.** Length: 2,500 words average; 1,000 words minimum; 3,500 words maximum. Publishes short shorts. Length: 500 words. Often critiques or comments on rejected ms.

How to Contact: Send complete ms with a cover letter. Include estimated word count. Reports in 3 weeks on queries; 6 weeks on mss. Send SASE for reply, return of ms or send a disposable copy of ms. Reprint submissions OK. Sample copy for $3.95. Reviews novel, short story collections and nonfiction books of interest to writers. Send books to editor.

Payment/Terms: Pays 1/2-3¢/word and 5 contributor's copies on publication for first North American serial rights; additional copies $2.

Advice: "The first paragraph needs to grab us and help lead us into the story. We look for finely-tuned writing void of unnecessary run-on sentences. Manuscripts must be unique. Always include a SASE and refrain from telling the editor how new you are (save that for later). Don't say something like 'your fine publication.' It tells us you've never read the magazine. And, by all means, don't tell us the magazine 'lacks substance' so you're sending a story that will be much better."

★ ✓ ◎ **MEDICINAL PURPOSES, Literary Review**, Poet to Poet Inc., 86-37 120 St., #2D, % Catterson, Richmond Hill NY 11418. (718)776-8853, (718)847-2150. E-mail: scarptp@worldnet.att.com. Website: poettopoet.com (includes writer's guidelines, samples of published work and announcements for open readings). **Editors:** Robert Dunn and Thomas M. Catterson. Magazine: 8½×5½; 64 pages; illustrations. "*Medicinal Purposes* publishes quality work that will benefit the world, though not necessarily through obvious means." Triannually. Estab. 1995. Circ. 1,000.

Needs: Adventure, erotica, ethnic/multicultural, experimental, fantasy, feminist, gay, historical, horror, humor/satire, lesbian, literary, mainstream/contemporary, mystery/suspense, psychic/supernatural/occult, regional, romance, science fiction, senior citizen/retirement, sports, westerns, young adult/teen. "Please no pornography, or hatemongering." Receives 15 unsolicited mss/month. Accepts 2-3 mss/issue; 8 mss/year. Publishes ms up to four issues after acceptance. Published work by Lisa Meyer and David Huberman. **Publishes 100 new writers/year.** Length: 2,000 words average; 50 words minimum; 3,000 words maximum. "We prefer maximum of 10 double-spaced pages." Publishes short shorts. Also publishes literary essays, literary criticism, poetry. Sometimes critiques or comments on rejected mss.

How to Contact: Send complete ms with a cover letter. Include estimated word count, brief bio, Social Security number. Reports in 6 weeks on queries; 8 weeks on mss. SASE. Simultaneous and electronic submissions (modem through e-mail) OK. Sample copy for $6, 6×9 SAE and 4 first-class stamps. Fiction guidelines free for #10 SASE.

Payment/Terms: Pays 2 contributor's copies. Acquires first rights.

Advice: "One aspect of the better stories we've seen is that the writer enjoys (or, at least, believes in) the tale being told. Also, learn the language—good English can be a beautiful thing. We long for stories that only a specific writer can tell, by virtue of experience or style. Expand our horizons. Clichés equal death around here."

★ ◎ ◎ **MEDIPHORS, A Literary Journal of the Health Professions**, P.O. Box 327, Bloomsburg PA 17815. E-mail: mediphor@ptd.net. Website: www.mediphors.org (includes writer's guidelines, names of editors, samples of short stories, essays, poetry, photography, covers and current contents, art and more). **Editor:** Eugene D. Radice, MD. Magazine: 8½×11; 73 pages; 20 lb. white paper; 70 lb. cover; illustrations and photos. "We publish broad work related to medicine and health including essay, short story, commentary, fiction, poetry. Our audience: general readers and health care professionals." Semiannually. Estab. 1993. Circ. 900.

Needs: "Short stories related to health." Adventure, experimental, historical, humor/satire, literary, mainstream/contemporary, science fiction (hard science, soft/sociological), medicine. "No religious, romance, suspense, erotica, fantasy." Receives 50 unsolicited mss/month. Accepts 14 mss/issue; 28 mss/year. Publishes ms 10 months after acceptance. Agented fiction 2%. **Publishes 10 new writers/year.** Length: 2,500 words average; 4,500 words maximum. Publishes short shorts. Also publishes literary essays and poetry. Sometimes critiques or comments on rejected mss.

How to Contact: Send complete ms with a cover letter. Include estimated word count, bio (paragraph) and any experience/employment in the health professions. Reports in 4 months on mss. Send SASE for reply, return of ms or send a disposable copy of ms. No simultaneous submissions. Sample copy for $6. Fiction guidelines for #10 SASE.

Payment/Terms: Pays 2 contributor's copies; additional copies for $5.50 Acquires first North American serial rights.

Advice: Looks for "high quality writing that shows fresh perspective in the medical and health fields. Accurate knowledge of subject material. Situations that explore human understanding in adversity. Order a sample copy for examples of work. Start with basic quality writing in short story and create believable, engaging stories concerning medicine and health. Knowledge of the field is important since the audience includes professionals within the medical field. Don't be discouraged. We enjoy receiving work from beginning writers."

$ ◎ **THE MIRACULOUS MEDAL**, The Central Association of the Miraculous Medal, 475 E. Chelten Ave., Philadelphia PA 19144. (215)848-1010. **Editor:** Rev. William J. O'Brien, C.M. Magazine. Quarterly.

Needs: Religious/inspirational. Receives 25 unsolicited fiction mss/month. Accepts 2 mss/issue; 8 mss/year. Publishes ms up to two years or more after acceptance.

How to Contact: Query first with SASE. Sample copy and fiction guidelines free.

Payment/Terms: Pays 2¢/word minimum. Pays on acceptance for first rights.

◻ **MOUNTAIN LUMINARY**, P.O. Box 1187, Mountain View AR 72560-1187. (870)585-2260. Fax: (870)269-4110. E-mail: ecomtn@mvtel.net. **Editor:** Anne Thiel. Magazine; photos. "*Mountain Luminary* is dedicated to bringing information to people about the Aquarian Age; how to grow with its new and evolutionary energies and how to work with the resultant changes in spirituality, relationships, environment and the planet. *Mountain Luminary* provides a vehicle for people to share ideas, philosophies and experiences that deepen understanding of this evolutionary process and humankind's journey on Earth." International quarterly. Estab. 1985.

Needs: Humor/satire, metaphor/inspirational/Aquarian-Age topics. Accepts 8-10 mss/year. Publishes ms 6 months after acceptance. Published work by Gerald Lewis, Robert L. Mayne and Anne Brewer. **Publishes 6 new writers/year.**

How to Contact: Query with clips of published work. SASE for return of ms. Accepts queries/mss by fax and e-mail. Simultaneous and electronic submissions (Mac IIci, Quark XP) OK. Sample copy and writer's guidelines free.

Payment/Terms: Pays 1 contributor's copy. "We may offer advertising space as payment." Acquires first rights.

Advice: "We look for stories with a moral—those with insight to problems on the path which raise the reader's awareness. Topical interests include: New Age/Aquarian Age, astrology, crystals, cultural and ethnic concerns, dreams, ecosystems, the environment, extraterrestrials, feminism, folklore, healing and health, holistic and natural health, inspiration, juvenile and teen issues, lifestyle, meditation, men's issues, metaphysics, mysticism, nutrition, parallel dimensions, prayer, psychic phenomenon, self-help, spirituality and women's issues."

⊠ $◻◎▨ **MURDEROUS INTENT, Mystery Magazine** Madison Publishing Company. (360)695-9004. Fax: (360)693-3354. E-mail: madison@teleport.com. Website: www.teleport.com/~madison (includes writer's guidelines, short fiction, articles, interviews, table of contents, minisynopsis corner, subscription and convention information). **Editor:** Margo Power. Magazine: 8½×11; 64 pages; newsprint; glossy 2-color cover; illustrations; photos, cozy/soft boiled mystery magazine publishing fiction, nonfiction and interviews. Quarterly. Estab. 1995. Circ. 7,000.

• *Murderous Intent* ranked #5 in *Writer's Digest* Fiction 50 list of top markets for fiction writers. Several authors have been short fiction Derringer Award recipients, Edgar nominees, and one story was purchased for a film.

Needs: Mystery/suspense (amateur sleuth, cozy, police procedural, private eye), psychic/supernatural/occult, science fiction (with mystery) "occasionally." No true crime, no cannibal stories, no stories with excessive violence, language or sex. (Nothing but mystery/suspense with a little ghostly presence now and then). Receives 200 unsolicited queries/month. Accepts 10-14 mss/issue; 40-48 mss/year. Publishes ms up to 1 year after acceptance. Published work by Robert Randell, Toni L.P. Kelner, Carol Cail, Michael Mallory, Seymour Shubin and L.L. Thrasher. Publishes 10 or more new writers/year. **Publishes 30% new writers/year.** Length: 2,000-4,000 words average; 250 words minimum; 5,000 words maximum. Publishes short shorts. Length: 250-400 words. Also publishes mystery-related essays and poetry. Sometimes critiques or comments on rejected mss. Annual contest, 2,000 words, mystery. Deadline: August 1. $10 entry fee. SASE. E-mail for guidelines, different theme each year.

How to Contact: Email queries only. Include a brief story synopsis, word count, telephone number, e-mail and address. "If it looks like something that fits the magazine we will send guidelines for submitting the story. All snail mail submissions will be returned unopened." Only 1 story/submission. Reports in 1 week on queries, 1-2 weeks on mss. Sample copy for $5.95, 9×12 SAE and 4 first-class stamps. Guidelines for #10 SASE. "Minisynopsis Corner" for authors to submit minisynopses of their new mystery novels (free).

Payment/Terms: Pays $10 and 2 contributor's copies on acceptance; additional copies for $3.50 (issue their story appears in). Acquires first North American serial rights.

Advice: "The competition is tough so write the mystery you love—build characters people will remember— and surprise us."

◪ **MY LEGACY,** Weems Concepts, HCR-13, Box 21AA, Artemas PA 17211-9405. (814)458-3102. **Editor:** Kay Weems. Magazine: digest size; 125-150 pages; white paper; 20 lb. colored paper cover; illustrations. "Work must be in good taste. No bad language. Audience is from all walks of life," adults and children. Quarterly. Estab. 1991. Circ. 200.

Needs: Adventure, children's/juvenile (10-12 years), fantasy (children's fantasy, science fantasy), historical, horror, humor/satire, mainstream/contemporary, mystery/suspense (amateur sleuth, cozy, police procedural, private eye/hardboiled, romantic suspense), regional, religious/inspirational, romance (contemporary, futuristic/time travel, gothic, historical), science fiction (hard science, soft/sociological), senior citizen/retirement, westerns (frontier, traditional), young adult/teen (adventure, mystery, science fiction, western). No porno. List of upcoming themes available for SASE. Publishes special fiction issues or anthologies. Receives 15-30 unsolicited mss/month. Accepts 30-35 mss/issue; 120-140 mss/year. Publishes ms within 1 year after acceptance. Published work by Peter Gauthier, Jel D.Lewis (Jones); Brucie Jacobs, Joseph Farley, Mark Scott and Gerri George. Length: 2,500 words average. Publishes short shorts. Very seldom critiques or comments on rejected mss; "usually don't have time."

How to Contact: Send complete ms with a cover letter. Include estimated word count, bio (short paragraph) and list of publications. Reports within 1 year on mss. Send SASE for reply, return of ms or send a disposable copy of ms (preferable). Simultaneous and reprint submissions OK. Sample copy for $3.50, 9×6½ SAE and $1.70 postage. Fiction guidelines for #10 SASE.

Payment/Terms: Acquires one-time rights.

Advice: Looks for "a good beginning, tight writing, good conversations, believable characters and believable ending."

$☐ MYSTERY TIME, An Anthology of Short Stories, Hutton Publications, P.O. Box 2907, Decatur IL 62524. **Editor:** Linda Hutton. Booklet: 5½×8½; 52 pages; bond paper; illustrations. "Semiannual collection of short stories with a suspense or mystery theme for mystery buffs, with an emphasis on women writers and women protagonists." Estab. 1983.
Needs: Mystery/suspense only. Features older women as protagonists. Receives 10-15 unsolicited fiction mss/month. Accepts 20-24 mss/year. Published work by Patricia Crandall, Marian Poe and Vera Searles. **Published new writers within the last year.** Length: 1,500 words maximum. Occasionally critiques rejected mss and recommends other markets.
How to Contact: Send complete ms with SASE. "No cover letters." Simultaneous and previously published submissions OK. Reports in 1 month on mss. Publishes ms an average of 6-8 months after acceptance. Reprint submissions OK. Sample copy for $4. Fiction guidelines for #10 SASE.
Payment/Terms: Pays ¼-1¢/word and 1 contributor's copy; additional copies $2.50. Acquires one-time rights.
Advice: "Study a sample copy and the guidelines. Too many amateurs mark themselves as amateurs by submitting blindly."

$☑ NEW ENGLAND WRITERS' NETWORK, P.O. Box 483, Hudson MA 01749-0483. (978)562-2946. Fax: (978)568-0497. E-mail: newn4u@aol.com. Editor: Glenda Baker. **Fiction Editor:** Liz Aleshire. Poetry Editor: Judy Adourian. Magazine: 8½×11; 24 pages; coated cover. "We are devoted to helping new writers get published and to teaching through example and content. We are looking for well-written stories that grab us from the opening paragraph." Quarterly. Estab. 1994. Circ. 200.
• *New England Writers' Network* has a new feature called First Fiction. A story by a previously unpublished fiction writer is spotlighted under the heading First Fiction.
Needs: Adventure, condensed/excerpted novel, ethnic/multicultural, humor/satire, literary, mainstream/contemporary, mystery/suspense, religious/inspirational, romance. "We will consider anything except pornography or extreme violence." Accepts 5 mss/issue; 20 mss/year. Reads mss only from June 1 through September 1. Publishes ms 4-12 months after acceptance. Published work by Arline Chase, James Calandrillo, Edward Allen Faine, Nick Hubacker and Steve Burt. **Publishes 4-6 new writers/year.** Length: 2,000 words maximum. Publishes short shorts. Also publishes poetry and 3-4 personal essays per issue. Always critiques or comments on rejected mss.
How to Contact: Send complete ms with a cover letter. Include estimated word count. Bio on acceptance. Reports in 4 months. SASE for return of ms. No simultaneous submissions. Sample copy for $5.50. Fiction guidelines free. "We do not review story collections or novels. We do publish 2,000 words (maximum) novel excerpts. Writer picks the excerpt—do not send novel."
Payment/Terms: Pays $10 for fiction, $5 for personal essays, $3 per poem on publication and 1 contributor's copy. Acquires first North American serial rights.
Advice: "Give us a try! Please send for guidelines and a sample."

$☑ NEWFANGLED FAIRY TALES and GIRLS TO THE RESCUE, Meadowbrook Press, 5451 Smetana Dr., Minnetonka MN 55343. (612)930-1100. **Editor:** Bruce Lansky. Assistant Editor: Jason Sanford. Anthology series for children ages 8-12. Each book is published semiannually.
Needs: Children's/juvenile short stories (8-12 years). No novels or picture books. Receives 50-60 unsolicited submissions/month for each series. Accepts 10 mss/issue; 20 mss/year/book. Publishes ms 1 year after acceptance. **Publishes 10-15 new writers/year.** Length: 1,200-1,500 words average; 1,800 words maximum. Sometimes comments on or critiques rejected mss.
How to Contact: Query first. Include estimated word count and list of publications. Reports in 3 months. Send SASE for reply, return of ms or send disposable copy of ms. Simultaneous submissions and reprints OK. Fiction guidelines for #10 SASE. Address all submissions to Jason Sanford, assistant editor.
Payment/Terms: Pays $500 on publication for nonexclusive worldwide rights. Sends galleys to author.
Advice: "Read our guidelines before submitting. All our anthology series for children have very strict guidelines. Also, please read the books to get a feel for what types of stories we publish. Our series consistently feature short stories by previously unpublished writers—we consider stories on their own merits, not on the reputations of the authors."

★ $☑ ▼ NIGHT TERRORS, 1202 W. Market St., Orrville OH 44667-1710. (330)683-0338. E-mail: ded3548@aol.com. Website: users.aol.com/NTMagazine/ (includes updated guidelines, bios of the editor and writers, short fiction, order info, links to other sites of interest to writers and readers of horror). **Editor/Publisher:** D.E. Davidson. Magazine: 8½×11; 52 pages; 80 lb. glossy cover; illustrations and photographs. *Night Terrors* publishes quality horror fiction for literate adults. Quarterly. Estab. 1996. Circ. 1,000.
• *Night Terrors* has had 19 stories listed in the Honorable Mention section of *The Year's Best Fantasy and Horror, Annual Collections.* Five *Night Terrors* stories were nominated for the Horror Writer's Association's Bram Stoker Award for Short Fiction 1997, 1998.
Needs: Horror, psychic/supernatural/occult. "Night Terrors does not accept stories involving abuse, sexual

mutilation or stories with children as main characters. We publish traditional supernatural/psychological horror for a mature audience. Our emphasis is on literate work with a chill." Receives 50 unsolicited mss/month. Accepts 12 mss/issue; 46 mss/year. Publishes ms 2-6 months after acceptance. Published work by A.R. Morlan, J.N. Williamson, Hugh B. Cave, Don D'Ammassa and Dominick Cancilla. **Publishes 12 new writers/year.** Length: 3,000 words average; 2,000 words minimum; 5,000 words maximum. Often critiques or comments on rejected mss.

How to Contact: Send complete ms with a cover letter. Include estimated word count, 50-word bio and list of publications. Reports in 1 week on queries; 3 months on mss. Send SASE for reply, return of ms or send a disposable copy of ms. Simultaneous submissions and reprints OK. Sample copy for $6 (make checks to D.E. Davidson). Fiction guidelines free for #10 SASE.

Payment/Terms: Pays up to $100 on publication and 1-2 contributor's copy; additional copies for $4.50. Acquires first North American serial rights or second rights for reprints. Sends galleys to author.

Advice: "I publish what I like. I like stories which involve me with the viewpoint character and leave me with the feeling that his/her fate could have or might be mine. Act professionally. Check your work for typos, spelling, grammar, punctuation, format. Send your work flat. And if you must, paper clip it, don't staple. Include a brief, to-the-point cover letter."

THE NOCTURNAL LYRIC, Box 115, San Pedro CA 90733. (310)519-9220. E-mail: nlyric@webtv.net. Website: www.Angelfire.com/ca/nocturnallyric (includes fiction guidelines, upcoming authors, sample poetry and links to similar sites). **Editor:** Susan Moon. Digest: 5½×8½; 40 pages; illustrations. "We are a non-profit literary journal, dedicated to printing fiction by new writers for the sole purpose of getting read by people who otherwise might have never seen their work." Bimonthly. Estab. 1987. Circ. 400.

Needs: Experimental, horror, humor/satire, psychic/supernatural/occult, bizarre, poetry. Nothing graphically pornographic. "We will give priority to unusual, creative pieces. We would like to see more thought-provoking fiction." Receives 50 unsolicited mss/month. Publishes ms 10-12 months after acceptance. Recently published work by John Charles Galvin, Lugen Rosen and Janet Paszkowski. **Publishes 20 new writers/year.** Length: 2,000 words maximum. Publishes short shorts. Also publishes poetry.

How to Contact: Send complete ms with cover letter. Accepts queries by e-mail. Include "something about the author, areas of fiction he/she is interested in." Reports in 2 weeks on queries; 6-8 months on mss. SASE. Simultaneous and reprint submissions OK. Sample copy for $3 (checks to Susan Moon). For outside US, sample copy for $4 and use American stamps for SASE. No IRCs. Fiction guidelines for #10 SASE.

Payment/Terms: Pays in gift certificates for subscription discounts. Publication not copyrighted.

Advice: "Please stop wasting your postage sending us things that are in no way bizarre. Do send us your weirdest, most unique creations. Don't pretend you've read us when you haven't! I can usually tell! We're getting more into strange, surrealistic horror and fantasy, or silly, satirical horror. If you're avant-garde, we want you! We're mainly accepting things that are bizarre all the way through, as opposed to ones that only have a surprise bizarre ending."

THE OAK, 1530 Seventh St., Rock Island IL 61201. (309)788-3980. **Editor:** Betty Mowery. Magazine: 8½×11; 8-20 pages. "To provide a showcase for new authors while showing the work of established authors as well; to publish wholesome work, something with a message." Bimonthly. Estab. 1991. Circ. 300.

● "The Gray Squirrel," a section in *Oak*, uses fiction and poetry only from authors age 60 and up.

Needs: Adventure, contemporary, experimental, fantasy, humor, mainstream, prose poem. No erotica or love poetry. Receives 25 mss/month. Accepts up to 12 mss/issue. Publishes ms within 3 months of acceptance. Published 25 new writers/year. **Publishes 10 new writers/year.** Length: 500 words maximum. Publishes short shorts. Length: 200 words.

How to Contact: Send complete ms. Reports in 1 week. SASE. Simultaneous and reprint submissions OK. Sample copy for $3. Subscription $10 for 4 issues.

Payment/Terms: None, but not necessary to buy a copy in order to be published. Acquires first rights.

Advice: "I do not want erotica, extreme violence or killing of humans or animals the sake of killing. Just be yourself when you write. Please include SASE or manuscripts will be destroyed. Be sure name and address are on the manuscript. Study the markets for length of manuscript and what type of material is wanted."

ON SPEC, Box 4727, Edmonton, Alberta T6E 5G6 Canada. Phone/fax: (403)413-0215. E-mail: onspec@earthling.net. Website: www.icomm.ca/onspec (includes writer's guidelines, past editorials, excerpts from published fiction, links to writer's Internet resources). **Contact:** The Editors. Magazine: 5¼×8; 112 pages; illustrations. "Provides a venue for Canadian speculative writing—science fiction, fantasy, horror, magic realism." Quarterly. Estab. 1989. Circ. 2,000.

Needs: Fantasy and science fiction. No condensed or excerpted novels, no religious/inspirational stories. "We would like to see more horror, fantasy, science fiction—well-developed stories with complex characters and strong plots." Receives 50 mss/month. Buys 10 mss/issue; 40 mss/year. "We read manuscripts during the month after each deadline: February 28/May 31/August 31/November 30." Publishes ms 6-12 months after acceptance. **Publishes new writers, number varies.** Length: 4,000 words average; 1,000 words minimum; 6,000 words maximum. Also publishes poetry. Often critiques or comments on rejected mss.

How to Contact: Send complete ms with a cover letter. No submissions by e-mail or fax. Include estimated word count, 2-sentence bio and phone number. Reports in 5 months on mss. SASE for return of ms or send a disposable copy of ms plus #10 SASE for response. Include Canadian postage or IRCs. Simultaneous submissions OK. Sample copy for $6. Fiction guidelines for #10 SASE.

Payment/Terms: Pays $40-180 and 2 contributor's copies; additional copies for $4. Pays on acceptance for first North American serial rights.

Advice: "We're looking for original ideas with a strong SF element, excellent dialogue, and characters who are so believable, our readers will really care about them."

N ◑ PAPYRUS MAGAZINE, Papyrus Literary Enterprises, P.O. Box 270797, West Hartford CT 06127-0797. E-mail: gwhitaker@imagine.com. Website: www.readersndex.com/papyrus (includes writer's guidelines, contest rules, samples of *Papyrus* fiction, nonfiction and poetry). Editor-in-Chief: Ginger Whitaker. Magazine: 8½×11; 32 pages. "*Papyrus* is a quarterly periodical for the cultivation of creative works by black writers but we publish work from anyone interested in writing for a black audience. We seek, in particular, work from the unknown, underpublished or unpublished talented writer." Quarterly. Estab. 1994.

Needs: Ethnic/multicultural. Published work by Niama Leslie Williams, Melanie Hatter, Evelyn Palfrey, P.J. Jason, Eddie L. Myers, Allison Whittenberg and Priya Satia. Length: 1,500 words minimum; 3,500 words maximum. Also publishes literary essays and poetry. "Looking for insightful book reviews of serious fiction and nonfiction. Pays for book reviews, craft articles."

How to Contact: Send complete ms on 3.5 disk along with a printed copy. Macintosh users should submit files in ClarisWorks, Microsoft Word, WordPerfect or MacWrite II format. IBM users should submit files saved in ASCII or RTF format. SASE. No simultaneous submissions. Electronic submissions OK, query first. Sample copy for $2.20 (back copy) or $2.20 (current issue). Fiction guidelines for #10 SASE.

Payment/Terms: Pays contributor's copies. Acquires first rights.

Advice: "Make sure it is literate, easily accessible (on disk), and of interest to African Americans."

◎ PARADOXISM, Anti-literary Journal, University of New Mexico, Gallup NM 87301. Fax: (505)863-7532 (Attn. Dr. Smarandache). E-mail: smarand@unm.edu. Website: www.gallup.unm.edu/~smarandache/. **Editor:** Florentin Smarandache. Magazine: 8½×11; 100 pages; illustrations. "The paradoxism is an avant-garde movement set up by the editor in the 1980s in Romania. It tries to generalize the art, to make the unliterary become literary." Annually. Estab. 1993. Circ. 500.

Needs: "Crazy, uncommon, experimental, avant-garde"; also ethnic/multicultural. Plans specific themes in the next year. Publishes annual special fiction issue or anthology. Receives 3-4 unsolicited mss/month. Accepts 10 mss/issue. Published work by Dan Topa and Anatol Ciocanu. Length: 500 words minimum; 1,000 words maximum. Publishes short shorts. Also publishes literary essays, literary criticism and poetry. Focus on new literary terms such as paradoxist distich, tautological distich, dual distich

How to Contact: Query with clips of unpublished work. Reports in 2 months on mss. Send a disposable copy of ms. Sample copy for $19.95 and 8½×11 SASE.

Payment/Terms: Pays 1 contributor's copy. Not copyrighted.

Advice: "The Basic Thesis of the paradoxism: everything has a meaning and a non-meaning in a harmony each other. The Essence of the paradoxism: a) the sense has a non-sense, and reciprocally b) the non-sense has a sense. The Motto of the paradoxism: 'All is possible, the impossible too!' The Symbol of the paradoxism: (a spiral—optic illusion, or vicious circle)."

❦ ✔ $ ◑ PARSEC, the Alternative View of Sci-Fi, Parsec Publishing Company, % Plaza 69, 1935 Paris St., P.O. Box 21019, Sudbury Ontario P3E 6G6 Canada. (705)523-1831. Fax: (705) 523-5276. E-mail: parsec@isys.on.ca. Website: www.parsec.on.ca. **Editor:** Chris Krejlgaard. Magazine: 8×10¾; 60 pages; newsprint; illustrations and photos. "We accentuate the Canadian content in science fiction, fantasy and horror media projects." Quarterly. Estab. 1995. Circ. 6,000.

● Member of the Canadian Magazine Publishers Association.

Needs: Fantasy (science fantasy, sword and sorcery), horror, science fiction. "No first-person narratives." Publishes special fiction issues or anthologies. Accepts 16 mss/issue. Publishes ms 6-9 months after acceptance. Length: 2,500 words average; 1,500 words minimum; 7,000 words maximum. Often critiques or comments on rejected mss.

How to Contact: Query first; no unsolicited mss accepted. Include estimated word count. Reports in 3 months on queries. Include SASE for reply. Simultaneous and electronic submissions OK. Sample copy for $3. Fiction guidelines for 4×9 SASE. Reviews novels and short story collections. Send books to editor.

Payment/Terms: Pays $75 minimum; $125 maximum on publication plus 2 contributor's copies for first rights.

Advice: "The writer has four paragraphs to hook me. After that it's an uphill climb. A story must be compelling and relevant. Psuedo-science is frowned upon, but well-researched work that follows current work or trends through to a logical end is applauded. Read and know what type of work appears in *Parsec*. Too many authors submit work that clearly isn't suitable in terms of style and genre."

PENNY-A-LINER, P.O. Box 2163, Wenatchee WA 98807-2163. (509)662-7858. E-mail: ptl2163@aol.com. Website: maxpages.com/redrosebushpre (includes writer's guidelines, names of editors, short fiction, letters). **Editor:** Ella M. Dillon. Magazine: 8½×11; 44 pages; book stock paper; coated cover; illustrations and photos. "*Penny-a-Liner* features family reading—positive, entertaining." Triannually.

Needs: Adventure, children's/juvenile (adventure, animal, easy-to-read, fantasy, historical, mystery, preschool, series, sports, all ages), comics/graphic novels, ethnic/multicultural (general), experimental, family saga, fantasy (space fantasy, sword and sorcery), feminist, historical (general), horror (dark fantasy, futuristic, psychological, supernatural), humor satire, literary, mainstream, military/war, mystery/suspense (amateur sleuth, cozy, police procedural, private eye/hardboiled), regional, religious (children's religious, general religious, inspirational, religious fantasy, religious mystery/suspense, religious thriller, religious romance), romance (contemporary, futuristic/time travel, gothic, historical, regency period, romantic suspense), science fiction (hard science/technological, soft/sociological), short story collections, thriller/espionage, translations, western (frontier saga, traditional), young adult/teen (adventure, easy-to-read, fantasy/science fiction, historical, horror, mystery/suspense, problem novels, romance, series, sports, western). "No pornography or explicit sexual content." **Publishes "as many new writers as possible."** Length: 500-2,000 words average; 10-15 words minimum; 3,500 words maximum. Publishes short shorts. Also publishes literary essays, literary criticism and poetry.

How to Contact: Send complete ms with cover letter. Accepts queries/mss by e-mail. Include name and address on each page. Reports in 1 month on queries/mss. SASE for reply or send a disposable copy of ms. Simultaneous submissions and reprints OK. Sample copy and fiction guidelines free.

Payment/Terms: Pays 1¢/word, 1 contributor's copy; additional copies $4 each. Pays on publication. Acquires one-time rights.

Advice: "We encourage submissions from previously unpublished authors. Please type and double space your manuscript, and include year, name and address on each page. Neatness counts. Be friendly and courteous—do not make demands."

THE PIPE SMOKER'S EPHEMERIS, The Universal Coterie of Pipe Smokers, 20-37 120 St., College Point NY 11356-2128. **Editor:** Tom Dunn. Magazine: 8½×11; 84-96 pages; offset paper and cover; illustrations; photos. Pipe smoking and tobacco theme for general and professional audience. Irregular quarterly. Estab. 1964.

Needs: Pipe smoking related: historical, humor/satire, literary. Publishes ms up to 1 year after acceptance. Length: 2,500 words average; 5,000 words maximum. Also publishes short shorts. Occasionally critiques rejected mss.

How to Contact: Send complete ms with cover letter. Reports in 2 weeks on mss. Simultaneous and reprints OK. Sample copy for 8½×11 SAE and 6 first-class stamps.

Payment/Terms: Acquires one-time rights.

PIRATE WRITINGS, Tales of Fantasy, Mystery & Science Fiction, DNA Publications, P.O. Box 2988, Radford, VA 24143. Editorial Address: P.O. Box 329, Brightwaters NY 11718. E-mail: pwpubl@aol.com. **Editor:** Edward J. McFadden. Assistant Editor: Patrick Thomas. Magazine: full size, saddle stapled. "We are looking for poetry and short stories that entertain." Quarterly. Estab. 1992. Circ. 3,500.

Needs: Fantasy (dark fantasy, science fantasy, sword and sorcery), mystery/suspense, science fiction (all types). Receives 300-400 unsolicited mss/month. Accepts 8 mss/issue; 30-40 mss/year. Publishes ms 1-2 years after acceptance. Length: 3,000 words average; 750 words minimum; 8,000 words maximum. Also publishes poetry. Sometimes critiques or comments on rejected mss.

How to Contact: Send complete ms with cover letter. Include estimated word count, 1 paragraph bio, Social Security number, list of publications with submission. Reports in 1 week on queries; 2 months on mss. Send SASE for reply or return of ms or disposable copy of ms. Will consider simultaneous submissions. Sample copy for $5 (make check payable to Pirate Writings). Fiction guidelines for #10 SAE.

Payment/Terms: Pays 1-5¢/word for first North American serial rights.

Advice: "My goal is to provide a diverse, entertaining and thought-provoking magazine featuring all the above stated genres in every issue. Hints: I love a good ending. Move me, make me laugh, surprise me, and you're in. Read *PW* and you'll see what I mean."

POSKISNOLT PRESS, Yesterday's Press, Yesterday's Press, JAF Station, Box 7415, New York NY 10116-4630. **Editor:** Patricia D. Coscia. Magazine: 7×8½; 20 pages; regular typing paper. Estab. 1989. Circ. 100.

FOR EXPLANATIONS OF THESE SYMBOLS,
SEE THE INSIDE FRONT AND BACK COVERS OF THIS BOOK.

Needs: Contemporary, erotica, ethnic, experimental, fantasy, feminist, gay, humor/satire, lesbian, literary, mainstream, prose poem, psychic/supernatural/occult, romance, senior citizen/retirement, western, young adult/teen (10-18 years). "X-rated material is not accepted!" Plans to publish a special fiction issue or anthology in the future. Receives 50 unsolicited mss/month. Accepts 30 mss/issue; 100 mss/year. Publishes ms 6 months after acceptance. Length: 200 words average; 100 words minimum; 500 words maximum. Publishes short shorts. Length: 100-500 words. Sometimes critiques rejected mss and recommends other markets.
How to Contact: Query first with clips of published work or send complete ms with cover letter. Reports in 1 week on queries; 6 months on mss. SASE. Accepts simultaneous submissions. Sample copy for $5 with #10 SAE and $2 postage. Fiction guidelines for #10 SAE and $2 postage.
Payment/Terms: Pays with subscription to magazine or contributor's copies; charges for extras. Acquires all rights, first rights or one-time rights.

$ ◑ THE POST, Publishers Syndication International, P.O. Box 6218, Charlottesville VA 22906-6218. (804)964-1194. Fax: (804)964-0096. E-mail: asam@hombuslib.com. Website: www.hombuslib.com/. **Editor:** A.P. Samuels. Magazine: 8½×11; 32 pages. Monthly. Estab. 1988.
Needs: Adventure, mystery/suspense (private eye), romance (romantic suspense, historical, contemporary), western (traditional). "No explicit sex, gore, weird themes, extreme violence or bad language." Receives 35 unsolicited mss/month. Accepts 1 ms/issue; 12 mss/year. Time between acceptance and publication varies. Agented fiction 10%. **Publishes 1-3 new writers/year.** Length: 10,000 words average.
How to Contact: Send complete ms with cover letter. Reports on mss in 5 weeks. No simultaneous submissions. Fiction guidelines for #10 SASE.
Payment/Terms: Pays ½¢ to 4¢/word on acceptance for all rights.
Advice: "Manuscripts must be for a general audience."

Ⓝ ◯ PRAYERWORKS, Encouraging, God's people to do the real work of ministry—intercessory prayer, The Master's Work, P.O. Box 301363, Portland OR 97294-9363. (503)761-2072. Fax: (503)760-1184. E-mail: jayforpryr@aol.com. **Editor:** V. Ann Mandeville. Newsletter: 5½×8; 4 pages; bond paper. "Our intended audience is 70% retired Christians and 30% families. We publish 300-500 word devotional material—fiction, nonfiction, biographical poetry, clean quips and quotes. Our philosophy is evangelical Christian serving the body of Christ in the area of prayer." Estab. 1988. Circ. 650.
Needs: Religious/inspirational. "Subject matter may include anything which will build relationship with the Lord—prayer, ways to pray, stories of answered prayer, teaching on a Scripture portion, articles that will build faith, or poems will all work. We even use a series occasionally." Publishes 2-6 months after acceptance. Published work by Barb Marshal, Mary Hickey and Vann Mandeville. Length: 350-500 words average; 350 words minimum; 500 words maximum. Publishes short shorts. Also publishes poetry. Often critiques or comments on rejected mss.
How to Contact: Send complete ms with a cover letter. Include estimated word count and a very short bio. Reports in 1 month. Send SASE for reply, return of ms or send a disposable copy of ms. Simultaneous submissions and reprints OK. Sample copy and fiction guidelines for #10 SASE.
Payment/Terms: Pays free subscription to the magazine and contributor's copies on publication. Writer retains all rights. Not copyrighted.
Advice: Stories "must have a great take-away—no preaching; teach through action. Be thrifty with words—make them count."

$ ◐ ◎ PRISONERS OF THE NIGHT, An Adult Anthology of Erotica, Fright, Allure and . . . Vampirism, MKASHEF Enterprises, P.O. Box 688, Yucca Valley CA 92286-0688. E-mail: alayne@inetworld.net. **Editor:** Alayne Gelfand. Magazine: 8½×11; 50-80 pages; 20 lb. paper; slick cover; illustrations. "An adult, erotic vampire anthology of original character stories and poetry. Heterosexual and homosexual situations." Annually. Estab. 1987. Circ. 5,000.
Needs: "All stories must be erotic vampire stories, with unique characters, unusual situations." Adventure, contemporary, erotica, fantasy, feminist, gay, lesbian, literary, mystery/suspense, prose poem, psychic/supernatural/occult, science fiction (soft/sociological). No fiction that deals with anyone else's creations, i.e., no "Dracula" stories. No traditional Gothic, humor. Receives 100-150 unsolicited fiction mss/month. Buys 5-12 mss/issue. Publishes ms 1-11 months after acceptance. Published work by Keil Stuart, Steve Eller, James Dorr and Charles Jacob. **Publishes 1-5 new writers/year.** Length: under 8,000 words. Publishes short shorts. Sometimes critiques rejected mss.
How to Contact: Send complete ms with short cover letter. "A very brief introduction of author to the editor; name, address, *some* past credits if available." Reports in 1-3 weeks on queries; 2-4 months on mss. Reads *only* September through March. SASE. No simultaneous submissions. Accepts electronic submissions via Word, Word for Windows, ASCII disk. Sample copy #1-4, $15; #5, $12; #6-#9, $9.95, #10, $7.95, #11, $9.95. Fiction guidelines for #10 SASE.
Payment/Terms: Pays 1¢/word for fiction on acceptance for first North American serial rights.
Advice: Looks for "clean, professional presentation. Interesting writing style that flows from word-one and sucks the reader in. An interesting idea/concept that appears at the beginning of a story. Read at least the most

current issue of the publication to which you submit and read the guidelines before submitting. Know your market!''

$ ⊘ PSI, P.O. Box 6218, Charlottesville VA 22906-6218. (804)964-1194. Fax: (804)964-0096. E-mail: asam @esinet.net. **Editor:** A.P. Samuels. Magazine: 8½×11; 32 pages; bond paper; self cover. "Mystery and romance." Bimonthly. Estab. 1987.
Needs: Adventure, romance (contemporary, historical, young adult), mystery/suspense (private eye), western (traditional). No ghoulish, sex, violence. Wants to see more believable stories. Receives 35 unsolicited mss/month. Accepts 1-2 mss/issue. **Publishes 1-3 new writers/year.** Length: 10,000 (stories) and 30,000 (novelettes) words average. Critiques rejected mss "only on a rare occasion."
How to Contact: Send complete ms with cover letter. Reports in 2 weeks on queries; 4-6 weeks on mss. SASE. No simultaneous submissions. Accepts electronic submissions via disk.
Payment/Terms: Pays 1-4¢/word plus royalty on acceptance for all rights.
Advice: "Manuscripts must be for a general audience. Just good plain story telling (make it compelling). No explicit sex or ghoulish violence."

⊘ ♛ QUEEN OF ALL HEARTS, Queen Magazine, Montfort Missionaries, 26 S. Saxon Ave., Bay Shore NY 11706-8993. (516)665-0726. Fax: (516)665-4349. E-mail: pretre@worldnet.att.net. **Managing Editor:** Roger M. Charest, S.M.M. Magazine: 7¾×10¾; 48 pages; self cover stock; illustrations and photos. Magazine of "stories, articles and features on the Mother of God by explaining the Scriptural basis and traditional teaching of the Catholic Church concerning the Mother of Jesus, her influence in fields of history, literature, art, music, poetry, etc." Bimonthly. Estab. 1950. Circ. 2,500.
  • *Queen of All Hearts* received a Catholic Press Award for General Excellence (third place) and a Prayer and Spirituality Journalism Award.
Needs: Religious/inspirational. "No mss not about Our Lady, the Mother of God, the Mother of Jesus." Recently published work by Richard O'Donnell and Jackie Clements-Marenda. **Publishes 6 new writers/year.** Length: 1,500-2,000 words. Sometimes recommends other markets.
How to Contact: Send complete ms with SASE. Accepts queries/mss by e-mail and fax (mss by permission only). No simultaneous submissions. Reports in 1 month on mss. Publishes ms 6-12 months after acceptance. Sample copy for $2.50 with 9×12 SAE.
Payment/Terms: Varies. Pays 6 contributor's copies.
Advice: "We are publishing stories with a Marian theme."

⚎ ✓ $⃝ ◎ QUEEN'S QUARTERLY, A Canadian Review, Queen's University, Kingston, Ontario K7L 3N6 Canada. Phone/fax: (613)533-2667. Fax: (613)533-6822. E-mail: qquartly@post.queensu.ca. Website: info.queensu.ca./quarterly. **Editor:** Boris Castel. Magazine: 6×9; 800 pages/year; illustrations. "A general interest intellectual review, featuring articles on science, politics, humanities, arts and letters. Book reviews, poetry and fiction." Quarterly. Estab. 1893. Circ. 3,000.
Needs: Adventure, contemporary, experimental, fantasy, historical, humor/satire, literary, mainstream, science fiction and women's. "*Special emphasis on work by Canadian writers.*" Accepts 2 mss/issue; 8 mss/year. Published work by Gail Anderson-Dargatz, Mark Jarman, Rick Bowers and Dennis Bock; **published new writers within the last year.** Length: 2,000-3,000 words. Also publishes literary essays, literary criticism, poetry.
How to Contact: "Send complete ms with SASE." No simultaneous or multiple submissions. Reports within 3 months. Sample copy for $6.50. Reviews novels and short story collections. Electronic submissions OK.
Payment/Terms: Pays $100-300 for fiction, 2 contributor's copies and 1-year subscription; $5 charge for extras. Pays on publication for first North American serial rights. Sends galleys to author.

⊘ ◎ RFD, A Country Journal for Gay Men Everywhere, Short Mountain Collective, P.O. Box 68, Liberty TN 37095. (615)536-5176. **Contact:** The Collective. Magazine: 8½×11; 64-80 pages. "Focus on radical faeries, gay men's spirituality—country living." Quarterly. Estab. 1974. Circ. 3,600.
Needs: Gay: Erotica, ethnic/multicultural, experimental, fantasy, feminist, humor/satire, literary, mainstream/ contemporary, mystery/suspense, psychic/supernatural/occult, regional, romance. Receives 10 unsolicited mss/month. Accepts 3 mss/issue; 12 mss/year. Length: open. Publishes short shorts. Also publishes literary essays, literary criticism and poetry.
How to Contact: Send complete ms with cover letter and estimated word count. Usually reports in 6-9 months. Send SASE for reply, return of ms or send disposable copy of ms. Sample copy for $6. Free fiction guidelines.
Payment/Terms: Pays 1 or 2 contributor's copies. Not copyrighted.

★ ⊘ ◎ ROMANTIC HEARTS, A Magazine Dedicated to Short Romantic Fiction, P.O. Box 450669, Westlake OH 44145-0612. **Editor:** Debra L. Krauss. Magazine: 5¼×8; 48 pages; 20 lb. paper; 20 lb. color cover; illustrations and photographs. "Romantic Hearts is dedicated to publishing the finest romantic short fiction written today. Our audience is romance readers and writers. We also publish short romantic essays (500-1,500 words) and love poems of 25 lines of less." Bimonthly. Estab. 1996.
Needs: Romance (contemporary, futuristic/time travel, gothic, historical, all types). Wants more historical fiction.

No erotica or pornography. Receives 40 unsolicited mss/month. Accepts 5-7 mss/issue; 36-40 mss/year. Publishes ms 8-14 months after acceptance. Recently published work by Holly J. Fuhrmann, Penelope A. Marzec, Margaret Marr, Dawn Davis and Sheri Cobb South. **Publishes 20 new writers/year.** Length: 2,500 words average; 1,500 words minimum; 4,000 words maximum. Also publishes literary essays (must have a romantic theme), poetry. Occasionally critiques or comments on rejected mss.

How to Contact: Send complete ms with a cover letter. Include estimated word count. Reports in 6-8 weeks. Send SASE for reply, return of ms or send a disposable copy of ms. No simultaneous submissions. Sample copy for $4 ppd. Fiction guidelines free for #10 SASE.

Payment/Terms: Pays 3 contributor's copies on publication; additional copies for $2. Acquires first North American serial rights. "Send #10 SASE with request for contest guidelines."

Advice: "The stories I select are uplifting and positive. They must also be a 'romance.' A standout manuscript is one that contains strong characterization and lots of emotion. Always include a cover letter and correctly format your manuscript. Please be sure your story is a romance with a happy ending or the promise of one."

★ **$** ⊘ **ROSEBUD℗, For People Who Enjoy Writing,** P.O. Box 459, Cambridge WI 53523. Phone/fax: (608)423-9609. Website: www.hyperionstudio.com/rosebud (includes writer's guidelines, contests, preview, *Rosebud* bulletin board, teachers guide to current issue, outreach programs and advertising rates). **Editor:** Roderick Clark. Magazine: 7×10; 136 pages; 60 lb. matte; 100 lb. cover; illustrations. Quarterly. Estab. 1993. Circ. 11,000.

● *Rosebud* ranks #19 on *Writer's Digest* "Fiction 50" list of top fiction markets.

Needs: Adventure, condensed/excerpted novel, ethnic/multicultural, experimental, historical (general), humor/satire, literary, mainstream/contemporary, psychic/supernatural/occult, regional, romance (contemporary), science fiction (soft/sociological), serialized novel, translations. Each submission must fit loosely into one of the following categories to qualify: City and Shadow (urban settings), Songs of Suburbia (suburban themes), These Green Hills (nature and nostalgia), En Route (any type of travel), Mothers, Daughters, Wives (relationships), Ulysses' Bow (manhood), Paper, Scissors, Rock (childhood, middle age, old age), The Jeweled Prize (concerning love), Lost and Found (loss and discovery), Voices in Other Rooms (historic or of other culture), Overtime (involving work), Anything Goes (humor), I Hear Music (music), Season to Taste (food), Word Jazz (wordplay), Apples to Oranges (miscellaneous, excerpts, profiles). Publishes annual special fiction issue or anthology. Receives 1,200 unsolicited mss/month. Accepts 16 mss/issue; 64 mss/year. Publishes ms 1-3 months after acceptance. Published work by Seamus Heany, Louis Simpson, Allen Ginsberg and Philip Levine. **Publishes 70% new writers.** Length: 1,200-1,800 words average. Occasionally uses longer pieces and novel excerpts (prepublished). Publishes short shorts. Also publishes literary essays. Often critiques or comments on rejected mss.

How to Contact: Send complete ms with a cover letter. Include estimated word count and list of publications. Reports in 3 months on mss. SASE for return of ms. Simultaneous and reprints submissions OK. Sample copy for $6.95. Fiction guidelines for legal SASE.

Payment/Terms: Pays $45 and 3 contributor's copies on publication for one-time rights; additional copies for $4.40.

Advice: "Each issue will have six or seven flexible departments (selected from a total of sixteen departments that will rotate). We are seeking stories, articles, profiles, and poems of: love, alienation, travel, humor, nostalgia and unexpected revelation. Something has to 'happen' in the pieces we choose, but what happens inside characters is much more interesting to us than plot manipulation. We like good storytelling, real emotion and authentic voice."

★ ⊘ ▼ **SKIPPING STONES: A Multicultural Children's Magazine,** P.O. Box 3939, Eugene OR 97403-0939. (541)342-4956. E-mail: skipping@efn.org. Website: www.nonviolence.org/skipping (includes writer's guidelines). **Executive Editor:** Arun N. Toké. Magazine: 8½×11; 36 pages; recycled 50 lb. halopaque paper; 100 lb. text cover; illustrations and photos. "*Skipping Stones* is a multicultural, international, nature awareness magazine for children 8-16, and their parents and teachers." Published 5 times a year. Estab. 1988. Circ. 3,000.

● *Skipping Stones* received the 1997 National Association for Multicultural Education, Name Award.

Needs: Children's/juvenile (8-16 years): ethnic/multicultural, feminist, religious/inspirational, young adult/teen, international, nature. No simplistic, fiction for the sake of fiction, mystery, violent/abusive language or science fiction. "We want more authentic pieces based on truly multicultural/intercultural/international living experiences of authors. We welcome works by people of color." Upcoming themes: "Living Abroad," "Crosscultural Communications," "Life in the Year 2000," "Humor Unlimited," "Folktales," "Turning Points in Life . . .," "Raising Children: Rewards, Punishments." List of upcoming themes available for SASE. Receives 50 mss/month. Accepts 5-8 mss/issue; 25-30 mss/year. Publishes ms 3-6 months after acceptance. Published work by Victoria Collett, Charles Curatalo, Anjali Amit, Lily Hartmann and Peter Chase. **Publishes up to 100 new writers/year.** Length: 750 words average; 250 words minimum; 1,000 words maximum. Publishes short shorts. Also publishes literary essays and poetry (by youth under 18). Often critiques or comments on rejected mss. Sponsors contests and awards for writers under 17 years of age.

How to Contact: Send complete ms with a cover letter. Accepts queries/mss by e-mail. Include 50- to 100-word bio with background, international or intercultural experiences. Reports in 1 month on queries; 4 months on mss. Send SASE for reply, return of ms or send a disposable copy of ms. Simultaneous submissions OK. Sample copy for $5, and 4 first-class stamps. Fiction guidelines for #10 SASE.

Payment/Terms: Pays 1-3 contributor's copies; additional copies for $3. Acquires first North American serial rights and nonexclusive reprint rights.

Advice: Looking for stories with "multicultural/multiethnic theme. Realistic and suitable for 8 to 16 year olds (with use of other languages when appropriate). Promoting social and nature awareness. In addition to encouraging children's creativity, we also invite adults to submit their own writing and artwork for publication in *Skipping Stones*. Writings and artwork by adults should challenge readers to think and learn, cooperate and create."

✓ ◯ ◎ **SLATE AND STYLE, Magazine of the National Federation of the Blind Writers Division**, NFB Writer's Division, 2704 Beach Dr., Merrick NY 11566. (516)868-8718. Fax: (516)868-9076. E-mail: loristay@aol.com. **Fiction Editor:** Tom Stevens. Newsletter: 8 × 10; 32 print/40 Braille pages; cassette and large print. "Articles of interest to writers, and resources for blind writers." Quarterly. Estab. 1982. Circ. 200.

Needs: Adventure, contemporary, fantasy, humor/satire, blindness. No erotica. "Avoid theme of death." Does not read mss in June or July. Recently published work by Alma Hinkle, Marie Anna Pape and Lois Wencil. **Publishes 8-10 new writers/year.** Length: 3,000 words maximum. Publishes short shorts. Also publishes literary criticism and poetry. Critiques rejected mss only if requested.

How to Contact: Reports in 3-6 weeks. Accepts queries by e-mail. Large print sample copy for $2.50.

Payment/Terms: Pays in contributor's copies. Acquires one-time rights. Publication not copyrighted. Sponsors contests for fiction writers.

Advice: "Keep a copy. Editors can lose your work. Consider each first draft as just that and review your work before you send it. SASE a must. Although we circulate to blind writers, I do not wish to see articles on blindness by sighted writers unless they are married to, or the son/daughter/parent of a blind person. In general, we do not even print articles on blindness, preferring to publish articles on alternate techniques a blind writer can use when writing."

✓ ◯ **SPACE AND TIME,** 138 W. 70th St. (4B), New York NY 10023-4468. Website: www.bway.net/~natalia/space&time.html (includes guidelines, staff, current and future contents, back issues/books for sale, schedule of our reading series). Editor: Gordon Linzner. **Fiction Editor:** Gerard Hovarner. Magazine: 8½ × 11; 48 pages; 50 lb. paper; index card cover stock; illustrations and photos. "We publish science fiction, fantasy, horror and our favorite, that-which-defies-categorization." Biannually. Estab. 1966. Circ. 2,500. Member of the Small Press Center and the Small Press Genre Organization.

Needs: Fantasy (science, sword and sorcery, undefinable), horror, science fiction (hard science, soft/sociological, undefinable). Receives 100 unsolicited mss/month. Accepts 12 mss/issue; 24 mss/year. Publishes ms 6-18 months after acceptance. Recently published work by Robin Spriggs, Trey R. Barker, Stephen Antczak and Laurel Anne Mill. Length: 5,000 words average; 10,000 words maximum. Publishes short shorts. Also publishes literary essays, literary criticism and poetry. Send poems to Linda D. Addison. Often critiques or comments on rejected mss.

How to Contact: Send complete ms. Include estimated word count. Reports in 1 week on queries; 2-3 months on mss. Send SASE for reply, return of ms or send a disposable copy of ms. Sample copy for $6.50 and 9 × 12 SAE. Fiction guidelines for #10 SASE or SAE and 1 IRC.

Payment/Terms: Pays 1¢/word, $5 minimum and 2 contributor's copies on acceptance; additional copies $3. Acquires first North American serial rights and option to reprint in context of magazine.

Advice: Looks for "good writing, strong characterization and unusual plot or premise."

◪ ◯ **THE STORYTELLER, For Amateur Writers,** 2441 Washington Rd., Maynard AR 72444. (870)647-2137. **Editor:** Regina Williams. Tabloid: 8½ × 11; 50-60 pages; typing paper; illustrations. "This magazine is open to all new writers regardless of age. I will accept short stories in any genre and poetry in any type. Please keep in mind, this is a family publication." Quarterly. Estab. 1996.

Needs: Adventure, historical, humor/satire, literary, mainstream/contemporary, mystery/suspense, regional, religious/inspirational, romance, science fiction (soft/sociological), senior citizen/retirement, sports, westerns, young adult/teen. "I will not accept pornography, erotica, foul language, horror or graphic violence." Wants more well-plotted mysteries. Publishes ms 3-9 months after acceptance. Published work by Randy Offner, Otis Lawson, Bryan Byrd and Gracie Cauble. **Publishes approximately 100 new writers/year.** Length: 1,500 words maximum; 200 words minimum. Publishes short shorts. Also publishes literary essays and poetry. Sometimes critiques or comments on rejected mss.

How to Contact: Nonsubscribers must pay reading fee: $1/poem, $2/short story. Send complete ms with a cover letter. Include estimated word count and 5-line bio. Reports 2-4 weeks on queries; 1-2 months on mss. Send SASE for reply, return of ms or send a disposable copy of ms. Simultaneous and reprint submissions OK. Sample copy for $6. Fiction guidelines for #10 SASE.

Payment/Terms: "Readers vote quarterly for their favorites in all categories. Winning authors receive certificate of merit and free copy of issue in which their story or poem appeared."

Advice: Looks for "professionalism, good plots and unique characters. Purchase a sample copy so you know the kind of material we look for. Even though this is for amateur writers, don't send us something you would not send to paying markets." Would like more "well-plotted mysteries and suspense and a few traditional westerns. Avoid sending anything that children or young adults would not (or could not) read, such as really bad language."

STUDIO: A JOURNAL OF CHRISTIANS WRITING, 727 Peel St., Albury 2640 Australia. **Managing Editor:** Paul Grover. Circ. 300. Quarterly. Averages 20-30 stories/year.

Needs: "*Studio* publishes prose and poetry of literary merit, offers a venue for new and aspiring writers, and seeks to create a sense of community among Christians writing." Length: 500-5,000 words.

Payment/Terms: Pays in copies. Sample copy available for $8 (Australian). Subscription $40 (Australian) for 4 issues (1 year). International draft in Australian dollars and IRC required.

TALEBONES, Fiction on the Dark Edge, Fairwood Press, 5203 Quincy Ave. SE, Auburn WA 98092. E-mail: talebones@nventure.com. Website: www.nventure.com/talebones (includes guidelines, submission requirements, excerpts, news about the magazine, bios). **Editors:** Patrick and Honna Swenson. Magazine: digest size; 72 pages; standard paper; glossy cover stock; illustrations and photos. "We like stories that have punch, but still entertain. We like dark science fiction and dark fantasy, humor, psychological and experimental works." Quarterly. Estab. 1995. Circ. 400.

● *Talebones* was nominated for the International Horror Guild Award for Best Publication.

Needs: Fantasy (dark), humor/satire, science fiction (hard science, soft/sociological, dark). "No straight slash and hack horror. No cat stories or stories told by young adults. Would like to see more science fiction." Receives 200 mss/month. Accepts 6-7 mss/issue; 24-28 mss/year. Publishes ms 3-4 months after acceptance. Recently published work by Patrick O'Leary, Bruce Boston, Larry Tritten, Mark Rich, Hugh Cook and Uncle River. **Publishes 2-3 new writers/year.** Length: 3,000-4,000 words average; 500 words minimum; 6,000 words maximum. Publishes short shorts. Length: 1,000 words. Also publishes poetry.

How to Contact: Send complete ms with a cover letter. Accepts queries/mss by e-mail. Include estimated word count and 1-paragraph bio. Reports in 1 week on queries; 1-3 weeks on mss. Send SASE for reply, return of ms or send a disposable copy of ms. No simultaneous submissions. No reprints. Electronic submissions (e-mail) OK. Sample copy for $4.50. Fiction guidelines for SASE. Reviews novels and short story collections.

Payment/Terms: Pays $10-100 on acceptance and 1 contributor's copy; additional copies for $3. Acquires first North American serial rights. Sends galleys to author.

Advice: "The story must be entertaining, but should blur the boundary between science fiction and horror. Most of our stories have a dark edge to them, but often are humorous or psychological. Be polite and know how to properly present a manuscript. Include a cover letter, but keep it short and to the point."

TERRA INCOGNITA, A New Generation of Science Fiction, 52 Windermere Ave., Lansdowne PA 19050-1812. E-mail: terraincognita@writeme.com. Editor: Jan Berrien Berends. Magazine: 64 pages; e-brite paper; full-color glossy cover; illustrations; photos. "*Terra Incognita* is devoted to earth-based science fiction stories and relevant nonfiction articles. Readers of quality fiction—even those who are not science fiction fans—enjoy *TI*. Audience ranges from ages 18 and upward. We encourage feminist and socially conscious submissions." Quarterly. Estab. 1996.

Needs: Science fiction (hard science, soft/sociological). "No sexism and gratuitous sex and violence, racism or bias; avoid prose poems and vignettes. We prefer character-driven stories with protagonists and plots." Receives 200-300 unsolicited mss/month. Accepts 6-10 mss/issue; 25-35 mss/year. Publishes ms 3 months to 1 year after acceptance. Published work by L. Timmel Duchamp, Sue Storm, Timons Esais, W. Gregory Stewart, Nicola Griffith, Brian Stableford, Kandis Elliot and Darrell Schweitzer. Length: 5,000 words average; 100 words minimum; 15,000 words maximum. Publishes short shorts. Also publishes literary essays, literary criticism and poetry.

How to Contact: Send complete ms with cover letter. Include estimated word count and anything you think might be interesting in a cover letter. Reports in 1-2 weeks on queries; 4-12 weeks on mss. Send SASE for reply, return of ms or send a disposable copy of ms. "A cover letter is optional; a SASE is not." Sample copy for $5; $6 overseas. Fiction guidelines for #10 SASE. Reviews novels and short story collections.

Payment/Terms: Pays at least 3¢/word and 2 contributor's copies; additional copies $5. Pays on acceptance. Acquires first North American serial rights.

Advice: Looks for "good writing and literary merit; a story that grabs our interest and holds it straight through to the end. Write as well as you can (which means—don't overwrite, but do use the words themselves to advance your story), and tell us a story—preferably one we haven't heard before. Don't get your great idea rejected on account of lousy grammar or poor manuscript format. We take all submissions seriously."

THE THRESHOLD, Crossover Press, P.O. Box 101362, Pittsburgh PA 15237. (412)559-2269. E-mail: lazarro@aol.com. Website: members.aol.com/lazarro/threshold/home.htm. **Editors:** Don H. Laird and Michael Carricato. Magazine: 8½ × 11; 48 pages; colored bond paper; card cover; illustrations. "We truly are a magazine 'for writers, by writers.' Our audience is both young and old and they are in search of one thing: imaginative stories and poetry." Quarterly. Estab. 1996. Circ. 1,000.

Needs: Adventure, condensed/excerpted novel, erotica, experimental, fantasy, gay, horror, humor/satire, lesbian, literary, mainstream/contemporary, mystery/suspense, psychic/supernatural/occult, romance (contemporary, futuristic/time travel/gothic), science fiction, serialized novel, westerns. Publishes special fiction issues or anthologies. Receives 100 unsolicited mss/month. Accepts 6-8 mss/issue, 24-32 mss/year. Publishes ms up to 5 months after acceptance. Recently published work by Ben Boardman, M.E. Mitchell, Rhonda Nolan, Clay Chapman, Gustav Richar, Laura Capewell and Michael Kent. Length: 3,000-5,000 words average; 8,000 words maximum. Publishes short shorts. Also publishes poetry.

How to Contact: Send complete ms with a cover letter. Include estimated word count and 2-paragraph bio. Reports in 2 weeks on queries; 4-6 months on mss. Send SASE for reply, return of ms or send disposable copy of ms. Simultaneous and electronic submissions OK. Sample copy for $5.95. Fiction guidelines for #10 SASE.

Payment/Terms: Pays 1 contributor's copy for one-time rights.

Advice: "If we like it, we print it. Period. If it needs some changes, we send a letter recommending where some revisions would help. It is an open forum between writer and editor. Send in the work."

THRESHOLDS QUARTERLY, School of Metaphysics Associates Journal, SOM Publishing, School of Metaphysics National Headquarters, HCR1, Box 15, Windyville MO 65783. (417)345-8411. Fax: (417)345-6688 (call first, computerized). Website: www.som.org. **Editor:** Dr. Barbara Condron. Senior Editor: Dr. Laurel Fuller Clark. Magazine: 7 × 10; 32 pages; line drawings and b&w photos. "The School of Metaphysics is a nonprofit educational and service organization invested in education and research in the expansion of human consciousness and spiritual evolution of humanity. For all ages and backgrounds. Themes: dreams, healing, science fiction, personal insight, morality tales, fables, humor, spiritual insight, mystic experiences, religious articles, creative writing with universal themes." Quarterly. Estab. 1975. Circ. 5,000.

Needs: Adventure, fantasy, humor, psychic/supernatural, religious/inspirational, science fiction. Upcoming themes: "Dreams, Visions, and Creative Imagination" (February); "Health and Wholeness" (May); "Intuitive Arts" (August); "Man's Spiritual Consciousness" (November). Receives 5 unsolicited mss/month. Length: 4-10 double-spaced typed pages. Publishes short shorts. Also publishes literary essays and poetry. Often critiques or comments on rejected mss.

How to Contact: Query with outline; will accept unsolicited ms with cover letter; no guarantee on time length to respond. Include bio (1-2 paragraphs). Send SASE for reply, return of ms or send a disposable copy of ms. Sample copy for 9 × 12 SAE and $1.50 postage. Fiction guidelines for #10 SASE.

Payment/Terms: Pays up to 5 contributor's copies. Acquires all rights.

Advice: "We encourage works that have one or more of the following attributes: uplifting, educational, inspirational, entertaining, informative and innovative."

UP DARE?, la Pierna Tierna Press, P.O. Box 100, Shartlesville PA 19554. (610)488-6894. **Editors:** Mary M. Towne and Loring D. Emery. "The only requirement is that all submitted material must pertain to folks with physical or psychological handicaps-fiction or non-fiction." Magazine: digest-sized; 48 pages; illustrations. Bi-monthly. Estab. 1997.

Needs: Fiction and poetry. Looks for "honesty, plain language and message." No smut. Published work by Dan Buck, Annette Wilson, Sylvia Mais-Harak, Betty Jung Silconas and Denise Corrigan.

How to Contact: "We will take single-spaced and even double-sided submissions so long as they are legible. We prefer to optically scan all material to avoid typos. We will not insist on an SASE if you truly have financial limitations. We're trying to make it as easy as possible. We will take short (250 words or less) pieces in Braille." Sample copy for $2.50. Fiction guidelines for #10 SASE.

Advice: "We will not use euphemisms—a chair with a leg missing is a 'three-legged chair,' not a 'challenged seat.' We would like to hear from folks who are handicapped, but we aren't closing the door to others who understand and help or just have opinions to share. We will take reprints if the original appearance is identified."

VINTAGE NORTHWEST, Box 193, Bothell WA 98041. (425)823-9189. **Editors:** Jane Kaake and Sylvia Tacker. Magazine: 7 × 8½; 68 pages; illustrations. "We are a senior literary magazine, published by Northshore Senior Center, but our focus is to appeal to all ages. All work done by volunteers except printing." Published winter and summer. Estab. 1980. Circ. 300.

Needs: Adventure, comedy, fantasy, historical, humor/satire, inspirational, mystery/suspense, nostalgia, poetry, western (frontier). No religious or political mss. Receives 10-12 unsolicited mss/month. **Publishes as many new writers as possible.** Length: 1,000 words maximum. Also publishes literary essays. Occasionally critiques rejected mss.

How to Contact: Send complete ms. SASE. Simultaneous and previously published submissions OK. Reports in 3-6 months. Sample copy for $4.25 (postage included). Guidelines with SASE.

Payment/Terms: Pays 1 contributor's copy.

Advice: "Our only requirement is that the author be over 50 when submission is written."

$ **VIRGINIA QUARTERLY REVIEW,** One West Range, Charlottesville VA 22903. (804)924-3124. Fax: (804)924-1397. **Editor:** Staige Blackford. "A national magazine of literature and discussion. A lay, intellectual audience; people who are not out-and-out scholars but who are interested in ideas and literature." Quarterly. Estab. 1925. Circ. 4,000.

Needs: Adventure, contemporary, ethnic, feminist, humor, literary, romance, serialized novels (excerpts) and translations. "No pornography." Buys 3 mss/issue, 20 mss/year. Length: 3,000-7,000 words.

How to Contact: Query or send complete ms. SASE. No simultaneous or electronic submissions. Reports in 2 weeks on queries, 2 months on mss. Sample copy for $5.

Payment/Terms: Pays $10/printed page on publication for all rights. "Will transfer upon request." Offers Emily Clark Balch Award for best published short story of the year.

Advice: Looks for "stories with a somewhat Southern dialect and/or setting. Humor is welcome; stories involving cancer and geriatrics are not."

✔ ⊘ ◎ ▣ **VQ, The Village Square of Volcanodom**, (formerly *Volcano Quarterly*), 8009 18th Lane SE, Lacey WA 98053. (360)455-4607. E-mail: jmtanaka@webtv.net. **Editor:** Janet Tanaka.
• *Volcano Quarterly* has ceased print publication, and plans to publish online in January 2000. Please contact for updated writer's guidelines.

Ⓝ $ ⊘ ◎ **WEBER STUDIES: Vices and Viewpoints of the Contemporary West**, 1214 University Circle, Ogden UT 84408-1214. (801)626-6616. Website: weberstudies.weber.edu (includes full web edition of journal). **Editor:** Sherwin W. Howard. Magazine: 7½×10; 120-140 pages; coated paper; 4-color cover; illustrations; and photos. *Weber Studies* publishes work that "provides insight into the culture and environment (both broadly defined) of the contemporary western United States." Triannually "with occasional 4th issues." Estab. 1984. Circ. 1000.

Needs: Adventure, comics/graphic novels, ethnic/multicultural, experimental, fantasy (space fantasy), feminist, gay, historical, humor satire, lesbian, literary, mainstream, military/war, mystery/suspense, New Age, psychic/supernatural/occult, regional (contemporary western US), science fiction, short story collections, translations, western (frontier saga, traditional, contemporary). No children's/juvenile, erotica, religious or young adult/teen. Receives 50 unsolicited mss/month. Accepts 3-6 mss/issue; 9-18 mss/year. Publishes ms up to 18 months after acceptance. **Publishes "few" new writers/year.** Recently published work by Henry Hughes, David Kraues, Louise Farmer Smith, Branded Cesmet and Mo Lee. Word length: 5,000 words maximum. Publishes short shorts. Also publishes literary essays, poetry and personal narrative. Sometimes comments on or critiques rejected ms.

How to Contact: Send complete ms with a cover letter. Include estimated word count, bio (not necessary), and list of publications (not necessary). Reports on mss in 3 months. Send SASE for return of ms or disposable copy of ms. Sample copy for $7.

Payment/Terms: Pays $70-100, free subscription to the magazine and 1 contributor's copy on publication. Acquires first serial rights, electronic edition rights and requests electronic archive permission. Sends galleys to author.

Advice: "Is it true? Is it new? Is it interesting? Will the story appeal to educated readers who are concerned with the contemporary western United States? Declining public interest in reading generally is of concern. We publish both in print media and electronic media because we believe the future will expect both options."

$ ⊘ **WEIRD TALES**, Terminus Publishing Co., Inc., 123 Crooked Lane, King of Prussia PA 19406-2570. (610)275-4463. E-mail: owlswick@netaxs.com. **Editors:** George H. Seithers and Darrell Schweitzer. Magazine: 8½×11; 68 pages; white, non-glossy paper; glossy 4-color cover; illustrations. "We publish fantastic fiction, supernatural horror for an adult audience." Quarterly. Estab. 1923. Circ. 10,000.

Needs: Fantasy (sword and sorcery), horror, supernatural/occult, translations. "We want to see a wide range of fantasy, from sword and sorcery to supernatural horror. We can use some unclassifiables." No hard science fiction or non-fantasy. Receives 400 unsolicited mss/month. Accepts 8 mss/issue; 32 mss/year. Publishes ms 6-18 months after acceptance. Agented fiction 10%. Published work by Tanith Lee, Thomas Ligotti, Ian Watson and Lord Dunsany. **Publishes 6 new writers/year.** Length: 4,000 words average; 10,000 words maximum (very few over 8,000). "No effective minimum. Shortest we ever published was about 100 words." Publishes short shorts. Also publishes poetry. Always critiques or comments on rejected mss.

How to Contact: Send complete ms. Include estimated word count. Reports in 2-3 weeks on mss. Send SASE for reply, return of ms or send a disposable copy of ms with SASE. No simultaneous submissions. No reprint submissions, "but will buy first North American rights to stories published overseas." Sample copy for $4.95. Fiction guidelines for #10 SASE. Reviews novels and short story collections relevant to the horror/fantasy field.

Payment/Terms: Pays 3¢/word minimum and 2 contributor's copies for first North American serial rights plus anthology option. Sends galleys to author.

Advice: "We look for imagination and vivid writing. Read the magazine. Get a good grounding in the contemporary horror and fantasy field through the various 'best of the year' anthologies. Avoid the obvious cliches of technicalities of the hereafter, the mechanics of vampirism, generic Tolkien-clone fantasy. In general, it is better

---

VISIT THE WRITER'S DIGEST WEBSITE at www.writersdigest.com for hot new markets, daily market updates, writers' guidelines and much more.

to be honest and emotionally moving rather than clever. Avoid stories which have nothing of interest save for the allegedly 'surprise' ending."

WESTERN DIGEST, Crossbow Publications, 400 Whiteland Dr. NE, Calgary, Alberta T1Y 3M7 Canada. (403)280-3424. E-mail: crossbow@cadvision.com. Website: www.westerndigest.com (includes sample issue, stories, profile and links, comment page). **Publisher:** Douglas Sharp. Newsletter: 8½×11; 20 pages. Publishes Western fiction and cowboy poetry only. Estab. 1995. Circ. 200.

Needs: Westerns (frontier, traditional). "Do not combine westerns with science fiction. Would like to see more humorous stories." Receives 8 unsolicited mss/month. Accepts 5-8 mss/issue; 50 mss/year. Publishes ms 18 months after acceptance. Recently published work by John M. Floyd, Troy D. Smith, Bill Garwood and R.C. House. **Publishes 10 new writers/year.** Length: 3,000 words average; 1,000 words minimum; 5,000 words maximum. Publishes short shorts. Length: 1,000 words. Also publishes literary criticism and poetry. Always critiques or comments on rejected mss.

How to Contact: Send complete ms with a cover letter. Accepts queries/mss by e-mail. Include 10- to 30-word bio. Reports in 1 week on queries; 2 weeks on mss. Send SAE and 2 IRCs for return of ms. Simultaneous submissions, reprints and electronic (Macintosh disk, Word 5.1) submissions OK. Sample copy for $4. Fiction guidelines free. Reviews novels or short story collections.

Payment/Terms: Pays $10-60 (Canadian funds) and free subscription to the magazine on publication. Acquires one-time rights.

Advice: "I enjoy stories with humorous, ironic or surprise endings. I would like to read more humorous stories. Avoid shoot-'em-ups. One gets tired of reading stories where the fastest gun wins in the end. There are other stories to be told of the pioneers. Rewrite your story until it is perfect. Do not use contractions in narration unless the story is written in first person. Do not send three consecutive pages of dialogue. Be sure to identify the speaker after three or four paragraphs. A reader should not have to reread a passage to understand it. Please, no sex or heavy duty swearing."

THE WHITE CROW, Osric Publishing, P.O. Box 4501, Ann Arbor MI 48106. E-mail: chris@osric.com. **Editor:** Christopher Herdt. Zine: 5½×8; 32 pages; 20 lb. white paper; 60 lb. cover stock; illustrations and photos. "We seek solid literary works which will appeal to an intelligent but not necessarily literary audience." Quarterly. Estab. 1994. Circ. 200.

Needs: Ethnic/multicultural, experimental, humor/satire, literary, translations. Receives 3 mss/month. Accepts 1-2 mss/issue; 6 mss/year. Publishes ms up to 4 months after acceptance. Length: 2,500 words average; 300 words minimum; 3,000 words maximum. Publishes short shorts. Also publishes literary essays and poetry. Always critiques or comments on rejected mss.

How to Contact: Send complete ms with cover letter. Include estimated word count and a 30-word bio. Reports in 4 months. Send SASE for return of ms. Simultaneous submissions and reprints OK. Sample copy for $2.

Payment/Terms: Pays 1 contributor's copy; additional copies for $1. Acquires one-time rights. Not copyrighted.

Advice: "Is the story focused? Is it driven by a coherent, meaningful idea that can be grasped by an intelligent (but not literary) reader? We're here to edit a publication, not your writing, so please proof-read your ms. Running spell check is a fabulous idea too."

$ WICKED MYSTIC, FTWS Press, 532 La Guardia Place #371, New York NY 10012. (718)638-1533. E-mail: wickedmyst@aol.com. Website: www.wickedmystic.com (includes writer's guidelines, names of editors, short fiction, interviews with authors and chat line). **Editor:** Andre Scheluchin. Magazine: full size; 80 pages; standard paper; standard cover stock; illustrations; and photos. Publishes "extreme horror." Quarterly. Estab. 1990. Circ. 10,000.

Needs: Comics/graphic novels, erotica, experimental, fantasy, horror (dark fantasy, futuristic, psychological, supernatural, erotic), mystery/suspense, psychic/supernatural/occult, science fiction, thriller/espionage. List of upcoming themes available for SASE. Receives 500 unsolicited mss/month. Accepts 10 mss/issue; 40 mss/year. Publishes ms 2-4 months after acceptance. **Publishes 10 new writers/year.** Recently published work by James S. Dorr, Tony Plank, Mikael Fenner, Charlee Jacob, Joe Priody and Nicole Ludwig. Word length: 3,000 words average; 500 words minimum; 5,000 words maximum. Also publishes literary essays and poetry. Sometimes comments on or critiques rejected ms.

How to Contact: Send complete ms with a cover letter. Inquiries by e-mail OK. Includes estimated word count, 1 page bio and list of publications. Reports in 1 month. Send SASE for reply, return of ms or send a disposable copy of ms. No simultaneous submissions. Sample copy for $6. Guidelines free. Reviews novels, short story collections and nonfiction books of interest to writers. Send books to editor.

Payment/Terms: Pays $30-100 and 5 contributor's copies; additional copies $3. Payment on publication. Acquires first rights. Sends galleys to the author.

Advice: Looks for stories "full of psychotic twists. Keep the story moving at a quick pace."

WISCONSIN ACADEMY REVIEW, Wisconsin Academy of Sciences, Arts & Letters, 1922 University Ave., Madison WI 53705-4099. (608)263-1692. Fax: (608)265-3039. Magazine: 8½×11; 48-52 pages; 75 lb. coated paper; coated cover stock; illustrations; photos. "The *Review* reflects the focus of the sponsoring institution with its editorial emphasis on Wisconsin's intellectual, cultural, social and physical environment. It features short fiction, poetry, essays, nonfiction articles and Wisconsin-related art and book reviews for people interested in furthering regional arts and literature and disseminating information about sciences." Quarterly. Estab. 1954. Circ. approximately 1,800.

Needs: Experimental, historical, humor/satire, literary, mainstream, prose poem. "Author must have a Wisconsin connection or fiction must be set in Wisconsin." Receives 5-6 unsolicited fiction mss/month. Accepts 1-2 mss/issue; 6-8 mss/year. **Published new writers within the last year.** Length: 1,000 words minimum; 3,500 words maximum. Also publishes poetry; "will consider" literary essays, literary criticism.

How to Contact: Send complete ms with SAE and state author's connection to Wisconsin, the prerequisite. Sample copy for $3. Fiction guidelines for SASE. Reviews books on Wisconsin themes.

Payment/Terms: Pays 3-5 contributor's copies. Acquires first rights on publication.

Advice: "Manuscript publication is at the discretion of the editor based on space, content and balance. We prefer previously unpublished poetry and fiction. We publish emerging as well as established authors; fiction and poetry, without names attached, are sent to reviewers for evaluation."

N ✠ $◻ XODDITY, A Magazine of Speculative Fiction, P.O. Box 61736, Boulder City NV 89006. (702)293-3039. E-mail: xoddity@aol.com. Website: www.agoldmine.com (includes writer's guidelines, names of editors, short fiction, products). **Editors:** Carol C. MacLeod & M. Cathy Strachar. Magazine: 5½×8½; 40-70 pages; white offset paper; slick cover; illustrations and photos. Bimonthly science fiction magazine. Estab. 1998. Circ. 200.

Needs: Fantasy (space fantasy, sword and sorcery, cross genre), horror (dark fantasy, futuristic, psychological, supernatural), romance (futuristic/time travel), science fiction (hard science/technological, soft/sociological). "Try us with things that may seem off the wall. Horror and romance should be mainly science fiction and fantasy." List of upcoming themes available for SASE. Receives 100-150 unsolicited mss/month. Accepts 4-6 mss/issue; 36 mss/year. Publishes ms 2-6 months after acceptance. **Publishes 75% new writers/year.** Recently published work by T. Lynn Neal, Kelly Ferjutz, Louise Feaver Crawford, Paul E. Martens, Elizabeth Pearl and Cynthia Ward. Length: 3,500 words average; 100 words minimum; 5,000 words maximum. Publishes short shorts. Length: 250 words. Also publishes literary essays, literary criticism and poetry. Always critiques or comments on rejected ms.

How to Contact: Send complete ms with a cover letter. Include estimated word count, bio, social security number and list of publications. Reports in 6 weeks on queries; 3 months on mss. Send SASE for reply, return of ms or send a disposable copy of ms. Sample copy for $4 and 6×9 SAE with 78¢ postage. Guidelines for SASE. Reviews novel, short story collections and nonfiction books of interest to writers. Send books to editor.

Payment/Terms: Pays $5-75 on publication for first North American serial rights. Sometimes buys electronic rights. Sends prepublication galleys to author.

Advice: "Our criteria are straightforward—a professional looking manuscript written will in the genre of our magazine. The writing must grab us on page one and compel us to read more. Please read our magazine first. Get our guidelines. We've had to reject a lot of great writing recently because the author hadn't read our guidelines."

N $◻ YELLOW STICKY NOTES, P.O. Box 452, Greenfield IN 46140. (317)462-0037. E-mail: suwk@aol.com. Website: www.wordmuseum.com (includes writer's guidelines, editors, list of articles in upcoming issue). **Editor:** Su Kopil. Magazine: 8×11; 60 pages; paper varies; glossy cover; illustrations and photos. "*Yellow Sticky Notes* is a multi-genre magazine for writers and readers. It includes articles, interviews, short fiction and poetry. Semiannually. Estab. 1999. Circ. 2,000.

Needs: Adventure, children's/juvenile (adventure, animal, easy-to-read, fantasy, historical, mystery, preschool, series, sports), comics, ethnic/multicultural, fantasy (space fantasy, sword and sorcery, romance), historical, horror (psychological, supernatural), literary, mainstream, military/war, mystery/suspense (amateur sleuth, cozy, police procedural, private eye/hardboiled), regional, religious (children's religious, general religious, inspirational, religious fantasy, religious mystery/suspense, religious thriller, religious romance), romance (contemporary, futuristic/time travel, gothic, historical, regency period, romantic suspense), science fiction (hard science/technological, soft/sociological), thriller/espionage, western (frontier saga, traditional), young adult/teen (adventure, easy-to-read, fantasy/science fiction, historical, horror, mystery/suspense, problem novels, romance, series, sports, western. "We are a family oriented publication. No inappropriate themes or issues. Accepts 2 mss/issue; 4 mss/year. Does not read from August-Nov. or from Feb.-April. Publishes ms 6 months after acceptance. Agented fiction 2%. **Publishes 1 new writer/year.** Recently published work by Vicki Nince, Lori Soard, Cathy McDavid and Hilary Anne Brown. Length: 2,000 words average; 1,000 words minimum; 2,500 words maximum. Publishes short shorts. Length: 500 words. Also publishes literary essays and poetry. Sometimes critiques or comments on rejected ms.

How to Contact: Query first by e-mail. "No postal submissions." Include estimated word count, 1-2 paragraph bio and list of publications. Reports in 6 weeks on queries. Simultaneous and reprint submissions OK. Sample copy for $8.99. Guidelines free on website or for SASE.

Payment/Terms: Pays $1-10 and 1 contributor's copy on publication for first rights. Sends prepublication galleys to author.

Advice: "We like stories that are unique. Make us laugh, cry or smile. Make certain the manuscript is clean. Watch for spelling and grammatical errors. Clean up passive writing."

◎ **YOUNG JUDAEAN**, Hadassah Zionist Youth Commission, 50 W. 58th St., New York NY 10019. (212)303-4575. **Editor:** Debra Neufeld. Magazine: 8½ × 11; 16 pages; illustrations. "*Young Judaean* is for members of the Young Judaea Zionist youth movement, ages 8-13." Quarterly. Estab. 1910. Circ. 4,000.

Needs: Children's fiction including adventure, ethnic, fantasy, historical, humor/satire, juvenile, prose poem, religious, science fiction, suspense/mystery and translations. "All stories must have Jewish relevance." Receives 10-15 unsolicited fiction mss/month. Publishes ms up to 2 years after acceptance. Accepts 1-2 mss/issue; 10-20 mss/year. Length: 750 words minimum; 1,000 words maximum.

How to Contact: Send complete ms with SASE. Reports in 3 months on mss. Sample copy for 75¢. Free fiction guidelines.

Payment/Terms: Pays five contributor's copies.

Advice: "Stories must be of Jewish interest—lively and accessible to children without being condescending."

Zines

Vastly different from one another in appearance and content, the common source of zines seems to be a need for self-expression. Although this need to voice opinions has always been around, it was not until the '70s, and possibly beginning with the social upheaval of the '60s, that the availability of photocopiers and computers provided an easy, cheap way to produce the self-published and usually self-written "zines." And now, with the cyberspace explosion, an overwhelming number of "e-zines" are springing up in an electronic format every day.

SELF-EXPRESSION AND ARTISTIC FREEDOM

The editorial content of zines runs the gamut from traditional and genre fiction to personal rants and highly experimental work. Artistic freedom, however, is a characteristic of all zines. Although zine editors are open to a wide range of fiction that more conventional editors might not consider, don't make the mistake of thinking they expect any less from writers than the editors of other types of publications. Zine editors look for work that is creative and well presented and that shows the writer has taken time to become familiar with the market. And since most zines are highly specialized, familiarity with the niche markets they offer is extremely important.

Some of the zines listed here have been published since the early '80s, but many are relatively new and some were just starting publication as they filled out the questionnaire to be included in this edition of *Novel & Short Story Writer's Market*. Unfortunately, due to the waning energy and shrinking funds of their publishers (and often a lack of material), few last for more than several issues. Fortunately, though, some have been around since the late '70s and early '80s, and hundreds of new ones are launched every day.

While zines represent the most volatile group of publications in *Novel & Short Story Writer's Market*, they are also the most open to submissions by beginning writers. As mentioned above, the editors of zines are often writers themselves and welcome the opportunity to give others a chance at publication.

SELECTING THE RIGHT MARKET

Your chance for publication begins as you zero in on the zines most likely to be interested in your work. Begin by browsing through the listings. This is especially important since zines are the most diverse and specialized markets listed in this book. If you write genre fiction, check out the specific sections for lists of magazines publishing in that genre (mystery, page 52; romance, page 64; science fiction and fantasy, page 76). For other types of fiction, check the Category Index (starting on page 632) for the appropriate subject heading.

In addition to browsing through the listings and using the Category Index, check the ranking codes at the beginning of listings to find those most likely to be receptive to your work. Most all zines are open to new writers ($\square$) or to both new and established writers ($\blacksquare$). For more explanation about these codes, see the inside front and back covers of this book.

Once you have a list of zines you might like to try, read their listings carefully. Zines vary greatly in appearance as well as content. Some paper zines are photocopies published whenever the editor has material and money, while others feature offset printing and regular distribution schedules. And a few have evolved into four-color, commercial-looking, very slick publications. The physical description appearing near the beginning of the listings gives you clues about the size and financial commitment to the publication. This is not always an indication of quality, but chances are a publication with expensive paper and four-color artwork on the cover has more prestige than a photocopied publication featuring a clip art self-cover. If you're a new writer or your work is considered avant garde, however, you may be more interested in the photocopied zine or one of the electronic zines. For more information on some of the paper, binding and printing terms used in these descriptions, see Printing and Production Terms Defined on page 627. Also, The "Quick Start" Guide to Publishing Your Fiction, starting on page 2, describes in detail the listing information common to all markets in our book.

FURTHERING YOUR SEARCH

Reading the listings is only the first part of developing your marketing plan. The second part, equally important, is to obtain fiction guidelines and a copy of the actual zine. Reading copies of the publication helps you determine the fine points of the zine's publishing style and philosophy. Especially since zines tend to be highly specialized, there is no substitute for this hands-on, eyes-on research. With e-zines, all the information you need is available on their websites.

Unlike commercial periodicals available at most newsstands and bookstores, it requires a little more effort to obtain most of the paper zines listed here. You will probably need to send for a sample copy. We include sample copy prices in the listings whenever possible.

N ⭐ $⭘ 🔲 ANOTHEREALM, 287 Gano Ave., Orange Park FL 32073-4307. (904)269-5429. E-mail: goldstrm@tu.infi.net. Website: www.anotherealm.com. **Editor:** Jean Goldstrom. E-zine specializing in science fiction, fantasy and horror. Weekly. Estab. 1998.

● *Anotherealm* is a member of the Zine Guild.

Needs: Fantasy (space fantasy, sword and sorcery), horror (dark fantasy, futuristic, psychological, supernatural), science fiction (hard science/technological, soft/sociological). Receives 40 unsolicited mss/month. Accepts 8 mss/issue; 96 mss/year. Publishes ms "usually 2-6 months" after acceptance. **Publishes 40 new writers/year.** Word length: 5,000 words maximum. Always comments on or critiques rejected ms.

How to Contact: Send complete ms with a cover letter by e-mail. Include estimated word count and 50 word bio. Reports on mss in 2 months. No simultaneous submissions. Sample copy and guidelines free on website.

Payment/Terms: Pays $5 on acceptance. Acquires first rights.

Advice: "Same as everyone else—editor's prejudice view of 'the best.' Read my book *How to Write Creatively for Internet Magazines.*"

N ⭐ ⭘ ARTISAN, a journal of craft, P.O. Box 157, Wilmette IL 60091. E-mail: artisanjnl@aol.com. Website: members.aol.com/artisanjnl. **Editor:** Joan Daugherty.

Needs: "We'd love to see more 'literary' stories that appeal to a general audience-stories that are well written and sophisticated without being stuffy. Nothing sexually or violently graphic or with foul language unless it clearly contributes to the story." Recently published work by J.B. Powell, Frank Scozzari, Jean Ryan and Melanie Barton. **Publishes 16 new writers/year.** Annual fiction contest.

How to Contact: Electronic and traditional submissions accepted. E-mail submissions should be in ASCII text format; traditional submissions should include a SASE for reply. Sample copies $4.50. Subscriptions $15.

Advice: "Send us stories that have well-defined plots, believable characters and a definable 'turning point,' written with just enough words to get the job done-nothing longer than 4,000 words, preferably around 3,000."

⭘ ART:MAG, P.O. Box 70896, Las Vegas NV 89170. (702)734-8121. **Editor:** Peter Magliocco. Zine: 7×8½×8½, 8½×14, also 8½×11; 70-90 pages; 20 lb. bond paper; b&w pen and ink illustrations and photographs. Publishes "irreverent, literary-minded work by committed writers," for "small press, 'quasi-art-oriented' " audience. Annually. Estab. 1984. Circ. under 500.

Needs: Condensed/excerpted novel, confession, contemporary, erotica, ethnic, experimental, fantasy, feminist, gay, historical (general), horror, humor/satire, lesbian, literary, mainstream, mystery/suspense, prose poem, psychic/supernatural/occult, regional, science fiction, translations and arts. Wants to see more "daring and thought-provoking" fiction. No "slick-oriented stuff published by major magazines." Receives 1 plus ms/month. Accepts 1-2 mss/year. Does not read mss July-October. Publishes ms within 3-6 months of acceptance. Recently published work by Darren Delmore, Edward R. Dumont, Andy Mingo, R. Daniel Evans and the Mag Man. **Publishes 2 new writers/year.** Length: 2,000 words preferred; 250 words minimum; 3,000 words maximum. Also publishes literary essays "if relevant to aesthetic preferences," literary criticism "occasionally," poetry. Sometimes critiques rejected mss.

How to Contact: Send complete ms with cover letter. Reports in 3 months. SASE for ms. Simultaneous submissions OK. Sample copy for $5, 6×9 SAE and 79¢ postage. Two-year subscription for $10. Fiction guidelines for #10 SASE.

Payment/Terms: Pays contributor's copies. Acquires one-time rights.

Advice: "Seeking more novel and quality-oriented work, usually from solicited authors. Magazine fiction today needs to be concerned with the issues of fiction writing itself—not just with a desire to publish or please the largest audience. Think about things in the fine art world as well as the literary one and keep the hard core of life in between."

★ ◑ ATROCITY, Publication of the Absurd Sig, 2419 Greensburg Pike, Pittsburgh PA 15221. E-mail: rollh@juno.com. Website: www.geocities.com/Eureka/Park/3517 (includes samples). Editor: Hank Roll. **Editorial contact:** Tinker. Zine: 5½×8½; 30 pages; offset 20 lb. paper and cover; illustrations. Humor and satire for "high IQ-Mensa" members. Monthly. Estab. 1976. Circ. 250.
Needs: Humor/satire: Liar's Club, parody, jokes, funny stories, comments on the absurdity of today's world. Receives 30 unsolicited mss/month. Accepts 2 mss/issue. Publishes ms 6-12 months after acceptance. Published work by John Smethers, Sheryll Watt, Dolph Wave and Ellen Warts. **Published 12 new writers/last year.** Length: 50-150 words preferred; 650 words maximum.
How to Contact: Send complete ms. "No cover letter necessary if ms states what rights (e.g. first North American serial/reprint, etc.) are offered." Accepts queries/mss by e-mail. Reports in 1 month. SASE. Simultaneous and reprint submissions OK. Sample copy for $1.
Payment/Terms: Pays contributor's copies. Acquires one-time rights.
Advice: Do not submit mss exceeding 650 words. Manuscript should be single-spaced and copy ready in a horizontal format to fit on one 5½×8½ sheet. "If you don't read the specs, you get it back. Don't waste our time."

◑ ▣ AURICULAR IMMERSION MEDIA ONLINE MAGAZINE, 2434 21st Ave., San Francisco CA 94116. (415)664-6302. E-mail: aherrick@auricular.com. Website: www.auricular.com/AIM. **Editor:** Alan Herrick. Electronic zine. "An online magazine fueled mostly by submissions and developed as a support mechanism for beginning and experienced writers and reporters. Very little editorial discretion is exercised making this sort of an open forum, or testing ground for many contributors. Intended audience is 18-45. Magazine offers fiction, serial fiction, reviews (film and music) political articles, rants, raves and the like. Much of the reported material has a sarcastic edge."
Needs: "Completely open. Nothing offensively hateful. We would like to see more women writers' works." Published work by Ted Rosen, Ben Ohmart, Henry Warwick, John Humphries, Alan Herrick, Cliff Neighbors. Publishes as many new writers "as are willing to contribute material."
How to Contact: Electronic submissions only. Send mss via email in ASCII format or as a MS word RTF attachment.
Advice: "Be open minded, have an edge, and be willing to see your material presented in a fashion that is unconventional to other publications in attitude and appearance. Quite a few of our writers have scored weekly columns and paid publishing ventures with their submission to AIM on their CV. Although we can't afford to pay . . . we update the publication online regularly . . . all past submissions are available as archived material and we do our best to get word of our publication out to the masses without cluttering it with advertising and fluff."

Ⓝ ▣ BABEL, the Multilingual, Multicultural Online Journal of Arts and Ideas, E-mail: malcolm@to werofbabel.com. Website: www.towerofbabel.com. **Editor:** Malcolm Lawrence. Electronic zine. Publishes "regional reports from international stringers all over the planet, as well as features round table discussions, fiction, columns, poetry, erotica, travelogues, reviews of all the arts and editorials. We are an online community involving an extensive group of over 50 artists, writers and programmers, and over 150 translators representing (so far) 35 of the world's languages."
Needs: "There are no specific categories of fiction that we are not interested in. Possible exceptions: lawyers/vampires, different genders hailing from different planets, cold war military scenarios and things that go bump in the suburban night." Recently published work by Nicholas P. Snoek, Yves Jaques, Doug Williamson, A.L. Fern, Laura Feister, Denzel J. Hankinson, Pete Hanson and Malcolm Lawrence.
How to Contact: Send queries/mss by e-mail. "Please send submissions with a résumé/cv or biography, as Microsoft Word attached to e-mail." Reviews novels and short story collections.
Advice: "We would like to see more fiction with first-person male characters written by female authors as well as more fiction with first-person female characters written by male authors. The best advice we could give to writers wanting to be published in our publication is simply to know what you're writing about and to write passionately about it. We should also mention that the phrase 'dead white men' will only hurt your chances. The Internet is the most important invention since the printing press and will change the world in the same way. One look at *Babel* and you'll see our predictions for the future of electronic publishing."

◑ babysue, P.O. Box 8989, Atlanta GA 31106-8989. (404)875-8951. Website: www.babysue.com (includes comics, poetry, fiction and a wealth of music reviews). **Editor:** Don W. Seven. Zine: 8½×11; 32 pages; illustrations and photos. "*babysue* is a collection of music reviews, poetry, short fiction and cartoons for anyone who can think and is not easily offended." Biannually. Estab. 1983. Circ. 5,000.
  ● Sometimes funny, very often perverse, this 'zine featuring mostly cartoons and "comix" definitely is not for the easily offended.

Needs: Erotica, experimental and humor/satire. Receives 5-10 mss/month. Accepts 3-4 mss/year. Publishes ms within 3 months of acceptance. Published work by Daniel Lanette, Massy Baw, Andrew Taylor and Barbara Rimshaw. Publishes short shorts. Length: 1-2 single-spaced pages.

How to Contact: Query with clips of published work. SASE. Simultaneous submissions OK. No submissions via e-mail.

Payment/Terms: Pays 1 contributor's copy.

Advice: "Create out of the love of creating, not to see your work in print!"

N ○ **BACKSPACE, A Collection of Queer Poetry**, Lock the Target Media, 25 Riverside Ave., Gloucester MA 01930-2552. (978)282-5422. E-mail: bkspqpj@aol.com. Editor: Kimberley Smith. **Fiction Editor:** Charlotte Stratton. Zine: 5½×8½; 28 pages; copy paper; glossy cover; illustrations and photos. "*Backspace* is a literary zine for the gay, lesbian, bisexual and transgender community." Quarterly. Estab. 1991. Circ. 400-600.

Needs: Experimental, gay, humor/satire, lesbian, literary. "No sexually explicit or violent material." Plans to publish special fiction issues or anthologies. Receives 8-10 unsolicited mss/month. Accepts 4-8 mss/issue; 16-20 mss/year. Publishes ms 6 months after acceptance. Agented fiction 85%. Published work by B.Z. Niditch, Beth Brant, Monika Arnett, Robert Klein Engler and Leah Erickson. Also publishes literary essays, poetry.

How to Contact: Send complete ms with a cover letter. Include estimated word count, 25-word bio, list of publications. Reports in 2 weeks on queries; 3-6 weeks on mss. Send SASE for reply, return of ms or send a disposable copy of ms. Simultaneous, reprint, electronic submissions (3.5 diskette, Word, QuarkXPress, Pagemaker, ASCII; or e-mail) OK. Sample copy for $2.50. Fiction guidelines for #10 SASE. Reviews novels and short story collections. Send books to Charlotte Stratton.

Payment/Terms: Pays 1 contributor's copy; additional copies $5. Acquires one-time rights. Not copyrighted.

Advice: "Fully formed characters are important; topical allusions are distracting."

N ★ **BEEF: the meat**, (218)838-8333. E-mail: joymiller@uchicago.edu. Website: www.purdueonline.com~joyous. **Editor:** Joy Olivia Miller. Electronic zine. *BEEF* is "high brow content hidden in fun articles, reviews, stories and poetry. The point of *BEEF* is to entertain."

Needs: "No historical melodramatic pieces or pornographic work. Would like to see more dark comedy first person or modern and sci-fi." **Publishes 10 new writers/year.** Recently published work by Michelle Trella, Brian Zomchek and Christina Walker.

How to Contact: Accepts queries/mss by e-mail.

Advice: "Entertaining commentary on pop culture issues is a major theme . . . *BEEF* is mainly reviews and essays; however, fiction that would be appropriate/interesting to an audience of those age 18-28 is printed. Tends to be a college-educated crowd. Make your work fun and true to life. Honesty pays off. Although print will never die, the electronic publishing arena IS the future."

○ ▼ **THE BITTER OLEANDER**, 4983 Tall Oaks Dr., Fayetteville NY 13066-9776. (315)637-3047. Fax: (315)637-5056. E-mail: bones44@ix.netcom.com. Website: www.bitteroleander.com. **Editor:** Paul B. Roth. Zine specializing in poetry and fiction: 6×9; 128 pages; 55 lb. paper; 12 pt. CIS cover stock; photos. "We're interested in the surreal; deep image; particularization of natural experiences." Semiannually. Estab. 1974. Circ. 1,500.

• In 1998 *The Bitter Oleander* received a Hemingway grant from the French Ministry of Culture.

Needs: Experimental, new age/mystic/spiritual, translations. "No pornography; no confessional; no romance." Receives 12 unsolicited mss/month. Accepts 1-2 mss/issue; 2-4 mss/year. Does not read mss in July. Publishes ms 4-6 months after acceptance. Recently published work by Robert Bly, Charles Wright, Louis Simpson, Marjorie Agosín, Duane Locke and Alan Britt. Length: 1,000 words minimum; 2,000 words maximum. Publishes short shorts. Length: 1,500 words. Also publishes literary essays, poetry. Always critiques or comments on rejected ms.

How to Contact: Send complete ms with a cover letter. Include estimated word count, 50-word bio and list of publications. Reports in 1 week on queries; 1 month on mss. Send SASE for reply, return of ms. Sample copy for $8, 7×10 SAE with 4 first-class stamps. Fiction guidelines for #10 SASE.

Payment/Terms: Pays 1 contributor's copy; additional copies $8. Acquires first rights.

Advice: "We're interested in originality."

★ ✓ ○ **BLACK PETALS**, 708 S. 15th St., Manitowoc WI 54220. E-mail: subs@lsol.net. Website: www.netcom.com/~corwin/blackpetals/. **Editor:** D.M. Yortom. Zine specializing in horror/fantasy: full size; over 100 pages; photocopied; illustrations; movie and book reviews. "A little something special for those special readers of oddity and terror." Quarterly. Estab. 1997. Circ. 200.

Needs: Experimental, horror, psychic/supernatural/occult; science fiction (soft/sociological). Wants more hard core horror. No children's or romance. Contests every issue. Receives over 100 unsolicited mss/month. Accepts 14-20 mss/issue. Recently published work by Kent Robinson, C.B. Thatcher, James Patterson and Greg Gifune. **Publishes 10 new writers/year.** Length: 1,500 words average; no minimum; 2,500 words maximum. Publishes short shorts. Also publishes poetry. Always critiques or comments on rejected mss.

How to Contact: Send complete ms. Include estimated word count and list of publications. Reports in 2-4 weeks on queries and mss. "Disposable copies please. No e-mail submissions, query first." Simultaneous submissions and reprints OK. Sample copy for $5.50. Fiction guidelines for #10 SASE.

Payment/Terms: Pays contributor's copies; additional copies $5.50.

Advice: "My best advice—submit! How do you know if you'll get published unless you submit! Also, obtain a sample copy, follow guidelines and don't watch the mailbox. New unpublished writers are high on my list. If I have time I'll even help edit a manuscript. If I reject a manuscript, I encourage writers to send something else. Don't ever be discouraged, and don't wallpaper your office with rejection notes—toss them!"

N ⬡ ▣ **BLOODY MUSE**, 7085 15th St., Manitowoc WI 54220. E-mail: subs@1sol.net or drkwrtr@c2i2.c om. Website: westwood.fortunecity.com/chanel/338/bm/bm.htm. **Editors:** D.M. Yorton and Weston Ochse. Electronic zine. "*Bloody Muse* is the stories that your mother warned you against. Some of the darkest fiction on the web today. Stories and poetry that holds you tight and doesn't let go."

Needs: Horror (dark fantasy, psychological). "No romance or children or animals used in profane ways that don't have a credit to the story. No children's stories at all, this is an adult e-zine only. Want more psychological horror (thrillers)." **Publishes 5-6 new writers/year.** Recently published work by David Whitman, Greg Gifune, Durant, Sandra Fritz, Weston Ochse, S.L. Robinson and Sandra Deluca.

How to Contact: "Send queries/mss by e-mail only please. Send in the body of the e-mail. No attachments ever! Send to subs@1sol.net with title of e-zine in subject line."

Payment/Terms: "You will receive credit with an e-zine that has been in the top ten of www.goth.net plus in the top five for the best e-zine on the web. Once in a while we do have certain themes—when we do, payment is a subscription to one of the sister print zines."

Advice: "*Bloody Muse* is a hard e-zine to get into. Send your best hard gore horror. I look for harsh atmosphere that chills me while I am reading it and after I read it."

N **$** ⬡ ▣ **THE BLUE ROSE BOUQUET**, (419)394-5838. E-mail: ricehahn@bright.net. Website: www. blueroses.com. **Editor:** Pamela Rice Hahn. Electronic zine. Publishes "for general audiences who enjoy reading good humor or escaping into a good story."

Needs: Humor, satire, mainstream. "We occasionally run non-PG (but far from anything r-rated) humor and mark it "Adult Content" in the Index/Table of Contents for the issue; adult content is usually innuendo. I've told writers 'we don't publish explicit, but innuendo and out the other is okay.' We like puns." Publishes 5 new writers/issue. Recently published works by Troy More, Margaret Chittenden, Richard Montanari, Luanne Oleas, Larisa Dawn Sutton and Pamela Rice Hahn.

How to Contact: Send queries/mss by e-mail. "Initial submissions should be sent pasted in the body of an e-mail. Should we accept the submission, we may ask the author to send the manuscript as an attachment; we prefer Word format."

Payment & Terms: "Many of our authors write for fame—the opportunity to promote their work. However, we also select several stories or essays per issue for which the author is offered the choice between pay (usually $10 U.S.) or a book."

Advice: Looks for fiction "with good humor! We love it when a story makes us laugh out loud. We strongly believe in celebrating one another's writing successes. We maintain a 'wOOhOO & Congrats!!!' section on our online magazine for this purpose. Keeping with this philosophy, we're generous in the amount of bio space we allow our authors; bios can include links to the author's website as well as e-mail address and book purchase information, if applicable. Read the guidelines. And, please be patient. *The Blue Rose Bouquet* is a labor of love for myself and my co-editors Keith Giddeon and RJ Corradino. Therefore, response time to a submission is sometimes immediate; other times months can pass before we have a chance to review them. It depends on our own deadline schedules on other projects."

N ⬡ ◎ **BOTH SIDES NOW, Journal of Spiritual Alternatives**, Free People Press, 10547 State Highway 110 N., Tyler TX 75704-3731. (903)592-4263. Editor: Elihu Edelson. Zine: 8½×11; 10 pages; bond paper and cover; b&w line illustrations. "*Both Sides Now* explores the Aquarian frontier as the world witnesses the end of an old order and enters a New Age. Its contents include opinion, commentary, philosophy and creative writing for all who are interested in New Age matters." Published irregularly. Estab. 1969. Circ. 200.

Needs: Material with New Age slant, including fables, fantasy, humor/satire, myths, parables, psychic/supernatural, religious/inspirational, romance (futuristic/time travel), science fiction (utopian, soft/sociological). Length: "about 2 magazine pages, more or less." Also publishes literary essays, book reviews and poetry. Often comments on rejected mss with "brief note."

How to Contact: Send complete ms with SASE. Include brief bio and list of publications. Simultaneous submissions and previously published work OK. Reports in 3 months on mss. Send SASE for reply, return of ms or send a disposable copy of ms. Sample copy for $1. Reviews "New Age fiction."

CHECK THE CATEGORY INDEXES, located at the back of the book, for publishers interested in specific fiction subjects.

Payment/Terms: Pays 5 contributor's copies plus subscription. "Authors retain rights."
Advice: Looks for "tight, lucid writing that leaves the reader with a feeling of delight and/or enlightenment. Heed our editorial interests. Short pieces preferred as space is very limited. We plan to publish more fiction; emphasis has been on nonfiction to date."

THE BROBDINGNAGIAN TIMES, 96 Albert Rd., Cork, Ireland. Phone: (21)311227. **Editor:** Giovanni Malito. Zine specializing in short international work: $6 \times 8\frac{1}{2}$; 8 pages; 80 gramme paper; illustrations. "There are no obvious editorial slants. We are interested in any prose from anyone anywhere provided it is short (1,000 words maximum)." Quarterly. Estab. 1996. Circ. 250.
Needs: Ethnic/multicultural, experimental, horror, humor/satire, literary, romance (contemporary), science fiction (hard science/technological, soft/sociological). "No ghost stories/dysfunctional family stories/first sex stories." Receives 4-6 unsolicited mss/month. Accepts 2 mss/issue; 8 mss/year. Publishes ms in next issue after acceptance. **Publishes 2-3 new writers/year.** Published work by D.F. Lewis, Christopher Woods, Michael Wynne, Laura Lush, Ruba Neda and Jon Rourke. Length: 600 words average; 50 words minimum; 1,000 words maximum. Publishes short shorts. Length: 500 words. Also publishes literary essays, poetry. Always critiques or comments on rejected ms.
How to Contact: Send complete ms with a cover letter. Include estimated word count. Reports in 1 week on queries; 3 weeks on mss. Send SASE (IRCs) for reply, return of ms or send a disposable copy of ms. Simultaneous and reprint submissions OK. Sample copy for #10 SAE and 2 IRCs. Fiction guidelines for #10 SAE and 1 IRC.
Payment/Terms: Pays 2 contributor's copies; additional copies for postage. Acquires one-time rights for Ireland/U.K. Sends galleys to author if required. Copyrighted Ireland/U.K.
Advice: "Crisp language. Economy of language. These are important, otherwise almost anything goes."

BURNING SKY: Adventures in Science Fiction Terror, Thevin' Kitty Publications, P.O. Box 341, Marion MA 02738. E-mail: theedge@capecod.net. Website: www.capecod.net/thevinkitty (includes guidelines, current and back issue information, cover art, ordering information, information on editors). **Editor:** Greg F. Gifune. Associate editors: Carla Gifune and Chuck Deude. Zine specializing in science fiction horror: digest; 30-40 pages; white bond; glossy card cover. *Burning Sky* publishes "sci/fi horror blends ONLY." Triannually. Estab. 1998. Circ. 250.
- "In the Ending" by James H. Bearden was recommended for the Stoker Award.
Needs: Horror and science fiction blends. Receives more than 100 unsolicited mss/month. Accepts 5-6 mss/issue; 15-18 mss/year. Does not read January, May and September. Publishes ms 1-4 months after acceptance. Agented fiction 1-2%. **Publishes 1-3 new writers/year.** Recently published work by D. F. Lewis, Michael Laimo, Suzanne Donahue, Christopher Stires, Denis Kirk and Stephen van Maanen. Length: 2,000-3,000 words average; 500 words minimum; 3,500 words maximum. Also publishes literary criticism. Often critiques or comments on rejected ms.
How to Contact: Send complete ms with a cover letter. Accepts queries by e-mail, but no mss. Include estimated word count, bio, list of publications and cover letter. Reports in 1 week on queries; 1 week-2 months on mss. Send SASE for reply, return of ms or send a disposable copy of ms. No simultaneous submissions. Sample copy for $3 in US, $4 elsewhere. Reviews novels, short story collections and nonfiction books of interest to writers. Send books to editor.
Payment/Terms: Pays 1 contributor's copy; additional copies $3. Payment on publication. Sends galleys to author on request.
Advice: "We like strong, concise, lean writing, stories that follow our very specific guidelines of blending sci-fi and horror, stories with an 'edge of your seat' quality. Thought-provoking, tension filled and genuinely frightening stories with realistic dialogue and a gritty style. Do not send straight sci-fi or horror stories. We need elements of both. Read a copy. *Burning Sky* is a very particular market, but we are proud to have published three first stories in our first three issues, along with more established writers. Send us a well written story in proper manuscript format that fits our guidelines. We don't want highly technical or introverted ramblings—we want exciting, highly entertaining and frightening stories."

CETERIS PARIBUS. E-mail: ceteris@intrepid.net. Website: www.intrepid.net/ceteris/paribus.htm. **Editors:** Jim Carls, Jeff Edmonds, John Edwards and Roger Jones. Electronic zine. "Good writing with heart. Works by a circle of core writers, supplemented by select unsolicited contributions, have sustained a warm and entertaining intellectual and cultural exchange. The magazine strives to be unique, not bizarre; thought provoking, not iconoclastic; hospitable, not factional; literate, but not pedantic." Cumulative annual—works are posted on a continuing basis.
Needs: "Fiction, poetry, personal narratives, topical essays, reviews and criticism for the discerning reader. Our editors are not usually enthusiastic about experimental fiction or writing that is weird for weird's sake. We will consider any well written story with the almost hypnotic ability to transport the reader into its world. We favor traditional literary fiction, but we also welcome genre fiction." **Publishes at least 6 new writers/year.**
How to Contact: Electronic and traditional submissions accepted. "Manuscripts should be copied and pasted into e-mail. Don't use attachments! For the internet-impaired, paper manuscripts can be sent to Ceteris Paribus,

236 Snug Harbour Dr., Shalimar FL 32579-1261—but the response time will unavoidably be longer for such submissions."

Advice: "First, send only material that has not appeared previously. We are a unique Web magazine, not a recycling center. Second, we look for more than clever word-spinning. Style should be cultivated to enhance content; it can never compensate the lack. Write about what matters to you, not what might excite others. We look for writers who, through humor or drama, have something of value to say about the human experience."

✓ ◑ ◎ **A COMPANION IN ZEOR**, 307 Ashland Ave., Egg Harbor Township NJ 08234-5568. (606)645-6938. Fax: (606)645-8084. E-mail: klitman323@aol.com or karenlitman@juno.com. Website: www.simegen. com/in-t/virtualtecton/CZ. (includes guidelines, back issue flyers, etc.). **Editor:** Karen Litman. Fanzine: 8½ × 11; 60 pages; "letter" paper; heavy blue cover; b&w line illustrations; occasional b&w photographs. Publishes science fiction based on the various Universe creations of Jacqueline Lichtenberg. Occasional features on Star Trek, and other interests, convention reports, reviews of movies and books, recordings, etc. Published irregularly. Estab. 1978. Circ. 300.

  ● *Companion in Zeor* is one fanzine devoted to the work and characters of Jacqueline Lichtenberg. Lichtenberg's work includes several future world, alien and group culture novels and series including the Sime/Gen Series and The Dushau trilogy. She's also penned two books on her own vampire character and she co-authored *Star Trek Lives*.

Needs: Fantasy, humor/satire, prose poem, science fiction. "No vicious satire. Nothing X-rated. Homosexuality prohibited unless *essential* in story. We run a clean publication that anyone should be able to read without fear." Occasionally receives one manuscript a month." Publication of an accepted ms "goes to website posting. " Occasionally critiques rejected mss and recommends other markets.

How to Contact: Query first or send complete ms with cover letter. "Prefer cover letters about any writing experience prior, or related interests toward writing aims." Reports in 1 month. SASE. Simultaneous submissions OK. Sample copy price depends on individual circumstances. Fiction guidelines for #10 SASE. "I write individual letters to all queries. No form letter at present." SASE for guidelines required. Reviews science fiction/fantasy collections or titles. "We can accept e-mail queries and manuscripts through AOL providers."

Payment/Terms: Pays in contributor's copies. Acquires first rights. Acquires website rights as well.

Advice: "Send concise cover letter asking what the author would like me to do for them if their manuscript can not be used by my publication. They should follow guidelines of the type of material I use, which is often not done. I have had many submissions I can not use as it is general fiction which was sent instead. Ask for guidelines before submitting to a publication. Write to the best of your ability and work with your editor to develop your work to a higher point than your present skill level. Take constructive criticism and learn from it. Electronic web publishing seems the way the industry is heading. I would not have thought of a website a few years ago. Guidelines can be sent by e-mail. Receipt of manuscripts can only be through klitman323@aol.com. Juno cannot handle attachments. People can learn more through the domain—www.simegen.com/index.html."

✪ ◯ **CURRICULUM VITAE**, Simpson Publications, Grove City Factory Stores, P.O. Box 1309, Grove City PA 16127. (814)671-1361. E-mail: simpub@hotmail.com. Website: www.geocities.com/soho/cafe/2550 (includes guidelines, contacts, fiction, interviews). **Editor:** Michael Dittman. Zine: digest-sized; 75-100 pages; standard paper; card cover stock; illustrations. "We are dedicated to new, exciting writers. We like essays, travelogues and short stories filled with wonderful, tense, funny work by writers who just happen to be underpublished or beginners. Our audience is young and overeducated." Quarterly. Estab. 1995. Circ. 2,000.

Needs: Condensed/excerpted novel, erotica, ethnic/multicultural, experimental, humor/satire, literary, mainstream/contemporary, serialized novel, sports, translations. Wants to see more hyper realism, magic realism and translations. "No sentimental 'weepers' or Bukowski-esque material." List of upcoming themes available for SASE. Publishes special fiction issues or anthologies. Receives 45 unsolicited mss/month. Accepts 7 mss/issue; 28 mss/year. Publishes mss 12 months after acceptance. Published work by Amber Meadow Adams and Carl Hoffman. **Publishes 25 new writers/year.** Publishes short shorts. Also publishes literary essays, literary criticism, poetry. Often critiques or comments on rejected mss.

How to Contact: Send complete ms with cover letter. Accepts queries/mss by e-mail. Reports in 1 month on queries and mss. Send SASE for reply, return of ms or send a disposable copy of ms. Simultaneous, reprint and electronic submissions OK. Sample copy for $3. Fiction guidelines for #10 SASE. Reviews novels and short story collections. Send books to Amy Dittman.

Payment/Terms: Pays minimum 2 contributor's copies to $125 maximum on publication. Acquires one-time rights.

Advice: "Looks for quality of writing, a knowledge of past works of literature and a willingness to work with our editors. Submit often and take criticism with a grain of salt."

Ⓝ ◯ ▣ **DARGONZINE**. E-mail: dargon@shore.net. Website: www.dargonzine.org. **Editor:** Ornoth D.A. Liscomb. Electronic zine specializing in fantasy. "*DargonZine* is a collaborative anthology, designed to give aspiring amatuer writers the opportunity to interact with a live readership as well as other writers. Our goal is to write fantasy fiction that is mature, emotionally compelling and professional."

Needs: Fantasy. "We only accept fantasy fiction that is developed within our common milieu. We would like to see more fantasy stories with characters who are easy to identify with, which offer the reader an emotionally compelling experience, and restore a sense of wonder that modern fantasy has lost. Membership in the Dargon Project is a requirement for publication." **Publishes 6-10 new writers/year.** Recently published work by Bryan Read, Mark A. Murray, Dafydd Cyhoeddwr, Jim Ownes and Max Khaytsus.

How to Contact: Guidelines available on website.

Payment/Terms: "Authors retain all rights to their stories, and our only compensation is the growth and satisfaction that comes with working with other writers through peer review and close collaboration."

Advice: "Start by reading or readers' and writers' FAQs on our website. We have a strong idea of what makes good fantasy fiction, and we live with certain restrictions as a part of our collaborative milieu. Furthermore, writing for *DargonZine* requires a nontrivial commitment of time."

N ★ ⊘ ▣ DARK MOON RISING, c/o Angela Silliman, P.O. Box 42844, Cincinnati, OH 45242. E-mail: editor@darkmoonrising.com. Website: www.darkmoonrising.com. **Senior Editor:** Angela Silliman. "*DMR* is committed to publishing well-written science fiction, fantasy, horror and related genre fiction, poetry and artwork on the World Wide Web. We are interested in new writers trying to break into the field, but published writers are welcome. We try to convey an attitude of scholarship, quality, interactivity and fun in our publication." Published 6 times/year.

Needs: "We publish short (less than 5,000 words) science fiction, fantasy, horror and related genre fiction, as well as poetry and artwork fitting these genres. Our readership ranges in age and both genders, and come from around the world. The attitude of the e-zine is to maintain something around the level of PG-13 for all published materials. We are not interested in anything with excessive strong language, intensive gore or pornography. We are also not looking for anything in the mystery or romance genres." Would like to see more "character driven fantasy." Publishes 5-10 mss/issue. **Publishes 20-30 new writers/year.** Recently published work by Myth Spinner, TJ Radus, Mark A. Revera, Mike Oakwood, Kim Guilbeau, Jason W. Brick and Stephen Harley.

How to Contact: Query by e-mail. E-mail short stories (less than 5,000 words) and poetry without query. Guidelines on website. "If e-mail is not available to a writer, he or she may submit work to our land mail address. However, reply times will take longer, and writers should check out our submission guidelines before sending anything via land mail."

Payment/Terms: "We currently offer no compensation, but we do not ask for any rights, other than 60 day publication rights. After 60 days, the author may request that the story be removed if rights are sold elsewhere."

Advice: "Read what we have online already to get a feel for what we generally publish what we like, etc. If we like a story we'll work with you to get it just right. Have someone else read over your story for typos and missing words. As a writer, I know that when you've worked on a piece for a while, and you know what it's supposed to say, you may overlook errors. Reading out loud also helps in the revision process. Don't be afraid to submit your work! Electronic publishing is a great place for new and beginning authors to have a chance to get their work published. Though I don't think that electronic publishing will ever replace print publishing, it's a great place to get off to a good start. Also, it's a great way to see what works, and what doesn't—usually for free. I think that the online world is a booming market for short fiction and most magazines, zines, and other short story markets will be moving into the arena in the future."

◐ DEADLY NIGHTSHADE, P.O. Box 50174, Minneapolis MN 55405. (612)822-4252. E-mail: femmegothi que@interzone.org. **Editor:** Angela M. Bacon. Zine: 5½ × 8½; 40-50 pages; regular paper; 67 lb. cover stock; illustrations and photos. "A zine for the darker side of life. *Deadly Nightshade* specializes in publishing horror, themes based on the gothic/industrial subculture, but will accept other literary work outside the genre based on quality." Quarterly. Estab. 1997. Circ. 50-100.

Needs: Fantasy (sword and sorcery), horror, psychic/supernatural/occult. "No sexually explicit (bordering on porn) material; no sports-related, children's/juvenile, religious." Receives 1-2 unsolicited mss/month. Accepts 1-2 mss/issue. Publishes ms 1-3 months after acceptance. Published work by Greg Moore and Alexander Bledsoe. Length: 2,500 words average; 500 words minimum; 2,500 words maximum. Publishes short shorts. Also publishes poetry.

How to Contact: Query first with or without clips of published work. Include estimated word count, 1-page bio. Reports in 2-3 weeks. Send SASE for reply, return of ms or send a disposable copy of ms. Simultaneous and reprint submissions OK. Electronic submissions (disk or modem) OK. Sample copy for $4 (U.S. currency only; contact for Canada/Mexico/overseas pricing). Fiction guidelines for #10 SASE.

Payment/Terms: Pays 1 contributor's copy; additional copies $4 (Canada/Mexico/overseas prices are higher).

N $ ▣ DEEP OUTSIDE SFFH, C&C Clocktower Fiction, Box 260, 6549 Mission Gorge Rd., San Diego CA 92120. (619)582-6852. Website: www.clocktowerfiction.com/Outside. **Editors:** John Cullen and Brian Callahan. Online magazine offering science fiction and dark imaginative horror. Estab. 1998.

Needs: Horror, science fiction. "We seek well-written, character-driven fiction that is tightly plotted, professionally executed, with attention to basics—grammar, punctuation, usage. No sword and sorcery, shared worlds, porno of any kind, excessive violence or gore beyond legitimate needs of a story, no vulgarity unless it furthers the story (sparingly at that). No derivative works emulating TV shows or movies (e.g. Star Trek)." Buys 12 mss/year. Publishes ms an average of 3 months after acceptance. Length: 1,500-5,000 words.

How to Contact: Send complete ms. Reports in 3 months on mss. Sample copy and guidelines on website.
Payment/Terms: Pays 3¢/word. Buys first North American serial and first North American electronic serial rights.
Advice: "Please read the tips and guidelines on the magazine's website for further and up-to-the-moment details. Submissions by mail only. Traditional format, #10 SASE minimum for reply."

DEVIL BLOSSOMS, P.O. Box 5122, Seabrook NJ 08302-3511. Phone/fax: (609)451-6139. E-mail: devilblossoms@hotmail.com. **Editor:** John C. Erianne. Zine specializing in fiction and poetry: 8½ × 11; 24 pages; 20-50 lb. paper; card stock. "*Devil Blossoms* seeks dark, twisted fiction, abnormal psychological. Black comedy. Explicit work willing to push the envelope. I don't think anyone will confuse *Devil Blossoms* with a story from *Atlantic Monthly*." Publishes 1-3 issues/year. Established 1998. Circ. 500.
Needs: Erotica, experimental, horror, humor satire, literary, private eye/hardboiled, science fiction (soft/sociological). "No mainstream PC crap. Nothing formulaic or predictable. No romance or religion unless you are poking fun at both." Receives 100-150 unsolicited mss/month. Accepts 2-3 mss/issue. Publishes ms 8-12 months after acceptance. Recently published work by Wanda Rimsek, Carolyn Light Bell and Leslie Wolf Hodley. Length: 1,500 words average; 250 words minimum; 2,500 words maximum. Publishes short shorts and poetry. Sometimes critiques or comments on rejected mss.
How to Contact: Send complete ms with a cover letter. Accepts queries/mss by e-mail. Include estimated word count, SASE and/or valid e-mail address. Reports in 1 week on queries/mss. Send SASE for reply, return of ms or send a disposable copy of ms. Simultaneous submissions OK. Sample copy for $3. Fiction guidelines for #10 SAE and 1 first-class stamp or 1 IRC.
Payment/Terms: Pays 1-2 contributor's copies. Pays on publication. Acquires first rights. Sends galleys to author, "if they request it."
Advice: "If you submit something that makes me uneasy yet is well-written enough that I don't immediately shove it in the return envelope it will at least make the first cut. Read a sample copy before submitting. Follow my guidelines. Don't believe you're Faulkner just because your English teacher gave you a gold star. Writing has always been about crossing boundaries, revealing human nature as we interact with our environment. A lot of the fiction I read in the literary journals tries too hard to be inoffensive. What is acceptable isn't necessarily good for literature. Don't be afraid to unlock doors."

DISENCHANTED: beyond happily every after, P.O. Box 924, Colonial Heights VA 23834-0924. (978)383-6436. E-mail: disenchanted@postmark.net. Website: disenchanted.cjb.net. "Disenchanted is an online publication." **Editor:** Jeanette Snyder. "Disenchanted is a fantasy publication that looks beyond happily ever after. Dark tales with sad endings. If it's depressing, chances are it's for us." Quarterly. Estab. 1999.
Needs: Adventure, Children's/juvenile (adventure, fantasy), comics/graphic novels, fantasy (space fantasy, sword and sorcery), feminist, gay, historical (general), horror (dark fantasy), humor satire, lesbian, literary, mainstream, New Age, psychic/supernatural/occult, religious (religious fantasy), romance (gothic, historical), science fiction (soft/sociological), translations, young adult/teen (adventure, fantasy/science fiction). "Nothing that doesn't have an aspect of fantasy." Receives 10-20 unsolicited mss/month. Accepts up to 10 mss/issue; more than 40 mss/year. Publishes ms 1-2 issues after acceptance. **Always publishes new writers.** Recently published work by Jeanette Snyder. Length: 5,000 words average; 200 words minimum; 10,000 words maximum. Publishes short shorts. Length: 250 words. Also publishes literary essays, literary criticism and poetry. Often critiques or comments on rejected ms.
How to Contact: "Send complete manuscript, bio, and any previous publications by e-mail only." Include estimated word count and 100 word bio. Reports in 1-4 weeks. No simultaneous submissions, but reprints OK. Sample copy and fiction guidelines free.
Payment/Terms: Acquires first rights. "Stories kept online for 2 months and then archived for download."
Advice: "Must be fantasy; must look 'beyond happily every after.' I can tell when you don't read the guidelines. I'll accept a story that's relevant to the theme before I'll accept a story that's well-written but not right for us. Don't give up. If you've been told your work is too depressing, too dark, it might be just what I'm looking for."

DIXIE PHOENIX, Exploration in Spirituality, Silliness, the Civil War and So Much More, 3888 N. 30th St., Arlington VA 22207. E-mail: jsmosby@gateway.net. Website: www.concentric.net/~yamyak/dixiephoenix/frontporch.html (includes writer's guidelines, zine history, selected articles, collected reviews, a few recipes and a growing number of links). **Editors:** Mike & Bjorn Munson. Zine specializing in literature/essays: 5½ × 8½; 40-52 pages; 60 lb. standard paper; 60-70 lb. color cover; illustrations, photographs. "Our audience appears to be of all religious and political persuasions from fringe to mainstream. We try to make each issue intriguing, informative, edifying and entertaining. We're a 'Mom & Pop publication' not a corporate operation." Semiannually. Estab. 1992. Circ. 500.
Needs: Historical (general), humor/satire, literary, mainstream/contemporary, regional, religious/inspirational, translations, travel essays, Celtic and Southern themes, Southern ghost stories, regional from all walks of life; folklore from around the world. Wants more "transcendental, regional" fiction. No children's/juvenile, erotica (no profanity in general), psychic/occult, romance. Receives 16-25 unsolicited mss/month. Accepts 1-2 mss/issue; 3-4 mss/year. Publishes ms 6-18 months after acceptance. Recently published Errol Miller, Patricia G.

Rourke and James C. Sullivan. Length: 1,500 words average; 250 words minimum; 7,000 words maximum. Publishes short shorts. Also publishes literary essays, literary criticism, poetry. "We have regular columns concerning history, culture and spirituality." Sometimes critiques or comments on rejected mss.

How to Contact: Query first or e-mail. Include a "nice friendly letter telling us about themselves and/or their writing." Reports in 1 month on queries; e-mail queries are often quicker; 3-4 months on mss. Send a disposable copy of ms. Simultaneous submissions, reprints and electronic submissions OK. Sample copy for $2. Reviews novels and short story collections (also music).

Payment/Terms: Pays 3 contributor's copies on publication; additional copies for $2. Acquires one-time rights.

Advice: "We value sincerity over shock value. Fiction with a 'Phoenix Flavor' has a subject of personal exploration/discovery/epiphany/subjectivity whether spiritual, emotional, intellectual, etc. Definitely get a sample copy of our publication to get an idea of what we're about. Do many drafts and learn to critique your own work. Polish, polish, polish. No work is ever completely done."

N $ ☺ DREAMS & NIGHTMARES, The Magazine of Fantastic Poetry, 1300 Kicker Rd., Tuscaloosa AL 35404. (205)553-2284. E-mail: dragontea@earthlink.net. Website: home.earthlink.net/~dragontea/index .html. ourworld.compuserve.com/homepages/Anamnesis/dn.htm (includes guidelines, poetry, bibliographic archive of magazine). Editor: David C. Kopaska-Merkel. Zine: 5½×8½; 24 pages; ink drawing illustrations. "*DN* is mainly a poetry magazine, but I *am* looking for short-short stories. They should be either fantasy or science fiction." Estab. 1986. Circ. 250.

Needs: Experimental, fantasy, humor/satire, science fiction. "Try me with anything *except*: senseless violence, misogyny or hatred (unreasoning) of any kind of people, sappiness." Receives 5-10 unsolicited fiction mss/ month. Accepts 1-2 mss/issue; 3-6 mss/year. Publishes ms 1-9 months after acceptance. Recently published work by Nancy Bennett, D.F. Lewis, William John Watkins. Length: 500 words average; 1,000 words maximum. Publishes short shorts. Length: 500 or fewer words. Sometimes critiques rejected mss. Also publishes poetry.

How to Contact: Send complete ms. Reports in 1-3 weeks on queries; 1-6 weeks on mss. SASE. No simultaneous submissions. Electronic submissions (ASCII or RTF) OK. Sample copy for $3. Fiction guidelines for #10 SASE.

Payment/Terms: Pays $5 on acceptance and 2 contributor's copies for one-time rights.

Advice: "I don't want pointless violence or meandering vignettes. I do want extremely short science fiction or fantasy fiction that engages the reader's interest from word one. I want to be *involved*. Start with a good first line, lead the reader where you want him/her to go and end with something that causes a reaction or provokes thought."

◯ ◼ THE DRINKIN' BUDDY MAGAZINE: A Magazine for Art and Words, P.O. Box 720608, San Jose CA 95172. (408)397-8226. E-mail: editor@drinkinbuddy.com. Website: www.drinkinbuddy.com (includes names of editors, short fiction, interviews with authors, interviews with bands, reviews, fashion, food, movies, art, poetry, games). **Editor:** Mike. Webzine. Weekly. Estab. 1994. Circ. Worldwide.

Needs: Adventure, condensed/excerpted novel, erotica, ethnic/multicultural, fantasy, gay, historical, horror, humor, lesbian, literary, mainstream, mystery/suspense, psychic/supernatural, regional, romance, science fiction, sports, westerns. They would like to see more "drug-induced fiction. No father/son stories." Receives 30-40 unsolicited mss/month. Publishes short shorts.

How to Contact: Send 8-10 typewritten pgs. maximum. Send a disposable copy of the ms. Simultaneous, electronic submissions OK.

Payment/Terms: Acquires one-time rights.

Advice: "Looking for submissions in avant-garde, macabre, banal. Good characters and a snappy title make a manuscript stand out."

N ★ ◑ ◼ DUCT TAPE PRESS. E-mail: ducttape@geocities.com. Website: www.io.com/~crberry/Duct Tape. **Editor:** Josh Wardrip. Electronic zine. "We seek writing that is perhaps riskier than what mainstream journals typically publish but we also demand the writing be very well crafted."

Needs: Experimental, literary. "No genre fiction that fails to challenge the conventions of the given genre." **Publishes 50-60 new writers/year.** Recently published work by Michael Largo, Jay Marvin, Michael Rothenberg, Rich Logsdon and Anjana Basu. Also publishes poetry.

How to Contact: Send queries/mss by e-mail.

Advice: Looks for "daring, envelope-pushing writing that displays intelligence, attention to craft and imagination. We see a lot of writing that combines a few of these attributes, but rarely all of them. Familiarize yourself with the publication. A casual perusal should give you a general indication of the kind of material we favor. Don't assume that because we are a non-paying electronic zine we set lower standards than print publications. Please send your best work."

◒ THE EDGE, TALES OF SUSPENSE, Thievin' Kitty Publications, P.O. Box 341, Marion MA 02738. E-mail: theedge@capecod.net. **Editor:** Greg F. Gifune. Associate Editors: Carla S. Gifune, Chuck A. Deude. Zine specializing in varied genre suspense: digest-sized; 80-88 pages; heavy stock paper; heavy card cover. "We publish a broad range of genres, subjects and styles. While not an easy magazine to break into, we offer thrilling, 'edge of your seat' fiction from both seasoned and newer writers. We focus on the writing, not illustrations or distracting bells and whistles. Our goal is to present a quality, entertaining publication." Triannually. Estab. 1998. Circ. 1,000.

Needs: Adventure, erotica, gay, horror, lesbian, mystery/suspense (police procedural, private eye/hardboiled, noir), psychic/supernatural/occult, westerns with supernatural or horror element only. "Emphasis is on horror, crime and blends." No children's, young adult, romance, humor. Receives over 100 unsolicited mss/month. Accepts 10-12 mss/issue; 30-36 mss/year. Publishes ms 1-4 months after acceptance. Agented fiction 1-2%. Recently published work by Ken Goldman, John Roux, Scott Urgan, Stefano Donati, Suzanne Donahue, Robert Dunbar and Michael Laimo. Length: 2,500-4,500 words average; 700 words minimum; 8,000 words maximum. Also publishes poetry. Always critiques or comments on rejected ms.

How to Contact: Send complete ms with a cover letter. Include estimated word count, brief bio and list of publications. Reports in 1-8 weeks. Send SASE for reply, return of ms or send a disposable copy of ms. Simultaneous submissions OK but not preferred. Sample copy for $6 U.S., $7 elsewhere (includes postage). Fiction guidelines for #10 SASE.

Payment/Terms: Pays 1 contributor's copy; additional copies $5. Acquires one-time rights.

Advice: "We look for taut, tense thrillers with realistic dialogue, engaging characters, strong plots and endings that are both powerful and memorable. Graphic violence, sex and profanity all have their place but do not have to be gratuitous. We will not accept anything racist, sexist, sacrilegious, or stories that depict children or animals in violent or sexual situations!"

EIDOS: Sexual Freedom and Erotic Entertainment for Consenting Adults, P.O. Box 96, Boston MA 02137-0096. (617)262-0096. Fax: (617)364-0096. E-mail: eidos@eidos.org. Website: www.eidos.org (includes feature articles, interviews, poetry, short fiction, photos). **Editor:** Brenda Loew. Magazine: 8½×11; 40 pages; offset lithography; illustrations and photos. Magazine specializing in erotica for women, men and couples of all sexual orientations, preferences and lifestyles. "Explicit material regarding language and behavior formed in relationships, intimacy, moment of satisfaction—sensual, sexy, honest. For an energetic, well informed, international erotica readership." Quarterly. Estab. 1984. Circ. 12,000.

Needs: Erotica. Upbeat erotic fiction is especially wanted. Publishes at least 10-12 pieces of fiction/year. Published work by Mykola Dementuk, Jennifer Cole and Cliff Burns. Length: 1,000 words average; 500 words minimum; 2,000 words maximum. Also publishes literary criticism, poetry. Occasionally critiques rejected mss.

How to Contact: Send complete ms with SASE. "Cover letter with history of publication or short bio is welcome." Accepts queries/mss by e-mail. Reports in 1 month on queries; 1 month on mss. Simultaneous submissions OK. Sample copy for $5. Fiction guidelines for #10 SASE. Reviews novels and short story collections, "if related to subject of erotica (sex, politics, religion, etc.)."

Payment/Terms: Pays in contributor's copies. Acquires first North American serial rights.

Advice: "We receive more erotic fiction manuscripts now than in the past. Most likely because both men and women are more comfortable with the notion of submitting these manuscripts for publication as well as the desire to see alternative sexually-explicit fiction in print. Therefore we can publish more erotic fiction because we have more material to choose from. There is still a lot of debate as to what erotic fiction consists of. This is a tough market to break into. Manuscripts must fit our editorial needs and it is best to order a sample issue prior to writing or submitting material. Honest, explicitly pro-sex, mutually consensual erotica lacks unwanted power, control and degradation—no unwanted coercion of any kind."

ENTERZONE. E-mail: editor@ezone.org. Website: http//ezone.org/ez. **Story Editor:** Martha Conway. "*Enterzone* is a hyperzine of writing, art and new media publishing fiction and nonfiction stories, essays, criticism, personal commentary, poetry, computer-generated and scanned artwork, photography, audio art, comics, and cartoons for the internet-enabled adult reading public." Published work by David Alexander, Levi Asher, Frederick Barthelme, Milorad Pavic and Lisa Solod. **Publishes 4-8 new writers/year.**

Needs: Would like to see more short stories and hyperfiction. No science fiction or fantasy.

How to Contact: Query through e-mail: query@ezone.org.

Advice "We like stories that ring true. We like nonfiction that transcends the personal. We like our prose poetic and our poetry focused."

ETERNAL VOICE, E-mail: kurokuma@home.com. Website: homes.arealcity.com/blackrose/poetry.html. **Editor:** Cassia. Electronic zine. "*Eternal Voice* celebrates the darker side of poetry and fiction. It is intended to be a place for work that doesn't always fit into other markets."

Needs: Dark fiction. No "pornographic or tasteless work." Want more fantasy and science fiction.

How to Contact: Send queries/mss by e-mail or through website.

ETERNITY MAGAZINE, An online journal of the speculative imagination, Eternity Press, P.O. Box 930068, Norcross GA 30003. E-mail: editor@pulpeternity.com. Website: www.pulpeternity.com. **Editor:** Steve Algieri. Electronic zine specializing in science fiction, fantasy, mystery and horror. Illustrations. "Cutting-edge speculative fiction and poetry that matters. Embraces controversy, alternative views and new styles." Monthly. Estab. 1997. Circ. 10,000 page hits.

Needs: Ethnic/multicultural, experimental, fantasy (science, sword and sorcery), horror, psychic/supernatural/occult, romance (futuristic/time travel, gothic), science fiction (hard science, soft/sociological), mystery/suspense. "No pornographic, senseless violence and gore, child abuse and stories that perpetuate hate. We would like to see more gay/lesbian and ethnic fiction with a fantastic theme." List of upcoming themes for SASE. Receives 200 unsolicited mss/month. Accepts 6-7 mss/issue; 80 mss/year. Publishes ms 1 year after acceptance. Published work by Brian A. Hopkins, Loren W. Cooper, Elizabeth Barrette and Stella Atrium. Length: 2,000-5,000 words average; 15,000 maximum. Publishes short shorts. Also publishes literary essays, literary criticism, poetry. Always critiques or comments on rejected ms.

How to Contact: Send complete ms with a cover letter. Include estimated word count, bio (under 100 words) and list of publications. Reports in 2 weeks on queries; 10 weeks on mss. SASE for reply. Send a disposable copy of ms. Electronic submissions (disk or modem) OK. Reviews novels and short story collections.

Payment/Terms: Pays $2-50 on publication for first electronic rights. Sends galleys to author. Not copyrighted.

Advice: "We like clean manuscripts that start strong and end with a bang. We tend to select stories with strong conflict and that deal with issues. We love controversy and unique styles."

N ◯ FAYRDAW, P.O. Box 100, Shartlesville PA 19554. (610)488-6894. **Editors:** Loring D. Emery and Mary M. Towne. Zine: 5½×8½; 40 pages; 20 lb. paper; saddle-stitched; illustrations. Bimonthly. Estab. 1994. Circ. 50.

Needs: Adventure, experimental, historical, humor/satire, literary, mainstream/contemporary. "Nothing derivative or overly cute." Receives 10-20 unsolicited mss/month. Accepts 0-3 mss/issue; 20-25 mss/year. Publishes ms 3-4 months after acceptance. Recently published work by D'Amadeus, Karen Elkus, Sheryll Watt and Eddy Thomas. Length: 1,500 words maximum. Publishes short shorts. Also publishes literary essays, literary criticism. Often critiques or comments on rejected mss.

How to Contact: Send complete ms with a cover letter. Include estimated word count, bio (3-5 lines) and list of publications. "Anything chatty." Reports in 1 month. SASE for reply or send a disposable copy of ms. Simultaneous, reprint and electronic (3.5 or 5.25 disk) submissions OK. Sample copy for $2.50. Fiction guidelines for #10 SASE.

Payment/Terms: Pays $5 (fiction only). Pays on acceptance for one-time rights. Not copyrighted.

Advice: "Look at a sample. Read our guidelines. Fayrdaw is for scratching that itch, bitching that bitch, spreading oil on burning waters, a forum where you can rant in prose about things that really tee you off. With luck it will become the literary 'bird' to all the stupidity, cruelty, injustice and just plain cussedness in our world. We are ultra-Conservative but welcome Progressive contributions, warning the submitter that his work may be set against critical contrary commentary."

N ★ $ ◯ THE FUNNY TIMES, 2176 Lee Rd., Cleveland Heights OH 44118. (216)371-8600. E-mail: ft@funnytimes.com. Website: www.funnytimes.com (includes information about *The Funny Times*, cartoon of the week and laugh links). **Editors:** Ray Lesser and Susan Wolpert. Zine specializing in humor: tabloid; 24 pages; newsprint; illustrations. *The Funny Times* is a "liberal-left monthly humor review." Estab. 1985. Circ. 55,000.

Needs: "Anything funny." Receives hundreds of unsolicited mss/month. Accepts 5 mss/issue; 60 mss/year. Publishes ms 1-6 months after acceptance. Agented fiction 10%. **Publishes 10 new writers/year.** Length: 500-700 words average. Publishes short shorts.

How to Contact: Send complete ms with a cover letter. Include list of publications. Reports in 1-3 months. Send SASE for return of ms or disposable copy of ms. Simultaneous and reprint submissions OK. Sample copy for $3, 11×14 SAE and 77¢ 1st class postage. Guidelines for #10 SASE.

Payment/Terms: Pays $50, free subscription to the zine and 5 contributor's copies. Payment on publication. Acquires one-time rights.

Advice: "It must be funny."

◯ GOTTA WRITE NETWORK LITMAG, Maren Publications, 515 E. Thacker, Hoffman Estates IL 60194-1957. E-mail: netera@aol.com. Website: members.aol.com/gwnlitmag/. **Editor:** Denise Fleischer. Magazine: 8½×11; 48-84 pages; saddle-stapled ordinary paper; matte card or lighter weight cover stock; illustrations. Magazine "serves as an open forum to discuss new markets, successes and difficulties. Gives beginning writers their first break into print and promotionally supports established professional novelists." Distributed through the US, Canada and England. Semiannually. Estab. 1988. Circ. 200-300.

• In addition to publishing fiction, *Gotta Write Network Litmag* includes articles on writing techniques, small press market news, writers' seminar reviews, science fiction convention updates, and features a "Behind the Scenes" section in which qualified writers can conduct mail interviews with small press editors and professional writers. Writers interviewed in this manner in the past have included Katherine Elisha Kimbriel, Fern Michaels, Joseph A. Citro, R. Barri Flowers, Patti Berg and J.G. Passarella.

Needs: Adventure, contemporary, fantasy, historical, humor/satire, literary, mainstream, prose poem, romance (gothic), science fiction (hard science, soft/sociological). "Currently seeking work with a clear-cut message or a twist at the very end. All genres accepted with the exception of excessive violence, sexual overtones or obscenity." Receives 75-150 unsolicited mss per month. Accepts 1-6 mss per issue; up to 20 mss a year. Publishes mss 6-

12 months after acceptance. Recently published work by Bess M. Tittle, Raven, John Murphy, Nancee Harrison, Michael De Phillips, Kathie Hokren, Allen Woods and Allan Ringley. Length: 10 pages maximum for short stories. Also publishes poetry.

How to Contact: Send complete ms with cover letter. Include "who you are, genre, previous publications and focused area of writing." Reports in 2-4 months (later during publication months). SASE ("no SASE, no response"). Reports on fax submissions within days. Responds by fax. No simultaneous submissions or reprints. Electronic (e-mail) submissions OK. Sample copy for $6. Fiction guidelines for SASE.

Payment/Terms: Pays $10 or 2 contributor's copies for first North American serial rights.

Advice: "If I still think about the direction of the story after I've read it, I know it's good. Organize your thoughts on the plot and character development (qualities, emotions) before enduring ten drafts. Make your characters come alive by giving them a personality and a background, and then give them a little freedom. Let them take you through the story."

INSTANT CLASSICS, (617)859-9900. Fax: (617)734-1425. E-mail: kane@gamesville.com. Website: www.gamesville.com. **Editor:** Steven Kane. Electronic zine.

Needs: Recently published works by Harlan Ellison, Arthur C. Clarke, Bruce Benderson and Barry Yourgrau. **Publishes "dozens" of new writers/year.**

How to Contact: Send queries/mss by e-mail.

Advice: "Looks for work that has brevity and wit. Be brief and patient. It may take us a while to respond to submissions."

INTERTEXT. (415)389-1223. E-mail: editors@intertext.com. Website: www.intertext.com. **Editor:** Jason Snell. Electronic zine. "Our readers are computer literate (because we're online only) and appreciate entertaining fiction. They're usually accepting of different styles and genres—from mainstream to historical to science fiction to fantasy to horror to mystery—because we don't limit ourselves to one genre. They just want to read a story that makes them think or transports them to an interesting new place."

> ● *Intertext* author Stan Houston's *Bite Me, Deadly* was named one of the top net fiction stories of the year by *Pulp Eternity Magazine.*

Needs: "Well-written fiction from any genre or setting." Especially looking for intelligent science fiction. No "exploitative sex or violence. We will print stories with explicit sex or violence, but not if it serves no purpose other than titillation." No pornography, fan fiction, novels or by-the-book swords and sorcery. Published work by E. Jay O'Connell, Richard Kadrey, Levi Asher, Marcus Eubanks and William Routhier. **Publishes 16 new writers/year.**

How to Contact: Electronic submissions only. Stories should be in ASCII, HTML, or Microsoft Word formats.

Advice: "Have a clear writing style—the most clever story we've seen in months still won't make it if it's written badly. Try to make our readers think in a way they haven't before, or take them to a place they've never thought about before. And don't be afraid to mix genres—our readers have come to appreciate stories that aren't easily labeled as being part of one genre or another."

IVY, Queer Writers & Poets Journal, 25 Riverside Ave., Gloucester MA 01930-2552. (978)282-5422. E-mail: ivyzine@aol.com. Editor: Kimberley Smith. **Fiction Editor**: Charlotte Stratton. Zine specializing in poetry and short fiction: 5½ × 8½; 36 pages. Quarterly. Estab. 1999.

Needs: Gay, lesbian, literary. "Nothing sexually explicit or violent." Receives 40 unsolicited mss/month. Accepts 2-3 mss/issue; 10-12 mss/year. Publishes ms 1-2 months after acceptance. **Publishes 7-9 new writers/year.** Length: 2,000 words maximum; 500 words minimum. Publishes short shorts. Also publishes literary essays, criticism and poetry. Never critiques or comments on rejected ms.

How to Contact: Send complete ms with a cover letter. Include estimated word count, 25-word bio and list of publications. Reports in 2 weeks on mss. Send SASE for reply, return of ms or send a disposable copy of ms. Simultaneous and reprint submissions OK. Sample copy for $2 and 6 × 9 SAE with 2 first-class stamps. Guidelines for SASE. Reviews novels, short story collections or nonfiction books of interest to writers. Send books to Charlotte Stratton.

Payment/Terms: Pays 1 contributor's copy; additional copies $5. Acquires one-time rights.

Advice: Looks for "strong, concise writing, avoidance of cliché, nothing overwrought. Length does not equal quality. This publication is biased against explicit sex and violence."

JACK MACKEREL MAGAZINE, Rowhouse Press, P.O. Box 23134, Seattle WA 98102-0434. **Editor:** Greg Bachar. Zine: 5½ × 8½; 40-60 pages; Xerox bond paper; glossy card cover stock; b&w illustrations and photos. "We publish unconventional art, poetry and fiction." Quarterly. Estab. 1993. Circ. 1,000.

Needs: Condensed/excerpted novel, erotica, experimental, literary, surreal, translations. Publishes occasional chapbooks and anthologies. Receives 20-100 unsolicited mss/month. Accepts 10-20 mss/issue; 40-75 mss/year. Published work by David Berman, William Waltz, Heather Hayes, Brett Ralph, Ann Miller, Paul Dickinson and John Rose. Length: 250 words minimum; 5,000 words maximum. Publishes short shorts. Also publishes literary essays, literary criticism and poetry.

How to Contact: Send complete ms with a cover letter. Include bio with submission. Send SASE for reply,

return of ms or send a disposable copy of ms. Sample copy for $5 (make checks or money order out to Greg Bachar). Reviews novels and short story collections.
Payment/Terms: Pays in contributor's copies.

N ★ $ ○ ☑ ▣ JACKHAMMER E-ZINE, 9220 Jill Lane #2E, Schiller Park IL 60176. (847)928-9925. E-mail: jackhammer@eggplant-productions.com. Website: www.eggplant-productions.com. "The entire content of *Jackhammer E-zine* (including limited archives) can be found on the website, writer's guidelines, submission information and submission addresses are also available." **Editor:** Raechel Henderson. E-zine specializing in science fiction, fantasy, horror and nonfiction. "*Jackhammer E-zine* is a weekly themed e-zine. Each week we propose a 'Question of the Week' and all fiction and nonfiction published in that issue touches upon the 'Question of the Week.' We publish short fiction and short articles, preferring informative and personal essays over 'rants.' Our intended audience is anyone who likes to ask 'What if?' " Estab. 1997. Circ. 1,000.
- *Jackhammer E-zine* is a member of the Zine Association, for e-zines in the science fiction, fantasy, horror genres. *Jackhammer E-zine* has received the Page One Award for Literary Contribution in 1999, the Blue Moon Award for Website Excellence in 1999 and Eternity Online's Best of the Web: Editor of the Year award in 1999.

Needs: Fantasy (space fantasy, sword and sorcery, magic realism, modern fantasy), horror (dark fantasy, futuristic, psychological, supernatural), science fiction (soft/sociological), speculative fiction. "Other categories such as ethnic/multicultural, feminist, gay and occult would also be considered if they fall under the umbrella of speculative fiction. No splatterpunk, gore, straight erotica, anything that could be considered R-rated material." List of upcoming themes available at www.eggplant-productions.com/jackhammer/guidelines.html. Receives 80 unsolicited mss/month. Accepts 3 mss/issue; 156 mss/year. Publishes ms 1-12 months after acceptance. **Publishes 80 new writers/year.** Word length: 1,500 words average; 175 words minimum; 2,000 words maximum. Publishes short shorts. Length: 375 words. Often critiques or comments on rejected ms.
How to Contact: Send complete ms by e-mail. "We only accept e-mail submissions. Snail mail submissions are returned unread to the sender." Include estimated word count, 50 word bio, the question the story is being submitted for and a valid e-mail address. Reports in 1-2 weeks. Simultaneous and reprint submissions OK. Sample copy and guidelines free.
Payment/Terms: Pays $5-20. Payment on publication. Acquires first Worldwide electronic rights or Worldwide Electronic rights if applicable. "Eggplant Productions holds the rights up until 90 days after publication during which the work can not appear anywhere else on the Web."
Advice: "A properly formatted manuscript is always appreciated. What I really want in a story is to feel something after reading it. If a story makes me laugh, grin, cry or shudder, I'm going to buy it. If the story doesn't affect me one way or the other I'll pass it on. Read the guidelines carefully. Read them a third time. If you still have a question then you can e-mail me. Electronic publishing is still struggling for respectability and so my goal with *Jackhammer E-zine* is to provide quality short stories to readers. By 'quality' I mean stories that elicit an emotional response in readers. Also, by 'quality' I mean polished stories. Many places on the Web post stories that are still in the rough draft stage. Make sure your work is ready to be viewed by others before you send it out."

N ★ ◐ JUPITER'S FREEDOM, P.O. Box 110217, Palm Bay FL 32911-0217. (407)725-6243. E-mail: j5fm@hotmail.com. Website: members.xoom.com/j5fm (includes entire magazine, writer's guidelines, subscription, news, how to contact and more). **Editor:** Christine Smalldone. Zine: 8½×11; 20-30 pages; 20 lb. paper, 70 lb. cover stock; illustrations and photos. Quarterly science fiction zine "that tries to flow and grow in the sci-fi, horror, fantasy and surreal aspects of this mixed genre, trying to publish the best in these areas that have shown a new direction or approach in the realm of sci-fi, to engulf those who love sci-fi and all its elements in a visual landscape of words." Estab. 1998.
Needs: Fantasy (space fantasy), horror (dark fantasy, futuristic, psychological), science fiction (hard science/technological, soft/sociological). Receives 10-20 unsolicited mss/month. Accepts 3-5 mss/issue; 12-16 mss/year. Publishes ms 2-4 months after acceptance. **Publishes 20-30 new writers/year.** Recently published work by Suzi Kosturin, Joe Wocoski, Tom Brinck. Length: 10,000 words average; 5,000 words minimum; 15,000 words maximum. Publishes short shorts. Length: 500 words. Also publishes poetry. Often critiques or comments on rejected ms.
How to Contact: Send complete ms with a cover letter. Accepts queries/mss by e-mail. Include estimated word count, bio, list of publications. Reports in 1-2 weeks on queries; 3-4 weeks on mss. Send SASE for reply, return of ms or send a disposable copy of ms. Simultaneous submissions OK. Sample copy for $4 and 9½×11 envelope with 3 first-class stamps. Guidelines for #10 SASE.
Payment/Terms: Pays 1 contributor's copy; additional copies $1. Acquires one-time rights.
Advice: "Stay true and close to yourself, your style and your goals. Even if your story is bizarre and abstract, always write from your heart and talent, but don't be afraid to be different."

N ○ ▣ KASPER ZINE: Powerful Imaginations, Silly and Strange, %AKP, P.O. Box 2474, Athens GA 30612-0474. E-mail: kasper@akp.cc. Website: www.kasper.cc (includes writer's guidelines and a discussion board). **Editor:** Adrian Pritchett. Electronic zine specializing in humor. Publishes "prose, photography, and artwork that is weird, silly, or wonderful." Estab. 1996.

Needs: Humor satire. Accepts 3 mss/year. Publishes ms 2 months after acceptance. Recently published works by Matt Wixon, Heidi Sulzdorf, Brian Morton, Nestor Fabal, Fan Frank and David Lee. Length: 200 words minimum; 5,000 words maximum. Publishes short shorts. Length: 200 words.

How to Contact: Query first. Send queries/mss by e-mail. Include 75 word bio; e-mail and website addresses. Reports in 1 week on queries; 2 months on mss. Simultaneous submissions and reprints OK. Fiction guidelines for #10 SASE.

Advice: "A manuscript stands out if it balances nonsense with enough plot to be readable and hilarious."

N ⬤ **KIDS' WORLD, The Magazine That's All Kids!**, Stone Lightning Press, 1300 Kicker Rd., Tuscaloosa AL 35404. (205)553-2284. Editor: Morgan Kopaska-Merkel. Zine: digest size; 16-24 pages; standard white Xerox paper; card stock cover; illustrations. Publishes stories written by children under 17: "fantasy and 'kid stuff'—themes by kids, about kids and for kids." Quarterly. Estab. 1992. Circ. 60-80.

Needs: Children's/juvenile (4-12 years): adventure, fantasy (children's), mystery/suspense (amateur sleuth), science fiction (hard science, soft/sociological); young adult/teen (adventure, mystery, science fiction). No horror or romance. Receives 18-24 unsolicited mss/month. Accepts 30 mss/issue; 70-100 mss/year. Publishes ms from 1-24 months after acceptance. Recently published work by Brianne Butler, Betsy Champagne, McKay Talley and Michelle Tran. Length: 300 words average, 75 words minimum; 500 words maximum. Publishes short shorts. Length: 150-200 words. Also publishes poetry.

How to Contact: Send complete ms with a cover letter including your age. Reports in 2-12 weeks on mss. Send SASE for reply, return of ms or send a disposable copy of ms. Simultaneous and reprint submissions OK. Sample copy for $1.50 and SAE. Fiction guidelines for SASE.

Payment/Terms: Pays 1 contributor's copy. Acquires first North American serial rights.

Advice: "Stories must be appropriate for kids. Have an adult check spelling, grammar and punctuation."

N ⬤ **LIME GREEN BULLDOZERS**, Oyster Publications, P.O. Box 4333, Austin TX 78765. E-mail: oystapress@tab.com. Editor: Alaina Duro. Zine: 8½×11; 50 pages; regular white paper; illustrations and photos. Zine specializing in literature and artwork. "*LGB* looks for honest works of short fiction. Anything with a degree of integrity is sought." Annually. Estab. 1986. Circ. 250.

Needs: Condensed/excerpted novel, feminist, gay, historical, horror, humor/satire, lesbian, literary, mainstream/contemporary, mystery/suspense, psychic/supernatural/occult, serialized novel. "Nothing religious." Publishes annual special fiction issue or anthology. Published work by Judson Crews, Sigmund Weiss, Allyson Shaw and Harland Ristau. Receives 2-3 unsolicited mss/month. Accepts 2-3 mss/issue; 2-3 mss/year. Publishes ms 1 year after acceptance. Publishes short shorts. Also publishes literary essays, poetry. Sometimes critiques or comments on rejected mss.

How to Contact: Query first. Should include a "nice, personal letter." Reports in 1 month. Send SASE for reply, return of ms or send a disposable copy of ms. Simultaneous, reprint and electronic submissions (modem) OK. Sample copy for $5. Reviews novels and short story collections. Send books to Drucilla B. Blood.

Payment/Terms: Pays 1 contributor's copy.

Advice: "I'm tired of boring, one-dimensional stories with mundane plots. I like true stories and interesting twists."

⭐ ✅ ⬤ **LIQUID OHIO, Voice of the Unheard**, Grab Odd Dreams Press, P.O. Box 60265, Bakersfield CA 93386-0265. (805)871-0586. E-mail: liquidohio@aol.com. **Editor:** Amber Goddard. Magazine: 8×11; 13-25 pages; copy paper; illustrations and photos. "*Liquid Ohio* is a fairly new publication whose goal is to publish new writers that others might toss in the trash. Our main audience is creatively eccentric people who feel what they do." Quarterly. Estab. 1995. Circ. 500.

Needs: Experimental, humor/satire, literary. Receives 15-20 unsolicited mss/month. Accepts 2 mss/issue; 24-30 mss/year. Publishes ms 1-3 months after acceptance. Recently published work by Janet Kuypers, Peter Gorman and Christine Brandel. **Publishes 40-60 new writers/year.** Length: 1,500-1,800 words average; 2,500-3,000 words maximum. Publishes short shorts. Also publishes literary essays, literary criticism, poetry.

How to Contact: Send complete ms with a cover letter. Should include estimated word count. Reports in 3-4 weeks on queries; 3 months on mss. Send SASE for reply, return of ms or send a disposable copy of ms. Simultaneous submissions, reprint and electronic submissions OK. Sample copy for $3, 11×14 SAE and 3 first-class stamps. Fiction guidelines for #10 SASE.

Payment/Terms: Pays 3 contributor's copies. Acquires one-time rights.

Advice: "We like things that are different, but not too abstract or 'artsy' that one goes away saying, 'huh?'"

⬤ **A BULLET INTRODUCES COMMENTS** by the editor of *Novel & Short Story Writer's Market* indicating special information about the listing.

Write what you feel, not necessarily what sounds deep or meaningful—it will probably be that naturally if it's real. Send in anything you've got—live on the edge. Stories that are relatable, that deal with those of us trying to find a creative train in the world. We also love stories that are extremely unique e.g., talking pickles, etc."

N **M** **E** **LITERARY WITCHES**, 522 Kinsmoor Ave., Ft. Wayne IN 46807. (219)745-9616. E-mail: novaq ueer@aol.com. Website: members.aol.com/MeierAvila/index.html. **Fiction Editor:** Sabrina Counts. Electronic zine. "A postmodern journal exploring diverse literary art, rooted in feminist and literary theory. *Literary Witches* publishes work that reflects and explores post-modernism, reconstruction, hypertext, transgendered experimentation, multiculturalism, queer theory, feminism, postfeminism. *Literary Witches* is a journal of the mind and body, a cyber-gathering of academic theory and experimental fiction."

Needs: Ethnic/multicultural, experimental, feminist, gay, lesbian, literary. "Please do not send fantasy, vampire stories. Wants postmodern literature and fiction. We are especially interested in work exploring queer discourse, the body and postmodern piracy." **Publishes "a few" new writers/year.** Recently published works by Kathy Acker, Doug Rice, Cheryl Meier and Marita Avila.

How to Contact: Accepts queries/mss by e-mail. "Please submit your work in the body of e-mail along with your address and phone number or send in hardcopy."

Advice: "We feature literary art by the best American authors as well as diverse or new writers. Published work has been in the form of poetry, essays, short shorts, novel excerpts, hypertext, interviews, plays, listserve or e-mail excerpts. Our journal has a diverse audience of feminists, queers, scholars, artists, activists and is suggested reading for numerous university courses. We have had over 10,000 hits during the two years our publication has been in cyberspace. Read *Literary Witches* before sending your work for consideration. Electronic publishing is very important right now. For example, *Literary Witches* is becoming involved with an electronic journal that was just awarded the first Guggenheim grant for a cyber publication. And because of continuing accessibility to cyberspace, electronic journals can be reached by diverse groups of people. Work previously available only in hardcopy can be remade in cyberspace and remain in publication for long periods. Artists and audiences find one another."

N **E** **MILLENNIUM: A Journal for Tomorrowland**, E-mail: dsp@ctel.net. Website: www.etext.org/Zi nes/Millenium. **Editor:** Douglas Thornsjo. Electronic zine. "Our theme, if there is one, is 'Look ahead into the past,' or 'Don't be fooled by the present,' or 'Don't let some suited corporate bastard dictate the future. If it's possible to be respectful and revolutionary at the same time, that's what *Millennium* tries for."

Needs: Literary. "No aimless meta-fiction; religious or propagandistic; emotionally trite; graphically violent (sex is OK though!); stories that aren't about anything; stories that are about too much; stories by authors who can't be bothered to think about their readers. Interested in all genres, but the story and characters should be larger than the genre. The qualities we most value are grace, substance, character and sense of purpose that isn't overblown or sententious." Recently published works by Bruce Canwell and Richard Nostbakken.

How to Contact: Accepts queries/mss by e-mail only. "No paper submissions will be considered. Plain text preferred, but MS Word5 or earlier is OK."

Advice: "Always keep in mind Mark Twain's rules for short fiction especially including this one: 'A tale should arrive somewhere and accomplish something.' Editorial writers: our editorial bias is 'slightly left of center,' but we will not publish propaganda or religious material of any sort. Be familiar with (and follow) Mark Twain's rules for story-writing. Read good writers and try to be as good as what you read. Download and read the magazine (it is always free, so you have no excuse not to: if you can't be bothered to download and read a free magazine then you are not really a part of the electronic revolution and we don't want to hear from you.)"

N **O** **E** **MILLENNIUM SCIENCE FICTION & FANTASY**, P.O. Box 8118, Roswell NM 88202-8118. E-mail: jopoppub@jopoppub.com. Website: www.jopoppub.com (includes guidelines, short fiction, writers' pages, news, chatroom, sagas, poetry, flash fiction, art). Editor: S. Joan Popek. **Fiction Editor**: Diana R. Moreland. E-zine with print "Best Of" quarterly. Monthly e-zine publishes science fiction, fantasy and psychological horror, "offering the best of short speculative fiction we can find." Estab. 1993. Circ. 2,000. Member of the Horror Zine Association.

Needs: Fantasy (space fantasy), horror (dark fantasy, futuristic, psychological, supernatural, humor satire, science fiction (hard science/technological, soft/sociological), young adult (fantasy/science fiction, horror). "No explicit language, sex or violence. No graphic blood, guts or exploitation pieces." List of upcoming themes available for SASE. Receives 100 unsolicited mss/month. Accepts 4-5 mss/issue; 48-60 mss/year. Does not read mss October 31-January 1. Publishes ms 2-8 months after acceptance. **Publishes 1-3 new writers/year.** Recently published Greg F. Giyune and Patricia L. White. Length: 2,000 words average; 50 words minimum; 2,500 words maximum. Publishes short shorts. Length: 100 words. Also publishes literary criticism and poetry. Often critiques or comments on rejected ms.

How to Contact: Send complete ms with a cover letter. Accepts queries/mss by e-mail. Include estimated word count, 50-100 word bio and list of publications. Reports in 2 weeks to 4 months on queries; 2 weeks to 3 months on mss. Send SASE for reply, return of ms or send a disposable copy of ms. Reprint submissions OK. Sample copy for $6.50. Guidelines for #10 SASE. Reviews novels, short story collections and nonfiction books of interest to writers. Send books to Editor.

Payment/Terms: Pays $0-10 and 1 contributor's copy on acceptance; additional copies $3. Acquires one-time rights. Sponsors contest: see website for details.

Advice: "We have a standard rule-three grammar errors in the first paragraph is an automatic reject. We are leaning more towards e-mail submissions and welcome electronic copies of accepted manuscripts."

N **$** ◯ **MINDMARES MAGAZINE**, 18503 NE 158th St., Brush Prairie WA 98606-9615. E-mail: twisted mind@uswest.net. Website: www.twistedmind.net/mindmares (includes guidelines, previous issues, story excerpts, subscription and editor information). **Editor:** Tracy Martin. Zine specializing in horror: digest; 84 pages; glossy cover; illustrations. "*MindMares* is devoted to bringing the best new and published horror writers together for an exceptionally scary read." Quarterly. Estab. 1998. Circ. 500-700.

• A story from *MindMares*'s issue 2 received an honorable mention in Ellen Datlow's *Year's Best Horror* anthology.

Needs: Horror (dark fantasy, futuristic, psychological, supernatural). "No fantasy horror stories, no child sexual abuse." Receives 100 unsolicited mss/month. Accepts 13-15 mss/issue; 52-60 mss/year. Publishes ms 6-9 months after acceptance. **Publishes 4-6 new writers/year.** Recently published work by Charlee Jacob, Shikhar Dixit, Michael Kelly, Jeffrey Thomas, Weston Ochse, Anthony Armstrong and Scott Urban. Length: 3,000 words average; 300 words minimum; 5,000 words maximum. Publishes short shorts. Length: 480 words. Also publishes poetry. Always critiques or comments on rejected ms.

How to Contact: Send complete ms with a cover letter. Inquiries by e-mail OK. Include estimated word count, 50 word bio and list of publications. Reports on queries "immediately"; 3-4 weeks on mss. Send SASE for reply, return of ms or send a disposable copy of ms. Simultaneous and reprint submissions OK. Sample copy for $4. Fiction guidelines free. Reviews novels, short story collections and nonfiction books of interest to writers. Send books to editor.

Payment/Terms: Pays ¼-1¢/word and 1 contributor's copy; additional copies $3. Pays on publication. Acquires first North American serial rights. Sponsors contest: annual contest with cash prizes. Guidelines for SASE.

Advice: "I like to see really shocking horror fiction—not gore—but shocking and psychologically thrilling. Make me think, make me worry, scare me and shock me. Put me on the edge of my seat and make me sleep with the lights on! Keep writing. If I reject your work, I'll critique it. Take that advice and send it elsewhere. Then send me something else. But always keep submitting."

◯ **THE MONTHLY INDEPENDENT TRIBUNE TIMES JOURNAL POST GAZETTE NEWS CHRONICLE BULLETIN, The Magazine to Which No Superlatives Apply**, 80 Fairlawn Dr., Berkeley CA 94708-2106. Editor: T.S. Child. **Fiction Editor:** Denver Tucson. Zine: 5½×8; 8 pages; 60 lb. paper; 60 lb. cover; illustrations and photographs. "We publish short stories, short short stories, plays, game show transcriptions, pictures made of words, teeny-weeny novelinis." Published irregularly. Estab. 1983. Circ. 500.

• The editor would like to see more "discombobulating" stories.

Needs: Adventure, experimental, humor/satire, mystery/suspense (amateur sleuth, private eye), psychic/supernatural/occult. "If it's serious, literary, perfect, well-done or elegant, we don't want it. If it's bizarre, unclassifiable, funny, cryptic or original, we might." Nothing "pretentious; important; meaningful; honest." Receives 20 unsolicited mss/month. Accepts 3-4 mss/issue. Accepted manuscripts published in next issue. Length: 400 words preferred; 1,200 words maximum. Publishes short shorts. Length: 400 words. Sometimes critiques rejected mss.

How to Contact: Send complete ms with cover letter. Reports in 1 month. SASE. "May" accept simultaneous submissions. Sample copy for 50¢, and SASE.

Payment/Terms: Pays subscription (2 issues); 3 contributor's copies. Not copyrighted.

Advice: "First of all, stories must be *short*—1,200 words maximum, but the shorter the better. They must make us either laugh or scream or scratch our heads, or all three. Things that are slightly humorous, or written with any kind of audience in mind, are returned. If you can think of another magazine that might publish your story, send it to them, not us. Send us your worst, weirdest stories, the ones you're too embarrassed to send anywhere else."

⬛ ◼ **moonbomb press,** E-mail: moonbomb@hooked.net. Website: www.hooked.net/users/moonbomb. **Editor:** Paul C. Choi. Electronic zine. "We are contemporary, urban, irreverent, ethnic, random."

Needs: Short stories, poetry, short plays, any fictional format, autobiographical non-fiction, fictional journalism. No children's fiction. Wants more fictional realism and essays. "The main thing we seek in any piece of writing is a clear, identifiable voice. If this voice is also unique, we are even more pleased." Recently published work by Eve Pearlman and Sheryl Ridenour. **Publishes 2 new writers/year.**

How to Contact: Electronic submissions only.

Advice: "Be bold. Do not try to be what you are not. Anything so contrived is obviously so. Content and structure are important, but the voice, the heart behind the writing is even more essential."

N ★ **$** ◼ **NEVERWORLDS,** E-mail: editor@neverworlds.com. Website: www.neverworlds.com. **Editor:** Kevin L. McPherson. Electronic zine. "*Neverworlds* is dedicated to publishing quality speculative fiction and art from today's best up-and-coming talents."

Needs: Science fiction (hard science/technological), speculative fiction. "We publish everything from cross-genre fiction to speculative science articles and movie/book reviews. Our guidelines try to steer submissions away from erotica and splatter punk, but we're not completely adverse to these genres. Material based on previously done books or shows (Star Wars, Star Trek, etc.) will not be accepted. Would like to see more hard, technical science fiction." **Publishes 20 new writers/year.** Recently published works by Andrew Burt, Marcie Lynn Tentchoff, Will Sand, Corey Kellgren, David L. Felts, Jonathon M. Sullivan, Jeff Verona and Patricia Spork. Also publishes poetry.

How to Contact: Send queries/mss by e-mail. "E-mail submission to the editor can be in any format, the most popular being MS Word (doc) or WordPerfect (.wpd) file attachments. Plain text (.txt) files are acceptable, as well as including the submissions within the body of the message."

Payment/Terms: Pays $15 for short fiction; $20-30 for novellas and novelettes; and $5 for selected poetry.

Advice: "Make me think, or speculate, or dream, or wonder about what I've read. Keep me guessing—I love surprise and twist endings. Above all, entertain me."

N ★ ▣ NEWS OF THE BRAVE NEW WORLD, 200 Barnes St., Apt. E20, Carrboro NC 27510. Fax: (919)962-7576. E-mail: olaf@indy95.chem.unc.edu. Website: indy95.chem.unc.edu. Website: indy95.chem.unc.edu. **Editor:** Olaf Kohlmann. Electronic zine. "We serve as a platform for fresh, new authors in need of an outlet for their creative work without the usual rip-off practices, Therefore, this magazine is free of charge for readers and writers. It is published in two languages, i.e. English and German, with different material in each section."

Needs: Erotica, humor, short stories, poems, essays, reviews and novels (no excerpts, only complete works). Want more "dark and/or intelligent humor, erotic (not porn) and everything that offers surprises. No badly written fiction, extremely conservative writings, copycats of bestseller authors, predictable and boring stuff. We believe in a sparse layout to focus attention to the written word. There is no specific theme, because we do not want to tell the contributors what they have to write about." **Publishes 20-50 new writers/year.** Recently published work by Rich Logsdon, Vasilis Afxentiou, Holly Day, Josh Wardrip, Sherri Jilek, Quinn Nelson and Richard Fein.

How to Contact: Accepts queries/mss by e-mail. "Send as e-mail attachments, Word 6.0 documents or Text-only files. No Macintosh please. We cannot read it."

Advice: "Read your submissions at least twice. Correct spelling and grammar mistakes. We publish your work as it is submitted, and part of our philosophy is not to edit anything. It certainly is embarassing for the auhor and the publisher if a work is full of mistakes."

N ▣ NIGHTLY GATHERING: The E-Zine for SF & Beyond!, 3205 Waldron Rd., Camden NY 13316. (315)245-0553. E-mail: mjgcnys@aol.com. Website: www.ixtreme.com/nightlygathering. **Editor:** Michael James. Electronic zine. "*Nightly Gathering* is an independently published/edited electronic zine that showcases new and aspiring writers of the science fiction and fantasy genres. The goal/future of *Nightly Gathering* is to inspire new and creative ideas to keep alive the imagination that denotes the core value of science in an ever changing world."

Needs: Fantasy, science fiction, speculative. No erotic science fiction. Want more "speculative science fiction, more specifically centered towards time travel and the implicated changes dealt when tampering with an existing timeline." Recently published works by Steven L. Shiff, K. Tolman and Christina Zodiatris.

How to Contact: Send queries/mss by e-mail.

Advice: "Write from your heart. Simply put, do not let the pressures of a generic storyline (i.e., the latest meteor to wipe out all humanity, etc.) be the motivating factor in your story. Envision the story as it happens, allow the plot to develop in a traditional way instead of jumping from one facet to the other. Don't dwell on one particular character, leave the reader wanting to know more. Unfold the details within the story about the lead character or characters at certain intervals that pertain to events as they happen. Also, study grammatical structure and proper punctuation."

N ★ ◑ ▣ NOIR MECHANICS, a literary rag, Fax: (562)920-0250. E-mail: info@noirmechanics.com. Website: www.noirmechanics.com. **Editor:** Spyder Bytes (noir@primenet.com). Managing Editor: Brick Rage (brickrange@aol.com). Electronic zine. "If it makes you feel all dark inside, you're on the right track. Features short unpublished (either electronically or hard copy) new fiction in an ironic and often bizzare vein. Intended for anyone who appreciates well-crafted prose and also has a sense of humor."

Needs: Literary. Does not want "anything warm and fuzzy. No bunny rabbits. No idyllic afternoons in the park listening to Yanni. You get my drift." **Publishes 8-10 new writers/year.** "Since many of our contributors are well known award-winning novelists, playwrights and screenwriters, everyone writes under a pseudonym and includes a fabulous phony bio (á la *Granta*). We found this to be a very liberating format, and an age old tradition. As you know many writers get stuck in a genre and their publishers/producers don't want to see anything that strays from that." Length: 1,500 words.

How to Contact: Accepts queries/mss by e-mail.

Advice: "Would like to see more good stuff: things that are funny, scary and sexy. Not necessarily hard-boiled but fiction that hits you like a hot kiss at the end of a wet fist. Wear your mittens, keep your nose clean and commit random acts of coolness. My bookshelves have always threatened to crowd me out of wherever I live. It took me a while to get into web publishing, but now I'm a convert. There's nothing like holding a well-bound, fine paper volume in your hand, but distribution was always a problem. Anything that gets people reading good fiction, especially on a world-wide basis, has got to be good."

◐ NUTHOUSE, Essays, Stories and Other Amusements, Twin Rivers Press, P.O. Box 119, Ellenton FL 34222. E-mail: nuthous499@aol.com. Website: members.aol.com/Nuthous499/index.html (includes writer's guidelines, readers' letters, excerpts). **Chief of Staff:** Dr. Ludwig "Needles" Von Quirk. Zine: digest-sized; 12-16 pages; bond paper; illustrations and photos. "Humor of all genres for an adult readership that is not easily offended." Published every 6 weeks. Estab. 1993. Circ. 100.
Needs: Humor/satire: erotica, experimental, fantasy, feminist, historical (general), horror, literary, main-stream/contemporary, mystery/suspense, psychic/supernatural/occult, romance, science fiction and westerns. Plans annual "Halloween Party" issue featuring humorous verse and fiction with a horror theme. Receives 12-30 unsolicited mss/month. Accepts 3-5 mss/issue; 30 mss/year. Publishes ms 6-12 months after acceptance. Published work by Dale Andrew White, Mitchell Nathanson, Rob Loughran, Vanessa Dodge, Ken Rand, Don Hornbostel and Michael McWey. Length: 500 words average; 100 words minimum; 1,000 words maximum. Publishes short shorts. Length: 100-250 words. Also publishes literary essays, literary criticism and poetry. Often critiques or comments on rejected mss.
How to Contact: Send complete ms with a cover letter. Include estimated word count, bio (paragraph) and list of publications. Reports in 2-4 weeks on mss. SASE for return of ms or send disposable copy of ms. Simultaneous and reprint submissions OK. Sample copy for $1 (payable to Twin Rivers Press). Fiction guidelines for #10 SASE.
Payment/Terms: Pays 1 contributor's copy. Acquires one-time rights. Not copyrighted.
Advice: Looks for "laugh-out-loud prose. Strive for original ideas; read the great humorists—Saki, Woody Allen, Robert Benchley, Garrison Keillor, John Irving—and learn from them. We are turned off by sophomoric attempts at humor built on a single, tired, overworked gag or pun; give us a story with a beginning, middle and end."

Ⓝ ▣ NUVEIN ONLINE, (626)401-3466. Fax: (626)401-3460. E-mail: ediaz@earthlink.net. Website: www.nuvein.com. **Editor:** Enrique Diaz. Electronic zine. "We are open to short works of fiction which explore topics divergent from the mainstream. Especially welcome are stories with a point of view opposite traditional and stereotypical views of minorities, including women and gays. Our philosophy is to provide a forum for voices rarely heard in other publications."
Needs: Short fiction, serials, graphic e-novels and poetry. Wants more "experimental, cyberfiction, ethnic, as well as pieces dealing with the exploration of sexuality." **Publishes 4 new writers/year.** Recently published work by Ronald L. Boerem, Holly Day, Enrique Diaz and Rick Stepp-Boling.
How to Contact: Send queries/mss by e-mail.
Advice: "Read over each submission before sending it, and if you, as the writer, find the piece irresistible, e-mail it to us immediately!"

☑ $ ◖ ◎ OF UNICORNS AND SPACE STATIONS, %Gene Davis, P.O. Box 200, Bountiful UT 84011-0200. Website: www.genedavis.com/magazine. **Senior Editor:** Gene Davis. Zine: 5½×8½; 60 pages; 20 lb. white paper; card cover stock; illustrations. "We want science fiction and fantasy of a positive nature, that gives us ideas, that warns us about the future and gives potential answers. It should be for adults, though graphic sex, violence and offensive language are not considered." Biannual. Estab. 1994. Circ. 100.
Needs: Fantasy (science fantasy, sword and sorcery), science fiction (hard science, soft/sociological, utopian). Wants "clear writing that is easy to follow." Receives 20 unsolicited mss/month. Accepts 9-13 mss/issue; approximtely 25 mss/year. Publishes ms 6-12 months after acceptance. **Publishes approximately 5 new writers/year.** Length: 3,000 words average. Publishes short shorts. Also publishes poetry. Sometimes critiques or comments on rejected mss.
How to Contact: Send complete ms (clean, well-written, not stapled) with a cover letter. Include estimated word count, bio (75 words or less) and writer's classification of the piece (science fiction, fantasy, poetry). Reports in 3 months. Send SASE for reply, return of ms or send a disposable copy of ms. Simultaneous, reprint and electronic (disk only) submissions OK. If a subscriber, e-mail submissions OK. Sample copy for $4. Fiction guidelines for #10 SASE.
Payment/Terms: Pays 1¢/word and 1 contributor's copy for stories; $5/poem and 1 contributor's copy for poetry; additional copies for $4. Acquires one-time rights.
Advice: "Keep trying. It may take several tries to get published. Most stories I see are good. You just need to find an editor that goes ga-ga over your style."

Ⓝ ◐ OFFICE NUMBER ONE, 2111 Quarry Rd., Austin TX 78703. E-mail: onocdingus@aol.com. Editor: Carlos B. Dingus. Zine: 8½×11; 12 pages; 60 lb. standard paper; b&w illustrations and photos. "I look for short stories, imaginary news stories or essays (under 400 words) that can put a reader on edge—avoid profanity or obscenity, make a point that frees the reader to see several worlds." Biannual zine specializing in satire, humor and views from alternate realities. Estab. 1989. Circ. 1,000.
Needs: Fictional news articles, experimental, fantasy, horror, humor/satire, literary, psychic/supernatural/occult,

also fictional reviews, limericks. Receives 16 unsolicited mss/month. Buys 1-3 mss/issue; 16 mss/year. Publishes ms 6-12 months after acceptance. **Publishes 10-15 new writers/year.** Length: 400 words maximum, 150 best. Also publishes literary essays and poetry. Sometimes critiques or comments on rejected mss if requested.

How to Contact: Send complete ms with optional cover letter. Should include estimated word count with submission. Reports in 6-8 weeks on mss. Send SASE for reply, return of ms or send disposable copy of ms. Will consider simultaneous submissions, reprints. Sample copy for $2 with SAE and 3 first-class stamps. Fiction guidelines for SASE.

Payment/Terms: Pays 1 contributor's copy. Additional copies for $1 plus $1.50 postage and 9×12 SASE. Acquires one-time rights.

Advice: "Clean writing, no unnecessary words, clear presentation. Express *one* good idea. Write for an audience that you can identify. I'm planning to publish more *shorter* fiction. I plan to be more up-beat and to focus on a journalistic style—and broaden what can be accomplished within this style. It seems like the Internet is taking away from print media. However, I also think the Internet cannot replace print media for fiction writing."

N ◎ ONCE UPON A WORLD, 6300 W. Lake Mead #1058, Las Vegas NV 89108-6418. E-mail: 107753.2 174@compuserve.com. Editor: Emily Alward. Zine: 8½×11; 80-100 pages; white paper; card stock cover; pen & ink illustrations. "A science fiction and fantasy zine with emphasis on alternate-world cultures and stories of idea, character and interaction. Also publishes book reviews and poems for an adult audience, primarily readers of science fiction and fantasy. We're known for science fiction and fantasy stories with excellent wordbuilding and a humanistic emphasis." Annually. Estab. 1988. Circ. 100.

• The science fiction and fantasy published in *Once Upon a World* tends to be "centered on the human element" and explores the individual in society. The editor would like to see more stories set in worlds with alternate political, economic or family arrangements.

Needs: Fantasy, science fiction. No realistic "stories in contemporary settings"; horror; stories using Star Trek or other media characters; stories with completely negative endings. List of upcoming themes available for SASE. Receives 20 unsolicited mss/month. Accepts 8-12 mss/issue; per year "varies, depending on backlog." Publishes ms from 2 months to 1½ years after acceptance. Recently published work by Jon C. Picciuolo, Tamela Viglione and Patricia Mathews. **Publishes 5 new writers/year.** Length: 3,000 words average; 400 words minimum; 10,000 words maximum. Publishes short shorts. Also publishes poetry. Sometimes critiques rejected mss and recommends other markets.

How to Contact: Send complete manuscript. Reports in 2-4 weeks on queries; 2-16 weeks on mss. SASE. "Reluctantly" accepts simultaneous submissions. Sample copy for $9. Make checks payable to Emily Alward. Fiction guidelines for #10 SASE. Reviews novels and short story collections.

Payment/Terms: Pays contributor's copies. Acquires first rights. "Stories copyrighted in author's name; copyrights not registered."

Advice: "Create your own unique universe, and then show its texture and how it 'works' in the story. This is a good way to try out a world that you're building for a novel. But, don't forget to also give us interesting characters with believable problems. Submit widely, but pay attention to editors' needs and guidelines—don't scattershot. Take on new challenges—i.e., never say 'I only write science fiction, romance, or even fiction in general—you never know where your 'sideline' work is going to impress an editor. We aim to fill some niches not necessarily well-covered by larger publishers currently: science fantasy; cross-genre; SF love stories; and non-cyber centered futures."

N ★ $ ◎ ▣ THE ORPHIC CHRONICLE: The Online Magazine of SF, Fantasy and Horror, P.O. Box 171202, Arlington TX 76003-1202. (818) 457-4436. E-mail: editor@orphic-chronicle.com. Website: www.orphic-chronicle.com. "This is an online magazine. The entire issue: short fiction, poetry, reviews, features and our SF autograph section is on the WWW." **Editor:** S. Kay Elmore. E-zine specializing in science fiction, fantasy and horror. Quarterly. Estab. 1996. Circ. 3,000.

• The Orphic Chronicle is a member of the Zine Association, for e-zines in the science fiction, fantasy and horror genres.

Needs: Fantasy (space fantasy, sword and sorcery), horror (dark fantasy, futuristic, psychological, supernatural), psychic/supernatural/occult, science fiction (hard science/technological, soft/sociological, space opera). "No vampire fiction, no fan fiction, no serial killers." Upcoming themes: "Halloween mini-issue" (October 15, 2000). Accepts 6-8 mss/issue, 24-30 ms/year. Publishes ms 2-6 month after acceptance. **Publishes 10-15 new writers/ year.** Recently published work by Dean Loftis, Michael Williams, Sephera Giron, John Shanadan, Robert J. Tiess, Tom Gerencer and Bob Barrett. Length: 4,000 words average; no minimum; 10,000 words maximum. Publishes short shorts. Also publishes poetry. Sometimes critiques or comments on rejected ms.

How to Contact: Send complete ms via e-mail. Include estimated word count, 1 paragraph bio, list of publications, mailing address and your website and e-mail addresses. Reports in 1-3 months. Send SASE for reply, return of ms or send a disposable copy of ms. No simultaneous submissions; reprints OK. Sample copy free. Guidelines free for SAE. Reviews novels, short story collections and nonfiction books of interest to writers. Send books to above address.

Payment/Terms: Pays $5 on publication. Acquires first rights and reprint (one-time) rights if applicable.

Advice: "A strong, believable plot and traditional story forms are preferred. Give me good characters, readable dialogue and use your best English skills. Violence and gore must be justified, and your horror had better be horrific. Back up the science in your fiction, and make your fantasy truly fantastic. Send your best work. I suggest you have a friend help you double-check it for simple errors. Online science fiction/speculative fiction genre e-zines are the future of the small press short fiction market. Where once people ran a few thousand copies and begged distributors to carry them, we now publish online and reach worldwide with our publications—for a fraction of the cost."

OUTER DARKNESS, Where Nightmares Roam Unleashed, Outer Darkness Press, 1312 N. Delaware Place, Tulsa OK 74110. (918)832-1246. **Editor:** Dennis Kirk. Zine: 8½×5½; 60-80 pages; 20 lb. paper; 90 lb. glossy cover; illustrations. Specializes in imaginative literature. "Variety is something I strive for in *Outer Darkness*. In each issue we present readers with great tales of science fiction and horror along with poetry, cartoons and interviews/essays. I seek to provide readers with a magazine which, overall, is fun to read." Quarterly. Estab. 1994. Circ. 500.

• Fiction published in *Outer Darkness* has received honorable mention in *The Year's Best Fantasy and Horror.*

Needs: Fantasy (science), horror, mystery/suspense (with horror slant), psychic/supernatural/occult, romance (gothic), science fiction (hard science, soft/sociological). No straight mystery, pure fantasy—works which do not incorporate elements of science fiction and/or horror. Wants more "character driven tales—especially in the genre of science fiction." "I do not publish works with children in sexual situations and graphic language should be kept to a minimum." Receives 50-75 unsolicited mss/month. Accepts 7-9 mss/issue; 20-50 mss/year. Recently published work by Uncle River, Stefano Donati, Charlee Jacob and Ken Abner. **Publishes 4-6 new writers/year.** . Length: 3,000 words average; 1,000 words minimum; 5,000 words maximum. Also publishes literary essays and poetry. Always critiques or comments on rejected mss.

How to Contact: Send complete ms with a cover letter. Include estimated word count, 50- to 75-word bio, list of publications and "any awards, honors you have received." Reports in 1 week on queries; 1-2 months on mss. Send SASE for reply, return of ms or send a disposable copy of ms. Simultaneous submissions OK. Sample copy for $3.95. Fiction guidelines for #10 SASE.

Payment/Terms: Pays 3 contributor's copies for fiction, 2 for poetry and art. Pays on publication. Acquires one-time rights.

Advice: "Suspense is one thing I look for in stories. I want stories which grab the reader early on . . . and don't let go. I want stories which start off on either an interesting or suspenseful note. Read the works of Alan Dean Foster. Don't be discouraged by rejections. The best writers have received their share of rejection slips. Be patient. Take time to polish your work. Produce the best work you can and continue to submit, regardless of rejections. New writers now have more markets than ever before. I believe readers are searching for more 'traditional' works—and less 'experimental' styles. And while I have published works of an experimental nature, I like to give readers good, solid traditional fiction, for which I feel there is a definite demand."

PABLO LENNIS, The Magazine of Science Fiction, Fantasy and Fact, Etaoin Shrdlu Press, Fandom House, 30 N. 19th St., Lafayette IN 47904. **Editor:** John Thiel. Zine: 8½×11; 26 pages; standard stock; illustrations and "occasional" photos. "Science fiction, fantasy, science, research and mystic for scientists and science fiction and fantasy appreciators." Monthly.

Needs: Fantasy, science fiction. Receives 50 unsolicited mss/year. Accepts 4 mss/issue; 48 mss/year. Publishes ms 4 months after acceptance. Published work by Michael Lohr, Arthur Winfield Knight, Joanne Tolson and C.B. Thatcher. **Publishes 36 new writers/year.** Length: 1,500 words average; 3,000 words maximum. Also publishes literary criticism, poetry. Occasionally critiques rejected mss and recommends other markets.

How to Contact: "Method of submission is author's choice but he might prefer to query. No self-statement is necessary." No simultaneous submissions. Reports in 2 weeks. Does not accept computer printouts.

Payment/Terms: Pays 1 contributor's copy. Publication not copyrighted.

Advice: "I have taboos against unpleasant and offensive language and want material which is morally or otherwise elevating to the reader. I prefer an optimistic approach and favor fine writing. With a good structure dealt with intelligently underlying this, you have the kind of story I like. I prefer stories that have something to say to those which have something to report."

PAPYRUS JOURNAL: The Post-Contemporary Journal of Literature and Art, 650 Landfair Ave #106, Los Angeles CA 90024. E-mail: lmoskow@aol.com. Website: www.geocities.com/SoHo/Coffeehouse/2176/index.html (includes writer's guidelines). Electronic zine. **Editor:** Lee Moskow. Publishes "eclectic and experimental fiction, poetry, photography and art to a varied audience."

Needs: Experimental. No "sentimentality and trite love stories." Publishes new writers. Recently published work by Holly Day, Robert Klein Engler and Ben Ohmart. Also publishes poetry.

How to Contact: Send queries/mss by e-mail. Include bio and list of publications. Send submissions according to guidelines on website.

Advice: "Please follow the guidelines and check spelling and grammar for a better chance at publication. Include a brief bio in the e-mail listing any prior publication and something interesting about yourself that makes you stand apart from any other writer. I see stories as a stepping stone to print journal publication and I hope that all writers seen on *Papyrus* will one day become famous and remember where they were first published. *Papyrus Journal* and its sister e-zines will grow dramatically in the future."

★ ⊘ ▣ **PBW**, 130 W. Limestone, Yellow Springs OH 45387. (513)767-7416. E-mail: rianca@aol.com. **Editor:** Richard Freeman. Electronic disk zine: 700 pages; illustrations. "*PBW* is an experimental floppy disk that 'prints' strange and 'unpublishable' in an above-ground-sense writing." Quarterly electronic zine. Featuring avant-garde fiction and poetry. Estab. 1988.

● *PBW* is an electronic zine which can be read on a Macintosh or available over modem on BBS. Write for details.

Needs: Erotica, experimental, gay, lesbian, literary. No "conventional fiction of any kind." Receives 3 unsolicited mss/month. Accepts 40 mss/issue; 160 mss/year. Publishes ms within 3 months after acceptance. Published work by Dave Castleman, Marie Markoe and Henry Hardee. **Publishes 10-15 new writers/year.** Length: open. Publishes short shorts and novels in chapters. Publishes literary essays, literary criticisms and poetry. Always critiques or comments on rejected mss.

How to Contact: Send complete ms with a cover letter. Accepts queries by e-mail. "Manuscripts are only taken if sent on disk." Reports in 2 weeks. Send SASE for reply, return of ms or send a disposable copy of ms. Simultaneous, reprint and electronic (Mac or modem) submissions OK. Sample copy for $2. Reviews novels and short story collections.

Payment/Terms: Pays 1 contributor's copy. All rights revert back to author. Not copyrighted.

★ ◯ ▣ **PEN & SWORD**. (415)626-5179. E-mail: jag@rahul.net. Website: www.rahul.net/jag/. **Editor:** Jim Gardner. Electronic zine. "The best in modern and post-modern fiction, poetry, essays, criticism and reviews."

Needs: "*Pen & Sword* is an equal opportunity publisher and especially welcomes work from the gay/lesbian/bisexual community." Recently published work by Aldo Alvarez and Jim Tushinski. **Publishes 6-10 new writers/year.**

How to Contact: "Electronic submissions to the editor in MS Word, FrameMaker, HTML (preferred) or ASCII text are acceptable."

✓ ⊘ ◎ ♈ **PENNY DREADFUL, Tales & Poems of Fantastic Terror**, Pendragon Publications, P.O. Box 719, New York NY 10101-0719. **Editor:** Michael Pendragon. Zine specializing in horror: 8½×5½; 52 pages; illustrations and photos. Publication to "celebrate the darker aspects of man, the world and their creator. We seek to address a highly literate audience who appreciate horror as a literary art form." Triannually. Estab. 1996. Circ. 500.

● Penny Dreadful won several Honorable Mentions in St. Martin's Press's *The Year's Best Fantasy and Horror* competition.

Needs: Fantasy (dark symbolist), horror, psychic/supernatural/occult. Wants more "tales set in and in the style of the 19th century." No modern science fiction "constantly referring to 20th century persons, events, products, etc." List of upcoming themes available for SASE. Receives 100 unsolicited mss/month. Accepts 5-10 mss/issue; 15-30 mss/year. "*Penny Dreadful* reads all year until we have accepted enough submissions to fill more than one year's worth of issues." Recently published work by James S. Dorr, Scott Thomas, D.M. Yorton, Paul Bradshaw, Nancy Bennett and John Light. **Publishes 6 new writers/year.** Length: 500 words minimum; 2,500 words maximum. Publishes short shorts. Also publishes poetry. Always critiques or comments on rejected mss.

How to Contact: Send complete ms with a cover letter. Include estimated word count, bio and list of publications. Reports in up to 3 months on queries and mss. Send SASE for reply, return of ms or send disposable copy of ms. Simultaneous submissions and reprints OK. Sample copy for $5. Subscription for $12. Fiction guidelines for #10 SASE.

Payment/Terms: Pays 1 contributor copy for one-time rights. Sends galleys to author. Not copyrighted.

Advice: Whenever possible, try to submit to independent zines specializing in your genre. Be prepared to spend significant amounts of time and money. Expect only one copy as payment. Over time—if you're exceptionally talented and/or lucky—you may begin to build a small following."

★ ◎ ▣ **PEOPLENET DISABILITY DATENET HOME PAGE, "Where People Meet People,"**, Box 897, Levittown NY 11756-0897. (516)579-4043. E-mail: mauro@idt.net. Website: idt.net/~mauro (includes writer's guidelines, articles, stories, poems). **Editor:** Robert Mauro. "Romance stories featuring disabled characters." Estab. 1995.

Needs: Romance, contemporary and disabled. Main character must be disabled. Upcoming theme: "Marriage between disabled and non-disabled." Accepts 3 mss/year. Publishes immediately after acceptance. **Publishes 21 new writers/year.** Length: 1,500 words. Publishes short shorts. Length: 750 words. Also publishes poetry. Especially looking for book reviews on books dealing with disabled persons and sexuality.

How to Contact: Send complete ms by e-mail. No simultaneous submissions. Fiction guidelines online.

Payment/Terms: Acquires first rights.

Advice: "We are looking for romance stories of under 1,000 words on romance with a disabled man or woman as the main character. No sob stories or 'super crip' stories. Just realistic romance. No porn. Erotica okay. Love, respect, trust, understanding and acceptance are what I want."

★ $○ ▣ **PIF.** (360)493-0596. E-mail: editor@pifmagazine.com. Website: www.pifmagazine.com. Editor: Richard Luck. **Fiction Editor:** Jennifer Bergmark (fiction@pifmagazine.com). Electronic zine. "Starting point for the Literary E-press, *Pif* believes that electronic publishing will revolutionize the industry as profoundly as the printing press did, and we aim to usher in this new era with the best and the brightest the Net has to offer. Our audience is a cross-section of the global community. We're read in over 87 different countries. The majority of our readers tend to be educated, culturally aware and open-minded. Quite a few of our readers are writers as well."

Needs: "We publish a wide range of material, including: poetry, fiction, commentary and original artwork. We also include book, movie and music reviews. We are open to most anything, as long as it is well-written and shows a real love for the craft. We especially seek contemporary literary-quality fiction in the style of Douglas Coupland, Erica Jong, Henry Miller, et al. We're particularly interested in writers who are willing to break boundaries, who are honest and believe in themselves and the characters they create." Recently published work by Richard K. Weems, Karen Essex, Seth Brady Tucker, Leo Haber, Daniel Weinshenker and Michael Largo. "We are the premier publisher of new and unpublished writers on the Net. Several of the writers we originally introduced have, as a result of appearing in *Pif*, subsequently published novels or collections of poetry with mainstream publishers." **Publishes 10-12 new fiction writers/year.** Length: 5,000 words maximum; "Microfiction": 1,000 words maximum; "Hyper-fiction": 500 words maximum.

How to Contact: Electronic submissions only. "Submit via e-mail, pasting your submission into the body of the e-mail. Online submissions form is at www.pifmagazine.com/editor.shtml. Always send submissions to the proper editor. E-mail subs@pifmagazine.com for a complete listing of e-mail addresses."

Advice: "Be honest and be yourself. Take a chance and see where it leads you. Above all, believe in your characters and the story you're telling. If you're bored while writing the piece, chances are we'll be bored reading it. So be enthusiastic. Be brave. Be willing to go out on a limb."

〔N〕 ▣ **PILLOW SCREAMS,** 708 S. 15th, Manitowoc WI 54220. E-mail: subs@lsol.net. Website: members.spree.com/SIP/forevernight/pscreams/pillow1.htm. **Editor:** Nell Harmon (Naughty Nell). Electronic zine. "*Pillow Screams* features erotic horror where sex isn't the whole theme or plot of the story. No harsh porno here, only that sensual touch that scares you out of your pants. Adults only. Those who like to read the *Hot Blood Series* edited by Michael Garrett and Jeff Gelb will enjoy the stories published here."

Needs: Erotic horror. "No harsh horror, overdone vampire themes, anything reading like porno, childrens or sappy romance stories." Want more "sensual horror and less pushy sexual stories." **Publishes 1-2 new writers/year.** Recently published work by P.D. Cacek, M. Christian, Greg Gifune, David Whitman, Jason Tucker, Carol McCallister, Jason Duke and Rain Graves.

How to Contact: Accepts queries/mss by e-mail. "E-mail submissions only, in body only please, not attachments. Please put *Pillow Screams* in subject line."

Advice: "*Pillow Screams* gets over 100 submissions per issue and only six to eight are published per issue. Looking for sensual horror, no porno. If I start seeing the 'F' word every other sentence, expect a rejection and never ever use that awful 'C' word when submitting to me, it wouldn't even pass a first glance. Erotic horror is just that, erotic, not porno, don't pass off a bunch of 'ohs and ahs' and jump in the sack and get killed off, leave that for the bad horror movies. I want a hit, a remark, a whisper of what could be."

★ ✓ $○ **PLAY THE ODDS,** P.O. Box 55948, Little Rock AR 72215-5948. (501)228-5237. Editor: Tom Raley. **Fiction Editor:** Barbra Stone. Zine specializing in gaming/gambling: 8½×11; 16 lb. paper; illustrations and photos. "We cover gambling activities all across the country. We offer tips, reviews, instructions and advice. We also cover cruise lines since most have casinos on board." Monthly. Estab. 1997.

● *Play the Odds* ranked #2 on *Writer's Digest's* Fiction 50 list of top fiction markets.

Needs: Adventure, fantasy (science fantasy), horror, mystery/suspense (cozy, private eye/hardboiled, romantic suspense), science fiction (soft sociological), senior citizen/retirement, sports, westerns (traditional). "Must be gambling type story!" Receives 20-25 unsolicited mss/month. Accepts 1-2 mss/issue; 12-20 mss/year. Publishes ms 2-4 months after acceptance. Published work by Jennifer Sinclair and Gary Lewis. Length: 600 words average; 800 words maximum. Publishes short shorts. Also publishes literary criticism and poetry. Always critiques or comments on rejected mss.

How to Contact: Send complete ms with a cover letter. Include estimated word count and 100 word bio. Reports in 1 month on queries; 8-10 weeks on mss. Send SASE for reply, return of ms or send disposable copy of ms. Simultaneous submissions OK. Sample copy for $3. Fiction guidelines for #10 SASE. Reviews novels and short story collections. Send books to D.A. Rogers.

Payment/Terms: Varies on acceptance for one-time rights.

Advice: "We look for fast paced stories with real characters. The stories should be fun, enjoyable and the main character doesn't need to be trying to save the world. Few, if any of us, do that. We do however get in bad situations. You must write what you enjoy writing about. If you don't want to write a story about gambling or a gambler, it will show in your work. If it is something you do want, that will also show in your work and we will notice it."

[N] [★] [○] BERN PORTER INTERNATIONAL, 50 Salmond St., Belfast ME 04915. (207)338-4303. E-mail: bpinternational@hotmail.com. **Editors:** Natasha Bernstein and Sheila Holtz. Magazine: 8½ × 11; 8 pages; illustrations and photographs. "Experimantal prose and poetry at the edge of established literary forms." Bimonthly. Estab. 1997.

Needs: Experimental, literary, prose poem, translations, international. "No long conventional narratives. Want more short vignettes and surreal prose-poems." Receives 30-50 unsolicited mss/month. Publishes ms immediately after acceptance. Recently published work by Stephen Jama, Natasha Bernstein, C.A. Conrad, T. Anders Carson and Anne Welsh. **Publishes 12 new writers/year.** Length: 2 pages or less. Publishes short shorts.

How to Contact: Query first. Accepts queries by e-mail. Reports in 1 week. Simultaneous and reprint submissions OK. Sample copy $2, fiction guidelines free.

Payment/Terms: Pays in copies.

Advice: "Do not compromise your style and vision for the sake of the market. Megamarketing of authors by big mega publishers sucks. We seek to counter this trend by giving voice to authors who would not be heard in that world."

[★] [○] [◎] QECE, Question Everything Challenge Everything, 406 Main St. #3C, Collegeville PA 19426. E-mail: qece@aol.com. **Editor:** Larry Nocella. Zine: 5½ × 8½; 60 pages; copy paper; copy paper cover; illustrations and photographs. Zine "seeking to inspire free thought and action by encouraging a more questioning mentality. Intended for dreamers and quiet laid-back rebels." Biannually. Estab. 1996. Circ. 300.

Needs: Experimental. "Anything that inspires others to question and challenge conventions of fiction. Aggressive, compelling, short, fun is OK too. No lame stuff. Be wary of anything too foo-foo literary." No genre fiction, no formulas. Receives 15 unsolicited mss/month. Accepts 1 ms/issue; 3 mss/year. Publishes ms 6 months after acceptance. **Publishes 12 new writers/year.** Length: 1,000 words average. Publishes short shorts. Always critiques or comments on rejected mss.

How to Contact: Send complete ms with a cover letter. Include estimated word count and 25 words or less bio. Reports in 4 months. Send SASE for reply, return of ms or send a disposable copy of ms. Simultaneous and e-mail submissions OK. Sample copy for $3. Fiction guidelines free for #10 SASE.

Payment/Terms: Pays 2 contributor's copies; additional copies for $3 (make checks out to Larry Nocella). Acquires one-time rights.

Advice: "Ignore 'trends'; be yourself as much as possible and you'll create something unique. Be as timeless as possible. Avoid obscure, trendy references. Tie comments about a current trend to timeless observation. If it's in the 'news' chances are it won't be in QECE, The 'news' is a joke. Tell me something I need to know. Favor anecdotes and philosophy over intense political opinions. I'd prefer to hear about personal experiences and emotions everyone can relate to. Criticism is welcome, though. QECE can be negative, but remember it is positive too. Just go for it! Send away and let me decide! Get busy!"

[★] [✓] [◖] [▣] RENAISSANCE ONLINE MAGAZINE, (formerly *Renaissance Magazine*), 168 Orient Ave., Pawtucket RI 02861. E-mail: submit@renaissancemag.com. Website: www.renaissancemag.com. **Editor:** Kevin Ridolfi. Electronic zine. "*Renaissance* provides an open forum and exchange for an online community seeking for diversity on the jumbled and stagnant Internet. Works should be well-written and should deal with the effective resolution of a problem."

Needs: Short fiction, serial fiction, poetry, essays, humor, young adult. "No lewd, adult fiction." Recently published work by George Kashdan, Jennifer Maine, Elizabeth Dumont and Bonnie Nay. **Publishes 24 new writers/year.** Length: 3,000 words maximum.

How to Contact: Electronic and traditional submissions accepted, electronic (e-mail) submissions preferred.

Advice: "Browse through *Renaissance*'s past issues for content tendencies and submission requirements. Don't be afraid to go out on a short limb, but please limit yourself to our already existing categories."

[★] [○] S.L.U.G. FEST, LTD., A Magazine of Free Expression, SF, Ltd., P.O. Box 1238, Simpsonville SC 29681-1238. Editor: M.T. Nowak. **Fiction Editor:** M. Tatlow. Zine: 8½ × 11; 70 pages; 20 lb. paper; 30 lb. cover stock; illustrations. "We are dedicated to publishing the best poetry and fiction we can find from writers who have yet to be discovered." Quarterly. Estab. 1991. Circ. 1,000.

Needs: Adventure, ethnic/multicultural, experimental, feminist, historical, humor/satire, literary, mainstream/contemporary, regional, "philosophies, ramblings." "No poor writing." Receives 30 unsolicited mss/month. Accepts 5-10 mss/issue; 20-40 mss/year. Publishes mss 3 months after acceptance. **Publishes 50% new writers.** Length: 7,000-10,000 words preferred. Publishes short shorts. Also publishes literary essays, literary criticism and poetry. Often critiques and comments on rejected mss.

How to Contact: Send complete ms with a cover letter. Include estimated word count. Reports in 5 weeks. Send SASE for reply, return of ms or send a disposable copy of ms. Simultaneous, reprint and electronic submissions OK. Sample copy for $5. Fiction guidelines free. Reviews novels and short story collections.

Payment/Terms: Pays 1 contributor's copy. Rights revert to author upon publication.

Advice: "We look for humor, quality of imagery. Get our interest. Style and content must grab our editors. Strive for a humorous or unusual slant on life."

✓ ▢ ◎ **SEDUCTIVE TORTURE, Vampire Tales**, Vamp, Inc., 708 S. 15th St., Manitowoc WI 54220. **Editor:** D.M. Yorton. Zine specializing in vampire tales: full-size, 40-60 pages; illustrations. "Dark moody stories dealing with vampires." Adult audience. Triannually. Estab. 1998.
Needs: Erotica (soft!), fantasy, horror (soft), psychic/supernatural/occult. Receives 12-20 unsolicited mss/month. Accepts 4-8 mss/issue. Publishes ms 1-6 months after acceptance. Recently published work by Alex Bledsoe, Gary Jurechka and Sandra Deluca. Fowler. Length: 1,100 words average; 2,500 words maximum. Publishes short shorts. Also publishes poetry. Always critiques or comments on rejected ms.
How to Contact: Send complete ms with a cover letter. Include estimated word count, 1-paragraph bio and list of publications. Reports in 1 week on queries; 1-4 weeks on mss. Send SASE for reply, send a disposable copy of ms. Simultaneous and reprint submissions OK. Sample copy for $6.50. Fiction guidelines for #10 SASE.
Payment/Terms: Pays 1 contributor's copy; additional copies $6.25. Acquires one-time rights. Not copyrighted.
Advice: "We're looking for more new age and present-time vampire stories, not gothic unless well written, not punk-rock or vampire kills or vampire jumps in bed. *Seductive* is a hard magazine to get into but I highly encourage writers to keep trying."

✓ ▢ ◎ **SEPULCHRE**, Koshkovich Press, P.O. Box 429, Ft. Meade MD 20755-0429. E-mail: sepulchr97@aol.com. Website: www.members.aol.com/sepulchr97 (includes writer's guidelines, links to contributors' websites, graphic of current issue's cover, along with contributor list). **Editor:** Scot H.P. Drew. Zine: digest size; approximately 40 pages; 28 lb. paper; 67 lb. coverstock; illustrations and photos. "Quarterly zine devoted to bringing new writers of dark fantasy and imaginative horror out into the sunlight of the small press literary scene." Publishes fiction and poetry. Estab. 1997.
Needs: Fantasy (dark), horror, psychic/supernatural/occult. "No urban horror, sociological science fiction. We would like to see more classic horror akin to Poe, Lovecraft, Bierce." Receives 50 unsolicited mss/month. Accepts 5-10 mss/issue; 20-40 mss/year. Recently published work by Scott Urban, Anke Kriske and Cindy Main. **Publishes up to 10 new writers/year.** Length: 2,000-5,000 words average; 10,000 words maximum. Publishes short shorts. Also publishes poetry. Sample copy for $3 (make checks payable to Scot Drew). Fiction guidelines for #10 SASE.
How to Contact: Send complete ms with a cover letter. Accepts queries by e-mail. Include 2-5 line bio for inclusion with piece. Send disposable copy of ms. Reports in 1 month on mss. Simultaneous submissions OK.
Payment/Terms: Pays 1 contributor's copy.
Advice: "Send your darkest, most disturbing pieces."

N ▢ **SHADOW VOICES**, E-mail: phantomlady@geocities.com. Website: www.geocities.com/Athens/styx/1713/index.html. **Editor:** Vida Janulaitis. Electronic zine. "If you speak of the unknown and reach into the darkness of your soul, share your deepest thoughts. Send me your poetry and short stories."
Needs: "Any fiction or poetry that reveals your inner thoughts. No pornography, or racist material, or any material that may inspire someone to do harm to any form of life or property." Wants more fiction that "allows the writer to reveal a different side of life and themselves and put those feelings into words." Recently published work by Taylor Grahm, J.H.B. Maryann Hazen, Mike Harwood, Rich Logsdon, Vanessa Hawskworth and Vida Janulaitis.
How to Contact: Accepts queries/mss by e-mail. "Each and every submission should be sent on a separate e-mail, no file attachments please. At the top of each page place 'the title of the work,' your real name, complete e-mail address and a short bio. Please indicate submission in the e-mail subject line."
Advice: "Please edit your work carefully. I will assume poetic license. Most of all, write what's inside of you and be sincere about it."

N ✦ ▢ ▣ **SHORT STORY WRITERS SHOWCASE**, E-mail: ssweditor@yahoo.com. Website: www.geocities.com/Paris/Metro/3296. **Editor:** Melissa K. Beynon. Electronic zine specializing in literary short stories. "Post stories in a variety of genres with one goal in mind: entertain an intelligent population with the written word. If readers learn, feel, and come again, the site is a success." Estab. 1997.
Needs: Fantasy, romance, science fiction. "Want all genres of short stories that are written with intelligence, honesty and with the readers entertainment always in mind. Visitors to *SSWS* range in age from 8 to over 100. I accept stories written by all ages. I will not accept stories with explicit sex, unnecessary violence or harsh language, prejudice without change or involving a subject that could prove dangerous to young readers (like hopelessness). I would love to see more fantasy, romance and science fiction on *SSWS* in the future." **Publishes 100 new writers/year.** Recently published work by David R. Dixon, Lance Grim, Ross Hunter, Dan Kelly, Matt Mitchell, Bill Monks, Rhonda L. Nolan and Mike Oakwood. Length: 10,000 words maximum. Often critiques or comments on rejected mss.
How to Contact: Accepts queries/mss by e-mail. "I use Microsoft Word (the latest version) to read e-mailed contributions, usually as an attachment. If I can't read the format, I always reply to the contributor with suggestions on how to make it so I can read it."
Advice: "Read, read and re-read your work. Have friends, teachers and anyone who'll sit still long enough to read it. Listen to their advice. If you confuse, frustrate, or bore them, you'll confuse, frustrate or bore me. And pay attention to your word processor's spelling and grammar checker please, it isn't perfect."

SPUNK, The Journal of Spontaneous Creativity, P.O. Box 55336, Hayward CA 94545. (510)278-6689. **Editor:** Sean Reinhart. Zine: 5½ × 8½; 30 pages; photocopied; illustrations and photos. "*Spunk* is dedicated to the publication of short creative outbursts with no pretensions or apprehensions—somewhere along the fine line between matter and energy lies *Spunk*." Semiannually. Estab. 1997. Circ. 500.

Needs: Experimental, literary. List of upcoming themes available for SASE. Receive 50 unsolicited mss/month. Accepts to 15-20 mss/issue; 30-40 mss/year. Publishes ms 6-12 months after acceptance. Recently published work by Violet Jones, Stephen Gutierrez, B.Z. Niditch, Errol Miller and C.C. Russell. Length: 1,000 words average. "We love really good one-pagers." Also publishes literary essays and poetry. Sometimes critiques or comments on rejected mss.

How to Contact: Send complete ms with a cover letter. Reports in 6 months on mss. Send SASE for reply, return of ms. Simultaneous submissions OK. Sample copy for $2. Fiction guidelines for #10 SASE.

Payment/Terms: Pays 1 contributor's copy for first North American serial rights.

Advice: "All work should be short, unique and above all Spunky. Obtain a sample copy, not necessarily to emulate our style, but to know if we're on the same planet or not."

N ★ ⊘ ▣ STATE OF BEING, 214 River Bow, Georgetown TX 78628. (512)517-0880. E-mail: clock@apoculpro.org or kilgore@eden.com. Website: www.apoculpro.org (includes writer's guidelines, editor names, contributors, fiction, past issues, interviews with authors, history, special events, mailing list information, illumination, every answer). **Editor:** Kilgore Trout. E-zine. "We thrive off the new, fresh, unique-absurdity is worshipped, everything is embraced. If you are four years old and wield a crayon, write and submit." Monthly. Estab. 1994. Circ. "several hundred."

Needs: Adventure, erotica, ethnic/multicultural, experimental, family saga, fantasy, feminist, gay, glitz, historical, horror, humor satire, lesbian, literary, mainstream, military/war, mystery/suspense, New Age, psychic/supernatural/occult, regional, religious, romance, science fiction, short story collections, thriller/espionage, translations, western. No children's or young adult. Receives 5-20 unsolicited mss/month. Accepts 5-20 mss/issue; 60-100 mss/year. Publishes ms 1-2 months after acceptance. **Publishes 20 new writers/year.** Recently published work by Robert James Berry, Holly Day and D.L. Brown. Length: 1,200 words average; 3 words minimum. Also publishes literary essays, criticism and poetry. Sometimes critiques or comments on rejected ms.

How to Contact: Query or send complete ms with a cover letter. Accepts queries and mss by e-mail. Include bio. Reports in 1 month on queries and mss. Send SASE for reply, return of ms or send disposable copy of ms. Simultaneous and reprint submissions OK.

Payment/Terms: Acquires one-time rights.

Advice: We look for writing that is "nonstandard, unique, things I will not read about in *Reader's Digest*. Don't think, write."

N ★ ⊘ ▣ STORY BYTES—Very Short Stories, E-mail: editor@storybytes.com. Website: www.storybytes.com. **Editor:** M. Stanley Bubien. Electronic zine. "*Story Bytes—Very Short Stories* is strictly an electronic publication, appearing on the Internet in three forms. First, the stories are sent to an electronic mailing list of readers. They also get placed on the *Story Bytes* website, in both HTML and PDF format."

Needs: "Stories must be very short—having a length that is the power of 2 specifically: 2, 4, 8, 16, 32, 64, 128, 256, 512, 1,024 and 2,048 words long." No sexually explicit material. "Would like to see more material dealing with religion. Not necessarily 'inspirational' stories, but those that show the struggles of living a life of faith in a realistic manner." **Publishes 33% new writers.** Recently published work by Richard K. Weems, Joseph Lerner, Lisa Cote, Thomas Sennet, Mark Hansen and Wendy Williams. Preferred length: 256-512 words. Publishes short shorts.

How to Contact: Accepts queries/mss by e-mail. "I prefer plain text with story title, authorship and word count. Only accepts electronic submissions."

Advice: "In *Story Bytes*, the very short stories themselves range in topic. Many explore a brief event—a vignette of something unusual, unique and, at times, something even commonplace. Some stories can be bizarre, while others quite lucid. Some are based on actual events, while others are entirely fictional. Try to develop conflict early on (in the first sentence if possible!), and illustrate or resolve this conflict through action rather than description. I believe we'll find an audience for electronic published works primarily in the short story realm. Very few people want to sit in front of their computer to read *War and Peace!* But, most people gladly read e-mail, and messages in this form can easily range from 2 to 1,000 words."

✓ $⊘ SYNAESTHESIA PRESS CHAPBOOK SERIES, P.O. Box 1763, Tempe AZ 85280-1763. (602)280-9092. E-mail: books@synaesthesia.com. Website: www.synaesthesiapress.com (includes publication, bookstore, links). **Editor:** Jim Camp. Zine specializing in fiction: 16 pages; 50 lb. paper; card cover. Publishes

---

SENDING TO A COUNTRY other than your own? Be sure to send International Reply Coupons instead of stamps for replies or return of your manuscript.

fiction by new and established authors "writing outside the margin." Quarterly. Estab. 1995. Circ. 500.
Needs: Erotica, experimental, literary. No romance, children's, westerns, science fiction. Receives 10 unsolicited mss/month. Accepts 10 mss/year. Publishes ms 1-6 months after acceptance. Recently published work by Barry Gifford, Jack Micheline and A.D. Michele. **Publishes 1 new writer/year.** Length: 2,500 words maximum. Publishes short shorts. Also publishes literary essays, literary criticism and poetry.
How to Contact: Query first. Accepts queries/mss by e-mail. Include estimated word count. Reports in 1 week on queries. Send SASE for reply. Simultaneous, reprint and electronic submissions OK. Sample copy for $10. Fiction guidelines free. Reviews novels or short story collections. Send books to editor.
Payment/Terms: Pays $200 plus 6 contributor's copies. Sends galleys to author.
Advice: "Make it stand out. Hopefully, you are over 'anxiety of influence.' "

THE TALE SPINNER, Glasgow Publishing, P.O. Box 336, Bedford IN 47421. (812)279-8863. E-mail: 103273.134.compuserve.com. **Editor:** Joe Glasgow. Zine: 8½ × 11; 32 pages; illustrations. "As a multi-genre magazine we try to give our readers a variety of their favorite genre styles." Bimonthly. Estab. 1995. Circ. 200.
Needs: Adventure, erotica, ethnic/multicultural, fantasy (science, sword and sorcery), historical, humor/satire, mystery/suspense (amateur sleuth, cozy, police procedural, private eye/hardboiled, romantic suspense), romance (contemporary, futuristic/time travel, gothic, historical), science fiction (hard science, soft/sociological), sports, westerns (frontier, traditional), young adult/teen (science fiction). Receives 60 unsolicited mss/month. Accepts 10 mss/issue; 60 mss/year. Publishes ms 6 months after acceptance. Published work by John B. Rosenman, Larry Tritten, Ardath Mayhar, Tom Piccirilli, Lyn McConchie, O'Neil DeNoux and Lee Paul. Length: 800 words average; 4,000 words maximum. Publishes short shorts. Length: 250-500 words. Also publishes poetry. Often critiques or comments on rejected mss.
How to Contact: Send complete ms with cover letter. Include estimated word count and 1- to 2-paragraph bio. Reports in 3 weeks on queries; 1 month on mss. Send SASE for reply, return of ms or send a disposable copy of ms. Simultaneous and reprint submissions OK. Sample copy for $3.95 and 9 × 12 SASE. Fiction guidelines for #10 SASE.
Payment/Terms: Pays ½¢/word minimum; 3¢/word maximum and 1 contributor's copy; additional copies $2.50. Pays on publication. Acquires first North American serial rights or one-time rights.
Advice: "The writer must give me a reason for turning the page. I like a story that gets my attention from the opening paragraphs. Read a sample issue. Write! Write! Write!"

A TASTE FOR FLESH, 1 Massey Square #1217, East York, Ontario M4C 5L4 Canada. (416)699-6471. E-mail: theswan@geocities.com. Website: www.geocities.com/Athens/Troy/1541. **Editor:** Andrew R. Crow. Electronic zine. Publishes "horror poetry, fiction and ranting and raving for adult audiences. It's a place for those with a predilection for pain, poetry and the dark side of life."
Needs: Horror. No romance, westerns. "Want more psychological horror." **Publishes over 20 new writers/ year.** Recently published work by Brian Knight, Robert James Berry, Scott C. Holstad, Andrew R. Crow and Holly Day.
How to Contact: Send queries/mss by e-mail (plain text in e-mail or WordPerfect attachments).
Advice: "Read the masters of horror first. Make me squirm."

TRANSCENDENT VISIONS, Toxic Evolution Press, 251 S. Olds Blvd., 84-E, Fairless Hills PA 19030-3426. (215)547-7159. **Editor:** David Kime. Zine: letter size; 24 pages; xerox paper; illustrations. "*Transcendent Visions* is a literary zine by and for people who have been labeled mentally ill. Our purpose is to illustrate how creative and articulate mental patients are." Quarterly. Estab. 1992. Circ. 200.
• *Transcendent Visions* has received excellent reviews in many underground publications.
Needs: Experimental, feminist, gay, humor/satire, lesbian. Especially interested in material dealing with mental illness. "I do not like stuff one would find in a mainstream publication. No porn." Receives 5 unsolicited mss/ month. Accepts 7 mss/issue; 20 mss/year. Publishes ms 3-4 months after acceptance. Published work by Jim Reagan and Mike Stickel. Length: under 10 pages typed, double-spaced. Publishes short shorts. Also publishes poetry.
How to Contact: Send complete ms with cover letter. Include half-page bio. Reports in 2 weeks on queries; 1 month on mss. Send disposable copy of ms. Simultaneous submissions and reprints OK. Sample copy for $2.
Payment/Terms: Pays 1 contributor's copy on publication. Acquires one-time rights.
Advice: "We like unusual stories that are quirky. Please do not go on and on about what zines you have been published in or awards you have won, etc. We just want to read your material, not know your life story. Please don't swamp me with tons of submissions. Send up to five stories. Please print or type your name and address."

TROUT. E-mail: editor@troutmag.org. Website: www.troutmag.org. **Editor:** Robin Parkinson. E-zine. *Trout* is "slightly fishy, but never coarse."
Needs: "We publish humorous fiction, with a strong British slant. Our material ranges from themed collections of one-liners to a novel-length multi-threaded serial. The intended audience is composed of intelligent, articulate, literate people with a sense of humor and enough understanding of British culture to follow the jokes. No non-

humorous fiction." Would like to see more "humorous short stories." **Publishes 3-4 new writers/year.** Recently published work by Joann L. Dominik, Ric Craig, Andy Gittins, Elly Kelly, Steve Lewin, Sue McCoan and Alexander MacDonald.

How to Contact: "*Trout* does not accept unsolicited manuscripts, manuscript fragments or synopses. Writers who might wish to contribute to *Trout* should contact the editor by e-mail and be prepared to show a sample of their work."

Payment/Terms: " *Trout* is entirely noncommercial. We receive no payment so we have none to pass on."

Advice: "Read us. If you find what you read amusing and feel that you are capable of writing material in a similar vein then talk to us. However, if you don't understand what we're getting at, we would not recommend that you attempt to 'slant' your material to fit what you perceive *Trout* 's philosophy to be. We are interested in writers whose natural 'voice' matches what we are doing."

N ★ **$** ◑ ▢ **TWILIGHT SHOWCASE**, 1436 Fifth St., Waynesboro VA 22980. (540)949-4294. E-mail: gconn@rica.net. Website: home.rica.net/gconn. **Editor:** Gary W. Conner. Electronic zine. "We're interested in growing various subgenres of fantasy, those mainly being horror, dark fantasy and speculative fiction. We like a nice mix of writers you've read within these genres and writers you've never heard of." Monthly.

Needs: Fantasy (dark), horror, speculative fiction. **Publishes 75% new writers.** Recently published work by Philip Nutman, David Niall Wilson, Brett A. Savory, Patricia Lee Macomber, Mehitobel Wilson, D.F. Lewis, David Whitman, Weston Ochse, Ken Goldman and Michael Laimo.

How to Contact: Prefers queries/mss by e-mail. "Submissions should be carefully edited and e-mailed to strangeconcepts@rica.net. They may be sent in the body of the e-mail, in MSWord, MS Works, .rtf, or HTML formats.

Payment/Terms: Writers receive ½¢/word. Pays on publication.

Advice: "Read the magazine. Won't cost you a thing. Web fiction is flourishing, as it gives any number of new writers an opportunity to make themselves heard. I have read so many incredible stories on the internet that I am actually a fan of people I've never seen in print. There are some great e-zines out there."

N ★ ◑ ▢ **UNLIKELY STORIES**, 209 W. Dixie Ave., Marietta GA 30008. (770)422-9731. E-mail: unlikely@flash.net. Website: www.flash.net/~unlikely. **Editor:** Jonathan Penton. Electronic zine. "*Unlikely Stories* uses the internet to bring new forms of literature to people that don't necessarily have a great deal of literary exposure."

Needs: Literary. All genres. "Actively solicits quality works that cannot find publication due to their strange or adult nature. No weak characterizations. No form over substance, such as when metafiction writers use their style and/or Vonnegut references as an excuse not to develop characters or a plot." **Publishes 10-15 new writers/year.** Recently published work by Alan Kaufman, Elisha Porat and Laurel Ann Bogen. Also publishes poetry.

How to Contact: Prefers queries/mss by e-mail. Simultaneous submissions, reprints OK.

Advice: Wants more "fiction that seeks deeper truths. Art is an exploration and exposure of the thoughts and feelings that are hidden from everyday view. I like fiction that questions what is accepted as truth. Write from the heart, if you must, but mostly write something unique. I'm looking for stuff that only the author can express; unique and personal viewpoints on the nature of humans. The growing number of people who read electronic literature know which publications are quality and which are not. Although most of these publications do not pay, they often offer more exposure than the small print 'zines of the same exclusivity. There are now Internet poets with significant reputations, and many sites such as mine are regularly examined by print publications for new talent. However, the primary purpose of e-publishing is to have fun. There's not enough money in it to build a career, nor will there by anytime soon. Internet writers should do what gives them personal satisfaction, if it's money you're after, go bug *Atlantic Monthly*."

N ◑ **UNO MAS MAGAZINE**, P.O. Box 1832, Silver Spring MD 20915. E-mail: unomasmag@aol.com. Website: www.unomas.com. Editor: Jim Saah. **Fiction Editor:** Ron Saah. Zine: 8½×11; 50 pages; 60 lb. offset paper; glossy cover; illustrations and photos. "*Uno Mas Magazine* specializes in popular culture. Bringing new and established artists of all dimensions (music, literature, photography, poetry, etc.) together in one magazine." Quarterly. Estab. 1990. Circ. 3,500.

● *Uno Mas* has received excellent reviews in *factsheet 5*, *The Washington Post* and *Pulse Magazine*.

Needs: Condensed/excerpted novel, erotica, ethnic/multicultural, experimental, feminist, gay, historical, humor/satire, lesbian, literary, mystery/suspense (private eye/hardboiled, romantic suspense). Plans special fiction issue or anthology. Receives 4 unsolicited mss/month. Buys 2 mss/issue; 8 mss/year. Publishes ms 1-3 months after acceptance. Agented fiction 20%. Recently published work by George Logothetis and P.J. Jason. Length: 1,500-3,000 words average; 500 words minimum; 3,500 words maximum. Publishes short shorts. Also publishes literary essays, literary criticism and poetry. Sometimes critiques or comments on rejected ms.

How to Contact: Send complete ms with a cover letter. Include estimated word count, short bio and SASE. Reports in 2 weeks on queries; 1-3 months on mss. Send SASE for reply, return of ms or send a disposable copy of ms. Simultaneous, reprint and electronic submissions OK. Sample copy for $3, 9×11 SAE and 5 first-class stamps. Fiction guidelines free for #10 SASE. Reviews novels or short story collections.

Payment/Terms: Pays 3 contributor's copies; additional copies for $1.50. Acquires one-time rights. Sends galleys to author, "if requested."

Advice: "Short, tight pieces have the best chance of being published. Include word count and address on manuscript. Read *Uno Mas* before submitting anything."

☑ ◻ ▣ **VOIDING THE VOID**℗, 8 Henderson Place, New York NY 10028. (212)628-2799. E-mail: mail@vvoid.com. Website: www.vvoid.com. **Editor:** E. Lippincott. Electronic zine and hard copy specializing in personal world views: 11×17; 1 page; mock newsprint for hard copy. "A small reader specializing in individuals' fictional and nonfictional views of the world around them—as they personally experience it." Published monthly. Estab. 1997. Circ. 300 both in US and UK.

Needs: All categories. "We will consider anything the potential contributor feels is appropriate to the theme 'tangibility.' All fiction genres OK." Publishes holiday issues; submit at least 1 month prior to holiday. Receives 10-20 unsolicited mss/month. Accepts 3-10 mss/issue; 120 mss/year. Publishes ms immediately to 3 months after acceptance. Recently published work by Andrew Tiffen (UK), Brian Stuss, Barbara Lopez, Carey Lippincott, Erik Seims, Dan Budnik and Jenny Wu. Length: 5,000 words maximum. Publishes short shorts. Also publishes literary essays, literary criticism, poetry. Always critiques or comments on rejected ms.

How to Contact: Send complete ms with a cover letter; send electronic submissions via website or direct e-mail. Include estimated word count. Report in 2 weeks on queries; 6 weeks on mss. Send SASE for reply or return of ms. Simultaneous and reprint (with date and place indicated) submissions OK. Sample copy and fiction guidelines for #10 SASE. Reviews novels and short story collections

Payment/Terms: Pays 5 contributor's copies; additional copies 25¢. Acquires one-time rights. Not copyrighted.

Advice: "*Voiding the Void* is small and has a very particular slant. This publication is not about the 'writing' or the 'art' so much as it is about the human being behind it all."

N◻ ▣ **WILMINGTON BLUES.** E-mail: editor@wilmingtonblues.com. Website: www.wilmingtonblues .com. **Editor:** Trace Ramsey. Electronic zine. "New online publication dedicated to new writers and essayists."

Needs: Adventure, experimental, horror (dark fantasy, psychological), humor satire, literary, mainstream, mystery/suspense, psychic/supernatural/occult, religious (religious thriller), science fiction (soft/sociological), thriller/espionage. Receives 10-20 unsolicited mss/month. Publishes ms 1-2 months after acceptance. **Publishes as many new writers as possible.** Recently published work by Keith Kincaid and Jennifer Smith. Length: 2,500 words average; 250 words minimum; 10,000 words maximum. Publishes short shorts. Length: 250 words. Also publishes essays, poetry. Often critiques or comments on rejected mss.

How to Contact: Electronic submission only. "Please submit work as a text attachment to an e-mail." Include estimated word count, bio, e-mail address. Reports in 2 weeks on queries; 1 month on mss. Simultaneous submissions and reprints OK.

Payment/Terms: Acquires one-time rights.

Advice: "*Wilmington Blues* is brand new, so we know what it's like to be starting out. If you are a new writer of any skill level, please submit. If your work has something to offer, it will be published. We offer comments on work that isn't accepted, and we encourage resubmissions!"

N ☆ ◻ ▣ **THE WRITER'S HEAD,** 403 Harlon Dr., Suite B-7, Cary NC 27511. Fax: (919)872-4053. E-mail: jmason@writershood.com. Website: www.WritersHood.com. **Editor:** Jeff Mason. Electronic zine. "We are an online magazine whose mission is to publish and assist primarily amateur fiction writers. We publish eleven different fiction genres monthly, and our editors strive to help amateur writers hone their craft. By assisting and publishing both amateur and veteran writers we can provide a magazine with top quality fiction writing for our readers."

Needs: Adventure, children's/juvenile, fantasy, horror, humor satire, mainstream, mystery/suspense, romance, science fiction. No erotica, pornographic. "Our goal is to reach a family audience. Would like to see more mysteries, performing arts (including stage and screen plays) and action/adventure stories." **Publishes 200-300 new writers/year.** Recently published work by Steve Lazorwitz, Harry Buschman, Tony Chandler, Brian Lee, Susan Zoon and Susan Sterling.

How to Contact: Contact via online form or e-mail.

Advice: "Follow online submission guide and be prepared to work with our editors. Currently online publishing is in its infancy. It does not get the same type of recognition as the traditional print media. But this will change in time. Online publishing allows almost anyone to get their work published, which can dilute the effectiveness of online publications. However, once the public finds that they can read top-quality work online, I think they'll be more inclined to use all of the emerging technology."

N ☆ ◻ ▣ **XENITH,** 8963 Crane Rd., Milan MI 48160. E-mail: centaurus7@aol.com. Website: www.xenith.net. **Editor:** Kelly Phelan. Electronic zine. "*Xenith* allows young writers a welcoming place to flourish and develop their talents."

Needs: Young adult/teen. "All writing published is by teens or written for teens. The actual types of writing vary greatly as we welcome diversity: fiction of all genres, serials, poetry, essays, plays, articles, reviews, etc. No excessively dark fiction or fiction with gratuitous violence, profanity or sex. Want more speculative fiction (sci-fi, fantasy, magical realism, etc.). We would also welcome intelligent humor stories, satire, dark humor, anything with an edgy viewpoint." **Publishes 80-90% new writers.** Recently published works by Vasilis Afxentiou, Ben Bradley, Jami Amstone and Maynel Lorie.

How to Contact: Prefers queries/mss by e-mail (in ASCII text format, if possible). "You can also snail mail us your submissions. Include SASE, cover letter. Submissions on disk welcome (ASCII, MSWord 97 or compatible)."

Advice: "Its unbelievable how many sloppy, unproofread submissions we receive. First impressions are important! A writer is ten times more likely to be accepted if he or she simply proofreads or edits his or her work. Send us your finished, polished work—not your first draft! And even if you've been rejected before, don't be afraid to send us another submission—or even a revised and polished copy of something we've rejected in the past. We admire persistence! I think the serious, dramatic growth of electronic publishing is inevitable. As the expenses of paper and printing continue to mount, I believe more and more traditional publications will turn to the Internet. Not only is electronic publishing cost-efficient, but it also opens one to an astonishingly vast and diverse new audience that traditional publishers wouldn't normally have access to."

Consumer Magazines

In this section of *Novel & Short Story Writer's Market* are consumer magazines with circulations of more than 10,000. Many have circulations in the hundreds of thousands or millions. Among the oldest magazines listed here are ones not only familiar to us, but also to our parents, grandparents and even great-grandparents: *The Atlantic Monthly* (1857); *Christian Century* (1900); *Redbook* (1903); *The New Yorker* (1925); *Analog Science Fiction & Fact* (1930); *Esquire* (1933); and *Jack and Jill* (1938).

Consumer periodicals make excellent markets for fiction in terms of exposure, prestige and payment. Because these magazines are well-known, however, competition is great. Even the largest consumer publications buy only one or two stories an issue, yet thousands of writers submit to these popular magazines.

Despite the odds, it is possible for talented new writers to break into print in the magazines listed here. Your keys to breaking into these markets are careful research, professional presentation and, of course, top-quality fiction.

TYPES OF CONSUMER MAGAZINES

In this section you will find a number of popular publications, some for a broad-based, general-interest readership and others for large but select groups of readers—children, teenagers, women, men and seniors. There are also religious and church-affiliated magazines, publications devoted to the interests of particular cultures and outlooks, and top markets for genre fiction.

SELECTING THE RIGHT MARKET

Unlike smaller journals and publications, most of the magazines listed here are available at newsstands and bookstores. Many can also be found in the library, and guidelines and sample copies are almost always available by mail. Start your search, then, by familiarizing yourself with the fiction included in the magazines that interest you.

Don't make the mistake of thinking, just because you are familiar with a magazine, that their fiction isn't any different today than when you first saw it. Nothing could be further from the truth—consumer magazines, no matter how well established, are constantly revising their fiction needs as they strive to reach new readers and expand their audience base.

In a magazine that uses only one or two stories an issue, take a look at the nonfiction articles and features as well. These can give you a better idea of the audience for the publication and clues to the type of fiction that might appeal to them.

If you write genre fiction, check out the specific sections for lists of magazines publishing in that genre (mystery, page 52; romance, page 64; science fiction and fantasy, page 76). For other types of fiction look in the Category Index beginning on page 632. There you will find a list of markets that say they are looking for a particular subject.

You may want to use our ranking codes as a guide, especially if you are a new writer. At the end of this introduction is a list of the Roman numeral codes we use and what they mean.

FURTHERING YOUR SEARCH

See The "Quick Start" Guide to Publishing Your Fiction (page 2) for information about the material common to all listings in this book. In this section in particular, pay close attention to the number of submissions a magazine receives in a given period and how many they publish in the same period. This will give you a clear picture of how stiff your competition can be. Also, the ⭐ symbol before a listing identifies markets that offer writers greater opportunities by buying a large amount of freelance/unagented manuscripts.

While many of the magazines listed here publish one or two pieces of fiction in each issue, some also publish special fiction issues once or twice a year. We have indicated this in the listing information. We also note if the magazine is open to novel excerpts as well as short fiction and we advise novelists to query first before submitting long work.

The Business of Fiction Writing, beginning on page 104, covers the basics of submitting your work. Professional presentation is a must for all markets listed. Editors at consumer magazines are especially busy, and anything you can do to make your manuscript easy to read and accessible will help your chances of being published. Most magazines want to see complete manuscripts, but watch for publications in this section that require a query first. Also read Elements of the All Important Query Letter, beginning on page 81.

As in the previous section, we've included our own comments in many of the listings, set off by a bullet (●). Whenever possible, we list the publication's recent awards and honors. We've also included any special information we feel will help you in determining whether a particular publication interests you.

The maple leaf symbol (🍁) identifies our Canadian listings. You will also find some English-speaking markets from around the world. These foreign magazines are denoted with 🌐 at the beginning of the listings. Remember to use International Reply Coupons rather than stamps when you want a reply from a country other than your own.

For More Information

For more on consumer magazines, see issues of *Writer's Digest* and *Fiction Writer* (both by F&W Publications) and industry trade publications available in larger libraries.

For news about some of the genre publications listed here and information about a particular field, there are a number of magazines devoted to genre topics, including *The Mystery Review*, *Locus* (for science fiction); *Science Fiction Chronicle*; and *Romance Writers' Report* (available to members of Romance Writers of America). Addresses for these and other industry magazines can be found in the Publications of Interest section of this book.

Membership in the national groups devoted to specific genre fields is not restricted to novelists and can be valuable to writers of short fiction in these fields. Many include awards for "Best Short Story" in their annual contests. For information useful to genre writers, see For Mystery Writers, page 46; For Romance Writers, page 55; and For Science Fiction & Fantasy Writers, page 67. Also see the Organizations section of this book.

⭐ ✅ $📀 **AFRICAN VOICES, The Art and Literary Publication With Class & Soul,** African Voices Communications, Inc., 270 W. 96th St., New York NY 10025. (212)865-2982. Fax: (212)316-3335. Website: www.africanvoices.com. Editor: Carolyn A. Butts. Managing Editor: Layding Kaliba. **Fiction Editor**: Kim Horne. Magazine: 32 pages; illustrations and photos. "*AV* publishes enlightening and entertaining literature on the varied lifestyles of people of color." Quarterly. Estab. 1993. Circ. 20,000.
Needs: African-American: children's/juvenile (10-12 years), condensed/excerpted novel, erotica, ethnic/multi-cultural, gay, historical (general), horror, humor/satire, literary, mystery/suspense, psychic/supernatural/occult, religious/inspirational, science fiction, young adult/teen (adventure, romance). List of upcoming themes available for SASE. Publishes special fiction issue. Receives 20-50 unsolicited mss/month. Accepts 20 mss/issue. Publishes ms 3-6 months after acceptance. Agented fiction 5%. Published work by Junot Díaz, Michel Marriott and Carol Dixon. Length: 2,000 words average; 500 words minimum; 3,000 words maximum. Occasionally publishes short shorts. Also publishes literary essays and poetry.
How to Contact: Query with clips of published work. Include short bio. Reports in 6-12 weeks depending on backlog of queries; 2-3 months on mss. Send SASE for return of ms. Simultaneous, reprint and electronic

submissions OK. Sample copy for $5 and 9×12 SASE. Free fiction guidelines. Reviews novels and short story collections. Send books to Book Editor.

Payment/Terms: Pays $25 maximum on publication for first North American serial rights, free subscription and 5 contributor's copies.

Advice: "We are interested in more horror, erotic and drama pieces. *AV* wants to highlight the diversity in our culture. Stories must touch the humanity in us all."

⊠ $⊘ AIM MAGAZINE, P.O. Box 1174, Maywood IL 60153. (773)874-6184. Fax: (206)543-2746. Editor: Myron Apilado, EdD. **Fiction Editor:** Mark Boone. Magazine: 8½×11; 48 pages; slick paper; photos and illustrations. Publishes material "to purge racism from the human bloodstream through the written word—that is the purpose of *Aim Magazine*." Quarterly. Estab. 1973. Circ. 10,000.

● *Aim* sponsors an annual short story contest.

Needs: Open. No "religious" mss. Published special fiction issue last year; plans another. Receives 25 unsolicited mss/month. Buys 15 mss/issue; 60 mss/year. Recently published work by Christina Touregny, Thomas Lee Harris, Michael Williams and Jake Halpern. **Publishes 40 new writers/year.** Length: 800-1,000 words average. Publishes short shorts. Sometimes comments on rejected mss.

How to Contact: Send complete ms. Include SASE with cover letter and author's photograph. Simultaneous submissions OK. Reports in 1 month. Sample copy for $4 with SAE (9×12) and $1.80 postage. Fiction guidelines for #10 SASE.

Payment/Terms: Pays $15-25 on publication for first rights.

Advice: "Search for those who are making unselfish contributions to their community and write about them. Write about your own experiences. Be familiar with the background of your characters." Known for "stories with social significance, proving that people from different ethnic, racial backgrounds are more alike than they are different."

☑ $⊘ AMAZING® STORIES, Wizards of the Coast, P.O. Box 707, Renton WA 98057-0707. (425)204-6500. Website: www.amazingstoriesmagazine.com/ (includes fiction guidelines, short features and teasers for coming and current issues). **Editor:** Mr. Kim Mohan. Magazine: 8⅜×10¾; 100 pages; saddle-stitched; color illustrations; rarely photos. Magazine of science fiction stories for adults and young adults. Quarterly. Estab. 1926. Circ. 30,000.

● Due to a backlog, *Amazing Stories* will not be accepting unsolicited mss for some time. Check their website for updates.

Needs: Science fiction (hard science, soft/sociological), occasionally fantasy, rarely horror. "We prefer science fiction to dominate our content, but we will not turn away a well-written fantasy or horror piece. Low priority to heroic, pseudo-Medieval fantasy and stories derivative of folk tales; no gratuitous gore or offensive language." Receives 250-300 unsolicited fiction mss/month. Accepts 6-8 mss/issue. Publishes ms 4-8 months after acceptance. Agented fiction less than 5%. Published work by Orson Scott Card, Kristine Kathryn Rusch, Ben Bova, Ursula K. Le Guin, Neal Barrett, Jr. and Jack Williamson; **published new writers within the last year.** Length: 1,000 words minimum; 8,000 words maximum; can go to 10,000 words for work of exceptional merit. Not actively seeking serializations or excerpts from longer works. Usually critiques rejected ms.

How to Contact: Send complete ms with a cover letter. Include list of other professional credits in the genre. Reports in 60 days. SASE. No simultaneous submissions. Sample copy for $8 (includes first-class postage and handling). Fiction guidelines for #10 SASE or available at website.

Payment/Terms: Pays 6-10¢/word on acceptance for first worldwide rights in the English language. Sends comp copies to author.

Advice: "*AMAZING® Stories* resumed publication last year after a three-year suspension. This incarnation of the magazine contains some media-related fiction based on properties such as *Star Trek* and *Babylon 5*, but we are not open to unsolicited submissions of this type of material. The bulk of the magazine continues to be devoted to original, non-media-related science fiction. Our taste is eclectic, but our standards are high—we appreciate innovations in style or content, as long as the work is internally consistent and comprehensible."

Ⓝ $ THE AMERICAN CITIZEN ITALIAN PRESS, 13681 "V" St., Omaha NE 68137. (402)896-0403. Fax: (402)891-9430. Editor: Diana C. Failla. Magazine. Quarterly.

Needs: Ethnic, historical (general), sports, celebrity, human interest, mainstream and translations. "Will assign stories to corresponding writers." Buys 1-2 mss/issue. Length: 80 words minimum; 1,200 words maximum. Publishes short shorts.

How to Contact: Send complete ms with cover letter. Reports in 2 months on queries. Simultaneous submissions OK. "Send photo(s) to accompany story if possible. Pays $5/photo. Poetry also welcome." Sample copy and fiction guidelines for 9×12 SAE.

Payment/Terms: Pays $30-35 on publication for one-time rights.

☑ $◙ AMERICAN GIRL, Pleasant Company Publications, 8400 Fairway Place, Middleton WI 53562. (608)836-4848. E-mail: readermail.ag.pleasantco.com. Website: www.americangirl.com. **Editor:** Kristi Thom. Contact: Magazine Department Assistant. Magazine: 8½×11; 52 pages; illustrations and photos. "Four-color bimonthly magazine for girls age 8-12." Estab. 1991. Circ. 700,000.

• Pleasant Company is known for its series of books featuring girls from different periods of American history.

Needs: Children's/juvenile (girls 8-12 years): "contemporary, realistic fiction, adventure, historical, problem stories." No romance, science fiction, fantasy. Receives 100 unsolicited mss/month. Accepts 1 ms/year. Length: 2,300 words maximum. Publishes short shorts. Also publishes literary essays and poetry (if age appropriate). Recently published work by Susan Katz, Connie Porter, Sarah Masters Buckey, Jacqueline Wilson, Valerie Tripp and Anna Quindlen.

How to Contact: Query with published samples. Include bio (1 paragraph). Send SASE for reply, return of ms or send a disposable copy of ms. Simultaneous submissions OK. Send SASE for guidelines. Sample copy for $3.95 plus $1.93 postage.

Payment/Terms: Pays in cash; amount negotiable. Pays on acceptance for first North American serial rights. Sends galleys to author.

⭐ ✅ $ 📄 🔲 **ANALOG SCIENCE FICTION & FACT**, Dell Magazines, 475 Park Ave. S., Floor 11, New York NY 10016-6901. (212)686-7188. Fax: (212)686-7414. E-mail: analog@dellmagazines.com. Website: www.analogsf.com. **Editor:** Stanley Schmidt. Magazine: 5⅜ × 8½; 140 pages; illustrations (drawings); photos. "Well-written science fiction based on speculative ideas and fact articles on topics of the present and future frontiers of research. Our readership includes intelligent laymen and/or those professionally active in science and technology." Published 11 times yearly. Estab. 1930. Circ. 60,000.

• *Analog* is considered one of the leading science fiction publications. The magazine has won a number of Hugos, Chesleys and Nebula Awards. *Analog* ranked #12 on the *Writer's Digest*'s Fiction 50 list of top markets for fiction writers.

Needs: Science fiction (hard science, soft sociological) and serialized novels. "No stories which are not truly science fiction in the sense of having a plausible speculative idea *integral to the story*. We would like to see good humor that is also good, solid science fiction. We do one double-size issue per year (July)." Receives 300-500 unsolicited fiction mss/month. Accepts 4-8 mss/issue. Agented fiction 20%. Recently published work by Joan Slonczewski, Ben Bova, Maya Kathryn Bonnhoff, Jerry Oltion, Paul Levinson and Timothy Zahn. **Publishes 5-10 new writers/year.** Length: 2,000-80,000 words. Publishes short shorts. Critiques rejected mss "when there is time." Sometimes recommends other markets.

How to Contact: Send complete ms with SASE. Include cover letter with "anything that I need to know before reading the story, e.g. that it's a rewrite I suggested or that it incorporates copyrighted material. Otherwise, no cover letter is needed." Query with SASE only on serials. Reports in 1 month on both query and ms. No simultaneous submissions. Fiction guidelines for SASE. Sample copy for $5. Reviews novels and short story collections. Send books to Tom Easton.

Payment/Terms: Pays 5-8¢/word on acceptance for first North American serial rights and nonexclusive foreign rights. Sends galleys to author.

Advice: Mss are rejected because of "inaccurate science; poor plotting, characterization or writing in general. We literally only have room for 1-2% of what we get. Many stories are rejected not because of anything conspicuously *wrong*, but because they lack anything sufficiently *special*. What we buy must stand out from the crowd. Fresh, thought-provoking ideas are important. Familiarize yourself with the magazine—but don't try to imitate what we've already published."

🦋 $ 📄 **THE ANNALS OF ST. ANNE DE BEAUPRÉ**, Redemptorist Fathers, P.O. Box 1000, St. Anne de Beaupré, Quebec G0A 3C0 Canada. (418)827-4538. Fax: (418)827-4530. **Editor:** Father Roch Achard, C.Ss.R. Magazine: 8 × 11; 32 pages; glossy paper; photos. "Our aim is to promote devotion to St. Anne and Catholic family values." Monthly. Estab. 1878. Circ. 50,000.

Needs: Religious/inspirational. "We only wish to see something inspirational, educational, objective, uplifting. Reporting rather than analysis is simply not remarkable." Receives 50-60 unsolicited mss/month. Published work by Beverly Sheresh, Eugene Miller and Aubrey Haines. Publishes short stories. Length: 1,500 maximum. Always critiques or comments on rejected ms.

How to Contact: Send complete, typed, double spaced ms with a cover letter. Include estimated word count. Reports in 3 weeks. Send SASE for reply or return of ms. No simultaneous submissions. Free sample copy and guidelines.

Payment/Terms: Pays 3-4¢/word on acceptance and 3 contributor's copies on publication for first North American rights.

📄 🎯 **APPALACHIA JOURNAL**, Appalachian Mountain Club, 5 Joy St., Boston MA 02108. (617)523-0636. Editor: Sandy Stott. Magazine: 6 × 9; 160 pages; 60 lb. recycled paper; 10 pt. CS1 cover; 5-10 illustrations; 20-30 photographs. "*Appalachia* is the oldest mountaineering and conservation journal in the country. It specializes in backcountry recreation and conservation topics (hiking, canoeing, cross-country skiing, etc.) for outdoor (including armchair) enthusiasts." Semiannually (June and December). Estab. 1876. Circ. 15,000.

Needs: Prose, poem, sports. Receives 5-10 unsolicited mss/month. Accepts 1-2 mss/issue; 2-4 mss/year. Publishes ms 6-12 months after acceptance. Length: 500-4,000 words average. Publishes short shorts.

How to Contact: Send complete ms with cover letter. No simultaneous submissions. Reports in 1 month on

queries; 3 months on mss. SASE (or IRC) for query. Sample copy for $5. Fiction guidelines for #10 SAE.
Payment/Terms: Pays contributor's copies. Occasionally pays $100-300 for a feature—usually assigned.
Advice: "All submissions should be related to conservation, mountaineering, and/or backcountry recreation both in the Northeast and throughout the world. Most of our journal is nonfiction. The fiction we publish is mountain-related and often off-beat. Send us material that says, I went to the wilderness and *thought* this; not I went there and did this."

$ **☑** **ART TIMES, Commentary and Resources for the Fine and Performing Arts**, P.O. Box 730, Mt. Marion NY 12456. Phone/fax: (914)246-6944. **Editor:** Raymond J. Steiner. Magazine: 12×15; 24 pages; Jet paper and cover; illustrations; photos. "Arts magazine covering the disciplines for an over-40, affluent, arts-conscious and literate audience." Monthly. Estab. 1984. Circ. 20,000.
Needs: Adventure, contemporary, ethnic, fantasy, feminist, gay, historical, humor/satire, lesbian, literary, mainstream and science fiction. "We seek quality literary pieces. Nothing violent, sexist, erotic, juvenile, racist, romantic, political, etc." Receives 30-50 mss/month. Accepts 1 ms/issue; 11 mss/year. Publishes ms within 48-60 months of acceptance. **Publishes 1-5 new writers/year.** Length: 1,500 words maximum. Publishes short shorts.
How to Contact: Send complete ms with cover letter. Simultaneous submissions OK. Reports in 6 months. SASE. Sample copy for $1.75, 9×12 SAE and 3 first-class stamps. Fiction guidelines for #10 SASE.
Payment/Terms: Pays $25, free one-year subscription to magazine and 6 contributor's copies on publication for first North American serial rights.
Advice: "Competition is greater (more submissions received), but keep trying. We print new as well as published writers."

★ **✓** **$** **☑** **♈** **ASIMOV'S SCIENCE FICTION**, 475 Park Ave. S., Floor 11, New York NY 10016-6901. (212)686-7188. Fax: (212)686-7414. E-mail: asimovs@dellmagazines.com. Website: www.asimovs.com (includes guidelines, names of editors, short fiction, interviews with authors, editorials, and more). **Editor:** Gardner Dozois. Executive Editor: Sheila Williams. Magazine: 5¼×8¼ (trim size); 144 pages; 30 lb. newspaper; 70 lb. to 8 pt. C1S cover stock; illustrations; rarely photos. Magazine consists of science fiction and fantasy stories for adults and young adults. Publishes "the best short science fiction available." Estab. 1977. Circ. 50,000. 11 issues/year (one double issue).

● Named for a science fiction "legend," *Asimov's* regularly receives Hugo and Nebula Awards. Editor Gardner Dozois has received several awards for editing including Hugos and those from *Locus* and *Science Fiction Chronicle* magazines. This publication ranked #6 on *Writer's Digest*'s Fiction 50 list of top markets for fiction writers.

Needs: Science fiction (hard science, soft sociological), fantasy. No horror or psychic/supernatural. Receives approximately 800 unsolicited fiction mss each month. Accepts 10 mss/issue. Publishes ms 6-12 months after acceptance. Agented fiction 10%. Published work by Robert Silverberg, Connie Willis and Greg Egan. **Publishes 6 new writers/year.** Length: up to 20,000 words. Publishes short shorts. Critiques rejected mss "when there is time."
How to Contact: Send complete ms with SASE. No simultaneous submissions. Reports in 2-3 months. Fiction guidelines for #10 SASE. Sample copy for $5 and 9×12 SASE. Reviews novels and short story collections. Send books to Book Reviewer.
Payment/Terms: Pays 6-8¢/word for stories up to 7,500 words; 5¢/word for stories over 12,500; $450 for stories between those limits. Pays on acceptance for first World English serial rights plus specified foreign rights, as explained in contract. Very rarely buys reprints. Sends galleys to author.
Advice: "We are looking for character stories rather than those emphasizing technology or science. New writers will do best with a story under 10,000 words. Every new science fiction or fantasy film seems to 'inspire' writers—and this is not a desirable trend. Be sure to be familiar with our magazine and the type of story we like; workshops and lots of practice help. Try to stay away from trite, cliched themes. Start in the middle of the action, starting as close to the end of the story as you possibly can. We like stories that extrapolate from up-to-date scientific research, but don't forget that we've been publishing clone stories for decades. Ideas must be fresh."

$ **☑** **◎** **THE ASSOCIATE REFORMED PRESBYTERIAN**, The Associate Reformed Presbyterian, Inc., 1 Cleveland St., Greenville SC 29601. (864)232-8297. **Editor:** Ben Johnston. Magazine: 8½×11; 32-48 pages; 50 lb. offset paper; illustrations; photos. "We are the official magazine of our denomination. Articles generally relate to activities within the denomination—conferences, department work, etc., with a few special articles that would be of general interest to readers." Monthly. Estab. 1976. Circ. 6,100.

READ THE BUSINESS OF FICTION WRITING section for information on manuscript preparation, mailing tips, rights and more.

Needs: Contemporary, juvenile, religious/inspirational, spiritual, young adult/teen. "Stories should portray Christian values. No retelling of Bible stories or 'talking animal' stories. Stories for youth should deal with resolving real issues for young people." Receives 30-40 unsolicited fiction mss/month. Accepts 10-12 mss/year. Publishes ms within 1 year after acceptance. Published work by Lawrence Dorr, Jan Johnson and Deborah Christensen. Length: 300-750 words (children); 1,250 words maximum (youth). Sometimes critiques rejected mss.

How to Contact: Include cover letter. Reports in 6 weeks on queries and mss. Simultaneous submissions OK. Sample copy for $1.50; fiction guidelines for #10 SASE.

Payment/Terms: Pays $20-75 for first rights and contributor's copies.

Advice: "Currently we are seeking stories aimed at the 10 to 15 age group. We have an oversupply of stories for younger children."

$ ◑ ◎ BALLOON LIFE, The Magazine for Hot Air Ballooning, 2336 47th Ave., SW, Seattle WA 98116. (206)935-3649. Fax: (206)935-3326. E-mail: tom@balloonlife.com. Website: www.balloonlife.com/ (includes guidelines, sample issues). **Editor:** Tom Hamilton. Magazine: 8½×11; 48 pages; color, b&w photos. Publishes material "about the sport of hot air ballooning. Readers participate in hot air ballooning as pilots, crew, official observers at events and spectators."

Needs: Humor/satire, related to hot air ballooning. "Manuscripts should involve the sport of hot air ballooning in any aspect. Prefer humor based on actual events; fiction seldom published." Accepts 4-6 mss/year. Publishes ms within 3-4 months after acceptance. Length: 800 words minimum; 1,500 words maximum; 1,200 words average. Publishes short shorts. Length: 400-500 words. Sometimes critiques rejected mss and recommends other markets.

How to Contact: Send complete ms with cover letter that includes Social Security number. Accepts queries/mss by e-mail and fax (ms by permission only). Reports in 3 weeks on queries; 2 weeks on mss. SASE. Simultaneous and reprint submissions OK. Sample copy for 9×12 SAE and $1.94 postage. Guidelines for #10 SASE.

Payment/Terms: Pays $25-75 and contributor's copies on publication for first North American serial, one-time or other rights.

Advice: "Generally the magazine looks for humor pieces that can provide a light-hearted change of pace from the technical and current event articles. An example of a work we used was titled 'Balloon Astrology' and dealt with the character of a hot air balloon based on what sign it was born (made) under."

$ ◑ THE BEAR DELUXE MAGAZINE, Orlo, 2516 NW 29th, P.O. Box 10342, Portland OR 97296. (503)242-1047. Fax: (503)243-2645. E-mail: bear@orlo.org. Website: www.orlo.org (writing and contest guides). **Editor:** Thomas L. Webb. Magazine: 11×14; 60 pages; newsprint paper; Kraft paper cover; illustrations and photos. "*The Bear Deluxe* has an environmental focus, combining all forms and styles. Fiction should have environmental thread to it and should be engaging to a cross-section of audiences. The more street-level, the better." Quarterly. Estab. 1993. Circ. 17,000.

● *The Bear Deluxe* has received a publishing grant from the Oregon Council for the Humanities.

Needs: Environmentally focused: humor/satire, literary, science fiction. "We would like to see more nontraditional forms." No childrens or horror. List of upcoming themes available for SASE. Receives 20-30 unsolicited mss/month. Accepts 2-3 mss/issue; 8-12 mss/year. Publishes ms 2 months after acceptance. Recently published work by Kevin Burke, Rocco Lo Bosco, Gina Ochsuer, Art Gibney, Martin John Brocon and Sara Bucker. **Publishes 3-5 new writers/year.** Length: 2,500 words average; 900 words minimum; 4,000 words maximum. Publishes short shorts. Also publishes literary essays, literary criticism, poetry, reviews, opinion, investigative journalism, interviews and creative nonfiction. Sometimes critiques or comments on rejected mss.

How to Contact: Send complete ms with a cover letter. Include estimated word count, 10 to 15-word bio, list of publications, copy on disk, if possible. Accepts queries/mss by e-mail (mss by permission only). Reports in 1 month on queries; 3 months on mss. Send a disposable copy of mss. Simultaneous and electronic (disk is best, then e-mail) submissions OK. Sample copy for $3, 7½×11 SAE and 5 first-class stamps. Fiction guidelines for #10 SASE. Reviews novels and short story collections. Send SASE for "Edward Abbey" fiction contest and guidelines.

Payment/Terms: Pays free subscription to the magazine, contributor's copies and 5¢ per published word; additional copies for postage. Acquires first or one-time rights. Not copyrighted. Sponsors contests and awards for fiction writers.

Advice: "Keep sending work. Write actively and focus on the connections of man, nature, etc., not just flowery descriptions. Urban and suburban environments are grist for the mill as well. Have not seen enough quality humorous and ironic writing. Interview and artist profile ideas needed. Juxtaposition of place welcome. Action and hands-on great. Not all that interested in environmental ranting and simple 'walks through the park.' Make it powerful, yet accessible to a wide audience."

$ ◑ BOMB MAGAZINE, New Art Publications, 594 Broadway, Suite 905, New York NY 10012. (212)431-3943. Fax: (212)431-5880. E-mail: bomb@echonyc.com. **Editor-in-Chief:** Betsy Sussler. Associate Editor: Suzan Sherman. Magazine: 11×14; 104 pages; 70 lb. glossy cover; illustrations and photographs. Publishes "work which is unconventional and contains an edge, whether it be in style or subject matter." Quarterly. Estab. 1981.

Needs: Contemporary, experimental, novel excerpts. No genre: romance, horror, western. Receives 50 unsolicited mss/week. Accepts 6 mss/issue; 24 mss/year. Publishes ms 3-6 months after acceptance. Agented fiction 70%. Published work by Jim Lewis, AM Homes, Sandra Cisneros, Rick Bass and Denis Johnson. **Publishes 8 new writers/year.** Length: 10-12 pages average. Publishes interviews.

How to Contact: Send complete ms up to 25 pages in length with cover letter. Reports in 4 months on mss. SASE. Sample copy for $4.50 with $1.67 postage.

Payment/Terms: Pays $100 and contributor's copies on publication for first or one-time rights. Sends galleys to author.

Advice: "We are committed to publishing new work that commercial publishers often deem too dangerous or difficult. The problem is, a lot of young writers confuse difficult with dreadful. Read the magazine before you even think of submitting something."

$ ☑ ▼ BOSTON REVIEW A political and literary forum, Boston Critic Inc., E53-407, MIT, Cambridge MA 02139. (617)253-3642. Fax: (617)252-1549. E-mail: bostonreview@mit.edu. Website: www-polisci.m it.edu/bostonreview/ (includes full issue 1 month after publication, poetry and fiction links page, guidelines and contests guidelines, bookstore listing and subscription info). Editor: Joshua Cohen. **Fiction Editor:** Jodi Daynard. A bimonthly magazine "providing a forum of ideas in politics, literature and culture. Essays, reviews, poetry and fiction are published in every issue. Audience is well educated and interested in under recognized writers." Magazine: 10¾×14¾; 56 pages; newsprint. Estab. 1975. Circ. 30,000.

 • *Boston Review* is the recipient of a Pushcart Prize in poetry.

Needs: Contemporary, ethnic, experimental, literary, prose poem, regional, translations. No romance, erotica, genre fiction. Receives 150 unsolicited fiction mss/month. Buys 4-6 mss/year. Publishes ms an average of 4 months after acceptance. Recently published work by David Mamet, Rhoda Stamell, Jacob Appel, Elisha Porat and Diane Williams. Length: 4,000 words maximum; 2,000 words average. Occasionally critiques rejected ms.

How to Contact: Send complete ms with cover letter and SASE. "You can almost always tell professional writers by the very thought-out way they present themselves in cover letters. But even a beginning writer should find some link between the work (its style, subject, etc.) and the publication—some reason why the editor should consider publishing it." No queries or manuscripts by e-mail. Reports in 2-4 months. Simultaneous submissions OK (if noted). Sample copy for $4.50. Reviews novels and short story collections. Send books to Matthew Howard, managing editor.

Payment/Terms: Pays $50-100 and 5 contributor's copies after publication for first rights.

Advice: "I'm looking for stories that are emotionally and intellectually substantive and also interesting on the level of language. Things that are shocking, dark, lewd, comic, or even insane are fine so long as the fiction is *controlled* and purposeful in a masterly way. Subtlety, delicacy and lyricism are attractive too. Work tirelessly to make the work truly polished before you send it out. Make sure you know the publication you're submitting— don't send blind."

☑ $ ◎ BOWHUNTER MAGAZINE, The Number One Bowhunting Magazine, Primedia Special Interest Publications, 6405 Flank Dr., Harrisburg PA 17112. (717)657-9555. Fax: (717)657-9552. Founder/Editor-in-Chief: M.R. James. Associate Publisher/Editorial Director: Richard Cochran. **Editor:** Dwight Schuh. Magazine: 8×10½; 150 pages; 75 lb. glossy paper; 150 lb. glossy cover stock; illustrations and photographs. "We are a special interest publication for people who hunt with the bow and arrow. We publish hunting adventure and how-to stories. Our audience is predominantly male, 30-50, middle income." Bimonthly. Circ. 200,000.

 • Themes included in most fiction considered for *Bowhunter* are pro-conservation as well as pro-hunting.

Needs: Bowhunting, outdoor adventure. "Writers must expect a very limited market. We buy only one or two fiction pieces a year. Writers must know the market—bowhunting—and let that be the theme of their work. No 'me and my dog' types of stories; no stories by people who have obviously never held a bow in their hands." Receives 25 unsolicited fiction mss/month. Accepts 30 mss/year. Publishes ms 3 months to 2 years after acceptance. Length: 1,500 words average; 500 words minimum; 2,000 words maximum. Publishes short shorts. Length: 500 words. Sometimes critiques rejected mss and recommends other markets.

How to Contact: Query first or send complete ms with cover letter. Reports in 2 weeks on queries; 1 month on mss. Sample copy for $2 and 8½×11 SAE with appropriate postage. Fiction guidelines for #10 SASE.

Payment/Terms: Pays $100-350 on acceptance for first worldwide serial rights.

Advice: "We have a resident humorist who supplies us with most of the 'fiction' we need. But if a story comes through the door which captures the essence of bowhunting and we feel it will reach out to our readers, we will buy it. Despite our macho outdoor magazine status, we are a bunch of English majors who love to read. You can't bull your way around real outdoor people—they can spot a phony at 20 paces. If you've never camped out under the stars and listened to an elk bugle and try to relate that experience without really experiencing it, someone's going to know. We are very specialized; we don't want stories about shooting apples off people's heads or of Cupid's arrow finding its mark. James Dickey's *Deliverance* used bowhunting metaphorically, very effectively . . . while we don't expect that type of writing from everyone, that's the kind of feeling that characterizes a good piece of outdoor fiction."

☑ $ ⬚ ◎ **BUGLE, Journal of Elk and the Hunt**, Rocky Mountain Elk Foundation, P.O. Box 8249, Missoula MT 59807-8249. (406)523-4570. Fax: (406)523-4550. E-mail: bugle@rmef.org. Website: www.rmef.o rg. **Editor:** Dan Crockett. Editorial Assistant: Lee Cromrich. Magazine: 8½×11; 114-172 pages; 55 lb. Escanaba paper; 80 lb. sterling cover; b&w, 4-color illustrations and photographs. "The Rocky Mountain Elk Foundation is a nonprofit conservation organization established in 1984 to help conserve critical habitat for elk and other wildlife. *BUGLE* specializes in research, stories (fiction and nonfiction), art and photography pertaining to the world of elk and elk hunting." Bimonthly. Estab. 1984.

Needs: Elk-related adventure, children's/juvenile, historical, human interest, natural history, conservation. "We would like to see more humor. No formula outdoor or how-to writing." Upcoming themes; "Bowhunting" and "Women in the Outdoors." Receives 10-15 unsolicited mss/month. Accepts 5 mss/issue; 18-20 mss/year. Publishes ms 6 months after acceptance. Published work by Don Burgess and Mike Logan. Publishes 10 new writers/ year. Length: 2,500 words preferred; 1,500 words minimum; 5,000 words maximum. Publishes short shorts. Also publishes literary essays and poetry.

How to Contact: Query first or send complete ms with a cover letter. Accepts queries/mss by e-mail and fax (ms by permission only). Include estimated word count and bio (100 words). Reports in 2-4 weeks on queries; 10-12 weeks on ms. Send SASE for reply, return of ms or send a disposable copy of ms. Sample copy for $5. Writers guidelines free.

Payment/Terms: Pays 20¢/word maximum on acceptance for one-time rights.

Advice: "We accept fiction and nonfiction stories about elk that show originality, and respect for the animal and its habitat."

☑ ⬚ ♟ **CAMPUS LIFE MAGAZINE**, Christianity Today, Inc., 465 Gundersen Dr., Carol Stream IL 60188. (630)260-6200. Fax: (630)260-0114. E-mail: cledit@aol.com. Website: www.campuslife.net. **Managing Editor:** Christopher Lutes. Magazine: 8¼×11¼; 100 pages; 4-color and b&w illustrations; 4-color and b&w photos. "Teen magazine with a Christian point of view." Articles "vary from serious to humorous to current trends and issues, for teen readers." Bimonthly. Estab. 1942. Circ. 100,000.

● *Campus Life* regularly receives awards from the Evangelical Press Association.

Needs: "All fiction submissions must be contemporary, reflecting the teen experience in the '90s. We are a Christian magazine but are *not* interested in sappy, formulaic, sentimentally religious stories. We *are* interested in well-crafted stories that portray life realistically, stories high school and college youth relate to. Writing must reflect a Christian world view. If you don't understand our market and style, don't submit." Accepts 5 mss/year. Reading and response time slower in summer. **Published new writers within the last year.** Length: 1,000-2,000 words average, "possibly longer."

How to Contact: Query with short synopsis of work, published samples and SASE. Does not accept unsolicited mss. Reports in 4-6 weeks on queries. Sample copy for $2 and 9½×11 envelope.

Payment/Terms: Pays "generally" 15-20¢/word; 2 contributor's copies on acceptance for one-time rights.

Advice: "We print finely-crafted fiction that carries a contemporary teen (older teen) theme. First person fiction often works best. Ask us for sample copy with fiction story. We want experienced fiction writers who have something to say to young people without getting propagandistic."

★ $ ⬚ **CAPPER'S**, Ogden Publications, Inc. 1503 S.W. 42nd St., Topeka KS 66609-1265. (785)274-4346. Fax: (785)274-4305. E-mail: cappers@kspress.com. Website: www.cappers.com (includes sample items from publication and subscription information). **Editor:** Ann Crahan. Magazine: 36-56 pages; newsprint paper and cover stock; photos. A "clean, uplifting and nonsensational newspaper for families, from children to grandparents." Biweekly. Estab. 1879. Circ. 250,000.

● *Capper's* is interested in longer works of fiction, 7,000 words or more. They would like to see more stories with older characters. *Capper's* ranked #47 on *Writer's Digest*'s Fiction 50 list of top markets for fiction writers.

Needs: Serialized novels suitable for family reading. "We accept novel-length stories for serialization. No fiction containing violence, sexual references or obscenity. We would like to see more western romance, pioneer stories." Receives 2-3 unsolicited fiction mss each month. Accepts 4-6 stories/year. Recently published work by C.J. Sargent and Mona Exinger. Published new writers within the last year. Length: 7,000 words minimum; 40,000 words maximum.

How to Contact: Send complete ms with SASE. Cover letter and/or synopsis helpful. Reports in 6-8 months on ms. Sample copy for $2.

Payment/Terms: Pays $75-300 for one-time serialization and contributor's copies (1-2 copies as needed for copyright) on acceptance for second serial (reprint) rights and one-time rights.

Advice: "Since we publish in serialization, be sure your manuscript is suitable for that format. Each segment needs to be compelling enough so the reader remembers it and is anxious to read the next installment. Please proofread and edit carefully. We've seen major characters change names partway through the manuscript."

🌐 $ **CHAT**, King's Reach Tower, Stamford St., London SE1 9LS England. **Fiction Editor:** Olwen Rice. Weekly. Circ. 520,000.

Needs: Publishes mysteries, thrillers, science fiction and romance. Publishes 1 story/issue; 1/Christmas issue; 1/Summer special. Length: 800 words maximum.

How to Contact: "I accept and buy fiction from anyone, anywhere. Send material with reply coupons if you want your story returned."

Payment/Terms: Payment "negotiated with the fiction editor and made by cheque." Write editor for sample copy. Writer's guidelines available for SAE and IRCs.

CHICKADEE, Owl Communications, 179 John St., Suite 500, Toronto, Ontario M5T 3G5 Canada. (416)340-2700. Fax: (416)340-9769. E-mail: owl@owlkids.com. Website: www.owl.on.ca. **Editor:** Hilary Bain. Magazine: 8½ × 11¾; 36 pages; glossy paper and cover stock; illustrations and photographs. "*Chickadee* is created to give children aged 6-9 a lively, fun-filled look at the world around them. Each issue has a mix of activities, puzzles, games and stories." Published 9 times/year. Estab. 1979. Circ. 110,000.

• *Chickadee* has won several awards including the Ed Press Golden Lamp Honor award and the Parents' Choice Golden Seal awards.

Needs: Juvenile. No religious material. Accepts 1 ms/issue; 9 mss/year. Publishes ms an average of 1 year after acceptance. **Published new writers within the last year.** Length: 300-900 words.

How to Contact: Send complete ms and cover letter with $1 or IRC to cover postage and handling. Simultaneous submissions OK. Reports in 2 months. Sample copy for $4.50. Fiction guidelines for SAE and IRC.

Payment/Terms: Pays $25-250 (Canadian); 2 contributor's copies on acceptance for all rights. Occasionally buys reprints.

Advice: "Read back issues to see what types of fiction we publish. Common mistakes include loose, rambling, and boring prose; stories that lack a clear beginning, middle and end; unbelievable characters; and overwriting."

$⊘ CHILDREN'S DIGEST, Children's Better Health Institute, P.O. Box 567, 1100 Waterway Blvd., Indianapolis IN 46206. (317)634-1100. **Editor:** Mark Tipton. Magazine: 7 × 10⅛; 36 pages; reflective and preseparated illustrations; color and b&w photos. Magazine with special emphasis on health, nutrition, exercise and safety for preteens.

• Other magazines published by Children's Better Health Institute and listed in this book are *Children's Playmate, Humpty Dumpty's Magazine, Jack and Jill* and *Turtle.*

Needs: "Realistic stories, short plays, adventure and mysteries. Humorous stories are highly desirable. We especially need stories that *subtly* encourage readers to develop better health or safety habits. Stories should not exceed 1,500 words." Receives 40-50 unsolicited fiction mss each month. Published work by Judith Josephson, Pat McCarthy and Sharen Liddell; **published new writers within the last year.**

How to Contact: Currently not accepting unsolicited mss. Sample copy for $1.75. Fiction guidelines for SASE.

Payment/Terms: Pays 12¢/word minimum with up to 10 contributor's copies on publication for all rights.

Advice: "We try to present our health-related material in a positive—not a negative—light, and we try to incorporate humor and a light approach wherever possible without minimizing the seriousness of what we are saying. Fiction stories that deal with a health theme need not have health as the primary subject but should include it in some way in the course of events. Most rejected health-related manuscripts are too preachy or they lack substance. Children's magazines are not training grounds where authors learn to write 'real' material for 'real' readers. Because our readers frequently have limited attention spans, it is very important that we offer them well-written stories."

CHILDREN'S PLAYMATE, Children's Better Health Institute, P.O. Box 567, 1100 Waterway Blvd., Indianapolis IN 46206. (317)636-8881. **Editor:** Terry Harshman. Magazine: 7½ × 10; 48 pages; preseparated and reflective art; b&w and color illustrations. Juvenile magazine for children ages 6-8 years. Published 8 times/year.

• *Children's Digest, Humpty Dumpty's Magazine Jack and Jill* and *Turtle* magazines are also published by Children's Better Health Institute and listed in this book.

Needs: Juvenile with special emphasis on health, nutrition, safety and exercise. "Our present needs are for short, entertaining stories with a subtle health angle. Seasonal material is also always welcome." No adult or adolescent fiction. Receives approximately 150 unsolicited fiction mss each month. Published work by Batta Killion, Ericka Northrop, Elizabeth Murphy-Melas; **published new writers within the last year.** Length: 300-700 words.

How to Contact: Send complete ms with SASE. Indicate word count on material and date sent. Reports in 3 months. Sample copy for $1.75. Writer's guidelines for SASE.

Payment/Terms: Pays up to 17¢/word and 10 contributor's copies on publication for *all* rights.

Advice: "Stories should be kept simple and entertaining. Study past issues of the magazine—be aware of vocabulary limitations of the readers."

THE CHRISTIAN CENTURY, An Ecumenical Weekly, 407 S. Dearborn St., Chicago IL 60605. (312)427-5380. Fax: (312)427-1302. **Editor/Publisher:** John M. Buchanan. Magazine: 8¼ × 10⅞; 24-40 pages; illustrations and photos. "A liberal Protestant magazine interested in the public meaning of Christian faith as it applies to social issues, and in the individual appropriation of faith in modern circumstances." Weekly (sometimes biweekly). Estab. 1884. Circ. 35,000.

- *Christian Century* has received many awards each year from the Associated Church Press, including: best critical review, best written humor, best feature article, best fiction, etc.

Needs: Inspirational: feminist, mainstream/contemporary. "We are interested in articles that touch on religious themes in a sophisticated way; we are not interested in simplistic pietistic pieces." Receives 80 unsolicited mss/month. Accepts 10% of unsolicited mss. Publishes ms 1-3 months after acceptance. Published work by David Borofka and Doris Betts. Length: 2,500 words average; 1,500 words minimum; 3,000 words maximum. Also publishes literary essays and poetry.

How to Contact: Send complete ms with a cover letter. Include bio (100 words). Reports in 1 week on queries; 1 month on mss. Send a disposable copy of ms. No simultaneous submissions. Sample copy for $3. Reviews novels and short story collections.

Payment/Terms: Pays $200 maximum and 1 contributor's copy (additional copies for $1) on publication for all rights. Sends galleys to author.

N ◯ ◎ **CITYCYCLE MOTORCYCLE NEWS MAGAZINE,** Motormag Corp., P.O. Box 808, Nyalk NY 10960-0808. (914)353-MOTO. Fax: (914)353-5240. E-mail: motomag@aol.com. Website: www.moto-mag.com (includes short fiction, interviews with authors). **Editor:** Anne Pihzow. Magazine: tabloid; 64 pages; newsprint; illustrations and photos. Monthly magazine about motorcyling. Estab. 1990. Circ. 50,000.

Needs: "Anything about motorcycles." No "sexual fantasy." Accepts 10 mss/year. Publishes ms 2-6 months after acceptance. Length: 750-2,000 words average. Publishes short shorts. Also publishes literary essays, literary criticism and poetry. Sometimes critiques or comments on rejected mss.

How to Contact: Query with clips of published work. Reports in 4 weeks on queries. Send SASE for reply. Reprints OK. Sample copy for $3 and 9×12 SAE. Fiction guidelines for #10 SASE. Reviews novels and short story collections. Send books to editor.

Payment/Terms: Pays $10 minimum, $75 maximum on publication for one-time rights.

Advice: "Articles, stories and poetry can be about any subject, fiction or non-fiction, as long as the subject pertains to motorcycles or the world of motorcycling. Examples would include fiction or non-fiction stories about traveling cross-country on a motorcycle, biker lifestyle or perspective, motorcycling/biker humor, etc. Stories should reflect the love of riding motorcycles and the experience of what riding is like. Romance is fine. Science fiction is fine as long as it will interest our mostly male audience."

$ ◉ **CLUBHOUSE, Focus on the Family,** 8605 Explorer Dr., Colorado Springs CO 80920. (719)531-3400. **Editor:** Jesse Florea. Associate Editor: Annette Brashler Bourland. Magazine: 8×11; 24 pages; illustrations and photos. Publishes literature for kids aged 8-12. "Stories must have moral lesson included. *Clubhouse* readers are 8- to 12-year-old boys and girls who desire to know more about God and the Bible. Their parents (who typically pay for the membership) want wholesome, educational material with Scriptual or moral insight. The kids want excitement, adventure, action, humor or mystery. Your job as a writer is to please both the parent and child with each article." Monthly. Estab. 1989. Circ. 110,000.

Needs: Children's/juvenile (8-12 years), religious/inspirational, young adult/teen (adventure, western). No science fiction. Receives 150 unsolicited ms/month. Accepts 3-4 mss/issue. Agented fiction 15%. **Publishes 5 new writers/year.** Published work by Sigmund Brower and Nancy Rue. Length: 1,200 words average; 800 words minimum; 1,600 words maximum.

How to Contact: Send complete ms with cover letter. Include estimated word count, bio and list of publications. Reports in 8-10 weeks. Send SASE for reply, return of ms or send a disposable copy of ms. Sample copy for $1.50. Guidelines free.

Payment/Terms: Pays $400 maximum on acceptance and 2 contributor's copies; additional copies for $1.50. Acquires all rights, first rights, first North American serial rights or one-time rights.

Advice: Looks for "humor with a point, historical fiction featuring great Christians or Christians who lived during great times; contemporary, exotic settings; holiday material (Christmas, Thanksgiving, Easter, President's Day); parables; fantasy (avoid graphic descriptions of evil creatures and sorcery); mystery stories; choose-your-own adventure stories and westerns. No contemporary, middle-class family settings (we already have authors who can meet these needs) or stories dealing with boy-girl relationships."

≈ ✓ **$** ◉ **COMPANION MAGAZINE,** Convenutal Franciscan Friars, 695 Coxwell Ave., Suite 600, Toronto, Ontario M4C 5R6 Canada. (416)690-5611. Fax: (416)690-3320. **Editor:** Fr. Phil Kelly, OFM. Conv. Publishes material "emphasizing religious and human values and stressing Franciscan virtues—peace, simplicity, joy." Publication "directed toward Roman Catholics who seek encouragement, challenge and reconciliation." Monthly. Estab. 1936. Circ. 5,000.

Needs: Adventure, humor, mainstream, religious. Canadian settings preferred. Wants more stories about "people dealing with homosexuality, alcoholism, sexual abuse, marital infidelity and reconciliation." No evangelism. Receives 50 unsolicited fiction mss/month. Accepts 2 mss/issue. Time varies between acceptance and publication. Length: 1,200 words maximum. Publishes short shorts.

How to Contact: Send complete mss. Accepts mss by fax. Reports in 3 weeks to 1 month on mss. SAE with "cash to buy stamps" or IRC. Sample copy and fiction guidelines free.

Payment/Terms: Pays 6¢/word (Canadian funds) on publication for first North American serial rights.

Advice: "Keep it brief—1,200 words, up-beat, real, not preachy and judgemental. No miracles. Want originality and non-judgementality; no magic solutions to real problems and facing difficult situations in a christian manner."

CONTACT PUBLICATIONS, (formerly Contact Advertising), Box 3431, Ft. Pierce FL 34948. (561)464-5447. E-mail: nietzche@cadv.com. Website: www.cadv.com (includes short fiction club information). **Editor:** Herman Nietzche. Magazines and newspapers. Publications vary in size, 56-80 pages. "Group of 26 erotica, soft core publications for swingers, single males, married males, gay males, transgendered and bisexual persons." Bimonthly, quarterly and monthly. Estab. 1975. Circ. combined is 2,000,000.
• This is a group of regional publications with explicit sexual content, graphic personal ads, etc. Not for the easily offended.
Needs: Erotica, fantasy, swinger, fetish, gay, lesbian. Receives 8-10 unsolicited mss/month. Accepts 1-2 mss/issue; 40-50 mss/year. Publishes ms 1-3 months after acceptance. **Publishes 3-6 new writers/year.** Length: 2,000 words minimum; 3,500 words maximum. Sometimes critiques rejected mss.
How to Contact: Query first, query with clips of published work or send complete ms with cover letter. SASE. Simultaneous and reprint submissions OK. Sample copy for $7. Fiction guidelines with SASE.
Payment/Terms: First submission, free subscription to magazine; subsequent submissions $25 on publication for all rights or first rights; all receive 3 contributor's copies.
Advice: "Know your grammar! Content must be of an adult nature but well within guidelines of the law. Fantasy, unusual sexual encounters, swinging stories or editorials of a sexual bent are acceptable. Read Henry Miller!"

CORNERSTONE MAGAZINE, Cornerstone Communications, Inc., 939 W. Wilson Ave., Chicago IL 60640. (773)561-2450 ext. 2394. Fax (773)989-2076. Editor: Jon Trott. **Contact:** Submission Editor. Magazine: 8½×11; 64 pages; 35 lb. coated matie paper; self cover; illustrations and photos. "For adults, 18-45. We publish nonfiction (essays, personal experience, religious), music interviews, current events, film and book reviews, fiction, poetry. *Cornerstone* challenges readers to look through the window of biblical reality. Known as avant-garde, yet attempts to express orthodox belief in the language of the nineties." Approx. quarterly. Estab. 1972. Circ. 38,000.
• *Cornerstone Magazine* has won numerous awards from the Evangelical Press Association.
Needs: Ethnic/multicultural, fantasy (science fantasy), humor/satire, literary, mainstream/contemporary, religious/inspirational. Special interest in "issues pertinent to contemporary society, seen with a biblical worldview." No "pornography, cheap shots at non-Christians, unrealistic or syrupy articles." Receives 60 unsolicited mss/month. Accepts 1 mss/issue; 3-4 mss/year. Does not read mss during Christmas/New Year's week and the month of July. Published work by Dave Cheadle, C.S. Lewis and J.B. Simmonds. Length: 1,200 words average; 250 words minimum; 2,500 words maximum. Publishes short shorts. Length: 250-450 words. Also publishes literary essays, literary criticism and poetry.
How to Contact: Send complete ms. Include estimated word count, bio (50-100 words), list of publications, and name, address, phone and fax number on every item submitted. Send disposable copy of the ms. Will consider simultaneous submissions and reprints. No electronic or disk submissions. Reports in up to 6 months, only on acceptance. Sample copy for 8½×11 SAE and 6 first-class stamps. Reviews novels and short story collections.
Payment/Terms: Pays 8-10¢/word maximum; also 6 contributor's copies on publication. Purchases first serial rights.
Advice: "Articles may express Christian world view but shouldn't be unrealistic or syrupy. We're looking for high-quality fiction with skillful characterization and plot development and imaginative symbolism." Looks for "mature Christian short stories, as opposed to those more fit for church bulletins. We want fiction with bite and an edge but with a Christian worldview."

COSMOPOLITAN MAGAZINE, The Hearst Corp., 224 W. 57th St., New York NY 10019. (212)649-2000. Editor: Kath White. **Books Editor:** John Searles. "Most novel excerpts feature young, contemporary female protagonists and traditional plots, characterizations." Single career women (ages 18-34). Monthly. Circ. just under 3 million.
Needs: Adventure, contemporary, mystery and romance. Buys current novel or book excerpts. Agented fiction 98%. Published excerpts by Danielle Steel, Mario Puzo, Louise Erdrich and Lisa Scottoline.
How to Contact: Accepts submissions from agents and publishers only. Guidelines for #10 SASE. Reports in 8-10 weeks.
Payment/Terms: Open to negotiation with author's agent or publisher.

COUNTRY WOMAN, Reiman Publications, Box 643, Milwaukee WI 53201. (414)423-0100. Editor: Ann Kaiser. **Executive Editor:** Kathleen Pohl. Magazine: 8½×11; 68 pages; excellent quality paper; excellent cover stock; illustrations and photographs. "Stories should have a rural theme and be of specific interest to women who live on a farm or ranch, or in a small town or country home, and/or are simply interested in country-oriented topics." Bimonthly. Estab. 1971.
Needs: Fiction must be upbeat, heartwarming and focus on a country woman as central character. "Many of our stories and articles are written by our readers!" Published work by Edna Norrell, Millie Thomas Kearney and Rita Peterson. **Published new writers within last year.** Publishes 1 fiction story/issue. Length: 1,000 words.

How to Contact: Send $2 and SASE for sample copy and writer's guidelines. All manuscripts should be sent to Kathy Pohl, Executive Editor. Reports in 2-3 months. Include cover letter and SASE. Simultaneous and reprint submissions OK.

Payment/Terms: Pays $90-125 on acceptance for one-time rights.

Advice: "Read the magazine to get to know our audience. Send us country-to-the-core fiction, not yuppie-country stories—our readers know the difference! Very traditional fiction—with a definite beginning, middle and end, some kind of conflict/resolution, etc. We do not want to see contemporary avant-garde fiction—nothing dealing with divorce, drugs, etc., or general societal malaise of the '90s."

☑ ◯ ◎ ⽖ **CREATIVE KIDS,** Prufrock Press, P.O. Box 8813, Waco TX 76714-8813. (254)756-3337. Fax: (254)756-3339. E-mail: creative_kids@prufrock.com. Website: www.prufrock.com (includes catalog, submission guidelines and information about our staff). **Editor:** Libby Lindsey. Magazine: 7×10½; 36 pages; illustrations; photos. Material by children for children. Published 4 times/year. Estab. 1980. Circ. 45,000.

● *Creative Kids* featuring work by children has won Ed Press and Parents' Choice Gold and Silver Awards.

Needs: "We publish work by children ages 8-14." Publishes short stories, essays, games, puzzles, poems, opinion pieces and letters. Accepts 3-4 mss/issue; 12-16 mss/year. Publishes ms up to 2 years after acceptance. Published new writers within the last year. No novels.

How to Contact: Send complete ms with cover letter, include name, age, birthday, home address, school name and address, grade, statement of originality signed by teacher or parent. Must include SASE for response. Do not query. Reports in 1 month on mss. SASE. No simultaneous submissions. Sample copy for $3. Guidelines for SASE.

Payment/Terms: Pays 1 contributor's copy. Acquires all rights.

Advice: "*Creative Kids* is designed to entertain, stimulate and challenge the creativity of children ages 8 to 14, encouraging their abilities and helping them to explore their ideas, opinions and world. Your work reflects you. Make it neat, have it proofread and follow ALL guidelines."

$ ◯ ⽖ **CRICKET MAGAZINE,** Carus Corporation, P.O. Box 300, Peru IL 61354. (815)224-6656. Editor-in-Chief: Marianne Carus. Magazine: 8×10; 64 pages; illustrations; photos. Magazine for children, ages 9-14. Monthly. Estab. 1973. Circ. 70,000.

● *Cricket* has received a Parents Choice Award, Paul A. Witty Short Story Awards and awards from Ed Press. Carus Corporation also publishes *Spider, the Magazine for Children*, *Ladybug, the Magazine for Young Children*, and *Babybug*.

Needs: Adventure, contemporary, ethnic, fantasy, historic fiction, folk and fairytales, humorous, juvenile, mystery, science fiction and translations. No adult articles. All issues have different "mini-themes." Receives approximately 1,100 unsolicited fiction mss each month. Publishes ms 6-24 months or longer after acceptance. Accepts 180 mss/year. Agented fiction 1-2%. Published work by Peter Dickinson, Mary Stolz and Jane Yolen. **Published new writers within the last year.** Length: 500-2,000 words.

How to Contact: Do not query first. Send complete ms with SASE. List previous publications. Reports in 3 months on mss. Sample copy for $5; guidelines for SASE.

Payment/Terms: Pays up to 25¢/word; 2 contributor's copies; $2 charge for extras on publication for first rights. Sends edited mss for approval. Buys reprints.

Advice: "Do not write *down* to children. Write about well-researched subjects you are familiar with and interested in, or about something that concerns you deeply. Children *need* fiction and fantasy. Carefully study several issues of *Cricket* before you submit your manuscript." Sponsors contests for readers of all ages.

$ ◯ **CRUSADER MAGAZINE,** Calvinist Cadet Corps, Box 7259, Grand Rapids MI 49510-7259. (616)241-5616. **Editor:** G. Richard Broene. Magazine: 8½×11; 24 pages; 50 lb. white paper and cover stock; illustrations; photos. Magazine "for boys (ages 9-14) who are members of the Calvinist Cadet Corps. *Crusader* publishes stories and articles that have to do with the interests and concerns of boys, teaching Christian values subtly." 7 issues/year. Estab. 1958. Circ. 12,000.

Needs: Adventure, comics, juvenile, religious/inspirational, spiritual and sports. No fantasy, science fiction, fashion, horror or erotica. List of upcoming themes available for SASE. Receives 60 unsolicited fiction mss/month. Buys 3 mss/issue; 18 mss/year. Publishes ms 4-11 months after acceptance. Published work by Sigmund Brouwer, Douglas DeVries and Betty Lou Mell. **Publishes 0-3 new writers/year.** Length: 800 words minimum; 1,500 words maximum; 1,200 words average. Publishes short shorts.

How to Contact: Send complete ms and SASE with cover letter including theme of story. Reports in 1-3 months. Simultaneous and previously published submissions OK. Sample copy with a 9×12 SAE and 4 first-class stamps. Fiction guidelines for #10 SASE.

Payment/Terms: Pays 4-6¢/word and 1 contributor's copy. Pays on acceptance for one-time rights. Buys reprints.

Advice: "On a cover sheet, list the point your story is trying to make. Our magazine has a theme for each issue, and we try to fit the fiction to the theme. All fiction should be about a young boy's interests—sports, outdoor activities, problems—with an emphasis on a Christian perspective. No simple moralisms. Avoid simplistic answers to complicated problems."

insider report

Writing for the hearts and minds of men at *Esquire*

Pinckney Benedict, Arthur Bradford, Tony Early, Heidi Julavits. If these names aren't familiar to you, chances are you haven't picked up a copy of *Esquire* lately.

While today's *Esquire* still publishes fiction by familiar names like Martin Amis, Raymond Carver, Don DeLillo and John Updike, you're just as likely to see stories by names you *don't* recognize. Fresh, young voices in the magazine's venerable literary choir.

"We have a wonderful smattering of the old guard plus some new blood," Literary Editor Adrienne Miller says. "And that's what we try to do here. We try to mix it up. We try to keep the readers of our short stories guessing."

Miller herself is a fresh young voice. She started out in publishing as an editorial assistant at *GQ*, her first job after graduating from Oxford, Ohio's Miami University, where she majored in English Literature. Her boss at *GQ* was David Granger, then executive editor. Miller stayed at *GQ* for three years, moving up the ladder to assistant editor. Then Granger left the magazine to become editor-in-chief of *Esquire*, and in May of 1997, hired Miller as literary editor.

Since that time, Miller has been selecting fiction that continues *Esquire*'s mission to "challenge men's minds, touch their hearts and stir their souls." This is one of the aspects of her job she enjoys the most. "It's a great joy to work with art that has a kind of transcendent quality to it," she says. "I think that publishing fiction is a moral good, because through these stories, we have the chance to provoke people. These stories have redemptive qualities. They're meaningful in people's lives. I know I'm doing my job well when someone tells me that they really loved a story they read a couple of months ago, and they ripped it out and put it in their journal. Or they keep the issue by their bed and look at it every night before they go to sleep." That, Miller says, is the standard by which we judge good art.

To find such stories, Miller works with agents that represent well-known, established writers. But she also reads unrepresented, unsolicited manuscripts. "One of the great things about *Esquire* is we seriously consider unsolicited fiction. I have plenty of correspondence with writers whose stories I've read here, but who don't have agents and haven't been published. And I try to read everything with a blind eye to who wrote it. The worst thing possible would be for me to publish substandard work by a big name writer. I would much, much rather publish an A-plus story by an unknown instead of a C-level story by somebody famous."

When asked for examples of these A-plus unknowns, Miller mentions Heidi Julavits and Arthur Bradford. Bradford's story, "Dogs," is one of Miller's favorites of all time. "He has this fantastic, easygoing, very simple style. It's almost like naive art. It's just hilarious, and people seem to love the story."

But it's Heidi Julavits who takes the prize for garnering the most success after being published in *Esquire*. Her story, "Marry the One Who Gets There First," appeared in the April, 1998 issue, and will appear again in the 1999 edition of the yearly anthology, *The Best American Short Stories*. "This story was a risk for us, because it was a story by a young, unknown woman, and it's not a straight narrative; it has a very complicated architecture. But it was an incredible success." So incredible, in fact, that a couple weeks after it was published, Julavits landed a lucrative book contract for a novel of which she'd only written the first 50 pages. Miller credits the sale to the strength of those 50 pages, and the strength of "Marry."

When considering stories for publication, Miller looks for stories that speak to her. "The *only* thing you can ask for in a short story is for it to have life. For it to take wing and lift off the page. That's what I look for—a story that makes the hair on my arms stand up."

Here is where Thoreau's advice—"Simplify, simplify,"—goes right out the window. The most common problem Miller sees is that writers tend to *un*complicate life, rather than complicate it. "We go to art and to literature to ennoble us and to give us a transcendent experience. When I'm reading something, I know I'm really getting something out of it if I end up with the thought that life is far stranger and far more complicated than I thought it was."

This applies even to short-shorts, which *Esquire* publishes as its monthly Snap Fiction feature on the final page of each issue. "I tend to think of these stories as novelistic in scope," Miller says. "They are all rich, dense, complicated 500- to 800-word mini-novels. They're very traditional narratives; on that page, we don't really publish stories that are abstract or seem like exercises."

For a good example of what a Snap Fiction story should do, check out any of Tony Early's offerings. "We published five or six of his short-shorts in the last year and a half," she says. "He's the master of that form." Other talented Snappers are John Updike, Tim O'Brien, David Foster Wallace and newer writer Jon Billman, whom Miller describes as "incredibly talented."

No matter the length, though, the bottom line is that it has to be a good story. And, while it doesn't have to be a "man's story," it does have to appeal to *Esquire*'s average reader— which is a 39 year-old, middle-to-upper class male. "Do we only publish swaggering, macho fiction? No. Conversely, though, we would never publish a quiet, domestic, ladies' drawing room story." *Esquire* stories also must involve men in some way, Miller says. "We wouldn't publish a sister drama or a mother-daughter story, no matter how good. It's just not something our readers are interested in."

Looking down the road to the New Millennium, Miller finds it impossible to predict what's around the bend. "What's the new big trend? I can't even answer that. I know that we're waiting for the next big, important writer. The James Joyce of the late 20th, early 21st century isn't around yet, but we're all waiting for him or her. I think in the next couple of years, a lot of exciting things are going to happen in fiction." American readers want something different, she says. "We're all sick of reading about a plumber in a trailer park. We want a big, bold new thing. We're all hungering for that."

If you're wanting to write that bold new thing, Miller has some advice to offer. "Set yourself down at your desk and write. You have to be incredibly disciplined about it. Ninety percent of it is hard work, no excuses allowed." The rest, she says, is simple. "You just pop something in an envelope, sent it out and try not to cry if you get a rejection letter. Everybody gets rejected. If the faceless literary titans don't like your work, don't let it destroy you. Keep writing."

"On a happy note," Miller says, "I honestly think that all good, hardworking writers will be rewarded. I sit at a desk and plow through manuscripts every day, waiting for the good stories. Every editor I know does the same thing. Good writers will be rewarded. It's as simple as that."

—*David Borcherding*

$ ○ DIALOGUE, A World of Ideas for Visually Impaired People of All Ages, Blindskills Inc., P.O. Box 5181, Salem OR 97304-0181. (800)860-4224. (503)581-4224. Fax: (503)581-0178. E-mail: blindskl@telepo rt.com. Website: www.teleport.com/~blindski. **Editor/Publisher:** Carol McCarl. Magazine: 9×11; 130 pages; matte stock. Publishes information of general interest to visually impaired. Quarterly. Estab. 1961. Circ. 15,000.
Needs: Adventure, contemporary, fantasy, humor/satire, literary, mainstream, mystery/suspense, romance, science fiction, senior citizen/retirement. No erotica, religion, confessional or experimental. Receives approximately 10 unsolicited fiction mss/month. Accepts 3 mss/issue, 12 mss/year. Publishes ms an average of 6 months after acceptance. Published work by Kim Rush, Diana Braun and Eric Cameron. **Published new writers within the last year.** Length: 1,000 words average; 500 words minimum; 1,500 words maximum. Publishes short shorts. Occasionally critiques rejected mss. Sometimes recommends other markets. "We give top priority to blind or visually impaired (legally blind) authors."
How to Contact: Query first or send complete ms with SASE. Also send statement of visual disability. Reports in 2 weeks on queries; 6 weeks on mss. Accepts electronic submissions on disk; IBM and compatible; Word Perfect 5.1 or 6.0 preferred. Sample copy for $6 and #10 SAE with 1 first-class stamp. Fiction guidelines free.
Payment/Terms: Pays $5-35 and contributor's copy on acceptance for first rights.
Advice: "Authors should be blind or visually impaired. We prefer contemporary problem stories in which the protagonist solves his or her own problem. We are looking for strongly-plotted stories with definite beginnings, climaxes and endings. Characters may be blind, sighted or visually in-between. Because we want to encourage any writer who shows promise, we may return a story for revision when necessary."

$ ○ DISCOVERIES, WordAction Publishing Company, 6401 The Paseo, Kansas City MO 64131. (816)333-7000 ext. 2359. Fax: (816)333-4439. Contact: Assistant Editor. Story paper: 8½×11; 4 pages; illustrations. "Committed to reinforce the Bible concept taught in Sunday School curriculum, for ages 8-10 (grades 3-4)." Weekly.
Needs: Religious, puzzles, Bible trivia, 100-200 words. "Avoid fantasy, science fiction, personification of animals and cultural references that are distinctly American." Accepts 1-2 stories and 1-2 puzzles/issue. Publishes ms 1-2 years after acceptance. **Publishes 5-10 new writers/year.** Length: 500 words.
How to Contact: Send complete ms with cover letter and SASE. Send SASE for sample copy and guidelines.
Payment/Terms: Pays 5¢/word for multiple rights on acceptance or on publication.
Advice: "Stories should vividly portray definite Christian emphasis or character building values, without being preachy."

$ ○ DISCOVERY TRAILS, Gospel Publishing House, 1445 Boonville Ave., Springfield MO 65802-1894. (417)862-2781. Fax: (417)862-6059. E-mail: discoverytrails@ag.org. Website: www.home.ag.org. **Upper Elementary Editor:** Sinda S. Zinn. Magazine: 8×10; 4 pages; coated offset paper; art illustrations; photos. "A Sunday school take-home paper of articles and fictional stories that apply Christian principles to everyday living for 10- to 12-year-old children." Weekly. Estab. 1954. Circ. 40,000.
Needs: Contemporary, juvenile, religious/inspirational, spiritual, sports. Adventure stories and serials are welcome. No Biblical fiction or science fiction. Accepts 2 mss/issue. Recently published work by Lucinda J. Rollings, Karen Cogan, A.J. Sckut and Terry Miller Shannon. **Published new writers within the last year.** Length: 800-1,000 words. Publishes short shorts.
How to Contact: Send complete ms with SASE. Reports in 4-6 weeks. Free sample copy and guidelines with SASE.
Payment/Terms: Pays 7-10¢/word and 3 contributor's copies on acceptance.
Advice: "Know the age level and direct stories or articles relevant to that age group. Since junior-age children (grades 5 and 6) enjoy action, fiction provides a vehicle for communicating moral/spiritual principles in a dramatic framework. Fiction, if well done, can be a powerful tool for relating Christian principles. It must, however, be realistic and believable in its development. Make your children be children, not overly mature for their age. We would like more serial stories. Write for contemporary children, using setting and background that includes various ethnic groups."

◎ EMPHASIS ON FAITH AND LIVING, Missionary Church, Inc., P.O. Box 9127, Fort Wayne IN 46899-9127. (219)747-2027. Fax: (219)747-5331. **Editor:** Robert L. Ransom. Magazine: 8½×11; 16 pages; offset paper; illustrations and photos. "Religious/church oriented." Bimonthly. Estab. 1969. Circ. 14,000.
Needs: Religious/inspirational. Receives 10-15 unsolicited mss/month. Accepts 2 mss/year. Publishes ms 3-6 months after acceptance. Published work by Debra Wood and Denise George. Length: 500 words average; 200 words minimum; 1,000 words maximum. Publishes short shorts. Length: 200-250 words.
How to Contact: Send complete ms with a cover letter. Include estimated word count, bio and Social Security number. Reports in 2-3 months on mss. Send SASE for reply, return of ms or send a disposable copy of ms. Simultaneous reprint and electronic submissions OK. Sample copy for 9×12 SAE.
Payment/Terms: Pays $10-50 and 5 contributor's copies on publication.

$ ○ ESQUIRE, The Magazine for Men, Hearst Corp., 250 W. 55th St., New York NY 10019. (212)649-4020. Editor: David Granger. **Literary Editor:** Adrienne Miller. Magazine: Monthly. Estab. 1933. Circ. 750,000.

General readership is college educated and sophisticated, between ages 30 and 45.

• *Esquire* is well-respected for its fiction and has received several National Magazine Awards. Work published in *Esquire* has been selected for inclusion in the *Best American Short Stories* anthology.

Needs: No "pornography, science fiction or 'true romance' stories." Publishes special fiction issue in July. Receives "thousands" of unsolicited mss/year. Rarely accepts unsolicited fiction. Published work by David Foster Wallace, Tony Earley, Elizabeth McCracken, Heidi Jularits, Martin Amis, Don DeLillo.

How to Contact: Send complete ms with cover letter or submit through an agent. Simultaneous submissions OK. Fiction guidelines for SASE.

Payment/Terms: Pays in cash on acceptance, amount undisclosed. Publishes ms an average of 2 months after acceptance.

Advice: "Submit one story at a time. Worry a little less about publication, a little more about the work itself."

$ **EVANGEL,** Light & Life Communications, P.O. Box 535002, Indianapolis IN 46253-5002. (317)244-3660. **Editor:** Julie Innes. Sunday school take-home paper for distribution to adults who attend church. Fiction involves people coping with everyday crises, making decisions that show spiritual growth. Magazine: 5½×8½; 8 pages; 2- and 4-color illustrations; color and b&w photos. Weekly. Estab. 1897. Circ. 22,000.

Needs: Religious/inspirational. "No fiction without any semblance of Christian message or where the message clobbers the reader." Receives approximately 300 unsolicited fiction mss/month. Accepts 3-4 mss/issue, 156-200 mss/year. Recently published work by Karen Leet and Dennis Hensley. **Publishes 40% new writers.** Length: 500-1,200 words.

How to Contact: Send complete ms with SASE. Reports in 2 months. Electronic submissions (3½ inch disk-WordPerfect) OK; send hard copy with disk. Sample copy and writer's guidelines with #10 SASE.

Payment/Terms: Pays 4¢/word and 2 contributor's copies on publication.

Advice: "Choose a contemporary situation or conflict and create a good mix for the characters (not all-good or all-bad heroes and villains). Don't spell out everything in detail; let the reader fill in some blanks in the story. Keep him guessing." Rejects mss because of "unbelievable characters and predictable events in the story."

FIRST HAND, Experiences for Loving Men, First Hand Ltd., Box 1314, Teaneck NJ 07666. (201)836-9177. Fax: (201)836-5055. E-mail: firsthand3@aol.com. **Editor:** Bob Harris. Magazine: digest size; 130 pages; illustrations. "Half of the magazine is made up of our readers' own gay sexual experiences. Rest is fiction and columns devoted to health, travel, books, etc." Publishes 16 times/year. Estab. 1980. Circ. 60,000.

Needs: Erotica, gay. "Should be written in first person." No science fiction or fantasy. Erotica should detail experiences based in reality. Receives 75-100 unsolicited mss/month. Accepts 6 mss/issue; 72 mss/year. Publishes ms 9-18 months after acceptance. Length: 3,000 words preferred; 2,000 words minimum; 3,750 words maximum. Sometimes critiques rejected mss.

How to Contact: Send complete ms with cover letter. Include name, address, telephone and Social Security number and "advise on use of pseudonym if any. Also whether selling all rights or first North American rights." No simultaneous submissions. Reports in 1-2 months. SASE. Sample copy for $5. Fiction guidelines for #10 SASE.

Payment/Terms: Pays $100-150 on publication for all rights or first North American serial rights.

Advice: "Avoid the hackneyed situations. Be original. We like strong plots."

FLORIDA WILDLIFE, Florida Fish and Wildlife Conservation, 620 S. Meridian St., Tallahassee FL 32399-1600. (850)488-5563. Fax: (850)488-1961. Website: www.state.Fl.us/FWC/. **Editor:** Dick Sublette. Associate Editor: James Call. Magazine: 8½×11; 32 pages. "Conservation-oriented material for an 'outdoor' audience." Bimonthly. Estab. 1947. Circ. 26,000.

• *Florida Wildlife* has received the Florida Magazine Association and Association of Conservation Information awards.

Needs: "Florida-related adventure, natural history, volunteers and conservation/environmental work. Freshwater and saltwater subjects welcome." Accepts 24 mss/year. Length: 1,200 words average; 500 words minimum; 2,000 words maximum.

How to Contact: Send complete ms, double spaced, with cover letter including Social Security number. "We prefer to review article. Response time varies with amount of material on hand." Sample copy for $3.50. Will send writer's guidelines and how to submit memo upon request.

Payment/Terms: Pays minimum of $55 per published page on publication for one-time rights.

Advice: "Send your best work. It must *directly* concern Florida wildlife."

$ **THE FRIEND MAGAZINE,** The Church of Jesus Christ of Latter-day Saints, 50 E. North Temple, Salt Lake City UT 84150-3226. (801)240-2210. **Editor:** Vivian Paulsen. Magazine: 8½×10½; 50 pages; 40 lb. coated paper; 70 lb. coated cover stock; illustrations; photos. Publishes for 3- to 11-year-olds. Monthly. Estab. 1971. Circ. 275,000.

Needs: Children's/juvenile: adventure, ethnic, some historical, humor, mainstream, religious/inspirational, nature. Length: 1,000 words maximum. Publishes short shorts. Length: 250 words.

Playing with form in short stories and novels

By all rights, Heidi Julavits should still be publishing in obscure literary journals. After all, she's had only five short stories published—a mere beginning compared to most writers' careers. And at the beginning of a writing career, you publish in obscure literary journals, right?

Not Julavits. Her first story, "Penny Dreadfuls," was selected by Ethan Canin for the *Writer's Harvest 2* anthology. She jumped from there to score at three top magazines: *Story*, *Esquire* and *Zoetrope: All Story*, bypassing the obscure journal circuit altogether. Her *Esquire* story, "Marry the One Who Gets There First," was chosen for *The Best American Short Stories 1999*, and her first novel, *The Mineral Palace*, is an April 2000 release from Penguin Putnam. But while she's proud and honored to have

Heidi Julavits

appeared in such prestigious publications, Julavits is also quick to boast of having published her fifth story in *Timothy McSweeney's Quarterly Concern*—an obscure New York 'zine. When asked why, Julavits says, "I'm very proud to be in *McSweeney's* for reasons other than publishing prestige, and I guess it's because the magazine is so subversive and naughty, two things I've always secretly wanted to be."

If the architecture of Julavits's career path strikes you as odd, it seems appropriate once you read her work; her stories, too, have strange constructions. "Marry the One Who Gets There First," for example, is told as if you are looking through a photo album of wedding pictures. "Falling Man" jumps around in time, telling the story much more effectively than if the events had been placed chronologically.

Part of the reason for these structural devices, Julavits says, is because she doesn't like to read short stories, and therefore doesn't quite know how to write them. "I've always been a reader of novels, and I feel because that's what I've read, my imagination has been trained to think with that kind of scope and range. So I had a really difficult time when I started to write short stories, which you have to do in graduate school. I would try to cram too much stuff into them; I could never limit my focus to the classic short story. I couldn't write about two people in a room and one situation, and not have everything else in their lives be part of the story. I had imagined everything else about their lives and everyone else in their lives."

Julavits tried to write many straightforward short stories and "failed quite miserably. They all ended up being nearly 40 pages long." Then she found if she broke the story into small parts and arranged them in a non-linear way, her stories began to shrink. Much of the information she felt compelled to include in the story came to the reader in the spaces in between.

"Settling on these structural devices enabled me to satisfy my craving for more information. When you have a story that has all these different parts, you get a lot of tension *between* the parts. There's much that can happen as these parts rub together, and you get even more story existing in those spaces."

Julavits first hit on this method of storytelling with "The Penny Dreadfuls." Written while she was still in graduate school and working several jobs, it is composed of short blocks of story. "At that time, I literally only had ten minutes to sit down and write between jobs and classes. But I would have finished one block of story every time." Julavits wrote "Marry the One Who Gets There First" in a similar mode, while she was planning her *own* wedding. "It was the same kind of harried feeling, and there were all sorts of things going on in my head. I don't think I would have been able to write something long and connected and narrative and linear, because I was not living in either a narrative or a linear fashion at the time."

Julavits doesn't usually start with characters, which is another way she differs from the average writer. "I can more easily access a situation through the weather, the landscape, the things on the table. I'm very much a detail and atmosphere person. That's what first draws me into a scene. It's only after I understand the details that I can move in and start to see the people who would live in this place and what they would be like."

This, in fact, is how she started developing her novel, *The Mineral Palace*. After years of hearing her grandmother curse Pueblo, Colorado, Julavits was inspired to set a story there. Unlike her short work, however, *The Mineral Palace* does not have an unusual structure. "When I've talked to people about my novel, I've been apologetic, in a way, because I'm not playing with form in the same way that I've played with form in my short stories. I saw myself as the kind of writer who came up with clever structural devices, and so I put several in the book. But they weren't really working, and I realized part of the reason why was because they weren't necessary. It wasn't a question of economy anymore. I wasn't limited to 18 pages. I had 400 pages I could fill up with this stuff."

On the heels of this realization came the revelation that she was writing the type of book that first drew her to reading. "When I was growing up, my favorite books were adventure/discovery stories. I loved *The Chronicles of Narnia* and Enid Blyton's Famous Five series. And I discovered they were influencing what I was writing. I was trying to recreate the thing that attracted me to those books—the possibility of unknown, possibly magical things existing in the very dull real world."

Julavits believes writers need to find an occupation that gives them the time and emotional space to do their work. Six years ago, she quit her job as a fashion copywriter and took a job waitressing. "I never wrote less than when I was writing copy," she says. "The last thing I wanted to do when I got home was write, because I'd been writing all day." Waitressing, it turned out, was the perfect job for Julavits. "I'm a morning person, and waitressing at night gave me my mornings, when I am freshest, to write. I was by myself all day. But I don't like being alone all the time, which for a writer is a fairly unfortunate affliction. So I'd get to go out at night, I'd make money, I'd get to talk to people. And I happen to love food and wine, so it was almost the perfect existence for me."

This is not to say Julavits thinks all writers should take part-time waiter or waitress jobs. "Figure out how you work and what *you* need to give yourself the time and emotional space to write. Then get a job that enables you to have that. That way, you're not under any pressure, and your life is set up so everything is complementary. Otherwise, I think writing can be very frustrating. It can become a thing that gets squeezed out of your life pretty easily."

And don't think of writing as a career, she adds. "I don't think anyone should be drawn to it as a career. The thing that enabled me to keep going in the face of rejection and almost insurmountable odds was not to think of it as a career. It's just something I love to do. Therefore, if I wasn't making any money from my writing, that was OK, because it's just the thing I love to do the most."

HEIDI JULAVITS'S WRITING DAY

"I'm very, very proud of my writing day. It's something I've been trying to have for five or six years. In all that time, I've tried every conceivable arrangement for writing. I've written in cafés, I've written at home, I've written at friends' houses. I've written in the morning, in the evening, in the afternoon. I've gone running first, I've drunk coffee, I haven't drunk coffee. I've eaten, I haven't eaten. I've talked to people first, I haven't talked to people. Just every single thing to figure out what was going to enable me to write.

"It's hard to get yourself to sit down and do that every day. So I essentially ran six years of controlled experiments on myself. And finally, I figured out, OK, I can't drink coffee, I can't write at home, I can't talk on the phone before I write. Things that you don't know until you're faced with trying to figure out how you work. I found that I can write about a thousand words a day, but not really more than that. I mean, I *could*, but I end up having to cut them the next day; they're not inspired, they're kind of dull. You have to learn about your process of regeneration. You have to figure out at what point you use up whatever gas you have, and to push yourself any further just doesn't make any sense.

"My writing day turned out to be like a regular work day for me. I get up, I go into the city on the train with everyone else. I sort of barricade myself in a place where there isn't a phone and write. Before I got my book deal, I wrote Monday to Friday. I tried to keep to that schedule afterwards, but when it became clear to me that I wasn't going to be able to deliver the book on time, I began writing every day. I don't know what's going to happen when I finish the book. I'm so used to working every day that if I take a day off or a vacation, it's very strange.

"But mostly I write Monday to Friday, and it's part of the 'go to work with the masses' way I try to make writing a normal activity. I don't want to feel like I'm living in contrast to everybody else. I feel like I'm a person who works, the same way everyone else does."

—*David Borcherding*

How to Contact: Send complete ms. "No query letters please." Reports in 6-8 weeks. SASE. Sample copy for $1.50 with 9½×11 SAE and four 33¢ stamps.

Payment/Terms: Pays 10-13¢/word on acceptance for all rights.

Advice: "The *Friend* is particularly interested in stories with substance for tiny tots. Stories should focus on character-building qualities and should be wholesome without moralizing or preaching. Boys and girls resolving conflicts is a theme of particular merit. Since the magazine is circulated worldwide, the *Friend* is interested in stories and articles with universal settings, conflicts and character. Other suggestions include rebus, picture, holiday, sports, and photo stories, or manuscripts that portray various cultures. Very short pieces (up to 250 words) are desired for younger readers and preschool children. Appropriate humor is a constant need."

☑ $⊘ **THE GEM**, Churches of God, General Conference, Box 926, Findlay OH 45839. (419)424-1961. E-mail: communications@cggc.org. Website: www.cggc.org. **Editor:** Mac Cordell. Magazine: 6×9; 8 pages; 50 lb. uncoated paper; illustrations (clip art). "True-to-life stories of healed relationships and growing maturity in the Christian faith for senior high students through senior citizens who attend Churches of God, General Conference Sunday Schools." Weekly. Estab. 1865. Circ. 7,000.

Needs: Adventure, humor, mainstream, religious/inspirational, senior citizen/retirement. Nothing that denies or ridicules standard Christian values. No science fiction or Y2K stories. Prefers personal testimony or nonfiction short stories. Receives 45 unsolicited fiction mss/month. Accepts 1 ms every 2-3 issues; 20-25 mss/year. Publishes ms 4-12 months after submission. Length: 1,500 words average; 500 words minimum; 1,700 words maximum.

How to Contact: Send complete ms with cover letter ("letter not essential, unless there is information about author's background which enhances story's credibility or verifies details as being authentic"). Reports in 6 months. SASE. Simultaneous and reprint submissions OK. Sample copy and fiction guidelines for #10 SASE. "If more than one sample copy is desired along with the guidelines, will need 2 oz. postage."

Payment/Terms: Pays $10-15 and contributor's copies on publication for one-time rights. Charge for extras (postage for mailing more than one).

Advice: "There is not shortcut. The key to writing well is to read everything you can and then to write and write and write."

✅ $🖉 **GENT,** Dugent Corp., 14411 Commerce Way, Suite 420, Miami Lakes FL 33016. (305)557-0071. **Editor:** Fritz Bailey. "Men's magazine designed to have erotic appeal for the reader. Our publications are directed to a male audience, but we do have a certain percentage of female readers. For the most part, our audience is interested in erotically stimulating material, but not exclusively." Monthly. Estab. 1959. Circ. 175,000.

Needs: Erotica. *Gent* specializes in "D-Cup cheesecake," and fiction should be slanted accordingly. "Most of the fiction published includes several sex scenes. No fiction that concerns children, religious subjects or anything that might be libelous." Accepts 1 mss/issue; 13 mss/year. Publishes ms an average of 3 months after acceptance. **Published new writers within the last year.** Length: 2,500 words.

How to Contact: Send complete ms with SASE. Reports in 1 month. Sample copy for $7. Fiction guidelines for #10 SASE.

Payment/Terms: Pays $200 minimum on publication and 1 contributor's copy for first North American serial rights.

Advice: "Since *Gent* magazine is the 'Home of the D-Cups,' stories and articles containing either characters or themes with a major emphasis on large breasts will have the best chance for consideration. Study a sample copy first." Mss are rejected because "there are not enough or ineffective erotic sequences, plot is not plausible, wrong length, or not slanted specifically for us."

$🖉 **GOLF JOURNAL,** United States Golf Assoc., Golf House, P.O. Box 708, Far Hills NJ 07931-0708. (908)234-2300. Fax: (908)781-1112. **Editor:** Brett Avery. Managing Editor: Rich Skyzinski. Magazine: 48-56 pages; self cover stock; illustrations and photos. "The magazine's subject is golf—its history, lore, rules, equipment and general information. The focus is on amateur golf and those things applying to the millions of American golfers. Our audience is generally professional, highly literate and knowledgeable; they read *Golf Journal* because of an interest in the game, its traditions, and its noncommercial aspects." Published 9 times/year. Estab. 1948. Circ. 650,000.

Needs: Poignant or humorous essays and short stories. "Golf jokes will not be used." Accepts 12 mss/year. **Published new writers within the last year.** Length: 1,000-2,000 words.

How to Contact: Send complete ms with SASE. Reports in 2 months on mss. Sample copy for SASE.

Payment/Terms: Pays $500-1,000 on acceptance and 5 contributor's copies.

Advice: "Know your subject (golf); familiarize yourself first with the publication." Rejects mss because "fiction usually does not serve the function of *Golf Journal*, which, as the official magazine of the United States Golf Association, deals chiefly with the history, lore and rules of golf."

⭐ ✅ $🖉 **GRIT, American Life & Traditions**, Ogden Publications, Inc., 1503 S.W. 42nd St., Topeka KS 66609-1265. (913)274-4300. Fax: (785)274-4305. E-mail: grit@cjnetworks.com. Website: www.grit.com (includes cover story from current issue plus titles of other features and book and products store). **Editor-in-Chief:** Donna Doyle. Note on envelope: Attn: Fiction Department. Tabloid: 50 pages; 30 lb. newsprint; illustrations and photos. "*Grit* is a 'good news' publication and has been since 1882. Fiction should be 1,200 words or more and interesting, inspiring, perhaps compelling in nature. Audience is *conservative*; readers tend to be 40+ from smaller towns, rural areas." Biweekly. Estab. 1882. Circ. 200,000.

• *Grit* is considered one of the leading family-oriented publications.

Needs: Adventure, nostalgia, condensed novelette, mainstream/contemporary (conservative), mystery/suspense, light religious/inspirational, romance (contemporary, historical), science fiction, westerns (frontier, traditional). "No sex, violence, drugs, obscene words, abuse, alcohol, or negative diatribes." Upcoming themes: "Gardening" (January/February); "Love & Romance" (February); "Presenting the Harvest" (June); "Back to School" (August); "Health Issue" (September); "Home for the Holidays" (November); "Christmas Theme" (December). Buys 1 mss/issue; 26 mss/year. Recently published work by Adelaide Ferguson, Helen Folsom, Wendy Doggett, Eileen McGoffin and George Chaffee. **Publishes 20 new writers/year.** Length: 1,500 words average; 1,200 words minimum; 2,500 words maximum for serials. Also publishes poetry.

How To Contact: Send complete ms with cover letter. Include estimated word count, brief bio, Social Security number, list of publications with submission. Send SASE for return of ms. No simultaneous submissions. Sample copy for $4 postage/appropriate SASE.

Payment/Terms: Pays up to 22¢/word.

Terms: Purchases first North American serial or one-time rights.

Advice: Looks for "well-written, fast-paced adventures, lessons of life, wholesome stories with heart. Especially need serials with cliffhangers. Prefer western, historical with romantic interest."

GUIDEPOSTS FOR KIDS, P.O. Box 638, Chesterton IN 46304. Website:www.gp4k.com (for children, includes sample stories, games, interactives). **Editor-in-Chief:** Mary Lou Carney. Magazine: 8¼×10¾; 32 pages. "Value-centered bimonthly for kids 7-12 years old. Not preachy, concerned with contemporary issues." Bimonthly. Estab. 1990. Circ. 200,000.

● The magazine publishes many new writers but is primarily a market for writers who have already been published. *Guideposts for Kids* received Awards of Excellence from the Ed Press Association in 1995-1998, and also has received from SCBWI the Angel Awards.

Needs: Children's/juvenile: fantasy, historical (general), humor, mystery/suspense, holidays. "No 'adult as hero' or 'I-prayed-I-got' stories." Upcoming features: Materialism, Cheating, Self-esteem, Joke Writing. Receives 200 unsolicited mss/month. Accepts 1-2 mss/issue; 6-10 mss/year. Recently published work by Beverly Patt and Lisa Harkrader. Length: 1,300 words preferred; 600 words minimum; 1,400 words maximum. Publishes short shorts. Also publishes small amount of poetry. Sometimes critiques rejected mss; "only what shows promise."

How to Contact: Send complete ms with cover letter. Include estimated word count, Social Security number, phone number and SASE. Reports in 6-8 weeks. Send SASE for reply, return of ms or send disposable copy of ms. Simultaneous submissions OK. Sample copy for $3.25. Fiction guidelines for #10 SASE.

Payment/Terms: $250-600 on acceptance for all rights; 2 contributor's copies. Additional copies available.

Advice: "We're looking for the good stuff. Fast-paced, well-crafted stories aimed at kids 8-12 years of age. Stories should reflect strong traditional values. Don't preach. This is not a Sunday School handout, but a good solid piece of fiction that reflects traditional values and morality. Build your story around a solid principle and let the reader gain insight by inference. Don't let adults solve problems. While adults can appear in stories, they can't give the characters life's answers. Don't make your kid protagonist grateful and awed by sage, adult advice. Be original. We want a good mix of fiction—contemporary, historical, fantasy, sci-fi, mystery—centered around things that interest and concern kids. A kid reader should be able to identify with the characters strongly enough to think. '*I know just how he feels!*' Create a plot with believable characters. Here's how it works: the story must tell what happens when someone the reader likes (character) reaches an important goal (climax) by overcoming obstacles (conflict). Let kids be kids. Your dialogue (and use plenty of it!) should reflect how the kids sound, think and feel. Avoid slang, but listen to how real kids talk before you try and write for them. Give your characters feelings and actions suitable for the 4th to 6th grader."

HARPER'S MAGAZINE, 666 Broadway, 11th Floor, New York NY 10012. (212)614-6500. Website: www.harpers.org (includes submission guidelines). **Editor:** Lewis H. Lapham. Magazine: 8×10¾; 80 pages; illustrations. Magazine for well-educated, widely read and socially concerned readers, college-aged and older, those active in political and community affairs. Monthly. Circ. 218,000.

● This is considered a top but tough market for contemporary fiction.

Needs: Contemporary and humor. Stories on contemporary life and its problems. Receives 600 unsolicited fiction mss/year. Accepts 1 ms/year. Recently published work by David Guterson, David Foster Wallace, Johnathan Franzen, Steven Millhauser, Lisa Roney, Rick Moody and Steven Dixon. **Published new writers within the last year.** First published David Foster Wallace. Length: 1,000-5,000 words.

How to Contact: Query to managing editor, or through agent. Reports in 6 weeks on queries.

Payment/Terms: Pays $500-1,000 on acceptance for rights, which vary on each author materials and length. Sends galleys to author.

Advice: Buys very little fiction but *Harper's* has published short stories traditionally.

HIGHLIGHTS FOR CHILDREN, 803 Church St., Honesdale PA 18431. (570)253-1080. **Editor:** Kent L. Brown, Jr. Address fiction to: Beth Troop, **Manuscript Coordinator.** Magazine: 8½×11; 42 pages; uncoated paper; coated cover stock; illustrations; photos. Monthly. Circ. 2.8 million. Highlights publishes "general interest for children between the ages of 2 and 12. Our philosophy is 'fun with a purpose.' "

● *Highlights* is very supportive of writers. The magazine sponsors a contest and a workshop each year at Chautauqua (New York). Several authors published in *Highlights* have received SCBWI Magazine Merit Awards. *Highlights* ranked #7 on the *Writer's Digest*'s Fiction 50 list of top markets for fiction writers.

Needs: Juvenile (ages 2-12). Unusual stories appealing to both girls and boys; stories with good characterization, strong emotional appeal, vivid, full of action. "Begin with action rather than description, have strong plot, believable setting, suspense from start to finish." Length: 400-900 words. "We also need easy stories for very young readers (100-400 words)." No war, crime or violence. Receives 600-800 unsolicited fiction mss/month. Accepts 6-7 mss/issue. Also publishes rebus (picture) stories of 125 words or under for the 3- to 7-year-old child. Published work by Marianne Mitchell, Marty Kaminsky, Margaret Springer and Edmund Fortier. **Publishes 30 new writers/year.** Critiques rejected mss occasionally, "especially when editors see possibilities in story."

How to Contact: Send complete ms with SASE and include a rough word count and cover letter "with any previous acceptances by our magazine; any other published work anywhere." Reports in 1 month. Free guidelines on request.

Payment/Terms: Pays 14¢ and up/word on acceptance for all rights. Sends galleys to author.

Advice: "We accept a story on its merit whether written by an unpublished or an experienced writer. Mss are rejected because of poor writing, lack of plot, trite or worn-out plot, or poor characterization. Children *like* stories and learn about life from stories. Children learn to become lifelong fiction readers by enjoying stories. Feel passion for your subject. Create vivid images. Write a child-centered story; leave adults in the background."

✪ ✔ ◑ ⚇ **ALFRED HITCHCOCK MYSTERY MAGAZINE,** Dell Magazines, 475 Park Ave. S., New York NY 10016. (212)686-7188. Website: www.mysterypages.com (includes guidelines, story excerpts, subscription forms and logic puzzles). **Editor:** Cathleen Jordan. Mystery fiction magazine: 5¼ × 8⅜; 144 pages; 28 lb. newsprint paper; 60 lb. machine-/coated cover stock; illustrations; photos. Published 11 times/year, including 1 double issue. Estab. 1956. Circ. 615,000 readers.

• Stories published in *Alfred Hitchcock Mystery Magazine* have won Edgar Awards for "Best Mystery Story of the Year," Shamus Awards for "Best Private Eye Story of the Year" and Robert L. Fish Awards for "Best First Mystery Short Story of the Year." *Alfred Hitchcock Mystery Magazine* ranked #17 on the *Writer's Digest* Fiction 50 list of top markets for fiction writers.

Needs: Mystery and detection (amateur sleuth, private eye, police procedural, suspense, etc.). No sensationalism. Number of mss/issue varies with length of mss. Length: up to 14,000 words. Also publishes short shorts. Recently published work by Gary Alexander, Ron Goulart, Rob Kantner and Ann Ripley.

How to Contact: Send complete ms and SASE. Reports in 2 months. Guideline sheet for SASE. Sample issue for $5.

Payment/Terms: Pays 8¢/word on acceptance.

✪ $ ◑ ◎ **HOME TIMES,** Neighbor News, Inc., 3676 Collin Dr. #12, West Palm Beach FL 33406. (561)439-3509. E-mail: hometimes@aol.com. Editor: Dennis Lombard. Newspaper: tabloid; 24 pages; newsprint; illustrations and photographs. "Conservative news, views, fiction, poetry, sold to general public." Weekly. Estab. 1990. Circ. 3,000.

• The publisher offers "101 Reasons Why I Reject Your Manuscript," a 100-page report for a cost of $19.

Needs: Adventure, historical (general), humor/satire, literary, mainstream, religious/inspirational, sports. No romance. "All fiction needs to be related to the publication's focus on current events and conservative perspective—we feel you must examine a sample issue because *Home Times* is *different.*" Nothing "preachy or doctrinal, but Biblical worldview needed." Receives 40 unsolicited mss/month. Accepts 2-4 mss/issue. Publishes ms 1-9 months after acceptance. Published work by Cal Thomas, Chuck Colson, Armstrong Williams and Bruce Bartlett. **Publishes 10-15 new writers/year.** Length: 700 words average; 500 words minimum; 800 words maximum.

How to Contact: Send complete manuscript with cover letter including word count. "Absolutely no queries." Include in cover letter "One to two sentences on what the piece is and who you are." Reports on mss in 1 month. SASE. Simultaneous and reprint submissions OK. Sample current issues for $3. Guidelines for #10 SASE.

Payment/Terms: Pays $5-25 for one-time rights.

Advice: "We are very open to new writers, but read our newspaper—get the drift of our rather unusual conservative, pro-Christian, but non-religious content. Looks for "historical, issues, or family orientation; also like creative nonfiction on historical and issues subjects." Send $12 for a writer's 1-year subscription (12 current issues).

$ ◑ ◎ **HORIZONS, The Magazine of Presbyterian Women,** 100 Witherspoon St., Louisville KY 40202-1396. (502)569-5379. Fax: (502)569-8085. E-mail: lbradley@ctr.pcusa.org. **Associate Editor:** Leah Bradley. Magazine: 8 × 11; 40 pages; illustrations and photos. Magazine owned and operated by Presbyterian Women featuring "information, inspiration and education from the perspectives of women committed to Christ, the church and faithful discipleship." Bimonthly. Estab. 1988. Circ. 25,000.

Needs: Ethnic/multicultural, feminist, historical, humor/satire, literary, mainstream/contemporary, religious/inspirational, senior citizen/retirement, translations. "No sex/violence or romance." List of upcoming themes available for SASE. Receives 50 unsolicited mss/month. Accepts 1 ms/issue. Publishes ms 4 months after acceptance. **Publishes 6 new writers/year.** Length: 800-1,200 words maximum. Publishes short shorts. Length: 500 words. Also publishes literary essays, fiction and poetry. Sometimes critiques or comments on rejected mss.

How to Contact: Send complete ms with cover letter. Include estimated word count and Social Security number. Accepts queries and mss by e-mail and fax (mss by permission only). Reports in 1 week on queries; 2 weeks on mss. SASE or send a disposable copy of ms. Simultaneous submissions OK. Sample copy for 9 × 12 SAE. Fiction guidelines for #10 SASE. Reviews novels and short story collections. Send books to Leah Bradley.

Payment/Terms: Pays $50/page and 2 contributor's copies on publication for all rights; additional copies for $2.50.

Advice: "We are most interested in stories or articles that focus on current issues—family life, the mission of the church, and the challenges of culture and society—from the perspective of women committed to Christ."

$ ◑ **HUMPTY DUMPTY'S MAGAZINE,** Children's Better Health Institute, Box 567, 1100 Waterway Blvd., Indianapolis IN 46206. (317)636-8881. Fax: (317)684-8094. Website: www.satevepost.org/kidsonline. **Editor:** Nancy S. Axelrad. Magazine: 7⅝ × 10⅛; 36 pages; 35 lb. paper; coated cover; illustrations; some photos. Children's magazine "seeking to encourage children, ages 4-6, in healthy lifestyle habits, especially good nutrition and fitness." Publishes 8 issues/year.

• The Children's Better Health Institute also publishes *Children's Digest, Children's Playmate, Jack and Jill* and *Turtle,* also listed in this publication.

Needs: Juvenile health-related material and material of a more general nature. No inanimate talking objects, animal stories and science fiction. Wants more "health and fitness stories with a positive slant." Rhyming stories should flow easily with no contrived rhymes. Receives 100-200 unsolicited mss/month. Accepts 2-3 mss/issue. **Publishes 1-2 new writers/year.** Length: 300 words maximum.

How to Contact: Send complete ms with SASE. No queries. Reports in 3 months. Sample copy for $1.75. Editorial guidelines for SASE.

Payment/Terms: Pays up to 22¢/word for stories plus 10 contributor's copies on publication for all rights. (One-time book rights returned when requested for specific publication.)

Advice: "In contemporary stories, characters should be up-to-date, with realistic dialogue. We're looking for health-related stories with unusual twists or surprise endings. We want to avoid stories and poems that 'preach.' We try to present the health material in a positive way, utilizing a light humorous approach wherever possible." Most rejected mss "are too wordy or not age appropriate."

☑ $ ⊘ **IMPLOSION, A Journal of the Bizarre and Eccentric**, 1921 E. Colonial Dr., Orlando FL 32803. (407)898-5573. E-mail: cynthia@implosion-mag.com. Website: www.implosion-mag.com (includes guidelines, content samples, subscription info). **Editor:** Cynthia Conlin. Magazine: 8½×11; 64 pages; 50 lb. glossy paper; 80 lb. glossy cover stock; illustrations and photos. "*Implosion* explores the bizarre and eccentric. Publishes nonfiction features on travel, culture, art, film, music and more." Quarterly. Estab. 1995. Circ. 18,000.

Needs: Adventure, experimental (science fantasy), horror, humor, psychic/supernatural/occult, science fiction (hard science, soft/sociological). Especially interested in "material with weird and bizarre themes and overtones." No porn, children's. Receives 100 mss/month. Accepts 2-3 mss/issue; 8-15 mss/year. Publishes ms 4-7 months after acceptance. Published work by J. Spencer Dreischarf, Bert Benmeyer, D.F. Lewis and Rick Reed. **Publishes 5-8 new writers/year.** Length: 2,000 words average; 6,000 words maximum. Publishes short shorts. Also publishes literary criticism. Sometimes critiques or comments on rejected mss.

How to Contact: Send complete ms with cover letter. Include estimated word count and list of publications. Reports in 2-6 months on mss. Send SASE for reply, return of ms or send a disposable copy of ms. Simultaneous and reprint submissions OK. Sample copy for $5. Guidelines for SASE. Reviews novels and short story collections. Send books to editor.

Payment/Terms: Pays $15-30/story within 30 days of publication and 4 contributor's copies; additional copies for $3. Acquires first or one-time rights. Sends galleys to author if requested.

Advice: "We want new ideas and concepts, not clichéd rehashes of 'Twilight Zone' plots. A bit of humor doesn't hurt, either. Remember that 'bizarre' doesn't mean silly or pointless. Check your work for grammatical errors and the like—there's no greater turnoff than poorly constructed manuscripts."

★ $ ▢ ◎ **IN TOUCH FOR MEN**, 13122 Saticoy St., North Hollywood CA 91605-3402. (818)764-2288. Fax: (818)764-2307. E-mail: info@intouchformen.com. Website: www.intouchformen.com (includes information about current issues, subscription rates, hyperfiction, back issues and video reviews). **Editor:** Alan W. Mills. Magazine: 8×10¾; 100 pages; glossy paper; coated cover; illustrations and photographs. "*In Touch* is a magazine for gay men. It features six nude male centerfolds in each issue, but is erotic rather than pornographic. We include fiction. We also publish two other magazines, *Indulge* and *Blackmale*." Monthly. Estab. 1973. Circ. 70,000.

Needs: Confession, gay erotica, romance (contemporary, historical). All characters must be over 18 years old. Stories must have an explicit erotic content. No heterosexual or internalized homophobic fiction. Accepts 7 mss/month; 80 mss/year. Publishes ms 6 months after acceptance. **Publishes 20 new writers/year.** Length: 2,500 words average; up to 3,500 words maximum. Sometimes critiques rejected mss and recommends other markets.

How to Contact: Send complete ms with cover letter, name, address and Social Security number. Accepts queries and mss by e-mail and fax (mss by permission only). Reports in 2 weeks on queries; 2 months on mss. SASE. Simultaneous and reprint submissions, if from local publication, OK. Disk submissions OK (call before sending by modem). Sample copy for $6.95. Fiction guidelines free. Reviews novels and short story collections.

Payment/Terms: Pays $25-75 (except on rare occasions for a longer piece) on publication for one-time rights.

Advice: Publishes "primarily erotic material geared toward gay men. We sometimes run nonfiction or features about gay issues. I personally prefer (and accept) manuscripts that are not only erotic/hardcore, but show a developed story, plot and a concise ending (as opposed to just sexual vignettes that basically lead nowhere). If it has a little romance, too, that's even better. Emphasis still on the erotic, though. We now only use 'safe sex' depictions in fiction, hoping that it will prompt people to act responsibly. We have a new interest in experimental fiction as long as it does not violate the standards of the homoerotic genre. All fiction must conform to the basic rules of the genre. Beyond that, we look for inventive use of language, unique content, exciting themes and, on occasion, experimental structures or subversive issues. If you're writing for a genre, know that genre, but don't be afraid to twist things around just enough to stand out from the crowd. Our website is becoming increasingly important to us. We have our eyes open for interesting hyperfiction because we want people to keep returning to our site, hoping that they might subscribe to the magazine."

☑ ⊘ ◎ **INDIA CURRENTS, The Complete Indian American Magazine**, Box 21285, San Jose CA 95151. (408)274-6966. Fax: (408)274-2733. **Managing Editor:** Vandana Kumar. E-mail: editor@indiacurrents.c om. Magazine: 8½ × 11; 104 pages; newsprint paper; illustrations and photographs. "The arts and culture of India as seen in America for Indians and non-Indians with a common interest in India." Monthly. Estab. 1987. Circ. 25,000.

Needs: All Indian content: contemporary, ethnic, feminist, historical (general), humor/satire, literary, mainstream, regional, religious/inspirational, romance, translations (from Indian languages). "We seek material with insight into Indian culture, American culture and the crossing from one to another." Receives 12 unsolicited mss/month. Accepts 1 ms/issue; 12 mss/year. Publishes ms 2-6 months after acceptance. Published work by Chitra Divakaruni, Jyotsna Sreenivasan and Rajini Srikanth. **Published new writers within the last year.** Length: 2,000 words.

How to Contact: Send complete ms with cover letter and clips of published work. Reports in 2-3 months on mss. SASE. Simultaneous and reprint submissions OK. Accepts electronic submissions. Sample copy for $3.

Payment/Terms: Pays in subscriptions on publication for one-time rights (print and website).

Advice: "Story must be related to India and subcontinent in some meaningful way. The best stories are those which document some deep transformation as a result of an Indian experience, or those which show the humanity of Indians."

N ⬤ **INSIDE, The Magazine of the Jewish Exponent,** Jewish Federation, 226 S. 16th St., Philadelphia PA 19102. (215)893-5700. (215)546-3957. E-mail: editors@inside.com. **Editor-in-Chief:** Jane Biberman. Magazine: 175-225 pages; glossy paper; illustrations; photos. Aimed at middle- and upper-middle-class audience, Jewish-oriented articles and fiction. Quarterly. Estab. 1980. Circ. 75,000.

Needs: Contemporary, ethnic, humor/satire, literary and translations. No erotica. Receives approximately 10 unsolicited fiction mss/month. Buys 1-2 mss/issue; 4-8 mss/year. Recently published work by Jennifer Moses. **Published new writers within the last year.** Length: 1,500 words minimum; 3,000 words maximum; 2,000 words average. Occasionally critiques rejected mss.

How to Contact: Query first with clips of published work. Reports on queries in 3 weeks. SASE. Simultaneous submissions OK. Sample copy for $5 and 9 × 12 SAE. Fiction guidelines for SASE.

Payment/Terms: Pays $100-600 on acceptance for first rights. Sometimes buys reprints. Sends galleys to author.

Advice: "We're looking for original, avant-garde, stylish writing but we buy very little."

N 🌐 ⭐ ◎ **INTERZONE: Science Fiction and Fantasy,** 217 Preston Drove, Brighton BN1 6FL England. Website: www.sfsite.com/interzone (includes guidelines, subscription details). Editor: David Pringle. Monthly. Circ. 10,000. Publishes 5-6 stories/issue. "We're looking for intelligent science fiction in the 2,000-7,000 word range. Send two IRCs with 'overseas' submissions and a *disposable* ms." Pays £30 per 1,000 words on publication and 2 contributor's copies. "Please *read the magazine*—available through specialist science-fiction dealers or direct by subscription." Sample copies to USA: $6. Write for guidelines.

• *Interzone* ranked #43 on the *Writer's Digest* Fiction 50 list of top markets for fiction writers.

🌐 **$** ◎ **IRELAND'S OWN,** 1 North Main St., Wexford Ireland. **Editors:** Gerry Breen and Margaret Galvin. Weekly. Circ. 50,000. Publishes 3 stories/issue. "*Ireland's Own* is a homey family-oriented weekly magazine with a story emphasis on the traditional values of Irish society. Short stories must be written in a straightforward nonexperimental manner with an Irish orientation." Length: 1,800-2,000 words. Pays £40-50 on publication. "Study and know the magazine's requirements, orientation and target market. Guidelines and copies sent out on request."

$ ◎ ◎ **JACK AND JILL,** The Children's Better Health Institute, P.O. Box 567, 1100 Waterway Blvd., Indianapolis IN 46206. (317)636-8881. **Editor:** Daniel Lee. Children's magazine of articles, stories and activities, many with a health, safety, exercise or nutritional-oriented theme, ages 7-10 years. Monthly except January/February, April/May, July/August, October/November. Estab. 1938.

Needs: Science fiction, mystery, sports, adventure, historical fiction and humor. Health-related stories with a subtle lesson. **Published new writers within the last year.** Length: 500-800 words.

How to Contact: Send complete ms with SASE. Reports in 3 months on mss. Sample copy for $1.75. Fiction guidelines for SASE.

Payment/Terms: Pays up to 20¢/word on publication for all rights.

Advice: "Try to present health material in a positive—not a negative—light. Use humor and a light approach wherever possible without minimizing the seriousness of the subject. We need more humor and adventure stories."

N ⭐ **$** ⬤ **KIDZ CH@T,** 8121 Hamilton Ave., Cincinnati OH 45231-2396. (513)931-4050. **Editor:** Gary Thacker. Magazine (Sunday school take-home paper): 5⅜ × 8⅜; 8 pages; Choctaw matte 45 lb. paper; illustrations and photos. "*Kidz Ch@t* correlates with Standard Publishing's Middler Sunday school curriculum. Features tie into the theme of the Sunday school lesson each week." Weekly. Estab. 1999. Circ. 55,000.

• *Kidz Ch@t* replaced *R.A.D.A.R.* in Fall 1999. *Kidz Chat* ranked #13 on the *Writer's Digest* Fiction 50 list of top markets for fiction writers.

Needs: Children's/juvenile (adventure, animal, mystery), religious (children's religious). "All stories correlate with Standard Publishing's Middler Sunday school curriculum." No biblical fiction, science fiction or fantasy.

Receives 20 unsolicited mss/month. Accepts 1 ms/issue; 52 mss/year. Manuscripts are read following the deadline on the quarterly theme list. Publishes ms 1 year after acceptance. **Publishes 5 new writers/year.** Length: 475 words maximum.

How to Contact: Does not accept queries. Send SASE for theme list and guidelines. Include estimated word count and Social Security number. Reports in 4-5 weeks on mss after theme list deadline. SASE for return of ms. Simultaneous submissions and reprints OK. Sample copy and fiction guidelines free for #10 SAE, 1 first-class stamp or 1 IRC.

Payment/Terms: Writers receive 3-7¢/word and 4 contributor's copies. Pays on acceptance. Acquires one-time rights.

Advice: "Age-appropriateness is important. This includes language and the details of the story. Also, the time of year and the activities children are involved in at home and school should be considered. Send SASE for a sample copy, writers' guidelines, and theme list. Study these before submitting. From Standard Publishing's perspective, breaking *R-A-D-A-R* into two take-home papers has made a big difference. Now *R-A-D-A-R* has been replaced. *Kidz Ch@t* is for 3rd/4th graders and *Live Wire* is for 5th/6th graders. This has allowed more concentration on age-appropriateness of features in both publications."

$ ⬙ ◎ ☒ LADYBUG, The Cricket Magazine Group, P.O. Box 300, Peru IL 61354. (815)224-6656. Editor-in-Chief: Marianne Carus. Editor: Paula Morrow. Magazine: 8×10; 36 pages plus 4-page pullout section; illustrations. "*Ladybug* publishes original stories and poems by the world's best children's authors. For young children, ages 2-6." Monthly. Estab. 1990. Circ. 131,000.

   • *Ladybug* has received the Parents Choice Award; the Golden Lamp Honor Award and the Golden Lamp
   Award from Ed Press, and Magazine Merit awards from the Society of Children's Book Writers and
   Illustrators.

Needs: Fantasy (children's), folk tales, juvenile, picture stories, preschool, read-out-loud stories and realistic fiction. Length: 300-750 words preferred. Publishes short shorts.

How to Contact: Send complete ms with cover letter. Include word count on ms (do not count title). Reports in 3 months. SASE. Reprints are OK. Fiction guidelines for SASE. Sample copy for $4. For guidelines *and* sample send 9×12 SAE (no stamps required) and $4.

Payment/Terms: Pays up to 25¢/word (less for reprints) on publication for first publication rights or second serial (reprint) rights. For recurring features, pays flat fee and copyright becomes property of The Cricket Magazine Group.

Advice: Looks for "well-written stories for preschoolers: age-appropriate, not condescending. We look for rich, evocative language and sense of joy or wonder."

$ ◯ ◎ ☒ LIGUORIAN, "A Leading Catholic Magazine," Liguori Publications, 1 Liguori Dr., Liguori MO 63057-9998. (800)464-2555. Fax: (800)325-9526. E-mail: aweinert@liguori.org. Website: www.liguori.org. **Editor-in-Chief:** Allan Weinert, CSS.R. Magazine: 5×8½; 64 pages; b&w illustrations and photographs. "*Liguorian* is a Catholic magazine aimed at helping our readers to live a full Christian life. We publish articles for families, young people, children, religious and singles—all with the same aim." Monthly. Estab. 1913. Circ. 330,000.

   • *Liguorian* received Catholic Press Association awards for 1997 including Best Special Issue (September
   1997); Best Short Story (*Across the Clothesline*, by Kay Hogan); and an honorable mention (*In the Shadow
   of the Willows*, by Molly Glissner).

Needs: Religious/inspirational, young adult and senior citizen/retirement (with moral Christian thrust), spiritual. "Stories submitted to *Liguorian* must have as their goal the lifting up of the reader to a higher Christian view of values and goals. We are not interested in contemporary works that lack purpose or are of questionable moral value." Receives approximately 25 unsolicited fiction mss/month. Accepts 12 mss/year. Recently published work by Mel Morris, Perl Burke, Patricia Castle, Judy Case, Patricia Wyman and Helen Kronberg. **Publishes 5-6 new writers/year.** Length: 1,500-2,000 words preferred. Also publishes short shorts. Occasionally critiques rejected mss "if we feel the author is capable of giving us something we need even though this story did not suit us."

How to Contact: Send complete ms with SASE. Accepts disk submissions compatible with IBM, using a WordPerfect 5.1 program; prefers hard copy with disk submission. Reports in 10-12 weeks on mss. Sample copy and guidelines for #10 SASE.

Payment/Terms: Pays 10-12¢/word and 5 contributor's copies on acceptance for all rights. Offers 50% kill fee for assigned mss not published.

Advice: "First read several issues containing short stories. We look for originality and creative input in each story we read. Since most editors must wade through mounds of manuscripts each month, consideration for the editor requires that the market be studied, the manuscript be carefully presented and polished before submitting.

CHECK THE CATEGORY INDEXES, located at the back of the book, for publishers interested in specific fiction subjects.

Our publication uses only one story a month. Compare this with the 25 or more we receive over the transom each month. Also, many fiction mss are written without a specific goal or thrust, i.e., an interesting incident that goes nowhere is *not a story*. We believe fiction is a highly effective mode for transmitting the Christian message and also provides a good balance in an unusually heavy issue."

⭐ 💲 🔘 ◎ **LIVE,** Assemblies of God, 1445 Boonville, Springfield MO 65802-1894. (417)862-2781. Fax: (417)862-6059. E-mail: rl-live@gph.org. Website: www.home.ag.org/sscl/ (includes writer's guidelines, names of editors, short fiction and non-fiction and devotionals). **Editor:** Paul W. Smith. "A take-home story paper distributed weekly in young adult/adult Sunday school classes. *Live* is a story paper primarily. Stories in both fiction and narrative style are welcome. Poems, first-person anecdotes and humor are used as fillers. The purpose of *Live* is to present in short story form realistic characters who utilize biblical principles. We hope to challenge readers to take risks for God and to resolve their problems scripturally." Weekly. Circ. 115,000.

Needs: Religious/inspirational, prose poem and spiritual. "Inner city, ethnic, racial settings." No controversial stories about such subjects as feminism, war or capital punishment. Accepts 2 mss/issue. Recently published work by Sharon Lee Roberts, Robin Lee Shape, J. Grant Swank, Richard Maffeo, Leona A. Browning, Joe Seay, Sharon B. Miller and Paul Murrell. **Publishes 40 new writers/year.** Length: 500-1,700 words.

How to Contact: Send complete ms. Accepts queries by e-mail and fax. Social Security number and word count must be included. Simultaneous submissions OK. Reports in 6-8 weeks. Sample copy and guidelines for SASE.

Payment/Terms: Pays 10¢/word (first rights); 7¢/word (second rights) on acceptance.

Advice: "Study our publication and write good, inspirational true to life or fiction stories that will encourage people to become all they can be as Christians. Stories should go somewhere! Action, not just thought—life; interaction, not just insights. Heroes and heroines, suspense and conflict. Avoid simplistic, pietistic conclusions, preachy, critical or moralizing. We don't accept science or Bible fiction. Stories should be encouraging, challenging, humorous. Even problem-centered stories should be upbeat." Reserves the right to change titles, abbreviate length and clarify flashbacks for publication.

⭐ 💲 🔘 ▼ **MAGAZINE OF FANTASY AND SCIENCE FICTION,** P.O. Box 1806, New York NY 10159-1806. Phone/fax: (212)982-2676. E-mail: gordonfsf@aol.com. Website: www.sfsite.com/fsf (includes writer's guidelines, nonfiction features, current issue, information on back issues and links). **Editor:** Gordon Van Gelder. Magazine: illustrations on cover only. Publishes "science fiction and fantasy. Our readers are age 13 and up who are interested in science fiction and fantasy." Monthly. Estab. 1949. Circ. 50,000.

• *Magazine of Fantasy and Science Fiction* has won numerous awards including two Nebulas in 1997 and one in 1998 and 1999. The magazine ranks #4 on the latest *Writer's Digest* Fiction 50 list of top markets for fiction writers.

Needs: Fantasy and science fiction. Receives 500-600 unsolicited fiction submissions/month. Buys 8 fiction mss/issue ("on average"); 100-140 mss/year. Time between acceptance and publication varies; up to 3 years. Published work by Ray Bradbury, Esther M. Friesner, Stephen King and Gene Wolfe. **Publishes 3-8 new writers/ year.** Length: 25,000 words maximum. Publishes short shorts. Critiques rejected ms, "if quality warrants it." Sometimes recommends other markets.

How to Contact: Send complete ms with cover letter. Reports in 1 month on queries; 6-8 weeks on mss. SASE (or IRC). No simultaneous submissions. Sample copy for $5. Fiction guidelines for SASE.

Payment/Terms: Pays 5-8¢/word.

Terms: Pays on acceptance for first North American serial rights; foreign, option on anthology if requested.

Advice: "Our only real criterion for selecting fiction is how strongly it affects us when we read it. The manuscripts that stand out most are the ones that are prepared properly. Read a copy of the magazine first."

🔘 ▼ **MATURE LIVING,** Lifeway Christian Resources of the Southern Baptist Convention, MSN 140, 127 Ninth Ave. North, Nashville TN 37234-0140. (615)251-2191. Fax: (615)251-5008. E-mail: matureliving@bssb.com. **Editor:** Al Shackleford. Magazine: 8½ × 11; 52 pages; non-glare paper; slick cover stock; full color illustrations and photos. "Our magazine is Christian in content and the material required is what would appeal to 55 and over age group: inspirational, informational, nostalgic, humorous. Our magazine is distributed mainly through churches (especially Southern Baptist churches) that buy the magazine in bulk and distribute it to members in this age group." Monthly. Estab. 1977. Circ. 360,000.

• *Mature Living* received the gold award in the 1998 National Mature Media Awards.

Needs: Humor, religious/inspirational and senior citizen/retirement. Avoid all types of pornography, drugs, liquor, horror, science fiction and stories demeaning to the elderly. Receives 10 mss/month. Buys 1-2 mss/issue. Publishes ms an average of 1 year after acceptance. Published work by Burndean N. Sheffy, Pearl E. Trigg, Joyce M. Sixberry; **published new writers within the last year.** Length: 800-1,200 words (prefers 1,000).

How to Contact: Send complete ms with SASE. "No queries please." Include estimated word count and Social Security number. Reports in 2 months. Sample copy for $1. Guidelines for SASE.

Payment/Terms: Pays $75 on acceptance; 3 contributor's copies. $1 charge for extras. First rights if requested.

Advice: Mss are rejected because they are too long or subject matter unsuitable. "Our readers seem to enjoy an occasional short piece of fiction. It must be believable, however, and present senior adults in a favorable light."

$ Ⓛ Ⓞ MATURE YEARS, United Methodist Publishing House, 201 Eighth Ave. S., Nashville TN 37202. (615)749-6292. Fax: (615)749-6512. Editor: Marvin W. Cropsey. Magazine: 8½×11; 112 pages; illustrations and photos. Magazine "helps persons in and nearing retirement to appropriate the resources of the Christian faith as they seek to face the problems and opportunities related to aging." Quarterly. Estab. 1953.

Needs: Humor, intergenerational relationships, nostalgia, older adult issues, religious/inspirational, spiritual (for older adults). "We don't want anything poking fun at old age, saccharine stories or anything not for older adults. Must show older adults (age 55 plus) in a positive manner." Accepts 1 ms/issue, 4 mss/year. Publishes ms 1 year after acceptance. Published work by Ann S. Gray, Betty Z. Walker and Vickie Elaine Legg. **Published new writers within the last year.** Length: 1,000-1,800 words.

How to Contact: Send complete ms with SASE and Social Security number. No simultaneous submissions. Reports in 2 months. Sample copy for 10½×11 SAE and $5.

Payment/Terms: Pays 6¢/word on acceptance.

Advice: "Practice writing dialogue! Listen to people talk; take notes; master dialogue writing! Not easy, but well worth it! Most inquiry letters are far too long. If you can't sell me an idea in a brief paragraph, you're not going to sell the reader on reading your finished article or story."

Ⓝ Ⓛ Ⓨ MESSAGE MAGAZINE, Review and Herald Publishing Association, 55 W. Oak Ridge Dr., Hagerstown MD 21740. (301)393-4099. Fax: (301)393-4103. E-mail: message@rhpa.com. Website: www.messa gemagazine.org (abstracts, current cover, recipes, contact information and features). **Editor:** Dr. Ron C. Smith. Magazine: 8½×11; 31 pages; illustrations and photos. *MESSAGE* is a "Christian outreach magazine dealing with a variety of topics. Our primary audience is African-American." Bimonthly. Estab. 1798. Circ. 70,000.

• *MESSAGE* is the recipient of numerous awards from the Evangelical Press Association.

Needs: Religious/inspirational, young adult/teen. Upcoming theme: "Educational Issue" (importance of education). Receives 5 mss/month. Accepts 1 ms/issue; 7 mss/year. Length: 500-700 words average.

How to Contact: Send complete ms with cover letter. SASE. Include maximum 40-word bio, Social Security number, address and telephone number. Reports in 6-10 months on mss. Send a disposable copy of ms or SASE for return of ms. Electronic submissions OK. "We prefer not to reprint articles." Sample copy and fiction guidelines free.

Payment/Terms: Pays $50-300 and 3 contributor's copies on acceptance. Acquires first North American serial rights.

Advice: "*MESSAGE* does not accept a lot of fiction. The one department we might accept fiction for is our MESSAGE Jr. section. This department is for elementary-aged children and usually teaches some sort of biblical or moral lesson. However, the lessons are sometimes taught via fictitious stories."

✤ $ Ⓛ MESSENGER OF THE SACRED HEART, Apostleship of Prayer, 661 Greenwood Ave., Toronto, Ontario M4J 4B3 Canada. (416)466-1195. **Editors:** Rev. F.J. Power, S.J. and Alfred DeManche. Magazine: 7×10; 32 pages; coated paper; self-cover; illustrations; photos. Magazine for "Canadian and U.S. Catholics interested in developing a life of prayer and spirituality; stresses the great value of our ordinary actions and lives." Monthly. Estab. 1891. Circ. 14,000.

Needs: Religious/inspirational. Stories about people, adventure, heroism, humor, drama. No poetry. Accepts 1 ms/issue. Length: 750-1,500 words. Recommends other markets.

How to Contact: Send complete ms with SAE. No simultaneous submissions. Reports in 1 month. Sample copy for $1.50 (Canadian).

Payment/Terms: Pays 6¢/word, 3 contributor's copies on acceptance for first North American serial rights. Rarely buys reprints.

Advice: "Develop a story that sustains interest to the end. Do not preach, but use plot and characters to convey the message or theme. Aim to move the heart as well as the mind. If you can, add a light touch or a sense of humor to the story. Your ending should have impact, leaving a moral or faith message for the reader."

✓ Ⓛ Ⓞ Ⓨ MIDSTREAM, A Monthly Jewish Review, Theodor Herzl Foundation, 633 Third Ave., 21st Floor, New York NY 10017-6706. (212)339-6046. **Editor:** Joel Carmichael. Magazine: 8½×11; 48 pages; 50 lb. paper; 65 lb. white smooth cover stock. "We are a Zionist journal; we publish material with Jewish themes or that would appeal to a Jewish readership." Published 8 times/year. Estab. 1954. Circ. 10,000.

• Work published in *Midstream* was included in the *O. Henry Award* prize anthology.

Needs: Historical (general), humor/satire, literary, mainstream, translations. Want to see more "serious short stories regarding themes of Jewish /Zionists intetest whether religious, secular or political. Also needs background. Upcoming themes: "April issue each year is devoted to Holocaust themes. But since we publish only one piece of fiction per issue, there is a considerable backlog." Receives 15-20 unsolicited mss/month. Accepts 1 mss/issue; 10 mss/year. Publishes ms 6-18 months after acceptance. Agented fiction 10%. Recently published work by Curt Leviant, Leo Haber, Larry Lederman and Ira Gold. Length: 2,500 words average; 1,500 words minimum; 4,500 words maximum. Sometimes critiques rejected mss.

How to Contact: Send complete ms with cover letter, which should include "address, telephone, or affiliation of author; state that the ms is fiction." Reports in "up to 6 months." SASE.

Payment/Terms: Pays 5¢/word and contributor's copies on publication for first rights.

Advice: "Be patient—we publish only one piece of fiction per issue and we have a backlog. A writer may have to wait two or three years before publication."

$ ◐ ◎ MONTANA SENIOR NEWS, Barrett-Whitman Co., Box 3363, Great Falls MT 59403. (406)761-0305. Fax: (406)761-8358. E-mail: montsrnews@imt.net. **Editor:** Jack Love. Tabloid: 11×17; 60-80 pages; newsprint paper and cover; illustrations; photos. Publishes "everything of interest to seniors, except most day-to-day political items like Social Security and topics covered in the daily news. Personal profiles of seniors, their lives, times and reminiscences." Bimonthly. Estab. 1984. Circ. 27,000.
Needs: Historical, senior citizen/retirement, western (historical or contemporary). No fiction "unrelated to experiences to which seniors can relate." Buys 1 or fewer mss/issue; 4-5 mss/year. Length: 500-800 words preferred. Publishes short stories. Length: under 500 words.
How to Contact: Send complete ms with cover letter and phone number. Only responds to selected mss. Simultaneous and reprint submissions OK. Accepts queries by e-mail. Sample copy for 9×12 SAE and $2 postage and handling.
Payment/Terms: Pays 4¢/word on publication for first rights or one-time rights.

☑ ◐ $ ☑ MY FRIEND, The Catholic Magazine for Kids, Pauline Books & Media, 50 St. Paul's Ave., Boston MA 02130. (617)522-8911. E-mail: myfriend@pauline.org. **Editor:** Sister Kathryn James Hermes. Magazine: 8½×11; 32 pages; smooth, glossy paper and cover stock; illustrations; photos. Magazine of "religious truths and positive values for children in a format which is enjoyable and attractive. Each issue contains lives of saints, short stories, science corner, contests, projects, etc." Monthly during school year (September-June). Estab. 1979. Circ. 12,000.
• *My Friend* received third place in the Catholic Press Association's Best Short Story competition in 1998.
Needs: Juvenile, religious/inspirational, spiritual (children), sports (children). Receives 60 unsolicited fiction mss/month. Accepts 3-4 mss/issue; 30-40 mss/year. Published work by Rita Robinson, Mary Elizabeth Anderson and Sandra Humphrey. **Published new writers within the past year.** Length: 200 words minimum; 900 words maximum; 600 words average.
How to Contact: Send complete ms with SASE. Reports in 1-2 months on mss. Publishes ms an average of 1 year after acceptance. Sample copy for $2 and 9×12 SAE ($1.24 postage).
Payment/Terms: Pays $20-150 (stories, articles).
Advice: "We are particularly interested in fun and amusing stories with backbone. Good dialogue, realistic character development, current lingo are necessary. We have a need for each of these types at different times. We prefer child-centered stories in a real-world setting."

N ⊕ ◯ MY WEEKLY, For Women Everywhere, 80 Kingsway East, Dundee DD4 8SL Scotland. 01382 223131. Fax: 01382 452471. E-mail: kmilne@dcthomsonco.uk. **Editor:** H.G. Watson.
Needs: "*My Weekly* is a widely read magazine aimed at 'young' women of all ages. We are read by busy young mothers, active middle-aged wives and elderly retired ladies." Historical, humor, mainstream/contemporary, romance, serialized novel. No science fiction, fantasy or gratuitously sexual stories. Wants more "historical short stories; and seasonal stories (not Christmas so much—more New Year, Mother's, Father's Day, Easter; Valentine Day, etc.)." Accepts 4-5 mss/issue. Agented fiction 10%. Recently published work by Lavyrle Spencer, Catherine Cookson and Nicholas Sparks. Fiction "should deal with real, down-to-earth themes that relate to the lives of our readers. Endings should always be hopeful. Complete stories can be of any length from 1,000 to 3,500 words. Serials from 3 to 10 installments."
How to Contact: Send complete ms with cover letter. Include estimated word count. Simultaneous submissions OK.
Payment/Terms: Our rates compare favourably with other British magazines. Sample copy and guidelines free. Pays in contributor's copies. Acquires first British rights.
Advice: *My Weekly* is looking for fiction that is "original, warm and sympathetic with credible characters, logical storylines and a gripping opening sentence. Study your market. Don't attempt to patronize your readers. Never upset the fiction ficton editor!"

$ ◎ NA'AMAT WOMAN, Magazine of NA'AMAT USA, The Women's Labor Zionist Organization of America, 200 Madison Ave., New York NY 10016-3903. (212)725-8010. **Editor:** Judith A. Sokoloff. "Magazine covering a wide variety of subjects of interest to the Jewish community—including political and social issues, arts, profiles; many articles about Israel; and women's issues. Fiction must have a Jewish theme. Readers are the American Jewish community." Published 4 times/year. Estab. 1926. Circ. 20,000.
Needs: Contemporary, ethnic, literary. Receives 10 unsolicited fiction mss/month. Accepts 3-5 fiction mss/year. Length: 1,500 words minimum; 3,000 words maximum. Also buys nonfiction.
How to Contact: Query first or send complete ms with SASE. Reports in 3 months on mss. Free sample copy for 9×11½ SAE and $1.20 postage.
Payment/Terms: Pays 10¢/word and 2 contributor's copies on publication for first North American serial rights; assignments on work-for-hire basis.
Advice: "No maudlin nostalgia or romance; no hackneyed Jewish humor and no poetry."

☑ $ ● **NEW MYSTERY**, The Best New Mystery Stories, 101 W. 23rd St., PMB#7, New York NY 10010-7703. (212)353-1582. Fax: (212)353-3495. E-mail: newmyste@erols.com. Website: www.NewMystery.com (includes book and film reviews and short shorts). **Editor:** Charles Raisch III. Magazine: 8½×11; 96 pages; illustrations and photographs. "Mystery, suspense and crime." Quarterly. Estab. 1990. Circ. 90,000.

• Fiction published in *New Mystery* has been nominated for Edgar, Blaggard Shamus, Macavity and Anthony awards for best short story of the year. Response time for this magazine seems to be slower in summer months. The mystery included here is varied and realistic.

Needs: Mystery/suspense (cozy to hardboiled). No horror or romance. Wants more suspense and espionage. Plans special annual anthology. Receives 350 unsolicited mss/month. Buys 6-10 ms/issue. Agented fiction 50%. Published work by Stuart Kaminsky, Andrew Greeley and Rosemary Santini. **Publishes 1 new writer/issue.** Length: 3,000-5,000 words preferred. Also buys short book reviews 500-3,000 words. Sometimes critiques rejected mss.

How to Contact: *New Mystery charges a $7 fee for purchase of a contributor's packet, which includes guidelines and 2 sample copies.* Send complete ms with cover letter. "We cannot be responsible for unsolicited manuscripts." Reports on ms in 1 month. SASE. Sample copy for $5, 9×12 SAE and 4 first-class stamps.

Payment/Terms: Pays $25-1,000 on publication for negotiated rights.

Advice: Stories should have "believable characters in trouble; sympathetic lead; visual language." Sponsors "Annual First Story Contest."

☑ ● **THE NEW YORKER**, The New Yorker, Inc., 4 Times Square, New York NY 10036. (212)536-5800. Fiction Department. A quality magazine of interesting, well-written stories, articles, essays and poems for a literate audience. Weekly. Estab. 1925. Circ. 750,000.

How to Contact: Send complete ms with SASE. Reports in 10-12 weeks on mss. Publishes 1 ms/issue.

Payment/Terms: Varies. Pays on acceptance.

Advice: "Be lively, original, not overly literary. Write what you want to write, not what you think the editor would like. Send poetry to Poetry Department."

☑ $ ◐ **NUGGET**, Dugent Corp., 14411 Commerce Way, Suite 420, Miami Lakes FL 33016. (305)362-5580. **Editor-in-Chief:** Christopher James. A newsstand magazine designed to have erotic appeal for a fetish-oriented audience. Published 13 times a year. Estab. 1956. Circ. 100,000.

Needs: Offbeat, fetish-oriented material encompassing a variety of subjects (B&D, TV, TS, spanking, amputeeism, golden showers, infantalism, catfighting, etc.). Most fiction includes several sex scenes. No fiction that concerns children or religious subjects. Accepts 2 mss/issue. Agented fiction 5%. Length: 2,000-3,500 words.

How to Contact: Send complete ms with SASE. Reports in 1 month. Sample copy for $5. Guidelines for legal-sized SASE.

Payment/Terms: Pays minimum $200 and 1 contributor's copy on publication for first rights.

Advice: "Keep in mind the nature of the publication, which is fetish erotica. Subject matter can vary, but we prefer fetish themes."

$ ◐ **ON THE LINE**, Mennonite Publishing House, 616 Walnut Ave., Scottdale PA 15683-1999. (724)887-8500. Website: www.mph.org (includes guidelines and general information). **Editor:** Mary Clemens Meyer. Magazine: 7×10; 28 pages; illustrations; some photos. "A Christian magazine with the goal of helping children grow in their understanding and appreciation of God, the created world, themselves and other people." For children ages 9-14. Weekly. Estab. 1970. Circ. 6,000.

Needs: Problem-solving stories with Christian values for older children and young teens (9-14 years). No fantasy or fictionalized Bible stories. Wants more mystery and humorous. Receives 50-100 unsolicited mss/month. Accepts 52 mss/year. Recently published work by Joyce Styron Madsen, Brenda A. Witmer, Virginia Kroll and Heather Klassen. **Publishes 10-20 new writers/year.** Length: 800-1,500 words.

How to Contact: Send complete ms noting whether author is offering first-time or reprint rights. Reports in 1 month. SASE. Simultaneous and previously published work OK. Free sample copy and fiction guidelines.

Payment/Terms: Pays on acceptance for one-time rights.

Advice: "We believe in the power of story to entertain, inspire and challenge the reader to new growth. Know children and their thoughts, feelings and interests. Be realistic with characters and events in the fiction. Stories do not need to be true, but need to *feel* true. We look for easy readibility, realistic kids and grownups, humor, fun characters and plot movement without excessive description. Watch kids, interact with kids, listen to kids. It will show up in your writing."

$ ◐ ◎ **OPTIONS, The *Bi*-Monthly**, AJA Publishing, Box 170, Irvington NY 10533. E-mail: dianaeditr@aol.com. Website: www.youngandtight.com/men (includes short fiction). **Associate Editor:** Diana Sheridan. Magazine: digest-sized; 114 pages; newsprint paper; glossy cover stock; illustrations and photos. Sexually explicit magazine for and about bisexuals. "Please read our Advice subhead." 10 issues/year. Estab. 1982. Circ. 100,000.

Needs: Erotica, bisexual, gay, lesbian. "First person as-if-true experiences." Accepts 6 unsolicited fiction mss/issue. "Very little" of fiction is agented. **Published new writers within the last year.** Length: 2,000-3,000 words. Sometimes critiques rejected mss.

How to Contact: Send complete ms with or without cover letter. No simultaneous submissions. Reports in approximately 3 weeks. SASE. Electronic submissions (disk or e-mail as textfiles) OK. "Submissions on disk welcome, but please include hard copy too." Sample copy for $2.95 and 6×9 SAE with 5 first-class stamps. Fiction guidelines for SASE.

Payment/Terms: Pays $100 on publication for all rights. Will reassign book rights on request.

Advice: "Read a copy of *Options* carefully and look at our spec sheet before writing anything for us. That's not new advice, but to judge from some of what we get in the mail, it's necessary to repeat. We only buy two bi/lesbian pieces per issue; need is greater for bi/gay male mss. Though we're a bi rather than gay magazine, the emphasis is on same-sex relationships. If the readers want to read about a male/female couple, they'll buy another magazine. Gay male stories sent to *Options* will also be considered for publication in *Beau*, or one of our other gay male magazines. Must get into the hot action by 1,000 words into the story. (Sooner is fine too!) *Most important:* We *only* publish male/male stories that feature 'safe sex' practices unless the story is clearly something that took place pre-AIDS."

PEOPLE'S FRIEND, D.C. Thomson & Co., Ltd., 80 Kingsway East, Dundee DD4 8SL Scotland. 01382 223131. Fax: 01382 452491. **Fiction Editor:** Margaret McCoy. Weekly. Circ. 470,000.

Needs: Specializes in women's fiction. "British backgrounds preferred (but not essential) by our readership. Quite simply, we aim to entertain. Stories should have believable, well-developed characters in situations our readers can relate to. Our readers tend to be traditionalists." No stories of the supernatural or extreme sex or violence. Published work by Betty McInnes, Shirley Worral and Christina Jones. "We actively encourage new authors and do our best to help and advise." Publishes 5 stories/issue. Length: 1,000-3,000 words.

Payment/Terms: Pays $75-85 and contributor's copies. Sample copy and guidelines available on application.

Advice: Looks for manuscript with "emotional content and characterization."

PLAYBOY MAGAZINE, 680 N. Lake Shore Dr., Chicago IL 60611. (312)751-8000. Contact: Fiction Editor. Monthly magazine. "As the world's largest general-interest lifestyle magazine for men, *Playboy* spans the spectrum of contemporary men's passions. From hard-hitting investigative journalism to light-hearted humor, the latest in fashion and personal technology to the cutting edge of the popular culture, *Playboy* is and always has been both guidebook and dream book for generations of American men . . . the definitive source of information and ideas for over 10 million readers each month. In addition, *Playboy*'s 'Interview' and '20 Questions' present profiles of politicians, athletes and today's hottest personalities." Estab. 1953, Circ. 3,283,000.

How to Contact: Query first. "Fiction manuscripts must be no longer than 7,500 words for acceptance."

Advice: "*Playboy* does not consider poetry, plays, story outlines or novel-length manuscripts."

POCKETS, Devotional Magazine for Children, The Upper Room, 1908 Grand Ave., Box 189, Nashville TN 37202. (615)340-7333. E-mail: pockets@upperroom.org. Website: www.upperroom.org/pockets (includes themes, guidelines and contest guidelines). Editor-in-Chief: Janet R. Knight. **Associate Editor:** Lynn W. Gilliam. Magazine: 7×9; 48 pages; 50 lb. white econowrite paper; 80 lb. white coated, heavy cover stock; color and 2-color illustrations; some photos. Magazine for children ages 6-12, with articles specifically geared for ages 8 to 11. "The magazine offers stories, activities, prayers, poems—all geared to giving children a better understanding of themselves as children of God." Published monthly except for January. Estab. 1981. Estimated circ. 99,000.

• *Pockets* has received honors from the Educational Press Association of America. The magazine's fiction tends to feature children dealing with real-life situations "from a faith perspective." *Pockets* ranked #15 on *Writer's Digest*'s Fiction 50 list of top markets for fiction writers.

Needs: Adventure, contemporary, ethnic, historical (general), juvenile, religious/inspirational and suspense/mystery. No fantasy, science fiction, talking animals. "All submissions should address the broad theme of the magazine. Each issue will be built around one theme with material which can be used by children in a variety of ways. Scripture stories, fiction, poetry, prayers, art, graphics, puzzles and activities will all be included. Submissions do not need to be overtly religious. They should help children experience a Christian lifestyle that is not always a neatly-wrapped moral package, but is open to the continuing revelation of God's will. Seasonal material, both secular and liturgical, is desired. No violence, horror, sexual and racial stereotyping or fiction containing heavy moralizing." No talking animal stories or fantasy. Receives approximately 200 unsolicited fiction mss/month. Accepts 4-5 mss/issue; 44-60 mss/year. Publishes short shorts. A peace-with-justice theme will run throughout the magazine. Published work by Peggy King Anderson, Angela Gibson and John Steptoe. Published new writers last year. Length: 600 words minimum; 1,600 words maximum; 1,200 words average.

How to Contact: Send complete ms with SASE. Previously published submissions OK, but no simultaneous or faxed submissions. Reports in 1 month on mss. Publishes ms 1 year to 18 months after acceptance. Sample

---

INTERESTED IN A PARTICULAR GENRE? Check our sections for: **Mystery/Suspense**, page 46; **Romance**, page 55; **Science Fiction & Fantasy**, page 67.

copy free with SAE and 4 first-class stamps. Fiction guidelines and themes with SASE. "Strongly advise sending for themes before submitting."

Payment/Terms: Pays 14¢/word and up and 2-5 contributor's copies on acceptance for first North American serial rights. $1.95 charge for extras; $1 each for 10 or more.

Advice: "Listen to children as they talk with each other. Please send for a sample copy as well as guidelines and themes. Many ms we receive are simply inappropriate. Each issue is theme-related. Please send for list of themes. New themes published in December of each year. Include SASE." Sponsors annual fiction writing contest. Deadline: Aug. 15. Send for guidelines. $1,000 award and publication.

PORTLAND MAGAZINE, Maine's City Magazine,, 578 Congress St., Portland ME 04101. (207)775-4339. **Editor:** Colin Sargent. Magazine: 56 pages; 60 lb. paper; 80 lb. cover stock; illustrations and photographs. "City lifestyle magazine—style, business, real estate, controversy, fashion, cuisine, interviews and art relating to the Maine area." Monthly. Estab. 1986. Circ. 100,000.

Needs: Contemporary, historical, literary. Receives 20 unsolicited fiction mss/month. Accepts 1 mss/issue; 10 mss/year. Publishes short shorts. Published work by Janwillem van de Wetering, Sanford Phippen and Mame Medwed. Length: 3 double-spaced typed pages.

How to Contact: Query first. "Fiction below 700 words, please." Send complete ms with cover letter. Reports in 6 months. SASE. Accepts electronic submissions.

Payment/Terms: Pays on publication for first North American serial rights.

Advice: "We publish ambitious short fiction featuring everyone from Frederick Barthelme to newly discovered fiction by Edna St. Vincent Millay."

★ ✔ $⊘ **POWER AND LIGHT,** Word Action Publishing Company, 6401 The Paseo, Kansas City MO 64131-1284. (816)333-7000. Fax: (816)333-4439. E-mail: mprice@nazarene.org. **Editor:** Beula J. Postlewait. Story paper: 5½×8; 8 pages; storypaper and newsprint; illustrations and photos. "Relates Sunday School learning to preteens' lives. Must reflect theology of the Church of the Nazarene." Weekly. Estab. 1993. Circ. 30,000.

• *Power and Light* would like to see fiction with more natural, contemporary, positive situations.

Needs: Children's/juvenile (1-4 years; 10-12 years): adventure, fantasy (children's fantasy), religious/inspirational. List of upcoming themes available for SASE. Receives 40 mss/month. Accepts 10 mss/year. Publishes ms 2 years after acceptance. Recently published work by Bob Hostetler and Evelyn Horan. **Publishes 10 new writers/year.** Length: 700 words average; 650-700 words minimum; 750 words maximum. Often critiques or comments on rejected mss.

How to Contact: Query first ("E-mail response is much quicker and more convenient for queries"). Include estimated word count and Social Security number. Reports in 1 month on queries; 3 months on mss. SASE for reply or return or ms. Simultaneous, reprint and electronic (IBM disk or e-mail) submissions OK. Sample copy for #10 SASE. Fiction guidelines for #10 SASE.

Payment/Terms: Pays 5¢/word and 4 contributor's copies on publication for multi-use rights.

Advice: Looks for "creativity—situations relating to preteens that are not trite such as shoplifting, etc."

[N] $⊘ ▼ **ELLERY QUEEN'S MYSTERY MAGAZINE,** Dell Magazines, 475 Park Ave. S., New York NY 10016. (212)686-7188. (212)686-7414. Website: www.mysterypages.com (includes writer's guidelines, short fiction, book reviews and magazine's history and awards). **Editor:** Janet Hutchings. Magazine: 5⅜×8½; 144 pages with special 240-page combined September/October issue. Magazine for lovers of mystery fiction. Published 11 times/year. Estab. 1941. Circ. 500,000 readers.

• *EQMM* has won numerous awards and sponsors its own award for Best Stories of the Year, nominated by its readership.

Needs: "We accept only mystery, crime, suspense and detective fiction." No explicit sex or violence. Wants more classical who-dun-its. Receives approximately 400 unsolicited fiction mss each month. Accepts 10-15 mss/issue. Publishes ms 6-12 months after acceptance. Agented fiction 50%. Recently published work by Laurence Block, Joyce Carol Oats, John Mortimer and Minette Walters. **Publishes 11 new writers/year.** Length: up to 7,000 words, occasionally longer. Publishes 1-2 short novels of up to 17,000 words/year by established authors; minute mysteries of 250 words; short, humorous mystery verse. Critiques rejected mss "only when a story might be a possibility for us if revised." Sometimes recommends other markets.

How to Contact: Send complete ms with SASE. Cover letter should include publishing credits and brief biographical sketch. Simultaneous submissions OK. Reports in 3 months or sooner on mss. Fiction guidelines with SASE. Sample copy for $5.

Payment/Terms: Pays 3¢/word and up on acceptance for first North American serial rights. Occasionally buys reprints.

Advice: "We have a Department of First Stories and usually publish at least one first story an issue—i.e., the author's first published fiction. We select stories that are fresh and of the kind our readers have expressed a liking for. In writing a detective story, you must play fair with the reader, providing clues and necessary information. Otherwise you have a better chance of publishing if you avoid writing to formula."

⊞ $⊘ **RADIANCE, The Magazine for Large Women,** Box 30246, Oakland CA 94604. (510)482-0680. Website: www.radiancemagazine.com. **Editor:** Alice Ansfield. Fiction Editors: Alice Ansfield and Catherine Taylor. Magazine: 8½×11; 64 pages; glossy/coated paper; 70 lb. cover stock; illustrations; photos. "Theme is to encourage women to live fully now, whatever their body size. To stop waiting to live or feel good about themselves until they lose weight." Quarterly. Estab. 1984. Circ. 17,000. Readership: 80,000.

Needs: Adventure, contemporary, erotica, ethnic, fantasy, feminist, historical, humor/satire, mainstream, mystery/suspense, prose poem, science fiction, spiritual, sports, young adult/teen. "Want fiction to have a larger-bodied character; living in a positive, upbeat way. Our goal is to empower women." Receives 150 mss/month. Accepts 40 mss/year. Publishes ms within 1-2 years of acceptance. Published work by Marla Zarrow, Sallie Tisdale and Mary Kay Blakely. **Publishes 15 new writers/year.** Length: 2,000 words average; 1,000 words minimum; 5,000 words maximum. Publishes short shorts. Sometimes critiques rejected mss.

How to Contact: Query with clips of published work and send complete ms with cover letter. Reports in 3-4 months. SASE. Reprint submissions OK. Sample copy for $3.50. Guidelines for #10 SASE. Reviews novels and short story collections "with at least one large-size heroine."

Payment/Terms: Pays $35-100 and contributor's copies on publication for one-time rights. Sends galleys to the author if requested.

Advice: "Read our magazine before sending anything to us. Know what our philosophy and points of view are before sending a manuscript. Look around your community for inspiring, successful and unique large women doing things worth writing about. At this time, prefer fiction having to do with a larger woman (man, child). *Radiance* is one of the leading resources in the size-acceptance movement. Each issue profiles dynamic large women from all walks of life, along with articles on health, media, fashion and politics. Our audience is the 30 million American women who wear a size 16 or over. Feminist, emotionally-supportive, quarterly magazine."

⊘ **REDBOOK**, The Hearst Corporation, 224 W. 57th St., New York NY 10019. (212)649-2000. **Fiction Editor:** Dawn Raffel. Magazine: 8×10¾; 150-250 pages; 34 lb. paper; 70 lb. cover; illustrations; photos. "*Redbook's* readership consists of American women, ages 25-44. Most are well-educated, married, have children and also work outside the home." Monthly. Estab. 1903. Circ. 3,200,000.

Needs: Query. *Redbook* was not accepting unsolicited mss at the time of publication.

✓ $⊘ ◎ ✓ **REFORM JUDAISM,** Union of American Hebrew Congregations, 633 3rd Ave., New York NY 10017. (212)650-4240. Website: www.uahc.org/rjmag/ (includes writer's guidelines, general information, past issues, and more). **Editor:** Aron Hirt-Manheimer. Managing Editor: Joy Weinberg. Magazine: 8×10¾; 96 pages; illustrations; photos. "We cover subjects of Jewish interest in general and Reform Jewish in particular, for members of Reform Jewish congregations in the United States and Canada." Quarterly. Estab. 1972. Circ. 310,000.

• Recipient of The Simon Rockower Award for Excellence in Jewish Journalism for feature writing, graphic design and photography. The editor says they would publish more stories if they could find excellent, sophisticated, contemporary Jewish fiction.

Needs: Humor/satire, religious/inspirational. Receives 75 unsolicited mss/month. Buys 3 mss/year. Publishes ms 6 months after acceptance. Recently published work by Frederick Fastow and Bob Sloan. Length: 1,500 words average; 600 words minimum; 3,500 words maximum.

How to Contact: Send complete ms with cover letter. Reports in 6 weeks. SASE for ms. "For quickest response send self addressed stamped postcard with choices: "Yes, we're interested in publishing; Maybe, we'd like to hold for future consideration; No, we've decided to pass on publication." Simultaneous submissions OK. Sample copy for $3.50.

Payment/Terms: Pays 30¢/word on publication for first North American serial rights.

⊞ ✓ $⊘ ✓ **ST. ANTHONY MESSENGER,**, 1615 Republic St., Cincinnati OH 45210-1298. E-mail: stanthony@americancatholic.org. Website: www.AmericanCatholic.org (includes Saint of the day, selected articles, product information). **Editor:** Father Jack Wintz, O.F.M., O.F.M. Magazine: 8×10¾; 60 pages; illustrations; photos. "*St. Anthony Messenger* is a Catholic family magazine which aims to help its readers lead more fully human and Christian lives. We publish articles which report on a changing church and world, opinion pieces written from the perspective of Christian faith and values, personality profiles, and fiction which entertains and informs." Monthly. Estab. 1893. Circ. 333,000.

• This is a leading Catholic magazine, but has won awards for both religious and secular journalism and writing from the Catholic Press Association, the International Association of Business Communicators and the Cincinnati Editors Association. *St. Anthony Messenger* ranked #41 on *Writer's Digest's* Fiction 50 list of top markets for fiction writers.

Needs: Contemporary, religious/inspirational, romance, senior citizen/retirement and spiritual. "We do not want mawkishly sentimental or preachy fiction. Stories are most often rejected for poor plotting and characterization; bad dialogue—listen to how people talk; inadequate motivation. Many stories say nothing, are 'happenings' rather than stories." No fetal journals, no rewritten Bible stories. Receives 70-80 unsolicited fiction mss/month. Accepts 1 ms/issue; 12 mss/year. Publishes ms up to 1 year after acceptance. Recently published work by Bette Ann Gibson-Rieth, Karen Muensterman, Jacquelin Guidry and Cherie Langlois. Length: 2,000-3,000 words.

insider report

St. Anthony Messenger publishes fiction for *today's* Catholics

Barbara Beckwith

One of the perks of being managing editor at the religious magazine *St. Anthony Messenger* is the travel. Just last year Barbara Beckwith journeyed to the breathtaking cities of Rome, Geneva, Paris and Montreal. Responsible for the book review section and composing two articles and three editorials a year, she declares the "plum" of her job is still the writing. "Although I now take some pride in being able to encourage the writing of others," adds Beckwith. "When I read great short stories that have come in to our magazine, I get a tingle in my spine—and that tingle is never wrong."

Fiction published in *St. Anthony Messenger* has made it into *Prize Stories: The O. Henry Awards* and received honors from the Catholic Press Association among others. Reaching a wider audience, a short story featured in the magazine was adapted into the movie *Testament*. Beckwith says, "When fiction is good, it can be really powerful: cathartic, thought-provoking, even humorous."

Beckwith supervises an editorial team of an assistant managing editor, four assistant editors and three editorial assistants to coordinate the copyediting and proofreading of the entire magazine. She collaborated on the following interview with her assistant editor in charge of fiction, Sandy Howison, acknowledging, "Frankly, Sandy sees more of the bad submissions than I do, thank heavens."

How is *St. Anthony Messenger* different from other publications?
We are a religious publication, Catholic to the core, but we view religion broadly, seeing how every aspect of life should be affected by one's faith. We are a popular (not academic) publication that focuses on the experiences of real people and uses many concrete examples and applications. We encourage dialogue with our readers and love to see letters to the editor; in fact, we want to take advantage of the interactivity of the Web to improve that two-way communication.

The magazine is owned by the Franciscan friars, and that sets our tone: Church builders—and not critics for criticism's sake, yet not afraid to criticize when necessary; pastoral and compassionate; peace-loving and concerned for ecology; engaged with the world but not overpowered by it; practical rather than theoretical; orthodox but not stuffy; part of the international Church with a strong social justice tradition.

We have a circulation of 338,000, which makes us the second largest, paid-subscription Catholic magazine. That gives us a major responsibility in faith formation and as a trendsetter.

Many other general interest magazines are deleting fiction from their regular contents, but we find fiction has a power that articles do not—when it's well-written. Just after Christmas, for instance, we were considering an article about a real Kentucky death-row execution and a short story from the perspective of a mother whose daughter was killed as a bystander in a robbery. Both were anti-death penalty in intent, but we chose to buy the short story, which conveyed the emotional anguish better without being argumentative.

Could you outline the editorial process?

Manuscripts go first to Sandy who for 15 years has pruned out about 80 percent of them. She combs through our manuscripts carefully, fairly and promptly, and always comes up with the gems. The remaining 20 percent go to all the editors (eight) for reading and critique. In the end, the senior editor decides which will be bought. I function as the second copyeditor on everything.

What does Sandy look for in fiction submissions?

1. A well-written story with three-dimensional characters and realistic dialogue.
2. A story that's emotional without being maudlin and religious without being preachy.
3. A story that's not offensive to Catholic doctrine or sensibilities.
4. A story that's suitable for our audience (mostly female, mostly over 50, yet contemporary).
5. Fresh ideas or new ways of looking at common plots.

Describe the mistakes you commonly see in submissions.

Many don't take time to make their manuscript the best it can be *before* submitting it to us. We get lots of manuscripts full of typos and grammatical errors. Those small things make an editor distrust the accuracy of the larger things, like keeping tenses consistent and making sure that the flowers mentioned bloom in the season of the story, etc.

Many don't research our magazine sufficiently, and don't take advantage of the free writer's guidelines and sample copies we send to any prospective writer. We accept religious pieces from other religious perspectives, but they need to acknowledge our prime audience: Catholics. We use Catholic language to talk about religion on such topics as sacraments. We've gotten some stories that deal with extramarital sex, for instance, or contain language that would be offensive to our readers. No way would we publish these.

Many fiction manuscripts employ predictable plots. Every Christmas we get several stories set in modern times with "Joe" and his pregnant wife "Maria," who are homeless and need a place to stay. Guess when she has the baby?

We also get children's stories and retold Bible stories—which, if writers studied our guidelines, we say we don't publish.

What do writers do that is unprofessional?

They tell us this submission is a sure-fire hit, it can't miss, our readers are sure to love it. They know it's either too long or not the kind of thing we usually publish, but send it anyway and tell us we can fix it up as we see fit. Or they start talking about payment when the manuscript is sent unsolicited, send a handwritten cover letter, or tell us a mother/grandfather/best friend/priest/writing teacher liked this manuscript and said it should be published. Some even say God told them to write it and send it to us.

I particularly hate phone calls that ask after two weeks if we're buying a manuscript. Our delines warn writers it takes us six to eight weeks to get manuscripts back. Not just to allow time for our team of readers but the U.S. Postal Service, which is not swifter than eagles.

Phone queries are difficult, as are e-mail queries, because it's hard to judge the caliber of the writing. And most queries on fiction are meaningless, because reducing a story to its simplest terms loses too much—just send it.

What's the biggest misconception about *St. Anthony Messenger*?

I think it's the belief that being religious means being overly holy, devout or preachy. Our fiction is geared toward Catholics living in the world today, not 40 years ago.

How often do you receive submissions that are *too* religious?

We see them all the time. They are full of holier-than-thou characters who quote Scripture at every turn. We want characters who talk and act like real people, who struggle with contemporary moral dilemmas, who try to do the right thing and may or may not fully succeed.

Strive for a realistic tone. Ask yourself: Is this believable? Would real people talk and act like this? Don't end the story with a paragraph that tells what the character learned or what the moral is. If it's good fiction, the reader will get the message without being hit over the head with it.

How can writers best prepare for publication in *St. Anthony Messenger*?

Prospective writers should take the time to know who we are and what kinds of fiction we publish. They should concentrate on telling a good story. If it's well-written, with three dimensional characters and realistic dialogue, that's half the battle.

—*Tara Horton*

Critiques rejected mss "when there is time." Sometimes recommends other markets.
How to Contact: Send complete ms with SASE. No simultaneous submissions. Accepts queries by e-mail and fax. Reports in 6-8 weeks. Sample copy and guidelines available. Reviews novels and short story collections. Send books to Barbara Beckwith, book review editor.
Payment/Terms: Pays 15¢/word maximum and 2 contributor's copies on acceptance for first serial rights; $1 charge for extras.
Advice: "We publish one story a month and we get up to 1,000 a year. Too many offer simplistic 'solutions' or answers. Pay attention to endings. Easy, simplistic, deus ex machina endings don't work. People have to feel characters in the stories are real and have a reason to care about them and what happens to them. Fiction entertains but can also convey a point and sound values."

$ SATURDAY NIGHT, Saturday Night Magazine Ltd., 184 Front St. E, Suite 400, Toronto, Ontario M5A 4N3 Canada. (416)368-7237. Fax: (416)368-5112. E-mail: editorial@saturdaynight.ca. **Editor:** Paul Tough. Contact: Tara Ariano, assistant to the editor. Monthly magazine. Readership is urban concentrated. Well-educated, with a high disposable income. Average age is 43. Estab. 1887. Circ. 410,000.
Needs: Publishes novel excerpts.
How to Contact: Submit seasonal material 3-4 months in advance. Accepts simultaneous submissions. Sample copy for $3.50. Writer's guidelines free.
Payment/Terms: Pays on receipt of a publishable ms. Buys first North American serial rights.

$ SEEK, Standard Publishing, 8121 Hamilton Ave., Cincinnati OH 45231-2396. (513)931-4050. Fax: (513)931-0950. Website: www.standardpub.com. **Editor:** Eileen H. Wilmoth. Magazine: 5½ × 8½; 8 pages; news-print paper; art and photos in each issue. "Inspirational stories of faith-in-action for Christian young adults; a Sunday School take-home paper." Weekly. Estab. 1970. Circ. 40,000.
• *Seek* ranked #38 on the *Writer's Digest*'s Fiction 50 list of top markets for fiction writers.
Needs: Religious/inspirational. Accepts 150 mss/year. Publishes ms an average of 1 year after acceptance. 20% of work published is by new writers. Length: 500-1,200 words.

How to Contact: Send complete ms with SASE. No simultaneous submissions. No queries by fax or e-mail. Reports in 2-3 months. Free sample copy and guidelines.
Payment/Terms: Pays 5¢/word on acceptance. Buys reprints.
Advice: "Write a credible story with Christian slant—no preachments; avoid overworked themes such as joy in suffering, generation gaps, etc. Most manuscripts are rejected by us because of irrelevant topic or message, unrealistic story, or poor character and/or plot development. We use fiction stories that are believable."

★ $⊘ **SEVENTEEN**, III Magazine Corp., 850 Third Ave., New York NY 10022-6258. **Fiction Editor:** Ben Schrank. Magazine: 8½×11; 125-400 pages; 40 lb. coated paper; 80 lb. coated cover stock; illustrations; photos. A general interest magazine with fashion; beauty care; pertinent topics such as current issues, attitudes, experiences and concerns of teenagers. Monthly. Estab. 1944. Circ. 2.5 million.
• *Seventeen* sponsors an annual fiction contest for writers age 13-21. *Seventeen* ranked #1 on *Writer's Digest*'s Fiction 50 list of top fiction markets.
Needs: High-quality literary fiction. No science fiction, action/adventure or pornography. Receives 200 unsolicited fiction mss/month. Accepts 6-12 mss/year. Agented fiction 50%. Published work by Margaret Atwood, Edna O'Brien, Blake Nelson, Joyce Carol Oates, Ellen Gilchrist and Pagan Kennedy. **Publishes 4-5 new writers/year.** Length: approximately 750-3,500 words.
How to Contact: Send complete ms with SASE and cover letter with relevant credits. Reports in 3 months on mss. Guidelines for submissions with SASE.
Payment/Terms: Pays $700-2,500 on acceptance for one-time rights.
Advice: "Respect the intelligence and sophistication of teenagers. *Seventeen* remains open to the surprise of new voices. Our commitment to publishing the work of new writers remains strong; we continue to read every submission we receive. We believe that good fiction can move the reader toward thoughtful examination of her own life as well as the lives of others—providing her ultimately with a fuller appreciation of what it means to be human. While stories that focus on female teenage experience continue to be of interest, the less obvious possibilities are equally welcome. We encourage writers to submit literary short stories concerning subjects that may not be immediately identifiable as 'teenage,' with narrative styles that are experimental and challenging. Too often, unsolicited submissions possess voices and themes condescending and unsophisticated. Also, writers hesitate to send stories to *Seventeen* which they think too violent or risqué. Good writing holds the imaginable and then some, and if it doesn't find its home here, we're always grateful for the introduction to a writer's work. We're more inclined to publish cutting edge fiction than simple, young adult fiction."

N ★ ○ ◎ **SKIN ART,** Outlaw Biker Enterprises, Inc., Box 447, Voorhees NJ 08043. **Editor:** Casey Exton. Magazine: 8½×11; 96 pages; 50 lb. coated paper; 80 lb. cover stock; illustrations; photos. "Art magazine devoted to showcasing the very best of modern tattooing." Published 9 times/year. Estab. 1988. Circ. 100,000.
Needs: Fiction pertaining to subject matter (tattooing). Receives 20 unsolicited mss/month. Publishes 1 fiction ms/issue. Publishes mss 2-8 months after acceptance. Length: 1,000-2,500 words. "Very open to freelance writers and unpublished writers. Freelance photographers also needed send SASE for guidelines and needs."
How to Contact: Send complete ms with cover letter and SASE. Responds to queries within 6 weeks. Sample copy for $5 and 8½×11 SAE with 2 first-class stamps.
Payment/Terms: Payment on publication varies according to quality of work. Buys all rights.
Advice: "Very targeted market, strongly suggest you read magazine before submitting work."

○ ◎ **SOJOURNER, The Women's Forum**, 42 Seaverns Ave., Jamaica Plain MA 02130. (617)524-0415. E-mail: info@sojourner.org. Website: www.sojourner.org. **Editor:** Stephanie Poggi. Magazine: 11×17; 48 pages; newsprint; illustrations; photos. "Feminist journal publishing interviews, nonfiction features, news, viewpoints, poetry, reviews (music, cinema, books) and fiction for women." Published monthly. Estab. 1975. Circ. 45,000.
Needs: "Writing on race, sex, class and queerness." Experimental, fantasy, feminist, lesbian, humor/satire, literary, prose poem and women's. Query for upcoming themes. Receives 20 unsolicited fiction mss/month. Accepts 10 mss/year. Agented fiction 10%. Published work by Ruth Ann Lonardelli and Janie Adams. **Published new writers within the last year.** Length: 1,000 words minimum; 4,000 words maximum; 2,500 words average.
How to Contact: Send complete ms with SASE and cover letter with description of previous publications; current works. Simultaneous submissions OK. Reports in 6-8 months. Publishes ms an average of 6 months after acceptance. Sample copy for $3 with 10×13 SASE. Fiction guidelines for SASE.
Payment/Terms: Pays subscription to magazine and 2 contributor's copies, $15 for first rights. No extra charge up to 5 contributor's copies; $1 charge each thereafter.
Advice: "Pay attention to appearance of manuscript! Very difficult to wade through sloppily presented fiction, however good. Do write a cover letter. If not cute, it can't hurt and may help. Mention previous publication(s)."

$⊘ **SPIDER, The Magazine for Children,** Carus Publishing Co./Cricket Magazine Group, P.O. Box 300, Peru IL 61354. 1-800-588-8585. **Editor-in-Chief:** Marianne Carus. Senior Editor: Laura Tillotson. Magazine: 8×10; 33 pages; illustrations and photos. "*Spider* publishes high-quality literature for beginning readers, mostly children ages 6 to 9." Monthly. Estab. 1994. Circ. 80,000.

• Carus Publishing also publishes *Cricket* magazine, *Ladybug, the Magazine for Young Children* and *Babybug*.

Needs: Children's/juvenile (6-9 years), fantasy (children's fantasy). "No religious, didactic, or violent stories, or anything that talks down to children." Accepts 4 mss/issue. Publishes ms 2-3 years after acceptance. Agented fiction 2%. Published work by Lissa Rovetch, Ursula K. LeGuin and Eric Kimmel. Length: 775 words average; 300 words minimum; 1,000 words maximum. Publishes short shorts. Also publishes poetry. Often critiques or comments on rejected ms.

How to Contact: Send complete ms with a cover letter. Include exact word count. Reports in 3 months. Send SASE for return of ms. Simultaneous and reprint submissions OK. Sample copy for $5. Fiction guidelines for #10 SASE.

Payment/Terms: Pays 25¢/word and 2 contributor's copies on publication for first rights or one-time rights; additional copies for $2.

Advice: "Read back issues of *Spider*." Looks for "quality writing, good characterization, lively style, humor."

$◻ SPIRIT,, Good Ground Press, 1884 Randolph Ave., St. Paul MN 55105. (612)690-7012. Fax: (612)690-7039. Website: www.goodgroundpress.com. **Editor:** Joan Mitchell. Magazine: 8 ½×11; 4 pages; 50 lb. paper. Religious education magazine for Roman Catholic teens. "Stories must be realistic, not moralistic or pietistic. They are used as catalysts to promote teens' discussion of their conflicts." Biweekly (28 issues). Estab. 1988. Circ. 25,000.

Needs: Feminist, religious/inspirational, young adult/teen. Upcoming themes: Christmas and Easter. List of upcoming themes available for SASE. Receives 20 unsolicited mss/month. Accepts 1 mss/issue; 12 mss/year. Publishes ms 6-12 months after acceptance. Published work by Margaret McCarthy, Kathleen Y Choi, Heather Klassen, Kathleen Cleberg, Bob Bartlett and Ron LaGro. Length: 1,000 words minimum; 1,200 words maximum. Sometimes critiques or comments on rejected mss.

How to Contact: Send complete ms with a cover letter. Include estimated word count. Reports in 6 months on mss. SASE for return of ms or send a disposable copy of ms. Simultaneous submissions and reprints OK. Sample copy and fiction guidelines free.

Payment/Terms: Pays $200 minimum on publication and 5 contributor's copies. Acquires first North American serial rights.

Advice: Looks for "believable conflicts for teens. Just because we're religious, don't send pious, moralistic work."

★ ◻ ◎ STANDARD, Nazarene International Headquarters, 6401 The Paseo, Kansas City MO 64131. (816)333-7000. **Editor:** Everett Leadingham. Magazine: 8½×11; 8 pages; illustrations; photos. Inspirational reading for adults. Weekly. Estab. 1936. Circ. 165,000.

• *Standard* ranked #9 on the *Writer's Digest*'s Fiction 50 list of top markets for fiction writers.

Needs: "Looking for stories that show Christianity in action." Publishes ms 14-18 months after acceptance. **Published new writers within the last year.** Length: 1,200 words average; 500 words minimum; 1,200 words maximum.

How to Contact: Send complete ms with name, address and phone number. Reports in 2-3 months on mss. SASE. Simultaneous submissions OK but will pay only reprint rates. Sample copy and guidelines for SAE and 2 first-class stamps.

Payment/Terms: Pays 3½¢/word; 2¢/word (reprint) on acceptance; contributor's copies on publication.

★ $◻ STORY FRIENDS, Mennonite Publishing House, 616 Walnut Ave., Scottdale PA 15683-1999. (724)887-8500. Fax: (724)887-3111. E-mail: rstutz@mph.org. **Editor:** Rose Mary Stutzman. A magazine which portrays Jesus as a friend and helper. Nonfiction and fiction for children 4-9 years of age. Monthly.

• The Mennonite Publishing House also published *On the Line*, *Purpose* and *With* magazines.

Needs: Juvenile. Stories of everyday experiences at home, in church, in school or at play, which provide models of Christian values. "Wants to see more fiction set in African-American, Latino or Hispanic settings. No stories about children and their grandparents or children and their elderly neighbors. I have more than enough." Recently published work by Virginia Kroll and Lisa Harkrader. **Publishes 10-12 new writers/year.** Length: 300-800 words.

How to Contact: Send complete ms with SASE. Seasonal or holiday material should be submitted 6 months in advance. Free sample copy with SASE.

Payment/Terms: Pays 3-5¢/word on acceptance for one-time rights. Buys reprints. Not copyrighted.

Advice: "I am buying more 500-word stories since we switched to a new format. It is important to include relationships, patterns of forgiveness, respect, honesty, trust and caring. Prefer exciting yet plausible short stories which offer varied settings, introduce children to wide ranges of friends and demonstrate joys, fears, temptations and successes of the readers. Read good children's literature, the classics, the Newberry winner and the Caldecott winners. Respect children you know and allow their resourcefulness and character to have a voice in your writing."

⭐ 💲 🔲 📺 **THE SUN,** The Sun Publishing Company, Inc., 107 N. Roberson St., Char⋯
(919)942-5282. Website: www.thesunmagazine.org (includes guidelines, staff list and orde⋯
Safransky. Magazine: 8½×11; 48 pages; offset paper; glossy cover stock; illustrations; ⋯
magazine of ideas. While we tend to favor personal writing, we're open to just about anyth⋯
writing, if it doesn't make us feel stupid. Surprise us; we often don't know what we⋯
Monthly. Estab. 1974. Circ. 45,000.

- *The Sun* ranked #35 on *Writer's Digest*'s Fiction 50 list of top markets for fict⋯
  had a story anthologized in *Best American Short Stories 1998*.

Needs: Open to all fiction. Receives approximately 500 unsolicited fiction mss each month. ⋯
Recently published work by Poe Ballantine, Sybil Smith and Gillian Kendall. Publishes 2-3 pre⋯
lished writers/year. **Publishes 4-6 new writers/year.** Length: 7,000 words maximum. Also publishes⋯
How to Contact: Send complete ms with SASE. Reports in 3 months. Publishes ms an average of 6-12 ⋯
after acceptance. Sample copy for $5
Payment/Terms: Pays up to $500 on publication, plus 2 contributor's copies and a complimentary one-year⋯
subscription for one-time rights. Publishes reprints.
Tips: "We favor honest, personal writing with an intimate point of view."

🅽 ⭐ ⬭ ◎ **TATTOO REVUE,** Outlaw Biker Enterprises, Inc., Box 447, Voorhees NJ 08043. **Publisher:**
Casey Exton. Magazine: 8½×11; 96 pages; 50 lb. coated paper; 80 lb. cover stock; illustrations and photos.
"Art magazine devoted to showcasing the very best of modern tattooing." Published 10 times/year. Estab. 1988.
Circ. 180,000.
Needs: Fiction pertaining to subject matter (tattooing). Receives 20 unsolicited mss/month. Publishes 1 fiction
ms/issue. Publishes ms 2-8 months after acceptance. Length: 1,000-2,500 words. "Very open to freelance writers
and unpublished writers. Freelance photographers also needed."
How to Contact: Send complete ms with cover letter and SASE. Sample copy for $5 and 8½×11 SAE with
2 first-class stamps.
Payment/Terms: Payment varies according to length and quality of work; pays on publication. Acquires all
rights.
Advice: "Very targeted market, strongly suggest you read magazine before submitting work."

🅽 ⬭ **TOGETHER TIME,** 6401 The Paseo, Kansas City MO 64131. (816)333-7000. Fax: (816)333-4439.
E-mail: kjohnson@nazarene.org. **Editor:** Melissa Hammer. Take-home paper (story paper) for 3-4 year olds—
correlates with Sunday school curriculum. 8½×11; 4 pages; newprint; illustrations. *"Together Time* is a full-
color weekly story paper for three- and four-year-olds which correlates directly with the Word Action Sunday
school curriculum. It is designed to connect Sunday School learning with the daily living experiences and growth
of the child." Weekly.
Needs: Children's/juvenile (adventure, animal, easy-to-read, preschool, sports), religious (children's religious).
No "stories about God creating the world or golden rule stories—we see too many of these." List of upcoming
themes available for SASE. Receives 30 unsolicited mss/month. Accepts 1 mss/issue. Publishes ms 1-2 years
after acceptance. Agented fiction 50%. **Publishes 7 new writers/year.** Length: 200 words average; 175 minimum;
275 words maximum. Also publishes poetry. Often critiques or comments on rejected mss.
How to Contact: Send complete ms with a cover letter. Accepts queries/mss by e-mail. Include estimated word
count. Reports in 3 weeks on queries; 5 weeks on mss. SASE for reply to query or mss or return of ms. Sample
copy, guidelines for #10 SASE and 1 first-class stamp.
Payment/Terms: Pays $15-25 and 3 contributor's copies. Pays on publication. Acquires multi-use rights.
Advice: "Write a believable story that follows guidelines and fits our theme list. Send SASE for guidelines and
theme list. Study those and follow them when writing."

🅽 ⬭ 📺 **TOUCH,** GEMS (Girls Everywhere Meeting the Savior) Girls' Clubs, Box 7259, Grand Rapids
MI 49510. (616)241-5616. Editor: Jan Boone. Magazine: 8½×11; 24 pages; 50 lb. paper; 50 lb. cover stock;
illustrations and photos. "Our purpose is to lead girls into a living relationship with Jesus Christ and to help
them see how God is at work in their lives and the world around them. Puzzles, poetry, crafts, stories, articles,
and club input for girls ages 9-14." Monthly. Circ. 16,000.

- *Touch* has received awards for fiction and illustration from the Evangelical Press Association. Each year
  Touch selects a theme. The theme for 2000-2001 is "Danger Ahead! Join the Rescue Squad." While
  writers should not write for this theme, the editors say they should keep it in the back of their minds as
  they write.

Needs: Adventure, ethnic, juvenile and religious/inspirational. Write for upcoming themes. Receives 50 unsolic-
ited fiction mss/month. Buys 3 mss/issue; 30 mss/year. Published work by A.J. Schut; **published new writers
within the last year.** Length: 400 words minimum; 1,000 words maximum; 800 words average.
How to Contact: Send complete ms with 8×10 SASE. Cover letter with short description of the manuscript.
Reports in 2 months. Simultaneous and previously published submissions OK. Sample copy for 8×10 SASE.
Free guidelines.
Payment/Terms: Pays 3-5¢/word on publication for simultaneous, first or second serial rights.

ce: "Try new and refreshing approaches. The one-parent, new girl at school is a bit overdone in our ket. We have been dealing with issues like AIDS, abuse, drugs, and family relationships in our stories—more areness-type articles."

✓ $ ☑ ⛉ **TROIKA MAGAZINE, Wit, Wisdom, and Wherewithal**, Lone Tout Publications, Inc., P.O. Box 1006, Weston CT 06883. (203)227-5377. Fax: (203)222-9332. E-mail: etroika@aol.com. Website: wwwtroikamagazine.com. **Editor:** Celia Meadow. Magazine: 8⅛×10⅝; 100 pages; 45 lb. Expression paper; 100 lb. Warren cover; illustrations and photographs. "Our general interest magazine is geared toward an audience aged 30-50 looking to balance a lifestyle of family, community and personal success." Quarterly. Estab. 1994. Circ. 100,000.

• *Troika* received 1995 *Print Magazine* Awards for Excellence (design) and two Ozzie Silver Awards for Excellence (design).

Needs: Humor/satire, literary, mainstream/contemporary. No genre, experimental or children's. List of upcoming themes available for SASE. Receives 200 unsolicited mss/month. Accepts 2-5 mss/issue; 8-20 mss/year. Publishes ms 3-6 months after acceptance. **Publishes 40-50 new writers/year.** Recently published work by Daniel Etessani, J.P. Maney and Olivia Goldsmith. Length: 2,000-3,000 words. Also publishes literary essays and literary criticism. Sometimes critiques or comments on rejected ms.

How to Contact: Send complete ms with a cover letter giving address, phone/fax number and e-mail address. Accepts queries/mss by e-mail. Include estimated word count, brief bio, SASE and list of publications with submission. Reports in 1-3 months. Send SASE for reply to query. Send a disposable copy of ms. Simultaneous and electronic submissions OK. Sample copy for $5. Guidelines for #10 SASE.

Payment/Terms: Pays $250 maximum on publication for first North American serial rights.

Tips: "What makes a manuscript stand out? An authentic voice, an original story, a strong narrative, a delight in language, a sharp eye for detail, a keen intelligence. But proper grammar and spelling don't hurt either."

☑ **TURTLE MAGAZINE FOR PRESCHOOL KIDS**, Children's Better Health Institute, Benjamin Franklin Literary & Medical Society, Inc., Box 567, 1100 Waterway Blvd., Indianapolis IN 46206. (317)636-8881. **Editor:** Terry Harshman. Magazine of picture stories and articles for preschool children 2-5 years old.

• The Children's Better Health Institute also publishes *Child's Life, Children's Digest, Children's Playmate, Jack and Jill* and *Humpty Dumpty's Magazine*, also listed in this section.

Needs: Juvenile (preschool). Special emphasis on health, nutrition, exercise and safety. Also has need for "action rhymes to foster creative movement, very simple science experiments, and simple food activities." Receives approximately 100 unsolicited fiction mss/month. **Published new writers within the last year.** Length: 300 words.

How to Contact: Send complete ms with SASE. No queries. Reports in 8-10 weeks. Send SASE for Editorial Guidelines. Sample copy for $1.75.

Payment/Terms: Pays up to 22¢/word (approximate); varies for poetry and activities; includes 10 complimentary copies of issue in which work appears. Pays on publication for all rights.

Advice: "Become familiar with recent issues of the magazine and have a thorough understanding of the preschool child. You'll find we are catering more to our youngest readers, so think simply. Also, avoid being too heavy-handed with health-related material. First and foremost, health features should be fun! Because we have developed our own turtle character ('PokeyToes'), we are not interested in fiction stories featuring other turtles."

Ⓝ $ ☑ **THE WAR CRY**, 615 Slaters Lane, Alexandria VA 22313. (703)684-5500. Fax: (703)684-5539. Website: www.publications.salvationarmyusa.org (includes forum, selected articles from *War Cry* and *Young Salvationist*, devotional page, guidelines, letters to the editor form, information on journals and books). **Editor:** Lt. Colonel Marlene Chase. Magazine: 8½×11; 24 pages; glossy; illustrations; and photos. "*The War Cry* is the national biweekly publication of the Salvation Army. Publishes articles of interest to the Army and the Christian community." Estab. 1883. Circ. 300,000.

• *The War Cry* is a member of the Evangelical Press Association.

Needs: Children's/juvenile, family saga, religious (children's religious, general religious, inspirational). No fantasy, science fiction or New Age. Upcoming themes available for #10 SASE. Receives 30 unsolicited mss/month. Accepts 1 ms/issue; 10 mss/year. Publishes ms 6 weeks-1 year after acceptance. **Publishes 15 new writers/year.** Word length: 800 words average; 300 words minimum; 1,200 words maximum. Publishes short shorts. Also publishes poetry. Sometimes comments on or critiques rejected ms.

How to Contact: Send complete ms with a cover letter. Inquiries by fax and e-mail OK. Include estimated word count and social security number. Reports in 3 weeks on queries; 6-8 weeks on mss. Send SASE for return of ms or disposable copy of ms. Simultaneous and reprint submissions OK. Sample copy and guidelines for #10 SAE.

Payment/Terms: Pays 10-20¢/word; 12¢ for reprints and 2 contributor's copies. Payment on acceptance. Acquires first rights and one-time rights.

Advice: "We publish limited amounts of fiction, so it must be outstanding. No 'flights of fancy.' Make sure fiction is realistic and involving with good characterization. Get a sample copy."

★ $ ▨ ◎ ▧ **WITH: The Magazine for Radical Christian Youth,** Faith & Life Press, Box 347, Newton KS 67114-0347. (316)283-5100. **Editor:** Carol Duerksen. Editorial Assistant: Delia Graber. Magazine: 8½×11; 32 pages; 60 lb. coated paper and cover; illustrations and photos. "Our purpose is to help teenagers understand the issues that impact them and to help them make choices that reflect Mennonite-Anabaptist understandings of living by the Spirit of Christ. We publish all types of material—fiction, nonfiction, teen personal experience, etc." Published 8 times/year. Estab. 1968. Circ. 6,100.

• *With* won several awards from the Associated Church Press and the Evangelical Press Association, including the 1997 Award of Excellence in Youth Category for best youth magazine. *With* ranked #42 on the *Writer's Digest's* Fiction 50 list of top markets for fiction writers.

Needs: Contemporary, ethnic, humor/satire, mainstream, religious, young adult/teen (15-18 years). "We accept issue-oriented pieces as well as religious pieces. No religious fiction that gives 'pat' answers to serious situations." Would like to see more humor. Receives about 50 unsolicited mss/month. Accepts 1-2 mss/issue; 10-12 mss/year. Publishes ms up to 1 year after acceptance. Published work by Shirley Byers Lalonde. **Publishes 1-3 new writers/year.** Length: 1,500 words preferred; 400 words minimum; 2,000 words maximum. Rarely critiques rejected mss.

How to Contact: Send complete ms with cover letter, include short summary of author's credits and what rights they are selling. Reports in 1-2 months on mss. SASE. Simultaneous and reprint submissions OK. Sample copy for 9×12 SAE and $1.21 postage. Fiction guidelines for #10 SASE.

Payment/Terms: Pays 4¢/word for reprints; 6¢/word for simultaneous rights (one-time rights to an unpublished story); 6-10¢/word for assigned stories (first rights). Supplies contributor's copies; charge for extras.

Advice: "Each story should make a single point that our readers will find helpful through applying it in their own lives. Request our theme list and detailed fiction guidelines (enclose SASE). All our stories are theme-related, so writing to our themes greatly improves your odds."

$ ⊕ **WOMAN'S WEEKLY,** IPC Magazines, King's Reach, Stamford St., London SE1 9LS England. **Fiction Editor:** Gaynor Davies. Circ. 700,000. Publishes 1 serial and at least 2 short stories/week. "Short stories can be on any theme, but must have warmth. No explicit sex or violence. Serials need not be written in installments. They are submitted as complete manuscripts and we split them up, or send first installment of serial (4,500 words) and synopsis of the rest." Length: 1,000-3,500 words for short stories; 11,500-22,000 words for serials. Short story payment starts at £100 and rises as writer becomes a more regular contributor. Serial payments start at around £600/installment. Writers also receive contributor's copies. "Read the magazine concerned and try to understand who the publication is aimed at." Writers' guidelines available. Write to "Fiction Department."

★ ✓ $ ◯ **WOMAN'S WORLD MAGAZINE, The Woman's Weekly,** 270 Sylvan Ave., Englewood Cliffs NJ 07632. E-mail: wwweekly@aol.com. **Fiction Editor:** Johnene Granger. Magazine; 9½×11; 54 pages. We publish short romances and mini-mysteries for all women, ages 18-68." Weekly. Estab. 1980. Circ. 1.5 million.

Needs: Romance (contemporary), mystery. "We buy contemporary romances of 1,500 words. Stories must revolve around a compelling, true-to-life relationship dilemma; may feature a male or female protagonist, and may be written in either the first or third person. We are *not* interested in stories of life-or-death, or fluffy, fly-away style romances. When we say romance, what we really mean is relationship, whether it's just beginning or is about to celebrate its 50th anniversary." Receives 2,500 unsolicited mss/month. Accepts 2 mss/issue; 104 mss/year. Publishes mss 2-3 months after acceptance. Recently published work by Linda S. Reilly, Linda Yellin and Tim Myers. Length: romances—1,500 words; mysteries—1,000 words.

How to Contact: Send complete ms, "double spaced and typed in number 12 font." Cover letter not necessary. Include name, address, phone number and fax on first page of mss. *No queries.* Reports in 4-8 months. SASE. Fiction guidelines free.

Payment/Terms: Romances—$1,000, mysteries—$500. Pays on acceptance for first North American serial rights only.

Advice: "Familiarize yourself totally with our format and style. Read at least a year's worth of *Woman's World* fiction. Analyze and dissect it. Regarding romances, scrutinize them not only for content but tone, mood and sensibility."

**FOR EXPLANATIONS OF THESE SYMBOLS,
SEE THE INSIDE FRONT AND BACK COVERS OF THIS BOOK.**

◖ **WONDER TIME**, WordAction Publications, 6401 The Paseo, Kansas City MO 64131. (816)333-7000. Fax: (816)333-4439. **Editor:** Diane Fillmore. Magazine: 8¼ × 11; 4 pages; self cover; color illustrations. Hand-out story paper published through WordAction Publications; stories follow outline of Sunday School lessons for 6-8 year-olds. Weekly. Circ. 45,000.

Needs: Religious/inspirational and juvenile. Wants more "really good Christian fiction with a true story line, not just a narration of moralistic events." Stories must have first- to second-grade readability. No fairy tales or science fiction. Receives 50-75 unsolicited fiction mss/month. Accepts 1 ms/issue. Recently published work by Ruth Blount and Shirley Smith. Length: 250-350 words.

How to Contact: Send complete ms with SASE. Reports in 6 weeks. Sample copy and curriculum guide with SASE.

Payment/Terms: Pays $25 minimum on acceptance for multi-use rights.

Advice: "Basic themes reappear regularly. Please write for a theme list. Also, be familiar with what *Wonder Time* is all about. Ask for guidelines, sample copies, theme list before submitting."

N ⊕ **THE WORLD OF ENGLISH**, P.O. Box 1504, Beijing China. Chief Editor: Yu-Lun Chen. Monthly. Circ. 300,000.

Needs: "We welcome contributions of short and pithy articles that would cater to the interest of our reading public, new and knowledgeable writings on technological finds, especially interesting stories and novels, etc.

Payment/Terms: "As our currency is regrettably inconvertible, we send copies of our magazines as the compensation for contributions."

Advice: "Aside from literary works, we put our emphasis on the provision of articles that cover various fields in order to help readers expand their vocabulary rapidly and enhance their reading level effectively, and concurrently to raise their level in writing. Another motive is to render assistance to those who, while learning English, are able also to enrich their knowledge and enlarge their field of vision."

◖ **WY'EAST HISTORICAL JOURNAL**, Crumb Elbow Publishing, P.O. Box 294, Rhododendron OR 97049. (503)622-4798. Editor: Michael P. Jones. Journal: 5½ × 8½; 60 pages; top-notch paper; hardcover and softbound; illustrations and photographs. "The journal is published for Cascade Geographic Society, a nonprofit educational organization. Publishes historical or contemporary articles on the history of Oregon's Mt. Hood, the Columbia River, the Pacific NW, or the Old Oregon Country that includes Oregon, Washington, Idaho, Wyoming, Montana, Alaska, Northern California and British Columbia and sometimes other areas. For young adults to elderly." Quarterly. Estab. 1992. Circ. 2,500.

Needs: Open. Special interests include wildlife and fisheries, history of fur trade in Pacific Northwest, the Oregon Trail and Indians. "All materials should relate—somehow—to the region the publication is interested in." Publishes annual special fiction issue in winter. Receives 10 unsolicited mss/month. Accepts 1-2 mss/issue; 22-24 mss/year. Publishes ms up to one year after acceptance. Published work by Joel Palmer. **Publishes 5-10 new writers/year.** Publishes short shorts. Recommends other markets. "We have several other publications through Crumb Elbow Publishing where we can redirect the material."

How to Contact: Query with clips of published work or send complete ms with cover letter. Reports in 2 months "depending upon work load." SASE (required or material will *not* be returned). Simultaneous and reprint submissions OK. Sample copy for $7. Fiction guidelines for #10 SASE.

Payment/Terms: Pays contributor's copies on publication. Acquires one-time rights.

Advice: "A ms has to have a historical or contemporary tie to the Old Oregon Country, which was the lands that lay west of the Rocky Mountains to the Pacific Ocean, south to and including Northern California, and north to and including Alaska. It has to be about such things as nature, fish and wildlife, the Oregon Trail, pioneer settlement and homesteading, the Indian wars, gold mining, wild horses, Native American way of life and culture—which are only a few ideas. It has to be written in a non-offensive style, meaning please remove all four-letter words or passages dealing with loose sex and racist comments. Do not be afraid to try something a little different. If you write for the marketplace you might get published, but you loose something in the creative presentation. Write to please yourself and others will recognize your refreshing approach."

★ ✓ ◖ **YANKEE MAGAZINE**, Yankee Publishing Inc., P.O. Box 520, Dublin NH 03444. (603)563-8111. Fax: (603)563-8252. E-mail: queries@yankeepub.com. Editor: Judson D. Hale. **Contact:** Jeanne Tyrrell, editorial assistant. Magazine: 6 × 9; 176 pages; glossy paper; 4-color glossy cover stock; illustrations; color photos. "Entertaining and informative New England regional on current issues, people, history, antiques and crafts for general reading audience." Monthly. Estab. 1935. Circ. 700,000.

● *Yankee* ranked #16 in *Writer's Digest*'s Fiction 50 list of top fiction markets.

Needs: Literary. Fiction is to be set in New England or compatible with the area. No religious/inspirational, formula fiction or stereotypical dialect, novels or novellas. Accepts 3-4 mss/year. Published work by Andre Dubus, H. L. Mountzoures and Fred Bonnie. **Published new writers within the last year.** Length: 2,500 words. Publishes short shorts.

How to Contact: Send complete ms with SASE and previous publications. "Cover letters are important if they provide relevant information: previous publications or awards; special courses taken; special references (e.g.

'William Shakespeare suggested I send this to you. . . .')" Simultaneous submissions OK, "within reason." Reports in 2-8 weeks.

Payment/Terms: Pays $1,000 on acceptance; rights negotiable. Makes "no changes without author consent." Supplies contributor copies; sends galleys to authors.

Advice: "Read previous ten stories in *Yankee* for style and content. Fiction must be realistic and reflect life as it is—complexities and ambiguities inherent. Our fiction adds to the 'complete menu'—the magazine includes many categories—humor, profiles, straight journalism, essays, etc. Listen to the advice of any editor who takes the time to write a personal letter. Go to workshops; get advice and other readings before sending story out cold."

$ ◖ ◎ YOUNG SALVATIONIST, The Salvation Army, P.O. Box 269, 615 Slaters Lane, Alexandria VA 22313. (703)684-5500. Fax: (703)684-5539. E-mail: ys@usn.salvationarmy.org. Website: publications.salvationa rmyusa.org (includes selected articles, writer's guidelines and discussion forums). **Managing Editor:** Tim Clark. Magazine: 8×11; 24 pages; illustrations and photos. Christian emphasis articles for youth members of The Salvation Army. 10 issues/year. Estab. 1984. Circ. 50,000.

Needs: Religious/inspirational, young adult/teen. No historical. Would like to see "contemporary, real-life stories that don't preach or talk down to readers." Receives 60 unsolicited mss/month. Buys 9-10 ms/issue; 90-100 mss/ year. Publishes ms 3-4 months after acceptance. **Publishes 5 new writers/year.** Recently published work by Teresa Cleory and Betty Stock Everett. Length: 1,000 words preferred; 600 words minimum; 1,200 words maximum. Publishes short shorts. Sometimes critiques rejected mss and recommends other markets.

How to Contact: Send complete ms. Accepts queries/mss by fax and e-mail. Reports in 1-2 weeks on queries; 2-4 weeks on mss. SASE. Simultaneous and reprint submissions OK. Sample copy for 9×12 SAE and 3 first-class stamps. Fiction guidelines and theme list for #10 SASE. Address submissions to Tim Clark.

Payment/Terms: Pays 15¢/word on acceptance for all rights, first rights, first North American serial rights and one-time rights. Pays 10¢/word for reprint rights.

Advice: "Don't write about your high school experience. Write about teens now. Know the magazine, its readers and its mission."

Book Publishers

In this section, you will find many of the "big-name" book publishers. Many of these publishers remain tough markets for new writers or for those whose work might be considered literary or experimental. Indeed, some only accept work from established authors, and then often only through an author's agent. However, although having your novel published by one of the big commercial publishers listed in this section is difficult, it is not impossible. The trade magazine *Publishers Weekly* regularly features interviews with writers whose first novels are being released by top publishers. Many editors at large publishing houses find great satisfaction in publishing a writer's first novel.

Also listed here are "small presses" publishing four or more titles annually. Included among them are small and mid-size independent presses, university presses and other nonprofit publishers. Introducing new writers to the reading public has become an increasingly more important role of these smaller presses at a time when the large conglomerates are taking less chances on unknown writers. Many of the successful small presses listed in this section have built their reputations and their businesses in this way and have become known for publishing prize-winning fiction.

These smaller presses also tend to keep books in print longer than larger houses. And, since small presses publish a smaller number of books, each title is equally important to the publisher, and each is promoted in much the same way and with the same commitment. Editors also stay at small presses longer because they have more of a stake in the business—often they own the business. Many smaller book publishers are writers themselves and know first-hand the importance of a close editor-author or publisher-author relationship.

At the end of this section, we've included information on a number of "micropresses," small presses publishing three or fewer books per year.

TYPES OF BOOK PUBLISHERS

Large or small, the publishers in this section publish books "for the trade." That is, unlike textbook, technical or scholarly publishers, trade publishers publish books to be sold to the general consumer through bookstores, chain stores or other retail outlets. Within the trade book field, however, there are a number of different types of books.

The easiest way to categorize books is by their physical appearance and the way they are marketed. Hardcover books are the more expensive editions of a book, sold through bookstores and carrying a price tag of around $20 and up. Trade paperbacks are soft-bound books, also sold mostly in bookstores, but they carry a more modest price tag of usually around $10 to $20. Today a lot of fiction is published in this form because it means a lower financial risk than hardcover.

Mass market paperbacks are another animal altogether. These are the smaller "pocket-size" books available at bookstores, grocery stores, drug stores, chain retail outlets, etc. Much genre or category fiction is published in this format. This area of the publishing industry is very open to the work of talented new writers who write in specific genres such as science fiction, romance and mystery.

At one time publishers could be easily identified and grouped by the type of books they do. Today, however, the lines between hardcover and paperback books are blurred. Many publishers known for publishing hardcover books also publish trade paperbacks and have paperback imprints. This enables them to offer established authors (and a very few lucky newcomers) hard-soft deals in which their book comes out in both versions. Thanks to the mergers of the past decade, too, the same company may own several hardcover and paperback subsidiaries and imprints, even though their editorial focuses may remain separate.

CHOOSING A BOOK PUBLISHER

In addition to checking the bookstores and libraries for books by publishers that interest you, you may want to refer to the Category Index at the back of this book to find publishers divided by specific subject categories. If you write genre fiction, check our new genre sections for lists of book publishers: (mystery, page 52; romance, page 64; science fiction and fantasy, page 76). The subjects listed in the Indexes are general. Read individual listings to find which subcategories interest a publisher. For example, you will find several romance publishers listed in the For Romance Writers Section, but read the listings to find which type of romance is considered— gothic, contemporary, Regency or futuristic. See How to Use This Book to Publish Your Fiction for more on how to refine your list of potential markets.

The icons appearing before the names of the publishers will also help you in selecting a publisher. These codes are especially important in this section, because many of the publishing houses listed here require writers to submit through an agent. A 🔘 icon identifies those that mostly publish established and agented authors, while a 🔘 points to publishers most open to new writers. See the inside front and back covers of this book for a complete list and explanations of symbols used in this book.

IN THE LISTINGS

As with other sections in this book, we identify new listings with a 🅽 symbol. In this section, most with this symbol are not new publishers, but instead are established publishers who decided to list this year in the hope of finding promising new writers.

In addition to the 🅽 symbol indicating new listings, we include other symbols to help you in narrowing your search. English-speaking foreign markets are denoted by a 🌐 . The maple leaf symbol 🍁 identifies Canadian presses. If you are not a Canadian writer, but are interested in a Canadian press, check the listing carefully. Many small presses in Canada receive grants and other funds from their provincial or national government and are, therefore, restricted to publishing Canadian authors.

We continue to include editorial comments set off by a bullet (●) within listings. This is where we include information about any special requirements or circumstances that will help you know even more about the publisher's needs and policies. The 🏆 symbol identifies publishers who have recently received honors or awards for their books. And the 🅰 symbol indicates that a publisher accepts agented submissions only.

Each listing includes a summary of the editorial mission of the house, an overarching principle that ties together what they publish. Under the heading **Acquisitions**: we list one or more editors, often with their specific area of expertise. An imprint listed in boldface type means there is an independent listing arranged alphabetically within this section.

Book editors asked us again this year to emphasize the importance of paying close attention to the Needs and How to Contact subheads of listings for book publishers. Unlike magazine editors who want to see complete manuscripts of short stories, most of the book publishers listed here ask that writers send a query letter with an outline and/or synopsis and several chapters of their novel. The Business of Fiction Writing, beginning on page 104 of this book, outlines how to prepare work to submit directly to a publisher.

There are no subsidy book publishers listed in *Novel & Short Story Writer's Market*. By subsidy, we mean any arrangement in which the writer is expected to pay all or part of the cost of producing, distributing and marketing his book. We feel a writer should not be asked to share in any cost of turning his manuscript into a book. All the book publishers listed here told us that they *do not charge writers* for publishing their work. *If any of the publishers listed here ask you to pay any part of publishing or marketing your manuscript, please let us know.*

A NOTE ABOUT AGENTS

Many publishers are willing to look at unsolicited submissions, but most feel having an agent is to the writer's best advantage. In this section more than any other, you'll find a number of publishers who prefer submissions from agents. That's why we've included a section of agents open to submissions from fiction writers (page 115).

For listings of more agents and additional information on how to approach and deal with them, see the 2000 *Guide to Literary Agents*, published by Writer's Digest Books. The book separates nonfee- and fee-charging agents. While many agents do not charge any fees up front, a few charge writers to cover the costs of using outside readers. Be wary of those who charge large sums of money for reading a manuscript. Reading fees do not guarantee representation. Think of an agent as a potential business partner and feel free to ask tough questions about his or her credentials, experience and business practices.

I   For More Information

Some of the mystery, romance and science fiction publishers included in this section are also included in *Mystery Writer's Sourcebook*, *Romance Writer's Sourcebook* or *Science Fiction and Fantasy Writer's Sourcebook* (all published by Writer's Digest Books). These books include in-depth interviews with editors and publishers. Also check issues of *Publishers Weekly* for publishing industry trade news in the U.S. and around the world or *Quill & Quire* for book publishing news in the Canadian book industry.

For more small presses see the *International Directory of Little Magazines and Small Presses* published by Dustbooks (P.O. Box 100, Paradise CA 95967). To keep up with changes in the industry throughout the year, check issues of two small press trade publications: *Small Press Review* (also published by Dustbooks) and *Independent Publisher* (Jenkins Group, Inc., 121 E. Front St., 4th Floor, Traverse City MI 49684).

✔ ◑ ⛉ **ABSEY & CO., INC.,** 23011 Northerest Dr., Spring TX 77389. (281)257-2340. Fax: (281)251-4676. E-mail: abseyandco@aol.com. Website: www.absey.com (includes authors, titles and descriptions, contact information). **Acquisitions:** Trey Hall, editor-in-chief. "We are interested in book-length fiction of literary merit with a firm intended audience." Publishes hardcover and paperback originals. Publishes 6-10 titles/year. Receives 1,500 submissions/year. **Accepts 50% of books from first-time authors** and unagented writers.
● Two Absey books were named to the American Library Association's Best Books for Young Adults for 1998.
Needs: Juvenile, mainstream/contemporary, short story collections. Also publishes poetry. Recently published *The Legacy of Roxaboxen*, by Alice McLerran; *Where I'm From*, by George Ella Lyon; *Brothers of the Bat*, by James LeBuffe; *Phonics Friendly Books*, by Joyce Armstrong Carroll; and *Phonics Friendly Families*, by Kelley R. Smith.
How to Contact: Query with SASE. Reports in 3 months on queries, 6-9 months on mss. No e-mail submissions.
Terms: Pays 8-15% royalty on wholesale price. Publishes ms 1 year after acceptance. Writer's guidelines for #10 SASE.
Advice: "Since we are a small, new press looking for good manuscripts with a firm intended audience, we tend to work closely and attentively with our authors. Many established authors who have been with the large New York houses have come to us to publish their work because we work closely with them. We allow them input."

✔ ◑ **ACADEMY CHICAGO PUBLISHERS**, 363 W. Erie St., Chicago IL 60610. (312)751-7300. **Acquisitions**: Anita Miller, senior editor. Estab. 1975. Midsize independent publisher. Publishes hardcover and paperback originals and paperback reprints.
Needs: Biography, history, academic and anthologies. Only the most unusual mysteries, no private-eyes or thrillers. No explicit sex or violence. Serious fiction, not romance/adventure. "We will consider historical fiction that is well researched. No science fiction/fantasy, no religious/inspirational, no how-to, no cookbooks. In general,

we are very conscious of women's roles. We publish very few children's books." Published *The Man Who Once Played Catch with Nellie Fox*, by John Mandarino; *Glass Hearts*, by Terri Paul; and *Murder at Heartbreak Hospital*, by Henry Slesar.

How to Contact: Accepts unsolicited queries. Query and submit first three consecutive chapters, triple spaced, with SASE and a cover letter briefly describing the content of your work. No simultaneous submissions. "Manuscripts without envelopes will be discarded. *Mailers* are a *must*."

Terms: Pays 5-10% on net in royalties; no advance. Publishes ms 18 months after acceptance. Sends galleys to author.

Advice: "At the moment we are swamped with manuscripts and anything under consideration can be under consideration for months."

ACE SCIENCE FICTION, Berkley Publishing Group, 375 Hudson St., New York NY 10014. (212)366-2000. **Acquisitions**: Susan Allison, editor-in-chief; Anne Sowards, assistant editor. Estab. 1948. Publishes paperback originals and reprints and 6-10 hardcovers per year. Number of titles: 6/month. Buys 85-95% agented fiction.

Needs: Science fiction and fantasy. No other genre accepted. No short stories. Published *Forever Peace*, by Joe Haldeman; and *Neuromancer*, by William Gibson.

How to Contact: Submit outline/synopsis and 3 sample chapters with SASE. No simultaneous submissions. Reports in 2 months minimum on mss. "Queries answered immediately if SASE enclosed." Publishes ms an average of 18 months after acceptance.

Terms: Standard for the field. Sends galleys to author.

Advice: "Good science fiction and fantasy are almost always written by people who have read and loved a lot of it. We are looking for knowledgeable science or magic, as well as sympathetic characters with recognizable motivation. We are looking for solid, well-plotted science fiction: good action adventure, well-researched hard science with good characterization and books that emphasize characterization without sacrificing plot. In fantasy we are looking for all types of work, from high fantasy to sword and sorcery." Submit fantasy and science fiction to Anne Sowards.

ADAEX EDUCATIONAL PUBLICATIONS, P.O. Box AK188, Kumasi, Ghana. Fax: 233-51-30282. **Acquisitions**: Asare Konadu Yamoah, publisher, George Apraku Dentu, fiction editor. Distributes titles through bookstores. Promotes titles through advertising, direct mail.

Needs: Looks for cultural development, romance, literary translators and copyright brokers. "Publication development organization for Ghanaian, African and world literature: novels, workbooks, language development, etc." Published *Strange Happenings* and *Creatures of Circumstance*, by Asare Konadu. Average 5-10 fiction titles/year. Length: 8-250 typed pages.

How to Contact: Send brief summary and first and last chapter.

Terms: Pays advance and royalties.

Advice: "Manuscripts should be very clear in terms of language, the message it conveys should be universal."

ADVOCACY PRESS, Box 236, Santa Barbara CA 93102-0236. (805)962-2728. Fax: (805)963-3580. E-mail: advpress@impulse.net. **Acquisitions**: Ruth Vitale, curriculum specialist. Estab. 1983. "We promote gender equity and positive self-esteem through our programs and publications." Small publisher with 3-5 titles/year. Hardcover and paperback originals. Books: perfect or Smyth-sewn binding; illustrations; average print order: 5,000-10,000 copies; first novel print order: 5,000-10,000. Averages 2 children's fiction (32-48 pg.) titles per year. Promotes titles through catalogs, distributors, schools and bookstores.

• Advocacy Press books have won the Ben Franklin Award and the Friends of American Writers Award. The press also received the Eleanor Roosevelt Research and Development Award from the American Association of University Women for its significant contribution to equitable education.

Needs: Juvenile. Wants only gender equity/positive esteem messages to boys or girls—picture books; self-esteem issues. Published *Minou*, by Mindy Bingham (picture book); *Kylie's Song*, by Patty Sheehan (picture book); *Nature's Wonderful World in Rhyme*, by William Sheehan.

How to Contact: Submit complete manuscript with SASE for return. Reports in 3 months on queries. Simultaneous submissions OK.

Terms: Pays in royalties of 5-10%. Book catalog for SASE.

Advice: Wants "stories for children that give messages of self-sufficiency/self esteem. Please review some of our publications *before* you submit to us. For layout and writing guidelines, we recommend that you read *The Children's Book: How to Write It, How to Sell It* by Ellen Roberts, Writer's Digest Books. *Because of our limited focus, most of our titles have been written inhouse.*"

ALASKA NATIVE LANGUAGE CENTER, University of Alaska, P.O. Box 757680, Fairbanks AK 99775-7680. (907)474-7874. **Acquisitions**: Tom Alton, editor. Estab. 1972. Small education publisher limited to books in and about Alaska native languages. Generally nonfiction. Publishes hardcover and paperback originals. Books: 60 lb. book paper; offset printing; perfect binding; photos, line art illustrations; average print order: 500-1,000 copies. Averages 6-8 total titles each year.

Needs: Ethnic. Publishes original fiction only in native language and English by Alaska native writers. Published *A Practical Grammar of the Central Alaskan Yup'ik Eskimo Language*, by Steven A. Jacobson; *One Must Arrive With a Story to Tell*, by the Elders of Tununak, Alaska.
How to Contact: Does not accept unsolicited mss. Electronic submissions via ASCII for modem transmissions or Macintosh compatible files on 3.5 disk.
Terms: Does not pay. Sends galleys to author.

☑ ⊘ ◎ **ALEXANDER BOOKS**, Subsidiary of Creativity, Inc., 65 Macedonia Rd., Alexander NC 28701. (828)252-9515. E-mail: editor@abooks.com. Website: www.abooks.com (includes writer's guidelines, authors and titles). **Acquisitions:** Pat Roberts, editorial director. Publishes hardcover originals, and trade paperback and mass market paperback originals and reprints. Publishes primarily reprints; "very little" new fiction. Publishes 8-10 fiction titles/year.
Imprint(s): Farthest Star.
Needs: Historical, mainstream/contemporary, mystery, science fiction, western. "We prefer local or well-known authors or local interest settings." Recently published *Birthright: The Book of Man*, by Mike Resnick (science fiction); and *Compleat Chance Perdue*, by Ross H. Spencer (mystery).
How to Contact: Query or submit synopsis and 3 sample chapters with SASE. Reports in 1-2 months on queries.
Terms: Pays 12-15% royalty on wholesale price. Advances seldom given (minimum $100). Publishes ms 1-2 years after acceptance. Book catalog and writer's guidelines for 8½×11 SASE with $1.01 in first-class stamps.
Advice: "Your cover letter is very important. Most acquisition editors don't get past the letter. Make sure the letter makes the editor want to go further into the query package."

☑ ⊘ **ALYSON PUBLICATIONS, INC.**, 6922 Hollywood Blvd., Suite 1000, Los Angeles CA 90028. (323)871-1225. Fax: (323)467-6805. Website: www.alyson.com (includes guidelines, calls for submissions, synopses of books and mission statement). **Acquisitions**: Scott Brassart and Angela Brown, fiction editors. Estab. 1979. Medium-sized publisher specializing in lesbian- and gay-related material. Publishes paperback originals, reprints and some hardcover. Books: paper and printing varies; trade paper, perfect-bound; average print order: 8,000; first novel print order: 6,000. **Published new writers within the last year.** Plans 50 total titles, 25 fiction titles each year.
Imprint(s): Alyson Wonderland, Alyson Classics Library.
• In addition to adult titles, Alyson Publications has been known for its line of young adult and children's books.
Needs: "We are interested in all categories; *all* materials must be geared toward lesbian and/or gay readers. No poetry." Recently published *Fool's Errand*, by Louis Bayard (gay); *The Blue Lawn*, by William Taylor (gay); and *Looking Glass Lives*, by Felice Picano (gay). Publishes anthologies. Authors may submit to them directly.
How to Contact: Query first with SASE. Reports in 3-12 weeks.

⊘ **AMERICAN DIABETES ASSOCIATION**, 1660 Duke St., Alexandria VA 22314. (703)549-1500. Website: www.diabetes.org. **Acquisitions:** Robert J. Anthony, acquisitions editor. "The mission of the American Diabetes Association is to prevent and cure diabetes and to improve the lives of all people affected by diabetes." Publishes hardcover originals and trade paperback originals. Publishes 15 titles/year.
Needs: Juvenile. "We publish very little fiction—all for juveniles with diabetes." Published *The Dinosaur Tamer*, by Marcia Levine Mazur (juvenile fiction).
How to Contact: Query with synopsis and 2 sample chapters. Reports in 2 months.
Terms: Pays 7-10% royalty on retail price. Offers $3,000 advance. Publishes ms 9 months after acceptance. Book catalog free.
Advice: "Our audience consists primarily of consumers with diabetes who want to better manage their illness. Obtain a few of our books to better understand our target audience and appropriate reading level."

⬍ ◎ **ANNICK PRESS LTD.**, 15 Patricia Ave., Willowdale, Ontario M2M 1H9 Canada. (416)221-4802. Publisher of children's books. Publishes hardcover and paperback originals. Books: offset paper; full-color offset printing; perfect and library bound; full-color illustrations. Average print order: 9,000. First novel print order: 7,000. Plans 18 first picture books this year. Averages approximately 25 titles each year, both fiction and nonfiction. Average first picture book print order 2,000 cloth, 12,000 paper copies. Distributes titles through Firefly Books Ltd.
Needs: Children's books only.

READ THE BUSINESS OF FICTION WRITING section for information on manuscript preparation, mailing tips, rights and more.

How to Contact: "Annick Press publishes only work by Canadian citizens or residents." Does not accept unsolicited mss. Query with SASE. Free book catalog. Occasionally critiques rejected mss.
Terms: No terms disclosed.

◖ ARCADE PUBLISHING, 141 Fifth Ave., New York NY 10010. (212)475-2633. Fax: (212)353-8148. President, Editor-in-Chief: Richard Seaver. **Acquisitions:** Richard Seaver, Jeannette Seaver, Cal Barksdale and Coates Bateman. Estab. 1988. Independent publisher. Publishes hardcover originals and paperback reprints. Books: 50-55 lb. paper; notch, perfect-bound; illustrations; average print order: 10,000; first novel print order: 3,500-7,500. Published new writers within the year. Averages 40 total titles, 12-15 fiction titles each year. Distributes titles through Time Warner Trade Publishing.
Needs: Literary, mainstream/contemporary, mystery/suspense, translations. No romance, science fiction, young adult. Published *Trying to Save Piggy Sneed*, by John Irving; *Europa*, by Tim Parks; *Dreams of My Russian Summers*, by Andrei Makine; *The Brush-Off*, by Shane Maloney; and *The Queen's Bastard*, by Robin Maxwell.
How to Contact: No unsolicited mss; unsolicited mss will be returned (SASE or IRC). Submit through an agent only. Agented fiction 100%. Reports in 2 weeks on queries; 3-4 months on mss. Does not comment on rejected ms.
Terms: Pays negotiable advances and royalties and 10 author's copies. Writer's guidelines and book catalog for SASE.

◖ ARCHWAY PAPERBACKS, Imprint of Pocket Books for Young Readers, 1230 Avenue of the Americas, New York NY 10020. (212)698-7669. Website: www.simonsayskids.com. **Acquisitions:** Patricia MacDonald, vice president/editorial director. Published by Pocket Books. Publishes paperback originals and reprints. **Published new writers this year.**
Imprint(s): Minstrel Books (ages 7-12); and Archway (ages 12 and up).
Needs: Young adult: horror, mystery, suspense/adventure, thrillers. Young readers (80 pages and up): adventure, animals, humor, family, fantasy, friends, mystery, school, etc. No picture books. Published *Fear Street: The New Boy*, by R.L. Stine; and *Aliens Ate My Homework*, by Bruce Coville.
How to Contact: Submit query first with outline; SASE "mandatory. If SASE not attached, query letter will not be answered."
Payment/Terms: Pays royalties of 6% minimum; 8% maximum. Publishes ms 2 years after acceptance.

◖ ◎ ▼ ARTE PUBLICO PRESS, University of Houston, 4800 Calhoun, Houston TX 77204-2090. (713)743-2847. **Acquisitions:** Dr. Nicolás Kanellos, publisher. Estab. 1979. "Small press devoted to the publication of contemporary U.S.-Hispanic literature. Mostly trade paper; publishes 4-6 clothbound books/year. Publishes fiction and belles lettres." Publishes 36 paperback originals and occasionally reprints. Average print order 2,000-5,000. First novel print order 2,500-5,000.
Imprint(s): Piñata Books featuring children's and young adult literature by U.S.-Hispanic authors and *The Americas Review*.
● Arte Publico Press received the 1994 American Book Award for *In Search of Bernabé*, by Graciela Limón; the Thorpe Menn Award for Literary Achievement; the Southwest Book Award and others. Arte Publico Press is the oldest and largest publisher of Hispanic literature for children and adults in the United States.
Needs: Childrens/juvenile, contemporary, ethnic, feminist, literary, short story collections, young adult written by US-Hispanic authors. Published *A Perfect Silence*, by Alba Ambert; *Song of the Hummingbird*, by Graciela Limón; and *Little Havana Blues: A Cuban-American Literature Anthology*.
How to Contact: Accepts unsolicited mss. Submit outline/synopsis and sample chapters or complete ms with cover letter and SASE. Agented fiction 1%. Reports in 1 month on queries; 4 months on mss. Sometimes critiques rejected mss.
Terms: Offers $1,000-3,000 advance. Pays 10% royalty on wholesale price. Provides 20 author's copies; 40% discount on subsequent copies. Sends galleys to author. Publishes ms minimum 2 years after acceptance. Guidelines for SASE; book catalog free on request.
Advice: "Include cover letter in which you 'sell' your book—why should we publish the book, who will want to read it, why does it matter, etc."

◖ ▼ ATHENEUM BOOKS FOR YOUNG READERS, Imprint of the Simon & Schuster Children's Publishing Division, 1230 Avenue of the Americas, New York NY 10022. (212)698-2721. Vice President/Editorial Director: Jonathan J. Lanman. Editorial Coordinator: Howard Kaplan. **Acquisitions:** Marcia Marshall, executive director; Caitlyn Dlouhy, senior editor; Anne Schwartz, editorial director, Anne Schwartz Books. Second largest imprint of large publisher/corporation. Publishes hardcover originals. Books: Illustrations for picture books, some illustrated short novels. Average print order: 6,000-7,500. First novel print order: 5,000. Averages 50 total titles, 25 middle grade and YA fiction titles each year.
● Books published by Atheneum Books for Children have received the Newbery Medal (*The View From Saturday*, by E.L. Konigsburg) and the Christopher Award (*The Gold Coin*, by Alma Flor Ada, illustrated

by Neal Waldman). Because of the merger of Macmillan and Simon & Schuster, Atheneum Books has absorbed the Scribners imprint of Macmillan.

Needs: Juvenile (adventure, animal, contemporary, fantasy, historical, sports), preschool/picture book, young adult/teen (fantasy/science fiction, historical, mystery, problem novels, sports, spy/adventure). No "paperback romance type" fiction. Published *Lottie's New Beach Towel*, by Petra Matthers (3-8, picture book); *Achingly Alice*, by Phyllis Reynolds Naylor (10-14, middle grade novel); and *Rearranging*, by David Gifaldi (12 & up young adult fiction).

How to Contact: Accepts queries only. SASE. Agented fiction 40%. Reports in 4-6 weeks on queries. Simultaneous submissions OK "if we are so informed and author is unpublished." Very rarely critiques rejected mss.

Terms: Pays in royalties of 10%. Average advance: $3,000 "along with advance and royalties, authors receive ten free copies of their book and can purchase more at a special discount." Sends galleys to author. Writer's guidelines for #10 SASE.

Advice: "We publish all hardcover originals, occasionally an American edition of a British publication. Our fiction needs have not varied in terms of quantity—of the 50-60 titles we do each year, 25 are fiction in different age levels. We are less interested in specific topics or subject matter than in overall quality of craftsmanship. First, know your market thoroughly. We publish only children's books, so caring for and *respecting* children is of utmost importance. Also, fad topics are dangerous, as are works you haven't polished to the best of your ability. (Why should we choose a 'jewel in the rough' when we can get a manuscript a professional has polished to be ready for publication?) The juvenile market is not one in which a writer can 'practice' to become an adult writer. In general, be professional. We appreciate the writers who take the time to find out what type of books we publish by visiting the libraries and reading the books. Neatness is a pleasure, too."

AUNT LUTE BOOKS, P.O. Box 410687, San Francisco CA 94141. (415)826-1300. Fax: (415)826-8300. E-mail: books@auntlute.com. Website: www.auntlute.com. **Acquisitions:** Shahara Godfrey, first reader. Small feminist and women of color press. Publishes hardcover and paperback originals. Publishes 4 total titles/year.

Needs: Ethnic/multicultural, feminist, lesbian.

How to Contact: Accepts unsolicited mss. Query with outline/synopsis and sample chapters. Send SASE for return of ms. Reports in 4 months.

Terms: Pays in royalties. Guidelines and catalog for free.

Advice: "We seek manuscripts, both fiction and nonfiction, by women from a variety of cultures, ethnic backgrounds and subcultures; women who are self-aware and who, in the face of all contradictory evidence, are still hopeful that the world can reserve a place of respect for each woman in it. We seek work that explores the specificities of the worlds from which we come, and which examines the intersections between the borders which we all inhabit."

AVALON BOOKS, Imprint of Thomas Bouregy Company, Inc., 401 Lafayette St., New York NY 10003. (212)598-0222. **Editorial**: Ms. Veronica Mixon. Publishes hardcover originals. Averages 60 titles/year.

Needs: "Avalon Books publishes wholesome romances, mysteries, westerns. Intended for family reading, our books are read by adults as well as teenagers, and their characters are all adults. There is no graphic sex in any of our novels. Currently, we publish 10 books bi-monthly: four romances, two mysteries, two career romances and two westerns. All the romances are contemporary; all the westerns are historical." Published *In A Wink*, by Lacey Green (career romance); *Cyber Bride*, by Annette L. Couch-Jareb (romance); *Endangered*, by Charles Evans (mystery); and *Hannah and the Horseman*, by Johnny D. Boggs (western). Books range in length from a minimum of 40,000 words to a maximum of 50,000 words.

How to Contact: Submit the first three chapters. "We'll contact you if we're interested." Publishes many first novels. Enclose ms-size SASE. Reports in about 3 months. "Send SASE for a copy of our tip sheet."

Terms: The first half of the advance is paid upon signing of the contract; the second within 30 days after publication. Usually publishes within 6 to 8 months.

AVON BOOKS, Imprint of HarperCollins, 1350 Avenue of the Americas, New York NY 10019. (212)261-6800. Website: www.avonbooks.com. Senior Vice President/Publisher: Lou Aronica. Estab. 1941. Large hardcover and paperback publisher. Publishes hardcover and paperback originals and reprints. Averages more than 400 titles a year.

Imprint(s): Avon, **Avon Eos**, Tempest.

Needs: Literary fiction and nonfiction, health, history, mystery, science fiction, romance, young adult, pop culture.

How to Contact: Query letters only. SASE to insure response.

Terms: Vary.

AVON BOOKS FOR YOUNG READERS, Imprint of HarperCollins Children's Book Group, 1350 Avenue of the Americas, New York NY 10019. (212)261-6800. Fax: (212)261-6895. **Acquisitions:** Elise Howard, editor-in-chief; Ruth Katcher, senior editor. Avon BFYR publishes fiction and non-fiction for children ages 7 and up. Publishes hardcovers, paperback originals and reprints. Publishes 80-100 titles/year.

• At press time HarperCollins announced that Flare and Camelot would cease publishing.

Imprint(s): Avon Tempest (for ages 12 and up).

Needs: Subjects include adventure, humor, juvenile mainstream, mystery, ("very selective with mystery"), and literary fiction for teens. Avon does not publish picture books. Recently published *SMACK*, by Melvin Burgess.

How to Contact: Submit query letter and 3 chapters plus a synopsis. Reports back in 3 months.

Terms: Pays 6-8% royalty on retail price. Offers $2,000 minimum advance. Publishes ms 2 years after acceptance. Writer's guidelines and book catalog for 8×10 SAE with 5 first-class stamps.

AVON EOS, Imprint of HarperCollins, 1350 Avenue of the Americas, New York NY 10019. (212)261-6821. Fax: (212)261-6895. **Acquisitions:** Jennifer Brehl, executive editor. Diana Gill, associate editor. Imprint estab. 1998. Science fiction and fantasy imprint for serious readers. Imprint of major general trade publisher. Publishes trade hardcover, trade paperback (original and reprint), mass market paperback (original and reprint). **Published new writers within the last year.** Publishes 48 total titles/year, all fiction.

Needs: Fantasy, science fiction. Recently published *Ends of Days*, by Dennis Danvers; *Krondor: The Betrayal*, by Raymond E. Feist; and *Singer From the Sea*, by Sheri S. Tepper.

How to Contact: Send query with outline/synopsis and 3 sample chapters. Do not send full ms. Include estimated word count, bio and list of publishing credits. Send SASE for reply. Agented fiction 99%. Reports in 1 month on queries. Simultaneous submissions OK.

Terms: Pays negotiable advance. Sends galleys to author.

Advice: "Get an agent."

BAEN BOOKS, P.O. Box 1403, Riverdale NY 10471. (718)548-3100. Website: www.baen.com (includes writer's guidelines, chat line, annotated catalog, author bios, tour information). Publisher and Editor: Jim Baen. **Acquisitions:** Toni Weisskopf, executive editor. Estab. 1983. "We publish books at the heart of science fiction and fantasy." Independent publisher. Publishes hardcover and paperback originals and paperback reprints. Published new writers within the last year. **Plans 2-3 first novels this year.** Averages 60 fiction titles each year. Distributes titles through Simon & Schuster.

Imprint(s): Baen Science Fiction and Baen Fantasy.

Needs: Fantasy and science fiction. Interested in science fiction novels (based on real science) and fantasy novels "that at least strive for originality." Published *A Civil Campaign*, by Lois McMaster Bujold; *Four and Twenty Blackbirds*, by Mercedes Lachey; and *Echoes of Honor*, by David Weber.

How to Contact: Accepts unsolicited mss. Submit ms or outline/synopsis and 3 consecutive sample chapters with SASE (or IRC). Reports in 6-9 months. Will consider simultaneous submissions, "but grudgingly and not as seriously as exclusives." Occasionally critiques rejected mss.

Terms: Pays in royalties; offers advance. Sends galleys to author. Writer's guidelines for SASE.

Advice: "Keep an eye and a firm hand on the overall story you are telling. Style is important but less important than plot. Good style, like good breeding, never calls attention to itself. Read *Writing to the Point*, by Algis Budrys. We like to maintain long-term relationships with authors."

BAKER BOOKS, a division of Baker Book House, P.O. Box 6287, Grand Rapids MI 49516-6213. (616)676-9185. Fax: (616)676-9573. Website: www.bakerbooks.com (includes guidelines, "Meet Our Editors," book excerpts and features, company history, advance info. on future releases). **Acquisitions:** Rebecca Cooper, fiction editor. Estab. 1939. "Midsize Evangelical publisher." Publishes hardcover and paperback originals. Books: web offset print; average print order: 5,000-10,000; first novel print order: 5,000. Averages 130 total titles.

Needs: "We are mainly seeking fiction of two genres: contemporary women's fiction and mystery." No fiction that is not written from a Christian world view or of a genre not specified. Published *Praise Jerusalem!* and *Resting in the Bosom of the Lamb*, by Augusta Trobaugh (contemporary women's fiction); and *The Secrets of Barneveld Calvary*, by James Schaap (contemporary women's fiction).

How to Contact: Submit query letter, outline/synopsis and 3 sample chapters. SASE. Reports in 4-8 months on queries. Simultaneous submissions OK. Sometimes comments on rejected ms.

Terms: Pays royalties of 14% (of net). Sometimes offers advance. Sends galleys to author. Publishes ms 1 year

FOR EXPLANATIONS OF THESE SYMBOLS,
SEE THE INSIDE FRONT AND BACK COVERS OF THIS BOOK.

insider report

Leslie Pietrzyk has a bestseller on her hands—a Dutch bestseller

Leslie Pietrzyk

Photo by Donna Rowe

Leslie Pietrzyk's first novel *Pears on a Willow Tree*, an ambitious exploration into the lives of four generations of Polish matriarchs, was published in fall 1998 by Avon Books. "The title is a Polish expression," Pietrzyk explains; "it's a thing you say to someone who wishes for something she can't have." Though the novel's narrative weaves back and forth from the early part of the century to the present day, the story's tension centers around the relationship between the black sheep of the Marchewka family, Ginger, and her more responsible daughter, Amy. Both of these characters seem to want more than the other can give. Ginger feels smothered by the tightly-knit traditions of her Polish Catholic upbringing and finds her only sense of independence by drinking too much. Because Ginger was determined to move far away from her home in Detroit, Amy is left alone to cope with her mother's alcoholism. Amy finds herself desperately clutching to her richly-textured memories of Polish funerals, weddings, family reunions, and especially the food—fat *pierogis* and *kielbasa*—that sustains such a family through good times and bad.

Here in the U.S., *Pears On a Willow Tree* was greeted with good reviews and solid sales. But no one, especially not the author, predicted the huge success a book about American immigrants would have overseas. "The book is doing well in England, but it's Holland where it's really taken off. For the life of me I can't figure out why."

Here Pietrzyk talks about receiving her first taste of success and now being able to fulfill her lifelong ambition of writing full time.

Were you prepared for your success overseas?
I was pleased that my agent was able to sell the foreign rights in England and The Netherlands, but I never gave any thought to the possibility that there would be anything beyond that. It just seemed so out of my reality—I couldn't even imagine my words translated into Dutch. So I was quite thrilled when my agent called me one morning and said, "Leslie, you're my first best-selling author in The Netherlands."

Who was responsible for the Dutch translation? Do you think your book will be translated into any other languages?
At this point, the likelihood of additional foreign sales is quite unlikely unless the paperback becomes a big seller in the U.S. or someone makes a movie.

I'm not sure if my translation experience is the norm or not, but I imagined that someone would contact me at some point and perhaps ask questions about odd Americanisms in the book (e.g., what is a dork?). Instead I went to my mailbox one day, and there was a copy of the book—translated, published, out in the world.

Have you thought about going overseas to promote the book?
At one point there was talk about my going to Amsterdam, but that didn't come to pass. I would've loved to have gone.

What kind of work have you done to promote the book at home?
I've been a shameless maniac about promoting the book here. I sent postcards to everyone I know and asked close friends to send postcards to everyone they know. I printed up business cards that I give to everyone I meet. Yesterday I gave one to the man next to me at the car service center (his wife was Polish and he seemed very interested). I've spoken to book clubs; I've been on a library panel; and I've arranged readings for myself at bookstores and through various Polish-American organizations. So far my travels have taken me to Detroit, Baltimore, Connecticut, Boston, Savannah, Rochester, Minneapolis, Iowa City, all over. It's a lot of time and energy—both the organization and the traveling—but I think it's worthwhile. I very much enjoy connecting with readers.

My mother was kind enough to produce a website for the book, which has been surprisingly useful for readers wanting more information and people inviting me to give readings. She's posted reviews and an essay I wrote for the publisher's newsletter about where I got the idea for the book. If anyone is interested the address is *http://members/aol.com.willowpear/pears.htm*.

Who do you imagine your readers are?
I never really imagine my readers as I'm writing. While it feels that this is the type of book that appeals mainly to women, I've found that men enjoy it as well. Often they are reminded of their mothers or family growing up or they like the insight into the mother-daughter relationship. And though it's a book about Polish-Americans—and that community has been very welcoming and supportive—I've also met people from other ethnic backgrounds who relate to the dilemmas these women face. It's a universal story in many ways—mothers and daughters trying to get along, a family struggling to find its place in America.

Your book includes your e-mail address along with your biographical information. Tell me about your favorite e-mails from fans. Any from Holland or England?
My editor thought I was a nut for putting my e-mail address on the book cover, but I thought it would be fun to see what sort of responses I'd get. And it has been interesting—nobody too kooky! I've gotten loads of messages from women who grew up in Polish families similar to the one I write about. I like it when they share stories about their childhoods and families. Perhaps my favorite e-mail was from a group of high school girls who were writing about me and my book as a project for a world literature class. I've also had a number of people contact me because they wanted more information for their book clubs—that's also nice. The e-mail address wasn't on the Dutch version (which may have been for the best since I wouldn't know how to respond in Dutch). There are two versions in England, sort of like a trade paperback

and a mass market version. The e-mail wasn't on the first, but it is on the mass market version, so we will see what happens. I think including an e-mail is a good idea, and I wish more authors would try it.

What have you learned about the business side of writing?
I feel very fortunate that I worked at a local Chamber of Commerce for seven years and was able to learn a lot about sales and marketing from expert sales people. That experience also made me more comfortable with the whole idea of having to sell yourself and your "product"— something I, like many writers, had no skills or interest in for a long time. What I've really learned is that it requires a lot of work and follow-up; marketing a book can almost become a full time job.

When does *Pears on a Willow Tree* go into paperback in America? And what are your expectations? Do you think this will change the life of your book?
The book comes out in paperback in July of '99. At this point, I'm trying not to have any expectations. It's so much simpler that way. But I've heard a book really "lives" in paperback— that book stores are much more prone to have paperback copies of your book for longer than they have hardcovers. I've found that to be true—six or seven months after the book came out in hardcover, it was hard to find in bookstores. A hardcover's life is very short—I suppose because not too many people buy hardcovers on impulse. They buy them because they've just read a review or they've heard about it from someone or it's an author they already like. I think people are much more willing to take a chance on a paperback because the cost is so much less. It will be interesting to see whether the rise of online bookstores will prolong the lives of hardcover books.

What will you do differently when your next book comes out?
Overall, I was very happy with my whole experience with *Pears on a Willow Tree*. I think with the next book, I will be more mentally prepared for the big commitment all the promotion requires. And I think the second book is always different than a first. With a first book there is the sense that "I've completed my life's goal," that getting that book published means it's the answer to everything. It's an amazing, wonderful experience to be sure—but it isn't the answer to everything. There's another book to write and another one after that. The first novel is just one exciting step in a long journey.
    —*Brad Vice*

after acceptance. Writer's guidelines for #10 SASE. Book catalog for 9½ × 12½ SAE and 3 first-class stamps. **Advice:** "We are not interested in historical fiction, romances, science fiction, Biblical narratives, or spiritual warfare novels. Please write for further information regarding our fiction lines. Send a cover letter describing your novel and your credentials as an author. Do not call to 'pass by' your idea. Do not send complete manuscripts."

BALLANTINE BOOKS, 201 E. 50th St., New York NY 10022. Subsidiary of Random House. **Acquisitions**: Leona Nevler, editor (all fiction); Peter Borland, executive editor (commercial fiction); Elisa Wares, senior editor (romance, mystery); Joe Blades, associate publisher (mystery). Publishes originals (general fiction, mass-market, trade paperback and hardcover). **Published new writers this year.** Averages over 120 total titles each year.
Needs: Major historical fiction, women's mainstream and general fiction.
How to Contact: Submit query letter or brief synopsis and first 100 pages of ms. SASE required. Reports in 2 months on queries; 4-5 months on mss.
Terms: Pays in royalties and advance.

◎ **BANKS CHANNEL BOOKS,** P.O. Box 4446, Wilmington NC 28406. (910)762-4677. Fax (910)762-4677. E-mail: bankschan@aol.com. Managing Editor: E.R. Olefsky. Estab. 1993. "We are a regional press doing books *by Carolina authors only*. We look at fiction through our novel contest only." Publishes hardcover and paperback originals and paperback reprints. Books: 50-60 lb. paper; perfect or hardcase bound; illustrations sometimes. Average print order: 3,000. First novel print order: 3,000-5,000. **Published new writers within the last year.** Plans 3 novels this year.
Needs: Literary. Recently published *Styles by Maggie Sweet*, by Judith Minthorn; *Takedown*, by E.M.J. Benjamin; and *Festival in Fire Season* (reprint), by Ellyn Bache.
How to Contact: Charges entry fee for contest. Send query letter first. Include 1-paragraph bio and list of publishing credits with submission. SASE for reply or return of ms. Reports in 1 week on queries; 2 months on mss. No simultaneous submissions.
Payment/Terms: Pays royalties of 6% minimum; 10% maximum. Sends galleys to author. Publishes ms 1 year after acceptance. Contest guidelines for #10 SASE.
Advice: "We are seeing work that ten years ago would have been snapped up by the big New York presses—and we are delighted to have it. Send a beautifully crafted piece of literary fiction to our contest. It doesn't need to have a Carolina setting, but it helps."

◪ **BANTAM BOOKS,** Division of Bantam Dell Publishing Group, Inc. 1540 Broadway, New York NY 10036. (212)354-6500. Fax: (212)782-9523. **Acquisitions:** Toni Burbank, Ann Harris, executive editors. Estab. 1945. Complete publishing: hard-cover, trade, mass market. Publishes 350 titles/year.
Imprint(s): Crime Line, Domain, **Fanfare, Loveswept, Spectra**.
Needs: Contemporary, literary, mystery, historical, western, romance, science fiction, fantasy, adventure, horror, gay, lesbian. Published *The Story of B*, by Daniel Quinn; and *The Burning Man*, by Phillip M. Margolin.
How to Contact: Query letter only first. No unsolicited mss. Include estimated word count and list of publishing credits. Simultaneous submissions OK. Reports on queries in 2-3 months.
Terms: Individually negotiated. Publishes ms 1 year after acceptance. Writer's guidelines (for romance only) free for SASE.

◖ **BANTAM/DOUBLEDAY/DELL BOOKS FOR YOUNG READERS DIVISION,** Random House Children's Publishing, 1540 Broadway, New York NY 10036. Division of Random House. Estab. 1945. Complete publishing: hardcover, trade, mass market.
Imprint(s): Delacorte Press Books for Young Readers, Doubleday Picture Books; Paperback line: Dell Yearling, Laurel-Leaf, Star Fire, Sweet Dreams, Sweet Valley High.
• The Young Readers Division offers two contests, the Delacorte Press Annual Prize for a First Young Adult Novel and the Marguerite DeAngeli Prize.
Needs: Childrens/juvenile, young adult/teen. Published *Baby*, by Patricia MacLachlan; *Whatever Happened to Janie*, by Caroline Cooney; *Nate the Great and the Pillowcase*, by Marjorie Sharmat.
How to Contact: Send query letter. Does not accept unsolicited mss. Submit through agent. Agented fiction 100%. Reports on queries "as soon as possible."
Terms: Individually negotiated; offers advance.

🌑◖ **BEACH HOLME PUBLISHERS LTD.,** 226-2040 W. 12th Ave., Vancouver, British Columbia V6J 2G2 Canada. (604)773-4868. Fax: (604)733-4860. E-mail: bhp@beachholme.bc.ca. Website: www.beachholme.bc.ca (includes guidelines, authors, excerpts, titles, ordering information). **Acquisitions:** Joy Gugeler, managing editor; Phil Ditomaso, Marketing Manager. Estab. 1971. Publishes trade paperback originals. Publishes 14 titles/year. "Accepting only Canadian submissions." **Publishes 40% previously unpublished writers/year.**
Needs: Adult literary fiction from authors published in Canadian literary magazines. Young adult (Canada historical/regional). "Interested in excellent quality, imaginative writing." Recently published *We Could Stay Here All Night*, by Debbie Howlett (short fiction).
How to Contact: Send cover letter, SASE, outline and two chapters. Reports in 2 months. Simultaneous submissions OK, if so noted.
Terms: Pays 10% royalty on retail price. Offers $500 average advance. Publishes ms 1 year after acceptance. Writer's guidelines free.
Advice: "Make sure the manuscript is well written. We see so many that only the unique and excellent can't be put down. Prior publication is a must. This doesn't necessarily mean book length manuscripts, but a writer should try to publish his or her short fiction."

◖ **FREDERIC C. BEIL, PUBLISHER, INC.,** 609 Whitaker St., Savannah GA 31401. E-mail: beilbook@beil.com. Website: www.beil.com. **Acquisitions:** Frederic C. Beil III, president; Mary Ann Bowman, editor. Estab. 1983. "Our objectives are (1) to offer to the reading public carefully selected texts of lasting value; (2) to adhere to high standards in the choice of materials and in bookmarking craftsmanship; (3) to produce books that exemplify good taste in format and design; and (4) to maintain the lowest cost consistent with quality." General trade publisher. Publishes hardcover originals and reprints. Books: acid-free paper; letterpress and offset printing;

Smyth-sewn, hardcover binding; illustrations. Average print order: 3,000. First novel print order: 3,000. **Plans 2 first novels this year.** Averages 14 total titles, 4 fiction titles each year.

Imprint(s): The Sandstone Press, Hypermedia, Inc.

Needs: Historical, biography, literary, regional, short story collections, translations. Published *A Woman of Means*, by Peter Taylor; *An Exile*, by Madison Jones; and *Delirium of the Brave*, by William C. Harris, Jr.

How to Contact: Does not accept unsolicited mss. Query first. Reports in 1 week on queries.

Terms: Payment "all negotiable." Sends galleys to author. Book catalog free on request.

THE BERKLEY PUBLISHING GROUP, Subsidiary of Penguin Putnam, 375 Hudson St., New York NY 10014. (212)366-2000. Publisher/Editor-in-Chief: Leslie Gelbman. Associate Director, Editorial: Susan Allison. Fiction Editors: Natalee Rosenstein, Judith Palais, Tom Colgan, Gail Fortune, Ginjer Buchanan, Lisa Considine, Denise Silvestro and Christine Zika. Nonfiction: Lisa Considine, Denise Silvestro and Christine Zika. Large commercial category line. Publishes paperback originals, trade paperbacks and hardcover and paperback reprints. Books: Paperbound printing; perfect binding; average print order: "depends on position in list." **Plans approximately 10 first novels this year.** Averages 1,180 total titles, 1,000 fiction titles each year.

Imprint(s): Berkley, Jove, Boulevard, **Ace Science Fiction.**

Needs: Fantasy, mainstream, mystery/suspense, romance (contemporary, historical), science fiction. Published works by Tom Clancy and Patricia Cornwell.

How to Contact: *Strongly* recommends agented material. Queries answered if SASE enclosed. Accepts simultaneous submissions. Reports in 3 months minimum on mss.

Terms: Pays royalties of 4-10%. Provides 10 author's copies. Publishes ms 2 years after acceptance. Writer's guidelines and book catalog not available.

Advice: "Aspiring novelists should keep abreast of the current trends in publishing by reading *The New York Times* Bestseller Lists, trade magazines for their desired genre and *Publishers Weekly.*"

BETHANY HOUSE PUBLISHERS, Subsidiary of Bethany Fellowship, Inc., 11400 Hampshire Ave. S., Minneapolis MN 55438. (612)829-2500. **Acquisitions:** Sharon Madison, review department. "The purpose of Bethany House Publishers' publishing program is to relate biblical truth to all areas of life, whether in the framework of a well-told story, a challenging book for spiritual growth, or a Bible reference work." Publishes hardcover and trade paperback originals, mass market paperback reprints. Publishes 120-150 titles/year.

Imprint(s): Bethany Backyard (Rochelle Glöege, editor).

Needs: Adventure, historical, mainstream/contemporary, religious (romance), young adult. Recently published *A Quiet Strength*, by Janette Oke; *The Postcard*, by Beverly Lewis; *Mandie & the Buried Stranger*, by Lois Gladys Leppard; and *Ephesus Fragment*, by Gary Parker.

How to Contact: Submit proposal package to Sharon Madison, review department, including synopsis, 3 sample chapters, author information, educational background and writing experience with SASE. Reports in 3 months. Simultaneous submissions OK.

Terms: Pays negotiable royalty on wholesale price. Offers negotiable advance. Publishes ms 1 year after acceptance. Writer's guidelines free. Book catalog for 9×12 SAE with 5 first-class stamps.

BIRCH BROOK PRESS, P.O. Box 81, Delhi NY 13753. (212)353-3326. Fax: (607)746-7453. **Acquisitions**: Tom Tolnay, publisher. Estab. 1982. Small publisher of popular culture and literary titles in handcrafted letterpress editions. Specializes in fiction anthologies with specific theme. Books: 80 lb. vellum paper; letterpress printing; wood engraving illustrations. Average print order: 500-1,000. Averages 4-6 total titles; 2-3 fiction titles each year. Distributes titles through Ingram, Baker and Taylor, Barnes & Noble On-Line, amazon.com. Promotes titles through catalogs, direct mail and group ads.

Imprint(s): Birch Brook Press, Persephone Press and Birch Brook Impressions.

Needs: Literary. "We make specific calls for fiction when we are doing an anthology." Plans to publish literary-quality anthology of mystery short stories. Published *Magic & Madness in the Library*, edited by Eric Graeber (fiction collection); *Kilimanjaro Burning*, by John Robinson (novella); *Autobiography of Maria Callas: A Novel*, by Alma Bond; and *The Derelict Genius of Martin M*, by Frank Fagan.

How to Contact: Prefers samples with query letter and SASE. Reports on queries in 2-6 weeks; mss 2-3 months. Simultaneous submissions OK. Sometimes critiques or comments on rejected mss.

Terms: Modest flat fee as advance against royalties. Writers guidelines and catalog for SASE.

Advice: "Write well on subjects of interest to BBP such as outdoors, fly fishing, baseball, music and literary mysteries."

BkMk PRESS, UMKC, University House, 5100 Rockhill Rd., Kansas City MO 64110-2499. (816)235-2558. Fax: (816)235-2611. E-mail: bkmk@umkc.edu. **Acquisitions**: James McKinley, director. Estab. 1971. Small independent press. "Mostly short story collections." Publishes hardback and paperback originals. Books: standard paper; offset printing; perfect- and case-bound; average print order: 600. **Publishes 0-1 previously unpublished authors/year.** Averages 6 total titles, 1 fiction title each year. Distributes titles through direct mail and wholesalers (Books in Print). Promotes titles through Books in Print, some magazine/journal advertising, brochure mailings, readings and appearances.

Needs: Contemporary, ethnic, experimental, literary, translations. "Fiction publishing limited to short stories and novellas. Ordinarily prints anthologies or collections by one writer. BkMk Press does not publish commercial novels." Published *Drive Dive Dance & Fight*, by Thomas E. Kennedy (short stories); *Body and Blood*, by Philip Russell (episodic novel); and *Mustaches & Other Stories*, by G.W. Clift (short stories).

How to Contact: Query first or submit 2 sample chapters with SASE. Reports in 2-3 months on queries; 6 months on mss.

Terms: Pays royalties of 10% and 20 author's copies. Sends galleys to author. Free book catalog.

Advice: "We value the exceptional, rare, well-crafted and daring. Please pursue magazine/journal publication of individual stories before you query us. The object is to hone your craft before you place it before a publication." Especially interested in Midwestern writers.

BLACK HERON PRESS, P.O. Box 95676, Seattle WA 98145. **Acquisitions**: Jerry Gold, publisher. Estab. 1984. One-person operation; no immediate plans to expand. "We're known for literary fiction. We've done several Vietnam War titles and several surrealistic fictions." Publishes paperback and hardback originals. Average print order: 2,000; first novel print order: 1,500. Averages 4 fiction titles each year. Distributes titles nationally.

• Four books published by Black Heron Press have won awards from King County Arts Commission. This press received Bumbershoot Most Significant Contribution to Literature in 1996.

Needs: Adventure, contemporary, experimental, humor/satire, literary, science fiction. Vietnam war novel—literary. "We don't want to see fiction written for the mass market. If it sells to the mass market, fine, but we don't see ourselves as a commercial press." Recently published *Charlie & The Children*, by Joanna C. Scott; *The Fruit 'N Food*, by Leonard Chang; and *In A Cold Open Field*, by Sheila Solomon Klass.

How to Contact: Query with first 50 pages only. Reports in 3 months on queries. Simultaneous submissions OK.

Terms: Pays standard royalty rates. No advance.

Advice: "A query letter should tell me: 1) number of words; 2) number of pages; 3) if ms is available on floppy disk; 4) if parts of novel have been published; 5) if so, where?"

JOHN F. BLAIR, PUBLISHER, 1406 Plaza Dr., Winston-Salem NC 27103. (910)768-1374. Fax: (910)768-9194. **Acquisitions**: Carolyn Sakowski, president. Estab. 1954. Small independent publisher. Publishes hardcover and paperback originals. Books: Acid-free paper; offset printing; illustrations. Average print order: 5,000. Number of titles: 17 in 1996, 20 in 1997, 20 in 1999. "Among our 17-20 books, we do one novel a year."

Needs: Prefers regional material dealing with southeastern U.S. No confessions or erotica. "Our editorial focus concentrates mostly on nonfiction." Published *Freedom's Altar*, by Charles Price; *Caveat*, by Laura Kalpakian; and *Something Blue*, by Jean Spaugh.

How to Contact: Query or submit with SASE. Simultaneous submissions OK. Reports in 1 month. Publishes ms 1-2 years after acceptance. Free book catalog.

Terms: Negotiable.

Advice: "We are primarily interested in nonfiction titles. Most of our titles have a tie-in with North Carolina or the southeastern United States. Please enclose a cover letter and outline with the manuscript. We prefer to review queries before we are sent complete manuscripts. Queries should include an approximate word count."

THE BLUE SKY PRESS, Imprint of Scholastic Inc., 555 Broadway, New York NY 10012. (212)343-6100. Fax: (212)343-4535. Website: www.scholastic.com. **Acquisitions:** Editorial Director. Blue Sky Press publishes primarily juvenile picture books. Publishes hardcover originals. Publishes 15 titles/year.

• Because of a long backlog of books, The Blue Sky Press is not accepting unsolicited submissions.

Needs: Juvenile: adventure, fantasy, historical, humor, mainstream/contemporary, picture books, multicultural, folktales. Published *Bluish*, by Virginia Hamilton (novel); *No, David!*, by David Shannon (picture book); and *To Every Thing There is a Season*, by Leo and Diane Dillon (multicultural/historical).

How to Contact: Agented fiction 25%. Reports in 6 months on queries.

Terms: Pays 10% royalty on wholesale price, between authors and illustrators. Publishes ms 2½ years after acceptance.

BOREALIS PRESS, 110 Bloomingdale St., Ottawa, Ontario K2C 4A4 Canada. Fax: (613)829-7783. E-mail: borealis@istar.ca. Website: www.borealispress.com (includes names of editors, authors, titles). **Acquisitions**: Frank Tierney, editor; Glenn Clever, fiction editor. Estab. 1970. "Publishes Canadiana, with an emphasis on titles suitable for adoption at senior high school/university levels." Publishes hardcover and paperback originals and reprints. Books: standard book-quality paper; offset printing; perfect and cloth binding. Average print order: 1,000. Buys juvenile mss with b&w illustrations. Averages 4 total titles each year. Promotes titles through website, catalogue distribution, fliers for titles, ads in media.

Imprint(s): *Journal of Canadian Poetry*, Tecumseh Press Ltd., Canadian Critical Editions Series.

• Borealis Press has a "New Canadian Drama," with six books in print. The series won Ontario Arts Council and Canada Council grants.

Needs: Contemporary, literary, juvenile, young adult. "Must have a Canadian content or author; query first." Published *Jamie of Fort William*, by Elizabeth Kouhi; *Sunshine Sketches of a Little Town*, by Stephen Leacock; and *Tribe of Star Bear*, Victoria Mihaly.

How to Contact: Submit query with SASE (Canadian postage). No simultaneous submissions. Reports in 2 weeks on queries, 3-4 months on mss. Publishes ms 1-2 years after acceptance.

Terms: Pays 10% royalties and 3 free author's copies; no advance. Sends galleys to author. Publishes ms 18 months after acceptance. Free book catalog with SASE.

Advice: "Have your work professionally edited. Our greatest challenge is finding good authors, i.e., those who submit innovative and original material."

BOYDS MILLS PRESS, Subsidiary of Highlights for Children, 815 Church St., Honesdale PA 18431. (800)490-5111. **Acquisitions**: Beth Troop, manuscript coordinator. Estab. 1990. "Independent publisher of quality books for children of all ages." Publishes hardcover. Books: Coated paper; offset printing; case binding; 4-color illustrations; average print order varies. Plans 4 fiction titles (novels). Distributes titles through independent sales reps and via order line directly from Boyds Mills Press. Promotes titles through sales and professional conferences; sales reps; reviews. **Publishes 2 previously unpublished writers/year.**

- Boyds Mills Press author Jan Cheripko won the Young Adults Choices for 1998 and the 1997 Joan Fassler Memorial Book Award for *Imitate the Tiger*.

Needs: Juvenile, young adult (adventure, animal, contemporary, ethnic, historical, sports). Recently published *Kat's Surrender*, by Theresa Martin Golding (YA); *Barn Savers*, by Linda Oatman High (picture book); and *It's Just a Game*, by John Farrell (picture book).

How to Contact: Accepts unsolicited mss. Send first three chapters and synopsis. Reports in 1 month. Simultaneous submissions OK.

Terms: Pays standard rates. Sends pre-publication galleys to author. Time between acceptance and publication depends on "what season it is scheduled for." Writer's guidelines for #10 SASE.

Advice: "Read through our recently published titles and review our catalogue. If your book is too different from what we publish, then it may not fit our list. Feel free to query us if you're not sure."

BRANDEN PUBLISHING CO., Subsidiary of Branden Press, Box 843, 17 Station St., Brookline Village MA 02447. Fax: (617)734-2046. E-mail: branden@branden.com. Website: www.branden.com. **Acquisitions**: Adolph Caso, editor. Estab. 1967. Publishes hardcover and paperback originals and reprints. Books: 55-60 lb. acid-free paper; case- or perfect-bound; illustrations; average print order: 5,000. **Plans 5 first novels this year.** Averages 15 total titles, 5 fiction titles each year.

Imprint(s): I.P.L.

Needs: Ethnic, historical, literary, military/war, short story collections and translations. Looking for "contemporary, fast pace, modern society." No porno, experimental or horror. Published *I, Morgain*, by Harry Robin; *The Bell Keeper*, by Marilyn Seguin; and *The Straw Obelisk*, by Adolph Caso.

How to Contact: Does not accept unsolicited mss. Query *only* with SASE. Reports in 1 week on queries, with either "we cannot use," or "send entire manuscript."

Terms: Pays royalties of 5-10% minimum. Advance negotiable. Provides 10 author's copies. Sends galleys to author. Publishes ms "several months" after acceptance.

Advice: "Publishing more fiction because of demand. *Do not make phone, fax or e-mail inquiries.* Do not oversubmit; single submissions only; do not procrastinate if contract is offered. Our audience is a well-read general public, professionals, college students, and some high school students. We like books by or about women."

GEORGE BRAZILLER, INC., 171 Madison Ave., Suite 1103, New York NY 10016. (212)889-0909. **Acquisitions:** Mary Taveros, production editor. Publishes hardcover and trade paperback originals and reprints. Publishes 25 titles/year.

Needs: Ethnic, gay, lesbian, literary. "We rarely do fiction but when we have published novels, they have mostly been literary novels." Published *Blindsight*, by Herve Guibert; and *Papa's Suitcase*, by Gerhard Kopf (literary fiction).

How to Contact: Submit 4-6 sample chapters with SASE. Agented fiction 20%. Reports in 3 months on proposals.

Terms: Pays standard royalty: 8% paperback; 10-15% hardback. Publishes ms 10 months after acceptance. Writer's guidelines and book catalog free.

BRIDGE WORKS PUBLISHING CO., 221 Bridge Lane, Box 1798, Bridgehampton NY 11932. (516)537-3418. Fax: (516)537-5092. E-mail: bap@hamptons.com. **Acquisitions**: Barbara Phillips, editorial director. Estab. 1992. "We are very small, doing only 4-6 books a year. We publish quality fiction and nonfiction. Our books are routinely reviewed in major publications." Publishes hardcover originals. Average print order: 5,000. **Published new writers within the last year.** Plans 4 novels this year. Averages 4-6 total titles (75% fiction) each year. Distributes titles through National Book Network.

- Bridge Works author Ann Mohin received the 1998 *New York Times* Notable Book of the Year Award for *The Farm She Was.*

Needs Humor/satire, literary, translations. Recently published *Free Reign*, by Rosemary Aubert; and *Duty*, by Jim R. Lane.

How to Contact: Accepts unsolicited mss, but "must send query letter first." Query with outline/synopsis and 4 sample chapters. "If you are a first-time writer, do not query or send manuscripts unless work has been edited by a freelance editor." Include estimated word count and list of publishing credits. Send SASE for reply, return of ms or send a disposable copy of ms. Agented fiction 50%. Reports in 2 weeks on queries; 2 months on mss. Sometimes critiques or comments on rejected mss.

Payment/Terms: Pays royalties of 10% maximum "based on cover price with a reserve against returns." Average advance: $1,000. Sends galleys to author. Publishes ms 1 year after acceptance.

Advice: "We are very interested in discovering new writers and we work closely with our authors in both the editorial and marketing processes. This has proved invaluable to new authors."

⊞ ◯ THE BRITISH BOOK COMPANY, INC., 149 Palos Verdes Blvd., Suite B, Redondo Beach CA 90277. (310)373-5917. Fax: (310)373-7342. E-mail: th@malvernfirst.com. Website: www.malvernfirst.com (includes writer's guidelines, names of editors, book catalog, interviews with authors and chat line). **Acquisitions:** Tony Harold (general adult); Kelli Cordray (general and short stories). Estab. 1998 (in UK for 20 years). "Midsized independent." Publishes hardcover originals. Books: 100 gsm paper; sheet fed printing; cased seon binding. First novel print order: 2,000-5,000. **Published 10 new writers within the last year.** Plans 8 first novels this year. Averages 20-30 total titles, 15-20 fiction titles/year. Always critiques or comments on rejected ms.

Imprint: The Malvern Publishing Co. Ltd. (first novels).

Needs: Adventure, family saga, historical (general), horror, humor satire, lesbian, literary, mainstream, military/war, mystery/suspense, romance, short story collections, thriller/espionage. "Want more general mainstream adult fiction. Publishes short story anthologies. Writers may submit to Kelli Cordray. Recently published *Making It*, by Ira Skutch (mainstream); *Over Under Sideways Down*, by Gordon Skene (mainstream); and *L.A. Breakdown*, by Lou Mathews (literary). Publishes the *Another Great American First Novel* series.

How to Contact: Accepts unsolicited mss. Query with outline/synopsis and 2-3 sample chapters (not first or last). Unsolicited queries/correspondence by e-mail and fax OK. Include estimated word count and 200 word bio. Send a disposable copy of the ms. Agented fiction 10%. Reports in 2 weeks on queries; 2-3 months on mss. No simultaneous submissions.

Terms: Pays royalties of 7½% minimum; 15% maximum. Offers negotiable advance. Sends galleys to author. Publishes ms 6-18 months after acceptance. Writer's guidelines and book catalog free.

Advice: "Decline in first novels by major houses provides us with more writers to select from. Follow our guidelines when submitting. Don't tell us how good your novel is—let us read it. Manuscripts should be on one side of paper only and double spaced. Check for silly mistakes, write well, be prepared to revise if needed."

⊘ Ⓐ BROADWAY BOOKS, Division of Random House, Inc. 1540 Broadway, New York NY 10036. (212)354-6500. Website: www.broadwaybooks.com. Publisher/Editor-in-Chief: Robert Asahina. Broadway publishes general interest nonfiction and fiction for adults. Publishes hardcover and trade paperback originals and reprints.

Needs: Publishes commercial literary fiction. Recently published *Freedomland*, by Richard Price.

How to Contact: This publisher accepts agented fiction only.

✦ ✓ ⊘ BROKEN JAW PRESS, (formerly Maritimes Arts Projects Productions), Box 596, Stn. A, Fredericton, New Brunswick E3B 5A6 Canada. Phone/fax: (506)454-5127. E-mail: jblades@nbnet.nb.ca. Website: www.brokenjaw.com. **Acquisitions:** Joe Blades, publisher. "We are a small, mostly literary, Canadian publishing house. We accept only Canadian authors." Publishes Canadian-authored trade paperback originals and reprints. **Publishes 1 previously unpublished fiction writer/year.** Publishes 12 titles/year, plus *New Muse of Contempt* magazine. Distributes titles through General Distribution Services Ltd. (Toronto, Vancouver and Lewiston, NY).

● Broken Jaw Press is not currently accepting unsolicited submissions or queries. Only accepting mss or queries pertaining to the contest for first book for unpublished fiction writers (New Muse Award). Query with SASE for details or visit website.

Imprint(s): Book Rat, SpareTime Editions, Dead Sea Physh Products, Maritimes Arts Projects Productions.

Needs: Literary. Published *Rum River*, by Raymond Fraser; *Herbarium of Souls*, by Vladimir Tasic; and *Like Minds*, by Shannon Friesen.

How to Contact: Not currently accepting unsolicited book mss or queries.

Terms: Pays 10% royalty on retail price. Offers $0-100 advance. Publishes ms 1 year after acceptance. Writer's guidelines for #10 SASE (Canadian postage or IRC). Book catalog for 9 × 12 SAE with $1.25 Canadian stamps or 2 IRCs or visit website.

✦ ✓ ◎ CANADIAN INSTITUTE OF UKRAINIAN STUDIES PRESS, CIUS Toronto Publications Office, University of Toronto, Dept. of Slavic Languages and Literatures, 21 Sussex Ave., Toronto, Ontario M5S 1A1 Canada. (780)978-8240. Fax: (780)978-2672. E-mail: cius@chass.utoronto.ca. Website: www.utoronto.ca/cius. **Acquisitions:** Maxim Tarnawsky, director. Estab. 1976. "We publish scholarship about Ukraine and Ukrainians in Canada." Publishes hardcover and trade paperback originals and reprints. Publishes 5-10 titles/year.

Needs: Ukrainian literary works. "We do not publish fiction except for use as college textbooks." Recently published *The Word and War*, by Rener Jeanne Hanchuk; *Between Kyiv and Constantinople*, by Andre Partykevich Zustrichi; and *Proshchannia Kryha Druka*, by Hrykory Kostiuk.

How to Contact: Query or submit complete ms. Reports in 1 month on queries, 3 months on mss.

Terms: Nonauthor-subsidy publishes 20-30% of books. Pays 0-2% royalty on retail price. Publishes ms 2 years after acceptance. Writer's guidelines and book catalog free.

Advice: "We are a scholarly press and do not normally pay our authors. Our audience consists of university students and teachers and the general public interested in Ukrainian and Ukrainian-Canadian affairs."

CANDLEWICK PRESS, Subsidiary of Walker Books Ltd. (London), 2067 Massachusetts Ave., Cambridge MA 02140. (617)661-3330. Fax: (617)661-0565. **Acquisitions:** Liz Bicknell, editor-in-chief (picture books/poetry/fiction); Mary Lee Donovan, executive editor (nonfiction/fiction); Gale Pryor, editor (nonfiction/fiction); Amy Ehrlich, editor at large (picture books); Kara LaReau, assistant editor (fiction/poetry); Cynthia Platt (fiction/nonfiction). Candlewick Press publishes high-quality illustrated children's books for ages infant through young adult. "We are a truly child-centered publisher." Estab. 1991. Publishes hardcover originals, trade paperback originals and reprints. Publishes 200 titles/year.

Needs: Juvenile. Recently published *Dove Song*, by Kristine Franklin; and *Burger Wuss*, by M.T. Anderson.

How to Contact: Agented submissions only. Reports in 10 weeks on mss. Simultaneous submissions OK, if so noted.

Terms: Pays 10% royalty on retail price. Advance varies. Publishes ms 3 years after acceptance for illustrated books, 1 year for others.

CAROLRHODA BOOKS, INC., Division of the Lerner Publishing Group, 241 First Ave. N., Minneapolis MN 55401. (612)332-3344. Fax: (612)332-7615. Website: www.lernerbooks.com. **Acquisitions:** Rebecca Poole, submissions editor. Estab. 1969. Carolrhoda Books seeks creative K-6 children's nonfiction and historical fiction with unique and well-developed ideas and angles. Publishes hardcover originals. Publishes 50-60 titles/year.

Needs: Juvenile, historical, picture books, multicultural, fiction for beginning readers. "We continue to add fiction for middle grades and 1-2 picture books per year. Not looking for folktales or anthropomorphic animal stories." Published *Come Morning*, by Leslie Davis Guccione (historical); *Fire in the Sky*, by Candice Ransom (historical); and *Fire at the Triangle Factory*, by Holly Littlefield (easy reader historical).

How to Contact: "Submissions are accepted in the months of March and October only. Submissions received in any other month will be returned unopened." Query with SASE or send complete ms for picture books. Include SASE for return of ms. Reports in 2-6 months. Simultaneous submissions OK.

Terms: Pays royalty on wholesale price, makes outright purchase or negotiates payments of advance against royalty. Advance varies. Publishes ms 18 months after acceptance. Writer's guidelines and book catalog for 9×12 SASE with $3 in postage. No phone calls.

Advice: "Our audience consists of children ages four to eleven. We publish very few picture books. We prefer manuscripts that can fit into one of our series. Spend time developing your idea in a unique way or from a unique angle; avoid trite, hackneyed plots and ideas."

CARROLL & GRAF PUBLISHERS, INC., Avalon Publishing Group, 19 W. 21st St., Suite 601, New York NY 10010. (212)627-8590. Fax: (212)627-8490. **Acquisitions:** Kent Carroll, publisher/executive editor. Estab. 1983. "Carroll and Graf is one of the few remaining independent trade publishers and is therefore able to publish successfully and work with first-time authors and novelists." Publishes hardcover and paperback originals and paperback reprints. **Plans 5 first novels this year.** Averages 120 total titles, 75 fiction titles each year. Average first novel print order 7,500 copies.

Needs: Contemporary, erotica, fantasy, science fiction, literary, mainstream and mystery/suspense. No romance.

How to Contact: Does not accept unsolicited mss. Query first or submit outline/synopsis and sample chapters. SASE. Reports in 2 weeks. Occasionally critiques rejected mss.

Terms: Pays in royalties of 6% minimum; 15% maximum; advance negotiable. Sends galleys to author. Publishes ms 9 months after acceptance. Free book catalog on request.

CARTWHEEL BOOKS, Imprint of Scholastic, Inc., 555 Broadway, New York NY 10012. (212)343-6100. Fax: (212)343-4444. Website: www.scholastic.com. **Acquisitions:** Lisa Baker, editor; Sonia Black, editor; Diane Muldrow, editor. Estab. 1991. "Cartwheel Books publishes innovative books for children, ages 3-9. We are looking for 'novelties' that are books first, play objects second. Even without its gimmick, a Cartwheel Book should stand alone as a valid piece of children's literature." Publishes hardcover originals. Publishes 85-100 titles/year.

Needs: Fantasy, humor, juvenile, mystery, picture books, science fiction. "The subject should have mass market appeal for very young children. Humor can be helpful, but not necessary. Mistakes writers make are a reading level that is too difficult, a topic of no interest or too narrow, or manuscripts that are too long." Published *Little Bill (series)*, by Bill Cosby (picture book); *Dinofours* (series), by Steve Metzger (picture book); and *The Haunted House*, by Fiona Conboy (3-D puzzle storybook).

How to Contact: Agented submissions or previously published authors only. Reports in 2 months on queries; 6 months on mss. Simultaneous submissions OK.

Terms: Pays royalty on retail price. Offers advance. Publishes ms 2 years after acceptance. Book catalog for 9×12 SAE. Writer's guidelines free.

Advice: Audience is young children, ages 3-9. "Know what types of books the publisher does. Some manuscripts that don't work for one house may be perfect for another. Check out bookstores or catalogs to see where your writing would 'fit' best."

CATBIRD PRESS, 16 Windsor Rd., North Haven CT 06473-3015. E-mail: catbird@pipeline.com. Website: www.catbirdpress.com (includes writer's guidelines, book information and excerpts). Publisher: Robert Wechsler. **Acquisitions:** Hrissi Haldezos. Estab. 1987. Small independent trade publisher. "Catbird Press specializes in sophisticated, imaginative prose humor as well as humorous fiction and Central European literature in translation." Publishes cloth and paperback originals. Books: acid-free paper; offset printing; paper binding; illustrations (where relevant). Average print order: 4,000. First novel print order: 3,000. **Publishes 0-1 previously unpublished writers/year.** Averages 4 total titles, 1-2 fiction titles each year. Promotes books through reviews, publicity, advertising, readings and signings.

- Catbird Press's *It Came With the House*, by Jeffrey Shaffer, was a finalist in the Best Humor Book category of the Small Press Book Awards.

Needs: Humor (specialty); literary, translations (specialty Czech, French and German read in-house). No thriller, historical, science fiction, or other genre writing; only writing with a fresh style and approach. Recently published *Coast to Coast*, by Frederic Raphael; *City, Sister, Silver*, by Jachym Topol; and *The Cornerstone*, by Randall Beth Platt.

How to Contact: Accepts unsolicited mss but no queries. Submit outline/synopsis with sample chapter. Accepts queries (but no mss) by e-mail. SASE. Reports in 2-4 weeks on mss. Simultaneous submissions OK, "but let us know if simultaneous."

Terms: Pays royalties of 7½-10%. Average advance: $2,000; offers negotiable advance. Sends galleys to author. Publishes ms approximately 1 year after acceptance. Terms depend on particular book. Writer's guidelines for #10 SASE or available at website.

Advice: "Book publishing is a business. If you're not willing to learn the business and research the publishers, as well as learn the craft, you should not expect much from publishers. It's a waste of time to send genre or other derivative writing to a literary press. We are interested in novelists who combine a sense of humor with a true knowledge of and love for language, a lack of ideology, care for craft and self-criticism."

CENTENNIAL PUBLICATIONS, 256 Nashua Ct., Grand Junction CO 81503. (970)243-8780. **Acquisitions:** Dick Spurr, publisher. Publishes hardcover and trade paperback originals and reprints. Publishes 4-5 titles/year.

Needs: Humor, mystery. "We are very selective in this market." Published *In Over My Waders*, by Jack Sayer (humor).

How to Contact: Submit synopsis. Reports in 1 week on queries, 1 month on mss.

Terms: Pays 8-10% royalty on retail price. Offers average of $1,000 advance. Publishes ms 8 months after acceptance. Book catalog free.

CENTER PRESS, P.O. Box 16452, Encino CA 91416-6452. (818)377-4301. Website: members.xoom. com/CenterPress. **Acquisitions:** Gabriella Stone, managing editor. Estab. 1979. "Small three-person publisher with expansion goals." Publishes hardcover and paperback originals, especially short story and poetry collections. Plans 1-2 novels this year. Averages 6 total titles.

- Center Press sponsors the Masters Literary Award.

Needs: Erotica, historical, humor/satire, literary, short story collections. *List for novels filled for next year or two.*

How to Contact: Does not accept unsolicited mss. Query through agent only. SASE. Agented fiction 90%. Reports in 2 months on queries. Simultaneous submissions OK. Occasionally critiques or comments on rejected mss; fee varies.

Terms: Payment rate is "very variable." Sends galleys to author.

Advice: "Be competent, be solvent. Know who you are. Target your market."

CHARIOT VICTOR PUBLISHING, 4050 Lee Vance View, Colorado Springs CO 80918. (719)536-3280. **Acquisitions:** Submit all one-page query letters to Melissa Borger. Estab. 1875. Publishes hardcover and paperback originals.

Imprint(s): Faith Parenting, **Faith Kids**, Victor Books, Faithful Woman, Lion Publishing.

Needs: Religious/inspirational, juvenile, adult, sports, Biblical, Bible studies, parenting, picture book and easy-to-read. Published *A Woman's Journey* series, by Dee Brestin; and *Oceans and Rivers*, by Michael Carroll. Published new writers within the last year.

How to Contact: No unsolicited mss. Only accepted agented and requested submissions. All unsolicited mss are returned unopened.

Terms: Royalties vary ("depending on whether it is trade, mass market or cloth and whether children's or adults"). Offers advance. Writer's guidelines with SASE.

Advice: "Focus on family spiritual growth in four areas: parent, child, personal, women. Strong focus on discipleship. Publishes books toddler through adult. Not accepting fiction at this time."

CHARLESBRIDGE PUBLISHING, 85 Main St., Watertown MA 02472. (617)926-0329, ext. 140. Website: www.charlesbridge.com (includes writer's guidelines, names of editors, authors, titles, chat lines). **Acquisitions:** Elena Dworkin Wright, editorial director. Estab. 1980. "We are looking for fiction to use as literature in the math and physical science curriculum." **Published 1 previously unpublished writer/year.** Publishes school programs and hardcover and trade paperback originals. Publishes 20 books/year. Promotes titles through catalogs, trade shows, education conventions, author presentations through our speaker's bureau.

Imprint: *Talewinds* (fiction).

Needs: Math concepts in nonrhyming story. Published *Sir Cumference and the First Round Table*, by Cindy Neuschwander (a math adventure/picture book); *Turn of the Century*, by Ellen Jackson; and *Once Upon a Dime*, by Nancy Kelly Allen (picture books).

How to Contact: Reports in 2 months.

Terms: Publishes ms 1 year after acceptance.

Advice: "We market through schools, book stores and specialty stores at museums, science centers, etc."

CHINOOK PRESS, 1432 Yellowstone Ave., Billings MT 59102. (406)245-7704. Editor/Publisher: Mary Ellen Westwood. Estab. 1996. "One-person operation on a part-time basis just starting out. I hope to have a catalog of equal parts fiction, nonfiction and poetry." Publishes paperback originals. Books: acid-free paper; printing and binding suitable to product; illustrations. Average print order: 2,000-5,000. First novel print order: 2,000-5,000. Plans 1 first novel this year. Averages 4 total titles, 2 fiction titles each year. Sometimes critiques or comments on rejected mss.

Needs: Adventure, childrens/juvenile (all types), ethnic/multicultural, experimental, family saga, fantasy (all types), feminist, historical, humor/satire, literary, mainstream/contemporary, mystery/suspense (all types), regional (the West), science fiction (all types), short story collections, translations, young adult/teen (all types). "I want fiction that educates and uplifts, that shows real human beings in real or imagined situations that aid in human advancement. I do not want fiction that titillates for the sole purpose of titillation. I want fiction with a definite message and purpose."

How to Contact: Accepts unsolicited mss. Submit complete ms with cover letter. Include estimated word count, 1-page bio, Social Security number, list of publishing credits and "brief explanation of why you wrote what you wrote." Send SASE for return of ms. Reports in 2 months on queries and mss. Simultaneous submissions OK "if identified as such."

Terms: "We make individual arrangements with each author depending on book, but author must provide promotion time." Sends galleys to author. Publishes ms 2 months to 2 years after acceptance. Writer's guidelines for #10 SASE.

Advice: "I am a well-trained and well-practiced editor with 29 years experience in both journalism and law. Bad spelling, incorrect grammar and muddy thinking will not sell your work to me. But your best effort will receive attentive and enthusiastic handling here. I want more new and creative solutions to the human condition. I want fewer 'Oh, woe is me! I just can't do anything with my life.' stories."

CIRCLET PRESS, 1770 Massachusetts Ave., #278, Cambridge MA 02140. (617)864-0492 (noon-4p.m. EST). Fax: (617)864-0663, call before faxing. E-mail: circlet-info@circlet.com. Website: www.circlet.com/ (includes previews of upcoming books, catalog of complete books in print, links to authors' web pages and other publishers). **Acquisitions:** Cecilia Tan, publisher. Estab. 1992. Small, independent specialty book publisher. "We are the only book publisher specializing in science fiction and fantasy of an erotic nature." Publishes paperback originals. Books: perfect binding; illustrations sometimes; average print order: 2,500. **Publishes 50 previously unpublished writers/year.** Averages 6-8 anthologies each year. Distributes titles through the LPC Group in the US/Canada, Turnaround UK in the UK and Bulldog Books in Australia. Promotes titles through reviews in book trade and general media, mentions in Publishers Weekly, Bookselling This Week and regional radio/TV.

● Nominated titles from Circlet Press were finalists in the Small Press Book Award, Firecracker Alternative Book Award and Lambda Literary Award in 1998.

Imprints: The Ultra Violet Library (non-erotic lesbian/gay fantasy and science fiction).

Needs: "We publish only short stories of erotic science fiction/fantasy, of all persuasions (gay, straight, bi, feminist, lesbian, etc.). No horror! No exploitative sex, murder or rape. No degradation." No novels. All books are anthologies of short stories. Recently published *Through a Brazen Minor*, by Delia Sherman (fantasy); *Things Invisible to See*, edited by Lawrence Schimel (fantasy); and *Fetish Fantastic*, edited by Cecilia Tan (science fiction erotica).

How to Contact: Accepts unsolicited mss between April 15 and August 31. Accepts queries (no mss) by e-mail. "Any manuscript sent other than this time period will be returned unread or discarded." Submit complete short story with cover letter. Include estimated word count, 50-100 word bio, list of publishing credits. Send SASE for reply, return of ms or send a disposable copy of ms. Agented fiction 5%. Reports in 6-12 months.

Simultaneous submissions OK. Always critiques or comments on rejected mss.

Terms: Pays minimum ½¢/word for 1-time anthology rights only, plus 2 copies; author is free to sell other rights. Sends galleys to author. Publishes ms 1-24 months after acceptance. Writer's guidelines for #10 SASE. Book catalog for #10 SAE and 2 first-class stamps.

Advice: "Read what we publish, learn to use lyrical but concise language to portray sex positively. Make sex and erotic interaction integral to your plot. Stay away from genre stereotypes. Use depth of character, internal monologue and psychological introspection to draw me in." Note: "We do not publish novels."

✓ ⊘ **CLARION BOOKS,** Imprint of Houghton Mifflin Company, 215 Park Ave. S., New York NY 10003. **Acquisitions:** Dinah Stevenson, editorial director; Michele Coppola, editor. Estab. 1965. Clarion is a strong presence when it comes to books for young readers. Publishes hardcover originals. Publishes 50 titles/year.
● Clarion is swamped with submissions and is not accepting manuscripts at this time.

✓ ⊘ ▼ **CLEIS PRESS,** P.O. Box 14684, San Francisco CA 94114. E-mail: fdcleis@aol.com. **Acquisitions:** Frederique Delacoste, editor. Estab. 1980. Midsize independent publisher. Publishes paperback originals. Published new writers within the last year. **Plans 1 first novel every other year.** Averages 15 total titles, 5 (3 are anthologies) fiction titles/year.
● Cleis Press has received the Best Fiction Firecracker Award for *The Leather Daddy and the Femme,* by Carol Queen, the Fab Award, and the Firecracker for Outstanding Press for 1999.

Needs: Comics/graphic novels, erotica, ethnic/multicultural (gay/lesbian), feminist, gay, historical (gay/lesbian), human rights, humor/satire, lesbian, novels, thriller/espionage, translations. Published *Sexually Speaking: Collected Sex Writings,* by Gore Vidal (essays); and *A Fragile Union,* by Joan Nestle (essays), which won a Lambda Literary Award.

How to Contact: Accepts unsolicited mss with SASE. Accepts unsolicited queries by E-mail. Submit complete ms with a cover letter. Include 1- or 2-page bio, list of publishing credits. Send SASE for reply or send a disposable copy of ms. Agented fiction 25%. Reports in 6 weeks. No simultaneous submissions.

Payment/Terms: Pays royalty of 7%. Advance is negotiable. Sends galleys to author. Publishes ms 12-18 months after acceptance. Catalogue for SASE and 2 first-class stamps.

⊘ ▼ **COFFEE HOUSE PRESS,** 27 N. Fourth St., Minneapolis MN 55401. (612)338-0125. **Acquisitions:** Allan Kornblum and Chris Fischbach, editors. Estab. 1984. "Nonprofit publisher with a small staff. We publish literary titles: fiction and poetry." Publishes paperback originals. Books: acid-free paper; cover illustrations; average print order: 2,500. First novel print order: 3,000-4,000. **Published new writers within the last year.** Plans 2 first novels this year. Averages 12 total titles, 6 fiction titles each year.
● This successful nonprofit small press has received numerous grants from various organizations including NEA, the Mellon Foundation and Lila Wallace/Readers Digest.

Needs: Contemporary, ethnic, experimental, literary. Looking for "non-genre, contemporary, high quality, unique material." No westerns, romance, erotica, mainstream, science fiction or mystery. Publishes anthologies, but they are closed to unsolicited submissions. Also publishes a series of short-short collections called "Coffee-to-Go." Published *Ex Utero,* by Laurie Foos (first novel); *Gunga Din Highway,* by Frank Chin (novel); and *A .38 Special & a Broken Heart,* by Jonis Agee (short short stories).

How to Contact: Accepts unsolicited mss. Submit samples with cover letter. SASE. Agented fiction 10%. Reports in 2 months on queries; 7 months on mss.

Terms: Pays royalties of 8%. Average advance: $3,000. Provides 15 author's copies. Writer's guidelines for #10 SASE with 55¢ postage.

✓ ⊘ ▼ **CONCORDIA PUBLISHING HOUSE,** 3558 S. Jefferson Ave., St. Louis MO 63118-3968. (314)268-1187. Fax: (314)268-1329. Website: www.cphmall.com (includes guidelines, editorial contacts, products, question/answer). Children's Editor: Jane Wilke. Adult and Youth Editor: Rachel Hoyer. Estab. 1869. "We publish Protestant, inspirational, theological, family and juvenile books. All manuscripts should conform to the doctrinal tenets of The Lutheran Church—Missouri Synod." Publishes hardcover and trade paperback originals. Publishes 160 titles/year.
● Concordia was a finalist for the Gold Medallion in the picture book category of the CBA awards program.

Needs: Juvenile novels. "We will consider fiction for the following age ranges: 4-7, 6-9, 8-12, 10-14, and children's picture books. All books must contain Christian content. No adult Christian fiction." Recently pub-

READ THE BUSINESS OF FICTION WRITING section for information on manuscript preparation, mailing tips, rights and more.

lished *Ask Willie*, by Paul Buchanan (juvenile); and *Desert Dictives*, by Mona Gainsburg Hodgson.

How to Contact: No phone queries, please. Send a query with SASE first. Reports in 2-3 months on queries. Simultaneous submissions discouraged.

Terms: Pays royalty or makes outright purchase. Publishes ms 18 months after acceptance. Writer's guidelines for #10 SASE.

Advice: "Do not fictionalize Bible stories."

CONSTABLE AND COMPANY, 3 The Lanchesters, 162 Fulham Palace Rd., London W6 9ER England. Crime Fiction Editor: Tara Lawrence. Averages 30 fiction titles/year. Publishes "crime fiction (mysteries)." Length: 60,000 words minimum; 100,000 words maximum. Recently published *Dead Innocent*, by Maureen O'Brien (crime); *The Swarm of Heaven*, by Derek Wilson (crime); and *Candles for the Dead*, by Frank Smith (crime).

How to Contact: Send brief summary, 3 sample chapters and return postage. Pays advance and royalties. Write to publishers for catalog.

Advice: Constable and Company is looking for "crime novels with good, strong identities. Think about what it is that makes your book(s) stand out from the others."

COTEAU BOOKS, Thunder Creek Publishing Co-operative Ltd., 401-2206 Dewdney Ave., Regina, Saskatchewan S4R 1H3 Canada. (306)777-0170. Fax: (306)522-5152. E-mail: coteau@coteau.unibase.com. Website: coteau.unibase.com. **Acquisitions:** Barbara Sapergia, acquisitions editor. Estab. 1975. "Coteau Books publishes the finest Canadian fiction, poetry drama and children's literature, with an emphasis on western writers." Independent publisher. Publishes paperback originals. Books: #2 offset or 60 lb. hi-bulk paper; offset printing; perfect bound; 4-color illustrations. Average print order: 1,500-3,000; first novel print order: approx. 1,500. **Published new writers within the last year.** Publishes 14 total titles, 6-8 fiction titles each year. Distributed by General Distribution Services.

- Books published by Coteau Books have received awards including the City of Edmonton Book Prize for *Banjo Lessons*, Jubilee Fiction Award for *In the Misleading Absence of Light*, and the Danuta Gleed Literary Award for *The Progress of an Object in Motion*.

Needs: Novels, short fiction, middle years and young adult fiction. No science fiction. No children's picture books. Publishes Canadian authors only.

How to Contact: *Canadian writers only.* Send submissions with query letter and résumé to Acquisitions Editor. SASE. No simultaneous or multiple submissions. Fiction 10%. Responds to e-mail queries. Reports on queries in 2-3 months; 2-3 months on mss. Sometimes comments on rejected mss.

Terms: "We're a co-operative and receive subsidies from the Canadian, provincial and local governments. We do not accept payments from authors to publish their works." Sends galleys to author. Publishes ms 1-2 years after acceptance. Book catalog for 8½×11 SASE.

Advice: "We publish short-story collections, novels, drama, nonfiction and poetry collections, as well as literary interviews and children's books. This is part of our mandate. The work speaks for itself! Be bold. Be creative. Be persistent!"

CREATIVE WITH WORDS PUBLICATIONS, Box 223226, Carmel CA 93922. Fax: (831)655-8627. E-mail: cwwpub@usa.net. Website: members.tripod.com/~CreativeWithWords (includes guidelines, themes, submittal form, catalog, editor's notes, editing tips, mission statement, "Best of the month" salute to writers and winning entry). **Acquisitions:** Brigitta Geltrich (general); Bert Hower (nature), fiction editor. Estab. 1975. Staff works on part-time basis "with guest editors, artists and readers from throughout the U.S. We try to publish clean prose and poetry with family appeal." Books: bond and stock paper; mimeographed printing; saddle-stitched binding; illustrations and photographs. **Publishes 50-70% new writers.** Average print order varies. Publishes paperback anthologies of new and established writers. Averages 12-14 anthologies each year. Distributes titles through author, schools and libraries.

Needs: Humor/satire, juvenile (easy-to-read, fantasy), nature. "Editorial needs center on folkloristic items (according to themes): tall tales and such for annual anthologies." Needs seasonal short stories, stories on values and human relationships appealing to general public; "tales" of folklore nature, appealing to all ages, poetry, prose and language art works by children. Published anthologies, *Humor, School, Love, Folklore*."

How to Contact: Accepts unsolicited mss. Query first; submit complete ms (prose no more than 1,500 words) with SASE and cover letter. Electronic submissions (3.5 diskette) OK. Reports in 1 month on queries; 2-4 weeks on mss after deadline. Publishes ms 1-2 months after deadline. Writer's guidelines and theme list (1 oz.) for SASE. No simultaneous submissions, "no previously published material." *Critiques rejected mss; $10 for short stories (less than 1,000 words); $20 for longer stories, folklore items; $5 for poetry* (up to 20 lines).

Terms: Pays in 20% reduced author copies (20%: 1-9 copies; 30%: 10 copies); Best of the Month (1 free copy) and winning entry published on the Web.

Advice: "Our fiction appeals to general public: children—senior citizens. Follow guidelines and rules of Creative With Words Publications and not those the writer feels CWW should have. We only consider fiction along the lines of folklore, seasonal genres and annual themes set by CWW. Be brief, sincere, well-informed, patient and proficient! Look at the world from a different perspective, research your topic thoroughly, apply brevity, and write your story through a viewpoint character, whether antagonist, protagonist or narrator."

◐ ◎ ▼ **CROSSWAY BOOKS,** Division of Good News Publishers, 1300 Crescent, Wheaton IL 60187-5800. Fax: (630)682-4785. **Acquisitions**: Jill Carter. Estab. 1938. " 'Making a difference in people's lives for Christ' as its maxim, Crossway Books lists titles written from an evangelical Christian perspective." Midsize independent evangelical religious publisher. Publishes paperback originals. Average print order 5,000-10,000 copies. Averages 75 total titles, 10-15 fiction titles each year. Distributes through Christian bookstores and catalogs.

● Crossway Books is known as a leader in Christian fiction. Several of their books have received "Gold Medallion" awards from the Evangelical Christian Publishers Association.

Needs: Contemporary, adventure, historical, literary, religious/inspirational, young adult. "All fiction published by Crossway Books must be written from the perspective of evangelical Christianity. It must understand and view the world through a Christian worldview." No sentimental, didactic, "inspirational" religious fiction, heavy-handed allegorical or derivative fantasy. Recently published *Never Forsaken*, by Kathleen Jacobs (historical); *The Chairman*, by Harry Lee Kraus, Jr. (medical thriller); and *All That Glitters*, by Gilbert Morris (contemporary).

How to Contact: Does not accept unsolicited mss. Send query with synopsis and sample chapters only. Reports in 6-8 weeks on queries. Publishes ms 1-2 years after acceptance.

Terms: Pays in royalties and negotiates advance. Writer's guidelines for SASE. Book catalog for 9×12 SAE and 6 first-class stamps.

Advice: "We feel called to publish fiction in the following categories: Christian realism, historical fiction, intrigue, western fiction and children's fiction. All fiction should include explicit Christian content, artfully woven into the plot, and must be consistent with our statements of vision, purpose and commitment. Crossway can successfully publish and market *quality* Christian novelists. Also read John Gardner's *On Moral Fiction*. We require a minimum word count of 25,000 words."

◐ **CUMBERLAND HOUSE PUBLISHING,** 431 Harding Industrial Dr., Nashville TN 37211. (615)832-1171. Fax: (615)832-0633. E-mail: cumbhouse@aol.com. **Acquisitions**: Ron Pitkin, president. "We look for unique titles with clearly defined audiences." Publishes hardcover and trade paperback originals, and hardcover and trade paperback reprints. Publishes 35 titles/year. Imprint publishes 5 titles/year.

Imprint(s): Cumberland House Hearthside; Julia M. Pitkin, editor-in-chief.

Needs: Mystery, historical. Recently published *Skeleton Crew*, by Beverly Connor (mystery); and *Manassas*, by James Reasoner.

How to Contact: Query first. Writers should know "the odds are really stacked against them." Agented fiction 20%. Reports in 2 months on queries; 4 months on mss. Simultaneous submissions OK.

Terms: Pays 10-20% royalty on wholesale price. Offers $1,000-10,000 advance. Publishes ms an average of 8 months after acceptance. Book catalog for 8×10 SAE and 4 first-class stamps. Writer's guidelines free.

Advice: Audience is "adventuresome people who like a fresh approach to things. Writers should tell what their idea is, why it's unique and why somebody would want to buy it—but don't pester us."

◐ **DANTE UNIVERSITY OF AMERICA PRESS, INC.**, P.O. Box 843, Brookline Village MA 02147-0843. Fax: (617)734-2046. E-mail: danteu@usa1.com. Website: www.danteuniversity.org/dpress.html. **Acquisitions**: Adolph Caso, president. "The Dante University Press exists to bring quality, educational books pertaining to our Italian heritage as well as the historical and political studies of America. Profits from the sale of these publications benefit the Foundation, bringing Dante University closer to a reality." Estab. 1975. Publishes hardcover and trade paperback originals and reprints. Publishes 5 titles/year. Average print order for a first book is 3,000.

Needs: Translations from Italian and Latin. Recently published *Rogue Angel*, by Carol Damioli.

How to Contact: Query first with SASE. Agented fiction 50%. Reports in 2 months.

Terms: Pays royalty. Negotiable advance. Publishes ms 10 months after acceptance.

◐ **MAY DAVENPORT, PUBLISHERS,** 26313 Purissima Rd., Los Altos Hills CA 94022. (650)948-6499. Fax: (650)947-1373. E-mail: robertd@whidbey.com. Website: www.maydavenportpublishers.com (includes catalog, author information). **Acquisitions**: May Davenport, editor/publisher. Estab. 1976. "We prefer books which can be *used* in high schools as supplementary readings in English or creative writing courses. Reading skills have to be taught, and novels by humorous authors can be more pleasant to read than Hawthorne's or Melville's novels, war novels, or novels about past generations. Humor has a place in literature." Publishes hardcover and trade paperback originals. Publishes 4 titles/year. Distributes titles through direct mail order.

Imprint(s): md Books (nonfiction and fiction).

Needs: Humor, literary. "We want to focus on novels junior and senior high school teachers can share with their reluctant readers in their classrooms." Recently published *Magda Rose*, by Paul Lauria (fiction novel); and *Boudreau of de Bayou*, by Philip Stonecipher (picture book); and *Windriders*, by Blake Grant (fiction novel).

How to Contact: Query with SASE. Reports in 1 month.

Terms: Pays 15% royalty on retail price. No advance. Publishes ms 1 year after acceptance. Book catalog and writer's guidelines for #10 SASE.

Advice: "Just write humorous fictional novels about today's generation with youthful, admirable, believable characters to make young readers laugh. TV-oriented youth need role models in literature, and how a writer uses descriptive adjectives and similes enlightens youngsters who are so used to music, animation, special effects with stories."

DAW BOOKS, INC., Distributed by Penguin Putnam Inc., 375 Hudson St., New York NY 10014. Fax: (212)366-2090. Publishers: Elizabeth R. Wollheim and Sheila E. Gilbert. **Acquisitions:** Peter Stampfel, submissions editor. Estab. 1971. Publishes paperback originals and hardcover originals. Books: Illustrations sometimes; average print and number of first novels published per year vary widely. Averages 40 new titles plus 40 or more reissues, all fiction, each year. Occasionally critiques rejected mss.
Needs: Science fiction (hard science, soft sociological), fantasy and mainstream thrillers only. Recently published *The Black Swan*, by Mercedes Lackey; *OTHERLAND: Mountain of Black Grass*, Vol. 3, by Tad Williams; and *Precursor*, by C.J. Cherryh. Publishes many original anthologies including *Sword & Sorceress* (edited by Marion Zimmer Bradley); *Cat Fantastic* (edited by Andre Norton and Martin H. Greenberg). "You may write to the editors (after looking at the anthology) for guidelines % DAW."
How to Contact: Submit complete ms with return postage and SASE. Usually reports in 3-5 months on mss, but in special cases may take longer. "No agent required."
Terms: Pays an advance against royalties. Sends galleys to author.
Advice: "We strongly encourage new writers. Research your publishers and submit only appropriate work."

✔ ◖ DEL REY BOOKS, Subsidiary of Ballantine Publishing Group, 201 E. 50 St., New York NY 10022-7703. (212)572-2677. E-mail: delray@randomhouse.com. Website: www.randomhouse.com/delrey/. Editorial Director: Shelly Shapiro. Senior Editor: Veronica Chapman. Estab. 1977. "In terms of mass market, we basically created the field of fantasy bestsellers. Not that it didn't exist before, but we put the mass into mass market." Publishes hardcover originals and paperback originals and reprints. **Plans 6-7 first novels this year.** Publishes 70 titles each year, all fiction. Sometimes critiques rejected mss.
Needs: Fantasy and science fiction. Fantasy must have magic as an intrinsic element to the plot. No flying-saucer, Atlantis or occult novels. Published *First King of Shamara*, by Terry Brooks; *The Demon Awakens*, by R.A. Salvatore; *The Chronicles of Pern*, by Anne McCaffrey (science fiction/hardcover original); *The Shining Ones*, by David Eddings (fantasy/hardcover original); and *Jack the Bodiless*, by Julian May (science fiction/paperback reprint).
How to Contact: Query first with detailed outline and synopsis of story from beginning to end. No unsolicited mss. Reports in 6 months, occasionally longer.
Terms: Pays royalty on retail price; "advance is competitive." Publishes ms 1 year after acceptance. Sends galleys to author. Writer's guidelines for #10 SASE.
Advice: Has been publishing "more fiction and hardcovers, because the market is there for them. Read a lot of science fiction and fantasy, such as works by Anne McCaffrey, David Eddings, Larry Niven, Arthur C. Clarke, Terry Brooks, Frederik Pohl, Barbara Hambly. When writing, pay particular attention to plotting (and a satisfactory conclusion) and characters (sympathetic and well-rounded) because those are what readers look for."

◖ DELACORTE PRESS, Imprint of Dell Publishing, Division of Bantam Dell Publishing Group, 1540 Broadway, New York NY 10036. (212)354-6500. Editor-in-Chief: Leslie Schnur. **Acquisitions:** (Ms.) Jackie Cantor (women's fiction); Tom Spain (commercial nonfiction and fiction). Publishes hardcover and trade paperback originals. Publishes 36 titles/year.
Needs: Mainstream/contemporary. No mss for children's or young adult books accepted in this division. Published *Killing Time in St. Cloud*, by Judith Guest; *The Horse Whisperer*, by Nicholas Evans; *Hardcase*, by Bill Pronzin; and *Be Cool*, by Elmore Leonard.
How to Contact: Query with outline, first 3 chapters or brief proposal. Accepts simultaneous submissions. Reports in 4 months.
Terms: Pays 7½-12½ royalty. Advance varies. Publishes ms 2 years after acceptance, but varies. Guidelines for 9 × 12 SASE.

◖ DELL PUBLISHING ISLAND, Imprint of Dell Publishing, Division of Bantam Dell Publishing Group, 1540 Broadway, New York NY 10036. (212)354-6500. **Acquisitions:** Tom Spain, editorial director. Publishes trade paperback originals and reprints. Publishes bestseller fiction and nonfiction. Publishes 12 titles/year.
Needs: Mystery, romance, suspense. Published *Runaway Jury*, by John Grisham (suspense).
How to Contact: Reports in 4-6 months on queries. Agented fiction 95%. Simultaneous submissions OK.
Terms: Pays 7½-12½% royalty on retail price. Advance varies. Simultaneous submissions OK. Publishes ms 1 year after acceptance. Book catalog for 9 × 12 SAE and 3 first class stamps.

◖ DELTA TRADE PAPERBACKS, Imprint of Dell Publishing, Division of Bantam Dell Publishing Group, 1540 Broadway, New York NY 10036. (212)354-6500. **Acquisitions:** Tom Spain, editorial director. Publishes trade paperback originals, mostly light, humorous material and books on pop culture. Publishes 36 titles/year.

Needs: Erotica, literary, short story collections. Recently published *Fast Greens*, by Turk Pipkin; *Last Days of the Dog Men*, by Brad Watson (stories); and *Charming Billy*, by Alice McDermott.

How to Contact: Query with synopsis, 2-3 sample chapters or complete ms and SASE. Agented fiction 95%. Reports in 4-6 months on queries. Simultaneous submissions OK.

Terms: Pays 7½-12½% royalty on retail price. Advance varies. Publishes ms 1 year after acceptance. Book catalog for 9 × 12 SAE and 3 first class stamps.

☑ ⊘ **DIAL BOOKS FOR YOUNG READERS**, Division of Penguin Putnam Inc., 375 Hudson St., 3rd Floor, New York NY 10014. (212)366-2800. President/Publisher: Nancy Paulsen. Assistant Editor: Jocelyn Wright. Editorial Assistant: Victoria Wells. **Acquisitions**: Submissions Editor. Estab. 1961. Trade children's book publisher, "looking for agented picture book mss and novels." Publishes hardcover originals. **Plans 1 first novel this year.** Averages 100 titles, mainly fiction.

Imprint(s): Pied Piper Books, Easy-to-Read Books.

Needs: Juvenile (1-9 yrs.) including: animal, fantasy, spy/adventure, contemporary and easy-to-read; young adult/teen (10-16 years) including: fantasy/science fiction, literary and commercial mystery and fiction. Published *Sam and the Tigers*, by Julius Lester and Jerry Pinckney; *Language of Doves*, by Rosemary Wells; and *Great Interactive Dream Machine*, by Richard Peck.

How to Contact: Does not accept unsolicited mss. Query with SASE. Occasionally critiques or comments on rejected ms.

Terms: Pays advance against royalties.

Advice: "To agents: We are publishing more fiction books than in the past, and we publish only hardcover originals, most of which are fiction. At this time we are particularly interested in both fiction and nonfiction for the middle grades, and innovative picture book manuscripts. We also are looking for easy-to-reads for first and second graders. Plays, collections of games and riddles, and counting and alphabet books are generally discouraged. Before submitting a manuscript to a publisher, it is a good idea to request a catalog to see what the publisher is currently publishing. We will send a catalog to anyone who sends 4 first-class stamps with a self-addressed, 9 × 12 envelope."

⊘ Ⓐ **DIAL PRESS**, Imprint of Dell Publishing, 1540 Broadway, New York NY 10036. (212)354-6500. Fax: (212)782-9698. Website: www.bbd.com. **Acquisitions**: Susan Kamil, vice president, editorial director. Estab. 1924. "Dial Press is dedicated to the publication of quality fiction and nonfiction." Publishes 6-12 titles/year.

Needs: Ethnic, literary. Published *Pack of Two*, by Caroline Knapp (memoir); *Kaaterskill Falls*, by Allegra Groodman (literary novel); and *City of Light*, by Lauren Belfer (literary novel).

How to Contact: Agented submissions only. Reports in 2 months. Simultaneous submissions OK.

Terms: Pays royalty on retail price. Publishes ms 1-2 years after acceptance.

◖ Ⓐ **DOUBLEDAY ADULT TRADE**, a division of Doubleday Broadway Publishing Group, Inc., 1540 Broadway., New York NY 10036. (212)782-9911. Fax: (212)782-9700. Website: www.bdd.com. **Acquisitions**: William Thomas, vice president/editor-in-chief. Estab. 1897. Publishes hardcover and paperback originals and paperback reprints.

Imprint(s): Anchor Press (contact Gerald Howard); Currency (contact Roger Scholl); Main Street (contact Gerald Howard); **Nan A. Talese** (contact Nan A. Talese); Religious Division (contact Eric Major); Image (contact Trace Murphy).

Needs: "Doubleday is not able to consider unsolicited queries, proposals or manuscripts unless submitted through a bona fide literary agent."

Terms: Pays in royalties; offers advance. Publishes ms 1 year after acceptance.

◖ **DOWN EAST BOOKS**, Division of Down East Enterprise, Inc., P.O. Box 679, Camden ME 04843-0679. Fax: (207)594-7215. E-mail: adevine@downeast.com. Senior Editor: Karin Womer. **Acquisitions**: Acquisitions Editor. Estab. 1954. "We are primarily a regional publisher concentrating on Maine or New England." Publishes hardcover and trade paperback originals and trade paperback reprints. Publishes 20-24 titles/year. Average print order for a first book is 3,000.

● Down East Books has published Elisabeth Ogilvie, Michael McIntosh, Louise Dickinson Roch and John N. Cole.

MARKET CONDITIONS are constantly changing! If you're still using this book and it is 2001 or later, buy the newest edition of *Novel & Short Story Writer's Market* at your favorite bookstore or order from Writer's Digest Books at (800)289-0963.

Imprint(s): Silver Quill (outdoor sportsmen market).

Needs: Juvenile, regional. "We publish 1-2 juvenile titles/year (fiction and non-fiction), and 1-2 adult fiction titles/year." Recently published *Tides of the Heart*, by Thomas M. Sheehan (novel); *Day Before Winter*, by Elisabeth Ogilvie (novel); and *My Brothers' Keeper*, by Nancy Johnson (young adult novel).

How to Contact: Query first with small sample of text, outline and SASE. Reports in 2 months. Simultaneous submissions OK.

Terms: Pays 10-15% on receipts. Offers $200 average advance. Publishes ms 1 year after acceptance. Writer's guidelines for 9×12 SAE with 3 first-class stamps.

DUFOUR EDITIONS, P.O. Box 7, Chester Springs PA 19425. (610)458-5005. Fax: (610)458-7103. E-mail: dufour8023@aol.com. **Acquisitions:** Thomas Lavoie, associate publisher. Estab. 1940s. Small independent publisher, tending toward literary fiction. Publishes hardcover and paperback originals and reprints. Publishes 6-7 total titles/year; 1-2 fiction titles. Promotes titles through catalogs, reviews, direct mail, sales reps, Book Expo and wholesalers.

Needs: Literary, short story collections, translations. Published *Last Love in Constantinople*, by Milorad Pavic.

How to Contact: Send query letter only first. Include estimated word count, bio and list of publishing credits. Include SASE for reply. Reports in 2-3 weeks on queries; 2-3 months on mss.

THOMAS DUNNE BOOKS, Imprint of St. Martin's Press, 175 Fifth Ave., New York NY 10010. (212)674-5151. **Acquisitions:** Tom Dunne. Publishes wide range of fiction and nonfiction. Publishes hardcover originals, trade paperback originals and reprints. Publishes 90 titles/year.

Needs: Mainstream/contemporary, mystery/suspense, "women's" thriller. Recently published *Brandenburg*, by Glenn Meade (thriller); and *Birds of Prey*, by Wilbur Smith.

How to Contact: Query or submit synopsis and 100 sample pages with SASE. Reports in 2 months on queries. Simultaneous submissions OK.

Terms: Pays 10-15% royalty on retail price for hardcover, 7½% for paperback. Advance varies with project. Publishes ms 1 year after acceptance. Book catalog and writer's guidelines free.

DUTTON CHILDREN'S BOOKS, Imprint of Penguin Putnam Inc., 345 Hudson St., New York NY 10014. (212)414-3700. **Acquisitions:** Lucia Monfried, associate publisher and editor-in-chief. Estab. 1852. Dutton Children's Books publishes fiction and nonfiction for readers ranging from preschoolers to young adults on a variety of subjects. Publishes hardcover originals. Publishes 80 titles/year.

Needs: Dutton Children's Books has a complete publishing program that includes picture books; easy-to-read books; and fiction for all ages, from "first-chapter" books to young adult readers. Published *The Iron Ring*, by Lloyd Alexander; *How Yussei Caught the Gefilte Fish*, by Charlotte Herman, illustrated by Katya Krenina.

How to Contact: Query with SASE.

Terms: Pays royalty on retail price.

DUTTON PLUME, Division of Penguin Putnam Inc., 375 Hudson St., New York NY 10014. (212)366-2000. **Acquisitions:** Lori Lipsky, publisher (mainstream fiction); Brian Tart, editor-in-chief (commercial fiction); Rosemary Ahern, senior editor (literary fiction). Estab. 1948. Publishes hardcover and paperback originals and paperback reprints. **Published new writers within the last year.**

Imprint(s): Onyx, Topaz, Mentor, Signet Classic, Plume, Plume Fiction, Meridian, **Roc.**

Needs: "All kinds of commercial and literary fiction, including mainstream, historical, Regency, New Age, western, thriller, science fiction, fantasy, gay. Full length novels and collections." Published *Trial by Fire*, by Nancy Taylor Rosenberg; *Black Cross*, by Greg Iles; and *The Takeover*, by Stephen Frey.

How to Contact: Agented mss only. Queries accepted with SASE. "State type of book and past publishing projects." Simultaneous submissions OK. Reports in 3 months.

Terms: Pays in royalties and author's copies; offers advance. Sends galleys to author. Publishes ms 18 months after acceptance. Book catalog for SASE.

Advice: "Write the complete manuscript and submit it to an agent or agents. We publish The Trailsman, Battletech and other western and science fiction series—all by ongoing authors. Would be receptive to ideas for new series in commercial fiction."

E.M. PRESS, INC., P.O. Box 4057, Manassas VA 20108. (540)349-9958. E-mail: empress2@erols. com. Website: www.empressinc.com. **Acquisitions:** Phoebe Tufts, fiction editor. Estab. 1991. "Expanding small press." Publishes paperback and hardcover originals. Books: 50 lb. text paper; offset printing; perfect binding; illustrations. Average print order: 1,200-5,000. Averages 8 total titles, fiction, poetry and nonfiction, each year. Distributes titles through wholesalers and direct sales. Promotes titles through radio and TV, Interview Report, direct mailings and Ingram's catalogs.

Needs: "We are focusing more on Virginia/Maryland/DC authors and subject matter. We're emphasizing nonfiction and we're launching a new children's line, though we still consider 'marketable' fiction. Published *The Relationship*, by John Hyman (young adult); *Santa's New Reindeer*, by Judie Schrecker; *I, Anna Kerry*, by William Giannini (literary); and *How Will They Get That Heart Down Your Throat*, by Karen Walton.

How to Contact: Accepts unsolicited mss. Submit outline/synopsis and sample chapters or complete ms with cover letter. Include estimated word count. Send a SASE for reply, return of ms or send a disposable copy of the ms. Agented fiction 10%. Reports in 3 months on queries; 3 months on mss. Simultaneous submissions OK.

Terms: Amount of royalties and advances varies. Sends galleys to author. Publishes ms 18 months after acceptance. Writer's guidelines for SASE.

Advice: Publishing "less fiction, more regional work, though we look for fiction that will do well in secondary rights sales."

EAKIN PRESS, P.O. Box 90159, Austin TX 78709-0159. (512)288-1771. Fax: (512)288-1813. **Acquisitions**: Edwin M. Eakin, editorial director; Melissa Roberts, Virginia Messer. Estab. 1978. Eakin specializes in Texana and Western Americana for juveniles.

Imprint(s): Nortex.

Needs: Juvenile. Specifically needs historical fiction for school market, juveniles set in Southwest for Southwest grade schoolers. Published *Inside Russia*, by Zoya Zarubona.

How to Contact: Prefers queries, but accepts unsolicited mss. Send SASE for guidelines. Agented fiction 5%. Simultaneous submissions OK. Reports in 3 months on queries.

Terms: Pays royalties; no advance. Sends galleys to author. Publishes ms 1-1½ years after acceptance. Writers guidelines for #10 SASE. Book catalog for 75¢.

Advice: "Juvenile fiction only with strong Southwest theme. We receive around 1,200 queries or unsolicited mss a year."

THE ECCO PRESS, HarperCollins, 10 E. 53rd St., New York NY 10022. (212)207-7000. Website: www.harpercollins.com. **Acquisitions**: Daniel Halpern, editor-in-chief. Estab. 1970. Publishes hardcover and paperback originals and reprints. Books: acid-free paper; offset printing; Smythe-sewn binding; occasional illustrations. Averages 60 total titles, 20 fiction titles each year. Average first novel print order: 3,000 copies.

Needs: "We can publish possibly one or two original novels a year." Literary, short story collections. No science fiction, romantic novels, western (cowboy) or historical novels. Recently published *Summer at Gaglow*, by Esther Freud; *Hell*, by Kathryn Davis; and *Vast Emotions and Imperfect Thoughts*, by Ruben Fonseca.

How to Contact: Accepts unsolicited mss. Query first with SASE and 1-page bio. Send all queries to submissions editor. Reports in 3-6 months, depending on the season.

Terms: Pays in royalties. Advance is negotiable. Publishes ms 1 year after acceptance. Writer's guidelines for SASE. Book catalog free on request.

Advice: "We are always interested in first novels and feel it's important they be brought to the attention of the reading public."

WM. B. EERDMANS PUBLISHING CO., 255 Jefferson Ave. SE, Grand Rapids MI 49503-4570. (800)253-7521. Fax: (616)459-6540. **Acquisitions**: Jon Pott, editor-in-chief, fiction editor (adult fiction); Judy Zylstra, fiction editor (children); Gwen Penning, assistant to the editor-in-chief. Estab. 1911. "Although Eerdmans publishes some regional books and other nonreligious titles, it is essentially a religious publisher whose titles range from the academic to the semi-popular. Our children's fiction is meant to help a child explore life in God's world and to foster a child's exploration of her or his faith. We are a midsize independent publisher. We publish the occasional adult novel, and these tend to address spiritual issues from a Christian perspective." Publishes hardcover and paperback originals and reprints. **Publishes 1 previously unpublished writer/year.** Averages 140 total titles, 6-8 fiction titles (mostly for children) each year. Sometimes critiques or comments on rejected ms.

Imprint(s): Eerdmans Books for Young Readers.

  ● Wm. B. Eerdmans Publishing Co.'s titles have won awards from the American Library Association and The American Bookseller's Association.

Needs: Religious (children's, general, fantasy). Published *At Break of Day*, by Nikki Grimes (children's); *The Goodbye Boat*, by Mary Joslin (children's); and *A Traitor Among Us*, by Elizabeth Van Steenwyk (middle reader).

How to Contact: Accepts unsolicited mss. Query with outline/synopsis and 2 sample chapters. Accepts unsolicited queries and correspondence by fax. Include 150- to 200-word bio and list of publishing credits. SASE for reply or send a disposable copy of ms. Agented fiction 25%. Reports in 3-4 weeks on queries; 2-3 months on mss. Simultaneous submissions OK, "if notified." Electronic submission (fax) OK.

Terms: Pays royalties of 7% minimum. Offers negotiable advance. Sends galleys to author. Publishes ms 12-18 months after acceptance. Writer's guidelines and book catalog free.

Advice: "Our readers are educated and fairly sophisticated, and we are looking for novels with literary merit."

EMPYREAL PRESS, P.O. Box 1746, Place Du Parc, Montreal, Quebec H2W 2R7 Canada. Website: www.3.sympatico.ca/empyreal. **Acquisitions**: Colleen B. McCool. "Our mission is the publishing of literature which doesn't fit into any standard 'mold'—writing which is experimental yet grounded in discipline, imagination." Publishes trade paperback originals. **Publishes 50% previously unpublished writers/year.** Publishes 1-4 titles/year.

  ● Empyreal Press is currently not accepting unsolicited manuscripts.

How to Contact: No unsolicited mss. Book catalog for #10 SASE.

Advice: "Seriously consider self-publication: for instance, Roddy Boyle's *The Commitments* was published by the author himself. Talk about a success. Small and large presses, Empyreal included, are overloaded, some with waiting lists up to 5 years long. By publishing one's own work, one maintains full control, especially if the work is a commercial success."

PAUL S. ERIKSSON, PUBLISHER P.O. Box 125, Forest Dale VT 05745. (802)247-4210 Fax: (802)247-4256. **Acquisitions:** Paul S. Eriksson, editor; Peggy Eriksson, associate publisher/co-editor. Estab. 1960. "We look for intelligence, excitement and saleability." Publishes hardcover and paperback originals. First novel print order: 3,000-5,000.
Needs: Mainstream. Published *The Headmaster's Papers*, by Richard A. Hawley; *The Year that Trembled*, by Scott Lax; and *Hand in Hand*, by Tauno Yliruusi.
How to Contact: Query first. Publishes ms an average of 6 months after acceptance.
Terms: Pays 10-15% in royalties; advance offered if necessary. Free book catalog.
Advice: "Our taste runs to serious fiction."

M. EVANS & CO., INC., 216 E. 49th St., New York NY 10017. (212)688-2810. Fax: (212)486-4544. E-mail: mevans@sprynet.com. Contact: Editor. Estab. 1960. Publishes hardcover and trade paper nonfiction and a small fiction list. Publishes 30-40 titles each year.
Needs: "Small general trade publisher specializing in nonfiction titles on health, nutrition, diet, cookbooks, parenting, popular psychology." Published *The Kill Boy*, by Chris Stewart; *Down the Common*, by Ann Baer; and *Presumption*, by Julia Barnett.
How to Contact: Query first with outline/synopsis and 3 sample chapters. SASE. Agented fiction: 100%. Simultaneous submissions OK.
Terms: Pays in royalties and offers advance; amounts vary. Sends galleys to author. Publishes ms 6-12 months after acceptance.

FAITH KIDS℠, (formerly Chariot Children's Books), Imprint of Cook Communications Ministries, 4050 Lee Vance View, Colorado Springs CO 80918. (719)536-3271. Fax: (719)536-3269. **Acquisitions:** Karen Artl, children's product manager. "Faith Kids Books publishes works of children's inspirational titles, ages 1-12, with a clear 'God print' or value to influence children's spiritual growth." Publishes hardcover and trade paperback originals. Publishes 40 titles/year.
Needs: "Toddler, picture books, devotionals, Bible storybooks, for an age range of 1-12. We're particularly interested in materials for beginning readers." Recently published *Deserts and Jungles*, by Michael Carroll.
How to Contact: "Faith Kids is not accepting unsolicited manuscripts at this time." Queries from previously published authors only. Query with SASE. Reports in 4 months on queries. Simultaneous submissions OK if so noted.
Terms: Pays variable royalty on retail price. Offers advance. Publishes ms 2 years after acceptance. Writer's guidelines for #10 SASE. Book catalog on request.

FANFARE, Imprint of Bantam Books, Division of Bantam Doubleday Dell, 1540 Broadway, New York NY 10036. (212)354-6500. Fax: (212)782-9523. **Acquisition:** Beth de Guzman, senior editor; Wendy McCurdy, senior editor; Kara Cesare, associate editor. Fanfare's mission is "to publish a range of the best voices in women's fiction from brand new to established authors." **Publishes 10-15% previously unpublished writers/year.** Publishes 30 titles/year.
Needs: Publishes only romance and women's contemporary fiction. Adventure/romance, historical/romance, suspense/romance, western/romance. Length: 90,000-120,000 words. Recently published *The Accidental Bride*, by Jane Feather (historical romance); *The Other Daughter*, by Lira Gardner (romantic suspense); and *Stolen Hearts*, by Michelle Martin (contemporary romance).
How to Contact: Agented submissions only. Agented fiction 95%. Reports in 2-3 months on queries; 3-4 months on mss (accepted only upon request). Simultaneous submissions OK.
Terms: Royalty and advance negotiable. Publishes ms 1-2 years after acceptance.
Advice: "Be aware of what we publish and what our needs are in terms of length and content of manuscripts."

FANTAGRAPHICS BOOKS, 7563 Lake City Way NE, Seattle WA 98115. (206)524-1967. Fax: (206)524-2104. Publisher: Gary Groth. Estab. 1976. Publishes comic books, comics series and graphic novels. Books: offset printing; saddle-stitched periodicals and Smythe-sewn books; heavily illustrated. Publishes originals and reprints. Publishes 25 titles each month.
Needs: Comic books and graphic novels (adventure, fantasy, horror, mystery, romance, science, social parodies). "We look for subject matter that is more or less the same as you would find in mainstream fiction." Published *Blood of Palomar*, by Gilbert Hernandez; *The Dragon Bellows Saga*, by Stan Sakai; *Death of Speedy*; *Housebound with Rick Geary*; and *Little Nemo in Slumberland*.
How to Contact: Send a plot summary, pages of completed art (photocopies only) and character sketches. May send completed script if the author is willing to work with an artist of the publisher's choosing. Include cover letter and SASE. Reports in 1 month.

Terms: Pays in royalties of 8% (but must be split with artist) and advance.

FARRAR, STRAUS & GIROUX, 19 Union Square W., New York NY 10003. (212)741-6900. Fax: (212)633-2427. **Acquisitions:** Jonathan Galassi, editor-in-chief; Elisabeth Sifton, publisher, Hill & Wang (European literature, German literature in translation); John Glusman, executive editor (literary fiction); Rebecca Saleton, editorial director, North Point Press; Elisabeth Dyssegard, executive editor, Noonday; Ethan Nosowsky, editor (literary fiction); Rebecca Kurson, assistant editor (fiction). Publishes hardcover originals. **Published new writers within the last year.** Plans 2 first novels this year. Averages 120 hardcover titles/year. Receives 5,000 submissions/year.
Imprint(s): Hill & Wang, Farrar, Straus-Giroux Paperbacks, North Point Press and **Farrar, Straus & Giroux/ Children's Books** (Sunburst Books, Aerial Fiction, Mirasol).
Needs: Open. No genre material.
How to Contact: Does not accept unsolicited mss. Query first (outline/synopsis and sample chapters). "Vast majority of fiction is agented." Reports in 2-3 months. Simultaneous submissions OK.
Terms: Pays royalties (standard, subject to negotiation). Offers advance. Sends galleys to author. Publishes ms 18 months after acceptance. Catalog for 9×12 SAE with 3 first class stamps.
Tips: "Study our style and list."

FARRAR, STRAUS & GIROUX PAPERBACKS, (formerly Noonday Press), Imprint of Farrar Straus Giroux, LLC, a division of Von Holtzbrinck Publishing, 19 Union Square W., New York NY 10003. (212)741-6900. Fax: (212)633-2427. **Acquisitions:** Linda Rosenberg, director. FSG Paperbacks emphasizes literary nonfiction and fiction, as well as poetry. Publishes trade paperback originals and reprints.
Needs: Literary. Mostly reprints of classic authors. Recently published *Opened Ground*, by Seamus Heaney; and *The Magic Barrel*, by Bernard Malamud.
How to Contact: Query with outline to editorial department. Reports in 2-3 months on queries.

FARRAR, STRAUS & GIROUX/CHILDREN'S BOOKS, 19 Union Square W., New York NY 10003. (212)741-6900. **Acquisitions:** Margaret Fergus, editor-in-chief. Estab. 1946. "We publish original and well-written material for all ages." Number of titles: 70. **Published new writers within the last year.** Buys 25% agented fiction.
Needs: Children's picture books, juvenile novels, nonfiction. Published *Holes*, by Louis Sacher; *The Trolls*, by Polly Horvath; and *Tribute to Another Dead Rock Star*, by Randy Powell.
How to Contact: Submit outline/synopsis and 3 sample chapters, summary of ms and any pertinent information about author, author's writing, etc. "No submissions by fax or e-mail." Reports in 1 month on queries, 3 months on mss. Publishes ms 18-24 months after acceptance.
Terms: Pays in royalties; offers advance. Publishes ms 18 months after acceptance. Book catalog with 9×12 SASE and $1.87 postage.
Advice: "Study our list to avoid sending something inappropriate. Send query letters for long manuscripts; don't ask for editorial advice (just not possible, unfortunately); and send SASEs!"

FARTHEST STAR, Imprint of Alexander Books, 65 Macedonia Rd., Alexander NC 28701. (828)252-9515. Fax: (828)255-8719. E-mail: pat@abooks.com. Website: www.abooks.com (includes titles). **Acquisitions:** Pat Roberts, editor. Publishes trade paperback originals and reprints. Publishes 4 titles/year. Distributes titles through major distributors, mail order catalog and on the Web.
Needs: Science fiction. Recently published *Birthright: The Book of Man*, by Mike Resnick (science fiction reprint); and *Galactic Midway*, by Mike Resnick (science fiction).
How to Contact: Query or submit 3 sample chapters with SASE. Reports in 1-2 months on queries. Simultaneous submissions OK.
Terms: Pays 12-15% royalty on wholesale price. Seldom offers advance. Publishes ms 1-2 years after acceptance. Writer's guidelines for #10 SASE with 2 first-class stamps. Book catalog for 8½×11 SASE with $1.01 first-class stamps.
Tips: "Your cover letter is very important. Most acquisition editors don't go past the cover letter."

FAWCETT, Division of Random House/Ballantine, 201 E. 50th St., New York NY 10022. (212)751-2600. **Acquisitions:** Leona Nevler, editor-in-chief. Estab. 1955. Major publisher of mass market and trade paperbacks. Publishes paperback originals and reprints. Prints 160 titles annually. **Encourages new writers.** "Always looking for *great* first novels."
Imprint(s): Ivy, Crest, Gold Medal, Columbine and Juniper and Ballantine.
Needs: Mysteries. Published *Noelle*, by Diana Palmer; *Writing for the Moon*, by Kristin Hannah.
How to Contact: Agented material only.
Terms: Pays usual advance and royalties. Publishes ms 1 year after acceptance.
Advice: "Gold Medal list consists of four paperbacks per month—usually three are originals."

insider report

Journalism plus fiction writing equals success for Bob Shacochis

Give award-winning writer Bob Shacochis a reason to write, and he is out the door.

As a journalist, he may be heading to Russia for *Outside Magazine* to salmon fish and unexpectedly link up with the Russian mafia. Or, he may head to Haiti for *Harper's Magazine* to cover a war zone, which he did in 1994. For *Outside*, Shacochis has written about the island of Providencia, off the coast of Colombia, where he once spent many months in his early twenties fishing with a master spear-fisherman named Raimundo. This is where his fictional instinct took root: he felt that this real person, "Mundo," would surface in his first book of short fiction, *Easy in the Islands*.

And this is part of Shacochis's dilemma as a fiction writer. His gifts for fiction—as reflected in the National Book Award for First Fiction in 1985 for *Easy in the Islands*—are frequently shelved so he can pay the bills, as he says, with the highly-touted journalism assignments he gets.

But do the forms complement each other in the long run? Does he get equal satisfaction shifting between genres? "There are many similar elements in *both* genres, like characterization, tone and language that are integrated into a work," he says. "I write lengthy investigative journalism, so, like the fiction writer I also am, I strive to hear the voices of my fact-ridden characters talking. The journalism will conjure a factual atmosphere given what the factual characters and story present. In fiction, atmosphere and characters would be totally imagined, of course."

Regardless of genre, Shacochis insists a story must be told. The threads of a narrative must be tied together, he says, and that means paying close attention to character, storyline and pacing. "One genre is fact and truth, and the other genre is imagination and truth. When I write journalism I'm as deep into story and language as I am writing fiction."

Shacochis emerged as a rising star of fiction in his early thirties, after a year stint in the Peace Corps as an agricultural journalist and then as a copy editor at the *Palm Beach Evening Times*. Born in 1951 in Virginia to a family whose roots are in Lithuania, Shacochis was weaned as a journalist, first writing for his high school newspaper and later earning a journalism degree at the University of Missouri.

Shacochis savored his years in the Iowa Writers' Workshop (1980-1983) largely because of the connections it afforded. But his decision to apply to Iowa happened literally overnight. He pulled a story off the wire at the *Evening Times* only to discover that James Michener had donated one million dollars to the Writer's Workshop. "I called them up and said, 'I hear Mr. Michener left you some money to give to me. How can I get it?'" A few months later he was studying with esteemed writers James Alan McPherson and Barry Hannah via a Michener Fellowship.

Shacochis eagerly signed up to meet each editor and agent that came though the Iowa program. "I didn't want to miss a beat," he says. "While I loved Iowa, my aim was to get stories published in major commercial magazines and literary magazines, as soon as possible. When it looked bleak at first, it all of a sudden materialized," he adds, referring to his success in landing, through his agent, stories in *Playboy* and *Esquire* magazines.

Since Iowa is so competitive, as are most university graduate writing programs, does Shacochis advocate writers enter such a program to succeed? "A writer can learn and hone his or her craft anywhere," he says. "It doesn't have to be through a degree program. You should seek out writers' conferences or community writing programs, some sort of collective where you're trading manuscripts and getting feedback. At all costs."

This far-out ride, as Shacochis calls his full-time career as a writer, is due in great part to his winning the National Book Award for First Fiction in 1985. The doors to recognition flew open, but Shacochis was tentative in snatching up every available literary opportunity. "I think I did it wisely. I did accept what I knew I could do, namely work for *Harper's* and *Outside* magazines. And I had to focus on my novel *Swimming in the Volcano*—that was the major priority."

But, one asks, why did it take ten years to produce his novel? That answer lies in Shacochis's pains to get his fiction right. "I go very deeply into my stories, fiction or journalism. I'm not happy if I go at it too quickly. You're supposed to get your work right and that takes considerable time."

This is sound advice for any fiction writer, he says. "Take your time getting a story right, but work as much and as long on it as possible—until your gut feeling says, 'It's done, it needs to go out now.'" Being flexible with a piece of writing is what helped Shacochis find the right publisher early on. An aspect of a nonfiction piece he wrote for *Playboy* magazine (which was never published) turned out to become the opening part of his first novel.

Between *Easy in the Islands* and *Swimming in the Volcano* (1993) came his 1989 collection, *The Next New World*, which won the Prix de Rome. He'd worked sporadically on *Swimming . . .*, but the tug of journalism and teaching persisted. "A writer has to have great patience with the whole machine involved with writing, revising, submitting, waiting and hoping. And I'm a working writer—the advances on the fiction went quickly. That's still the case today." This need for patience affected his entire relationship with the novel. While slaving over it, at one point he tossed away 500 pages out of sheer dissatisfaction with the characters' voices and lack of resonance, and started over.

Voice is the key to Shacochis's fiction, especially when it's first person point-of-view. Shacochis must often hear a character's voice before he worries about other elements. He likens this to an actor. "The actor gets the script from the director who says, 'This is what this character sounds like.' The actor works on speaking that voice. As in a lot of my fiction, once I get to that voice, I start knowing what's in that character's mind and heart."

"I get that voice going before I work on getting sentences or language true right away," he says. "Once the voice is rolling, then the lyricism in that voice takes over." Shacochis's fiction is textured and layered, and he never seems reluctant to diversify his characters and settings. "I usually have a real person in mind when I create characters, but usually it's just an image: the way someone cooks or sways a hip, someone's mannerisms. I use this as a seed to build the characters."

But this is only one way Shacochis has begun writing short stories. He suggests working "from an immediate image that opens the door to your writing fiction that day—if you need a start. Also, I've written shorter fiction as a response to a mood: it may be a gleeful, upbeat mood or a more elegaic one. You can get into a story that way," he says.

His most recent book, *The Immaculate Invasion*, is a testament to his risk-taking as a writer, in a physical and literary sense. Although it's journalism, chronicling Shacochis living with American military during its 1994 peace-keeping invasion of Haiti and the fear of being shot at by anti-American factions, he knew the story would have to be told in a novel-like way, with a focus on character, tone, language and storyline.

He would come back to the lessons of fiction. "I make judgements about people and events in the book—I go after truth—just like I make judgements on characters in my fiction. In this way the book is more like a seriously extended essay and fact upon fact upon fact." Such range is the offspring of Shacochis's reading habits, too. He suggests a writer "read everything around you. Latch onto books you may not otherwise think are important. They are. And then write, write, write. It's the only way to advance your craft."

—*Jeffrey Hillard*

N **FC2**, Dept. of English, FSU, Tallahassee FL 32306-1580. (850)644-2260. E-mail: fc2@english.fsu.edu. Publishers: R.M. Berry, Jeffrey DeShell. Estab. 1974. Publisher of innovative fiction. Publishes hardcover and paperback originals. Books: perfect/Smyth binding; illustrations. Average print order: 2,200. First novel print order: 2,200. **Published new writers within the last year.** Plans no first novels, 2 first story collections this year. Averages 6 total titles, 6 fiction titles each year. Often critiques or comments on rejected mss.
Needs: Formally innovative, experimental, modernist/postmodern, avant-garde, anarchist, feminist, gay, minority, cyberpunk. Published *Book of Lazarus*, by Richard Grossman; *Is It Sexual Harassment Yet?*, by Cris Mazza; *Nature Studies*, by John Henry Ryskamp; and *Latino Heretics Anthology*, edited by Tony Diaz.
How to Contact: Accepts unsolicited mss. Query first with outline/synopsis. Include 1-page bio, list of publishing credits. SASE with ms. Agented fiction 5%. Reports on queries in 3 weeks; mss in 2-4 months. Simultaneous submissions OK. Send queries to: FC2, Unit for Contemporary Literature, Illinois State University, 109 Fairchild Hall, Normal IL 61790-4241.
Terms: Pays royalties of 7½%. Sends galleys to author. Publishes ms 1 year after acceptance.
Advice: "Be familiar with our list."

✓ **THE FEMINIST PRESS AT THE CITY UNIVERSITY OF NEW YORK**, 365 Fifth Ave., New York NY 10016. Website: www.feministpress.org (includes writer's guidelines, online catalog, teacher's resources). **Acquisitions**: Jean Casella, senior editor; Florence Howe, publisher; Sara Cahill, editor; Marna Miller, editor. Estab. 1970. "Nonprofit, tax-exempt, education and publishing organization interested in changing the curriculum, the classroom and consciousness." Publishes hardcover and paperback reprints. "We use an acid-free paper, perfect-bind our books, four color covers; and some cloth for library sales if the book has been out of print for some time; we shoot from the original text when possible. We always include a scholarly and literary afterword, since we are introducing a text to a new audience. Average print run: 4,000." Publishes no original fiction; exceptions are anthologies and international works. Averages 10-15 total titles/year; 4-8 fiction titles/year (reprints of feminist classics only). Distributes titles through Consortium Book Sales and Distribution. Promotes titles through author tours, advertising, exhibits and conferences.
Needs: Contemporary, ethnic, feminist, gay, lesbian, literary, regional, science fiction, translations, women's. Published *Apples From the Desert*, by Savyon Liebrecht (short stories, translation); *Confessions of Madame Psyche*, by Dorothy Bryant (novel); and *Mulberry and Peach*, by Hualing Nen (novel, translation).
How to Contact: Accepts unsolicited mss. Query first. Submit outline/synopsis and 1 sample chapter. Accepts queries/correspondence by fax. SASE. Reports in 1 month on queries; 3 months on mss. Simultaneous submissions OK.
Terms: Pays royalties of 10% of net sales; $100 advance; 10 author's copies. Sends galleys to author. Book catalog free on request.

◑ ▼ **FIREBRAND BOOKS**, 141 The Commons, Ithaca NY 14850. (607)272-0000. Website: www.firebrandbooks.com. **Acquisitions**: Nancy K. Bereano, publisher. Estab. 1985. "Our audience includes feminists, lesbians, ethnic audiences, and other progressive people." Independent feminist and lesbian press. Publishes quality trade paperback originals. Averages 6-8 total titles each year.
● Firebrand has won the Lambda Literary Award Organization's Publisher's Service Award.
Needs: Feminist, lesbian. Published *The Gilda Stories*, by Jewelle Gomez (novel); and *Stone Butch Blues*, by Leslie Feinberg (novel).

How to Contact: Accepts unsolicited mss. Submit outline/synopsis and sample chapters or send complete ms with cover letter. SASE. Reports in 2 weeks on queries; 2 months on mss. Simultaneous submissions OK with notification.
Terms: Pays royalties. Publishes ms 1 year after acceptance.

FOCUS PUBLISHING, INC., 502 Third St. N.W., Bemidji MN 56601. (218)759-9817. Website: www.paulbunyan.net/focus. **Acquisitions:** Jan Haley, president. "Focus Publishing is a small press primarily devoted to Christian books appropriate to children and home-schooling families." Publishes hardcover and trade paperback originals and reprints. Publishes 4-6 titles/year.
Needs: Juvenile, picture books, religious, young adult. "We are looking for Christian books for men and young adults. Be sure to list your target audience." Published *The Gift*, by Jan Haley.
How to Contact: Query and submit synopsis with SASE. Reports in 2 months.
Terms: Pays 7-10% royalty on retail price. Publishes ms 1 year after acceptance. Book catalog free.
Advice: "I prefer SASE inquiries, synopsis and target markets. Please don't send 5 lbs. of paper with no return postage."

FORGE BOOKS, Tom Doherty Associates, St. Martin's Press, 175 5th Ave., New York NY 10010. (212)388-0100. Fax: (212)388-0191. **Acquisitions**: Melissa Ann Singer, senior editor; Natalia Aponte, editor. Estab. 1993. "Midsize company that specializes in genre fiction, mainly thrillers, historicals and mysteries." Publishes hardcover and paperback originals. **Published new writers within the last year.** Plans 2-3 first novels this year. Averages 130 total titles, 129 fiction titles each year. Sometimes critiques or comments on rejected mss.
Imprint(s): Tor Books, Orb.
Needs: Erotica, historical, horror, mainstream/contemporary, mystery/suspense (amateur sleuth, cozy, police procedural, private eye/hardboiled), thriller/espionage, western (frontier saga, traditional). Plans anthology. Published *Relic*, by Douglas Preston and Lincoln Child (thriller); *Mirage*, by Soheir Khashoggi (contemporary fiction); *1812*, by David Nevin (historical); and *Billy Gashade*, by Loren D. Estleman.
How to Contact: Accepts unsolicited mss. Query with outline/synopsis and first 3 sample chapters. Include estimated word count, bio and list of publishing credits. SASE for reply. Agented fiction 95%. Reports in 4 months on proposals. Simultaneous submissions OK.
Terms: Pays royalties. Advance $7,000 and up. Sends galleys to author. Publishes ms 9-12 months after acceptance.
Advice: "The writing mechanics must be outstanding for a new author to break into today's market."

FOUL PLAY PRESS, Imprint of W.W. Norton, 500 Fifth Ave., New York NY 10110. (212)354-5500. Fax: (212)869-0856. Website: www.wwnorton.com. **Acquisitions:** Candace Watt, editor. Estab. 1996. Publishes hardcover originals and paperback reprints. Publishes 6 titles/year.
Needs: Mystery, suspense.
How to Contact: Agented mss only.

FRIENDS UNITED PRESS, 101 Quaker Hill Dr., Richmond IN 47374-1980. (765)962-7573. Fax: (765)966-1293. Website: www.fum.org. **Acquisitions:** Barbara Bennett Mays, editor/manager. Estab. 1973. "Friends United Press commits itself to energize and equip Friends and others through the power of the Holy Spirit to gather people into fellowship where Jesus Christ is known, loved and obeyed as teacher and Lord." Quaker Denominated House. Publishes paperback originals. Books: 60 lb. paper; perfect bound. Average print order: 1,000. Averages 7 total titles, 1-2 fiction titles each year. Member of Protestant Church Publishers Association. Promotes titles through magazines.
Needs: Historical (Friends' history), religious (children's, inspirational). Recently published *For The Gift of A Friend*; *For the Love of a Friend*; and *For the Call of a Friend*, by Susan McCracken.
How to Contact: Submit query letter only. Send SASE for reply. Reports in 1 month.
Terms: Pays royalties of 7½% maximum. Sends galleys to author. Publishes ms 1 year after acceptance. Writer's guidelines for #10 SASE.
Advice: "Membership in the Society of Friends (Quakers) is preferred. Manuscript should be about Quakers, Quaker history or theology, or about theology or spirituality that is in the realm of the theology and spirituality of Friends."

FRONT STREET BOOKS, 20 Battery Park Ave., #403, Asheville NC 28801. (828)236-3097. Fax: (828)236-3098. E-mail: nhz@frontstreetbooks.com. Website: www.frontstreetbooks.com. **Acquisitions:** Stephen Roxburgh. Estab. 1994. "Small independent publisher of high-quality picture books and literature for children and young adults." Publishes hardcover originals.
● Front Street Books has published several award-winning books including a Newbery Honor Book and two National Book Award Finalists.
Needs: Children's/juvenile (adventure, animal, easy-to-read, fantasy, historical, mystery, preschool/picture book,

sports), young adult/teen (adventure, fantasy/science fiction, historical, horror, mystery/suspense, problem novels, romance, sports, western).

How to Contact: Accepts unsolicited mss. Query first, submit outline/synopsis and a few sample chapters or submit complete ms with cover letter. Unsolicited queries/correspondence by e-mail and fax OK. Include short bio and list of publishing credits. Send SASE for reply, return of ms or send disposable copy of ms. Agented fiction 10%. Reports in 2 weeks on queries; 2 months on mss. Simultaneous submissions OK. No electronic submissions.

Terms: Pays royalties. Offers negotiable advance.

GAY SUNSHINE PRESS AND LEYLAND PUBLICATIONS, P.O. Box 410690, San Francisco CA 94141. Fax: (415)626-1802. Website: www.gaysunshine.com. **Acquisitions**: Winston Leyland, editor. Estab. 1970. Midsize independent press. Publishes hardcover and paperback originals. Books: natural paper; perfect-bound; illustrations. Average print order: 5,000-10,000.

- Gay Sunshine Press has received a Lambda Book Award for *Gay Roots* (volume 1), named "Best Book by a Gay or Lesbian Press," and received grants from the National Endowment for the Arts.

Needs: Literary, experimental, translations—all gay male material only. "We desire fiction on gay themes of *high* literary quality and prefer writers who have already had work published in literary magazines. We also publish erotica—short stories and novels." Published *Partings at Dawn: An Anthology of Japanese Gay Literature from the 12th to the 20th Centuries*; and *Out of the Blue: Russia's Hidden Gay Literature—An Anthology*.

How to Contact: "Do not send an unsolicited manuscript." Query with SASE. Reports in 3 weeks on queries; 2 months on mss. Send $1 for catalog.

Terms: Negotiates terms with author. Sends galleys to author. Pays royalties or by outright purchase.

Advice: "We continue to be interested in receiving queries from authors who have book-length manuscripts of high literary quality. We feel it is important that an author know exactly what to expect from our press (promotion, distribution, etc.) before a contract is signed. Before submitting a query or manuscript to a particular press, obtain critical feedback on your manuscript from knowledgeable people. If you alienate a publisher by submitting a manuscript shoddily prepared/typed, or one needing very extensive rewriting, or one which is not in the area of the publisher's specialty, you will surely not get a second chance with that press."

LAURA GERINGER BOOKS, Imprint of HarperCollins Children's Books, 10 E. 53rd St., New York NY 10022. (212)207-7000. Website: www.harpercollins.com. **Acquisitions:** Laura Geringer, senior vice president/publisher. "We look for books that are out of the ordinary, authors who have their own definite take, and artists that add a sense of humor to the text." Publishes hardcover originals. **Published 5% previously unpublished writers/year.** Publishes 15-20 titles/year.

Needs: Adventure, fantasy, historical, humor, literary, picture books, young adult. Recently published *Zoe Rising*, by Pam Conrad (novel); *Rolie Polie Olie*, by William Joyce (picture book); and *If You Give a Pig a Pancake*, by Laura Numeroff.

How to Contact: Query with SASE for picture books; submit complete ms with SASE for novels. Agented fiction 75%. Reports in 4 months on queries.

Terms: Pays 10-12½% on retail price. Advance varies. Publishes ms 6-12 months after acceptance for novels, 1-2 years after acceptance for picture books. Writer's guidelines for #10 SASE. Book catalog for 8 × 10 SAE with 3 first-class stamps.

Advice: "A mistake writers often make is failing to research the type of books an imprint publishes, therefore sending inappropriate material."

GESSLER PUBLISHING COMPANY, 10 E. Church Ave., Roanoke VA 24011. (703)345-1429. Fax: (540)342-7172. E-mail: gesslerco@aol.com. Website: www.gessler.com (includes company info., teacher activities, links). **Acquisitions:** Richard Kurshan, CEO. Estab. 1932. "Publisher/distributor of foreign language educational materials (primary/secondary schools)." Publishes paperback originals and reprints, videos and software. Averages 75 total titles each year. Distributes titles through education dealers and catalog.

Needs: "Foreign language or English as a Second Language." Needs juvenile, literary, preschool/picture book, short story collections, translations. Published *Don Quixote de la Mancha* (cartoon version of classic, in Spanish); *El Cid* (prose and poetry version of the classic, In Spanish); and *Les Miserables* (simplified version of Victor Hugo classic, in French).

How to Contact: Query first, then send outline/synopsis and 2-3 sample chapters; complete ms with cover letter. Agented fiction 10%. Reports on queries in 1 month; on mss in 6 weeks. Simultaneous and electronic (e-mail, fax) submissions OK. Sometimes comments on rejected ms.

Terms: Pay varies with each author and contract. Sends galleys to author. "Varies on time of submission and acceptance relating to our catalog publication date." Publishes ms 9 months after acceptance. Writer's guidelines not available. Book catalog free on request.

Advice: "We specialize in the foreign language market directed to teachers and schools. A book that would interest us has to be attractive to the market. A teacher would be most likely to create a book for us."

✿ ☑ ◎ ☙ **GOOSE LANE EDITIONS,** 469 King St., Fredericton, New Brunswick E3B 1E5 Canada. (506)450-4251. **Acquisitions**: Laurel Boone, acquisitions editor. Estab. 1957. Publishes hardcover and paperback originals and occasional reprints. Books: some illustrations. Average print run: 3,000. First novel print order: 1,500. Averages 14 total titles, 4-5 fiction titles each year. Distributes titles through General Distribution Services. Sales through Literary Press Group (Canada) and Stoddart (US).

• Goose Lane author Lynn Coady won the Dartmouth Book Award, the Thomas Raddal Award and the Atlantic Booksellers' Association Bookseller's Choice Award for *Strange Heaven*. Alan Cumyn won the Ottawa-Carleton Book Award for *Man of Bone*.

Needs: Contemporary, historical, literary, short story collections. "Not suitable for mainstream or mass-market submissions. No genres i.e.: modern and historical adventure, crime, modern and historical romance, science fiction, fantasy, westerns, confessional works (fictional and autobiographical), and thrillers and other mystery books." Recently published *Close to the Fire*, by David Helwig; *The Summer of Apartment X*, by Lesley Choyce; and *Luther Corhern's Salmon Camp Chronicles*, by Herb Curtis.

How to Contact: Considers unsolicited mss; outline or synopsis and 30-50 page sample. Query first. SASE "with Canadian stamps, International Reply Coupons, cash, check or money order. No U.S. stamps please." Reports in 6 months.

Terms: Pays royalties of 8% minimum; 12% maximum. Average advance: $100-200, negotiable. Sends galleys to author. Writers guidelines for SAE and IRC or Canadian stamps.

Advice: "We do not consider submissions from outside Canada."

☑ ◎ ☙ **GRAYWOLF PRESS,** 2402 University Ave., Suite 203, St. Paul MN 55114. (651)641-0077. Fax: (651)641-0036. E-mail: wolves@graywolfpress.org. Website: www.graywolfpress.org (includes writers' guidelines, information about titles and authors, staff roster, general information about the press). Editor/Publisher: Fiona McCrae. **Acquisitions**: Anne Czarniecki and Katie Dublinski. Estab. 1974. "Graywolf Press is an independent, nonprofit publisher dedicated to the creation and promotion of thoughtful and imaginative contemporary literature essential to a vital and diverse culture." Growing small literary press, nonprofit corporation. Publishes hardcover and paperback originals. Books: acid-free quality paper; offset printing; hardcover and soft binding; illustrations occasionally. Average print order: 3,000-10,000. First novel print order: 2,000-6,000. Averages 14-16 total titles, 4-6 fiction titles each year.

• Graywolf Press books have won numerous awards.

Needs: Literary, and short story collections. Literary fiction; no genre books (romance, western, science fiction, suspense). Published *How the Body Prays*, by Peter Weltner (novel); *The Wedding Jester*, by Steve Stern (short stories); and *A Four Sided Bed*, by Elizabeth Searle (novel).

How to Contact: Query with SASE. Reports in 3 months. Simultaneous submissions OK. Occasionally critiques rejected mss.

Terms: Pays in royalties of 7½-10%; negotiates advance and number of author's copies. Sends galleys to author. Publishes ms 18 months after acceptance. Free book catalog. Guidelines for #10 SASE.

Advice: "Please review the catalog and submission guidelines before submitting your work. We rarely publish collections or novels by authors who have not published work previously in literary journals or magazines."

◐ **GREENE BARK PRESS,** P.O. Box 1108, Bridgeport CT 06601. (203)372-4861. E-mail: greenebark@aol.com. Website: www.bookworld.com/greenebark. **Acquisitions:** Michele Hofbauer, associate publisher. "We only publish children's fiction—all subjects, but in reading picture book format appealing to ages 3-9 or all ages." Publishes hardcover originals. **Publishes 60% previously unpublished writers/year.** Publishes 5 titles/year. Distributes titles through Baker & Taylor, Partners Book Distributing and Quality Books. Promotes titles through ads, trade shows (national and regional), direct mail campaigns.

Needs: Juvenile. Published *Molly Meets Mona & Friends*, by Gladys Walker (hardcover picture book).

How to Contact: Submit complete ms with SASE. Does not accept queries or ms by e-mail. Reports in 3 months on mss. Simultaneous submissions OK.

Terms: Pays 10-15% royalty on wholesale price. Publishes ms 1 year after acceptance. Writer's guidelines and book catalog with SASE.

Advice: Audience is "children who read to themselves and others. Mothers, fathers, grandparents, godparents who read to their respective children, grandchildren. Include SASE, be prepared to wait, do NOT inquire by telephone, fax or e-mail."

◐ **GREENWILLOW BOOKS,** Imprint of HarperCollins Children's Book Group, 1350 Avenue of the Americas, New York NY 10019. (212)261-6500. Website: www.williammorrow.com. Estab. 1974. "Greenwillow Books publishes quality hardcover books for children." Publishes hardcover originals and reprints. **Publishes 1% previously unpublished writers/year.** Publishes 70-80 titles/year.

Needs: Juvenile, picture books: fantasy, historical, humor, literary, mystery. Recently published *Beyond the Mango Tree*, by Amy Bronwen Zemser; *No Pretty Pictures: A Child of War*, by Anita Lobel; and *The Gargoyle on the Roof*, by Jack Prelutsky.

How to Contact: Reports in 3 months on mss. Agented fiction 70%. Simultaneous submissions OK.

Terms: Pays 10% royalty on wholesale price for first-time authors. Advance varies. Publishes ms 2 years after acceptance. Writer's guidelines for #10 SASE. Book catalog for $2 and 9×12 SAE.

☑ ◐ GROLIER PUBLISHING, Grolier Inc., Sherman Turnpike, Danbury CT 06816. (203)797-3500. Fax: (203)797-3197. Estab. 1895. "Grolier Publishing is a leading publisher of reference, educational and children's books. We provide parents, teachers and librarians with the tools they need to enlighten children to the pleasure of learning and prepare them for the road ahead." Publishes hardcover and trade paperback originals.
Imprint(s): Children's Press, Franklin Watts, **Orchard Books**.
Needs: Juvenile, picture books.
How to Contact: Prefers to work with unagented authors. Reports in 4 months on proposals. Simultaneous submissions OK.
Terms: Pays royalty for established authors; makes outright purchase for first-time authors. Advance varies. Publishes ms 18 months after acceptance. Writer's guidelines free. Book catalog for 9×12 SAE and $3 postage.

◐ GRYPHON PUBLICATIONS, P.O. Box 209, Brooklyn NY 11228. (718)646-6126 (after 6 pm EST). **Acquisitions:** Gary Lovisi, owner/editor. Estab. 1983. Publishes paperback originals and trade paperback reprints. Books: bond paper; offset printing; perfect binding. Average print order: 500-1,000. **Published new writers within the last year.** Plans 2 first novels this year. Averages 10-15 total titles, 12 fiction titles each year.
Imprint(s): Gryphon Books, Gryphon Doubles, Gryphon SF Rediscovery Series.
Needs: Mystery/suspense (private eye/hardboiled, crime), science fiction (hard science/technological, soft/sociological). No supernatural, horror, romance or westerns. Published *The Dreaming Detective*, by Ralph Vaughn (mystery-fantasy-horror); *The Woman in the Dugout*, by Gary Lovisi and T. Arnone (baseball novel); and *A Mate for Murder*, by Bruno Fischer (hardboiled pulp). Publishes Gryphon Double novel series.
How to Contact: "I am not looking for novels now but will see a *1-page synopsis* with SASE." Include estimated word count, 50-word bio, short list of publishing credits, "how you heard about us." Send SASE. Do not send ms. Agented fiction 5-10%. Reports in 2-4 weeks on queries; 1-2 months on mss. Simultaneous and electronic submissions OK (with hard copy—disk in ASCII). Often critiques or comments on rejected mss.
Terms: For magazines, $5-45 on publication plus 2 contributor's copies; for novels/collections payment varies and is much more. Sends galleys to author. Publishes ms 1-3 years after acceptance. Writers guidelines and book catalog for SASE.
Advice: "I am looking for better and better writing, more cutting-edge material with *impact*! Keep it lean and focused."

◼ ◯ ◎ GUERNICA EDITIONS, P.O. Box 117, Station P, Toronto, Ontario M63 2WC Canada. (416)658-9888. Fax: (416)657-8885. Website: www.ourworld.compuserve.com/Homepages/Guernica (includes authors, titles). **Acquisitions:** Antonio D'Alfonso, editor. Umberto Claudio, fiction editor. Estab. 1978. Publishes paperback originals. Books: offset printing; perfect binding. Average print order: 1,500. Average first novel print order: 1,000. **Publishes 1 previously unpublished writer/year.** Plans to publish 1 first novel this year. Publishes 16-20 total titles each year. Promotes titles through direct mail and advertising.
Needs: Contemporary, ethnic, literary, translations of foreign novels. Looking for novels about women and ethnic subjects. No unsolicited works. Recently published *Feast of the Dead*, by Anthony Fragola (short stories); *Impala*, by Carole David (novel); and *A House on the Piazza*, by Kenny Marotta (short stories).
How to Contact: Query first. Does not accept or return unsolicited mss. IRCs. Reports in 6 months. Electronic submissions via IBM WordPerfect disks.
Terms: Pays royalties of 7-10% and 10 author's copies. Book catalog for SAE and $5 postage. (Canadian stamps only).
Advice: Publishing "short novels (150 pages or less)."

⊕ ◐ ROBERT HALE LIMITED, Clerkenwell House, 45/47 Clerkenwell Green, London EC1R 0HT England. Fax: 0171-490-4958. Publishes hardcover and trade paperback originals and hardcover reprints. **Publishes approximately 50 previously unpublished writers/year.**
Needs: Historical (not U.S. history), mainstream and western. Length: 40,000-150,000 words. Published *The Big Brown Bear*, by Robert Elegant (mainstream); *Mexican Hat*, by Michael McGarrity (crime); and *Mischief*, by Amanda Quick (historical romance).
How to Contact: Send cover letter, synopsis or brief summary and 2 sample chapters. Unsolicited queries/ correspondence by fax OK.
Advice: "Write well and have a strong plot!"

◐ ◎ HAMPTON ROADS PUBLISHING COMPANY, INC., 134 Burgess Ln., Charlottesville VA 22902. (804)296-2772. Fax: (804)296-5096. E-mail: hrpc@hrpub.com. Website: www.hrpub.com (includes writer's guidelines, authors, titles, synopsis of books, message board, guest book). **Acquisitions:** Frank DeMarco, chairman and chief editor. Estab. 1989. Publishes and distributes hardcover and paperback originals on subjects including metaphysics, health, complementary medicine, visionary fiction and other related topics. "We work as a team to produce the best books we are capable of producing which will impact, uplift and contribute to positive change in the world. We publish what defies or doesn't quite fit the usual genres. We are noted for visionary fiction." Average print order: 3,000-5,000. **Publishes 6-10 previously unpublished writers/year.** Averages 30 total titles/year, 5-6 fiction titles/year. Distributes titles through distributors. Promotes titles through advertising, representatives, author signings and radio-TV interviews with authors.

Needs: Literary, New Age/mystic/spiritual, psychic/supernatural/occult. Looking for "visionary fiction, past-life fiction, based on actual memories." Recently published *Astral Dynamics*, by Robert Bruce; *Infinite Grace*, by Diane Goldner (healing); and *Judas the Gentile*, by D.S. Uliteras (fiction).

How to Contact: Accepts unsolicited proposals. Query first. Unsolicited queries/correspondence by e-mail and fax OK. Include description of book. Send SASE for reply, return of ms or send disposable copy of ms (preferred). Agented fiction 5%. Reports in 3-4 weeks on queries; 3-5 months on mss. Simultaneous submissions OK.

Terms: Pays in royalties; advance is negotiable. Sends galleys to author.

Advice: "Send us something new and different. Be patient. Sometimes we are slow."

☑ ☺ Ⓐ Ⓨ HARCOURT INC., (formerly Harcourt Brace & Co.) 525 B St., Suite 1900, San Diego CA 92101. (619)231-6616. Fax: (619)699-6777. Website: www.harcourt.com. Publisher: Louise Pelan. **Acquisitions**: Jeannette Larson, editor (general fiction); Allyn Johnston, editorial director of Harcourt Brace Children's Books; Linda Zuckerman, editorial director of Browndeer Press; Elizabeth Van Doren, editorial director of Gulliver Books; Anne Davies, senior editor of Gulliver Books; Paula Wiseman, editorial director of Silver Whistle. Publishes hardcover originals and paperback reprints. Averages 150 titles/year. **Publishes "very few" new writers/year.**

Imprint(s): Harcourt Inc. Children's Books, Gulliver Books, Browndeer Press, Red Wagon Books and Silver Whistle.

● Books published by Harcourt Trade Publishers have received numerous awards including the Caldecott and Newbery medals and selections as the American Library Association's "Best Books for Young Adults." Note that the publisher only accepts manuscripts through an agent. Unagented writers may query only.

Needs: Nonfiction for all ages, picture books for very young children, historical, mystery. Published *To Market, To Market*, by Ann Miranda; *Antarctic Antics*, by Judy Sierra; *Armageddon Summer*, by Bruce Coville and Jan Yolen; and *Count On Me*, by Alice Provensen.

How to Contact: Query first. Submit through agent only. No unsolicited mss.

Terms: Terms vary according to individual books; pays on royalty basis. Catalog for 9 × 12 SASE.

Advice: "Read as much current fiction as you can; familiarize yourself with the type of fiction published by a particular house; interact with young people to obtain a realistic picture of their concerns, interests and speech patterns."

☺ HARCOURT INC., CHILDREN'S BOOKS DIVISION, (formerly Harcourt Brace & Company, Children's Book Division), 525 B St., Suite 1900, San Diego CA 92101. (619) 231-6616. Fax: (619)699-6777. Website: www.harcourt.com. **Acquisitions:** Manuscript Submissions. "Harcourt Inc. owns some of the world's most prestigious publishing imprints—which distinguish quality products for the juvenile, educational, scientific, technical, medical, professional and trade markets worldwide." Publishes hardcover originals and trade paperback reprints.

Imprint(s): Harcourt Brace Children's Books, Gulliver Books, Gulliver Green, Silver Whistle, Red Wagon, Voyager and Odyssey Paperbacks, Magic Carpet, Libros Viajeros and Green Light Readers.

Needs: Childrens/juvenile, young adult. Published *The Many Troubles of Andy Russell*, by David Adler (middle grade); *Armageddon Summer*, by Bruce Coville and Jane Yolen (young adult); and *Pictures 1918*, by Jeanette Ingold (young adult).

How to Contact: Query first. No phone calls.

🌱 ☑ ◑ ◎ HARLEQUIN ENTERPRISES, LTD., 225 Duncan Mill Rd., Don Mills, Ontario M3B 3K9 Canada. (416)445-5860. Website: www.romance.net (includes product listings, author information, a full range of related information). Chairman and CEO: Brian E. Hickey. President and COO: Stuart J. Campbell. Vice President Editorial: Isabel Swift. Editorial Director Harlequin, Gold Eagle, Worldwide Library: Randall Toye; Silhouette, Steeple Hill: Tara Gavin; MIRA: Diane Maggy. Estab. 1949. Publishes paperback originals and reprints. Books: Newsprint paper; web printing; perfect-bound. Published new writers within the last year. Number of titles: Averages 700/year. Distributes titles through retail market, direct mail market and overseas through operating companies. Promotes titles through trade and consumer advertising: print, radio, TV. Buys agented and unagented fiction.

Imprint(s): Harlequin, Silhouette, MIRA, Gold Eagle, Worldwide Mysteries, Steeple Hill.

Needs: Romance, heroic adventure, mystery/suspense (romantic suspense *only*). Will accept nothing that is not related to the desired categories.

How to Contact: Send query letter or send outline and first 50 pages (2 or 3 chapters) or submit through agent with SASE (Canadian). No simultaneous submissions. Reports in 6 weeks on queries; 2 months on mss.

Terms: Offers royalties, advance. Must return advance if book is not completed or is unacceptable. Sends galleys to author. Publishes ms 1 year after acceptance. Guidelines available.

Advice: "The quickest route to success is to follow directions for submissions: Query first. We encourage first novelists. Before sending a manuscript, read as many current Harlequin titles as you can. It's very important to know the genre and the series most appropriate for your submission." Submissions for Harlequin Romance and Harlequin Presents should go to: Mills & Boon Limited Eton House, 18-24 Paradise Road, Richmond, Surrey TW9 1SR United Kingdom, Attn: Karin Stoecker; Superromances: Paula Eykelhof, senior editor, (Don Mills address above); Temptation: Birgit Davis-Todd, senior editor (Don Mills address). Intrigue: Denise O'Sullivan, associate editor, Harlequin Books, 6th Floor, 300 E. 42 Street, New York, NY 10017. Silhouette and Steeple Hill submissions should also be sent to the New York office, attention Tara Gavin. MIRA submissions to Dianne Maggy, senior editor (Don Mills address); Gold Eagle and Worldwide Mysteries submissions to Feroze Moham-med, senior editor (Don Mills address). "The relationship between the novelist and editor is regarded highly and treated with professionalism."

N: ⊕ ◐ HARLEQUIN MILLS & BOON LTD., Subsidiary of Harlequin Enterprises Ltd., Eton House, 18-24 Paradise Rd., Richmond, Surrey TW9 1SR United Kingdom. (44)0181-948-0444. Website: www.romance. net (includes forthcoming titles and author profiles). **Acquisitions:** K. Stoecker, editorial director; Tessa Shapcott, senior editor (Harlequin Presents®); Linda Fildew, senior editor (Harlequin Romance®). Estab. 1908-1909. "World's largest publisher of brand name category romance; books are available for translation into more than 20 languages and distributed in more than 100 international markets." Publishes paperback originals. Published new writers within the last year. Plans 3-4 first novels this year.
Imprint(s): Harlequin, Silhouette, MIRA, Mills & Boon.
Needs: Romance (contemporary, historical, regency period, medical). Publishes Christmas anthologies. Closed to outside submissions. Publishes Harlequin Romance, Harlequin Presents (historical romance, medical romance in the UK). Recently published *Outback Wife and Mother*, by Barbara Hannay (Harlequin Romance/Mills & Boon); *A Convenient Bridegroom*, by Helen Bianchin (Harlequin Presents); and *The Mistress Assignment*, by Penny Jordan (Harlequin Presents).
How to Contact: Does not accept unsolicited mss; returns unsolicted mss. Query with outline/synopsis. Unso-licited queries/correspondence by fax OK. Include estimated word count, 1-2 paragraph bio, list of publishing credits and why the story is targeted at the series. Send SASE for reply, return of ms. Agented fiction less than 50%. Reports in 1 month on 12-14 weeks on mss. No simultaneous submissions. Often critiques or comments on rejected mss.
Terms: Advance against royalty. Sends galleys to author. Publishes ms up to 3 years after acceptance. Writer's guidelines free.
Advice: "Study a wide selection or our current paperbacks to gain an understanding of our requirements—then write from the heart."

◐ ♥ HARPERCOLLINS CHILDREN'S BOOKS GROUP, HarperCollins Publishers, 1350 Avenue of the Americas, New York NY 10019. (212)261-6800. Website: www.harpercollins.com. President/Publisher: Susan Katz. Senior Vice President/Associate Publisher/Editor-in-Chief: Kate Morgan Jackson. **Acquisitions:** Joanna Cotler, vice president/editorial director, Joanna Cotler Books; Laura Geringer, vice president/editorial director, Laura Geringer Books; Mary Alice Moore, VP Director of Brand Publishing; Suzanne Daghlian, editorial director, HarperFestival; Ginee Seo, editorial director, Harper Trophy; Executive Editors: Phoebe Yeh, Robert O. Warren and Alix Reid. Publishes hardcover trade titles, paperbacks and novelty books.
  ● HarperCollins Children's Books received the 1998 Newbery Honor for *Ella Enchanted*, by Gail Levine; the 1998 Newbery Honor for *Wringer*, by Jerry Spinelli; and the 1999 Coretta Scott King Honor for *I Have Heard of a Land*, by Joyce Carol Thomas and Floyd Cooper.
Imprint(s): Avon, Joanna Cotler Books, **Laura Geringer Books, Greenwillow Books, HarperCollins,** Harper-Festival, HarperTrophy, Tempest.
Needs: Picture books, easy-to-read, middle-grade, teenage and young adult novels; fiction, fantasy, animal, sports, spy/adventure, historical, science fiction, problem novels and contemporary. Recently published *Ella Enchanted*, by Gail Carson Levine (middle grade); *Today I Feel Silly*, by Jamie Lee Curtis (picture book); and *This Little Piggy*, by Jane Manning (novelty).
How to Contact: Query; submit complete ms; submit outline/synopsis and sample chapters; submit through agent. SASE for query, ms. Please identify simultaneous submissions. Reports in 2-3 months.
Terms: Average 10% in royalties. Royalties on picture books shared with illustrators. Offers advance. Publishes novel 1 year; picture books 2 years after acceptance. Writer's guidelines and book catalog for SASE.
Advice: "Write from your own experience and the child you once were. Read widely in the field of adult and children's literature. Realize that writing for children is a difficult challenge. Read other young adult novelists as well as adult novelists. Pay attention to styles, approaches, topics. Be willing to rewrite, perhaps many times. We have no rules for subject matter, length or vocabulary but look instead for ideas that are fresh and imaginative. Good writing that involves the reader in a story or subject that has appeal for young readers is also essential. One submission is considered by all imprints."

⊘ Ⓐ HARPERCOLLINS PUBLISHERS, 10 E. 53rd St., New York NY 10022. (212)207-7000. Website: www.harpercollins.com. "HarperCollins, one of the largest English language publishers in the world, is a broad-based publisher with strengths in academic, business and professional, children's, educational, general interest, and religious and spiritual books, as well as multimedia titles." Publishes hardcover and paperback originals and paperback reprints. Trade publishes 120-150 titles/year.

Imprint(s): Harper Adult Trade; Harper Audio, Harper Business, **HarperLibros**, **HarperPaperbacks**, **Harper-Perennial**, **Harper Children's Books**, HarperSan Francisco, Regan Books, Cliff Street Books, HarperEntertainment, HarperResource, HarperVoyager, **Ecco Press**, **Zondervan Publishing House**.

Needs: Adventure, fantasy, gothic, historical, mystery, science fiction, suspense, western, literary. "We look for a strong story line and exceptional literary talent." Published *The Tennis Partner*, by Abraham Verghese; *The Professor and the Madman*, by Simon Winchester; *I Know This Much Is True*, by Wally Lamb; *The Antelope Wife*, by Louise Erdrich; *Cloudsplitter*, by Russell Banks; and *The Soul of Sex*, by Thomas Moore.

How to Contact: *No unsolicited queries or mss.* Agented submissions only. Reports on solicited queries in 6 weeks.

Terms: Pays standard royalties. Advance negotiable.

Advice: "We do not accept any unsolicited material."

HARPERCOLLINS PUBLISHERS (NEW ZEALAND) LIMITED, P.O. Box 1, Auckland, New Zealand. **Acquisitions:** Ian Watt, publisher. Averages 4-6 fiction titles/year (20-25 nonfiction).

Imprint(s): Flamingo, HarperCollins.

Needs: Adult fiction: Flamingo and HarperCollins imprints; Junior fiction: 8-11 years. Length: Flamingo and HarperCollins: 40,000+ words; Junior: 15-17,000 words.

How to Contact: Full ms preferred.

Terms: Pays royalties. "Write and ask for guidelines."

Advice: "It helps if the author and story have New Zealand connections/content."

HARPERPAPERBACKS, Division of HarperCollins Publishers, 10 E. 53rd St., New York NY 10022. (212)207-7000. Fax: (212)207-7759. **Acquisitions:** Carolyn Marino, editorial director; Jessica Lichtenstein, fiction editor; Laura Cifelli, fiction editor (romantic fiction); Leslie Stern, fiction editor. Publishes paperback originals and reprints. Published new writers within the last year.

Imprint(s): HarperChoice.

Needs: Mainstream/contemporary, mystery/suspense, romance (contemporary, historical, romantic suspense), thriller/espionage.

How to Contact: Query by letter or agent. No unsolicited mss accepted.

Terms: Pays advance and royalties.

HARPERPERENNIAL, Imprint of HarperCollins Publishers, 10 E. 53rd St., New York NY 10022. (212)207-7000. Website: www.harpercollins.com. **Acquisitions:** Susan Weinberg, senior vice president/publisher. Estab. 1963. "HarperPerennial publishes a broad range of adult fiction and nonfiction paperbacks." Publishes trade paperback originals and reprints. Publishes 100 titles/year.

Needs: Ethnic, feminist, literary. "Don't send us novels—go through hardcover." Published *Lying On the Couch*, by Irwin D. Yalom (psycho-thriller novel); *American Pie*, by Michael Lee West (novel); and *Bird Girl and the Man Who Followed the Sun*, by Velma Wallis (fiction/native American studies).

How to Contact: Agented submissions only.

Terms: Pays 5-7½% royalty. Advance varies. Publishes ms 6 months after acceptance. Book catalog free.

Advice: Audience is general reader—high school, college. "Call and get the name of an editor and they will look at it. Usually an editor is listed in a book's acknowledgments. You should address your submission to an editor or else it will probably be returned."

HARVEST HOUSE PUBLISHERS, 1075 Arrowsmith, Eugene OR 97402-9197. (541)343-0123. Editorial Managing Director: LaRae Weikert. Vice President of Editorial: Carolyn McCready. Estab. 1974. "The foundation of our publishing program is to publish books that 'help the hurts of people' and nurture spiritual growth." Midsize independent publisher. Publishes hardcover and paperback originals and reprints. Books: 40 lb. ground wood paper; offset printing; perfect binding; average print order: 10,000; first novel print order: 10,000-15,000. Averages 120 total titles, 6 fiction titles each year.

How to Contact: No longer accepting unsolicited ms. Recommends using Evangelical Christian Publishers Association website (www.ecpa.org) or the Writer's Edge.

HELICON NINE EDITIONS, Subsidiary of Midwest Center for the Literary Arts, Inc., P.O. Box 22412, Kansas City MO 64113. (816)753-1095. **Acquisitions:** Gloria Vando Hickok, publisher/editor; Pat Breed (general fiction); Ann Slegman (general fiction); Steve Shapiro (general fiction). Estab. 1990. Small press publishing poetry, fiction, creative nonfiction and anthologies. Publishes paperback originals. Books: 60 lb. paper; offset printing; perfect-bound; 4-color cover. Average print order: 1,000-5,000. **Published 1 new writer within the last year.** Plans 4 total titles, 2-4 fiction titles this year. Also publishes one-story chapbooks called *feuillets*, which come with envelope, 250 print run. Distributes titles through Baker & Taylor, The Booksource, Brodart, Ingrams, Follett (library acquisitions), Midwest Library Service. Promotes titles through reviews, readings, radio and television interviews.

• Helicon Nine Editions sponsors the annual Willa Cather Fiction Prize—a $1,000 prize plus publication. Send a SASE for guidelines. Helicon Nine author Anne Whitney Pierce won the O'Henry Award for *Galaxy Girls: Wonder Woman.*

Needs: Contemporary, ethnic, experimental, literary, short story collections, translations. "We're only interested in fine literature." Nothing "commercial." Recently published *Climbing the God Tree,* by Jamie Wriston Colbert; and *One Girl,* by Sheila Kohler (short stories).

How to Contact: Does not accept unsolicited mss. Query first. SASE. Reports in 1 week on queries.

Terms: Pays advance and royalties, author's copies. "Individual arrangement with author." Sends galleys to author. Publishes ms 6-12 months after acceptance.

Advice: "We accept short story collections. We welcome new writers and first books. Submit a clean, readable copy in a folder or box—paginated with title and name on each page. Also, do not pre-design book, i.e., no illustrations. We'd like to see books that will be read 50-100 years from now."

HOHM PRESS, P.O. Box 2501, Prescott AZ 86302. (520)717-1779. E-mail: pinedr@goodnet.com. **Acquisitions:** Regina Sara Ryan, managing editor. Estab. 1975. "Our offerings include a range of titles in the areas of psychology and spirituality, herbistry, alternative health methods and nutrition, as well as distinctive children's books. Hohm Press is proud to present authors from the U.S. and Europe who have a clarity of vision and the mastery to communicate that vision." Publishes hardcover and trade paperback originals. Publishes 6-8 titles/year. **50% of books from first-time authors.**

How to Contact: Reports in 3 months on queries. Simultaneous submissions OK.

Terms: Pays 10-15% royalty on net sales. No advance. Publishes ms 18 months after acceptance. Book catalog for $1.50.

HOLIDAY HOUSE, INC., 425 Madison, New York NY 10017. (212)688-0085. Fax: (212)421-6134. Editor-in-Chief: Regina Griffin. **Acquisitions:** Michelle Frey, associate editor. Estab. 1935. "Holiday House has a commitment to publishing first-time authors and illustrators." Independent publisher of children's books, picture books, nonfiction and novels for young readers. Publishes hardcover originals and paperback reprints. **Published new writers within the last year.** Number of titles: Approximately 50 hardcovers and 15 paperbacks each year.

• *The Wright Brothers: How They Invented the Airplane* by Russell Freedman and published by Holiday House is a Newbery Honor Book.

Needs: Children's books only: literary, contemporary, Judaica and holiday, adventure, humor and animal stories for young readers. Published *The Life and Death of Crazy Horse,* by Russell Freedman; *The Golen,* by Barbara Rogasky, illustrated by Trina Schart Hyman; and *The Magic Dreidels,* by Eric A. Kimmel, illustrated by Katya Krenina. "We're not in a position to be too encouraging, as our list is tight, but we're always open to good writing."

How to Contact: "We ask for query letters only with SASE. We do not accept simultaneous submissions. No phone calls, please."

Terms: Advance and royalties are flexible, depending upon whether the book is illustrated. Publishes ms 1-2 years after acceptance.

Advice: "Please submit only one project at a time."

HENRY HOLT & COMPANY, 115 W. 18th St., 6th Floor, New York NY 10011. (212)886-9200. **Acquisitions:** Sara Bershtel, editorial director (Metropolitan Books); (Mr.) Tracy Brown, executive editor (adult literary fiction). Publishes hardcover and paperback originals and reprints. Averages 80-100 total original titles, 35% of total is fiction each year.

Imprint(s): Owl (paper), John Macrae Books, Metropolitan Books, **Henry Holt & Company Books for Young Readers**.

How to Contact: Accepts queries; no unsolicited mss. Agented fiction 95%.

Terms: Pays in royalties of 10% minimum; 15% maximum; advance. Sends galleys to author.

HENRY HOLT & COMPANY BOOKS FOR YOUNG READERS, Imprint of Henry Holt & Co., Inc., 115 W. 18th St., New York NY 10011. (212)886-9200. Fax: (212)633-0748. **Acquisitions:** Laura Godwin, vice president and associate publisher; Nina Ignatowicz, executive editor; Marc Aronson, senior editor (young adult nonfiction and fiction); Christy Ottaviano, senior editor (picture books, middle grade fiction). Estab. 1866 (Holt). Henry Holt Books for Young Readers publishes excellent books of all kinds (fiction, nonfiction, illustrated) for all ages, from the very young to the young adult. Publishes hardcover and trade paperback originals. Publishes 50-60 titles/year.

CHECK THE CATEGORY INDEXES, located at the back of the book, for publishers interested in specific fiction subjects.

Imprint(s): Edge Books (Marc Aronson, senior editor, "a high caliber young adult fiction imprint"); Red Feather Books ("covers a range between early chapter and younger middle grade readers"); Owlet Paperbacks.
Needs: Juvenile: adventure, animal, contemporary, fantasy, history, humor, multicultural, religion, sports, suspense/mystery. Picture books: animal, concept, history, humor, multicultural, religion, sports. Young adult: contemporary, fantasy, history, multicultural, nature/environment, problem novels, sports. Recently published *Smack*, by Melvin Burgess; and *Whirligig*, by Paul Fleischman (both young adult).
How to Contact: Query with SASE. Reports in 5 months on queries and mss. No longer accepts multiple simultaneous submissions.
Terms: Pays royalty and advance. Publishes ms 18 months after acceptance. Book catalog and writer's guidelines upon request with SASE.

✓ ◙ ▼ **HOUGHTON MIFFLIN BOOKS FOR CHILDREN,** Imprint of Houghton Mifflin Company, 222 Berkeley St., Boston MA 02116-3764. (617)351-5000. Fax: (617)351-1111. E-mail: hmco.com. Website: www.hmco.com (includes titles, job postings, etc.) **Acquisitions:** Amanda Sullivan, submissions coordinator; Margaret Raymo, senior editor; Amy Flynn, associate editor. "Houghton Mifflin gives shape to ideas that educate, inform, and above all, delight." Publishes hardcover and trade paperback originals and reprints. **Publishes 12 previously unpublished writers/year.** Firm publishes approximately 60 titles/year. Promtoes titles through author visits, advertising, reviews.
Imprint(s): Clarion Books, New York City (contact: Dinah Stevenson); Walter Lorraine Books (contact: W. Lorraine).
● Houghton Mifflin Books for Children received the Caldecott Award in 1999 for *Snowflake Bently.*
Needs: Adventure, ethnic, historical, humor, juvenile (early readers), literary, mystery, picture books, suspense, young adult, board books. Recently published *Dare Truth or Promise*, by Paula Boock (young adult); *Signs and Wonders*, by Pat Lowery Collins; and *The Circuit*, by Francisco Jimenez.
How to Contact: Submit complete ms with appropriate-sized SASE. Reports in 2 months. Simultaneous submissions OK. Mss and proposals in the following format are not considered: e-mail, fax, disk, website.
Terms: Pays 5-10% royalty on retail price. Advance dependent on many factors. Publishes ms 18 months after acceptance. For writer's guidelines need small SASE. For book catalog need 9×12 SASE with 3 first-class stamps.

◙ Ⓐ **HOUGHTON MIFFLIN COMPANY,** 222 Berkeley St., Boston MA 02116. (617)351-5000. Fax: (617)351-1202. Website: www.hmco.com. **Acquisitions:** Submissions Editor. Estab. 1832. Publishes hardcover and paperback originals and paperback reprints. Averages 100 total titles, 50 fiction titles each year. **10% of books by new authors.**
Needs: Adventure, confession, ethnic, fantasy, feminist, gay/lesbian, historical, humor, literary, mainstream contemporary, mystery/suspense. Agented fiction 80%.
Terms: Pays royalties of 10% minimum; 15% maximum. Advance varies. Publishes ms 1-2 years after acceptance.
How to Contact: Does not accept unsolicited mss. Query with 3 sample chapters, SASE.

[N] **HOWELLS HOUSE,** P.O. Box 9546, Washington DC 20016-9546. (202)333-2182. **Acquisitions:** W.D. Howells, publisher. Estab. 1988. "Our interests are institutions and institutional change." Publishes hardcover and trade paperback originals and reprints. Publishes 4 titles/year; each imprint publishes 2-3 titles/year.
Imprint(s): The Compass Press, Whalesback Books.
Needs: Historical, literary, mainstream/contemporary.
How to Contact: Query first. Reports in 2 months on proposals.
Terms: Pays 15% net royalty or makes outright purchase. May offer advance. Publishes ms 8 months after ms development completed.

[N] ◙ **HUNTINGTON HOUSE PUBLISHERS,** P.O. Box 53788, Lafayette LA 70505. (318)237-7049. Fax: (318)237-7060. E-mail: ladawn@eatel.net. Website: www.huntingtonhousebooks.com. **Acquisitions:** editorial department. Estab. 1983. **Published 9 new writers within the last year.** Plans 4 first novels this year. Publishes 30 total titles, 10 fiction titles/year.
Needs: Young adult/teen (adventure, easy-to-read, fantasy/science fiction, historical, mystery/suspense, series). Recently published *High On Adventure III*, by Steve Arrington; *Patriots*, by James Wesley Rawles (first novel); *Slash Brokers*, by Jeff Barganier (first novel).
How to Contact: Accepts unsolicited mss. Query with outline/synopsis and sample chapters. Include estimated word count and brief bio. Send a disposable copy of the ms. Agented fiction 5%. Reports in 3 weeks on mss. Simultaneous submissions OK.
Terms: Pays royalties of 10-15%. Sends prepublication galleys to author. Writer's guidelines for SASE.
Advice: "Submit an outline (two to four pages) and chapter by chapter synopsis of your idea. Even if the breakdown is still only tentative, this provides us with the information we need to determine which of our series your piece could join. Note any previously published material and include excerpts (no more than two pages each). Enclose any peer reviews, recommendations, and references in the proposal package."

⊘ Ⓐ HYPERION BOOKS FOR CHILDREN, Imprint of Hyperion, 114 Fifth Ave., New York NY 10011. (212)633-4400. Fax: (212)633-4833. **Acquisitions:** Editorial Director. "The aim of Hyperion Books for Children is to create a dynamic children's program informed by Disney's creative vision, direct connection to children, and unparalleled marketing and distribution." Publishes hardcover and trade paperback originals. Publishes 210 titles/year.

Needs: Juvenile, picture books, young adult. Published *McDuff*, by Rosemary Wells and Susan Jeffers (picture book); and *Split Just Right*, by Adele Griffin (middle grade).

How to Contact: Agented submissions only. Reports in 1 month. Simultaneous submissions OK.

Terms: Pays royalty, "varies too widely to generalize." Advance varies. Publishes ms 1 year after acceptance. Writer's guidelines and book catalog free.

Advice: "Hyperion Books for Children are meant to appeal to an upscale children's audience. Study your audience. Look at and research current children's books. Who publishes what you like? Approach them. We are Disney and are always looking for Disney material."

⊘ Ⓐ IDEALS CHILDREN'S BOOKS, Imprint of Hambleton-Hill Publishing, Inc., 1501 County Hospital Rd., Nashville TN 37218. **Acquisitions:** Bethany Snyder, editor. Ideals Children's Books publishes some fiction and nonfiction for toddlers to 8-year-olds. Publishes children's hardcover and trade paperback originals. Publishes 40 titles/year.

Needs: Childrens/juvenile. Recently published *Outside*, by Joseph S. Bonsall, illustrated by Erin M. Mauterer; and *Just Right*, by Alan Osmond, illustrated by Thomas A. Arrestad.

How to Contact: This publisher only accepts unsolicited mss from agents and members of the Society of Children's Book Writers & Illustrators, and previously published book authors may submit with a list of writing credits.

Terms: Pay determined by individual contract. Publishes ms up to 2 years after acceptance. Writer's guidelines for #10 SASE.

Advice: Audience is children in the toddler to 8-year-old range. "We are seeking original, child-centered fiction for the picture book format. *We do not publish chapter books.* We are not interested in alphabet books or anthropomorphism."

⊘ INTERLINK PUBLISHING GROUP, INC., 46 Crosby St., Northampton MA 01060-1804. (413)582-7054. Fax: (413)582-7057. E-mail: interpg@aol.com. Contemporary fiction in translation published under Emerging Voices: New International Fiction. **Acquisitions:** Michel Moushabeck, publisher; Pam Thompson, fiction editor. Estab. 1987. "Midsize independent publisher specializing in world travel, world literature, world history and politics." Publishes hardcover and paperback originals. Books: 55 lb. Warren Sebago Cream white paper; web offset printing; perfect binding; average print order: 5,000; first novel print order: 5,000. Distributes titles through distributors such as Baker & Taylor. Promotes titles through book mailings to extensive, specialized lists of editors and reviewers, authors read at bookstores and special events across the country. Published new writers within the last year. **Publishes 0-2 previously unpublished writers/year.** Plans 2 first novels this year. Averages 30 total titles, 2-6 fiction titles each year.

Imprint(s): Interlink Books, Olive Branch Press and Crocodile Books USA.

Needs: "Adult translated fiction from around the world." Published *House of the Winds*, by Mia Yun (first novel, first translation in English); *The Gardens of Light*, by Amin Maalouf (novel translated from French); and *War in the Land of Egypt*, by Yusef Al-Qaid (novel translated from Arabic). Publishes the International Folk Tales series.

How to Contact: Does not accept unsolicited mss, e-mail or fax queries. Submit query letter and brief sample only. SASE. Reports within 6 weeks on queries.

Terms: Pays royalties of 6% minimum; 7% maximum. Sends galleys to author. Publishes ms 1-1½ years after acceptance.

Advice: "Our Emerging Voices Series is designed to bring to North American readers the once-unheard voices of writers who have achieved wide acclaim at home, but were not recognized beyond the borders of their native lands. We are also looking for folktale collections (for adults) from around the world that fit in our International Folk Tale Series."

⊘ IRONWEED PRESS, P.O. Box 754208, Parkside Station, Forest Hills NY 11375. (718)544-1120. Fax: (718)268-2394. E-mail: iwpress@aol.com. **Acquisitions:** Robert Giannetto, fiction editor. Estab. 1996. Small independent publisher. Publishes hardcover and paperback originals. **Plans 1 first novel this year.** Averages 4 total titles, 4 fiction titles/year. Distributes titles through national wholesalers.

Needs: Ethnic/multicultural (Asian-American), experimental, humor/satire, literary. Published *Best Short Stories of Frank Norris* (literature).

How to Contact: Accepts unsolicited mss. Submit complete ms with a cover letter. Include list of publishing credits. SASE for return of ms. Reports in 3 months on queries; 4-6 months on mss. Simultaneous submissions OK. Sometimes critiques or comments on rejected mss.

Payment/Terms: Pays royalties of 8% minimum; offers advance; provides author's copies. Sends galleys to author. Publishes ms 18-24 months after acceptance.

⬛ ◎ **ITALICA PRESS,** 595 Main St., #605, New York NY 10044. (212)935-4230. Fax: (212)838-7812. E-mail: italica@idt.net. Website: www.italica.com (includes authors, titles). **Acquisitions**: Eileen Gardiner and Ronald G. Musto, publishers. Estab. 1985. Small independent publisher of Italian fiction in translation. Publishes paperback originals. Books: 50-60 lb. natural paper; offset printing; Smythe-sewn binding; illustrations. Average print order: 1,500. "First time translators published. We would like to see translations of Italian writers well-known in Italy who are not yet translated for an American audience." Publishes 6 total titles each year; 2 fiction titles. Distributes titles through direct mail. Promotes titles through catalogs and website.
Needs: Translations of 20th Century Italian fiction. Published *Bakunin's Son*, by Sergio Atzeni (experimental); *Otronto*, by Maria Corti; and *Sparrow*, by Giovanni Verga.
How to Contact: Accepts unsolicited mss. Query first. Queries by e-mail and fax OK. Reports in 3 weeks on queries; 2 months on mss. Simultaneous submissions OK. Electronic submissions via Macintosh disk. Sometimes critiques rejected mss.
Terms: Pays in royalties of 5-15% and 10 author's copies. Sends pre-publication galleys to author. Publishes ms 1 year after acceptance. Book catalog free on request.
Advice: "Remember we publish *only* fiction that has been previously published in Italian. A *brief* call saves a lot of postage. 90% of the proposals we receive are completely off base—but we are very interested in things that are right on target. Please send return postage if you want your manuscript back."

☑ ◨ ◎ **JAMESON BOOKS,** 722 Columbus St., P.O. Box 738, Ottawa IL 61350. (815)434-7905. Fax: (815)434-7907. E-mail: 72557.3635@compuserve.com. **Acquisitions**: Jameson G. Campaigne, Jr., publisher/editor Estab. 1986. "Jameson Books publishes conservative/libertarian politics and economics and pre-cowboy frontier novels (1750-1840)." Publishes hardcover and paperback originals and reprints. Books: free sheet paper; offset printing; average print order: 10,000; first novel print order: 5,000. Plans 6-8 novels this year. Averages 12-16 total titles, 4-8 fiction titles each year. Distributes titles through LPC Group/Chicago (book trade). Occasionally critiques or comments on rejected mss.
Needs: Very well-researched western (frontier pre-1850). No cowboys, no science fiction, mystery, poetry, et al. Published *Yellowstone Kelly*, by Peter Bowen; *Wister Trace*, by Loren Estelman; and *One-Eyed Dream*, by Terry Johnston.
How to Contact: Does not accepted unsolicited mss. Submit outline/synopsis and 3 consecutive sample chapters. SASE. Agented fiction 50%. Reports in 2 weeks on queries; 2-5 months on mss. Simultaneous submissions OK.
Terms: Pays royalties of 5% minimum; 15% maximum. Average advance: $1,500. Sends galleys to author. Publishes ms 1-12 months after acceptance.

☑ ◨ **JOURNEY BOOKS,** a division of Bob Jones University Press, 1700 Wade Hampton Blvd., Greenville SC 29614. (864)242-5100, ext. 4316. Website: www.bju.edu/press/freelnce.html. **Acquisitions**: Mrs. Gloria Repp, editor. Estab. 1974. "Small independent publisher." Publishes paperback originals and reprints. Books: 50 lb. white paper; Webb lithography printing; perfect-bound binding. Average print order: 5,000. First novel print order: 5,000. **Published new writers within the last year.** Plans 3 first novels this year. Averages 12 total titles, 10 fiction titles each year.
Needs: Children's/juvenile (adventure, animal, easy-to-read, historical, mystery, series, sports), young adults (adventure, historical, mystery/suspense, series, sports, western). Published *The Rivers of Judah*, by Catherine Farnes (contemporary teen fiction); *Arby Jenkins*, by Sharon Hambric (contemporary ages 9-12); and *The Treasure Keeper*, by Anita Williams, (adventure ages 6-10).
How to Contact: Accepts unsolicited mss. Query with outline and 5 sample chapters. Submit complete ms with cover letter. Include estimated word count, short bio, Social Security number and list of publishing credits. Send SASE for reply, return of ms or send a disposable copy of ms. Reports in 3 weeks on queries; 6 weeks on mss. Simultaneous and disk submissions (IBM compatible preferred) OK. "Check our webpage for guidelines." Sometimes comments on rejected mss.
Terms: "Pay flat fee for first-time authors; royalties for established authors." Sends final ms to author. Publishes ms 12-18 months after acceptance. Writer's guidelines and book catalog free.
Advice: Needs "more upper-elementary adventure/mystery or a good series. No picture books. No didactic stories. Read guidelines carefully. Send SASE if you wish to have ms returned. Give us original, well-developed characters in a suspenseful plot with good moral tone."

◨ **KAEDEN BOOKS,** 19915 Lake Rd., Box 16190, Rocky River OH 44116. (440)356-0030. Fax: (440)356-5081. E-mail: kaeden01@aol.com. Website: www.kaeden.com (includes samples of books, reviews and titles). **Acquisitions**: Kathleen Urmston, fiction editor (children's K-3); Karen Tabak, fiction editor (children's grades 3-6). Estab. 1990. "Children's book publisher for education K-6 market: reading stories, science, math and social studies materials, also poetry." Publishes paperback originals. Books: offset printing; saddle binding; illustrations. Average print order: 5,000. First novel print order: 5,000. **Published more than 20 new writers within the last year.** Plans 2 first novels in 1999. Averages 50 total titles, 40 fiction titles/year.
Needs: Adventure, children's/juvenile (adventure, animal, easy-to-read, fantasy, historical, mystery, preschool/picture book, series, sports), ethnic/multicultural, fantasy (space fantasy), historical (general), humor/satire, mys-

tery/suspense (amateur sleuth), romance (romantic suspense), science fiction (soft/sociological), short story collections, thriller/espionage. Plans a poetry anthology/associated stories. Submit stories and poetry to editor.

How to Contact: Accepts unsolicited mss. Query with outline/synopsis. Include 1-page bio and list of publishing credits. Send a disposable copy of ms. Reports in 1 year.

Terms: Negotiable, either royalties or flat fee by individual arrangement with author depending on book. No advance. Publishes ms 6-24 months after acceptance.

Advice: "Our line is expanding with particular interest in poetry and fiction/nonfiction for grades three to six. Material must be suitable for use in the public school classroom, be multicultural and be high interest with appropriate word usage and a positive tone for the respective grade."

KAYA PRODUCTION, 373 Broadway, Suite E-2, New York NY 10013. (212)343-9503. Fax: (212)343-8291. E-mail: kaya@kaya.com. Website: www.kaya.com. **Acquisitions:** Sunyoung Lee, editor. "Kaya is a small independent press dedicated to the publication of innovative literature from the Asian diaspora." Publishes hardcover originals and trade paperback originals and reprints.

Needs: Ethnic, regional. "Kaya publishes Asian, Asian-American and Asian diasporic materials. We are looking for innovative writers with a commitment to quality literature." Recently published *East Goes West*, by Younghill Kang (novel reprint).

How to Contact: Submit synopsis and 2-4 sample chapters with SASE. Reports in 6 months on mss. Simultaneous submissions OK.

Terms: Guidelines available at website. Book catalog free.

Advice: Audience is people interested in a high standard of literature and who are interested in breaking down easy approaches to multicultural literature. "Authors should be aware they should either be Asian or should be writing about Asian or Asian-American issues."

KENSINGTON PUBLISHING CORP., 850 Third Ave., 16th Floor, New York NY 10022. (212)407-1500. Fax: (212)935-0699. **Acquisitions**: Karen Thomas, senior editor (Arabesque); Tracy Bernstein, editorial director (Kensington Trade Paperbacks); Paul Dinas, editor-in-chief (Pinnacle Books); Ann La Farge, executive editor (Zebra Books and Kensington Mass Market). Estab. 1975. "Kensington focuses on profitable niches and uses aggressive marketing techniques to support its books." Publishes hardcover originals, trade paperbacks and mass market originals and reprints. Averages 300 total titles/year.

Needs: Adventure, contemporary, erotica, mysteries, nonfiction, romance (contemporary, historical, regency, multicultural), thrillers, true crime, women's. No science fiction. Published *Destiny Mine*, by Janelle Taylor; *The Fall Line*, by Mark T. Sullivan; *Cemetary of Angels*, by Noel Hynd; and "Bride Price," in *Irish Magic II*, by Roberta Gellis. Ms length ranges from 100,000 to 125,000 words.

How to Contact: Contact with agent. Reports in 3-5 months.

Terms: Pays royalties and advances. Publishes ms 18 months after acceptance. Free book catalog.

Advice: "We want fiction that will appeal to the mass market and we want writers who want to make a career."

ALLEN A. KNOLL, PUBLISHERS, 200A W. Victoria St., Suite 3, Santa Barbara CA 93101-3627. Fax: (805)966-6657. E-mail: aaknoll@aol.com. Estab. 1990. Small independent publisher. "We publish books for intelligent people who read for fun." Publishes hardcover originals. Books: Offset printing; sewn binding. Member PMA, SPAN, ABA. Distributes titles through Ingram, Baker & Taylor, Brodart, Sunbelt. Promotes titles through advertising in specialty publications, direct mail, prepublication reviews and advertising.

Needs: Published *Flip Side*, by Theodore Roosevelt Gardner II (suspense); *The Unlucky Seven*, by Alistair Boyle (mystery); and *Phantom Virus*, by David Champion (courtroom drama). Publishes A Bomber Hanson Mystery (courtroom drama series) and A Gil Yates Private Investigator Novel (P.I. series).

How to Contact: Does not accept unsolicited mss. Book catalog free.

ALFRED A. KNOPF, Division of Random House, 201 E. 50th St., New York NY 10022. (212)751-2600. **Acquisitions:** Senior Editor. Estab. 1915. Publishes hardcover originals. Number of titles: approximately 200 each year. Buys 90% agented fiction. **Published new writers in the last year.** Also publishes nonfiction.

Needs: Contemporary, literary and spy. No western, gothic, romance, erotica, religious or science fiction. Published new writers within the last year.

How to Contact: Submit outline or synopsis with SASE. Reports within 3 months on mss. Publishes ms an average of 1 year after acceptance.

Terms: Pays 10-15% in royalties; offers advance. Must return advance if book is not completed or is unacceptable. Publishes ms 1 year after acceptance.

Advice: Publishes book-length fiction of literary merit by known and unknown writers.

KNOPF BOOKS FOR YOUNG READERS, Division of Random House, 201 E. 50th St., New York NY 10022. (212)751-2600. Website: www.randomhouse.com. **Acquisitions:** Sinion Boughton, publishing director. "Knopf is known for high quality literary fiction, and is willing to take risks with writing styles. It publishes for children ages 5 and up." Publishes hardcover and paperback originals and reprints. Averages 30 total titles, approximately 7 fiction titles each year.

Imprint(s): Dragonfly Books (picture books) and Knopf paperbacks (fiction).

Needs: "High-quality contemporary, humor, picture books, middle grade novels." Published *Merl and Jasper's Supper Caper*, by Laura Rankin, *The Squiggle*, by Carole Lexa Shaefer and Piers Morgan; *Crash*, by Jerry Spinelli; and *The Golden Compass*, by Philip Pullman.

How to Contact: Query with outline/synopsis and 2 sample chapters with SASE. Simultaneous submissions OK. Reports in 4 months.

Terms: Pays royalties of 4% minimum; 10% maximum. Average advance: $3,000 and up. Sends galleys to author. Publishes ms 1-2 years after acceptance.

LAUGHING OWL PUBLISHING, INC., 12610 Highway 90, Grand Bay AL 36541. (334)865-5177. Fax: (334)865-6252. E-mail: laughingowl@juno.com. Website: www.laughingowl.com (includes online bookstore, catalog, first chapters, writer's guidelines). **Acquisitions:** Heather Wilkinson, fiction editor. "Publisher of multi-genre fiction with a fresh new voice." Publishes paperback originals. Books: 50 lb. paper; offset printing; perfect binding. Average print order: 3,000-5,000. First novel print order: 2,000-3,000. Averages 5 fiction titles/ year.

Needs: Historical, horror (dark fantasy), psychic/supernatural/occult, regional (Southern). *"Fully contracted until 2003."* Published *Angel Fire*, by Ron Franscell (contemporary literary fiction); *The Beloved*, by M.D. Gray (occult suspense); and *The Labyrinth of the Grail*, by William Mann (historical).

How to Contact: Query with outline synopsis. Unsolicited queries/correspondence by e-mail and fax OK. Include exact word count. Send SASE for reply. Agented fiction 25%. Reports in 2 months on queries; 3-6 months on mss. Electronic submissions 92,000-97,000 words (disk or modem) OK.

Terms: Pays royalties of 6% minimum; 12% maximum; standard royalty contract. Sends galleys to author. Writer's guidelines and book catalog free; available on website.

Advice: "Follow our writer's guidelines. We give equal consideration to first-time writers as to established writers. Be professional; take the query letter seriously. A synopsis is not the first 20 pages. We want work that is available on disk to save on typesetting costs."

✓ ◐ Ⓐ LAUREL BOOKS, Imprint of Dell Publishing, Division of Bantam Doubleday, 1540 Broadway, New York NY 10036. (212)354-6500. **Acquisitions:** Maggie Crawford, editorial director. Publishes trade paperback originals, mostly light, humorous material and books on pop culture. Publishes 4 titles/year.

Needs: Literary.

How to Contact: Agented submissions only.

Terms: Pays 7½-12½% royalty on retail price. Advance varies. Publishes ms 1 year after acceptance. Book catalog for 9×12 SAE and 3 first class stamps.

◐ LEE & LOW BOOKS, 95 Madison Ave., New York NY 10016. (212)779-4400. Fax: (212)683-1894. Website: www.leeandlow.com. **Publisher:** Philip Lee. Estab. 1991. "Our goals are to meet a growing need for books that address children of color, and to present literature that all children can identify with. We only consider multicultural children's picture books. Of special interest are stories set in contemporary America." Publishes hardcover originals—picture books only. Averages 8-12 total titles each year.

Needs: Children's/juvenile (historical, multicultural, preschool/picture book for children ages 2-10). "We do not consider folktales, fairy tales or animal stories." Published *Dear Ms. Parks: A Dialogue With Today's Youth*, by Rosa Parks (collection of correspondence); *Giving Thanks: A Native American Good Morning Message*, by Chief Jake Swamp (picture book); and *Sam and the Lucky Money*, by Karen Chinn (picture book).

How to Contact: Accepts unsolicited mss. Send complete ms with cover letter or through an agent. Send SASE for reply, return of ms or send a disposable ms. Agented fiction 30%. Reports in 2-4 months. Simultaneous submissions OK. Sometimes critiques or comments on rejected mss.

Terms: Pays royalties. Offers advance. Sends galleys to author. Writer's guidelines for #10 SASE or on website. Book catalog for SASE with $1.43 postage.

Advice: "Writers should familiarize themselves with the styles and formats of recently published children's books. Lee & Low Books is a multicultural children's book publisher. We would like to see more contemporary stories set in the U.S. Animal stories and folktales are not considered at this time."

✓ ◐ LEISURE BOOKS, Division of Dorchester Publishing Co., Inc., 276 Fifth Ave., Suite 1008, New York NY 10001. (212)725-8811. Fax: (212)532-1054. E-mail: dorchedit@aol.com. Website: www.dorchesterpub.com (includes writer's guidelines, names of editors, authors, titles, etc.). **Acquisitions**: Jennifer Bonnell, Kate Seaver. Mass-market paperback publisher—originals and reprints. Publishes romances, westerns, horrors and technothrillers only. Books: Newsprint paper; offset printing; perfect-bound; average print order: variable; first novel print order: variable. **Plans 25 first novels this year.** Averages 150 total titles, 145 fiction titles each year. Promotes titles through ads in *Romantic Times*, author readings, promotional items.

Imprint(s): Leisure Books (contact: Alicia Condon), **Love Spell Books** (contact: Christopher Keeslar).

Needs: Historical romance, horror, technothriller, western. Looking for "historical romance (90,000-115,000 words)." Published *Pure Temptation*, by Connie Mason (historical romance); and *Frankly My Dear*, by Sandra Hill (time-travel romance).

How to Contact: Accepts unsolicited mss. Query first. No electronic submissions. SASE. Agented fiction 70%. Reports in 1 month on queries; 3-4 months on mss. "All mss must be typed, double-spaced on one side and left unbound." Comments on rejected ms "only if requested ms requires it."

Terms: Offers negotiable advance. Payment depends "on category and track record of author." Sends galleys to author. Publishes ms within 2 years after acceptance. Romance guidelines for #10 SASE.

Advice: Encourages first novelists "if they are talented and willing to take direction, *and* write the kind of genre fiction we publish. Please include a brief synopsis if sample chapters are requested."

✓ ◑ **LERNER PUBLICATIONS COMPANY**, 241 First Ave. N., Minneapolis MN 55401. (612)332-3344. Fax: (612)332-7615. **Acquisitions**: Jennifer Zimian, submissions editor. Estab. 1959. "Midsize independent *children's* publisher." Publishes hardcover originals and paperback reprints. Books: Offset printing; reinforced library binding; perfect binding; average print order: 5,000-7,500; first novel print order: 5,000. Averages 70 total titles, 1-2 fiction titles each year.

Imprint(s): First Avenue Editions.

Needs: Young adult: general, problem novels, sports, adventure, mystery (young adult). Looking for "well-written middle grade and young adult. No *adult fiction* or single short stories." Published *Dancing Pink Flamigos and Other Stories*, by Maria Testa.

How to Contact: "Submissions are accepted in the months of March and October only. Work received in any other month will be returned unopened. Accepts unsolicited mss. Query first or submit outline/synopsis and 2 sample chapters. Reports in 2-6 months. Simultaneous submissions OK.

Terms: Pays royalties. Offers advance. Provides author's copies. Sends galleys to author. Publishes ms 12-18 months after acceptance. Writer's guidelines for #10 SASE. Book catalog for 9 × 12 SAE with $3.20 postage.

Advice: Would like to see "less gender and racial stereotyping; protagonists from many cultures."

◑ **LINTEL**, 24 Blake Lane, Middletown NY 10940. (212)674-4901. Editorial Director: Walter James Miller. Estab. 1977. Two-person organization on part-time basis. Books: 90% opaque paper; photo offset printing; perfect binding; illustrations. Average print order: 1,000. First novel print order: 1,200. Publishes hardcover and paperback originals. Occasionally comments on rejected mss.

Needs: Experimental, feminist, gay, lesbian, regional short fiction. Published second edition (fourth printing) of *Klytaimnestra Who Stayed at Home*, mythopoeic novel by Nancy Bogen; and *The Mountain,* by Rebecca Rass.

How to Contact: Accepts unsolicited mss. Query with SASE. Simultaneous and photocopied submissions OK. Reports in 2 months on queries; 3 months on mss. Publishes ms 6-8 months after acceptance.

Terms: Negotiated. No advance. Sends galleys to author. Free book catalog.

Advice: "Lintel is devoted to the kinds of literary art that will never make The Literary Guild or even the Book-of-the-Month Club: that is, literature concerned with the advancement of literary art. We still look for the innovative work ignored by the commercial presses. We consider any ms on its merits alone. We encourage first novelists. Be innovative, advance the *art* of fiction, but still keep in mind the need to reach reader's aspirations as well as your own. Originality is the greatest suspense-building factor. Consistent spelling errors, errors in grammar and syntax can mean only rejection."

✓ ◑ ⵖ **LIONHEARTED PUBLISHING, INC.,** P.O. Box 618, Zephyr Cove NV 89448-0618. (775)588-1388. Fax: (775)588-1386. E-mail: admin@lionhearted.com. Website: www.LionHearted.com (includes writer's guidelines, authors, titles, articles and writing tips for authors). **Acquisitions**: Historical or Contemporary Acquisitions Editor. Estab. 1994. Independent. "We publish entertaining, fun, romantic genre fiction—single title releases." Publishes paperback originals. Books: mass market paperback; perfect binding. Also expanded romance into e-book formats. **Published new writers within the last year.** Plans 12 first novels this year. Averages 12-72 fiction titles/year. Distributes titles through amazon.com; all Barnes & Noble store computer systems. Promotes titles through direct mail and advertising.

● LionHearted Publishing is mentioned in the *Wall Street Journal's 1998 Almanac for Women Entrepreneurs* and has received two Holt Medallion Awards for *Oracle*, by Katherine Greyle.

Needs: Romance (contemporary, futuristic/time travel, historical, regency period, romantic suspense; over 65,000 words only). Published *Isn't It Romantic?*, by Ronda Thompson (romance); *Oracle*, by Katherine Greyle (romance); and *P.S. I've Taken a Lover*, by Ronda Thompson.

How to Contact: Accepts unsolicited mss. Query with outline/synopsis and 3 sample chapters. Include estimated word count, list of publishing credits, cover letter and 1 paragraph story summary in cover or query letter. Send SASE for reply, return of ms or send disposable copy of ms. Agented fiction less than 10%. Reports in 1 month on queries; 3 months on mss. No simultaneous submissions. Always critiques or comments on rejected mss.

Terms: Pays royalties of 10% maximum on paperbacks; 10-25% on electronic books. Average advance: $1,000. $5,000 minimum guarantee on royalties. Sends galleys to author. Publishes ms 18-24 months after acceptance. Writer's guidelines free for #10 SASE. Book catalog available for SASE.

Advice: "If you are not an avid reader of romance, don't attempt to write romance, and don't waste your time or an editor's by submitting to a publisher of romance."

◑ **LITTLE, BROWN AND COMPANY**, 1271 Avenue of the Americas, New York NY 10020 and 3 Center Plaza, Boston MA 02108. (212)522-8700 and (617)227-0730. Fax: (212)522-2067. **Acquisitions**: Editorial Department. Estab. 1837. "The general editorial philosophy for all divisions continues to be broad and flexible, with high quality and the promise of commercial success always the first considerations." Medium-size house. Publishes adult and juvenile hardcover and paperback originals. **Published new writers within the last year.** Averages 125 total adult titles/year. Number of fiction titles varies.
Imprint(s): Little, Brown; Back Bay; Bulfinch Press.
 • Send children's submissions to Submissions Editor, Children's Books, at Boston address. Send Bulfinch submissions to Submissions Editor, Bulfinch Press, at Boston address. Include SASE.
Needs: Open. No science fiction. Published *When the Wind Blows*, by James Patterson; *Angels Flight*, by Michael Connelly; and *The Pilot's Wife*, by Anita Shreve.
How to Contact: Does not accept unsolicited adult mss or proposals.
Terms: "We publish on a royalty basis, with advance."

☑◑Ⓐ♆ **LITTLE, BROWN AND COMPANY CHILDREN'S BOOKS,** Trade Division; Children's Books, 3 Center Plaza, Boston MA 02108. (617)227-0730. Website: www.littlebrown.com. Maria Modugno, editorial director and associate publisher. **Acquisitions**: Megan S. Tingley, executive editor. Estab. 1837. Books: 70 lb. paper; sheet-fed printing; illustrations. Sometimes buys juvenile mss with illustrations "if by professional artist." **Published "a few" new writers within the last year.** Distributes titles through sales representatives. Promotes titles through author tours, book signings, posters, press kits, magazine and newspapers and Beacon Hill Bookbay.
 • *Maniac Magee*, by Jerry Spinelli and published by Little, Brown and Company Children's Books, received a Newbery Award. *Toot and Puddle*, by Holly Hobbie was named an ABBY Honor Book.
Needs: Middle grade fiction and young adult. Recently published *The Tale I Told Sasha*, by Nancy Willard, illustrated by David Christiana; *Look-Alikes*, by Joan Steiner (picture book); and *Romance of the Snob Squad*, by Julie Anne Peters (middle grade novel). Publishes 3 previously unpublished writers/year.
How to Contact: Submit through agent only.
Terms: Pays on royalty basis. Sends galleys to author. Publishes ms 1-2 years after acceptance.
Advice: "We are looking for trade books with bookstore appeal. We are especially looking for young children's (ages 3-5) picture books. New authors should be aware of what is currently being published. We recommend they spend time at the local library and bookstore familiarizing themselves with new publications." Known for "humorous middle grade fiction with lots of kid appeal. Literary, multi-layered young adult fiction with distinctive characters and complex plots."

☑◑ **LITTLE SIMON**, Imprint of Simon & Schuster Children's Publishing Division, 1230 Avenue of the Americas, New York NY 10022. (212)698-7200. Website: www.simonsays.com. **Acquisitions**: Submissions Editor. "Our goal is to provide fresh material in an innovative format for pre-school age. Our books are often, if not exclusively, illustrator driven." Averages 120 total titles/year. This imprint publishes novelty books only (pop-ups, lift-the-flaps board books, etc).
How to Contact: Query for more information. Does not accept unsolicited mss. Reports in 8 months. Accepts simultaneous submissions.
Terms: Negotiable.

◐ **LIVINGSTON PRESS**, Station 22, University of Alabama, Livingston AL 35470. Fax: (205)652-3717. E-mail: jwt@uwamail.westal.edu. Website: www.livingstonpress (includes catalog). **Acquisitions**: Joe Taylor, editor. Estab. 1982. "Literary press. We publish offbeat and/or southern literature. Emphasis on offbeat." Publishes hardcover and paperback originals. Books: acid-free paper; offset printing; perfect binding. Average print order: 1,500. First novel print order: 1,500. Published new writers within the last year. Plans 2 first novels this year. Averages 4-6 total titles, 5 fiction titles each year. Distributes titles through Yankee Book, Baker & Taylor, Blackwell North America. Promotes titles through catalogs, readings, postcards, 75-100 review copies. Sometimes critiques or comments on rejected mss.
Imprint(s): Swallows Tale Press.
Needs: Literary, short story collections. No genre. Recently published *Detecting Metal*, by Fred Bonnie (novel).
How to Contact: Does not accept unsolicited mss. Query first. Include bio, list of publishing credits. Send SASE for reply, return of ms or send a disposable copy of ms. Reports in 3 weeks on queries; 6 months on mss. Simultaneous submissions OK.
Terms: Pays 12% of press run in contributor's copies. Sends galleys to author. Publishes ms 1-2 years after acceptance. Book catalog free.
Advice: "Our readers are interested in literature, often quirky literature."

◎ **LLEWELLYN PUBLICATIONS**, Llewellyn Worldwide, Ltd., P.O. Box 64383, St. Paul MN 55164-0383. (612)291-1970. Fax: (612)291-1908. E-mail: lwlpc@llewellyn.com. Website: www.llewellyn.com. **Acquisitions:** Nancy Mostad, acquisitions and development manager. Midsize publisher of New Age/occult fiction and nonfic-

insider report

Perseverance pays off for bestselling novelist

In the middle of the night on her 21st birthday Janet Fitch decided she wanted to write fiction. "Before I'd ever written a page I called myself a writer," says Fitch. But it took 12 years of writing and rejection before this Los Angeles native sold her first story to a literary journal. "It took me years to get published because nobody told me not to send every story to *Harpers* and *The New Yorker!*"

Janet Fitch

Fitch went on to publish several short stories in journals and a young adult novel, but when it came time to publish her first full-length novel, *White Oleander* (Little, Brown & Company), she sold it to the first editor she sent it to. And then Oprah Winfrey borrowed an advanced copy of the book from a friend while on a beach vacation according to *Publisher's Weekly*, and *White Oleander* became Oprah's 24th book club pick. In fact, Oprah loved it so much, she called Fitch's editor to ask if she could be the reader for the audio book version. And if that wasn't enough to celebrate, Warner Bros. bought the film rights to the novel.

Despite the success of *White Oleander*, Fitch hasn't let the media hype go to her head. "The work of writing has nothing to do with that," says Fitch. "The further away from being a regular private citizen people get, the more writing suffers from it. The regular human experience is the richest part." It is Fitch's exploration of the essence of being human through vivid poetic writing that has reaped praise for *White Oleander* from readers and critics alike. *White Oleander* tells the story of a dynamic mother-daughter relationship between Ingrid, an uncompromising artist, and her teenage daughter Astrid. When Ingrid is put in jail for murder, Astrid must survive a series of dysfunctional foster homes, meeting an eclectic array of personalities that catapult her through a poignant coming-of-age story.

To insure her book's palpable emotional realism, Fitch interviewed women who had been foster daughters. "I put up flyers around town asking foster daughters to share their story. It was a blind process, just a voice mail exchange, only first names, very confidential. I talked to women about their experiences and the stories were phenomenal," she says. Fitch began her research only after her novel was well underway. "I start on the writing before doing any research and then I know what I'm looking for. If I do the research first it prevents me from imagining. I was checking what I had already done to see if it conformed to what I was hearing."

It took Fitch four years to write and research *White Oleander*, but when she submitted it to her editor, he challenged her to create the book's emotionally anticipated climax where Astrid confronts her mother in prison. "It was a scene I was afraid to write," says Fitch. "I didn't want to write it because if I blew it I knew I would ruin the book. So I thought of a smaller scene that was less definitive but I thought I could handle. Often writers are afraid to do the big scene for fear it will be obvious, for fear we won't do it well, that we'll bungle it and it will be glaringly bad." Her editor gave her just the push she needed to give her characters the ending they deserved.

Critics and audiences have been seduced by Fitch's stylish use of language and metaphor. But Fitch, who admits she "didn't come out of the womb writing," had to learn how to infuse her writing with lyricism. Her early literary influences included Poe, Doestoevsky, Faulkner and Joyce Carol Oates, but it wasn't until she met author Kate Braverman that she found a teacher to take her writing to an artistic level. "I could always tell a good story, but I needed to learn the poetry of it," says Fitch. "I had the craft but I didn't have the art yet. I wasn't really working on that word-by-word level. I read Braverman's *Lithium for Medea* and her other works and sought her out as a teacher. That brought me the rest of the way."

After two years of study with Braverman, Fitch joined a writing group, the Hardwords Collective. "They helped me bridge the gap between what I was doing and what I wanted to do in my writing," she says. The writing group provided Fitch with invaluable support and criticism, but she cautions writers to listen only to people who really appreciate your work. "Someone who doesn't like your work will never be a good critic of it," says Fitch. "Listen to the people who like your work and their criticism will make it more of what they want. It will help the writing be more of what it is."

After 20 years of writing, Fitch knows there's "nothing more embarrassing than being an unpublished writer." And often friends and family don't understand the compelling desire to write and keep writing. "The truth is your family and friends generally don't care if you write or not," says Fitch. "Your family just sees it as this weird thing you do that takes time away from them and their needs. They can't see the point to it. Even when you do start publishing, often they still don't understand it, which is good and bad. They like you whether or not you write and that's comforting. But it's lonely. When people talk about the loneliness of writers, it's not being alone in a room writing, it's that nobody cares if you write or not. Your support system as a writer comes from other writers who are struggling like you."

In addition to writing, Fitch teaches fiction, reviews books in assorted publications and has a husband and nine-year-old daughter. She writes every day whether she's inspired or not. "I tell my students it's better to write 15 minutes a day than write for 5 hours on a Saturday. Your book is alive and you have to keep it on life support." Fitch, who already has ideas for her next novel, is not daunted by the task of following up her first book's success. "What's intimidating is writing for 20 years thinking maybe nothing will ever happen," she says. "That's what takes the endurance, the nerve. To have a book do well and everyone's waiting for a second book, that's not a problem."

—*Tricia Waddell*

tion. Publishes paperback originals. Plans 1-2 first novels this year. Publishes 100 total titles/year; 10 fiction titles/year.
Needs: New Age/mystic/spiritual, psychic/supernatural/occult. Published *Soothsayer*, by D.J. Conway (occult); and *Ronin*, by D.A. Heeley (fantasy).
How to Contact: Query with outline/synopsis and 3 sample chapters or submit complete ms with a cover letter. Include estimated word count and bio. Send SASE for reply, return of ms or send disposable copy of ms. Replies in 3 months. Simultaneous submissions OK.
Terms: Pays 10% royalty on money received both retail and wholesale. Sends galleys to author. Publishes ms 1 year after acceptance. Fiction guidelines free. Book catalog $3.

JAMES LORIMER & CO., PUBLISHERS, 35 Britain St., Toronto, Ontario M5A 1R7 Canada. (416)362-4762. Fax: (416)362-3939. E-mail: jlc@sympatico.ca. **Acquisitions:** Diane Young, editor-in-chief.

"James Lorimer & Co. publishes Canadian authors only, on Canadian issues/topics. For juvenile list, realistic themes only, especially mysteries and sports." Publishes trade paperback originals. **Publishes 10% previously unpublished writers/year.** Publishes 30 titles/year.

Needs: Juvenile, young adult. "No fantasy, science fiction, talking animals; realistic themes only. Currently seeking sports novels for ages 9-13 (Canadian writers only)."

How to Contact: Submit synopsis and 2 sample chapters. Reports in 4 months.

Terms: Pays 5-10% royalty on retail price. Offers negotiable advance. Publishes ms about 1 year after acceptance. Book catalog for #10 SASE.

LOTHROP, LEE & SHEPARD BOOKS, Imprint of HarperCollins Children's Book Group, 1350 Avenue of the Americas, New York NY 10019. (212)261-6641. Fax: (212)261-6648. Website: www.william morrow.com.

   • At press time, HarperCollins announced that the Lothrop Lee & Shepard imprint would cease publishing.

LOVE SPELL, Leisure Books, Division of Dorchester Publishing Co., Inc., 276 Fifth Ave., Suite 1008, New York NY 10001-0112. (212)725-8811. **Acquisitions:** Christopher Kessler, editor; Jennifer Bonnell and Kate Seaver, editorial assistants. "Love Spell publishes quirky sub-genres of romance: time-travel, paranormal, futuristic, lighthearted contemporaries and historicals. Despite the exotic settings, we are still interested in character-driven plots." Mass market paperback publisher—originals and reprints. Books: newsprint paper; offset printing; perfect-bound; average print order: varies; first novel print order: varies. **Plans 15 first novels this year.** Averages 45 titles/year.

Needs: Romance (futuristic, time travel, paranormal, historical). Looking for romances of 90,000-115,000 words. Recently published *Hidden Heart*, by Anne Avery (futuristic romance).

How to Contact: Accepts unsolicited mss. Query first. "All mss must be typed, double-spaced on one side and left unbound." SASE for return of ms. Agented fiction 70%. Reports in 3-6 months. Comments "only if requested ms requires it."

Terms: Offers negotiable advance. "Payment depends on category and track record of author." Sends galleys to author. Publishes ms within 2 years after acceptance. Writer's guidelines for #10 SASE.

Advice: "The best way to learn to write a Love Spell Romance is by reading several of our recent releases. The best written stories are usually ones writers feel passionate about—so write from your heart! Also, the market is very tight these days so more than ever we are looking for refreshing, standout original fiction."

THE LYONS PRESS, 31 W. 21st St., New York NY 10010. (212)929-1836. **Acquisitions:** Lilly Golden and Bryan Oettel. Estab. 1984. Publishes hardcover and paperback originals and paperback reprints. **30% of books from first-time authors.** Averages 110-120 total titles.

Needs: Adventure (sports), short story collections, western, outdoors. Published *Guiding Elliott*, by Robert Lee (fiction); *Travers Corners*, by Scott Waldie (short stories); and *Dry Rain*, by Pete Fromm (short stories).

How to Contact: Accepts unsolicited mss. Query with outline/synopsis. Include bio and list of publishing credits. Send SASE for reply. Agented fiction 60%. Reports in 2 months. Simultaneous submissions OK. Critiques or comments on rejected mss.

Terms: Pays royalties; offers advance. Sends galleys to author.

Advice: The Lyons Press has teamed up to develop books with L.L. Bean, *Field & Stream*, The Nature Conservancy and *Golf Magazine*.

MACMURRAY & BECK, INC., 1490 Lafayette St., Suite 108, Denver CO 80218. (303)832-2152. Fax: (303)832-2158. E-mail: koffler@macmurraybeck.com. Website: www.macmurraybeck.com (includes writer's guidelines, authors, titles). **Acquisitions:** MacMurray & Beck submissions or Divina submissions. Estab. 1991. "We are interested in reflective personal narrative of high literary quality." Publishes hardcover and paperback originals. Books: average print order: 4,000; first novel print order: 4,000. Published new writers within the last year. Plans 6-8 novels this year. Averages 8-10 total titles. Distributes titles through major wholesalers and the Internet. Promotes titles through national advertising, direct mail and the Internet.

**FOR EXPLANATIONS OF THESE SYMBOLS,
SEE THE INSIDE FRONT AND BACK COVERS OF THIS BOOK.**

Imprint(s): Divina—a speculative fiction imprint.

Needs: Contemporary, literary, short story collections, translations. Looking for "reflective fiction with high literary quality and commercial potential. No genre fiction, plot-driven, traditional, frontier western or mainstream." Recently published *Horace Afoot*, by Frederick Reuss; *Celibates and Other Lovers*, by Walter Keady; and *The Oxygen Man*, by Steve Yarbrough.

How to Contact: Does not accept unsolicited mss. Query first with outline/synopsis and 15 sample pages. Include 1-page bio, list of publishing credits, any writing awards or grants. SASE for reply. Agented fiction 75%. Reports in 3 months on queries. Simultaneous submissions OK. Sometimes critiques or comments on rejected mss.

Terms: Pays royalties; offers negotiable advance. Publishes ms 18 months after acceptance. Book catalog for $2.

Advice: "We are most interested in manuscripts that reflect carefully and emotionally on the ways we live our lives, on the things that happen to us, on what we know and believe. Our editors are also drawn to works that contemplate the roles that geography, culture, family and tradition play in all our efforts to define ourselves. We search for works that are free of the modern habit of accepting the world without thought. We publish a very limited number of novels each year and base our selection on literary quality first. Submit a concise, saleable proposal. Tell us why we should publish the book, not just what it is about."

JOHN MACRAE BOOKS, Imprint of Henry Holt & Co., Inc., 115 W. 18th St., New York NY 10011. (212)886-9200. Estab. 1991. "We publish literary fiction and nonfiction. Our primary interest is in language; strong, compelling writing." Publishes hardcover originals. Publishes 20-25 titles/year.

Needs: Literary, mainstream/contemporary. Published *Burning Their Boats*, by Angela Carter (novel).

How to Contact: Does not accept unsolicited mss or queries.

Terms: Pays standard hardcover royalty. Advance varies. Publishes ms 1 year after acceptance.

MAGE PUBLISHERS, 1032 29th St. NW, Washington DC 20007. (202)342-1642. Fax: (202)342-9269. E-mail: info@mage.com. Website: www.mage.com. **Acquisitions**: Amin Sepehri, assistant to publisher. Estab. 1985. "Small independent publisher." Publishes hardcover originals. Averages 4 total titles, 1 fiction title each year.

Needs: "**We publish only books on Iran and Persia and translations of Iranian fiction writers.**" Ethnic (Iran) fiction. Published *My Uncle Napoleon*, by Iraj Pezeshkzad; *King of the Benighted*, by M. Irani; and *Sutra and Other Stories*, by Simin Daneshvar.

How to Contact: Query first. SASE. Reports in 3 months on queries. Simultaneous and electronic submissions OK.

Terms: Pays royalties. Publishes ms 1 year after acceptance. Writer's guidelines on website.

Advice: "If it isn't related to Persia/Iran, don't waste our time or yours."

MAIN STREET BOOKS, Imprint of Doubleday Adult Trade, Broadway Publishing Group, Random House, 1540 Broadway, New York NY 10036. (212)354-6500. **Acquisitions:** Gerald Howard, editor-in-chief. Estab. 1992. "Main Street Books continues the tradition of Dolphin Books of publishing backlists, but we are focusing more on 'up front' books and big sellers in the areas of self-help, fitness and popular culture." Publishes hardcover originals, trade paperback originals and reprints. Publishes 20-30 titles/year.

Needs: Literary, pop, commercial. Published *Outside Providence*, by Peter Farrelly; and *Beeperless Remote*, by Van Whitfield.

How to Contact: Agented submissions only. Reports in 1 month on queries; 6 months on mss. Simultaneous submissions OK, if so noted.

Terms: Offers advance and royalties. Publishes ms 18 months after acceptance. Doubleday book catalog and writer's guidelines free.

Advice: "We have a general interest list."

MARCH STREET PRESS, 3413 Wilshire, Greensboro NC 27408-2923. Phone/fax: (336)282-9754. E-mail: rbixby@aol.com. Website: users.aol.com/marchst (includes writer's guidelines; names of editors, authors, titles). **Acquisitions:** Robert Bixby, editor/publisher. Estab. 1988. Publishes paperback originals. Books: vellum paper; photocopy; saddle-stitch binding. Averages 4-6 total titles, 1 or fewer fiction titles/year.

Needs: Literary. Short story collections. Published *Jailer's Inn*, by Deborah Bayer (very short fiction).

How to Contact: *"Accepts unsolicited mss if $10 reading fee enclosed."* Submit complete ms with a cover letter and reading fee. Send SASE for reply, return of ms or send a disposable copy of ms. Reports in 1 week on queries; 6 months on mss. Simultaneous submissions OK. Sometimes critiques or comments on a rejected ms.

Terms: Pays royalty of 15%. Provides 10 author's copies. Sends galleys to author. Publishes ms 6-12 months after acceptance. Writer's guidelines for #10 SASE; also on website.

MARINER BOOKS, Imprint of Houghton Mifflin, 222 Berkeley St., Boston MA 02116. (617)351-5000. Fax: (617)351-1202. Website: www.hmco.com. **Acquisitions:** Paperback Direct. Estab. 1997. Publishes trade paperback originals and reprints.

● Mariner Books' *The Blue Flower*, by Penelope Fitzgerald, received the National Book Critics Circle Award.

Needs: Literary, mainstream/contemporary. Recently published *The Blue Flower*, by Penelope Fitzgerald (historical fiction).

How to Contact: Prefers agented submissions.

Terms: Pays royalty on retail price or makes outright purchase. Advance varies. Book catalog free.

⊘ MARGARET K. McELDERRY BOOKS, Imprint of the Simon & Schuster Children's Publishing Division, 1230 Sixth Ave., New York NY 10020. (212)698-2761. **Acquisitions:** Emma D. Dryden, senior editor. Estab. 1971. Publishes hardcover originals. Books: High quality paper; offset printing; cloth and three-piece bindings; illustrations; average print order: 10,000; first novel print order: 6,000. Published new writers within the last year. Averages 25 total titles each year. Buys juvenile and young adult mss, agented or non-agented. Query first.

● Books published by Margaret K. McElderry Books have received numerous awards including the Newbery and the Caldecott Awards, and a *Boston Globe-Horn Book* honor award. Because of the merger between Macmillan and Simon & Schuster this imprint (still intact) is under a new division (see above).

Needs: All categories (fiction and nonfiction) for juvenile and young adult: adventure, contemporary, early chapter books, fantasy, literary, mystery and picture books. "We will consider any category. Results depend on the quality of the imagination, the artwork and the writing." Recently published *A Summertime Song*, written and illustrated by Irene Haas; *Dog Friday*, by Hilary McKay; and *The Moorchild*, by Eloise McGraw.

Terms: Pays in royalties; offers advance. Publishes ms 18 months after acceptance.

Advice: "Imaginative writing of high quality is always in demand; also picture books that are original and unusual. Picture book manuscripts written in prose are totally acceptable. Keep in mind that McElderry Books is a very small imprint which only publishes 12 or 13 books per season, so we are very selective about the books we will undertake for publication. The YA market is tough right now, so we're being very picky. We try not to publish any 'trend' books. Be familiar with our list and with what is being published this year by all publishing houses."

⊘ MEADOWBROOK PRESS, 5451 Smetana Dr., Minnetonka MN 55343. (612)930-1100. Fax: (612)930-1940. Website: www.meadowbookpress.com. **Acquisitions:** Jason Sanford, fiction editor. Estab. 1975. Publishes trade paperback originals. Publishes 20 titles/year.

Needs: Childrens/juvenile. "We have very specific guidelines for children's fiction. Send for guidelines before submitting. We do not accept unsolicited picture books or novel-length submissions." Published *Girls to the Rescue*, Book #5, edited by Bruce Lansky (a collection of stories featuring courageous, clever and determined girls); and *Newfangled Fairy Tales*.

How to Contact: Query first. Reports in 3 months on queries. Simultaneous submissions OK.

Terms: Publishes ms 1 year after acceptance. Writer's guidelines and book catalog for #10 SASE.

Advice: "We publish several fiction anthologies for children and are always on the lookout for quality short stories. We are especially willing to work with new writers—we consider stories on their own merits, not on the reputations of the authors."

✔ ⊘ ⅄ MERCURY HOUSE, 736 Clementina St., Suite 300, San Francisco CA 94103. (415)626-7874. Fax: (415)626-7875. E-mail: mercury@hooked.net. Website: www.wenet.net/~mercury/. **Acquisitions:** K. Janene-Nelson, managing editor. Estab. 1985. Small nonprofit literary house publishing outstanding work overlooked by mainstream presses, especially with a minority viewpoint. Publishes paperback originals. Books: acid-free paper; notch binding; some illustrations. Average print order: 4,000; first novel print order: 3,500. Averages 8 total titles, 2 fiction titles/year. Member of Consortium Book Sales & Distribution.

● Recent recognition of Mercury House includes a 1998 PEN Oakland Josephine Miles Award for *House With A Blue Bed*, by Alfred Arteaga, and a 1997 French/American Translation Award finalist for *Masters & Servants*, by Pierre Michon, translated by Wyatt Alexander Mason.

Needs: Ethnic/multicultural, experimental, feminist, gay, lesbian, literary, regional (western), translations. Recently published *A Girl with a Monkey: New & Selected Stories*, by Leonard Michaels; *The Temple of Iconclasts*, by Juan Rodolfo Wilcock, translated by Lawrence Venufi; and *Writing Jazz*, by David Meltzer (jazz anthology).

How to Contact: Does not accept unsolicited mss.

Terms: Pays royalties of 10% minimum. Average advance is low. Provides 10 author's copies. Sends galleys to author. Publishes ms in the same season after acceptance. Writer's guidelines free for #10 SASE. Book catalog for 55¢ postage or 6½×8½ SAE and $1.01 postage.

✔ ⊘ ⅄ MILKWEED EDITIONS, 430 First Ave. N., Suite 668, Minneapolis MN 55401-1743. (612)332-3192. Fax: (612)332-6248. E-mail: books@milkweed.org. Website: www.milkweededitions.org (includes writer's guidelines, mission statement, catalog, poem of day, excerpts from titles). **Acquisitions:** Emilie Buchwald, publisher; Elisabeth Fitz, manuscript coordinator. Estab. 1984. Nonprofit publisher. Publishes hardcover and paperback originals. Books: book text quality—acid-free paper; offset printing; perfect or hardcover binding. Average print order: 4,000. First novel print order depends on book. **Publishes 1-3 new writers/year.** Averages 17 total titles/year. Number of fiction titles "depends on manuscripts." Large orders distributed through Publishers Group West, individual orders handled in-house. Promotes titles through author tours, readings, reviews in media publications, mass and individual mailings of catalogs, trade shows.

• Milkweed Editions books have received numerous awards, including Finalist, *LMP* Individual Achievement Award for Editor Emilie Buchwald, awards from the American Library Association a *New York Times* Notable, and several Pushcarts.

Needs: For adult readers: literary fiction, nonfiction, poetry, essays; for children (ages 8-12): fiction and biographies. Translations welcome for both audiences. No legends or folktales for children. No romance, mysteries, science fiction. Recently published *Trip Sheets*, by Ellen Hawley (literary novel); *Thirst*, by Ken Kalfus (literary short stories); and *Hunting Down Home*, by Jean McNeil (literary novel).

How to Contact: Send for guidelines first, then submit complete ms. Reports in 1 month on queries; 6 months on mss. Simultaneous submissions OK. "Send for guidelines. Must enclose SASE."

Terms: Authors are paid in royalties of 7½%; offers negotiable advance; 10 author's copies. Sends galleys to author. Publishes ms 1 year after acceptance. Book catalog for $1.50 postage.

Advice: "Read good contemporary literary fiction, find your own voice, and persist. Familiarize yourself with our list before submitting."

⃠ ◎ Ⓐ MINOTAUR, (formerly Dead Letter), Imprint of St. Martin's Press, 175 Fifth Ave., New York NY 10010. (212)674-5151. **Acquisitions:** Joe Veltre, editor. Publishes trade hardcover and paperback originals and reprints, commercial non-fiction, literary fiction and mass market paperback originals and reprints. Publishes 36 titles/year.

Needs: Mystery.

How to Contact: Query with synopsis, 3 sample chapters and SASE. Agented fiction 99.9%. Simultaneous submissions OK.

Terms: Pays variable royalty on net price. Advance varies.

⃠ MINSTREL BOOKS, Imprint of Pocket Books for Young Readers, Imprint of Simon & Schuster, 1230 Avenue of the Americas, New York NY 10020. (212)698-7000. Website: www.simonandschuster.com. Editorial director: Patricia McDonald. **Acquisitions:** Attn: Manuscript proposals. Estab. 1986. "Minstrel publishes fun, kid-oriented books, the kinds kids pick for themselves, for middle grade readers, ages 8-12." Publishes hardcover originals and reprints, trade paperback originals. Publishes 125 titles/year.

Needs: Middle grade fiction for ages 8-12: animal stories, fantasy, humor, school stories, mystery, suspense. No picture books. Recently published *Upchuck and the Rotten Willy*, by Bill Wallace; *The Flood Disaster*, by Peg Kehret; and *I Was A Sixth Grade Alien*, by Bruce Coville.

How to Contact: Query with synopsis/outline, sample chapters and SASE. Reports in 3 months on queries. Simultaneous submissions OK.

Terms: Pays 6-8% royalty on retail price. Advance varies. Publishes ms 2 years after acceptance. Writer's guidelines and book catalog free.

Advice: "Hang out with kids to make sure your dialogue and subject matter are accurate."

⃠ MOREHOUSE PUBLISHING CO., 4475 Linglestown Rd., Harrisburg PA 17112. Fax: (717)541-8136. Website: www.morehousegroup.com. **Acquisitions:** Debra K. Farrington, editorial director. Estab. 1884. Morehouse publishes a wide variety of religious nonfiction and fiction with an emphasis on the Anglican faith. Publishes hardcover and paperback originals. Publishes 35 titles/year.

Needs: Christian picture books for ages 3-8. Artwork essential. Published *Bless All Creatures Here Below*, by Judith Gwyn Brown; and *Angel and Me*, by Sara Maitland.

How to Contact: Submit entire ms (1,500 words maximum), résumé and SASE. Note: Manuscripts from outside the US will not be returned. Please send copies only. Reports in 2 months. Simultaneous submissions OK.

Terms: Pays 7-10% royalty. Offers $500-1,000 advance. Publishes ms 18 months after acceptance. Book catalog for 9×12 SAE with $1.01 in postage stamps.

⃠ Ⓐ WILLIAM MORROW AND COMPANY, INC., Division of HarperCollins, 1350 Avenue of the Americas, New York NY 10019. (212)261-6500. Fax: (212)261-6595. **Acquisitions:** Lisa Queen, vice president, editorial director (William Morrow); Susan Pearson, editor-in-chief (Lothrop, Lee & Shepard Books); Barbara Lalicki, senior vice president and publisher (Morrow Junior Books); Toni Sciarra, editor (Quill Trade Paperbacks); Susan Hirschman (Greenwillow Books). Estab. 1926. Approximately one fourth of books published are fiction.

Imprint(s): Greenwillow Books; Hearst Books; Hearst Marine Books; Morrow; Quill Trade Paperbacks.

Needs: "Morrow accepts only the highest quality submissions" in contemporary, literary, experimental, adventure, mystery/suspense, spy, historical, war, feminist, gay/lesbian, science fiction, horror, humor/satire and translations. Juvenile and young adult divisions are separate.

How to Contact: Submit through agent. All unsolicited mss are returned unopened. "We will accept queries, proposals or mss only when submitted through a literary agent." Simultaneous submissions OK.

Terms: Pays in royalties; offers advance. Sends galleys to author. Publishes ms 2 years after acceptance. Free book catalog.

Advice: "The Morrow divisions of Greenwillow Books; Lothrop, Lee & Shepard; Mulberry Books and Morrow Junior Books handle juvenile books. We do five to ten first novels every year and about one-fourth of the titles are fiction. Having an agent helps to find a publisher."

☑ ◎ ▼ **MULTNOMAH PUBLISHERS, INC.**, P.O. Box 1720, Sisters OR 97759. (541)549-1144. Fax: (541)549-0260. **Acquisitions:** Editorial Dept. Estab. 1987. Midsize independent publisher of evangelical fiction and nonfiction. Publishes paperback originals. Books: perfect binding; average print order: 12,000. Averages 120 total titles, 20-25 fiction titles each year.
  • Multnomah Books has received several Gold Medallion Book Awards from the Evangelical Christian Publishers Association.

Needs: Literary, mystery/suspense, religious/inspirational issue or thesis fiction. Published *Margaret's Peace*, by Linda Hall (suspese); and *A Gathering of Finches*, by Jane Kirkpatrick (historical novel).

How to Contact: Submit outline/synopsis and 3 sample chapters. "Include a cover letter with any additional information that might help us in our review." Send SASE for reply, return of ms or send a disposable copy of ms. Reports in 10 weeks. Simultaneous submissions OK.

Terms: Pays royalties. Provides 100 author's copies. Sends galleys to author. Publishes ms 1-2 years after acceptance. Writer's guidelines for SASE.

Advice: "Looking for clean, moral, uplifting fiction. We're particularly interested in contemporary women's fiction, historical fiction, superior romance, mystery/suspense and thesis fiction."

🇳 ◉ ◎ **MY WEEKLY STORY COLLECTION,** (formerly My Weekly Story Library), D.C. Thomson and Co., Ltd., 22 Meadowside, Dundee DD19QJ, Scotland. Fiction Editor: Mrs. D. Hunter. Publishes 48, 30,000-word romantic novels/year. "Cheap paperback story library with full-colour cover. Material should not be violent, controversial or sexually explicit." Length: approximately 30,000 words. Writers are paid on acceptance. "Send the opening 3 chapters and a synopsis. Avoid too many colloquialisms/Americanisms. Stories can be set anywhere but local colour not too 'local' as to be alien." Both contemporary and historical novels considered. Guidelines available on request.

◐ Ⓐ ▼ **THE MYSTERIOUS PRESS,** Crime and mystery fiction imprint for Warner Books, 1271 Avenue of the Americas, New York NY 10120. (212)522-7200. Website: www.warnerbooks.com. (includes authors, titles, guidelines, bulletin board, tour info., contests). **Acquisitions:** Sara Ann Freed, editor-in-chief. William Malloy, executive editor. Estab. 1976. Publishes hardcover and paperback originals and paperback reprints. Books: Hardcover (some Smythe-sewn) and paperback binding; illustrations rarely. Average first novel print order: 10,000 copies. **Published new writers within the last year.**

Needs: Mystery/suspense. Published *Freezer Burn*, by Joe R. Lansdale; *A Walk Through Fire*, by Marcia Muller; *The Ax* by Donald E. Westlake; and *The Hours of the Virgin*, by Loren D. Estleman.

How to Contact: Agented material only.

Terms: Pays in royalties of 10% minimum; offers negotiable advance. Sends galleys to author. Buys hard and softcover rights. Publishes ms 1 year after acceptance.

Advice: "Write a strong and memorable novel, and with the help of a good literary agent, you'll find the right publishing house. Don't despair if your manuscript is rejected by several houses. All publishing houses are looking for new and exciting crime novels, but it may not be at the time your novel is submitted. Hang in there, keep the faith—and good luck."

☑ ◎ **THE NAUTICAL & AVIATION PUBLISHING CO. OF AMERICA INC.**, 1250 Fairmont Ave., Mt. Pleasant SC 29464. (843)856-0561. Fax: (843)856-3864. President: Jan Snouck-Hurgronje. **Acquisitions:** Rebecca Irish, editor. Estab. 1979. Small publisher interested in quality military history and literature. Publishes hardcover originals and reprints. Averages 10 total titles, 1-4 fiction titles each year.

Needs: Military/war (especially military history and Civil War). Looks for "novels with a strong military history orientation." Published *Normandy*, by VADM William P. Mack (military fiction); *Straits of Messina*, by VADM William P. Mack (military fiction); and *The Captain*, by Jan De Hartog (military fiction).

How to Contact: Accepts unsolicited mss. Query first or submit cover letter with 2 chapters or brief synopsis. SASE necessary for return of mss. Agented fiction "miniscule." Reports on queries in 2-3 weeks; on mss in 3 weeks. Simultaneous submissions OK. Sometimes comments on rejected mss.

 A BULLET INTRODUCES COMMENTS by the editor of *Novel & Short Story Writer's Market* indicating special information about the listing.

Terms: Pays royalties of 10-15% on selling price. Advance negotiable. After acceptance publishes ms "as quickly as possible—next season." Book catalog free on request.

Advice: Publishing more fiction. Encourages first novelists. "We're interested in good writing—first novel or last novel. Keep it historical, put characters in a historical context. Professionalism counts. Know your subject. *Convince us.*"

✓ ◐ **NAVAL INSTITUTE PRESS** Imprint of U.S. Naval Institute, 291 Wood Rd., Annapolis MD 21402-5034. Fax: (410)295-1084. E-mail: esecunda@usni.org. Website: www.nip.org. Press Director: Ronald Chambers.

Acquisitions: Paul Wilderson, executive editor; Tom Cutler, senior acquisitions editor; Eric Mills, acquisitions editor. Estab. 1873. The Naval Institute Press publishes general and scholarly books of professional, scientific, historical and literary interest to the naval and maritime communities. Publishes 80 titles/year. Average print order for a first book is 2,500.

Imprint(s): Bluejacket Books (paperback reprints).

Needs: Limited fiction on military and naval themes. Recently published *Captain Kilburnie*, by William P. Mack (Age of Sail historical novel).

How to Contact: Query letter strongly recommended.

Terms: Pays 5-10% royalty on net sales. Publishes ms 1 year after acceptance. Writer's guidelines for #10 SASE. Book catalog free with 9×12 SASE.

◐ ◎ **NEW VICTORIA PUBLISHERS,** P.O. Box 27, Norwich VT 05055-0027. Phone/fax: (802)649-5297. E-mail: newvic@aol.com. Website: www.opendoor.com/NewVic/ (includes list of titles). **Acquisitions:** Claudia Lamperti, editor; ReBecca Béguin, editor. Estab. 1976. Small, three-person operation. Publishes trade paperback originals. Plans 2-5 first novels this year. **Publishes approximately 3 previously unpublished writers/ year.** Averages 8-10 titles/year. Distributes titles through Inbook/LPC Group.

● Books published by New Victoria Publishers have been nominated for Lambda Literary Awards and the Vermont Book Publishers Special Merit Award.

Needs: Lesbian/feminist: adventure, fantasy, historical, humor, mystery (amateur sleuth), romance. Looking for "strong feminist characters, also strong plot and action. We will consider most anything if it is well written and appeals to a lesbian/feminist audience." Publishes anthologies or special editions. Query for guidelines. Published *Rafferty Street*, by Lee Lynch (novel); *Killing At the Cat*, by Carlene Miller (mystery); and *Skin to Skin*, by Martha Miller (erotic short fiction).

How to Contact: Submit outline/synopsis and sample chapters. SASE. Unsolicited queries/correspondence by e-mail and fax OK. Reports in 2 weeks on queries; 1 month on mss.

Terms: Pays royalties of 10%. Publishes ms 1 year after acceptance. Book catalog free.

Advice: "We are especially interested in lesbian or feminist mysteries, ideally with a character or characters who can evolve through a series of books. Mysteries should involve a complex plot, accurate legal and police procedural detail, and protagonists with full emotional lives. Pay attention to plot and character development. Read guidelines carefully."

🍁 ✓ ◎ **NEWEST PUBLISHERS LTD.,** 201, 8540-109 St., Edmonton, Alberta T6G 1E6 Canada. (780)432-9427. Fax: (780)433-3179. E-mail: newest@planet.eon.net. **Acquisitions:** Liz Grieve, general manager. Estab. 1977. Publishes trade paperback originals. **Published new writers within the last year.** Averages 8 total titles, fiction and nonfiction. Distributes titles through General Distribution Services. Promotes titles through book launches, media interviews, review copy mailings and touring.

Needs: Literary. "Our press is interested in western Canadian writing." Recently published *The Widows*, by Suzette Mayr (novel); *The Blood Girls*, by Meira Cook (novel); and *Baser Elements*, by Murray Malcolm (crime fiction). Publishes the Nunatak New Fiction Series.

How to Contact: Accepts unsolicited mss. Accepts queries by e-mail. SASE necessary for return of ms. Reports in 2 months on queries; 4-6 months on mss. Rarely offers comments on rejected mss.

Terms: Pays royalties of 10% minimum. Sends galleys to author. Publishes ms at least 1 year after acceptance. Book catalog for 9×12 SASE.

Advice: *"We publish western Canadian writers only or books about western Canada. We are looking for excellent quality and originality."*

✓ ◐ ▼ **NORTHLAND PUBLISHING CO., INC.,** P.O. Box 1389, Flagstaff AZ 86002-1389. (520)774-5251. Fax: (520)774-0592. E-mail: editorial@northlandpub.com. Website: www.northlandpub.com. **Acquisitions:** Brad Melton, Northland Publishing editor; Aimee Jackson, Rising Moon editor. Estab. 1958. Publishes hardcover and trade paperback originals. **Publishes 30% previously unpublished writers/year.** Averages 10 titles/year per imprint.

● This publisher has received the following awards for fiction titles: Smithsonian's Notable Books for Children (*The Unbreakable Code*); Western Writers of America Storyteller Award Winner (*Slim and Miss Prim*); 1998 Parent's Choice Recommendation (*Old Jake's Skirts*); *Small Press* Children's Book Award Winner.

Imprint(s): Rising Moon (books for young readers).

Needs: Children's picture book and middle reader chapter book stories. Picture book mss should be 350-1,500 words; chapter book mss should be approximately 20,000 words. Recently published *Fiddlin' Sam*, by Marianna Dengler, illustrated by Sibyl Graber Gerig; and *Missing in the Mountains*, by T.S. Fields.

How to Contact: Query or submit outline and 3 sample chapters. Reports in 1 month on queries; 3 months on mss. No fax or e-mail submissions. Simultaneous submissions OK if so noted.

Terms: Pays 5-12% royalty on net receipts, depending upon terms. Offers $4,000-5,000 average advance. Publishes ms 2 years after acceptance. Writer's guidelines and book catalog for 9 × 12 SAE with $1.50 in postage.

Advice: "We only publish general interest fiction for young readers."

◑ Ⓐ NORTH-SOUTH BOOKS, affiliate of Nord-Sud Verlag AG, 1123 Broadway, Suite 800, New York NY 10010. (212)463-9736. Website: www.northsouth.com. **Acquisitions:** Julie Amper. Estab. 1985. "The aim of North-South is to build bridges—bridges between authors and artists from different countries and between readers of all ages. We believe children should be exposed to as wide a range of artistic styles as possible with universal themes." **Publishes 5% previously unpublished writers/year.** Publishes 100 titles/year.

• North-South Books is the publisher of the international bestseller, *The Rainbow Fish*.

Needs: Picture books, easy-to-read. "We are currently accepting only picture books; all other books are selected by our German office." Published *The Rainbow Fish & the Big Blue Whale*, by Marcus Pfister (picture); *The Other Side of the Bridge*, Wolfram Hänel (easy-to-read); and *A Mouse in the House*, by G. Wagener.

How to Contact: Agented fiction only. Query. Does not respond unless interested. All unsolicited mss returned unopened. Returns submissions accompanied by SASE.

Terms: Pays royalty on retail price. Publishes ms 2 years after acceptance.

☑ ◑ ⚕ W.W. NORTON & COMPANY, INC., 500 Fifth Ave., New York NY 10110. (212)354-5500. Website: www.wwnorton.com. Estab. 1924. Midsize independent publisher of trade books and college textbooks. Publishes literary fiction. Publishes hardcover originals. Occasionally comments on rejected mss.

• *Ship Fever*, by Andrea Barrett, published by W.W. Norton & Company, Inc., won the National Book Award.

Needs: High-quality literary fiction. No occult, science fiction, religious, gothic, romances, experimental, confession, erotica, psychic/supernatural, fantasy, horror, juvenile or young adult. Published *Ship Fever*, by Andrea Barrett; *Oyster*, by Jannette Turner Hospital; and *Power*, by Linda Hogan.

How to Contact: Submit query letter to "Editorial Department" listing credentials and briefly describing ms. SASE. Simultaneous submissions OK. Reports in 8-10 weeks. Packaging and postage must be enclosed to ensure safe return of materials.

Advice: "We will occasionally encourage writers of promise whom we do not immediately publish. We are principally interested in the literary quality of fiction manuscripts. A familiarity with our current list of titles will give you an idea of what we're looking for. If your book is good and you have no agent you may eventually succeed; but the road to success will be easier and shorter if you have an agent backing the book."

◑ ONE WORLD, Imprint of Ballantine Publishing, Random House, Inc., 201 E. 50th St., New York NY 10022. (212)572-2620. Fax: (212)940-7539. Website: www.randomhouse.com. **Acquisitions:** Cheryl Woodruff, publisher; Gary Brozek, editor. Estab. 1992. "One World's list includes books written by and focused on African Americans, Native Americans, Asian Americans and Latino Americans. We concentrate on *American* multicultural experiences." Publishes hardcover and trade paperback originals, trade and mass market paperback reprints. **Publishes 25% previously unpublished writers/year;** 5% from unagented writers.

Needs: "We are looking for good contemporary fiction. In the past, topics have mostly been 'pre-Civil rights era and before.'" Published *Kinfolks*, by Kristin Hunter Lattany (novel).

How to Contact: Query with synopsis, 3 sample chapters (100 pages) and SASE. Reports in 4 months.

Terms: Pays 8-12% royalty on retail price, varies from hardcover to mass market. Advance varies. Publishes ms 2 years after acceptance. Writer's guidelines and book catalog for #10 SASE.

Advice: "For first-time authors, have a completed manuscript. You won't be asked to write on speculation."

♣ ☑ ◐ ◎ ORCA BOOK PUBLISHERS LTD., P.O. Box 5626, Station B, Victoria, British Columbia V8R 6S4 Canada. (250)380-1229. Fax: (250)380-1892. E-mail: orca@orcabook.com. Website: www.orcabooks.c om. Publisher: R.J. Tyrrell. Estab. 1984. **Acquisitions:** Ann Featherstone, children's book editor. Publishes hardcover and paperback originals. Books: quality 60 lb. book stock paper; illustrations Average print order: 3,000-5,000. First novel print order: 3,000-5,000. **Plans 1-2 first novels this year.** Averages 20-25 total titles, 1-2 fiction titles each year. Sometimes comments on rejected mss.

Needs: Contemporary, juvenile (5-9 years), literary, mainstream, young adult/teen (10-18 years). Looking for "contemporary fiction." No "romance, science fiction."

How to Contact: Query first, then submit outline/synopsis and 1 or 2 sample chapters. SASE. Agented fiction 20%. Reports in 2 weeks on queries; 1-2 months on mss. Publishes Canadian authors only.

Terms: Pays royalties of 10%; $500 average advance. Sends galleys to author. Publishes ms 6 months-1 year after acceptance. Writer's guidelines for SASE. Book catalog for 8½ × 11 SASE.

Advice: "We are looking to promote and publish Canadians."

◑ ORCHARD BOOKS, A Grolier Publishing Company, 95 Madison Ave., New York NY 10016. (212)951-2600. **Acquisitions:** Sarah Caguiat, editor; Ana Cerro, editor. Orchard specializes in children's illustrated and picture books. Publishes hardcover and trade paperback originals. **Publishes 25% previously unpublished writers/year.**
Needs: Picture books, young adult, middle reader, board book, novelty and some nonfiction. Published *The Pig Who Ran a Red Light*, by Paul Brett Johnson; and *One Seal*, by John Stadler.
How to Contact: No unsolicited mss. Query with SASE. Reports in 3 months on queries.
Terms: Pays 7½-10% royalty on retail price. Advance varies. Publishes ms 1 year after acceptance.
Advice: "Go to a bookstore and read several Orchard Books to get an idea of what we publish. Write what you feel and query us if you think it's 'right.' It's worth finding the right publishing match."

⊕ ◑ ORIENT PAPERBACKS, A division of Vision Books Pvt Ltd., Madarsa Rd., Kashmere Gate, Delhi 110 006 India. Editor: Sudhir Malhotra. Publishes 10-15 novels or story collections/year. "We are one of the largest paperback publishers in S.E. Asia and publish English fiction by authors from this part of the world."
Needs: Length: 40,000 words minimum.
Terms: Pays royalty on copies sold.
How to Contact: Send cover letter, brief summary, 1 sample chapter and author's bio data. "We send writers' guidelines on accepting a proposal."

✿ ✓ ◑ ORPHEUS ROMANCE, Red Merle Ltd., Pinegrove Box 64004, Oakville, Ontario L6K 2C0 Canada. (905)337-2188. Fax: (905)337-0999. E-mail: info@orpheusromance.com. Website: www.OrpheusRomance.com and www.iReadRomance.com (includes submission guidelines; online/downloadable romance short stories; online zine; "Orpheus Romancer"; chat rooms; forums; profiles; etc.). **Acquisitions:** Marybeth O'Halloran, fiction editor (Orpheus Romance—classic/modern/chimeric/period, including Bittersweets); Maralyn Ellis, fiction editor (Retrospective Romance [1900-1960s]); Stacey Doherty, fiction editor (Orpheus Romancer—Bedtime Bites). Estab. 1966. "Orpheus Romance publishes fresh, first-rate romantic fiction, including: Bittersweets (less traditional endings); Retrospectives (1900-1960s romances) and all other traditional romance categories in both novel and shorter lengths." Publishes paperback originals and online/downloadable originals. Books: 50 lb. book newsprint; sheet-fed offset; perfect binding; cover duotone illustrations. **Published 5 new writers within the last year.** Averages 6 fiction titles/year.
Needs: Romance (contemporary, futuristic/time travel, gothic, historical, regency period, romantic suspense), young adult/teen (romance). Especially looking for Retrospective (1900-1960s), Bittersweets, Generationals (sagas) and Englightenments. Published *True Love*, by Flora Kidd and *Cheyenne Moon*, by Karlyn Thayer (online short stories); and *Stand & Deliver*, by Kat McBride (novelette). Publishes Generationals series (family sagas; stories through time).
How to Contact: Accepts unsolicited mss. Query with outline/synopsis and 3 sample chapters. Unsolicited queries/correspondence by e-mail and fax OK. Include estimated word count, 200-word bio and list of publishing credits. Send SASE for reply; send a disposable copy of ms. Reports in 6 weeks on queries; 2 months on mss. Electronic submissions (disk or modem) OK. Sometimes critiques or comments on rejected ms.
Terms: Pays royalties for novels. Advance negotiable. Pays 5¢/word for short stories. "Payment by individual arrangement with author." Sends galleys to author. Publishes ms up to one year after acceptance. Writer's guidelines for SASE (1 IRC). Book catalog for #10 SASE (1 IRC).
Advice: "We are looking for professional, polished manuscripts with strong elements of characterization, setting, plot and resolution. We are publishing topics and themes that are a little broader than traditional mainstream romance but the romance must still be central."

ℕ ⊕ PETER OWEN PUBLISHERS, 73 Kenway Rd., London SW5 0RE England. E-mail: admin@peterowen.u-net.com. **Acquisitions:** Antonia Owen, fiction editor. Averages 15 fiction titles/year.
Needs: "Independent publishing house now 45 years old. Publish fiction from around the world, from Russia to Japan. Publishers of Shusaku Endo, Paul and Jane Bowles, Hermann Hesse, Octavio Paz, Colette, etc." Does not accept short stories, only excerpts from novels of normal length."
How to Contact: Send cover letter, synopsis and/or sample chapter. Please include SASE (or IRC).
Terms: Pays advance and standard royalty.
Advice: "Be concise. Always include SASE and/or international reply coupon. Best to work through agent. Writers can obtain copy of our catalogue by sending SASE, and/or international reply coupon. It would help greatly if author was familiar with the list. U.K. bookselling, especially since end of net book agreement, is making new fiction very hard to sell. It is also hard to get fiction reviewed. At the moment we are publishing less fiction than nonfiction."

◑ RICHARD C. OWEN PUBLISHERS INC., P.O. Box 585, Katonah NY 10536. Fax: (914)232-3903. **Acquisitions:** Janice Boland, director of children's books. "Our focus is literacy education with a meaning-centered perspective. We believe students become enthusiastic, independent, life-long learners when supported and guided by skillful teachers. The professional development work we do and the books we publish support these beliefs." Publishes hardcover and paperback originals. **Publishes 15 previously unpublished writers/**

year. Distributes titles to schools via mail order. Promotes titles through data base mailing, reputation, catalog, brochures, appropriate publications—magazines, etc.

- "We are also seeking manuscripts for our new collection of short, snappy stories for 8-9-year-old children (3rd grades). Subjects include humor, careers, mysteries, science fiction, folktales, women, fashion trends, sports, music, myths, journalism, history, inventions, planets, architecture, plays, adventure, technology, vehicles."

Needs: Picture books. "Brief, strong story line, real characters, natural language, exciting—child-appealing stories with a twist. No lists, alphabet or counting books." Recently published *The Dollar*, by Nathan Zimelman; *Who Cleans the Museum*, by Lisa Brochu; and *Pancakes*, by Wendi J. Silvano.

How to Contact: Send for ms guidelines, then submit full ms with SASE. Reports in 1 month on queries; 2 months on mss. Simultaneous submissions OK, if so noted.

Terms: Pays 5% royalty on wholesale price. Publishes ms 3 years after acceptance. Writer's guidelines for SASE with 52¢ postage.

Advice: "We don't respond to queries. Because our books are so brief it is better to send entire ms. Write clear simple strong stories with memorable characters and with a big wind up finish."

OWL BOOKS, Imprint of Henry Holt & Co., Inc., 115 W. 18th St., New York NY 10011. (212)886-9200. **Acquisitions:** David Sobel, senior editor. Estab. 1996. "We are looking for original, great ideas that have commercial appeal, but that you can respect." **Publishes 30% previously unpublished writers/year.**

Needs: Literary mainstream/contemporary. Published *White Boy Shuffle*, by Paul Beatty; and *The Debt to Pleasure*, by John Lanchester.

How to Contact: Query with synopsis, 1 sample chapter and SASE. Reports in 2 months. Simultaneous submissions OK.

Terms: Pays 6-7½% royalty on retail price. Advance varies. Publishes ms 1 year after acceptance.

PANTHEON BOOKS, Subsidiary of Random House, 201 E. 50th St., 25th Floor, New York NY 10022. (212)751-2600. Fax: (212)572-6030. Editorial Director: Dan Frank. Senior Editor: Shelley Wagner. Executive Editor: Erroll McDonald. **Acquisitions:** Editorial Department. Estab. 1942. "Small but well-established imprint of well-known large house." Publishes hardcover and trade paperback originals and trade paperback reprints. Averages 75 total titles, about one-third fiction, each year.

Needs: Quality fiction and nonfiction. Published *Crooked Little Heart*, by Anne Lamott.

How to Contact: Query letter and sample material. SASE.

Payment/Terms: Pays royalties; offers advance.

PAPIER-MACHE PRESS, 627 Walker St., Watsonville CA 95076-4119. (408)763-1420. Fax: (408)763-1422. Website: www.ReadersNdex.com/papiermache. **Acquisitions:** Shirley Coe, acquisitions editor. Estab. 1984. "Small women's press." Publishes anthologies, novels. Books: 60-70 lb. offset paper; perfect-bound or case-bound. Average print order: 25,000. Published new writers within the last year. Publishes 4-6 total titles/year.

- Papier-Mache Press author Molly Giles won the Small Press Book Award for Fiction and the California Book Award for Fiction for *Creek Walk and Other Stories*.

Needs: Contemporary, short stories on announced themes. Published *At Our Core: Women Writing About Power*, by Sandra Martz (anthology); and *Generation to Generation*, by Sandra Martz and Shirley Coe (anthology).

How to Contact: Send SASE for current submission guidelines.

Terms: Standard royalty agreements and complimentary copy. Publishes ms 18 months after acceptance. Writer's guidelines and book catalog free.

Advice: "Request submission guidelines regarding upcoming anthology themes and submission periods."

PASSEGGIATA PRESS, INC., P.O. Box 636, Pueblo CO 81002. (719)544-1038. Fax: (719)544-7911. **Acquisitions:** Donald Herdeck, publisher/editor-in-chief. Estab. 1973. "We search for books that will make clear the complexity and value of non-Western literature and culture." Small independent publisher with expanding list. Publishes hardcover and paperback originals and reprints. Books: library binding; illustrations. Average print order: 1,000-1,500. First novel print order: 1,000. Averages 15 total titles, 6-8 fiction titles each year. **15% of books from first-time authors; 99% from unagented writers.**

- Passeggiata, formerly Three Continents Press, has published three authors awarded the Nobel Prize in Literature.

Needs: "We publish original fiction only by writers from Africa, the Caribbean, the Middle East, Asia and the Pacific. No fiction by writers from North America or Western Europe." Published *Lina: Portrait of a Damascene Girl*, by Samar Altar; *The Native Informant*, by Ramzi Salti (stories); and *Repudiation*, by Rachid Boudjedra.

How to Contact: Query with outline/synopsis and sample pages with SASE. State "origins (non-Western), education and previous publications." Reports in 1 week on queries; 1 month on mss. Simultaneous submissions OK. Occasionally critiques ("a few sentences") rejected mss.

Terms: "Send inquiry letter first and ms only if so requested by us. We are not a subsidy publisher, but do a few specialized titles a year with grants. In those cases we accept institutional subventions. Foundation or institution receives 20-30 copies of book and at times royalty on first printing. We pay royalties twice yearly (against advance) as a percentage of net paid receipts." Royalties of 5% minimum; 10% maximum. Offers negotiable advance, $300 average. Provides 10 author's copies. Sends galleys to author. Free book catalog available; inquiry letter first and ms only if so requested by us.

Advice: "Submit professional work (within our parameters of interest) with well worked-over language and clean manuscripts prepared to exacting standards."

PEACHTREE PUBLISHERS, LTD., 494 Armour Circle NE, Atlanta GA 30324. (404)876-8761. Fax: (404)875-2578. Website: www.peachtree-online.com (includes writer's guidelines, current catalog of titles, upcoming promotional events, behind-the-scenes look at creating a book). President: Margaret Quinlin. **Acquisitions:** Sarah Smith and Helen Harriss, fiction editors. Estab. 1977. Small, independent publisher specializing in general interest publications, particularly of Southern origin. Publishes hardcover and paperback originals and hardcover reprints. Average first novel print run 3,000. Averages 18-20 total titles, 1-2 fiction titles each year. **Publishes 2 previously unpublished writers/year.** Plans 0 first novels this year. Promotes titles through review copies to appropriate publications, press kits and book signings at local bookstores.

Imprint(s): Freestone and Peachtree Jr.

• Peachtree has received the 1998 Books for the Teen Age and the 1998 Oklahoma Book Award for *Hero*, by S.L. Rottman. They recently put a stronger emphasis on books for children and young adults.

Needs: Young adult and juvenile fiction. Contemporary, literary, mainstream, regional. No adult science fiction/ fantasy, horror, religious, romance, historical or mystery/suspense. "We are seeking YA and juvenile works including mystery and historical fiction, however." Recently published *Older But Wilder*, by Effie Wilder.

How to Contact: Accepts unsolicited mss. Query, submit outline/synopsis and 50 pages, or submit complete ms with SASE. Reports in 1 month on queries; 3 months on mss. Simultaneous submissions OK. Do not fax or e-mail queries, manuscripts or submissions

Terms: Pays in royalties. Sends galleys to author. Free writer's guidelines. Publishes ms 2 years after acceptance. Book catalog for 2 first-class stamps.

Advice: "We encourage original efforts in first novels."

PEEPAL TREE PRESS, 17 King's Ave., Leeds LS6 1QS England. E-mail: submissions@peepal.demon.co.uk. **Acquisitions:** Jeremy Poynting, fiction editor. **Publishes 3 previously unpublished writers/year.** Averages 12-14 fiction titles/year.

Needs: "Peepal Tree publishes primarily Caribbean and Black British fiction, though it has begun to expand into African and South Asian writing. We publish both novels and collections of short stories." Recently published *Wheel and Come Again* (anthology of reggae poetry); and *Mapmakers of Spitalfields* (British/Asian short stories). Length: 25,000 words minimum; 100,000 words maximum.

How to Contact: Send a cover letter, synopsis and 3 sample chapters.

Terms: Pays 10% royalties, in general no advances.

Advice: "We suggest that authors send for a copy of our catalog to get some sense of the range and parameters of what we do." Peepal Tree publishes an annual catalog from the address above. Catalog is also available by e-mail: hannah@peepal.demon.co.uk.

PELICAN PUBLISHING COMPANY, Box 3110, Gretna LA 70054-3110. (504)368-1175. Website: www.pelicanpub.com (includes writer's guidelines, featured book, index of Pelican books). **Acquisitions:** Nina Kooij, editor-in-chief. Estab. 1926. "We seek writers on the cutting edge of ideas. We believe ideas have consequences. One of the consequences is that they lead to a bestselling book." Publishes paperback reprints and hardcover originals. Books: Hardcover and paperback binding; illustrations sometimes. Buys juvenile mss with illustrations. Distributes titles internationally through distributors, bookstores, libraries. Promotes titles at reading and book conventions, in trade magazines, in radio interviews, print reviews and TV interviews.

Needs: Juvenile fiction, especially with a regional and/or historical focus. No young adult fiction, contemporary fiction or fiction containing graphic language, violence or sex. Also no "psychological" novels. Recently published *Unforgotten*, by D.J. Meador (adult historical fiction); and *Jolie Blonde and the Three Héberts: A Cajun Twist to an Old Tale*, by Sheila Hébert Collins (children's regional fairytale).

How to Contact: Prefers query. May submit outline/synopsis and 2 sample chapters with SASE. No simultaneous submissions. "Not responsible if writer's only copy is sent." Reports in 1 month on queries; 3 months on mss. Publishes ms 9-18 months after acceptance. Comments on rejected mss "infrequently."

Terms: Pays 10% in royalties; 10 contributor's copies; advance considered. Sends galleys to author. Catalog of titles and writer's guidelines for SASE.

Advice: "Research the market carefully. Request our catalog to see if your work is consistent with our list. For ages 8 and up, story must be planned in chapters that will fill at least 90 double-spaced manuscript pages. Topic for ages 8-12 must be Louisiana related and historical. We look for stories that illuminate a particular place and time in history and that are clean entertainment. The only original adult work we might consider is historical fiction, preferably Civil War (not romance). Please don't send three or more chapters unless solicited. Follow our guidelines listed under 'How to Contact.' "

⤴ ◐ ◎ PEMMICAN PUBLICATIONS, 1635 Burrows Ave., Unit 2, Winnipeg, Manitoba R2X 3B5 Canada. (204)589-6346. Fax: (204)589-2063. E-mail: pemmican@pemmican.mb.ca. Website: www.pemmican.m b.ca. **Acquisitions:** Sue Maclean, managing editor. Estab. 1980. Metis and Aboriginal children's books, some adult. Publishes paperback originals. Books: stapled binding and perfect-bound; 4-color illustrations. Average print order: 2,500. First novel print order: 1,000. **Published new writers within the last year.** Averages 9 total titles each year. Distributes titles through Pemmican Publications. Promotes titles through press releases, fax, catalogues and book displays.

Needs: Children's/juvenile (American Indian, easy-to-read, preschool/picture book); ethnic/multicultural (Native American). Published *Red Parka Mary*, by Peter Eyvindson (children's); *Nanabosho & Kitchie Odjig*, by Joe McLellan (native children's legend); and *Jack Pine Fish Camp*, by Tina Umpherville (children's). Also publishes the Builders of Canada series.

How to Contact: Accepts unsolicited mss. Submit complete ms with cover letter. Send SASE (or IRC) for reply, return of ms or send a disposable copy of ms. Reports in 1 year. Simultaneous submissions OK.

Terms: Pays royalties of 10% minimum. Average advance: $350. Provides 10 author's copies.

◐ ◎ PERFECTION LEARNING CORP., 10520 New York Ave., Des Moines IA 50322. (515)278-0133. Fax: (515)278-2980. E-mail: perflern@netins.net. **Acquisitions:** Sue Thies, senior editor K-12 books—Cover-to-Cover imprint. Midsize, supplemental publisher of educational materials. Publishes hardcover and paperback originals. **Publishes 10-15 previously unpublished writers/year.** Publishes 50-75 total titles/year, fiction and nonfiction. Distributes titles through catalog and sales reps. Promotes titles through educational conferences, brochures, sales calls.

Imprint(s): Cover-to-Cover (contact: Sue Thies, senior editor, all genres).

Needs: Hi/lo mss in all genres. Readability of ms should be at least two grade levels below interest level. Please do not submit mss with fewer than 4,000 words or more than 20,000 words. Recently published *Tall Shadow*, by Bonnie Highsmith Taylor (Native American); *The Rattlesnack Necklace*, by Linda Baxter (historical fiction); and *Tales of Mark Twain*, by Peg Hall (retold short stories)."

How to Contact: Query with outline/synopsis and 3-4 sample chapters or submit complete ms with a cover letter. Unsolicited queries/correspondence by e-mail or fax OK. Include 1-page bio, estimated word count and list of publishing credits. Send SASE for reply, return of ms or send a disposable copy of the ms. Simultaneous submissions OK.

Terms: Publishes ms 6-8 months after acceptance. Fiction guidelines free.

Advice: "We are an educational publisher. Check with educators to find out their needs, their students' needs and what's popular.

◐ PHILOMEL BOOKS, Imprint of Penguin Putnam Inc., 345 Hudson St., New York NY 10014. (212)414-3610. **Acquisitions:** Patricia Lee Gauch, editorial director; Michael Green, senior editor. Estab. 1980. "A high-quality oriented imprint focused on stimulating picture books, middle-grade novels, and young adult novels." Publishes hardcover originals and paperback reprints. Averages 25 total titles, 5-7 novels/year.

Needs: Adventure, ethnic, family saga, fantasy, historical, juvenile (5-9 years), literary, preschool/picture book, regional, short story collections, translations, western (young adult), young adult/teen (10-18 years). Looking for "story-driven novels with a strong cultural voice but which speak universally." No "generic, mass-market oriented fiction." Published *The Long Patrol*, by Brian Jacques; *I Am Mordred*, by Nancy Springer; and *Choosing Up Sides*, by John H. Ritter.

How to Contact: Accepts unsolicited mss. Query first or submit outline/synopsis and first 3 chapters. SASE. Agented fiction 40%. Reports in 8-10 weeks on queries; 12-16 weeks on mss. Simultaneous submissions OK. Sometimes comments on rejected ms.

Terms: Pays royalties, negotiable advance and author's copies. Sends galleys to author. Publishes ms anywhere from 1-3 years after acceptance. Writer's guidelines for #10 SASE. Book catalog for 9×12 SASE.

Advice: "We are not a mass-market publisher and do not publish short stories independently. In addition, we do just a few novels a year."

◐ PICADOR USA, Distributed by St. Martin's Press, 175 Fifth Ave., New York NY 10010. **Acquisitions:** George Witte. Estab. 1994. "We publish high-quality literary fiction and nonfiction. We are open to a broad range of subjects, well written by authoritative authors." Publishes hardcover originals and trade paperback originals and reprints. **Publishes 30% previously unpublished writers/year.**

Needs: Literary. Published *The Lazarus Rumba*, by Ernesto Mestre; *Mr. White's Confession*, by Robert Clark; and *A Short History of Rudeness*, by Mark Caldwell.

How to Contact: Query only with SASE. Reports in 2 months on queries. Simultaneous submissions OK.

Terms: Pays 7½-12½% royalty on retail price. Advance varies. Publishes ms 18 months after acceptance. Writer's guidelines for #10 SASE. Book catalog for 9×12 SASE and $2.60 postage.

☑ ◐ PIÑATA BOOKS, Imprint of Arte Publico Press, University of Houston, Houston TX 77204-2174. (713)743-2841. Fax: (713)743-3080. **Acquisitions:** Nicolas Kanellos, director. Estab. 1994. "We are dedicated to the publication of children's and young adult literature focusing on U.S. Hispanic culture." Publishes hardcover

and trade paperback originals. **Publishes 60% previously unpublished writers/year.**
Needs: Adventure, juvenile, picture books, young adult. Recently published *Trino's Choice*, by Diane Gonzales Bertrand (ages 11-up); *Delicious Hullabaloo/Pachanga Deliciosa*, by Pat Mora (picture book); and *The Year of Our Revolution*, by Judith Ortiz Cofer (young adult).
How to Contact: Query with synopsis, 2 sample chapters and SASE. Reports in 1 month on queries, 6 months on mss. Simultaneous submissions OK.
Terms: Pays 10% royalty on wholesale price. Offers $1,000-3,000 advance. Publishes ms 2 years after acceptance. Writer's guidelines for #10 SASE. Book catalog free.
Advice: "Include cover letter with submission explaining why your manuscript is unique and important, why we should publish it, who will buy it, relevance to the U.S. Hispanic culture, etc."

PINEAPPLE PRESS, P.O. Box 3899, Sarasota FL 34230-3899. (941)953-2797. E-mail: info@pineapplepress.com. Website: www.pineapplepress.com (includes searchable database of titles, news events, featured books, company profile, and option to request a hard copy of catalog). **Acquisitions:** June Cussen, executive editor. Estab. 1982. Small independent trade publisher. Publishes hardcover and paperback originals and paperback reprints. Books: quality paper; offset printing; Smyth-sewn or perfect-bound; illustrations occasionally. Average print order: 5,000. First novel print order: 2,000-5,000. **Published new writers within the last year.** Plans 1-2 first novels this year. Averages 20 total titles each year. Distributes titles through Pineapple, Ingram and Baker & Taylor. Promotes titles through reviews, advertising in print media, direct mail, author signings and the World Wide Web.
Needs: "We prefer to see only novels set in Florida." Recently published *Myra Sims*, by Janis Owens; and *Bridger's Run*, by Jon Wilson.
How to Contact: Prefers query, cover letter listing previous publications, outline or one-page synopsis with sample chapters (including the first) and SASE. Then if requested, submit complete ms with SASE. Reports in 2 months. Simultaneous submissions OK.
Terms: Pays royalties of 7½-15%. Advance is not usually offered. "Basically, it is an individual agreement with each author depending on the book." Sends galleys to author. Publishes ms 18 months after acceptance. Book catalog sent if label and $1.24 postage enclosed.
Advice: "Quality first novels will be published, though we usually only do one or two novels per year. We regard the author/editor relationship as a trusting relationship with communication open both ways. Learn all you can about the publishing process and about how to promote your book once it is published."

PIPPIN PRESS, 229 E. 85th Street, Gracie Station Box 1347, New York NY 10028. (212)288-4920. Fax: (732)225-1562. **Acquisitions:** Barbara Francis, publisher; Joyce Segal, senior editor. Estab. 1987. "Small, independent children's book company, formed by the former editor-in-chief of Prentice Hall's juvenile book division." Publishes hardcover originals. Books: 135-150 GSM offset-semi-matte paper (for picture books); offset, sheet-fed printing; Smythe-sewn binding; full color, black and white line illustrations and half tone, b&w and full color illustrations. Averages 5-6 titles each year. Sometimes comments on rejected mss.
Needs: Juvenile only for ages 4-12. "I am interested in humorous novels for children of about 7-12. Also interested in autobiographical novels for 8-12 year olds and selected historical fiction for the same age group. Less interested in picture books at this time."
How to Contact: No unsolicited mss. Query first. SASE. Reports in 2-3 weeks on queries. Simultaneous submissions OK.
Terms: Pays royalties. Sends galleys to author. Publication time after ms is accepted "depends on the amount of revision required, type of illustration, etc." Writer's guidelines for #10 SASE.

PLEASANT COMPANY PUBLICATIONS, Subsidiary of Pleasant Company, 8400 Fairway Place, Middleton WI 53528. (608)836-4848. Fax: (608)836-1999. **Acquisitions:** Jennifer Hirsch, submissions editor. Estab. 1986. Midsize independent publisher. Publishes hardcover and paperback originals. Averages 30-40 total titles, 3 fiction titles/year.
Imprints: The American Girls Collection and American Girl Library.
Needs: Children's/juvenile (historical, mystery, contemporary for girls 8-12). Pleasant Company Publications also seeks mss for its contemporary fiction imprint. "Novels should capture the spirit of contemporary American girls and also illuminate the ways in which their lives are personally touched by issues and concerns affecting America today. We are looking for thoughtfully developed characters and plots, and a discernible sense of place." Stories must feature an American girl, aged 11-12; reading level 4th-6th grade. No science fiction or first-romance stories. Recently published *The Smuggler's Treasure*, by Sarah Masters Buckley; *Ceiling of Stars*, by Ann Howard Creel; and *A Song for Jeffrey*, by Constance M. Roland.
How to Contact: Accepts unsolicited mss. Query with outline/synopsis and 3 sample chapters or send entire ms. Include list of publishing credits. "Tell us why the story is right for us." Send SASE for reply, return of ms or send a disposable copy of ms. Agented fiction 5%. Reports in 8-10 weeks on queries; 3-4 months on mss. Simultaneous submissions OK.
Payment/Terms: Vary. Publishes ms 3-12 months after acceptance. Writer's guidelines for SASE.
Advice: For historical fiction "your story *must* have a girl protagonist age 8-12. No early reader. Our readers

are girls 10-12, along with parents and educators. We want to see character development and strong plotting."

PRESIDIO PRESS, 505B San Marin Dr., Suite 300, Novato CA 94945. (415)898-1081, ext. 125. Fax: (415)898-0383. **Acquisitions:** E.J. McCarthy, editor-in-chief. Estab. 1976. Small independent general trade—specialist in military. Publishes hardcover originals. Publishes an average of 2 works of fiction per list. **Regularly publishes new writers.** Averages 24 new titles each year.

Needs: Historical with military background, war, thriller/espionage. Published *Synbat*, by Bob Mayer; *Proud Legions*, by John Antal; and *A Murder of Crows*, by Steve Shepard.

How to Contact: Accepts unsolicited mss. Query first. SASE. Reports in 2 weeks on queries; 2-3 months on mss. Simultaneous submissions OK. Critiques or comments on rejected ms.

Terms: Pays in royalties of 15% of net minimum; advance: $1,000 average. Sends edited manuscripts and page proofs to author. Publishes ms 12-18 months after acceptance. Book catalog and guidelines free on request. Send 9 × 12 SASE with $1.30 postage.

Advice: "Think twice before entering any highly competitive genre; don't imitate; do your best. Have faith in your writing and don't let the market disappoint or discourage you."

PRIDE & IMPRINTS, (formerly Pride Publications and Imprints), 7419 Ebbert Drive SE, Port Orchard WA 98367. **Acquisitions:** Cris Newport, senior editor. Large independent publisher specializing in cutting edge novels and children's books. Publishes paperback originals and reprints. Average and first novel print orders: 5,000. **Published new writers within the last year.** Averages 20 total titles/year, 12 fiction titles/year.

● Chosen as the "Best Example of an Independent Publisher" by BookWatch (Midwest Book Review).

Needs: Adventure, children's/juvenile (adventure, easy-to-read, fantasy, historical, mystery, series), comics/graphic novels, erotica, ethnic/mulitcultural, experimental, fantasy (space fantasy, sword and sorcery), feminist, gay, historical, humor/satire, lesbian, literary, mystery/suspense (amateur sleuth), psychic/supernatural/occult, science fiction (hard science, soft/sociological, cyberfiction), young adult/teen (adventure, easy-to-read, fantasy/science fiction, historical, horror, mystery/suspense, problem novels, series). Published *Still Life with Buddy*, by Leslie Newman (novel told in poetry); *Shadows of Aggar*, by Chris Anne Wolfe (fantasy); and *The White Bones of Truth*, by Cris Newport (future fiction). Publishes mystery and science fiction series.

How to Contact: "Send a one page synopsis of the manuscript; a one page letter which lists the manuscript's title, its genre, word count, the author's name, the Pride & Imprints title you have read which inspired you to send your work to us and why you think we should publish your work; and a postcard (available from any postoffice) on which you write: your name, the title of the work and the following: *Please send the first 50 pages and a detailed plot synopsis with a SASE for reponse* and, on a separate line: *Thank you, but we are not interested in this work."*

Terms: Pays royalties of 10% minimum. Publishes ms 12 months after acceptance. Guidelines online only.

Advice: "Read our books before you even query us."

PUFFIN BOOKS, Imprint of Penguin Putnam Inc., 345 Hudson St., New York NY 10014-3657. (212)414-3481. Website: www.penguinputnam.com. **Acquisitions:** Sharyn November, senior editor; Kristin Gilson, executive editor; Joy Peskin, assistant editor. "Puffin Books publishes high-end trade paperbacks and paperback reprints for preschool children, beginning and middle readers, and young adults." Publishes trade paperback originals and reprints.

Needs: Picture books, young adult novels, middle grade and easy-to-read grades 1-3. "We publish mostly paperback reprints. We do few original titles." Published *A Gift for Mama*, by Esther Hautzig (Puffin chapter book).

How to Contact: Submit picture book ms or 3 sample chapters with SASE. Reports in 1 month on mss. Simultaneous submissions OK, if so noted.

Terms: Royalty and advance vary. Publishes ms 1 year after acceptance. Book catalog for 9 × 12 SASE with 7 first-class stamps; send request to Marketing Department.

Advice: "Our audience ranges from little children 'first books' to young adult (ages 14-16). An original idea has the best luck."

G.P. PUTNAM'S SONS, Imprint of Penguin Putnam Inc., 375 Hudson St., New York NY 10016. (212)951-8405. Fax: (212)951-8694. Website: www.putnam.com. **Acquisitions:** Acquisitions Editor. Publishes hardcover originals. **Published new writers within the last year.**

Imprint(s): Grosset, Philomel, Price Stern Sloan, Putnam, Riverhead, Jeremy P. Tarcher.

Needs: Adventure, literary, mainstream/contemporary, mystery/suspense, women's. Published *Executive Orders*, by Tom Clancy (adventure); *Small Vices*, by Robert B. Parker (mystery/thriller); and *Chromosome 6*, by Robin Cook (medical thriller).

How to Contact: Does not accept unsolicited mss. Prefers agented submissions. Reports in 6 months on queries. Simultaneous submissions OK.

Payment/Terms: Pays variable royalties on retail price. Advance varies. Writer's guidelines free.

QUIXOTE PRESS, 1854 345th Ave., Wever IA 52658. (319)372-7480. Fax: (319)372-7485. E-mail: madd mack@interl.net. **Acquisitions:** Bruce Carlson, president. Quixote Press specializes in humorous regional folklore and special interest cookbooks. Publishes trade paperback originals and reprints. **Publishes 90% previously unpublished writers/year.**

Needs: Adventure, ethnic, experimental, humor, short story collections, children's. Recently published *Eating Ohio*, by Rus Pishnery (short stories about Ohio); *Lil' Red Book of Fishing Tips*, by Tom Whitecloud (fishing tales); and *How to Talk Hoosier*, by Netha Bell (humor).

How to Contact: Query with synopsis and SASE. Reports in 2 months. Simultaneous submissions OK.

Terms: Pays 10% royalty on wholesale price. No advance. Publishes ms 1 year after acceptance. Writer's guidelines and book catalog for #10 SASE.

Advice: "Carefully consider marketing considerations. Audience is women in gift shops, on farm site direct retail outlets Contact us at *idea* stage, not complete ms. stage. Be receptive to design input by us."

RAGWEED PRESS INC./gynergy books, P.O. Box 2023, Charlottetown, Prince Edward Island C1A 7N7 Canada. (902)566-5750. Fax: (902)566-4473. E-mail: editor@ragweed.com. **Acquisitions:** Managing Editor. Estab. 1980. "Independent Canadian-owned feminist press." Publishes paperback originals. Books: 60 lb. paper; perfect binding. Average print order: 2,000. Averages 8 total titles, 3 fiction titles each year. **Published new writers within the last year.**

Needs: *Canadian-authors only.* "We do accept submissions to anthologies from U.S. writers." Children's/juvenile (adventure, picture book, girl-positive), feminist, lesbian, regional, young adult. Recently published *The Dog Wizard*, by Anne Louise MacDonald (children's picture book); and *Fragment by Fragment*, by Margo Rivera.

How to Contact: Accepts unsolicited mss with cover letter, brief bio, list of publishing credits. SASE for reply. Reports in 6 months. Simultaneous submissions OK.

Terms: Pays royalties of 10%; offers negotiable advance. Provides 5 author's copies. Sends galleys to author. Publishes ms 1-2 years after acceptance. Writer's guidelines for #10 SASE. Book catalog for large SAE and 2 first-class stamps.

Advice: "Send us your full manuscript, and be patient. Please remember SASE—no phone calls or e-mail."

RAINBOW BOOKS, INC., P.O. Box 430, Highland City, FL 33846. (800)613-BOOK. Fax: (941)648-4420. E-mail: naip@aol.com. **Acquisitions:** Besty Lampe, editorial director. Estab. 1979. Midsize press. Trade sort and hardcover originals. Books: 60 lb. paper; perfect binding. Average print order: 10,000. First novel print order: 2,000-5,000. Distributes titles through Ingram Books, Baker & Taylor Books, amazon.com, barnesandnoble.com, as well as other regional distributors. Promotes titles through advance bound galleys to hi-profile reviewers well in advance of publication, advertising.

Imprints: Rainbow Mystery (book-length mystery).

- Member of Publishers Association of the South, Florida Publishers Association, National Association of Independent Publishers, Association of American Publishers, Publishers Marketing Association.

Needs: Mystery (amateur sleuth, cozy, police procedural). "We would like to see well-written mysteries." Recently published *Biotechnology is Murder*, a Ben Candidi Mystery by Dirk Wyle; and *Revenge of the Gypsy Queen*, A Tracy Eaton Mystery by Kris Neri.

How to Contact: Query first for guidelines. Include estimated word count, bio of 3 pages or less, synopsis, opening 2 chapters and list of publishing credits. Send SASE for reply, return of materials or send disposable copy. Reports in 2-3 weeks on queries; 8-10 weeks on mss. Simultaneous submissions OK.

Terms: Pays in royalties plus advance and 50 author's copies. Negotiates all arrangements. Sends galleys to author. Publishes ms 1-2 years after acceptance.

Advice: "Since we are just beginning to publish mystery fiction, the future is hard to read. We feel that the very large publishers have closed their doors to the unpublished author—that poor soul who writes well but doesn't have a track record. We'd like to find those folks and give them an opportunity to be published and perhaps find an audience that would follow them through the years. In other words, we're going to look very carefully at each manuscript we call for. Be professional. Come in with that manuscript looking like a pro's manuscript. Please don't tell us, 'I have a great idea for a mystery novel and I've got it on paper. You can clean it up however you want.' That's not to say that we won't help the author that's 'almost there'; we will. Meanwhile, be prepared. If we decide to take on the novel, provide a PC compatible diskette of the book."

RANDOM HOUSE BOOKS FOR YOUNG READERS, (formerly Random House Children's Publishing), 201 E. 50th St., New York NY 10022. (212)751-2600. Fax: (212)940-7685. Website: www.randomho use.com/kids (includes catalog, contests, new books, author information, CD-ROM store, Magic Tree House, Thomas the Tank Engine, Arthur the Aardvark & Seussville websites.) Publishing Director: Kate Klimo. **Acquisitions:** Mallory Loehr, assistant publishing director (First Chapter—Young Adult); Heidi Kilgras, senior editor (Board Books—Beginning Readers); Naomi Kleinberg, executive editor (mass market); Alice Alfonsi, publishing director (Star Wars); and Lawrence David, director of licensing. Estab. 1935. Publishes hardcover, trade paperback, and mass market paperback originals and reprints. **Publishes 1-5 previously unpublished writers/year.** "Random House Children's Books aims to create books that nurture the hearts and minds of children, providing and promoting quality books and a rich variety of media that entertain and educate readers from 6 months to 12

years." Distributes titles to trade and mass markets. Promotes titles through magazine ads, in-store promotions.
- Random House Children's Publishing received American Bookseller, Children's Pick of the Lists award for *Toots & the Upside Down House*, 1997.

Needs: Humor, juvenile, mystery, picture books, young adult. Recently published *Magic Tree House* series, by Mary Pope Osborne; *Mice Are Nice*, by Charles Gigna (ages 4-6); *First Test*, by Tamora Pierce (YA fantasy); and *Dinovease*, by Scott Ciencin (middle grade science fiction).
How to Contact: Agented fiction only. Reports in 3-24 weeks. Simultaneous submissions OK.
Terms: Pays 1-6% royalty or makes outright purchase. Advance varies. Publishes ms 1-3 years after acceptance.
Advice: "Familiarize yourself with our list. We look for original, unique stories. Do something that hasn't been done."

◯ RANDOM HOUSE, INC., 201 E. 50th St., 11th Floor, New York NY 10022. (212)751-2600. Website: www.randomhouse.com. **Acquisitions:** Sandy Fine, submissions coordinator. Estab. 1925. Publishes hardcover and paperback originals. **Encourages new writers.**
Imprint(s): Pantheon Books, Vintage Books, Times Books, Villard Books and **Knopf**.
Needs: Adventure, contemporary, experimental, fantasy, historical, horror, humor, literary, mainstream, short story collections, mystery/suspense. "We publish fiction of the highest standards." Authors include James Michener, Robert Ludlum, Mary Gordon.
How to Contact: Query with SASE. Simultaneous submissions OK. Reports in 4-6 weeks on queries, 2 months on mss. Rarely comments on rejected mss.
Terms: Payment as per standard minimum book contracts. Free writer's guidelines and book catalog.
Advice: "Please try to get an agent because of the large volume of manuscripts received, agented work is looked at first."

◯ Ⓐ RANDOM HOUSE, INC. JUVENILE BOOKS, 201 E. 50th St., New York NY 10022. (212)572-2600. **Acquisitions:** (Juvenile Division): Kate Klimo, vice president publishing director, Random House; Mallory Loehr, assistant publishing director; Simon Boughton, vice president/publishing director, Andrea Cascardi, associate publishing director, Crown/Knopf. Managing Editor (all imprints): Sue Malone Barber. Publishes hardcover, trade paperback and mass market paperback originals, mass market paperback reprints.
Imprint(s): Random House Books for Young Readers, **Alfred A. Knopf**, Crown Children's Books, Dragonfly Paperbacks.
Needs: Adventure, young adult (confession), fantasy, historical, horror, humor, juvenile, mystery/suspense, picture books, science fiction (juvenile/young adult), young adult.
How to Contact: Agented fiction only.

🍁 ◯ Ⓐ RANDOM HOUSE OF CANADA, Division of Random House, Inc., 33 Yonge St., Suite 210, Toronto, Ontario M5E 1G4 Canada. Publishes hardcover and paperback originals. Publishes 56 titles/year. No unsolicited mss. Agented fiction only. All unsolicited mss returned unopened. "We are *not* a mass market publisher."
Imprint(s): Vintage Canada.

🍁 ◯ ◎ ♟ RED DEER PRESS, (formerly Red Deer College Press), Box 5005, Red Deer, Alberta T4N 5H5 Canada. (403)342-3321. Fax: (403)357-3639. E-mail: cdearden@rdc.ab.ca. **Acquisitions:** Dennis Johnson, managing editor; Aritha van Herk, fiction editor. Estab. 1975. Publishes adult and young adult hardcover and paperback originals "focusing on books by, about, or of interest to Western Canadians." Books: offset paper; offset printing; hardcover/perfect-bound. Average print order: 5,000. First novel print order: 2,500. Averages 14-16 total titles, 2 fiction titles each year. Distributes titles in Canada, the US and the UK.
Imprint(s): Roundup Books (edited by Ted Stone), Inprints (fiction reprint series, edited by Aritha van Herk).
- Red Deer Press has received numerous honors and awards from the Book Publishers Association of Alberta, Canadian Children's Book Centre, the Governor General of Canada and the Writers Guild of Alberta. *Mamie's Children: Three Generations of Prairie Women*, by Judy Schultz received the Georges Bugnet Award for Best Novel.
Needs: Contemporary, experimental, literary, young adult. No romance, science fiction. Published anthologies under Roundup Books imprint focusing on stories/poetry of the Canadian and American West. Recently published *Great Stories of the Sea*, edited by Norma Ravvin (anthology); *A Fine Daughter*, by Catherine Simmons Niven (novel); and *Great Tales of the Goldrush*, by Ted Stone (anthology).
How to Contact: *Canadian authors only*. Does not accept unsolicited mss in children's and young adult genres. Query first or submit outline/synopsis and 2 sample chapters. SASE. Reports in 6 months on queries; in 6 months on mss. Simultaneous submissions OK. Final mss must be submitted on Mac disk in MS Word.
Terms: Pays royalties of 8-10%. Advance is negotiable. Sends galleys to author. Publishes ms 1 year after acceptance. Book catalog for 9×12 SASE.
Advice: "We're very interested in literary and experimental fiction from Canadian writers with a proven track record (either published books or widely published in established magazines or journals) and for manuscripts with regional themes and/or a distinctive voice. We publish Canadian authors almost exclusively."

◑ RED DRAGON PRESS, 433 Old Town Court, Alexandria VA 22314-3545. **Acquisitions**: Laura Qa, publisher. David Alan, editor. Estab. 1993. "Small independent publisher of innovative, progressive and experimental works." Publishes paperback originals. Books: quality paper; offset printing; perfect binding; some illustrations. Average print order: 500. **Publishes 2-3 previously unpublished writers/year.** Plans 1 first novel this year. Averages 4 total titles, 1-2 fiction titles/year. Member of Women's National Book Association. Distributes titles through amazon.com, Borders, Barnes & Noble, retail and wholesale, special order and direct mail order. Promotes titles through arts reviews, journals, newsletters, special events, readings and signings.
Needs: Experimental, fantasy (space fantasy), horror (dark fantasy, futuristic, psychological, supernatural), literary, psychic/supernatural/occult, science fiction (hard science/technological, soft/sociological), short story collections. Recently published *True Stories: Fiction by Uncommon Women*, by Grace Cavalieri, Susan Cole, Jean Russell, Laura Qa and Dee Snyder.
How to Contact: Accepts unsolicited mss. Submit query letter. Unsolicited queries/correspondence by fax OK. Include 1 page bio, list of publishing credits and 1-3 sample stories (up to 36 pages). Send reading fee of $5 for short fiction and $10 for novels and SASE for reply, return of ms or send disposable copy of ms. Reports in 6 weeks. Simultaneous submissions OK. Often critiques or comments on rejected mss *for various fee*.
Terms: Publishes ms 6-12 months after acceptance. Writer's guidelines free for #10 SASE. Book catalog for #10 SASE.
Advice: "Red Dragon Press is undertaking to promote authors of innovative, progressive, and experimental works, who aspire to evoke the emotions of the reader by stressing the symbolic value of language, and in the creation of meaningful new ideas, forms, and methods. We are proponents of works that represent the nature of man as androgynous, as in the fusing of male and female symbolism, and we support works that deal with psychological and parapsychological topics."

✓ ◐ REVELL PUBLISHING, Subsidiary of Baker Book House, P.O. Box 6287, Grand Rapids MI 49516-6287. (616)676-9185. Fax: (616)676-9573. E-mail: lholland@bakerbooks.com or petersen@bakerbooks.com. Website: www.bakerbooks.com. **Acquisitions**: Sheila Ingram, assistant to the editorial director; Jane Campbell, senior editor (Chosen Books). Estab. 1870. Midsize publisher. "Revell publishes to the heart (rather than to the head). For 125 years, Revell has been publishing evangelical books for personal enrichment and spiritual growth of general Christian readers." Publishes hardcover, trade paperback and mass market originals and reprints. Average print order: 7,500. **Published new writers within the last year.** Plans 1 first novel this year. Averages 60 total titles, 8 fiction titles each year. 10% of books from first-time authors.
Imprint(s): Spire Books.
Needs: Religious/inspirational (general). Published *Triumph of the Soul*, by Michael R. Joens (contemporary); *Daughter of Joy*, by Kathleen Morgan (historical); and *Blue Mist on the Danube*, by Doris Eliane Fell (contemporary).
How to Contact: Query with outline/synopsis. Include estimated word count, bio and list of publishing credits. Send SASE for reply, return of ms or send a disposable copy of ms. Agented fiction 20%. Reports in 3 weeks on queries; 2 weeks on mss. Simultaneous submissions OK. Sometimes comments on rejected mss.
Terms: Pays royalties. Sends galleys to author. Publishes ms 1 year after acceptance. Writer's guidelines for SASE.

◑ REVIEW AND HERALD PUBLISHING ASSOCIATION, 55 W. Oak Ridge Dr., Hagerstown MD 21740. (301)393-3000. **Acquisitions**: Jeannette R. Johnson, editor. "Through print and electronic media, the Review and Herald Publishing Association nurtures a growing relationship with God by providing products that teach and enrich people spiritually, mentally, physically and socially as we near Christ's soon second coming." Publishes hardcover, trade paperback and mass market paperback originals and reprints. **Publishes 50% previously unpublished writers/year.**
Needs: Adventure, historical, humor, juvenile, mainstream/contemporary, religious, all Christian-living related. Published *Shadow Creek Ranch*, by Charles Mills (juvenile adventure series); *The Liberation of Allyson Brown*, by Helen Godfrey Pyke (inspirational); and *The Appearing*, by Penny Estes Wheeler (inspirational).
How to Contact: Submit synopsis and complete ms or 3 sample chapters. Reports in 1 month on queries; 2 months on mss. Simultaneous submissions OK.
Terms: Pays 7-15% royalty. Offers $500-1,000 advance. Publishes ms 18 months after acceptance. Writer's guidelines for #10 SASE. Book catalog for 10×13 SASE.
Advice: "We publish for a wide audience, preschool through adult."

Ⓝ ◐ RIO GRANDE PRESS, 4320 Canyon, Ste. A12, Amarillo TX 79109. Website: www.poetpantry.com/se_la_vie/ (includes guidelines, contests and book list). **Acquisitions**: Rosalie Avara, publisher. Estab. 1989. "One-person operation on a half-time basis." Publishes paperback originals. Books: offset printing; saddle-stitched binding. Average print order: 100. **Published new writers within the last year.** Averages 7 total titles, 2 fiction titles each year.
Imprint(s): *Se La Vie Writer's Journal*.
• The publisher also sponsors a short short story contest quarterly.

Needs: Adventure, contemporary, ethnic, family saga, fantasy, humor/satire, literary, mystery/suspense (amateur sleuth, private eye, romantic suspense), regional, short story collections. Looking for "general interest, slice of life stories; good, clean, wholesome stories about everyday people. No sex, porn, science fiction (although I may consider flights of fantasy, daydreams, etc.), or religious. Any subject within the 'wholesome' limits. No experimental styles, just good conventional plot, characters, dialogue." Published *The Story Shop* I-VII (short story anthologies; 15 stories by individual authors).

How to Contact: Submit story after June 1. SASE. Reports in 2 weeks on queries or acceptance. Sometimes comments on rejected mss. Word limit: 2,000. Samples available.

Terms: Pays, if contest is involved, up to $15 plus honorable mention coupons.

Advice: "I enjoy working with writers new to fiction, especially when I see that they have really worked hard on their craft, i.e., cutting out all unnecessary words, using action dialogue, interesting descriptive scenes, thought-out plots and well-rounded characters that are believable. Please read listing carefully noting what type and subject of fiction is desired. Best to send SASE for general guidelines."

◯ RISING TIDE PRESS, 3831 N. Oracle Rd., Tucson AZ 85705. (520)888-1140. E-mail: rtpress@aol.com. **Acquisitions**: Lee Boojamra, editor; Alice Frier, senior editor (romance, literary and erotica); Lee Boojamra, editor (mystery/adventure); Lee Ferris, editor (science fiction/fantasy/horror). Estab. 1988. "Independent women's press, publishing lesbian nonfiction and fiction—novels only—no short stories." Publishes paperback trade originals. Books: 60 lb. vellum paper; sheet fed and/or web printing; perfect-bound. Average print run: 5,000. First novel print run: 4,000-6,000. **Publishes 4-5 previously unpublished writers/year.** Plans 10-12 first novels this year. Averages 12 total titles. Distributes titles through Bookpeople, Koen Books, Baker & Taylor, Alamo Square, Marginal (Canada), Turnaround (UK) and Banyon Tree (Pacific Basin). Promotes titles through magazines, journals, newspapers, *PW*, Lambda Book Report, distributor's catalogs, special publications.

Needs: Lesbian adventure, contemporary, erotica, fantasy, feminist, romance, science fiction, suspense/mystery, western. Looking for romance and mystery. "Minimal heterosexual content." Recently published *Deadly Gamble*, by Diane Davidson (mystery); *Cloud Nine Affair*, by Katherine Kreuter (mystery); and *Coming Attractions*, by Bobbi Marolt (romance). Developing a dark fantasy and erotica line.

How to Contact: Accepts unsolicited mss with 1-page outline/synopsis and SASE. Reports in 1 week on queries; 2-3 months on mss. Comments on rejected mss.

Terms: Pays 10-15% royalties. "*We will assist writers who wish to self-publish for a nominal fee.*" Sends galleys to author. Publishes ms 6-18 months after acceptance. Writer's guidelines for #10 SASE. Book catalog for $1.

Advice: "Outline your story to give it boundaries and structure. Find creative ways to introduce your characters and begin the story in the middle of some action and dialogue. Our greatest challenge is finding quality manuscripts that are well plotted and not predictable, with well-developed, memorable characters."

◯ ROC, Imprint of New American Library, a division of Penguin Putnam, Inc., 375 Hudson St., New York NY 10014. (212)366-2000. Fax: (212)366-2888. **Acquisitions**: Laura Anne Gilman, executive editor; Jennifer Heddle, assistant editor. Publishes hardcover, trade paperback and mass market originals and reprints. **Published new writers within the last year.** Averages 40 (all fiction) titles each year.

Needs: Fantasy, horror (dark fantasy) and science fiction. Anthologies by invitation only. Published *Island in the Sea of Time*, by S.M. Stirling (science fiction); *Into the Fire*; by Dennis McKiernan (fantasy); and *Silk*, by Caitlin Kiernan (horror). Publishes the Battletech® and Shadowrun® series.

How to Contact: Query with outline/synopsis and 3 sample chapters. Include list of publishing credits. Not responsible for return of submission if no SASE is included. Agented fiction 99%. Reports in 1 month on queries; 4-6 months on mss. Simultaneous submissions OK. Sometimes comments on rejected ms.

Terms: "Competitive with the field."

◯ Ⓐ ST. MARTIN'S PRESS, 175 Fifth Ave., New York NY 10010. (212)674-5151. Chairman and CEO: John Sargent. President: Roy Gainsburg. Publishes hardcover and paperback reprints and originals.

Imprint(s): Thomas Dunne, Picador USA, Stonewall Inn, Minotaur and Griffin.

Needs: Contemporary, literary, experimental, adventure, mystery/suspense, spy, historical, war, gothic, romance, confession, feminist, gay, lesbian, ethnic, erotica, psychic/supernatural, religious/inspirational, science fiction, fantasy, horror and humor/satire. No plays, children's literature or short fiction. Published *The Silence of the Lambs*, by Thomas Harris; *The Shell Seekers* and *September* by Rosamunde Pilcher.

How to Contact: St. Martin's Press only considers manuscripts and proposals submitted by literary agents.

Terms: Pays standard advance and royalties.

AN IMPRINT LISTED IN BOLDFACE TYPE means there is an independent listing arranged alphabetically within this section.

◐ ▼ **SARABANDE BOOKS, INC.**, 2234 Dundee Rd., Suite 200, Louisville KY 40205-1845. Fax: (502)458-4065. E-mail: sarabandek@aol.com. Website: www.SarabandeBooks.org (includes authors, forthcoming titles, backlist, writer's guidelines, names of editors, author interviews and excerpts from their work and ordering and contest information). **Acquisitions**: Sarah Gorham, editor-in-chief; Kirby Gann, fiction editor. Estab. 1994. "Small literary press publishing poetry and short fiction." Publishes hardcover and paperback originals. **Publishes 2-3 previously unpublished writers/year.** Averages 8 total titles, 4-5 fiction titles each year. Distributes titles through Consortium Book Sales & Distribution. Promotes titles through advertising in national magazines, sales reps, brochures, newsletters, postcards, catalogs, press release mailings, sales conferences, book fairs, author tours and reviews.

  • Books published by Sarabande Books have received the following awards: 1997/98 Society of Midland Authors Award and 1997 Carl Sandburg Award—Sharon Solwitz, *Blood & Milk*; 1997 Poetry Center Book Award and First Annual Levis Reading Prize—Belle Waring, *Dark Blonde*; GLCA New Writers Award—Becky Hagenston, *A Gram of Mars*.

Needs: Short story collections, 300 pages maximum (or collections of novellas, or single novellas of 150 pages). "Short fiction *only*. We do not publish full-length novels." Published *Mr. Dalloway*, by Robin Lippincott (novella); *A Gram of Mars*, by Becky Hagenston (short stories); and *The Baby Can Sing and Other Stories*, by Judith Slater.
How to Contact: Submit (in September only). Query with outline/synopsis and 1 sample story or 10-page sample. Include 1 page bio, listing of publishing credits. SASE for reply. Reports in 3 months on queries; 6 months on mss. Simultaneous submissions OK.
Terms: Pays in royalties, author's copies. Sends galleys to author. Writer's guidelines available for contest only. Send #10 SASE. Book catalog available.
Advice: "Make sure you're not writing in a vacuum, that you've read and are conscious of your competition in contemporary literature. Have someone read your manuscript, checking it for ordering, coherence. Better a lean, consistently strong manuscript than one that is long and uneven. Old fashioned as it sounds, we like a story to have good narrative, or at least we like to be engaged, to find ourselves turning the pages with real interest."

⊘ ▼ **SCHOLASTIC INC.**, 555 Broadway, New York NY 10012-3999. (212)343-6100. Website: www.scholastic.com (includes general information about Scholastic). Scholastic Inc. **Acquisitions:** Jean Feiwel, senior vice president/publisher, Book Group Scholastic Inc. Estab. 1920. Publishes books for children ages 4-young adult. "We are proud of the many fine, innovative materials we have created—such as classroom magazines, book clubs, book fairs, and our new literacy and technology programs. But we are most proud of our reputation as 'The Most Trusted Name in Learning.' " Publishes juvenile hardcover picture books, novels and nonfiction. Distributes titles through Scholastic Book Clubs, Scholastic Book Fairs, bookstores and other retailers.
Imprint(s): Blue Sky Press (contact: Bonnie Verberg, editorial director); Cartwheel Books (contact: Bernette Ford, editorial director); Arthur Levine Books (contact: Arthur Levine, editorial director); Mariposa (Spanish language contact: Susana Pasternac, editorial director); **Scholastic Press** (contact: Elizabeth Szabla); Scholastic Trade Paperbacks (contact: Craig Walker, editorial director; Maria Weisbin, assistant to Craig Walker); Scholastic Reference (contact: Wendy Barish, editorial director).

  • Scholastic published *Out of the Dust*, by Karen Hesse winner of the Newbery Medal.

Needs: Hardcover—open to all subjects suitable for children. Paperback—family stories, mysteries, school, friendships for ages 8-12, 35,000 words. Young adult fiction, romance, family and mystery for ages 12-15, 40,000-45,000 words for average to good readers. Published *Her Stories: African American Folktales, Fairy Tales and True Tales*, by Virginia Hamilton, illustrated by Leo and Diane Dillon; and *Pigs in the Middle of the Road*, by Lynn Plourde.
How to Contact: No unsolicited submissions. Submissions (agented) may be made to the Editorial Director. Reports in 6 months.
Terms: Pays advance and royalty on retail price. Writer's guidelines for #10 SASE.
Advice: "Be current, topical and get an agent for your work."

✔ ⊘ Ⓐ **SCHOLASTIC PRESS**, Imprint of Scholastic Inc., 555 Broadway, New York NY 10012. (212)343-6100. Website: www.scholastic.com. **Acquisitions:** Elizabeth Szabla, editorial director. Scholastic Press publishes a range of picture books, middle grade and young adult novels. Publishes hardcover originals. **Publishes 5% previously unpublished writers/year.**
Needs: Juvenile, picture books. Published *Perloo the Bold*, by Ari; and *Riding Freedom*, by Pam Nuñoz Ryan.
How to Contact: Agented submissions only. Reports in 6 months on queries from previously published authors.
Terms: Pays royalty on retail price. Royalty and advance vary. Publishes ms 18 months after acceptance.

⊘ Ⓐ **SCRIBNER'S**, Unit of Simon & Schuster, 1230 Avenue of the Americas, New York NY 10020. (212)698-7000. **Acquisitions:** Jillian Blake, editor. Publishes hardcover originals. **Published new writers within the last year.** Averages 70-75 total titles/year.
Imprint(s): Rawson Associates; Lisa Drew Books.
Needs: Literary, mystery/suspense. Published *Accordion Crimes*, by E. Annie Proulx (novel, Pulitzer Prize winning author); *Underworld*, by Don Delillo; and *Go Now*, by Richard Hell (novel).
How to Contact: Submit through agent. Reports in 3 months on queries. Simultaneous submissions OK.

Terms: Pays royalties of 7½% minimum; 12½% maximum. Advance varies. Publishes ms 9 months after acceptance.

✓ ◯ ◎ ▼ **SEAL PRESS**, 3131 Western Ave., Suite 410, Seattle WA 98121. (206)283-7844. Fax: (206)285-9410. E-mail: sealprss@scn.org. Website: www.sealpress.com. **Acquisitions**: Faith Conlon, president. Estab. 1976. "Midsize independent feminist book publisher interested in original, lively, radical, empowering and culturally diverse books by women." Publishes hardcover and trade paperback originals. Books: 55 lb. natural paper; Cameron Belt, Web or offset printing; perfect binding; illustrations occasionally; average print order: 6,500; first novel print order: 4,000-5,000. Averages 15 total titles, 2 fiction titles each year. Receives 500 queries and 250 mss/year. **25% of books from first-time authors; 80% from unagented writers.** Sometimes critiques rejected ms "very briefly."

● Seal has received numerous awards including Lambda Literary Awards for mysteries, humor and translation.

Needs: Fiction by lesbians and/or women of color. "We publish women only. Work must be feminist, non-racist, non-homophobic." Publishes anthologies. Send SASE for list of upcoming projects. Published *An Open Weave*, by Devorah Major (literary novel); *Faint Praise*, by Ellen Hart (mystery novel); and *The Lesbian Parenting Book*, by D. Menlee Clunis and G. Dorsey Green.
How to Contact: Query with outline/synopsis and 2 sample chapters. SASE. Reports in 2 months.
Terms: Pays royalties; offers negotiable advance. Publishes ms 1-2 years after acceptance. Writer's guidelines and book catalog are free.

◑ ▼ **SECOND CHANCE PRESS AND THE PERMANENT PRESS,** 4170 Noyac Rd., Sag Harbor NY 11963. (516)725-1101. Fax: (516)725-8215. E-mail: shepard@thepermanentpress.com. Website: www.theper manentpress.com (includes titles, authors, descriptions of backlist and frontlist titles and an order form). **Acquisitions**: Judith and Martin Shepard, publishers. Estab. 1977. Mid-size, independent publisher of literary fiction. Publishes hardcover originals and trade paperbacks. Average print order: 1,500-2,000. First novel print order: 1,500-2,000. Published new writers within the last year. **Publishes 75% previously unpublished writers/year.** Averages 12 total titles, all fiction, each year. Distributes titles through Ingram, Baker & Taylor and Brodart. Promotes titles through reviews.

● This publisher received a Literary Marketplace Award for Editorial Excellence and a Small Press Book Award for Best Gay/Lesbian Title for Elise O'Haene's *Licking Our Wounds*.

Needs: Contemporary, erotica, ethnic/multicultural, experimental, family saga, literary, mainstream. "We like novels with a unique point of view and a high quality of writing." No genre novels. Recently published *A Soldier's Book*, by Joanna Higgins; *Ohio Angels*, by Harriet Scott Chessman; *Fluke*, by Martin Blinder; and *Irregulars*, by Marilyn Jacovsky.
How to Contact: Query with outline and no more than 2 chapters. SASE. No queries by e-mail or fax. Agented fiction 35%. Reports in 6 weeks on queries; 6 months on mss. Simultaneous submissions OK.
Terms: Pays royalties of 10-20%. Advance: $1,000. Sends galleys to author. Book catalog for $3.
Advice: "We are looking for good books, be they tenth novels or first ones, it makes little difference. The fiction is more important than the track record. Send us the beginning of the story, it's impossible to judge something that begins on page 302. Also, no outlines and very short synopsis—let the writing present itself."

✓ ◑ ◎ ▣ **SERENDIPITY SYSTEMS**, P.O. Box 140, San Simeon CA 93452. (805)927-5259. E-mail: bookware@thegrid.net. Website: www.s-e-r-e-n-d-i-p-i-t-y.com (includes guidelines, sample books, writer's manuscript help, catalog). **Acquisitions**: John Galuszka, publisher. Estab. 1985. "Electronic publishing for IBM-PC compatible systems." Publishes "electronic editions originals and reprints." Books on disk. **Published new writers within the last year.** Averages 36 total titles, 15 fiction titles each year (either publish or distribute). Often comments on rejected mss.
Imprint(s): Books-on-Disks™, Bookware™ and Rocket e Books™.
Needs: "Works of fiction which use, or have the potential to use, hypertext, multimedia or other computer-enhanced features. We cannot use on-paper manuscripts." No romance, religion, New Age, children's, young adult, occult. Published *Costa Azul*, by C.J. Newton (humor); *Sideshow*, by Marian Allan (science fiction); and *Silicon Karma*, by Tom Easton (science fiction).
How to Contact: Query by e-mail. Submit complete ms with cover letter and SASE. *IBM-PC compatible disk required.* ASCII files required unless the work is hypertext or multimedia. Send SASE for reply, return of ms or send disposable copy of ms. Reports in 2 weeks on queries; 1 month on mss.
Terms: Pays royalties of 25%. Publishes ms 2 months after acceptance. Writer's guidelines on website.
Advice: "We are interested in seeing multimedia works suitable for Internet distribution. Would like to see: more works of serious literature—novels, short stories, plays, etc. Would like to not see: right wing adventure fantasies from 'Tom Clancy' wanna-be's."

◑ **SEVEN BUFFALOES PRESS**, Box 249, Big Timber MT 59011. **Acquisitions**: Art Cuelho, editor/publisher. Estab. 1975. Publishes paperback originals. Averages 4-5 total titles each year.
Needs: Contemporary, short story collections, "rural, American Hobo, Okies, Native-American, Southern Appa-

lachia, Arkansas and the Ozarks. Wants farm- and ranch-based stories.'' Published *Rig Nine*, by William Rintoul (collection of oilfield short stories).

How to Contact: Query first with SASE. Reports in 1 month. Sample copy $7 postpaid.

Terms: Pays royalties of 10% minimum; 15% on second edition or in author's copies (10% of edition). No advance. Writer's guidelines and book catalog for SASE.

Advice: ''There's too much influence from TV and Hollywood, media writing I call it. We need to get back to the people, to those who built and are still building this nation with sweat, blood and brains. More people are into it for the money, instead of for the good writing that is still to be cranked out by isolated writers. Remember, I was a writer for ten years before I became a publisher.''

☑ ◐ ▼ **SEVEN STORIES PRESS,** 140 Watts St., New York NY 10013. (212)226-8760. Fax: (212)226-1411. E-mail: info@sevenstories.com. Website: www.sevenstories.com. **Acquisitions**: Daniel Simon and Paul Abruzzo. Estab. 1995. ''Publishers of a distinguished list of authors in fine literature, journalism, contemporary culture and alternative health.'' Publishes hardcover and paperback originals and paperback reprints. Average print order: 5,000. **Publishes 15% of books from first-time authors.** Averages 20 total titles, 10 fiction titles/year. Sometimes critiques or comments on rejected mss.

● See interview with Seven Stories author Octavia Butler on page 70. Seven Stories Press received Firecracker Alternative Book Awards (nonfiction), 1996 through 1999; the Will Eisner Comic Industry Award (Best Graphic Album-New) 1997; nomination for Best Books for Young Adults by ALA 1997; Nebula Award Finalist, 1995, 1996; and two *New York Times* Notables.

Needs: Literary. Plans anthologies. Ongoing series of short story collections from other cultures (e.g., *Contemporary Fiction from Central America*; from Vietnam, etc. Published *Barney Polan's Game*, by Charley Rosen (novel); *Grand Central Winter*, by Lee Stringer (memoir); and *Shame*, by Annie Ernaux (novel).

How to Contact: Query with outline/synopsis and 1 sample chapter. Include list of publishing credits. SASE for reply. Agented fiction 60%. Reports in 1 month on queries; 4 months on mss. Simultaneous submissions OK.

Payment/Terms: Pays standard royalty; offers advance. Sends galleys to author. Publishes ms 1-2 years after acceptance. Free book catalog.

Advice: ''Writers should only send us their work after they have read some of the books we publish and find our editorial vision in sync with theirs.''

☑ ◐ **17TH STREET PRODUCTIONS,** (formerly Daniel Weiss Associates, Inc.), 33 W. 17th St., New York NY 10011. Fax: (212)633-1236. **Acquisitions**: Jennifer Klein, editorial assistant; Kieran Scott, editor (YA romance); Cecily von Ziegesar (middle grade horse series); Melissa Senate, senior editor (YA romance). Estab. 1987. ''Packager of 140 titles a year including juvenile, young adult, and adult fiction as well as nonfiction titles. We package for a range of publishers within their specifications.'' Publishes paperback originals. All titles by first-time writers are commissioned for established series.

Needs: Juvenile (friendship, horse), mainstream, preschool/picture book, beginning readers and young adult (continuity series, romance, romantic suspense, thriller). Publishes Sweet Valley Jr. High, Sweet Valley Senior Year and Sweet Valley University series. Published *Thoroughbred*, by Joanna Campbell (juvenile horse series); *Love Stories* (YA romance series); and *Countdown*, by Daniel Parker (YA science fiction series).

How to Contact: Send SASE for guidelines to series currently in production. Unsolicited queries/correspondence by fax OK.

Terms: Pays advance royalty. Advance is negotiable. Publishes ms 1 year after acceptance. Writer's guidelines for #10 SASE.

Advice: ''We are always happy to work with and encourage first-time novelists. Being packagers, we often create and outline books by committee. This system is quite beneficial to writers who may be less experienced.''

☑ ◐ ◎ **HAROLD SHAW PUBLISHERS,** Box 567, Wheaton IL 60189. (603)665-6700. Estab. 1968. ''Small, independent religious publisher with expanding fiction line.'' Publishes trade paperback originals and reprints. Average print order: 4,000. Averages 40 total titles, 1-2 fiction titles each year. Receives 1,000 submissions/year. **10-20% of books from first-time authors; 90% from unagented writers.**

Needs: Literary, religious/inspirational. Looking for religious literary novels for adults. No short stories, romances, children's fiction. Recently published *The Other Side of the Sun* and *Love Letters*, by Madeleine L'Engle; and *The Tower, the Mask, and the Grave*, by Betty Smartt Carter (mystery). Published new writers within the last year.

How to Contact: Accepts unsolicited mss. Query first. Submit outline/synopsis and 2-3 sample chapters. SASE. Reports in 4-6 weeks on queries; 3-4 months on mss. No simultaneous submissions. Sometimes critiques rejected mss. No fax or e-mail queries.

Terms: Pays royalties of 5-10%. Provides 10 author's copies. Sends pages to author. Publishes ms 12-18 months after acceptance. Writer's guidelines for #10 SASE. Book catalog for 9×12 SAE and 5 first-class stamps.

Advice: ''Character and plot development are important to us. We look for quality writing in word and in thought. 'Sappiness' and 'pop-writing' don't go over well at all with our editorial department.''

SILHOUETTE BOOKS, 300 E. 42nd St., 6th Floor, New York NY 10017. (212)682-6080. Fax: (212)682-4539. Website: www.romance.net. Editorial Director: Tara Gavin. Executive Senior Editor: Leslie J. Wainger. **Acquisitions:** Mary-Theresa Hussey, senior editor (Silhouette Romance); Joan Marlow Golan, senior editor (Silhouette Desire); Karen Taylor Richman, senior editor (Silhouette Special Edition); Tracy Farrell, Senior Editor and Editorial Coordinator (Harlequin Historicals, Love Inspired); Melissa Jeglinski, associate senior editor (Harlequin American Romance); Denise O'Sullivan, associate senior editor (Harlequin Intrigue). Editors: Gail Chasan, Karen Kosztolnyik, Margaret Marbury and Lynda Curnyn. Estab. 1979. Publishes paperback originals. **Published 10-20 new writers within the last year.** Buys agented and unagented adult romances. Averages 360 total titles each year.

Imprint(s): Silhouette Romance, Silhouette Special Edition, Silhouette Desire, Silhouette Intimate Moments, Silhouette Yours Truly, Harlequin Historicals.

* Books published by Silhouette Books have received numerous awards including Romance Writers of America's Rita Award, awards from Romantic Times and best selling awards from Walden and B. Dalton bookstores.

Needs: Contemporary romances, historical romances. Recently published *Callaghan's Bride*, by Diana Palmer (SR); *Rio: Man of Destiny*, by Cait London (SD); and *The Perfect Neighbor*, by Nora Roberts (SSE).

How to Contact: Submit query letter with brief synopsis and SASE. No unsolicited or simultaneous submissions. Publishes ms 9-36 months after acceptance. Occasionally comments on rejected mss.

Terms: Pays in royalties; offers advance (negotiated on an individual basis). Must return advance if book is not completed or is unacceptable. Publishes ms 3 years after acceptance.

Advice: "You are competing with writers that love the genre and know what our readers want—because many of them started as readers. Please note that the fact that our novels are fun to read doesn't make them easy to write. Storytelling ability, clean compelling writing and love of the genre are necessary."

SIMON & SCHUSTER BOOKS FOR YOUNG READERS, Subsidiary of Simon & Schuster Children's Publishing Division, 1230 Avenue of the Americas, New York NY 10020. (212)698-2851. Fax: (212)698-2796. Website: www.simonsayskids.com. **Acquisitions:** Stephanie Owens Lurie, vice president/editorial director; David Gale, executive editor; Kevin Lewis, senior editor; Amy-Hampton Knight, associate editor. "We're looking for complex, challenging YA novels and middle-grade fiction with a fresh, unique slant." Publishes hardcover originals. **Publishes 2-3 previously unpublished writers/year.** Plans 4 first novels this year. Averages 80 total titles, 20 fiction titles each year. Promotes titles through trade magazines, conventions and catalog.

* Books from Simon & Schuster Books for Young Readers have received the following awards: 1999 Coretta Scott King Author Award and ALA Best Book for Young Adults for *Heaven* by Angela Johnson; *School Library Journal* Best Book of 1998 for *The Wild Kid*, by Harry Mazer; and ALA BestBook for Young Adults for *Among the Hidden*, by Margaret Peterson Haddix; and *1 Horn Book*—Fanfare List.

Needs: Children's/juvenile, young adult/teen (adventure, historical, mystery, contemporary fiction). No problem novels. No anthropomorphic characters. Publishes anthologies; editor solicits from established writers. Recently published *The Landry News*, by Andrew Clements (middle-grade fiction); *The Raging Quiet*, by Sheryl Jordan (young adult fiction); and *Hard Love*, by Ellen Wittlinger (young adult fiction).

How to Contact: *Does not accept unsolicited mss.* Submit query letter and SASE. Agented fiction 90%. Reports in 2 months on queries. Simultaneous submissions OK.

Terms: Pays royalties. Offers negotiable advance. Sends galleys to author. Publishes ms within 2 years of acceptance. Writer's guidelines for #10 SASE. Book catalog available in libraries.

Advice: "Study our catalog and read books we have published to get an idea of our list. The fiction market is crowded and writers need a strong, fresh, original voice to stand out."

GIBBS SMITH, PUBLISHER/PEREGRINE SMITH, P.O. Box 667, Layton UT 84041. (801)544-9800. Fax: (801)544-5582. Website: www.gibbs~smith.com. **Acquisitions:** Gail Yngve, editor (gift books, poetry); Suzanne Taylor, children's editor; Madge Baird, editorial director (humor, westerns). Estab. 1969. Small independent press. "We publish books that make a difference." Publishes hardcover and paperback originals and reprints. Averages 40-60 total titles, 1-2 fiction titles each year. Receives 1,500-2,000 submissions/year. **Publishes 8-10% of books from first-time authors; 50% from unagented writers.**

* Gibbs Smith is the recipient of a Western Writers Association Fiction Award.

Needs: Only short works oriented to gift market. Publishes *The Peregrine Reader*, a series of anthologies based upon a variety of themes. Published *The White Rooster and Other Stories*, by Robert Bausch (literary); and *Last Buckaroo*, by Mackey Hedges (western).

How to Contact: Accepts unsolicited mss. Query with outline/synopsis and 2 sample chapters. Include estimated word count, 1-paragraph bio and list of publishing credits. SASE for reply. Reports in 3-4 weeks on queries; 2-4 months on mss. Simultaneous submissions OK. Sometimes critiques or comments on rejected mss.

Terms: Pays royalties; amount depends on author and author's publishing history. Provides 10 author's copies. Sends galleys to author. Publishes ms 1-2 years after acceptance. Writer's guidelines and book catalog for #10 SASE.

⬤ **SOHO PRESS**, 853 Broadway, New York NY 10003. (212)260-1900. Website: www.sohopress.com. **Acquisitions**: Juris Jurjevics, Laura M.C. Hruska and Melanie Fleishman, editors. Publishes hardcover originals and trade paperback reprints. **Publishes 7-10 previously unpublished writers/year.** Averages 32 titles/year. Distributes titles through Farrar, Straus & Giroux. Promotes titles through readings, tours, print ads, reviews, interviews, advance reading copies, postcards and brochures.
Imprint(s): Soho Crime, edited by Laura Hruska and Juris Jurjevics (mystery); and Hera, edited by Laura Hruska (women's historical fiction).
Needs: Ethnic, literary, mainstream, mystery/espionage, suspense. "We do novels that are the very best of their kind." Recently published *The Farming of Bones*, by Edwidge Danticat; *The Long Firm*, by Jake Arnott; and *Murder in the Marais*, by Cara Black. Also publishes the Hera series (serious historical fiction reprints with strong female leads).
How to Contact: Submit query with SASE. Reports in 1 month on queries; 6 weeks on mss. Simultaneous submissions OK.
Terms: Pays royalties of 10-15% on retail price. For trade paperbacks pays 7½%. Offers advance. Publishes ms 10 months after acceptance. Book catalog plus $1 for SASE.
Advice: Greatest challenge is "introducing brand new, untested writers. We do not care if they are agented or not. Half the books we publish come directly from authors. We look for a distinctive writing style, strong writing skills and compelling plots. We are not interested in trite expression of mass market formulae."

⬤ **SOUNDPRINTS**, Division of Trudy Corporation, 353 Main Ave., Norwalk CT 06851. Fax: (203)846-1776. E-mail: sndprnts@ix.netcom.com. Website: www.soundprints.com. **Acquisitions**: Editorial Assistant. Publishes hardcover originals. **Publishes 20% previously unpublished writers/year.** Publishes 20 titles/year.
Needs: Juvenile.
How to Contact: Query first. Reports on queries in 3 months. Simultaneous submissions OK.
Terms: Makes outright purchase. No advance. Publishes ms 2 years after acceptance. Book catalog for 9 × 12 SASE with $1.33 postage. Writer's guidelines for #10 SASE.
Advice: "Our books are written for children from ages 4-8. Our most successful authors can craft a wonderful story which is derived from authentic wildlife facts. First inquiry to us should ask about our interest in publishing a book about a specific animal or habitat. When we publish juvenile fiction, it will be about wildlife and all information in the book *must* be accurate."

⬤ **SOUTHERN METHODIST UNIVERSITY PRESS,** P.O. Box 415, Dallas TX 75275. (214)768-1433. Fax: (214)768-1428. **Acquisitions**: Kathryn M. Lang, senior editor. Estab. 1936. "Small university press publishing in areas of film/theater, Southwest life and letters, religion/medical ethics and contemporary fiction." Publishes hardcover and paperback originals and reprints. Books: acid-free paper; perfect-bound; some illustrations. Average print order 2,000. **Publishes 2 previously unpublished writers/year.** Averages 10-12 total titles; 3-4 fiction titles each year. Sometimes comments on rejected mss. Distributes titles through Texas A&M University Press Consortium. Promotes titles through writers' publications.
Needs: Contemporary, ethnic, literary, regional, short story collections. "We are always willing to look at 'serious' or 'literary' fiction." No "mass market, science fiction, formula, thriller, romance." Published *The Earth & the Sky*, by Debbie Lee Wesselmann; *Lost and Old Rivers*, by Alan Cheuse; and *Polonaise*, by Tony Bukoski (short story collections).
How to Contact: Accepts unsolicited mss. Query first. Submit outline/synopsis and 3 sample chapters. SASE. Reports in 3 weeks on queries; 6-12 months on mss. No simultaneous submissions.
Terms: Pays royalties of 10% net, negotiable small advance, 10 author's copies. Publishes ms 1 year after acceptance. Book catalog free.
Advice: "We view encouraging first time authors as part of the mission of a university press. Send query describing the project and your own background. Research the press before you submit—don't send us the kinds of things we don't publish." Looks for "quality fiction from new or established writers."

✅ ⬤ ◎ ▼ **SPECTRA BOOKS**, Subsidiary of Random House, Inc., 1540 Broadway, New York NY 10036. (212)782-9418. Fax: (212)782-9523. Website: www.randomhouse.com. Senior Editor: Patrick Bruttoj. Editor: Anne Lesley Groell. Estab. 1985. Large science fiction, fantasy and speculative fiction line. Publishes hardcover originals, paperback originals and trade paperbacks. Averages 60 total titles, all fiction.
● Many Bantam Spectra Books have received Hugos and Nebulas.
Needs: Fantasy, literary, science fiction. Needs include novels that attempt to broaden the traditional range of science fiction and fantasy. Strong emphasis on characterization. Especially well written traditional science fiction and fantasy will be considered. No fiction that doesn't have at least some element of speculation or the fantastic. Published *A Clash of Kings*, by George R. Martin (medieval fantasy); *Ship of Magic*, by Robin Hobb (coming of age fantasy); and *Antarctica*, by Stanley Robinson (science fiction).
How to Contact: Query first with 3 chapters and a short (no more than 3 pages double-spaced) synopsis. SASE. Agented fiction 90%. Reports in 6 months. Simultaneous submissions OK if noted.
Terms: Pays in royalties; negotiable advance. Sends galleys to author. Writer's guidelines for #10 SASE.
Advice: "Please follow our guidelines carefully and type neatly."

insider report

Author shares lessons learned from writing a first novel

Frank Dobson

"He didn't want to die. I couldn't kill him off," Frank Dobson says about the protagonist of his first novel, *The Race is Not Given*. A PBS special about the artist Jo Roman's decision to commit "rational suicide" after being diagnosed with terminal cancer inspired Dobson to begin what he assumed would be a short story. Stan Thompson, the "young, gifted African-American protagonist," is a former college track star. When his cancer returns, he leaves a prestigious job to return to his family home in Buffalo, New York, and a position as assistant manager of a shoe store. Before committing suicide, Stan feels compelled to help his parents, who have drifted apart, either come together as a couple again or separate for good.

"After about the first 30 pages or so, I knew it had to be a novel because there was no end in sight," Dobson says. That readers who had seen a draft asked him, "Where's the rest?" also encouraged him to continue.

Although, like Stan, Dobson is a native of Buffalo and ran track in high school, he says he was "very conscious of not making it autobiographical. Stan's not me." Other characters, however, are "imbued with spirits of people I've met." Stan's mother, who spends much of her time at BB's Bar, "is based on the mom of a woman I dated years ago." Stan's deeply religious father, members of the track team, and Stan's lovers are also in many ways composites of people he has known. The funeral of Stan's close friend and teammate is based on a funeral Dobson really attended.

Although one of Dobson's stories won the national Bessie Head/Zora Neale Hurston Fiction Writers Award from Chicago State University in 1994, Dobson, who has a Ph.D. in literature from Bowling Green State University, realized soon that he was more interested in writing in longer forms. "The first story I ever wrote was 30 pages long, which is pretty darn long. As I've matured as a writer I've realized my wont is to write longer stuff." Before *The Race is Not Given*, though, Dobson had never attempted a novel.

While the idea of rational suicide inspired the novel, Dobson says he spent a lot of time letting the characters talk to him before deciding on many of the novel's key plot elements. The dramatic and unexpected penultimate scene of *The Race is Not Given*, for example, occurs in BB's Bar. Stan does not, finally, commit suicide, but there is a shooting. Dobson says, "I did not know they were all going to end up in the bar. There were three or four locations that seemed they could have been the setting for the final scene." Dobson "toyed with other endings, one of which was running in front of a car," before realizing that Stan really did not want to take his own life.

Over the course of a writing and revision process Dobson estimates at six to eight years, the novel's characters and events evolved significantly. Stan was given an ex-wife, for example, and became older than he was in the original manuscript. At one point Dobson had eliminated Stan's cancer; but "then life intervened, when my dad was diagnosed with prostate cancer." Dobson read a great deal about cancer because of his father and ended up keeping cancer in the novel as well.

Dobson's closest reader of the novel before it was published was Jimmy Cheshire, a colleague in the English Department at Wright State University, in Dayton, where Dobson teaches creative writing and literature. Dobson says, "It's important to me that my readers are not simply loved ones. I'm going to get a different reading from my wife, and that's OK, but that's not going to help me in the same way as someone who understands the rigors of writing life, who can say, 'this is working and this is not.'"

Dobson says he worked on *The Race is Not Given* in fits and starts, and he "could probably write a book on how not to write a novel." Midway through the book, he wrote an outline, and "a timeline, which would allow me to adhere to some sense of chronology," but this did not happen until he had developed considerable knowledge of the characters. There were periods of prolonged "inspiration and professionalism where I did write every darn day," but also stretches when the work was put aside because events of life—parenting and working in particular—simply intervened.

"I thought it was finished in '93 or so and had secured an agent after sending it out a little myself," he says. After a year during which the agent sent out the manuscript and received interest but no buyers, Dobson rewrote and revised the novel and began again looking for a publisher on his own. Before he severed relations with the agent, he says, she had started to suggest he begin other projects, but Dobson felt, "I could not rest—or let the characters rest—until they found a home. I need to deal with this one."

The book had been rejected 20 or 30 times, he estimates, before he found Sterling House, a Pittsburgh publisher, through a listing in *Writer's Digest* magazine. Dobson sent a cover letter, sample chapter, "and maybe a query letter, maybe a bio," and the novel was finally accepted within three months after he submitted it. There were not many revisions to be made, since he had already rewritten the novel so much. One difficulty arose when Dobson was unable to get permission from publishers to quote certain song lyrics and had to remove them from his manuscript. He lamented the loss at first but says he is "now at peace. Maybe the allusion is all you need." Accepted in September of 1997, the book was published in February of 1999.

Dobson believes the writer's labor should not end with the book's publication. It's important for the writer to assist as much as possible with the book's marketing and promotion, since the writer may well have contacts the publisher does not. Local churches, for example, have offered to host readings of Dobson's work. Before *The Race is Not Given*, was published, he compiled a list of professional and personal contacts and had Sterling House send out complimentary copies, to encourage reviews and other attention to the book. He says, too, that he has taken it upon himself to promote the book in local and regional papers and at writer's conferences. He recently arranged, for himself, a mini-tour, reading and signing books at a black cultural festival in Indianapolis and later in Texas.

Dobson is about 150 pages into a new novel, *Climbing*, which follows members of an inner-city gospel choir in Buffalo over a 20-year period. He feels he has learned much from the experience of writing his first novel. This time, he began by creating a character sketch for each choir member and has also "sketched out the chronology of the novel." This prewriting has allowed Dobson to "get to the center of this novel a lot faster than I did with the first."

Dobson suggests writers carry a hardbound journal everywhere in order to write whenever time and inspiration permit. "All I have to worry about is pen and paper, as opposed to a laptop or suchlike, which are wonderful but not as portable." He also urges writers to "know as much about your ending as is possible. I don't know the ending of *Climbing*, but I know where everyone's going to be at the end, even the minor characters. I did not know with the other novel."

Above all, Dobson emphasizes the importance of perseverance and faith. Because the writing and marketing process can take years, "you have to believe in the project, make necessary revisions and be flexible." He admits that although he wouldn't have said so at the time, the revisions he made along the way were necessary ones. "*The Race is Not Given* is a better book now," he says, "than it would be if it had been accepted in '94 or '95 as opposed to '97."

—*Laurie Henry*

SPINSTERS INK, 32 E. First St., #330, Duluth MN 55802. Fax: (218)727-3119. E-mail: spinster@ spinsters-ink.com. Website: www.spinsters-ink.com (includes online catalog, writer's guidelines, staff list, chat rooms, excerpts from books, discussion forums). **Acquisitions**: Nancy Walker. Estab. 1978. Moderate-size women's publishing company growing steadily. "We are committed to publishing works by women writing from the periphery: fat women, Jewish women, lesbians, poor women, rural women, women of color, etc." Publishes paperback originals and reprints. Books: 55 lb. acid-free natural paper; photo offset printing; perfect-bound; illustrations when appropriate. Average print order: 5,000. **Published new writers within the last year.** Plans 2 first novels this year. Averages 6 total titles, 3-5 fiction titles each year. Distributes titles through Words Distributing and all wholesalers. Promotes titles through Women's Review of Books, Feminist Bookstore News, regional advertising, author interviews and reviews.

● Spinsters Ink won a 1997 Minnesota Women's Consortium Award. They published *Silent Words*, by Joan Drury, which received a 1997 Minnesota Book Award, a 1997 PMA Benjamin Franklin Award and a 1997 Northeastern Minnesota Book Award.

Needs: Feminist, lesbian. Wants "full-length quality fiction—thoroughly revised novels which display deep characterization, theme and style. We *only* consider books by women. No books by men, or books with sexist, racist or ageist content." Published *Silent Words*, by Joan Drury (feminist mystery); *The Activist's Daughter*, by Ellyn Bache (feminist); and *Living at Night*, by Mariana Romo-Carmona (lesbian). Publishes anthologies. Writers may submit directly.

How to Contact: Query or submit outline/synopsis and 2-5 sample chapters not to exceed 50 pages with SASE. Reports in 1 month on queries; 3 months on mss. Simultaneous submissions OK. Prefers hard copy submission. Occasionally critiques rejected mss.

Terms: Pays royalties of 7-10%, plus 10 author's copies; unlimited extra copies at 40% discount. Publishes ms 18 months after acceptance. Free book catalog.

Advice: "In the past, lesbian fiction has been largely 'escape fiction' with sex and romance as the only required ingredients; however, we encourage more complex work that treats the lesbian lifestyle with the honesty it deserves. Look at our catalog and mission statement. Does your book fit our criteria?"

STARBURST PUBLISHERS, P.O. Box 4123, Lancaster PA 17604. (717)293-0939. Fax: (717)293-1945. E-mail: starburst@starburstpublishers.com. Website: www.starburstpublishers.com (includes writer's guidelines, authors, titles, editorial information, catalog, rights, distribution, etc.). **Acquisitions**: David A. Robie, editorial director. Estab. 1982. Midsize independent press specializing in inspirational and self-help books. Publishes trade paperback and hardcover originals and trade paperback reprints. Receives 1,000 submission/year. 60% of books by first-time authors. **Publishes 1-2 previously unpublished writers/year.** Averages 10-15 total titles each year. Distributes titles through all major distributors and sales reps. Promotes titles through print, radio, and major distributors.

Needs: Religious/inspirational: Adventure, contemporary, fantasy, historical, horror, military/war, psychic/supernatural/occult, romance (contemporary, historical), spiritual, suspense/mystery, western. Wants "inspirational material." Published *The Fragile Thread*, by Aliske Webb; and *The Miracle of the Sacred Scroll*, by Johan Christian.

How to Contact: Submit outline/synopsis, 3 sample chapters, bio and SASE. Unsolicited queries/correspondence by e-mail OK. Agented fiction less than 25%. Reports in 6-8 weeks on manuscripts; 1 month on queries.

Accepts electronic submissions via disk and modem, "but also wants clean double-spaced typewritten or computer printout manuscript."

Terms: Pays royalties of 6% minimum; 16% maximum. "Individual arrangement with writer depending on the manuscript as well as writer's experience as a published author." Publishes ms up to one year after acceptance. Writer's guidelines for #10 SASE. Book catalog for 9 × 12 SAE and 4 first-class stamps.

Advice: "50% of our line goes into the inspirational marketplace; 50% into the general marketplace. We are one of the few publishers that has direct sales representation into both the inspirational and general marketplace."

☑ ◉ **STEEPLE HILL,** 300 E. 42nd Street, 6th Floor, New York NY 10017. (212)682-6080. Fax: (212)682-4539. Steeple Hill publishes Love Inspired, a line of inspirational contemporary romances with stories designed to lift readers spirits and gladden their hearts. These books feature characters facing the challenge of today's world and learning important lessons about life, love and faith. Editorial Manager: Tara Gavin. **Acquisitions:** Tracy Farrell, senior editor and editorial coordinator; Melissa Endlich, associate editor; Patience Smith, assistant editor; Ann Leslie Tutle, associate editor. Publishes paperback originals and reprints. Buys agented and unagented inspirational love stories.

• Authors who write for Steeple Hill are a combination of celebrated authors in the Christian women's fiction market such as Jane Peart, Carole Gift Page, and Irene Brand, as well as talented newcomers to the field of inspirational romance.

Needs: "Wholesome contemporary tales of inspirational romance that include strong family values and high moral standards. Drama, humor and a touch of mystery all have a place in the series."

How to Contact: Submit query letter with brief synopsis and SASE or write for detailed submission guidelines/tip sheets. No simultaneous submissions. Publishes 9-36 months after acceptance. Occasionally comments on rejected mss.

Terms: Royalties paid twice-yearly; offers advance (negotiated on an individual basis). Must return advance if book is not completed or unacceptable. Writer's guidelines for #10 SASE.

Advice: "Although the element of faith must be clearly present, it should be well-integrated into the characterizations and plot. Children and humor are welcome; family values and traditional morals are imperative. While there is no premarital sex between characters, a vivid, exciting romance that is presented with a mature prespective is essential."

◎ ⬛ **STONE BRIDGE PRESS,** P.O. Box 8208, Berkeley CA 94707. (510)524-8732. Fax: (510)524-8711. E-mail: sbp@stonebridge.com. Website: www.stonebridge.com (includes complete catalog, contact information, related features, submission guidelines and excerpts). **Acquisitions:** Peter Goodman, publisher. Estab. 1989. "Independent press focusing on books about Japan in English (business, language, culture, literature)." Publishes paperback originals and reprints. Books: 60-70 lb. offset paper; web and sheet paper; perfect-bound; some illustrations. Averages 6 total titles, 2 fiction titles, each year. Distributes titles through Consortium. Promotes titles through Internet announcements, special-interest magazines and niche tie-ins to associations.

Imprint(s): Rock Spring Collection of Japanese Literature, edited by Peter Goodman.

• Stone Bridge Press received a PEN West Literary Award for Translation and a Japan-U.S. Friendship Prize for *Still Life*, by Junzo Shono, translated by Wayne P. Lammers.

Needs: Japan-themed. No poetry. If not translation, interested in the expatriate experience. "Primarily looking at material relating to Japan. Mostly translations, but we'd like to see samples of work dealing with the expatriate experience." Also Asian- and Japanese-American. Published *The Broken Bridge*, edited by Suzanne Kamata (anthology).

How to Contact: Accepts unsolicited mss. Query first. Unsolicited queries/correspondence by e-mail and fax OK. Submit 1-page cover letter, outline/synopsis and 3 sample chapters. SASE. Agented fiction 25%. Reports in 1 month on queries; 6-8 months on mss. Simultaneous submissions OK. Sometimes comments on rejected ms.

Terms: Pays royalties, offers negotiable advance. Publishes ms 18-24 months after acceptance. Catalog for 1 first-class stamp.

Advice: "As we focus on Japan-related material there is no point in approaching us unless you are very familiar with Japan. We'd especially like to see submissions dealing with the expatriate experience. Please, absolutely no commercial fiction."

◙ **STONEWALL INN,** Imprint of St. Martin's Press, 175 Fifth Ave., New York NY 10010. (212)674-5151. Website: www.stonewallinn.com. **Acquisitions:** Keith Kahla, general editor. "Stonewall Inn is the only gay and lesbian focused imprint at a major house . . . and is more inclusive of gay men than most small presses." Publishes trade paperback originals and reprints. Publishes 20-23 titles/year. Receives 3,000 queries/year. **Publishes 40% previously unpublished writers/year.**

Needs: Gay, lesbian, literary, mystery. Recently published *An Arrows Flight*, by Mark Merlis; and *Some Men Are Lookers*, by Ethan Mordden.

How to Contact: Query with SASE. Reports in 6 months on queries. Simultaneous submissions OK.

Terms: Pays standard royalty on retail price. Pays $5,000 advance (for first-time authors). Publishes ms 1 year after acceptance. Book catalog free.

Advice: "Anybody who has any question about what a gay novel is should go out and read half a dozen. For example, there are hundreds of 'coming out' novels in print."

☑ ⊘ ☒ STORY LINE PRESS, Three Oaks Farm, P.O. Box 1240, Ashland OR 97520-0055. (541)512-8792. Fax: (541)512-8793. E-mail: mail@storylinepress.com. Website: www.storylinepress.com. **Acquisitions:** Robert McDowell, editor. Estab. 1985. "Nonprofit literary press." Publishes hardcover and paperback originals and hardcover and paperback reprints. **Published new writers within the last year.** Plans 1 first novel this year. Averages 12 total titles, 3 fiction titles each year.
   • Story Line Press books have received awards including the Oregon Book Award.
Needs: Adventure, ethnic/multicultural, literary, mystery/suspense, regional, short story collections, translations. Recently published *Home Ground* and *The Bungalow*, by Lynn Freed; *Quit Monks or Die!*, by Maxine Kumin; and *Memoirs of a Minotaur*, by Robin Magowan. Publishes Stuart Mallory Mystery series.
How to Contact: Accepts unsolicited mss. Returns mss "if postage is included." Query with outline. Include bio, list of publishing credits and description of work. Send SASE for reply, return of ms or send a disposable copy of ms. Agented fiction 2.7%. Reports in 9-12 weeks on queries; 6-9 months on mss. Simultaneous submissions OK. No electronic submissions.
Terms: Provides author's copies; payment depends on grant/award money. Sends galleys to author. Publishes ms 1-3 years after acceptance. Book catalog for 7×10 SASE.
Advice: "Patience . . . understanding of a nonprofit literary presses' limitations. Be very familiar with our list and only submit accordingly."

◎ ☒ SUNSTONE PRESS, P.O. Box 2321, Santa Fe NM 87504-2321. (505)988-4418. Contact: James C. Smith, Jr. Estab. 1971. Midsize publisher. Publishes hardcover and paperback originals. Average first novel print order: 2,000. **Published new writers within the last year.** Plans 2 first novels this year. Averages 16 total titles, 2-3 fiction titles, each year.
   • Sunstone Press published *Ninez*, by Virginia Nylander Ebinger which received the Southwest Book Award from the Border Regional Library Association.
Needs: Western. "We have a Southwestern theme emphasis. Sometimes buys juvenile mss with illustrations." No science fiction, romance or occult. Published *Apache: The Long Ride Home*, by Grant Gall (Indian/Western); *Sorrel*, by Rita Cleary; and *To Die in Dinetah*, by John Truitt.
How to Contact: Accepts unsolicited mss. Query first or submit outline/synopsis and 2 sample chapters with SASE. Reports in 2 weeks. Simultaneous submissions OK. Publishes ms 9-12 months after acceptance.
Terms: Pays royalties, 10% maximum, and 10 author's copies.

⊘ TAB BOOK CLUB, (TEEN AGE BOOK CLUB), Scholastic Inc., 555 Broadway, New York NY 10012. Senior Editor: Greg Holch. **Published new writers within the last year.**
Needs: "TAB Book Club publishes novels for young teenagers in seventh through ninth grades. At the present time these novels are all reprints from Scholastic's trade division or from other publishers. The Tab Book Club is not currently publishing original novels."
How to Contact: "We are not looking at new manuscripts this year."
Advice: "The books we are publishing now are literary works that we hope will become the classics of the future. They are novels that reveal the hearts and souls of their authors."

☑ ⊘ Ⓐ NAN A. TALESE, Imprint of Doubleday, 1540 Broadway, New York NY 10036. (212)782-8918. Fax: (212)782-9261. Website: www.nanatalese.com. **Acquisitions:** Nan A. Talese, editorial director. "Nan A. Talese publishes nonfiction with a powerful guiding narrative and relevance to larger cultural trends and interests, and literary fiction of the highest quality." Publishes hardcover originals. Publishes 15 titles/year. Receives 400 queries and mss/year.
Needs: Literary. Published *Alias Grace*, by Margaret Atwood (novel); *Desire of Everlasting Hills*, by Thomas Cahill; *Amsterdam*, by Ian McEwan; and *Great Shame*, by Thomas Keneally.
How to Contact: Agented fiction only. Reports in 1 week on queries, 1 month on mss. Simultaneous submissions OK.
Terms: Pays royalty on retail price, varies. Advance varies. Publishes ms 8 months after acceptance.
Advice: "We're interested in literary narrative, fiction and nonfiction—we're not interested in genre fiction. No low-market stuff. Audience is highly literate people interested in good story-telling, intellectual and psychologically significant. We want well-written material."

☑ ⊘ TEXAS CHRISTIAN UNIVERSITY PRESS, P.O. Box 298300, TCU, Fort Worth TX 76129. (817)257-7822. Fax: (817)257-5075. E-mail: j.alter@tcu.edu. Website: www.prs.tcu.edu/prs/ (includes staff, awards, authors' guidelines, catalog, ordering general info). Director: Judy Alter. **Acquisitions:** Tracy Row, editor. Estab. 1966. Texas Christian publishes "scholarly monographs, other serious scholarly work and regional titles of significance focusing on the history and literature of the American." Publishes hardcover originals, some reprints. **Publishes 10% previously unpublished writers/year.** Publishes 10 titles/year. Receives 100 submissions/year. Distributes titles through consortium headquarted at Texas A&M.

Needs: Regional fiction. Published *Understanding Women*, by C.W. Smith; *Tales from the Sunday House*, by Minetta Altgelt Goyne (history); and *Manhunters*, by Elmer Keigh.
How to Contact: Considers mss by invitation only. Please do not query. Reports in 3 months.
Terms: Nonauthor-subsidy publishes 10% of books. Pays 10% royalty on net price. Publishes ms 16 months after acceptance.
Advice: "Regional and/or Texana nonfiction or fiction have best chance of breaking into our firm."

⊚ **THORNDIKE PRESS**, Division of Macmillan U.S.A., Box 159, Thorndike ME 04986. (800)223-6121.
Acquisitions: Jamie Knobloch. Estab. 1979. Midsize publisher of hardcover and paperback large print *reprints*. Books: alkaline paper; offset printing; Smythe-sewn library binding; average print order: 1,000. Publishes 907 total titles each year.
Needs: Original romances. Call Hazel Rumney at ext. 223 for submission requirements.
How to Contact: Query for romances only.
Terms: Pays 10% in royalties.
Advice: "We do not accept unpublished works other than romances."

◉ **TIDEWATER PUBLISHERS,** Imprint of Cornell Maritime Press, Inc., P.O. Box 456, Centreville MD 21617-0456. (410)758-1075. Fax: (410)758-6849. **Acquisitions:** Charlotte Kurst, managing editor. Estab. 1938. "Tidewater Publishers issues adult nonfiction works related to the Chesapeake Bay area, Delmarva or Maryland in general. The only fiction we handle is juvenile and must have a regional focus." Publishes hardcover and paperback originals. **Publishes 41% previously unpublished writers/year.** Publishes 7-9 titles/year.
Needs: Regional juvenile fiction only. Published *Toulouse: The Story of a Canada Goose*, by Priscilla Cummings (picture book); and *Oyster Moon*, by Margaret Meacham (adventure).
How to Contact: Query or submit outline/synopsis and sample chapters. Reports in 2 months.
Terms: Pays 7½-15% royalty on retail price. Publishes ms 1 year after acceptance. Book catalog for 10×13 SAE with 5 first-class stamps.
Advice: "Our audience is made up of readers interested in works that are specific to the Chesapeake Bay and Delmarva Peninsula area."

◉ **TOR BOOKS**, Tom Doherty Associates, 175 Fifth Ave., New York NY 10010. (212)388-0100. **Acquisitions**: Patrick Nielsen Hayden, manager of science fiction; Melissa Singer (Forge Books). Estab. 1980. Publishes hardcover and paperback originals, plus some paperback reprints. Books: 5 point Dombook paper; offset printing; Bursel and perfect binding; few illustrations. Averages 200 total titles, mostly fiction, each year. Some nonfiction titles.
Imprint(s): Forge Books.
Needs: Fantasy, mainstream, science fiction and horror. Published *The Path of Daggers*, by Robert Jordan; *1916*, by Morgan Llywelyn; *The Predators*, by Harold Robbins; and *Darwinia*, by Robert Charles Wilson.
How to Contact: Agented mss preferred. Buys 90% agented fiction. No simultaneous submissions. Address manuscripts to "Editorial," *not* to the Managing Editor's office.
Terms: Pays in royalties and advance. Writer must return advance if book is not completed or is unacceptable. Sends galleys to author. Free book catalog on request. Publishes ms 1-2 years after acceptance.

⦂Ⓝ⦂ ◉ **TRICYCLE PRESS**, Subsidiary of Ten Speed Press, P.O. Box 7123, Berkeley CA 94707. (510)559-1600. Fax: (510)559-1637. Website: www.tenspeed.com (includes ms guidelines, book catalog and excerpts).
Acquisitions: Nicole Geiger. Estab. 1993. "Tricycle Press looks for books that are slightly out of the mainstream, and books that encourage children to develop their potential." Publishes hardcover and paperback originals and hardcover and paperback reprints. **Published 2 new writers within the last year.** Plans 0-1 first novel this year. Plans 15-16 total titles; 0-1 novel titles/year; 7-8 picture books/year. Rarely critiques/comments on rejected ms.
Needs: Children's/juvenile (adventure, fantasy, mystery, preschool/picture book, series). Publishes anthology, *The Stone Soup Book of Animal Stories*. Stories selected by magazine editors. Recently published *The Diary of Chickabiddy Baby*, by Emma Kallok (novel, middle-grade reader); *Hurry Granny Annie*, by Arlene Alda (picture book); and *Never Let Your Cat Make Lunch for You*, by Lee Harris (picture book). "We would like to publish a children's fiction series."
How to Contact: Accepts unsolicited mss. Query with outline/synopsis and 3 sample chapters. Include bio and list of publishing credits. Send SASE for reply, return of ms or send a disposable copy of ms. Reports in 4 months on mss. Simultaneous submissions OK.
Terms: Pays royalties, advance and in author's copies. Sends galleys to author. Publishes ms 1 year after acceptance. Writer's guidelines for SASE and 1 first-class stamp. Book catalog for 8½×11 SAE and 99¢ postage.
Advice: "We have published our first children's novel, and are looking for new novels for middle-age readers (ages 9-11)."

TSR, INC., Wizards of the Coast, P.O. Box 707, Renton WA 98057-0707. (425)226-6500. Executive Editor: Mary Kirchoff. **Acquisitions**: Submissions Editor. Estab. 1974. "We publish original paperback and hardcover novels and 'shared world' books." TSR publishes games as well, including the Dungeons & Dragons® role-playing game. Books: standard paperbacks; offset printing; perfect binding; b&w (usually) illustrations; average first novel print order: 40,000. Averages 40-50 fiction titles each year. Receives 600 queries and 300 mss/year. **Publishes 10% previously unpublished writers.**

Imprint(s): Dragonlance® series, Forgotten Realms™ series, Dungeons & Dragons® Books, Dark Sun Books, **TSR™ Books**, Ravenloft™ Books, Magic: The Gathering, Legend of the Rings, Star*Drive and Dark Matter.
 • TSR also publishes the magazine *Amazing Stories* listed in this book.

Needs: "We most often publish character-oriented fantasy and science fiction; all horror must be suitable for line of Ravenloft™ Books. We work with authors who can deal in a serious fashion with the genres we concentrate on and can be creative within the confines of our work-for-hire contracts." Published *The Legacy*, by R.A. Salvatore; *The Valorian*, by Mary H. Herbert; and *Before the Mask*, by Michael and Teri Williams.

How to Contact: "Because most of our books are strongly tied to our game products, we expect our writers to be very familiar with those products."

Terms: Pays royalties of 4% of cover price. Offers advances. "Commissioned works, with the exception of our TSR™ Books line, are written as work-for-hire, with TSR, Inc., holding all copyrights." Publishes ms 1 year after acceptance.

Advice: "With the huge success of our Dragonlance® series and Forgotten Realms™ books, we expect to be working even more closely with TSR-owned fantasy worlds. Be familiar with our line and query us regarding a proposal."

TYNDALE HOUSE PUBLISHERS, P.O. Box 80, 351 Executive Drive, Wheaton IL 60189-0080. (630)668-8300. Fax: (630)668-8311. Website: www.tyndale.com. Vice President of Editorial: Ron Beers. **Acquisitions**: Ken Petersen, acquisition director. Manuscript Review Committee. Estab. 1962. Privately owned religious press. Publishes hardcover and trade paperback originals and paperback reprints. Averages 100 total titles, 20-25 fiction titles each year. Average first novel print order: 5,000-15,000 copies. Distributes titles through catalog houses, rackers and distributors. Promotes titles through prints ads in trade publications, radio, point of sale materials and catalogs.

Imprint(s): Lining Books.
 • Three books published by Tyndale House have received the Gold Medallion Book Award. They include *The Last Sin Eater*, by Francine Rivers; *The Sword of Truth*, by Gilbert Morris; and *A Rose Remembered*, by Michael Phillips.

Needs: Religious: historical, romance. "We primarily publish Christian historical romances, with occasional contemporary, suspense or standalones." Published *Treasure of Zanzibar*, by Catherine Palmer (adventure romance); *The Atonement Child*, by Francine Rivers (general); and *Left Behind* series, by Jerry Jenkins and Tim Lattaye (prophecy fiction). Publishes 1 previously unpublished writer/year.

How to Contact: Does not accept unsolicited mss. Queries only. Reports in 6-10 weeks. Publishes ms an average of 9-18 months after acceptance.

Terms: Royalty and advance negotiable. Publishes ms 18 months after acceptance. Writer's guidelines and book catalog for 9×12 SAE and $2.40 for postage.

Advice: "We are a religious publishing house with a primarily evangelical Christian market. We are looking for spiritual themes and content within established genres."

UNITY BOOKS, Unity School of Christianity, 1901 NW Blue Parkway, Unity Village MO 64065-0001. (816)524-3550 ext. 3190. Fax: (816)251-3552. E-mail: ~books@unityworldhq.org. Website: www.unityworldhq.org. **Acquisitions**: Michael Maday, editor; Raymond Teague, associate editor. "We are a bridge between traditional Christianity and New Age spirituality. Unity School of Christianity is based on metaphysical Christian principles, spiritual values and the healing power of prayer as a resource for daily living." Publishes hardcover and trade paperback originals and reprints. **Publishes 50% previously unpublished writers/year.** Publishes 18 titles/year.

Needs: Spiritual, inspirational, metaphysical.

How to Contact: Query with synopsis and sample chapter. Reports in 1 month on queries; 2 months on mss.

Terms: Pays 10-15% royalty on net receipts. Publishes ms 13 months after acceptance of final ms. Writer's guidelines and book catalog free.

UNIVERSITY OF GEORGIA PRESS, 330 Research Dr., Athens GA 30602-4901. (706)369-6130. Fax: (706)369-6131. E-mail: ugapress@uga.edu. **Acquisitions:** David Dejardines, acquisition editor. Estab. 1938. University of Georgia Press is a midsized press. "We publish one or two original works of fiction/year. Those with which we have had the greatest success are literary novels, with southern settings and themes. We do not publish mainstream fiction in general, particularly historical or adventure/action novels. We publish short fiction (two collections/year) *only* through our Flannery O'Connor award for short fiction competition." Occasionally publishes previously unpublished authors. Publishes 85 titles/year.

Imprint(s): Brown Thrasher Books, David Dejardines, acquisition editor (paperback originals and reprints, Southern history, literature and culture).

Needs: Literary. Recently published *Survival Rates: Stories*, by Mary Clyde; and *The Edge of Marriage: Stories*, by Hester Kaplan.

How to Contact: Query with 1-2 sample chapters and SASE. Reports in 2 months on queries.
Terms: Pays 7-10% royalty on net price. Rarely offers advance; amount varies. Publishes ms 1 year after acceptance. Writer's guidelines for #10 SASE. Book catalog free.

UNIVERSITY OF IOWA PRESS, 119 W. Park Rd., Iowa City IA 52242-1000. (319)335-2000. Fax: (319)335-2055. Website: www.uiowa.edu/~uipress. **Acquisitions:** Holly Carver, interim director. Estab. 1969. Publishes hardcover and paperback originals. Publishes 35 titles/year. Average print run for a first book is 1,000-1,500.
Needs: Currently publishes the Iowa Short Fiction Award selections.
How to Contact: Query first. Reports within 4 months.
Terms: Pays 7-10% royalty on net price. Publishes ms 1 year after acceptance. Writer's guidelines and book catalog free.

UNIVERSITY OF NEBRASKA PRESS, 312 N. 14th St., P.O. Box 880484, Lincoln NE 68588-0484. (402)472-3581. Fax: (402)472-0308. E-mail: press@unlinfo.unl.edu. Website: www.unl.edu./UP/home.htm. **Acquisitions:** Daniel Ross, director. Estab. 1941. "The University of Nebraska Press seeks to encourage, develop, publish and disseminate research, literature and the publishing arts. The Press maintains scholarly standards and fosters innovations guided by referred evaluations." Publishes hardcover and paperback originals and reprints. **Publishes 25% previously unpublished writers/year.** Average print order for a first book is 900.
Imprint(s): Bison Books (paperback reprints).
• University of Nebraska Press has published such authors as N. Scott Momaday, Diane Glancy and Gerald Vizenor.
Needs: Accepts fiction translations but no original fiction. Published *School Days*, by Patrick Chamoiseau (Caribbean childhood memoir); *Rue Ordener, Rue Labat*, Sarah Kofman (France-Judaism, 20th century); and *Celebration in the Northwest*, by Ana Maria Matute (contemporary Spanish women's fiction).
How to Contact: Query first with outline/synopsis, 1 sample chapter and introduction. Reports in 4 months.
Terms: Pays graduated royalty from 7% on original books. Occasional advance. Writer's guidelines and book catalog for 9×12 SAE with 5 first-class stamps.

UNIVERSITY OF TEXAS PRESS, P.O. Box 7819, Austin TX 78713-7819. Fax: (512)320-0668. E-mail: utpress@uts.cc.utexas.edu. Website: www.utexas.edu/utpress/. **Acquisitions:** Theresa May, assistant director/executive editor (social sciences, Latin American studies); James Burr, acquisitions editor (humanities, classics). Contact: Acquisitions Editor (science). Estab. 1952. **Publishes 50% previously unpublished writers/year.** Publishes 80 titles/year. Average print order for a first book is 1,000.
Needs: Latin American and Middle Eastern fiction only in translation. Published *Lost in the City: Tree of Desire* and *Serafin*, by Ionacio Solares (novels).
How to Contact: Query or submit outline and 2 sample chapters. Reports in up to 3 months.
Terms: Pays royalty usually based on net income. Offers advance occasionally. Publishes ms 18 months after acceptance. Writer's guidelines and book catalog free.
Advice: "It's difficult to make a manuscript over 400 double-spaced pages into a feasible book. Authors should take special care to edit out extraneous material. Looks for sharply focused, in-depth treatments of important topics."

UNIVERSITY PRESS OF NEW ENGLAND, (includes Wesleyan University Press), 23 S. Main St., Hanover NH 03755-2048. (603)643-7100. Fax: (603)643-1540. E-mail: university.press@dartmouth.edu. Website: www.dartmouth.edu/acad-inst/upne/ (includes writer's guidelines, names of editors, authors, titles, etc.). Director: Richard M. Abel. **Acquisitions:** Phil Pochoda, editorial director (literary, New England); Phyllis Deutsch, editor. Estab. 1970. "University Press of New England is a consortium of six university presses. Some books—those published for one of the consortium members—carry the joint imprint of New England and the member: Wesleyan, Dartmouth, Brandeis, Tufts, University of New Hampshire and Middlebury College." Publishes hardcover originals; New England settings only. Publishes 85 titles/year; 6 fiction titles/year. Promotes titles through catalog, magazine advertisements, trade journal ads, mailings.
Imprint(s): HardScrabble.
• University Press of New England books received the Bakeless Literary Publication Prize for *What She Left Me: Stories and a Novella*, by Judy Doenges; and the Strauss Living Award/A.A. of Arts & Letters for *Wherever That Great Heart May Be*, by W.D. Wetherell.
Needs: Literary, regional (New England) novels and reprints. Recently published *Leaving Rico*, by Frank X. Garpar; *Where the Time Goes*, by R.D. Skillings; and *The Salt House*, by Cynthia Huntington.
How to Contact: Query first. Unsolicited queries/correspondence by e-mail and fax OK. Submit outline, list of publishing credits, 1-2 sample chapters with SASE. Agented fiction 50%. Simultaneous submissions OK. Reports in 2 months. Sometimes comments on rejected mss.
Terms: Pays standard royalty. Offers advance occasionally. Writer's guidelines and book catalog for 9×12 SAE with 5 first-class stamps.

insider report

A funny book, a serious writer: Melissa Bank and *The Girls' Guide to Hunting and Fishing*

Melissa Bank

Melissa Bank had few publishing credits when her story collection, *The Girls' Guide to Hunting and Fishing*, was sold by agent Molly Friedrich to Viking Press for $275,000. No overnight sensation, Bank worked on her craft for many years before being recognized. She became interested in fiction in college, and began writing because she wanted to make sense of things she didn't understand. "I felt that I was an outsider—I'm sure other writers feel this way—not listened to, not heard. Becoming a writer or artist is a way of respecting yourself and what you have to say." Bank continued to write while working as an editorial assistant at Berkley Books, and later as director of foreign rights at Aaron Priest Agency. "I got into publishing because I liked the tradition," she says, "and I loved to read." Her favorite writers include "Richard Ford, especially *Rock Springs*; also Pam Houston, Tim O'Brien and Nick Hornby. I'm a big Tolstoy fan . . . Fitzgerald . . . probably the world's only female Hemingway fan . . . Edith Wharton . . . George Eliot." While at Aaron Priest, Bank applied to Cornell and was offered a two-year fellowship.

"It was the first time I took myself seriously as a writer." Bank says. "I had good teachers, Lamar Herrin and Stephanie Vaughn in particular. Early on, I spent a lot of time writing serious stories on subjects I knew nothing about—incest, poverty—close-to-the-bone issues. It took me a long time to 'write what I knew' because my own life didn't seem worth writing about." Bank spent two years in the MFA program and an additional two years teaching creative writing. "I wrote 'The Floating House' (which appears in *The Girls' Guide* . . .) at Cornell, though I revised it every year for the last 12 or 13 years; I don't know if it was dedication or neurotic compulsion. I didn't write the current ending until just before it was published."

When Bank left Cornell, she became a copywriter. "I worked in advertising for eight years, writing fiction at night and on weekends. It was draining, but the way I thought of it, fiction writing was my real job. It never occurred to me that I'd be able to make a living at it. I thought I'd always need a second job. There are so many good—*really* good—writers out there, all with second jobs. The only full-time writers I knew worked as journalists to support their fiction. For me, writing fiction was a reward in itself, and at some point, I realized it had better be enough, because I might never be successful. It's a good thing to think that way. Otherwise, there's too much pressure—waiting for writing to save your life." She wrote the majority of the stories appearing in her collection during her advertising years, hoping if she published a book, she'd be able to go back to teaching. Thanks to the record-breaking sale of *The Girls' Guide* . . ., she's achieved what she once considered impossible.

Much of the value of the book, according to Viking Press, is due to the linking of the stories. "Four of the stories started out separately. I began to see them as linked together—part of a continuum—two years before the book was published," says Bank. The main character, Jane, is an adolescent who grows up during the course of the book. "I was very attached to Jane at each stage of life. It was a listening-to-your-character, hands-on thing. I never think about my characters in the abstract; it's more like writing out their lives. When the right lines come, I pay attention." Bank was motivated to write stories that captured an essential truth. "I was after a realistic type of fiction about perpetually growing up. It seems to me that we're continually having revelations, whether we're 14 or 84." Her storytelling has a definite style and rhythm, a way of expression that evolved in the course of writing. "The best way for me to write a story is to get it down all at once—have it develop evenly across so that it's liquid—then rewrite it. If I try to perfect a story as I go, the prose hardens, and I become enamored of my own words before I even know what the story is about. I'll use a baking metaphor (though honestly, fixing corn flakes is about as far as I go): When you put a cake in the oven, you want it to cook evenly. If you keep opening the oven door and fussing with it, it'll go flat. Editing during the first draft is my personal definition of writer's block."

Bank's stories contain great phrases, funny lines and lots of little truths. In the book, these lines pop into the main character's head, but the conception is more complicated. "I'll write something down and the core idea or phrase is there, but it's not quite right. I do a lot of rewriting. I think the first thought is the best thought, though it often needs honing. But it's important not to labor over something too much, which can take you further away from the truth.

"It's difficult to come out with a revelation that's true but not obvious. The type of revelation that interests me isn't the great rumbling of an epiphany, but the quiet thing you realize by yourself. I test the revelation or joke through the character—would she/he really say/know this?"

The Girls' Guide . . . reflects an insider's knowledge of the New York publishing industry. Bank is continually surprised that people try to link her life with Jane's, but she is pleased readers believe in the character she has created. "Even though writing is a public act, I'm a private person. My writing reflects what I value and cherish, my view of how the world works. But it's Jane's autobiography, not mine." In the story "My Old Man," Jane is mentored in her career by an older and quite successful lover. Bank has a definite opinion on the subject: "A mentor can save you a lot of time, but there are dangers. One of the real requirements of being a writer is learning to trust your own judgement, and the danger of having a mentor is that you'll turn that over to him or her, and won't recognize or trust yourself."

In the book's acknowledgments, Melissa Bank thanked 19 readers, many of whom supported her work all along: a mixed group of relatives, fellow students at Cornell and nonwriting friends. "I used readers a lot in my early years," she says. "Good readers are hard to find. I told a group at a writers' workshop recently that the readers they met there might be their readers for life."

Bank just finished a screenplay of the last story in the book for Francis Ford Coppola, and is preparing to start on the rewrite. "He has a lot of respect for writers and always goes for the original idea." The script is officially in development with Disney. When asked for words of advice for other writers, Bank says, "Don't listen to advice! I mean advice that *discourages* you. If something or someone makes you feel you shouldn't be writing, don't listen." It's a matter of self-respect.

—Joanne Miller

N. ◯ VAGABOND PRESS, Subsidiary of Phony Lid Publications, P.O. Box 2153, Rosemead CA 91770. (626)572-9476. E-mail: phonylid@earthlink.net. Website: www.FyVoCuk.com (includes information on Phony Lid Publications, *Vagabond Magazine*, excerpts from the magazine, guidelines and available titles). **Acquisitions**: Kelly Dessaint, fiction editor. Estab. 1998. "Publisher of aggressive, gut-instinct short fiction with a focus on post punk, urban gore themes and ideas." Publishes paperback originals. Books: glossy cover, standard inside; doutech printing; perfect/flat binding; illustrations. Average print order: 300-500. **Published more than 30 new writers within the last year.** Plans 1-3 first novels this year. Averages 20 total titles, 10 fiction titles/year. Always critiques/comments on rejected mss.

Needs: Experimental, humor, satire, literary. "We are looking for short novels 100-200 pages, aggressive, post-punk, urban gore. We read everything but prefer a literary bent on the pulp genre." Recently published *Everything Falls Apart Then Back Together Just to Fall Apart Again*, by Louis Baudrey (short stories).

How to Contact: Accepts unsolicited mss. Submit complete ms with cover letter. Unsolicited queries/correspondence by e-mail OK. Include estimated word count and 1 paragraph bio. Send SASE for reply, return of ms or send a disposable copy of ms. Reports in 2 weeks on queries; 2 months on mss. Simultaneous submissions OK.

Terms: Pays in author's copies (25% of print order). Sends galleys to author. Publishes ms 2-4 months after acceptance. Writer's guidelines for SAE and 2 IRCs. Book catalog free.

Advice: "We publish more fiction in our magazine *Vagabond* because we are finally receiving the type of material we want to use. In this process, we are coming in contact with writers that have novels or short story collections that fit our criteria. The principle trend we have noticed is that the type of fiction that is selling is not the type of work that is being published by the literary journals. We focus on works that entertain, present them with illustrations and pursue larger works from these writers. As the popularity of the magazine grows so does the market for collections and novels that we wish to publish. Don't try to be another Charles Bukowski or Jack Kerouac. Find a voice through these writers. Recognize that it's not the themes that appeal to us, but the honest approach to subjects that entertain and challenge the reader."

◆ ◯ VANWELL PUBLISHING LIMITED, 1 Northrup Crescent, P.O. Box 2131, St. Catharines, Ontario L2R 7S2 Canada. (905)937-3100. Fax: (905)937-1760. **Acquisitions:** Angela Dobler, general editor; Simon Kooter, editor (military). Estab. 1983. Publishes trade originals and reprints. **Publishes 85% previously unpublished writers/year.** Publishes 5-7 titles/year.

- Vanwell Publishing Ltd. has received awards from Education Children's Book Centre and Notable Education Libraries Association.

Needs: Historical, military/war. Recently published *The Stone Orchard*, by Susan Merritt (historical fiction); *The Wagner Whacker*, by Joseph Romain (baseball, historical fiction).

How to Contact: "Not accepting unsolicited manuscripts at present."

Terms: Pays 8-15% royalty on wholesale price. Offers $200 average advance. Publishes ms 1 year after acceptance. Book catalog free.

Advice: "The writer has the best chance of selling a manuscript to our firm which is in keeping with our publishing program, well written and organized. Our audience: older male, history buff, war veteran; regional tourist; students. *Canadian* only military/aviation, naval, military/history and children's nonfiction have the best chance with us."

◯ Ⓐ VIKING, Imprint of Penguin Putnam Inc., 375 Hudson St., New York NY 10014. (212)366-2000. **Acquisitions:** Barbara Grossman, publisher. Publishes a mix of academic and popular fiction and nonfiction. Publishes hardcover and trade paperback originals.

Needs: Literary, mainstream/contemporary, mystery, suspense. Published *Out to Canaan*, by John Karon (novel).

How to Contact: Agented fiction only. Reports in 4-6 months on queries. Simultaneous submissions OK.

Terms: Pays 10-15% royalty on retail price. Advance negotiable. Publishes ms 1 year after acceptance.

Advice: "Looking for writers who can deliver a book a year (or faster) of consistent quality."

◯ VIKING CHILDREN'S BOOKS, Imprint of Penguin Putnam Inc., 375 Hudson St., New York NY 10014-3657. (212)366-2000. Fax: (212)414-3399. Website: www.penguinputnam.com (includes online catalog of all imprints, feature articles and interviews, young readers site, order information, education and teacher's resources). **Acquisitions:** Melanie Cecka, editor. "Viking Children's Books publishes the highest quality trade books for children including fiction, nonfiction, and novelty books for pre-schoolers through young adults." Publishes hardcover originals. **Publishes 1-5 previously unpublished writers/year.** Publishes 80 books/year. Promotes titles through press kits, institutional ads.

Needs: Juvenile, young adult. Recently published *Someone Like You*, by Sarah Dessen (novel); *Window Music*, by Anastasia Suen/Wade Zahares (picture book); and *Spotlight on Cody*, by Betsy Duffey (chapter book).

How to Contact: Picture books and novels submit entire ms. Reports in 2-3 months on queries. No simultaneous submissions. SASE mandatory for return of materials.

Terms: Pays 10% royalty on retail price. Advance negotiable. Publishes ms 12-18 months after acceptance.

Advice: No "cartoony" or mass-market submissions for picture books.

⊕ ⊘ **VISION BOOKS PVT LTD.,** Madarsa Rd., Kashmere Gate, Delhi 110006 India. **Acquisitions**: Sudhir Malhotra, fiction editor. Publishes 25 titles/year.
Needs: "We are a large multilingual publishing house publishing fiction and other trade books."
How to Contact: "A brief synopsis should be submitted initially. Subsequently, upon hearing from the editor, a typescript may be sent."
Terms: Pays royalties.

◯ ◎ **VISTA PUBLISHING, INC.,** 422 Morris Ave., Suite One, Long Branch NJ 07740-5901. (732)229-6500. Fax: (732)229-9647. E-mail: czagury@vistapubl.com. Website: www.vistapubl.com (includes titles, authors, editors, pricing and ordering information). **Acquisitions**: Carolyn Zagury, president. Estab. 1991. "Small, independent press, owned by women and specializing in fiction by nurses and allied health professional authors." Publishes paperback originals. **Publishes 3 previously unpublished writers/year.** Plans 3 first novels this year. Averages 12 total titles, 6 fiction titles each year. Distributes titles through catalogs, wholesalers, distributors, exhibits, website, trade shows, book clubs and bookstores. Promotes titles through author signings, press releases, author speakings, author interviews, exhibits, website, direct mail and book reviews.
Needs: Adventure, humor/satire, mystery/suspense, romance, short story collections. Recently published *Eucarion*, by Curt Samlaska (action thriller); *Deathtone*, by John Riva (mystery thriller); and *Memories of the Dance*, by Keith Neely (action).
How to Contact: Accepts unsolicited mss. Query with complete ms. E-mail and fax query letter/correspondence OK. Include bio. Send SASE for reply, return of ms or send disposable copy of ms. Reports in 2 months on mss. Simultaneous submissions OK. Comments on rejected mss.
Terms: Pays royalties. Sends galleys to author. Publishes ms 2 years after acceptance. Writer's guidelines and book catalog for SASE.
Advice: "We prefer to read full mss. Authors should be nurses or allied health professionals."

◯ ▨ **WALKER AND COMPANY,** 435 Hudson St., New York NY 10014. Fax: (212)727-0984. **Acquisitions**: Michael Seidman (mystery), Emily Easton (young adult). Estab. 1959. Midsize independent publisher with plans to expand. Publishes hardcover and trade paperback originals. Average first novel print order: 2,500-3,500. Number of titles: 70/year. **Published many new writers within the last year.**
• Books published by Walker and Company have received numerous awards including the Spur Award (for westerns) and the Shamus Awards for Best First Private Eye Novel and Best Novel.
Needs: Nonfiction, sophisticated, quality mystery (amateur sleuth, cozy, private eye, police procedural), and children's and young adult nonfiction. Published *The Killing of Monday Brown*, by Sandra West Prowell; *Murder in the Place of Anubis*, by Lynda S. Robinson; and *Who In Hell Is Wanda Fuca*, by G.M. Ford.
How to Contact: *Does not accept unsolicited mss.* Submit outline and chapters as preliminary. Query letter should include "a concise description of the story line, including its outcome, word length of story (we prefer 70,000 words), writing experience, publishing credits, particular expertise on this subject and in this genre. Common mistakes: Sounding unprofessional (i.e. too chatty, too braggardly). Forgetting SASE." Agented fiction 50%. Notify if multiple or simultaneous submissions. Reports in 3-5 months. Publishes ms an average of 1 year after acceptance. Occasionally comments on rejected mss.
Terms: Negotiable (usually advance against royalty). Must return advance if book is not completed or is unacceptable.
Advice: "As for mysteries, we are open to all types, including suspense novels and offbeat books that maintain a 'play fair' puzzle. We are always looking for well-written western novels that are offbeat and strong on characterization. Character development is most important in all Walker fiction. We expect the author to be expert in the categories, to know the background and foundations of the genre. To realize that just because some subgenre is hot it doesn't mean that that is the area to mine—after all, if everyone is doing female p.i.s, doesn't it make more sense to do something that isn't crowded, something that might serve to balance a list, rather than make it top heavy? Finally, don't tell us why your book is going to be a success; instead, show me that you can write and write well. It is your writing, and not your hype that interests us."

☑ ▨ ⊘ Ⓐ **WARNER ASPECT,** Imprint of Warner Books, 1271 Avenue of the Americas, New York NY 10020. Fax: (212)522-7990. Website: twbookmark.com (includes each month's new titles, advice from writers, previous titles and interviews with authors, "hot news," contests). **Acquisitions**: Betsy Mitchell, editor-in-chief. "We're looking for 'epic' stories in both fantasy and science fiction." Publishes hardcover, trade paperback, mass market paperback originals and mass market paperback reprints. **Publishes 2 previously unpublished writers/year.** Distributes titles through nationwide sales force.
• Warner Aspect published *Brown Girl in the Ring*, by Nalo Hopkinson, winner of Locus Award for Best First Novel.
Needs: Fantasy, science fiction. Recently published *The Naked God*, by Peter F. Hamilton (science fiction); and *A Cavern of Black Ice*, by J.V. Jones (fantasy).
How to Contact: Agented fiction only. Reports in 10 weeks on mss.
Terms: Pays royalty on retail price. Offers $5,000-up advance. Publishes ms 14 months after acceptance of ms.
Advice: "Think epic! Our favorite stories are big-screen science fiction and fantasy, with plenty of characters

and subplots. Sample our existing titles—we're a fairly new list and pretty strongly focused." Mistake writers often make is "hoping against hope that being unagented won't make a difference. We simply don't have the staff to look at unagented projects."

WARNER BOOKS, Time & Life Building, 1271 Avenue of the Americas, New York NY 10020. (212)522-7200. Publishes hardcover, trade paperback and mass market paperback originals and reprints. Warner publishes general interest fiction. Averages 350 total titles/year.
Imprint(s): Mysterious Press, Warner Aspect.
Needs: Fantasy, mainstream, mystery/suspense, romance, science fiction, thriller. Published *The Simple Truth*, by Daniel Baldaccci; *Nocturne*, by Ed McBain (mystery); *Where the Heart Is*, by Billie Letts; *Alibi*, by Sandra Brown; and *A Walk to Remember*, by Nicholas Sparks.

WESLEYAN UNIVERSITY PRESS, 110 Mount Vernon St., Middletown CT 06459. (860)685-2420.
Acquisitions: Suzanna Tamminen, editor-in-chief. "We are a scholarly press with a focus on cultural studies." Publishes hardcover originals. **Publishes 10% previously unpublished writers/year.** Publishes 20-25 titles/ year.
Needs: Science fiction. "We publish very little fiction." Recently published *Dhalgren*, by Samuel R. Delany.
How to Contact: Submit outline. Reports in 1 month on queries, 3 months on mss. Simultaneous submissions OK.
Terms: Pays 6% royalty. Publishes ms 1 year after acceptance. Writer's guidelines for #10 SASE. Book catalog free.
Advice: Audience is the informed general reader to specialized academic reader.

WILSHIRE BOOK CO., 12015 Sherman Rd., North Hollywood CA 91605-3781. (818)765-8579. Fax: (818)765-2922. E-mail: mpowers@mpowers.com. Website: www.mpowers.com (includes types of books published). **Acquisitions:** Melvin Powers, publisher. Marcia Powers, senior editor (adult fables). Estab. 1947. "You are not only what you are today, but also what you choose to become tomorrow. We are looking for adult fables that teach principles of psychological growth." Publishes trade paperback originals and reprints. **Publishes 80% previously unpublished writers/year.** Publishes 15 titles/year. Distributes titles through wholesalers, bookstores and mail order. Promotes titles through author interviews on radio and television.
Needs: Allegories that teach principles of psychological/spiritual growth or offer guidance in living. Min. 30,000 words. Published *The Princess Who Believed in Fairy Tales*, by Marcia Grad; *The Knight in Rusty Armor*, by Robert Fisher. Allegories only. No standard novels or short stories.
How to Contact: Requires synopsis, 3 sample chapters and SASE. Accepts complete mss. Unsolicited queries/ correspondence by e-mail OK. Reports in 2 months.
Terms: Pays standard royalty. Publishes ms 6 months after acceptance.
Advice: "We are vitally interested in all new material we receive. Just as you hopefully submit your manuscript for publication, we hopefully read every one submitted, searching for those that we believe will be successful in the marketplace. Writing and publishing must be a team effort. We need you to write what we can sell. We suggest that you read the successful books mentioned above or others that are similar: *Greatest Salesman in the World*, *Illusions*, *Way of the Peaceful Warrior*, *Celestine Prophecy*. Analyze them to discover what elements make them winners. Duplicate those elements in your own style, using a creative new approach and fresh material, and you will have written a book we can successfully market."

THE WOMEN'S PRESS, 34 Great Sutton St., London EC1V 0LQ England. **Acquisitions**: Elsbeth Lindner, Kirsty Dunseath and Charlotte Cole, fiction editors. Publishes approximately 50 titles/year.
Needs: "Women's fiction, written by women. Centered on women. Theme can be anything—all themes may be women's concern—but we look for political/feminist awareness, originality, wit, fiction of ideas. Includes literary fiction, crime, and teenage list *Livewire*."
Terms: Writers receive royalty, including advance.
Advice: Writers should ask themselves, "Is this a manuscript which would interest a feminist/political press?"

THE WONDERLAND PRESS, INC., 160 Fifth Avenue, Suite 723, New York NY 10010. (212)989-2550. E-mail: litraryagt@aol.com. Contact: John Campbell. Estab. 1985. Member of the American Book Producers Association. Represents 24 clients. Specializes in high-quality nonfiction, illustrated, reference, how-to and entertainment books. "We welcome submissions from new authors, but proposals must be unique, of high commercial interest and well written." Currently handles: 90% nonfiction books; 10% novels.
  ● The Wonderland Press is also a book packager and "in a very strong position to nurture strong proposals all the way from concept through bound books."
Needs: Considers these fiction areas: action/adventure; literary; picture book; thriller.
How to Contact: Send outline/proposal with SASE. Reports in 3-5 days on queries; 1-2 weeks on mss.
Needs: Does not want to receive poetry, memoir, children or category fiction.
Terms: Agent receives 15% commission on domestic sales. Offers written contract. 30-90 days notice must be

given to terminate contract. Offers criticism service, included in 15% commission. Charges for photocopying, long-distance telephone, overnight express-mail, messengering.

Tips: "Follow your talent. Write with passion. Know your market. Submit work in final form; if you feel a need to apologize for its mistakes, typos, or incompleteness, then it is not ready to be seen. We want to see your best work."

WORLDWIDE LIBRARY, Division of Harlequin Books, 225 Duncan Mill Rd., Don Mills, Ontario M3B 3K9 Canada. (416)445-5860. **Acquisitions:** Feroze Mohammed, senior editor/editorial coordinator. Estab. 1979. Large commercial category line. Publishes paperback originals and reprints. Averages 72 titles, all fiction, each year. "Mystery program is reprint; no originals please."

Imprint(s): Worldwide Mystery; Gold Eagle Books.

Needs: "Action-adventure series and future fiction."

How to Contact: Query first or submit outline/synopsis/series concept or overview and sample chapters. SAE. U.S. stamps do not work in Canada; use International Reply Coupons or money order. Reports in 10 weeks on queries. Simultaneous submissions OK.

Terms: Advance and sometimes royalties; copyright buyout. Publishes ms 1-2 years after acceptance.

Advice: "Publishing fiction in very selective areas."

WRITE WAY PUBLISHING, P.O. Box 441278, Aurora CO 80044. (800)680-1493. Fax: (303)617-1440. E-mail: writewy@aol.com. Website: www.writewaypub.com (includes first chapter, reviews and sales information on every title). **Acquisitions:** Dorrie O'Brien, owner/editor. Estab. 1993. "Write Way is a book-only, fiction-only small press concentrating on genre publications such as mysteries, soft science fiction, fairy tale/fantasy and horror/thrillers. Small press. Publishes hardcover originals. Average print order: 2,500. First novel print order: 1,000. Published new writers within the last year. **Publishes 40% previously unpublished writers/year.** Averages 10-12 total titles, all fiction, each year. Distributes titles through Midpoint Trade Books. Promotes titles through newspapers, magazines and trade shows.

Needs: Fantasy/fairy tale, horror (soft), mystery/suspense (amateur sleuth, cozy, police procedural, private eye/hardboiled), psychic/supernatural, science fiction (soft/sociological, space trilogy/series). Published *The Dead Past*, by Tom Piccirilli (mystery); *Fury's Children*, by Seymour Shubin (psychological suspense); and *Cheat the Devil*, by Jane Rubino (mystery).

How to Contact: Query with short outline/synopsis and 1-2 sample chapters. Include estimated word count, bio (reasonably short) and list of publishing credits. Send SASE for reply, return of ms or send a disposable copy of ms. Agented fiction 10%. Reports in 2-4 weeks on queries; 6-8 months on mss. Simultaneous submissions OK. Often comments on rejected mss.

Terms: Pays royalties of 8% minimum; 10% maximum. Does not pay advances. Sends galleys to author. Publishes ms within 3 years after acceptance. Writer's guidelines for SASE.

Advice: "Always have the query letter, synopsis and the first chapters edited by an unbiased party prior to submitting them to us. Remember: first impressions are just as important to a publisher as they might be to a prospective employer."

WRITERS PRESS, 2309 Mountainview Dr., Suite 220, Boise ID 83706. (208)327-0566. Fax: (208)327-3477. E-mail: writers@cyberhighway.net. Website: www.writerspress.com. **Acquisitions:** John Ybarra, editor. "By publishing high-quality children's literature that is both fun and educational, we are striving to make a difference in today's educational world." Publishes hardcover and trade paperback originals. **Publishes 60% previously unpublished writers/year.** Publishes 3-4 titles/year.

Needs: Adventure, historical, juvenile, picture books, young adult, inclusion, special education. Published *Eagle Feather*, by Sonia Gardner, illustrated by James Spurlock (picture book).

How to Contact: Query first. Reports in 1 month on queries, 4 months on mss.

Terms: Pays 4-12% royalty or makes outright purchase of up to $1,500. Publishes ms 6 months after acceptance. Writer's and catalog guidelines free.

YORK PRESS LTD., 152 Boardwalk Dr., Toronto, Ontario M4L 3X4 Canada. (416)690-3788. Fax: (416)690-3797. E-mail: yorkpress@sympatico.ca. Website: www3.sympatico.ca/yorkpress. **Acquisitions:** Dr. S. Elkhadem, general manager/editor. Estab. 1975. "We publish scholarly books and creative writing of an experimental nature." Publishes trade paperback originals. **Publishes 10% previously unpublished writers/year.** Publishes 10 titles/year.

Needs: "Fiction of an experimental nature by well-established writers." Published *The Moonhare*, by Kirk Hampton (experimental novel).

How to Contact: Query first. Reports in 2 months.

Terms: Pays 10-20% royalty on wholesale price. Publishes ms 6 months after acceptance.

ZEBRA BOOKS, Imprint of Kensington, 850 Third Ave., 16th Floor, New York NY 10022. (212)407-1500. Publisher: Lynn Brown. **Acquisitions:** Ann Lafarge, editor. "Zebra Books is dedicated to women's fiction, which includes, but is not limited to romance." Publishes hardcover originals, trade paperback and mass market

paperback originals and reprints. **Publishes 5% previously unpublished writers/year.** Publishes 140-170 titles/year.
Needs: Romance, women's fiction. Published *By Candelight*; *Love With a Stranger*, by Janell Taylor (romance); and *Darling Jasmine*, by Bertrice Small.
How to Contact: Query with synopsis and SASE. Not accepting unsolicited submissions. Reports in 1 month on queries, in 3 months on mss. Simultaneous submissions OK.
Terms: Pays variable royalty and advance. Publishes ms 18 months after acceptance. Book catalog for #10 SASE.

ZOLAND BOOKS, INC., 384 Huron Ave., Cambridge MA 02138. (617)864-6252. Fax: (617)661-4998. E-mail: info@zolandbooks.com. Website: www.zolandbooks.com. **Acquisitions:** Roland Pease, publisher/editor. Managing Editor: Michael Lindgren. Marketing Director: Stephen Hull. Estab. 1987. "We are a literary press, publishing poetry, fiction, nonfiction, photography, and other titles of literary interest." Publishes hardcover and paperback originals and reprints. Books: acid-free paper; sewn binding; some with illustrations. Average print order: 2,000-5,000. **Publishes 1-2 previously unpublished writers/year.** Averages 14 total titles each year. Distributes titles through Consortium Book Sales and Distribution. Promotes titles through catalog, publicity, advertisements, direct mail.
   • Awards include: Hemingway/PEN Award, Kafka Prize for Women's Fiction, National Book Award finalist, *New York Times* Notable Book, *Publishers Weekly* Best Book of the Year.
Needs: Contemporary, feminist, literary, African-American interest. Recently published *Courting Disaster*, by Julie Edelson (literary novel); *A Citizen of the World*, by Maclin Bocock (short stories); and *The Long Run of Myles Mayberry*, by Alfred Acorn (literary novel).
How to Contact: Accepts unsolicited mss. Query first, then send complete ms with cover letter. SASE. Reports in 4-6 weeks on queries; 3-6 months on mss.
Terms: Pays royalties of 5-8%. Average advance: $1,500; negotiable (also pays author's copies). Sends galleys to author. Publishes ms 1-2 years after acceptance. Book catalog for 6×9 SAE and 2 first-class stamps.
Advice: "Be original."

ZONDERVAN, Division of HarperCollins Publishers, 5300 Patterson SE, Grand Rapids MI 49530. (616)698-6900. E-mail: @zph.com. Website: www.zondervan.com. **Acquisitions:** Manuscript Review Editor. Estab. 1931. "Our mission is to be the leading Christian communication company meeting the needs of people with resources that glorify Jesus Christ and promote biblical principles." Large evangelical Christian publishing house. Publishes hardcover and paperback originals and reprints, though fiction is generally in paper only. Published new writers in the last year. Averages 150 total titles, 15-20 fiction titles each year. Average first novel: 5,000 copies.
Needs: Adult fiction, (mainstream, biblical, historical, suspense, mystery), "Inklings-style" fiction of high literary quality. Christian relevance necessary in all cases. Will *not* consider collections of short stories. Recently published *Glimpses of Truth*, by Jack Ceranaugh (historical); *Seasons Under Heaven*, by Terri Blackstock and Bev Lattaye (mainstream); and *Tonopah*, by Christopher Lane (suspense).
How to Contact: Accepts unsolicited mss. Write for writer's guidelines first. Include #10 SASE. Query or submit outline/synopsis and 2 sample chapters. Reports in 6-8 weeks on queries; 3-4 months on mss.
Terms: "Standard contract provides for a percentage of the net price received by publisher for each copy sold, usually 14-17% of net."
Advice: "Almost no unsolicited fiction is published. Send plot outline and one or two sample chapters. Editors will *not* read entire manuscripts. Your sample chapters will make or break you."

MICROPRESSES

The very small presses listed here are owned or operated by one to three people, often friends or family members. Some are cooperatives of writers and most of these presses started out publishing their staff members' books or books by their friends. Even the most successful of these presses are unable to afford the six-figure advances, lavish promotional budgets and huge press runs possible in the large, commercial houses. These presses can easily be swamped with submissions, but writers published by them are usually treated as "one of the family."

ACME PRESS, P.O. Box 1702, Westminster MD 21158. (410)848-7577. **Acquisitions:** Ms. E.G. Johnston, managing editor. Estab. 1991. "We operate on a part-time basis and publish 1-2 novels/year." Publishes hardcover and paperback originals. **Published new writers within the last year.** Averages 1-2 novels/year.
Needs: Humor/satire. "We publish only humor novels, so we don't want to see anything that's not funny." Published *She-Crab Soup*, by Dawn Langley Simmons (fictional memoir/humor); *Biting the Wall*, by J. M. Johnston (humor/mystery); and *Hearts of Gold*, by James Magorian (humor/mystery).
How to Contact: Accepts unsolicited mss. Query first, submit outline/synopsis and first 50 pages or submit complete ms with cover letter. Include estimated word count with submission. SASE for reply, return of ms or

send a disposable copy of ms. Agented fiction 25%. Reports in 1-2 weeks on queries; 4-6 weeks on mss. Simultaneous submissions OK. Always comments on rejected mss.

Terms: Provides 25 author's copies; pays 50% of profits. Sends galleys to author. Publishes ms 1 year after acceptance. Writer's guidelines and book catalog for #10 SASE.

N 🌐 THE AMERICAN UNIVERSITY IN CAIRO PRESS, 113 Kasr El Aini St., Cairo Egypt. Fax: +20 2 356-1440. E-mail: aucpress@aucegypt.edu. Website: www.aucpress.com. **Acquisitions**: Werner Mark Linz, director; Pauline Wickham, senior editor, translated Arabic fiction. Averages 2-4 fiction titles/year.
Needs: "Egyptology, Middle East studies, Islamic art and architecture, social anthropology, Arabic literature in translation. The press is the sole agent of Nobel laureate for literature, Naguib Mahjouz. Recently published *City of Love and Ashes*, by Yusef Idris; *The Tent*, by Miral Tahawy; and *The Other Place*, Ibrahim Abdel Meguid. The press publishes the journal *Cario Papers*, a quarterly monograph series in social studies. Special series, joint imprints, and/or copublishing programs: Numerous copublishing programs with U.S. and U.K. university presses and other U.S. and European publishers." Length: 30,000 words minimum; 75,000 words maximum.
How to Contact: Send a cover letter and entire ms.
Advice: "Manuscripts should deal with Egypt and/or Middle East."

🗾 ◖ ANVIL PRESS, Bentall Centre, P.O. Box 1575, Vancouver, British Columbia V6C 2P7 Canada; or Lee Building, #204-A, 175 E. Broadway, Vancouver, British Columbia V5T 1W2 Canada. (604)876-8710. Fax: (604)879-2667. E-mail: subter@pinc.com. **Acquisitions**: Brian Kaufman and Dennis E. Bolen, fiction editors. Estab. 1988. "1½ person operation with volunteer editorial board. Anvil Press publishes contemporary fiction, poetry and drama, giving voice to up-and-coming Canadian writers, exploring all literary genres, discovering, nurturing and promoting new Canadian literary talent." Publishes paperback originals. Books: offset or web printing; perfect-bound. Average print order: 1,000-1,500. First novel print order: 1,000. **Plans 2 first novels this year.** Averages 2-3 fiction titles each year. Often comments on rejected mss. Also offers a critique service for a fee.
● Anvil Press's *Monday Night Man*, by Grant Buday, was nominated for the City of Vancouver Book Prize. *Ivanhoe Station*, by Lyle Neff, was nominated for the British Columbia Book Prize in 1998.
Needs: Experimental, contemporary modern, literary, short story collections. Recently published *White Lung*, by Grant Buday (novel); *Aairborne Photo*, by Clint Burnham (contemporary); *The Underwood*, by P.G. Tarr; and *Salvage King, Ya*, by Mark Jarman (novel). Published new writers within the last year. Publishes the Anvil Pamphlet series: shorter works (essays, political tracts, polemics, treatises and works of fiction that are shorter than novel or novella form).
How to Contact: Canadian writers only. Accepts unsolicited mss. Query first or submit outline/synopsis and 1-2 sample chapters. Include estimated word count and bio with submission. Send SASE for reply, return of ms or a disposable copy of ms. Reports in 1 month on queries; 2-4 months on mss. Simultaneous submissions OK (please note in query letter that manuscript is a simultaneous submission).
Terms: Pays royalties of 15% (of final sales). Average advance: $400. Sends galleys to author. Publishes ms within contract year. Book catalog for 9×12 SASE and 2 first-class stamps.
Advice: "We are only interested in writing that is progressive in some way—form, content. We want contemporary fiction from serious writers who intend to be around for awhile and be a name people will know in years to come."

ARTEMIS CREATIONS PUBLISHING, 3395 Nostrand Ave., 2-J, Brooklyn NY 11229-4053. Fax: (718)648-8215. E-mail: artemispub@aol.com. Website: members.aol.com/artemispub. **Acquisitions**: Shirley Oliveira, president. Publishes trade paperback originals and reprints. Publishes 3-4 titles/year.
Imprint(s): Fem Suprem; *Matriarch's Way* (journal).
Needs: Erotica, experimental, fantasy, feminist, gothic, horror, occult, religious, science fiction. Recently published *Welts*, by Gloria and Dave Wallace (erotica).
How to Contact: Query or submit synopsis and 3 sample chapters with SASE. Reports in 3 days. Simultaneous submissions OK. *Charges $15 reading fee.* "We use part-time, freelance readers. The fee goes to them."
Terms: No advance. Publishes ms 18 months after acceptance. Writer's guidelines for #10 SASE.
Advice: "Our readers are looking for strong, powerful feminine archetypes in fiction and nonfiction—goddess, matriarchy, etc."

🌐 ◖ ◎ ATTIC PRESS, Crawford Business Park, Crosses Green, Cork, Ireland. Contact: Managing Editor. E-mail: e.ocarrol@ucc.ie. Website: www.iol.ie/~atticirl/. Averages 2-3 fiction titles/year. "Attic Press is an independent, export-oriented, Irish-owned publishing house with a strong international profile. The press specializes in the publication of women's fiction, politics, sociology, narratives and current affairs." Publishes an award-winning series of teenage fiction, Bright Sparks. Query. "Unsolicited proposals will be returned without acknowledgement." Pays advance on signing contract and royalties. Write for catalog.

N ◖ Ⓐ BANCROFT PRESS, P.O. Box 65360, Baltimore MD 21209. (410)358-0658. Fax: (410)764-1967. E-mail: sazizi@bancroftpress.com. Website: www.bancroftpress.com (includes booklist, guidelines and mission statement). **Acquisitions:** Sarah Azizi, editor. Estab. 1991. "Small independent press publishing literary and commercial fiction, often by journalists." Publishes hardcover and paperback originals. First novel print order: 5,000-7,500. **Published 4 new writers within the last year.** Plans 2 first novels in 2000. Averages 4-6 total titles, 2-4 fiction titles/year. Sometimes critiques/comments on rejected mss.

Needs: Ethnic/multicultural (general), family saga, feminist, gay, glitz, historical, horror (dark fantasy, futuristic, psychological, supernatural), humor satire, lesbian, literary, mainstream, military/war, mystery/suspense (amateur sleuth, cozy, police procedural, private eye/hardboiled), New Age/mystic, psychic/supernatural, regional, science fiction (hard science/technological, soft/sociological), short story collections, thriller/espionage, translations, western (frontier saga, traditional), young adult/teen (historical, problam novels, series). Recently published *Those Who Trespass*, by Bill O'Reilly (thriller); *The Re-Appearance of Adam Weldser*, by Scott Fuqua (literary); and *Malicious Intent*, by Mike Walker (Hollywood).

How to Contact: Accepts unsolicited mss. Query with outline/synopsis and 3 sample chapters. Unsolicited queries/correspondence by e-mail and fax OK. Include bio and list of publishing credits. Send SASE for reply, return of ms or send a disposable copy of ms. Agented fiction 100%. Reports in 3 months. Simultaneous submissions OK. No electronic submissions.

Terms: Pays royalties of 8% minimum; 12½% maximum. Average advance: $7,500. Sends galleys to author. Publishes ms 18 months after acceptance. Writer's guidelines and book catalog free.

Advice: "Be patient, send a sample, know your book's audience."

BEGGAR'S PRESS, 8110 N. 38th St., Omaha NE 68112-2018. (402)455-2615. Publisher: Richard R. Carey. Imprints are Lamplight, Raskolnikov's Cellar, Beggar's Review. Estab. 1952. Small independent publisher. "We are noted for publishing books and periodicals in the styles of the great masters of the past. We publish three periodicals (literary) and novels, poetry chapbooks, and collections of short stories." Publishes paperback originals. Books: 20 lb. paper; offset; perfect binding; some illustrations. Average print order: 500-700. First novel print order: 500. **Published new writers within the last year.** Plans 2 first novels this year. Averages 3-5 total titles, 4 fiction titles/year. Charges "reasonable rate" for complete ms critique. Member of International Association of Independent Publishers and Federation of Literary Publishers.

Needs: Adventure, historical (general, 1800's), horror (psychological), humor/satire, literary, mystery/suspense, romance (gothic, historical), short story collection. Published *An Evening Studying the Anatomy of Jena Kruger*, by Richard Carey; *My Doorknob Is Female*, by Diane Jensen; and *Seduction of An Olive*, by Debra Knight. Plans series.

How to Contact: "We are not accepting queries or manuscripts at the present time. We are completely scheduled for the next two years." No unsolicited submissions.

Payment/Terms: Pays royalties of 10% minimum; 15% maximum; provides 2 author's copies

BILINGUAL PRESS/EDITORIAL BILINGÜE, Hispanic Research Center, Arizona State University, Tempe AZ 85287-2702. (480)965-3867. Editor: Gary Keller. Estab. 1973. "University affiliated." Publishes hardcover and paperback originals, and reprints. Books: 60 lb. acid-free paper; single sheet or web press printing; case-bound and perfect-bound; illustrations sometimes; average print order: 4,000 copies (1,000 case-bound, 3,000 soft cover). **Published new writers within the last year.** Plans 2 first novels this year. Averages 12 total titles, 6 fiction each year. Sometimes comments on rejected ms.

Needs: Ethnic, literary, short story collections, translations. "We are always on the lookout for Chicano, Puerto Rican, Cuban-American or other U.S.-Hispanic themes with strong and serious literary qualities and distinctive and intellectually important themes. We have been receiving a lot of fiction set in Latin America (usually Mexico or Central America) where the main character is either an ingenue to the culture or a spy, adventurer or mercenary. We don't publish this sort of 'Look, I'm in an exotic land' type of thing. Also, novels about the Aztecs or other pre-Columbians are very iffy." Published *MotherTongue*, by Demetria Martinez (novel); *Rita and Los Angeles*, by Leo Romero (short stories); and *Sanctuary Stories*, by Michael Smith (stories and essays).

How to Contact: Query first. SASE. Reports in 3 weeks on queries; 2 months on mss. Simultaneous submissions OK.

Terms: Pays royalties of 10%. Average advance $500. Provides 10 author's copies. Sends galleys to author. Publishes ms 1 year after acceptance. Writer's guidelines available. Book catalog free.

Advice: "Writers should take the utmost care in assuring that their manuscripts are clean, grammatically impeccable, and have perfect spelling. This is true not only of the English but the Spanish as well. All accent marks need to be in place as well as other diacritical marks. When these are missing it's an immediate first indication that the author does not really know Hispanic culture and is not equipped to write about it. We are interested in publishing creative literature that treats the U.S.-Hispanic experience in a distinctive, creative, revealing way. The kinds of books that we publish we keep in print for a very long time irrespective of sales. We are busy establishing and preserving a U.S.-Hispanic canon of creative literature."

BOOKS FOR ALL TIMES, INC., Box 2, Alexandria VA 22313. Website: www.bfat.com. **Acquisitions:** Joe David, publisher/editor. Estab. 1981. One-man operation. Publishes hardcover and paperback originals. Books: 60 lb. paper; offset printing; perfect binding. Average print order: 1,000. "No plans for new writers at present." Has published 2 fiction titles to date.

Needs: Contemporary, literary, short story collections. "No novels at the moment; hopeful, though, of someday soon publishing a collection of quality short stories. No popular fiction or material easily published by the major or minor houses specializing in mindless entertainment. Only interested in stories of the Victor Hugo or Sinclair Lewis quality."

How to Contact: Query first with SASE. Simultaneous submissions OK. Reports in 1 month on queries. Occasionally critiques rejected mss.

Terms: Pays negotiable advance. "Publishing/payment arrangement will depend on plans for the book." Book catalog free with SASE.

Advice: Interested in "controversial, honest books which satisfy the reader's curiosity to know. Read Victor Hugo, Fyodor Dostoyevsky and Sinclair Lewis, for example. I am actively looking for short articles (up to 3,000 words) on contemporary education. I prefer material critical of the public schools when documented and convincing."

N ◨ ◎ BREAKAWAY BOOKS, P.O. Box 24, Halcottsville NY 12438. Phone/fax: (212)898-0408. E-mail: editorial@breakawaybooks.com. Website: www.breakawaybooks.com. **Acquisitions**: Garth Battista, fiction editor (sports fiction). Estab. 1994. "Small press specializing in fine literary books on sports." Publishes hardcover originals and paperback reprints. **Published 3 new writers within the last year.** Plans 1 first novel in 2000. Averages 9 total titles, 8 fiction titles/year. Sometimes critiques/comments on rejected mss.

Needs: Sports.

How to Contact: Accepts unsolicited mss. Query with outline/synopsis and sample chapters. Submit complete ms with cover letter. Unsolicited queries/correspondence by e-mail OK. Include bio and list of publishing credits. Send SASE for reply, return of ms or send disposable copy of ms. Agented fiction 50%. Simultaneous and electronic submissions OK.

Terms: Pays royalties of 7.5% minimum; 10% maximum. Sends galleys to author. Publishes ms 9-18 months.

◨ BROWNOUT LABORATORIES, RD 2, Box 5, Little Falls NY 13365. **Acquisitions:** Michael Hanna, fiction editor. Estab. 1994. "Brownout Laboratories is a cultural metaproject that publishes the works of some of the young intelligentsia. Some of the common themes of the books are: the present condition of nihilism, ecology, counterculture, contemporary music, vegetarianism and writing." Publishes paperback originals. Books: 100% recycled, 75% post-consumer content paper; high-quality photocopying; hand-sewn saddle-stitch binding. Average print order: 50. Averages 2-3 total titles, 1 fiction title/year.

Needs: Erotica (no gratuitous violence), ethnic/multicultural, experimental, feminist, gay and bisexual (but not queer), lesbian and bisexual (but not queer), literary, mystery/suspense (hardboiled), science fiction (must be of high enough quality to be of interest to critics who have no particular penchant for science fiction), short story collections, translations (if translated by the author from French, German, Spanish or Croatian/Bosnian). Recently published *Fighting Gravity*, by Sarah Posner.

How to Contact: Accepts unsolicited mss. Query with cover letter, outline/synopsis, curriculum vitae and first 10 pages. Send SASE for reply, return of ms or send a disposable copy of ms. Reports in 3 weeks on queries; 2 months on mss. Simultaneous submissions OK. Always critiques or comments on rejected ms.

Terms: Pays royalty of 20%. "We publish the book and then pay royalties on each copy sold." Publishes ms 1-3 months after acceptance. Book catalog free.

◨ CALYX BOOKS, P.O. Box B, Corvallis OR 97339-0539. (503)753-9384. Fax: (541)753-0515. E-mail: calyx@proaxis.com. **Acquisitions**: M. Donnelly, director; Micki Reaman, managing editor. Estab. 1986. "Calyx exists to publish women's literary and artistic work and is committed to publishing the works of all women, including women of color, older women, lesbians, working-class women, and other voices that need to be heard." Publishes hardcover and paperback originals. Books: offset printing; paper and cloth binding. Average print order: 4,000-10,000 copies. First novel print order: 4,000-5,000. **Publishes approximately 1 previously unpublished writer/year.** Averages 3 total titles each year. Distributes titles through Consortium Book Sales and Distribution. Promotes titles through author reading tours, print advertising (trade and individuals), galley and review copy mailings, presence at trade shows, etc.

   ● Past anthologies include *Forbidden Stitch: An Asian American Women's Anthology*; *Women and Aging*; *Present Tense: Writing and Art by Young Women*; and *A Line of Cutting Women*.

Needs: Contemporary, ethnic, experimental, feminist, lesbian, literary, short story collections, translations. Published *Into the Forest*, by Jean Hegland (women's literature); *Switch*, by Carol Guess (lesbian literature); and *The End of the Class Wars*, by Catherine Brady (short stories).

How to Contact: Send SASE for submission guidelines. E-mail for guidelines OK.

Terms: Pays royalties of 10% minimum, author's copies, (depends on grant/award money). Average advance: $200-500. Sends galleys to author. Publishes ms 2 years after acceptance. Writer's guidelines for #10 SASE. Book catalog free on request.

Advice: "Read our book catalog and journal. Be familiar with our publications. Follow our guidelines. Please do *not* query. Pay attention to when we're open: In 2000 from January 1 to March 15. Post mark dates."

CHRISTCHURCH PUBLISHERS LTD., 2 Caversham St., London S.W.3, 4AH UK. Fax: 0044 171 351 4995. Fiction Editor: James Hughes. Averages 25 fiction titles/year. "Miscellaneous fiction, also poetry. More 'literary' style of fiction, but also thrillers, crime fiction etc." Length: 30,000 words minimum. Send a cover letter, synopsis, brief summary. "Preliminary letter and *brief* synopsis favored." Pays advance and royalties. "We have contacts and agents worldwide."

CROSS-CULTURAL COMMUNICATIONS, 239 Wynsum Ave., Merrick NY 11566-4725. (516)868-5635. Fax: (516)379-1901. E-mail: cccmia@juno.com. Editorial Director: Stanley H. Barkan. Estab. 1971. "Small/alternative literary arts publisher focusing on the traditionally neglected languages and cultures in bilingual and multimedia format." Publishes chapbooks, magazines, anthologies, novels, audio cassettes (talking books) and video cassettes (video books, video mags); hardcover and paperback originals. Publishes new women writers series, Holocaust series, Israeli writers series, Dutch writers series, Asian-, African- and Italian-American heritage writers series, Polish writers series, Armenian writers series, Native American writers series, Latin American writers series.

  ● Authors published by this press have received international awards including Nat Scammacca who won the National Poetry Prize of Italy and Gabriel Preil who won the Bialik Prize of Israel.

Needs: Contemporary, literary, experimental, ethnic, humor/satire, juvenile and young adult folktales, and translations. "Main interests: bilingual short stories and children's folktales, parts of novels of authors of other cultures, translations; some American fiction. No fiction that is not directed toward other cultures. For an annual anthology of authors writing in other languages (primarily), we will be seeking very short stories with original-language copy (other than Latin script should be print quality 10/12) on good paper. Title: *Cross-Cultural Review Anthology: International Fiction 1*. We expect to extend our *CCR* series to include 10 fiction issues: *Five Contemporary* (Dutch, Swedish, Yiddish, Norwegian, Danish, Sicilian, Greek, Israeli, etc.) *Fiction Writers*." Published *Sicilian Origin of the Odyssey*, by L.G. Pocock (bilingual English-Italian translation by Nat Scammacca); *Sikano L'Americano!* and *Bye Bye America*, by Nat Scammacca; and *Milkrun*, by Robert J. Gress.

How to Contact: Accepts unsolicited mss. Query with SAE with $1 postage to include book catalog. "Note: Original language ms should accompany translations." Simultaneous and photocopied submissions OK. Reports in 1 month.

Terms: Pays "sometimes" 10-25% in royalties and "occasionally" by outright purchase, in author's copies— "10% of run for chapbook series," and "by arrangement for other publications." No advance.

Advice: "Write because you want to or you must; satisfy yourself. If you've done the best you can, then you've succeeded. You will find a publisher and an audience eventually. Generally, we have a greater interest in nonfiction novels and translations. Short stories and excerpts from novels written in one of the traditional neglected languages are preferred—with the original version (i.e., bilingual). Our kinderbook series will soon be in production with a similar bilingual emphasis, especially for folktales, fairy tales, and fables."

DAN RIVER PRESS, Subsidiary of Conservatory of American Letters, P.O. Box 298, Thomaston ME 04861. (207)354-0998. Fax: (207)354-8953. E-mail: cal@americanletters.org. Website: www.americanletters.org. **Acquisitions**: Richard S. Dawburg III, fiction editor. Estab. 1979. "Small press publishing fiction and biographies." Publishes hardcover and paperback originals. Books: offset printing; perfect binding. Average print order: 1,000; first novel print order: 1,000. **Published 2 new writers within the last year.** Plans 1 first novel this year. Averages 3 total titles, 3 fiction titles/year.

Needs: Adventure, experimental, family saga, fantasy, historical (general), horror, humor satire, literary, mainstream, regional, romance, science fiction, short story collections, thriller/espionage, western, young adult/teen (adventure, historical). Publishes *Dan River Anthology 2000*. Writers may submit to Anthology Editor. Recently published *Wytopitloc*, by Ed Raur Jr. (hunting stories).

How to Contact: Accepts unsolicited mss. Submit complete ms with cover letter. Unsolicited queries/correspondence by e-mail and fax OK. Include estimated word count, Social Security number and list of publishing credits. Send SASE for reply, return of ms or send disposable copy of ms. Reports in 2 weeks on queries; 1 month on mss. Simultaneous submissions OK.

Terms: Pays royalties of 10% minimum; 15% maximum; negotiable advance. Sends galleys to author. Publishes ms 9-15 months after acceptance. Writer's guidelines for #10 SASE. Book catalog for 7½×10 SASE. "Both are free at our website."

DARKTALES PUBLICATIONS, P.O. Box 675, Grandview MO 64030. (718)889-3405. E-mail: dave @darktales.com. Website: www.darktales.com (includes an entire Web community for horror writers and fans—horror discussion listserve, webring, chatroom, fiction bulletin boards, book catalog, interviews and commentary in e-zine, *Sinister Element*, and more). **Acquisitions**: Butch Miller, fiction editor (noir, speculative fiction, horror); David Nordhaus (dark fantasy, horror). Estab. 1998. Small independent publisher. "Our publishing focus is on horror, from extreme to esoteric. We hope to add some truly wonderful new titles to the body of horror. What makes us unique is that so many of the authors we are working with are new names to the horror scene. We hope to make them succeed, or at least help them on their way." Publishes paperback originals. Books: trade paper; limited runs; perma-bound. Average print order: 750. **Publishes 50% new writers last year.** Plans 3 first novels this year. Plans 5 total titles, all fiction, this year. Always comments on rejected ms. Member of the Horror Writers Association.

Needs: Comics/graphic novels, erotica, horror (dark fantasy, futuristic, psychological, supernatural, extreme). "We are really searching for that new voice in horror or dark fiction." Publishes horror anthology, *Asylum Anthology* Series. Writers may submit to Anthology Editor Victor Heck. See website for details. Recently published *Scary Rednecks and Other Inbred Horrors*, by David Whitman and Weston Osche; *Demonesque*, by Steven L. Climer. Publishes the *Sinister Element* series.

How to Contact: Does not accept unsolicited mss. Query first with outline/synopsis and 3-5 sample chapters. Include estimated word count, bio, list of publishing credits, proposal if new concept. SASE for reply. Agented fiction 20%. Reports in 3-5 weeks on queries. Simultaneous submissions OK.

Terms: Pays royalties of 6-8%. Advance is negotiable. Publishes ms within 1 year of acceptance. Guidelines available on website.

Advice: "We are a new, but highly motivated, company who not only wants to work with newer writers, but who is bent on helping them succeed and in perpetuating horror as a genre. Don't assume anything with us. Send us your best work-not a first draft or something hurriedly thrown together. We're looking for new horror angles and new horror voices. Our mission statement: We are bringing horror to the world."

⊠◯ THE DESIGN IMAGE GROUP INC., 231 S. Frontage Rd., Suite 17, Burr Ridge IL 60521. (630)789-8991. Fax: (630)789-9013. Website: www.designimagegroup.com (includes book catalog and links). **Acquisitions**: Editorial Committee. Estab. 1998. "Horror/genre fiction micropublisher distributing exclusively through normal trade channels." Publishes paperback originals. Books: offset paper; offset printing; perfect binding. Average print order: 5,000. **Published 4 new writers within the last year.** Plans 4 first novels this year. Averages 6 total titles, 6 fiction titles/year. Often critiques/comments on rejected mss.
  ● The Design Image Group Inc. has been an International Horror Guild Award Nominee for First Novel and HWA Stoker Award Nominee for first novel. They are members of the Publishers Marketing Association and Horror Writers Association.

Needs: Horror, supernatural. Looking for "traditional supernatural horror fiction." Publishes horror anthology. Guidelines announced in writers' and genre publications in advance. Recently published *Carmilla: The Return*, by Kyle Marffin (vampire novel); *Night Prayers*, by P.D. Cacek (vampire novel); *Storytellers*, by Julie Anne Parks (horror novel); and *Shadow of the Beast*, by Margaret Carter (werewolf novel).

How to Contact: Accepts unsolicited mss. Query letter only first. Query with outline/synopsis and 3 sample chapters. Agented fiction 25%. Reports in 3-4 weeks. Simultaneous submissions OK.

Terms: Pays royalties of 10% minimum; 12% maximum. Average advance: $3,000. Provides 12 author's copies. Sends galleys to author. Publishes ms 3-4 months after acceptance. Writer's guidelines for SASE. Book catalog for 6×9 SASE.

Advice: "We publish traditional supernatural horror ONLY—vampires, ghosts, werewolves, witches, etc. No thrillers, serial killers, etc. Please send for writers guidelines they're quite specific and helpful."

⊠◑◎ DOWN THERE PRESS, Subsidiary of Open Enterprises Cooperative, Inc., 938 Howard St., #205, San Francisco CA 94103. (415)974-8985 ext 205. Fax: (415)974-8989. E-mail: goodvibe@well.com. Website: www.goodvibes/dtp/dtp.html (includes titles, author bios, excerpts, guidelines, calls for submissions). Imprints are Yes Press and Red Alder Books. Managing Editor: Leigh Davidson. Estab. 1975. Small independent press with part-time staff; part of a large worker-owned cooperative. Publishes paperback originals. Books: Web offset printing; perfect binding; some illustrations. Average print order: 5,000. First novel print order: 3,000-5,000. **Published new writers within the last year.** Averages 1-2 total titles, 1 fiction title each year. Sometimes critiques or comments on rejected mss. Member of Publishers Marketing Association and Northern California Book Publicity and Marketing Association.

Needs: Erotica, feminist, lesbian. Published *Herotica 6*, edited by Marcy Sheiner (anthology); *Sex Spoken Here: Erotic Reading Circle Stories*, edited by Carol Queen and Jack Davis (anthology); and *Sex Toy Tales*, edited by A. Semans and Cathy Winks.

How to Contact: Accepts unsolicited mss. Submit partial ms with cover letter, synopsized and table of contents (short stories for anthologies only). Include estimated word count. Accepts queries and correspondence by fax. Send SASE for reply, return of ms or send disposable copy of ms. Reports in 6-9 months on mss. Simultaneous submissions OK.

Terms: Pays royalties and author's copies. Sends galleys to author. Publishes ms 18 months after acceptance. Writer's guidelines and book catalog for #10 SASE.

⊠✂◯ EDGE SCIENCE FICTION AND FANTASY PUBLISHING, Box 75064, Cambrian P.O., Calgary, Alberta T2K 6J8 Canada. (403)254-0159. Fax: (403)254-0456. E-mail: editor@edgewebsite.com. Website: www.edgewebsite.com (includes writer's guidelines, upcoming books, book descriptions, sample chapters, author bios, writer's resources). **Acquisitions**: Jessie Tambay, Mike Bone, Roxanne Bennett (fiction editors). Estab. 1997. Small independent publisher of science fiction and fantasy novels. Publishes hardcover originals. Books: offset printing; case binding. Average print order: 5,000. **Plans 2 first novels in 2000.** Publishes 1-6 total titles, all fiction, each year. Sometimes critiques or comments on rejected ms. Member of the Publishers Marketing Association and Independent Publishers Association of Canada.

Needs: Fantasy, horror (dark fantasy), religious (religious fantasy), romance (futuristic/time travel), science fiction. Recently published *The Black Chalice*, by Marie Jakober (historical fantasy); *Throne Price*, by Lynda Jane Williamson and Alison Sinclair (science fiction epic, first novel), *Keeper's Child*, Leslie Davis (science fiction, first novel).

How to Contact: Accepts unsolicited mss. Query with outline/synopsis and 3 sample chapters. Include estimated word count and list of publishing credits. Send SASE for reply or send disposable copy of the ms. Agented fiction 20%. Reports in 3-12 weeks on queries, 6-20 weeks on mss. Simultaneous submissions OK.

Terms: Pays royalties of 10% plus negotiable advance. Sends prepublication galleys to author. Publishes ms within 3 years of acceptance. Writer's guidelines for SASE or SAE with 1 IRC.

Advice: "Polish your work before you submit it."

N: GASLIGHT, Empire Publishing Services, P.O. Box 1344, Studio City CA 91614. (818)784-8918. **Acquisitions:** Ian Wilkes, fiction editor (Sherlock Holmes only). Estab. 1960. Publishes hardcover and paperback originals and reprints. Publishes 4 novels/year.

Needs: Sherlock Holmes only.

How to Contact: Does not accept unsolicited mss. Query first. Include estimated word count, bio, list of publishing credits and a sample of the material. SASE for reply. Agented fiction 25%. Reports in 2 weeks on queries.

Terms: Pays royalties plus advance; negotiable. Sends prepublication galleys to author. Publishes ms 7 months-2 years after acceptance.

Advice: "Send only what we ask for."

N: GOLDENISLE PUBLISHERS, INC., 2395 Hawkinsville Hwy., Eastman GA 31023. (912)374-9455. Fax: (912)374-9720. **Acquisitions:** Tena Ryals and Fern Smith (Maryland office). Estab. 1998. "Small independent publisher." Publishes hardcover and paperback originals and hardcover reprints. Average print order: 1,000; first novel print order: 1,000. **Published 0 new writers within the last year.** Plans 1 first novel this year. Averages 3-5 total titles, 3 fiction titles/year. Sometimes critiques or comments on rejected mss.
• Member of PMA.

Needs: Historical (general), humor satire, mainstream, religious (inspirational), romance (historical), western (frontier saga). Recently published *The Third Season*, by Jack P. Jones (mainstream, contemporary); *Plantation*, by Fern Smith-Brown (historical romance); and *Brasada*, by Don Johnson (historical western).

How to Contact: Does not accept unsolicited mss. For return of ms "must include SASE." Query letter only first. Include estimated word count, 1 page bio and list of publishing credits. Send SASE for reply. Reports in 3-6 weeks on queries; 4 months on mss.

Terms: Pays royalties. Sends galleys to author. Publishes ms 1-2 years after acceptance.

Advice: "We do not publish material containing the 'f-word,' hard profanity, explicit sex or 'thrown-in violence.' Write what you enjoy writing and revise until it touches your heart."

N: GRADE SCHOOL PRESS, 3266 Yonge St., #1829, Toronto, Ontario M4N 3P6 Canada. Phone/fax: (416)784-2883. E-mail: jlastman@compuserve.com. Administrative Assistant: Ziny. Estab. 1990. "Part-time/small press." Publishes paperback originals. Averages 1-3 total titles, 0-1 fiction title/year. Member CANSCAP.

Needs: Children's/juvenile (historical, series, sports, hi/lo), family saga, feminist, historical (children's only), religious (Jewish only, children's), young adult/teen (easy-to-read, historical, problem novels, series), education (special needs, testing/advocacy).

How to Contact: Accepts unsolicited mss. Query with outline/synopsis and several sample chapters. Include estimated word count, list of publishing credits and general author goals. Send a disposable copy of ms. Sometimes critiques or comments on rejected mss.

Payment/Terms: Provides author's copies; payment depends on grants/awards. Sends galleys to author. Publishes ms 6-12 months after acceptance.

Advice: "Be interesting, original, polished, practical."

GRIFFON HOUSE PUBLICATIONS, 1401 Pennsylvania Ave., Wilmington DE 19806. Phone/fax: (302)656-3230. E-mail: griffonhse@aol.com. Director: John H. Ryan. Estab. 1976. Small press. Publishes paperback originals and reprints.

Needs: Contemporary, drama, ethnic (open), experimental, history, international politics, literary, multinational

---

INTERESTED IN A PARTICULAR GENRE? Check our sections for: **Mystery/Suspense**, page 46; **Romance**, page 55; **Science Fiction & Fantasy**, page 67.

theory, national sovereignty, poetry, political analysis/theory, reprints, theory, translations.
How to Contact: Query with SASE. No simultaneous submissions. Reports in 1 month.
Terms: Pays in author's copies. No advance.

HANDSHAKE EDITIONS, Atelier A2, 83 rue de la Tombe Issoire, 75014 Paris France. Fax: 33-1-4320-4195. E-mail: jim_haynes@wanadoo.fr. Editor: Jim Haynes. Publishes 4 story collections or novels/year. "Only face-to-face submissions accepted. More interested in 'faction' and autobiographical writing." Pays in copies. Writers interested in submitting a manscript should "have lunch or dinner with me in Paris."

HARRIS LITERARY AGENCY, P.O. Box 6023, San Diego CA 92166. (619)697-0600. Fax: (619)697-0610. E-mail: n@adnc.com. **Acquisitions:** Barbara Harris, president. Estab. 1996.
Needs: Adventure, mainstream/contemporary, mystery/suspense, science fiction. "No horror or erotica." Length: 60,000 words average; 45,000 words minimum.
How to Contact: Query first by e-mail or fax. Include 400-word bio and list of publications. Reports in 3 weeks on queries; 1 month on mss. Send SASE for reply, return of ms or send a disposable copy of ms. Simultaneous and electronic submissions OK.
Terms: Sends galleys to author. Not copyrighted.
Advice: "Looks for originality, quality writing and good plot. Avoid submitting unedited work."

HEARTSONG PRESENTS, Subsidiary of Barbour Publishing, Inc., P.O. Box 719, Uhrichsville OH 44683. (614)922-6045. Fax: (614)922-5948. E-mail: barbourbooks.com. Estab. 1992. Book publisher with book club. Member of Evangelical Christian Publishers Association.
Needs: Romance (contemporary, gothic, historical, romantic suspense, inspirational). Published work by Colleen L. Reece, Tracie J. Peterson, Peggy Darty, Sally Laity, Yvonne Lehman, Loree Lough, DeWanna Pace and Norma Jean Lutz.
How to Contact: Query with synopsis. Include estimated word count, list of publishing credits. Send SASE for reply, return of ms or send disposable copy of ms. Reports in 3 months on queries; 3-5 months on mss. Simultaneous submissions OK.
Terms: Pays average advance: $2,000. No royalty. Provides 10 author's copies. Sends galleys to author on request. Writer's guidelines free for #10 SASE and 1 IRC.
Advice: "We look for sweet romances that emphasize the need for God as part of lasting romance. We like a strong, entertaining story that has an inspirational theme gently woven throughout. Don't dwell on the physical side of romance. Don't preach your inspirational message, but demonstrate it through the lives of your characters. Study our guidelines and published titles."

HEMKUNT, Publishers A-78 Naraina Industrial Area Ph.I, New Delhi India 110028. **Acquisitions:** G.P. Singh, managing director; Deepinder Singh/Arvinder Singh, export directors.
Needs: "We would be interested in novels, preferably by authors with a published work. Would like to have distribution rights for US, Canada and UK beside India."
How to Contact: Send a cover letter, brief summary, 3 sample chapters (first, last and one other chapter). "Writer should have at least 1-2 published novels to his/her credit."
Terms: Catalog on request.

HOLLOW EARTH PUBLISHING, P.O. Box 1355, Boston MA 02205-1355. (617)746-3130. E-mail: hep2@hotmail.com. **Acquisitions:** Helian Grimes, editor/publisher. Estab. 1983. "Small independent publisher." Publishes hardcover and paperback originals and reprints. Books: acid-free paper; offset printing; Smythe binding.
Needs: Comics/graphic novels, fantasy (sword and sorcery), feminist, gay, lesbian, literary, New Age/mystic/spiritual, translations. Looking for "computers, Internet, Norse mythology, magic." Publishes various computer application series.
How to Contact: Contact by e-mail only. Does not accept unsolicited mss. Include estimated word count, 1-2 page bio, list of publishing credits. Agented fiction 90%. Reports in 2 months. Accepts disk submissions.
Terms: Pays in royalties. Sends galleys to author. Publishes ms 6 months after acceptance.
Advice: Looking for "less fiction, more computer information."

ILLUMINATION PUBLISHING CO., P.O. Box 1865, Bellevue WA 98009. (425)644-7185. Fax: (425)644-9274. E-mail: liteinfo@illumin.com. Website: www.illumin.com. **Acquisitions:** Ruth Thompson, editorial director. Estab. 1987. "Illumination Arts is a small company publishing high quality, enlightened children's picture books with spiritual and inspirational values." Publishes hardcover originals. Publishes 2 children's picture book/year. **Publishes 1-2 previously unpublished writers/year.** Distributes titles through Book World, New Leaf, De Vorss, Book People, Quality, Ingram, Baker & Taylor, Koen Pacific and bookstores. Promotes titles through direct mailings, website, book shows, flyers and posters, catalogs. Publisher arranges author and illustrators signings but expert authors/illustrators to actively promote. Enters many book award events. Member of Book Publishers of the Northwest.
• Illumination Publishing's *SAI Prophecy* was selected as best novel and *Dreambirds* was selected as

best children's book by The Coalition of Visionary Retailers at The International New Age Trade Show, 1998. *The Right Touch* was a finalist in 1998 Small Press Awards and a winner of the 1999 Ben Franklin Award (parenting).

Needs: Children's/juvenile (adventure, inspirational, preschool/picture books). Recently published *The Right Touch*, by Sandy Kleven and *Sky Castle*, by Sandra Hankey (children's picture books).

How to Contact: Accepts unsolicited mss. Query first or submit complete ms with cover letter. Unsolicited queries/correspondence by e-mail and fax OK. Include estimated word count, Social Security number and list of publishing credits. Send SASE for reply or return of ms. Reports in 1 week on queries; 1 month on mss. Simultaneous submissions OK. Often critiques or comments on rejected mss.

Terms: Pays royalties. Sends galleys to author. Publishes ms 18 months-2 years after acceptance. Writer's guidelines for SASE.

Advice: "Submit full manuscripts, neatly typed without grammatical or spelling errors. Expect to be edited many times. Be patient. We are very *painstaking*."

IVY LEAGUE PRESS, INC., P.O. Box 3326, San Ramon CA 94583-8326. (925)736-0601 or 800-IVY-PRESS. Fax: (925)736-0602 or (888)IVY-PRESS. E-mail: ivyleaguepress@worldnet.att.net. **Acquisitions**: Maria Thomas, editor. Publishes hardcover and paperback originals. Specializes in medical thrillers. Books: perfect binding. First novel print order: 5,000. Plans 1 novel this year. Averages 2 total titles, 1-2 fiction titles/year. Distributes titles through Baker & Taylor and Ingram. Promotes titles through TV, radio and print.

Needs: Mystery/suspense(medical). Published *Allergy Shots*, by Litman.

How to Contact: Accepts unsolicited mss. Query with outline/synopsis. Include estimated word count, bio and list of publishing credits. Send SASE or a disposable copy of the ms. Reports in 2 months on queries. Electronic submissions OK. Always critiques or comments on rejected mss.

Payment/Terms: Royalties vary. Sends galleys to author.

Advice: "If you tell a terrific story of medical suspense, one which is hard to put down, we may publish it."

JESPERSON PRESS LTD., 39 James Lane, St. John's, Newfoundland A1E 3H3 Canada. (709)753-0633. Editor: JoAnne Soper-Cook. Midsize independent publisher. Publishes hardcover and paperback originals. Averages 7-10 total titles, 1-2 fiction titles each year. Sometimes comments on rejected mss.

Needs: Solid contemporary fiction by Newfoundland authors about Newfoundland, preferably novel-length or short story collection. Not interested in young adult, childrens' or poetry of any kind.

How to Contact: Query with synopsis and SASE (Canadian postage or IRCs, please) only. No unsolicited mss. Reports in 3 months or less.

Terms: Pays negotiable royalties. Sends galleys to author. Book catalog free.

KAWABATA PRESS, Knill Cross House, Knill Cross, Millbrook, Torpoint, Cornwall PL10 1DX England. Fiction Editor: Colln Webb.

Needs: "Mostly poetry—but prose should be realistic, free of genre writing and clichés and above all original in ideas and content." Length: 2,000-4,000 words (for stories).

How to Contact: "Don't forget return postage (or IRC)."

Terms: Writers receive half of profits after print costs are covered. Write for guidelines and book list.

Advice: "Avoid clichés; avoid obnoxious plots; avoid the big themes (life, death, etc.); be original; find a new angle or perspective; try to be natural rather than clever; be honest."

LEAPFROG PRESS, P.O. Box 1495, 110 Commercial St., Wellfleet MA 02667-1495. (508)349-1925. Fax: (508)349-1180. E-mail: leapfrog@capecod.net. Website: www.leapfrogpress.com (includes description of press, mission statement, writer's guidelines, e-mail link, description of books, sample poems, link to distributor, cover designs). **Acquisitions:** David Witkowsky, acquisitions editor. Estab. 1996. "We publish book-length literary fiction and literate nonfiction that reflects a strong personal story. We publish books that are referred to by the large publishers as midlist but which we believe to be the heart and soul of literature. We're a small shop, so the small number of books we choose receive a lot of attention." Publishes hardcover and paperback originals and paperback reprints. Books: acid-free paper; sewn binding. Average print order: 3,000. First novel print order: 4,000 (average). Averages 2-3 total titles, 1-2 fiction titles/year. Distributes titles through Consortium Book Sales and Distribution, St. Paul, MN. Promotes titles through all national review media, bookstore readings, author tours, website, radio shows, chain store promotions, advertisements.

 • Member of the Publishers Marketing Association, Bookbuilders of Boston and PEN.

Needs: Erotica, ethnic (Jewish), feminist, gay, humor/satire, lesbian, literary, mainstream/contemporary, regional (Cape Cod), religious (Jewish). "Genres often blur; we're interested in good writing. We'd love to see memoirs as well as fiction that comments on the world through the lens of personal, political or family experience." Published *The Kitchen Man*, by Ira Wood; *The Dangerous Age*, by Anette Williams Jaffee; and *Leo@Fergusrules.-com*, by Anne Taugherlini.

How to Contact: Query first with outline/synopsis and 2-4 sample chapters (50 pages). Does not accept unsolicited mss. Unsolicited queries/correspondence by e-mail OK. Include bio, list of publishing credits and a brief description of the book with submission. Send SASE for reply, return of ms or send a disposable copy of ms. Reports in 2-3 months on queries; 6 months on mss. Simultaneous submissions OK. Sometimes critiques or comments on rejected mss.

Payment/Terms: Pays royalties of 4% minimum; 8% maximum. Offers negotiable advance. Provides negotiable number of author's copies. Sends galleys to author. Publishes ms 1-2 years after acceptance.

Advice: "Send us a manuscript that educates us somewhat about our world and does not dwell on personal problems only. And, it must be well written. We strongly push sales of secondary rights (translations, foreign sales) and expect the author and publisher to participate equally in the proceeds. Writers must be willing to accept and incorporate editorial advice and cannot shirk their responsibility to publicize their own work by giving readings, contacting book stores, drumming up local media attention, etc. We believe in strong marketing with an author who can publicize him/herself."

LEMEAC EDITEUR INC., 1124 Marie Anne Est, Montreal, Québec H2J 2B7 Canada. (514)524-5558. Fax: (514)524-3145. Directeur Littéraire: Pierre Filion. Estab. 1957. Publishes paperback originals. Books: offset #2 paper; offset printing; allemand binding; color/cover illustration. Average print order: 1,000. First novel print order: 1,000. **Published new writers within the last year.** Plans at least 1 first novel every year. Averages 25 total titles, 20 fiction titles each year. Often critiques or comments on rejected mss.

Needs: Literary, romance (contemporary, futuristic/time travel, historical), short story collections, translations. Writers submit to editor. Published *Un objet de beauté*, by Michel Tremblay (novel); and *L'Empeinte de l'ange*, by Nancy Huston (novel).

How to Contact: Accepts unsolicited mss. Submit complete ms with cover letter. Send a disposable copy of ms. Agented fiction 10%. Reports in 3 months on queries; 6 months on mss. No simultaneous submissions.

Terms: Pays royalties of 10%. Sends galleys to author. Publishes ms 1-2 years after acceptance.

LIGHTWAVE PUBLISHING INC., P.O. Box 160, Maple Ridge, British Columbia V2X 7G1 Canada. (804)462-7890. Fax: (604)462-8208. E-mail: christie@lightwavepublishing.com. Website: www.lightwavepublishing.com (includes book catalogs, children's activities, articles). **Acquisitions**: Christie Bowler, fiction editor (children's). Estab. 1991. "Small award-winning independant publisher of Christian children's and parenting material." Publishes hardcover originals.

● Lightwave has received three Angel Awards.

Needs: Children's/juvenile (religious), religious (children's religious, general religious). "We only hire 'work-for-hire' and look for good writers willing to work to detailed specifications."

How to Contact: Does not accept unsolicited mss. Query letter only first. Include bio and list of publishing credits. Send SASE with Canadian stamps for reply, return of ms or send disposable copy of ms. Reports in 1 month on queries. No simultaneous submissions.

Terms: Pays a lump sum. Finds writers on a work-for-hire basis. Publishes ms 8 months after acceptance. Writer's guidelines free. Book catalog on website.

Advice: "Writer must be a team player, willing to work for hire (no royalties, limited accreditation), versatile, professional, work well to instructions and deadlines."

THE LILLIPUT PRESS, 62-63 Sitric Rd., Arbour Hill, Dublin 7 Ireland. Fiction Editor: Antony Farrell. Averages 2-3 fiction titles/year. Length: 50,000 words minimum. Send a cover letter, brief summary and 1 sample chapter. Pays small advance and royalties. "Send double-spaced hard copy." Write for catalog.

LUCKY HEART BOOKS, Subsidiary of Salt Lick Press, Salt Lick Foundation, Inc., 1900 West Hwy. 6, Waco TX 76712. **Acquisitions**: James Haining, editor/publisher. Estab. 1969. Small press with significant work reviews in several national publications. Publishes paperback originals and reprints. Books: offset/bond paper; offset printing; hand-sewn or perfect-bound; illustrations. Average print order: 500. First novel print order: 500.

Needs: Open to all fiction categories. Published *Catch My Breath*, by Michael Lally.

How to Contact: Accepts unsolicited mss. SASE. Agented fiction 1%. Reports in 2 weeks to 4 months on mss. Sometimes critiques or comments on rejected mss.

Terms: Pays 10 author's copies. Sends galleys to author.

Advice: "Follow your heart. Believe in what you do. Use the head, but follow the heart."

THE LUTTERWORTH PRESS, P.O. Box 60, Cambridge CB1 2NT England. Fax: +44(0)1223 366951. E-mail: publishing@lutterworth.com. Website: lutterworth.com (includes catalogs, company résumé, order forms, selection of books with extra details). **Acquisitions**: Adrian Brink, fiction editor. "Two hundred-year-old small press publishing wide range of adult nonfiction, religious and children's books."

Imprint(s): Acorn Editions.

Needs: The only fiction we publish is for children: picture books (with text from 0-10,000 words), educational, young novels, story collections. Also nonfiction as well as religious children's books." Recently published *Carol Corsa and Mickey Morgan* by Claire Rosemary Jane (children's); and *Bravo, Persevere*, by Robert Spencer (children's).

How to Contact: Send synopsis and sample chapter. Unsolicited queries/correspondence by e-mail and fax OK. "Send IRCs. English language is universal, i.e., mid-Atlantic English."

Terms: Pays royalty.

MID-LIST PRESS, Jackson, Hart & Leslie, Inc., 4324-12th Ave. S., Minneapolis MN 55407-3218. (612)822-3733. Fax: (612)823-8387. E-mail: guide@midlist.org. Website: www.midlist.org (includes writer's guidelines, history/mission, authors and titles, ordering information). **Acquisitions**: Marianne Nora, associate publisher; Lane Stiles, senior editor. Estab. 1989. Nonprofit literary small press. Publishes hardcover originals and paperback originals and hardcover reprints. Books: acid-free paper; offset printing; perfect or Smyth-sewn binding. Average print order: 2,000. **Publishes 2 previously unpublished authors/year.** Plans 1 first novel this year. Averages 3 fiction titles each year. Rarely comments on rejected mss. Distributes titles through Small Press Distribution, Baker & Taylor, Ingram, Midwest Library Service, Every Pratt and Bookman. Promotes titles through publicity, direct mail, catalogs, reviews and awards, author's events.

● The publisher's philosophy is to nurture "mid-list" titles—books of literary merit that may not fit "promotional pigeonholes"—especially by writers who were previously unpublished.

Needs: General fiction. No children's/juvenile, romance, young adult, religious. Recently published *The View From Below: Stories*, by Lindsey Crittenden (short fiction collection); *The Last Cigarette*, by Jason Waldrop (novel); and *The Hand Before the Eye*, by Donald Friedman (novel). Publishes First Series Award for the Novel and First Series Award for Short Fiction. *There is a $20 reading fee for a First Series Award but no charge for publication.*

How to Contact: Accepts unsolicited mss. Query first for guidelines or visit website at www.midlist.org. Include #10 SASE. Send a disposable copy of the ms. Agented fiction less than 10%. Reports in 1-3 weeks on queries; 1-3 months on mss. Simultaneous submissions OK.

Terms: Pays royalty of 40% minimum; 50% maximum of profits. Average advance: $1,000. Sends galleys to author. Publishes ms 6-12 months after acceptance. Writer's guidelines for #10 SASE.

Advice: "Write first for guidelines before submitting a query, proposal or manuscript. And take the time to read some of the titles we've published."

MILKWEEDS FOR YOUNG READERS, Imprint of Milkweed Editions, 430 First Ave. N., Suite 668, Minneapolis MN 55401-1743. (612)332-3192. Fax: (612)332-6248. **Acquisitions:** Elisabeth Fitz, children's reader. Estab. 1984. "Milkweeds for Young Readers are works that embody humane values and contribute to cultural understanding." Publishes hardcover and trade paperback originals. **Publishes 25% previously unpublished writers/year.** Publishes 3 titles/year.

Needs: For ages 8-12: adventure, animal, fantasy, historical, juvenile and mainstream/contemporary. Recently published *The Spider's Web*, by Laura E. Williams; *No Place*, by Kay Hangaard; and *Treasure of Panther Peak*, by Aileen Kilgore Henderson.

How to Contact: Send copy of complete ms. Agented fiction 30%. Reports in 2-6 months on mss. Simultaneous submissions OK.

Terms: Pays 7½% royalty on retail price. Advance varies. Publishes ms 1 year after acceptance. Writer's guidelines for #10 SASE. Book catalog for $1.50.

MISTY HILL PRESS, 5024 Turner Rd., Sebastopol, CA 95472. (707)823-7437. **Acquisitions**: Sally C. Karste, managing editor. Estab. 1985. Two person operation on a part-time basis. Publishes paperback originals. Books: illustrations; average print order: 2,000; first novel print order: 500-1,000. **Plans 1 first novel this year.** Publishes 1 title each year.

Needs: Juvenile (historical). Looking for "historical fiction for children, well researched for library market." Published *Trails to Poosey*, by Olive R. Cook (historical fiction); and *Tales Fledgling Homestead*, by Joe Armstrong (nonfiction portraits).

How to Contact: Accepts unsolicited mss. Submit outline/synopsis and sample chapters. Reports within weeks. Simultaneous submissions OK. Sometimes critiques rejected mss; *$15/hour charge for critiques.*

Terms: Pays royalties of 5%. Sends prepublication galleys to author. Writer's guidelines and book catalog for SASE (or IRC).

MOUNTAIN STATE PRESS, 2300 MacCorkle Ave. SE, Charleston WV 25304. (304)357-4767. Fax: (304)357-4715. E-mail: msp1@newwave.net. **Acquisitions**: Lisa Contreras. Estab. 1978. "A small nonprofit press run by a Board of 13 members who volunteer their time. We specialize in books about West Virginia or by authors from West Virginia." Publishes paperback originals and reprints. **Published new writers within the last year.** Plans 2-3 first novels this year. Averages 3 total titles, 1-2 fiction titles each year. Promotes titles through newspapers, book signings and mailings.

Needs: Family saga, historical (West Virginia), military/war, New Age/mystic/spiritual, religious. Currently compiling an anthology. Recently published *The Roads That Brought Us Home*, by Morris, Edward, David and Roger (Appalachian memoir); *Reflections of a Nonagenarian*, by Sidney M. Kleeman (memoir-poetry); and *Mom & Ramps Forever*, by Barbara Beury McCallum (cookbook humor-Appalachian).

How to Contact: Accepts unsolicited mss. Query with outline/synopsis and 3 sample chapters or submit complete ms with cover letter. Include estimated word count and bio. Send SASE for reply, return of ms or send disposable copy of ms. Reports in 6 months on mss. Electronic submissions OK. Often critiques or comments on rejected mss.

Terms: Pays royalties.

Advice: "Send your manuscript in and it will be read and reviewed by the members of the Board of Mountain State Press."

N **NEW RIVERS PRESS**, 420 N. Fifth St., Suite 938, Minneapolis MN 55401. Fax: (612)339-9047. E-mail: newrivpr@mtn.org. Website: www.mtn.org/newrivpr (includes authors, titles, covers, guidelines, ordering information). Publisher: C.W. Truesdale. **Acquisitions**: Phyllis Jendro, executive director. Estab. 1968.
Needs: Contemporary, literary, experimental, translations. "No popular fantasy/romance. Nothing pious, polemical (unless other very good redeeming qualities). We are interested in only quality literature and always have been (though our concentration in the past has been poetry)." Recently published *The Dirty Shame Hotel*, by Ron Block; and *American Fiction Volume 10*, by Alan Davis and Michael White.
How to Contact: Query. SASE. Reports in 6 months on queries; within 6 months of query approval on mss. "No multiple submissions, please."
Terms: Minnesota Voices Project Series pays authors $500. Publishes ms 2 years after acceptance. Free book catalog.
Advice: "We read for quality, which experience has taught can be very eclectic and can come sometimes from out of nowhere. We are interested in publishing short fiction (as well as poetry and translations) because it is and has been a great indigenous American form and is almost completely ignored by the commercial houses. Find a *real* subject, something that belongs to you and not what you think or surmise that you should be doing by current standards and fads. Please send SASE for guidelines. At this time we cannot accept unsolicited submissions. You must submit through the Minnesota Voices Project, open to residents of Minnesota or the Headwaters Literary Contest, open to residents of North and South Dakota, Illinois, Michigan, Iowa and Wisconsin."

✓ **♀** **OUR CHILD PRESS**, P.O. Box 74, Wayne PA 19087-0074. (610)964-0606. Fax: (610)964-0938. E-mail: ocp98@aol.com. Website: members.aol/com/ocp98/index.html. CEO: Carol Hallenbeck. Estab. 1984. Publishes hardcover and paperback originals and reprints. **Plans 2 first novels this year.** Plans 2 titles this year.
   • Received the Ben Franklin Award for *Don't Call Me Marda*, by Sheila Welch.
Needs: Adventure, contemporary, fantasy, juvenile (5-9 yrs.), preschool/picture book and young adult/teen (10-18 years). Especially interested in books on adoption or learning disabilities. Published *Don't Call Me Marda*, by Sheila Welch (juvenile); *Oliver—An Adoption Story*, by Lois Wickstrom; and *Blue Ridge*, by Jon Patrick Harper.
How to Contact: Query first. Does not accept unsolicited mss. Reports in 2 weeks on queries; 2 months on mss. Simultaneous submissions OK. Sometimes comments on rejected mss.
Terms: Pays royalties of 5% minimum. Publishes ms up to 6 months after acceptance. Book catalog free.

◐ **OUTRIDER PRESS**, 937 Patricia Lane, Crete IL 60417. (708)672-6630. Fax: (708)672-5820. E-mail: outriderpr@aol.com. Website: www.outriderpress.com (includes info on titles, authors, editors, the Tallgrass Writer's Guild and Chicago's Printers Row Book Fair). **Acquisitions**: Phyllis Nelson, president; Whitney Scott, fiction editor. Estab. 1988. "Small operation to support the voices of freedom and equality regardless of race, gender, orientation. Known for publishing new authors." Publishes trade paper originals. Books: offset printing; perfect binding; average print order: under 5,000. Averages 2-3 total titles, 1 fiction title each year. Distributes titles through Baker & Taylor, amazon.com. Promotes titles through readings, book fairs, publishing parties, book stores, amazon.com and paid ads.
Needs: Feminist, literary, New Age/mystic/spiritual, gay, lesbian, short story collection. No Christian/religious work. Publishes anthologies. "Our anthologies are contests with $250 cash prizes in addition to publication and high-profile readings. We pay our judges and neither seek nor accept federal grant funding because we choose independence and self-sufficiency free of any sort of censorship. Therefore, we charge a $16 reading fee for poetry and fiction." Guidelines for SASE. Recently published *Finding a Home*, by Margaret Glass (humor/satire); *Geese*, by Gregory Stall; and *The Goat Goes Sightseeing*, by Dominique Slavin (humor/satire). Scheduled for 2000 publication: *Feathers, Fins & Fur* (anthology of poetry, short fiction and essays on animals); and *Scratching It Out—A Slightly Irreverent Writer's Manual*; and an anthology on nature and our planet: *Earth Beneath, Sky Beyond*. Scheduled for 2001: *A Kiss is Still a Kiss* (an anthology on love).
How to Contact: Accepts unsolicited mss with SASE. Submit complete ms with cover letter (with short stories). Include estimated word count and list of publishing credits. SASE for return of ms. Reports in 1 month on queries; 2 months on mss. Simultaneous submissions OK. Accepts electronic submissions (3.5 IBM compatible—WordPerfect 5.0, 5.1, 5.2 or 6.0 for DOS; Microsoft Word '97; Rich Text format. No ASCII, no Macs). Sometimes comments on rejected mss; *charges $2 double-spaced pages with 10-page minimum, prepaid and SASE for return*.
Terms: Payment depends on award money. Writer's guidelines for SASE.
Advice: "We have a need for short and super-short fiction with pace and flair and poetry with texture and imagery. Give me fresh, honest writing that reflects craft, focus and sense of place; character-driven writing that studies the terrain of human hearts exploring the non-traditional. Take risks, but know your craft. We favor work that's well-crafted, tightly-written and smoothly flowing. Read our publications to familiarize yourself with our preferences."

N **◐** **PALARI PUBLISHING**, P.O. Box 9288, Richmond VA 23227-0288. (804)264-4615. Fax: (804)266-6709. E-mail: palaripub@aol.com. Website: www.palari.net (includes writer's guidelines). **Acquisitions**: David Smitherman, fiction editor. Estab. 1998. Small publisher specializing in southern mysteries and nonfiction. Publishes hardcover and paperback originals. **Published 3 new writers within the last year.** Plans 2 first novels in 2000. Averages 4 total titles, 2 fiction titles/year. Often critiques or comments on rejected mss.

● Member of Publishers Marketing Association.

Needs: Adventure, erotica, gay, historical, horror, lesbian, literary, mainstream, mystery/suspense, thriller/espionage. Recently published *The Guessing Game*, by Ted Randler (mystery).

How to Contact: Accepts unsolicited mss. Query with outline/synopsis and 3 sample chapters. Query with outline/synopsis and 3 sample chapters. Accepts unsolicited queries/correspondence by e-mail. Include estimated word count, 1 page bio, Social Security number and list of publishing credits. Send SASE for reply, return of ms or send a disposable copy of ms. Reports in 1 month on queries; 2 months on mss. Simultaneous and electronic submissions OK.

Terms: Pays royalties. Publishes ms within 1 year after acceptance. Writer's guidelines available on website.

Advice: "Send a good bio. I'm interested in a writer's experience and unique outlook on life."

⊘ PAPYRUS PUBLISHERS & LETTERBOX SERVICE, (formerly Papyrus Publishers & Letterbox Literary Service), P.O. Box 27383, Las Vegas NV 89126-1383. (702)256-3838. Publicity and Promotion Director: Anthony Wade. **Acquisitions:** Geoffrey Hutchison-Cleaves, editor-in-chief; Jessie Rosé, fiction editor. Estab. London 1946; USA 1982. Mid-size independent press. Publishes hardcover originals. Audio books; average print order 2,500. Averages 3 total titles each year. Promotes titles through mail, individual author fliers, author tours.

Imprint(s): Letterbox Service; Difficult Subjects Made Easy To Understand.

Needs: No erotica, gay, feminist, children's, spiritual, lesbian, political. Published *Is Forever Too Long?* by Heather Latimer (romantic fiction); *Violet*, by Joan Griffith; and *Louis Wain—King of the Cat Artists 1860-1939*, by Heather Latimer (dramatized biography).

How to Contact: "Not accepting right now. Fully stocked."

Terms: Pays royalties of 10% minimum. Advance varies. Publishes ms 1 year after acceptance.

Advice: "Don't send it, unless you have polished and polished and polished. Absolutely no established author sends off a piece that has just been 'written' once. That is the first draft of many!"

◎ PIG IRON PRESS, 26 N. Phelps, Box 237, Youngstown OH 44501-0237. (330)747-6932. Fax: (330)747-0599. **Acquisitons:** Jim Villani, editor/publisher. Small independent publisher. Publishes hardcover originals, paperback originals and reprints. Books: 60 lb. offset paper; offset lithography; paper/casebound; illustration on cover only. Average print order: 1,000. First novel print order: 800. Averages 2 total titles, 1 fiction title/year.

Needs: Adventure, experimental, science fiction, short story collections. Published *The Harvest*, by Judith Hemschemeyer (social realism).

How to Contact: Include estimated word count and list of publishing credits. Send SASE for reply, return of ms or send a disposable copy of ms. Reports in 1 month on queries; 3 months on mss.

Terms: Sends galleys to author. Writer's guidelines for #10 SASE. Book catalog for SASE.

⊘ THE POST-APOLLO PRESS, 35 Marie St., Sausalito CA 94965. (415)332-1458. Fax: (415)332-8045. E-mail: tpapress@dnai.com. Website: www.dnai.com/~tpapress/ (includes excerpts, catalog, reviews and ordering links). **Acquisitions:** Simone Fattal, publisher. Estab. 1982. Specializes in "women writers published in Europe or the Middle East who have been translated into English for the first time." Publishes paperback originals. Book: acid-free paper; lithography printing; perfect-bound. Average print order: 1,000. First novel print order: 1,000. **Published new writers within the last year.** Averages 2 total titles each year. Distributes titles through Small Press Distribution, Berkeley, California. Promotes titles through advertising in selected literary quarterlies, SPD catalog, Feminist Bookstore News & Catalog, ALA and ABA and SF Bay Area Book Festival participation.

Needs: Feminist, lesbian, literary, spiritual, translations. No juvenile, horror, sports or romance. "Many of our books are first translations into English." Recently published *Josef Is Dying*, by Ulla Berkéwicz (novel); and *A Beggar At Damascus Gate*, by Yasmine Zahran.

How to Contact: "The Post-Apollo Press is not accepting manuscripts or queries currently due to a full publishing schedule."

Terms: Pays royalties of 6½% minimum or by individual arrangement. Sends galleys to author. Publishes ms 1½ years after acceptance. Book catalog free.

Advice: "We want to see serious, literary quality, informed by an experimental aesthetic."

▧ THE PRAIRIE PUBLISHING COMPANY, Box 2997, Winnipeg, Manitoba R3C 4B5 Canada. (204)837-7499. Publisher: Ralph Watkins. Estab. 1969. Buys juvenile mss with illustrations. Books: 60 lb. high-bulk paper; offset printing; perfect-bound; line-drawings. Average print order: 2,000. First novel print order: 2,000. **Published work by previously unpublished authors within the last year.**

● **A BULLET INTRODUCES COMMENTS** by the editor of *Novel & Short Story Writer's Market* indicating special information about the listing.

Needs: Open. Published: *The Homeplace*, (historical novel); *My Name is Marie Anne Gaboury*, (first French-Canadian woman in the Northwest); and *The Tale of Jonathan Thimblemouse*.

How to Contact: Query with SASE or IRC. No simultaneous submissions. Reports in 1 month on queries, 6 weeks on mss. Publishes ms 4-6 months after acceptance. Free book catalog.

Terms: Pays 10% in royalties. No advance.

Advice: "We work on a manuscript with the intensity of a Max Perkins. A clean, well-prepared manuscript can go a long way toward making an editor's job easier. On the other hand, the author should not attempt to anticipate the format of the book, which is a decision for the publisher to make. In order to succeed in today's market, the story must be tight, well written and to the point. Do not be discouraged by rejections."

PRESS GANG PUBLISHERS, 1723 Grant St., Vancouver, British Columbia V5L 2Y6 Canada. (604)251-3315. Fax: (604)251-3329. Website: www.pressgang.ca. Estab. 1974. Feminist press, 3 full-time staff. Publishes paperback originals and reprints. Books: paperback; offset printing; perfect-bound. Average print order: 3,500. First novel print order: 2,000.

● Press Gang Publishers received the Lambda Literary Award 1997 for *Beyond the Pale* by Elana Dykewoman and the Ferro-Grumley Prize 1997 for *Sunnybrook: A True Story with Lies* by Persimmon Blackbridge.

Needs: Feminist fiction, nonfiction, mystery, short stories. Subjects and themes include lesbian, women and psychiatry, women and the law, native studies, women of color, erotica, literary. No children/young adult/teen. No poetry. Priority given to Canadian writers. Recently published *Prozac Highway*, by Persimmon Blackridge; *Love Ruins Everything*, by Karen X. Tulchinsky; and *When Fox Is A Thousand*, by Larissa Lai.

How to Contact: Accepts unsolicited mss. Query first. SASE. Reports in 2 months on queries; 3-4 months on mss. Simultaneous submissions OK.

Terms: Pays 8-10% royalties. Sends galleys to author. Book catalog free on request.

PUBLISHERS SYNDICATION, INTERNATIONAL, P.O. Box 6218, Charlottesville VA 22906-6218. (804)964-1194. Fax: (804)964-0096. **Acquisitions:** A. Samuels. Estab. 1979.

Needs: Adventure, mystery/suspense (amateur sleuth, police procedural), thriller/espionage, western (frontier saga).

How to Contact: Accepts unsolicited mss. Submit complete ms with a cover letter. Include estimated word count. Send SASE for reply, return of ms. Reports in 3-4 weeks on mss.

Terms: Pays royalties of .05% minimum; 2% maximum. Advance is negotiable. Writer's guidelines for SASE.

Advice: "The type of manuscript we are looking for is devoid of references which might offend. Remember you are writing for a general audience."

RED SAGE PUBLISHING, INC., P.O. Box 4844, Seminole FL 33775-4844. Phone/fax: (727)391-3847. Website: www.RedSagePub.com (includes authors and guidelines). **Acquisitions:** Alexandria Kendall, editor (romance erotica). Estab. 1955. Publishes "romance erotica or ultra-sensual romance novellas written by romance writers." Publishes paperback originals. Books: perfect binding. **Published 3 new writers within the last year.** Averages 1 total title, 1 fiction title/year.

● Red Sage Publishing received the Fallot Literary Award for Fiction.

Imprint(s): The Secrets Collections (romance, ultra-sensual), edited by Alexandria Kendall.

Needs: Romance (ultra-sensual) novellas for The Secrets Collections: The Best in Women's Sensual Fiction anthology. Length: 20,000-30,000 words. Writers may submit to anthology editor. Recently published *Enslaved*, by Desireé Lindsey (historical/regency); *Blood & Kisses*, by Angela Knight (future/vampire); *The Spy Who Loved Me*, by Jeanie Cesarini (contemporary).

How to Contact: Accepts unsolicited mss. Query with outline/synopsis and 10 sample pages. Include estimated word count and list of publishing credits if applicable. Send SASE for return of ms. Reports in 3 months. Sometimes critiques or comments on rejected ms.

Terms: Pays advance and royalty. Sends galleys to author. Publishes ms 1-2 years after acceptance. Writer's guidelines for SASE.

RENDITIONS, Research Centre for Translation, Institute of Chinese Studies, Chinese University of Hong Kong, Shatin, New Territories, Hong Kong. Phone: 852-26097399. Fax: 852-26035110. E-mail: renditions @cuhk.edu.hk. Website: www.cuhk.edu.hk/renditions (includes sections about Research Centre for Translation, the Chinese University of Hong Kong, *Renditions* magazines, Renditions paperbacks, Renditions books, forthcoming, ordering information and related sites). **Acquisitions:** Dr. Eva Hung, editor. Averages 2 fiction titles annually. "Academic specialist publisher. Distributes titles through local and overseas distributors and electronically via homepage and amazon.com. Promotes titles through homepage, by exchange ads with *China Now* and *China Review International* and paid ads in *Feminist Bookstore News* and *Journal of Asian Studies* of AAS.

Needs: Will only consider English translations of Chinese fiction, prose, drama and poetry. Fiction published either in semiannual journal (*Renditions*) or in the Renditions Paperback series. Recently published *The Cockroach and Other Stories*, by Liu Yichang; *A Girl Like Me and Other Stories* and *Marvels of a Floating City*, by Xi Xi (Hong Kong stories).

How to Contact: For fiction over 5,000 words in translation, sample is required. Sample length: 1,000-2,000 words. Send sample chapter. "Submit only works in our specialized area. One copy of translation accompanied by one copy of original Chinese text." Fax and e-mail requests for information and guidelines OK.

Terms: Pays honorarium for publication in *Renditions*; royalties for paperback series.

RONSDALE PRESS, 3350 W. 21 Ave., Vancouver, British Columbia V6S 1G7 Canada. (604)738-4688. Fax: (604)731-4548. E-mail: ronhatch@pinc.com. Website: www.ronsdalepress.com (includes guidelines, catalog, events). **Acquisitions:** Ronald B. Hatch, president. Estab. 1988. Ronsdale Press is "dedicated to publishing books that give Canadians new insights into themselves and their country." Publishes paperback originals. Books: 60 lb. paper; photo offset printing; perfect binding. Average print order: 1,000. **Publishes 1-2 previously unpublished writers/year.** First novel print order: 1,500. Plans 1 first novel this year. Averages 3 fiction titles each year. Distributes titles through General Distribution and Partners West. Promotes titles through ads in BC Bookworld and Globe & Mail, and interviews on radio.

● Ronsdale author Jamie MacDonald won the Alberta Import Award for *The Ghoul's Night Out*.

Needs: Experimental and literary. Recently published *The City in the Egg*, by Michel Trembly (novel); *Tangled in Time*, by Lynne Fairbridge (children's); and *Daruma Days*, by Terry Watada (short stories).

How to Contact: *Canadian authors only.* Accepts unsolicited mss. Submit outline/synopsis and first 100 pages. SASE. Unsolicited queries/correspondence by e-mail and fax OK. Short story collections must have some magazine publication. Reports in 2 weeks on queries; 2 months on mss. Sometimes comments on rejected mss.

Terms: Pays royalties of 10%. Provides author's copies. Sends galleys to author. Publishes ms 6 months after acceptance.

Advice: "We publish both fiction and poetry. Authors *must* be Canadian. We look for writing that shows the author has read widely in contemporary and earlier literature. Ronsdale, like other literary presses, is not interested in mass-market or pulp materials."

ST. AUGUSTINE SOCIETY PRESS, 68 Kingsway Crescent, Etobicoke, Ontario M8X 2R6 Canada. (416)239-1670. **Acquisitions:** Frances Breckenridge, editor. Estab. 1994. "We are a small press, independent of any church. We seek manuscripts which can expand the circle of light detailed by St. Augustine, either fiction or nonfiction." Publishes paperback originals. Average print order: 500 (depends on the type of final product). Averages 1 total title, variable number of fiction titles each year. Member of Toronto Small Press Group.

Needs: Literary, mainstream/contemporary. Published *Maledetti (The Forsaken)*, by Michael Gualtieri (novel).

How to Contact: Accepts unsolicited mss. Query with outline/synopsis and 2 sample chapters. Send SASE for reply, return of ms or send a disposable copy of ms. Reports in 3 weeks on queries. Simultaneous submissions OK.

Payment/Terms: Negotiable. Sends galleys to author. Publishes ms 6 months after acceptance. Free writer's guidelines.

Advice: "We welcome works by writers who have, through years of study, gained insights into the human condition. A book that is just a 'good read' is of no interest to us."

THE SAVANT GARDE WORKSHOP, a privately-owned affiliate of The Savant Garde Institute, Ltd., P.O. Box 1650, Sag Harbor NY 11963-0060. Phone/fax: (516)725-1414. Website: www.savantgarde.org. **Acquisitions:** Vilna Jorgen II, publisher; Charles Collins, editor, literary futurist; Artemis Smith, editor, multimedia, philosophy, long poems. Estab. 1953. "Literary multiple-media publisher." Publishes hardcover and paperback originals and reprints. First novel print order: 1,000. Promotes archived titles through listing in R.R. Bowker, barnesandnoble.com, Borders.com, savantgarde.org, dustbooks, amazon.com, Baker & Taylor, word-of-mouth in world literary circles and academic/scientific associations and conferences.

● Be sure to look at this publishers' guidelines and webpage. Works could best be described as avant-garde/post modern, experimental.

Needs: Contemporary, futuristic, humanist, literary, philosophical. "We are open to the best, whatever it is." No "mediocrity or pot boilers." Published *01 or a Machine Called SKEETS*, by Artemis Smith (avant-garde). Series include "On-Demand Desktop Collectors' Editions," "Artists' Limited Editions," "Monographs of The Savant Garde Institute."

How to Contact: Do not send unsolicited mss. Query first by e-mail, include outline, URL, and complete verifiable vita. Reports in 6 weeks on queries ("during academic year"); 2 months on invited mss. Sometimes comments on rejected mss.

Terms: Average advance: $500, honorarium (depends on grant/award money). Terms set by individual arrangement with author depending on the book and previous professional experience. Sends galleys to author. Publishes ms 18 months after final acceptance. Writer's guidelines on website.

Advice: "We are looking for extremely rare offerings. We are not interested in the usual commercial submissions. Convince us you are a real artist, not a hacker." Would like to see more "thinking for the 21st Century of Nobel Prize calibre. We're expanding into multimedia, web and CD-ROM co-publishing and seek multitalented authors who can produce and perform their own multimedia work for web and CD-ROM release. We are overbought, understaffed and underfunded—don't expect a quick reply or fast publication date."

N ☐ **SCHERF BOOKS**, Subsidiary of Scherf, Inc., P.O. Box 80180, Las Vegas NV 89180-0180. (702)243-4895. Fax: (702)243-7460. E-mail: ds@scherf.com. Website: www.scherf.com (includes book catalog). **Acquisitions**: Dietmar Scherf (all fiction); Drew Janssen (mainstream, thrillers, mystery/suspense, action/adventure); Gail Kirby (mainstream, romance, family saga, literary, historical). Estab. 1990. "Small publisher concentrating on selective titles. We want to discover the next John Grisham, Danielle Steel, Nora Roberts, Tom Clancy, Michael Crichton, Ernest Hemingway, Anne Rice, Stephen King, etc. Based on our parent company we have vast resources and are known to get behind our books and authors just like a major publishing house would." Publishes hardcover and paperback originals. Average print order: 2,500-50,000; first novel print order: 2,500-20,000. **Plans 10 first novels in 2000.** Averages 4-6 total titles, 2 fiction titles/year.

Needs: Adventure, children's/juvenile (adventure, animal, easy-to-read, fantasy, historical, mystery, series), ethnic/multicultural (general), family saga, fantasy (space fantasy, sword sorcery), historical (general), horror (dark fantasy, futuristic, psychological, supernatural), literary, mainstream, mystery/suspense, religious (inspirational, religious mystery/suspense, religious thriller), romance (contemporary, gothic, historical), science fiction (soft/sociological), thriller/espionage, young adult/teen (adventure, easy-to-read, fantasy/science fiction, historical, horror, mystery/suspense, series). "We consistently look for thrillers and mystery/suspense novels that appeal to a broad audience. But also quality literary fiction is very interesting. We're searching for great unpublished writers and new ideas."

How to Contact: Does not accept or return unsolicted mss. Query letter only first. Include estimated word count and 1 paragraph bio. Send SASE for reply, return of ms or send disposable copy of ms. Reports in 3-4 weeks on queries; 2-4 months on mss. Simultaneous submissions OK. Sometimes critiques or comments on rejected mss.

Terms: Pays royalties of 5% minimum; 15% maximum. Offers negotiable advance. Sends galleys to author. Publishes ms 12-18 months after acceptance.

Advice: "We're concentrating on novels, now. There are many manuscripts out there, but it is difficult to find an excellent piece of work. But once we find that certain exceptional novel, we're getting behind it full throttle. Write the greatest book possible about a story that you love and are truly excited about. Learn some writing skills, especially grammar, characterizations, dialogue or strong narrative qualities, plot, etc. A great story is a beginning, but the writer has to have excellent writing skills. Read books from authors that you like, but develop your own unique voice and style. Polish your manuscript the best way you know how. Have your query letter to the point and no longer than two pages, and always include a SASE. Make sure your manuscript is completed before you contact us, and respond promptly when we request your material."

✔ ☑ ◎ **THE SENIORS MARKET**, 652 Treece Gulch, Stevensville MT 59870. (406)777-5191. Fax: (406)777-7206. E-mail: cotton@bigsky.net. Website: missoula.bigsky.net/coveandcloister (includes guidelines, rates and testimonial). **Acquisitions:** James L. Cotton, editor. "We will consider other submissions, but strongly prefer material written *by* seniors (over 50) *for* seniors."

Needs: Adventure, historical, humor/satire, literary, mainstream/contemporary, mystery/suspense (amateur sleuth, cozy), regional, religious/inspirational, romance (contemporary, gothic, historical, frontier), senior citizen/retirement, sports, westerns (frontier, traditional). Publishes ms 1 year after acceptance. Will consider short story collection for anthology. "*Always comments on rejected ms. Will critique or line edit for a fee.*"

How to Contact: Query first. Inquiries by fax and e-mail OK. Include estimated word count. "Don't submit if you expect us to do this without your involvement." Reports in 3 weeks on queries; 2 months on mss. Send SASE for reply; send a disposable copy of ms. Simultaneous submissions OK.

Terms: Pays advance and royalty. Sends galleys to author. Publishes ms 1 year after acceptance.

Advice: "Remember we prefer senior writers. Whether literary or genre, your work must be genuine, not imitative nor trendy. Time is precious, and if you ask seniors to spend it with your work, it must add meaning and pleasure to their lives."

◆ ☑ **SNOWAPPLE PRESS**, P.O. Box 66024, Heritage Postal Outlet, Edmonton, Alberta T6J 6T4 Canada. (403)437-0191. **Acquisitions**: Vanna Tessier, editor. Estab. 1991. "We focus on topics that are interesting, unusual and controversial." Small independent literary press. Publishes hardcover and paperback originals. Books: non-acid paper; offset printing; perfect binding; illustrations. Average print order: 500. First novel print order: 500. **Plans 1 first novel this year.** Averages 3-4 total titles, 1-2 fiction titles each year. Distributes titles through bookseller and library wholesalers. Promotes titles through press releases and reviews.

Needs: Adventure, children's/juvenile (adventure, fantasy, mystery), experimental, historical, literary, mainstream/contemporary, short story collections, translations, young adult/teen (adventure, mystery/suspense). Recently published *A Crop Of Stones: Graphic Means*, by Vanna Tessier (short stories); *The Last Waltz Of Chopin*, translated by Gilberto Finzi (novel).

How to Contact: Does not accept unsolicited mss. Query first with 1-page cover letter. Include estimated word count, 300-word bio and list of publishing credits. SASE with sufficient IRCs. Reports in 3-4 weeks on queries; 3 months on mss. Simultaneous submissions OK.

Terms: Pays honorarium; provides 10-25 author's copies. Sends galleys to author. Publishes ms 12-18 months after acceptance.

Advice: "Query first to obtain guidelines with proper SASE and IRCs."

THE SPIRIT THAT MOVES US PRESS, P.O. Box 720820-N, Jackson Heights NY 11372-0820. (718)426-8788. E-mail: msklar@mindspring.com. **Acquisitions**: Morty Sklar, editor/publisher. Estab. 1974. Small independent literary publisher. Publishes hardcover and paperback originals. "We do, for the most part, simultaneous clothbound and trade paperbacks for the same title." Books: 60 lb. natural acid-free paper; mostly photo-offset, some letterpress; cloth and perfect binding; illustrations. Average print order: 3,000. Published new writers within the last year. **Publishes 75% previously unpublished writers/year.** Averages 2 fiction titles, mostly multi-author. Distributes titles directly and through wholesalers. Promotes titles through direct mail and review copies, as well as advertisements in trade and consumer publications.

• *Patchwork Of Dreams*, was awarded a grant by New York City Council representative to place this book in several schools for classroom use. The Spirit That Moves Us Press is known for our having been the first U.S. publisher of Jaroslav Seifert, who won the Nobel Prize a year after they published his *The Casting Of Bells*.

Needs: Literary. "Our choice of 'literary' does not exclude almost any other category—as long as the writing communicates on an emotional level, and is involved with people more than things. Nothing sensational or academic." Published *Patchwork of Dreams: Voices from the Heart of the New America*, a multiethnic collection of fiction and other genres; *Editor's Choice III: Fiction, Poetry & Art from the U.S. Small Press*, biennally, and *Free Parking*, all edited by Morty Sklar.

How to Contact: Accepts unsolicited mss. "We are undergoing major changes. Please query before sending work." Query letter only first "unless he/she sees an announcement that calls for manuscripts and gives a deadline." Include estimated word count, bio and whether or not ms is a simultaneous submission. SASE for reply or return of ms. Reports on mss "if rejected, soon; if under consideration, from 1-3 months." Comments on rejected mss "when author requests that or when we are compelled to by the writing (good or bad)."

Terms: Pays royalties of 10% net and authors copies, also honorarium, depends on finances. Sends galleys to author. Publishes up to 1 year after acceptance. Plans and time-frames for #10 SASE "but the guidelines are only for certain books; we don't use general guidelines." Catalog for 6×9 SAE and 2 first-class stamps.

Advice: "We are interested in work that is not only well written, but that gets the reader involved on an emotional level. No matter how skilled the writing is, or how interesting or exciting the story, if we don't care about the people in it, we won't consider it. Also, we are open to a great variety of styles, so just be yourself and don't try to second-guess the editor. You may have our newest collection *Patchwork of Dreams* as a sample, for $10 (regularly $14.50 with postage)."

[N] STORM PEAK PRESS, 2629 Nob Hill Ave. N., Seattle WA 98109. (206)223-0162. Publishes trade paperback originals and reprints. Publishes 3 books/year.

Needs: Recently published *Summer of the Hunters*, by John Dashney.

How to Contact: Query with SASE. Reports in 2 months.

Terms: Pays royalty on retail price or net revenues.

Advice: "Get editorial help before sending a manuscript. Be confident the material is well-written."

STORMLINE PRESS, P.O. Box 593, Urbana IL 61801. Publisher: Raymond Bial. Estab. 1985. "Small independent literary press operated by one person on a part-time basis, publishing one or two books annually." Publishes hardcover and paperback originals. Books: acid-free paper; paper and cloth binding; b&w illustrations. Average print order: 1,000-2,000. First novel print order: 1,000-2,000. **Published new writers within the last year.** Averages 1-2 total titles, all fiction each year.

• Stormline's title, *First Frost*, was selected for a Best of the Small Presses Award.

Needs: Literary. Looks for "serious literary works, especially those which accurately and sensitively reflect rural and small town life." Published *Silent Friends: A Quaker Quilt*, by Margaret Lacey (short story collection).

How to Contact: No longer considers unsolicited submissions.

Terms: Pays royalties of 10% maximum. Provides author's copies. Sends galleys to author. Publishes ms 6-12 months after acceptance. Writer's guidelines for SASE. Book catalog free.

Advice: "We look for a distinctive voice and writing style. We are always interested in looking at manuscripts of exceptional literary merit. We are not interested in popular fiction or experimental writing. Please review other titles published by the press, notably *Silent Friends: A Quaker Quilt*, to get an idea of the type of books published by our press."

[N] TAILORED TOURS PUBLICATIONS, INC., Box 22861, Lake Buena Vista FL 32830. (407)354-3070. Fax: (407)248-8504. **Acquisitions**: Jenny Caneen (Southern fiction); S. Lee (children's fiction, grades 4 and up, Southern themes only). Estab. 1992. "Small independent press specializing in books for children and adults about the South—and particularly Florida." Publishes paperback originals. **Published 3 new writers within the last year.** Plans 2 first novels this year. Averages more than 10 total titles, more than 2 fiction titles/year.

Needs: Children's/juvenile (historical), historical (general, Florida related), mystery/suspense (Florida related), regional (Southern), young adult/teen (adventure, historical). Recently published *Ponce de Leon Sails Again*, by Susan Grohmann (young readers).

How to Contact: Accepts unsolicited mss. Query letter only first or query with outline/synopsis and sample chapters. Send SASE for reply, return of ms or send disposable copy of ms. Reports in 1 month. Simultaneous

submissions OK. Sometimes critiques or comments on rejected mss, if the work is exceptional.
Terms: Pays royalties, depending on title. Sends galleys to author. Publishes ms 2-3 months after final acceptance. Writer's guidelines for SASE. Book catalog for $1, 9 × 12 SAE and 3 first-class stamps.

THIRD WORLD PRESS, P.O. Box 19730, Chicago IL 60619. (773)651-0700. Fax: (773)651-7286. Publisher/Editor: Haki Madhubuti. Fiction Editors: Gwendolyn Mitchell, Melissa Moore. Estab. 1967. Black-owned and operated independent publisher of fiction and nonfiction books about the black experience throughout the Diaspora. Publishes paperback originals. **Plans 1 first novel this year,** as well as short story collections. Averages 10 total titles, 3 fiction titles each year. Average first novel print order 15,000 copies. Distributes titles through Partners, Baker & Taylor and bookstores. Promotes titles through direct mail, catalogs and newspapers.
Needs: Ethnic, historical, juvenile (animal, easy-to-read, fantasy, historical, contemporary), preschool/picture book, short story collections, and young adult/teen (easy-to-read/teen, folktales, historical). Recently published *In the Shadow of the Son*, by Michael Simanga. "We primarily publish nonfiction, but will consider fiction by and about blacks."
How to Contact: Accepts unsolicited mss January and July only. Query or submit outline/synopsis and 1 sample chapter with SASE. Reports in 6 weeks on queries; 5 months on mss. Simultaneous submissions OK. Accepts computer printout submissions.
Terms: Individual arrangement with author depending on the book, etc.

THISTLEDOWN PRESS, 633 Main St., Saskatoon, Saskatchewan S7H 0J8 Canada. (306)244-1722. Fax: (306)244-1762. E-mail: thistle@sk.sympatico.ca. Website: www.thistledown.sk.ca (includes guidelines, catalog, teaching materials). Editor-in-Chief: Patrick O'Rourke. **Acquisitions**: Jesse Stothers. Estab. 1975. Publishes paperback originals—literary fiction, young adult fiction, poetry. Books: Quality stock paper; offset printing; perfect-bound; occasional illustrations. Average print order 1,500-2,000. First novel print order: 1,000-1,500. **Publishes 4 previously unpublished writers/year.** Publishes 12 titles, 6 or 7 fiction, each year. Distributes titles through General Distribution Services. Promotes titles through intensive school promotions, online, advertising, special offers.
 • Thistledown received a Saskatchewan Book Award-Publishing in Education in 1998 for *Takes: Stories for Young Adults*, by R.P. MacIntyre, editor.
Needs: Literary, experimental, short story collections, novels.
How to Contact: Query first with SASE. No unsolicited mss. Unsolicited queries/correspondence by e-mail and fax OK. "We *only* want to see Canadian-authored submissions. We will *not* consider multiple submissions." Photocopied submissions OK. Reports in 2 months on queries. Publishes anthologies. "Stories are nominated." Recently published *Prisoner in a Red-Rose Chain*, by Jeffrey Moore (literary/novel); *Aphid & the Shadow Drinkers*, by Steven Lattey (short fiction); and *The Lady at Batoche*, by David Richards (young adult historical novel). Also publishes The Mayer Mystery Series (mystery novels for young adults) and The New Leaf Series (first books for poetry and fiction—Saskatchewan residents only).
Payment/Terms: Pays standard royalty on retail price. Publishes ms 1-2 years after acceptance. Writer's guidelines and book catalog for #10 SASE.
Advice: "We are primarily looking for quality writing that is original and innovative in its perspective and/or use of language. Thistledown would like to receive queries first before submission—perhaps with novel outline, some indication of previous publications, periodicals your work has appeared in. *We publish Canadian authors only.* We are continuing to publish more fiction and are looking for new fiction writers to add to our list. New Leaf Editions line is first books of poetry or fiction by emerging Saskatchewan authors. Familiarize yourself with some of our books before submitting a query or manuscript to the press."

THORNGATE ROAD, Campus Box 4240, English Department, Illinois State University, Normal IL 61790-4240. (309)438-7705. Fax: (309)438-5414. E-mail: jmelled@ilstu.edu. **Acquisitions**: Jim Elledge, director. Estab. 1996. Thorngate Road is a small, one-person operation publishing cross-genre/experimental texts by gays, lesbians or bisexuals only. Publishes paperback originals. Books: 70 lb. paper; offset printing; saddle stitched; cover only illustrations. Average print order: 300. Averages 2 total titles, 1 prose poetry title/year.
Imprint(s): Berdache Chapbook Series and Frank O'Hara Award Chapbook Series.
 • Thorngate Road also sponsors the Frank O'Hara Award Chapbook Competition.
Needs: Experimental, feminist, gay, lesbian, literary, prose poetry, short shorts. Recently published *Two Girls*, by Kristy Nielsen (prose poems); *Essay with Movable Parts*, by David Trinidad (prose poem); *Miss Molly Rockin'*, by Maureen Seaton (prose poems). Publishes the Frank O'Hara Chapbook Series and Berdache Chapbook Series.
How to Contact: Accepts unsolicited mss only if submitted to the Frank O'Hara Award Chapbook Competition. Query letter only. Unsolicited queries/correspondence by e-mail OK. Include list of publishing credits. Acknowledgements page should accompany submissions to the O'Hara contest. Send SASE for reply. Reports in 1 week on queries. Simultaneous submissions OK.
Terms: Pays in 25 author's copies; pays honorarium of $200 for winners of the Frank O'Hara Award Chapbook Competition. Sends galleys to author. Writer's guidelines free for #10 SASE by September 1 annually.
Advice: Support lesbigay presses and journals by buying copies of their books and issues or with cash donations,

even if the donations are small. Don't support us in hopes of getting your work published but because it's a noble endeavor—and because it's necessary in order to get lesbigay voices heard.

THE TOBY PRESS LTD., 146 New Cavendish St., London W1M 7FG England. Phone: (011)44-188-0001. Fax: (011)44-188-0002. E-mail: toby@tobypress.com. Website: www.tobypress.com. **Acquisitions**: Matthew Miller, director. Estab. 1999. "Small, independent publisher, selling directly to consumers in U.K. and U.S." Publishes hardcover originals. First novel print order: 5,000-8,000. **Published 2 new writers within the last year.** Plans 6 first novels in 2000. Publishes 20 total titles/year. Sometimes critiques or comments on rejected ms.

Needs: Ethnic/multicultural (general), historical (general), literary, mystery/suspense, short story collections, thriller/espionage. Recently published *Failing Paris*, by Samantha Dunn (first novel); *Absence*, by Raymond Tallis; *Cardiofitness*, by Alessandra Montrucchio.

How to Contact: Query with outline/synopsis and 1-2 sample chapters. Include estimated word count, bio and list of publishing credits. Agented fiction 80%. Reports in 1 month on queries. Simultaneous submissions OK.

Terms: Pays royalties of 10-15% plus negotiable advance. Send prepublication galleys to author. Publishes ms within 1 year after acceptance.

Advice: "We only want writing of a high standard."

TROPICAL PRESS, INC., P.O. Box 161174, Miami FL 33116-1174. Fax: (305)378-1595. E-mail: tropicbook@aol.com. Website: www.tropicalpress.com. **Acquisitions**: Susan Diez and Gordon Witherspoon (fiction editors). Estab. 1997. Independent publisher. Publishes paperback originals. **Published 2 new writers within the last year.** Plans 1 first novel this year. Averages 4 total titles, 2 fiction titles/year.

Needs: Adventure, historical (general), mystery/suspense.

How to Contact: Accepts unsolicited mss. Query with outline/synopsis and 1 sample chapter. Send SASE for reply. Agented fiction 50%. Reports in 1 month on queries. Simultaneous submissions OK. Sometimes critiques or comments on rejected mss.

Terms: Pays royalties of 5% minimum. Pay depends on grants/awards. Sends galleys to author. Publishes ms 1 year after acceptance. Writer's guidelines for #10 SASE.

Advice: "We see a niche for all good writing that doesn't require the sale of 25,000 copies to break even. Present a clean, well conceived presentation. Give us your credits, if any, and let the writing speak for itself."

TURNSTONE PRESS, 607-100 Arthur St., Winnipeg, Manitoba R3B 1H3 Canada. (204)947-1555. Fax: (204)942-1555. E-mail: editor@turnstonepress.mb.ca. **Acquisitions**: Manuela Dias, editor. Estab. 1976. "Turnstone Press is a literary press that publishes Canadian writers with an emphasis on writers from, and writing on, the Canadian west." Canadian literary press focusing on eclectic new writing, prairie writers and travel writing. Books: Offset paper; perfect-bound; average first novel print order: 1,500. **Publishes 3 previously unpublished writers/year.** Averages 10-12 total titles/year. Distributes titles through General Distribution Services (Canada and US). Promotes titles through Canadian national and local print media and select US print advertising.

●   Turnstone Press received the Manitoba Book Design of the Year Award. *Summer of My Amazing Luck*, by Miriam Toews was nominated for the Stephen Leacock Award for Humor and the John Hirsch Award for Most Promising Writer. *Bread, Wine and Angels*, by Anna P. Zurzolo was runner-up for the Commonwealth Writer's Prize for Best First Book.

Imprints: Ravenstone.

Needs: Experimental, literary, regional (Western Canada), mystery, gothic, noir. "We will be doing only 4-5 fiction titles a year. Interested in new work exploring new narrative/fiction forms, travel/adventure writing of a literary nature and writing that pushes the boundaries of genre." Published *How to Get There From Here*, by Michelle Berry (short stories); and *Summer of My Amazing Luck*, by Miriam Toews (comic novel).

How to Contact: *Canadian authors only.* Accepts unsolicited mss. Query first with 20-40 sample pages and SASE. Include estimated word count and list of publishing credits. Reports in 2 months on queries; 2-4 months on mss.

Terms: Pays royalties of 10%; 10 author's copies. Average advance: $500. Publishes ms 1 year after acceptance. Sends galleys to author. Book catalog free with SASE. Simultaneous submissions OK if notified.

Advice: "Like most Canadian literary presses, we depend heavily on government grants which are not available for books by non-Canadians. Do some homework before submitting work to make sure your subject matter/

**FOR EXPLANATIONS OF THESE SYMBOLS,
SEE THE INSIDE FRONT AND BACK COVERS OF THIS BOOK.**

genre/writing style falls within the publishers area of interest. Specializes in prairie writing."

◎ **ULTRAMARINE PUBLISHING CO., INC.**, Box 303, Hastings-on-the-Hudson NY 10706. (914)478-1339. Fax: (914)478-1365. Publisher: Christopher P. Stephens. Estab. 1973. Small publisher. "We have 200 titles in print. We also distribute for authors where a major publisher has dropped a title." Averages 15 total titles, 12 fiction titles each year. Buys 90% agented fiction. Occasionally critiques rejected mss.
Needs: Experimental, fantasy, mainstream, science fiction, short story collections. No romance, westerns, mysteries.
How to Contact: Does not accept unsolicited mss.
Terms: Pays royalties of 10% minimum; advance is negotiable. Publishes ms an average of 8 months after acceptance. Free book catalog.

◐ **UNIVERSITY OF MISSOURI PRESS**, 2910 LeMone Blvd., Columbia MO 65201-8227. (573)882-7641. Fax: (573)884-4498. E-mail: willcoxc@ext.missouri.edu. Website: www.system.missouri.edu.upress (includes authors, titles, book descriptions). **Acquisitions**: Clair Willcox, editor. Estab. 1958. "Mid-size university press." Publishes paperback originals and reprints (short story collections only). **Published new writers within the last year.** Publishes 1 previously unpublished writer/year. Averages 52 total titles, 4 short story collections each year. Distributes titles through direct mail, bookstores, sales reps.
   • The University of Missouri Press is a member of the Association of American University Presses.
Needs: Short story collections. No children's fiction. Recently published *The Angel of the Garden*, by Scott Ely (short story collection); *Doors*, by William Hoffman (short story collection); *Blue Money*, by Susan Hubbard (short story collection).
How to Contact: Accepts unsolicited mss. Query first. Queries/correspondence by e-mail and fax OK. Submit cover letter and sample story or two. Include bio/publishing credits. SASE for reply. Reports in 2 weeks on queries; 3 months on mss. Simultaneous submissions OK. Sometimes comments on rejected ms.
Terms: Pays royalties of 6%. Sends galleys to author. Publishes ms 1-1½ years after acceptance. Book catalogs are free.

◪ ◎ **UNIVERSITY OF NEVADA PRESS**, MS 166, Reno NV 89557-0076. (702)784-6573. Fax: (702)784-6200. E-mail: dalrympl@scs.unr.edu. Director: Ronald E. Latimer. Editor-in-Chief: Margaret Dalrymple. Estab. l961. "Small university press. Publishes fiction that focuses primarily on the American West." Publishes hardcover and paperback originals and paperback reprints. Books: acid-free paper. Publishes approximately 25 total titles, 2 fiction titles/year. Member AAUP.
Needs: Ethnic/multicultural (general), family saga, historical (American West), humor/satire, mystery/suspense (U.S. West), regional (U.S. West). Published *Wild Indians & Other Creatures*, by Adrian Louis (short stories); *Bad Boys and Black Sheep*, by Robert Franklin Gish (short stories); and *The Measurable World*, by Katharine Coles (novel). "We have series in Basque Studies, Gambling Studies, history and humanities, ethnonationalism, Western literature."
How to Contact: Accepts unsolicited mss. Query with outline/synopsis and 2-4 sample chapters. E-mail and fax OK. Include estimated word count, 1-2 page bio and list of publishing credits. Send SASE for reply, return of ms or send a disposable copy of ms. Agented fiction 20%. Reports in 2-3 weeks on queries; 2-4 months on mss. Sometimes critiques or comments on rejected mss.
Payment/Terms: Pays royalties; negotiated on a book-by-book basis. Sends galleys to author. Publishes ms 9-24 months after acceptance. Writer's guidelines for #10 SASE.
Advice: "We are not interested in genre fiction."

✓ ◎ ⛟ **UNIVERSITY PRESS OF COLORADO**, P.O. Box 849, Niwot CO 80544. (303)530-5337. Fax: (303)530-5306. E-mail: prattd@stripe.colorado.edu. **Acquisitions**: Darrin Pratt, acquisitions editor; Luther Wilson, director. Estab. 1965. "Small, independent, scholarly publisher, nonprofit." Publishes hardcover and paperback originals and reprints. Books: acid-free paper; offset printing; case bound. Average print order: 1,000. First novel print order: 1,500. **Publishes 1 previously unpublished writer/year.** Averages 30 total titles, 2 fiction titles each year. Member of The Association of American University Presses.
   • *Mari: A Novel*, by Jane Valentine Barker, published by the University of Colorado Press, received the 1998 Colorado Book Award in Fiction and the Colorado Author's League 1997 and the Top Hand Award for Best Fiction.
Needs: Regional (western), western (modern). Recently published *The Circle Leads Home*, by Mary Anderson Parks (20th century Native American); *The Meade Solution*, by Robert Conley (contemporary fiction); and *Roll On Columbia I, II, & III*, by Bill Gulick (western history).
How to Contact: Query with outline/synopsis and 3 sample chapters. Include estimated word count, bio and list of publishing credits. Unsolicited queries/correspondence by e-mail and fax OK. Send SASE for reply, return of ms or send disposable copy of ms. Agented fiction 90%. Reports in 3 weeks on queries; 4 months on mss. Sometimes critiques or comments on rejected mss.
Terms: Pays royalties of 12% maximum. Provides 10 author's copies. Sends galleys to author. Publishes ms within 2 years after acceptance. Writer's guidelines and book catalog free.

Advice: "We look for high quality fiction that might not appeal to the larger trade houses. We are interested in publishing fiction that fits into our series *Women's West*. Generally, our authors are responsible for proofreading and indexing their own manuscripts. If they do not wish to do so, we will hire proofreaders and/or indexers at the author's expense."

☑ ◔ **VAN NESTE BOOKS**, 12836 Ashtree Rd., Midlothian VA 23113-3095. Phone/fax: (804)897-3568. E-mail: kvno@aol.com. Website: members.aol.com/kvno/vbooks/van_neste_books.htm (current and backlist books, author information and contact information). **Acquisitions:** Karen Van Neste Owen, publisher. Estab. 1996. "We are a small independent publisher interested in publishing serious fiction." Publishes hardcover originals. Books: 55 lb. acid-free paper; cloth binding; illustrations (cover only). Average print order: 1,200. **Publishes 2 previously unpublished writers/year.** Plans 2-4 first novels per year. Averages 2-4 total titles, 2-4 fiction titles each year. Distributes titles through Van Neste Books. Promotes titles through bound galleys mailed to book reviewers throughout the U.S. and representation by the Permanent Press's foreign and Hollywood agents.
Needs: Feminist, historical, humor/satire, literary, mainstream/contemporary, mystery/suspense, regional (southern), thriller/espionage. Recently published *Lumen*, by Ben Pastor (historical mystery); *Floating in a Most Peculiar Way*, by David Racine (mainstream contemporary); *The Edge of Things*, by Richard Lyons (psychological thriller); and *One August Day*, by Charlotte Morgan (mainstream contemporary).
How to Contact: Accepts unsolicited mss. Query with "brief" synopsis and 3 sample chapters. Include estimated word count, 2-paragraph bio, Social Security number and list of publishing credits. Unsolicited queries/correspondence by e-mail OK. Send SASE for reply, return of ms or send disposable copy of ms. Reports in 2 months on queries; 6 months on mss. Sometimes critiques or comments on rejected mss.
Terms: Pays royalties of 10-15% minimum on print runs of more than 2,500 copies; half that on print runs under 2,500 copies. Average advance: $500 for finished disk. Sends galleys to author. Publishes ms 12-18 months after acceptance.
Advice: "I am looking for serious, mainstream contemporary fiction and will consider first-time novelists. However, because the business is so small, I need the copy to be as clean (free of mistakes) as possible. No collections of short stories, poetry or juvenile fiction, please. Because of the difficulty for first-time and midlist authors to find a publisher, we like to think that we offer a chance for quality fiction to see the light—to publish an author's novel that might not be published otherwise."

Ⓝ ◎ **VANESSAPRESS**, P.O. Box 82761, Fairbanks AK 99708. (907)452-5070. Website: www.mosquitonet. com/~inkworks/vanessapress.html (includes names of editors, authors, titles, general contact information and prices). **Acquisitions:** Sue Mitchell. Estab. 1984. "Vanessapress is Alaska's only women's publishing company. Our focus is on work by Alaskan women authors. We publish fiction, nonfiction and poetry." Publishes paperback originals and reprints. Average print order: 1,000. **Published 1 new writer within the last year.** Publishes 1 title/year. Sometimes critiques or comments on rejected ms.
Needs: "We accept manuscripts of all genres."
How to Contact: Accepts unsolicited mss. Query with outline/synopsis and 3 sample chapters. Include list of publishing credits and marketing plan. SASE for return of ms. Reports in 2 months on queries; 3 months on mss. Publishes ms 1-2 years after acceptance.
Advice: "We only accept submissions from Alaskan women authors."

Ⓝ 🍁 ◎ 🏆 **VÉHICULE PRESS**, Box 125, Place du Parc Station, Montreal, Quebec H2W 2M9 Canada. Imprint: Signal Editions for poetry. Publisher/Editor: Simon Dardick. Estab. 1973. Small publisher of scholarly, literary and cultural books. Publishes hardcover and paperback originals. Books: good quality paper; offset printing; perfect and cloth binding; illustrations. Average print order: 1,000-3,000. Averages 13 total titles each year.
● A Véhicule Press book, *Friends & Marriages*, by George Szanto received the QSPELL Prize for Fiction.
Needs: Feminist, literary, regional, short story collections, translations—"*by Canadian residents only.*" No romance or formula writing. Published *Evil Eye*, by Ann Diamond; *Strange and Familiar Places*, by Kenneth Radu; *Friends & Marriages*, by George Szanto; and *Rembrandt's Model*, by Yeshim Ternar.
How to Contact: Query first or send sample chapters. SASE ("no U.S. stamps, please"). Reports in 3 months on mss.
Terms: Pays in royalties of 10% minimum; 12% maximum. "Depends on press run and sales." Sends galleys to author. "Translators of fiction can receive Canada Council funding, which publisher applies for." Book catalog for 9×12 SASE.
Advice: "Quality in almost any style is acceptable. We believe in the editing process."

Ⓝ ◙ ◎ **VOICES FROM MY RETREAT**, P.O. Box 1077, S, Fallsburg NY 12779. (914)436-7455. Fax: (718)885-0066. E-mail: myretreat2@aol.com. **Acquisitions:** Marian Butler, fiction editor (literary fiction). Estab. 1999. "Small independent publisher focusing on novels and short story collections with an international slant, i.e. characters, setting, themes." Publishes paperback originals. Plans 1 first novel this year. Averages 2 total titles, 2 fiction titles/year.

• Voices From My Retreat is a member of Small Press (NYC) and the International Womens Writing Guild.

Needs: Ethnic/multicultural (general), experimental, feminist, historical (general), humor satire, literary, mainstream, short story collections, international slant. Recently published *Beneath the Hill*, by Pat Carr (literary).

How to Contact: Accepts unsolicited mss. Submit complete ms with cover letter. Include estimated word count, and 1-page bio. Send SASE for reply, return of ms or send disposable copy of ms. Reports in 2 months on mss. Simultaneous submissions and electronic submissions OK. Sometimes critiques or comments on rejected mss.

Terms: Pays royalties of 10% minimum. Publishes ms 6 months after acceptance.

Advice: "Be gut level honest. We are not interested in fiction in which the author uses a point of view of the opposite sex or of a race, class, or nationality which he/she is not. We are looking for both experience and authenticity."

☑ ◎ **W.W. PUBLICATIONS**, 4108 Menton, Flint MI 48507. Also publishes *Minas Tirith Evening Star*. **Acquisitions**: Philip Helms, editor. Estab. 1967. One-man operation on part-time basis. Publishes paperback originals and reprints. Books: typing paper; offset printing; staple-bound; black ink illustrations. Average print order: 500. First novel print order: 500. Averages 1 title (fiction) each year.

Needs: Fantasy, science fiction. "Specializes in Tolkien-related or middle-earth." Published *The Adventures of Fungo Hafwirse*, by Philip W. Helms and David L. Dettman.

How to Contact: Accepts unsolicited mss. Submit complete ms with SASE. Reports in 1 month. "Submit hardy copy by mail only. No phone inquiries, no fax and no e-mail. No exceptions." Occasionally critiques rejected mss.

Terms: Individual arrangement with author depending on book, etc.; provides 5 author's copies.

Advice: "We are publishing more fiction and more paperbacks. The author/editor relationship: a friend and helper."

Ⓝ ◐ ◎ **WAVERLY HOUSE PUBLISHING**, P.O. Box 1053, Glenside PA 19038. (215)884-5873. E-mail: info@natsel.com. Website: www.natsel.com (includes book catalog and interviews with authors). **Acquisitions**: Nora Wright. Estab. 1997. 'Small independent publisher publishing works of high entertainment value which also convey a message of social significance to the African-American community." Publishes hardcover and paperback originals. Books: offset printing; casebound with perfect binding. Average print order: 2,000; first novel print order: 2,000. **Published 1 new writer within the last year.** Plans 1 first novel this year. Averages 2-3 total titles, 2-3 fiction titles/year.

• Waverly is a member of PMA and SPAN.

Needs: Ethnic/multicultural (specific culture, African-American). Recently published *Damaged!*, by Bernadette Y. Connor (novel).

How to Contact: No unsolicited mss. Query letter only first. Accepts unsolicited queries by e-mail. Include estimated word count and 50-word bio. Send SASE for reply, return of ms or send disposable copy of ms. Reports in 3-4 weeks on queries; 2 months on mss. Simultaneous submissions OK.

Terms: Pays royalties of 6% minimum. Sends galleys to author. Publishes ms 9-12 months after acceptance.

◎ **WOODLEY MEMORIAL PRESS**, English Dept., Washburn University, Topeka KS 66621. (785)234-1032. E-mail: zzlaws@washburn.edu.Website: www.wuacc.edu/reference/woodley-press/index.html (includes writer's guidelines, editors, authors, titles). Editor: Robert N. Lawson. Estab. 1980. "Woodley Memorial Press is a small, nonprofit press which publishes book-length poetry and fiction collections by Kansas writers only; by 'Kansas writers' we mean writers who reside in Kansas or have a Kansas connection." Publishes paperback originals. Averages 2 titles each year.

Needs: Contemporary, experimental, literary, mainstream, short story collection. "We do not want to see genre fiction, juvenile, or young adult." Recently published *Gathering Reunion*, by David Tangeman (stories and poetry); *The Monday, Wednesday, Friday Girl*, by Stuart Levine (short stories); and *Rudolph, Encouraged by His Therapist*, by Eugene Bales (satiric).

How to Contact: *Charges $5 reading fee.* Accepts unsolicited mss. Accepts unsolicited queries and correspondence by e-mail. Send complete ms. SASE. Reports in 2 weeks on queries; 2 months on mss. Sometimes comments on rejected ms.

Terms: "Terms are individually arranged with author after acceptance of manuscript." Publishes ms one year after acceptance. Writer's guidelines available at above website address.

Advice: "We only publish one work of fiction a year, on average, and definitely want it to be by a Kansas author. We are more likely to do a collection of short stories by a single author."

Ⓝ ◐ ▼ **WRITERS DIRECT**, Subsidiary of Titlewaves Publishing, 1351 Kuhio Highway, Kapaa HI 96746. (808)822-7449. Fax: (808)822-2312. E-mail: rs@hshawaii.com. Website: www.bestplacesonearth.com (includes book catalog). **Acquisitions**: Rob Sanford, editor. Estab. 1985. "Small independent publishing house founded and run by published authors." Publishes hardcover and paperback originals and hardcover and paperback reprints. Books: recycled paper; digital printing; perfect binding; illustrations. **Published 4 new writers within**

the last year. Plans 1 first novel this year. Averages more than 6 total titles, 2 fiction titles/year.

● Writers Direct author David Penhallow received the Maui Writers Conference Novel of the Year, 1996. Member of the Hawaii Publishers Association.

Needs: Adventure, children's/juvenile, humor satire, literary, mainstream, New Age/mystic, psychic/supernatural, regional (Hawaii), religious (children's religious, inspirational, religious mystery/suspense, religious thriller), science fiction, thriller/espionage. Recently published *After the Ball*, by David Penhallow (coming of age novel).

How to Contact: Accepts unsolicited mss. Query with outline/synopsis and 3 sample chapters. Include estimated word count, 1-page bio, list of publishing credits, why author wrote book, marketing plan. Send SASE for reply, return of ms or send disposable copy of ms. Reports in 1 month on queries; 3 months on mss. Simultaneous submissions OK. Sometimes critiques or comments on rejected mss.

Terms: Pays royalties of 15% minimum; 35% maximum. Sometimes sends galleys to author. Book catalog for legal-size SASE.

Advice: "Do what you do best and enjoy most. Your writing is an outcome of the above."

Screenwriting

BY KIRSTEN C. HOLM

Practically everyone you meet in Los Angeles, from your airport cabbie on, is writing a script. It might be a feature film, movie of the week, TV series or documentary, but the sheer amount of competition can seem overwhelming. Some will never make a sale, while others make a decent living on sales and options without ever having any of their work produced. But there are those writers who make a living doing what they love and see their names roll by on the credits. How do they get there? How do *you* get there?

First, work on your writing. You'll improve with each script, so there is no way of getting around the need to write and write some more. It's a good idea to read as many scripts as you can get your hands on. Check your local bookstores and libraries. Script City (8033 Sunset Blvd., Suite 1500, Hollywood CA 90046, (800)676-2522, www.scriptcity.net) carries thousands of movie and TV scripts, classics to current releases, as well as books, audio/video seminars and software in their $2 catalog. Book City (6631 Hollywood Blvd., Hollywood CA 90028, (800)4-CINEMA, www.hollywoodbookcity.com) has film and TV scripts in all genres and a large selection of movie books in their $2.50 catalog.

There are lots of books that will give you the "rules" of format and structure for writing for TV or film. Samuel French (7623 Sunset Blvd., Hollywood CA 90046 (213)876-0570, www.sam uelfrench.com) carries a number of how-to books and reference materials on these subjects. The correct format marks your script as a professional submission. Most successful scriptwriters will tell you to learn the correct structure, internalize those rules—and then throw them away and write intuitively.

WRITING FOR TV

To break into TV you must have spec scripts—work written for free that serves as a calling card and gets you in the door. A spec script showcases your writing abilities and gets your name in front of influential people. Whether a network has invited you in to pitch some ideas, or a movie producer has contacted you to write a first draft for a feature film, the quality of writing in your spec script got their attention and that may get you the job.

It's a good idea to have several spec scripts, perhaps one each for three of the top five shows in the format you prefer to work in, whether it's sitcom (half-hour comedies), episodic (one hour series) or movie of the week (two hour dramatic movies). Perhaps you want to showcase the breadth of your writing ability; some writers have a portfolio of a few eight o'clock type shows (i.e., *Friends, Everybody Loves Raymond, Smart Guy*), a few nine-o'clock shows (i.e., *Frasier, Just Shoot Me, The X-Files*) and one or two episodics (i.e., *The Practice, Law & Order, NYPD Blue*). These are all "hot" shows for writers and can demonstrate your abilities to create believable dialogue for characters already familiar to your intended readers. For TV and cable movies you should have completed original scripts (not sequels to existing movies) and you might also have a few for episodic TV shows.

In choosing the shows you write spec scripts for you must remember one thing: don't write a script for a show you want to work on. If you want to write for *NYPD Blue*, for example, you'll send a *Law & Order* script and vice versa. It may seem contradictory, but it is standard

---

KIRSTEN C. HOLM *is editor of* Writer's Market.

practice. It reduces the chances of lawsuits, and writers and producers can feel very proprietary about their show and their stories. They may not be objective enough to fairly evaluate your writing. In submitting another similar type of show you'll avoid those problems while demonstrating comparable skills.

In writing your TV script you must get *inside* the show and understand the characters' internal motivations. You must immerse yourself in how the characters speak, think and interact. Don't introduce new characters in a spec script for an existing show—write believable dialogue for the characters as they are portrayed. Be sure to choose a show that you like—you'll be better able to demonstrate your writing ability through characters you respond to.

You must also understand the external factors. How the show is filmed bears on how you write. Most sitcoms are shot on videotape with three cameras, on a sound stage with a studio audience. Episodics are often shot on film with one camera and include on-location shots. *Dharma & Greg* has a flat, evenly-lit look and takes place in a limited number of locations. *NYPD Blue* has a gritty realism with varying lighting and a variety of settings.

Another important external influence in writing for TV is the timing of commercials in conjunction with the act structure. There are lots of sources detailing the suggested content and length of acts, but generally a sitcom has a teaser (short opening scene), two acts and a tag (short closing scene), and an episodic has a teaser, four acts and a tag. Each act closes with a turning point. Watching TV analytically and keeping a log of events will reveal some elements of basic structure. *Successful Scriptwriting*, by Wolff & Cox (Writer's Digest Books), offers detailed discussions of various types of shows.

WRITING FOR THE MOVIES

With feature films you may feel at once more liberated and more bound by structure. An original movie script contains characters you have created, with storylines you design, allowing you more freedom than you have in TV. However, your writing must still convey believable dialogue and realistic characters, with a plausible plot and high-quality writing carried through the roughly 120 pages. The characters must have a problem that involves the audience. When you go to a movie you don't want to spend time watching the *second* worst night of a character's life. You're looking for the big issue that crystallizes a character, that portrays a journey with important consequences.

At the same time you are creating, you should also be constructing. Be aware of the basic three act structure for feature films. Scenes can be of varying lengths, but are usually no longer than three to three and a half pages. Some writers list scenes that must occur, then flesh them out from beginning to end, writing with the structure of events in mind. The beginning and climactic scenes are the easiest; it's how they get there from here that's difficult.

Many novice screenwriters tend to write too many visual cues and camera directions into their scripts. Your goal should be to write something readable, like a "compressed novella." Write succinct resonant scenes and leave the camera technique to the director and producer. In action/adventure movies, however, there needs to be a balance since the script demands more visual direction.

It seems to be easier for TV writers to cross over to movies. Cable movies bridge the two, and are generally less derivative and more willing to take chances with a higher quality show designed to attract an audience not interested in network offerings. Cable is also less susceptible to advertiser pullout, which means it can tackle more controversial topics.

Feature films and TV are very different and writers occupy different positions. TV is a medium for writers and producers; directors work for them. Many TV writers are also producers. In feature films the writers and producers work for the director and often have little or no say about what happens to the work once the script has been sold. For TV the writer pitches the idea; for feature films generally the producer pitches the idea and then finds a writer.

MARKETING YOUR SCRIPTS

If you intend to make writing your profession you must act professionally. Accepted submission practices should become second nature.

- The initial pitch is made through a query letter, which is no longer than one page with a one paragraph synopsis and brief summary of your credits if they are relevant to the subject of your script.
- Never send a complete manuscript until it is requested.
- Almost every script sent to a producer, studio or agent must be accompanied by a release form. Ask for that company's form when you receive an invitation to submit the whole script. Mark your envelope "release form enclosed" to prevent it being returned unread.
- Always include a self-addressed stamped envelope (SASE) if you want your work returned; a disposable copy may be accompanied by a self-addressed stamped postcard for reply.
- Allow four to six weeks from receipt of your manuscript before writing a follow-up letter.

When your script is requested, be sure it's written in the appropriate format. Unusual binding, fancy covers or illustrations mark an amateur. Three brass brads with a plain or black cover indicate a pro.

There are a limited number of ideas in the world, so it's inevitable that similar ideas occur to more than one person. Hollywood is a buyer's market and a release form states that pretty clearly. An idea is not copyrightable, so be careful about sharing premises. The written expression of that idea, however, can be protected and it's a good idea to do so. The Writers Guild of America can register scripts for television and theatrical motion pictures, series formats, storylines and step outlines. You need not be a member of the WGA to use this service. Copyrighting your work with the Copyright Office of the Library of Congress also protects your work from infringement. Contact either agency for more information and an application form.

For More Information

If you are a writer, you should write—all the time. When you're not writing, read. There are numerous books on the art, craft and business of screenwriting. Industry trade papers such as *Daily Variety* and *Hollywood Reporter* can keep you in touch with the day to day news and upcoming events. Specialty newsletters such as *Hollywood Scriptwriter* (P.O. Box 10277, Burbank CA 91510, (818)845-5525, www.hollywoodscriptwriter.com) offer tips from successful scriptwriters and agents. The *Hollywood Creative Directory* (3000 W. Olympic Blvd., Suite 2525, Santa Monica CA 90404, (800)815-0503, fax: (310)315-4816, e-mail: hcd@hollyvision.com, website: www.hollyvision.com) is an extensive list of production companies, studios and networks that also lists companies and talent with studio deals. Excellent resources on the craft of screenwriting include *The Insider's Guide to Writing for Screen and Television*, by Ronald Tobias (Writer's Digest Books), *Successful Scriptwriting*, by Jurgen Wolff and Kerry Cox (Writer's Digest Books, 1507 Dana Ave., Cincinnati OH 45207, (800)289-0963), *Story: Substance, Structure, Style and the Principles of Screenwriting*, by Robert McKee (HarperCollins, 10 E. 53rd St., New York NY 10036) and *Making a Good Script Great*, by Linda Seger (Samuel French, 45 W. 25th St., New York NY 10010).

Computer services have various bulletin boards and chat hours for scriptwriters that provide contact with other writers and a chance to share information and encouragement.

It may take years of work before you come up with a script someone is willing to take a chance on. Those years need to be spent learning your craft and understanding the business. Polishing scripts, writing new material, keeping current with the industry and networking constantly will keep you busy. When you do get that call you'll be confident in your abilities and know that your hard work is beginning to pay off.

ALEXANDER/ENRIGHT AND ASSOCIATES, 201 Wilshire Blvd., 3rd Floor, Santa Monica CA 90401. Contact: Sarah Koepple, development associate. Produces for a general television audience. Buys 3 scripts/year. Works with many writers/year. Buys TV and film rights only. Accepts previously produced material. Reports in 1 month on queries; 6 weeks on submissions. Query with synopsis. Pays in accordance with Writer's Guild standards.
Needs: Women-driven dramas, but will accept others. No extreme violence, horror or stalkers.

N ▢ ALLIED ARTISTS, INC., 859 N. Hollywood Way, Suite 377, Burbank CA 91505. (818)594-4089. Contact: John Nichols, vice president, development. Estab. 1990. Produces material for broadcast and cable television, home video and film. Buys 3-5 scripts/year. Works with 10-20 writers/year. Buys first rights or all rights. Accepts previously produced material. Reports in 2 months on queries; 3 months on scripts. Submit synopsis/outline. Pays in accordance with Writers Guild standards (amount and method negotiable). Written queries only—*no phone pitches.*
Needs: Films, videotapes. Social issue TV special (30-60 minutes); special interest home video topics; instruction and entertainment; positive values feature screenplays.
Tips: "We are looking for positive, up-lifting dramatic stories involving real people situations. Future trend is for more reality-based programming, as well as interactive television programs for viewer participation."

☑ AMERICAN CLASSICS, (formerly Three Guys From Verona Inc.), 5746 Rhodes Ave., Valley Village CA 91607. (818)980-9777. Partner: Clancy Grass. Estab. 1993. Buys 3 scripts/year. Works with 7-8 writers/year. Buys first and all rights. Accepts previously produced material. Reports in 1 month on queries; 3 months on submissions. Catalog for #10 SASE. "Query with 2-3 page synopsis with 2-3 ideas of the dialogue." Pays in accordance with Writer's Guild standards excluding synopsis.
Needs: Films (16 & 35mm), videotapes. Looking for great idea, nothing specific.

THE AMERICAN MOVING PICTURE COMPANY INC., 838 N. Doheny Dr., #904, Los Angeles CA 90069. (310)276-0750. E-mail: mazutzky@juno.com. Contact: Isabel Casper, vice president, creative affairs. Estab. 1979. Theatrical motion picture audience. Buys screenplay rights and ancillaries. Produced four theatrical motion pictures. Does not return submissions. Reports in 1 month. Query with synopsis. Pays in accordance with Writers Guild standards or more.
Needs: Films (35mm), commercial. "We want commercial and unique material."

ANGEL FILMS, 967 Highway 40, New Franklin MO 65274-9778. Phone/fax: (573)698-3900. E-mail: angelfilm @aol.com. Vice President Production: Matthew Eastman. Estab. 1980. Produces material for feature films, television. Buys 10 scripts/year. Works with 20 writers/year. Buys all rights. Accepts previously published material (if rights available). Reports in 1 months on queries; 1-2 months on scripts. Query with synopsis. Makes outright purchase. "Our company is a low-budget producer, which means people get paid fairly, but don't get rich."
Needs: Films (35mm), videotapes. "We are looking for projects that can be used to produce feature film and television feature film and series work. These would be in the areas of action adventure, comedy, horror, thriller, science fiction, animation for children." Also looking for direct to video materials.
Tips: "Don't copy others. Try to be original. Don't overwork your idea. As far as trends are concerned, don't pay attention to what is 'in.' By the time it gets to us it will most likely be on the way 'out.' And if you can't let your own grandmother read it, don't send it. Slow down on western submissions. They are not selling. If you wish material returned, enclose proper postage with all submissions. Send SASE for response to queries and return of scripts."

ANGEL'S TOUCH PRODUCTIONS, 22906 Calabash St., Woodland Hills CA 91364. Contact: Phil Nemy, director of development. Estab. 1986. Professional screenplays and teleplays. Send synopsis. Reports in 8 months. Rights negotiated between production company and author. Payment negotiated.
Needs: All types, all genres, only full-length teleplays and screenplays—no one-acts.
Tips: "We only seek feature film screenplays, television screenplays, and episodic teleplays. *No phone calls!*"

☑ THE BADHAM COMPANY, 3344 Clerendon Rd., Beverly Hills CA 90210. (818)990-9495. Fax: (818)981-9163. Estab. 1991. Theatrical audience. Buys 1 script/year. Works with 2 writers/year. Buys first rights. Accepts previously produced material. Reports in 1 month. Query with synopsis. We go to studio and they purchase option. Will read projects already set up with producer and/or studio.
Needs: Films (35mm).
Tips: "It's too easy to write action and ignore characters."

BARNSTORM FILMS, 73 Market St., Venice CA 90291. (310)396-5937. Fax: (310)450-4988. Contact: Tony Bill, president. Estab. 1969. Produces feature films. Buys 2-3 scripts/year. Works with 4-5 writers/year.

Tips: Looking for strong, character-based commercial scripts. Not interested in science fiction or fantasy. Must send SASE with synopsis. Query first, do not send script unless we request it!"

☑ ☐ **BIG EVENT PICTURES**, (formerly StoneRoad Production, Inc.), 11288 Ventura Blvd., #909, Studio City CA 91604. E-mail: bigevent1@hotmail.com. Contact: Michael Cargile, president. Produces feature films for theaters, cable TV and home video. PG, R, and G-rated films. Reports in 1 month on queries if interested; 2 months requested on submissions. Query with SASE and synopsis.
Needs: Films. All genres. Looking for good material from writers who have taken the time to learn the unique and difficult craft of scriptwriting.
Tips: "Interesting query letters intrigue us—and tell us something about the writer. Query letter should include a short 'log line' or 'pitch' encapsulating 'what this story is about.' We look for unique stories and strong characters. We would like to see more action and science fiction submissions. We make movies that we would like to see. Producers are known for encouraging new (e.g. unproduced) screenwriters and giving real consideration to their scripts."

☐ Ⓐ **BIG STAR MOTION PICTURES LTD.**, 13025 Yonge St., #201, Richmond Hill, Ontario L4E 1Z5 Canada. (416)720-9825. Fax: (905)773-3153. E-mail: bigstar@pathcom.com. Contact: Frank A. Deluca. Estab. 1991. Buys 5 scripts/year. Works with 5-10 writers/year. Reports in 3 months on queries; 3 months on scripts. Submit synopsis first. Scripts should be submitted by agent or lawyer.
Needs: Films (35mm). "We are very active in all medias, but are primarily looking for television projects, cable, network, etc. Family Films are of special interest."

☑ **BOZ PRODUCTIONS**, 1632 N. Sierra Bonita Ave., Los Angeles CA 90046. (323)876-3232. Fax: (323)876-3231. E-mail: boz51@aol.com. Director of Development: Jeff Monarch. Estab. 1987. All audiences. Buys 3-5 scripts/year. Works with several writers/year. Buys all rights. Accepts previously produced material. Reports in 1 month on queries; 1-2 months on scripts. Query with synopsis and résumé. Pay varies.
Needs: Films (35mm). Feature-length film scripts or rights to real stories for MOW's.

CANVAS HOUSE FILMS, 3671 Bear St., #E, Santa Ana CA 92704. Contact: Mitch Teemley, producer. Estab. 1994. General audience. Buys 2-3 scripts/year. Works with 10-15 writers/year. Buys first rights, all rights. Accepts previously produced material. Reports in 1 month on queries; 4 months on submissions. Query with detailed (2-4 page) synopsis and résumé or list of credits. Pays in accordance with Writers Guild standards.
Needs: Films (35mm). "Quality feature-length filmscripts—all types, but no lurid, 'hard-R'-rated material."
Tips: "Know proper formatting and story structure. There is a need for 'family' material that can appeal to *grown-ups* as well as children."

CINE/DESIGN FILMS, INC., P.O. Box 6495, Denver CO 80206. (303)777-4222. E-mail: jghusband@aol.com. Producer/Director: Jon Husband. Produces educational material for general, sales-training and theatrical audiences. 75% freelance written; 90% unagented submissions. "Original, solid ideas are encouraged." Rights purchased vary.
Needs: Films (16, 35mm). "Motion picture outlines in the theatrical and documentary areas. We are seeking theatrical scripts in the low-budget area that are possible to produce for under $2 to 3 million. We seek flexibility and personalities who can work well with our clients." Send 8-10-page outline before submitting ms. Pays $100-200/screen minute on 16mm productions. Theatrical scripts negotiable.
Tips: "Understand the marketing needs of film production today. Materials will not be returned."

☑ **CODIKOW FILMS**, 8899 Beverly Blvd., #719, Los Angeles CA 90048. (310)246-9388. Fax: (310)246-9877. E-mail: codikowflm@aol.com. Website: www.codikowfilms.com. Director of Development: Lara Moon. Estab. 1990. Buys 6 scripts/year. Works with 12 writers/year. Buys all rights. Reports in 2 months on submissions. Query or résumé. Pays in accordance with Writer's Guild standards.
Needs: Films (35mm). Commercial and independent screenplays; good writing—all subjects.

☑ **CPC ENTERTAINMENT**, 840 N. Larrabee St., #2322, Los Angeles CA 90069. (310)652-8194. Fax: (310)652-4998. E-mail: 74151.1117@compuserve.com. Producer/Director: Peggy Chene. Vice President, Creative Affairs: Sylvie de la Riviere. Development Associate: Barbara Kerr Condon. Feature and TV. Buys 15 scripts/year. Works with 24 writers/year. Buys all rights. Recent production: "In the Eyes of a Stranger," CBS-TV thriller starring Richard Dean Anderson, CBS-TV. Reports in 2 months on written queries; 3 months on submissions. Query with 1 sentence premise, 3 sentence synopsis and résumé. Prefers queries by e-mail. Outright purchase WGA minimum; and up.
   • CPC Entertainment is looking for scripts of wider budget range, from low independent to high studio.
Needs: Needs feature and TV movie screenplays: small independent, or any budget for thrillers, true stories, action/adventure, character driven stories of any genre.

EAST EL LAY FILMS, 12041 Hoffman St., Studio City CA 91604. (818)769-4565. (818)769-1917. Contact: Daniel Kuhn, president. Co-President: Susan Coppola (director). Estab. 1992. Low-budget feature films for television markets. Buys 2 scripts/year. Works with many writers/year. Buys first rights and options for at least 1 year with refusal rights. Reports in 3-4 weeks on queries. Query with synopsis and résumé. Pays royalty, makes outright purchase or option fee.
Needs: Film loops (35mm), videotapes.

ENTERTAINMENT PRODUCTIONS, INC., 2118 Wilshire Blvd., Suite 744, Santa Monica CA 90403. (310)456-3143. Fax: (310)456-8950. Producer: Edward Coe. Contact: Story Editor. Estab. 1971. Produces films for theatrical and television (worldwide) distribution. Reports in 1 month only if SASE enclosed.
Needs: Screenplay originals. Query with synopsis and SASE. Price negotiated on a project-by-project basis. Writer's release in any form will be acceptable.
Tips: "State what genre the script is and why it has great potential."

N: FRONT STREET PRODUCTIONS, (formerly Water Street Pictures), 2656 29th St., #208, Santa Monica CA 90405. Vice President, Development: Tim Fortona. Estab. 1994. General entertainment, television and feature. Buys 5 scripts/year. Works with 5 writers/year. Buys all rights. Reports in 6 months on queries; 1 year on submissions. Query with synopsis. Unsolicited scripts will be thrown away. Pays in accordance with Writer's Guild standards.
Needs: Films (35mm). "We are not interested in the ordinary, even if it's a wonderfully written script. Your concept must be surprising enough to capture our eye by the first sentence of your synopsis."
Tips: "Never pester overworked development executives. Write only from your own experience or research and always look to be different then what's in theaters now."

N: GREEN GRASS BLUE SKY COMPANY, 5168 Otis Ave., Tarzana CA 91356. Fax: (818)705-7366. Contact: Frank Catalano, president. Estab. 1997. General audience. Buys all rights. Accepts previously produced material. Query only (no scripts). Reports in 2 months on queries. Pay varies depending upon project.
Needs: Films.
Tips: "Seeks projects with poetry and spirit. No shoot-em ups."

BETH GROSSBARD PRODUCTIONS, 5168 Otis Ave., Tarzana CA 91356. Fax: (818)705-7366. Producer: Beth Grossbard. Contact: M. Habash, development associate. Estab. 1994. Buys 6 scripts/year. Works with 20 writers/year. First rights and true life story rights. Reports in 3 months or less on queries; 4 months on submissions. Query with synopsis or treatment/outline. Pays in accordance with Writer's Guild standards.
Needs: Films (35mm).
Tips: "Looking for material to be developed for television, cable and feature film markets. Subject matters of interest include: true stories, family dramas, social issues, young adult/children's stories, historical/biographical accounts and high concept pieces. Will also consider outline/treatments for unpublished manuscripts or small press books."

HANDPRINT ENTERTAINMENT, 8436 W. 3rd St., Suite #650, Los Angeles CA 90036. Fax: (323)655-8555. Contact: Carr D'Angelo, executive vice president of production. Estab. 1997. Young adult to adult 18-40. Buys 10 scripts/year. Works with 40 writers/year. Buys first or all rights. "We are submit to Miramax/Dimension to buy or seek our own means." Accepts previously produced material. Reports in 1 month. Query with synopsis. Pays in accordance with Writer's Guild standards.
Needs: "Commerically-minded material with an edge—thrillers, action, romantic comedy. Push the envelope of your genre."

HBO PICTURES, 2049 Century Park E., Suite 3600, Los Angeles CA 90067. Fax: (310)201-9552. Contact: Bettina Moss, story editor. Contact by fax or mail only. Reports in 1 month. Query with synopsis one page or shorter. Payment varies.
Needs: Features for TV. Looks at all genres except family films or films with children as main protagonists. Focus on socially relevant material.
Tips: "Letter should be individualized, no 'clear executive' salutation. Check spelling and grammar usage in cover letter and synopsis. I will not read a synopsis if cover letter has glaring typos."

IFM FILM ASSOCIATES INC., 1541 N. Gardner St., Los Angeles CA 90046. (323)874-4249. Fax: (323)874-2654. E-mail: alyonsifmfilm@aol.com. Executive Vice President: Ann Lyons. Estab. 1994. Film and television all media world wide. Buys 10 scripts/year. Works with 30 writers/year. Buys all rights. No previously produced material. No submissions will be returned. Reports in 1 month on queries; 1-3 months on submissions. Catalog for SAE with $3. Query with synopsis. Pays in accordance with Writer's Guild standards, or so otherwise negotiated.

Needs: Film (35mm). Thrillers, family, action.

☑ **INTERNATIONAL HOME ENTERTAINMENT**, 1440 Veteran Ave., Suite 650, Los Angeles CA 90024. (213)663-6940. Contact: Jed Leland, Jr., assistant to the president. Estab. 1976. Buys first rights. Reports in 2 months. Query. Pays in accordance with Writers Guild standards.
   ● Looking for material that is international in scope.
Tips: "Our response time is faster on average now (3-6 weeks), but no replies without a SASE. *No unsolicited scripts*. We do not respond to unsolicited phone calls."

MARTY KATZ PRODUCTIONS, 1250 6th St., Suite 205, Santa Monica CA 90401. (310)260-8501. Fax: (310)260-8502. Contact: Frederick Levy, vice president, development. Estab. 1992. Produces material for all audiences. Buys first, all and film rights. Accepts previously produced material. Reports in 1 month. "One page query letter by fax or mail. We will respond if interested in reading."
Needs: Films (35mm).

KN'K PRODUCTIONS INC., 5230 Shira Dr., Valley Village CA 91607-2300. (818)760-3106. Fax: (818)760-2478. Creative Director: Katharine Kramer. Estab. 1992. "Looking for film material with strong roles for mature women (ages 40-55 etc.). Also roles for young women and potential movie musicals, message movies." Buys 3 scripts/year. Works with 5 writers/year. Buys all rights. No previously produced material. Reports in 2-3 months. Catalog for #10 SASE. Submit synopsis, complete script and résumé. Pays in accordance with Writers Guild standards or partnership.
Needs: Multimedia kits. "Doing more partnerships with writers as opposed to just Writers Guild minimum. Concentration on original vehicles for the mature actress to fill the gap that's missing from mainstream cinema."
Tips: "We are primarily looking for women's projects, for female-driven vehicles for mature actresses, 45-55, but we are emphasizing music-driven projects more and more. We are also looking for strong male-driven vehicles (emphasis on mature actors). We are focusing on character-driven, original material." Also looking for "rock driven musicals and strong roles for men (40-65) beside women. Also we have a keen interest in film projects about the music business or sports."

☑ **LANCASTER GATE ENTERTAINMENT**, 16001 Ventura Blvd. #110, Encino CA 91436. (818)995-6000. Fax: (818)386-2612. Contact: Brian K. Schlichter, vice president, development and production. Estab. 1989. Theatrical and television. Works with dozens of writers/year. Rights purchased negotiable. Recently produced projects: *Grumpy Old Men*, *Grumpier Old Men*, *Angel Flight Down*, *Deadly Web*, *December*. Reports in 1 month on queries. Query. Pays in accordance with Writer's Guild standards.
Needs: Films (35mm-70mm). Feature and television scripts, pitches.

☑ **ANDREW LAUREN PRODUCTIONS**, 36 E. 23rd St. #6F, New York City NY 10010. (212)475-1600. Fax: (212)475-2225. E-mail: alprod@earthlink.net. Director of Development: Jordon Hoffman. Estab. 1996. Produces for theatrical audiences. Buys all rights. Reports in 1 month on queries; 4 months on submissions. Query. Pays in accordance with Writer's Guild standards.
Needs: Films (35mm). "We are looking for original feature length screenplays or a writer who can adapt one."

☑ **LICHT/MUELLER FILM CORP.**, 132A S. Lasky Dr., Suite #200, Beverly Hills CA 90212. Fax: (310)205-5590. Creative Assistant: Winston Stromberg. Estab. 1983. Produces material for all audiences. Accepts previously produced material. Reports in 1 month on queries; 3 months on submissions. Query with synopsis.
Needs: Films (35mm). "Scripts for feature films."
Tips: "We tend to focus on comedy, but are open to most other genres."

☑ **LOCKWOOD FILMS (LONDON) INC.**, 12569 Boston Dr., RR #41, London, Ontario N6H 5L2 Canada. (519)434-6006. Fax: (519)645-0507. E-mail: mark.mccurdy@odyssey.on.ca. President: Nancy Johnson. Estab. 1974. Audience is entertainment and general broadcast for kids 9-12 and family viewing. Works with 5-6 writers/year. Submit query with synopsis, résumé or sample scripts. "Submissions will not be considered unless a proposal submission agreement is signed. We will send one upon receiving submissions." Negotiated fee.
Needs: Family entertainment: series, seasonal specials, mini-series, and movies of the week. Also feature films, documentaries.
Tips: "Potential contributors should have a fax machine and should be prepared to sign a 'proposal submission agreement.' We are in development with national broadcaster on live-action family drama series. Looking for international co-production opportunities."

■ **MEDIACOM DEVELOPMENT CORP.**, P.O. Box 6331, Burbank CA 91510-6331. (818)594-4089. Contact: Felix Girard, director/program development. Estab. 1978. 80% freelance written. Buys 8-12 scripts/year from unpublished/unproduced writers. 50% of scripts produced are unagented submissions. Query with samples. Reports in 1 month. Buys all rights or first rights. Written query only. Please do not call.
Needs: Produces films, multimedia kits, tapes and cassettes, slides and videotape with programmed instructional print materials, broadcast and cable television programs. Publishes software ("programmed instruction training courses"). Negotiates payment depending on project. Looking for new ideas for CD-ROM titles.
Tips: "Send short samples of work. Especially interested in flexibility to meet clients' demands, creativity in treatment of precise subject matter. We are looking for good, fresh projects (both special and series) for cable and pay television markets. A trend in the audiovisual field that freelance writers should be aware of is the move toward more interactive video disc/computer CRT delivery of training materials for corporate markets."

MILWAUKEE FILMWORKS, 4218 Whitsett Ave., Suite 4, Studio City CA 91604. (818)762-9080. Fax: (310)278-2632. Contact: Douglas Gardner. Estab. 1991. Film and TV audience. Works with 4 writers/year. Buys screenplays-option. *Feature scripts only*. Returns submissions on a case to case basis. Reports in up to 4 months. Query with complete script. Pay varies in accordance with Writers Guild standards.

MNC FILMS, P.O. Box 16195, Beverly Hills CA 90209-2195. E-mail: mncfilms@aol.com. Contact: Mark Cohen, producer. Estab. 1991. Feature film audience. Buys 2 scripts/year. Works with 3 writers/year. Buys all rights or purchases option on screenplay. Accepts previously produced material. Query with synopsis only. Prefers e-mail queries. Pays in accordance with Writers Guild standards (work for hire) or variable fee for option of material.
Needs: Feature length films. "I'm looking for story-driven films with well-developed characters. Screenplays or books easily adaptable for lower- to mid-range budget."
Tips: "In the past I have received many submissions from writers who do not pay attention to the type of material that I am looking for. I am looking for character-driven stories with an emphasis on individuals and relationships."

✓ ■ **MOUNTAIN DRIVE**, 625 Arizona Ave., Santa Monica CA 90401. (310)587-1250. Fax: (310)458-6664. Development Director: John G. Otto. Estab. 1980. Film and TV audience. Works with 10-15 writers/year. Buys all rights. Accept previously produced material. Reports in 2 months on queries; 1 month on submissions. Catalog for #10 SASE. Query with synopsis or completed script. Pays by royalty, outright purchase or in accordance with Writer's Guild standards.
Needs: Films (35mm), videotapes. "Mini-series-historical, contemporary dramas. Children's programming, family films, as well as Satuday morning. Sci-fi stories. Action-adventure-syndication."
Tips: "Please ensure that script/treatment is registered. Receive thousands of scripts each year with no return information. Trends seem to go with character-driven material. Effects important in some respect, but good story is what counts."

✓ **MOVIE REPS INTERNATIONAL**, 7135 Hollywood Blvd., #104, Los Angeles CA 90046. (213)876-4052. Fax: (213)876-4052. Contact: Danny Bohbot, story editor. Estab. 1989. US and foreign audiences. Buys 4 scripts/year. Works with 2 writers/year. Buys first or all rights. No previously produced material. Reports in 1 month on queries. Free catalog. Query with synopsis. Pays royalty or makes outright purchase.
Needs: Films (35mm). Feature film script, minimum 100 pages. Genres: action/thriller, romantic comedy, adventure, art type of film. Looking for: fresh ideas, no holds bar kind of script, extremely original.
Tips: Originality is key; and combine it with high concept.

✓ **OPEN DOOR ENTERTAINMENT**, 162 N. Doheny Dr., Beverly Hills CA 90211. (310)777-8851. Fax: (310)777-8861. E-mail: opendoorkai@compuserve.com. President: Kai Schoenhals. Estab. 1997. Feature films. Global distribution all ages. Buys 4-7 scripts/year. Works with 15-20 writers/year. Buys first rights, all rights and film rights, limited options. Accept previously produced material. Reports in 1 month, depending on where we are in terms of production and travel. Query with synopsis, completed script or resume. Pays 2-5% dependent, once we begin principle photography.
Needs: Films (35mm).
Tips: "We have offices in LA, NYC, London, Copenhagen and Warsaw. We are interested in crossing the Atlantic gap. We are most interested in bringing projects to Poland to be put into production there (i.e., genre, sci-fi, fantasy, horror, epic, comedy, drama, action)."

✓ ■ **TOM PARKER MOTION PICTURES**, 3941 S. Bristol, #285, Santa Ana CA 92704. (714)545-2887. Fax: (714)545-9775. President: Tom Parker. Contact: Jennifer Phelps, script/development. Produces and distributes feature-length motion pictures worldwide for theatrical, home video, pay and free TV. Also produces short subject special interest films (30, 45, 60 minutes). Works with 5-10 scripts/year. Previously produced and distributed "Amazing Love Secret" (R), and "The Sturgis Story" (R). Reports in 6 months. "Follow the instructions herein and do not phone for info or to inquire about your script."
Needs: "Complete script *only* for low budget (under $1 million) "R" or "PG" rated action/thriller, action/

adventure, comedy, adult romance (R), sex comedy (R), family action/adventure to be filmed in 35mm film for the theatrical and home video market. (Do not send TV movie scripts, series, teleplays, stage plays). *Very limited dialogue*. Scripts should be action-oriented and fully described. Screen stories or scripts OK, but no camera angles please. No heavy drama, documentaries, social commentaries, dope stories, weird or horror. Violence or sex OK, but must be well motivated with strong story line." Submit synopsis and description of characters with finished scripts. Makes outright purchase: $5,000-25,000. Will consider participation, co-production.
Tips: "Absolutely will not return scripts or report on rejected scripts unless accompanied by SASE."

N PICTURE ENTERTAINMENT CORPORATION, 8332 Melrose, Hollywood CA 90069. (310)858-8300. President/CEO: Lee Caplin. Vice President Development: Sonia Mintz. Produces feature films for theatrical audience and TV audience. Buys 2 scripts/year. Works with 10 writers/year. Buys all rights. Reports on submissions in 2 months.
Needs: Films (35mm); videotapes. Feature scripts 100-120 pages. Submit completed script. "Pays on a deal by deal basis; some WGA, some not."
Tips: "Don't send derivitive standard material. Emphasis on unique plot and characters, realistic dialogue. *Discourage* period pieces, over-the-top comedy, graphic sex/violence, SciFi. *Encourage* action, action/comedy, thriller, thriller/comedy." No summaries or treatments; completed screenplays only.

POP/ART FILM FACTORY, 513 Wilshire Blvd., #215, Santa Monica CA 90401. Mailing address: 300 Carlsbad Village Dr., Suite 108A-65, Carlsbad CA 92008. E-mail: dzpff@earthlink.net. Website: www.molotovpictures .com, click on "directors, Daniel Zirilli." Contact: Daniel Zirilli. Estab. 1990. Produces material for "all audiences/features films." Query with synopsis. Pays on per project basis.
Needs: Film (35mm), documentaries, multimedia kits. "Looking for interesting productions of all kinds. We are producing 3 feature films per year, and 15-20 music-oriented projects. Also looking for exercise and other special interest videos."
Tips: "Be original. Do not play it safe. If you don't receive a response from anyone you have ever sent your ideas to, or you continually get rejected, don't give up if you believe in yourself. Good luck and keep writing!" Will look at "reels" ¾ or VHS.

O PROMARK ENTERTAINMENT GROUP, 3599 Cahuenga Blvd. W., Los Angeles CA 90026. (213)878-0404. Fax: (213)878-0486. Contact: Gil Adrienne Wishnick, vice president Creative Affairs. Promark is a foreign sales company, producing theatrical films for the foreign market. Buys 8-10 scripts/year. Works with 8-10 writers/year. Buys all rights. Reports in 1 month on queries, 2 months on submissions. Query with synopsis. Makes outright purchase.
 • Promark is concentrating on action-thrillers in the vein of *The Net* or *Marathon Man*. They are not looking for science fiction/action as much this year, as they have a rather full production slate with many sci-fi and techno-thrillers.
Needs: Film (35mm). "We are looking for screenplays in the action thriller genres. Our aim is to produce lower budget (3 million and under) films that have a solid, novel premise—a smart but smaller scale independent film. Our films are male-oriented, urban in setting and hopefully smart. We try to find projects with a fresh premise, a clever hook and strong characters. We will also consider a family film, but not a drama or a comedy. Again, these family films need to have an element of action or suspense. We are not interested in comedies, dramas or erotic thrillers. Among the films we produced are: *Angel's Dance*, a twist on conventional hitman films, with Jim Belushi and Sheryl Lee; *A Breed Apart*, a psychological thriller with Andrew McCarthy; *The Invader*, a sci-fiction action/drama, starring Sean Young, Ben Cross and Nick Mancuso. We are currently looking for suspenseful thrillers with interesting, even quirky characters. We are also looking for family films, specifically adventure yarns for and about kids (ages 8-13) in which the kids are the action heroes. The budgets are low (750,000), so special effects are out. Otherwise, our needs remain roughly the same."

THE PUPPETOON STUDIOS, P.O. Box 80141, Las Vegas NV 89180. E-mail: director@scifistation.com. Website: www.scifistation.com. Contact: Arnold Leibovit, president. Estab. 1987. "Broad audience." Works with 2 writers/year. Reports in 1 month on queries; 2 months on scripts. Query with synopsis. Submit complete script. A Submission Release *must* be included with all queries. Currently producing the animated feature, "Moby Dick: The Whale's Tale." SASE required for return of all materials. Pays in accordance with Writers Guild standards. No novels, plays, poems, treatments; no submissions on computer disk. Unsolicited scripts must have release. Must include release form.
Needs: Films (35mm). "We are seeking animation properties including presentation drawings and character designs. The more detailed drawings with animation scripts the better. Always looking for fresh broad audience material."

N RED HOTS ENTERTAINMENT, 634 N. Glen Oaks Blvd., #374, Burbank CA 91502-1024. (818)954-0092. Senior Vice President/Development: Chip Miller. Contact: Kit Gleason, director of story and development. Estab. 1990. Options 1 script/year. Works with 2-3 writers/year. Buys first rights, all rights, "short and long term options, as well." No previously produced material. Reports in 14 weeks on queries; 4 months on mss. Query with synopsis and SASE. Pays in accordance with Writer's Guild standards. "Negotiable on writer's previous credits, etc."

Needs: Film loops (16mm), films (35mm), videotapes. "We are a feature film, television and music video production company and have no audiovisual material needs."

Tips: "Best advice possible: originality, uniqueness, write from your instincts and *don't* follow trends. Send synopsis or 1-page pitch with SASE and release form as well as a personal bio. No hi-tech stories, fatal disease things or yuppie stories. Looking for youth-driven material with unique premise and characters with substance."

▢ REEL LIFE WOMEN, 10158 Hollow Glew Circle, Bel Air CA 90077. (310)271-4722. E-mail: reellifewom en@compuserve.com. Co-President: Joanne Parrent. Estab. 1996. Mass audiences. Buys 3-4 scripts/year. Accepts previously produced material. Reports in 2 months. Query with synopsis, résumé or SASE for response to query. Pays in accordance with Writer's Guild standards.

Needs: Films. Looking for full-length scripts for feature films or television movies only. (No series or episode TV scripts.) Must be professionally formatted (courier 12pt.) and under 130 pages. All genres considered particularly drama, comedy, action, suspense.

Tips: "Must be professional screenwriters. We are not interested in writers who don't know their craft well. That said, we are looking for interesting, unique stories, which have good roles for actresses. We are not interested in women in stereotypical roles, as the male hero's sidekick, as passive helpmates, etc."

RICHULCO, INC., 11041 Santa Monica Blvd., Suite 511, Los Angeles CA 90025. Contact: Richard Hull. Estab. 1993. All audiences. Buys 2 scripts/year. Works with 10-15 writers/year. Buys all rights. Accepts previously produced material. Reports in 1 month on queries; 3 month on submissions. Query with synopsis or résumé.

Needs: Films (35mm), videotapes. High concept, excellent dialogue, screenplays.

Ⓝ ▢ ROSEMONT PRODUCTIONS, 16255 Ventura Blvd., Suite 900, Encino CA 91436. Fax: (818)528-2301. Contact: Sheri Brummond, manager of development. Buys all rights. Accepts previously produced material. Reports in 2 months. Query with synopsis and résumé. Pays royalty or makes outright purchase in accordance with Writer's Guild standards.

Needs: Films, videotapes, multimedia kits. Network and cable movies. Looks at scripts, treatments, books, short stories, novellas, true stories and life rights attached, etc.

THE SHELDON/POST COMPANY, 1437 Rising Glen Rd., Los Angeles CA 90069. Producers: David Sheldon, Ira Post. Estab. 1989. Produces theatrical motion pictures, movies and series for television. Options and acquires all rights. Reports in 2 months. Query with 1-2 page synopsis, 2-3 sample pages and SASE. "Do not send scripts or books until requested. If the synopsis is of interest, you will be sent a release form to return with your manuscript. No phone inquiries." Pays in accordance with Writers Guild standards.

Needs: "We look for all types of material, including comedy, family stories, suspense dramas, horror, sci-fi, thrillers, action-adventure." True stories should include news articles or other documentation.

Tips: "A synopsis should tell the entire story with the entire plot—including a beginning, a middle and an end. During the past three years, the producers have been in business with 20th Century Fox, Paramount Pictures, Columbia Pictures and currently have contracts with Magic Johnson Entertainment, Producers Entertainment Group and Cosgrove-Meuer Productions. Most recent productions: "Grizzly Adams and the Legend of Dark Mountain" and "Secrets of a Small Town.""

▢ SKYLARK FILMS, 1123 Pacific St., Santa Monica CA 90405. (310)396-5753. Fax: (310)396-5753. E-mail: skyfilm@aol.com. Contact: Brad Pollack, producer. Estab. 1990. Buys 6 scripts/year. Buys first or all rights. Accepts previously produced material. Reports in 2-4 weeks on queries; 1-2 months on submissions. Query with synopsis. Option or other structures depending on circumstances. Pays in accordance with Writer's Guild standards.

Needs: Films (TV, cable, feature).

● Skylark Films is now seeking action, suspense, thrillers and science fiction.

Tips: "True stories of romance or tragedy/redemption stories and contemporary issues for TV mows and cable. High concept, high stakes, action or romantic comedy for feature film."

SKYLINE PARTNERS, 10550 Wilshire Blvd., #304, Los Angeles CA 90024. (310)470-3363. Fax: (310)470-0060. E-mail: fkuehnert@netscape.com. Contact: Fred Kuehuert. Estab. 1990. Produces material for theatrical, television, video audiences. Buys 3 scripts/year. Buys all rights. Accepts previously produced material. Reports in 2 months on queries. Query with synopsis. Pays per negotiation.
Needs: Films (35mm).
Tips: "First, send a treatment so a determination can be made if the genre is something we're looking for. Secondly, we will contact the writer if there is preliminary interest. Third, send compiled script plus release form."

◻ **ALAN SMITHEE FILMS**, 7510 Sunset Blvd., Suite #525, Hollywood CA 90046. Website: www.smithee.com/films. Director: Fred Smythe. Contact: Cinjun Sinclair, story analyst. Estab. 1990. Mass, cable television and theatrical releases. Buys 1 script/year. Works with 5 writers/year. Buys first time rights, all rights or options short-term. No previously produced material. No submissions will be returned. Reports in 2 months. Query with synopsis. Pays in accordance with Writer's Guild standards.
Needs: Films (35mm), videotapes. No specific needs, varies constantly with market. Wants internationally marketable material.
Tips: "Strong dialogue. Fresh angles in storylines. It's all been told before, so tell it well."

🄽 **SOUTH FORK PRODUCTIONS**, P.O. Box 1935, Santa Monica CA 90406-1935. Fax: (310)829-5029. Contact: Jim Sullivan, producer. Estab. 1980. Produces material for TV and film. Buys 2 scripts/year. Works with 4 writers/year. Buys all rights. No previously produced material. Send synopsis/outline and motion picture treatments, plus previous credits, with SASE. No complete scripts. Pays in accordance with Writers Guild Standards.
• South Fork is currently looking for Irish-based scripts.
Needs: Films (16, 35mm), videotapes.
Tips: "Follow established formats for treatments. SASE for return."

SPECTACOR FILMS, 9000 Sunset Blvd., #1550, West Hollywood CA 90069. Director of Development: Jonathan Mundale. Estab. 1988. HBO audiences. Buys 3-4 scripts/year. Works with 10-12 writers/year. Buys all rights. Reports in 1 month on queries; 3 months on submissions. Query with synopsis or completed script. Pays small option money applicable to $40-50,000 purchase price.
Needs: Films. Low budget action scripts. Should be 105 pages or less. Cop/action stories, buddy action stories. Unique hook or idea. Hero should be male in his 30's.
Tips: "Have an action script with something truly unique. Keep it proper script format. Keep as few attachments as possible."

STRATUM ENTERTAINMENT, 747 Tearwood Rd., Los Angeles CA 90049. (310)472-4217. President: Dianne Mandell. Estab. 1995. Buys 2-3 scripts/year. Works with 20 writers/year. Buys first and all rights. Reports immediately on queries; 1 month on submissions. Complete script. Pays in accordance with Writer's Guild standards.
Needs: Films.

🅰 **STUDIO MERRYWOOD**, 85 Putnam Ave., Hamden CT 06517-2827. Phone/fax: (203)407-1834. E-mail: merrywood@compuserve.com. Website: ourworld.compuserve.com/homepages/Merrywood. Contact: Raul daSilva, creative director. Estab. 1984. Produces animated and live action motion pictures for entertainment audiences. "We are planning to severely limit but not close out freelance input. Will be taking roughly 5-7%. We will accept only material which we request from agent. Cannot return material or respond to direct queries."
• The Merrywood Studio is no longer producing children's animation of any kind.
Needs: Proprietary material only. Human potential themes woven into highly entertaining drama, high adventure, comedy. This is a new market for animation with only precedent in the illustrated novels published in France and Japan. Cannot handle unsolicited mail/scripts and will not return mail. Open to *agented* submissions of credit sheets, concepts and synopses only. Profit sharing depending upon value of concept and writer's following. Pays at least Writers Guild levels or better, plus expenses.
Tips: "This is *not a market for beginning writers*. Established, professional work with highly unusual and original themes is sought. If you love writing, it will show and we will recognize it and reward it in every way you can imagine. We are not a 'factory' and work on a very high level of excellence."

TALKING RINGS ENTERTAINMENT, P.O. Box 80141, Las Vegas NV 89180. E-mail: director@scifistation.com. Website: www.scifistation.com. President/Artistic Director: Arnold Leibovit. Contact: Barbara Schimpf, vice president, production. Estab. 1988. "Produces material for motion pictures and television. Works with 2 writers/year. Reports on submissions in 2 months. No treatments, novels, poems or plays, no submissions on computer disk. Query with logline and synopsis. A Submission Release *must* be included with all queries. Produced and directed "The Fantasy Film Worlds of George Pal," "The Puppetoon Movie." Currently producing a remake of "The Time Machine," "7 Faces of Dr. Lao." SASE required for return of all materials. Pays in accordance with Writers Guild Standards.

Needs: "Prefers high concept, mixed genres, comedy, adventure, sci-fi/fantasy, as well as unusual visually rich character driven smaller works with unusual twists, comic sensibility, pathos and always always the unexpected." Films (35mm), videotapes. Must include release form.

Tips: "New policy: submission of logline and synopsis for evaluation first. Do not send scripts until we ask for them. A Talking Rings Entertainment release form must be completed and returned with material. Accepting loglines via e-mail at director@scifistation.com."

UNIFILMS, INC., 22931 Sycamore Creek Dr., Valencia CA 91354-2050. (805)297-2000. Vice President, Development: Jack Adams. Estab. 1984. Buys 0-5 scripts/year. Reports in 2 weeks on queries.

Needs: Feature films *only*. Looking for feature film screenplays, current format, 100-120 pages long; commercial but not stupid, dramatic but not "artsy," funny but not puerile. Query with synopsis and SASE. "If you don't include a SASE, we won't reply. We do not accept unsolicited scripts. Save your postage; if you send us a script we'll return it unopened."

Tips: "If you've taken classes, read books, attended seminars and writers' workshops all concerned with script-writing and read hundreds of produced studio screenplays *prior* to seeing the film and you're still convinced you've got a wonderful script, we might want to see it. But desire and enthusiasm are not enough; you have to have independent corroboration that your work is as good as you think it is. If you've got someone else in the entertainment industry to recommend your script, we might be more interested in seeing it. But if you waste our time with a project that's not yet ready to be seen, we're not going to react well. Your first draft is not usually the draft you're going to show to the industry. *Get a professional opinion first*, then rewrite before you submit to us. Very few people care about synopses, outlines or treatments for sales consideration. THE SCRIPT is the basic blueprint, and everyone in the country is working on a script. Ideas are a dime a dozen. If you can *execute* that idea well and get people *excited* about that idea, you've got something. But most writers are wanna-bes, who submit scripts that need a lot more work just to get to the 'promising' stage. Scripts are *always* rewritten. If you can't convince us you're a *writer*, we don't care. But if you *can* write and you've got a *second* wonderful script we might talk. But don't send a 'laundry list' of your scripts; pick the best one and pitch it to us. If it's not for us, then maybe come back with project number two. More than one project at a time confuses Hollywood; make it easy for us and you'll make it easy for yourself. And if you do it in a professional manner, you'll convince us sooner. Good luck, and keep writing (rewriting)."

VANGUARD PRODUCTIONS, 12111 Beatrice St., Culver City CA 90230. Website: www.emamulti. com/vanguard. Contact: Terence M. O'Keefe, president. Estab. 1985. Buys 1 script/year. Buys all rights or options rights. Accepts previously produced material. Reports in 3 months on queries; 6 months on scripts. Query with synopsis, résumé and SASE. Pays in accordance with Writers Guild standards or negotiated option.

Needs: Films (35mm), videotapes.

WONDERLAND ENTERTAINMENT GROUP, 1255 E. Valley Rd., Santa Barbara CA 93108. (805)565-0802. Fax: (805)565-3858. E-mail: wl1@gte.net. Contact: Emmanuel Itier, president. Estab. 1989. Produces material for any audience. Buys 5 scripts/year. Works with 4 writers/year. Buys all rights. Reports in 1 month. Submit complete script and résumé. Pays in accordance with Writers Guild standards.

Needs: Films. "We are seeking any screenplay for full-length motion pictures."

Tips: "Be patient but aggressive enough to keep people interested in your screenplay."

WORLD FILM SERVICES, 630 Fifth Ave., Suite 1505, New York NY 10111. (212)632-3456. Director of Development: David Laserson. Estab. 1963. Mainstream, family, adult. Buys 5 scripts/year. Works with 5-20 writers/year. Buys all rights. Reports in 1 month on queries; 2 months on submissions. Query. Pays in accordance with Writer's Guild standards. "Productions include *The Dresser* and *Passage to India*."

Needs: Films (35mm). "We are looking for beautifully written, character-driven screenplays that can play big. Scripts A-list talent would give their *** to star in."

Tips: "Never assume the director will ameliorate the weak spots in your script. Try to really write a film on paper, to the tiniest detail. Leave the reader reeling from your VISION."

ZACHARY ENTERTAINMENT, 273 S. Swall Dr., Beverly Hills CA 90211-2612. Fax: (310)289-9788. E-mail: zacharyent@aol.com. Development Associate: David O. Miller. Estab. 1981. Audience is film goers of all ages, television viewers. Buys 5-10 scripts/year. Works with 30 writers/year. Rights purchased vary. Produced *The Tie That Binds*, feature film for Hollywood Pictures, a division of Walt Disney Studios and *Carriers*, CBS-TV movie. Reports in 2 weeks on queries; 3 months on submissions. Query with synopsis. Pay varies.

Needs: Films for theatrical, cable and network television release.

Tips: "Submit logline (one line description) and a short synopsis of storyline. Short biographical profile, focus on professional background. SASE required for all mailed inquiries. If submissions are sent via e-mail, subject must include specific information or else run the risk of being deleted as junk mail. All genres accepted but ideas must be comercially viable, high concept, original and marketable."

☑ **ZIDE ENTERTAINMENT/ZIDE/PERRY FILMS**, 9100 Wilshire Blvd., Suite 615E, Beverly Hills CA 90212. (310)887-2990. Fax: (310)887-2995. E-mail: jfrankel@zide.com. Contact: Jennie Frankel, creative executive. Estab. 1994. All audiences. "We set up about 20 projects a year, 2000 should be even bigger." Works with 50 writers/year. Buys management/production company rights. Reports in 1 month. Query with synopsis. We keep a management percentage.

Needs: Films (35mm). Scripts, books, comic books, treatments. "We are looking for examples of strong writing over a commercial idea."

Contests & Awards

In addition to honors and, quite often, cash awards, contests and awards programs offer writers the opportunity to be judged on the basis of quality alone without the outside factors that sometimes influence publishing decisions. New writers who win contests may be published for the first time, while more experienced writers may gain public recognition of an entire body of work.

Listed here are contests for almost every type of fiction writing. Some focus on form, such as short stories, novels or novellas, while others feature writing on particular themes or topics. Still others are prestigious prizes or awards for work that must be nominated such as the Pulitzer Prize in Fiction. Chances are no matter what type of fiction you write, there is a contest or award program that may interest you.

SELECTING AND SUBMITTING TO A CONTEST

Use the same care in submitting to contests as you would sending your manuscript to a publication or book publisher. Deadlines are very important and where possible we've included this information. At times contest deadlines were only approximate at our press deadline, so be sure to write or call for complete information.

Follow the rules to the letter. If, for instance, contest rules require your name on a cover sheet only, you will be disqualified if you ignore this and put your name on every page. Find out how many copies to send. If you don't send the correct amount, by the time you are contacted to send more it may be past the submission deadline. An increasing number of contests invite writers to query by e-mail and many post contest information on their websites. Check listings for e-mail and website addresses.

One note of caution: Beware of contests that charge entry fees that are disproportionate to the amount of the prize. Contests offering a $10 prize, but charging $7 in entry fees, are a waste of your time and money.

If you are interested in a contest or award that requires your publisher to nominate your work, it's acceptable to make your interest known. Be sure to leave the publisher plenty of time, however, to make the nomination deadline.

ADVENTURES IN STORYTELLING MAGAZINE'S NATIONAL STORIES INTO PRINT WRITING CONTEST, *Adventures in Storytelling Magazine*, 1702 Eastbrook Dr., Columbus OH 43223. Contact: Chris Irvin. Annual competition with theme for stories 500 words or less. Prizes: 1st, 2nd and 3rd place winner and 3 honorable mentions. Cash awards are given based on total entry fees. First place will receive 25% of total entry fees; 2nd place, 15%; and 3rd place, 10%. Entry fee $3 per entry. Competition recieves approximately 25 submissions. Guidelines for SASE. Inquiries by e-mail OK. Deadline: November 1. Winners announced by January 31. "Follow guidelines carefully. Be sure your story does not exceed word limit and conforms to contest themes."

AIM MAGAZINE SHORT STORY CONTEST, P.O. Box 1174, Maywood IL 60153. Fax: (206)543-2746. Website: www.aimmagazine.org. Contact: Myron Apilado, publisher/editor; Ruth Apilado, associate editor; Mark Boone, fiction editor. Estab. 1984. "To encourage and reward good writing in the short story form. The contest is particularly for new writers." Award: $100 plus publication in fall issue. Competition receives 40 submissions. "Judged by *AIM*'s editorial staff." Sample copy for $4 or on website. Contest rules for SASE. Deadline: August 15. Unpublished submissions. "We're looking for compelling, well-written stories with lasting social significance." Winners announced September 1.

AKC GAZETTE, 260 Madison Ave., New York NY 10016. (212)696-8333. Features Editor: Josh Adams. Annual contest for short stories under 2,000 words. Award: Prizes of $350, $250 and $150 for top three entries.

Top entry published in magazine. Judges: Panel. Contest requirements available for SASE. "The *Gazette* sponsors an annual fiction contest for short short stories on some subject relating to purebred dogs. Fiction for our magazine needs a slant toward the serious fancier with real insight into the human/dog bond and breed-specific purebred behavior." Deadline: September 30. Winners announced in May. Winners notified by phone and mail. List of winners available for SASE.

⬤ **AKRON MANUSCRIPT CLUB ANNUAL FICTION CONTEST**, Akron Manuscript Club and A.U., Falls Writer's Workshop, and Taylor Memorial Library, P.O. Box 1101, Cuyahoga Falls OH 44223-0101. (330)923-2094. Contest Director: M.M. LoPiccolo. Award to "encourage writers with cash prizes and certificates and to provide in-depth critique that most writers have never had the benefit of seeing." Annual competition for short stories. Award: Certificates to $50 (1st Prize in three fiction categories dependent on funding); certificates for 2nd and 3rd Prizes. Competition receives 20-50 submissions per category. Judge: M.M. LoPiccolo. Entry/critique fee $25 for each entry in one category. Guidelines will be sent *only* with SASE. Inquiries by e-mail OK. Deadline: January 1-March 15. Unpublished submissions. Word length: 2,500 words (12-13 pages). Send all mail to: Fiction Contest, P.O. Box 1101, Cuyahoga Falls OH 44223-0101, Attn: M.M. LoPiccolo. "Send *no* manuscript without obtaining current guidelines. *Nothing* will be returned without SASE." Winners announced May 2000. Winners notified by mail. List of winners available after May for SASE.

✔⬤◎ **ALLIGATOR JUNIPER NATIONAL WRITING CONTEST**, Prescott College, 220 Grove Ave., Prescott AZ 86301. (520)778-2090, ext. 2012. Fax: (520)776-5137. Annual competition for fiction, creative nonfiction, poetry. "We aim to publish work that is original, graceful, skillful, authentic, moving, and memorable." Award: $500 plus publication for 1st place in each category. Non-winners chosen for publication paid in copies. Competition receives 250 submissions. Fiction is judged by editors and staff of *Alligator Juniper*. Entry fee $10 for each story up to 30 pages. Additional entries require additional fee. All entrants receive the next issue, a $7.50 value. Guidelines available for SASE. Deadline: October. Winners announced January. Winners notified by phone. List of winners mailed to all entrants.

⬤ *AMELIA* **MAGAZINE AWARDS**, 329 "E" St., Bakersfield CA 93304. (805)323-4064. Contact: Frederick A. Raborg, Jr., editor. The Reed Smith Fiction Prize; The Willie Lee Martin Short Story Award; The Cassie Wade Short Fiction Award; The Patrick T. T. Bradshaw Fiction Award; and four annual genre awards in science fiction, romance, western and fantasy/horror. Estab. 1984. Annual. "To publish the finest fiction possible and reward the writer; to allow good writers to earn some money in small press publication. *Amelia* strives to fill that gap between major circulation magazines and quality university journals." Unpublished submissions. Length: The Reed Smith—3,000 words maximum; The Willie Lee Martin—3,500-5,000 words; The Cassie Wade—4,500 words maximum; The Patrick T. T. Bradshaw—25,000 words; the genre awards—science fiction, 5,000 words; romance, 3,000 words; western, 5,000 words; fantasy/horror, 5,000 words. Award: "Each prize consists of $200 plus publication and two copies of issue containing winner's work." The Reed Smith Fiction Prize offers two additional awards when quality merits of $100 and $50, and publication; Bradshaw Fiction Award: $250, 2 copies. Deadlines: The Reed Smith Prize—September 1; The Willie Lee Martin—March 1; The Cassie Wade—June 1; The Patrick T. T. Bradshaw—February 15; *Amelia* fantasy/horror—February 1; *Amelia* western—April 1; *Amelia* romance—October 1; *Amelia* science fiction—December 15. Entry fee: $7.50. Sample copies: $9.95. Bradshaw Award fee: $10. Contest rules for SASE. Looking for "high quality work equal to finest fiction being published today."

✔⬤◎ *ANALECTA* **COLLEGE FICTION CONTEST**, The Liberal Arts Council, FAC 17, Austin TX 78712. (512)471-6563. Fax: (512)471-4518. Website: www.utexas.edu/cola/depts/lac/analecta.html. Editor: Alice Wang. Purpose to "give student writers, at the University of Texas and universities across the country, a forum for publication. We believe that publication in a journal with the quality and reputation of *Analecta* will benefit student writers." Annual competition for short stories, poetry, drama, nonfiction, visual art (submit slides). Award: $100 for featured artist in each genre. Competition receives approximately 1,500 submissions. Judges: Student editorial board of approximately 25 people. No entry fee. Guidelines for SASE. Deadline: mid-October. Unpublished submissions. Limited to college students. Length: 5,000 words or less. "*Analecta* is distributed to 300 university writing programs across the country." Winners announced in early May. Winners notified by phone and mail. List of winners available by e-mail.

⬤ **SHERWOOD ANDERSON SHORT FICTION AWARD**, *Mid-American Review*, Dept. of English, Bowling Green State University, Bowling Green OH 43403. (419)372-2725. Contact: Michael Czyzniejewski, fiction editor. Annual. "Contest is open to all writers. It is judged by a well-known writer, e.g., June Spence. Editors choose the top five entries, then the winner is selected by judge and guaranteed publication in the spring issue of *Mid-American Review*, plus $300. All entrants receive a copy of the issue where the winners are printed." Competition receives 100-200 submissions. $10 entry fee per story. Guidelines available for SASE. Deadline: October 1. Unpublished material. Winners notified by phone or mail.

⊕ ◐ ◎ **ANDREAS-GRYPHIUS-PREIS (LITERATURPREIS DER KÜNSTLERGILDE)**, Die Kunstlergilde e.V., Hafenmarkt 2, D-73728 Esslingen a.N., Germany. Phone: 0049/711/3969010. Fax: 0049/711/39690123. Chief Secretary: Ramona Rauscher-Steinebrunner. "The prize is awarded for the best piece of writing or for complete literary works." Annual competition for short stories, novels, story collections, translations. Award: 1 prize of DM 25,000; 1 prize of DM 7,000. Competition receives 50 entries. Inquiries by fax OK. Judges: Jury members (7 persons). Guidelines available. Fiction should be published in German in the last 5 years. Deadline: October. "The prize is awarded to writers who are dealing with the particular problems of the German culture in eastern Europe." Winners announced beginning of 2000. Winners notified by mail.

✔ **ANNUAL FICTION CONTEST**, (formerly Spring Fantasy Fiction Contest), Women In The Arts, P.O. Box 2907, Decatur IL 62524. (217)872-0811. Contact: Vice President. Award to "encourage new writers, whether published or not." Annual competition for short stories. Award: At least $30. Competition receives 25-30 submissions. Judges: WITA members who are professional writers. Entry fee $2 for each story submitted. Guidelines available for SASE. Deadline: November 15 annually. Published or previously unpublished submissions. Open to anyone. Word length: 1,500 words maximum. "Entrants must send for our contest rules and follow the specific format requirements."

✔ **ANNUAL JUVENILE-FICTION CONTEST**, (formerly Spring Fantasy Juvenile-Fiction Contest), Women In The Arts, P.O. Box 2907, Decatur IL 62524. (217)872-0811. Contact: Vice President. Award to "encourage writers of children's literature, whether published or not." Annual competition for short stories. Award: At least $30. Competition receives 10-15 submissions. Judges: WITA members who are professional writers. Entry fee $2 for each story submitted. Guidelines available for SASE. Deadline: November 15 annually. Published or previously unpublished submissions. Open to anyone. Word length: 1,500 words maximum. "Entrants must send for our contest rules and follow the specific format requirements."

❧ ✔ ◐ ◎ **THE ANNUAL/ATLANTIC WRITING COMPETITIONS**, Writers' Federation of Nova Scotia, 1113 Marginal Rd., Halifax, Nova Scotia B3H 4P7 Canada. (902)423-8116. E-mail: writers1@fox.nstn.ca. Website: www.chebucto.ns.ca/Culture/WFNS/. Executive Director: Jane Buss. "To recognize and encourage unpublished writers in the region of Atlantic Canada. (Competition only open to residents of Nova Scotia, Newfoundland, Prince Edward Island and New Brunswick, the four Atlantic Provinces.)" Annual competition for short stories, novels, poetry, children's writing and drama. Award: Various cash awards. Competition receives approximately 10-12 submissions for novels; 75 for poetry; 75 for children's; 75 for short stories; 10 for nonfiction. Judges: Professional writers, librarians, booksellers. Entry fee $15/entry. Guidelines available after May 1999 for SASE. Inquiries by fax or e-mail OK. Deadline: July 31. Unpublished submissions. Winners announced February 2001. Winners notified by mail. List of winners available by request from office.

✔ ◐ **ANTHOLOGY ANNUAL CONTEST**, P.O. Box 4411, Mesa AZ 85201. (602)461-8200. E-mail: guidelines@inkwellpress.com. Contest Coordinator: Sharon Skinner. Annual competition for short stories. Awards: 1st Prize $150, *Anthology* t-shirt, 1-year subscription; 2nd Prize, $20 gift certificate to inkwellpress.com website, *Anthology* T-shirt, 1-year subscription; 3rd Prize, $10 gift certificate to inkwellpress.com website, *Anthology* t-shirt, 1-year subscription. All prize-winning stories are published in January/February of following year. Entry fee $5/short story. Maximum number of entries: 2/writer. "All stories submitted to contest are eligible to be printed in upcoming issues of *Anthology*, regardless of finish, unless author specifies otherwise. We ask for one-time rights. All copyrights are held by their original owner." Guidelines for SASE. Simultaneous and prepublished submissions OK. Any subject, any genre. Word length: 1,000-6,000 words.

▣ *ANTIETAM REVIEW* **LITERARY AWARD**, *Antietam Review*, 41 S. Potomac St., Hagerstown MD 21740. Phone/fax: (301)791-3132. Contact: Susanne Kass, executive editor. Annual award to encourage and give recognition to excellence in short fiction. Open to writers from Maryland, Pennsylvania, Virginia, West Virginia, Washington DC and Delaware. "We consider only previously unpublished work. We read manuscripts between June 1 and September 1." Award: $100 for the story; the story is printed as lead in the magazine with citation as winner of Literary Contest. Competition receives 100 submissions. "We consider all fiction mss sent to *Antietam Review* Literary Contest as entries for inclusion in each issue. We look for well-crafted, serious literary prose fiction under 5,000 words." Entry fee $10 for each story submitted. Guidelines available after January for #10 SASE. Deadline: September 1. Winners announced October. Winners notified by phone and mail. List of winners available for SASE.

❧ ◯ **ANVIL PRESS INTERNATIONAL 3-DAY NOVEL WRITING CONTEST**, Anvil Press, 204-A 175 E. Broadway, Vancouver, British Columbia V5T 1W2 Canada. (604)876-8710. Fax: (604)879-2667. E-mail: subter@pinc.com. Publisher: Brian Kaufman. Annual prize for best novel written in 3 days, held every Labor Day weekend. Award: Offer of publication with percentage of royalties (grand prize); $500 Canadian (1st runner up); $250 Canadian (2nd runner up). Competition receives 400-500 submissions. Judges: Anvil Press Editorial Board. Entry fee: $25. Guidelines available June 1 for SASE. Inquiries by fax and e-mail OK. Deadline: September 3. "Runner up categories may not be offered every year. Please query." Winners announced November

30. Winners notified by phone and mail. List of winners available November 30 for SASE. "This is a short novel and should contain all the ingredients found in any good novel: character development, a strong story plot line and dramatic action. Don't think of a movie treatment or TV-style scenario and read past winners!"

✓ ○ ◎ **ARIZONA COMMISSION ON THE ARTS CREATIVE WRITING FELLOWSHIPS**, 417 W. Roosevelt St., Phoenix AZ 85003. (602)255-5882. E-mail: general@arizonaarts.org. Website: az.arts.asu.edu/artscomm. Contact: Jill Bernstein, literature director. Fellowships awarded in alternate years to fiction writers and poets. Award: $5,000-7,500. Competition receives 120-150 submissions. Judges: Out-of-state writers/editors. Guidelines available for SASE. Inquiries by fax and e-mail OK. Deadline: September 16. Arizona resident poets and writers over 18 years of age only. Winners announced by April 2000. Winners notified in writing. List of winners available for SASE.

✓ ◐ ◎ **ARTIST TRUST ARTIST FELLOWSHIPS; GAP GRANTS**, Artist Trust, 1402 Third Ave., Suite 404, Seattle WA 98101-2118. (206)467-8734. Fax: (206)467-9633. E-mail: info@artisttrust.org. Program Director: Heather Dwyer. Artist Trust has 2 grant programs for generative artists in Washington State; the GAP and Fellowships. The GAP (Grants for Artist's Projects) is an annual award of up to $1,200 for a project proposal. The program is open to artists in all disciplines. The Fellowship grant is an award of $5,500 in unrestricted funding. Fellowships for Craft, Media, Literature and Music was awarded in 1999, and Fellowships for Dance, Design, Theater and Visual Art will be awarded in 2000. Competition receives 600 (GAP) submissions; 500 (Fellowship 1999). Judges: Fellowship—Peer panel of 3 professional artists and arts professionals in each discipline; GAP—Interdisciplinary peer panel of 5 artists and arts professionals. Guidelines available in December for GAP grants; April for Fellowship for SASE. Inquiries by fax and e-mail OK. Deadline: late February (GAP), mid-June (Fellowship). Winners announced December (Fellowship), May (GAP). Winners notified by mail. List of winners available by mail.

◐ ◎ **ASF TRANSLATION PRIZE**, American-Scandinavian Foundation, 725 Park Ave., New York NY 10021. (212)879-9779. Fax: (212)249-3444. E-mail: agyongy@amscan.org. Website: www.amscan.org. Contact: Publishing office. Estab. 1980. "To encourage the translation and publication of the best of contemporary Scandinavian poetry and fiction and to make it available to a wider American audience." Annual competition for poetry, drama, literary prose and fiction translations. Award: $2,000, a bronze medallion and publication in *Scandinavian Review*. Competition receives 20-30 submissions. Competition rules and entry forms available with SASE. Inquiries by fax and e-mail OK. Deadline: June 1, 2000. Submissions must have been previously published in the original Scandinavian language. No previously translated material. Original authors should have been born within past 200 years. Winners announced in September. Winners notified by mail. List of winners available for SASE. "Select a choice literary work by an important Scandinavian author whose work has not yet been translated into English."

✓ ○ ◎ **THE ISAAC ASIMOV AWARD**, International Association for the Fantastic in the Arts and *Asimov's* magazine, School of Mass Communications, U. of South Florida, 4202 E. Fowler, Tampa FL 33620. (813)974-6792. Fax: (813)974-2591. E-mail: rwilber@chuma.cas.usf.edu. Administrator: Rick Wilber. "The award honors the legacy of one of science fiction's most distinguished authors through an award aimed at undergraduate writers." Annual award for short stories. Award: $500 and consideration for publication in *Asimov's*. Competition receives 100-200 submissions. Judges: *Asimov's* editors. Entry fee: $10 for up to 3 submissions. Guidelines available for SASE. Inquiries by fax and e-mail OK. Deadline: December 15. Unpublished submissions. Full-time college undergraduates only. Winners announced in February. Winners notified by telephone. List of winners available in March for SASE.

❧ ✓ **ASTED/GRAND PRIX DE LITTERATURE JEUNESSE DU QUEBEC-ALVINE-BELISLE, (III, IV)**, Association pour l'avancement des sciences et des techniques de la documentation, 3414 Avenue du Parc, Bureau 202, Montreal, Quebec H2X 2H5 Canada. (514)281-5012. Fax: (514)281-8219. E-mail: info@asted.org. Website: www.asted.org. President: Micheline Patton. "Prize granted for the best work in youth literature edited in French in the Quebec Province. Authors and editors can participate in the contest." Annual competition for fiction and nonfiction for children and young adults. Award: $500. Deadline: June 1. Contest entry limited to editors of books published during the preceding year. French translations of other languages are not accepted.

◐ ◎ **THE ATHENAEUM LITERARY AWARD**, The Athenaeum of Philadelphia, 219 S. Sixth St., Philadelphia PA 19106. (215)925-2688. Fax: (215)925-3755. Website: www.libertynet.org/athena. Contact: Literary Award Committee. Annual award to recognize and encourage outstanding literary achievement in Philadelphia and its vicinity. Award: A bronze medal bearing the name of the award, the seal of the Athenaeum, the title of the book, the name of the author and the year. Competition receives 10-20 submissions. Judged by committee appointed by Board of Directors. Deadline: December. Submissions must have been published during the preceding year. Nominations shall be made in writing to the Literary Award Committee by the author, the publisher or a member of the Athenaeum, accompanied by a copy of the book. The Athenaeum Literary Award is granted for a work of general literature, not exclusively for fiction. Juvenile fiction is not included. Winners announced spring 2002. Winners notified by mail. List of winners available on website.

AUTHORS IN THE PARK/*FINE PRINT* CONTEST, P.O. Box 85, Winter Park FL 32790-0085. (407)658-4520. Fax: (407)275-8688. E-mail: foley@magicnet.net. Contact: David Foley. Annual competition. Award: $1,000 (1st Prize), $500 (2nd Prize), $250 (3rd Prize). Competition receives 200 submissions. Guidelines for SASE. Read guidelines before sending ms. Deadline: April 31. Word length: 5,000 words maximum. Winners announced in short story collection, *Fine Print*, before December.

AWP AWARD SERIES IN POETRY, CREATIVE NONFICTION AND SHORT FICTION, AWP/ Thomas Dunne Books Novel Award, The Associated Writing Programs, Tallwood House, Mail Stop 1E3, George Mason University, Fairfax VA 22030. (703)993-4301. Fax: (703)993-4302. E-mail: awp@gmu.edu. Website: www.gmu.edu/departments/awp. Contact: David Sherwin, editor. Annual award. The AWP Award Series was established in cooperation with several university presses in order to publish and make fine fiction available to a wide audience. The competition is open to all authors writing in English. Winners receive $2,000. Awards: $2,000 honorarium and publication with a university press. In addition, AWP tries to place mss of finalists with participating presses. Competition receives 300-400 novel and 200-300 short fiction submissions. Judges: Distinguished writers in each genre. Entry fee $20 nonmembers, $10 AWP members. Contest/award rules and guidelines for business-size SASE or visit our website. No phone calls please. Mss must be postmarked between January 1-February 28. Only book-length mss in the novel and short story collections are eligible. Manuscripts previously published in their entirety, including self-publishing, are not eligible. No mss returned. Winners announced in August. Winners notified by phone or mail. List of winners available on website.

AWP INTRO JOURNALS PROJECT, Tallwood House, Mail Stop 1E3, George Mason University, Fairfax VA 22030. Contact: David Sherwin. "This is a prize for students in AWP member university creative writing programs only. Authors are nominated by the head of the creative writing department. Each school may send 2 nominated short stories." Annual competition for short stories and poetry. Award: $50 plus publication in participating journal. 1998 journals included *Puerto del Sol*, *Quarterly West*, *Mid-American Review*, *Cimmaron Review*, *The Metropolitan Review*, *Willow Springs* and *Hayden's Ferry Review*. Judges: AWP. Deadline: December. Unpublished submissions only.

EMILY CLARK BALCH AWARDS, *The Virginia Quarterly Review*, One West Range, Charlottesville VA 22903. Editor: Staige D. Blackford. Annual award "to recognize distinguished short fiction by American writers." For stories published in *The Virginia Quarterly Review* during the calendar year. Award: $500.

BARRINGTON AREA ARTS COUNCIL/WHETSTONE PRIZES, Box 1266, Barrington IL 60010-1266. (847)382-5626. Fax: (847)382-3685. Co-editors: Sandra Berris, Marsha Portnoy and Jean Tolle. Annual competition "to encourage and reward works of literary excellence." Awards: The Whetstone Prize, usually $500 to a single author for best fiction, nonfiction or poetry selected for publication in *Whetstone* (an annual literary journal); The John Patrick McGrath Award, $250 to a single author, for fiction. Competition receives hundreds of entries; all submissions to *Whetstone* are eligible. Judges: Co-editors of *Whetstone*. Guidelines available by mail or fax query. Deadline: open until publication; "we read all year." Unpublished submissions. Length: prose up to 25 pages; poetry, 3-5 poems. Sample copies with guidelines $5 postpaid. Winners announced December. Winners notified by letter. List of winners available in January for SASE. Winners announced in front of *Whetstone* as well as press releases, etc.

MILDRED L. BATCHELDER AWARD, Association for Library Service to Children/American Library Association, 50 E. Huron St., Chicago IL 60611. (312)944-6780, ext. 2163. Fax: (312)280-3257. E-mail: alsc@ala.org. Website: www.ala.org/alsc. Program Officer: Linda Bostrom. To encourage international exchange of quality children's books by recognizing US publishers of such books in translation. Annual competition for translations. Award: Citation. Judge: Mildred L. Batchelder award committee. Guidelines available February 1 by phone, mail or e-mail. Deadline: December. Books should be US trade publications for which children, up to and including age 14, are potential audience. Winners announced in mid-January. Winners notified by phone. List of winners available by website, phone.

**FOR EXPLANATIONS OF THESE SYMBOLS,
SEE THE INSIDE FRONT AND BACK COVERS OF THIS BOOK.**

🌐 **BCLT/BCLA TRANSLATION COMPETITION**, British Centre for Literary Translation/British Comparative Literature Association, % BCLT, University of East Anglia, Norwich NR4 7TJ England. Phone/fax: +44 1603 592785. E-mail: c.c.wilson@uea.ac.uk. Contact: Christine Wilson, publicity coordinator. Annual competition for translations. Award: £350 (1st Prize); £200 (2nd Prize); £100 (3rd Prize). Judges: A panel. Entry fee £5 sterling only. Guidelines available for SASE. Deadline: early 2000. Word length: maximum of 25 double-spaced A4 single-sided pages. Winners announced July or August. Winners notified by mail.

⭕ **GEORGE BENNETT FELLOWSHIP**, Phillips Exeter Academy, 20 Main St., Exeter NH 03833-2460. (603)772-4311. Coordinator, Selection Committee: Charles Pratt. "To provide time and freedom from monetary concerns to a person contemplating or pursuing a career as a professional writer. The committee favors applicants who have not yet published a book-length work with a major publisher." Annual award of writing residency. Award: A stipend ($6,000 at present), plus room and board for academic year. Competition receives approximately 125 submissions. Judges are a committee of the English department. Entry fee $5. Application form and guidelines for SASE, or obtain from the Academy website: www.exeter.edu. Deadline: December 1. Winners announced in March. Winners notified by letter or phone. List of winners available in March. All applicants will receive an announcement of the winner.

▥ **BERTELSMANN'S WORLD OF EXPRESSIONS SCHOLARSHIP PROGRAM**, Bertelsmann USA, 1540 Broadway, New York NY 10036. (212)930-4978. Fax: (212)930-4783. E-mail: bwoesp@bmge.com. Website: www.worldofexpression.org. Program Manager: Melanie Fallon-Houska. Annual competition for short stories and poems. Award: $1,000-10,000, 46 awards total. Competition receives 2,000 submissions per category. Judges: Various city officials, executives, authors, editors. Guidelines for SASE. Deadline: March 15. All the winners must be public New York City high school seniors. Word length: 2,500 words or less.

⭕ ◎ **"BEST OF OHIO WRITERS" CONTEST**, *Ohio Writer Magazine*, P.O. Box 91801, Cleveland OH 44101. (216)932-8444. Executive Director: Darlene Montonaro. Award "to encourage and promote the work of writers in Ohio." Annual competition for short stories. Awards: $150 (1st Prize), $50 (2nd Prize). Competition receives 200-300 submissions. Judges: "A selected panel of prominent Ohio writers." Entry fee $10; includes subscription to *Ohio Writer*. Guidelines available after January 1 for SASE. Deadline: July 31. Unpublished submissions. Ohio writers only. Length: 2,500 words. "No cliché plots; we're looking for fresh, unpublished voices." Winners announced November 1. Winners are notified by phone; confirmed by mail. List of winners available November 1 for SASE.

▥ ◐ ◎ **BEST OF SOFT SCIENCE FICTION CONTEST**, Soft SF Writers Assoc., 1277 Joan Dr., Merritt Island FL 32952. Contest Director: Lela E. Buis. Award to "encourage the publication of science fiction styles in which emotional content and artistic effect are emphasized rather than plot and deterministic science. Adult issues are encouraged, but gratuitous violence and graphic sex are not the emotional impacts we want." Annual award for short stories. Awards: $100 (1st Prize), $50 (2nd Prize), $25 (3rd Prize). Judges: Members of the Soft SF Writers Association. No entry fee. Guidelines for SASE. Entries accepted October 1 through December 15. Entries must have been submitted for publication or published between January 1 and December 15. Word length: 7,000 words. Story must have elements of science fiction, though cross-genre stories are acceptable. Judging criteria: emotional impact, artistic style, clarity, originality, characterization, theme weight, imagery, sensuality; violence or sex added for shock value are discouraged. Format: Send disposable manuscript in standard format. Securely attach name and address.

✅ ◎ **DORIS BETTS FICTION PRIZE**, (formerly NCWN Fiction Competition), North Carolina Writers' Network, 3501 Hwy. 54 W., Studio C, Chapel Hill NC 27516. (919)967-9540. Fax: (919)929-0535. E-mail: mail@ncwriters.org. Website: www.ncwriters.org. Program Coordinator: Frances Dowell. Award to "encourage and recognize the work of emerging and established North Carolina writers." Annual competition for short stories. Awards: $150 1st Place, $100 2nd Place, $50 3rd Place. Competition receives 100-150 submissions. Judges change annually. Entry fee $4 for NCWN members; $6 for nonmembers. Guidelines for SASE. Deadline: February 27. Unpublished submissions. "The award is available only to legal residents of North Carolina or out-of-state NCWN members." Word length: 6 double-spaced pages (1,500 words maximum). Winners announced in May. Winners notified by phone and letter. List of winners available for SASE.

🍁 ✅ ◐ ◎ **THE GEOFFREY BILSON AWARD FOR HISTORICAL FICTION FOR YOUNG PEOPLE**, The Canadian Children's Book Centre, 35 Spadina Rd., Toronto, Ontario M5R 2S9 Canada. (416)975-0010. Fax: (416)975-1839. E-mail: ccbc@sympatico.ca. Website: www3.sympatico.ca/ccbc. Contact: Hadley Dyer, library coordinator. "Award given for best piece of historical fiction for young people." Annual competition for novels. Award: $1,000 (Canadian). Competition receives approximately 8-12 submissions. Judged by a jury of five people from the children's literature community. Previously published submissions. Canadian authors only. "Publishers of Canadian children's books regularly submit copies of their books to the Centre for our library collection. From those books, selections are made for inclusion in the Our Choice list of recommended Canadian children's books each year. The shortlist for the Bilson Award is created after the selections have been made for Our Choice, as the book must first be selected for Our Choice to be part of the Bilson shortlist."

☑ ◎ **IRMA S. AND JAMES H. BLACK CHILDREN'S BOOK AWARD**, Bank Street College, 610 W. 112th St., New York NY 10025-1898. (212)875-4450. Fax: (212)875-4558. E-mail: lindag@bnkst.edu. Website: www.bankstreet.edu/html/library/isb.html. Award Director: Linda Greengrass. Annual award "to honor the young children's book published in the preceding year judged the most outstanding in text as well as in art. Book must be published the year preceding the May award." Award: Press function at Harvard Club, a scroll and seals by Maurice Sendak for attaching to award book's run. Judges: Adult children's literature experts and children 6-10 years old. No entry fee. Inquiries by fax and e-mail OK. Deadline: December 15. "Write to address above. Usually publishers submit books they want considered, but individuals can too. No entries are returned." Winners announced in May. Winners notified by phone.

☑ ◎ ◎ **JAMES TAIT BLACK MEMORIAL PRIZES**, Department of English Literature, University of Edinburgh, Edinburgh EH8 9JX Scotland. Phone: 44 131 650 3617. Fax: 44 131 650 6898. E-mail: communications.office@ed.ac.uk. Website: www.ed.ac.uk. Contact: Anne McKelvie, Deputy Director of Communications and Public Affairs. "Two prizes are awarded: one for the best work of fiction, one for the best biography or work of that nature, published during the calendar year: October 1st to September 30th." Annual competition. Award: £3,000 each. Competition receives approximately 300 submissions. Judge: Professor R.D.S. Jack, Dept. of English Literature. Guidelines for SASE or SAE and IRC. Guildlines available Sept. 30. Deadline: September 30. Previously published submissions. "Eligible works are those written in English, originating with a British publisher, and first published in Britain in the year of the award. Works should be submitted by publishers." Winners announced in January. Winners notified by phone, via publisher. Contact Department of English Literature for list of winners.

☑ ◎ **THE BLACK WARRIOR REVIEW LITERARY AWARD**, P.O. Box 862936, Tuscaloosa AL 35486-0277. (205)348-4518. Website: www.sa.ua.edu/osm/bwr. Editor: Laura Didyk. "Award is to recognize the best fiction published in *BWR* in a volume year. Only fiction accepted for publication is considered for the award." Competition is for short stories and novel chapters. Award: $500. Competition receives approximately 3,000 submissions. Prize awarded by an outside judge. Guidelines available for SASE. Winners announced in the Fall. Winners notified by phone or mail. List of winners available for purchase in Fall issue.

⊕ ◎ ◎ **BOARDMAN TASKER PRIZE**, 14 Pine Lodge, Dairyground Rd., Bramhall, Stockport, Cheshire SK7 2HS United Kingdom. Phone/fax: 0161 439 4624. Contact: Mrs. Dorothy Boardman. "To reward a book which has made an outstanding contribution to mountain literature. A memorial to Peter Boardman and Joe Tasker, who disappeared on Everest in 1982." Award: £2,000. Competition receives 20 submissions. Judges: A panel of 3 judges elected by trustees. Guidelines for SASE. Deadline: August. Limited to works published or distributed in the UK for the first time between November 1 and October 31. Publisher's entry only. "May be fiction, nonfiction, poetry or drama. Not an anthology. Subject must be concerned with a mountain environment. Previous winners have been books on expeditions, climbing experiences; a biography of a mountaineer; novels." Winners announced October or November. Winners notified by mail. Short list, available in September, will be sent to all publishers who have entered books.

☑ ◎ ◎ **BOOK PUBLISHERS OF TEXAS AWARD, The Texas Institute of Letters**, Center for the Study of the Southwest, Flowers Hall 327, Southwest Texas State University, San Marcos TX 78666. (512)245-2232. Fax: (512)245-7462. E-mail: mb13@swt.edu. Website: www.english.swet.edu/css/TIL/index. Secretary: Mark Busby. "Award to honor the best book written for children or young people that was published the year prior to that in which the award is given." Annual competition for children's literature. Award: $250. Competition receives approximately 40 submissions. Judges: Committee selected by TIL. Guidelines available after June 2000 for SASE. Inquiries by e-mail and fax OK. Deadline: January 14, 2000. Previously published submissions from January 1 through December 31 of the year prior to the award. "To be eligible, the writer must have been born in Texas or have lived in the state for two years at some time, or the subject matter of the work must be associated with Texas." Winners announced April 15, 2001. Winners notified by phone. List of winners available on website.

⬚ ⊕ **BOOKER PRIZE FOR FICTION**, Book Trust, Book House, 45 E. Hill, London SW18 2QZ England. Phone: 0181 516 2973. Fax: 0181 516 2978. Prizes Manager: Sandra Vince. Award to the best novel of the year. Annual competition for novels. Award: £20,000. Each of the short listed authors receive £1,000. Competition receives 100 submissions. Judges: Five judges appointed by the Booker Management Committee. Deadline: July 1. Published submissions. A full-length novel written in English by a citizen of the Commonwealth or Republic of Ireland.

☑ ◎ **BOSTON GLOBE-HORN BOOK AWARDS**, *Horn Book Magazine, Inc.*, 56 Roland St., Suite 200, Boston MA 02129. (617)628-0225. Fax: (617)628-0882. E-mail: info@hbook.com. Website: www.hbook.com. Contact: Karen Walsh, marketing manager. Annual award. "To honor excellence in children's fiction or poetry, picture and nonfiction books published within the US." Award: $500 and engraved silver bowl first prize in each category; engraved silver plate for the 2 honor books in each category. Competition receives 2,000 submissions. No entry fee. Guidelines available after January for SASE. Inquiries by fax and e-mail OK. Entry forms or rules for SASE. Deadline: May 15. Previously published material between June 1, 1998-May 31, 1999. Books are submitted by publishers. Winners announced in August. Winners notified by phone. List of winners available in September by telephone or e-mail.

BOSTON REVIEW SHORT STORY CONTEST, *Boston Review*, E53-407, MIT, Cambridge MA 02139. (617)494-0108. E-mail: review@mit.edu. Website: bostonreview.mit.edu. Annual award for short stories. Award: $300. Processing fee $10. Deadline: October 1. Unpublished submissions. Competition receives 500 entries. No restrictions on subject matter. Inquiries by e-mail OK. Deadline September 1. Word length: 4,000 words. Winning entry published in December issue. All entrants receive a 1-year subscription to the *Boston Review* beginning with the December issue. Stories not returned. Winners announced December 1. Winner notified by mail.

BRAZOS BOOKSTORE (HOUSTON) AWARD (SINGLE SHORT STORY), The Texas Institute of Letters, Center for the Study of the Southwest, Flowes Hall 327, Southwest Texas State University, San Marcos TX 78666. (512)245-2232. Fax: (512)245-7462. E-mail: mb13@swt.edu. Website: www.english.swt. edu/css/TIL/index. Secretary: Mark Busby. Award to "honor the writer of the best short story published for the first time during the calendar year before the award is given." Annual competition for short stories. Award: $750. Competition receives approximately 40-50 submissions. Judges: Panel selected by TIL Council. Guidelines for SASE. Inquiries by e-mail OK. Deadline: January 14. Previously published submissions. Entries must have appeared in print between January 1 and December 31 of the year prior to the award. "Award available to writers who, at some time, have lived in Texas at least two years consecutively or whose work has a significant Texas theme. Entries must be sent directly to the three judges. Their names and addresses are available from the TIL office. Include SASE. Winners announced April 15. Winners notified by phone."

BRODY ARTS FUND, California Community Foundation, 606 S. Olive St., Suite 2400, Los Angeles CA 90014. (213)413-4042. Website: www.calfund.org. Contact: Cindy DiGiampaolo, senior program secretary. "To recognize and support the work of emerging writers resident in Los Angeles County, California, whose work reflects the ethnic and cultural diversity of the region." Award granted every 3 years for short stories, novels, poetry, plays and screenplays. Award: $5,000 unrestricted fellowship (approximately 5-7 awarded once every 3 years). Competition receives approximately 150 submissions. Guidelines available after March for SASE. Judges: A peer panel of local writers and editors. Probable deadline in mid-March 2000. Previously published or unpublished submissions. All applicants must be based in Los Angeles County, California. Guidelines and application forms can be requested by phone or letter, but not until February, 2000.

BRONX RECOGNIZES ITS OWN (B.R.I.O.), Bronx Council on the Arts, 1738 Hone Ave., Bronx NY 10461-1486. (718)931-9500. Fax: (718)409-6445. E-mail: bronxart@artswire.org. Website: www.bron xarts.org. Director, Community Arts Services: Ed Friedman. Award to "recognize artistic talent in Bronx County." Annual competition for novels. Award: $1,500 (awards 12/year in visual, media, performing and literary arts). Competition receives approximately 20 literary submissions. Judges: Peer panel of non-Bronx artists. Guidelines available mid-December by a phone call, written request or on website. Inquiries by fax and e-mail OK. Deadline: March. Only Bronx artists may apply. Proof of Bronx residency required. Word length: 20 typed pages of ms. Winners announced in May. Winners notified 2 months after deadline by mail.

GEORGES BUGNET AWARD FOR THE NOVEL, Writers Guild of Alberta, 3rd Floor, Percy Page Centre, 11759 Groat Rd., Edmonton, Alberta T5M 3K6 Canada. (780)422-8174. Fax: (780)422-2663. Contact: Miki Andrejevic, executive director. "To recognize outstanding books published by Alberta authors each year." Annual competition for novels. Award: $500 (Canadian) and leather-bound book. Judges: Selected published writers across Canada. Guidelines for SASE. Deadline: December 31. Previously published submissions. Must have appeared in print between January 1 and December 31. Open to Alberta authors only.

BURNABY WRITERS' SOCIETY ANNUAL COMPETITION, 6584 Deer Lake Ave., British Columbia V5G 3T7 Canada. (604)435-6500. Annual competition to encourage creative writing in British Columbia. "Category varies from year to year." Award: $200, $100 and $50 (Canadian) prizes. Receives 400-600 entries for each award. Judge: "Independent recognized professional in the field." Entry fee $5. Contest requirements after March for SASE. Deadline: May 31. Open to British Columbia authors only. Winners announced in September. Winners notified by phone or mail. List of winners available for SASE.

BUSH ARTIST FELLOWS PROGRAM, (formerly Bush Artist Fellowships), Bush Foundation, E-900 First Nat'l Bank Building, 332 Minnesota St., St. Paul MN 55101-1387. (651)227-5222. Fax: (651)297-6485. E-mail: kpolley@bushfound.org. Program Assistant: Kathi Polley. Award to "provide artists with significant financial support that enables them to further their work and their contribution to their communities. Fellows may decide to take time for solitary work or reflection, engage in collaborative or community projects, or embark on travel or research." Annual grant. Award: $40,000 for 12-18 months. Competition receives 200-300 submissions. Literature (fiction, creative nonfiction, poetry) offered every other year. Next offered 2001 BAF. Applications available August 2000. Inquiries by fax and e-mail OK. Deadline: October 2000. Must meet certain publication requirements. Judges: A panel of artists and arts professionals who reside outside of Minnesota, South Dakota, North Dakota or Wisconsin. Applicants must be at least 25 years old, and Minnesota, South Dakota, North Dakota or Western Wisconsin residents. Students not eligible. Winners announced in Spring 2001. Winners notified by letter. List of winners available in May; will be sent to all applicants.

BYLINE MAGAZINE LITERARY AWARDS, P.O. Box 130596, Edmond OK 73013-0001. (405)348-5591. E-mail: bylinemp@aol.com. Website: www.bylinemag.com. Contact: Marcia Preston, executive editor/publisher. "To encourage our subscribers in striving for high quality writing." Annual awards for short stories and poetry. Award: $250 in each category. Competition receives approximately 200 submissions in each category. Judges are published writers not on the *ByLine* staff. Entry fee $5 for stories; $3 for poems. Guidelines available for SASE. Postmark deadline: November 1. "Judges look for quality writing, well-drawn characters, significant themes. Entries should be unpublished and not have won money in any previous contest. Winners announced in February issue and published in February or March issue with photo and short bio. Open to subscribers only."

CALIFORNIA BOOK AWARDS, The Commonwealth Club of California, 595 Market St., San Francisco CA 94105. (415)597-6700. (415)597-6729. E-mail: cwc@sirius.com. Website: www.commonwealthclub.org. Book Award Coordinator: Jim Wilson. Annual competition for novels and story collections. Award: $2,000 (1st Prize); $300 (2nd Prize). Competition receives 25-45 submissions. Judges: Panel of jurors. Guidelines for SASE. Inquiries by fax and e-mail OK. Deadline: January 31. Previously published submissions that appeared in print between January 1 and December 30. "Writers must have been legal residents of California when manuscript was accepted for publication. Enter as early as possible—supply three copies of book." Winners announced in the summer. Winners notified by phone, mail or through publisher. List of winners available for SASE or on website.

CALIFORNIA WRITERS' CLUB CONTEST, California Writers' Club, P.O. Box 1281, Berkeley CA 94701. Contact: Contest Coordinator. Cash awards "to encourage writing." Competition is held annually. Competition receives varying number of submissions. Judges: Professional writers, members of California Writers' Club. Entry fee to be determined. Guidelines available January 1 through March 30 by mail or on website. Inquiries by fax or e-mail OK. Deadline: May 1. Unpublished submissions. "Open to all." Winners announced at annual conference. Winners notified by mail, fax or phone. List of winners available July 1.

JOHN W. CAMPBELL MEMORIAL AWARD FOR THE BEST SCIENCE-FICTION NOVEL OF THE YEAR; THEODORE STURGEON MEMORIAL AWARD FOR THE BEST SCIENCE FICTION SHORT FICTION, Center for the Study of Science Fiction, English Dept., University of Kansas, Lawrence KS 66045. (785)864-3380. Fax: (785)864-4298. E-mail: jgunn@falcon.cc.ukans.edu. Website: www.falcon.cc.ukans.edu/~sfcenter/. Professor and Director: James Gunn. "To honor the best novel and short science fiction of the year." Annual competition for short stories and novels. Award: Certificate. "Winners' names are engraved on a trophy." Campbell Award receives approximately 200 submissions. Judges: 2 separate juries. Inquiries by e-mail and fax OK. Deadline: December 31. For previously published submissions. "Ordinarily publishers should submit work, but authors have done so when publishers would not. Send for list of jurors." Entrants for the Sturgeon Award are selected by nomination only. Winners announced July 14. List of winners available for SASE.

CANADA COUNCIL GOVERNOR GENERAL'S LITERARY AWARDS, Canada Council for the Arts, 350 Albert St., P.O. Box 1047, Ottawa, Ontario K1P 5V8 Canada. (613)566-4414, ext. 5576. E-mail: josiane.polidori@canadacouncil.ca. Contact: Writing and Publishing Section. "Awards of $10,000 each are given annually to the best English-language and best French-language Canadian work in each of seven categories: children's literature (text) and children's literature (illustration), drama, fiction, poetry, nonfiction and translation." Canadian authors, illustrators and translators only. Books must be submitted by publishers (4 copies must be sent to the Canada Council) and accompanied by a Publisher's Submissions Form, available from the Writing and Publishing Section. Self-published books are not eligible.

CAPTIVATING BEGINNINGS CONTEST, *Lynx Eye*, 1880 Hill Dr., Los Angeles CA 90041-1244. (323)550-8522. E-mail: pamccully@aol.com. Co-editor: Pam McCully. Annual award for stories "with engrossing beginnings, stories that will enthrall and absorb readers." Award: $100 plus publication, 1st Prize; $10 each for 4 honorable mentions plus publication. Competition receives 6,000 submissions. Judges: *Lynx Eye* editors. Entry fee $5/story. Guidelines available for SASE. Unpublished submissions. Length: 7,500 words or less. "The stories will be judged on the first 500 words." Deadline: January 31. Winners announced March 15. Winners notified by phone or e-mail. List of winners available March 31 for SASE.

N ◎ THE CAROLINA NOVEL AWARD, Banks Channel Books, P.O. Box 4446, Wilmington NC 28406. Biennial award to encourage excellence in fiction-writing by Carolina authors. Competition for original novels. Award: $1,000 advance against royalties and publication by Banks Channel Books. Judges: Banks Channel Books staff. Entry fee: $35. Guidelines for SASE. Deadline varies. Unpublished submissions. Limited to North and South Carolina residents. Length: 200-400 pages. Winner announced in December. Contest results available for SASE.

◻ ◎ RAYMOND CARVER SHORT STORY CONTEST, Dept. of English, Humboldt State University, Arcata CA 95521. (707)826-5946, ext. 1. Fax: (707)826-5939. E-mail: kce1@axe.humboldt.edu. Contact: Student Coordinator. Annual award for previously unpublished short stories. Award: $1,000 and publication in *Toyon* (1st Prize). $500 and honorable mention in *Toyon* (2nd Prize). Honorable mention in *Toyon* (3rd Prize). Competition receives 400 submissions. Entry fee $10/story. Guidelines available June 1 for #10 SASE. Deadline: December 1. For US citizens only. Send 2 copies of story; author's name, address, phone number and title of story on separate cover page only. Story must be no more than 6,000 words. For notification of receipt of ms, include self-addressed, stamped postcard. For Winners List include SASE. For a copy of the *Toyon*, send $2. "Follow directions and have faith in your work." Winners announced June 1. Winners notified by mail. List of winners available June 1.

N ◻ ◎ WILLA CATHER FICTION PRIZE, Helicon Nine Editions, 3607 Pennsylvania, Kansas City MO 64111. (816)753-1095. Fax: (816)753-1016. Contact: Gloria Vando Hickok, publisher. Annual competition for novels, story collections and novellas. Award: $1,000. Competition receives 300-350 submissions. Winners chosen by nationally recognized writers. Entry fee $20. Guidelines for SASE. Deadline: May 1. Unpublished submissions. Open to all writers residing in the US and its territories and Canada. Mss will not be returned. Past judges include William Gass, Robley Wilson, Daniel Stern, Leonard Michaels, Carolyn Doty. Winners announced in the fall. Winners notified by phone. Finalists notified by mail with critique of ms. List of winners available in November for SASE.

◐ THE *CHELSEA* AWARDS, P.O. Box 773, Cooper Station, New York NY 10276-0773. E-mail: rafoerster@ aol.com. *Mail entries to*: Chelsea Awards, %Richard Foerster, Editor, P.O. Box 1040, York Beach ME 03910-1040. Annual competition for short stories. Award: $1,000 and publication in *Chelsea* (all entries are considered for publication). Competition receives 300 submissions. Judges: The editors. Entry fee $10 (for which entrants also receive a subscription). Guidelines available for SASE. Deadline: June 15. Unpublished submissions. Manuscripts may not exceed 30 typed pages or about 7,500 words. The stories must not be under consideration elsewhere or scheduled for book publication within 8 months of the competition deadline. Include separate cover sheet; no name on ms. Mss will not be returned; include SASE for notification of results. Winners announced August 15. Winners notified by telephone. List of winners available August 20 for SASE.

✓ ◻ ◎ CHICANO/LATINO LITERARY CONTEST, Dept. of Spanish & Portuguese, University of California-Irvine, Irvine CA 92697. (949)824-5443. Fax: (949)824-2803. E-mail: rubyt@uci.edu. Website: www. humanities.hnet.uci.edu/spanishandportuguese/contest.html. Coordinator: Ruby Trejo. Annual award for novels, short stories, poetry and drama (different genre every year). Award: Usually $1,000. Guidelines for SASE. Deadline: May 15. Inquiries by fax and e-mail OK. Unpublished submissions. Winners notified by letter in October.

⊕ ◐ THE CHILDREN'S BOOK AWARD, Federation of Children's Book Groups, The Old Malt House, Aldbourne, Marlborough, Wilts SN8 2DW England. Award to "promote good quality books for children." Annual award for short stories, novels, story collections and translations. Award: "Portfolio of children's writing and drawings and a magnificent trophy of silver and oak." Judges: Thousands of children from all over the United Kingdom. Guidelines for SASE or SAE and IRC. Deadline: December 31. Published and previously unpublished submissions (first publication in UK). "The book should be suitable for children."

N ◎ CHILDREN'S WRITERS FICTION CONTEST, Goodin Williams Goodwin Literary Associates, P.O. Box 8863, Springfield MO 65801-8863. (417)863-7670. Fax: (417)864-4745. Coordinator: V.R. Williams. Award to "promote writing for children by encouraging children's writers and giving them an opportunity to submit their work in competition." Annual competition for short stories and translations. Award: $150 and/or publication in *Hodge Podge*. Competition receives 100 submissions. "Judged by Goodin Williams and Goodwin. Entries are judged for clarity, grammar, punctuation, imagery, content and suitability for children." Entry fee $5. Guidelines available February 2000 for SASE. Inquiries by fax OK. Deadline: July 31, 2000. Previously unpublished submissions. Word length: 1,000 words. "Work submitted on colored paper, book format or illustrated is not acceptable. Stories should have believable characters." Winners announced approximately 1 month after deadline. Winner notified by mail 4-6 weeks after deadline. List of winners available in September 2000 for SASE.

THE CHRISTOPHER AWARD, The Christophers, 12 E. 48th St., New York NY 10017. (212)759-4050. Contact: Ms. Peggy Flanagan, awards coordinator. Annual award "to encourage creative people to continue to produce works which affirm the highest values of the human spirit in adult and children's books." Published submissions only. Award: Bronze medallion. "Award judged by a grassroots panel and a final panel of experts. Juvenile works are 'children tested.' " Examples of books awarded: *The Silver Balloon*, by Susan Bonners, and *Minty: A Story of Young Harriet Tubman*, by Alan Schroeder.

CNW/FFWA FLORIDA STATE WRITING COMPETITION, Florida Freelance Writers Association, P.O. Box A, North Stratford NH 03590. (603)922-8338. Fax: (603)922-8339. E-mail: danakcnw@ncia.net. Website: www.writers-editors.com. Executive Director: Dana K. Cassell. Award "to recognize publishable writing." Annual competition for short stories and novels. Competition receives 50-100 submissions. Judges: Published authors, teachers, editors. Entry fee varies with membership status. Guidelines available for SASE or on website. Deadline: March 15. Previously unpublished submissions. Winners will be notified by mail by May 31.

COMMONWEALTH CLUB OF CALIFORNIA, California Book Awards, 595 Market St., San Francisco CA 94105. (415)597-6700. Fax: (415)597-6729. E-mail: cwcu@sirius.com. Website: www.commonwealthclub.org. Book Awards Coordinator: James R. Wilson. Main contest established in 1931. Annual. "To encourage California writers and honor literary merit." Awards: Gold and silver medals. Judges: Jury of literary experts. For books published during the year preceding the particular contest. Three copies of book and a completed entry form required. Inquiries by fax and e-mail OK. Deadline: January. Winners announced in summer. Winners announced by phone and mail. "Write or phone asking for the forms. Either an author or publisher may enter a book. We usually receive over 300 entries."

CONSEIL DE LA VIE FRANCAISE EN AMÉRIQUE/PRIX CHAMPLAIN, (II, IV), Conseil de la vie Française en Amérique, 150 Boul René-Lévesque Est, Rez-De-Chaussee, Quebec G1R 2B2 Canada. (418)646-9117. Fax: (418)644-7670. E-mail: cvfa@cvfa.ca. Website: www.cvfa.ca. Prix Champlain estab. 1957. Annual award to encourage literary work in novel or short story in French by Francophiles living outside Quebec, in the US or Canada. "There is no restriction as to the subject matter. If the author lives in Quebec, the subject matter must be related to French-speaking people living outside of Quebec." Award: $1,500 in Canadian currency. The prize will be given alternately; one year for fiction, the next for nonfiction. Next fiction award in 1999. 3 different judges each year. Guidelines for SASE or IRC. Deadline: December 31. For previously published or contracted submissions, published no more than 3 years prior to award. Author must furnish 4 examples of work, curriculum vitae, address and phone number.

CROSSING BOUNDARIES WRITING AWARDS, *International Quarterly*, P.O. Box 10521, Tallahassee FL 32302-2521. (850)224-5078. Fax:(850)224-5127. E-mail: vbrock@mailer.fsu.edu. Editor-in-chief/President: Van K. Brock. Award to "reward original creative excellence in two separate categories: fiction/creative nonfiction; poetry." Annual competition for short stories and translations. Awards: Publication plus $1,000 each genre. Competition receives 350 submissions. Judges: *International Quarterly* editors. Entry fee $10 for nonmembers, $5 for members. Guidelines for SASE. Deadline: March 1. "Early submissions appreciated—submissions accepted year round." Unpublished submissions. Word length: 5,000 for prose, no requirement for poetry. "Original translations into English are also eligible, judged by accuracy and fidelity to original (original and permission should be included), and excellence in English." Winners announced August 31. Winners notified by mail. List of winners available for SASE.

THE *CRUCIBLE* POETRY AND FICTION COMPETITION, *Crucible*, Barton College, College Station, Wilson NC 27893. Annual competition for short stories. Award: $150 (1st Prize); $100 (2nd Prize) and publication in *Crucible*. Judges: The editors. Guidelines for SASE. Deadline: April. "The best time to submit is December through April." Unpublished submissions only. Fiction should be 8,000 words or less.

DANA AWARD IN SPECULATIVE FICTION, 7207 Townsend Forest Court, Browns Summit NC 27214-9634. (336)656-7009. E-mail: danaawards@pipeline.com. Website: danaawards.home.pipeline.com. Chair, Dana Awards: Mary Elizabeth Parker. Award "to reward work that has been previously unrecognized in the area of speculative fiction (fantasy, horror, science fiction, surrealism). No work for or by children/young adults. Let authors be aware work must meet standards of literary complexity and excellence. That is, character development, excellence of style are as important as the plot line." Annual competition for short stories. Award: $500. Competition receives 100-200 submissions. Entry fee $10/short story. Make checks payable to Dana Awards. Guidelines for SASE, by e-mail or on website. Inquiries by e-mail OK. Unpublished submissions and not under contract to any publisher. Word length: no minimum, but no longer than 10,000 words. 3,000 word average preferred. Postmark deadline: October 31. Winners announced early Spring. Winners notified by phone; then by letter. Send SASE with submissions to receive competition results letter.

DANA AWARD IN THE NOVEL, 7207 Townsend Forest Court, Browns Summit NC 27214-9634. (336)656-7009. E-mail: danaawards@pipeline.com. Website: danaawards.home.pipeline.com. Chair, Dana Awards: Mary

Elizabeth Parker. Award to "reward work that has not yet been recognized, since we know from firsthand experience how tough the literary market is." Annual competition for novels. Award: $1,000. Competition receives 200-300 submissions. Judges: Nationally-published novelists. Entry fee $20 for each submission. Guidelines for SASE. Postmark deadline October 31. Unpublished submissions and not under contract to be published. "Novelists should submit first 50 pages only of a novel either completed or in progress. No novels for or by children/young adults. In-progress submissions should be as polished as possible. Multiple submissions accepted, but each must include a separate $20 entry fee. Make checks payable to Dana Awards. Winners announced early spring. Winners notified by phone; then by letter. List of winners available early spring. Send SASE for results letter along with submissions.

THE DOROTHY DANIELS ANNUAL HONORARY WRITING AWARD, National League of American Pen Women, Simi Valley Branch, P.O. Box 1485, Simi Valley CA 93062. Contest Chair: Diane Reichick. Award "to honor excellent writing." Annual competition for short stories. Award: $100 (1st Place). Judges: Pen Women members. Competition receives approximately 150 entries. Entry fee $5/short story. Rules for SASE. Deadline: July 30. Unpublished submissions: not currently submitted elsewhere; entries must have received no prior awards. No limit on number of entries. Any person except Simi Valley Pen Women, interns, and their immediate families are eligible. Any genre. Word length: 2,000 words maximum. "Entries must follow rules exactly." Winners announced November 1. Winners notified by mail. List of winners available for SASE.

○ **MARGUERITE DE ANGELI PRIZE,** Bantam Doubleday Dell Books for Young Readers, 1540 Broadway, New York NY 10036. (212)782-8633. Fax: (212)782-9452. Editorial assistant: Pearl N. Young. "To encourage the writing of fiction for middle grade readers (either contemporary or historical) in the same spirit as the works of Marguerite de Angeli." Open to US and Candian writers. Annual competition for first novels for middle-grade readers (ages 7-10). Award: One BDD hardcover and paperback book contract, with $1,500 cash prize and $3,500 advance against royalties. Competition receives 350 submissions. Judges: Editors of BDD Books for Young Readers. Guidelines for SASE. Deadline: Submissions must be postmarked between April 1 and June 30. Previously unpublished (middle-grade) fiction. Length: 40-144 pages. Winners announced October. Winners notified by phone and letter. List of winners available on back of guidelines.

DEAD METAPHOR PRESS CHAPBOOK CONTEST, Dead Metaphor Press, P.O. Box 2076, Boulder CO 80306-2076. (303)417-9398. E-mail: dmetaphorp@aol.com. Contact: Richard Wilmarth. Award to "promote quality writing." Annual competition for short stories. Award: 10% of the press run. Competition receives 100 submissions. Judge: Richard Wilmarth. Entry fee $10. Guidelines available in October for SASE. Deadline: October 31. Word length: 24 page limit. Winners announced at end of February.

☑ ○ **DELACORTE PRESS ANNUAL PRIZE FOR A FIRST YOUNG ADULT NOVEL**, Delacorte Press, Department BFYR, 1540 Broadway, New York NY 10036. (212)782-9062. Fax: (212)782-9452. Contact: Wendy Lamb, executive editor. Estab. 1983. Annual award "to encourage the writing of contemporary young adult fiction." Award: Contract for publication of book; $1,500 cash prize and a $6,000 advance against royalties. Competition receives 500 submissions. Judges are the editors of Delacorte Press Books for Young Readers. Contest rules for SASE. Inquiries by fax OK. Unpublished submissions; fiction with a contemporary setting that will be suitable for ages 12-18. Deadline: December 30 (no submissions accepted prior to October 1). Writers may be previously published, but cannot have published a young adult novel before. Winners announced April. Winners notified by phone and letter. List of winners available for SASE.

⬚ ○ ◎ **DELAWARE DIVISION OF THE ARTS,** 820 N. French St., Wilmington DE 19801. (302)577-8284. Fax: (302)577-6561. E-mail: bking@state.de.us. Website: www.artsdel.org Coordinator: Barbara R. King. "To help further careers of emerging and established professional artists." Annual awards for Delaware residents only. Awards: $5,000 for established professionals; $2,000 for emerging professionals. Competition receives 100 submissions. Judges are out-of-state professionals in each division. Entry forms or rules available after January 1 for SASE. Inquiries by fax or e-mail OK. Deadline: August 2. Winners announced in December. Winners notified by mail.

☑ **DOBIE/PAISANO FELLOWSHIPS**, Texas Institute of Letters, Center for the Study of the Southwest, Flowers Hall 327, Southwest Texas State University, San Marcos TX 78666. (512)245-2232. Fax: (512)245-7462. E-mail: mb13@swt.edu. Website: www.english.swt.edu/css/TIL/index. Secretary: Mark Busby. Award to "honor the achievement and promise of two writers." Annual competition for fiction, poetry or nonfiction. Award: $1,200/month for six months and rent-free stay at Paisano ranch southwest of Austin, TX. Judges: Committee from Texas Institute of Letters and the University of Texas. Guidelines available June 2000 for SASE. Inquiries by e-mail and fax OK. Deadline: January 14, 2001. "To be eligible, a writer must have been born in Texas or have lived in the state for at least two consecutive years at some point. The winners usually have notable publishing credits behind them in addition to promising work that is under way." Winners announced April 15, 2001. List of winners available on website.

○ JACK DYER FICTION PRIZE, *Crab Orchard Review*, English Dept., Southern Illinois University, Carbondale IL 62901-4503. (618)453-6833. Website: www.siu.edu/~crborchd. Managing Editor: Jon Tribble. Award to "reward and publish exceptional fiction." Annual competition for short stories. Award: $1,000 and publication. Competition receives approximately 200 submissions. Judges: Pre-screened by *Crab Orchard* staff; winner chosen by outside judge. Entry fee $10; year's subscription included. Guidelines available after January 2000 for SASE. Deadline March 15, 2000. Previously unpublished submissions. Word length: 6,000. "Please note that no stories will be returned." Winners announced by June 1, 2000. Winners notified by phone. List of winners available for SASE.

○ EATON LITERARY ASSOCIATES' LITERARY AWARDS PROGRAM, Eaton Literary Associates, P.O. Box 49795, Sarasota FL 34230. (941)366-6589. Fax: (941)365-4679. E-mail: eatonlit@aol.com. Website: www.eatonliterary.com. Contact: Richard Lawrence, vice president. Biannual award for short stories and novels. Award: $2,500 for best book-length ms, $500 for best short story. Competition receives approx. 2,000 submissions annually. Judges are 2 staff members in conjunction with an independent agency. Entry forms or rules for SASE. Inquiries by fax and e-mail OK. Deadline: March 31 for short stories; August 31 for book-length mss. Winners announced April and September. Winners notified by mail.

☆ ✓ ◑ ◎ ARTHUR ELLIS AWARDS, Crime Writers of Canada, Box 113, 3007 Kingston Rd., Scarborough, Ontario M1M 1P1 Canada. (416)461-9846. Fax: (416)461-4489. E-mail: ap113@torfree.net.on.ca. Website: www.swifty.com/cwc/cwchome.htm. Contact: Secretary-Treasurer. "To recognize excellence in all aspects of crime-writing." Annual competition for short stories and novels. Award: Statuette (plus *maybe* cash or goods). Judges: Panels of members and experts. Guidelines for SASE. Inquiries by mail or fax OK. Deadline: January 31, 2000 for published submissions that appeared in print between January 1 and December 31 of previous year. Open to Canadian residents (any citizenship) or Canadian citizens living abroad. Four complete copies of each work must be submitted. Every entry must state category entered. Categories include Best Novel, Best First Novel, Best Short Story, Best Nonfiction, Best Play and Best Juvenile. Winners announced May 2000. Winners notified by phone, mail or fax. List of winners available by phone, mail or fax after May.

✓ ◑ ◎ EMERGING LESBIAN WRITERS FUND AWARDS, (II), Astraea National Lesbian Action Foundation, 116 E. 16th St., 7th Floor, New York NY 10003. (212)529-8021. Fax: (212)982-3321. E-mail: info@astraea.org. Website: www.astraea.org. Executive Director: Katherine Acey. Award to "recognize and encourage new/emerging lesbian writers and poets." Annual competition for fiction and poetry. Award: $10,000 (one time only grantees). Competition receives 600 submissions. Judges: Established writers/poets (2 each category). Entry fee $5. Guidelines for SASE (application form required). Deadline: March 8. Previously published submissions. U.S. residents only. Write for guidelines. "Must have at least one published work. No submissions accepted without application form." Winners announced in July. Winners notified in June by mail and phone.

EVERGREEN CHRONICLES NOVELLA CONTEST, Evergreen Chronicles, P.O. Box 8939, Minneapolis MN 55408-0939. (612)823-6638. E-mail: evergchron@aol.com. Managing Editor: Cynthia Fogard. Award to "promote work on novellas of gay, lesbian, bisexual or transgender (GLBT) themes/content/experience." Annual competition for novellas. Award: $500/1st Prize, $100/2nd Prize. Competition receives 50 submissions per category. Judges: Nationally acclaimed GLBT writers. Guidelines for SASE. Inquiries by e-mail OK. Deadline: September 30. Previously unpublished submissions. Word length: novellas with GLBT themes between 15,000-30,000 words. Winners announced in May. Winners notified by phone or mail in January. List of winners available for SASE.

◑ VIRGINIA FAULKNER AWARD FOR EXCELLENCE IN WRITING, Prairie Schooner, 201 Andrews Hall, University of Nebraska, Lincoln NE 68588-0334. (402)472-0911. Fax: (402)472-9771. E-mail: lrando lp@unlinfo.unl.edu. Website: www.unl.edu/schooner/psmain.htm. Contact: Hilda Raz, editor. "An award for writing published in *Prairie Schooner* in the previous year." Annual competition for short stories, novel excerpts and translations. Award: $1,000. Judges: Editorial Board. Guidelines for SASE. Inquiries by fax and e-mail OK. "We only read mss from September through May." Work must have been published in *Prairie Schooner* in the previous year. Winners will be notified by mail. List of winners will be published in spring *Prairie Schooner*.

○ WILLIAM FAULKNER COMPETITION IN FICTION, The Pirate's Alley Faulkner Society Inc., 632 Pirate's Alley, New Orleans LA 70116-3254. (504)586-1612. Fax: (504)522-9725. Website: www.wordsandmusic .org or www.members.aol.com/faulkhouse. Contest Director: R. James. "To encourage publisher interest in writers with potential." Annual competition for short stories, novels, novellas, personal essays and poetry. Award: $7,500 for novel, $2,500 for novella, $1,500 for short story, $1,000 personal essay, $750 poetry and gold medals, plus trip to New Orleans for presentation. Competition receives 200-300 submissions per category. Judges: Professional writers, academics. Entry fee $25 for each poem, essay, short story; $30 for novella; $35 for novel. Guidelines for SASE. Inquiries by fax OK but guidelines won't be faxed. Guidelines on website. Deadline: April 15. Unpublished submissions. Word length: for novels, over 50,000; for novellas, under 50,000; for short stories, under 20,000. All entries must be accompanied by official entry form which is provided with guidelines. Winners announced in September. Winners notified by telephone. List of winners available in October for SASE.

N **FEMINIST WRITER'S CONTEST**, NW Suburban Chicago NOW Chapter, % Kate Hutchinson, Buffalo Grove H.S., 1100 W. Dundee, Buffalo Grove IL 60089. (847)718-4075. E-mail: khutchin@dist214.k12.il.us. Contest Director: Kate Hutchinson. "To encourage, to reward feminist writers, and to be published in our chapter newsletter." Annual competition for short stories and essays. Award: $100 (1st place), $50 (2nd place). Competition receives approximately 50-60 submissions. Judges are feminist teachers, writers, political activists, social workers and entrepeneurs. Entry fee $10. Guidelines available after January for SASE. Inquiries by e-mail OK. Deadline: August 31 of each year. May be either published or unpublished. "We accept both foreign or domestic entries. Stories/essays may be on any subject, but should reflect feminist awareness." Word length: 3,000 words or less. Winners announced January. Winners notified by phone and letter. List of winners available for SASE.

N **FIRST IMPRESSIONS**, Tampa Area Romance Authors, P.O. Box 1481, Oldsmar FL 34677-1481. E-mail: sscherdin@aol.com. Website: www.sdogmedia.com/tara. Contact: Sharon Scherdin, contest coordinator. Award for "editor recognition." Annual competition for novels. Award: Editor critique. Competition has maximum of 5 entries/category. Judges: Qualified judges and published authors. "Critiques will be given." Entry fee $20. Guidelines available February 1, 2000 for SASE. Inquiries by e-mail OK. Deadline: May 1, 2000. Previously unpublished submissions. Award for "romance genre only. Categories include: long contemporary, short contemporary and paranormal/time travel." Word length: 25 page maximum; prologue and 1 chapter only. "Enter a well-written first chapter where the hero and heroine meet, the characters are well-rounded, and their goals, motivation and conflicts are present or insinuated, along with a hint of the romance." Winners announced in September 2000. Winners notified by mail. "Top 5 finalists will be given the opportunity to revise the first chapter before it's sent to the editor for final judging." List of winners available mid-September 2000 for SASE.

N **ROBERT L. FISH MEMORIAL AWARD**, Mystery Writers of America, Inc., 17 E. 47th St., 6th Floor, New York NY 10017. Website: www.mysterywriters.org. Estab. 1984. Annual award "to encourage new writers in the mystery/detective/suspense short story—and, subsequently, larger work in the genre." Award: $500 and plaque. Judges: The MWA committee for best short story of the year in the mystery genre. Deadline: November 30. Previously published submissions published the year prior to the award. Looking for "a story with a crime that is central to the plot that is well written and distinctive." Guidelines and application for SASE or on website.

DOROTHY CANFIELD FISHER AWARD, Vermont Dept. of Libraries, 109 State St., Montpelier VT 05609-0601. (802)828-3261. Fax: (802)828-2199. E-mail: ggreene@dol.state.vt.us. Website: www.dol.state.vt.us. Contact: Grace Greene, Children's Services Consultant. Estab. 1957. Annual award. "To encourage Vermont schoolchildren to become enthusiastic and discriminating readers and to honor the memory of one of Vermont's most distinguished and beloved literary figures." Award: Illuminated scroll. Publishers send the committee review copies of books to consider. Only books of the current publishing year can be considered for next year's master list. Master list of titles is drawn up in March each year. Children vote each year in the spring and the award is given before the school year ends. Submissions must be "written by living American authors, be suitable for children in grades 4-8, and have literary merit. Can be nonfiction also." Inquiries by e-mail OK. Deadline: December 1. Winners announced in April. Call, write or e-mail for list of winners.

N **FLORIDA FIRST COAST WRITERS' FESTIVAL NOVEL, SHORT FICTION & POETRY AWARDS**, Writers' Festival & Florida Community College at Jacksonville, FCCJ North Campus, 4501 Capper Rd., Jacksonville FL 32218-4499. (904)766-6559. Fax: (904)766-6654. E-mail: hdenson@fccj.org. Website: astro.fccj.org/wf/. Festival Contest Directors: Howard Denson and Brian Hale. Conference and contest "to create a healthy writing environment, honor writers of merit, select some stories for *The State Street Review* (a literary magazine) and find a novel manuscript to recommend to St. Martin's Press for 'serious consideration.' " Annual competition for short stories and novels. Competition receives 65 novel, 150-250 short fiction and 300-600 poetry submissions. Judges: University faculty and freelance and professional writers. Entry fees $30 (novels), $10 (short fiction), $5 (poetry). Guidelines available in the fall for SASE. Inquiries by fax and e-mail OK. Deadlines: November 1 all categories. Unpublished submissions. Word length: none for novel; short fiction, 6,000 words. Winners announced at the Florida First Coast Writers' Festival held in May.

THE FLORIDA REVIEW EDITORS' AWARDS, *The Florida Review*, Department of English, UCF, Orlando FL 32816. (407)823-2038. Fax: (407)823-6582. Website: pegasus.cc.ucf.edu/-english/floridareview/home.htm. Editor: Russell Kesler. Annual competition for short stories, essays, creative nonfiction, poetry. Awards: $500 for each category and publication in summer issue. Competition receives 200 submissions. Judges: *The Florida Review* editorial staff. Entry fee $10 for each entry. Guidelines for SASE after January 1, 2000. Deadline: entries are accepted January through March only. Unpublished submissions. Word length: 7,500 words/prose; grouping of 3-5 poems up to 40 lines maximum. "All submissions must contain a SASE if the contest entrant wants to know the outcome of the Editors' Awards." Winners announced May 31.

FLORIDA STATE WRITING COMPETITION, Florida Freelance Writers Association, P.O. Box A, North Stratford NH 03590-0167. (603)922-8338. Fax: (603)922-8339. E-mail: danakcnw@ncia.net. Website: www.writers-editors.com. Executive Director: Dana K. Cassell. "To offer additional opportunities for writers to earn income and recognition from their writing efforts." Annual competition for short stories and novels. Award: Varies from $25-100. Competition receives approximately 100 short stories; 50 novels. Judges: Authors, editors and teachers. Entry fee from $5-20. Guidelines for SASE. Deadline: March 15. Unpublished submissions. Categories include literary, genre and novel chapter. "Guidelines are revised each year and subject to change. New guidelines are available in summer of each year." Inquiries by fax and e-mail OK. Winners announced May 31. Winners notified by mail. List of winners available for SASE marked "winners" and on website.

FOOD, RECIPES, WINES & SUCH, Creative With Words Publications, P.O. Box 223226, Carmel CA 93922. (831)655-8627. E-mail: cwwpub@usa.net. Website: members.tripod.com/~CreativeWithWords. Editor and Publisher: Brigitta Geltrich. 25th Anniversary award. Competition for short stories, poetry and recipes. Award: $25 (1st Prize); $10 (2nd Prize); $5 (3rd Prize); $1 (4rd-13th Prizes); small gift (3 honorable mentions). "We will close the competition when 300 manuscripts from 300 individual writers have been received." Judges: CWW editors and readers. Guidelines for SASE. Inquiries by e-mail OK with e-mail return address. Previously unpublished submissions. Word length: 800 words or less. "Recipes must be tried and approved; stories/poetry must be original (the old told in a new exciting way); guidelines must be followed." Winners announced one month after contest closes. Winners notified by mail and e-mail. List of winners available on website.

FOOL FOR LOVE FIRST CHAPTER CONTEST, Virginia Romance Writers, P.O. Box 35, Midlothian VA 23113. E-mail: romancewriters@excite.com. Website: www.geocities.com/SoHo/Museum/2164. Contact: Lori Stacy. Award to "recognize unpublished writers in romance fiction." Annual competition for novels. Award: $25; certificate. Competition receives 33 awards/category; 100 awards for 3 categories. Judges: Experienced critiquers and/or published romance authors. Final judges are acquiring editors. Entry fee $25. Guidelines for SASE or on website. Inquiries by e-mail OK. Deadline: April 1, 2000. Previously unpublished submissions. Award is for romance only. Categories include historical/regency; long contemporary; story contemporary. Word length: prologue/ first chapter up to 20 pages. "Know your market and genre." Winners announced August 2000. Winners notified by e-mail and mail. List of winners available August 2000 on website.

FOSTER CITY INTERNATIONAL WRITERS' CONTEST, Foster City Arts & Culture Committee, 650 Shell Blvd., Foster City CA 94404. (415)345-3751. Chairman: Clarke N. Simm. Award "to encourage and support new writers." Annual competition for short stories. Award: $250 (first); certificate of merit (second-fifth). Competition receives approx. 2,500 submissions. Judges: Peninsula Press Club. Entry fee $10. Guidelines for SASE. Deadline: November 1st each year. Unpublished submissions. Word length: no more than 3,000 words.

H.E. FRANCIS SHORT STORY AWARD, Ruth Hindman Foundation, University of Alabama, English Department, Patricia Sammon, Huntsville AL 35899. Fax: (256)533-6893. Chairperson: Patricia Sammon. Annual short story competition to honor H.E. Francis, retired professor of English at the University of Alabama in Huntsville. Award: $1,000. Competition receives approximately 500 submissions. Judges: Distinguished writers. Entry fee. Guidelines for SASE. Deadline: December 31. Unpublished submissions. Winners announced March. Winners notified by mail. List of winners available for SASE.

MILES FRANKLIN LITERARY AWARD, Arts Management Pty. Ltd., Station House, Rawson Place, 790 George St., Sydney NSW 2000 Australia. Fax: 61-2-92117762. E-mail: enquiries@artsmanagement.com.au "For the advancement, improvement and betterment of Australian literature." Annual award for novels. Award: AUS $28,000 (in 1999), to the author "who presents the novel which is of the highest literary merit and which must present Australian life in any of its phases." Competition receives 60 submissions. Judges: Peter Rose, Dagmar Schmidmaier, Jill Kitson, Professor Elizabeth Webby, Associate Professor Adrian Mitchell and Hilary McPhee (in 1999). Guidelines for SASE. Inquiries by fax and e-mail OK. Deadline: January 31. Previously published submissions. "The novel must have been published in the year prior to competition entry and must present Australian life in any of its phases." Winners announced May/June. Winners notified at award ceremony.

SOUERETTE DIEHL FRASER AWARD, The Texas Institute of Letters, Center for the Study of the Southwest, Flowers Hall 327, Southwest Texas State University San Marcos TX 78666. (512)245-2232. Fax: (512)245-7462. E-mail: mb13@swt..edu. Website: www.english.swt.edu/css/TIL/index. Secretary: Mark Busby. "To recognize the best literary translation of a book into English, the translation published between January 1 and December 30 of the year prior to the award's announcement in the spring." Annual competition for translations. Award: $1,000. Judges: Committee of three. Guidelines available June 2000 for SASE. Inquiries by fax and e-mail OK. Deadline: January 14 2001. "Award available to translators who were born in Texas or who have lived in the state at some time for two consecutive years." Winners announced in April 15, 2001. Winners notified by phone or mail. List of winners available on website.

FRENCH BREAD AWARDS, *Pacific Coast Journal*, P.O. Box 23868, San Jose CA 95153. Contact: Stillson Graham, editor. Award with the goal of "finding the best fiction and poetry out there." Annual competition for short stories and poetry. Award: $50 (1st Prize), $25 (2nd Prize). Competition receives approximately 50 submissions. Judges: Editorial staff of *Pacific Coast Journal*. Entry fee $6. Guidelines for SASE. Deadline: September 1. Unpublished submissions. Length: 4,000 words. "Manuscripts will not be returned. Send SASE for winners' list. All entrants will receive issue in which first place winners are published." Winners announced in December. Winners notified by phone and mail. List of winners available for SASE.

◻ **GLIMMER TRAIN'S FALL SHORT-STORY AWARD FOR NEW WRITERS,** Glimmer Train Press, Inc., 710 SW Madison St., Suite 504, Portland OR 97205-2900. (503)221-0836. Fax: (503)221-0837. Website: www.glimmertrain.com (includes writers' guidelines and a Q&A section for writers). Contest Director: Linda Burmeister Davies. Contest offered for any writer whose fiction hasn't appeared in a nationally-distributed publication with a circulation over 5,000. "Send original, unpublished short (1,200-8,000 words) story with $12 reading fee for each story entered. Guidelines available for SASE. Inquiries by fax OK. Must be postmarked between August 1 and September 30. Title page to include name, address, phone, and Short Story Award for New Writers must be written on outside of envelope. No need for SASE as materials will not be returned. Notification on January 2. Winner receives $1,200, publication in *Glimmer Train Stories* and 20 copies of that issue. First/second runners-up receive $500/$300, respectively, and consideration for publication. All applicants receive a copy of the issue in which winning entry is published and runners-up announced."

◻ **GLIMMER TRAIN'S FICTION OPEN,** Glimmer Train Press, Inc., 710 SW Madison St., Suite 504, Portland OR 97205-2900. (503)221-0836. Fax: (503)221-0837. Website: www.glimmertrain.com (includes writers' guidelines and a Q&A section for writers). Contest Director: Linda Burmeister Davies. Contest for short story, open to all writers. Award: First place $2,000, publication in *Glimmer Train Stories* (circ. 13,000) and 20 copies of that issue. First/second runners-up receive $1,000/$600 respectively and consideration for publication. Reading fee $15 for each story submitted. Guidelines for SASE. Must be postmarked between May 1 and June 30 and please write "FICTION OPEN" on the outisde of the envelope. Unpublished submissions. No theme or word-count limitations. Winners will be called by October 15. List of winners available for SASE with story.

◻ **GLIMMER TRAIN'S SPRING SHORT-STORY AWARD FOR NEW WRITERS,** Glimmer Train Press, Inc., 710 SW Madison St., Suite 504, Portland OR 97205-2900. (503)221-0836. Fax: (503)221-0837. Website: www.glimmertrain.com (includes writers' guidelines and a Q&A section for writers). Contest Director: Linda Burmeister Davies. Contest offered for any writer whose fiction hasn't appeared in a nationally-distributed publication with a circulation over 5,000. "Send original, unpublished short (1,200-8,000 words) story with $12 reading fee for each story entered. Guidelines available for SASE. Inquiries by fax OK. Must be postmarked between February 1 and March 31. Title page to include name, address, phone, and Short Story Award for New Writers must be written on outside of envelope. No need for SASE as materials will not be returned. Notification on July 1. Winner receives $1,200, publication in *Glimmer Train Stories* and 20 copies of that issue. First/second runners-up receive $500/$300, respectively, and consideration for publication. All applicants receive a copy of the issue in which winning entry is published and runners-up announced."

N **✷** **◎** **GOD USES INK ANNUAL CHRISTIAN WRITERS' CONTEST**, *Faith Today*, M.I.P. Box 3745, Markham, ONT L3R 0Y4 Canada. (905)479-5885. Fax (905)479-4742. E-mail: ft@efc-canada.com. Website: www. efc-canada.com. Contact: Bill Fledderus, contest director. Award "to encourage Canadian Christian writers in the pursuit of excellence in the craft of print communication." Annual competition for short stories, articles, non-fiction books and novels. Awards: From $150-$250. Entry fee $20/book, $15/article. Maximum 3 entries/person. Competition receives 6 short story and 13 novel submissions. Guidelines for SASE/IRC. Inquiries by fax or e-mail OK. Published submissions. Published entries must have appeared in print between January 1, 1999 and December 31, 1999. Canadian Christian writers only. Writers may submit their own fiction or publisher may nominate the writer's work. "Read entry guidelines and form carefully. Winners announced June 18 (at our writers' conference in Guelph)." Winners notified after June 20 by mail. List of winners available after June 20.

N **◒** **GOLD MEDALLION BOOK AWARDS**, Evangelical Christian Publishers Association, 1969 East Broadway Rd. #2, Tempe AZ 85282. (480)966-3998. Fax: (480)966-1944. E-mail: jmeegan@ecpa.org. Website: www.ecpa.org. President: Doug Ross. Award to "recognize quality/encourage excellence." Annual competition for 20 categories including fiction. Award: Gold Medallion plaque. Competition receives approximately 43 submission in the fiction category. Judges: "Two rounds of judges—first round primarily Christian bookstore owners, managers and book buyers; second round primarily editors, book reviewers, industry leaders and selected Christian bookstore leaders. First round will determine five finalists in each of the 20 categories. Second round judges the finalists in each category." Entry fee of $300 for non-members. Guidelines available October 1, 1999. Inquiries by fax and e-mail OK. Deadline: December 1. Previously published submissions appearing during the calendar year preceding the year in which the award are to be presented. Entries must be submitted by the publisher. Winners announced in July at the Annual Gold Medallion Book Awards Banquet. List of winners available by contacting the ECPA offices.

N ☐ ◎ GOLDEN CHANCE, Central Florida Romance Writers, 3880 South Washington, #212, Titusville FL 32780. E-mail: sandi53@hotmail.com. Website: www.geocities.com/Athens/Aegean/7389/cfrwmain.html. Contact: Sandi Haddad. Award to promote excellence in romance genre. Annual competition for novels. Award: $150 (1st prize); $100 (2nd prize); $50 (3rd prize). Competition limited to first 50 submissions. Judges: 3 experienced writers; finalists ranked by romance editor. Entry fee $25. Guidelines available after January, 2000 for SASE. Inquiries by e-mail OK. Deadline May 20. Unpublished submissions. Limited to Romance Writers of America members only. Length: first 30 pages of ms plus up to 12-page synopsis. "Read and understand target market." Finalists announced in September. Winners notified by phone. List of winners available for SASE or by e-mail after December.

N ☐ GOTCHA! CATCH THAT EDITOR'S ATTENTION, Silicon Valley Chapter Romance Writers of America, P.O. Box 875, Brisbane CA 94005-0875. (415)587-1115. E-mail: ncochranrodigy.net. Website: www. slip.net/~nissen/rwa. Contest Chair: Nancy Cochran. Award to "give feedback to writers." Annual competition for novels. Award: Top 3 winners in each category will have their entry sent to an editor for evaluation. Competition receives 10 submissions in historical; 20 submissions in specialty; 55 submissions in contemporary. Judges: Published and unpublished members of the Romance Writers of America Chapter. Entry fee $15. Guidelines available March 2000 for SASE or on website. Inquiries by e-mail OK. Deadline: June 2000. Previously unpublished submissions. "Romance genre only." Word length: 15 pages maximum of opening scene. "Make sure you are submitting the best work you can and follow the rules." Winners announced in August 2000. Winners notified by mail or phone. List of winners available September 2000 for SASE.

◪ ☐ ◎ GOVERNMENT OF NEWFOUNDLAND AND LABRADOR ARTS AND LETTERS COMPETITION Government of Newfoundland and Labrador Dept. of Tourism and Culture, P.O. Box 1854, St. John's, Newfoundland A1C 5P9 Canada. (709)729-5253. Fax: (709)729-5952. Co-ordinator: Regina Best. Award "to encourage the creative talent of people of the Province of Newfoundland and Labrador." Annual competition for arts and letters. Award: Senior division: $600 (1st Prize), $300 (2nd Prize), $150 (3rd Prize); Junior division: $300 (1st Prize), $200 (2nd Prize), $100 (3rd Prize). Competition receives approximately 1,000 submissions and 60-70 fiction entries. Judges: Blind judging by outside people who are professionals in their field. Guidelines for SASE. Deadline: February. Unpublished submissions. Competition is only open to residents of this province. "There are two divisions in this competition: Junior (12-18 years) and Senior (19-on). Each entry receives a written adjudication. There are prizes in several categories; fiction; nonfiction; poetry; dramatic script; painting; 3-D art; drawing and print-making; photography; musical composition. Categories in the Junior division are poetry, prose and visual arts. Applications and rules and regulations for entering are available at the above address." Winners announced in May. Winners notified by press release. List of winners available.

N ◪ GREAT AMERICAN BOOK CONTEST, Book Deals, Inc., 20 Wacker Dr., Suite 1928, Chicago IL 60606. (312)372-0227. Fax: (312) 372-0249. E-mail: bookdeals@aol.com. President: Caroline Francis Carney. Award to "discover American authors of exceptional talent whose work equals or surpasses the finest of American's past and future." Annual competition for novels and narrative nonfiction. Award: Two Grand Prizes of $1,500 each for one fiction and one nonfiction work and a meeting with a book editor and a film scout; $750 honorable mention for an author 30 years or younger whose "strong voice exhibits the next generation's literary promise." Judges: Jury of authors, literary experts, academics. Entry fee $30. Guidelines available January 2000 for SASE. Inquiries by fax and e-mail OK. Deadline: December 31. Previously unpublished submissions. "Story must have an American setting, authors most have an exceptional narrative voice and the recommended length is between 45,000-300,000 words." Winners announced on or by April 1, 2001. Winners notified by phone. List of winners available after April 1, 2001 for SASE.

N ☐ *THE GREAT BLUE BEACON SHORT-STORY CONTEST*, 1425 Patriot Dr., Melbourne FL 32940. (407)253-5869. E-mail: ajircc@juno.com. Editor/Publisher: A. J. Byers. Award to "recognize the best short-short fiction and encourage young and beginning writers." Quarterly award for short stories. Award: $50; $25; $10. Competition receives more than 50 submissions. Judges: Professional, published writers. Judges for "writing style, traditional short-story attributes, enjoyment." Entry fee $5/story ($4 for newsletter subscribers). Guidelines available early 2000 for SASE. Inquiries by e-mail OK. Previously unpublished submissions. Word length: 750 words maximum. "Edit stories carefully. Stories should follow standard guidelines for good fiction." Winners announced approximately 2 months after submission deadline. Winners announced by mail with certificate and payment. List of winners available for SASE or by e-mail.

SENDING TO A COUNTRY other than your own? Be sure to send International Reply Coupons instead of stamps for replies or return of your manuscript.

☑ ◎ GREAT LAKES BOOK AWARDS, Great Lakes Booksellers Awards, 509 Lafayette St., Grand Haven MI 49417. (616)847-2460. Fax: (616)842-0051. Award to "recognize and reward excellence in the writing and publishing of books that capture the spirit and enhance awareness of the region." Annual competition for fiction, children's and nonfiction. Award: $500 plus bookstore promotion. Competition receives approximately 40 submissions. Five judges each category. No entry fee. Guidelines available. Deadline: May 31, 2000. Writer must be nominated by members of the GLBA. Winners announced September 2000.

☑ GREAT LAKES COLLEGES ASSOCIATION NEW WRITERS AWARD, Great Lakes Colleges Association Inc., 535 W. William, Suite 301, Ann Arbor MI 48103. (734)761-4833. Fax: (734)761-3939. E-mail: mitroi@glca/org. Annual award. Winners are invited to tour the GLCA colleges. An honorarium of at least $300 will be guaranteed the author by each of the GLCA colleges they visit. Receives 30-40 entries in each category annually. Judges: Professors from member colleges. No entry fee. Guidelines available after August 1. Inquiries by fax and e-mail OK. Deadline: February 21. Unpublished submissions. First publication in fiction or poetry. Writer must be nominated by publisher. Four copies of the book should be sent to: Director, New Writers Award. Winners announced in May. Letters go to publishers who have submitted.

☑ ◑ GREAT PLAINS STORYTELLING & POETRY READING CONTEST, P.O. Box 492, Anita IA 50020. Phone/fax: (712)762-4363. Director: Robert Everhart. Estab. 1976. Annual award "to provide an outlet for writers to present not only their works but also to provide a large audience for their presentation *live* by the writer. Attendance at the event, which takes place annually in Avoca, Iowa, is *required*." Award: 1st Prize $50; 2nd Prize $25; 3rd Prize $15; 4th Prize $10; and 5th Prize $5. Entry fee: $5. Entry forms available at contest only. Deadline is day of contest, which takes place over Labor Day Weekend. Previously published or unpublished submissions.

☑ ◐ THE GREENSBORO REVIEW LITERARY AWARDS, English Dept., 134 McIver Bldg, UNC-Greensboro, P.O. Box 26170, Greensboro NC 27402-6170. (336)334-5459. E-mail: jlclark@uncg.edu. Website: www.uncg.edu/eng/mfa. Editor: Jim Clark. Annual award. Award: $250. Competition receives 1,000 submissions. Guidelines for SASE. Inquiries by e-mail OK. Deadline: September 15. Unpublished submissions. "All manuscripts meeting literary award guidelines will be considered for cash award as well as for publication in *The Greensboro Review*." Winners notified in December. List of winners published in the Spring issue of *The Greensboro Review*.

◐ HACKNEY LITERARY AWARDS, Box 549003, Birmingham Southern College, Birmingham AL 35254. (205)226-4921. Fax: (205)226-4931. E-mail: dcwilson@bsc.edu. Website: www.bsc.edu. Contact: Dr. Myra Crawford, Hackney award chairman. Annual award for previously unpublished short stories, poetry and novels. Award: $5,000 (novel); $5,000 (poetry and short stories; 6 prizes). Competition receives approx. 500 submissions. Award chairman appoints judges and supervises the competition. Entry fee: $25 novel; $10 poetry and short story. Rules/entry form for SASE. Inquiries by fax and e-mail OK. Novel submissions must be postmarked on or before September 30. Short stories and poetry submissions must be postmarked on or before December 31. Winners announced at Writing Today Writers' Conference April 17-18, 2000. List of winners available for SASE.

Ⓝ ◐ ◎ HEADWATERS LITERARY COMPETITION, New Rivers Press, 420 N. 5th St. #938, Minneapolis MN 55401. (612)339-7114. Fax: (612)339-9047. E-mail: newrivpr@mtn.org. Website: www.mtn.org/newri vpr. Editorial Assistant: Eric Braun. Award to "find and publish the best creative prose book-length manuscripts in the upper Midwest (excluding Minnesota, for which we have a separate contest, the *Minnesota Voices Project*)." Annual competition for novels or story collections. Award: $500 and publication of book. Competition receives 100 prose and 100 poetry submissions. Judges: "We hire outside judges who work together with our Senior Editor, C.W. Truesdale." Entry fee $10. Guidelines available April 2000 for SASE. Deadline: September 4. Previously unpublished submissions. "Individual stories may have been published, but not as a book length collection. Open to all writers residing in North or South Dakota, Illinois, Iowa, Michigan and Wisconsin. Short fiction, novellas, memoirs, personal essays and other forms of creative prose." Word length: 100-200 pages for prose; 40-60 pages for poetry. "Look at recent NRP books, particularly contest winners." Winners announced May/June 2001. "All entrants will receive letter notifying them of the panelists' decisions." List of winners available for SASE.

Ⓝ ◐ DRUE HEINZ LITERATURE PRIZE, University of Pittsburgh Press, 3347 Forbes Ave., Pittsburgh PA 15261. (412)383-2456. Fax: (412)383-2466. E-mail: presst@pitt.edu. Website: www.pitt.edu/~press. Annual award "to support the writer of short fiction at a time when the economics of commercial publishing make it more and more difficult for the serious literary artist working in the short story and novella to find publication." Award: $10,000 and publication by the University of Pittsburgh Press. "It is imperative that entrants request complete rules of the competition by sending an SASE before submitting a manuscript." Submissions will be received only during the months of May and June. Postmark deadline: June 30. Manuscripts must be unpublished in book form. The award is open to writers who have published a book-length collection of fiction or a minimum of three short stories or novellas in commercial magazines or literary journals of national distribution. Winners announced in February. Winners notified by phone or mail. List of winners available for SASE sent with manuscript.

N ◐ ERNEST HEMINGWAY FOUNDATION/PEN AWARD FOR FIRST FICTION, PEN New England, P.O. Box 725, North Cambridge MA 02140. Awards Coordinator: Mary Louise Sullivan. Annual award "to give beginning writers recognition and encouragement and to stimulate interest in first novels among publishers and readers." Award: $7,500. Novels or short story collections must have been published during calendar year under consideration. Entry form or rules for SASE. Deadline: December 15. "The Ernest Hemingway Foundation/PEN Award For First Fiction is given to an American author of the best first-published book-length work of fiction published by an established publishing house in the US each calendar year."

◐ LORIAN HEMINGWAY SHORT STORY COMPETITION, P.O. Box 993, Key West FL 33041-0993. (305)294-0320. Fax: (305)292-3653. E-mail: calico2419@aol.com. Contact: Carol Shaughnessy, co-director. Award to "encourage literary excellence and the efforts of writers who have not yet had major-market success." Annual competition for short stories. Awards: $1,000 (1st Prize); $500 (2nd Prize); $500 (3rd Prize); honorable mentions. Competition receives approximately 850 submissions. Judges: A panel of writers, editors and literary scholars selected by novelist Lorian Hemingway. Entry fee $10 for each story postmarked by June 1, 2000; $15 for each story postmarked between June 1 and June 15, 2000. Guidelines for SASE after February 1. Inquiries by fax and e-mail OK. Deadline: June 1, 2000 and June 15, 2000. Unpublished submissions. "Open to all writers whose fiction has not appeared in a nationally distributed publication with a circulation of 5,000 or more." Word length: 3,000 words maximum. "We look for excellence, pure and simple—no genre restrictions, no theme restrictions—we seek a writer's voice that cannot be ignored." Winners announced before August 1. Winners notified by phone. "All entrants will receive a letter from Lorian Hemingway and a list of winners by October 1."

✔ ◑ ◎ HIGHLIGHTS FOR CHILDREN, 803 Church St., Honesdale PA 18431. (570)253-1080. Manuscript Coordinator: Beth Troop. Award "to honor quality stories (previously unpublished) for young readers." Three $1,000 awards. Competition receives 1,000 submissions. Judges: *Highlights* editors. Stories: up to 500 words for beginning readers (to age 8) and 900 words for more advanced readers (ages 9 to 12). No minimum word length. No entry form necessary. Guidelines for SASE. To be submitted between January 1 and February 29 to "Fiction Contest" at address above. "No violence, crime or derogatory humor. Obtain a copy of the guidelines, since the theme changes each year." Nonwinning entries returned in June if SASE is included with ms. Winners announced in June. Winners notified by phone or letter. List of winners will be sent with returned mss.

N ◐ THE ALFRED HODDER FELLOWSHIP, The Council of the Humanities, Princeton University, 122 E. Pyne, Princeton NJ 08544. Program Manager: Marjorie Asbury. "This fellowship is awarded for the pursuit of independent work in the humanities. The recipient is usually a writer or scholar in the early stages of his or her career, a person 'with more than ordinary learning' and with 'much more than ordinary intellectual and literary gifts.' " Traditionally, the Hodder Fellow has been a humanist outside of academia. Candidates for the Ph.D. are not eligible. Award: $45,600. The Hodder Fellow spends an academic year in residence at Princeton working independently. Competition receives 300 submissions. Judges: Princeton Committee on Humanistic Studies. Deadline: November 1. Applicants must submit a résumé, a sample of previous work (10 page maximum, not returnable), and a project proposal of 2 to 3 pages. Letters of recommendation are not required.

N ◯ ◎ HONOLULU MAGAZINE/BORDERS BOOKS & MUSIC FICTION CONTEST, *Honolulu* Magazine, 36 Merchant St., Honolulu HI 96813. (808)524-7400. Contact: A. Kam Napier, associate editor. "We do not accept fiction except during our annual contest, at which time we welcome it." Annual award for short stories. Award: $1,000 and publication in the April issue of *Honolulu* Magazine. Competition receives approximately 400 submissions. Judges: Panel of well-known Hawaii-based writers. Rules for SASE. Deadline: early December. "Stories must have a Hawaii theme, setting and/or characters. Author should enclose name and address in separate small envelope. Do not put name on story."

N ◯ ◎ L. RON HUBBARD'S WRITERS OF THE FUTURE CONTEST, P.O. Box 1630N, Los Angeles CA 90078. (323)466-3310. Fax: (323)466-6474. Website: www.authorservicesinc.com/wof_home.htm. Contest Administrator: Nathalie Cordebard. Estab. 1984. Quarterly. "Foremost contest for new writers of science fiction, fantasy and horror, short stories and novelettes. Awards $2,250 in quarterly prizes, annual $4,000 Grand Prize, five-day Writer's Workshop with major authors, publication in leading international anthology. Outstanding professional judges panel. No entry fee. Entrants retain all rights. For explicit instructions on how to enter send SASE to the above address." Winners announced quarterly. Winners notified by phone and mail.

✔ ◯ ◎ ZORA NEALE HURSTON/RICHARD WRIGHT AWARD, Zora Neale Hurston/Richard Wright Foundation, English Dept., Virginia Commonwealth University, P.O. Box 842005, Richmond VA 23284-2005. (804)225-4729. Fax: (804)828-8684. E-mail: hurstonwright@yahoo.com. Website: www.has.vcu.edu/

HWF. Workshop Director: Donna Champ Banks. President/Founder: Marita Golden. "Awards excellence in fiction for writing by students of African descent enrolled full time as an undergraduate or graduate student in any college or university in the U.S." Annual award for previously unpublished short stories and novel excerpts. Award: $1,000 (1st Place); $500 (2nd and 3rd Place). Competition receives 50-75 submissions. Judges: Published writers. Guidelines available in September for SASE. Deadline: postmarked no later than December 10. Unpublished submissions. Word length: 25 pages maximum. Winners announced in March. Winners notified by mail. List of winners available in April.

✓ ◯ **INDIANA REVIEW FICTION PRIZE**, *Indiana Review*, Ballantine Hall 465, 1020 E. Kirkwood Ave., Bloomington IN 47405-7103. Website: www.indiana.edu/~inreview. Contest for fiction in any style and on any subject. Alternates each year with poetry contest. Award: $500, publication in the *Indiana Review* and contributor's copies (1st Place). Each entrant will receive the prize issue. Competition receives 300 submissions. Guidelines for SASE after May 2000. No previously published works, or works forthcoming elsewhere, are eligible. Simultaneous submissions acceptable, but in event of entrant withdraw, contest fee will not be refunded. Length: 40 pages maximum, double spaced. SASE for outcome.

INDIVIDUAL ARTIST FELLOWSHIP, Nebraska Arts Council, 3838 Davenport, Omaha NE 68131-2329. (402)421-3627. Fax: (402)595-2334. E-mail: stwnac@infobridge.com. Website: www.nebraskaartscouncil.org. Program Manager: Suzanne Wise. Award to "recognize outstanding achievement by Nebraska writers." Competition every third year for short stories and novels. Award: $5,000 Distinguished Achievement; $1,000-2,000 Merit Awards. Competition receives 70-80 submissions per category. Judges: Panel of 3. Deadline: November 15, 1999. Next deadline for literature: November 15, 2002. Published or previously unpublished submissions. Nebraska residents only. Word length: 50 pages.

Ⓝ **INDIVIDUAL ARTIST FELLOWSHIP PROGRAM**, Florida Department of State, Division of Cultural Affairs, The Capitol, Tallahassee FL 32399-0250. (904)487-2980. Arts Adminstrator: Valerie Ohlsson. Annual competition for $5,000 fellowship award. Judges: A peer review panel. Guidelines available. Deadline: February 1. Published or previously unpublished submissions. Residents of Florida only; in fiction, short story, poetry and children's literature. Word length: up to 30 pages.

INDIVIDUAL ARTIST FELLOWSHIPS, Maine Arts Commission, 25 State House Station, Augusta ME 04333-0025. (207)287-2750. Fax: (207)287-2335. E-mail: kathy.jones@state.me.us. Website: www.mainearts.com. Associate for Contemporary Arts: Kathy Ann Jones. Unrestricted funds ($3,000) awarded for artistic excellence. Biannual competition for fiction, children's literature, creative nonfiction and poetry. Award: $3,000. Competition receives 80-100 submissions per category. Judges: A jury of experts is selected each time. Guidelines available September 1. Inquiries by fax and e-mail OK. Deadline: February 2, 1999 and every other year. Published or previously unpublished submissions. Artists must be Maine residents. Word length: fiction or creative nonfiction (maximum 20 pages of prose). Winners announced in June. Winners notified by phone, followed by mail. List of winners available in June for SASE.

Ⓝ ◯ **INTERNATIONAL WRITERS CONTEST,** Foster City Arts and Culture Committee, 650 Shell Blvd., Foster City CA 94404. (415)345-5731. Contact: Contest chairman. Annual. "To foster and encourage aspiring writers." Unpublished submissions. Award: 1st Prize in each of 4 categories $250, Honorable Mention $125. The 4 categories are: Best Fiction, Best Humor, Best Story for Children, Best Poem. Deadline: November 30. Winners announced January. English language entries only. Entry fee $10 to City of Foster City. Contest rules for SASE.

◯ **IOWA SCHOOL OF LETTERS AWARD FOR SHORT FICTION, THE JOHN SIMMONS SHORT FICTION AWARD**, Iowa Writers' Workshop, 102 Dey House, 507 N. Clinton St., Iowa City IA 52242-1000. Annual awards for short story collections. To encourage writers of short fiction. Award: Publication of winning collections by University of Iowa Press the following fall. Entries must be at least 150 pages, typewritten, and submitted between August 1 and September 30. Stamped, self-addressed return packaging must accompany manuscript. Rules for SASE. Iowa Writer's Workshop does initial screening of entries; finalists (about 6) sent to outside judge for final selection. "A different well-known writer is chosen each year as judge. Any writer who has not previously published a volume of prose fiction is eligible to enter the competition for these prizes. Revised manuscripts which have been previously entered may be resubmitted."

Ⓝ 🌐 **THE IRISH TIMES LITERATURE PRIZES**, The Irish Times Limited, 10-16 D'Olier St., Dublin 2 Ireland. (01)6792022. Fax: (01)6709383. E-mail: gcavanagh@irish-times.ie. Administrator: Gerard Cavanagh. Co-ordinator: Eleanor Walsh. Biannual competition for novels and story collections. Guidelines available. Deadline: between August 1, 1999 and July 31, 2001. Previously published submissions between August 1, 1995-July 31, 1997. Author must have been born in Ireland. Writer must be nominated by screening panel.

☑ ◯ ◎ **JOSEPH HENRY JACKSON AWARD**, Intersection for the Arts/The San Francisco Foundation, 446 Valencia St., San Francisco CA 94103. (415)626-2787. E-mail: intrsect@wenet.net. Website: www.wenet.net/ ~intrsect. Contact: Awards Coordinator. Award "to encourage young, unpublished writers." Annual award for short stories, novels and story collections. Award: $2,000. Competition receives 150-200 submissions. Entry form and rules available in mid-October for SASE. Deadline: January 31. Unpublished submissions only. Applicant must be resident of northern California or Nevada for 3 consecutive years immediately prior to the deadline date. Age of applicant must be 20 through 35. Work cannot exceed 100 double-spaced, typed pages. "Submit a serious, ambitious portion of a book-length manuscript." Winners announced June 15. Winners notified by mail. "Winners will be announced in letter mailed to all applicants."

☑ ◎ **JAPAN FOUNDATION ARTISTS FELLOWSHIP PROGRAM**, 152 W. 57th St., 39th Floor, New York NY 10019. (212)489-0299. Fax: (212)489-0409. E-mail: yuika_goto@jfny.org. Website: www.jfny.org. Program Assistant: Yuika Goto. "This program provides artists and specialists in the arts with the opportunity to pursue creative projects in Japan and to meet and consult with their Japanese counterparts." Annual competition. Several artists fellowships from two to six months' duration during the 1998 Japanese fiscal year (April 1-March 31) are available to artists, such as writers, musicians, painters, sculptors, stage artists, movie directors, etc.; and specialists in the arts, such as scenario writers, curators, etc. Benefits include transportation to and from Japan; settling-in, research, activities and other allowances and a monthly stipend. See brochure for more details. Competition receives approximately 30-40 submissions. Judges: Foundation staff in Japan. Guidelines available after August. Inquiries by fax and e-mail OK. Deadline: December 1. "Work should be related to Japan. Applicants must be accredited artists or specialists. Affiliation with a Japanese artist or institution is required. Three letters of reference, including one from the Japanese affiliate must accompany all applications. Winners announced April 2000. Winners notified by mail. List of winners available by phone.

◖ ◎ *JAPANOPHILE* **SHORT STORY CONTEST**, *Japanophile*, P.O. Box 7977, Ann Arbor MI 48107-7977. (734)930-1553. Fax: (734)930-9968. E-mail: jpnhand@japanophile.com. Website: www.japanophile.com. Editor: Susan Aitken Lapp. Estab. 1974. Annual award "to encourage quality writing on Japan-America understanding." Award: $100 plus possible publication. Competition receives 200 submissions. Entry fee: $5. Send $4 for sample copy of magazine. Guidelines available by August for SASE, e-mail or on website. Inquiries by fax and e-mail OK. Deadline: December 31. Prefers unpublished submissions. Stories should involve Japanese and non-Japanese characters, maximum 5,000 words. Winners notified in March. Winners notified by mail. List of winners available in March for SASE.

◑ ◎ **JEFFERSON CUP**, Virginia Library Association, P.O. Box 8277, Norfolk VA 23503-0277. (757)583-0041. Fax: (757)583-5041. E-mail: hahne@bellatlantic.net. Website: www.vla.org. Annual competition for U.S. history, historical fiction or biography for young people. Award: Cup and $500. Judges: Jefferson Cup Committee. Previously published one year prior to selection. Writer must be nominated by publisher.

☑ ◖ ◎ **JESSE JONES AWARD FOR FICTION (BOOK)**, The Texas Institute of Letters, Center for the Study of the Southwest, Flowers Hall 327, Southwest Texas State University, San Marcos TX 78666. (512)245-2232. Fax: (512)245-7462. E-mail: mb12@swt.edu. Website: www.english.swt.edu/css/TIL/index. Secretary: Mark Busby. "To honor the writer of the best novel or collection of short fiction published during the calendar year before the award is given." Annual award for novels or story collections. Award: $6,000. Competition receives 30-40 entries per year. Judges: Panel selected by TIL Council. Guidelines available in June 2000 for SASE. Inquiries by fax and e-mail OK. Deadline: January 14, 2001. Previously published fiction, which must have appeared in print between January 1 and December 31 of the prior year. "Award available to writers who, at some time, have lived in Texas at least two years consecutively or whose work has a significant Texas theme." Winners announced April 15, 2001. Winners notified by phone or mail. List of winners available on website.

☑ ◯ **JAMES JONES FIRST NOVEL FELLOWSHIP**, James Jones Society, Wilkes University, Wilkes-Barre PA 18766. (570)408-4530. Fax: (570)408-7829. E-mail: english@wilkesl.wilkes.edu. Website: wilkes.edu/ ~english/jones.html. English Department Professor: Patricia B. Heaman. Award to "honor the spirit of unblinking honesty, determination, and insight into modern culture exemplified by the late James Jones by encouraging the work of an American writer who has not published a book-length work of fiction." Annual award for unpublished novel, novella, or collection of related short stories in progress. Award: $5,000. Receives approximately 500 applications. Judges: "A collection of writers and members of the James Jones Society." Application fee: $15. Guidelines for SASE. Inquiries by e-mail and fax OK. Deadline: March 1. Unpublished submissions. "Award is open to American writers." Word length: 50 opening pages and a two-page thematic outline. "Name, address, telephone number on title page only." Winners announced early September. Winners notified by mail and phone. List of winners available early October for SASE. "For more information, visit us on the Web."

KATHA: INDIAN AMERICAN FICTION CONTEST, *India Currents* Magazine, P.O. Box 21285, San Jose CA 95151. (408)274-6966. Fax: (408)274-2733. E-mail: mgeditor@indiacurrents.com. Website: www.indiacurrents.com. Managing Editor: Vandana Kumar. Award "to encourage creative writing which has as its focus India,

Indian culture, Indian-Americans and America's views of India." Annual competition for short stories. Awards: $100 (1st Prize), $75 (2nd Prize), $50 (3rd Prize), 2 honorable mentions. All entrants receive a 1-year subscription to *India Currents*. Competition received 45 submissions last year. Judges: "A distinguished panel of Indian-American authors. Guidelines for SASE. Inquiries by e-mail and fax OK. Deadline: December 31. Unpublished submissions. Length: 3,000 words maximum. "Write about something you have experienced personally or do extensive research, so that you can write knowledgebly."

✔ 🖉 ◎ **ROBERT F. KENNEDY BOOK AWARDS**, 1367 Connecticut Ave. NW, Suite 200, Washington DC 20036. (202)463-7575. Fax: (202)463-6606. E-mail: info@rfkmemorial.org. Website: www.rfkmemorial.org. Contact: Director of the Book Award. Endowed by Arthur Schlesinger, Jr., from proceeds of his biography, *Robert Kennedy and His Times*. Annual. "To award the author of a book which most faithfully and forcefully reflects Robert Kennedy's purposes." For books published during the calendar year. Award: $2,500 cash prize awarded in the spring. Guidelines available in the fall. Inquiries by fax and e-mail OK. Deadline: January 2. Looking for "a work of literary merit in fact or fiction that shows compassion for the poor or powerless or those suffering from injustice." Four copies of each book submitted should be sent, along with a $25 entry fee. Winners announced Spring 2000. Winners notified by phone. List of winners available by phone, fax or e-mail.

[N] 🔘 ◎ **KENTUCKY ARTS COUNCIL, KENTUCKY ARTISTS FELLOWSHIPS,** 31 Fountain Place, Frankfort KY 40601. (502)564-3757. Fax: (502)564-2839. E-mail: lmeadows@mail.state.ky.us. "To encourage and assist the professional development of Kentucky artists." 10-15 writing fellowships offered every other (or even-numbered) year in fiction, poetry, playwriting. Award: $5,000. Competition receives 175 submissions. Judges are out-of-state panelists (writers, editors, playwrights, etc.) of distinction. Open only to Kentucky residents (minimum one year). Entry forms available for *Kentucky residents in July 2000*." Inquiries by fax and e-mail OK. Deadline: September 2000. Winners announced December 2000. Winners notified by mail.

[N] 💟 **KIRIYAMA PACIFIC RIM BOOK PRIZE**, Kiriyama Pacific Rim Foundation and University of San Francisco Center for the Pacific Rim, 2130 Fulton St., San Francisco CA 94117-1080. (415)422-5984. Fax: (415)422-5933. E-mail: cuevas@usfca.edu. Website: www.usfca.edu/pac_rim/kiriyama. Project Coordinator: Jeannine Cuevas. Annual competition for full-length books, fiction or non-fiction. Award: $30,000 divided equally between authors of one fiction and one nonfiction work. Competition receives 200 submissions. Judges: 2 panels of 3 judges (one panel for fiction and one for nonfiction). Guidelines available in February. Inquiries by fax and e-mail OK. Deadline: July 1. All works should be published. Published entries must have appeared in print between November 1, 1999 and October 31, 2000. "The prize is open to publishers/writers world wide. Entries must concern the Pacific Rim. Writer must be nominated by publisher. Writers should prompt their publishers to do so." Winners announced Fall of 2000. Winner notified by phone. Winners announced on website and live radio program.

✔ 🔘 **LAGNIAPPE FOR LITERACY**, Southern Louisiana Romance Writers (a chapter of Romance Writers of America), P.O. Box 1743, Metairie LA 70004-1743. (504)835-6760. E-mail: jwilsonwv@aol.com. Contest Coordinators: Jean Wilson and Brenda Howard. Award "to offer unpublished authors feedback from published authors; to offer unpublished authors help getting published; to raise money for YMCA Educational Services' literacy training programs." Annual award for novels. Award: Entire winning ms read by an editor attending The New Orleans Popular Fiction Conference (1st Prize); 3 chapters and synopsis of winning ms read by an attending literary agent (2nd Prize). Competition receives approximately 100 submissions. Judges: First round by 3 published authors; finalists judged by editors and agents. Entry fee $15. Guidelines for SASE. Inquiries by fax and e-mail OK. Deadline: August 31. Unpublished submissions. Award available to writers 18 years of age and older from any region; any genre except short stories or children's literature. Novels only. Length: Send first 5 pages of novel. Winners announced at conference in November and/or by mail. List of winners available for SASE.

✔ 🔘 **LAWRENCE FOUNDATION PRIZE**, *Michigan Quarterly Review*, 3032 Rackham Bldg., Ann Arbor MI 48109-1070. (734)764-9265. Website: www.umich.edu/~mgr. Contact: Doris Knight, administrative assistant. "An annual cash prize awarded to the author of the best short story published in *Michigan Quarterly Review* each year." Annual competition for short stories. Award: $1,000. Competition receives approximately 500 submissions. "Stories must already be published in *MQR*; this is not a competition in which manuscripts are read outside of the normal submission process."

✿ ✔ 🖉 ◎ **STEPHEN LEACOCK MEDAL FOR HUMOUR**, Stephen Leacock Associates, P.O. Box 854, Orillia, Ontario L3V 6K8 Canada. (705)325-7972. Chairman, Award Committee: Judith Rapson. Award "to encourage writing of humour by Canadians." Annual competition for short stories, novels and story collections. Award: Stephen Leacock (silver) medal for humour and Laurentian Bank of Canada cash award of $5,000 (Canadian). Competition receives 50 submissions. Five judges selected across Canada. Entry fee $25 (Canadian). Guidelines for SASE. Deadline: December 30. Submissions should have been published in book form in the previous year. Open to Canadian citizens or landed immigrants only. Winners announced by April 1. Winners notified via publisher. List of winners available May 15 by mail or phone.

LEAGUE OF UTAH WRITERS CONTEST, League of Utah Writers, 4621 W. Harman Dr., West Valley City UT 84120-3752. (801)964-0861. E-mail: chetim@numucom.com. Website: www.desertonline/users/luwrite. President: Dorthy Crofts. "The annual LUW Contest has been held since 1935 to give Utah writers an opportunity to get their works read and critiqued. It also encourages writers to keep writing in an effort to get published." Annual competition for short stories and novels. Award: Twenty-nine categories, cash award of $30/$20/$10 ; children's book category, $50/$25/$15; full length book category $100/$50/$25; published writers category. Competition receives 10-100 submissions/category. Judges: Professional judges who are paid for their services. Entry fee $4, short story; $20, full length book. Guidelines available January 2000 for SASE. Inquiries by fax, e-mail and phone OK. Deadline: June 15, 2000. Both published and previously unpublished submissions. Published submissions much have appeared in print between June 1999 and June 2000. "For the first time since 1935, the LUW Contest was opened up to writers from the 10 western states. No specific genre, although we do have separate categories for speculative fiction, children's and teen's besides our full length book category on any subject." Word length: 1,500 words maximum, short short story; 3,000 words maximum, short story; 4,000 words maximum, speculative fiction; 75,000 word maximum, full length book; 3,500 words maximum children's story; 3,500 words maximum, teen story; 5,000 words maximum, Agnes Burke Short Story. "Participate every year—don't give up after one try, get involved with your local chapter of other writers, read all you can and write something everyday—regardless of what it is." Winners will be announced at the Annual Writers Round-up in September. List of winners available at Round-up or for SASE.

LINES IN THE SAND SHORT FICTION CONTEST, Le Sand Publications, 1252 Terra Nova Blvd., Pacifica CA 94044-4340. (650)355-9069. Contact: Barbara J. Less, associate editor. "To encourage the writing of good short fiction, any genre." Annual competition for short stories. Award: $50, $25, or $10 and publication in *Lines in the Sand*. January/February awards edition. Honorable mentions will be published as space allows. Competition receives approximately 100 submissions. Judges: The editors. Entry fee $5. Guidelines available January 2000 for SASE. Deadline: November 30, 2000. Previously published or unpublished submissions. Word length: 2,000 words maximum. Winners announced January 2001. Winners notified by mail December 1999. List of winners available for SASE.

LITERAL LATTÉ FICTION AWARD, *Literal Latté*, 61 E. 8th St., Suite 240, New York NY 10003. (212)260-5532. E-mail: litlatte@aol.com. Website: www.literal-latte.com. Contact: Jenine Gordon Bockman, editor/publisher. Award to "provide talented writers with three essential tools for continued success: money, publication and recognition." Annual competition for short stories. Award: $1,000 (1st Prize); $200 (2nd Prize); $100 (3rd Prize); up to 7 honorable mentions. Competition receives 400-600 submissions. Judges: The editors. Entry fee $10 ($15 includes subscription) for each story submitted. Guidelines available for SASE. Inquiries by e-mail OK. Deadline: mid-January. Previously unpublished submissions. Open to new and established writers worldwide. Word length: 6,000 words maximum. "The First Prize Story in the First Annual Literal Latté Fiction Awards has been honored with a Pushcart Prize." Winners notified by phone. List of winners available in late April for SASE.

LONG FICTION CONTEST INTERNATIONAL, White Eagle Coffee Store Press, P.O. Box 383, Fox River Grove IL 60021-0383. (847)639-9200. E-mail: wecspress@aol.com. Website: members.aol.com/wecspress. Contact: Publisher. To promote and support the long fiction form. Annual award for short stories. "Entries accepted from anywhere in the world; story must be written in English." Winning story receives A.E. Coppard Award—publication as chapbook plus $500, 25 contributor's copies; 40 additional copies sent to book publishers/agents and 10 press kits. Entry fee $15 US, ($5 for second story in same envelope). Must be in US funds. Competition receives 200 entries. Guidelines available in April. Inquiries by fax and e-mail OK. SASE for results. Deadline: December 15. Accepts previously unpublished submissions, but previous publication of small parts with acknowledgements is OK. Simultaneous submissions OK. No limits on style or subject matter. Length: 8,000-14,000 words (30-50 pages double spaced) single story; may have multiparts or be a self-contained novel segment. Send cover with title, name, address, phone; second title page with title only. Submissions are not returned; they are recycled. "Previous winners include Adria Bernardi, Doug Hornig, Christy Sheffield Sanford, Eleanor Swanson, Gregory J. Wolos and Joe Hill. SASE for most current information." Winners announced March 30, 2001. Winners notified by phone. List of winners available March 30 for SASE. "Write with richness and depth."

THE LONGMEADOW JOURNAL LITERARY COMPETITION, c/o Robert and Rita Morton, 6750 Longmeadow Ave, Lincolnwood IL 60646. (312)726-9789. Contact: Robert and Rita Morton. Award to "stimulate the young to write." Annual competition for short stories. Award: $175 (1st Prize); $100 (2nd Prize); 5 prizes of $50. Competition receives 700 submissions. Judges: Robert and Rita Morton. Guidelines for SASE. Award for "short story writers between the ages of 10-19." Word length: 3,000 words or less. Winners notified by June 15, 2000.

LOS ANGELES TIMES BOOK PRIZES, *L.A. Times*, % Public Affairs Dept. Times Mirror Square, Los Angeles CA 90053. (213)237-5775. Fax: (213)237-4609. E-mail: tom.crouch@latimes.com. Website: www.latim

es.com. Contact: Tom Crouch, administrative coordinator. Annual award. For books published between January 1 and December 31. Award: $1,000 cash prize in each of the following categories: fiction, first fiction (the Art Seidenbaum Award) and young adult fiction. In addition, the Robert Kirsch Award recognizes the body of work by a writer living in or writing on the American West. Entry is by nomination of juries—no external nominations or submissions are accepted. Juries appointed by the *L.A. Times*. No entry fee. "Works must have their first U.S. publication during the calendar year." Writers must be nominated by committee members. "The Times provides air fare and lodging in Los Angeles for the winning authors to attend the awards ceremony held in April on the eve of the *Los Angeles Times Festival of Books*."

✓ ◯ ◉ **LSU/SOUTHERN REVIEW SHORT FICTION AWARD**, *The Southern Review*, 43 Allen Hall, LSU, Baton Rouge LA 70803-5005. (225)388-5108. Fax: (225)388-5098. E-mail: bmacon@unix1.sncc.lsu.edu. Website: www.lsu.edu/guests/wwwtsm. Contact: Michael Griffith. Award "to recognize the best first collection of short stories published in the U.S. in the past year." Annual competition. Award: $500, possible reading. Competition receives approx. 35-40 submissions. Judges: A committee of editors and faculty members. Guidelines for SASE. Deadline: January 31. Submissions must have been published between January 1 and December 31 of previous year. Only books published in the US.

✓ ◯ ◉ **MALICE DOMESTIC GRANT**, % Shirley Smith, 5562 Brittany Court, Frederick MD 21703. (301)293-0020. Fax: (301)797-7567. E-mail: ssmith811@aol.com. Grants Chair: Shirley Smith. Given "to encourage unpublished writers in their pursuit—grant may be used to offset registration, travel or other expenses relating to attending writers' conferences, etc., within one year of award." Annual competition for novels and nonfiction. Award: $500. Competition receives 35-50 submissions. Judges: The Malice Domestic Board. Guidelines for SASE. Inquiries by e-mail OK. Deadline: December. Unpublished submissions. "Our genre is loosely translated as mystery stories of the Agatha Christie type, that is 'mysteries of manners.' These works usually feature amateur detective characters who know each other. No excessive gore or violence." Submit plot synopsis and 3 chapters of work in progress. Include résumé, a letter of reference from someone familiar with your work, a typed letter of application explaining qualifications for the grant and the workshop/conference to be attended or the research to be funded. Winners announced in May. Winers notified by e-mail and phone. List of winners for SASE.

◐ ◉ **MARIN ARTS COUNCIL INDIVIDUAL ARTIST GRANTS**, 251 N. San Pedro Rd., San Rafael CA 94903. (415)499-8350. Fax: (415)499-8537. Grants Coordinator: Alison DeJung. "For Marin County residents only. Award to provide unrestricted grants starting at $2,000 to individual artists in a variety of media." Every other year competition for short stories, novels, plays, poetry. Competition receives approx. 15-90 submissions. Judges: Professionals in the field. Guidelines for SASE. Previously published submissions and unpublished submissions.

🌐 ◯ ◉ **THE MARTEN BEQUEST TRAVELLING SCHOLARSHIP**, Arts Management Pty. Ltd., Station House Rawson Place, 790 George St., Sydney NSW 2000 Australia. Phone: +61-2-92125066. Fax: +61-2-9211-7762. E-mail: enquiries@artsmanagement.com. Artists and Projects Manager: Claudia Crosariol. "The Marten Bequest is intended to augment a scholar's own resources towards affording him or her a cultural education by means of a travelling scholarship, to be awarded to one or more applicants who fulfill the required conditions and who are of outstanding ability and promise in one or more categories of the arts. The scholarships shall be used for study, maintenance and travel either in Australia or overseas. One scholarship is granted in each of nine categories which rotate in two groups on an annual basis: instrumental music, painting, singing, prose, poetry, acting, architecture, sculpture and ballet." Award: AUS $18,000 payable in two installments of $9,000 per annum. Competition receives 120 submissions. Panel of 6 judges. Guidelines for SASE. Deadline: last Friday in October. Winners announced in March. Winners notified by phone and mail. List of winners available by phone in late March.

◯ ◉ **WALTER RUMSEY MARVIN GRANT**, Ohioana Library Association, 65 S. Front St., Room 1105, Columbus OH 43215-4163. (614)466-3831. Fax: (614)728-6974. E-mail: ohioana@winsto.state.on.us. Contact: Linda Hengst. "To encourage young unpublished (meaning not having a book published) writers (under age 30)." Annual competition for short stories. Award: $1,000. Guidelines for SASE. Deadline: January 31. Open to unpublished authors born in Ohio or who have lived in Ohio for a minimum of five years. Must be under 30 years of age. Up to six pieces of prose may be submitted; maximum 60 pages, minimum 10 pages.

ℕ ◯ **MASTERS LITERARY AWARD**, Center Press, P.O. Box 16452, Encino CA 91416-6452. Website: members.xoom.com/centerpress. "One yearly Grand Prize of $1,000, and four quarterly awards of 'Honorable Mention' each in either 1) fiction; 2) poetry and song lyrics; 3) nonfiction." Judges: Gabriella Stone, Scott A. Sonders and Sandra Gilbert. Entry fee $15. Awards are given on March 15, June 15, September 15 and December 15. Any submission received prior to an award date is eligible for the subsequent award. Submissions accepted throughout the year. Fiction and nonfiction must be no more than 20 pages (5,000 words); poetry no more than

150 lines. All entries must be in the English language. #10 SASE required for guidelines. "Be persistant, be consistent, be professional."

☑ ◻ ◎ **MARY MCCARTHY PRIZE IN SHORT FICTION**, Sarabande Books, Inc., P.O. Box 4999, Louisville KY 40204. (502)458-4028. Fax: (502)458-4065. E-mail: sarabandek@aol.com. Website: www.saraban debooks.org. Contact: Kirby Gann, managing editor. "To award publication and $2,000 to an outstanding collection of short stories and/or novellas, up to 300 pages; or single novella, 150 pages maximum." Competition receives 1,000-1,500 submissions. Judge: Nationally known writer, changes yearly. Entry fee $15. Guidelines for SASE. Deadline: February 15. Unpublished submissions. US citizens. Word length: 150-300 pages. "Writers must submit a required entry form and follow contest guildelines for ms submission. Writers must include a #10 SASE with their inquiries." Winners announced in June.

◻ **THE JOHN H. MCGINNIS MEMORIAL AWARD**, *Southwest Review*, P.O. Box 750374, 307 Fondren Library West, Southern Methodist University, Dallas TX 75275-0374. (214)768-1037. Contact: Elizabeth Mills, senior editor. Annual awards (fiction and nonfiction). Stories or essays must have been published in the *Southwest Review* prior to the announcement of the award. Awards: $1,000. Pieces are not submitted directly for the award but for publication in the magazine.

◑ **JENNY MCKEAN MOORE WRITER IN WASHINGTON**, Jenny McKean Moore Fund & The George Washington University, Dept. of English, George Washington University, Washington DC 20052. (202)994-6180. Fax: (202)994-7915. Professor of English: D. McAleavey. Annual award "of a teaching residency for a different genre each year." Award: $46,000 and an "attractive benefits package." Receives 200 submissions. Judges: George Washington University English faculty and members of the J.M. Moore Fund. Guidelines for SASE. Deadline: November 15. Previously published submissions. Winners announced in February. Winners notified by phone.

☑ ◻ ◎ **MCKNIGHT ARTIST FELLOWSHIPS FOR WRITERS, Administered by the Loft**, The Loft, Pratt Community Center, 1011 Washington Ave. S., Minneapolis MN 55416. (612)379-8999. Fax: (612)951-4423. Website: www.loft.org. Program Coordinator: Jerod Santek. "To give Minnesota writers of demonstrated ability an opportunity to work for a concentrated period of time on their writing." Annual awards of $10,000; 2 in poetry and 3 in creative prose; 2 awards of distinction of $20,000. Competition receives approximately 125-175 submissions/year. Judges are from out-of-state. Entry forms or rules available in October for SASE "or see website." Deadline: November. "Applicants *must* be Minnesota residents and must send for and observe guidelines." Winners announced by May 1. Winner notified by phone or mail. List of winners available in August for SASE.

◑ ◎ **MICHIGAN AUTHOR AWARD**, Michigan Library Association/Michigan Center for the Book, 6810 S. Cedar, Suite 6, Lansing MI 48911. (517)694-6615. Fax: (517)694-4330. E-mail: hartzelm@mlc.lib.mi.us. Executive Director: Marianne Hartzell. "Award to recognize an outstanding published body of fiction, nonfiction, poetry and/or playscript, by a Michigan author." Annual competition for short stories, novels, story collections. Award: $1,000. Competition receives 50 submissions. Judges: Panel members represent a broad spectrum of expertise in writing, publishing and book collecting. Guidelines available in February for SASE or by e-mail. Inquiries by fax and e-mail OK. Deadline: May. Previously published submissions. Eligibility: current Michigan resident; long-time resident, recently relocated; or author whose works identify with Michigan because of subject/ setting. Nominee must have 3 published works. Winners announced in July. Winners notified by phone.

◑ **MID-LIST PRESS FIRST SERIES AWARD FOR SHORT FICTION**, Mid-List Press, 4324-12th Ave. South, Minneapolis MN 55407-3218. (612)822-3733. Fax: (612)823-8387. E-mail: guide@midlist.org. Website: www.midlist.org. Contact: Lane Stiles, senior editor. To encourage and nurture short fiction writers who have never published a collection of fiction. Annual competition for fiction collections. Award: $1,000 advance and publication. Judges: Manuscript readers and the editors of Mid-List Press. Entry fee $20. Deadline: July 1. Previously published or unpublished submissions. Word length: 50,000 words minimum. "Application forms and guidelines are available for a #10 SASE or visit our website." Winners announced in December. Winners notified by phone and mail in December.

◻ **MID-LIST PRESS FIRST SERIES AWARD FOR THE NOVEL**, Mid-List Press, 4324-12th Ave. South, Minneapolis MN 55407-3218. (612)822-3733. Fax: (612)823-8387. E-mail: guide@midlist.org. Website: www.m idlist.org. Contact: Lane Stiles, senior editor. To encourage and nurture first-time novelists. Annual competition for novels. Award: $1,000 advance and publication. Competition receives approximately 500 submissions. Judges: Manuscript readers and the editors of Mid-List Press. Entry fee $20. Deadline: February 1. Unpublished submissions. Word length: minimum 50,000 words. "Application forms and guidelines are available for a #10 SASE, or visit our website." Winners announced in July. Winners notified by phone and mail. Winners' list published in *Poets & Writers* and *AWP Chronicle*.

✓ ⊘ **MILKWEED EDITIONS NATIONAL FICTION PRIZE**, Milkweed Editions, 430 First Ave. N., Suite 668, Minneapolis MN 55401-1743. (612)332-3192. Fax: (612)332-6248. Publisher: Emilie Buchwald. Annual award for a novel, a short story collection, one or more novellas, or a combination of short stories and novellas. The Prize will be awarded to the best work of fiction that Milkweed accepts for publication during each calendar year by a writer not previously published by Milkweed Editions. The winner will receive a $5,000 cash advance as part of any royalties agreed upon at the time of acceptance. Must request guidelines; send SASE. There is no deadline. Judged by Milkweed Editions. "Please look at previous winners: *The Empress of One*, by Faith Sullivan; *Confidence of the Heart*, by David Schweidel; *Montana 1948*, by Larry Watson; and *Aquaboogie*, by Susan Straight—this is the caliber of fiction we are searching for. Catalog available for $1.50 postage, if people need a sense of our list."

⊘ **MILKWEED EDITIONS PRIZE FOR CHILDREN'S LITERATURE**, Milkweed Editions, 430 First Ave. N., Suite 400, Minneapolis MN 55401. (612)332-3192. Fax: (612)332-6248. Website: www.milkweed.org. Publisher: Emilie Buchwald. "Our goal is to encourage writers to create books for the important age range of middle readers." Annual award for novels for children ages 8 to 12. The prize will be awarded to the best work for children ages 8 to 12 that Milkweed accepts for publication during each calendar year by a writer not previously published by Milkweed. The winner will receive $2,000 cash advance as a part of any royalties agreed upon at the time of acceptance. There is no deadline. Judges: Milkweed Editions. Guidelines for SASE. Unpublished in book form. Page length: 110-350 pages. "Send for guidelines for children's literature and check our website to review previous winners. Winners notified upon acceptance for publication."

N ⊘ ◎ **MIND BOOK OF THE YEAR—THE ALLEN LANE AWARD MIND**, Granta House, 15-19 Broadway, London E15 4BQ England. Contact: Ms. A. Brackx. "To award a prize to the work of fiction or nonfiction which outstandingly furthers public understanding of the causes, experience or treatment of mental health problems." Annual competition for novels and works of nonfiction. Award: £1,000. Competition receives approximately 50-100 submissions. Judges: A panel drawn from MIND's Council of Management. Deadline: December. Previously published submissions. Author's nomination is accepted. All books must be published in English in the UK.

N ◎ **MINNESOTA VOICES PROJECT**, New Rivers Press, 420 N. Fifth St., #910, Minneapolis MN 55401. (612)339-7114. Website: www.mtn.org/newrivpr. Contact: Eric Braun, editorial assistant. Annual award "to foster and encourage new and emerging regional writers of short fiction, novellas, personal essays and poetry." Requires entry form. Awards: $500 to each author published in the series plus "a generous royalty agreement if book goes into second printing." Competition receives 100 submissions. No entry fee. Send request with SASE for guidelines in October. Deadline: April 1. Restricted to new and emerging writers from Minnesota. Winners announced October. Winners notified by phone and mail. List of winners available for SASE.

✓ *MISSISSIPPI REVIEW* **PRIZE**, University of Southern Mississippi/Mississippi Review, P.O. Box 5144 USM, Hattiesburg MS 39406-5144. (601)266-4321. Fax: (601)266-5757. E-mail: rief@netdoor.com. Contact: Rie Fortenberry, managing editor. Annual award to "reward excellence in new fiction and poetry and to find new writers who are just beginning their careers." Award: $500 plus publication for the winning story and poem; publication for all runners-up. Prize issue $5 for contributor. Entry fee $10/story. No manuscripts returned. Deadline: May 31. Previously unpublished submissions. List of winners and runners-up for SASE.

N *THE MISSOURI REVIEW* **EDITORS' PRIZE CONTEST**, 1507 Hillcrest Hall, Columbia MO 65211. (573)882-4474. Fax: (573)884-4671. Website: www.missourireview.org. Contact: Greg Michalson, managing editor. Annual competition for short stories, poetry and essays. Award: Cash ($1,500 for fiction and poetry, $1,000 for essay) and publication in *The Missouri Review*. Competition receives more than 1,000 submissions. Judges: *The Missouri Review* staff. Page restrictions: 25 typed, double-spaced, for fiction and essays, 10 for poetry. Entry fee $15 for each entry (checks payable to *The Missouri Review*). Each fee entitles entrant to a one-year subscription to *The Missouri Review*, an extension of a current subscription, or a gift subscription. Guidelines available June for SASE. Deadline: October 15. Outside of envelope should be marked "Fiction," "Essay," or "Poetry." Enclose an index card with author's name, address, and telephone number in the left corner and, for fiction and essay entries only, the work's title in the center. Entries must be previously unpublished and will not be returned. Winners announced in January. Winners notified by phone and mail. List of winners available for SASE. No further guidelines necessary. "Send fully realized stories with a distinctive voice, style and subject."

N ◑ **MOBIL PEGASUS PRIZE**, Mobil Corporation, (Room 7P2114), 3225 Gallows Rd., Fairfax VA 22037-0001. (703)846-1004. E-mail: gail_campbell-wooley@email.mobil.com. Contact: Director. To recognize distinguished works of literature from around the globe. Award for novels. "Prize is given on a country-by-country basis and does not involve submissions unless requested by national juries." 1998 award: Venezuela.

◯ **MODEST CONTEST**, *New Stone Circle*, 1185 E. 1900 North Rd., White Heath IL 61884. (217)762-5801. Fax: (217)398-4096. E-mail: m-hays@uiuc.edu. Fiction Editor: Mary Lucille Hays. Award "to encourage good writing." Annual competition for short stories. Awards: $100 (1st Prize). All contestants receive a copy of the contest issue. Competition receives approximately 100 submissions. Judge: Mary Hays. Entry fee $10. Guidelines for SASE. Deadline: June 1. Unpublished submissions. Winners announced in September. Winners notified by mail.

MONEY FOR WOMEN, Money for Woman/Barbara Deming Memorial Fund, Inc., Box 630125, Bronx NY 10463. Administrator: Susan Pliner. "Small grants to individual feminists in the arts." Biannual competition. Award: $200-1,000. Competition receives approximately 150 submissions. Judges: Board of Directors. Guidelines for SASE. Deadline: December 31, June 30. Limited to US and Canadian citizens. Word length: 25 pages. May submit own fiction. "Only for feminists in the arts." Winners announced five months after deadline. Winners notified by mail.

☑ ◎ **MONTANA ARTS COUNCIL INDIVIDUAL ARTIST FELLOWSHIP**, 316 N. Park Ave., Room 252, Helena MT 59620. (406)444-6430. Executive Director: Arlynn Fishbaugh. Annual award of $2,000. Competition receives about 80-200 submissions/year. Panelists are professional artists. Contest requirements available for SASE or e-mail at mac@state.mt.us. Deadline each year. Restricted to residents of Montana; not open to degree-seeking students.

◯ **MYSTERY MAYHEM CONTEST**, *Mystery Time*/Hutton Publications, P.O. Box 2907, Decatur IL 62524. Contact: Linda Hutton, editor. Award "to encourage writers to have fun writing a mystery spoof." Annual competition for short stories. Award: $10 cash and publication in *Mystery Time*. Competition receives approximately 100 submissions. Judge: Linda Hutton, editor of *Mystery Time*. Guidelines for SASE. Deadline: September 15 annually. Unpublished submissions. Word length: Must be one sentence of any length. "One entry per person, of one sentence which can be any length, which is the opening of a mystery spoof. Must include SASE. Entry form not required. All material must be typed. Flyer of previous years' winners available for $1 plus #10 SASE." Winners announced in October in Mystery Time Anthology Autumn issue.

🍁 ◯ ◎ **THE NATIONAL CHAPTER OF CANADA IODE VIOLET DOWNEY BOOK AWARD**, The National Chapter of Canada IODE, 254-40 Orchard View Blvd., Toronto, Ontario M4R 1B9 Canada. (416)487-4416. Fax: (416)487-4417. Chairman, Book Award Committee: Marty Dalton. "The award is given to a Canadian author for an English language book suitable for children 13 years of age and under, published in Canada during the previous calendar year. Fairy tales, anthologies and books adapted from another source are not eligible." Annual competition for novels, children's literature. Award: $3,000. Competition receives 100-120 submissions. Judges: A six-member panel of judges including four National IODE officers and two non-members who are recognized specialists in the field of children's literature. Guidelines for SASE. Deadline: December 31. Previously published January 1, 1999 and December 31, 1999. "The book must have been written by a Canadian citizen and must have been published in Canada during the calendar year." Word length: Must have at least 500 words of text preferably with Canadian content.

☑ ◯ **NATIONAL FEDERATION OF THE BLIND WRITER'S DIVISION FICTION CONTEST**, National Federation of the Blind Writer's Division, 1203 Fairview Rd., Columbia MO 65203. (516)868-8718. Fax: (516)868-9076. President: Tom Stevens. First Vice President, Writer's Division: Lori Stayer. "To promote good writing for blind writers and Division members, blind or sighted." Annual competition for short stories. Award: $50, $40, $25, $15. Competitions receives 20 submissions. Entry fee $5/story. Guidelines for SASE. Inquiries by fax OK. Deadline: May 1, 2000 (contest opens 9/1/99). Unpublished submissions. "Entrant must be legally blind or a member of the National Federation of the Blind Writers' Division. Story must be in English, and typed. SASE necessary." Critique on request, $5. Word length: 3,000 maximum. Winners announced July 31. Winners notified by mail. List of winners available for SASE.

☑ ◯ **NATIONAL WRITERS ASSOCIATION ANNUAL NOVEL WRITING CONTEST**, National Writers Association, 3140 Peoria St., PMB 295, Aurora CO 80014. (303)841-0246. E-mail: sandywriter@aol.com. Website: www.nationalwriters.com. Contact: Sandy Whelchel, director. Annual award to "recognize and reward outstanding ability and to increase the opportunity for publication." Award: $500 (1st Prize); $300 (2nd Prize); $100 (3rd Prize). Award judged by successful writers. Entry fee: $35. Judges' evaluation sheets sent to each entry with SASE. Contest rules and entry forms available with SASE. Opens December 1. Deadline: April 1. Unpublished submissions, any genre or category. Length: 20,000-100,000 words.

☑ ◯ **NATIONAL WRITERS ASSOCIATION ANNUAL SHORT STORY CONTEST**, National Writers Association, 3140 S. Peoria #295, Aurora CO 80014-3155. (303)841-0246. Fax: (303)751-8593. E-mail: sandywrter@aol.com. Website: www.nationalwriters.com. Executive Director: Sandy Whelchel. Annual award to encourage and recognize writing by freelancers in the short story field. Award: $200 (1st Prize); $100 (2nd Prize); $50 (3rd Prize). Opens April 1. Entry fee $15. Guidelines available in January for SASE. All entries must be postmarked by July 1. Inquiries by fax and e-mail OK. Evaluation sheets sent to each entrant if SASE provided. Unpublished submissions. Length: No more than 5,000 words. Winners announced at the NWA Summer

Conference in June. Winners notified by phone or mail. List of winners published in *Authorship*.

○ ◎ **THE NATIONAL WRITTEN & ILLUSTRATED BY . . . AWARDS CONTEST FOR STU-DENTS**, Landmark Editions, Inc., P.O. Box 270169, Kansas City MO 64127-2135. (816)241-4919. Fax: (816)483-3755. Website: www.LandmarkEditions.com. Contact: Nan Thatch. "Contest initiated to encourage students to write and illustrate original books and to inspire them to become published authors and illustrators." Annual competition. "Each student whose book is selected for publication will be offered a complete publishing contract. To ensure that students benefit from the proceeds, royalties from the sale of their books will be placed in an individual trust fund, set up for each student by his or her parents or legal guardians, at a bank of their choice. Funds may be withdrawn when a student becomes of age, or withdrawn earlier (either in whole or in part) for educational purposes or in case of proof of specific needs due to unusual hardship. Reports of book sales and royalties will be sent to the student and the parents or guardians annually." Winners also receive an all-expense-paid trip to Kansas City to oversee final reproduction phases of their books. Books by students may be entered in one of three age categories: A—6 to 9 years old; B—10 to 13 years old; C—14 to 19 years old. Each book submitted must be both written and illustrated by the same student. "Any books that are written by one student and illustrated by another will be automatically disqualified." Book entries must be submitted by a teacher or librarian. Entry fee $2. For rules and guidelines, send a #10 SAE with 66¢ postage or on website: www.landmarkeditions.com. Deadline: May 1 of each year. Winners announced October. Winners notified by phone.

THE NEBRASKA REVIEW **AWARD IN FICTION**, The Nebraska Review, University of Nebraska at Omaha, Omaha NE 68182-0324. (402)554-3159. Managing Editor: James Reed. Award to "recognize short fiction of the highest possible quality." Annual competition for short stories. Award: Publication plus $500. Competition receives 400-500 submissions. Judges: Staff. Entry fee $10 for each story submitted. Guidelines for SASE. Deadline: November 30. Previously unpublished submissions. Word length: 5,000 words. Winners announced March 15. Winners notified by phone and/or mail in February.

🄽 ○ **NESFA SCIENCE FICTION SHORT STORY CONTEST**, New England Science Fiction Association, P.O. Box 809, Framingham MA 01701-0203. (617)625-2311. Fax: (617)776-3243. E-mail: info@nesfa.org. Website: www.nesfa.org. Conact: Suford Lewis. Contest to encourage people to write science fiction and fantasy short stories. Annual competition for short stories. Award: Plaque and $50 of NESFA merchandise. Competition receives 20-50 submissions. Judges: Well-known, professional science fiction and fantasy writers. Contest guidelines available for SASE. Inquiries by fax and e-mail OK. Deadline November 15. Unpublished submissions. Limited to writers who have had no fiction published. Word length: 7,500 words or less. "Read a lot of science fiction and fantasy. Write using good grammar. Have a plot, a beginning, middle and end." Winners announced at banquet in February. Winners notified by mail. List of winners will be send to all entrants at the end of February.

◉ **NEUSTADT INTERNATIONAL PRIZE FOR LITERATURE**, *World Literature Today*, 110 Monnet Hall, University of Oklahoma, Norman OK 73019-4033. Contact: William Riggan, director. Biennial award to recognize distinguished and continuing achievement in fiction, poetry or drama. Awards: $40,000, an eagle feather cast in silver, an award certificate and a special issue of *WLT* devoted to the laureate. "We are looking for outstanding accomplishment in world literature. The Neustadt Prize is not open to application. Nominations are made only by members of the international jury, which changes for each award. Jury meetings are held in February or March of even-numbered years. Unsolicited manuscripts, whether published or unpublished, cannot be considered."

✓ ○ ◎ **NEVADA ARTS COUNCIL ARTISTS' FELLOWSHIPS**, 602 N. Curry St., Carson City NV 89703. (775)687-6680. Fax: (775)687-6688. E-mail: sarosse@clan.lib.nv.us. Artists' Services Program: Sharon Rosse, coordinator. Award "to honor individual artists and their artistic achievements to support artists' efforts in advancing their careers." Annual competition for fiction, nonfiction, poetry, playwriting. Award: $5,000 ($4,500 immediately, $500 after public service event completed). Competition receives approximately 230 submissions. Judges: Peer panels of professional artists. Guidelines available, no SASE required. Deadline: April 25, 2000. "Only available to Nevada residents." Word length: 25 pages prose and plays, 10 pages poetry. Winners announced June. Winners notified by mail. Entrants receive list of winners. "Inquire about jackpot grants for Nevada residents' projects, up to $1,000."

○ ◎ *THE NEW ERA* **WRITING, ART, PHOTOGRAPHY AND MUSIC CONTEST**, *New Era Magazine* (LDS Church), 50 E. North Temple, Salt Lake City UT 84150. (801)240-2951. Contact: Larry A. Hiller, managing editor. "To encourage young Mormon writers and artists." Annual competition for short stories. Award: Partial scholarship to Brigham Young University or Ricks College or cash awards. Competition receives approximately 300 submissions. Judges: *New Era* editors. Guidelines for SASE. October 1999 issue will have ruler and entry form. Deadline: January 7, 2000. Unpublished submissions. Contest open only to 12-23-year-old members of the Church of Jesus Christ of Latter-Day Saints. Winners announced by April 15, 2000. Winners notified by letter. List of winners in the September 2000 issue.

NEW HAMPSHIRE STATE COUNCIL ON THE ARTS INDIVIDUAL ARTIST FELLOW-SHIP, 40 N. Main St., Concord NH 03301-4974. (603)271-2789. Website: www.state.nh.us/nharts. Artist Services Coordinator: Audrey V. Sylvester. Fellowship "recognizes artistic excellence and professional commitment of professional artists in literature who are legal/permanent residents of the state of New Hampshire. Individual artists fellowships are being reviewed as part of the council's five year plan. Please visit our website for current information."

NEW JERSEY STATE COUNCIL ON THE ARTS PROSE FELLOWSHIP, P.O. Box 306, Trenton NJ 08625. (609)292-6130. Annual grants for writers of short stories, novels, story collections. Past awards have ranged from $5,000-12,000. 1999 awards averaged $6,285. Judges: Peer panel. Guidelines for SASE. Deadline: mid-July. For either previously published or unpublished submissions. "Previously published work must be submitted as a manuscript." Applicants must be New Jersey residents. Submit copies of short fiction, short stories or prose not exceeding 15 pages and no less than 10 pages. For novels in progress, a one-page synopsis and sample chapter should be submitted.

NEW LETTERS LITERARY AWARD, UMKC, 5101 Rockhill Rd., Kansas City MO 64110-2499. (816)235-1168. Fax: (816)235-2611. E-mail: mccraryg@smptgate.umkc.edu. Awards Coordinator: Glenda McCrary. Award to "discover and reward unpublished work by new and established writers." Annual competition for short stories. Award: $1,000 and publication. Competition receives 600 entries/year. Entry fee $10. Guidelines for SASE. Inquiries by fax and e-mail OK. Deadline: May 15. Submissions must be unpublished. Length requirement: 5,000 words or less. Winners notified by personal letter in September. List of winners available for SASE.

NEW MILLENNIUM WRITING AWARDS, Room S, P.O. Box 2463, Knoxville TN 37901-2463. (423)428-0389. E-mail: donwill@aol.com. Website: www.mach2.com/books. Contact: Don Williams, editor. Award "to promote literary excellence in contemporary fiction." Semiannual competition for short stories. Award: $1,000 plus publication in *New Millennium Writings*. Competition receives approximately 1,000 submissions. Judges: Novelists and short story writers. Entry fee: $10. Guidelines for SASE available year round and on website. Inquiries by e-mail OK. Deadlines: June 15 and November 15. Unpublished submissions. No required word length. "Provide a bold, yet organic opening line, sustain the voice and mood throughout, tell an entertaining and vital story with a strong ending." Winners announced August and February. Winners notified by mail and phone. All entrants will receive a list of winners, plus a copy of the journal. Send letter-sized SASE with entry for list.

NEW WRITING AWARD, *New Writing Magazine*, PO Box 1812, Amherst NY 14226-7812. (716)834-1067. E-mail: info@newwriting.com. Website: www.newwriting.com. Director: Sam Meade. "We wish to reward *new* writing. Looking for originality in form and content." New and beginning writers encouraged. Annual open competition for prose (novel, novel excerpt, scripts, short story, essay, humor, other) and poetry. Deadline: Postmark by May 31 and December 31. Award: Up to $3,000 for best entry. Additional awards for finalists. Possible publication. Competition receives 500 submissions. Judges: Panel of editors. Entry fee $10 plus 10¢/page. Guidelines for SASE. Inquiries by e-mail OK. No application form required—simply send submission with reading fee, SASE for manuscript return or notification, and 3×5 card for each entry, including: story name, author and address. Winners announced in July and February. "For more information visit our website."

JOHN NEWBERY AWARD, American Library Association (ALA) Awards and Citations Program, Association for Library Service to Children, 50 E. Huron St., Chicago IL 60611. (312)280-2168. Fax: (312)944-7671. E-mail: alsc@ala.org. Website: www.ala.org/alsc. Executive Director: S. Roman. Annual award. Only books for children published in the US during the preceding year are eligible. Award: Medal. Entry restricted to US citizens-residents. Guidelines available February 1. Inquiries by fax and e-mail OK. Deadline: December. Winners announced in January. Winners notified by phone. List of winners available in February on website.

NFB WRITERS' FICTION CONTEST, The Writers' Division of the National Federation of the Blind, 1203 S. Fairview Rd., Columbia MO 65203-0809. (573)445-6091. President of Division: Tom Stevens. Award to "encourage members and other blind writers to write fiction." Annual competition for short stories. Award: Four prizes of $50, $35, $20, $10, plus honorable mentions and possible publication in *Slate & Style*. Competition receives 25 submissions. Entry fee $5 per story. Guidelines available August 1 for SASE. Deadline: May 1. Unpublished submissions. Word length: 2,000 words (maximum). "Send a 150-word bio with each entry. Please, no erotica." Winners announced July 15. Winners notified by letter. List of winners available in July for SASE. "Be a serious contestant. Too many entries received with a multitude of spelling and grammatical errors.

96 INC'S BRUCE P. ROSSLEY LITERARY AWARDS, 96 Inc., P.O. Box 15559, Boston MA 02215-0010. (617)267-0543. Fax: (617)262-3568. E-mail: to90inc@ici.net. Director: Vera Gold. Award "to increase the attention for writers of merit who have received little recognition." Biennial award for short stories, novels and story collections. Award: $1,000 for the literary award and $100 for Bruce P. Rossley New Voice Award. Competition receives 400-500 submissions. Judges: Professionals in the fields of writing, journalism and publishing. Entry fee $10. Guidelines available after July 1999 for SASE. Deadline: September 30. Published or unpublished submissions. "In addition to writing, the writer's accomplishments in the fields of teaching and community service will also be considered." Open to writers from New England. Work must be nominated by "someone familiar with the writer's work." Winners announced November. Winners notified by mail early November. Winners are honored at a reception near the end of the year. List of winners available in November for #10 SASE.

[N] [♥] [◎] THE NOMA AWARD FOR PUBLISHING IN AFRICA, P.O. Box 128, Witney, Oxon 0X9 5X4 United Kingdom. (44)1993-775235. Fax: (44)1993-709265. E-mail: maryljay@aol.com. Contact: Mary Jay. Sponsored by Kodansha Ltd. Award "to encourage publication of works by African writers and scholars in Africa, instead of abroad as is still too often the case at present." Annual competition for a new book in any of these categories: Scholarly or academic; books for children; literature and creative writing, including fiction, drama and poetry. Award: $10,000. Competition receives approximately 140 submissions. Judges: A committee of African scholars and book experts and representatives of the international book community. Chairman: Walter Bgoya. Guidelines for SASE. Deadline: February 28. Previously published submissions. Submissions are through publishers only. Winners announced September. Winners notified through publishers. List of winners available for SASE.

[N] [◎] NORTH CAROLINA ARTS COUNCIL FELLOWSHIP, 221 E. Lane St., Raleigh NC 27611. (919)733-2111 ext. 22. Literature Director: Deborah McGill. Grants program "to encourage the continued achievements of North Carolina's writers of fiction, poetry, literary nonfiction and literary translation." Biannual awards: Up to $8,000 each. Council receives approximately 200 submissions. Judges are a panel of editors and published writers from outside the state. Writers must be over 18 years old, not currently enrolled in degree-granting program, and *must have been a resident of North Carolina for 1 full year as of the application deadline.* Deadline: November 1, 2000.

[◎] NORTH CAROLINA ARTS COUNCIL WRITERS' RESIDENCIES, 221 E. Lane St., Raleigh NC 27601-2807. (919)733-2111, ext. 22. Fax: (919)733-4834. E-mail: dmcgill@ncacmail.dcr.state.nc.us. Website: www.ncarts.org. Literature Director: Deborah McGill. Award "to recognize and encourage North Carolina's finest creative writers. Every year we offer a two-month residency for one writer at the LaNapoule Art Foundation in southern France, a three-month residency for one writer at Headlands Center for the Arts (California), and a one-month residency for one writer at Vermont Studio Center." Judges: Panels of writers and editors convened by the residency centers. Guidelines available after March 1 by phone or mail. Inquiries by fax and e-mail OK. Deadline: early June. Writers must be over 18 years old, not currently enrolled in degree-granting program on undergraduate or graduate level and *must have been a resident of North Carolina for 1 full year as of application deadline.* Winners announced in the Fall. Winners notified by phone. List of winners available by phone, mail or on website.

[🌐] [✓] [○] NORWEGIAN LITERATURE ABROAD GRANT (NORLA), Bygdoy Allè 21, 0262 Oslo Norway. +47 2212 2540. Fax: +47 2212 2544. E-mail: firmapost@norla.no. Manager: Kristin Brudevoll. Award to "help Norwegian fiction to be published outside Scandinavia and ensure that the translator will be paid for his/her work." Annual compensation for translations, 50-60% of the translation's cost. Competition receives 40-50 submissions. Judges: An advisory (literary) board of 5 persons. Guidelines for SASE. Deadline: December 15. Previously published submissions. "Application form can be obtained from NORLA. Foreign (non-Scandanavian) publishers may apply for the award."

[N] NTPWA ANNUAL POETRY & FICTION CONTEST, North Texas Professional Writer's Association, P.O. Box 563, Bedford TX 76095-0563. (817)428-2822. Fax: (817)428-2181. E-mail: justel@cris.com. Website: www.startext.net/homes/prowritr. Contact: Elaine Lanmon. Award "to recognize and encourage previously unpublished writers." Annual competition for short stories, novels and poetry. Fiction awards: $50 (1st Prize), $25 (2nd Prize). Poetry awards: $25 (1st Prize), $10 (2nd Prize). Judges: Published writers. Entry fee: $5 fiction, $3/ 2 poems. Guidelines for SASE. Inquiries by fax and e-mail OK. Deadline: May 31, 2000. Unpublished submissions. Length: 25 pages (fiction); 25 lines (poetry). Winners announced July 15, 2000. List of winners available for SASE.

[N] [○] THE FLANNERY O'CONNOR AWARD FOR SHORT FICTION, The University of Georgia Press, 330 Research Dr., Athens GA 30602. (706)369-6135. Fax: (708)369-6131. E-mail: mnunnell@ugapress.uga.edu. Website: www.uga.edu/ugapress. Contact: Margaret Nunnelley, award coordinator. Annual award "to recognize outstanding collections of short fiction. Published and unpublished authors are welcome." Award: $1,000 and publication by the University of Georgia Press. Competition receives 330 submissions. Deadline: April 1-May 31. "Manuscripts cannot be accepted at any other time." Entry fee $15. Contest rules for SASE. Ms will not be returned. Winners announced November 2000. Winners notified by mail.

N ⊙ FRANK O'CONNOR FICTION AWARD, *descant*, Dept. of English, Texas Christian University, Fort Worth TX 76129. (817)921-7240. Business Manager: Claudia Knott. Estab. 1979 with *descant*; earlier awarded through *Quartet*. Annual award to honor the best published fiction in *descant* for its current volume. Award: $500 prize. No entry fee. "About 12 to 15 stories are published annually in *descant*. Winning story is selected from this group."

🍁 ✓ ⊘ ◎ HOWARD O'HAGAN AWARD FOR SHORT FICTION, Writers Guild of Alberta, 3rd Floor, Percy Page Centre, 11759 Groat Rd., Edmonton, Alberta T5M 3K6 Canada. (780)422-8174. Fax: (780)422-2663. Executive Director: Miki Andrejevic. "To recognize outstanding books published by Alberta authors each year." Annual competition for short stories. Award: $500 (Canadian) cash and leather bound book. Competition receives 20-30 submissions. Judges: Selected published writers across Canada. Guidelines for SASE. Deadline: December 31. Previously published submissions published between January and December 31. Open to Alberta authors only.

N FRANK O'HARA AWARD CHAPBOOK COMPETITION, Thorngate Road, Campus Box 4240, English Department, Illinois State University, Normal IL 61790-4240. (309)438-7705. E-mail: jmelled@ilstu.edu. Director/Publisher: Jim Elledge. Award to "publish a chapbook-length collection (20 pp. max.) of poetry, prose poems, or cross-genre work (e.g., short-short fiction) by lesbian, bisexual, transgendered or gay authors." Award: $500 plus 25 copies. Competition receives 150 submissions. Judge: An anonymous, nationally-recognized lesbian, bi, transgendered or gay author. Entry fee $15 for each ms. submitted. Guidelines available for SASE. Deadline: February 1. Published or previously unpublished submissions. "The contest is open to lesbian, bisexual, transgendered or gay authors for short (16 pp. max.) collections of poetry, prose poems or cross-genre texts (e.g., short-short fiction). Individuals may submit as many 16-page manuscripts as they want as long as each is accompanied by the $15 reading fee. Thus far, Larry Wayne Johns' *An Invisible Veil Between Us*, Ron Mohring's *Amateur Grief* and Brent Goodman's *Wrong Horoscope* have won. Each is available for $6. Thorngate Road has also published books by Kristy Nielsen, David Trinidad, Karen Lee Osborne, Reginald Shepherd and Maureen Seaton in its invitation only Berdache series.

✓ ⊘ OHIO STATE UNIVERSITY PRESS, 1070 Carmack Rd., Columbus OH 43210-1002. (614)292-6930. Fax: (614)292-2065. E-mail: ohiostatepress@osu.edu. Website: www.ohiostatepress.org. Contact: Jeanette Rivard. Estab. 1957. "Small-sized university press." Publishes "scholarly and trade books." Member of Association of American University Presses (AAUP), International Association of Scholarly Publishers (IASP) and Association of American Publishers (AAP). Publishes one annual winner of poetry contest and of short fiction prize. Guidelines available on website. Inquiries by e-mail and fax OK. Competition receives 400-500 submissions.

◎ OHIOANA AWARD FOR CHILDREN'S LITERATURE, ALICE WOOD MEMORIAL, Ohioana Library Association, 65 S. Front St., Room 1105, Columbus OH 43215-4163. (614)466-3831. Fax: (614)728-6974. E-mail: ohioana@winslo.state.oh.us. Director: Linda Hengst. Competition "to honor an individual whose body of work has made, and continues to make, a significant contribution to literature for children or young adults." Annual award of $1,000. Guidelines for SASE. Inquiries by fax and e-mail OK. Deadline: December 31 prior to year award is given. "Open to authors born in Ohio or who have lived in Ohio for a minimum of five years." Winners announced in summer. Winners notified by letter. Entrants can call, e-mail or check website for winner.

⊘ ◎ OHIOANA BOOK AWARDS, Ohioana Library Association, 65 S. Front St., Room 1105, Columbus OH 43215-4163. (614)466-3831. Fax: (614)728-6974. E-mail: ohioana@winslo.state.oh.us. Contact: Linda R. Hengst, director. Annual awards granted (only if the judges believe a book of sufficiently high quality has been submitted) to bring recognition to outstanding books by Ohioans or about Ohio. Five categories: Fiction, Nonfiction, Juvenile, Poetry and About Ohio or an Ohioan. Criteria: Books written or edited by a native Ohioan or resident of the state for at least 5 years; two copies of the book MUST be received by the Ohioana Library by December 31 prior to the year the award is given; literary quality of the book must be outstanding. Awards: Certificate and glass sculpture (up to 6 awards given annually). Each spring a jury considers all books received since the previous jury. Award judged by a jury selected from librarians, book reviewers, writers and other

MARKET CONDITIONS are constantly changing! If you're still using this book and it is 2001 or later, buy the newest edition of *Novel & Short Story Writer's Market* at your favorite bookstore or order from Writer's Digest Books at (800)289-0963.

knowledgeable people. No entry forms are needed, but they are available. "We will be glad to answer letters asking specific questions."

N ◎ OKLAHOMA BOOK AWARD, Oklahoma Center for the Book, 200 NE 18th, Oklahoma City OK 73105-3298. (405)522-3575. Fax: (405)525-7804. E-mail: gcarlile@oltn.odl.state.ok.us. Website: www.odl.state. ok.us/OCB. Executive Director: Glenda Carlile. Award to "recognize Oklahoma authors or books written about Oklahoma in the pervious year." Annual competition for novels and story collections. Award: Medal. Competition receives 25-80 submissions for fiction and non-fiction. Judges: A panel of 5 judges for each of 5 categories (fiction, non-fiction, children/young adult, poetry and design/illustration). Guidelines available August 1 for SASE. Inquiries by fax and e-mail OK. Deadline: January 10. Previously published submissions appearing between January 1 and December of the previous year. "Writers much live or have lived in Oklahoma or book must have an Oklahoma theme. Entry forms available after August 1. Mail entry along with 6 copies of book." Winners announced at book award ceremony March 11. Call for list of winners available March 13.

N ◯ THE CHRIS O'MALLEY PRIZE IN FICTION, The Madison Review, 600 North Park St., Madison WI 53706. (608)263-0566. Fiction Editors: Jennifer Dobbins and Sam Jackson. Award to "recognize emerging writers." Annual award for short stories. Award: $500; publication; 2 issues. Judges: "Entries go though an initial screening by staff members; final decision is made by editors." Entry fee $3. Guidelines for SASE. Deadline: entries only accepted during September 2000. Previously unpublished submissions. Word length: no more than 30 pages. Winners announced January 2001. Winners notified by phone by December 25, 2000.

N ◯ OPEN VOICE AWARDS, Westside YMCA—Writer's Voice, 5 W. 63rd St., New York NY 10023. (212)875-4124. E-mail: wtrsvoice@aol.com. Competition for fiction or poetry. Award: $1,000 honorarium and featured reading. Entry fee $15. Deadline: December 31. Unpublished submissions. "Submit a maximum of 15 double-spaced pages in a single genre. Enclose $10 entry fee." Guidelines for SASE.

✔ ◯ OPUS MAGNUM DISCOVERY AWARDS, C.C.S. Entertainment Group, 433 N. Camden Dr., #600, Beverly Hills CA 90210. (310)288-1881. Fax: (310)475-0193. E-mail: awards@screenwriters.com. President: Carlos Abreu. Award "to discover new unpublished manuscripts." Annual competition for novels. Award: Film rights options up to $10,000. Judges: Industry professionals. Entry fee $75. Deadline: August 1 of each year. Unpublished submissions.

◯ ORANGE BLOSSOM FICTION CONTEST, The Oak, 1530 Seventh St., Rock Island IL 61201. (309)788-3980. Contact: Betty Mowery, editor. "To build up circulation of publication and give new authors a chance for competition and publication along with seasoned writers." Award: Subscription to The Oak. Competition receives approximately 75 submissions. Judges: Various editors from other publications, some published authors and previous contest winners. Entry fee six 33¢ stamps. Guidelines available after January for SASE. Word length: 500 words maximum. "May be on any subject, but avoid gore and killing of humans or animals." Deadline: July 1. Winners announced mid-July. Winners notified by mail.

N ◎ OREGON BOOK AWARDS, Literary Arts, Inc., 720 SW Washington, Suite 700, Portland OR 97205. (503)227-2583. Fax: (503)241-7429. E-mail: la@literary-arts.org. Website: www.literary-arts.org. Program Director: Carrie Hoops. Annual award for outstanding authors of fiction, poetry, literary nonfiction, young readers and drama. Award: $1,000 in each category. Competition receives 20 submissions. Judges: Out-of-state experts. Guidelines available in February for SASE. Inquiries by fax and e-mail OK. Deadline: March 31. Limited to Oregon residents. Winners announced November 30. Winners are notified at an awards ceremony. List of winners available in November.

✔ ◯ ◎ OREGON INDIVIDUAL ARTIST FELLOWSHIP, Oregon Arts Commission, 775 Summer St. N.E., Salem OR 97310. (503)986-0082. Fax: (503)986-0260. E-mail: oregon.artscomm@state.or.us. Website: art.econ.state.or.us. Assistant Director: Michael Faison. "Award enables professional artists to undertake projects to assist their professional development." Biennial competition for short stories, novels, poetry and story collections. Award: $3,000. (Please note: ten $3,000 awards are spread over 5 disciplines—literature, music/opera, media arts, dance and theatre awarded in even-numbered years.) Competition receives 150 submissions. Guidelines available after March. Judges: Peer panel from outside the state. Deadline: September 1. Competition limited to Oregon residents. Winners announced December. Winners notified by mail. List of winners can be requested from Oregon Arts Commission or check the website.

◎ DOBIE PAISANO FELLOWSHIPS, Dobie House, 702 E. Dean Keeton St., Austin TX 78705. (512)471-8542. Fax: (512)471-9997. E-mail: aslate@mail.utexas.edu. Director: Audrey N. Slate. Annual fellowships for creative writing (includes short stories, novels and story collections). Award: 6 months residence at ranch; $1,200 monthly living stipend. Competition receives approximately 100 submissions. Judges: Faculty of University of Texas and members of Texas Institute of Letters. Entry fee: $10. Application and guidelines available in October on request by letter, fax or e-mail. "Open to writers with a Texas connection—native Texans, people who have lived in Texas at least two years, or writers with published work on Texas and Southwest." Deadline: January 21, 2000. Winners announced in May. Winners notified by telephone followed by mail. List of winners available by mail in late May.

KENNETH PATCHEN COMPETITION, Pig Iron Press, P.O. Box 237, Youngstown OH 44501. (330)747-6932. Fax: (330)747-0599. Contact: Jim Villani, publisher. Biannual. Awards works of fiction and poetry in alternating years. Award: Publication; $500. Judge with national visibility selected annually. Entry fee $10. Competition receives 100 submissions. Guidelines available for SASE. Reading period: January 1 to December 31. Award for fiction: 2001, 2003; fiction award for novel or short story collection, either form eligible. Previous publication of individual stories, poems or parts of novel OK. Ms should not exceed 500 typed pages. Winners announced June. Winners notified by mail. List of winners available in July for SASE. "Find a voice that is personal, informal, and original."

THE PATERSON FICTION PRIZE, The Poetry Center at Passaic County Community College, One College Boulevard, Paterson NJ 07505-1179. (973)684-6555. Fax: (973)684-5843. E-mail: m.gillan@pccc.cc.nj.us. Director: Maria Mazziotti Gillan. Award to "encourage recognition of high-quality writing." Annual competition for books of short stories and novels. Award: $1,000. Competition receives 400 submissions. Judge: A different one every year. Guidelines available for SASE. Deadline: April 1, 2000.

PEARL SHORT STORY CONTEST, *Pearl* Magazine, 3030 E. Second St., Long Beach CA 90803-5163. (562)434-4523. Contact: Marilyn Johnson, editor. Award to "provide a larger forum and help widen publishing opportunities for fiction writers in the small press; and to help support the continuing publication of *Pearl*." Annual competition for short stories. Award: $100, publication in *Pearl* and 10 copies. Competition receives approximately 100 submissions. Judges: Editors of *Pearl* (Marilyn Johnson, Joan Jobe Smith, Barbara Hauk). Entry fee $10 per story. Includes copy of magazine featuring winning story. Guidelines for SASE. Deadline: March 15. Unpublished submissions. Length: 4,000 words maximum. Include a brief biographical note and SASE for reply or return of manuscript. Accepts simultaneous submissions, but asks to be notified if story is accepted elsewhere. All submissions are considered for publication in *Pearl*. "Although we are open to all types of fiction, we look most favorably upon coherent, well-crafted narratives, containing interesting, believable characters and meaningful situations." Winners notified by mail June 2000. Winners notified by mail or phone. List of winners available for SASE.

JUDITH SIEGEL PEARSON AWARD, Wayne State University, Detroit MI 48202. Contact: Chair, English Dept. Competition "to honor writing about women." Annual award. Short stories up to 20 pages considered every third year (poetry and drama/nonfiction in alternate years). Fiction: 2000. Deadline: March 1, 2000. Award: Up to $400. Competition receives up to 100 submissions/year. Submissions are internally screened; then a noted writer does final reading. Entry forms for SASE. Winners announced mid-April by phone, mail and e-mail.

WILLIAM PEDEN PRIZE IN FICTION, *The Missouri Review*, 1507 Hillcrest Hall, University of Missouri, Columbia MO 65211. (573)882-4474. Website: www.missourireview.org. Contact: Speer Morgan, Greg Michalson, editors. Annual award "to honor the best short story published in *The Missouri Review* each year." Submissions are to be previously published in the volume year for which the prize is awarded. Award: $1,000. Competition receives 2,000 submissions. No entry deadline or fee. No rules; all fiction published in *MR* is automatically entered.

PEN CENTER USA WEST LITERARY AWARD IN FICTION, PEN Center USA West, 672 S. LaFayette Park Place, #41, Los Angeles CA 90057. (213)365-8500. Fax: (213)365-9616. E-mail: pen@pen-usa-west.org. Website: www.pen-usa-west.org. Executive Director: Sherrill Britton. To recognize fiction writers who live in the western United States. Annual competition for published novels and story collections. Award: $1,000, plaque, and honored at a ceremony in Los Angeles. Competition receives 150 submissions. Judges: Panel of writers, booksellers, editors. Entry fee $20 for each book submitted. Guidelines available in July for SASE. Inquiries by fax and e-mail OK. Deadline: December 31. Books published between January 1, 1999 and December 31, 1999. Open only to writers living west of the Mississippi. All entries must include 4 non-returnable copies of each submission and a completed entry form. Winners announced May 2000. Winners notified by phone and mail. Call or send SASE to request press release of winners or visit website.

PEN NEW ENGLAND/L.L. WINSHIP AWARD, P.O. Box 725, N. Cambridge MA 02140. (617)499-9550. Fax: (617)353-7136. E-mail: penne@bu.edu. Website: www.pen-ne.org. Coordinator: Mary L. Sullivan. Award to "acknowledge and praise a work of (published 1999) fiction, nonfiction or poetry with a New England topic and setting and/or by an author whose main residence is New England." Annual competition for novels and poetry. Award: $2,500. Competition receives 150 submissions. Five judges. 1999 judges included Jane G. Hawes, Bill Littlefield, Alexandra Marshall, Lloyd Schwartz and Jan Swafford. Guidelines available in October for SASE. Inquiries by fax and e-mail OK. Deadline: January 1. Previously published submissions that appeared between January 1 and December 31 of the preceeding year. Winners announced mid-March. Winners will be notified through publisher or PEN-NE Executive Board member. List of winners available in April by fax or phone.

PEN/BOOK-OF-THE-MONTH CLUB TRANSLATION PRIZE, PEN American Center, 568 Broadway, New York NY 10012. (212)334-1660. E-mail: jm@pen.org. Awards Coordinator: John Morrone. Award "to recognize the art of the literary translator." Annual competition for translations. Award: $3,000. Deadline: December 15. Previously published submissions within the calendar year. "Translators may be of any nationality, but book must have been published in the US and must be a book-length literary translation." Books may be submitted by publishers, agents or translators. No application form. Send three copies. "Early submissions are strongly recommended."

THE PEN/FAULKNER AWARD FOR FICTION, c/o The Folger Shakespeare Library, 201 E. Capitol St. SE, Washington DC 20003. (202)675-0345. Fax: (202)608-1719. E-mail: delaney@folger.edu. Website: www.folger.edu. Contact: Janice Delaney, PEN/Faulkner Foundation Executive Director. Annual award. "To award the most distinguished book-length work of fiction published by an American writer." Award: $15,000 for winner; $5,000 for nominees. Judges: Three writers chosen by the Trustees of the Award. Deadline: October 31. Published submissions only. Writers and publishers submit four copies of eligible titles published the current year. No juvenile. Authors must be American citizens.

PEN/NORMA KLEIN AWARD, PEN American Center, 568 Broadway, New York NY 10012. (212)334-1660. E-mail: jm@pen.org. Award Director: John Morrone. "Established in 1990 in memory of the late PEN member and distinguished children's book author, the biennial prize recognizes an emerging voice of literary merit among American writers of children's fiction. Candidates for the award are new authors whose books (for elementary school to young adult readers) demonstrate the adventuresome and innovative spirit that characterizes the best children's literature and Norma Klein's own work (but need not resemble her novels stylistically)." Award: $3,000. Judges: A panel of three distinguished children's authors. Guidelines for SASE. Previously published submissions. Writer must be nominated by other authors or editors of children's books. Next award: 2001.

JAMES D. PHELAN AWARD, Intersection for the Arts/The San Francisco Foundation, 446 Valencia St., San Francisco CA 94103-3415. (415)626-2787. Fax: (415)626-1636. E-mail: intrsect@wenet.net. Website: www.wenet.net/~intrsect. Program Director: Kevin B. Chen. Annual award "to author of an unpublished work-in-progress of fiction (novel or short story), nonfictional prose, poetry or drama." Award: $2,000 and certificate. Competition receives more than 160 submissions. All submissions are read by three initial readers (change from year to year) who forward ten submissions each onto three judges (change from year to year). Judges are established Bay Area writers with extensive publishing and teaching histories. Rules and entry forms available after October 15 for SASE. Deadline: January 31. Unpublished submissions. Applicant must have been born in the state of California, but need not be a current resident, and be 20-35 years old. Winners announced June 15. Winners notified by letter.

PLAYBOY COLLEGE FICTION CONTEST, *Playboy* Magazine, 680 N. Lake Shore Dr., Chicago IL 60611. (312)751-8000. Website: www.playboy.com. Award "to foster young writing talent." Annual competition for short stories. Award: $3,000 plus publication in the magazine. Competition receives 1,000 submissions. Judges: Staff. Guidelines available for SASE or on website. Deadline: January 1. Submissions should be unpublished. No age limit; college affiliation required. Stories should be 25 pages or fewer. "Manuscripts are not returned. Results of the contest will be sent via SASE." Winners announced in February or March. Winners notified by letter. List of winners available in February or March for SASE or on website.

POCKETS FICTION WRITING CONTEST, *Pockets Magazine*, Upper Room Publications, P.O. Box 189, Nashville TN 37202-0189. (615)340-7333. Fax: (615)340-7267. (Do not send submissions via fax.) E-mail: pockets@upperroom.org. Website: www.upperroom.org/pockets. Associate Editor: Lynn W. Gilliam. To "find new freelance writers for the magazine." Annual competition for short stories. Award: $1,000 and publication. Competition receives 600 submissions. Judged by *Pockets* editors and editors of other Upper Room publications. Guidelines available after February 1 for SASE or on website. Inquiries by e-mail and fax OK. Deadline: August 15. Former winners may not enter. Unpublished submissions. Word length: 1,000-1,600 words. "No historical fiction or fantasy." Winners announced November 1. Winners notified by mail or phone. List of winners available for SASE.

EDGAR ALLAN POE AWARDS, Mystery Writers of America, Inc., 17 E. 47th St., Sixth Floor, New York NY 10017. (212)888-8171. Fax: (212)888-8107. E-mail: mwa-org@earthlink.net. Website: www.mysterywriters.net. Executive Director: Mary Beth Becker. Annual awards to enhance the prestige of the mystery. For mystery works published or produced during the calendar year. Award: Bust of Poe. Awards for best mystery novel, best first novel by an American author, best softcover original novel, best short story, best critical/biographical work, best fact crime, best young adult, best juvenile novel, best play, best screenplay, best television feature and best episode in a series. Contact above address or check website for specifics. Deadline: November 30. Winners announced in February.

N POETRY AND FICTION CONTEST, *The Briar Cliff Review*, Briar Cliff College, 3303 Rebecca St., Sioux City IA 51104-0100. (712)279-5321. Fax: (712)279-5410. E-mail: currans@briar-cliff.edu. Website: www. briar-cliff.edu/bcreview. Contact: Tricia Currans-Sheehan, editor. Award "to reward good writers and showcase quality writing." Annual award for short stories and poetry. Award: $300 and publication in spring issue. Competition receives 100-125 submissions. Judges: Editors. "All entries are read by at least 3 editors." Entry fee $10. Guidelines for SASE. Deadline: submissions between August 1 and November 1. Previously unpublished submissions. Word length: 5,000 words maximum. "Send us your best work. We want stories with a plot." Winners announced December or January. Winners notified by letter. List of winners available for SASE sent with submission.

N ○ KATHERINE ANNE PORTER PRIZE FOR FICTION, *Nimrod International Journal of Prose and Poetry*, University of Tulsa, 600 S. College, Tulsa OK 74104. (918)584-3333. E-mail: nimrod@utulsa.edu. Website: www.utulsa.edu/nimrod. Editor: Francine Ringold. "To award promising young writers and to increase the quality of manuscripts submitted to *Nimrod*." Annual award for short stories. Award: $2,000 (1st Prize), $1,000 (2nd Prize) plus publication, two contributors copies and $5/page up to $25 total. Receives approximately 500 entries/year. Judge varies each year. Past judges: Ron Carlson, Rosellen Brown, Alison Lurie, Gordon Lish, George Garrett, Toby Olson, John Leonard and Gladys Swan. Entry fee: $20. Guidelines after January for #10 SASE. Deadline for submissions: April 30. Previously unpublished manuscripts. Length: 7,500 words maximum. "Must be typed, double-spaced. Our contest is judged anonymously, so we ask that writers take their names off of their manuscripts (need 2 copies total). Include a cover sheet containing your name, full address, phone and the title of your work. Include a SASE for notification of the results. We encourage writers to read *Nimrod* before submission to discern whether or not their work is compatible with the style of our journal. Single issues are $10 (book rate postage included)." Winners announced in July. Winners notified by mail. List of winners available for SASE with entry.

POTOMAC REVIEW FIFTH ANNUAL SHORT STORY CONTEST, P.O. Box 354, Port Tobacco MD 20677. (301)934-1412. Fax: (301)753-1648. E-mail: elilu@juno.com. Website: www.meral.com/potomac. Contact: Eli Flam, editor. Award to "prime the pump for top submissions, spread the word about our 'big little quarterly' and come up with winning entries to publish." Annual competition for short stories. Award: $300 and publication in the fall 2000 issue. Competition receives more than 50 submissions. Judge: A top writer or writers with no connection to the magazine. Reading fee $15; year's subscription included. Guidelines will be in the fall 1999 and winter 1999-2000 issues, or send SASE for guidelines or order sample copy ($5 ppd). Deadline: January-March 31. Previously unpublished submissions. There are no limitations of style or provenance. Word length: up to 3,000 words. "We may publish the first runner-up as well." Competition receives 90 submissions. Winners announced by June. Winners notified by phone and mail. List of winners available for SASE. "Tell a story that gets at 'the concealed' side of life, something that works for a quarterly with a conscience—and a lurking sense of humor."

○ PRAIRIE SCHOONER LAWRENCE FOUNDATION AWARD, 201 Andrews Hall, University of Nebraska, Lincoln NE 68588-0334. (402)472-0911. Fax: (402)472-9771. E-mail: lrandolp@unlinfo.unl.edu. Website: www.unl.edu/schooner/psmain.htm. Contact: Hilda Raz, editor. Annual award "given to the author of the best short story published in *Prairie Schooner* during the preceding year." Award: $1,000. Inquiries by fax and e-mail OK. "Only short fiction published in *Prairie Schooner* is eligible for consideration. Manuscripts are read September-May."

N ◎ PREMIO AZTLAN, University of New Mexico, Department of English Language and Literature, Albuquerque NM 87131. Contact: Rudolfo Anaya. "National literary prize established for the purpose of encouraging and rewarding new Chicano and Chicana writers." Annual competition. Award: $1,000. Guidelines for SASE. Deadline: December 1, 1999. "New writers are those who have published no more than two books of fiction. Any writer or publisher may submit five copies of a work of fiction published in 1999. The 1999 publication may serve as the second book. The writer's current vita must accompany the materials, which will not be returned." Award will be made in the spring of 2000, and the winner will be invited to read his or her work at the University of New Mexico.

✓ ○ ◎ THE PRESIDIO LA BAHIA AWARD, The Sons of the Republic of Texas, 1717 8th St., Bay City TX 77414. Phone/fax: (409)245-6644. E-mail: srttexas@srttexas.org. Website: www.srttexas.org. Contact: Melinda Williams. "To promote suitable preservation of relics, appropriate dissemination of data, and research into our Texas heritage, with particular attention to the Spanish Colonial period." Annual competition for novels. Award: "A total of $2,000 is available annually for winning participants, with a minimum first place prize of $1,200 for the best published book. At its discretion, the SRT may award a second place book prize or a prize for the best published paper, article published in a periodical or project of a nonliterary nature." Judges: Recognized authorities on Texas history. Guidelines available in June for SASE. Inquiries by mail, fax and e-mail OK. Entries will be accepted from June 1 to September 30. Previously published submissions and completed projects. Competition is open to any person interested in the Spanish Colonial influence on Texas culture. Winners announced December. Winners notified by phone and mail. List of winners available for SASE.

N © **PRISM: Futuristic, Fantasy and Paranormal Sub-Genre Chapter of Romance Writers of America**. E-mail: cyndee.somerville@juno.com. Website: www.sff.net/ffp. Secretary: Cyndee Somerville. Award to "recognize excellence in paranormal romances and paranormals with a strong romantic theme." Annual award for novels. Award: "PRISM award for 1st place in 4 categories, certificates for 2nd and 3rd place in each category." Competition receives approximately 40 submissions. Judges: "Entries judged on a scale of 1-10 in 3 categories (FF&P elements, writing & style, emotional impact); judged by published authors and readers." Entry fee $30. Guidelines available late 1999/early 2000 at website or by e-mail. Previously published submissions that appeared between January 1999-December 1999. "Books must be romances with paranormal elements (i.e., futuristic/fantasy, time travel, or paranormal), or be paranormals with strong romance theme. We accept both print and e-book entries. Romance must be central to the story, but the story much contain paranormal elements." Winner announced July 2000. Winners notified by mail or e-mail and on website.

✦ ✓ ○ PRISM INTERNATIONAL SHORT FICTION CONTEST, *Prism International*, Dept. of Creative Writing, University of British Columbia, E462-1866 Main Mall, Vancouver, British Columbia V6T 1Z1 Canada. (604)822-2514. Fax: (604)822-3616. E-mail: prism@interchange.ubc.ca. Website: www.arts.ubc.ca. Contest Manager: Nancy Lee. Award: $2,000 (1st Prize); five $200 consolation prizes. Competition receives 750 submissions. Deadline: December 31 of each year. Entry fee $17 plus $5 reading fee for each story; 1 year subscription included. Guidelines available in May 1999 for SASE. Inquiries by fax and e-mail OK. Winners announced in June. Winners notified by mail or e-mail. List of winners available in June for SASE, e-mail or on website. "Read a fiction contest issue of *PRISM International* to see what editors are looking for the fiction contest issue comes out each summer in July or August."

◐ ◎ PULITZER PRIZE IN FICTION, Columbia University, 709 Journalism Bldg., Mail Code 3865, New York NY 10027. (212)854-3841. Fax: (212)854-3342. E-mail: pulitzer-feedback@pulitzer.org. Website: www.pulitzer.org. Administrator: Seymour Topping. Annual award for distinguished short stories, novels and story collections *first* published in U.S. in book form during the year by an American author, preferably dealing with American life. Award: $5,000 and certificate. Competition receives 185 submissions. Guidelines and entry forms available for SASE or request by phone or e-mail or on website. Inquiries by fax and e-mail OK. Deadline: Books published between January 1 and June 30 must be submitted by July 1. Books published between July 1 and October 31 must be submitted by November 1; books published between November 1 and December 31 must be submitted in galleys or page proofs by November 1. Submit 4 copies of the book, entry form, biography and photo of author and $50 handling fee. Open to American authors. Winners announced in April. Winners notified by telegram.

N ○ **"PUT YOUR BEST HOOK FORWARD,"** Inland Valley Romance Writers of America, P.O. Box 1386, Corona CA 92878. (909)272-0728. Contact: Linda Carroll-Bradd. Contest to "perfect the opening hook of a romance novel and reward the top 3 submissions with a critique by an editor." Annual contest for the first 10 pages of a novel. Award: $50 (1st prize); $25 (2nd prize); $15 (3rd prize); top three entries in each category also receive a critique from a romance editor. Categories are contemporary and historical/paranormal. Competition receives 30-50 submission per category. Judges: 1 published romance author and 1 experienced critic. Entry fee $15. Guidelines available for SASE or on website in late 1999. Inquiries by e-mail OK. Deadline April 1. Unpublished submissions. Contest only open to unpublished members of Romance Writers of America. Length: 2,500 words or 10 pages maximum. "Send us the start of your romance novel. Be sure you do all you can to 'hook' an editor's interest." Winners announced August 2000. Winners notified by phone and follow-up letter.

✦ ◐ ◎ QSPELL BOOK AWARDS/HUGH MACLENNAN FICTION AWARD, Quebec Writers' Federation, 1200 Atwater, Montreal, Quebec H3Z 1X4 Canada. (514)933-0878. Fax: (514)934-2485. E-mail: qspell@total.net. Website: www.qwf.org.QWF. Coordinator: Diana McNeil. Award "to honor excellence in writing in English in Quebec." Annual competition for short stories, novels, poetry, nonfiction, first book and translation. Award: $2,000 (Canadian) in each category; $500 for first book. Competition receives 15-20 submissions. Judges: Panel of 3 jurors, different each year. Entry fee $10 (Canadian) per title. Guidelines for SASE. Inquiries by fax and e-mail OK. Deadlines: May 31, 2000 (for works published October 1, 1999 to May 15, 2000); August 15, 2000 (for works published May 16, 2000 to September 30, 2000). "Writer must have resided in Quebec for three of the past five years." Books may be published anywhere. Page length: more than 48 pages. Winners announced in December. Winners notified at an awards gala in December. List of winners available for SASE.

O **QUARTERLY WEST NOVELLA COMPETITION**, University of Utah, 200 S. Central Campus Dr., Room 317, Salt Lake City UT 84112-9109. (801)581-3938. Website: www.chronicle.utah.edu/QW/QW.html. Contact: Margot Schilpp, editor. Biennial award for novellas. Award: 2 prizes of $500 and publication in *Quarterly West*. Competition receives 300 submissions. Send SASE for contest rules available in June 2000. Deadline: Postmarked by December 31, 2000. Winners announced in May or June. Winners notified by phone. List of winners available for SASE.

O **QUINCY WRITERS GUILD ANNUAL CREATIVE WRITING CONTEST**, P.O. Box 433, Quincy IL 62306-0433. "A contest to promote new writing." Annual competition for short stories, nonfiction, poetry. Awards: Cash for 1st, 2nd, 3rd Place entries; certificates for honorable mention. Competition receives approximately 150 submissions. Judges: Writing professionals not affiliated with Quincy Writers Guild. Entry fee $4 (fiction and nonfiction, each entry); $2 (poetry each entry). Guidelines for SASE. Deadline: April 1, 2000. Unpublished submissions. Word length: Fiction: 3,000 words; Nonfiction: 2,000 words; Poetry: 3 pages maximum, any style. "Guidelines are very important and available for SASE. Guidelines also available by e-mail from chillebr@adams.net. No entry form is required. Entries accepted after January 1." Winners announced July 2000. Winners notified by mail in June. List of winners available after July 2000 for SASE.

☑ ◐ ◎ **SIR WALTER RALEIGH AWARD**, North Carolina Literary and Historical Association, 4610 CMS Center., Raleigh NC 27699-4610. (919)733-9375. Awards Coordinator: Jerry C. Cashion. "To promote among the people of North Carolina an interest in their own literature." Annual award for novels. Award: Statue of Sir Walter Raleigh. Competition receives 8-12 submissions. Judges: University English and history professors. Guidelines available in August for SASE. Inquiries by fax OK. Deadline: July 15, 2000. Book must be an original work published during the 12 months ending June 30 of the year for which the award is given. Writer must be a legal or physical resident of North Carolina for the three years preceding the close of the contest period. Authors or publishers may submit 3 copies of their book to the above address. Winners announced November. Winners notified by mail. List of winners available for SASE.

◎ **THE REA AWARD FOR THE SHORT STORY**, Dungannon Foundation, 53 W. Church Hill Rd., Washington CT 06794. (860)868-9455. Contact: Elizabeth Rea, president. Annual award for "a writer who has made a significant contribution to the short story form." Award: $30,000. Judges: 3 jurors. Work must be nominated by the jury. Award announced in spring annually. "This award cannot be applied for."

♡ **REGINA MEDAL AWARD**, Catholic Library Association, 100 North St., Suite 224, Pittsfield MA 01201-5109. E-mail: cla@vgernet.com. Website: www.cathla.org. Contact: Jean R. Bostley, SSJ executive director. Annual award. To honor continued distinguished lifetime contribution to children's literature. Award: Silver medal. Award given during Easter week. Selection by a special committee; nominees are suggested by the Catholic Library Association Membership.

☑ O ◎ **RHODE ISLAND STATE COUNCIL ON THE ARTS**, Individual Artist's Fellowship in Literature, 95 Cedar St., Suite 103, Providence RI 02903-1062. (401)222-3880. Fax: (401)521-1351. Website: www.RISCA.state.ri.us. Executive Director: Randall Rosenbaum. Biennial fellowship. Award: $5,000; runner-up $1,000. Competition receives approximately 50 submissions. In-state panel makes recommendations to an out-of-state judge, who recommends finalist to the council. Entry forms and guidelines for SASE. Inquiries by e-mail and fax OK. Deadline: April 1. Artists must be Rhode Island residents and not undergraduate or graduate students. "Program guidelines may change. Prospective applicants should contact RISCA prior to deadline." Winners announced in July. Winners notified by mail.

◐ ◎ **HAROLD U. RIBALOW PRIZE**, *Hadassah Magazine*, 50 W. 58th St., New York NY 10019. (212)688-0227. Fax: (212)446-9521. E-mail: hadamag@aol.com. Contact: Alan M. Tigay, executive editor. Estab. 1983. Annual award "for a book of fiction on a Jewish theme. Harold U. Ribalow was a noted writer and editor who devoted his time to the discovery and encouragement of young Jewish writers." Book should have been published the year preceding the award. Award: $1,000 and excerpt of book in *Hadassah Magazine*. Deadline is April of the year following publication.

Ⓝ ♡ **THE MARY ROBERTS RINEHART FUND**, Mail Stop Number 3E4, English Dept., George Mason University Creative Writing Program, 4400 University Dr., Fairfax VA 22030-4444. (703)993-1185. E-mail: engl.grad@gmu.edu. Director: William Miller. Annual award in fiction, nonfiction and poetry by unpublished writers (that is, writers ineligible to apply for NEA grants). Award: Three awards, one in each category each year (about $2,000 each). Competition receives approximately 75-100 submissions. Rules for SASE. Inquiries by e-mail OK. Next fiction deadline November 30. Writers must be nominated by a sponsoring writer, writing teacher, editor or agent. Winners announced in Spring. Winners notified by mail. List of winners available for SASE.

Ⓝ O **RIVER CITY WRITING AWARD IN FICTION**, *River City*, Dept. of English, The University of Memphis, Memphis TN 38152. (901)678-4591. Awards Coordinator: Thomas Russell. "Annual award to reward the best short stories." Award: $2,000 (1st Prize); $500 (2nd Prize); $300 (3rd Prize). Competition receives approximately 600 submissions. Judge: To be announced. Entry fee $10 which includes a subscription to *River City*. Guidelines available with SASE. Deadline: January 20. Unpublished fiction. Open to all writers. Word length: 7,500 maximum. Winners announced in June. Winners notified by phone and mail.

ROTTEN ROMANCE, Hutton Publications, P.O. Box 2907, Decatur IL 62524. Contact: Linda Hutton, editor. Award to "have fun writing a spoof of genre fiction." Annual competition for short stories. Award: $10 and publication. Competition receives 100 submissions. Judge: Linda Hutton, editor. Guidelines available for SASE. Inquiries by fax OK. Deadline: Valentine's Day annually. Previously unpublished submissions. Open to anyone. Word length: no more than 1 sentence, any length. "An entry form is available, but not required. Handwritten envelopes and/or entries will be discarded; all material must be typed. SASE required with entry. Tickle your sense of humor and ally it with your best writing. Study paperback romances to get a feel for the genre." Winners announced March 1. Winners notified by mail.

◎ **PLEASANT T. ROWLAND PRIZE FOR FICTION FOR GIRLS**, Pleasant Company Publications, 8400 Fairway Place, Middleton WI 53562. (608)836-4848. Fax: (608)836-1999. Contact: Submissions Editor. Award to "encourage writers to turn their talents to the creation of high-quality fiction for girls and to reward talented authors of novels that successfully capture the spirit of contemporary American girls and illuminate the ways in which their lives may be personally touched by events and concerns shaping the United States today." Sponsored by Pleasant Company, publisher of The American Girls Collection series of historical fiction, American Girl Library advice and activity books, and *American Girl* magazine. Annual competition for novels appealing to girls ages 8-12. Award: $10,000. Winning author will be offered a standard contract with an advance and royalty payments for publication of the book under Pleasant Company's new contemporary fiction imprint, AG Fiction. All entries considered for possible publication by Pleasant Company. Judges: Editors of Pleasant Company Publications. No entry fee; 1 entry/person. Guidelines for SASE. Deadline: September 1. Unpublished submissions. No simultaneous submissions. US residents only. Authors whose work is now being published by Pleasant Company not eligible. Employees, their immediate family and suppliers of materials or services to Pleasant Company not eligible. Void where prohibited by law. Word length: 100-200 pages, double spaced. Submissions by authors or agents. "Stories should feature female protagonists between the ages of 10 and 12. We welcome characters of varying cultural backgrounds and family situations." Winner announced shortly after December 31. Include self-addressed stamped postcard with entry for list of winners.

✓ **RENEE SAGIV FICTION PRIZE**, (formerly Phoebe Fiction Prize), *Phoebe*, MSN 2D6 George Mason University, 4400 University Dr., Fairfax VA 22030-4444. (703)993-2915. E-mail: phoebe@gmu.edu. Contact: Peter C. Riebling, editor. Award to "find and publish new and exciting fiction." Annual competition for short stories. Award: $500 and publication. Competition receives 200 submissions. Judges: Known fiction writers. Entry fee $10 for each story submitted. Guidelines available after July for SASE. Deadline: December 15. Previously unpublished submissions. Word length: maximum of 25 pages. "Guidelines only (no submissions) may be requested by e-mail." Winners announced March. Winners notified by mail. List of winners available for SASE. "Phoebe encourages experimental writing."

🌐 **THE IAN ST. JAMES AWARDS**, P.O. Box 60, Cranbrook, Kent TN17 2ZR United Kingdom. 01580 212626. Fax: 01580 212041. Director: Merric Davidson. Award to "provide a better way for a writer to take a first step towards a literary career." Annual competition for short stories. Award: £2,000 top prize. Competition receives 2,500-3,000 submissions. Judges: Writers, publishers. Entry fee £5 per story. Guidelines available after January 1999 for SASE with either IRCs stamps or IRSc. Deadline: April 30. Previously unpublished submissions. Winners announced in July. Winners notified by mail. List of winners available September 1999 for SAE.

Ⓝ 🍁 **SALIVAN SHORT STORY CONTEST**, Salivan Enterprises, 1692 Place de Lierre, #300, Laval Quebec H7G 4X7 Canada. (514)683-6767. Fax: (450)668-1679. E-mail: salivan@hotmail.com. Website: www.ne tcom.ca/~salivan or www.salivan.com. Contact: Tammy Mackenzie, contest coordinator. Award "to promote excellence in short stories and to see them published." Biannual award for short stories. Three categories include science fiction/fantasy, horror and romance. Award: For each category, 40% of category winnings and 90 day publication on the website (1st Prize); 90 day publication (2nd and 3rd Prizes); top 15-20 stories published in annual anthology. Competition receives 150-500 entries. Judges: Editors and publishes in the given genre. Entry fee $5 US. Guidelines for SASE or on website. Inquiries by fax and e-mail OK. Deadlines: February 28 and October 31. Submissions should be the exclusive property of the author, published or unpublished. "Only stories in science fiction/fantasy, horror or romance." Word length: 6,000 words maximum. "Know your genre and submit stories that stretch that genre." Winners announced within 3 months of deadline. Winners notified by mail, phone and e-mail. List of winners available three months after deadline for SASE, e-mail, fax or on website.

Ⓝ ◯ **THE SANDSTONE PRIZE IN SHORT FICTION**, Ohio State University Press, 1070 Carmack Rd., Columbus OH 43210-1002. Fax: (800) 678-6416. Website: www.ohiostatepress.org. Fiction Editor: Bill Roorbach. Competition for short stories or novellas. Award: $1,500; publication; invitation to direct a creative writing workshop at Ohio State; public reading. Judges: Independent judge. Entry fee $20. Guidelines on website. Deadline: January 31. Word length: 150-300 typed pages (approximately 40,000-80,000 words); novellas less than 125 pages (approximately 35,000 words). Winners announced in May. List of winners available for SASE included with entry.

SCIENCE FICTION WRITERS OF EARTH (SFWoE) SHORT STORY CONTEST, Science Fiction Writers of Earth, P.O. Box 121293, Fort Worth TX 76121-1293. (817)451-8674. E-mail: sfwoe@flash.net. Website: www.flash.net/~sfwoe. SFWoE Administrator: Gilbert Gordon Reis. Purpose "to promote the art of science fiction/fantasy short story writing." Annual award for short stories. Award: $200 (1st Prize); $100 (2nd Prize); $50 (3rd Prize). First place story is published by *Altair—Magazine of Speculative Fiction*. *Altair* also pays 3¢/word to the author of the winning story on publication. Competition receives approximately 200 submissions/year. Judge: Author Edward Bryant. Entry fee $5 for first entry; $2 for additional entries. Guidelines available after November for SASE (or print from website). Inquiries by e-mail OK. Deadline: October 30. Submissions must be unpublished. Stories should be science fiction or fantasy, 2,000-7,500 words. "Although many of our past winners are now published authors, there is still room for improvement. The odds are good for a well-written story. Contestants enjoy international competition." Winners announced January 31. Winners notified by phone. "Each contestant is mailed the contest results, judge's report, and a listing of contestant's entries."

SE LA VIE WRITER'S JOURNAL CONTEST, Rio Grande Press, 4320 Canyon, Suite A12, Amarillo TX 79109. Contact: Rosalie Avara, editor. Competition offered quarterly for short short stories with surprise ending. Award: Publication in the *Se La Vie Writer's Journal* plus up to $10 and contributor's copy. Judge: Editor. Entry fee $4 for each or $7 for two (payable to Rosalie Avara). Guidelines for SASE. Deadlines: March 31, June 30, September 30, December 31. Unpublished submissions. Themes: slice-of-life, mystery, adventure, social. Length: 800 words maximum, 200 words minimum.

SEATTLE ARTISTS PROGRAM, Seattle Arts Commission, 312 First Ave. N., Suite 200, Seattle WA 98109. (206)684-7310. Fax: (206)684-7172. Website: www.ci.seattle.wa.us/seattle/sac/home.htm. Project Manager: Irene Gómez. "Award to support development of new works by Seattle individual, generative literary artists." Biannual competition for poetry, prose/fiction, scriptwriting, screenwriting, critical writing and creative nonfiction. Award: $2,000 or $7,500. Competition receives approx. 150 submissions. Judges: Peer review panels. Guidelines/application available in May for 8½×11 SASE. Deadline: July 2000 (even numbered years). Previously published submissions or unpublished submissions. Only Seattle residents or individuals with a Seattle studio or office may apply. Word length: Word-length requirements vary; the guidelines must be read. Winners announced in October 2000. Winners notified by mail.

7 HILLS SHORT FICTION CONTEST, Tallahassee Writers Association, P.O. Box 6996, Tallahassee FL 32314. (850)222-8731. E-mail: verna@talstar.com. Website: www.twaonline.org. Fiction Chair: Verna Safran. Competition to "stimulate good writing, to use proceeds for book donations to library and to produce a literary magazine." Annual competition for short stories. 1999 Theme: "Family Ties." Awards: $100 (1st Prize); $75 (2nd Prize); $50 (3rd Prize); plus honorable mentions and publication. Competition receives 100-300 submissions. Judges: Different each year. Entry fee $10. Guidelines available in March for SASE. Inquiries by e-mail OK. Deadline: August 15. Unpublished submissions and not submitted elsewhere. "We want literary fiction, not genre fiction." Word length: 1,500-2,000. Winners announced in October. Winners notified at Fall Writer's Conference and by mail. List of winners available in October for SASE.

SEVENTEEN MAGAZINE FICTION CONTEST, *Seventeen Magazine*, 850 Third Ave., New York NY 10022-6258. Website: www.seventeen.com. Editor-in-Chief: Patti Adcroft. To honor best short fiction by a young writer. Competition receives 5,000 submissions. Guidelines for SASE. Rules published in the November issue. Contest for 13-21 year olds. Deadline: April 30. Submissions judged by a panel of outside readers, former winners and *Seventeen*'s editors. Competition receives 5,000 entries. Cash awarded to winners. First-place story published in the December or January issue. Winners announced in late 1999. Winners notified by phone or mail. List of winners available in an early issue in year 2000.

FRANCES SHAW FELLOWSHIP FOR OLDER WOMEN WRITERS, The Ragdale Foundation, 1260 N. Green Bay Rd., Lake Forest IL 60045-1106. (847)234-1063. Fax: (847)234-1075. E-mail: ragdale1@aol.com. Website: nsn.ns/silus.org/lfkhome/ragdale. Director of Programming and Marketing: Sylvia Brown. Award to "nurture and support older women writers who are just beginning to write seriously." Annual competition for short stories, novels and poetry. Award: 2 months free residency at Ragdale, plus domestic travel. Competition receives 150 submissions. Judges: A panel of four anonymous women writers. Guidelines for SASE. Inquiries by fax or e-mail OK. Deadline: February 1. Previously unpublished submissions. Females over 55. Word length: 20 pages/12 short poems. "Make your letter of application interesting, covering your desire to write and the reasons you have been thwarted to this point." Winners announced in April. Winners notified by phone.

N ◯ SHORT FICTION CONTEST, Le Sand Publication, 1252 Terra Nova Blvd., Pacifica CA 94044-4340. (650)355-9069. Associate Editor: Barbara J. Less. Award to "encourage writing good short stories." Annual competition for short stories. Award: $50; $25; $10; publication. Contest receives 100 submissions. Judges: Nina Z. Sanders and Barbara J. Less. Submissions judged for "interesting writing." Entry fee $5. Guidelines for SASE. Deadline: November 30, 2000. Previously unpublished submissions. Word length: 2,000 maximum. "Have a hook beginning, good middle and satisfying conclusion. No porn or excessive use of bad language unless needed." Winners announced in January. Winners and honorable mentions published in January/February awards edition of *Lines in the Sand*. List of winners available January 2000 for SASE.

N ✿ ◯ SHORT GRAIN CONTEST, Box 1154, Regina, Saskatchewan S4P 3B4 Canada. (306)244-2828. Fax: (306)244-0255. E-mail: grain.mag@sk.sympatico.ca. Website: www.skwriter.com. ("E-mail entries not accepted.") Contact: Elizabeth Philips. Annual competition for postcard stories, prose poems, dramatic monologues and creative non-fiction. Awards: $500 (1st Prize), $300 (2nd Prize); $200 (3rd Prize) in each category. "All winners and Honourable Mentions will also receive regular payment for publication in *Grain*." Competition receives approximately 900 submissions. Judges: Canadian writers with national and international reputations. Query first. Entry fee $22 for 2 entries in one category (includes one-year subscription); each additional entry in the same category $5. U.S. and International entries in U.S. dollars. U.S. writers add $4 U.S. postage. International writers add $6 U.S. postage. Guidelines for SASE or SAE and IRC. Deadline: January 31. Unpublished submissions. Contest entries must be either an original postcard story (a work of narrative fiction written in 500 words or less) or a prose poem (a lyric poem written as a prose paragraph or paragraphs in 500 words or less), or a dramatic monologue (a self-contained speech given by a single character in 500 words or less). Winners announced April. Winners notified by phone, e-mail and mail. List of winners available for SASE.

◯ SHORT, SHORT FICTION CONTEST, New England Writers, P.O. Box 483, Windsor VT 05089-0483. (802)674-2315. E-mail: newvtpoets@juno.com. Editor: Frank Anthony. Competition for publication in annual *Anthology of New England Writers*. Annual competition for short stories. Award: $500. Competition receives 150 submissions. Judge: TBA, 2000. Entry fee $6. Guidelines available January 2000 for SASE. Inquires by e-mail OK. Deadline: June 15, 2000. Unpublished submissions. Word length: 1,000 words maximum. "We want well-crafted stories written for an audience with high standards." Winners announced at annual N.E.W. conference in July. List of winners available for SASE.

✓ ◯ SIDE SHOW 8TH SHORT STORY CONTEST, Somersault Press, P.O. Box 1428, El Cerrito CA 94530-1428. (510)215-2207. E-mail: jisom@crl.com. Editor: Shelley Anderson. Award "to attract quality writers for our 300-odd page paperback fiction anthology." Awards: $200 (1st Prize); $100 (2nd Prize); $75 (3rd Prize); $5/printed page paid to all accepted writers (on publication). Competition receives 1,000 submissions. Judges: The editors of *Side Show*. Entry fee $10; year's subscription included. Leaflet available but no guidelines or restrictions on length, subject or style. Inquiries by e-mail OK. Sample copy for $10 plus $2 postage. Multiple submissions (in same mailing envelope) encouraged (only one entry fee required for each writer). Will critique if requested. No deadline. Book published when we accept 20-25 stories. "A story from *Side Show* was selected for inclusion in *Pushcart Prize XVIII: Best of the Small Presses*."

N ◎ SKIPPING STONES HONOR AWARDS, P.O. Box 3939, Eugene OR 97403-0939. (541)342-4956. Fax: (541)342-4956. E-mail: skipping@efn.org. Website: www.nonviolence.org/skipping. Executive Editor: Arun N. Toke. Award to "promote multicultural and/or nature awareness through creative writings for children and teens." Annual competition for short stories, novels, story collection and translation. Award: Honor certificates; seals; reviews; press release/publicity. Competition receives 125 submissions. Judges: "A multicultural committee of readers, reviewers and editors." Entry fee $50 ($25 for small/low income publishers/self-publishers). Guidelines for SASE. Inquiries by e-mail OK. Deadline: January 15, 2001. Previously published submissions that appeared in print between January 1999 and January 2001. Writer may submit own work or can be nominated by publisher, authors or illustrators. "We seek authentic, exceptional, child/youth friendly books that promote intercultural/international/intergenerational harmony and understanding through creative ways. Writings that come out of your own experiences/cultural understanding seem to have an edge." Winners announced April 2001. Winners notified through press release, personal notifications and by publishing reviews of winning titles.

◗ BERNICE SLOTE AWARD, *Prairie Schooner*, 201 Andrews Hall, University of Nebraska, Lincoln NE 68588-0334. (402)472-0911. Contact: Hilda Raz, editor. "An award for the best work by a beginning writer published in *Prairie Schooner* during the previous year." Annual award for short stories, novel excerpts and translations. Award: $500. Judges: Editorial board. Guidelines for SASE. Unpublished submissions. Must be beginning writers (not have a book published). "We only read mss September through May." The work must have been published in the magazine to be considered for the annual prizes.

◯ ◎ KAY SNOW CONTEST, Willamette Writers, 9045 SW Barbur Blvd., Suite 5-A, Portland OR 97219-4027. (503)452-1592. Fax: (503)452-0372. E-mail: wilwrite@teleport.com. Website: www.teleport.com/~wilwrite/. Contact: Bill Johnson, office manager. Award "to create a showcase for writers of all fields of literature."

Annual competition for short stories; also poetry (structured and nonstructured), nonfiction, juvenile and student writers and screenwriters. Award: $200 (1st Prize) in each category, second and third prizes, honorable mentions. Competition receives approximately 500 submissions. Judges: Nationally recognized writers and teachers. Entry fee $15, nonmembers; $10, members; $5, students. Guidelines for #10 SASE. Inquiries by fax and e-mail OK. Deadline: May 15 postmark. Unpublished submissions. Maximum 5 double-spaced pages or 1 poem with maximum 5 double-spaced pages per entry fee. Winners announced August. Winners notified by mail and phone. List of winners available for SASE. Prize winners will be honored at the two-day August Willamette Writers Conference. Press releases will be sent to local and national media announcing the winners, and excerpts from winning entries may appear in our newsletter.

☑ ☑ ⊚ **SOCIETY OF CHILDREN'S BOOK WRITERS AND ILLUSTRATORS GOLDEN KITE AWARDS,** Society of Children's Book Writers and Illustrators, 8271 Beverly Blvd., Los Angeles CA 90048. (323)782-1010. Contact: Mercedes Coats, chairperson. Annual award. "To recognize outstanding works of fiction, nonfiction and picture illustration for children by members of the Society of Children's Book Writers and Illustrators and published in the award year." Published submissions should be submitted from January to December of publication year. Deadline: December 15. Rules for SASE. Award: Statuette and plaque. Looking for quality material for children. Individual "must be member of the SCBWI to submit books."

☑ ◯ ⊚ **SOCIETY OF CHILDREN'S BOOK WRITERS AND ILLUSTRATORS WORK-IN-PROGRESS GRANTS,** 8271 Beverly Blvd., Los Angeles CA 90048. (323)782-1010. Contact: SCBWI. Annual grant for any genre or contemporary novel for young people; also nonfiction research grant and grant for work whose author has never been published. Award: $1,000 (1st Prize), $500 (2nd Prize). Work-in-progress. Competition receives approximately 180 submissions. Judges: Members of children's book field—editors, authors, etc. Guidelines for SASE. Deadline: February 1-May 1. Unpublished submissions. Applicants must be SCBWI members.

☑ ◯ *SONORA REVIEW* **SHORT STORY CONTEST,** Dept. of English, University of Arizona, Tucson AZ 85721-0067. (520)321-7759. E-mail: sonora@u.arizona.edu. Fiction Editor: Heather Hughes. Annual contest to encourage and support quality short fiction. $250 (1st Prize) plus publication in *Sonora Review*. All entrants receive copy of the magazine. Entry fee $10. Competition receives 200 submissions. Send SASE or inquire via e-mail for contest rules and deadlines.

◯ ⊚ **SOUTH CAROLINA ARTS COMMISSION AND** *THE POST AND COURIER* **NEWSPAPER (CHARLESTON, SC) SOUTH CAROLINA FICTION PROJECT,** 1800 Gervais St., Columbia SC 29201. (803)734-8696. Website: www.state.sc.us/arts. Director, Literary Arts Program: Sara June Goldstein. Award "to get money to fiction writers and to get their work published and read." Annual award for short stories. Award: $500 and publication in *The Post and Courier*. Competition receives between 150 and 300 submissions for 12 awards (up to 12 stories chosen). Judges: A panel of professional writers and Assistant Features Editor for *The Post and Courier*. Deadline: January 15. *South Carolina residents only.* Stories must not be over 2,500 words. Query for guidelines or visit website.

◯ ⊚ **SOUTH CAROLINA ARTS COMMISSION LITERATURE FELLOWSHIPS AND LITERATURE GRANTS, (I, IV),** 1800 Gervais St., Columbia SC 29201. (803)734-8696. Director, Literary Arts Program: Sara June Goldstein. "The purpose of the fellowships is to give a cash award to a deserving writer (alternating years: either poetry or prose) whose works are of the highest caliber." Award: $7,500 fellowship. Matching project grants up to $5,000. Judges: Out-of-state panel of professional writers and editors for fellowships, and panels and SCAC staff for grants. Query for entry forms or rules. Fellowship deadline February 15. Grants deadlines April 1 and September 1. *South Carolina residents only.* "The next deadline is for poetry (2000)."

⊚ **SOUTH DAKOTA ARTS COUNCIL,** 800 Governors Dr., Pierre SD 57501-2294. (605)773-3131. "Individual artist's project grants—ranging from $500 to $3,000—are planned for the fiscal year 1998 through 2000." Guidelines for SASE. Deadline: March 1. Grants are open only to residents of South Dakota.

☑ ◯ **SOUTHEASTERN REGIONAL WRITING COMPETITIONS,** (formerly Southeastern Regional Writing Competitions), Humpus Bumpus, P.O. Box 1303, Roswell GA 30077-1303. (770)781-9705. Fax: (770)781-4676. E-mail: paulcossman@mindspring.com. Website: www.humpusbumpus.com. Contact: Paul A. Cossman. Award to "identify and publish new writers in order to help them launch their writing careers." Annual competitions for adults and students (K-12th grade). Award: Publication in trade paperback book sold at Humpus Bumpus Books and Atlanta area Barnes & Noble stores. Contest receives 350-400 submissions. Entry fee: $10. Guidelines available on website or phone. Deadline: March 15. Winners announced June 30. Winners notified by mail. List of winners available. "Be original creative and fresh. Have good character development, good imagery, (good grammar and spelling)."

☑ ◎ *THE SOUTHERN REVIEW/LOUISIANA STATE UNIVERSITY ANNUAL SHORT FICTION AWARD*, *The Southern Review*, 43 Allen Hall, Louisiana State University, Baton Rouge LA 70803-5005. (225)388-5108. Fax: (225)388-5098. E-mail: bmacon@unix1.sncc.lsu.edu. Website: www.lsu.edu/guests/wwwt sm. Associate Editor: Michael Griffith. Annual award "to encourage publication of good fiction." For a first collection of short stories by an American writer published in the United States appearing during calendar year. Award: $500. Possible campus reading. Competition receives 100 submissions. Guidelines available for SASE. Inquiries by fax and e-mail OK. Deadline: January 31. Two copies to be submitted by publisher or author. Looking for "style, sense of craft, plot, in-depth characters." Winners announced summer. Winners notified by mail or phone.

▨: ◯ *STAND MAGAZINE* **SHORT STORY COMPETITION**, *Stand Magazine*, 179 Wingrove Road, Newcastle upon Tyne NE4 9DA England. Annual award for short stories. Award: £1,500 (1st Prize); £500 (2nd Prize); £250 (3rd Prize); £150 (4th Prize); £100 (5th Prize) (or US $ equivalent). Entry fee $8. Guidelines and entry form on receipt of UK SAE or 2 IRCs. Deadline: June 30.

◯ ◎ **WALLACE E. STEGNER FELLOWSHIP**, Creative Writing Program, Stanford University, Stanford CA 94305-2087. (650)723-2637. Fax: (650)723-3679. E-mail: gay-pierce@forsythe.stanford.edu. Website: www. stanford.edu/dept/english/cw. Program Administrator: Gay Pierce. Annual award for short stories, novels, poetry and story collections. Five fellowships in fiction ($15,000 stipend plus required tuition of approximately $5,700). Competition receives 600 submissions. Entry fee $40. Guidelines available in June for SASE. Inquiries by fax and e-mail OK. Deadline: December 1. For unpublished or previously published fiction writers. Residency required. Word length: 9,000 words or 40 pages. Winners announced April. Winners notified by telephone. All applicants receive notification of winners.

☑ ◎ **STONY BROOK $1,000 SHORT FICTION PRIZE**, State University of New York, Department of English, Humanities Bldg., Stony Brook NY 11794-5350. (516)632-7400. E-mail: cmcgrath@notes.cc.sunysb. edu. Website: naples.cc.sunysb.edu/CAS/fiction.nsf. Director: Carolyn McGrath. Award "to recognize excellent undergraduate fiction." Annual competition for short stories. Award: $1,000. Competition receives 250-300 submissions. Judges: Faculty of the Department of English & Creative Writing Program. No entry fee. Guidelines for SASE or on website. Inquiries by e-mail OK. Deadline: February 4, 2000. Unpublished submissions. "Only undergraduates enrolled full time in American or Canadian colleges and universities for the academic year 1999-2000 are eligible. Students with an Asian background are particularly encouraged to participate." Word length: 5,000 words or less. Winners announced by June 2000. Winners notified by phone. List of winners available on website, by e-mail or writing to Carolyn McGrath.

❀ ☑ ◯ **SUB-TERRAIN ANNUAL SHORT STORY CONTEST**, *sub-TERRAIN Magazine*, P.O. Box 1575, Bentall Center, Vancouver, British Columbia V6C 2P7 Canada. (604)876-8710. Fax: (604)879-2667. E-mail: subter@pinc.com. Website: www.anvilpress.com. Managing editor: Brian Kaufman. Award "to inspire writers to get down to it and struggle with a form that is condensed and difficult. To encourage clean, powerful writing." Annual award for short stories. Award: $500 and publication. Runners-up also receive publication. Competition receives 150-200 submissions. Judges: An editorial collective. Entry fee $15 for one story, $5 extra for each additional story (includes 3-issue subscription). Guidelines available in November for SASE. "Contest kicks off in November." Deadline: May 15. Unpublished submissions. Length: 2,000 words maximum. Winners announced in July issue. Winners notified by phone call and press release. "We are looking for fiction that has MOTION, that goes the distance in fewer words. Also, originality and a strong sense of voice are two main elements we look for."

☑ **THE RICHARD SULLIVAN PRIZE IN SHORT FICTION**, Creative Writing Program, Department of English and University of Notre Dame Press, Department of English, University of Notre Dame, Notre Dame IN 46556-0368. (219)631-7526. Fax: (219)631-8209. E-mail: english.righter1@nd.edu. Website: www.nd.edu. Director of Creative Writing: Sonia Gernes. Award to "publish the second (or later) volume of short stories by an author of demonstrated excellence." Biannual competition for short stories and story collections. Award: $1,000 ($500 award, $500 advance) and publication by University of Notre Dame Press. Competition receives 150 submissions. Judges: Faculty of the Creative Writing Program. Guidelines available for SASE. Inquiries by fax and e-mail OK. Deadline: May 1-August 31, 2002. Open to any writer who has published at least one previous volume of short stories. Winners announced January 2003. Winners notified by phone and mail. List of winners available end of January 2003 for SASE.

☑ ◯ **TALL GRASS WRITERS GUILD LITERARY ANTHOLOGY/CONTEST**, (formerly Feminist Writers Guild Literary Anthology/Contest), Outrider Press, 937 Patricia Lane, Crete IL 60417. (708)672-6630 or (800)933-4680 (code 03). E-mail: outriderpr@aol.com. Website: www.OutriderPress.com. Contact: Whitney Scott, Senior Editor. Competition to collect diverse writings by authors of all ages, genders and orientations on the theme of Nature: "Earth Beneath, Sky Beyond." Open to poetry, short stories and creative nonfiction. Award: Publication in anthology; free copy to all published contributors. $250 to the best in each category. Competition receives 400-600 submissions. Judges: Independent panel. Entry fee $16; $12 for members. Guidelines and entry form available for SASE. Inquiries by e-mail OK. Deadline: January 31. Unpublished and published submissions. Word length: 2,000 words or less. Maximum 2 entries per person. Include SASE. Winners announced in July. List of winners available for SASE.

SYDNEY TAYLOR MANUSCRIPT COMPETITION, Association of Jewish Libraries, 1327 Wyntercreek Lane, Dunwoody GA 30338. Fax: (770)671-8380. E-mail: m-psand@mindspring.com. Website: aleph.lib.ohio-state.edu/www/asl.html. Coordinator: Paula Sandfelder. Award to "deepen the understanding of Judaism for all children by helping to launch new writers of children's Jewish fiction." Annual competition for novels. Award: $1,000. Competition receives 25 submissions. Judges: 5 children's librarians. Guidelines for #10 SASE. Inquiries by fax and e-mail OK. Deadline: January 15. Previously unpublished submissions. "Children's fiction for readers 8-11 years with universal appeal and Jewish content. Writer must not have a previously published book." Word length: 64 page minimum-200 page maximum, double-spaced. Winners announced May 15. Winners notified by phone or mail. List of winners available by contacting the coordinator.

◐ ◎ **TENNESSEE ARTS COMMISSION LITERARY FELLOWSHIP**, 401 Charlotte Ave., Nashville TN 37243-0780. (615)741-1701. Fax: (615)741-8559. E-mail: aswanson@mail.state.tn.us. Director of Literary Arts: Alice Swanson. Award to "honor promising writers." Annual award for fiction or poetry. Award: $5,000. Competition receives approximately 30 submissions. Judges are out-of-state jurors. Previously published and unpublished submissions. Writers must be previously published writers and residents of Tennessee. Word length: 15 ms pages. Write for guidelines. Inquiries by fax and e-mail OK. This year's award is for poetry.

N: *TEXAS REVIEW* PRESS BOOK COMPETITIONS, Texas Review Press, English Department, Box 2146, Sam Houston State University, Huntsville TX 77341-2146. (409)294-1992. Assistant to the Director: Susan Nichols. Annual. The *Texas Review* has two competitions for fiction: the George Garrett Fiction Prize for a book of stories or short novel and the *Texas Review* Novella Prize for novellas. Competitions receive approximately 125 submissions. Judges: Final judges are George Garrett and X.J. Kennedy. Entry fee $20. Guidelines available for SASE. Inquiries by fax and e-mail OK. Deadline: George Garret Fiction Prize, September; *Texas Review* Novella Prize, October. Previously unpublished submissions. Word length: George Garret Fiction Prize, up to 250 pages; *Texas Review* Novella Prize, up to 150 pages. "Get your hands on previous winners and read them, but notice their diversity—we are not looking for the same thing twice." Winners announced by mail, time varies. Winners notified by phone.

◐ **THURBER HOUSE RESIDENCIES**, The Thurber House, 77 Jefferson Ave., Columbus OH 43215. (614)464-1032. Fax: (614)228-7445. Website: www.thurberhouse.org. Contact: Michael J. Rosen, literary director. "Four writers/year are chosen as writers-in-residence, one for each quarter." Award for writers of novels and story collections. Award: $6,000 stipend and housing for a quarter in the furnished third-floor apartment of James Thurber's boyhood home. Judges: Advisory panel. Guidelines available in August. To apply, send letter of interest and curriculum vitae. Deadline: December 15. "The James Thurber Writer-in-Residence will teach a class in the Creative Writing Program at The Ohio State University in either fiction, nonfiction or poetry and will offer one public reading and a short workshop for writers in the community. Significant time outside of teaching is reserved for the writer's own work-in-progress. Candidates should have published at least one book with a major publisher, in any area of fiction, nonfiction, or poetry and should possess some experience in teaching." Winners announced in March. Winners notified by mail and phone. List of winners available in April for SASE.

◖ **THE THURBER PRIZE FOR AMERICAN HUMOR**, The Thurber House, 77 Jefferson Ave., Columbus OH 43215. (614)464-1032. Fax: (614)228-7445. Literary Director: Michael J. Rosen. Award "to give the nation's highest recognition of the art of humor writing." Biannual competition for novels and story collections. Award: $5,000; Thurber statuette. Up to 3 Honor Awards may also be conferred. Judges: Well-known members of the national arts community. Entry fee $25/title. Guidelines for SASE. Published submissions or accepted for publication in US for first time. No reprints or paperback editions of previously published books. Word length: no requirement. Primarily pictorial works such as cartoon collections are not considered. Work must be nominated by publisher.

❋ ✓ ***TICKLED BY THUNDER* ANNUAL FICTION CONTEST**, Tickled By Thunder, 14076-86A Ave., Surrey, British Columbia V3W 0V9 Canada. (604)591-6095. E-mail: thunder@istar.ca. Website: home.istar.ca/~thunder. Contact: Larry Lindner, editor. "To encourage new writers." Annual competition for short stories. Award: 50% of all fees, $100 minimum (Canadian), 1 year's (4-issue) subscription plus publication. Competition

VISIT THE WRITER'S DIGEST WEBSITE at http://www.writersdigest.com for hot new markets, daily market updates, writers' guidelines and much more.

receives approximately 30 submissions. Judges: The editor and other writers. Entry fee $10 (Canadian) per entry (free for subscribers but more than one story requires $5 per entry). Guidelines available for SASE. Inquiries by e-mail OK. Deadline: February 15. Unpublished submissions. Word length: 2,000 words or less. Winners announced in May. Winners notified by mail. List of winners available for SASE.

☑ **LON TINKLE AWARD**, Texas Institute of Letters, Center for the Study of the Southwest, Flowers Hall 327, Southwest Texas State University, San Marcos TX 78666. (512)245-2232. Fax: (512)245-7462. E-mail: mb13@swt.edu. Website: www.english.swt.edu/css/TIL/index. Secretary: Mark Busby. Award to "honor a Texas writer for excellence sustained throughout a career." Annual competition for lifetime achievement. Award: $1,500. Competition receives 40 submissions. Judges: TIL Council. Guidelines available in June 2000 for SASE. Inquiries by e-mail OK. Deadline: January 14, 2001. To be eligible, the writer must have a notable association with Texas. Writer must be nominated by a member of TIL Council. "The TIL Council chooses the winner. Applications for the award are not made, through one might suggest possible candidates to an officer or member of the Council." Winners announced April 15, 2001. Winners notified by mail or phone. List of winners available on website.

◑ ◎ **TOWSON UNIVERSITY PRIZE FOR LITERATURE**, Towson University Foundation, Towson University, Towson MD 21252-0001. (410)830-2128. Fax: (410)830-6392. E-mail: djones@towson.edu. Dean, College of Liberal Arts: Dan L. Jones. Annual award for novels or short story collections, previously published. Award: $1,500. Competition receives 5-10 submissions. Requirements: Writer must not be over 40; must be a Maryland resident. Guidelines available spring 2000 for SASE. Inquiries by fax and e-mail OK. Deadline: May 15, 2000. Winners announced December 1999. Winners notified by letter. List of winners available by calling or writing Sue Ann Nordhoff-Klaus.

◰ ◯ **TROUBADOUR'S SHORT STORY CONTEST**, Troubadour's Writers Group, P.O. Box 138, Woodstock IL 60098. E-mail: ghstwn@aol.com. Website: www.owc.net/~mason/troubadours.html. Contest "for those who enjoy writing competitions and/or appreciate feedback from judges." Annual competition for short stories. Award: $75 (1st prize); $50 (2nd prize); $25 (3rd prize); each entry is given a written critique, which is returned to the author with SASE; winner are offered the opportunity to have their stories published in *The Lantern*. Competition receives 100 submissions. Judges: Published authors. Entry fee $5 per story; multiple entries OK if each is accompanied by $5 fee. Guidelines available for SASE or by e-mail. Deadline March 1, 2000. Unpublished submissions. "Follow the format guidelines and enter a complete story with a beginning, middle and end. No poetry, vignettes or essays." Winners announced before July, 2000. Winners notified by SASE.

☑ ◑ ◎ **STEVEN TURNER AWARD,** The Texas Institute of Letters, Center for the Study of the Southwest, Flowers Hall 327, Southwest Texas State University, San Marcos TX 78666. (512)245-2232. Fax: (512)245-7462. E-mail: mb13@swt.edu. Website: www.english.swt.edu/css/TIL/index. Secretary: Mark Busby. "To honor the best first book of fiction published by a writer who was born in Texas or who has lived in the state for two years at some time, or whose work concerns the state." Annual award for novels and story collections. Award: $1,000. Judges: Committee. Guidelines available in July for SASE. Inquiries by e-mail OK. Deadline: January 14. Previously published submissions appearing in print between January 1 and December 31. Winners announced in April. Winners notified by phone. List of winners available on website.

☑ ◯ **THE MARK TWAIN AWARD FOR SHORT FICTION**, *Red Rock Review*, NSSW English Dept., J2A, 3200 E. Cheyenne Ave., N. Las Vegas NV 89030-4296. (702)651-4005. Fax: (702)651-4639. E-mail: rich_logsdon@ccsn.nevada.edu. Website: www.ccsn.nevada.edu/academics/departments/English/redrock.htm (includes contest guidelines and general submissions guidelines). Contact: Rich Logsdon, editor. Award to "find and publish the best available works of short fiction." Annual competition for short stories. Awards: $1,000 and publication. Competition receives 250-300 entries. Judges: Pre-judging by magazine staff and readers; winner selected by guest judge (guest judge for 1997 contest was Ron Carlson). Entry fee: $10. Guidelines available November 1, 1999 for SASE. Inquiries by fax and e-mail OK. Deadline: October 31, 2000. Previously unpublished submissions. Word length: 3,500 words or less. "Author's name should not appear anywhere on manuscript. Submissions should include cover page with author's name, address and phone. No simultaneous submissions. Writing should grab the reader's attention early and show a freshness of language and voice." Winners announced Spring 2001. Winners notified by phone. List of winners available for SASE.

◖ ◎ **MARK TWAIN AWARD**, Missouri Association of School Librarians, 1552 Rue Riviera, Bonne Terre MO 63628-9349. Phone/fax: (573)358-1053. E-mail: masloffice@aol.com. Website: www.coe.missouri.edu/~mas/. Contact: Leah Murray. Estab. 1970. Annual award to introduce children to the best of current literature for children and to stimulate reading. Award: A bronze bust of Mark Twain, created by Barbara Shanklin, a Missouri sculptor. A committee selects pre-list of the books nominated for the award; statewide reader/selectors review and rate the books, and then children throughout the state vote to choose a winner from the final list. Books must be published two years prior to nomination for the award list. Publishers may send books they wish to nominate for the list to the committee members. 1) Books should be of interest to children in grades 4 through 8; 2) written by an author living in the US; 3) of literary value which may enrich children's personal lives. Inquiries by fax and e-mail OK. Winners announced in May. Winners notified in April by phone. List of winners available.

[N] THE UNDISCOVERED WRITER II, Rendezvous/Love Designers Writers' Club, Inc., 1507 Burnham Ave., Calumet City IL 60409. (708)862-9797. E-mail: vadew9340@aol.com. Contact: Virginia A. Deweese, editor. Award "to discover new writers in romance." Annual competition for novels. Award: Winners read by editors and agents. Competition limited to 150 submissions. Judges: Members of the Love Designers Writers' Club and reviewers for Rendezvous. Entry fee $20. Guidelines available for SASE. Inquiries by e-mail OK. Deadline: February 1. Previously unpublished submissions. Competition "for writers of romance fiction: contemporary, historical, regency, suspense, fantasy, etc." Word length: first 10 pages of the novel. "Follow the guidelines and write a great book." Winners notified by mail. List of winner available for SASE.

UPC SCIENCE FICTION AWARD, Universitat Politècnica de Catalunya Board of Trustees, gran capità 2-4, Edifici NEXUS, 08034 Barcelona Spain. Phone: 34 93 4016343. Fax: 34 93 4017766. E-mail: consell-social@rectorat.upc.es. Website: www.upc.es/op/english/sciencefiction/sciencefiction.htm. "The award is based on the desire for integral education at UPC. The literary genre of science fiction is undoubtedly the most suitable for a university such as UPC, since it unifies the concepts of science and literature." Annual award for short stories: 1,000,000 pesetas (about $10,000 US). Competition receives 140 submissions. Judges: Professors of the university and science fiction writers. Guidelines available in February by mail, e-mail, fax or phone. Deadline: September 15, 2000. Previously unpublished entries. Length: 70-115 pages, double-spaced, 30 lines/page, 70 characters/line. Submissions may be made in Spanish, English, Catalan or French. The author must sign his work with a pseudonym and enclose a sealed envelope with full name, a personal ID number, address and phone. The pseudonym and title of work must appear on the envelope. Winners announced December 2000. Winners notified by phone. List of winners sent to all entrants.

VERY SHORT FICTION SUMMER AWARD, *Glimmer Train Stories*, 710 SW Madison St., Suite 504, Portland OR 97205. (503)221-0836. Fax: (503)221-0837. Website: www.glimmertrain.com (includes writers' guidelines and Q&A section for writers). Contact: Linda Burmeister Davies, editor. Annual award offered to encourage the art of the very short story. Contest opens May 1 and ends July 31; entry must be postmarked between these dates. Awards: $1,200 and publication in *Glimmer Train Stories* (1st Place); $500 (2nd Place); $300 (3rd Place). Competition receives 1,500 submissions. Entry fee: $10 per story. Guidelines available for SASE or check website. Inquiries by fax OK. Word length: 2,000 words maximum. First page of story should include name, address, phone number and word count. "VSF AWARD" must be written on outside of envelope. Materials will not be returned. Include SASE for list of winning entries. Notification on November 1.

VERY SHORT FICTION WINTER AWARD, *Glimmer Train Stories*, 710 SW Madison St., Suite 504, Portland OR 97205. (503)221-0836. Fax: (503)221-0837. Website: www.glimmertrain.com (includes writer's guidelines and a Q&A section for writers). Contact: Linda Burmeister Davies, editor. Award offered to encourage the art of the very short story. Contest opens November 1 and ends January 31; entry must be postmarked between these dates. Awards: $1,200 and publication in *Glimmer Train Stories* (1st Place); $500 (2nd Place); $300 (3rd Place). Entry fee: $10 per story. Guidelines available for SASE or check website. Inquiries by fax OK. Word length: 2,000 words maximum. First page of story should include name, address, phone number and word count. "VSF AWARD" must be written on outside of envelope. Materials will not be returned. Include SASE for list of winners. Notification on May 1.

VIOLET CROWN BOOK AWARD, Austin Writers' League, 1501 W. Fifth St., Suite E-2, Austin TX 78703. (512)499-8914. Fax: (512)499-0441. E-mail: awl@writersleague.org. Website: www.writersleague.org. Executive Director: Jim Bob McMillan. Award "to recognize the best books published by Austin Writers' League members over the period July 1 to June 30 in fiction, nonfiction and literary (poetry, short story collections, etc.) categories." Award: Three $1,000 cash awards and trophies. Competition receives approximately 100 submissions. Judges: A panel of judges who are not affiliated with the Austin Writers' League or Barnes & Noble. Entry fee $10. Guidelines after January for SASE. Deadline: June 30. Previously published submissions between July 1 and June 30. "Entrants must be Austin Writers' League members. League members reside all over the U.S. and some foreign countries. Persons may join the League when they send in entries." Publisher may also submit entry in writer's name. Inquiries by fax and e-mail OK. Winners announced September 2000. Winners notified by phone and mail. List of winners available for SASE. "Awards are co-sponsored by Barnes & Noble Booksellers. Special citations are presented to finalists."

WALDEN FELLOWSHIP, Coordinated by: Extended Campus Programs, Southern Oregon University, 1250 Siskiyou Blvd., Ashland OR 97520-5038. (503)552-6901. Fax: (541)552-6047. E-mail: friendly@sou.edu. Arts Coordinator: Brooke Friendly. Award "to give Oregon writers the opportunity to pursue their work at a quiet, beautiful farm in southern Oregon." Annual competition for all types of writing. Award: 3-6 week residencies. Competition receives approximately 30 submissions. Judges: Committee judges selected by the sponsor. Guidelines for SASE. Inquiries by fax and e-mail OK. Deadline: end of November. Oregon writers only. Word length: maximum 30 pages prose, 8-10 poems. Winners announced in January. Winners notified by mail. List of winners available for SASE.

EDWARD LEWIS WALLANT MEMORIAL BOOK AWARD, 3 Brighton Rd., West Hartford CT 06117. Sponsored by Dr. and Mrs. Irving Waltman. Contact: Mrs. Irving Waltman. Annual award. Memorial to Edward Lewis Wallant offering incentive and encouragement to beginning writers, for books published the year before the award is conferred in the spring. Award: $500 plus award certificate. Books may be submitted for consideration to Dr. Sanford Pinsker, Department of English, Franklin & Marshall College, P.O. Box 3003, Lancaster PA 17604-3003. Deadline: December 31. "Looking for creative work of fiction by an American which has significance for the American Jew. The novel (or collection of short stories) should preferably bear a kinship to the writing of Wallant. The award will seek out the writer who has not yet achieved literary prominence." Winners announced January-February. Winners notified by phone.

WE DARE YOU CONTEST, Saskatchewan Romance Writers, 817 Cathcart St., Winnipeg Manitoba R3R 3C1 Canada. E-mail: sask.romance.writers@home.com. Website: www.members.home.net/sask.romance.writers/srw.htm. Contest Coordinator: Judy Reynolds. Award to "provide romance writers with an opportunity to be critiqued by experienced judges, with the five top entries read and ranked by Silhouette Books editor Mary-Theresa Hussey." Annual competition for novels. Award: Every entry receives 3 critiques of first 25 pages; top five will be read and ranked by a Silhouette editor; first place receives $50 (Canadian), a critique of the entire manuscript and a certificate; second to 5th receive a certificate. Competition accepts a maximum of 40 submissions. Judges: Three members of Saskatchewan Romance Writers. Judged on "hook, dialogue, characterization, conflict, and other essential writing elements." Entry fee $15 US or $20 Canadian. Guidelines available January 2000 for SASE. Inquiries by e-mail OK or check website. Deadline: July 1, 2000. Previously unpublished submissions. "The contest and awards are available to romance writers. Judging is based on standards and accepted practices used in the romance genre. Writers from any geographical area are welcome." Word length: submit the first 25 double-spaced pages. "Since the premise of the 'We Dare You' contest is to hook us on your story, the best tip I can give is to give us an interesting opening that grabs us and makes us want to continue reading. Also, please read and follow the competition guidelines carefully." Winners announced September 2000. Winners notified by phone or e-mail. List of winners available September 2000 for SASE or by e-mail.

WEATHERFORD AWARD, Appalachian Center, CPO 2336, Berea College, Berea KY 40404-2336. (606)986-9341 ext. 5140. Director: Gordon McKinney. Award to "select the best work about Appalachia, monograph, fiction or poetry." Annual competition for short stories, novels and story collections. Award: $500. Competition receives 15 submissions. Judges: Committee of Appalachian writers. Deadline: December 31. Published submissions. Available only to authors who write about the Appalachian Region. "The majority of the winners of the award have been authors of nonfiction works."

WESTERN HERITAGE AWARDS, National Cowboy Hall of Fame, 1700 NE 63rd St., Oklahoma City OK 73111. (405)478-2250. Fax: (405)478-4714. Contact: M.J. Van Deuenter, director of publications. Annual award "to honor outstanding quality in fiction, nonfiction and art literature." Submissions are to have been published during the previous calendar year. Award: The Wrangler, a replica of a C.M. Russell Bronze. Competition receives 350 submissions. Entry fee $35. Entry forms and rules available October 1 for SASE. Inquiries by fax OK. Deadline: November 30. Looking for "stories that best capture the spirit of the West. Submit five actual copies of the work." Winners announced April. Winners notified by letter.

WHITING WRITERS' AWARDS, Mrs. Giles Whiting Foundation, 1133 Avenue of the Americas, New York NY 10036-6710. Director, Writer's Program: Barbara K. Bristol. Annual award for writers of fiction, poetry, nonfiction and plays with an emphasis on emerging writers. Award: $30,000 (10 awards). Candidates are submitted by appointed nominators and chosen for awards by an appointed selection committee. Direct applications and informal nominations not accepted by the foundation. List of winners available October 30 by request.

WIND MAGAZINE SHORT STORY COMPETITION, P.O. Box 24548, Lexington KY 40524. Website: wind.wind.org. Editors: Charlie G. Hughes and Leatha F. Kendrick. Annual competition for short stories. Award: $500 and publication (1st Prize); finalists receive a 1-year subscription. Entry fee $10/story. Deadline: April 30. Word length: 5,000 words or less. List of winners available for SASE.

WISCONSIN ARTS BOARD INDIVIDUAL ARTIST PROGRAM, 101 E. Wilson St., First Floor, Madison WI 53702. (608)264-8191. Fax: (608)267-0380. E-mail: mark.fraire@arts.state.wi.us. Website: www.arts.state.wi.us. Contact: Mark J. Fraire. Biennial awards for short stories, poetry, novels, novellas, drama, essay/criticism. Awards: 5 awards of $8,000. Competition receives approximately 250 submissions. Entry forms or rules available in August upon request. Inquiries by fax and e-mail OK. Deadline: September 15 of even-numbered years (2000, 2002 etc.). Wisconsin residents only. Students are ineligible. Winners announced in late December. Winner notified by mail.

WISCONSIN INSTITUTE FOR CREATIVE WRITING FELLOWSHIP, University of Wisconsin—Creative Writing, English Department, 600 N. Park St., Madison WI 53706. Website: polyglot.lss.wisc.edu/english. Director: Jesse Lee Kercheval. Competition "to provide time, space and an intellectual community for writers working on first books." Six annual awards for short stories, novels and story collections. Awards: $22,000/9-month appointment. Competition receives 500 submissions. Judges: English Department faculty. Guidelines available for SASE; write to Ron Kuka or check website. Deadline: month of February. Published or unpublished submissions. Applicants must have received an M.F.A. or comparable graduate degree in creative writing and not yet published a book. Limit 1 story up to 30 pages in length. No name on writing sample. Two letters of recommendation and vita or resume required.

PAUL A. WITTY SHORT STORY AWARD, (II), International Reading Association, P.O. Box 8139, 800 Barksdale Rd., Newark DE 19714-8139. (302)731-1600, ext. 293. Fax: (302)731-1057. E-mail: jbutler @reading.org. Website: www.reading.org. Public Information Coordinator: Janet Butler. Annual award given to the author of an original short story published for the first time in 1999 in a periodical for children. Award: $1,000. "The short story should serve as a literary standard that encourages young readers to read periodicals." For guidelines write to: Executive Office. Deadline: December 1. Published submissions.

THOMAS WOLFE FICTION PRIZE North Carolina Writers' Network, 3501 Hwy. 54 W., Studio C, Chapel Hill NC 27510. (919)967-9540. Fax: (919)929-0535. E-mail: ncwn@sunsite.unc.edu. Website: sunsite.unc .edu/ncwriters. Program Coordinator: Frances Dovell. "Our international literary prizes seek to recognize the best in today's writing." Annual award for fiction. Award: $1,000 and winning entry will be considered for publication in *Carolina Quarterly*. Competition receives 800-900 submissions. Entry fee $7. Guidelines available in spring for SASE. Inquiries by e-mail OK. Deadline: August 31. Unpublished submissions. Length: 12 double-spaced pages maximum. Winners announced December 1999. Winners notified by phone in December. List of winners available for SASE.

TOBIAS WOLFF AWARD FOR FICTION, Mail Stop 9053, Western Washington University, Bellingham WA 98225. Annual competition for novels and short stories. Award: $1,000 (1st Prize); $250 (2nd Prize); $100 (3rd Prize). Judge: To be announced. Entry fee $10 for the first entry, $5/story or chapter thereafter. Guidelines for SASE. Deadline: March 1. Unpublished submissions. Length: 10,000 words or less per story or chapter. Winner announced July. List of winners available for SASE.

WORLD FANTASY AWARDS, World Fantasy Awards Association, P.O. Box 1666, Lynnwood WA 98046-1666. E-mail: sfexessec@aol.com. Contact: Peter Dennis Pautz, president. Award to "recognize excellence in fantasy literature worldwide." Annual competition for short stories, novels, story collections, anthologies, novellas and life achievement. Award: Bust of HP Lovecraft. Judge: Panel. Guidelines available for SASE. Deadline: June 30. Published submissions from previous calendar year. Word length: 10,000-40,000 novella; 10,000 short story. "All fantasy is eligible, from supernatural horror to Tolkienesque to sword and sorcery to the occult, and beyond." Winners announced November 1. List of winners available November 1.

THE WRITERS COMMUNITY RESIDENCY AWARDS, The YMCA National Writer's Voice of the YMCA of the USA. 101 N. Wacker Dr., Chicago IL 60606. (800)USA-YMCA #515. Program Director: Jennifer O'Grady. Offers semester-long residencies to mid-career writers at YMCAs nationwide. Biannual award for novels and story collections. Award: A semester-long residency. Residents conduct a master-level workshop and give a public reading at their host Writer's Voice center. Honorarium is $6,000. Judges: A committee at each Writer's Voice center. Deadlines vary. "Interested writers should contact their local writer's voice center for deadlines." Previously published submissions in book form. "Writers should apply directly to the Writer's Voice center, as application procedures vary. For a list of Writer's Voice center addresses, send SASE."

WRITER'S DIGEST ANNUAL WRITING COMPETITION, (Short Story Division), *Writer's Digest*, 1507 Dana Ave., Cincinnati OH 45207. (513)531-2690, ext. 328. E-mail: competitions@fwpubs.com. Website: www.writersdigest.com. Contact: Contest Director. Grand Prize is an expenses-paid trip to New York City with arrangements to meet editors/agents in winning writer's field. Other awards include cash, reference books and certificates of recognition. Names of grand prize winner and top 100 winners are announced in the November issue of *Writer's Digest*. Top entries published in booklet ($5.75). Send SASE to *WD* Writing Competition for rules and entry form, or see January through May issues of *Writer's Digest*. Deadline: May 31. Entry fee $10 per manuscript. All entries must be original, unpublished and not previously submitted to a *Writer's Digest* contest. Length: 4,000 words maximum. No acknowledgement will be made of receipt of mss nor will mss be returned. Three of the ten writing categories target short fiction: mainstream/literary, genre and children's fiction.

WRITER'S DIGEST NATIONAL SELF-PUBLISHED BOOK AWARDS, *Writer's Digest*, 1507 Dana Ave., Cincinnati OH 45207. (513)531-2690, ext. 328. E-mail: competitions@fwpubs.com. Website: www.writersdigest. com. Contact: Contest Director. Award to "recognize and promote excellence in self-published books." Annual competition with six categories: fiction (novel or short story collection), nonfiction, cookbooks, poetry, children's and young adult life stories, inspirational (spiritual, New Age) and reference books. Grand prize: $1,000 plus an ad in *Publishers Weekly* and promotion in *Writer's Digest*. Category winners receive $300 and promotion in Writer's Digest. Judges: Final judges are successful self-published authors and book editors. Entry fee $95 for each book submitted. Guidelines available for SASE. Deadline: December 15. Published submissions. Author must pay full cost and book must have been published in year of contest or two years prior.

N: WRITERS' FILM PROJECT, The Chesterfield Film Co., 1158 26th St., PMB 544, Santa Monica CA 90403. (213)683-3977. Fax: (310)260-6116. Website: www.chesterfield-co.com. Administrator: Doug Rosen. Award "provides up to 5 (20,000) dollar yearly stipends to promote and foster talented screenwriters, fiction writers and playwrights." Annual competition for short stories, novels and screenplays. Award: 5 $20,000 awards. Competition receives several thousand submissions. Judges: Mentors, panel of judges. Entry fee $39.50 US dollars for each story submitted. Guidelines available for SASE. Deadline: November 14, 2000. Published or previously unpublished submissions. "Program open to all age groups, race, religion, educational level etc. Past winners have ranged in age from early 20's to late 50's."

⬜ WRITERS' INTL FORUM WRITING COMPETITION, *Writers' Intl Forum*, P.O. Box 516, Tracyton WA 98393-0516. Website: www.bristolservicesintl.com. Editor: Sandra E. Haven. Award "to encourage strong storyline in a tight package." Four or more competitions per year for short stories. Award: Cash prizes, merchandise and certificates (amounts vary per competition). Competition receives over 200 entries. Judges: *Writers' Intl Forum* staff. Entry fees vary per competition. Guidelines available for SASE or on website. Previously unpublished submissions. "Length, theme, prizes, deadline, fee and other requirements vary for each competition. Entries are judged on creativity, technique, mechanics and appeal." List of winners available one month after closing. Automatically mailed with entrant's return SASE for manuscript.

✓ ⬜ WRITERS' JOURNAL ANNUAL FICTION CONTEST, Val-Tech Media, P.O. Box 394, Perham MN 56573-0394. (218)346-7921. Fax: (218)346-7924. E-mail: writersjournal@wadena.net. Website: www.sowas hco.com/writersjournal. Contact: Leon Ogroske, publisher/managing editor. Award: $50 (1st Place); $25 (2nd Place); $15 (3rd Place). Also gives honorable mentions and publishes prize winners. Competition receives approximately 300 submissions/year. Entry fee $5 each. Entry forms or rules available for SASE. Deadline: December 31. Maximum length is 2,000 words. Two copies of each entry are required—one *without* name or address of writer. Winners notified by mail.

✓ ⬜ WRITERS' JOURNAL ROMANCE CONTEST, *Writers' Journal*, Val-Tech Media, P.O. Box 394, Perham MN 56573-0394. (218)346-7921. Fax: (218)346-7924. E-mail: writersjournal@wadena.net. Website: www.sowashco.com/writersjournal. Contact: Leon Ogroske. Annual competition for short stories. Award: $50 (1st Prize); $25 (2nd Prize); $15 (3rd Prize); publishes prize winers plus honorable mentions. Competition receives 350 submissions. Entry fee $5/entry. Guidelines available for SASE (4 entries/person). Deadline: July 31. Unpublished submissions. Word length: 2,000 words maximum. Winners announced in December. Winners notified by mail and winners list published in *Writers' Journal Magazine*. "Enclose #10 SASE for winner's list."

✓ ⬜ THE WRITERS' WORKSHOP INTERNATIONAL FICTION CONTEST, The Writers' Workshop, 387 Beaucatcher Rd., Asheville NC 28805. Phone/fax: (828)254-8111. Executive Director: Karen Ackerson. Annual awards for fiction. Awards: $500 (1st Prize); $250 (2nd Prize); $100 (3rd Prize). Competition receives approximately 350 submissions. Past judges have been Peter Matthiessen, Kurt Vonnegut, E.L. Doctorow. Entry fee $18/$15 members. Guidelines for SASE. Deadline: February 25. Unpublished submissions. Length: 4,000 words typed, double-spaced pages per story. Multiple submissions are accepted.

N: ♥ YOUNG READER'S CHOICE AWARD, Pacific Northwest Library Association, Graduate School of Library and Information Sciences, P.O. Box 352930, FM-30, University of Washington, Seattle WA 98195. (206)543-1897. Annual award "to promote reading as an enjoyable activity and to provide children an opportunity to endorse a book they consider an excellent story." Award: Silver medal. Judges: Children's librarians and teachers nominate; children in grades 4-12 vote for their favorite book on the list. Guidelines for SASE. Deadline: February 1. Previously published submissions. Writers must be nominated by children's librarians and teachers. No unsolicited submissions.

N: ◎ YOUNG TEXAS WRITERS SCHOLARSHIPS, Austin Writers' League, 1501 W. Fifth St., Suite E-2, Austin TX 78703. (512)499-8914. Fax: (512)499-0441. E-mail: awl@writersleague.org. Website: www.write rsleague.org. Executive Director: Jim Bob McMillan. Award to "recognize outstanding young writing talent enrolled in grades 9-12 in Texas schools." Annual competition for short stories (other categories: essays, poetry, journalism). Awards: 12 cash awards ($50 to $150). Competition receives more than 500 submissions. Judges:

Experienced writers. Entry fee $5 (one time fee for multiple entries). Fee may be waived. Guidelines for SASE. Deadline: January 31. Entrants must be Texan. Word length: requirements specified on guidelines for each category. Winning entries are published in special anthology. Winners announced May. Winners notified by mail and phone. List of winners available for SASE.

N **ZOETROPE SHORT STORY CONTEST**, Zoetrope: All Story, 1350 Avenue of the Americas, 24th Floor, New York NY 10019. (212)696-5720. Fax: (212)696-5845. Website: www.zoetrope-stories.com. Contact: Adrienne Brodeur, editor-in-chief. Annual competition for short stories. Award: $1,000 (1st Prize); $500 (2nd Prize); $250 (3rd Prize). Judges: Editors of *Zoetrope: All-Story*. Entry fee $10. Guidelines available for SASE in May, 2000. Unpublished submissions. Word length: 5,000 words maximum. "Please mark envelope clearly 'contest.'" Winners announced November 15, 2000. Winners notified by phone. List of winners available for SASE.

Resources

Conferences & Workshops

Why are conferences so popular? Writers and conference directors alike tell us it's because writing can be such a lonely business otherwise—that at conferences writers have the opportunity to meet (and commiserate) with fellow writers, as well as meet and network with publishers, editors and agents. Conferences and workshops provide some of the best opportunities for writers to make publishing contacts and pick up valuable information on the business, as well as the craft, of writing.

The bulk of the listings in this section are for conferences. Most conferences last from one day to one week and offer a combination of workshop-type writing sessions, panel discussions, and a variety of guest speakers. Topics may include all aspects of writing from fiction to poetry to scriptwriting, or they may focus on a specific area such as those sponsored by the Romance Writers of America for writers specializing in romance or the SCBWI conferences on writing for children's books.

Workshops, however, tend to run longer—usually one to two weeks. Designed to operate like writing classes, most require writers to be prepared to work on and discuss their work-in-progress while attending. An important benefit of workshops is the opportunity they provide writers for an intensive critique of their work, often by professional writing teachers and established writers.

Each of the listings here includes information on the specific focus of an event as well as planned panels, guest speakers and workshop topics. It is important to note, however, some conference directors were still in the planning stages for 2000 when we contacted them. If it was not possible to include 2000 dates, fees or topics, we have provided information from 1999 so you can get an idea of what to expect. For the most current information, it's best to send a self-addressed, stamped envelope to the director in question about three months before the date(s) listed.

FINDING A CONFERENCE

Many writers try to make it to at least one conference a year, but cost and location count as much as subject matter or other considerations, when determining which conference to attend. There are conferences in almost every state and province and even some in Europe open to North Americans.

To make it easier for you to find a conference close to home—or to find one in an exotic locale to fit into your vacation plans—we've divided this section into geographic regions. The conferences appear in alphabetical order under the appropriate regional heading.

Note that conferences appear under the regional heading according to where they will be held, which is sometimes different than the address given as the place to register or send for information. The regions are as follows:

Northeast (pages 572-577): Connecticut, Maine, Massachusetts, New Hampshire, New York, Rhode Island, Vermont

Midatlantic (pages 577-579): Washington DC, Delaware, Maryland, New Jersey, Pennsylvania

Midsouth (pages 579-581): North Carolina, South Carolina, Tennessee, Virginia, West Virginia

Southeast (pages 581-585): Alabama, Arkansas, Florida, Georgia, Louisiana, Mississippi, Puerto Rico

Midwest (pages 586-590): Illinois, Indiana, Kentucky, Michigan, Ohio

North Central (pages 590-591): Iowa, Minnesota, Nebraska, North Dakota, South Dakota, Wisconsin

South Central (pages 591-596): Colorado, Kansas, Missouri, New Mexico, Oklahoma, Texas

West (pages 597-601): Arizona, California, Hawaii, Nevada, Utah

Northwest (pages 601-604): Alaska, Idaho, Montana, Oregon, Washington, Wyoming

Canada (pages 604-605)

International (pages 605-607)

LEARNING AND NETWORKING

Besides learning from workshop leaders and panelists in formal sessions, writers at conferences also benefit from conversations with other attendees. Writers on all levels enjoy sharing insights. Often, a conversation over lunch can reveal a new market for your work or let you know which editors are most receptive to the work of new writers. You can find out about recent editor changes and about specific agents. A casual chat could lead to a new contact or resource in your area.

Many editors and agents make visiting conferences a part of their regular search for new writers. A cover letter or query that starts with "I met you at the National Writers Association Conference," or "I found your talk on your company's new romance line at the Moonlight and Magnolias most interesting . . ." may give you a small leg up on the competition.

While a few writers have been successful in selling their manuscripts at a conference, the availability of editors and agents does not usually mean these folks will have the time there to read your novel or six best short stories (unless, of course, you've scheduled an individual meeting with them ahead of time). While editors and agents are glad to meet writers and discuss work in general terms, usually they don't have the time (or energy) to give an extensive critique during a conference. In other words, use the conference as a way to make a first, brief contact.

SELECTING A CONFERENCE

Besides the obvious considerations of time, place and cost, choose your conference based on your writing goals. If, for example, your goal is to improve the quality of your writing, it will be more helpful to you to choose a hands-on craft workshop rather than a conference offering a series of panels on marketing and promotion. If, on the other hand, you are a science fiction novelist who would like to meet your fans, try one of the many science fiction conferences or "cons" held throughout the country and the world.

Look for panelists and workshop instructors whose work you admire and who seem to be writing in your general area. Check for specific panels or discussions of topics relevant to what you are writing now. Think about the size—would you feel more comfortable with a small workshop of eight people or a large group of 100 or more attendees?

If your funds are limited, start by looking for conferences close to home, but you may want to explore those that offer contests with cash prizes—and a chance to recoup your expenses. A few conferences and workshops also offer scholarships, but the competition is stiff and writers interested in these should find out the requirements early. Finally, students may want to look for conferences and workshops that offer college credit. You will find these options included in the listings here. Again, send a self-addressed, stamped envelope for the most current details.

> ### For More Information
>
> For more information on conferences and even more conferences from which to choose, check the May issue of *Writer's Digest*. The Guide to Writers Conferences (ShawGuides, 10 W. 66th St., Suite 30H, New York NY 10023) is another helpful resource now available on the Writer's Digest website at www.writersdigest.com.

Northeast (CT, MA, ME, NH, NY, RI, VT)

BECOME A MORE PRODUCTIVE WRITER, P.O. Box 1310, Boston MA 02117-1310. (617)266-1613. E-mail: marcia@yudkin.com. Director: Marcia Yudkin. Estab. 1991. Workshop held approximately 3 times/year. Workshop held on one Saturday in May, October, February. Average attendance 15. "Creativity workshop for fiction writers and others. Based on latest discoveries about the creative process, participants learn to access their unconscious wisdom, find their own voice, utilize kinesthetic, visual and auditory methods of writing, and bypass longstanding blocks and obstacles. Held at a hotel in central Boston."
Costs: $149.
Accommodations: List of area hotels and bed & breakfasts provided.
Additional Information: Conference brochures/guidelines are available after August. Inquiries by mail, phone or e-mail OK. "Audiotapes of seminar information also available."

BREAD LOAF WRITERS' CONFERENCE, Middlebury College, Middlebury VT 05753. (802)443-5286. Fax: (802)443-2087. E-mail: blwc@mail.middlebury.edu. Administrative Coordinator: Carol Knauss. Estab. 1926. Annual. Conference held in late August. Conference duration: 11 days. Average attendance: 230. For fiction, nonfiction and poetry. Held at the summer campus in Ripton, Vermont (belongs to Middlebury College).
Costs: $1,730 (includes room/board) (1999).
Accommodations: Accommodations are at Ripton. Onsite accommodations $605 (1998).
Additional Information: Conference brochures/guidelines available January 2000. Inquiries by fax and e-mail OK.

☑ **DOWNEAST MAINE WRITER'S WORKSHOPS**, P.O. Box 446, Stockton Springs ME 04981. (207)567-4317. Fax: (207)567-3023. E-mail: redbaron@ime.net. Website: www.maineweb.com/writers/. Director: Janet J. Barron. Estab. 1994. Annual. Tentative dates 2000, last week in July and second week in August. Writing workshops geared towards aspiring writers. "We hold small, 3-day workshops during the summer each year. In intense, experimental hands-on workshops, we address, in-depth, the subject of 'How to Get Your Writing Published' and 'Writing for the Children's Market' via expert, individual, personalized, practical guidance and inside-the-industry info from a 30-year professional writer and acquisition editor of several well-known publishing houses. Upon registration, students receive a questionnaire requesting responses re: their writing level, writing interests, and expectations from the conference. From this information, we build the workshop which is entirely geared around participants' information and needs. Each workshop is limited to 12 students."
Costs: Tuition (includes lunch): 3-day, $295, $19.95 for 300-page textbook and $4 shipping and handling ("we accept Visa and MC"). Reasonable local accommodations and meals additional (except lunch during conference).
Accommodations: Upon registration, participants receive a list of local B&Bs and Inns, most of which include large, full breakfasts in their reasonable rates. They also receive a list of area activities and events.
Additional Information: Upon registration, students receive a comprehensive, confidential questionnaire. DEMWW workshops are completely constructed around participant's answers to questionnaires. Also offers a writer's clinic for writing feedback if participants seek this type of assistance. No requirements prior to registration. For more details and free brochures, contact DEMWW at any of the numbers listed. Conference brochures available April 2000.

☑ **EASTERN WRITERS' CONFERENCE**, English Dept., Salem State College, Salem MA 01970-5353. (978)542-6330. E-mail: suzanne.hennessey@salem.mass.edu. Conference Directors: Suzanne Hennessey and Regina Flynn. Estab. 1977. Annual. Conference held late June. Average attendance: 60. Conference to "provide a sense of community and support for area poets and prose writers. We try to present speakers and programs of interest, changing our format from time to time. Conference-goers have an opportunity to read to an audience or have manuscripts professionally critiqued. We tend to draw regionally." Previous speakers have included Nancy Mairs, Susanna Kaysen, Tim O'Brien, Linda Weltner.
Costs: "Under $100."

Accommodations: Available on campus.
Additional Information: Conference brochure/guidelines are available April 30. Inquiries by e-mail OK. "Optional manuscript critiques are available for an additional fee. E-mail in February for confirmation of date."

THE FOUNDATIONS OF CREATIVITY® WRITING WORKSHOP, The Elizabeth Ayres Center for Creative Writing, 155 E. 31st St., Suite 4-R, New York NY 10016-6830. (212)689-4692 or (800)510-1049. E-mail: eacenter@aol.com. Website: www.CreativeWritingCenter.com. Owner/Director: Elizabeth Ayres. Estab. 1990. Conference held 10 times/year. Workshops begin every 7 weeks, 1 time/week for 6 weeks. Average attendance: 10. "The purpose of the workshop is to help fledgling writers conquer their fear of the blank page; develop imaginative tools; capitalize on the strengths of their natural voice and style; develop confidence; and interact with other writers in a stimulating, supportive atmosphere." Writers' Retreats also offered 3-5 times/year in weekend and week-long formats. Average attendance: 15. "Retreats provide an opportunity for extended writing time in a tranquil setting with like-minded companions."
Costs: $255 (1999); retreats vary from $350-700 depending on duration.
Additional Information: Workshop brochures and guidelines free. Inquiries by mail, phone or e-mail.

☑ HOFSTRA UNIVERSITY SUMMER WRITERS' CONFERENCE, 250 Hofstra University, UCCE, Hempstead NY 11549. (516)463-5016. Fax: (516)463-4833. E-mail: dcekah@hofstra.edu. Director, Liberal Arts Studies: Kenneth Henwood. Estab. 1972. Annual (every summer, starting week after July 4). Conference to be held July 10-21, 2000. Average attendance: 50. Conference offers workshops in fiction, nonfiction, poetry, juvenile fiction, stage/screenwriting and, on occasion, one other genre such as detective fiction or science fiction. Site is the university campus, a suburban setting, 25 miles from NYC. Guest speakers are not yet known. "We have had the likes of Oscar Hijuelos, Robert Olen Butler, Hilma and Meg Wolitzer, Budd Schulberg and Cynthia Ozick."
Costs: Non-credit (no meals, no room): approximately $375 per workshop. Credit: Approximately $1,000/workshop (2 credits) undergraduate and graduate $2,000 (4 credits) undergraduate and graduate.
Accommodations: Free bus operates between Hempstead Train Station and campus for those commuting from NYC. Dormitory rooms are available for approximately $350 for the 2 week conference. Those who request area hotels will receive a list. Hotels are approximately $75 and above/night.
Additional Information: "All workshops include critiquing. Each participant is given one-on-one time of ½ hour with workshop leader. Only credit students must submit manuscripts when registering. We submit work to the Shaw Guides Contest and other Writer's Conferences and Retreats contests when appropriate." Conference brochures/guidelines available March 2000. Inquiries by fax and e-mail OK.

IWWG MEET THE AGENTS AND EDITORS: THE BIG APPLE WORKSHOPS, % International Women's Writing Guild, P.O. Box 810, Gracie Station, New York NY 10028-0082. (212)737-7536. Fax: (212)737-9469. E-mail: iwwg@iwwg.com. Website: www.iwwg.com. Executive Director: Hannelore Hahn. Estab. 1980. Biannual. Workshops held April 15-16, 2000 and October 14-15, 2000. Average attendance: 200. Workshops to promote creative writing and professional success. Site: Private meeting space of the City Athletic Club, mid-town New York City. Saturday: One day workshop. Sunday morning: open house/meet the authors and panel discussion with eight recently published authors. Sunday afternoon: open house/meet the authors, independent presses and editors.
Costs: $100 for the weekend.
Accommodations: Information on transportation arrangements and overnight accommodations made available.
Additional Information: Workshop brochures/guidelines are available for SASE. Inquires by fax and e-mail OK.

IWWG SUMMER CONFERENCE, % International Women's Writing Guild, P.O. Box 810, Gracie Station, New York NY 10028-0082. (212)737-7536. Fax: (212)737-9469. E-mail: iwwg@iwwg.com. Website: www.iwwg.com. Executive Director: Hannelore Hahn. Estab. 1977. Annual. Conference held August 11-18, 2000. Average attendance: 450, including international attendees. Conference to promote writing in all genres, personal growth and professional success. Conference is held "on the tranquil campus of Skidmore College in Saratoga Springs, NY, where the serene Hudson Valley meets the North Country of the Adirondacks." Sixty-five different workshops are offered everyday. Overall theme: "Writing Towards Personal and Professional Growth."
Costs: $700 for week-long program, plus room and board.
Accommodations: Transportation by air to Albany, New York, or Amtrak train available from New York City. Conference attendees stay on campus.
Additional Information: Conference brochures/guidelines available for SASE. Inquires by fax and e-mail OK.

MANHATTANVILLE COLLEGE WRITERS' WEEK, 2900 Purchase St., Purchase NY 10577-2103. (914)694-3425. Fax: (914)694-3488. E-mail: rdowd@mville. Website: www.manhattanville.edu. Dean, School of Graduate and Professional Studies: Ruth Dowd, R.S.C.J. Estab. 1982. Annual. Conference held last week of June 1999. Average attendance: 90. Workshops include children's literature, journal writing, creative nonfiction, personal essay, poetry, fiction, travel writing and short fiction. "The Conference is designed not only for writers

but for teachers of writing. Each workshop is attended by a Master teacher who works with the writers/teachers in the afternoon to help them to translate their writing skills for classroom use." Students do intensive work in the genre of their choice. Manhattanville is a suburban campus 30 miles from New York City. The campus centers around Reid Castle, the administration building, the former home of Whitelaw Reid. Workshops are conducted in Reid Castle. We feature a major author as guest lecturer during the Conference. Past speakers have included such authors as Toni Morrison, Mary Gordon, Gail Godwin, Pete Hamill and poet Mark Doty.
Costs: Conference cost was $560 in 1998 plus $30 fee.
Accommodations: Students may rent rooms in the college residence halls. More luxurious accommodations are available at neighboring hotels. In the summer of 1998 the cost of renting a room in the residence halls was $25 per night.
Additional Information: Conference brochures/guidelines are available for SASE in March. Inquiries by fax OK.

N NECRONOMICON: The Cthulhu Mythos Convention, P.O. Box 1038, Back Bay Annex, Boston MA 02117-1038. E-mail: necronomicon@necropress.com. Website: ww2.necropress.com/necronomicon. Estab. 1993. Conference held every two years (odd-numbered). Conference held in August. Conference duration: 3 days (Friday-Sunday). Average attendance: 300-400. Conference to "celebrate H.P. Lovecraft and the Cthulhu Mythos in all its forms (literature, TV and film, scholarly, role-playing gaming, artwork). Weird fiction in general." Conference held at the Marriot Hotel in Providence, RI. "Focuses on past and current writers (and others) who use Lovecraft's (and others') 'Cthulhu Mythos' themes and ideas in their works." Speakers include Fred Chappel, author and Jason Eckhardt, artist.
Costs: $75; $70 with early arrangements.
Accommodations: Special convention room-rate at the Marriott: $99 single/night, $119 double/night.
Additional Information: Inquiries by e-mail OK. "We are a very specialized-themed convention and draw the top names and people in the field. While the numbers are small, at the 1995 convention we had people from 12 different countries attend. It is a great place to network!"

☑ NEW ENGLAND WRITERS' WORKSHOP AT EMERSON COLLEGE, (formerly New England Writers' Workshop of Simmons College), 100 Beacon St., Boston MA 02116. (617)824-8570. Fax: (617)824-7857. Conference Administrator: Jena Schwartz. Estab. 1977. Annually in summer. Workshop held 1st week of June. Workshop lasts one week. Average attendance: 45. "Adult fiction: novel, short story. Boston and its literary heritage provide a stimulating environment for a workshop of writers. Emerson College is located in downtown Boston in the vicinity of Boston Commons. Our theme is usually fiction (novel or short story) with the workshops in the morning and then the afternoon speakers either talk about their own work or talk about the 'business' of publishing." Past speakers and workshop leaders have included John Updike, Anne Beattie and Jill McCorkle as well as editors from *The New Yorker*, *The Atlantic* and Houghton Mifflin.
Costs: $550 (includes full week of workshops and speakers, individual consultations, refreshments and 2 receptions).
Accommodations: Cost is $175 single, $150 double for Sunday to Friday on-campus housing. A list of local hotels is also available.
Additional Information: "Up to 30 pages of manuscript may be sent in prior to workshop to be reviewed privately with workshop leader during the week." Conference brochures/guidelines are available for SASE in March. Inquiries by fax OK.

ODYSSEY, 20 Levesque Lane, Mont Vernon NH 03057. Phone/fax: (603)673-6234. E-mail: jcavelos@empire.n et. Website: www.nhc.edu/odyssey/. Director: Jeanne Cavelos. Estab. 1995. Annual. Workshop to be held June 12 to July 21. Attendance limited to 20. "A workshop for fantasy, science fiction and horror writers that combines an intensive learning and writing experience with in-depth feedback on students' manuscripts. The only workshop to combine the overall guidance and in-depth feedback of a single instructor with the varied perspectives of guest lectures." Conference held at New Hampshire College in Manchester, New Hampshire. Previous guest lecturers included: Harlan Ellison, Ben Bova, Jane Yolen, Elizabeth Hand, Ellen Kushner, Craig Shaw Gardner, Melissa Scott, Patricia McKillip and John Crowley.
Costs: In 1999: $1,040 tuition, $337 housing (double room), $20 application fee, $525 food (approximate), $55 processing fee to receive college credit.
Accommodations: "Workshop students stay at New Hampshire College townhouses and eat at college."
Additional Information: Students must apply and include a writing sample. Students' works are critiqued throughout the 6 weeks. Workshop brochures and guidelines available for SASE after August. Inquiries by fax and e-mail OK.

N THE OLDERS' CHILDREN'S WRITING WORKSHOP, 84 New St., Albany VT 05820. (802)755-6774. E-mail: julvt@together.net. Contact: Jules Older. Estab. 1996. Annual. Workshop held in October in Vermont. Workshop duration: 1 full Saturday. Average attendance: 12. Workshop covers all aspects of writing for children. Workshop held in an inn in northern Vermont. Workshop speakers are Jules and Effin Older.
Costs: $200.

Accommodations: Information on overnight accommodations is available.

Additional Information: "We do include optional critiques." Workshop brochures available for SASE. Inquiries by e-mail OK.

N̄ THE OLDERS' TRAVEL WRITING WORKSHOP, 84 New St., Albany VT 05820. (802)755-6774. E-mail: julvt@together.net. Contact: Jules Older. Estab. 1988. Annual. Workshop held in the summer and occasionally winter. Workshop duration: 1 full Saturday. Average attendance: 12-16. Workshop on travel writing. Workshop held at mountain resorts in Vermont, New Hampshire and Cooperstown, NY. Themes include "Bringing Your Passions Into Travel Writing" and "Travel Writing in Fiction, for Adults and Kids." Workshop speakers are Jules and Effin Older.

Costs: $200.

Accommodations: Information on overnight accommodations is available.

Additional Information: "We do include optional critiques." Workshop brochures available year round. Inquiries by e-mail OK.

ROBERT QUACKENBUSH'S CHILDREN'S BOOK WRITING & ILLUSTRATING WORKSHOPS, 460 E. 79th St., New York NY 10021-1443. (212)744-3822. Fax: (212)861-2761. E-mail: rqstudios@aol.com. Website: www.rquackenbush.com. Instructor: Robert Quackenbush. Estab. 1982. Annual. Workshop held July 10-14, 2000. Average attendance: limited to 10. Workshops to promote writing and illustrating books for children. Held at the Manhattan studio of Robert Quackenbush, author and illustrator of over 170 books for young readers. "Focus is generally on picture books, easy-to-read and early chapter books. All classes led by Robert Quackenbush."

Costs: $650 tuition covers all costs of the workshop, but does not include housing and meals. A $100 nonrefundable deposit is required with the $550 balance due two weeks prior to attendance.

Accommodations: A list of recommended hotels and restaurants is sent upon receipt of deposit.

Additional Information: Class is for beginners and professionals. Critiques during workshop. Private consultations also available at an hourly rate. "Programs suited to your needs; individualized schedules can be designed. Write or phone to discuss your goals and you will receive a prompt reply." Conference brochures are available for SASE. Inquiries by fax OK, but please include mailing address with inquiries. No inquiries by e-mail.

☑ SCBWI MIDYEAR CONFERENCE, NYC, (formerly SCBWI Conference in Children's Literature, NYC), 8271 Broadway Blvd., Los Angeles CA 90048. (323)782-1010. Fax: (323)782-1892. E-mail: membership @scbwi.org. Website: scbwi.org. President: Stephen Mooser. Estab. 1975. Annual. Conference held February 5-6, 2000. Average attendance: 350. Conference is to promote writing for children: picture books; fiction; nonfiction; middle grade and young adult; meet an editor; meet an agent; financial planning for writers; marketing your book; children's multimedia; etc. Held at Roosevelt Hotel, 45 E. 45th St., New York.

Costs: See website for current cost.

Accommodations: Write for information; hotel names will be supplied.

Additional Information: Conference brochures/guidelines are available for SASE.

N̄ SCBWI/HOFSTRA CHILDREN'S LITERATURE CONFERENCE, Hofstra University, University College of Continuing Education, Republic Hall, Hempstead NY 11549. (516)463-5016. Co-organizers: Connie C. Epstein, Adrienne Betz and Kenneth Henwood. Estab. 1985. Annual. Conference to be held April 15, 2000. Average attendance: 150. Conference to encourage good writing for children. "Purpose is to bring together various professional groups—writers, illustrators, librarians, teachers—who are interested in writing for children. Each year we organize the program around a theme. Last year it was Using Those 26 Letters." The conference takes place at the Student Center Building of Hofstra University, located in Hempstead, Long Island. "We have two general sessions, an editorial panel and five break-out groups held in rooms in the Center or nearby classrooms." Last year's conference featured Paula Danziger and Anne M. Martin as the 2 general speakers, and 2 children's book editors critiqued randomly selected first-manuscript pages submitted by registrants. Special interest groups are offered in picture books, nonfiction and submission procedures with others in fiction.

Cost: $60 (previous year) for SCBWI members; $65 for nonmembers. Lunch included.

☑ STATE OF MAINE WRITERS' CONFERENCE, 18 Hill Rd., Belmont MA 02478. (617)489-1548. Co-chairs: June Knowles and Mary Pitts. Estab. 1941. Annual. Conference held August 15-18, 2000. Conference duration: 4 days. Average attendance: 40. "We try to present a balanced as well as eclectic conference. There is quite a bit of time and attention given to poetry but we also have children's literature, travel, novels/fiction and other issues of interest to writers. Other speakers are publishers, editors, illustrators and other professionals. Our concentration is, by intention, a general view of writing to publish. We are located in Ocean Park, a small seashore village 14 miles south of Portland. Ours is a summer assembly center with many buildings from the Victorian Age. The conference meets in Porter Hall, one of the assembly buildings which is listed on the National Register of Historic Places. Within recent years our guest list has included Lewis Turco, Amy MacDonald, Jeffrey Aronson, Wesley McNair, John N. Cole, Betsy Sholl, John Tagliabue, Roy Fairfield, Oscar Greene and many others. We usually have about 10 guest presenters a year."

Costs: $90-100 includes the conference banquet. There is a reduced fee, $45, for students ages 21 and under. The fee does not include housing or meals which must be arranged separately by the conferees.

Accommodations: An accommodations list is available. "We are in a summer resort area and motels, guest houses and restaurants abound."

Additional Information: "We have a list of about nine contests on various genres. The prizes, all modest, are awarded at the end of the conference and only to those who are registered." Send SASE for program guide and contest announcements.

☑ VASSAR COLLEGE CHILDREN'S BOOK INSTITUTE OF PUBLISHING AND WRITING,

(formerly Vassar College Institute of Publishing and Writing: Children's Books in the Marketplace), Vassar College, Box 300, Poughkeepsie NY 12604-0077. (914)437-5903. Fax: (914)437-7209. E-mail: mabruno@vassar .edu. Website: www.vassar.edu. Associate Director of College Relations: Maryann Bruno. Estab. 1983. Annual. Conference held mid to late June. Conference duration: 1 week. Average attendance: 25. Writing and publishing children's literature. "We offer the nuts and bolts of how to get your work published plus critiques of participants' writings." The conference is held at Vassar College, a 1,000-acre campus located in the mid-Hudson valley. The campus is self-contained, with residence halls, dining facilities, and classroom and meeting facilities. Vassar is located 90 miles north of New York City, and is accessible by car, train and air. Participants have use of Vassar's athletic facilities, including swimming, squash, tennis and jogging. Vassar is known for the beauty of its campus. "The Institute is directed by author/editor Jean Margollo and features top working professionals from the field of publishing."

Costs: $900, includes full tuition, room and three meals a day.

Accommodations: Special conference attendee accommodations are in campus residence halls.

Additional Information: Writers may submit a 10-page sample of their writing for critique, which occurs during the week of the conference. Artists' portfolios are reviewed individually. Conference brochures/guidelines are available March 1 or earlier upon request. Inquiries by fax and e-mail OK.

☑ WESLEYAN WRITERS CONFERENCE, Wesleyan University, Middletown CT 06459. (860)685-3604.

Fax: (860)685-2441. E-mail: agreene@wesleyan.edu. Website: www.wesleyan.edu/writing/conferen.html. Director: Anne Greene. Estab. 1956. Annual. Conference held the last week in June. Average attendance: 100. For fiction techniques, novel, short story, poetry, screenwriting, nonfiction, literary journalism, memoir. The conference is held on the campus of Wesleyan University, in the hills overlooking the Connecticut River. Meals and lodging are provided on campus. Features readings of new fiction, guest lectures on a range of topics including publishing and daily seminars. "Both new and experienced writers are welcome."

Costs: In 1998, day rate $660 (including meals); boarding students' rate $775 (including meals and room for 5 nights).

Accommodations: "Participants can fly to Hartford or take Amtrak to Meriden, CT. We are happy to help participants make travel arrangements." Overnight participants stay on campus.

Additional Information: Manuscript critiques are available as part of the program but are not required. Participants may attend seminars in several different genres. Scholarships and teaching fellowships are available, including the Jakobson awards for new writers and the Jon Davidoff Scholarships for journalists. Inquiries by e-mail and fax OK.

N: THE WRITER'S VOICE, 5 West 63rd St., New York NY 10023. (212)875-4124. Fax: (212)875-4176. E-

mail: wtrsvoice1@aol.com. Website: www.ymcanyc.org. Contact: Rory Tyler. Estab. 1981. Workshop held four times/year (summer, spring, winter and fall). Workshop duration: 6-10 weeks, two hours one night/week. Average attendance: 15. Workshop on "fiction, poetry, writing for performance, non-fiction, playwriting and writing for children." Workshop held at the Westside YMCA.

Costs: $300/workshop.

Additional Information: Sponsors several contests including awards for poetry, fiction and non-fiction. Guidelines for SASE. Workshop brochures/guidelines available for SASE. "The Writer's Voice of the Westside Y is the largest non-academic literary arts center in the U.S."

N: WRITING, CREATIVITY AND RITUAL: A WOMAN'S RETREAT, 995 Chapman Rd., Yorktown

Heights NY 10598. E-mail: ehanlon@bestweb.net. Contact: Emily Hanlon. Estab. 1998. Biannual. Retreat held July 24-July 31, 2000. Average attendance: 20 is the limit. Retreat for "fiction, memoir, creative nonfiction and the creative process." Location varies. "I try to find places conducive to creativity and the imagination. January 2000, an island off the coast of Mexico; July 2000, Glastonbury, England." The theme of the retreat is "the

---

CAN'T FIND A CONFERENCE? Conferences are listed by region. Check the introduction to this section for a list of regional categories.

passion and risk of the creative journey. Writing emphasis on the writer's voice through opening to characters that come from the writer's unconscious."

Costs: 1999 fees: $1,200-1,600 depending on choice of room. Includes workshop, room and all meals.
Additional Information: Brochures/guidelines free and available spring 2000. Inquiries by e-mail OK. "This retreat is open only to women. Enrollment is limited to 20. More than just a writing workshop or conference, the retreat is an exploration of the passion, the shadowland and dance of creativity."

N ZEN MOUNTAIN MONASTERY, Mt. Tremper NY 12457. (914)688-2228. Fax: (914)688-2415. E-mail: zmmtrain@zen-mtn.org. Website: www.sen-mtn.org/zmm. Contact: Training office. On-going writer retreats. Duration: 1 weekend. Average attendance: 15-20. Workshop on "Zen and its relation to the creative process. The retreat takes place within the context of Zen training. Participants will be introduced to Zazen (the formal seated meditation). We offer retreats in Haiku, poetry and journal writing." Workshops held at an American Zen Buddhist Monastery located in the Catskill Mountains retreat cabin. Speakers include Anne Waldman, Christian McEwen and Gabriel Rico ("Pain and Possibility").
Costs: $195 includes meals, lodging and Zen training.
Accommodations: Direct bus line for NY Port Authority Adirondack Trailways provided. "Participants are expected to stay here for the entirety of the retreat. Dormitory style lodging for men and women."
Additional Information: Workshop brochures/guidelines for SASE. Inquiries by fax and e-mail OK.

Midatlantic (DC, DE, MD, NJ, PA)

THE COLLEGE OF NEW JERSEY WRITERS' CONFERENCE, English Dept., The College of New Jersey, P.O. Box 7718, Ewing NJ 08628-0718. (609)771-3254. Fax: (609)771-3345. E-mail: write@tcnj.edu. Director: Jean Hollander. Estab. 1980. Annual. Conference held April 4, 2000. Conference duration: 9 a.m. to 10:30 p.m. Average attendance: 600-1,000. "Conference concentrates on fiction (the largest number of participants), poetry, children's literature, play and screenwriting, magazine and newspaper journalism, overcoming writer's block, nonfiction books. Conference is held at the student center at the college in two auditoriums and workshop rooms; also Kendall Theatre on campus." The focus is on various genres: romance, detective, mystery, TV writing, etc. Topics have included "How to Get Happily Published," "How to Get an Agent" and "Earning a Living as a Writer." The conference usually presents twenty or so authors, plus two featured speakers, who have included Arthur Miller, Saul Bellow, Toni Morrison, Joyce Carol Oates, Erica Jong and Alice Walker.
Costs: General registration $45, plus $10 for each workshop. Lower rates for students.
Additional Information: Brochures/guidelines available for SASE. Inquiries by e-mail or phone OK.

N MID-ATLANTIC MYSTERY BOOK FAIR & CONVENTION, Detecto Mysterioso Books at Society Hill Playhouse, 507 S. Eighth St., Philadelphia PA 19147. (215)923-0211. Fax: (923)923-1789. E-mail: shp@erols .com. Website: www.erols.com/SHP. Contact: Deen Kogan, chairperson. Estab. 1991. Annual. Convention held October 13-15, 2000. Average attendance: 450-500. Focus is on mystery, suspense, thriller, true crime novels. "An examination of the genre from many points of view." The convention is held at the Wyndham Franklin Plaza, located in the historic area of Philadelphia. Previous speakers included Lawrence Block, Jeremiah Healy, Neil Albert, Michael Connelly, Paul Levine, Eileen Dreyer, Earl Emerson, Wendy Hornsby.
Costs: $125 registration fee.
Accommodations: Attendees must make their own transportation arrangements. Special room rate available at convention hotel.
Additional Information: "The Bookroom is a focal point of the convention. Twenty-five specialty dealers are expected to exhibit and collectables range from hot-off-the-press bestsellers to 1930's pulp; from fine editions to reading copies. Conference brochures/guidelines are available by mail or telephone after June 15, 1999. Inquiries by e-mail and fax OK, provide address."

☑ MONTROSE CHRISTIAN WRITER'S CONFERENCE, 5 Locust St., Montrose Bible Conference, Montrose PA 18801-1112. (570)278-1001. (800)598-5030. Fax: (570)278-3061. E-mail: mbc@montrosebible.o rg. Website: www.montrosebible.org. Bible Conference Director: Jim Fahringer. Estab. 1990. Annual. Conference held July. Average attendance: 75. "We try to meet a cross-section of writing needs, for beginners and advanced, covering fiction, poetry and writing for children. We meet in the beautiful village of Montrose, Pennsylvania, situated in the mountains. The Bible Conference provides motel-like accommodations and good food. The main sessions are held in the chapel with rooms available for other classes. Fiction writing has been taught each year."
Costs: In 1999 registration was $100.
Accommodations: Will meet planes in Binghamton NY and Scranton PA; will meet bus in Great Bend PA. Information on overnight accommodations is available. On-site accommodations: room and board $225-$342/ week; $38-$57/day including food.
Additional Information: "Writers can send work ahead and have it critiqued for $20." Brochures/guidelines are available by e-mail and fax. "The attendees are usually church related. The writing has a Christian emphasis."

[N] JENNY McKEAN MOORE COMMUNITY WORKSHOPS, English Dept., George Washington University, Washington DC 20052. (202)994-8223. Fax: (202)363-8628. Professor: D. McAleavey. Estab. 1976. Workshop held each semester. Next semester begins August 1999. Length: semester. Average attendance: 15. Workshop concentration varies depending on professor—usually fiction or poetry. Workshop held at university.
Costs: Free.
Additional Information: Admission is competitive and by ms.

[N] OUTDOOR WRITERS ASSOCIATION OF AMERICA ANNUAL CONFERENCE, Rd. 1, Box 177, Spring Mills PA 16875. (814)364-9557. E-mail: eking4owaa@compuserve.com. Meeting Planner: Eileen King. Estab. 1927. Annual. Conference held in June. Will be held in Greensboro NC in 2000. Average attendance: 800-950. Conference concentrates on outdoor communications (all forms of media). Featured speakers have included Don Ranley, University of Missouri, Columbia; US Forest Service Chief Michael Dombeck; Nina Leopold Bradley (daughter of Aldo Leopold); Secretary of the Interior, Bruce Babbitt.
Costs: $140 for nonmembers; "applicants must have prior approval from Executive Director." Registration fee includes cost of most meals.
Accommodations: List of accommodations available after April. Special room rate for attendees.
Additional Information: Sponsors contests, "but all is done prior to the conference and you must be a member to enter them." Conference brochures/guidelines are available for SASE.

[N] PENNWRITERS CONFERENCE, RR #2, Box 241, Middlebury Center PA 16935. (717)871-0599. (717)871-6104. E-mail: elizwrite8@aol.com. Website: www.pennwriters.org. Contact: Elizabeth Darrach. Estab. 1987. Annual. Conference held May 19-20, 2000. Average attendance: 140. "We encompass all genres and will be aiming for workshops to cover many areas, including fiction (long and short), nonfiction, etc." Workshop held at the Holiday Inn Airport "a large hotel with many rooms for conferences and meetings in Harrisburg PA. Theme for 2000 is 'Tools for the 21st Century,' and we will be addressing e-publishing, webpages, etc." Speakers include Kathryn Falk, Michael Seidman, Jack Ketchum and Bonnee Pierson.
Costs: 1999 fees: $125 for members.
Accommodations: Special rate of $74/night if reservation is made by April 21.
Additional Information: "We will be having at least one critique session, limited to the first 15 submissions—for synopsis only." Sponsors contest: published authors judge fiction in 2 categories, short stories and Great Beginnings (novels). Conference brochures/guidelines for SASE. Inquiries by fax and e-mail OK. "Agent/editor appointments are available on a first-come, first serve basis."

ST. DAVIDS CHRISTIAN WRITERS CONFERENCE, 87 Pines Rd. E., Hadley PA 16130-1019. E-mail: audstall@nauticom.net. Registrar: Audrey Stallsmith. Estab. 1957. Annual. Conference held third week in June. "Located at picturesque Geneva College, Beaver Falls PA, north of Pittsburgh." Attendance: 100. "We have a 42 year history, and are known for our family-like atmosphere and quality programs." Conference will train writers in religious and general writing through workshops in fiction, nonfiction, beginning and advanced writing, poetry, children's writing, devotional/inspirational writing. Optional tutorials and market consultations. Recent workshop leaders have included Les Stobbe, Lurlene McDaniel and Shirley Brinkerhoff.
Cost: Tuition is $250; room and board is $225. Optional programs are extra.
Accommodations: College dormitory rooms with linens provided, excellent food in college cafeteria. "We provide transportation from the Pittsburgh airport if prior arrangements are made."
Additional Information: Small informal critique groups do not require pre-conference manuscript submission. Sponsors annual contest for registered conferees. Categories may include humorous poetry, serious poetry, fiction (short story), op-ed, children's lit, character sketch, personal experience, humorous prose. Judges are faculty members, editors or agents. Conference brochure available in March for SASE or request by e-mail.

[N] SUSPENSE, MYSTERY & INTRIGUE II, % Novel Explorations, Suite 350, 10705 Charter Dr., Columbia MD 21044. (800)432-6659. Fax: (410)964-0878. E-mail: novelexp@erols.com. Website: www.erols.com/novelexp. Contact: Patty Suchy. Estab. 1998. Conference held every 2 years. Next conference: 2001. Conference duration: one week in January. Average attendance: 60. Conference concentrates on fiction, mystery, suspense, romantic suspense, short stories and horror. Conference held aboard the SS Norwegian Sky. Workshops include "Murder With Only One Witness"; "Mind of a Serial Killer"; "PI's Real & Fictional"; "Balancing Plot and Characters"; "How to Get Happily Published"; "Can You Really Do That?"; and "From Book to Movie." Conference speakers are J.A. Jance, keynote speaker; Jeffrey Deaver, special guest of honor; Elaine Raco Chase; Kathleen Eagle; Jeremiah Healy; Laura Lippman; Robert J. Randisi; Marthayn Pelegrimas; Kelsey Roberts.
Costs: $100. Cabins start at $795 plus port charge and transportation.
Accommodations: Special cruise/air rates available. Conference is on board the SS Norwegian Sky cruising from Miami to Eleuthera, San Juan, St. Thomas, Stirrup Cay, Miami.
Additional Information: Brochures/guidelines available for SASE. Inquiries by fax and e-mail OK. "Books for sale on ship; ship board autographing; dinner with authors; relaxed, personal atmosphere."

WASHINGTON INDEPENDENT WRITERS (WIW) SPRING WRITERS CONFERENCE, #220, 733 15th St. NW, Suite 220, Washington DC 20005-2112. (202)347-4973. Fax:: (202)628-0298. E-mail: washwriter@aol.com. Website: www.washwriter.org. Executive Director: Isolde Chapin. Estab. 1975. Annual. Conference held May 14-15. Conference duration: Friday evening and Saturday. Average attendance: 250. "Gives participants a chance to hear from and talk with dozens of experts on book and magazine publishing as well as on the craft, tools and business of writing." National Press Club as conference site. Past keynote speakers include Erica Jong, Haynes Johnson, Diane Rehm and Kitty Kelley.
Costs: $125 members; $150 nonmembers; $185 membership and conference.
Additional Information: Brochures/guidelines available for SASE in February. Inquiries by fax and e-mail OK.

N WINTER POETRY & PROSE GETAWAY IN CAPE MAY, 18 North Richards Ave., Ventor NJ 08406-2136. (609)823-5076. E-mail: wintergetaway@hotmail.com. Website: www.wintergetaway.com. Contact: Peter E. Murphy. Estab. 1994. Annual. Workshop held January 14-17, 2000. Average attendance: 150. "Open to all writers, beginners and experienced over the age of 18. Prose workshops meet all day Saturday and Sunday and on Monday morning. Participants choose one workshop from among the following choices: short story (beginning and advanced), memoir, novel, drama, humor, nature writing, photography, story telling and pottery. Classes are small so each person receives individual attention for the new writing or work-in-progress that they are focusing on. The workshops are held at the Grand Hotel on the oceanfront in historic Cape May, New Jersey. Individual tutorials are available for fictions writers at an additional cost." 1999 speakers included Renee Ashley, Robert Carnevale, Cat Doty, Penny Dugan, Stephen Dunn and Amy Eshoo.
Costs: "Cost for 1999 was $350 which included breakfast and lunch for three days, all workshop session and evening activities, and a double room." Dinners are not included. Participants may choose a single room at an additional cost. Some workshops require additional material fees. Commuters who make their own arrangements are welcome. A $25 early bird discount is available if full payment is made by November 15.
Accommodations: "Participants stay in comfortable rooms, most with an ocean view, perfect for thawing out the muse. Hotel facilities include a pool, sauna and a whirlpool, as well as a lounge and disco for late evening dancing."
Additional Information: "Individual critiques are available to prose writers at an additional cost. Work in progress should be sent ahead of time." Conference brochures/guidelines free after September 15. Inquiries by e-mail OK. "The Writers Getaway is known for its challenging and supportive workshops that encourage imaginative risk-taking and promote freedom and transformation in the participants' writing."

N WRITING FOR PUBLICATION, Villanova University, Villanova PA 19085-1099. (215)645-4620. Fax: (610)519-4623. Director: Wm. Ray Heitzmann, Ph.D. Estab. 1975. Semiannual. Conference dates vary, held fall, spring. Average attendance: 15-20 (seminar style). Conference covers marketing one's manuscript (fiction, nonfiction, book, article, etc.); strong emphasis on marketing. Conference held in a seminar room at a university (easy access, parking, etc.). Panels include "Advanced Writing for Publication," "Part-time Writing," "Working With Editors." Panelists include Ray Heitzman, and others.
Costs: $385 (graduate credit); $100 (non-credit) plus $10 registration fee.
Accommodations: List of motels/hotels available, but most people live in area and commute. Special arrangements made on an individual basis.
Additional Information: Critiques available. Voluntary submission of manuscripts. Brochures/guidelines are available. Inquiries by fax OK. "Workshop graduates have been very successful." Emphasis: Non-fiction.

Midsouth (NC, SC, TN, VA, WV)

AMERICAN CHRISTIAN WRITERS CONFERENCES, P.O. Box 110390, Nashville TN 37222. (800)21-WRITE. Fax: (615)834-7736. E-mail: reqaforder@aol.com. Website: www.ECPA.ORG/ACW (includes schedule). Director: Reg Forder. Estab. 1981. Annual. Conference duration: 2 days. Average attendance: 100. To promote all forms of Christian writing. Conferences held throughout the year in over 2 dozen cities. Usually located at a major hotel chain like Holiday Inn.
Costs: Approximately $149 plus meals and accommodation.
Accommodations: Special rates available at host hotel.
Additional Information: Conference brochures/guidelines are available for SASE. Inquiries by fax and e-mail OK.

N CHATTANOOGA CONFERENCE ON SOUTHERN LITERATURE, c/o Arts & Education Council, P.O. Box 4203, Chattanooga TN 37405-0203. (423)267-1218. Fax: (423)267-1018. E-mail: artsed@bellsouth.com. Website: www.artsedcouncil.org. Contact: Susan Robinson. Estab. 1981. Biennial. Conference held April 19-21, 2001. Average attendance: 1,200. Conference on fiction, non-fiction, drama and poetry. Conference held in "downtown Chattanooga on the campus of the University of Tennessee in the historic Tivoli Theatre." 1999

panels included "Portrayal of Women in Southern Literature," "Southern Literature on the Edge of the Millennium" and "Fact or Fiction: Defining the Boundaries in Historical Writing." 1999 speakers included Ross Spears, Kaye Gibbons, Margaret Edson, Wilma Dykeman, Janice Daugharty and Barry Hannah.
Costs: 1999 fees: $35 (covers conference registration only).
Accommodations: "Radison Read House Hotel offers a rate of $82/night for conference attendees." Shuttle service provided from the Raddison Read House Hotel to the University of Tennessee at Chattanooga.
Additional Information: Conference brochures with schedule available in January 2001 for SASE. Inquiries by fax and e-mail OK.

☑ **DUKE UNIVERSITY WRITERS' WORKSHOP**, Box 90700, Durham NC 27708. (919)684-5375. Director: Georgann Eubanks. Estab. 1978. Annual. Workshop held in July. Average attendance: 50. To promote "creative writing: beginning, intermediate and advanced fiction; short story; scriptwriting; poetry; creative nonfiction." Workshop held at "at a beautiful retreat center on the North Carolina coast. Nationally recognized for its academic excellence, Duke sponsors this workshop annually for creative writers of various genres."
Costs: $695 (meals and room included).
Accommodations: Single and double rooms available.
Additional Information: Critiques available. "Works-in-progress requested 3 weeks before workshop. Each participant gets *private* consult plus small-group in-class critiques." Brochures/guidelines are available. Concentrated instruction plus time to work. No glitz. Hard work. Great results."

HIGHLAND SUMMER CONFERENCE, Box 7014, Radford University, Radford VA 24142-7014. (540)831-5366. Fax: (540)831-5004. E-mail: jasbury@runet.edu. Website: www.runet.edu/~arsc. Chair, Appalachian Studies Program: Dr. Grace Toney Edwards. Contact: Jo Ann Asbury, assistant to director. Estab. 1978. Annual. Conference held last 2 weeks of June 2000. Conference duration: 12 days. Average attendance: 25. Three hours graduate or undergraduate credit. "The HSC features one (two weeks) or two (one week each) guest leaders each year. As a rule, our leaders are well-known writers who have connections, either thematic, or personal, or both, to the Appalachian region. The genre(s) of emphasis depends upon the workshop leader(s). In the past we have had as guest lecturers Nikki Giovanni, Sharyn McCrumb, Gurney Norman, Denise Giardinia, George Ella Lyon, Jim Wayne Miller, Wilma Dykeman and Robert Morgan. The Highland Summer Conference is held at Radford University, a school of about 9,000 students. Radford is in the Blue Ridge Mountains of southwest Virginia about 45 miles south of Roanoke, VA."
Costs: "The cost is based on current Radford tuition for 3 credit hours plus an additional conference fee. On-campus meals and housing are available at additional cost. In 1999 conference tuition was $433 for instate undergraduates, $475 for graduate students."
Accommodations: "We do not have special rate arrangements with local hotels. We do offer accommodations on the Radford University Campus in a recently refurbished residence hall. (In 1999 cost was $19-28 per night.)"
Additional Information: "Conference leaders do typically critique work done during the two-week conference, but do not ask to have any writing submitted prior to the conference beginning." Conference brochures/guidelines are available after February, 2000 for SASE. Inquiries by e-mail and fax OK.

☑ **NORTH CAROLINA WRITERS' NETWORK FALL CONFERENCE**, P.O. Box 954, Carrboro NC 27510-0954. (919)967-9540. Fax: (919)929-0535. E-mail: mail@ncwriters.org. Website: www.ncwriters.org. Executive Director: Linda G. Hobson. Contact: Bobbie Collins-Perry, program and services director. Estab. 1985. Annual. 2000 conference will be held in Fayetteville, NC, November 10-12. Average attendance: 450. "The conference is a weekend full of workshops, panels, readings and discussion groups. It endeavors to serve writers of all levels of skill from beginning, to emerging, to established. We try to have *all* genres represented. In the past we have had novelists, poets, journalists, editors, children's writers, young adult writers, storytellers, playwrights, screenwriters, etc. We take the conference to a different location in North Carolina each year in order to best serve our entire state. We hold the conference at a conference center with hotel rooms available."
Costs: "Conference cost is approximately $175 and includes three to four meals."
Accommodations: "Special conference hotel rates are obtained, but the individual makes his/her own reservations. If requested, we will help the individual find a roommate."
Additional Information: Conference brochures/guidelines are available in late August for 2 first-class stamps. Inquiries by fax or e-mail OK, or look for the complete brochure and registration forms on website.

🆖 **POLICE WRITERS CONFERENCE**, P.O. Box 416, Hayes VA 23072-0416. (804)642-2343. E-mail: rfulton@policewriter.com. Website: www.policewriter.com. Contact: Roger Fulton, president. Estab. 1997. Annual. Conference held in November. Conference duration: 3 days. Average attendance: 50. Conference to "educate both experienced and novice fiction and nonfiction writers of police related work and networking, networking, networking among writers, editors and agents." Held at a hotel conference center. Courses for 1999 included "Trends in the Future Publishing Industry," "A Fiction Workshop" and "Writing With a Small Publishing House." 1999 speakers included Ed Dee, police novelist and Roger Fulton, nonfiction writer.
Costs: $225 for 3 days.
Accommodations: "Special discounts on airfare through our official travel agency." Shuttle services included

in conference fee. Special conference accommodations and prices available. On-site accommodation available for $95/night 'while they last."

Additional Information: Sponsors a contest for police related stories up to 1,500 words in fiction and nonfiction. Entry fee is included in the registration fee. Conference brochures/guidelines available for SASE. Inquiries by fax and e-mail OK. "The Police Writers Club sponsors this conference. Applications must be made and accepted, and other evidence of police affiliations or interest may be required."

SEWANEE WRITERS' CONFERENCE, 310 St. Luke's Hall, Sewanee TN 37383-1000. (931)598-1141. Fax: (931)598-1145. E-mail: cpeters@sewanee.edu. Website: www.sewanee.edu/writers_conference/home.html. Conference Coordinator: Cheri B. Peters. Estab. 1990. Annual. Conference held July 18-31, 2000. Conference duration: 12 days. Average attendance: 110. "We offer genre-based workshops in fiction, poetry, and playwriting. The Sewanee Writers' Conference uses the facilities of the University of the South. Physically, the University is a collection of ivy-covered Gothic-style buildings, located on the Cumberland Plateau in mid-Tennessee. We allow invited editors, publishers, and agents to structure their own presentations, but there is always opportunity for questions from the audience." The 1999 faculty included Rachel Hadas, Barry Hannah, Robert Hass, Amy Hempel, John Hollander, Andrew Hudgins, Charles Johnson, Diane Johnson, Romulus Linney, Margot Livesey, Alice McDermott, Rick Moody, Marsha Norman and Padgett Powell.

Costs: Full conference fee (tuition, board, and basic room) is $1,200; a single room costs an additional $50.

Accommodations: Complimentary chartered bus service is available, on a limited basis, on the first and last days of the conference. Participants are housed in University dormitory rooms. Motel or B&B housing is available but not abundantly so. Dormitory housing costs are included in the full conference fee.

Additional Information: "We offer each participant (excluding auditors) the opportunity for a private manuscript conference with a member of the faculty. These manuscripts are due one month before the conference begins." Conference brochures/guidelines are available after February, "but no SASE is necessary. The conference has available a limited number of fellowships and scholarships; these are awarded on a competitive basis." Inquiries by e-mail OK.

✔ **THE WRITERS' WORKSHOP**, 387 Beaucatcher Rd., Asheville NC 28805. (828)254-8111. Executive Director: Karen Tager. Estab. 1984. Held throughout the year. Conference duration: 1-3 days. Sites are throughout the South, especially North Carolina. Past guest speakers include John Le Carré, Peter Matthiessen and Eudora Welty.

Costs: Vary. Financial assistance available to low-income writers. Information on overnight accommodations is made available.

Southeast (AL, AR, FL, GA, LA, MS, PR [Puerto Rico])

N **ALABAMA WRITERS' CONCLAVE**, P.O. Box 230787, Montgomery AL 36123-0787. (334)244-8920. Fax: (334)387-9123. E-mail: poettennis@aol.com. Editor: D.J. Tennis. President: Kay Blankenship. Estab. 1923. Annual. Conference held for three days, the first week in August. Average attendance: 75-100. Conference to promote "all phases" of writing. Held at the Ramsay Conference Center (University of Montevallo). "We attempt to contain all workshops under this roof."

Costs: Fees for 3 days are $45 for members; $55 for nonmembers (which includes membership). Lower rates for 1- or 2-day attendence. Meals and awards banquet additional cost.

Accommodations: Accommodations available on campus. $18 for single, $36 for double.

Additional Information: "We have 'name' speakers and workshops with members helping members. We offer open mike readings every evening. We sponsor a contest each year with a published book of winners." Sponsors a contest. Conference brochures/guidelines available for SASE after June. Inquiries by fax and e-mail OK. Membership dues are $15 and include a quarterly newsletter. Membership information from Donna Jean Tennis at above address.

ARKANSAS WRITERS' CONFERENCE, 6817 Gingerbread, Little Rock AR 72204. (501)565-8889. Fax: (501)565-7220. E-mail: pvining@aristotle.net. Counselor: Peggy Vining. Estab. 1944. Annual. Conference held first weekend in June. Average attendance: 225. "We have a variety of subjects related to writing—we have some general sessions, some more specific, but try to vary each year's subjects."

Costs: Registration: $10; luncheon: $15; banquet: $17.50, contest entry $5.

Accommodations: "We meet at a Holiday Inn Select—rooms available at reasonable rate." Holiday Inn has a bus to bring anyone from airport. Rooms average $64.

Additional Information: "We have 36 contest categories. Some are open only to Arkansans, most are open to all writers. Our judges are not announced before conference but are qualified, many from out of state." Conference brochures are available for SASE after February 1. "We have had 226 attending from 12 states— over 3,000 contest entries from 43 states and New Zealand, Mexico and Canada. We have a get acquainted party Thursday evening for early arrivers."

insider report

The Sewanee Writers' Conference is looking for genius

Genius is the primary criteria for evaluating the hundreds of applications submitted to Sewanee Writers' Conference Director Wyatt Prunty who has been director since its first year in 1990. "It's a read-off, basically, for the strength of the application."

The Sewanee Writers' Conference, which takes place at The University of the South deep in the mountains of southern Tennessee each summer, has grown both in size and in reputation since it began. In 1999, over 1,300 applications were requested, and just under 600 were submitted to the conference, which admits roughly 110 writers each year. "The maximum application requests we had was 1,400 the year Derek Walcott was on staff," Prunty says. "We had already invited him, and then he won the Nobel Prize. But the fall-off rate is similar to what you get with

Wyatt Prunty

college applications—if a thousand people write for your applications, four hundred will actually apply, or around forty percent. We don't have that many applications this year, but the applications are much more savvy."

When the mounds of applications begin piling in the Sewanee offices in early spring, they are sent to readers—two for fiction, two for poetry, and one for playwriting—who evaluate the manuscripts. And although factors like letters of recommendation and the applicant's self-evaluation essay are taken into consideration, it's the strength of the applicant's writing that matters most. But even that, says Prunty, can be judged differently from year to year.

"What is looked for shifts slightly as the readers change," says Prunty. "And what determines who applies more than anything else is the faculty. You'll get some people who are interested in working with Anthony Hecht and have a certain aesthetic, and you'll have some people who want to work with Tim O'Brien and have a certain aesthetic." And so while the readers keep these factors in mind, the overall consideration, says Prunty, is "genius."

Sewanee receives more applications in fiction than in its other genres; because of this demand, the conference expanded from only two fiction workshops to four, while it holds at two for poetry and one for playwriting. "There's a space cap right now," Prunty says. "If we expand too much we'll take a good thing and create a crowding problem, and then you get the kind of edginess that happens when you take adults from established lives and put them into an undergraduate housing situation. They may be good campers and get along, but that's not the way you ought to treat them. If you really admire their work, you really ought to give them a little space. We really try to take care of people, feed them well, house them appropriately, and just make sure they know we're looking after them."

While maintaining its comfortable size, the conference manages to cram a dizzying number of activities into its two-week duration. Prunty says applicants should not apply solely to work

Photo © Miriam Berkley

with one faculty member, but to immerse themselves in all the conference has to offer. "You're not going there just to be with one person. You're going there for all the panel discussions, all the readings, all the lectures, all the guest writers who give readings, all the little social events that are there to make it easier for people to get to know each other. You wind up at meals seated beside a person you might not feel like walking up and introducing yourself to, but you might wind up talking over dinner. Food relaxes people; it makes them chat."

Other than possessing writing genius, what can writers do to make their applications more attractive to Sewanee's readers? "It all falls back to having good material, having something ready," Prunty says. "You might not be ready the first year you apply, but maybe you're ready the third year. The applications tend to be very competitive."

Once writers have been accepted to the conference, they have a lot to look forward to. "We just have so many things packed in, it's totally unrealistic to expect everybody to attend everything," Prunty says. Workshop attendance every other day is a given, as well as the evening readings by faculty and guests. In between are panel discussions and lectures by editors, agents and other writers—not to mention afternoon readings, receptions and meals. With so much going on, Prunty says, "sleep deficit can be a problem."

But the two weeks of sleep deprivation can have a big payoff. Through their contact with agents and editors at the conference, many writers are able to break into magazine publishing or have their manuscript read by an agent. In fact, the newsletter published each year has grown steadily fatter with the achievements of conference alumni.

"We have a lot more success than anybody at helping people get things first into magazines and then with publishers," Prunty says. "We've done particularly well helping poets get into magazines, and we've done pretty well getting fiction writers published. Bringing in editors does not lead to publication for fiction writers, but it may lead to wisdom. I do think bringing in agents helps. And the periodical editors can help fiction writers, putting them in touch with job contacts. We also get plays produced. That's fairly significant, too."

All this in addition to two weeks of workshop, an hour-long individual conference with a faculty member, and the opportunity to meet and learn from some of the best writers in the country. The list of fiction faculty from 1999 included Barry Hannah, Amy Hempel, Charles Johnson, Diane Johnson, Margot Livesey, 1999 National Book Award winner Alice McDermott, Rick Moody and Padgett Powell.

And there is one more thing, Prunty says, that conferees can expect from their Sewanee experience. "You can expect to meet like-minded souls who really are promising people of some ability, and you can carry a lot of that away in terms of friendships. Writers are a minority in this country, and they do tend to stay in touch. So it's a good splice into that world."

—*Juliana Gray Vice*

FLORIDA CHRISTIAN WRITERS CONFERENCE, 2600 Park Ave., Titusville FL 32780. (407)269-6702, ext. 202. Fax: (407)383-1741. E-mail: writer@digital.net. Website: www.kipertek.com/writer. Conference Director: Billie Wilson. Estab. 1988. Annual. Conference is held in late January. Conference duration: 5 days. Average attendance: 200. To promote "all areas of writing." Conference held at Park Avenue Retreat Center, a conference complex at a large church near Kennedy Space Center. Editors will represent over 30 publications and publishing houses.
Costs: Tuition $360, included tuition, room and board (double occupancy).
Accommodations: "We provide shuttle from the airport and from the hotel to retreat center. We make reservations at major hotel chain."
Additional Information: Critiques available. "Each writer may submit three works for critique. We have specialists in every area of writing to critique." Conference brochures/guidelines are available for SASE.

☑ **FLORIDA FIRST COAST WRITERS' FESTIVAL**, 101 W. State St., FCCJ Downtown Campus, Jacksonville FL 32202. (904)633-8327. Fax: (904)633-8435. E-mail: kclower@fccj.org. Website: www.fccj.org/wf/. Budget administrator: Kathy Clower. Estab. 1985. Annual. 2000 Festival: May 18-20. Average attendance: 300-350. All areas: mainstream plus genre. Held at Sea Turtle Inn on Atlantic Beach.
Costs: "Early bird special $145 for 2 days (including lunch) or $75 for each day; pre-conference workshops and banquet extra."
Accommodations: Sea Turtle Inn, (904)249-7402 or (800)874-6000, has a special festival rate.
Additional Information: Conference brochures/contest guidelines are available. Inquiries by e-mail and fax OK. Sponsors contests for short fiction, poetry and novels. Novel judges are David Poyer and Lenore Hart. Entry fees: $30, novels; $10, short fiction; $5, poetry. Deadline: November 1 for novels, short fiction, poems. E-mail contest inquiries to hdenson@fccj.org.

☑ **FLORIDA SUNCOAST WRITERS' CONFERENCE**, University of South Florida, Division of Lifelong Learning, 4202 E. Fowler Ave., MHH116, Tampa FL 33620-6610. (813)974-2403. Fax: (813)974-5732. E-mail: kiersty@admin.usf.edu. Website: www.contest.usf.edu/sce/lll/flcenter.htm. Directors: Steve Rubin, Ed Hirshberg, Betty Moss and Lagretta Lenker. Estab. 1970. Annual. Held February 3-5, 2000. Conference duration: 3 days. Average attendance: 350-400. Conference covers poetry, short story, novel and nonfiction, including science fiction, detective, travel writing, drama, TV scripts, photojournalism and juvenile. "We do not focus on any one particular aspect of the writing profession but instead offer a variety of writing related topics including marketing. The conference is held on the picturesque university campus fronting the bay in St. Petersburg, Florida." Features panels with agents and editors. Guest speakers have included Lady P.D. James, Carolyn Forche, Marge Piercy, William Styron, David Guterson, John Updike and Joyce Carol Oates.
Costs: Call for verification.
Accommodations: Special rates available at area hotels. "All information is contained in our brochure."
Additional Information: Participants may submit work for critiquing. Extra fee charged for this service. Conference brochures/guidelines are available in October. Inquiries by e-mail and fax OK.

Ⓝ **HAMBIDGE CENTER**, P.O. Box 339, Rabun Gap GA 30552. (706)746-5718. (706)746-9933. E-mail: hambidge@rabun.net. Website: www.rabun.net/~Hambidge. Contact: Bob Thomas. Estab. 1934. Workshops held year round. Application deadlines: May 1 for November-April sessions; November 1 for May-October sessions. Residencies are from 2 weeks-2 months. Average attendance: 8 residents. "Creative artists in all disciplines use uninterrupted time to create (writers included!)." Facility is located on "600 acres in north Georgia mountains. Rural, beautiful, private and semi-private cottage/studios. Dinner served May-October. On National Register of Historic Places."
Costs: $25/week.
Accommodations: "Artists stay in one of eight residence cottage-studios. Each living area is private and equipped with kitchen and bath facilities."
Additional Information: "Must submit an application ($20 application fee) and samples of work. Work is reviewed by a panel of professionals in each field." Workshop brochures/guidelines available for SASE upon request. Inquires by e-mail OK, but snail mail preferred.

Ⓝ **HOW TO BE PUBLISHED WORKSHOPS**, P.O. Box 100031, Birmingham AL 35210. (205)907-0140. E-mail: mgteach@earthlink.net. Website: home.earthlink.net/~mgteach. Contact: Michael Garrett. Estab. 1986. Workshops held "numerous times" during the year. Workshop duration: 1 day. Average attendance: 10-15. Workshop to "move writers of category fiction closer to publication." Workshop held at college campuses and universities. Themes include "Marketing," "Idea Development" and a manuscript critique.
Costs: "Price varies from school to school."
Additional Information: "Special critique is offered, but advance submission is not required." Brochures/guidelines available. Inquiries by e-mail OK.

Ⓝ **NEW ORLEANS POPULAR FICTION CONFERENCE**, P.O. Box 740113, New Orleans LA 70174-0113. (504)391-1320. E-mail: kathlisn@aol.com. Website: www.sola.org. Contact: Kathleen Nance. Estab. 1994. Annual. Conference held November, 2000. Conference lasts 2 days. Average attendance: 135. Conference for working writers of popular fiction held in downtown New Orleans hotel. 1999 speakers included Debbie Macomber and panels of editors and agents.
Costs: $155/2 days; includes 2 lunches and opening reception.
Accommodations: "We work with a travel agent to assist attendees in finding accommodations that meet their needs."
Additional Information: Sponsors a contest for popular fiction. Judged on first 5 pages by published authors, editors and agents. Conference brochure/guidelines available in summer. "We're a conference for writers of popular fiction-both unpublished and published."

Ⓝ **MARJORIE KINNAN RAWLINGS: WRITING THE REGION**, P.O. Box 12246, Gainesville FL 32604. (888)917-7001. Fax: (352)373-8854. E-mail: shakes@ufl.edu. Website: www.afn.org/~gaca/writers/writer

s.html. Contact: Norma M. Homan. Estab. 1997. Annual conference held in July/August 2000. Conference duration: 5 days. Average attendance: 100. Conference concentrates on fiction, writing for children, poetry, nonfiction, drama, screenwriting, writing with humor, setting, character, etc. Conference held at historic building, formerly the Thomas Hotel. 1999 panels included "Writing Children's Books"; "How Should I Tell My Life Story?"; "Character Development in the Novel"; "Freelancing with Magazines"; "Writing Historical Fiction." 1999 speakers included Marilyn Maple, Bill Maxwell, Walda Metcalf, Shelley Fraser Mickle, Robert Norman and Deborah Savage.

Costs: $355 for 5 days including meals; $325 "early bird" registration; $125 single day; $75 half day.

Accommodations: Special conference rates at area hotels available.

Additional Information: Manuscript consultation on an individual basis by application only and $100 additional fee. Sponsors essay contest for registrants on a topic dealing with Marjorie Kinnan Rawlings. Brochures/ guidelines available for SASE. Inquiries by fax and e-mail OK.

SCBWI/FLORIDA ANNUAL FALL CONFERENCE, 2158 Portland Ave., Wellington FL 33414. (561)798-4824. E-mail: barcafer@aol.com. Florida Regional Advisor: Barbara Casey. Estab. 1985. Annual. Conference held in September. Conference duration: one-half day. Average attendance: 70. Conference to promote "all aspects of writing and illustrating for children. The facilities include the meeting rooms of the Library and Town Hall of Palm Springs FL (near West Palm Beach)."

Costs: $50 for SCBWI members, $55 for non-SCBWI members. Ms and art evaluations, $30.

Accommodations: Special conference rates at Airport Hilton, West Palm Beach, Florida.

Additional Information: Conference brochures/guidelines are available in July for SASE. Inquiries by e-mail OK.

[N] WRITE IT OUT, P.O. Box 704, Sarasota FL 34230-0704. (941)359-3824. Fax: (941)359-3931. E-mail: rmillerwio@aol.com. Website: members.aol.com/rmillerwio/wiohome.html/. Contact: Ronni Miller. Estab. 1997. Workshops held 2-3 times/year in April, June and August, 2000. Duration: 5-10 days. Average attendance: 4-10. Workshops on "fiction, travel writing, poetry, memoirs." The workshops are held in Italy in a Tuscan villa, in Bermuda at a hotel or in Cape Cod at an inn. Theme: "Landscape—Horizon." 1999 speakers included Arturo Vivante, novelist.

Costs: 1999 fees: Italy $1,995; Bermuda $895; Cape Cod $595. Price includes tuition, room and board. Airfare not included.

Additional Information: "Critiques on work are given at the workshops." Brochures/guidelines for SASE. Inquiries by fax and e-mail OK. Workshops have "small groups, option to spend time writing and not attend classes with personal appointments made with instructors for feedback."

WRITING STRATEGIES FOR THE CHRISTIAN MARKET, 2712 S. Peninsula Dr., Daytona Beach FL 32118-5706. (904)322-1111. Fax: (904)322-1111*9. E-mail: romy14@juno.com. Website: www.amazon.com. Instructor: Rosemary Upton. Estab. 1991. Seminars given approximately 2 times a year. Conference duration: 3 hours. Average attendance: 10-20. Seminars include Basics I, Marketing II, Business III, Building the novel. Held in a conference room: instructor teaches from a podium. Question and answer session provided. Critique shop included once a month, except summer (July and August). Instructors include Rosemary Upton, novelist; Kistler London, editor. Write, phone, fax or e-mail to receive a writing strategies newsletter and brochure.

Costs: $30 for each 3-hour seminar.

Additional Information: "Designed for correspondence students as well as the classroom experience, the courses are economical and include all materials, as well as the evaluation of assignments." Those who have taken Writing Strategies instruction are able to attend an on-going monthly critiqueshop where their peers critique their work. Manual provided with each seminar. Conference brochures/guidelines are available for SASE. Inquiries by fax and e-mail OK. Independent study by mail also available.

[✓] WRITING TODAY—BIRMINGHAM-SOUTHERN COLLEGE, Box 549003, Birmingham AL 35254. (205)226-4921. Fax: (205)226-3072. E-mail: dcwilson@bsc.edu. Website: www.bsc.edu. Director of Special Events: Martha Ross. Estab. 1978. Annual. Conference held April 7-8, 2000. Average attendance: 400-500. "This is a two-day conference with approximately 18 workshops, lectures and readings. We try to offer workshops in short fiction, novels, poetry, children's literature, magazine writing, and general information of concern to aspiring writers such as publishing, agents, markets and research. The conference is sponsored by Birmingham-Southern College and is held on the campus in classrooms and lecture halls." The 1999 conference featured Pat Conroy, Richard North Patterson, Connie May Fowler and David Sedaris.

Costs: $120 for both days. This includes lunches, reception and morning coffee and rolls.

Accommodations: Attendees must arrange own transportation. Local hotels and motels offer special rates, but participants must make their own reservations.

Additional Information: "We usually offer a critique for interested writers. We have had poetry and short story critiques. There is an additional charge for these critiques." Sponsors the Hackney Literary Competition Awards for poetry, short story and novels. Guidelines available for SASE.

Midwest (IL, IN, KY, MI, OH)

ANTIOCH WRITERS' WORKSHOP, P.O. Box 494, Yellow Springs OH 45387. E-mail: info@antiochwriter sworkshop.com. Website: www.antiochwritersworkshop.com. Estab. 1984. Annual. Conference held from August 5-12. Average attendance: 80. Workshop concentration: poetry, nonfiction and fiction. Workshop located on Antioch College campus in the Village of Yellow Springs. Speakers have included Sue Grafton, Imogene Bolls, George Ella Lyon, Herbert Martin, John Jakes, Virginia Hamilton and Natalie Goldberg.
Costs: Tuition is $485—lower for local and repeat—plus meals.
Accommodations: "We pick up attendees free at the airport." Accommodations made at dorms and area hotels. Cost is $16-26/night (for dorms).
Additional Information: Offers mss critique sessions. Conference brochures/guidelines are available after March 2000.

THE COLUMBUS WRITERS CONFERENCE, P.O. Box 20548, Columbus OH 43220. (614)451-3075. Fax: (614)451-0174. E-mail: AngelaPL28@aol.com. Director: Angela Palazzolo. Estab. 1993. Annual. Confer-ence held in September. Average attendance: 200. "The conference covers a wide variety of fiction and nonfiction topics. Writing topics have included novel, short story, children's, young adult, poetry, historical fiction, science fiction, fantasy, humor, mystery, playwriting, screenwriting, travel, humor, cookbook, technical, queries, book proposals and freelance writing. Other topics have included finding and working with an agent, targeting markets, time management, obtaining grants, sparking creativity and networking." Speakers have included Lee K. Abbott, Lore Segal, Jack Matthews, Mike Harden, Oscar Collier, Maureen F. McHugh, Ralph Keyes, Stephanie S. Tolan, J. Patrick Lewis, Tracey E. Dils, Dennis L. McKiernan, Karen Harper, Melvin Helitzer, Susan Porter, Les Roberts, Tracey E. Dils, J. Patrick Lewis and many other professionals in the writing field.
Costs: Early registration fee is $134 for the full conference (Friday afternoon sessions, dinner, and Saturday program); otherwise fee is $150. Early registration for the Saturday program (includes continental breakfast, lunch, and afternoon refreshments) is $94; otherwise fee is $110.
Additional Information: Call, write, e-mail or send fax to obtain a conference brochure, available mid-summer.

GREEN RIVER WRITERS NOVELS-IN-PROGRESS WORKSHOP, 11906 Locust Rd., Middletown KY 40243-1413. (502)245-4902. E-mail: mary_odell@ntr.net. Director: Mary E. O'Dell. Estab. 1991. Annual. Con-ference held March 12-19, 2000. Conference duration: 1 week. Average attendance: 50. Open to persons, college age and above, who have approximately 3 chapters (60 pages) or more of a novel. Mainstream and genre novels handled by individual instructors. Short fiction collections welcome. "Each novelist instructor works with a small group (5-7 people) for five days; then agents/editors are there for panels and appointments on the weekend." Site is The University of Louisville's Shelby Campus, suburban setting, graduate dorm housing (private rooms available with shared bath for each 2 rooms). "Meetings and classes held in nearby classroom building. Grounds available for walking, etc. Lovely setting, restaurants and shopping available nearby. Participants carpool to restaurants, etc. This year we are covering mystery, fantasy, mainstream/literary, suspense, historical."
Costs: Tuition—$375, housing $22 per night private, $18 shared. Does not include meals.
Accommodations: "We do meet participants' planes and see that participants without cars have transportation to meals, etc. If participants would rather stay in hotel, we will make that information available."
Additional Information: Participants send 60 pages/3 chapters with synopsis and $25 reading fee which applies to tuition. Deadline will be in late January. Conference brochures/guidelines are available after January 1 for SASE. Inquiries by e-mail OK.

THE HEIGHTS WRITER'S CONFERENCE, 35 N. Chillicothe Rd., Suite D, Aurora OH 44202-8741. Fax: (330)562-1217. E-mail: writersword@juno.com. Director: Lavern Hall. Estab. 1992. Annual. Conference held first Saturday in May. Average attendance: 125. "Fiction, nonfiction, science fiction, poetry, children's, marketing, etc." The conference is sponsored by Writer's World Press and held at the Cleveland Marriott East, Beachwood OH. Offers seminars on the craft, business and legal aspects of writing plus 2 teaching, hands-on workshops. "No theme; published authors and experts in their field sharing their secrets and networking for success."
Additional Information: Conference brochure available March 1 for SASE. Inquiries by e-mail and fax OK.

✔ **IMAGINATION**, Cleveland State University, Division of Continuing Education, 2344 Euclid Ave., Cleve-land OH 44115. (216)687-4522. Director: Dan Chaon. Estab. 1990. Annual. Conference lasts 5 days and is held June 27-July 2, 2000. Average attendance: 60. "Conference concentrates on fiction, poetry and nonfiction. Held at Mather Mansion, a restored 19th Century Mansion on the campus of Cleveland State University." Past themes have included Writing Beyond Realism and Business of Writing. E-mail, fax or mail for brochure after January 2000.

✔ **INDIANA UNIVERSITY WRITERS' CONFERENCE**, 464 Ballantine Hall, Bloomington IN 47405. (812)855-1877. Fax: (812)855-9535. Managing Director: Romayne Rubinas. Estab. 1940. Annual. Conference/ workshops held from June 25-30. Average attendance: 100. "Conference to promote poetry, fiction and nonfiction (emphasis on poetry and fiction)." Located on the campus of Indiana University, Bloomington. "We do not have themes, although we do have panels that discuss issues such as how to publish. We also have classes that tackle just about every subject of writing. Rodney Jones, Mary Jo Salter, Allison Joseph, Brad Leithauser and Jessie Lee Kerchival spoke and taught workshops at the 1999 conference.

Costs: Approximately $300; does not include food or housing. This price does *not* reflect the cost of taking the conference for credit. "We supply conferees with options for overnight accommodations. We offer special conference rates for both the hotel and dorm facilities on site.

Additional Information: "In order to be accepted in a workshop, the writer must submit the work they would like critiqued. Work is evaluated before accepting applicant. Scholarships are available determined by an outside reader/writer, based on the quality of the manuscript." Conference brochures/guidelines available for SASE in February. Application deadline is in early May. Apply early as workshops fill up quickly. "We are the second oldest writer's conference in the country. We are in our 60th year."

N IRWA WRITER WORKSHOP, P.O. Box 36340, Indianapolis IN 46236-0340. (317)894-1853. Fax: (317)891-9938. Website: www.irwa.hypermart.com. Contact: Peggy Emard. Estab. 1994. Biannual. Workshop held in spring and fall. Duration: 1 day. Average attendance: 50. Workshop on "romantic fiction." 1999 panels included plot, characters and professional development. 1998 panels included character-based vs. plot-based fiction. 1999 speakers included Alicia Rasley and Susan Wiggs. 1998 speakers included Kathleen Eagle and Jennifer Crusie.

Costs: $50.

Accommodations: "All registered attendees receive hotel information, pre-conference welcome party and door prizes. Special conference hotel rates are usually less than $75."

Additional information: Conference brochures/guidelines for SASE four months prior to workshop. Inquiries by fax and e-mail OK. "These are hands-on, interactive workshops; come prepared to write. Most speakers are award-winning romance novelists with a professional teaching background."

THE MID AMERICA MYSTERY CONFERENCE, Magna cum Murder, The E.B. Ball Center, Ball State University, Muncie IN 47306. (765)285-8975. Fax: (765)747-9566. E-mail: kkenniso@wp.bsu.edu. Estab. 1994. Annual. Conference held from October 29-31. Average attendance: 400. Conference for crime and detective fiction held in the Horizon Convention Center and Historic Radisson Hotel Roberts. Past speakers included Mickey Spillane, Anne Perry, Jeremiah Healy, John Gilstrap and Tess Gerritsen.

Costs: $165, which includes continental breakfasts, boxed lunches, a reception and a banquet (1997).

Additional Information: Brochures or guidelines available for SASE. Inquiries by fax and e-mail OK.

N MIDLAND WRITERS CONFERENCE, Grace A. Dow Memorial Library, 1710 W. St. Andrews, Midland MI 48640-2698. (517)835-7151. Fax: (517)835-9791. E-mail: kred@vlc.lib.mi.us. Website: www.gracedowli brary.org. Conference Chair: Katherine Redwine. Estab. 1980. Annual. Conference held June 10, 2000. Average attendance: 100. "The Conference is composed of a well-known keynote speaker and workshops on a variety of subjects including poetry, children's writing, freelancing, agents, etc. The attendees are both published and unpublished authors. The Conference is held at the Grace A. Dow Memorial Library in the auditorium and conference rooms. Keynoters in the past have included Dave Barry, Pat Conroy, Kurt Vonnegut, Peggy Noonan, Roger Ebert."

Costs: Adult—$50 before May 26, $60 after May 27; students, senior citizens and handicapped—$40 before May 26, $50 after May 26. A box lunch is available. Costs are approximate until plans for upcoming conference are finalized.

Accommodations: A list of area hotels is available.

Additional Information: Conference brochures/guidelines are mailed mid-April. Call or write to be put on mailing list. Inquiries by e-mail and fax OK.

N MIDWEST WRITERS' CONFERENCE, 6000 Frank Ave. NW, Canton OH 44720-7599. (216)499-9600. Fax: (330)494-6121. E-mail: Druhe@Stark.Kent.Edu. Conference Director: Debbie Ruhe. Estab. 1968. Annual. Conference held in early October. Conference duration: 2 days. Average attendance: 350. "The conference provides an atmosphere in which aspiring writers can meet with and learn from experienced and established writers through lectures, workshops, competitive contest, personal interviews and informal group discussions. The areas of concentration include fiction, nonfiction, juvenile literature and poetry. The Midwest Writers' Conference is held on Kent State University Stark Campus in Canton, Ohio. This two-day conference is held in Main Hall, a four-story building and wheel chair accessible."

Costs: $125 includes Friday workshops, keynote address, Saturday workshops, box luncheon and manuscript entry fee (limited to two submissions); $70 for contest only (includes two manuscripts).

Accommodations: Arrangements are made with a local hotel which is near Kent Stark and offers a special reduced rate for conference attendees. Conferees must make their own reservations 3 weeks before the conference to be guaranteed this special conference rate.

Additional Information: Each manuscript entered in the contest will receive a critique. If the manuscript is selected for final judging, it will receive an additional critique from the final judge. Conference attendees are not required to submit manuscripts to the writing contest. Manuscript deadline is early August. For contest: A maximum of 1 entry for each category is permitted. Entries must be typed on 8½ × 11 paper, double-spaced. A separate page must accompany each entry bearing the author's name, address, phone, category and title of the work. Entries are not to exceed 3,000 words in length. Work must be original, unpublished and not a winner in any contest at the time of entry. Conference brochures and guidelines are available after June 2000 for SASE. Inquiries by e-mail and fax OK.

N MIDWEST WRITERS WORKSHOP, Dept. of Journalism, Ball State University, Muncie IN 47306. (765)285-5587. Fax: (765)285-5997. E-mail: econn@fsu.edu. Website: members.aol.com/midww/mww.html. Co-Director: Earl L. Conn. Estab. 1974. Annual. Workshop to be held July 26-29, 2000. Average attendance: 130. For fiction, nonfiction, poetry. Conference held at Hotel Roberts in downtown Muncie.

Costs: In 1999, cost was $205 including opening reception, hospitality room and closing banquet.

Accommodations: Special hotel rates offered.

Additional Information: Critiques available. $20 for individual critiquing. Conference brochures/guidelines are available for SASE.

N THE MINISTRY OF WRITING: AN ANNUAL COLLOQUIM, Earlham School of Religion, 228 College, Richmond IN 47374. (800)432-1377. E-mail: billbr@earlham.edu. Website: www.earlham.edu/esr. Contact: J. Brent Bill. Estab. 1992. Annual conference held October 27-28, 2000. Conference duration: 1½ days. Average attendance: 175. Conference "to encourage writers to see writing as ministry. Workshops are held on poetry, essay, marketing, etc. Varies from year to year." Held on the campus of Earlham School of Religion in Richmond, IN—using classrooms, worship spaces, etc. 1999 conference featured C. Michael Curtis, editor of the *Atlantic Monthly*, addressing themes of faith and fiction. Speakers included Mary Brown (poetry), Will Campbell (keynoter; story); Holly Miller (marketing); Larry Ingle (history); Jay Marshall (publishing); Peter Anderson (contemplative writing); Barbara Bennett Mays (editing).

Costs: $50 for entire conference (including meals); $45 for Saturday only; $20 student fee (graduate/undergrad).

Accommodations: List of hotels available.

Additional Information: Conference brochures/guidelines available for SASE after August 1999. Inquiries by e-mail OK.

MISSISSIPPI VALLEY WRITERS CONFERENCE, 3403 45th St., Moline IL 61265. (309)762-8985. E-mail: kimseuss@aol.com. Conference Founder/Director: David R. Collins. Estab. 1973. Annual. Conference held June 5-10, 2000. Average attendance: 80. "Conference for all areas of writing for publication." Conference held at Augustana College, a liberal arts school along the Mississippi River. 2000 workshop leaders will be bj elsner, Mel Boring, Max Collins, H.E. Francis, Bess Pierce, Karl Largent, Roald Tweet amd Rich Johnson.

Costs: $25 for registration; $50 for 1 workshop; $90 for two; plus $40 for each additional workshops; $25 to audit.

Accommodations: On-campus facitilites available. Accommodations are available at Erickson Hall on the Augustana College campus. Cost for 6 nights is $100; cost for 15 meals is $100.

Additional Information: Conferees may submit mss to workshop leaders for personal conferences during the week. Cash awards are given at the end of the conference week by workshop leaders based on mss submitted. Conference brochures/guidelines are available for SASE. "Conference is open to the beginner as well as the polished professional—all are welcome."

OAKLAND UNIVERSITY WRITERS' CONFERENCE, 231 Varner Hall, Rochester MI 48309-4401. (248)370-4386. Fax: (248)370-4280. E-mail: gjboddy@oakland.edu. Program Director: Gloria J. Boddy. Estab. 1961. Annual. Conference held in October. Average attendance: 400. Held at Oakland University: Oakland Center: Vandenburg Hall and O'Dowd Hall. Each annual conference covers all aspects and types of writing in 36 concurrent workshops on Saturday. Major writers from various genres are speakers for the Saturday conference and luncheon program. Individual critiques and hands-on writing workshops are conducted Friday. Areas: poetry, articles, fiction, short stories, playwriting, nonfiction, young adult, children's literature. Keynote speaker in 1999: Judith Guest.

Costs: 1999: Conference registration: $75; lunch, $12; individual ms, $48; writing workshop, $38.

Accommodations: List is available.

Additional Information: Conference brochure/guidelines available after August 2000 for SASE. Inquiries by e-mail and fax OK.

OF DARK & STORMY NIGHTS, Mystery Writers of America—Midwest Chapter, P.O. Box 1944, Muncie IN 47308-1944. (765)288-7402. E-mail: spurgeonmwa@juno.com. Workshop Director: W.W. Spurgeon.

Estab. 1982. Annual. Workshop held June 10. Workshop duration: 1 day. Average attendance: 200. Dedicated to "writing *mystery* fiction and crime-related nonfiction. Workshops and panels presented on techniques of mystery writing from ideas to revision, marketing, investigative techniques and more, by published writers, law enforcement experts and publishing professionals." Site is Holiday Inn, Rolling Meadows IL (suburban Chicago).
Costs: $125 for MWA members; $150 for non-members; $50 extra for ms critique.
Accommodations: Easily accessible by car or train (from Chicago) Holiday Inn, Rolling Meadows $89 per night plus tax; free airport bus (Chicago O'Hare) and previously arranged rides from train.
Additional Information: "We accept manuscripts for critique (first 30 pages maximum); $50 cost. Writers meet with critics during workshop for one-on-one discussions." Brochures available for SASE after February 1. Inquiries by e-mail OK.

ROPEWALK WRITERS' RETREAT, 8600 University Blvd., Evansville IN 47712. (812)464-1863. E-mail: lcleek.ucs@smtp.usi.edu. Conference Coordinator: Linda Cleek. Estab. 1989. Annual. Conference held in June. Average attendance: 42. "The week-long RopeWalk Writers' Retreat gives participants an opportunity to attend workshops and to confer privately with one of four or five prominent writers. Historic New Harmony, Indiana, site of two nineteenth century utopian experiments, provides an ideal setting for this event with its retreat-like atmosphere and its history of creative and intellectual achievement. At RopeWalk you will be encouraged to write—not simply listen to others talks about writing. Each workshop will be limited to twelve participants. The New Harmony Inn and Conference Center will be headquarters for the RopeWalk Writers' Retreat. Please note that reservations at the Inn should be confirmed by May 1." 1999 faculty Lynn Emanuel, Rodney Jones, Scott Sanders, Sigrid Nunez and Lucie Brock-Broido.
Costs: $425 (1999), includes breakfasts and lunches.
Accommodations: Information on overnight accommodations is made available. "Room-sharing assistance; some low-cost accommodations."
Additional Information: For critiques submit mss approx. 6 weeks ahead. Brochures are available after January 15.

SELF PUBLISHING YOUR OWN BOOK, 34200 Ridge Rd., #110, Willoughby OH 44094-2954. (440)943-3047 or (800)653-4261. E-mail address: fa837@cleveland.freenet.edu. Teacher: Lea Leever Oldham. Estab. 1989. Quarterly. Conferences usually held in February, April, August and October. Conference duration: 2½ hours. Average attendance: up to 25. Conference covers copyrighting, marketing, pricing, ISBN number, Library of Congress catalog number, reaching the right customers and picking a printer. Held at Lakeland Community College, Kirtland, OH (east of Cleveland off I-90) and other locations. Classrooms are wheelchair accessible.
Additional Information: Conference guidelines are available for SASE. Inquiries by e-mail OK.

WESTERN RESERVE WRITERS & FREELANCE CONFERENCE, 34200 Ridge Rd., #110, Willoughby OH 44094. (440)943-3047 or (800)653-4261. E-mail address: fa837@cleveland.freenet.edu. Coordinator: Lea Leever Oldham. Estab. 1984. Annual. Conference held every September. Conference duration: 1 day. Average attendance: 150. "Fiction, nonfiction, inspirational, children's, poetry, humor, scifi, copyright and tax information, etc." Held "at Lakeland Community College, Kirtland, OH. Classrooms wheelchair accessible. Accessible from I-90, east of Cleveland." Panels include "no themes, simply published authors and other experts sharing their secrets."
Costs: $59 including lunch.
Additional Information: Conference brochures/guidelines are available after July for SASE. Inquiries by e-mail OK.

WESTERN RESERVE WRITERS MINI CONFERENCE, 34200 Ridge Rd., #110, Willoughby OH 44094. (440)943-3047 or (800)653-4261. E-mail address: fa837@cleveland.freenet.edu. Coordinator: Lea Leever Oldham. Estab. 1991. Annual. Conference held in late March. Conference duration: ½ day. Average attendance: 175. Conference to promote "fiction, nonfiction, children's, poetry, science fiction, etc." Held at Lakeland Community College, Kirtland, OH (east of Cleveland off I-90). Classrooms are wheelchair accessible. "Conference is for beginners, intermediate and advanced writers." Past speakers have included Mary Grimm, Nick Bade, James Martin and Mary Ryan.
Costs: $39.
Additional Information: Conference brochures/guidelines are available after January 1999 for SASE. Inquiries by e-mail OK.

N WRITE-TO-PUBLISH CONFERENCE, 9731 N Fox Glen Dr. #6F, Niles IL 60714-5861. (847)296-3964. Fax: (847)296-0754. E-mail: linjohnson@compuserve.com. Contact: Lin Johnson. Estab. 1971. Annual. Conference held from June 7-10, 2000. Average attendance: 150. Conference on "writing all types of manuscripts for the Christian market." Held at Wheaton College (Chicago area). Novelist Jack Cavanaugh is scheduled to speak at next conference.
Costs: $325.

Accommodations: Shuttle service provided. Accommodations in campus residence halls or discounted hotel rates. Costs $180-$320.

Additional Information: Optional critiquing available. Conference brochures/guidelines available in February for SASE. Inquiries by fax and e-mail OK. The conference is "focused on the Christian market."

WRITING FOR MONEY WORKSHOP, 34200 Ridge Rd., #110, Willoughby OH 44094. (440)943-3047 or (800)653-4261. E-mail: fa837@cleveland.freenet.edu. Contact: Lea Leever Oldham. Conference held several times during the year. 2000 dates and locations available by e-mail and phone. Conference duration: one day. "Covers query letters, characterization for fiction, editing grammar, manuscript preparation and marketing saleable manuscripts." Held at Lakeland Community College, Kirtland, OH. Right off I-90 and in Mayfield, OH, east of Cleveland.

Costs: $39/day.

Additional Information: Workshop brochure/guidelines are available a month prior to class. Inquiries by e-mail OK.

North Central (IA, MN, NE, ND, SD, WI)

☑ **PETER DAVIDSON'S WRITER'S SEMINAR**, 982 S. Emerald Hills Dr., P.O. Box 497, Arnolds Park IA 51331-0497. (712)332-9329. Fax: (712)362-8363. Seminar Presenter: Peter Davidson. Estab. 1985. Seminars held about 30 times annually, in various sites. Offered year round. Seminars last 1 day, usually 9 a.m.-4 p.m. Average attendance: 35. "All writing areas including books of fiction and nonfiction, children's works, short stories, magazine articles, poetry, songs, scripts, religious works, personal experiences and romance fiction. All seminars are sponsored by community colleges or colleges across the U.S. Covers many topics including developing your idea, writing the manuscript, copyrighting, and marketing your work. The information is very practical— participants will be able to put into practice the principles discussed. The seminar is fast-paced and should be a lot of fun for participants."

Costs: Each sponsoring college sets own fees, ranging from $42-59, depending on location, etc.

Accommodations: "Participants make their own arrangements. Usually, no special arrangements are available."

Additional Information: "Participants are encouraged to bring their ideas and/or manuscripts for a short, informal evaluation by seminar presenter, Peter Davidson." Conference brochures/guidelines are available for SASE. No inquiries by fax or e-mail. "On even-numbered years, usually present seminars in Colorado, Wyoming, Nebraska, Kansas, Iowa, Minnesota and South Dakota. On odd-numbered years, usually present seminars in Illinois, Iowa, Minnesota, Arkansas, Missouri, South Dakota, Nebraska and Tennessee."

☑ **GREAT LAKES WRITER'S WORKSHOP**, Alverno College, 3400 S. 43 St., P.O. Box 343922, Milwaukee WI 53234-3922. (414)382-6176. Fax: (414)382-6332. Assistant Director: Cindy Jackson, Professional and Community Education. Estab. 1985. Annual. Workshop held the third Friday and Saturday in June. Average attendance: 150. "Workshops focus on a variety of subjects including fiction, writing for magazines, freelance writing, writing for children, poetry, marketing, etc. Participants may select a portion of the workshop or attend the full 2 days. Classes are held during the evening and weekend. The workshop is held in Milwaukee, WI at Alverno College."

Costs: In 1999, cost was $80 for entire workshop.

Accommodations: Attendees must make their own travel arrangments. Accommodations are available on campus; rooms are in residence halls and are not air-conditioned. Cost in 1997 was $25 for single, $20 per person for double. There are also hotels in the surrounding area. Call (414)382-6040 for information regarding overnight accommodations.

Additional Information: "Some workshop instructors may provide critiques, but this changes depending upon the workshop and speaker. This would be indicated in the workshop brochure." Brochures are available for SASE after March. Inquiries by fax OK.

IOWA SUMMER WRITING FESTIVAL, 116 International Center, University of Iowa, Iowa City IA 52242-1802. (319)335-2534. E-mail: peggy-houston@uiowa.edu; amy-margolis@uiowa.edu. Website: www.edu/~iswfe st. Directors: Peggy Houston, Amy Margolis. Estab. 1987. Annual. Festival held in June and July. Workshops are one week or a weekend. Average attendance: limited to 12/class—over 1,500 participants throughout the summer. "We offer courses in most areas of writing: novel, short story, essay, poetry, playwriting, screenwriting, humor, travel, writing for children, memoir, women's writing, romance and mystery." Site is the University of Iowa campus. Guest speakers are undetermined at this time. Readers and instructors have included Lee K. Abbott, Susan Power, Joy Harjo, Gish Jen, Abraham Verghese, Robert Olen Butler, Ethan Canin, Clark Blaise, Gerald Stern, Donald Justice, Michael Dennis Browne, Marvin Bell, Hope Edelman.

Costs: $400/week; $175, weekend workshop (1999 rates). Discounts available for early registration. Housing and meals are separate.

Accommodations: "We offer participants a choice of accommodations: dormitory, $27/night; Iowa House, $65/night; Holiday Inn, $70/night (rates subject to changes)."
Additional Information: Brochure/guidelines are available in February. Inquiries by fax and e-mail OK.

SPLIT ROCK ARTS PROGRAM, University of Minnesota, 335 Nolte Center, 315 Pillsbury Dr., SE, Minneapolis MN 55455. (612)624-6800. Fax: (612)624-5891. E-mail: srap@mail.cee.umn.edu. Estab. 1982. Annual. Workshops held in July and August. Over 40 one-week intensive residential workshops held. "The Split Rock Arts Program is offered through the University of Minnesota on its Duluth campus. Over 40 one-week intensive residential workshops in writing, visual arts, fine crafts and creativity enhancement are held for 5 weeks in July and August. This unique arts community provides a nurturing environment in a beautiful setting overlooking Lake Superior and the summer port city of Duluth. Courses, which can be taken for credit, are offered in poetry, stories, memoirs, novels and personal essays." Instructors in 1999 included Paulette Bates Alden, Carol Bly, Michael Dennis Browne, Ray Gonzalez, Susan Hubbard, Craig Lesley, Lawrence Sutin, Sylvia Watanabe and Catherine Watson.
Costs: $450, tuition (may vary with options). Moderately priced housing available for additional cost.
Accommodations: Campus apartments and dormitory available.
Additional Information: A limited number of scholarships are available based on qualification and need. Call for catalog.

UNIVERSITY OF WISCONSIN AT MADISON WRITERS INSTITUTE, 610 Langdon St., Madison WI 53703. (608)262-3447. Website: www.dcs.wisc.edu/lsa (includes classes and workshops, program and instructor descriptions, registration information and programs for children and teens). Director: Christine DeSmet. Estab. 1989. Annual. Conference held August 3-4, 2000. Average attendance: 175. Conference held at University of Wisconsin at Madison. Fiction and nonfiction workshops. Guest speakers are published authors, editors and agents.
Costs: $185 for 2 days; critique fees.
Accommodations: Info on accommodations sent with registration confirmation. Critiques available. Conference brochures/guidelines are available for SASE after June 2000. Inquiries by fax and e-mail OK.

N WISCONSIN REGIONAL WRITER'S ASSOCIATION CONFERENCE, 510 W. Sunset Ave., Appleton WI 54911-1139. (920)734-3724. E-mail: wrwa@lakeside.net. Website: www.inkwells.net/wrwa. Contact: Patricia Boverhuis. Estab. 1948. Semiannual. Conference held May 6, 2000 and September 23-24, 2000. Average attendance: 100-150. Conference for any and all areas of writing-nonfiction, journalism, screenwriting, etc. Conference facilities vary. Past conference topics included creative nonfiction, historical writing, outdoor writing, journalism and spiritual writing.
Costs: $35 for spring; $50 for fall.
Accommodations: Information about overnight accommodations is available. "We always negotiate a special conference rate for our attendees. Conference brochure/guidelines available for SASE. Inquiries by e-mail OK.

✓ WISCONSIN WRITERS' WORKSHOP, (formerly Redbird Writing Studios), 3195 S. Superior St., Milwaukee WI 53207-3074. (414)294-4688. E-mail: kathiell@aol.com. Director: Kathie Lokken. Estab. 1993. Average attendance: 6-15. "WWW offers beginning and continuing workshops plus an encouraging atmosphere for writers of all ages and genres. Year-round sessions provide peer critique and support as well as professional guidance. Topic-focused classes help the writer through specific challenges, such as writing the novel or short story, or marketing completed work. Private editing and consultations also available. All instructors are published authors. Classes and workshops are offered in a historic building overlooking Lake Michigan."
Costs: $50-$125.
Additional Information: Brochure available for SASE.

WRITING WORKSHOP, P.O. Box 65, Ellison Bay WI 54210. (920)854-4088. E-mail: clearing@mail.wiscnet .net. Resident Manager: Don Buchholz. Estab. 1935. Annual. Conference held in June. Average attendance: 16. "General writing journal, poetry as well as fiction and nonfiction." Held in a "quiet, residential setting in deep woods on the shore of Green Bay." Past guest speakers include Lowell B. Komie (short story), T.V. Olsen (novelist) and Barbara Vroman (novelist).
Costs: In 1999, cost was $589 (twin bed) or $549 (dormitory).
Accommodations: "Two to a room with private bath in rustic log and stone buildings. Great hall type of classroom for the conference."
Additional Information: Catalog (8½ × 11) available upon request.

South Central (CO, KS, MO, NM, OK, TX)

✓ ASPEN SUMMER WORDS WRITING RETREAT AND LITERARY FESTIVAL, (formerly Aspen Writers' Conference), Box 7726, Aspen CO 81612. (800)925-2526. Fax (970)920-5700. E-mail: aspenwrite@aol.

com. Executive Director: Jeanne McGovern. Estab. 1975. Annual. Writing retreat and literary festival held in late June at locations around Aspen. Average attendance: 150. Writing retreat for fiction, memoir and poetry; literary festival for craft lectures, industry talks, round table discussions and readings. 1999 festival featured Ron Carlson, fiction; Craig Nelson and Jim Hornfisher, agents; Tom Auer and John Lehman, editors; and Pam Houston. **Costs:** $300/retreat; $150/festival; $25/private meetings with agents and editors (1999)
Accommodations On-campus housing $110/night single; $55/night double. Off campus rates vary. Free shuttle.
Additional Information: Manuscripts to be submitted for review by faculty prior to conference. Brochures available for SASE.

AUSTIN WRITERS' LEAGUE WORKSHOPS/CONFERENCES/CLASSES, E-2, 1501 W. Fifth, Austin TX 78703. (512)499-8914. Fax: (512)499-0441. E-mail: awl@writersleague.org. Website: www.writersleague.org. Executive Director: Jim Bob McMillan. Estab. 1982. Conference scheduled for July 2000. Duration: varies according to program. Average attendance from 15 to 200. To promote "all genres, fiction and nonfiction, poetry, writing for children, screenwriting, playwriting, legal and tax information for writers, also writing workshops for children and youth." Programs held at AWL Resource Center/Library, other sites in Austin and Texas. Topics include: finding and working with agents and publishers; writing and marketing short fiction; dialogue; characterization; voice; research; basic and advanced fiction writing/focus on the novel; business of writing; also workshops for genres. Past speakers have included Dwight Swain, Natalie Goldberg, David Lindsey, Shelby Hearon, Gabriele Rico, Benjamin Saenz, Rosellen Brown, Sandra Scofield, Reginald Gibbons, Anne Lamott, Sterling Lord and Sue Grafton.
Costs: Varies from free to $185, depending on program. Most classes, $20-50; workshops $35-75; conferences: $125-185.
Accommodations: Special rates given at some hotels for program participants.
Additional Information: Critique sessions offered at some programs. Individual presenters determine critique requirements. Those requirements are then made available through Austin Writers' League office and in workshop promotion. Contests and awards programs are offered separately. Brochures/guidelines are available after May 2000 on request. Inquiries by fax and e-mail OK.

N: FLATIRONS BLUNT INSTRUMENT MYSTERY WORKSHOP, c/o Thora Chinnery, 415 Erie Dr., Boulder CO 80303. (303)499-0203. Fax: (303)494-5995. E-mail: chinnery@chisp.net. Website: bcn.boulder.co .us/arts/blunt. Contact: Thora Chinnery. Estab. 1996. Annual. Conference held June 24, 2000. Conference duration: 1 day. Average attendance: 70. Conference for "mystery writers and readers." Conference held in "two very large auditorium size rooms at the local Elks club." Panels for 1999 included "Taking a Stab at Plotting," "Cooking up a Character," "Avoiding Rigor Mortis in the Series," "Hands-on Writing," "Creativity" and "Humor." 2000 speakers will include Michael Siedman, Walker Press; Julie Kaewert and Christine Jorgensen. **Costs:** 1999 fees: $50 (included continental breakfast and buffet with lunch). "Out of town guests were given free bed and breakfast with local members."
Additional Information: "Limited critiquing is available from published authors on a first come basis." Conference brochures/guidelines available January 2000 for SASE. Inquiries by fax and e-mail OK. "It is the only genre specific mystery workshop in the Rocky Mountain area. The scenery is fabulous. The conference is sponsored by the Rocky Mountain Chapter of Sisters in Crime."

N: FRONTIERS IN WRITING CONFERENCE, P.O. Box 19303, Amarillo TX 79114. (806)354-2305. E-mail: cliff@nts-online.net. Website: users.arn.net/~ppw. President: Cliff Heffner. Sponsored by Panhandle Professional Writers, Amarillo College, West Texas A&M University with support from Austin Writers' League in cooperation with Texas Commission on the Arts. Annual conference held 2 days in June. For fiction, nonfiction and poetry. Conference held at the Amarillo College Business and Industry Center.
Costs: In 1999, cost was $80 for PPW members, $115 for nonmembers (meals included).
Accommodations: Special conference rates available at hotel.
Additional Information: Conference brochure/registration form available for SASE; includes information on contest for unpublished work. "Conference presenters include authors, editors and agents; appointments available."

✓ GOLDEN TRIANGLE WRITERS GUILD, 4245 Calder, Beaumont TX 77706. (409)898-4894. Advisor: D.J. Resnick. E-mail: gtwg@juno.com. Estab. 1983. Annual. Conference held during third weekend in October. Attendance limited to 350. Held at the Hilton Hotel on IH10 at Washington in Beaumont, Texas.
Costs: $210-235 before October 2nd; $235-260 after October 2nd. Cost includes meals and 1 year membership.
Accommodations: Special conference rates available at Holiday Inn (Beaumont).
Additional Information: Sponsors a contest. Attendance required. Preliminary judging done by published authors and/or specialists in each specific genre. Final judging done by editors and/or agents specializing in each specific area.

N: HARWELDEN LITERARY FESTIVAL, 2210 S. Main, Harwelden Mansion, Tulsa OK 74114. (918)584-3333. Fax: (918)582-2787. E-mail: ahct@swbell.net. Contact: Sarah Theobald-Hall. Estab. 1995. Annual. Festival held April 20-21, 2000. Average attendance: 150. Festival for poetry and fiction held in historic Tudor mansion overlooking Arkansas River. 1999 events included poetry master class, fiction master class, "Myths of Sex and Gender in Poetry," "Passionate Heartbeats in Plot and Dialogue." Guest speakers included John Koethe (poet) and Jewell Parker Rhodes (novelist).

Costs: $25 for members of the Arts and Humanities Council; $30 for nonmembers.

Accomodations: "Recommendations available from conference contact."

Additional Information: "Master Classes restricted to 10-12 writers who must submit an 8-10 page writing sample by April 14, 2000." Conference brochures/guidelines are available for SASE after March 1, 2000. Inquiries by fax and e-mail OK. "Festival has hands-on emphasis with focus on enriching craft and interaction with writing community in Tulsa."

N HEARTLAND WRITERS CONFERENCE, P.O. Box 652, Kennett MO 63857. (573)297-3325. Fax: (573)297-3352. E-mail: hwg@heartlandwriters.org. Website: www.heartlandwriters.org. Contact: HWG Steering Committee. Estab. 1990. Conference held biennially (even numbered years). Conference held June 6-8, 2002. Average attendance: 160. Conference concentrates on "multi-genre popular fiction and nonfiction, also includes poetry, children's and screenwriting." Conference is held at Best Western Coach House Inn, Sikeston, Missouri, reserved exclusively for the conference. Seminars at 1998 conference included "Identifying Your Genre"; "Getting Agented"; "Myth Adventures"; "Query Letters"; "Poisons for Fiction Writers"; "Characterization"; "Writing to Sell"; "Writing YA"; "Inspirational Romance Markets." 1998 speakers included Christopher Vogler, author of *The Writer's Journey*; agents: Alice Orr, Jennifer Jackson, Ricia Mainhardt and Christy Fletcher; editors: Caitlyn Dlouhy, Melissa Jeglinski, Kim Waltemyer and Joe Veltre.

Costs: 1998 fees were $175 early registration before March 20; $185 general registration until May 15; $225 thereafter if space is available. "Includes workshops and meals. Lodging is separate."

Accommodations: All travel arrangements are the responsibility of the writer. Special rates are available at Coach House Inn and other area hotels. Information is published in the brochure. Onsite accommodations for 1998 were $45/night for one bedroom suites; $70/night for two bedroom suites. There are only 57 units in the Coach House. When those rooms are all taken, rooms are available at the Holiday Inn Express $45/night.

Additional Information: "No fiction critiques. Entrants in the poetry division of the Great Beginnings Writing Competition receive one-on-one critiques." Sponsors writing contest with entries judged in final round by an agent or editor. See brochure for categories and requirements. Conference brochures/guidelines available for SASE after January 2000. Inquiries by e-mail OK. Also inquire about the What a Novel Idea workshop presented by Connie Bennett every 12 to 18 months in Southeastern Missouri at: What A Novel Idea, Connie Bennett, P.O. Box 14, Dexter MO 63841 or e-mail thewritr@hotmail.com.

N HOUSTON WRITERS CONFERENCE 2000, P.O. Box 742683, Houston TX 77274-2683. (281)342-5924. E-mail: houwrites@aol.com. Website: www.houstonwrites.com. Contact: Ted Simmons. Estab. 1997. Conference held annually March 16-19, 2000. Average attendance: 250. Conference includes all genres, fiction and nonfiction. Conference is held at the Houston Marriott Westside Hotel. 1999 dinner and luncheon speakers were Anita Richmond Bunkley, Melanie Lawson and Susan Wiggs. Every year there is also a agent/editor Q&A panel with 15 panelists in 1999.

Costs: $225 before November 1, 1999; $240 November 2-February 1, 2000; $255 after February 2, 2000.

Accommodations: Special rate for participants of $65 at Houston Marriott Westside. Check website for additional information.

Additional Information: E-mail or check website for contest information. Conference brochures/guidelines available for SASE after September 1999. Inquiries by e-mail OK. Conference includes "approximately 50 multi-track workshops over 2½ days, multi-genre, all experience levels, bookstore and author signings."

☑ MAPLE WOODS COMMUNITY COLLEGE WRITERS' CONFERENCE, 2601 NE Barry Rd., Kansas City MO 64156-1299. (816)437-3042. Fax: (816)437-0479. E-mail: schumacp@maplewoods.cc.mo.us. Website: www.kcmetro.cc.mo.us. Director, Community Education: Paula Schumacher. Conference held September 22-23, 2000. Average attendance: 300-350. Nonfiction, fiction, science fiction, mystery, romance, short story, magazine writing, essay writing, publishers, literary agents. Conference site: Country Club Plaza, Kansas City MO.

Costs: $35 (Friday), $79 (Saturday). Continental breakfast and break-time soft drinks included on Saturday.

Additional Information: Special hotel rates available. Request information through e-mail, fax or in writing.

☑ NATIONAL WRITERS ASSOCIATION CONFERENCE, 3140 S. Peoria, Suite 295, Aurora CO 80014. (303)841-0246. Fax: (303)751-8593. E-mail address: sandywriter@aol.com. Executive Director: Sandy Whelchel. Estab. 1926. Annual. Conference usually held in June in Denver, CO. Conference duration: 3 days. Average attendance: 200-300. General writing and marketing.

Costs: $300 (approx.).

Additional Information: Awards for previous contests will be presented at the conference. Conference brochures/guidelines are available for SASE.

☑ **THE NEW LETTERS WEEKEND WRITERS CONFERENCE**, University of Missouri-Kansas City, College of Arts and Sciences Continuing Ed. Division, 4825 Troost, Room 215, Kansas City MO 64110-2499. (816)235-2736. Fax: (816)235-5279. E-mail: mckinleym@umkc.edu. Estab. in the mid-70s as The Longboat Key Writers Conference. Annual. Runs during June. Conference duration is 3 days. Average attendance: 75. "The New Letters Weekend Writers Conference brings together talented writers in many genres for lectures, seminars, readings, workshops and individual conferences. The emphasis is on craft and the creative process in poetry, fiction, screenwriting, playwriting and journalism; but the program also deals with matters of psychology, publications and marketing. The conference is appropriate for both advanced and beginning writers. The conference meets at the beautiful Diastole conference center of The University of Missouri-Kansas City."
Costs: Several options are available. Participants may choose to attend as a non-credit student or they may attend for 1-3 hours of college credit from the University of Missouri-Kansas City. Conference registration includes continental breakfasts, Saturday and Sunday lunch. For complete information, contact the University of Missouri-Kansas City.
Accommodations: Registrants are responsible for their own transportation, but information on area accommodations is made available.
Additional Information: Those registering for college credit are required to submit a ms in advance. Ms reading and critique is included in the credit fee. Those attending the conference for non-credit also have the option of having their ms critiqued for an additional fee. Inquiries by e-mail and fax OK.

☑ **NORTHWEST OKLAHOMA WRITER'S WORKSHOP**, 1118 Lookout Dr., Enid OK 73701. Phone/fax: (580)237-6535. E-mail: enidwriters@hotmail.com. Website: welcome.to/EnidWritersClub. Workshop coordinator: Bev Walton-Porter. Estab. 1991. Annual. Conference held in April. Conference duration: 6 hours. Average attendance: 20-30. "Usually fiction is the concentration area. The purpose is to help writers learn more about the craft of writing and encourage writers 'to step out in faith' and submit." Held in Cherokee Strip Conference Center. Past speakers have been Norma Jean Lutz, inspirational and magazine writing; Deborah Bouziden, fiction and magazine writing; Anna Meyers, children's writing; Sondra Soli, poetry; Marcia Preston, magazines, Mary Lynn, manuscript preparation and submission protocol; Jean Hager, writing mysteries; Annie Jones, romance.
Costs: $40; includes catered lunch.
Additional Information: Conference guidelines are available for SASE. Inquiries by e-mail OK.

Ⓝ OKLAHOMA WRITERS' WORKSHOP, *Nimrod*, University of Tulsa, 600 S. College, Tulsa OK 74104. (918)631-3080. Fax: (918)631-3033. E-mail: ringoldfl@utulsa.edu. Website: www.utulsa.edu/nimrod. Editor-in-Chief: Francine Ringold, PhD. Estab. 1978. Workshop held annually in October. Workshop duration: 1 day. Average attendance: 100-150. Workshop in fiction and poetry. "Prize winners (Nimrod/Hardman Prizes) conduct workshops as do contest judges. Past judges: Rosellen Brown, Stanley Kunitz, Toby Olson, Lucille Clifton and W.S. Merwin."
Costs: Not yet determined; generally nominal. Lunch provided.
Additional Information: *Nimrod International Journal* sponsors *Nimrod*/Hardman Literary Awards: The Kathe rine Anne Porter Prize for fiction and The Pablo Neruda Prize for poetry. Poety and fiction prizes: $2,000 each and publication (1st prize); $1,000 each and publication (2nd prize). Deadline: must be postmarked no later than April 30. Guidelines for SASE.

☑ **GARY PROVOST'S WRITERS RETREAT WORKSHOP**, % Write It/Sell It, 2507 South Boston Place, Tulsa OK 74114. (978)368-0287 or phone/fax: (918)583-1471. E-mail: wrwwisi@aol.com. Website: www. channel1.com/wisi Director: Gail Provost Stockwell. Assistant Director: Lance Stockwell; Workshop Leader: Carol Dougherty. Estab. 1987. May 1999 workshop held at Marydale Retreat Center in Erlanger, KY (just south of Cincinnati, OH). Workshop held May 26-June 4, 2000. Workshop duration: 10 days. Average attendance: 30. Focus on fiction and narrative nonfiction books in progress. All genres. "The Writers Retreat Workshop is an intensive learning experience for small groups of serious-minded writers. Founded by the late Gary Provost, one of the country's leading writing instructors and his wife Gail, an award-winning author, the WRW is a challenging and enriching adventure. The goal of the WRW core staff and visiting agents/editors/authors is for students to leave with a solid understanding of the marketplace as well as the craft of writing a novel. In the heart of a supportive and spirited community of fellow writers, students learn Gary Provost's course and make remarkable leaps in their writing, editing and marketing skills."
Costs: Costs (discount for past participants) $1,620 for 10 days which includes all food and lodging. The Marydale Retreat Center is 5 miles from the Cincinnati airport and offers shuttle services.
Additional Information: Participants are selected based upon the appropriateness of this program for the applicant's specific writing project. Participants are asked to submit a brief overview and synopsis before the workshop and are given assignments and feedback during the 10-day workshop. Brochures/guidelines are available after December by calling 1-800-642-2494. Inquiries by fax and e-mail OK.

☑ **ROCKY MOUNTAIN BOOK FESTIVAL**, 2123 Downing St., Denver CO 80205. (303)839-8320. Fax: (303)839-8319. E-mail: ccftb@compuserve.com. Website: www.aclin.org/~ccftb. Executive Director: Christine Citrun. Estab. 1991. Annual. Festival held in November. Average attendance: 20,000. Festival promotes published

work from all genres. Held at Denver Merchandise Mart. Offers a wide variety of panels. Approximately 200 authors are scheduled to speak at the next festival.
Costs: $4 (adult); $2 (child).
Additional Information: Brochures/guidelines available. Inquiries by e-mail and fax OK.

■ **ROCKY MOUNTAIN CHILDREN'S BOOK FESTIVAL**, 2123 Downing St., Denver CO 80205-5210. (303)839-8320. Fax: (303)839-8319. E-mail: ccftb@compuserve.com. Program Coordinator: Anna Kaltenbach. Estab. 1996. Annual festival held in the fall. Festival duration: 2 days. Average attendance: 30,000. Festival promotes published work for and about children/families. It is solely for children's authors and illustrators— open to the public. Held at Denver Merchandise Mart. Approximately 100 authors speak annually. Past authors include Ann M. Martin, Sharon Creech, Nikki Grimes, T.A. Barron, Laura Numeroff, Jean Craighead George and Robert Munsch.
Costs: $2 children, $4 adults.
Accommodations: "Information on accommodations available."
Additional Information: Send SASE for brochure/guidelines. Inquiries by fax and e-mail OK.

■ **ROMANCE WRITERS OF AMERICA NATIONAL CONFERENCE**, 3707 FM 1960 West, Suite 555, Houston TX 77068. (281)440-6885, ext. 27. Fax: (281)440-7510. Website: www.rwanational.com. Executive Director: Allison Kelley. Estab. 1981. Annual. Conference held in late July or early August. Average attendance: 1,500. Over 100 workshops on writing, researching and the business side of being a working writer. Publishing professionals attend and accept appointments. Keynote speaker is renowned romance writer. Conference will be held in Washington, D.C. in 2000.
Costs: $300.
Additional Information: Annual RITA awards are presented for romance authors. Annual Golden Heart awards are presented for unpublished writers. Conference brochures/guidelines are available for SASE.

■ **SHORT COURSE ON PROFESSIONAL WRITING**, University of Oklahoma, Journalism, 860 Van Vleet Oval, Norman OK 73019-0270. (405)325-4171. Fax: (405)325-7565. E-mail: jmadisondavis@ou.edu. Estab. 1938. Annual conference held the second weekend in June. Average attendance: 200. Conference focuses on writing for publication—all paying markets. Held at the Holiday Inn in Norman. 1999 guest speakers included Robert J. Conley, Jean Hager, Carolyn G. Hart, Bill Wallace and others.
Costs: $195.
Accomodations: Provides special rates at the Holiday Inn.
Additional Information: "Critiques are optional, but we provide them. Manuscripts must be submitted ahead of time." Brochures available in March for SASE. Inquiries by fax and e-mail OK. "We have sixty years of success with editors, agents and authors. Many successful writers were 'discovered' at the Short Course."

■ **SOUTHWEST WRITERS WORKSHOP CONFERENCE**, 8200 Mountain Rd. NE, Suite 106, Albuquerque NM 87110. (505)265-9485. Fax: (505)265-9483. E-mail: swriters@aol.com. Website: www.us1.net1// SWW. Estab. 1983. Annual. Conference held in August. Average attendance: about 400. "Conference concentrates on all areas of writing." Workshops and speakers include writers and editors of all genres for all levels from beginners to advanced. The 1999 keynote speaker was Charles Johnson, author of *Middle Passages* and *Dreamer*.
Costs: $265 (members) and $320 (nonmembers); includes conference sessions, 2 luncheons, 2 banquets.
Accommodations: Usually have official airline and discount rates. Special conference rates are available at hotel. A list of other area hotels and motels is available.
Additional Information: Sponsors a contest judged by authors, editors and agents from New York, Los Angeles, etc., and from major publishing houses. Eighteen categories. Deadline: May 1. Entry fee is $29 (members) or $39 (nonmembers). Brochures/guidelines available for SASE. Inquiries by e-mail and fax OK. "An appointment (10 minutes, one-on-one) may be set up at the conference with editor or agent of your choice on a first-registered/first-served basis."

STEAMBOAT SPRINGS WRITERS GROUP, P.O. Box 774284, Steamboat Springs CO 80477. (970)879-8079. E-mail: freiberger@compuserve.com. Director: Harriet Freiberger. Estab. 1982. Annual. Conference held July 22, 2000. Conference duration: 1 day. Average attendance: 30. "Our conference emphasizes instruction within the seminar format. Novices and polished professionals benefit from the individual attention and the camaraderie which can be established within small groups. A pleasurable and memorable learning experience is guaranteed by the relaxed and friendly atmosphere of the old train depot. Registration is limited." Steamboat Arts Council sponsors the group at the restored Train Depot.
Costs: $35 before June 1, $45 after. Fee covers all conference activities, including lunch. Lodging available at Steamboat Resorts; 10% discount for participants. Optional dinner and activities during evening preceding conference.
Additional Information: Available April 15. Inquiries by e-mail, phone or mail OK.

WRITER'S ROUNDTABLE CONFERENCE, P.O. Box 461572, Garland TX 75046-1572. (800)473-2538 ext. 5. Fax: (972)414-2839. E-mail: directors@wrc-online.com. Website: wrc-online.com. Contact: Registrar. Estab. 1996. Annual. Conference held March 31-April 2, 2000. Average attendance: 200-250. Conference is "multi-genre—emphasis on marketing and writing career advancement rather than basic 'how to write.' Over 50% in attendance are full-time writers." Conference held at the Renaissance Dallas North Hotel. "New addition in 2000: Round-the-clock Pitching Panels in addition to comprehensive workshops and roundtables." Speakers include Leyla Aker, senior editor at Knopf; Diane Hess, senior editor at Scholastic; Charles Rosenbaum, editorial director at Broadman & Holman; Cindy Mintz, ICM Los Angeles; Bob Banner, producer/director; and Donna Gould, book publicist.

Costs: "Scale of discounts depending on how early people register. For weekend, registration costs range from $195 (early-early) to $325 (walk-up); for Saturday only it's less. All registrations include a full set of conference tapes."

Accommodations: Discounts available from American Airlines, Avis Car Rentals and the Renaissance Dallas North Hotel. Hotel rates for conference attendees are $119/night (single/double), $139/night (triple) and $159/night (quadruple).

Additional Information: Conference brochures/guidelines available August 15, 1999 for SASE. Inquiries by fax and e-mail OK. "WRC is geared toward professional writers seeking to advance their careers (both print and broadcast) and serious, informed writers wanting to break into the business. Not a 'Writers 101' type conference."

WRITERS WORKSHOP IN SCIENCE FICTION, English Department/University of Kansas, Lawrence KS 66045-2115. (785)864-3380. Fax: (785)864-4298. E-mail: jgunn@falcon.cc.ukans.edu. Website: falcon.cc.ukans.edu/~sfcenter/. Professor: James Gunn. Estab. 1985. Annual. Conference held July 3-16, 2000. Average attendance: 15. Conference for writing and marketing science fiction. "Housing is provided and classes meet in university housing on the University of Kansas campus. Workshop sessions operate informally in a lounge." The workshop is "small, informal and aimed at writers on the edge of publication or regular publication." 1999 guest writers: Frederik Pohl, SF writer and former editor and agent; John Ordover, writer and editor; Kij Johnson and Christopher McKittrick, writers.

Costs: Tuition: $400. Housing and meals are additional.

Accommodations: Several airport shuttle services offer reasonable transportation from the Kansas City International Airport to Lawrence. During past conferences, students were housed in a student dormitory at $12/day double, $22/day single.

Additional Information: "Admission to the workshop is by submission of an acceptable story. Two additional stories should be submitted by the end of June. These three stories are copied and distributed to other participants for critiquing and are the basis for the first week of the workshop; one story is rewritten for the second week." Brochures/guidelines are available after December 15 for SASE. Inquiries by phone, fax or e-mail OK. "The Writers Workshop in Science Fiction is intended for writers who have just started to sell their work or need that extra bit of understanding or skill to become a published writer."

NORMAN ZOLLINGER'S TAOS SCHOOL OF WRITING, (formerly Taos School of Writing), P.O. Box 20496, Albuquerque NM 87154-0496. (505)294-4601. Fax: (505)294-7049. E-mail: spletzer@swcp.com. Website: www.us1.net/zollinger. Administrator: Suzanne Spletzer. Estab. 1993 by Norman Zollinger. Annual. Conference held in mid-July. Conference duration: 1 week. Average attendance: 60. "All fiction, nonfiction and screenwriting. No poetry. Purpose—to promote good writing skills. We meet at the Thunderbird Lodge in the Taos Ski Valley, NM. (We are the only ones there.) No telephones or televisions in rooms. No elevator. Slightly rustic landscape. Quiet mountain setting at 9,000 feet." Conference focuses on writing fiction and nonfiction and publishing. Previous speakers include David Morrell, Suzy McKee Charnas, Stephen R. Donaldson, Norman Zollinger, Denise Chavez, Richard S. Wheeler, Max Evans and Tony Hillerman, plus editors amd agents.

Costs: $1,200; includes tuition, room and board.

Accommodations: "Travel agent arranges rental cars or shuttle rides to Ski Valley from Albuquerque Sunport."

Additional Information: "Acceptance to school is determined by evaluation of submitted manuscript. Manuscripts are critiqued by faculty and students in the class sessions." Conference brochures/guidelines are available after January. Visit website for most current information and registration form, or e-mail, call or send SASE.

**FOR EXPLANATIONS OF THESE SYMBOLS,
SEE THE INSIDE FRONT AND BACK COVERS OF THIS BOOK.**

West (AZ, CA, HI, NV, UT)

BE THE WRITER YOU WANT TO BE MANUSCRIPT CLINIC, 23350 Sereno Court, Villa 30, Cupertino CA 95014. (415)691-0300. Contact: Louise Purwin Zobel. Estab. 1969. Workshop held irregularly—usually semiannually at several locations. Workshop duration: 1-2 days. Average attendance: 20-30. "This manuscript clinic enables writers of any type of material to turn in their work-in-progress—at any stage of development— to receive help with structure and style, as well as marketing advice." It is held on about 40 campuses at different times, including University of California and other university and college campuses throughout the west.
Costs: Usually $45-65/day, "depending on campus."
Additional Information: Brochures/guidelines available for SASE.

CALIFORNIA WRITER'S CLUB CONFERENCE AT ASILOMAR, 3975 Kim Court, Sebastopol CA 95472. (707)823-8128. E-mail: gpmansergh@aol.com. Website: www.calwriters.com. Contact: Gil Mansergh, director. Estab. 1941. Annual. Held July 7-9, 2000. Conference duration: Friday afternoon through Sunday lunch. Average attendance: 350. Conference offers opportunity to learn from and network with successful writers, agents and editors in Asilomar's beautiful and historic beach side setting on the shores of Monterey Bay. Presentations, panels, hands-on workshops and agent/editor appointments focus on writing and marketing short stories, novels, articles, books, poetry and screenplays for children and adults.
Costs: $450 includes all conference privileges, shared lodging and 6 meals. There is a $90 surcharge for a single room.
Accommodations: Part of the California State Park system, Asilomar is rustic and beautiful. Julia Morgan designed redwood and stone buildings share 105 acres of dunes and pine forests with modern AIA and National Academy of Design winning lodges. Monterey airport is a 15 minute taxi drive away.
Additional Information: First prize winners in all 7 categories of the *California Writers' Club* writing competitions receive free registration to next conference. $10 entry fee. Contest deadline is May 1, 2000. Brochure and contest submission rules will be available in late February.

CANTERBURY SAILS—CREATIVE WRITING WORKSHOPS, 555 Bryant St. #368, Palo Alto CA 94301. (888)399-7245. (650)566-8289. E-mail: info@canterburysails.com. Website: www.canterburysails.com. Contact: Bree DeMoss. Estab. 1995. Conferences held year round. Conference held in the Mayan Riviera, January-April 2000; San Juan Islands, June-August/September 2000; and Turkish Coast, June/July 2000. Conference duration: 6 and 12 days. Average attendance: 8-14 passengers and instructor(s). Conference is "multi-genre; poetry; short story; fiction; creative nonfiction; travel writing; literature/classics." Conference held on an "80 foot luxury sailing yacht."
Costs: $1,475 for 6-day trip; $2,950 for 12-day trip. Includes all course instruction and materials, meals and lodging aboard the yacht, all tours, and use of snorkeling equipment and kayaks.
Accommodations: "Two to a state room with air-conditioning and in suite bathrooms and showers."
Additional Information: "We encourage writers to bring their materials and /or distribute it to other passengers/ students before the trip, but we do not require this." Conference brochures/guidelines free. Inquiries by fax and e-mail OK.

DESERT WRITERS WORKSHOP/CANYONLANDS FIELD INSTITUTE, P.O. Box 68, Moab UT 84532. (435)259-7750 or (800)860-5262. Fax: (435)259-2335. E-mail: cfiinfo@canyonlandsfieldinst.org. Website: www.canyonlandsfieldinst.org/. Executive Director and Conference Coordinator: Karla Vanderzanden. Estab. 1984. Annual. Held first weekend in November. Conference duration: 3 days. Average attendance: 30. Concentrations include fiction, nonfiction, poetry. Site is at a ranch near Moab, Utah. "Theme is oriented towards understanding the vital connection between the natural world and human communities." Faculty panel has included in past years Ann Zwinger, Pam Houston, Linda Hogan, Christopher Merrill, Terry Tempest Williams and Richard Shelton.
Costs: $525 (members of CFI, $510); $150 deposit, which includes meals Friday-Sunday, instruction, field trip, lodging.
Accommodations: At a guest ranch, included in cost.
Additional Information: Brochures are available for SASE. Inquiries by phone, fax or e-mail OK. "Participants may submit work in advance, but it is not required. Student readings, evaluations and consultations with guest instructors/faculty are part of the workshop. Desert Writers Workshop is supported in part by grants from the Utah Arts Council and National Endowment for the Arts. A partial scholarship is available. College credit is also available for an additional fee."

FILM SCHOOL FOR WRITERS, P.O. Box 481252, Los Angeles CA 90048. (323)933-3456. Fax: (323)933-1464. E-mail: filmschool@hollywoodu.com. Website: hollywoodu.com. Contact: Registration. Estab. 1986. Bimonthly. Conference duration: 1-3 weekends. Average attendance: 60. Conference to "teach writers how to produce or direct their novel/writing into a feature film." Conference held at teaching soundstage in Santa Monica. Panels planed for next conference include "Financing Feature Films," "Directing Feature Films" and "Writing Feature Films."

Costs: $299.
Additional Information: Conference brochures/guidelines are available for SASE. Inquiries by fax OK.

[N] INTERNATIONAL READERS THEATRE WORKSHOPS, P.O. Box 17193, San Diego CA 92177. (619)276-1948. Fax: (619)576-7369. Website: www.readers-theatre.com. Contact: Bill Adams, director. Estab. 1974. Workshop held July 10-22, 2000. Average attendance: 70. Workshop on "all aspects of Readers Theatre with emphasis on scriptmaking." Workshop held at Wellington Hall on King's College Campus in London.
Costs: "$1,395 includes housing for two weeks (twin accommodations), traditional English breakfast, complimentary mid-morning coffee break and all institute fees."
Additional Information: "One-on-one critiques available between writer and faculty (if members)." Conference brochures/guidelines available for SASE. Inquiries by fax OK. Conference offers "up to 9 credits in Theatre (Speech) and/or Education from the University of Southern Maine at $122/unit."

I'VE ALWAYS WANTED TO WRITE BUT . . ., 23350 Sereno Court, Villa 30, Cupertino CA 95014. (415)691-0300. Contact: Louise Purwin Zobel. Estab. 1969. Workshop held irregularly, several times a year at different locations. Workshop duration: 1-2 days. Average attendance: 30-50. Workshop "encourages real beginners to get started on a lifelong dream. Focuses on the basics of writing." Workshops held at about 40 college and university campuses in the West, including University of California.
Costs: Usually $45-65/day "depending on college or university."
Additional Information: Brochures/guidelines are available for SASE after August.

IWWG EARLY SPRING IN CALIFORNIA CONFERENCE, International Women's Writing Guild, P.O. Box 810, Gracie Station, New York NY 10028-0082. (212)737-7536. Fax: (212)737-9469. E-mail: iwwg@iwwg.com. Website: www.IWWG.com. Executive Director: Hannelore Hahn. Estab. 1982. Annual. Conference held March 11-12. Average attendance: 80. Conference to promote "creative writing, personal growth and empowerment." Site is a redwood forest mountain retreat in Santa Cruz, California.
Costs: $300 for weekend program, plus room and board; $65 per day for commuters, $125 for Saturday and Sunday only.
Accommodations: Accommodations are all at conference site.
Additional Information: Conference brochures/guidelines are available for SASE after August. Inquiries by e-mail and fax OK.

[N] LEAGUE OF UTAH WRITERS ROUND-UP, 4621 W. Harman Dr., W.V.C. UT 84120-3752. Phone/fax: (801)964-0861. E-mail: crofts@numucom.com. Website: users.deseretonline.com/luwrite. Contact: Dorothy Crofts. Estab. 1935. Annual. Conference held in September 2000. Conference duration: 2 days, Friday and Saturday. Average attendance: 200. "The purpose of the conference is to award the winners of our annual contest as well as instruction in all areas of writing. Speakers cover subjects from generating ideas to writing a novel and working with a publisher. We have something for everyone." Conference held at hotel conference rooms and ballroom facilities with view of lakeside for awards banquet. Dinner at poolside. 1999 themes included "Generating Ideas"; "25 Ideas on How to Work Well with a Publisher"; "Script to Screen"; "On Writing a Novel"; "What an Editorial Consultant Can Do For You." 1999 speakers included Jim Cypher, literary agent; Gerald Lund, historical novelist; Dick Siddoway, author; Dave Wolverton, author; Jennie Hansen, romance writer and Duane Crowther, publisher.
Costs: 1999 costs: $100 for LUW members ($80 if registered before August 31); $150 for nonmembers (fee includes 4 meals).
Accommodations: Shuttle service is available from Salt Lake International Airport to Salt Lake Airport Hilton. List of hotel/motel accommodations available. Special hotel rate for conference attendees $79.
Additional Information: Opportunity for writers to meet one-on-one with literary agent from New York, 10 pages of their novel will be read and reviewed with writer. Sponsors contests for eight fiction categories, three open to nonmembers of League. Word limits vary from 1,500 to 75,000. Conference brochures/guidelines available for SASE after January 2000. Inquiries by fax and e-mail OK.

[N] LOS ANGELES WRITERS CONFERENCE, Universal City Walk, Universal City CA 91608. (310)825-9415. Fax: (310)206-7382. E-mail: writers@unex.ucla.edu. Website: www.unex.edu/writers. Contact: Madaleine Laird. Estab. 1997. Annual. Conference held February 17-20, 2000. Average attendance: 150-200. Conference on "creative writing—memoir, novel, short story writing." Located in UCLA extension classrooms on Universal City Walk. Panels include "sources of motivation and inspiration for writers." Speakers include Ray Bradbury, Carolyn See and L.A. Theatresports.
Costs: $545 before December 1; $645 after December 1 (includes parking, one event with food each day and guest speakers).
Accommodations: "The workshops and special events are all held on City Walk, which is the equivalent of one city block." Information on overnight accommodations is available.
Additional Information: Conference brochures available late September for SASE. Inquiries by fax and e-mail OK. "Our conference focuses on the writing process, sources or motivation and inspiration."

"WE WANT TO PUBLISH YOUR WORK."

You would give anything to hear an editor speak those six magic words. So you work hard for weeks, months, even years to make that happen. You create a brilliant piece of work and a knock-out presentation, but there's still one vital step to ensure publication. You still need to submit your work to the right buyers. With rapid changes in the publishing industry it's not always easy to know who those buyers are. That's why each year thousands of writers, just like you, turn to the most current edition of this indispensable market guide.

Keep ahead of the changes by ordering *2001 Novel & Short Story Writer's Market* today! You'll save the frustration of getting manuscripts returned in the mail stamped MOVED: ADDRESS UNKNOWN. And of NOT submitting your work to new listings because you don't know they exist. All you have to do to order the upcoming 2001 edition is complete the attached order card and return it with your payment. Order now and you'll get the 2001 edition at the 2000 price—just $24.99—no matter how much the regular price may increase!

Completely Updated Each Year

Novel & Short Story Writer's Market

2000+ PLACES TO PUBLISH YOUR FICTION
- 500+ book publishers
- 700+ literary markets
- 500+ genre markets
- 450+ contemporary markets
- 200+ electronic markets
- 3,000 e-mail addresses & websites
- 2,000+ phone numbers

350 NEW MARKETS **75+ AGENTS**

2001 Novel & Short Story Writer's Market will be published and ready for shipment in January 2001.

Turn Over for More Great Books to Help Get Your Fiction Published!

☐ **Yes!** I want the most current edition of *Novel & Short Story Writer's Market*. Please send me the 2001 edition at the 2000 price–$24.99. (NOTE: *2001 Novel & Short Story Writer's Market* will be ready for shipment in January 2001.) #10682

Additional books from the back of this card:

Book	Price
#	$
#	$
#	$
#	$
Subtotal	$

*Add $3.50 postage and handling for one book; $1.50 for each additional book.

Postage & Handling	$

Payment must accompany order. Ohioans add 6% sales tax. Canadians add 7% GST.

Total	$

VISA/MasterCard orders call
TOLL FREE 1-800-289-0963
8:30 to 5:00 Mon.-Fri. Eastern Time
or FAX 1-888-590-4082

☐ Payment enclosed $_____ (or)
Charge my: ☐ Visa ☐ MasterCard Exp._____

Account #_____

Signature_____

Name_____

Address_____

City_____

State/Prov._____ Zip/PC _____

30-Day Money Back Guarantee on every book you buy!

6580

Mail to: Writer's Digest Books • 1507 Dana Avenue • Cincinnati, OH 45207

New Writer's Digest Books!

2000 Guide to Literary Agents
edited by Donya Dickerson
Team up with an agent using this invaluable directory (now in its
9th year). Over 500 listings of literary and script agents, plus
inside information on the industry will help you choose the right
agent to represent you.
#10627/$21.99/335p/pb

The Insider's Guide to Getting an Agent
Lori Perkins
Getting an agent is sometimes crucial to getting published.
But, how do you locate the one that's right for you? This New
York literary agent offers advice, sample queries and proposals
that provide the guidance you need to find an agent that suits
your needs.
#10630/$16.99/240p/pb

Your Novel Proposal: From Creation to Contract
Blythe Camenson & Marshall J. Cook
The only guide of its kind covering everything from the query
letter to the book deal! Drawing on the experience of authors,
editors and agents, this book provides the essential details needed
to get published in today's rapidly changing fiction industry.
#10628/$18.99/256p/hc

You Can Write a Romance
Rita Clay Estrada & Rita Gallagher
Discover superb instruction with exercises and examples, plus
true-life success stories that give you the skills and inspiration
to turn your romance writing dreams into a reality.
#10633/$12.99/128p/pb

You Can Write a Mystery
Gillian Roberts
This award-winning author takes the mystery out of the profitable whodunit market. Learn about the core elements of the
genre, from developing ideas and building character profiles to
researching crimes and selecting point of view.
#10634/$12.99/128p/pb

Facts in a Flash: A Research Guide for Writers
Ellen Metter
Take the frustration out or your research projects with this mix
of humor, data and savvy research techniques—from cruising the
stacks to surfing the net.
#10632/$24.99/432p/hc

ⓃⒾ ROBERT MCKEE'S STORY STRUCTURE, PMB 1007, 7095 Hollywood Blvd., Los Angeles CA 90028-8903. (888)676-2533. Fax: (323)650-4791. E-mail: mxla-mckee@labridge.com. Website: www.mckeestor y.com. Contact: Joe Cook, conference coordinator. Estab. 1983. Workshops held in March, June, September, December in Los Angeles and March and September in New York. Average attendance: 280 (LA), 215 (NY). "Primary emphasis of workshops is on screenwriting with applications for novels, playwriting and journalism." Workshops held in LA at Pacific Design Center (385 seat theatre) and in NY at Fashion Institute (305 seat lecture hall).
Costs: $495/person; group discounts available.
Accommodations: Discount hotel rates available.
Additional Information: Workshop brochures available in January.

☑ MOUNT HERMON CHRISTIAN WRITERS CONFERENCE, P.O. Box 413, Mount Hermon CA 95041-0413. (831)430-1238. Fax: (831)335-9218. E-mail: slist@mhcamps.org. Website: www.mounthermon.org. Director of Specialized Programs: David R. Talbott. Estab. 1970. Annual. Conference held Friday-Tuesday over Palm Sunday weekend, April 14-18, 2000. Average attendance: 250. "We are a broad-ranging conference for all areas of Christian writing, including fiction, children's, poetry, nonfiction, magazines, books, educational curriculum and radio and TV scriptwriting. This is a working, how-to conference, with many workshops within the conference involving on-site writing assignments. The conference is sponsored by and held at the 440-acre Mount Hermon Christian Conference Center near San Jose, California, in the heart of the coastal redwoods. Registrants stay in hotel-style accommodations, and full board is provided as part of conference fees. Meals are taken family style, with faculty joining registrants. The faculty/student ratio is about 1:6 or 7. The bulk of our faculty are editors and publisher representatives from major Christian publishing houses nationwide."
Costs: Registration fees include tuition, conference sessions, resource notebook, refreshment breaks, room and board and vary from $525 (economy) to $750 (deluxe), double occupancy (1999 fees).
Accommodations: Airport shuttles are available from the San Jose International Airport. Housing is not required of registrants, but about 95% of our registrants use Mount Hermon's own housing facilities (hotel-style double-occupancy rooms). Meals with the conference are required and are included in all fees.
Additional Information: Registrants may submit 2 works for critique in advance of the conference, then have personal interviews with critiquers during the conference. No advance work is required however. Conference brochures/guidelines are available in December for SASE or by calling (888)MH-CAMPS. Inquiries by e-mail and fax OK. "The residential nature of our conference makes this a unique setting for one-on-one interaction with faculty/staff. There is also a decided inspirational flavor to the conference, and general sessions with well-known speakers are a highlight."

ⓃⒾ NO CRIME UNPUBLISHED™ MYSTERY WRITERS' CONFERENCE, Sisters in Crime/Los Angeles, P.O. Box 251646, Los Angeles CA 90025. (213)694-2972. E-mail: sincla@email.com. Website: www.sis tersincrimela.com. Estab. 1995. Annual. Conference duration: 1 day. Average attendance: 200. Conference on mystery and crime writing. Usually held in hotel near Los Angeles airport. Two-track program: Craft and forensic sessions; keynote speaker, luncheon speaker, agent panel, book signings. In 1999: Earlene Fowler, keynote speaker; authors, agents, forensic experts, public defender.
Costs: $80, included continental breakfast, snacks, lunch, souvenir items and all sessions (1999).
Accommodations: Airport shuttle to hotel. Optional overnight stay available. Hotel conference rate available. Arrangements made directly with hotel.
Additional Information: Conference brochure available for SASE.

PASADENA WRITERS' FORUM, P.C.C. Extended Learning Dept., 1570 E. Colorado Blvd., Pasadena CA 91106-2003. (626)585-7608. Coordinator: Meredith Brucker. Estab. 1954. Annual. Conference held March 4, 2000. Average attendance: 200. "For the novice as well as the professional writer in any field of interest: fiction or nonfiction, including scripts, children's, humor and poetry." Conference held on the campus of Pasadena City College. A panel discussion by agents, editors or authors is often featured at the end of the day.
Costs: $100, including box lunch and coffee hour.
Additional Information: Brochure upon request, no SASE necessary. "Pasadena City College also periodically offers an eight-week class 'Writing for Publication'."

☑ SAN DIEGO STATE UNIVERSITY WRITERS' CONFERENCE, SDSU College of Extended Studies, 5250 Campanile Drive, San Diego State University, San Diego CA 92182-1920. (619)594-2517. E-mail: ppierce @mail.sdsu.edu. Website: www.ces.sdsu.edu. Contact: Diane Dunaway, conference coordinator. Assistant to Director of Extension and Conference Facilitator: Paula Pierce. Estab. 1984. Annual. Conference held on 3rd weekend in January. Conference duration: 2 days. Average attendance: approximately 400. "This conference is held in San Diego, California, at the Mission Valley Doubletree. Each year the SDSU Writers Conference offers a variety of workshops for the beginner and the advanced writer. This conference allows the individual writer to choose which workshop best suits his/her needs. In addition to the workshops, editor/agent appointments and office hours are provided so attendees may meet with speakers, editors and agents in small, personal groups to discuss specific questions. A reception is offered Saturday immediately following the workshops where attendees may socialize with the faculty in a relaxed atmosphere. Keynote speaker is to be determined."

Costs: Approximately $225. This includes all conference workshops and office hours, coffee and pastries in the morning, lunch and reception Saturday evening. Editor/agent appointments extra fee.

Accommodations: Doubletree Mission Valley, (619)297-5466. Conference rate available for SDSU Writers Conference attendees. Attendees must make their own travel arrangements.

Additional Information: Editor/Agent sessions are private, one-on-one opportunities to meet with editors and agents to discuss your submission. To receive a brochure, e-mail, fax, call or send a postcard to above address. No SASE required.

THE WILLIAM SAROYAN WRITER'S CONFERENCE, P.O. Box 5331, Fresno CA 93755-5331. Phone/fax: (559)224-2154. E-mail: law@pacbell.net. Contact: Linda West. Estab. 1991. Annual. Conference held April 7-9, 2000. Conference duration: "Friday noon to Sunday noon." Average attendance: 250. Conference on "how to write and how to get published." The conference is held at Piccadilly Inn which is "close to the airport, other hotels and all workshops in one section of the hotel." 1999 speakers included A. Scott Berg, Bill Brohaugh, Georgia Hughes, Libby Hall and Eva Shaw.

Costs: 1999 fees: $225 for all workshops (choice of 39), most meals, critique sessions, one-on-ones with agents, editors, etc. Overnight accommodations listed in brochure. On-site accommodations approximately $80/night.

Additional Information: Brochures/guidelines available for SASE. Inquiries by fax and e-mail OK. The conference is "small, intimate—easy to talk with agents, editors, etc."

SCBWI/NATIONAL CONFERENCE ON WRITING & ILLUSTRATING FOR CHILDREN, 8271 Beverly Blvd., Los Angeles CA 90048. (323)782-1010. Executive Director: Lin Oliver. Estab. 1972. Annual. Conference held in August. Conference duration: 4 days. Average attendance: 350. Writing and illustrating for children. Site: Century Plaza Hotel in Los Angeles. Theme: "The Business of Writing."

Costs: $320 (members); $340 (late registration, members); $360 (nonmembers). Cost does not include hotel room.

Accommodations: Information on overnight accommodations made available. Conference rates at the hotel about $135/night.

Additional Information: Ms and illustration critiques are available. Conference brochures/guidelines are available (after June) for SASE.

UCLA EXTENSION WRITERS' PROGRAM, 10995 Le Conte Ave., #440, Los Angeles CA 90024. (310)825-9415 or (800)388-UCLA. Fax: (310)206-7382. E-mail: writers@unex.ucla.edu. Website: www.unex.ucla.edu/writers. Conference Coordinator: Cindy Lieberman. Estab. 1891. Courses held year-round with one-day or intensive weekend workshops to 12-week courses. A year-long Master Sequence is also offered every fall. "The diverse offerings span introductory seminars to professional novel and script completion workshops. The annual Los Angeles Writers Conference and a number of 1, 2 and 4-day intensive workshops are popular with out-of-town students due to their specific focus and the chance to work with industry professionals. The most comprehensive and diverse continuing education writing program in the country, offering over 400 courses a year including: screenwriting, fiction, writing for young people, poetry, nonfiction, playwriting, publishing and writing for interactive multimedia. Courses are offered in Los Angeles on the UCLA campus, Santa Monica and Universal City as well as online over the internet. Adult learners in the UCLA Extension Writers' Program study with professional screenwriters, fiction writers, playwrights, poets, nonfiction writers, and interactive multimedia writers, who bring practical experience, theoretical knowledge, and a wide variety of teaching styles and philosophies to their classes." Call for details.

Costs: Vary from $75-425.

Accommodations: Students make own arrangements. The program can provide assistance in locating local accommodations.

Additional Information: Conference brochures/guidelines are available year-round. Inquiries by e-mail and fax OK. "Some advanced-level classes have manuscript submittal requirements; instructions are always detailed in the quarterly UCLA Extension course catalog. An annual fiction prize, The James Kirkwood Prize in Creative Writing, has been established and is given annually to one fiction writer who has produced outstanding work in a Writers' Program course."

VOLCANO WRITERS' RETREAT, P.O. Box 163, Volcano CA 95689-0163. (209)296-7945. E-mail: khexberg@volcano.net. Website: www.volcano.net/~khexberg. Contact: Karen Hexberg. Estab. 1998. Biannual. Retreat held in April and October, 2000. Duration: 3 days. Average attendance: 25-35 (limited). Retreat for writing "fiction, poetry, essay, memoir." Held at the St. George Hotel. Hotel is "150 years old and located in the most picturesque of all the gold country towns, Volcano."

Costs: 1999 fees: $200-250 (including lodging and some meals).

Accommodations: "Most attendees stay at the site, The St. George Hotel, although individuals may make other arrangements."

Additional Information: "Absolutely no critiquing. The purpose of this retreat is to create a non-competitive, non-judgmental, safe atmosphere where we are all free to write the worst stuff in the world." Brochures/guidelines for SASE. Inquiries by e-mail OK.

☑ **WORLD HORROR CONVENTION**, P.O. Box 32167, Aurora CO 80041. (303)480-5363. E-mail: trbark er@earthlink.net. Website: www.whc.2000.org. Chairman: Ted Bryant. Estab. 1991. Annual. Conference held in different cities. Held May 11-14, 2000. Average attendance: 500. Concentration on horror-related fiction. Includes readings, panels, presentations, autographings, art show, dealers room, video/animation room, hospitality suite, etc. Featured speakers/panelists for 2000 are Peter Straub, Melanie Tem, Harlan Ellison, J. Michael Straczyrski, Steve Rasnic Tem, Ellen Datlow and Dan Simmons..
Costs: Supporting membership $30; attending membership $75-100.
Accommodations: Special hotel rates are available.
Additional Information: Guidelines available for SASE. Inquiries by fax and e-mail OK. "Professionals wishing to participate in our program must obtain an Attending Membership." 2001 conference will be in Seattle.

☑ **WRANGLING WITH WRITING**, Society of Southwestern Authors, P.O. Box 30355, Tucson AZ 85751. (520)296-5299. E-mail: wporter202@aol.com. Director: Penny Porter. Estab. 1971. Annual. Conference held 3 days in January. Attendance: limited to 350. Conference "to assist writers in whatever ways we can. We cover all areas." Held at the Holiday Inn with hotel rooms available. Keynote speakers for 2000 conference will be Ray Bradbury, Andrew Greeley and Bud Gardner. Plus 36 workshops for all genres of writing.
Costs: $175; includes 4 meals.
Accommodations: Inn Suites Hotel in Tucson. Information included in brochure available for SASE.
Additional Information: Critiques given if ms sent ahead. Sponsors short story contest (2,500 words or less) separate from the conference. Deadline May 31. Awards given September 21. Brochures/guidelines available after October 15 for SASE. Requests accepted via e-mail.

WRITE YOUR LIFE STORY FOR PAY, 23350 Sereno Court, Villa 30, Cupertino CA 95014. (415)691-0300. Contact: Louise Purwin Zobel. Estab. 1969. Workshop held irregularly, usually semiannually at several locations. Workshop duration: 1-2 days. Average attendance: 30-50. "Because every adult has a story worth telling, this conference helps participants to write fiction and nonfiction in books and short forms, using their own life stories as a base." This workshop is held on about 40 campuses at different times, inluding University of California and other university and college campuses in the West.
Costs: Usually $45-65/day, "depending on campus."
Additional Information: Brochures/guidelines available for SASE.

WRITERS CONNECTION SELLING TO HOLLYWOOD, P.O. Box 24770, San Jose CA 95154-4770. (408)445-3600. Fax: (408)445-3609. E-mail: info@sellingtohollywood.com. Website: www.sellingtohollywood.c om. Directors: Steve and Meera Lester. Estab. 1988. Annual. Conference held in August in LA area. Conference duration: 3 days; August 6-8, 1999. Average attendance: 275. "Conference targets scriptwriters and fiction writers, whose short stories, books, or scripts have strong cinematic potential, and who want to make valuable contacts in the film industry. Full conference registrants receive a private consultation with the film industry producer or professional of his/her choice who make up the faculty. Panels, workshops, 'Ask a Pro' discussion groups and networking sessions include over 50 agents, professional film and TV scriptwriters, producers, attorneys, studio executives and consultants."
Costs: In 1999: full conference by July 15, $500, $525 after July 15. Includes some meals.
Accommodations: $90/night (in LA) for private room; $50/shared room. Discount with designated conference airline.
Additional Information: "This is the premier screenwriting conference of its kind in the country, unique in its offering of an industry-wide perspective from pros working in all echelons of the film industry. Great for making contacts." Conference brochure/guidelines available March; phone, e-mail, fax or send written request.

Northwest (AK, ID, MT, OR, WA, WY)

CENTRUMS PORT TOWNSEND WRITERS' CONFERENCE, Box 1158, Port Townsend WA 98368. (360)385-3102. Fax: (360)385-2470. E-mail: centrum@centrum.org. Website: www.centrum.org. Director: Sam Hamill. Estab. 1974. Annual. Conference held mid-July. Average attendance: 180. Conference to promote poetry, fiction, creative nonfiction. The conference is held at a 700-acre state park on the strait of Juan de Fuca. "The site is a Victorian-era military fort with miles of beaches, wooded trails and recreation facilities. The park is within the limits of Port Townsend, a historic seaport and arts community, approximately 80 miles northwest of Seattle, on the Olympic Peninsula." There will be 5 guest speakers in addition to 10 fulltime faculty.
Costs: Approximately $325-425 tuition and $200 room and board. Less expensive option available.
Accommodations: "Modest room and board facilities on site." Also list of hotels/motels/inns/bed & breakfasts/ private rentals available.

Additional Information: "Admission to workshops is selective, based on manuscript submissions." Brochures/guidelines available for SASE or on website. "The conference focus is on the craft of writing and the writing life, not on marketing."

CLARION WEST WRITERS' WORKSHOP, 340 15th Ave. E., Suite 350, Seattle WA 98112. (206)322-9083. E-mail: leijona@nwrain.com. Website: www.sff.net.clarionwest/. Administrator: Leslie Howle. Estab. 1983. Annual. Workshop held June 20-July 30. Workshop duration 6 weeks. Average attendance: 20. "Conference to prepare students for professional careers in science fiction and fantasy writing. Held at Seattle Central Community College on Seattle's Capitol Hill, an urban site close to restaurants and cafes, not too far from downtown." Deadline for applications: April 1.
Costs: Workshop: $1,400 ($100 discount if application received by March 1). Dormitory housing: $800, meals not included.
Accommodations: Students are strongly encouraged to stay on-site, in dormitory housing at Seattle University. Cost: $800, meals not included, for 6-week stay.
Additional Information: "This is a critique-based workshop. Students are encouraged to write a story a week; the critique of student material produced at the workshop forms the principal activity of the workshop. Students and instructors critique manuscripts as a group." Conference guidelines available for SASE. Inquiries by e-mail OK. Limited scholarships are available, based on financial need. Students must submit 20-30 pages of ms with $25 application fee to qualify for admission. Dormitory and classrooms are handicapped accessible.

☑ **FLIGHT OF THE MIND—SUMMER WRITING WORKSHOP FOR WOMEN**, 622 SE 29th Ave., Portland OR 97214. (503)233-3936. Fax: (503)233-0774. E-mail: soapston@teleport.com. Website: www.teleport.com/%7esoapston/Flight/. Director: Ruth Gundle. Estab. 1984. Annual. Workshops held June 17-24 and June 26-July 3, 2000. Conference duration: each workshop lasts 1 week. Average attendance: 70. "Conference held at rustic retreat center on the Mackenzie River in the foothills of the Oregon Cascades. Right on the river—hiking trails, hot springs nearby. Most students accommodated in single dorm rooms; a few private cabins available. We have our own cooks and provide spectacular food." Five classes—topics vary year to year; 1999 included fiction with Ursula K. LeGuin and poetry by Lucille Clifton.
Costs: Approximately $800 for tuition, board and single dorm room. Extra for private cabin; bunk room cheaper alternative.
Accommodations: Special arrangements for transportation: "We charter a bus to pick up participants in Eugene, OR, at airport, train station and bus station." Accommodations and meals are included in cost.
Additional Information: "Critiquing is part of most classes; no individual critiques. We require manuscript submissions for acceptance into workshop. (Receive about twice as many applications as spaces.)" Workshop brochures/guidelines are available after January for 1 first-class stamp (no envelope) plus name and address. Inquiries by e-mail OK. "This is a feminist-oriented workshop with a focus on work generated at the workshop. High level of seriousness by all participants."

☑ **HAYSTACK WRITING PROGRAM**, PSU Summer Session, P.O. Box 1491, Portland OR 97207-1491. (503)725-4186. Fax: (503)725-4840. E-mail: herrinm@pdx.edu. Website: www.haystackpdx.edu. Contact: Maggie Herrington. Estab. 1968. Annual. Program runs from last week of June through first week of August. Workshop duration varies; one-week and weekend workshops are available throughout the six-week program. Average attendance: 10-15/workshop; total program: 400. "The program features a broad range of writing courses for writers at all skill levels. Classes are held in Cannon Beach, Oregon." Past instructors have included William Stafford, Ursula K. LeGuin, Craig Lesley, Molly Gloss, Mark Medoff, Tom Spanbauer, Sallie Tisdale.
Costs: Approximately $380/course weeklong; $150 (weekend). Does not include room and board.
Accommodations: Attendees make their own transportation arrangements. Various accommodations available including: B&B, motel, hotel, private rooms, camping, etc. A list of specific accommodations is provided.
Additional Information: Free brochure available after March. Inquiries by e-mail and fax OK. University credit (graduate or undergraduate) is available.

☑ **PACIFIC NORTHWEST WRITERS SUMMER CONFERENCE**, 2608 3rd Ave., Suite B, Seattle WA 98121. (206)443-3807. E-mail: pnwa@pnwa.org. Website: www.pnwa.org. Contact: Office. Estab. 1955. Annual. Conference held July 13-16, 2000. Average attendance: 700. Conference focuses on "fiction, nonfiction, poetry, film, drama, self-publishing, the creative process, critiques, core groups, advice from pros and networking." Site is Tacoma Sheraton Convention Center. "Editors and agents come from both coasts. They bring lore from the world of publishing. The PNWC provides opportunities for writers to get to know editors and agents. The literary contest provides feedback from professionals and possible fame for the winners."
Costs: $300-400, some meals included.
Additional Information: On-site critiques are available in small groups. Literary contest in these categories: adult articles and essays, nonfiction book, adult non-genre novel, poetry, adult genre novel, juvenile/young adult, screenwriting, adult short story and Stella Cameron romance novel prize. Deadline: February 15. Up to $8,000 awarded in prizes. Send SASE for guidelines.

N: PORTLAND STATE UNIVERSITY HAYSTACK WRITING PROGRAM, PSU Summer Session, P.O. Box 1491, Portland OR 97207. (503)725-4186. Contact: Maggie Herrington. Estab. 1968. Annual. Conference held from late June to early August in one-week sessions meeting Monday through Friday; some weekend workshops. Average attendance: 10-15/class. Conference offers a selection of writing courses including fiction, nonfiction, poetry, essay and memoir—taught by well-known writers in small-group sessions. Classes are held in the local school with supplemental activities at the beach, community lecture hall, and other areas of the resort town. University credit available.
Costs: $185 (weekend)-$380 (weeklong). Participants locate their own housing and meals.
Accommodations: Housing costs are $50-400/week. Camping, bed and breakfasts and hotels are available.

N: WHIDBEY ISLAND WRITERS' CONFERENCE, 5456 Pleasant View Lane, Freeland WA 98249. (360)331-2739. E-mail: writers@whidbey.com. Website: www.whidbey.com/writers. Contact: Celeste Mergens. Annual. Conference held March 3-5, 2000. Conference held in "local homes by the sea on Whidbey Island. A variety of informative classes and hands-on interactive writing workshops are offered. Expert panel discussions will be held where agents and editors will share inside details, devulge what they are looking for and offer important how-to's in skill building sessions." Speakers include Christina Baldwin, Marian Blue, Margaret Chittenden, Aaron Elkins and Elizabeth Engstrom.
Costs: $258 for the weekend not including meals and lodging.
Accommodations: Shuttle from Sea-tac Airport to Mukilteo Ferry for Whidbey Island and from the ferry to the conference available. "We have an accommodations hotline available through the Langley Chamber of Commerce. When making lodging reservations please mention the conference to receive a participant discount."
Additional Information: "If registrant desires an agent/editor consultation, they must submit the first five pages for a chapter book or youth novel or entire picture book idea with a written one-page synopsis." Conference brochures/guidelines available July 15 for SASE. Inquiries by e-mail OK.

WILLAMETTE WRITERS CONFERENCE, 9045 SW Barbur, Suite 5-A, Portland OR 97219-4027. (503)452-1592. Fax: (503)452-0372. E-mail: wilwrite@teleport.com. Website: www.tele.com/~wilwrite/. Contact: Bill Johnson, office manager. Estab. 1968. Annual. Conference held in August. Average attendance: 320. "Willamette Writers is open to all writers, and we plan our conference accordingly. We offer workshops on all aspects of fiction, nonfiction, marketing, the creative process, etc. Also we invite top notch inspirational speakers for key note addresses. Most often the conference is held on a local college campus which offers a scholarly atmosphere and allows us to keep conference prices down. Recent theme was 'The Writers Way.' We always include at least one agent or editor panel and offer a variety of topics of interest to both fiction, nonfiction and screenwriters." Recent editors, agents and film producers in attendance have included: Wendy Hubbert, Penguin Putnam; Carrie McGinnis, St. Martin's Press; Leslie Meredith, Ballantine Books; Stanley Brooks, Once Upon a Time Films; Julian Fowles, Asparza-Katz Productions; David Gassman, ICM; Nancy Ellis, Nancy Ellis Literary Agency; and Linda Mead, Linda Mead Literary Agency.
Costs: Cost for full conference including meals is $210 members; $246 nonmembers.
Accomodations: If necessary, these can be made on an individual basis. Some years special rates are available.
Additional Information: Conference brochures/guidelines are available in May for catalog-size SASE. Inquiries by fax and e-mail OK.

WRITE ON THE SOUND WRITERS' CONFERENCE, 700 Main St., Edmonds WA 98020. (425)771-0228. Fax: (425)771-0253. E-mail: wots@ci.edmonds.wa.us. Cultural Resources Coordinator: Frances Chapin. Sponsored by Edmonds Arts Commission. Estab. 1986. Annual. Conference held October 7-8, 2000. Conference duration: 2 days. Average attendance: 160. "Workshops and lectures are offered for a variety of writing interests and levels of expertise. It is a high quality, affordable conference with limited registration."
Costs: $85 for 2 days, $50 for 1 day (1999); includes registration, morning refreshments and 1 ticket to keynote lecture.
Additional Information: Brochures available in July. Inquiries by e-mail and fax OK.

N: YELLOW BAY WRITERS' WORKSHOP, Center for Continuing Education, University of Montana, Missoula MT 59812-1990. (406)243-2094. Fax: (406)243-2047. E-mail: hhi@selway.umt.edu. Website: www.umt.edu/ccesp/yellowbay. Contact: Program Manager. Estab. 1988. Annual. Conference held mid August. Average attendance: 50-60. Includes four workshops: 2 fiction; 1 poetry; 1 creative nonfiction/personal essay. Conference "held at the University of Montana's Flathead Lake Biological Station, a research station with informal educational facilities and rustic cabin living. Located in northwestern Montana on Flathead Lake, the largest natural freshwater lake west of the Mississippi River. All faculty are requested to present a craft lecture—usually also have an editor leading a panel discussion." 1999 faculty included Pam Houston, Denis Johnson, Jane Miller and Fred Haefele.
Costs: In 1999, for all workshops, lodging (single occupancy) and meals $840; $815 with double occupancy; $495 for commuters.

Accommodations: Shuttle is available from Missoula to Yellow Bay for those flying to Montana. Cost of shuttle is $45.
Additional Information: Brochures/guidelines are available for SASE.

Canada

[N] BOOMING GROUND, Buch E-462, 1866 Main Mall, Creative Writing Program, UBC, Vancouver, British Columbia V6T 121 Canada. (604)822-2469. Fax: (604)822-3616. E-mail: bg@arts.ubc.ca. Website: www. arts.ubc.ca/bg. Contact: Andrew Gray. Estab. 1998. Annual. Conference held July 8-15, 2000. Average attendance: 70. Conference on "fiction, poetry, non-fiction, screenplays." Conference held at "Green College, a residential college at the University of Columbia, overlooking the ocean." 1999 panels included "Paths to Publication," "Writing and Adapting for the Screen," "The Writer/Editor Relationship" and "The Writing Life." 1999 speakers included Diane Ackerman, keynote speaker; Zsuzsi Gartner, Esta Spalding, Linda Svendsen and Carolyn Swayze, panelists.
Costs: 1999 fees: $645 (Canadian). Meals and accommodation separate. Some scholarships available.
Accommodations: "Information on overnight accommodations is available and students are encouraged to stay on-site at Green College." On site accommodations: $360 and $397 (Canadian) for 7 nights.
Additional information: "Workshops are based on works-in-progress. Writers must submit manuscript with application for jury selection." Conference brochures/guidelines available January 2000 for SASE. Inquiries by fax and e-mail OK. "Classes are offered in both standard level and master classes. Standard classes are aimed at early career writers, while master classes are intended for mid-career writers."

THE FESTIVAL OF THE WRITTEN ARTS, Box 2299, Sechelt, British Columbia V0N 3A0 Canada. (800)565-9631 or (604)885-9631. Fax: (604)885-3967. E-mail: written_arts@sunshine.net. Website: www.sunshine. net/rockwood. Festival Producer: Gail Bull. Estab. 1983. Annual. Festival held: August 10-13, 2000. Average attendance: 3,500. To promote "all writing genres." Festival held at the Rockwood Centre. "The Centre overlooks the town of Sechelt on the Sunshine Coast. The lodge around which the Centre was organized was built in 1937 as a destination for holidayers arriving on the old Union Steamship Line; it has been preserved very much as it was in its heyday. A new twelve-bedroom annex was added in 1982, and in 1989 the Festival of the Written Arts constructed a Pavilion for outdoor performances next to the annex. The festival does not have a theme. Instead, it showcases 20 or more Canadian writers in a wide variety of genres each year—the only all Canadian writer's festival."
Costs: $12 per event or $150 for a four-day pass (Canadian funds).
Accommodations: Lists of hotels and bed/breakfast available.
Additional Information: The festival runs contests during the 3½ days of the event. Prizes are books donated by publishers. Brochures/guidelines are available after mid-April. Inquiries by e-mail and fax OK.

MARITIME WRITERS' WORKSHOP, Extension & Summer Session, UNB Box 4400, Fredericton, New Brunswick E3B 5A3 Canada. Phone/fax: (506)474-1144. E-mail: k4jc@unb.ca. Website: www.unb.ca/web/coned/writers/marritrs.html. Coordinator: Rhona Sawlor. Estab. 1976. Annual. Conference held July 9-15, 2000. Average attendance: 50. "We offer small groups of ten, practical manuscript focus. Notice writers welcome. Workshops in four areas: fiction, poetry, nonfiction, writing for children." Site is University of New Brunswick, Fredericton campus.
Costs: $350, tuition; $135 meals; $125/double room; $145/single room (Canadian funds).
Accommodations: On-campus accommodations and meals.
Additional Information: "Participants must submit 10-20 manuscript pages which form a focus for workshop discussions." Brochures are available after March. No SASE necessary. Inquiries by e-mail and fax OK.

SAGE HILL WRITING EXPERIENCE, Box 1731, Saskatoon, Saskatchewan S7K 3S1 Canada. Phone/fax: (306)652-7395. E-mail: sage.hill@sk.sympatico.ca. Website: www.lights.com/sagehill. Executive Director: Steven Ross Smith. Annual. Workshops held in August and October. Workshop duration 10-21 days. Attendance: limited to 36-40. "Sage Hill Writing Experience offers a special working and learning opportunity to writers at different stages of development. Top quality instruction, low instructor-student ratio and the beautiful Sage Hill setting offer conditions ideal for the pursuit of excellence in the arts of fiction, poetry and playwriting." The Sage Hill location features "individual accommodation, in-room writing area, lounges, meeting rooms, healthy meals, walking woods and vistas in several directions." Seven classes are held: Introduction to Writing Fiction & Poetry; Fiction Workshop; Writing Young Adult Fiction Workshop; Poetry Workshop; Poetry Colloquium;

CAN'T FIND A CONFERENCE? Conferences are listed by region. Check the introduction to this section for a list of regional categories.

Fiction Colloquium; Playwriting Lab. 1999 faculty included Don McKay, Elizabeth Philips, Dennis Cooley, Myrna Kostash, Dianne Warren, Robert Kroetsch.
Costs: $595 (Canadian) includes instruction, accommodation, meals and all facilities. Fall Poetry Colloquium: $875.
Accommodations: On-site individual accommodations located at Lumsden 45 kilometers outside Regina. Fall Colloquium is at Muenster, Saskatchewan, 150 kilometers east of Saskatchewan.
Additional Information: For Introduction to Creative Writing: A five-page sample of your writing or a statement of your interest in creative writing; list of courses taken required. For intermediate and colloquium program: A resume of your writing career and a 12-page sample of your work plus 5 pages of published work required. Application deadline is May 1. Guidelines are available after January for SASE. Inquiries by e-mail and fax OK. Scholarships and bursaries are available.

[N] [icon] SUNSHINE COAST FESTIVAL OF THE WRITTEN ARTS, Box 2299, Sechelt, British Columbia V0N 3A0 Canada. (604)885-9631 or (800) 565-9631. Fax: (604)885-3967. E-mail: written_arts@sunshine.net. Website: www.sunshine.net/rockwood. Contact: Gail Bull. Estab. 1982. Annual. Festival held August 10-13, 2000. Average attendance: 9,500. Festival "tries to represent all genres." Held in a "500 seat pavilion set in the beautiful Rockwood Gardens in the seaside town of Sechelt, B.C." 1999 speakers included Maragret Atwood, Arthur Black, Andreas Schroeder, Bill Richardson, Anne Petrie and Margo Button.
Costs: Individual events, $12; Festival pass, $150; student discounts. Meals and lodging are not included.
Accommodations: Information on overnight accommodations is available.
Additional information: Conference brochures/guidelines available in May for SASE. Inquiries by fax and e-mail OK.

[N] [icon] THE VANCOUVER INTERNATIONAL WRITERS FESTIVAL, 1398 Cartwright St., Vancouver, British Columbia V6H 3R8 Canada. (604)681-6330. Fax: (604)681-8400. E-mail: alee@writersfest.bc.ca. Website: www.writersfest.bc.ca. Estab. 1988. Annual. Held October 18-22, 2000. Average attendance: 11,000. "This is a festival for readers and writers. The program of events is diverse and includes readings, panel discussions, seminars. Lots of opportunities to interact with the writers who attend." Held on Granville Island—in the heart of Vancouver. Two professional theaters are used as well as Performance Works (an open space). "We try to avoid specific themes. Programming takes place between February and June each year and is by invitation."
Costs: Tickets are $10-15 (Canadian).
Accommodations: Local tourist info can be provided when necessary and requested.
Additional Information: Brochures/guidelines are available for SASE after August. Inquiries by e-mail and fax OK. "A reminder—this is a festival, a celebration, not a conference or workshop."

[icon] THE VICTORIA SCHOOL OF WRITING, Box 8152, Victoria, British Columbia V8W 3R8 Canada. (250)598-5300. Fax: (250)598-0066. E-mail: writeawy@islandnet.com. Website: www.islandnet.com/vicwrite. Contact: Margaret Dyment. Conference held from July 18-21. "Four-day intensive workshop on beautiful Vancouver Island with outstanding author-instructors in fiction, poetry, historical fiction and nonfiction."
Cost: $475 (Canadian).
Accommodations: On site.
Additional Information: Workshop brochures available. Inquiries by e-mail and fax OK.

International

[icon] THE AEGEAN CENTER FOR THE FINE ARTS WORKSHOPS, Paros 84400, Cyclades, Greece. Phone/fax: (30)284-23287. E-mail: studyart@aegeancenter.org. Website: www.aegeancenter.org. Director: John A. Pack. Held 7 times/year. Workshop held May, June, September, October and November. Workshop duration: Spring—4-13 weeks; Summer sessions: 2-3 weeks; Fall—4-15 weeks. Average attendance: 15. "Creative writing in all its aspects." Spring workshop held at the Aegean Center "in a neoclassical 16th century townhouse in the village of Parikia with a gallery/lecture hall, well-equipped darkroom, modest library, rooms for studio space and classrooms." Location is on Paros, an island about 100 miles southeast of Athens. Fall workshop held in Italy starting in Pistoia in 16th century Villa Rospigliosi and includes travel to Pisa, Lucca, Prato, Siena, Venice, Florence and Rome in Italy as well as Athens and, finally, Paros.
Costs: For 13-week Spring workshop, tuition is $6,500 in 2000 or $2,500/monthly session (housing included). For 15-week Fall workshop, tuition is $7,500 in 2000, or $2,500 for monthly session ($2,500 Italy session only). Includes housing (villa accommodation and hotels in Italy); half board in Villa accommodation; travel while in Italy; museum entrance fees.
Accommodations: In Paros, accommodations (single occupancy apartment). All apartments have small equipped kitchen areas and private bathroom. Italy, villa accommodation and hotels.
Additional Information: College credit is available. Workshop brochures/guidelines are available for SASE or via website. Inquiries by e-mail and fax OK.

🌐 **ART WORKSHOPS IN GUATEMALA**, 4758 Lyndale Ave. S, Minneapolis MN 55409-2304. (612)825-0747. Fax: (612)825-6637. E-mail: info@artguat.org. Website: www.artguat.org. Conference Director: Liza Fourré. Estab. 1995. Annual. Maximum class size: 10 students per class. The conference is held in a private home. Workshop titles include: Creative Writing—Developing the Novel with Tessa Bridal (February 4-13, 2000).
Costs: $1,675 (includes tuition, air fare to Guatemala from USA, lodging and ground transportation).
Accommodations: All transportation included.
Additional Information: Conference brochures/guidelines are available. Inquiries by e-mail and fax are OK.

🌐 **THE ARVON FOUNDATION LTD. WORKSHOPS**, Totleigh Barton Sheepwash, Beaworthy, Devon EX21 5NS United Kingdom. Phone: 00 44 14 09231338. National Director: David Pease. Estab. 1968 (workshops). Workshops held April through November at 3 centers. Workshops last 4½ days. Average attendence: 16/workshop. Workshops cover all types of fiction writing. "Totleigh Barton in Devon was the first Arvon centre. Next came Lumb Bank (Hebden Bridge, West Yorkshire HX7 6DF) and now, 12 courses at Moniack Mhor (Moniack, Kirkhill, Inverness IV 5 7PQ)." Totleigh Barton is a thatched manor house. Lumb Bank is an 18th century mill owner's home and Moniack Mhor is a traditional croft house. All are in peaceful, rural settings. In the three houses there are living rooms, reading rooms, rooms for private study, dining rooms and well equipped kitchens."
Costs: In 1999 course fee will be £320 which includes food, tuition and accommodation. For those in need, a limited number of grants and bursaries are available from the Arvon Foundation.
Accommodations: There is sleeping accommodation for up to 16 course members, but only limited single room accommodation (there are 8 bedrooms at Lumb Bank, 12 bedrooms at Moniack Mhor and 13 bedrooms at Totleigh Barton). The adjacent barns at Lumb Bank and Totleigh Barton have been converted into workshop/studio space and there are writing huts in the garden.
Additional Information: Sometimes writers are required to submit work. Check for details. Conference brochure/guidelines available for SASE.

🌐 **EDINBURGH UNIVERSITY CENTRE FOR CONTINUING EDUCATION CREATIVE WRITING WORKSHOPS**, 11 Buccleuch Place, Edinburgh Scotland EH8 9LW. (131)650-4400. Fax: (131)667-6097. E-mail: cce@ed.ac.uk. Website: www.cce.ed.ac.uk. Administrative Director of International Summer Schools: Bridget M. Stevens. Contact: Ursula Michels. Estab. 1990. Introductory course June 24-30; short story course July 1-7; playwriting course July 17-21. Average attendance: 15. Courses cover "basic techniques of creative writing, the short story and playwriting. The University of Edinburgh Centre for Continuing Education occupies traditional 18th century premises near the George Square Campus. Located nearby are libraries, banks and recreational facilities. Free use of word-processing facilities."
Costs: In 1999 cost was £195 per one-week course (tuition only).
Accommodations: Information on overnight accommodations is available. Accommodations include student dormitories, self-catering apartment and local homes.
Additional Information: Conference brochures/guidelines available after December for SASE. Inquiries by e-mail and fax OK.

🌐 ✅ **PARIS WRITERS' WORKSHOP/WICE**, 20, Bd du Montparnasse, Paris, France 75015. (33-1)45.66.75.50. Fax: (33-1)40.65.96.53. E-mail: pww@wice-paris.org. Website: www.wice.org. Directors: Rose Burke and Marcia Lebre. Estab. 1987. Annual. Conference held first week in July. Average attendance: 40-50. "Conference concentrates on fiction, nonfiction creativity and poetry. Visiting lecturers speak on a variety of issues important to beginning and advanced writers. 1999 lecturers included Cole Swenson, chair of Creative Writing Department at the University of Denver; Bob Mohl, online author; David Smith, co-editor of the *Southern Review*; and Christopher Dickey, journalist and author. Located in the heart of Paris on the Bd. du Montparnasse, the stomping grounds of such famous American writers as Ernest Hemingway, Henry Miller and F. Scott Fitzgerald. The site consists of 4 classrooms, a resource center/library and private terrace."
Costs: $370—tuition only.
Additional Information: "Students submit 1 copy of complete ms or work-in-progress which is sent in advance to writer in residence. Each student has a one-on-one consultation with writer in residence concerning ms that was submitted." Conference brochure/guidelines are available winter 1999/2000. Inquiries by e-mail and fax OK. "Workshop attracts many expatriate Americans and other English language students from all over Europe and North America. We can assist with finding a range of hotels, from budget to more luxurious accommodations. We are an intimate workshop with an exciting mix of more experienced, published writers and enthusiastic beginners. Past writers include CK Williams, Carolyn Kizer, Grace Paley, Jayne Anne Phillips, Marilyn Hacker, Matthew Sweeney, Carol Shields, Isabelle Huggins and Gwen Davis.

🌐 ✅ **SUMMER IN FRANCE WRITING WORKSHOPS**, HCOI, Box 102, Plainview TX 79072. Phone/fax: (806)889-3533. E-mail: bettye@plainview.com. Website: www.parisamericanacademy.edu. Director: Bettye Givens. Annual. Conference: 27 days in July. Average attendance: 10-15. For fiction, poetry, nonfiction, drama. The classrooms are in the Val de Grace 277 Rue St. Jacques in the heart of the Latin Quarter near Luxeumbourg

Park in Paris. Guest speakers include Paris poets, professors and editors (lectures in English).

Costs: Costs vary. 1999 cost was $2,850. Costs includes literature classes, art history and the writing workshop and shared apartments.

Accommodations: Some accommodations with a French family.

Additional Information: Conference brochures/guidelines are available for SASE. Inquiries by e-mail and fax OK. "Enroll early. Side trips out of Paris are planned as are poetry readings at the Paris American Academy and at Shakespeare & Co."

TŶ NEWYDD WRITER'S CENTRE, Llanystumdwy, Cricieth Gwynedd LL52 OLW, United Kingdom. Phone: 01766-522811. Fax: 01766 523095. Director: Sally Baker. Estab. 1990. Regular courses held throughout the year. Every course held Monday-Saturday. Average attendance: 14. "To give people the opportunity to work side by side with professional writers, in an informal atmosphere." Site is Tŷ Newydd. Large manor house. Last home of the prime minister, David Lloyd George. Situated in North Wales, Great Britain-between mountains and sea." Past featured tutors include novelists Beryl Bainbridge and Bernice Rubens.

Costs: £295 for Monday-Saturday (includes full board, tuition).

Accommodations: Transportation from railway stations arranged. Accommodation in Tŷ Newydd (onsite).

Additional Information: Brochures/guidelines are available by mail, phone or fax after January. Inquiries by fax OK. "We have had several people from U.S. on courses here in the past three years. More and more people come to us from the U.S. often combining a writing course with a tour of Wales."

THE WRITERS' SUMMER SCHOOL, SWANWICK, The Rectory, Blisworth, NN7 3BJ England. Phone/fax: 07050-630949. E-mail: bcourtie@aol.com. Website: dspace.dial.pipex.com/roydev/. Secretary: Brenda Courtie. Estab. 1949. Annual. Conference held August 14-20, 1999. Average attendance: 300 plus. "Conference concentrates on all fields of writing." Speakers in 1999 included Bernard Cornwell and Deborah Moggach.

Costs: 1999: £198-£300 per person inclusive.

Accommodations: Buses from main line station to conference centre provided.

Additional Information: Conference brochures/guidelines are available after February. Inquiries by mail, e-mail and fax OK. "The Writers' Summer School is a nonprofit-making organization."

Organizations

When you write, you write alone. It's just you and the typewriter or computer screen. Yet the writing life does not need to be a lonely one. Joining a writing group or organization can be an important step in your writing career. By meeting other writers, discussing your common problems and sharing ideas, you can enrich your writing and increase your understanding of this sometimes difficult, but rewarding life.

The variety of writers' organizations seems endless—encompassing every type of writing and writer—from small, informal groups that gather regularly at a local coffee house for critique sessions to regional groups that hold annual conferences to share technique and marketing tips. National organizations and unions fight for writers' rights and higher payment for freelancers, and international groups monitor the treatment of writers around the world.

In this section you will find state-, province- and regional-based groups. You'll also find national organizations including the National Writers Association. The Mystery Writers of America and the Western Writers of America are examples of groups devoted to a particular type of writing. Whatever your needs or goals, you're likely to find a group listed here to interest you.

SELECTING A WRITERS' ORGANIZATION

To help you make an informed decision, we've provided information on the scope, membership and goals of the organizations listed on these pages. We asked groups to outline the types of memberships available and the benefits members can expect. Most groups will provide additional information for a self-addressed, stamped envelope, and you may be able to get a sample copy of their newsletter for a modest fee.

Keep in mind joining a writers' organization is a two-way street. When you join an organization, you become a part of it and, in addition to membership fees, most groups need and want your help. If you want to get involved, opportunities can include everything from chairing a committee to writing for the newsletter to helping set up an annual conference. The level of your involvement is up to you, and almost all organizations welcome contributions of time and effort.

Selecting a group to join depends on a number of factors. As a first step, you must determine what you want from membership in a writers' organization. Then send away for more information on the groups that seem to fit your needs. Start, however, by asking yourself:

• Would I like to meet writers in my city? Am I more interested in making contacts with other writers across the country or around the world?

• Am I interested in a group that will critique and give me feedback on work-in-progress?

• Do I want marketing information and tips on dealing with editors?

• Would I like to meet other writers who write the same type of work I do or am I interested in meeting writers from a variety of fields?

• How much time can I devote to meetings and are regular meetings important to me? How much can I afford to pay in dues?

• Would I like to get involved in running the group, working on the group's newsletters, planning a conference?

• Am I interested in a group devoted to writers' rights and treatment or would I rather concentrate on the business of writing?

For More Information

Because they do not usually have the resources or inclination to promote themselves widely, finding a local writers' group is usually a word-of-mouth process. If you would like to start a writers group in your area, read The How-Tos of Money & Meetings for Writers' Groups on page 613. Also ask your local libraries and bookstores if they sponsor writers' groups in conjunction with Writer's Digest Books. If they are not already, you or a representative of the library or bookstore may call (800)289-0963, ext. 424 for a free packet of information on starting a writers' group.

If you have a computer and would like to meet with writers in other areas of the country, you will find many commercial online services, such as GEnie and America Online, have writers' sections and "clubs" online. Many free online services available through Internet also have writers' "boards."

For more information on writers' organizations, check *The Writer's Essential Desk Reference: A Companion to Writer's Market*, 2nd edition (Writer's Digest Books, 1507 Dana Ave., Cincinnati OH 45207). Other directories listing organizations for writers include the *Literary Market Place* or *International Literary Market Place* (R.R. Bowker, 121 Chanlon Rd., New Providence NJ 07974). The National Writers Association also maintains a list of writers' organizations.

ASSOCIATED WRITING PROGRAMS, Tallwood House, Mail Stop 1E3, George Mason University, Fairfax VA 22030-9736. (703)993-4301. Fax: (703)993-4302. E-mail: awp@gmu.edu. Website: www.awpwriter. org (includes FAQ, membership information/ordering, award series guidelines, links to institutional members, AWP news). Contact: Membership Services. Estab. 1967. Number of Members: 5,000 individuals and 290 institutions. Types of Membership: Institutional (universities); graduate students; individual writers; and *Chronicle* subscribers. Open to any person interested in writing; most members are students or faculty of university writing programs (worldwide). Benefits include information on creative writing programs; grants, awards and publishing opportunities for writers; job list for academe and writing-related fields; a job placement service for writers in academe and beyond. AWP holds an Annual Conference in a different US city every spring; also conducts an annual Award Series in poetry, short story collections, novel and creative nonfiction, in which winner receives $2,000 honorarium and publication by a participating press. AWP acts as agent for finalists in Award Series and tries to place their manuscript with publishers throughout the year. Manuscripts accepted January 1-February 28 only. Novel competition; winner receives publication by St. Martin's Press and $10,000 in royalties. Send SASE for new guidelines. Publishes *The Writer's Chronicle* 6 times/year; 3 times/academic semester. Available to members for free. Nonmembers may order a subscription for $20/year; $25/year Canada; call for overseas rates. Also publishes the *AWP Official Guide to Writing Programs* which lists about 330 creative writing programs in universities across the country and in Canada. *Guide* is updated every 2 years; cost is $25.95, which includes shipping and handling. Dues: $57 for individuals; $37 students (must send copy of ID); additional $62 for full placement service. AWP keeps dossiers on file and sends them to school or organization of person's request. Holds two meetings per year for the Board of Directors. Send SASE for information. Inquiries by fax and e-mail OK.

AUSTIN WRITERS' LEAGUE, Austin Writers' League, 1501 W. Fifth, E-2, Austin TX 78703. (512)499-8914. Fax: (512)499-0441. Executive Director: Jim Bob McMillan. Estab. 1981. Number of Members: 1,600. Types of Memberships: Regular, student/senior citizen, family. Monthly meetings and use of resource center/library is open to the public. "Membership includes both aspiring and professional writers, all ages and all ethnic groups." Job bank is also open to the public. Public also has access to technical assistance. Partial and full scholarships offered for some programs. Of 1,600 members, 800 reside in Austin. Remaining 800 live all over the US and in other countries. Benefits include monthly newsletter, monthly meetings, study groups, resource center/library-checkout privileges, discounts on workshops, seminars, classes, job bank, discounts on books and tapes, participation in awards programs, technical/marketing assistance, copyright forms and information, Writers Helping Writers (mentoring program). Center has 5 rooms plus 2 offices and storage area. Public space includes reception and job bank area; conference/classroom; library; and copy/mail room. Library includes 1,000 titles. Sponsors fall and spring workshops, weekend seminars, informal classes, sponsorships for special events such as readings, production of original plays, media conferences, creative writing programs for children and youth; Violet Crown Book Awards, newsletter writing awards, Young Texas Writers awards, contests for various anthologies. Publishes *Austin Writer* (monthly newsletter), sponsors with Texas Commission on the Arts Texas Literary Touring Program. Administers literature subgranting program for Texas Commission on the Arts. Membership/

subscription: $40, $35-students, senior citizens, $60 family membership. Monthly meetings. Study groups set their own regular meeting schedules. Send SASE for information.

☑ **THE AUTHORS GUILD**, 330 W. 42nd St., 29th Floor, New York NY 10036-6902. (212)563-5904. Fax: (212)564-8363. E-mail: staff@authorsguild.org. Website: www.authorsguild.org (includes publishing industry news, business, legal and membership information). Executive Director: Paul Aiken. Contact: John McCloskey, membership coordinator. Inquiries by fax and e-mail OK. Purpose of organization: membership organization of 7,500 members offers services and information materials intended to help published authors with the business and legal aspects of their work, including contract problems, copyright matters, freedom of expression and taxation. Maintains staff of attorneys and legal interns to assist members. Group health insurance available. Qualifications for membership: book author published by an established American publisher within 7 years or any author who has had 3 works, fiction or nonfiction, published by a magazine or magazines of general circulation in the last 18 months. Associate membership also available. Annual dues: $90. Different levels of membership include: associate membership with all rights except voting available to an author who has a firm contract offer from an American publisher. Workshops/conferences: "The Guild and the Authors Guild Foundation conduct several symposia each year at which experts provide information, offer advice, and answer questions on subjects of concern to authors. Typical subjects have been the rights of privacy and publicity, libel, wills and estates, taxation, copyright, editors and editing, the art of interviewing, standards of criticism and book reviewing. Transcripts of these symposia are published and circulated to members." "The *Authors Guild Bulletin*, a quarterly journal, contains articles on matters of interest to published writers, reports of Guild activities, contract surveys, advice on problem clauses in contracts, transcripts of Guild and League symposia, and information on a variety of professional topics. Subscription included in the cost of the annual dues."

🌐 ☑ **THE BRITISH FANTASY SOCIETY**, 201 Reddish Rd., South Reddish, Stockport SK5 7HR United Kingdom. E-mail: syrinx.2112@btinternet.com. Website: www.herebedragons.co.uk/bfs (includes membership details, news, books for sale, fantasy conference details). Secretary: Robert Parkinson. Estab. 1971. Open to: "Anyone interested in fantasy. The British Fantasy Society was formed to provide coverage of the fantasy, science fiction and horror fields. To achieve this, the Society publishes its *Newsletter*, packed with information and reviews of new books and films, plus a number of other booklets of fiction and articles: *Winter Chills*, *Mystique*, *Masters of Fantasy* and *Dark Horizons*. The BFS also organises an annual Fantasy Conference at which the British Fantasy Awards are presented for categories such as Best Novel, Best Short Story and Best Film." Dues and subscription fees are £20 (UK); £25 (Europe), £40 (elsewhere). Payment in sterling only. Send SASE or IRC for information. Inquiries by e-mail OK.

☑ **CALIFORNIA WRITERS' CLUB**, P.O. Box 1281, Berkeley CA 94701. Website: www/calwriters.com. Estab. 1909. Ten branches. Number of Members: 900. Type of Memberships: Associate and active. Open to all writers. "Includes published authors, those actively pursuing a career in writing and those associated with the field of writing." Benefits include: CWC sponsors annual conference with writing contest. Publishes a monthly newsletter at state level and at branch level. Available to members only. Dues: $35/year. Send SASE for information. Inquiries by e-mail (through website OK).

☑ **CANADIAN SOCIETY OF CHILDREN'S AUTHORS, ILLUSTRATORS AND PERFORMERS (CANSCAIP)**, 35 Spadina Rd., Toronto, Ontario M5R 2S9 Canada. (416)515-1559. Fax: (416)515-7022. E-mail: canscaip@interlog.com. Website: www.interlog.com/~canscaip (includes children's authors, seminar information, art collection—samples [traveling]). Executive Secretary: Nancy Prasad. Estab. 1977. Number of Members: 1,100. Types of membership: Full professional member and friend (associate member). Open to professional active writers, illustrators and performers in the field of children's culture (full members); beginners and all other interested persons and institutions (friends). International scope, but emphasis on Canada. Benefits include quarterly newsletter, minutes of monthly meetings, marketing opportunities, publicity via our membership directory and our "members available" list, jobs (school visits, readings, workshops, residencies, etc.) through our "members available" list, mutual support through monthly meetings. Sponsors annual workshop, "Packaging Your Imagination," held every October. Publishes *CANSCAIP News*, quarterly, available to all (free with membership, otherwise $25 Canadian). Dues: professional fees: $60 Canadian/year; friend fees: $25/year; institutional $30/year. "Professionals must have written, illustrated or performed work for children commercially, sufficient to satisfy the membership committee (more details on request)." CANSCAIP National has open meetings from September to June, monthly in Toronto. CANSCAIP West holds bimonthly meetings in Vancouver. Also has a London, Ontario branch. Send SASE for information. Inquiries by fax and e-mail OK.

MARKET CONDITIONS are constantly changing! If you're still using this book and it is 2001 or later, buy the newest edition of *Novel & Short Story Writer's Market* at your favorite bookstore or order from Writer's Digest Books at (800)289-0963.

CINCINNATI WRITER'S PROJECT, 2592 Ferguson Rd., #9, Cincinnati OH 45238. (513)451-0410. E-mail: carolmarie_stock@mail.msj.edu. Contact: Carolmarie Stock. Estab. 1988. Organization of Cincinnati area writers. Members receive *Rough Draft*, the CWP monthly newsletter; general membership meeting held the third Thursday of each month. Members also participate in regularly scheduled workshops, critique sessions and readings in fiction, nonfiction, poetry and script/screen writing. Members' books are offered through the CWP book catalog and at other local writers' events. Dues for one year: $25, individual; $35 family. Send SASE for information. (See the interview with Dallas Wiebe, president and cofounder of CWP, in this section.)

FEDERATION OF BRITISH COLUMBIA WRITERS, MPO Box 2206, Vancouver, British Columbia V6P 6G5 Canada. (604)267-7087. Fax: (604)267-7086. E-mail: fedbcwrt@pinc.com. Website: www.swifty.com/bcwa. Coordinator of Administration and Member Services: Ana Torres. Executive Director: Corey Van't Haaff. Estab. 1982. Number of Members: 800. Types of Membership: regular. "Open to established and emerging writers in any genre, province-wide." Benefits include newsletter, liaison with funding bodies, publications, workshops, readings, literary contests, various retail and educational discounts. Sponsors readings and workshops. Publishes a newsletter 4 times/year, included in membership. Dues: $60 regular. Send SASE for information. Inquiries by fax and e-mail OK.

FEMINIST WRITERS GUILD, % Outrider Press, 937 Patricia Lane, Crete IL 60417. (708)672-6630. Fax: (708)672-5820 or toll free (800)933-4680 (code 03). E-mail: outriderpr@aol.com. President: Whitney Scott. Estab. 1977. Founded by outstanding writers including Adrienne Rich, Marge Piercy, Tillie Olsen and Valerie Miner. Number of members: 150. Open to: all who write seriously at any level regardless of age, gender, orientation. Benefits include formal readings, newsletters, monthly open mikes, two themed readings annually, publications, leadership opportunities and workshops in affiliation with Outrider Press, Inc. Sponsors an annual anthology contest with cash prizes and publication. 2000 theme is "Nature & Our Planet" (deadline: January 31, 2000). 2001 theme is Love Stories: "A Kiss is Still a Kiss" (deadline: January 31, 2001). Animal Stories: "Feathers, Fins and Fur." Send SASE for guidelines. Inquiries by e-mail OK. Dues for July 1, 1999 to June 30, 2000: $30.

HORROR WRITERS ASSOCIATION (HWA), P.O. Box 50577, Palo Alto CA 94303. E-mail: hwa@horror.org. Website: www.horror.org. President: S.P. Somtow. Estab. 1983. Number of Members: 850. Type of Memberships: Active—writers who have one published novel or three professional stories. Associate—non-writing professionals including editors, artists, agents and booksellers. Affiliate—beginning writers and others interested in the horror genre. Sponsors the "Bram Stoker Award" for excellence in horror writing. Publishes membership directory, handbook, and bimonthly newsletter with market reports. Dues: $55/year (US); $65/year (overseas); $75/year family membership; $100/year corporate membership. Meets once a year. Send SASE for information or visit website.

MANITOBA WRITERS' GUILD, 206-100 Arthur St., Winnipeg, Manitoba R3B, 1H3 Canada. (204)942-6134. Fax: (204)942-5754. E-mail: mbwriter@escape.ca. Number of members: approximately 550. Type of memberships: Regular, student, senior and fixed income. Open to anyone: writers, emerging and established; readers, particularly those interested in Manitoba literature. "Membership is provincial in general, although we have members from across Canada, USA and the world." Benefits include special discounts on programs, goods and services; regular mailings of program notices; and *WordWrap*, published 6 times/year, featuring articles, regular columns, information on current markets and competitions, announcements, and profiles of Manitoba writers. Programs include Mentor/Apprentice program, small resource center (2-staff, small resource library, nonlending); open workshops once a month in fall and winter; Annual spring conference, usually April; and Cafe Reading series. Dues: $40 regular; $20 seniors, students, fixed-income. Send SASE for information.

MYSTERY WRITERS OF AMERICA (MWA), 17 E. 47th St., 6th Floor, New York NY 10017. (212)888-8171. Fax: (212)888-8107. Website: www.mysterywriters.org (includes information about the newsletter, awards and membership). President: Barbara D'Amato. Estab. 1945. Number of Members: 2,600. Type of memberships: Active (professional, published writers of fiction or nonfiction crime/mystery/suspense); associate (professionals in allied fields, i.e., editor, publisher, critic, news reporter, publicist, librarian, bookseller, etc.); corresponding (writers qualified for active membership who live outside the US); affiliate (writers unpublished in the mystery field and those interested in the genre). Benefits include promotion and protection of writers' rights and interests, including counsel and advice on contracts, MWA courses and workshops, a national office, an annual conference featuring the Edgar Allan Poe Awards, the *MWA Anthology*, a national newsletter, regional conferences, insurance, marketing tools, meetings and research publications. Newsletter, *The Third Degree*, is published 10 times/year for members. Annual dues: $65 for US members; $32.50 for Corresponding members.

THE NATIONAL LEAGUE OF AMERICAN PEN WOMEN, INC., Headquarters: The Pen Arts Building, 1300 17th St., NW, Washington DC 20036-1973. (202)785-1997. Fax: (202)452-6868. E-mail: nlapw1@juno.com. Website: members.aol.com/penwomen/pen.htm. Contact: National President. Estab. 1897. Number of Members: 5,000. Types of Membership: Three classifications: Art, Letters, Music. Open to: Professional women. "Professional to us means our membership is open to women who sell their art, writings, or music compositions. We have over 175 branches in the mainland US plus Hawaii and the Republic of Panama. Some branches have as many as 100 members, some as few as 10 or 12. It is necessary to have 5 members to form a new branch." Benefits include a bimonthly magazine and local and national competitions. Our facility is The Pen Arts Building. It is a 20-room Victorian mansion. One distinguished resident was President Abraham Lincoln's son, Robert Todd Lincoln, the former Secretary of War and Minister of Great Britain. It has rooms available for Pen Women visiting the D.C. area, and for Board members in session 3 times a year. There are Branch and State Association competitions, as well as Biennial Convention competitions. Offers a research library of books by members and histories of the organization. Sponsors awards biennially to Pen Women in each classification: Art, Letters, Music, and $1,000 award biennially in even-numbered year to non-Pen Women in each classification for women age 35 and over who wish to pursue special work in art, music or letters field. *The Pen Woman* is the membership magazine, published 6 times a year, free to members, $18 a year for nonmember subscribers. Dues: $40/year for national organization, from $5-10/year for branch membership and from $1-5 for state association dues. Branches hold regular meetings each month, September through May except in northern states which meet usually March through September (for travel convenience). Send SASE for information. Inquiries via e-mail OK, but prefers SASE.

☑ **NATIONAL WRITERS ASSOCIATION**, 3140 S. Peoria, #295, Aurora CO 80014. (303)841-0246. Executive Director: Sandy Whelchel. Estab. 1937. Number of Members: 4,000. Types of Memberships: Regular membership for those without published credits; professional membership for those with published credits. Open to: Any interested writer. National/International plus we have 16 chapters in various states. Benefits include critiques, marketing advice, editing, literary agency, complaint service, chapbook publishing service, research reports on various aspects of writing, 4 contests, National Writers Press—self-publishing operation, computer bulletin board service, regular newsletter with updates on marketing, bimonthly magazine on writing related subjects, discounts on supplies, magazines and some services. Sponsors periodic conferences and workshops: short story contest opens April, closes July 1; novel contest opens December, closes April 1. Publishes *Flash Market News* (monthly publication for professional members only); *Authorship Magazine* (bimonthly publication available by subscription $20 to nonmembers). Dues: $65 regular; $85 professional. For professional membership requirement is equivalent of 3 articles or stories in a national or regional magazine; a book published by a royalty publisher, a play, TV script or movie produced. Send SASE for information. Chapters hold meetings on a monthly basis.

☑ **NEW HAMPSHIRE WRITERS' PROJECT**, P.O. Box 2693, Concord NH 03302-2693. (603)226-6649. Fax: (603)226-0035. E-mail: nhwp@nh.ultranet.com. Executive Director: Jackie E. Bonafide. Estab. 1988. Number of Members: 750. Type of Memberships: individual; senior/student. Open to anyone interested in the literary arts—writers (fiction, nonfiction, journalists, poets, scriptwriters, etc.), teachers, librarians, publishers and readers. Statewide scope. Benefits include a bimonthly publication featuring articles about NH writers and publishers; leads for writers, new books listings; and NH literary news. Also discounts on workshops, readings, conferences. Dues: $35 for individuals; $20 for seniors and full-time students; $250 for underwriters. Send SASE for information. Inquiries by fax and e-mail OK.

N **NORTH CAROLINA WRITERS' NETWORK**, P.O. Box 954, Carrboro NC 27510. (919)967-9540. Fax: (919)929-0535. Executive Director: Linda W. Hobson. Estab. 1985. Number of Members: 1,800. Open to: All writers, all levels of skill and friends of literature. Membership is approximately 1,600 in North Carolina and 200 in 33 other states and 5 other countries. Benefits include bimonthly newsletter, reduced rates for competition entry fees, fall and spring conferences, workshops, etc., use of critiquing service, use of library and resource center, press release and publicity service, information database(s). Sponsors annual Fall Conference for writers, Creative Nonfiction Competition, statewide workshops, Doris Betts Fiction Competition, Writers & Readers Series, Randall Jarrell Poetry Prize, Poetry Chapbook Competition, Thomas Wolfe Fiction Prize, Fiction Competition, Paul Green Playwright Prize. Publishes the 28-page bimonthly *Writers' Network News*, and *North Carolina's Literary Resource Guide*. Subscription included in dues. Dues: $40/year, $25/year (students enrolled in a degree-granting program, seniors 65+ and disabled). Events scheduled throughout the year. Send SASE for information.

N **ROMANCE WRITERS OF AMERICA (RWA)**, 3707 FM 1960 West, Suite 555, Houston TX 77068. (281)440-6885. Fax: (281)440-7510. E-mail: info@rwanational.com. Website: www.rwanational.com. Executive Manager: Allison Kelley. President: Jo Ann Ferguson. Estab. 1981. Number of members: over 7,500. Type of Memberships: General and associate. Open to: "Any person actively pursuing a writing career in the romance field." Membership is international. Benefits include annual conference, contests and awards, magazine, forums with publishing representatives, network for published authors, group insurance, regional newsletters and more. Dues: $70/new members; $60/renewal fee. Send SASE for information.

☑ **SCIENCE FICTION AND FANTASY WORKSHOP**, 1193 S. 1900 East, Salt Lake City UT 84108-1855. (801)582-2090. E-mail: workshop@burgoyne.com for more information. Website: www.sff.net/people/Dalton-Woodbury/sffw.htp. Director/Editor: Kathleen D. Woodbury. Estab. 1980. Number of members: 300. Type of memberships: "Active" is listed in the membership roster and so is accessible to all other members; "inactive" is not listed in the roster. Open to "anyone, anywhere. Our scope is international although over 96% of our members are in the US." Benefits include "several different critique groups: short stories, novels, articles, screenplays, poetry, etc. We also offer services such as copyediting, working out the numbers in planet building (give us the kind of planet you want and we'll tell you how far it is from the sun, etc.—or tell us what kind of sun you have and we'll tell you what your planet is like), brainstorming story, fragments or cultures or aliens, etc." Publishes *SF and Fantasy Workshop* (monthly); non-members subscribe for $15/year; samples are $1.50 and trial subscription: $8/6 issues. "We have a publication that contains outlines, synopses, proposals that authors submitted or used for novels that sold. The purpose is to show new and aspiring novelists what successful outlines, etc. look like, and to provide authors (with books coming out) advance publicity. Cost is $2.50/issue or $9/4 issues. We also publish a fiction booklet on an irregular basis. It contains one short story and three critiques by professional writers. Cost to anyone is $5/5 issues or $8/10 issues." Dues: Members pay a one-time fee of $5 (to cover the cost of the roster and the new-member information packet) and the annual $15 subscription fee. To renew membership, members simply renew their subscriptions. "Our organization is strictly by mail though that is now expanding to include e-mail." Or send SASE (or IRC).

SCIENCE FICTION WRITERS OF EARTH, P.O. Box 121293, Fort Worth TX 76121-1293. (817)451-8674. E-mail: sfwoe@flash.net. Website: www.flash.net/~sfwoe (includes contest rules, entry form, judge's report, contest results, list of writers who entered our contest, interviews with the winners, reviews of the top three stories, newsletter of interesting articles to our contestants and writers in general). Administrator: Gilbert Gordon Reis. Estab. 1980. Number of Members: 100-150. Open to: Unpublished writers of science fiction and fantasy short stories. "We have writers in Europe, Canada, Australia and several other countries, but the majority are from the US. Writers compete in our annual contest. This allows the writer to find out where he/she stands in writing ability. Winners often receive requests for their story from publishers. Many winners have told us that they believe that placing in the top ten of our contest gives them recognition and has assisted in getting their first story published." Dues: One must submit a science fiction or fantasy short story to our annual contest to be a member. Cost is $5 for membership and first story. $2 for each additional ms. The nominating committee meets several times a year to select the top ten stories of the annual contest. Author Edward Bryant selects the winners from the top ten stories. Contest deadline is October 30 and the cash awards and results are mailed out on January 31 of the following year. The first place story is published by *Altair*, magazine of speculative fiction. Information about the organization is available for SASE, by e-mail (no contest submissions) or from the Internet.

SCIENCE-FICTION AND FANTASY WRITERS OF AMERICA, INC., 532 La Guardia Place #632, New York NY 10012-1428. President: Michael Capobianco. Executive Director: Sharon Lee. Estab. 1965. Number of Members: 1,400. Type of Memberships: Active, associate, affiliate, institutional, estate and junior. Open to: "Professional writers, editors, anthologists, artists in the science fiction/fantasy genres and allied professional individuals and institutions. Our membership is international; we currently have members throughout Europe, Australia, Central and South America, Canada and some in Asia." We produce a variety of journals for our members, annual membership directory and provide a grievance committee, publicity committee, circulating book plan and access to medical/life/disability insurance. We award the SFWA Nebula Awards each year for outstanding achievement in the genre at novel, novella, novelet and short story lengths." Quarterly *SFWA Bulletin* to members; nonmembers may subscribe at $15/4 issues within US/Canada; $18.50 overseas. Bimonthly *SFWA Forum* for active and associate members only. Annual *SFWA Membership Directory* for members; available to professional organizations for $60. Active membership requires professional sale in the US of at least 3 short stories or 1 full-length book. Affiliate membership is open to professionals affiliated with science fiction writing. Associate membership require at least 1 professional sale in the US or other professional sale in the US or other professional involvement in the field respectively. Dues are pro-rated quarterly; info available upon request. Business meetings are held during Annual Nebula Awards weekend and usually during the annual World SF Convention. Send SASE for information.

☑ SISTERS IN CRIME, Box 442124, Lawrence KS 66044-8933. (785)842-1325. E-mail: sistersincrime@juno.com. Website: www.books.com/sinc. Contact: Beth Wasson, executive secretary. Estab. 1986. Number of Members: 3,200. The original purpose of this organization was to combat discrimination against women in the mystery field. Memberships are open to men as well as women, as long as they are committed to the organization and its goals. Offers membership assistance in networking and publicity.

🄽 SOCIETY OF MIDLAND AUTHORS, P.O. Box 10419, Fort Dearborn Station, Chicago IL 60610. Website: www.midlandauthors.com. President: Richard Lindberg. Estab. 1915. Number of Members: 260. Type of memberships: Regular, published authors and performed playwrights; Associate, librarians, editors, etc., others involved in publishing. Open to: Residents or natives of 12 midland states: Illinois, Iowa, Indiana, Michigan, Wisconsin, Nebraska, S. Dakota, N. Dakota, Ohio, Kansas, Missouri and Minnesota. Benefits include newsletter, listing in directory. Sponsors annual awards in 7 categories, with upwards of $300 prizes. Awards dinner in May at Cliff Dwellers Club, 200 S. Michigan Ave., Chicago IL 60603. Publishes newsletter several times/year. Dues: $25/year. Holds "5 program meetings/year, open to public at Cliff Dwellers Club, Chicago, featuring writers, editors, etc. on bookwriting subjects, theatrical subjects etc." Brochures are available for SASE.

 **SOCIETY OF SOUTHWESTERN AUTHORS**, P.O. Box 30355, Tucson AZ 85751-0355. (520)243-0940. Fax: (520)296-0409. E-mail: 4stern@azstarnet.com. President/Chairman: Chris Stern. Estab. 1972. Number of Members: 170. Memberships: Professional, Associate and Honorary. Professional: published authors of books, articles, poetry, etc.; Associate: aspiring writers not yet published; Honorary: one whose contribution to the writing profession or to SSA warrants such regonition. Benefits include conference, short story writing contest, critiques, marketing advice. Sponsors annual conference in January and annual short story writing contest. Publishes *The Write Word* which appears 6 times/year. Dues: $20/year. Meets monthly. Send SASE for information.

WESTERN WRITERS OF AMERICA, Office of the Secretary Treasurer, 1012 Fair St., Franklin TN 37064-2718. Phone/fax: (615)791-1444. E-mail: tncrutch@aol.com. Website: www.imt.net/~gedison/wwahome.html. Secretary Treasurer: James A. Crutchfield. Estab. 1953. Number of Members: 600. Type of Membership: Active, associate, patron. Open to: Professional, published writers who have multiple publications of fiction or nonfiction (usually at least three) about the West. Associate membership open to those with one book, a lesser number of short stories or publications or participation in the field such as editors, agents, reviewers, librarians, television producers, directors (dealing with the West). Patron memberships open to corporations, organizations and individuals with an interest in the West. Scope is international. Benefits: "By way of publications and conventions, members are kept abreast of developments in the field of Western literature and the publishing field, marketing requirements, income tax problems, copyright law, research facilities and techniques, and new publications. At conventions members have the opportunity for one-on-one conferences with editors, publishers and agents." Sponsors an annual four-day conference during fourth week of June featuring panels, lectures and seminars on publishing, writing and research. Includes the Spur Awards to honor authors of the best Western literature of the previous year. Publishes *Roundup Magazine* (6 times/year) for members. Available to nonmembers for $30. Publishes membership directory. Dues: $75 for active membership, $75 for associate membership, $250 for patron. For information on Spur Awards, send SASE. Inquiries by fax and e-mail OK.

WILLAMETTE WRITERS, 9045 SW Barbur Blvd., Suite 5A, Portland OR 97219. (503)452-1592. Fax: (503)452-0372. E-mail: wilwrite@teleport.com. Website: www.teleport.com/~wilwrite/. Office Manager: Bill Johnson. Estab. 1965. Number of members: 700. "Willamette Writers is a nonprofit, tax exempt corporation staffed by volunteers. Membership is open to both published and aspiring writers. WW provides support, encouragement and interaction for all genres of writers." Open to national membership, but serves primarily the Pacific Northwest. Benefits include a writers' referral service, critique groups, membership discounts, youth programs (4th-12th grades), monthly meetings with guest authors, intern program, annual writing contest, community projects, library and research services, as well as networking with other writing groups, office with writing reference and screenplay library. Sponsors annual conference held the second weekend in August; quarterly workshops; annual Kay Snow Writing Contest; and the Distinguished Northwest Writer Award. Publishes *The Willamette Writer* monthly: a 12-page newsletter for members and complimentary subscriptions. Information consists of features, how-to's, mechanics of writing, profile of featured monthly speaker, markets, workshops, conferences and benefits available to writers. Dues: $36/year; includes subscription to newsletter. Meets first Tuesday of each month; board meeting held last Tuesday of each month. Send SASE for information. Inquiries by fax and e-mail OK.

THE WRITER'S CENTER, 4508 Walsh St., Bethesda MD 20815. (301)654-8664. Website: www.writer.org. Executive E-mail: postmaster@writer.org. Director: Jane Fox. Estab. 1977. Number of Members: 2,200. Open to: Anyone interested in writing. Scope is regional DC, Maryland, Virginia, West Virginia, Pennsylvania. Benefits include newsletter, discounts in bookstore, workshops, public events, subscriptions to *Poet Lore*, use of equipment and annual small press book fair. Center offers workshops, reading series, equipment, newsletter and limited workspace. Sponsors workshops, conferences, award for narrative poem. Publishes *Writer's Carousel*, bimonthly. Nonmembers can pick it up at the Center. Dues: $30/year. Fees vary with service, see publications. Brochures are available for SASE. Inquiries by e-mail OK.

WRITERS' FEDERATION OF NEW BRUNSWICK, P.O. Box 37, Station A, Fredericton, New Brunswick E3B 4Y2 Canada. Phone/fax: (506)459-7228. E-mail: aa821@fan.nb.ca. Website: www.sjfn.nb.ca/communi

FOR EXPLANATIONS OF THESE SYMBOLS,
SEE THE INSIDE FRONT AND BACK COVERS OF THIS BOOK.

ty_hall/W/Writers_Federation_NB/index.htm. Project Coordinator: Anna Mae Snider. Estab. 1983. Number of Members: 230. Membership is open to anyone interested in writing. "This a provincial organization. Benefits include promotion of members' works through newsletter announcements and readings and launchings held at fall festival and annual general meeting. Services provided by WFNB include a Writers-in-Schools Program and manuscript reading. The WFNB sponsors a fall festival and an annual general meeting which feature workshops, readings and book launchings." There is also an annual literary competition, open to residents of New Brunswick only, which has prizes of $150, $75 and $50 in four categories: Fiction, nonfiction, children's literature and poetry; two $400 prizes for the best manuscript of poems (48 pgs.); the best short novel or collection of short stories and a category for young writers (14-18 years of age) which offers $150 (1st prize), $100 (2nd prize), $50 (3rd prize). Publishes a quarterly newsletter. Dues: $30/year; $20/year for students. Board of Directors meets approximately 5 times a year. Annual General Meeting is held in the spring of each year. Send SASE for information. Inquiries by e-mail and fax OK.

WRITERS' FEDERATION OF NOVA SCOTIA, 1113 Marginal Rd., Halifax, Nova Scotia B3H 4P7 Canada. Executive Director: Jane Buss. Estab. 1976. Number of Members: 500. Type of Memberships: General membership, student membership, Nova Scotia Writers' Council membership (professional), Honorary Life Membership. Open to anyone who writes. Provincial scope, with a few members living elsewhere in the country or the world. Benefits include advocacy of all kinds for writers, plus such regular programs as workshops and regular publications, including directories and a newsletter. Sponsors workshops, 2 annual conferences (one for general membership, the other for the professional wing), 4 book awards, one annual competition for unpublished manuscripts in various categories; a writers in the schools program, a manuscript reading service, reduced photocopying rates. Publishes *Eastword*, 6 issues annually, available by subscription for $35 (Canadian) to nonmembers. Dues: $35/year (Canadian). Holds an annual general meeting, an annual meeting of the Nova Scotia Writers' Council, several board meetings annually. Send 5×7 SASE for information.

WRITERS GUILD OF ALBERTA, Percy Page Centre, 11759 Groat Rd., 3rd Floor, Edmonton, Alberta T5M 3K6 Canada. (780)422-8174. Fax: (780)422-2663. E-mail: wga@oanet.com. Website: www.writers guild.ab.ca. Executive Director: Miki Andrejevic. Estab. 1980. Number of Members: 750. Membership open to current and past residents of Alberta. Regional (provincial) scope. Benefits include discounts on programs offered; manuscript evaluation service available; bimonthly newsletter; contacts; info on workshops, retreats, readings, etc. Sponsors workshops 2 times/year, retreats 3 times/year, annual conference, annual book awards program (Alberta writers only). Publishes *WestWord* 6 times/year; available for $60/year (Canadian) to nonmembers. Dues: $60/year for regular membership; $20/year senior/students/limited income; $100/year donating membership— charitable receipt issued (Canadian funds). Organized monthly meetings. Send SASE for information.

WRITERS INFORMATION NETWORK, P.O. Box 11337, Bainbridge Island WA 98110. (206)842-9103. Fax: (206)842-0536. E-mail: writersinfonetwork@juno.com or writersinfonetwork@cwix.com. Websites: www.bluejaypub.com/win or www.ecpa.org/win. Director: Elaine Wright Colvin. Estab. 1980. Number of members: 1,000. Open to: All interested in writing for religious publications/publishers. Scope is national and several foreign countries. Benefits include bimonthly magazine, *The WIN Informer*, market news, advocacy/grievance procedures, professional advice, writers conferences, press cards, author referral, free consultation. Sponsors workshops, conferences throughout the country each year—mailing list and advertised in *The WIN Informer* magazine. Dues: $33 US; $37 foreign/year. Holds quarterly meetings in Seattle, WA. Brochures are available for SASE. Inquiries by fax and e-mail OK.

THE WRITERS ROOM, INC., 10 Astor Place, 6th Floor, New York NY 10003. (212)254-6995. Fax: (212)533-6059. Website: www.writersroom@writersroom.org. Executive Director: Donna Brodie. Contact: Mariana Carreño, assistant to executive director. Estab. 1978. Number of Members: 200 fulltime and 40 part-time. Open to: Any writer who shows a serious commitment to writing. "We serve a diverse population of writers, but most of our residents live in or around the NYC area. We encourage writers from around the country (and world!) to apply for residency if they plan to visit NYC for a while." Benefits include 24-hour access to the facility. "We provide desk space, storage areas for computers, typewriters, etc., a kitchen where coffee and tea are always available, bathrooms and a lounge. We also offer in-house workshops on topics of practical importance to writers and monthly readings of work-in-progress." Dues: $175 per quarter year. Send SASE for application and background information. Inquiries by fax OK.

THE WRITERS' WORKSHOP, 387 Beaucatcher Rd., Asheville NC 28805. (828)254-8111. Executive Director: Karen Ackerson. Estab. 1984. Number of Members: 1,250. Types of Memberships: Student/low income $25; family/organization $65; individual $35. Open to all writers. Scope is national and international. Benefits include discounts on workshops, quarterly newsletter, critiquing services through the mail. Center offers reading room, assistance with editing your work. Publishes a newsletter; also available to nonmembers ($20). Offers workshops year-round in NC and the South; 2 retreats a year, 4 readings with nationally awarded authors. Contests and classes for children and teens as well. Advisory board includes Kurt Vonnegut, E.L. Doctorow, Peter Matthiessen, Reynolds Price, John Le Carre and Eudora Welty. Also sponsors international contests in fiction, memoirs, poetry and creative nonfiction. Brochures are available for SASE.

Publications of Interest

This section features listings for magazines and newsletters that focus on writing or the publishing industry. While many of these are not markets for fiction, they do offer articles, marketing advice or other information valuable to the fiction writer. Several magazines in this section offer actual market listings while others feature reviews of books in the field and news on the industry.

The timeliness factor is a primary reason most writers read periodicals. Changes in publishing happen very quickly and magazines can help you keep up with the latest news. Some magazines listed here, including *Writer's Digest* and *Fiction Writer*, cover the entire field of writing, while others such as *The Mystery Review*, *Locus* (science fiction) focus on a particular type of writing. We've also added publications which focus on a particular segment of the publishing industry.

Information on some publications for writers can be found in the introductions to other sections in this book. In addition, many of the literary and commercial magazines for writers listed in the markets sections are helpful to the fiction writer. Keep an eye on the newsstand and library shelves for others and let us know if you've found a publication particularly useful.

ABOUT CREATIVE TIME SPACES, ACT I Creativity Center, P.O. Box 30854, Palm Beach Gardens FL 33420. Editor: Charlotte Plotsky, M.S. International sourcebook of information, photos and other materials on retreats, colonies, communities, residencies and other programs for artists of all disciplines, including writers. Send SASE for details.

N. CANADIAN CHILDREN'S LITERATURE/LITTÉRATURE CANADIENNE POUR LA JEUNESSE, Slapsie, University of Guelph, Guelph, Ontario N1G 2W1 Canada. (519)824-4120, ext. 3189. Editors: Mary Rubio, Daniel Chouinard and Marie Davis. Administrator: Gay Christofides. Quarterly. "In-depth criticism of English and French Canadian literature for young people. Scholarly articles and reviews are supplemented by illustrations, photographs, and interviews with authors of children's books. The main themes and genres of children's literature are covered in special issues." Reviews novels and short story collections. Send review copies to the editors. Sample copies available; single copy price is $10 (Canadian). Subscriptions: $29 (Canadian), plus $10 for US, $16 for other non-Canadian addresses.

N. CANADIAN WRITER'S JOURNAL, Box 5180, New Liskeard, Ontario P0J 1P0 Canada. (705)647-5424. Fax: (705)647-8366. E-mail: cwj@ntl.sympatico.ca. Website: www.nt.net/~cwj/index.htm. Editor: Deborah Ranchuk. Quarterly. "Mainly short how-to and motivational articles related to all types of writing and of interest to both new and established writers. Fiction is published in limited quantities, and needs are fully supplied through an annual (fall) short fiction contest. SASE for contest rules." Lists markets for fiction. Sample copies available for $5 ($C for Canadian orders, $US for US orders). Subscription price: $15/year; $25/2 years ($C for Canadian orders, $US for US orders).

N. CHILDREN'S BOOK INSIDER, 901 Columbia Rd., Fort Collins CO 80525. E-mail: mail@write4kids.c om. Website: www.write4kids.com. Editor/Publisher: Laura Backes. Monthly. "Publication is devoted solely to children's book writers and illustrators. 'At Presstime' section gives current market information each month for fiction, nonfiction and illustration submissions to publishers. Other articles include writing and illustration tips for fiction and nonfiction, interviews with published authors and illustrators, features on alternative publishing methods (self-publishing, co-op publishing, etc.), how to submit work to publishers, industry trends. Also publishes books and writing tools for both beginning and experienced children's book writers." Sample copy and catalog for SASE with 55¢ postage or e-mail children@mailback.com for free online catalog. Single copy price: $3.25. Subscription price: $29.95/year (US); $35/year (Canadian).

FICTION WRITER, F&W Publications, 1507 Dana Ave., Cincinnati OH 45207. (513)531-2690. Fax: (513)531-1843. E-mail: peteb@fwpubs.com. Website: www.fictionwritermag.com. Editor: Peter Blocksom. Bimonthly. "*Fiction Writer* inspires beginning, intermediate and advanced writers through lively instruction on all aspects of fiction writing, combining within its pages the best qualities of a stimulating workshop, a challenging class and a supportive writing group. Through three key components—how-to features, essays on the craft of writing, and coverage of marketing trends—it supplies the tools every fiction writer needs. The magazine's writers include published authors and accomplished writing teachers, all of whom show readers the path to success— whether success be simply the pleasures of creation or the thrill of publication." Lists fiction markets. Sample copies available for $5.25. Subscriptions: (800)289-0963. Note: As with other listings in this section, this is not a market. Do not send mss.

☑ FICTION WRITER'S GUIDELINE, P.O. Box 72300, Albuquerque NM 87195. Editor: Blythe Camenson. Bimonthly. Our publication is "an eight page newsletter with agent/editor/author interviews, how-to articles on writing fiction and getting it published, fiction markets, conference listings, Q&A column, success stories and more." Sample copies available for $3.50. Subscriptions: $21/year; free to members of Fiction Writer's Connection. "Membership in FWC is $64/year; includes a free newsletter, free critiquing, and a toll-free hotline for questions and free advice. Send SASE for information."

☑ GILA QUEEN'S GUIDE TO MARKETS, P.O. Box 97, Newton NJ 07860-0097. (973)579-1537. Fax: (973)579-6441. E-mail: kathryn@gilaqueen.com. Website: www.gilaqueen.com. Editor: Kathryn Ptacek. "Includes complete guidelines for fiction (different genres), poetry, nonfiction, greeting cards, etc. Also includes 'theme section' each issue—science fiction/fantasy/horror, mystery/suspense, romance, western, Canadian, regional, women's markets, religious, etc. and 'mini-markets.' Regular departments include new address listings, dead/suspended markets, moving editors, anthologies, markets to be wary of, publishing news, etc. Every issue contains updates (of stuff listed in previous issues), new markets, conferences, contests. Publishes articles on writing topics, self-promotion, reviews of software and books of interest to writers, etc." Sample copy: $6. Subscriptions: $45/year (US); $49/year (Canada); $60/year (overseas).

LAMBDA BOOK REPORT, P.O. Box 73910, Washington DC 20056. (202)462-7924. Editor: Kanani Kauka. Monthly. "This review journal of contemporary gay and lesbian literature appeals to both readers and writers. Fiction queries published regularly." Lists fiction markets. Reviews novels, short story collections, poetry and nonfiction. Send review copies to Attn: Book Review Editor. Single copy price is $4.95/US. Subscriptions: $34.95/year (US); international rate: $58.95 (US $); Canada/Mexico: $46.95/year (US $).

LOCUS, The Newspaper of the Science Fiction Field, P.O. Box 13305, Oakland CA 94661. Editor: Charles N. Brown. Monthly. "Professional newsletter of science fiction, fantasy and horror; has news, interviews of authors, book reviews, column on electronic publishing, forthcoming books listings, monthly books-received listings, etc." Lists markets for fiction. Reviews novels or short story collections. Sample copies available. Single copy price: $4.95. Subscription price: $43/year, (2nd class mail) for US, $48 (US)/year, (2nd class) for Canada; $48 (US)/year (2nd class) for overseas.

MYSTERY READERS JOURNAL P.O. Box 8116, Berkeley CA 94707. E-mail: whodunit@murderonthemenu .com. Website: www.murderonthemenu.com/mystery. Contact: Editor. Estab. 1984. Includes interviews, essays, mystery news, new bookstores, overseas reports and convention listings. Quarterly review periodical which reviews books, both in and out of print, of different themes within mystery.

☑ THE MYSTERY REVIEW, A Quarterly Publication for Mystery & Suspense Readers, P.O. Box 233, Colborne, Ontario K0K 1S0 Canada. (613)475-4440. Editor: Barbara Davey. Quarterly. "Book reviews, information on new releases, interviews with authors and other people involved in mystery, 'real life' mysteries, out-of-print mysteries, mystery/suspense films, word games and puzzles with a mystery theme." Reviews mystery/suspense novels and short story collections. Send review copies to editor. Single copy price is $5.95 CDN in Canada/$5.95 US in the United States. Subscriptions: $21.50 CDN (includes GST) in Canada; $20 US in the US and $28 US elsewhere.

NEW WRITER'S MAGAZINE, P.O. Box 5976, Sarasota FL 34277. (941)953-7903. E-mail: newriters@aol.c om. Website: www.newriters.com. Editor: George J. Haborak. Bimonthly. "*New Writer's Magazine* is a publication for aspiring writers. It features 'how-to' articles, news and interviews with published and recently published authors. Will use fiction that has a tie-in with the world of the writer." Lists markets for fiction. Reviews novels and short story collections. Send review copies to Editor. Send #10 SASE for guidelines. Sample copies available;

FOR EXPLANATIONS OF THESE SYMBOLS, SEE THE INSIDE FRONT AND BACK COVERS OF THIS BOOK.

single copy price is $3. Subscriptions: $15/year, $25/2 years. Canadian $20 (US funds). International $35/year (US funds).

OHIO WRITER, P.O. Box 91801, Cleveland OH 44101. (216)932-8444. Editor: Ron Antonucci. Bimonthly. "Interviews with Ohio writers of fiction and nonfiction; current fiction markets in Ohio." Lists fiction markets. Reviews novels and short story collections. Sample copies available for $2.50. Subscriptions: $15/year; $40/3 years; $20/institutional rate.

N: POETS & WRITERS MAGAZINE, 72 Spring St., New York NY 10012. E-mail: pwsubs@pw.org. Website: www.pw.org. Covers primarily poetry and fiction writing. Bimonthly. "Includes profiles of noted authors and publishing professionals, practical how-to articles, a comprehensive listing of grants and awards for writers and special sections on subjects ranging from small presses to writers conferences." Lists markets for fiction. Sample copies available; single copy price is $4.95. Subscriptions: $19.95/year; $38/2 years. Subscriptions ordered through *Poets & Writers Magazine*, P.O. Box 543, Mount Morris IL 61054 or (815)734-1123.

THE REGENCY PLUME, 711 D. St. N.W., Ardmore OK 73401. E-mail: marilynclay@yahoo.com. Website: www.freetown.com/Picadilly/HydePark/1073/RegncyPlume.html. Editor: Marilyn Clay. Bimonthly. "The newsletter focus is on providing accurate historical facts relating to the Regency period: customs, clothes, entertainment, the wars, historical figures, etc. I stay in touch with New York editors who acquire Regency romance novels. Current market info appears regularly in newsletter—see Bits & Scraps." Current Regency romances are "Previewed." Sample copy available for $3.35; single copy price is $3, $5 outside US. Subscriptions: $18/year for 6 issues; $22 Canada; $28 foreign. ("Check must be drawn on a US bank. Postal money order okay.") Back issues available. Send SASE for subscription information, article guidelines or list of research and writing aids, such as audiotapes, historical maps, books on Regency period furniture and Regency romance writing contest.

☑ ROMANCE WRITERS REPORT, Romance Writers of America, 3707 F.M. 1960 W., Suite 555, Houston TX 77068. (281)440-6885. Fax: (281)440-7510. E-mail: infobox@rwanational.com. Editor: Charis McEachern. Monthly publication of Romance Writers of America, Inc. Subscriptions included as part of RWA membership. Includes articles, essays and tips written by established writers, contest and conference information and articles by romance editors.

ROMANTIC TIMES MAGAZINE, 55 Bergen St., Brooklyn NY 11201. (718)237-1097. Website: www.romant ictimes.com. Monthly. Features reviews, news and interviews of interest to the romance reader. Each issue also has special features such as photo tours of authors' houses, interviews with male cover models and articles on romantic pursuits (teas, salons, etc.) and mysteries. Subscriptions: $42/year in US; $66/year in Canada.

☑ SCAVENGER'S NEWSLETTER, 519 Ellinwood, Osage City KS 66523. (785)528-3538. Editor: Janet Fox. Monthly. "A market newsletter for SF/fantasy/horror/mystery writers with an interest in the small press. Articles about SF/fantasy/horror/mystery writing/marketing. Now using Flash fiction to 1,200 words, genres as above. No writing-related material for fiction. Payment for articles and fiction is $4 on acceptance." Lists markets for fiction. Sample copies available. Single copy price: $2.50. Subscription price: $22/year, $11/6 months. Canada: $21, $11.50. Overseas: $27, $13.50 (US funds only).

SCIENCE FICTION CHRONICLE, P.O. Box 022730, Brooklyn NY 11202-0056. (718)643-9011. Website: www.sfsite.com/sfc. Editor: Andrew I. Porter. Bimonthly. Publishes nonfiction, nothing about UFOs. "Bimonthly newsmagazine for professional writers, editors, readers of SF, fantasy, horror." Lists markets for fiction "updated every 6 months." Reviews novels, small press publications, audiotapes and short story collections. Send review copies to SFC and also to Don D'Ammassa, 323 Dodge St., E. Providence RI 02914. Sample copies available with 9×12 SAE with $1.43 postage; single copy price is $3.95 (US) or £3.50 (UK). Subscriptions: $25 first class US and Canada; $30 overseas. *Note: As with other listings in this section, this is not a "market"—Do not send mss or artwork.*

THE SMALL PRESS BOOK REVIEW, P.O. Box 176, Southport CT 06490. (203)332-7629. Editor: Henry Berry. Quarterly. "Brief reviews of all sorts of books from small presses/independent publishers." Addresses of publishers are given in reviews. Reviews novels and short story collections. Send review copies to editor. Published electronically via the Internet.

SMALL PRESS REVIEW/SMALL MAGAZINE REVIEW, P.O. Box 100, Paradise CA 95967. (916)877-6110. Editor: Len Fulton. Bimonthly. "Publishes news and reviews about small publishers, books and magazines." Lists markets for fiction and poetry. Reviews novels, short story and poetry collections. Sample copies available. Subscription price: $25/year.

☑ A VIEW FROM THE LOFT, 1011 Washington Ave. S, Minneapolis MN 55415. (612)379-8999, ext. 13. Editor: Ellen Hawley. Monthly. "Publishes articles on writing and list of markets for fiction, poetry and creative nonfiction." Sample copies available; single copy price is $4 US. Subscriptions: $40 in Twin Cities metro area; $25 elsewhere in US; $35 international, $20 low income/student. (Subscription available only as part of Loft membership; rates are membership rates.)

[N] WOW (Women on Writing), Newsletter For, By, About Woman Writers, (formerly Prosetry), P.O. Box 117727, Burlingame CA 94011-7727. E-mail: womenonwriting@USA.net. Editors: P.D. Steele and Bree LeMaire. Monthly. Estab. 1986. "We offer information relevant to writers, especially women: conferences, exercises, workshops, reviews on books, movies, videos, tips in all genres." Poetry 100% freelance. Guidelines for #10 SASE. E-mail for information.

THE WRITER, 120 Boylston St., Boston MA 02116-4615. Editor: Sylvia K. Burack. Monthly. Contains articles on improving writing techniques and getting published. Includes market lists of magazine and book publishers. Subscription price: $29/year, $54/2 years. Canadian: add $10/year. Foreign: add $30/year. Also publishes *The Writer's Handbook*, an annual book on all fields of writing plus market lists of magazine and book publishers.

WRITER'S CAROUSEL, The Writer's Center, 4508 Walsh St., Bethesda MD 20815-6006. (301)654-8664. Website: www.writer.org. Editor: Allan Lefcowitz. Bimonthly. "*Writer's Carousel* publishes book reviews and articles about writing and the writing scene." Lists fiction markets. Reviews novels and short story collections. Sample copies available. Subscriptions: $30 Writer's Center Membership.

☑ THE WRITER'S CHRONICLE, Associated Writing Programs, George Mason University, Tallwood House, Mail Stop 1E3, Fairfax VA 22030. (703)993-4301. E-mail: awp@gmu.edu. Website: www.awpwriter.org. Editor-in-Chief: D.W. Fenza. 6 times/year. Essays on contemporary literature and articles on the craft of creative writing only. Does *not* publish fiction. Lists fiction markets (back pages for "Submit"). Sample copies available; single copy price $5 (includes postage). Subscription: $20/year; $25/year Canada; check with office for overseas.

WRITER'S DIGEST BOOKS–MARKET BOOKS, 1507 Dana Ave., Cincinnati OH 45207. (513)531-2690. Website: www.writersdigest.com. Annual. In addition to *Novel & Short Story Writer's Market*, Writer's Digest Books also publishes *Writer's Market*, *Poet's Market*, *Children's Writer's & Illustrator's Market* and the *Guide to Literary Agents*. All include articles and listings of interest to writers. All are available at bookstores, libraries or through the publisher. (Request catalog.)

WRITER'S DIGEST, 1507 Dana Ave., Cincinnati OH 45207. (513)531-2690. Website: www.writersdigest.com. Associate Editor: Dawn Simonds Ramirez. Monthly. "*Writer's Digest* is a magazine of techniques and markets. We *inspire* the writer to write, *instruct* him or her on how to improve that work, and *direct* him or her toward appropriate markets." Lists markets for fiction, nonfiction, poetry. Single copy price: $4. Subscription price: $27.

☑ WRITERS' JOURNAL, Val-Tech Publishing, Inc., P.O. Box 394, Perham MN 56573-0394. (218)346-7921. Website: www.sowashco.com/writersjournal. Contact: Leon Ogroske. Bimonthly. "Provides a creative outlet for writers of fiction." Costs: $5/entry. Deadline: May 30. Annual. Guidelines for SASE. Award: $50 (1st prize); $25 (2nd prize); $15 (3rd prize). Buys one-time rights. Top three and selected honorable mentions will be published.

[N] WRITERS NEWS, P.O. Box 4, Nairn 1V12 4HU Scotland. "Practical advice for established and aspiring writers. How-to articles, news, markets and competitions." Overseas subscribers are now automatically enrolled in the British Overseas Writers Circle, which includes a newsletter of specialized information for writers outside Britain. Lists markets for fiction. Free trial issue available. Subscriptions: £44.90 (UK), £49.90 (Europe), £54.90 (rest of world).

☑ WRITER'S YEARBOOK, 1507 Dana Ave., Cincinnati OH 45207. (513)531-2690. Website: www.writersdigest.com. Executive Editor: Peter Blocksom. Annual. "A collection of the best writing *about* writing, with an exclusive survey of the year's 100 top markets for article-length nonfiction." Single copy price: $6.25.

Websites of Interest

BY MEGAN LANE

More and more these days, I find myself wondering how I ever lived without the Internet and the World Wide Web. I'm sure I got out more in those ancient times, but I never felt as powerful or as confident about being able to find the answer to any question my inquisitive brain might pose. Even if you refuse to use the Internet, it's virtually impossible to ignore it. Web addresses are popping up in the corners of TV screens, in print ads and even on the packaging of food we eat. But despite all the naying of the naysayers, there is useful information to be found in the vast network of cyberspace. So, enough with the excuses. Even if you don't own a computer, your local library does and now that you can easily access the Internet through your television, you'll have to find some more difficult bit of technology to shun. And even though my eyes are bloodshot from surfing for the past several hours (or is it days?), I've managed to compile a tiny and woefully incomplete listing of websites that fiction writers shouldn't miss.

WRITER'S DIGEST WEBSITE

www.writersdigest.com
This site includes daily markets, articles, interviews and information about writing books and magazines from *Writer's Digest*. It also has a huge, searchable database of writer's guidelines from thousands of publishers.

LITERARY FICTION

The English Server Fiction Collection: english-server.hss.cmu.edu/fiction/. "This site offers works of and about fiction collected from our members, contributing authors worldwide, and texts in the public domain." Includes: short fiction, novels, magazines of and about contemporary fiction and criticism, Internet sites publishing fiction, literary criticism, organizations which present awards for excellent fiction, plays, screenplays and dramatic criticism, epic and short verse, and poetic criticism.

Zuzu's Petals Literary Resources: www.zuzu.com. "With 700+ organized links to helpful resources for writers, artists, performers, and researchers, it is our goal to unearth and present some of the best links and information for the online creative community." Includes links to magazines, readings, conferences, workshops and more.

GENRE FICTION

Books and Writing Online: www.interzone.com/Books/books.html. This site includes links to helpful resources on writing, literature and publishing for science fiction and fantasy writers in addition to general book-related links useful to any writer regardless of genre.

Children's Literature Web Guide: www.ucalgary.ca/~dkbrown/index.html. "The Children's Literature Web Guide is an attempt to gather together and categorize the growing number of Internet resources related to books for children and young adults. Much of the information you can find through these pages is provided by others: fans, schools, libraries, and commercial enterprises involved in the book world." This comprehensive site for children's book writers and illustrators includes links to authors, publishers, booksellers, conferences and events, as well as other sites of interest.

Con-Tour: www.con-tour.com. "Con-Tour is a magazine for people who enjoy the fantasy, sci-fi, comic, gaming, and related conventions that are held all over the world. ConTour features listings of upcoming conventions, with highlights and reviews. We also have interviews with guests, fans, artists; and writers; pictures of fans, and nude pictorials of the women (and men) of fandom." The web version includes a list of conventions with hot links to their own websites. The website and magazine are not for the faint of heart, but true fanatics will have fun with what the zany editors throw at them.

The Market List: www.marketlist.com. Web magazine of genre fiction marketing information. "Each version includes over 100 current markets for genre fiction, with info on response times, genres accepted, payment rates and more."

The Mystery Writers' Forum: www.zott.com/mysforum/default.html. "This is a threaded bulletin board system geared specifically for writers and aspiring writers interested in gaining information about the publishing industry, writing advice and business information about the mystery genre." Discussions are separated into categories including agents, bookstores, contests, critique corner, death details and industry news.

Romance Central: romance-central.com. "Workshops are the heart of Romance Central. When we share knowlege and exchange ideas, we enhance our work and ourselves. Writers should view their peers as brothers and sisters, not competition. And by peers, I mean anyone who feels compelled to put words on paper." Great place for giving and receiving advice about romance writing.

Roundup Online Magazine: www.imt.net/~gedison/wwa.html. Official magazine of the Western Writers of America. Includes contest information, reviews of westerns and essays about the genre.

MAGAZINES
Electronic Newsstand: enews.com. Massive index of commercial magazines, searchable by title. Provides links to the magazine's website, description of current issue, subscription information and recommendations for similar magazines. A magazine in itself, this site also offers news about the magazine publishing industry and updates on the goings on at individual magazines.

John Hewitt's Writer's Resource Center: www.azstarnet.com/~poewar/writer/writer.html. Comprehensive writing site that includes links to consumer, trade and literary magazines. Also catalogs articles by Hewitt covering topics from overcoming writer's isolation to a directory of writers' colonies, associations and organizations of interest to writers.

BOOK PUBLISHERS
AcqWeb's Directory of Publisher and Vendors: www.library.vanderbilt.edu/law/acqs/pubr.html. Gigantic catalog of links to publishers. Subject headings include: general and multiple subject publishers, associations and institutes, electronic publications including online & CD-ROM, reprints, university presses, literature and fiction, children's literature, poetry, science fiction and fantasy.

Arachnoid Writer's Alliance: www.vena.com/arachnoid. This site "presents a collection of books for sale by independent and self-published authors." Gives you an idea of what struggling writers are up to. Includes author bios, contact information and short excerpts from books.

Books A to Z: http://www.booksatoz.com. "This site is intended to be a working tool to enable anyone to produce, distribute or find books. We will also list large numbers of resources for research in books and libraries. All of these areas are neglected and often overlooked in the commercial world. We will not attempt to make a gigantic site listing everything, but we will attempt to provide access to at least some resources in every area of book production, sales and research." Includes links to professional and creative services, production and technical info, bookmaking materials for sale, organizations and groups, events and news, book and music publishers, bookstores and searchers, marketing and distribution, academic and research tools.

Bookwire: www.bookwire.com. A gateway to finding information about publishers, booksellers, libraries, authors, reviews and awards. Also offers information about frequently asked publishing questions and answers, a calendar of events, a mailing list, and other helpful resources. Includes direct links to articles from *Publishers Weekly* and *Hungry Mind Review,* searchable databases from *Books In Print* and *Literary Market Place,* and links to over 7,000 book related sites.

Publishers' Catalogs: www.lights.com/publisher. This massive site includes a specific geographic index, which lists countries like Albania, Luxembourg, Thailand and Uruguay, as well as the US and UK. The alphabetical lists of publishers link with their websites. But what sets this site apart is its webhosting service for publishers. If a company doesn't have its catalog online, Northern Lights Internet Solutions can do it for them.

ORGANIZATIONS

Canadian Authors Association: www.islandnet.com/~caa/national.html. "The Association was founded to promote recognition of Canadian writers and their works, and to foster and develop a climate favorable to the creative arts. Its objectives:
To work for the encouragement and protection of writers.
To speak for writers before government and other inquires.
To sponsor awards and otherwise encourage work of literary and artistic merit.
To publish *Canadian Author, The Canadian Writer's Guide* and other publications designed to improve the professionalism of Canadian writers."

Horror Writers Association: www.horror.org. "The Horror Writers Association (HWA) was formed in the 1980s to bring together writers and others professionally interested in horror and dark fantasy, and to foster a greater appreciation of dark fiction among the general public. To this end, among other benefits, the organization issues a regular newsletter, presents the Bram Stoker Awards, and provides members with the latest news on paying markets. We have sponsored a series of successful members-only anthologies. Members also gain access to the private HWA areas on various online services, including Genie's Science Fiction Roundtables (especially SFRT4), Compuserve's SFLitForum 2, SFF-Net, and Dueling Modems, and can, if they choose, receive informational bulletins by e-mail."

National Writers Union: www.nwu.org/. "The National Writers Union (NWU) is the trade union for freelance writers of all genres. We are committed to improving the economic and working conditions of freelance writers through the collective strength of our members. We are a modern, innovative union offering grievance-resolution, industry campaigns, contract advice, health and dental plans, member education, job banks, networking, social events and much more. The NWU is affiliated with the United Automobile Workers (UAW) and through them with the AFL-CIO. Founded in 1983, the NWU has local and organizing committees throughout the country. Our 4,500 members include journalists, book authors, poets, copywriters, academic authors, cartoonists, and technical and business writers. The NWU has a Supporters Circle open to individuals or organizations who are not writers but wish to support the union."

PEN American Center: www.pen.org. "PEN American Center, the largest of nearly130 Centers worldwide that compose International PEN, is a membership association of prominent literary writers and editors. As a major voice of the literary community, the organization seeks to defend the freedom of expression wherever it may be threatened, and to promote and encourage the recognition and reading of contemporary literature."

Romance Writers of America: www.rwanational.com. "RWA is a non-profit professional/ educational association of 8,200 romance writers and other industry professionals. We are 'The Voice of Romance.' "

Society of Children's Book Writers and Illustrators: www.scbwi.org. "The only professional organization dedicated to serving the people who write, illustrate, or share a vital interest in children's literature. Whether you are a professional writer, a famous illustrator, a beginner with a good idea, or somewhere in between, SCBWI is here to serve you. Our website has a dual purpose: It exists as a service to our members as well as offering information about the children's publishing industry and our organization to non-members."

The Writers Guild of America: www.wga.org. "Home of the 8,500 professional writers who, since 1933, have created your favorite movies, television shows, and now, many of your favorite interactive games. All of these visions started with a script and a writer. In the beginning was the word. And the word was funny, dramatic, romantic, terrifying and dozens of other things that have entertained, moved and educated you. Here at our website, we hope to make film, television, interactive and other mass media writing—and writers—more familiar and accessible. Whether you are a writer, an aspiring writer, an entertainment professional or purely a member of the viewing public, we are happy to have you visit with us."

INSPIRATION

Authors: authors.about.com. "Expect to find the best links to sites about contemporary and classic authors. You'll also find original interviews and weekly features that focus on specific authors, period-specific projects, trends, and book reviews." This site also includes links to genre sites, playwrights, authors of all nationalities and an Authors Chat Room.

Creating a Celebration of Women Writers: www.cs.cmu.edu/afs/cs.cmu.edu/user/mmbt/www/ women/celebration.html. "While a number of original sources are already available on the World Wide Web, there are many gaps in the available material. We therefore hope to encourage many people to contribute texts and supporting information about women writers. We propose to make the construction of the exhibit a public process, providing a shared resource for information about the materials in preparation. An initial list of women writers and available online works is provided. We hope that people will commit to scanning or typing in specific works. People are welcome to suggest further additions to the list. We are looking for complete works (not excerpts or single chapters) that are either in the public domain, or authorized by the copyright holder. (Details about copyright restrictions and instructions for submitting works are provided.) As people agree to scan in resources, their names and the works they have agreed to enter will be annotated to the list." This site is an amazing resource of links to the works and biographies of women writers throughout history as well as other resources for and about women writers.

WRITING RULES

Elements of Style by William Strunk, Jr.: www.bartleby.com/141/index.html. The full text of the English language's most used guide to grammar.

Grammar Girl's Guide to the English Language: w3.one.net/~mslentz/grammar.girl. If

Strunk is too dry for you, try Grammar Girl—a supereditor with an attitude. She's compiled a mass of rules and pet peeves to steer any wayward writer back onto the good grammar track.

The Inkspot: www.inkspot.com. "Inkspot is a resource for writers. The Internet is a rich resource of information useful to writers but changes so quickly each day that it is often difficult to keep up with new developments. I started Inkspot for my own personal use but realized that other writers might benefit from it as well." Offers many, many links to writing resources on the Web. Definitely a good place to start looking for answers to any writing-related question.

William Safire's Rules for Writers: www.chem.gla.ac.uk/protein/pert/safire.rules.html. File this under great things to tape next to your computer—a tongue-in-cheek look at some important grammar rules.

RESEARCH RESOURCES

The Crime Writer: www.svn.net/mikekell/crimewriter.html. "If you are an author in the areas of true crime or criminology, published or not, this is your site. We hope to provide a meeting place and resources for authors in this genre who use the Internet as a primary source of information gathering, researching and networking." Includes links to resources that provide information on crime, current crime news and the criminal justice system, as well as general writing and news resources.

ViVa: A Current Bibliography of Women's History in Historical and Women's Studies Journals: www.iisg.nl/~womhist/. "ViVa is short for 'Vrouwengeschiedenis in het Vaktijdschrift', which is Dutch for 'Women's history in scholarly periodicals'. Articles in English, French, German and Dutch are selected for ViVa from more than 60 European and American periodicals." Great place to find details about the daily lives of women throughout history. Sample citation: "Anderson, Olive, 'Emigration and marriage break up in mid-Victorian England', Economic History Review 50 (1997) 1, 104-109."

Dr. Jim Weinrich's AIDS and Sexology Page: math.ucsd.edu/~weinrich. Don't snicker. This page of information and links is invaluable to any writer of contemporary fiction. The prime rule of fiction—write what you know—should really be write what you can learn a lot about. This site allows you to safely learn the how's and why's of human sexuality as well as its devastating modern consequences.

The best way to find information about specific research topics is through a search engine like Yahoo (www.yahoo.com) or Infoseek (www.infoseek.com). I did an exact phrase search on Yahoo for "life in" and came up with 478 matches. The websites covered everything from life in concentration camps to life in early Wisconsin to retired life in a motor home to life in ancient Egypt.

It still amazes me how much information waits at our fingertips. Certainly a vast portion of the Internet is taken up by commercial sites and time wasters, but the rest is filled with invaluable resources that are only a deep breath and a few mouse clicks away. If you lack experience with computers or the Internet, the library may be the best place to start. They can offer you friendly advice and a guiding hand. Otherwise, hop on board and start surfing. Your fiction will shine with the details you glean from cyberspace and every little touch can put you that much closer to your ultimate goal—publication.

◪ Canadian Writers Take Note

While much of the information contained in this section applies to all writers, here are some specifics of interest to Canadian writers:

Postage: When sending an SASE from Canada, you will need an International Reply Coupon. Also be aware, a GST tax is required on postage in Canada and for mail with postage under $5 going to destinations outside the country. Since Canadian postage rates are voted on in January of each year (after we go to press), contact a Canada Post Corporation Customer Service Division, located in most cities in Canada, for the most current rates.

Copyright: For information on copyrighting your work and to obtain forms, write Copyright and Industrial Design, Phase One, Place du Portage, 50 Victoria St., Hull, Quebec K1A 0C9 or call (819)997-1936. Website: www.cipo.gc.ca.

The public lending right: The Public Lending Right Commission has established that eligible Canadian authors are entitled to payments when a book is available through a library. Payments are determined by a sampling of the holdings of a representative number of libraries. To find out more about the program and to learn if you are eligible, write to the Public Lending Right Commission at 350 Albert St., P.O. Box 1047, Ottawa, Ontario K1P 5V8 or call (613)566-4378 for information. The Commission, which is part of The Canada Council, produces a helpful pamphlet, *How the PLR System Works,* on the program.

Grants available to Canadian writers: Most province art councils or departments of culture provide grants to resident writers. Some of these, as well as contests for Canadian writers, are listed in our Contests and Awards section. For national programs, contact The Canada Council, Writing and Publishing Section, P.O. Box 1047, Ottawa, Ontario K1P 5V8 or call (613)566-4338 for information. Fax: (613)566-4390. Website: www.canadacouncil.ca.

For more information: More details on much of the information listed above and additional information on writing and publishing in Canada are included in the *Writer's Essential Desk Reference: A Companion to Writer's Market*, 2nd edition, published by Writer's Digest Books. In addition to information on a wide range of topics useful to all writers, the book features a detailed chapter for Canadians, Writing and Selling in Canada, by Fred Kerner.

See the Organizations and Resources section of *Novel & Short Story Writer's Market* for listings of writers' organizations in Canada. Also contact The Writer's Union of Canada, 24 Ryerson Ave., Toronto, Ontario M5T 2P3; call them at (416)703-8982 or fax them at (416)703-0826. E-mail: twuc@the-wire.com. Website: www.swifty.com/twuc. This organization provides a wealth of information (as well as strong support) for Canadian writers, including specialized publications on publishing contracts; contract negotiations; the author/editor relationship; author awards, competitions and grants; agents; taxes for writers, libel issues and access to archives in Canada.

Printing & Production Terms Defined

In most of the magazine listings in this book you will find a brief physical description of each publication. This material usually includes the number of pages, type of paper, type of binding and whether or not the magazine uses photographs or illustrations.

Although it is important to look at a copy of the magazine to which you are submitting, these descriptions can give you a general idea of what the publication looks like. This material can provide you with a feel for the magazine's financial resources and prestige. Do not, however, rule out small, simply produced publications as these may be the most receptive to new writers. Watch for publications that have increased their page count or improved their production from year to year. This is a sign the publication is doing well and may be accepting more fiction.

You will notice a wide variety of printing terms used within these descriptions. We explain here some of the more common terms used in our listing descriptions. We do not include explanations of terms such as Mohawk and Karma which are brand names and refer to the paper manufacturer. *Getting it Printed*, by Mark Beach (Writer's Digest Books), is an excellent publication for those interested in learning more about printing and production.

PAPER

acid-free: Paper that has a low or no acid content. This type of paper resists deterioration from exposure to the elements. More expensive than many other types of paper, publications done on acid-free paper can last a long time.

bond: Bond paper is often used for stationery and is more transparent than text paper. It can be made of either sulphite (wood) or cotton fiber. Some bonds have a mixture of both wood and cotton (such as "25 percent cotton" paper). This is the type of paper most often used in photocopying or as standard typing paper.

coated/uncoated stock: Coated and uncoated are terms usually used when referring to book or text paper. More opaque than bond, it is the paper most used for offset printing. As the name implies, uncoated paper has no coating. Coated paper is coated with a layer of clay, varnish or other chemicals. It comes in various sheens and surfaces depending on the type of coating, but the most common are dull, matte and gloss.

cover stock: Cover stock is heavier book or text paper used to cover a publication. It comes in a variety of colors and textures and can be coated on one or both sides.

CS1/CS2: Most often used when referring to cover stock, CS1 means paper that is coated only on one side; CS2 is paper coated on both sides.

newsprint: Inexpensive absorbent pulp wood paper often used in newspapers and tabloids.

text: Text paper is similar to book paper (a smooth paper used in offset printing), but it has been given some texture by using rollers or other methods to apply a pattern to the paper.

vellum: Vellum is a text paper that is fairly porous and soft.

Some notes about paper weight and thickness: Often you will see paper thickness described in terms of pounds such as 80 lb. or 60 lb. paper. The weight is determined by figuring how many pounds in a ream of a particular paper (a ream is 500 sheets). This can be confusing, however, because this figure is based on a standard sheet size and standard sheet sizes vary depending on the type of paper used. This information is most helpful when comparing papers of the same type. For example, 80 lb. book paper versus 60 lb. book paper. Since the size of the paper is the same it would follow that 80 lb. paper is the thicker, heavier paper.

Some paper, especially cover stock, is described by the actual thickness of the paper. This is expressed in a system of points. Typical paper thicknesses range from 8 points to 14 points thick.

PRINTING

letterpress: Letterpress printing is printing that uses a raised surface such as type. The type is inked and then pressed against the paper. Unlike offset printing, only a limited number of impressions can be made, as the surface of the type can wear down.

offset: Offset is a printing method in which ink is transferred from an image-bearing plate to a "blanket" and from the blanket to the paper.

sheet-fed offset: Offset printing in which the paper is fed one piece at a time.

web offset: Offset printing in which a roll of paper is printed and then cut apart to make individual sheets.

There are many other printing methods but these are the ones most commonly referred to in our listings.

BINDING

case binding: In case binding, signatures (groups of pages) are stitched together with thread rather than glued together. The stitched pages are then trimmed on three sides and glued into a hardcover or board "case" or cover. Most hardcover books and thicker magazines are done this way.

comb binding: A comb is a plastic spine used to hold pages together with bent tabs that are fed through punched holes in the edge of the paper.

perfect binding: Used for paperback books and heavier magazines, perfect binding involves gathering signatures (groups of pages) into a stack, trimming off the folds so the edge is flat and gluing a cover to that edge.

saddle stitched: Publications in which the pages are stitched together using metal staples. This fairly inexpensive type of binding is usually used with books or magazines that are under 80 pages.

Smythe-sewn: Binding in which the pages are sewn together with thread. Smythe is the name of the most common machine used for this purpose.

spiral binding: A wire spiral that is wound through holes punched in pages is a spiral bind. This is the binding used in spiral notebooks.

Glossary

Advance. Payment by a publisher to an author prior to the publication of a book, to be deducted from the author's future royalties.

All rights. The rights contracted to a publisher permitting a manuscript's use anywhere and in any form, including movie and book club sales, without additional payment to the writer.

Anthology. A collection of selected writings by various authors.

Auction. Publishers sometimes bid against each other for the acquisition of a manuscript that has excellent sales prospects.

Backlist. A publisher's books not published during the current season but still in print.

Book producer/packager. An organization that may develop a book for a publisher based upon the publisher's idea or may plan all elements of a book, from its initial concept to writing and marketing strategies, and then sell the package to a book publisher and/or movie producer.

Cliffhanger. Fictional event in which the reader is left in suspense at the end of a chapter or episode, so that interest in the story's outcome will be sustained.

Clip. Sample, usually from a newspaper or magazine, of a writer's published work.

Cloak-and-dagger. A melodramatic, romantic type of fiction dealing with espionage and intrigue.

Commercial. Publishers whose concern is salability, profit and success with a large readership.

Contemporary. Material dealing with popular current trends, themes or topics.

Contributor's copy. Copy of an issue of a magazine or published book sent to an author whose work is included.

Copublishing. An arrangement in which the author and publisher share costs and profits.

Copyediting. Editing a manuscript for writing style, grammar, punctuation and factual accuracy.

Copyright. The legal right to exclusive publication, sale or distribution of a literary work.

Cover letter. A brief letter sent with a complete manuscript submitted to an editor.

"Cozy" (or "teacup") mystery. Mystery usually set in a small British town, in a bygone era, featuring a somewhat genteel, intellectual protagonist.

Cyberpunk. Type of science fiction, usually concerned with computer networks and human-computer combinations, involving young, sophisticated protagonists.

E-mail. Mail that has been sent electronically using a computer and modem.

Electronic submission. A submission of material by modem or on computer disk.

Experimental fiction. Fiction that is innovative in subject matter and style; avant-garde, non-formulaic, usually literary material.

Exposition. The portion of the storyline, usually the beginning, where background information about character and setting is related.

Fair use. A provision in the copyright law that says short passages from copyrighted material may be used without infringing on the owner's rights.

Fanzine. A noncommercial, small-circulation magazine usually dealing with fantasy, horror or science-fiction literature and art.

First North American serial rights. The right to publish material in a periodical before it appears in book form, for the first time, in the United States or Canada.

Galleys. The first typeset version of a manuscript that has not yet been divided into pages.

Genre. A formulaic type of fiction such as romance, western or horror.

Gothic. A genre in which the central character is usually a beautiful young woman and the setting an old mansion or castle, involving a handsome hero and real danger, either natural or supernatural.

Graphic novel. An adaptation of a novel into a long comic strip or heavily illustrated story of 40 pages or more, produced in paperback.

Hard-boiled detective novel. Mystery novel featuring a private eye or police detective as the protagonist; usually involves a murder. The emphasis is on the details of the crime.

Horror. A genre stressing fear, death and other aspects of the macabre.

Imprint. Name applied to a publisher's specific line (e.g. Owl, an imprint of Henry Holt).

Interactive fiction. Fiction in book or computer-software format where the reader determines the path the story will take by choosing from several alternatives at the end of each chapter or episode.

International Reply Coupon (IRC). A form purchased at a post office and enclosed with a letter or manuscript to a international publisher, to cover return postage costs.

Juvenile. Fiction intended for children 2-12.

Libel. Written or printed words that defame, malign or damagingly misrepresent a living person.

Literary. The general category of serious, non-formulaic, intelligent fiction, sometimes experimental, that most frequently appears in little magazines.

Literary agent. A person who acts for an author in finding a publisher or arranging contract terms on a literary project.

Mainstream. Traditionally written fiction on subjects or trends that transcend experimental or genre fiction categories.

Malice domestic novel. A traditional mystery novel that is not hard-boiled; emphasis is on the solution. Suspects and victims know one another.

Manuscript. The author's unpublished copy of a work, usually typewritten, used as the basis for typesetting.

Mass market paperback. Softcover book on a popular subject, usually around 4×7, directed to a general audience and sold in drugstores and groceries as well as in bookstores.

Ms(s). Abbreviation for manuscript(s).

Multiple submission. Submission of more than one short story at a time to the same editor. Do not make a multiple submission unless requested.

Narration. The account of events in a story's plot as related by the speaker or the voice of the author.

Narrator. The person who tells the story, either someone involved in the action or the voice of the writer.

New Age. A term including categories such as astrology, psychic phenomena, spiritual healing, UFOs, mysticism and other aspects of the occult.

Nom de plume. French for "pen name"; a pseudonym.

Novella (also novelette). A short novel or long story, approximately 7,000-15,000 words.

#10 envelope. 4×9½ envelope, used for queries and other business letters.

Offprint. Copy of a story taken from a magazine before it is bound.

One-time rights. Permission to publish a story in periodical or book form one time only.

Outline. A summary of a book's contents, often in the form of chapter headings with a few sentences outlining the action of the story under each one; sometimes part of a book proposal.

Payment on acceptance. Payment from the magazine or publishing house as soon as the decision to print a manuscript is made.

Payment on publication. Payment from the publisher after a manuscript is printed.

Pen name. A pseudonym used to conceal a writer's real name.

Periodical. A magazine or journal published at regular intervals.

Plot. The carefully devised series of events through which the characters progress in a work of fiction.

Proofreading. Close reading and correction of a manuscript's typographical errors.

Proofs. A typeset version of a manuscript used for correcting errors and making changes, often a photocopy of the galleys.

Proposal. An offer to write a specific work, usually consisting of an outline of the work and one or two completed chapters.

Protagonist. The principal or leading character in a literary work.

Public domain. Material that either was never copyrighted or whose copyright term has expired.

Pulp magazine. A periodical printed on inexpensive paper, usually containing lurid, sensational stories or articles.

Query. A letter written to an editor to elicit interest in a story the writer wants to submit.

Reader. A person hired by a publisher to read unsolicited manuscripts.

Reading fee. An arbitrary amount of money charged by some agents and publishers to read a submitted manuscript.

Regency romance. A genre romance, usually set in England between 1811-1820.

Remainders. Leftover copies of an out-of-print book, sold by the publisher at a reduced price.

Reporting time. The number of weeks or months it takes an editor to report back on an author's query or manuscript.

Reprint rights. Permission to print an already published work whose rights have been sold to another magazine or book publisher.

Roman à clef. French "novel with a key." A novel that represents actual living or historical characters and events in fictionalized form.

Romance. The genre relating accounts of passionate love and fictional heroic achievements.

Royalties. A percentage of the retail price paid to an author for each copy of the book that is sold.

SAE. Self-addressed envelope.

SASE. Self-addressed stamped envelope.

Science fiction. Genre in which scientific facts and hypotheses form the basis of actions and events.

Second serial (reprint) rights. Permission for the reprinting of a work in another periodical after its first publication in book or magazine form.

Self-publishing. In this arrangement, the author keeps all income derived from the book, but he pays for its manufacturing, production and marketing.

Sequel. A literary work that continues the narrative of a previous, related story or novel.

Serial rights. The rights given by an author to a publisher to print a piece in one or more periodicals.

Serialized novel. A book-length work of fiction published in sequential issues of a periodical.

Setting. The environment and time period during which the action of a story takes place.

Short short story. A condensed piece of fiction, usually under 700 words.

Simultaneous submission. The practice of sending copies of the same manuscript to several editors or publishers at the same time. Some people refuse to consider such submissions.

Slant. A story's particular approach or style, designed to appeal to the readers of a specific magazine.

Slice of life. A presentation of characters in a seemingly mundane situation which offers the reader a flash of illumination about the characters or their situation.

Slush pile. A stack of unsolicited manuscripts in the editorial offices of a publisher.

Social fiction. Fiction written with the purpose of bringing about positive changes in society.

Speculation (or Spec). An editor's agreement to look at an author's manuscript with no promise to purchase.

Speculative fiction (SpecFic). The all-inclusive term for science fiction, fantasy and horror.

Splatterpunk. Type of horror fiction known for its very violent and graphic content.

Subsidiary. An incorporated branch of a company or conglomerate (e.g. Alfred Knopf, Inc., a subsidiary of Random House, Inc.).

Subsidiary rights. All rights other than book publishing rights included in a book contract, such as paperback, book club and movie rights.

Subsidy publisher. A book publisher who charges the author for the cost of typesetting, printing and promoting a book. Also Vanity publisher.

Subterficial fiction. Innovative, challenging, nonconventional fiction in which what seems to be happening is the result of things not so easily perceived.

Suspense. A genre of fiction where the plot's primary function is to build a feeling of anticipation and fear in the reader over its possible outcome.

Synopsis. A brief summary of a story, novel or play. As part of a book proposal, it is a comprehensive summary condensed in a page or page and a half.

Tabloid. Publication printed on paper about half the size of a regular newspaper page (e.g. *The National Enquirer*).

Tearsheet. Page from a magazine containing a published story.

Theme. The dominant or central idea in a literary work; its message, moral or main thread.

Trade paperback. A softbound volume, usually around 5×8, published and designed for the general public, available mainly in bookstores.

Unsolicited manuscript. A story or novel manuscript that an editor did not specifically ask to see.

Vanity publisher. See Subsidy publisher.

Viewpoint. The position or attitude of the first- or third-person narrator or multiple narrators, which determines how a story's action is seen and evaluated.

Western. Genre with a setting in the West, usually between 1860-1890, with a formula plot about cowboys or other aspects of frontier life.

Whodunit. Genre dealing with murder, suspense and the detection of criminals.

Work-for-hire. Work that another party commissions you to do, generally for a flat fee. The creator does not own the copyright and therefore cannot sell any rights.

Young adult. The general classification of books written for readers 12-18.

Zine. Often one- or two-person operations run from the home of the publisher/editor. Themes tend to be specialized, personal, experimental and often controversial.

Category Index

Our Category Index makes it easy for you to identify publishers who are looking for a specific type of fiction. The index is divided into types of fiction, including a section of electronic magazines. Under each fiction category are magazines and book publishers looking for that kind of fiction. Publishers who are not listed under a fiction category either accept all types of fiction or have not indicated specific subject preferences. Also not appearing here are listings that need very specific types of fiction, e.g., "fiction about fly fishing only." To use this index to find a book publisher for your mainstream novel, for instance, go to the Mainstream/Contemporary section and look under Book Publishers. Finally, read individual listings *carefully* to determine the publishers best suited to your work.

For a listing of agents and the types of fiction they represent, see the Literary Agents Category Index beginning on page 137.

ADVENTURE

Magazines

ALL CATEGORIES OF FICTION
Magazines

CHILDREN'S/ JUVENILE
Magazines

COMICS/GRAPHIC NOVELS

Magazines

Book Publishers

CONDENSED NOVEL

Magazines

EXPERIMENTAL

Magazines

Chinook Press 418
Coffee House Press 419
Cross-Cultural Communications 488
Dan River Press 488
Empyreal 425
FC2 430
Gay Sunshine Press and Leyland Publications 432
Griffon House Publications 490
Helicon Nine Editions 437
Ironweed Press 440
Lintel 444
Mercury House 450
Morrow and Company, Inc., William 451
New Rivers Press 495
Pig Iron Press 496
Pride and Imprints 460
Quixote 461
Random House, Inc. 462
Red Deer Press 462
Red Dragon Press 463
Ronsdale Press 498
St. Martin's Press 464
Second Chance Press and The Permanent Press 466
Snowapple Press 499
Thistledown Press 501
Thorngate Road 501
Turnstone Press 502
Ultramarine Publishing 503
Vagabond Press 480
Voices from My Retreat 504
York Press 483

FAMILY SAGA
Magazines
Bibliophilos 158
Heist Magazine 307
Interbang 202
Penny-a-Liner 317
San Diego Writers' Monthly 258
State of Being 353
Storyboard 273
Talus & Scree 277
War Cry, The 396

Book Publishers
Bancroft Press 485
Bantam Books 411
British Book Company 415
Chinook Press 418
Dan River Press 488
Grade School Press 490
Harvest House Publishers 437
Mountain State Press 494
Philomel Books 458
Rio Grande Press 463
Scherf Books 499
Second Chance Press and The Permanent Press 466

University of Nevada Press 503

FANTASY
Magazines
About Such Things 143
Adventures of Sword & Sorcery 145
Advocate, PKA's Publication 145
Allegheny Review 147
Altair 296
Amazing Stories 360
Amelia 148
Anotherealm 329
Anthology 296
Armchair Aesthete, The 153
Art Times 362
Art:Mag 329
Asimov's Science Fiction 362
Axe Factory Review 154
Barbaric Yawp 155
Blue Skunk Companion, The 161
Brutarian 299
Cafe Irreal, The 167
Capers Aweigh 168
Challenging Destiny 299
Chiricú 172
Climbing Art, The 174
Companion in Zeor, A 334
Compleat Nurse, The 301
Contact Advertising 368
CZ's Magazine 302
Dagger of the Mind 302
Dan River Anthology 179
Dargonzine 334
Dark Moon Rising 335
Deadly Nightshade 335
Dialogue 372
Disenchanted 336
Dream International/Quarterly 303
Dreams & Nightmares 337
Dreams & Visions 304
Drinkin' Buddy Magazine, The 337
Eternal Voice 338
Eternity Magazine 338
Eureka Literary Magazine 182
Evansville Review 183
Faultline 185
Fish Drum Magazine 186
Flying Island, The 187
Forbidden Donut 188
Fugue 189
Gotta Write Network Litmag 339
Grasslands Review 193
Green's Magazine 195
Happy 196
Hawaii Pacific Review 307
Hayden's Ferry Review 197
Heist Magazine 307
Implosion 380

Indigenous Fiction 201
Interbang 202
Interzone 381
Jackhammer E-Zine 341
Jupiter's Freedom 341
Lamp-Post, The 209
Leapings Literary Magazine 210
Lines in the Sand 211
Lite 212
Lost Worlds 310
Lynx Eye 214
MacGuffin, The 215
Magazine of Fantasy & Science Fiction 383
Matriarch's Way: Journal of Female Supremacy 217
Medicinal Purposes 312
Merlyn's Pen 218
Millennium Science Fiction & Fantasy 343
Minas Tirith Evening-Star 219
Mind in Motion 219
Mississippi Review 222
Mobius 223
Musing Place, The 224
My Legacy 313
Nassau Review 224
Nightly Gathering 345
Northwoods Journal 231
Oak, The 315
Of Unicorns and Space Stations 346
Office Number One 346
Ohio Teachers Write 233
On Spec 315
Once Upon A World 347
Orphic Chronicle, The 347
Outer Darkness 348
Pablo Lennis 348
Palo Alto Review 236
Parsec 316
Penny Dreadful 349
Penny-a-Liner 317
Pirate Writings 317
Play the Odds 350
Playboy Magazine 387
Poetry Forum Short Stories 243
Poet's Fantasy 243
Portland Review 244
Poskisnolt Press 317
Potpourri 245
Primavera 247
Prisoners of the Night 318
Queen's Quarterly 319
Rag Mag 251
Reader's Break 252
Rejected Quarterly, The 254
Rockford Review, The 256
Rose & Thorn Literary E-Zine 257
Samsara 258

FEMINIST

Magazines

GAY

Magazines

HORROR

Magazines

CATEGORY INDEX

Book Publishers

LESBIAN

Magazines

Book Publishers

LITERARY

Magazines

Are You Ready to Write Better and Get Paid For What You Write?

At **Writer's Digest School,** we want you to have both a "flair for words" *and* the marketing know-how it takes to give your writing the best shot at publication. That's why you'll work with a professional, published writer who has already mastered the rules of the game firsthand. A savvy mentor who can show you, through detailed critiques of the writing assignments you send in, how to effectively target your work and get it into the hands of the right editor.

Whether you write articles or short stories, nonfiction or novels, **Writer's Digest School** has a workshop that's right for you. Each provides a wealth of expertise and one goal: helping you break into the writing market.

So if you're serious about getting published, you owe it to yourself to check out **Writer's Digest School**. To find out more about us, simply fill out and return the card below. There's absolutely no obligation!

Workshop descriptions on the back ➡

Send Me Free Information!

I want to write better and sell more with the help of the professionals at **Writer's Digest School**. Send me free information about the workshop I've checked below:

☐ Novel Writing Workshop   ☐ Writing & Selling Short Stories

☐ Writing & Selling Nonfiction Articles   ☐ Writing Your Life Stories

☐ Writer's Digest Criticism Service   ☐ The Elements of Effective Writing

☐ Getting Started in Writing   ☐ Marketing Your Nonfiction Book

                                         ☐ Screenwriting Workshop

Name _____

Address _____

City _____ State _____ ZIP _____

Phone: (Day) (_____)_____ (Eve.) (_____)_____

To get your package even sooner, call 1-800-759-0963
Outside the U.S. call 1-513-531-2690 ext. 342

INSXX1X0

Novel Writing Workshop: Iron out your plot, create your main characters, develop a dramatic background, and complete the opening scenes and summary of your novel's complete story. Plus, you'll pinpoint potential publishers for your type of book.

NEW! **Getting Started in Writing:** From short fiction and novels to articles and nonfiction books, we'll help you discover where your natural writing talents lie.

Writing & Selling Short Stories: Learn how to create believable characters, write vivid, true-to-life dialogue, fill your scenes with conflict, and keep your readers on the edge of their seats.

Writing & Selling Nonfiction Articles: Master the components for effective article writing and selling. You'll learn how to choose attention-grabbing topics, conduct stirring interviews, write compelling query letters, and slant a single article for a variety of publications.

Writing Your Life Stories: Learn how to weave the important events of your personal or family's history into a heartfelt story. You'll plan a writing strategy, complete a dateline of events, and discover how to combine factual events with narrative flow.

Writer's Digest Criticism Service: Have an experienced, published writer review your manuscripts before you submit them for pay. Whether you write books, articles, short stories or poetry, you'll get professional, objective feedback on what's working well, what needs strengthening, and which markets you should pursue.

The Elements of Effective Writing: Discover how to conquer the pesky grammar and usage problems that hold so many writers back. You'll refresh your basic English composition skills through step-by-step lessons and writing exercises designed to help keep your manuscripts out of the rejection pile.

Marketing Your Nonfiction Book: You'll work with your mentor to create a book proposal that you can send directly to a publisher, develop and refine your book idea, write a chapter-by-chapter outline of your subject, line up your sources and information, write sample chapters, and complete your query letter.

Screenwriting Workshop: Learn to write for the silver screen! Work step by step with a professional screenwriter to craft your script, find out how to research the right agent or producer for your work, and get indispensable information about the Hollywood submission process.

MAINSTREAM/ CONTEMPORARY

Magazines

NEW AGE/MYSTIC/ SPIRITUAL

Magazines

Book Publishers

PSYCHIC/ SUPERNATURAL/ OCCULT

Magazines

Book Publishers

REGIONAL

Magazines

Book Publishers

RELIGIOUS/ INSPIRATIONAL

Magazines

Book Publishers

ROMANCE

Magazines

SENIOR CITIZEN/ RETIREMENT

Magazines

WESTERN

Magazines

Book Publishers

General Index

Markets that appeared in the 1999 edition of *Novel & Short Story Writer's Market* but are not included in this edition are identified by a two-letter code explaining why the market was omitted: **(ED)**—Editorial Decision, **(NS)**—Not Accepting Submissions, **(NR)**—No (or late) Response to Listing Request, **(OB)**—Out of Business, **(RR)**—Removed by Market's Request, **(UC)**—Unable to Contact, **(UF)**—Uncertain Future.